Front and rear cover and front and rear internal flyleaf images
The Top Sale of the 2015-2016 season
1957 Ferrari 335 S
US$ 35.930.639
Artcurial, Paris (F) 5 February 2016
All images copyright and courtesy of Artcurial

ADOLFO ORSI   RAFFAELE GAZZI

CLASSIC CAR AUCTION
YEARBOOK 2015 2016

Sponsored by

Classic Car Auction 2015-2016 Yearbook

Published by:
Historica Selecta srl
Via Paussolo 14/a
41012 Carpi (Modena)
Italy

Edited by:
Adolfo Orsi
Raffaele Gazzi

Data processing by:
Historica Selecta srl

Iconography:
Historica Selecta srl
Archivio Adolfo Orsi

Historica Selecta thanks for their help:
Guido Aggazzotti Cavazza, Fiorenzo Fantuzzi, Katie Hellwig, Fausto Busato

© Copyright 2016 Historica Selecta

This book is copyrighted under the Berne Convention

All rights reserved. No part of this publication may be reproduced, stored, in a retrieval system, or transmitted in any form or by any mean, electronic, electrical, chemical, mechanical, optical, photocopying, recording or otherwise without prior written permission of Historica Selecta, Carpi.

The publisher refuses all responsibility about the data reported in this catalogue, directly coming from Auction Houses. Moreover, the publisher apologizes for any mistakes or omissions incurred in the laying-out of this catalogue. We shall be pleased to include any additions in the next edition.

Printing
Grafiche Zanini - Bologna - October 2016

Printed in Italy

978-88-96232-08-8

Introduction

Dear reader,

In 1986 when I decided to specialise in the field of collector's cars, I realized that a method for analysing market prices was missing. When from 1988 to 1991, in association with Finarte, I organized auctions of cars and automobilia in Modena, I started to gather data on the most important international sales.

In 1993 Raffaele Gazzi and I collaborated with Alberto Bolaffi in producing a yearbook, the Bolaffi Catalogue, which listed the data of cars offered for sale at international auctions, complete with prices in the leading currencies, with in-depth data on every single car. This became an essential tool for auction house managers, traders, specialized journalists and collectors alike, as well as for enthusiasts keen to be up-to-date with market values.

From the 2006-2008 edition, our company Historica Selecta took over the publishing of the Classic Car Auction Yearbook, which we increased every year with more data and graphics. This edition is the 21st (covering the 23th season) and it is the most comprehensive ever.

We are honoured to have Credit Suisse as our main sponsor and to count upon the faithful support of our advertisers, who understand the "raison d'être" of our publication.

Adolfo Orsi
President Historica Selecta

Dear Classic Car Auction Yearbook Enthusiast

Credit Suisse is delighted to sponsor the Classic Car Auction Yearbook once again, this being the eighth consecutive year we have partnered with what has become the trusted auction guide for classic car enthusiasts around the world.

Co-author Adolfo Orsi has become a part of the Credit Suisse Classic Car family, regularly joining us at our events such as the Goodwood Revival and the Grand Prix de Monaco Historique, where he delights guests with his valuable insights into the classic car world.

As a classic car collector and historic racer myself (the photo is taken before the Kinrara Trophy race at this year's Goodwood Revival), it is a real pleasure to represent Credit Suisse's involvement with the classic car world. In 2016, we attended the Grand Prix de Monaco Historique and reunited Sir Stirling Moss with his Maserati 250F, 60 years after his famous victory around the GP circuit. We also returned to Goodwood Revival where David Brabham joined the Credit Suisse racing legends, coinciding with the Goodwood Revival Jack Brabham celebrations, to take part in the 8th Credit Suisse Historic Racing Forum – along with Sir Stirling Moss OBE, Derek Bell MBE, Jochen Mass, Alain de Cadenet, and Dario Franchitti MBE.

If you would like to see more on our classic car program please visit: credit-suisse.com/classiccars

All that is left for me to do is to congratulate Adolfo and Raffaele on another fantastic Auction Yearbook.

Karsten Le Blanc
Credit Suisse (UK) Ltd.

HISTORICA SELECTA SRL

41012 CARPI (MODENA) - VIA PAUSSOLO, 14/A - ITALY
TEL +39 059 663955 - info@historicaselecta.it
www.classiccarauctionyearbook.com

Index

The 21th edition of the "Classic Car Auction Yearbook", edited by Adolfo Orsi and Raffaele Gazzi, and sponsored by Credit Suisse, covers the last classic car auction season, from 1st September 2015 to 31st August 2016, and will give the reader further information and useful data for a better comprehension of this important area of the antique market.

9 Market analysis of the 2015-2016 season

12 Authors' comment

18 Graphs of the prices achieved by cars offered and sold in earlier time

22 The Top 201 cars of the 2015-2016 season

28 Top 100 for make and country statistics

30 Statistics for period of manufacturing

34 Statistics for make

38 Average price achieved graphs

41 The 2015-2016 season "TOP TEN"

63 The 2015-2016 season case

65 Auction results from 1st September 2015 until 31st August 2016

391 23 years of TOP FIVE

405 23 years of TOP FIVE for Makes

410 TOP TWENTY of the last 23 seasons

412 Advertisers

413 Photo credits

414 Previous Yearbooks

416 About the authors

Market analysis of the 2015-2016 season

This chapter reports the classic car market analysis of the last auction season, carried out by the classic car department heads of Artcurial, Bonhams, Gooding & Company, RM Sotheby's and by the authors.

2016 was the Record Year for Artcurial Motorcars ! We are delighted and very proud to have held the sale of the Ferrari 335 S from the Pierre Bardinon Collection which set a new world record price for a car sold at auction (in euros and sterling). This sale is recompense for the car's racing pedigree, the famous drivers who have sat behind the wheel, its sculptural design, hugely powerful engine as well as its provenance. It is not easy to find such exclusive automobiles, but when they appear at auction, they obtain consistently high prices. The art world has adopted the term Blue Chip for such exceptional pieces. These are the ultimate art objects and there will always be buyers for such rare items.

During the last three years the market has been full of mass production models like the 911, Ferrari 512, Testarossa and 308, which have doubled if not tripled in value. For the first time in 15 years of continually rising prices, this sudden rise has halted, affecting those who have entered the market uninformed, hoping to profit from an easy investment and make a quick buck. These speculators have been punished for not buying with their heart. To buy what you love, with passion, is the best investment! And so the market has self-regulated and demonstrated its longevity. The 2015/2016 season has also seen increased demand for more recent models. There has been a considerable rise in prices for sports cars and exclusive models from the 1990s. In our Retromobile sale, the more recent cars such as the Bugatti EB110 and the ex-Gianni Agnelli Ferrari Testarossa Spider achieved strong prices. This rise is explained by the fact that buyers are younger than ever before, and are buying the car of their dreams earlier than preceding generations. This is undoubtedly due to the internet age and new sources of wealth. This is yet more evidence that the market is here to stay and is set to continue its inexorable progression. The secret continues to lie in finding automobiles that are new to the market with transparent histories. I sense the market becoming more specialised, with passionate collectors selecting cars according to their lifestyle and their areas of expertise. In brief, the market is structuring itself in a very positive way, with a view to the long-term.

MATTHIEU LAMOURE
Managing Director
Artcurial Motorcars

As another twelve months have passed since the last publication of the Yearbook we can for the first time in several years, probably six or seven actually notice that the market is behaving more rationally. Not everything is selling at vendor's expectations of tomorrow's prices to impatient buyers trying to jump on the band wagon while they still hope for their 'investment grade motor car' to bring them a better return than other commodities in their portfolio. This stabilization is truly good news not only for real enthusiasts but also the market because we all know that trees don't grow to the sky.

The actors in the market can these days be placed into three clear categories: the traditional enthusiast, the investor and the social animal.

The first will be delighted that he may again hope to be in a position to afford the cars he loves and wants to use, the second will be hedging his bets and if his purchases were wise he will be fine, the third will probably be the least affected as the purchase of the mid-range convertible he invested in will open the doors to rallies, events and social connections he had not made on the golf course, at pheasant shoots or while skiing in the alps.

As far as the product itself goes we can clearly define two emerging trends that have strengthened over the past twelve months. That the proof of collecting motor cars is based on nostalgia of what you loved when you were young and couldn't afford and the fact that like great art, a motor car is only original once, although it can be restored to concours condition as often as desired.

Results that back up these trends very clearly are some of the great cars from all periods that Bonhams were privileged to handle over the past year. Regarding the generational aspect we sold a Ferrari 575M Superamerica for £611,900 in London and a 575M coupé for €345,000 in Paris, both were in as new condition with manual transmission and not red. That was at the beginning of the period, more recently at Chantilly we sold a Porsche 928GTS again with manual gearbox for €101,200 and a 964/911 3.6 Turbo for €238,625 - prices unheard of only two years ago. What this shows us is a clear generational trend to the best examples with the most interesting specification in what some call the youngtimer category – watch this space before approximately 2005 when many models became too complicated with electronics and sometimes even hybrid technology.

As for originality, there can be no two better examples than the 1953 Jaguar works C-Type that had period Le Mans racing history, came from the same 53 year private ownership and sold at Monaco for €7,250,000 or the highly original Porsche 550RS that made £4,593,500 at Goodwood – both oozed irreplaceable patina and originality that you only find on a car once.

Although interest in more conventional prewar cars may be diminishing due to the same generational nostalgia, it's not the case when they 'tick all the boxes' such as the spectacular 1937 Bugatti T 57SC sports tourer with original coachwork by Vanden Plas that sold for $ 9,735,000 at Amelia Island or the magnificent 1935 Berlin Motor Show, Mercedes-Benz 500K Spezial Roadster at Chantilly offered through Bonhams by the grandson of the first owner. One of only two produced with cut down door coachwork and Mercedes Classic certified, this motoring icon sold for €5,290,000, both examples clearly proving that truly great cars continue to attract buyers of all ages even after over 80 years.

So to conclude for all of the above reasons it's been a good year for the market, sanity has prevailed and sometimes emotion has produced exceptional but justified results for very special motor cars.

With approximately twenty Bonhams collector car auctions scheduled before this important annual publication addresses the subject again, we look forward to being of assistance across the globe, in sharing our knowledge, passion and enthusiasm with all readers of the Classic Car Auction Yearbook.

PHILIP KANTOR
Head of Department Bonhams Motor Cars Europe
and Director European Board

Gooding & Company marked its highest sale total in the company history this year, garnering $233 million for 281 lots sold and posting a strong 85% sale rate. Our team curated a variety of exceptional cars at our three esteemed venues, and our clients recognized the quality offerings. Fifty collector cars sold above the $1 million mark and five rose above $10 million. Our events have become a destination for enthusiasts from around the world and this year, thousands tuned in from over 50 nations to witness the Gooding & Company auctions live via our HD webcast.

At our Scottsdale Auctions, we realized $43 million over two days. Numerous benchmarks were set and nine cars sold for over $1 million. We continued to see high demand for exceptional Ferraris from renowned Italian coachbuilders. Most notably, the 1950 Ferrari 166 MM/195 S Berlinetta Le Mans sold for a record price of $6,490,000. The remarkable coachbuilt 1967 Ferrari 330 GTC Speciale also prompted a rousing bidding war, selling for $3,410,000 and breaking a world-auction record for the model. We proudly offered Ferrari supercars from the Tony Shooshani Collection; Sue Callaway of *Fortune* describing Mr. Shooshani as "one of Ferrari's biggest and most loyal current collectors." The collection garnered strong results, which included the 2003 Ferrari Enzo (sold for $2,860,000), the 1995 Ferrari F50 (sold for $2,400,000) and the 1990 Ferrari F40 (sold for $1,534,000). Other prominent sales from the weekend: the stunning 1929 Duesenberg Model J Dual Cowl Phaeton (sold for $2,420,000) the bespoke 1948 Alfa Romeo 6C 2500 Super Sport Cabriolet (sold for $1,012,000) and the Boano-bodied 1955 Alfa Romeo 1900C SS Coupe Speciale (sold for: $990,000).

Following in March, at The Amelia Island Auction at the Omni Plantation's Racquet Park, we were honored to offer selections from the ultimate Porsche connoisseur, Mr. Jerry Seinfeld. "Next to Sunday's Amelia Island Concours, the Seinfeld show was the weekend's most eagerly anticipated event," stated Larry Webster, *Fox News*. Our Auctioneer, Charlie Ross, commanded an astounding price for the star of the day, the 1962 Ferrari 250 GT SWB California Spider, which sold for $17,160,000. The paddles went wild after Mr. Seinfeld joined me on stage for an introduction of his collection, with highpoints including the 1955 Porsche 550 Spyder (sold for $5,335,000), the 1974 Porsche 911 IROC RSR (sold for $2,310,000), the 1990 Porsche 962C (sold for $1,650,000), the 1958 Porsche 356 A 1500 GS/GT Carrera Speedster (sold for $1,540,000), and the 1994 Porsche 964 S Flachbau (sold for $1,017,500). "Mr. Ross wielded his magic," stated David Shaftel, *New York Times*, as $22.2 million was garnered by selections from The Jerry Seinfeld Collection. Overall, we realized over $60 million in a single day, achieving a one-day sale record for auctions held at Amelia Island, and selling 69 of 79 lots.

Gooding & Company is the official auction house of the Pebble Beach Concours d'Elegance®, and at this year's Pebble Beach Auctions we broke our two-day sale record, generating over $129 million. The sensational 1959 Ferrari 250 GT LWB California Spider Competizione sold for $18,150,000 – a new record for a Ferrari LWB California Spider and a new company record for a single lot sold at auction. This year at Pebble Beach I was proud to send 115 exceptional offerings to new homes with an average sale price of $1,128,606. We sold 26 cars for above $1 million, four cars above $10 million and broke numerous world records across multiple marques. These included the historic 1933 Alfa Romeo 8C 2300 Monza (sold for $11,990,000), the 1932 Bugatti Type 55 Roadster (sold for $10,400,000) driven by Achille Varzi in the 1932 Mille Miglia and "arguably the finest of its kind," said Mark Ewing, *Forbes*, the 1979 Porsche 935 (sold for $4,840,000) driven by Paul Newman at the 1979 24 Hours of Le Mans, the beautiful 1957 Maserati A6G/54 Frua Spider (sold for $3,300,000) and the superb 1930 Packard 734 Speedster Runabout (sold for $2,090,000).

In the coming year we anticipate an even greater sophistication in the global car community, with strong demand for respected marques and models that have unique specifications, documented provenance and are the best in their categories. From all of us at Gooding & Company, we look forward to seeing you at our auctions in 2017.

DAVID GOODING
President
Gooding & Company

Each year the introductions in this Yearbook tout records and report a stable, vibrant market. This season, while perhaps not as bullish as the 2014 peak, has continued the trend, with another incredible roster of motor cars coming to market and numerous auction benchmarks set. RM Sotheby's proudly accounted for five of the top 10 sales this season, including the most valuable car sold not only in 2015, but RM history: the Ferrari 290 MM for $28m. Monterey saw more records tumble, led by the Le Mans-winning Jaguar D-Type: the top seller of this year's Monterey week, its $21.7m price makes it the most valuable British car sold at auction. It was certainly refreshing to see the D-Type, along with the Alfa 2.9 ($19.8m) join the all-time top 10 most valuable cars sold at auction – a list almost exclusively dominated by Ferraris in recent years. Exceptional motor cars with indisputable history and provenance continue to lead the market, as do cars coming out of long-term ownership. While 50s/60s cars once dominated auction offerings, we're seeing greater diversity in sale catalogues. In Monterey this year, there were fewer 1950s / 60s vehicles on offer, modern classics (1980 and up) represented almost 25% of total cars presented, and there were almost twice as many vehicles from 2010 and later than the preceding two years. Worthy of mention is the ongoing rise of modern supercars. Limited, low-production examples from the 80s-2000s are now particularly in demand. Low mileage, single ownership and great maintenance history are crucial, but clients are digging deep for the right cars.

It would be remiss not to mention the changing market conditions of the past 12 months, with value adjustments recorded for select marques and models. Cars that have regularly traded hands, and/or were mass-produced are seeing a – possibly overdue – market correction. There is no reason for alarm – this is good news and suggests that the market is stabilising and maturing. The rate of return for such vehicles over the last five years was extraordinary, and as a result, unsustainable, should it have continued. What does this mean for auction houses? Sales percentages have been down a few points with cars that should have sold, failing to do so, something that can be attributed to sellers who have been slow to accept the current correction and are still hoping for top dollar on recently acquired cars. The ongoing challenge is to ensure entries are priced correctly for the market, not always easy when it comes to an enthusiast's prized possession!

The health of the market should not be judged on values alone. Like any market, there will be peaks and troughs. A thorough analysis on the state of the hobby should also be measured by event attendance, website views, magazine sales – the aspiration to own collector cars and participate in our great hobby is ever-growing and becoming more mainstream. Whether this is via the multitude of specialist rallies, Concours d'Elegance, historic race meetings, or even local Cars & Coffee events, the burgeoning lists of entrants and spectators at such events really should be factored in when analyzing the health of our industry, and by all accounts, it appears the appetite to enter into classic car ownership is very healthy.

In summary, good cars that are fresh to market, well presented, event-eligible and priced sensibly are selling strongly, but more importantly, the depth of interest and enthusiasm for the hobby as a whole remains at an all-time high. This is good news for the continued health of the industry we all cherish so much.

PETER WALLMAN
Managing Director
RM Sotheby's - Europe

Authors' comment

Galileo Galilei wrote "*measure what is measurable, and make measureable what is not so.*"

The newest edition of our Yearbook presents various new features. New indices and graphs have been added, and historical data from different periods has been reworked. As a consequence, the data and statistics of the preceding Yearbooks is slightly different than the current set of data because they considered a season that began August 1st and ended on July 31st, including the American August auctions as part of the beginning of the year, rather than at the end as we do now.

The final results of the last season represent a reality much better than the perceptions we and many other experts felt from the auction rooms.

The two fundamental measures of the market are the overall turnover and the percentage of lots sold. The turnover of the world's leading auctions [1] for the 2015-2016 season remained practically unchanged in Dollar terms (-1.5%, $1,211 million versus $1,229 million in 2014-2015), as well as in Euro (+0.5%, €1,086 million versus €1,080 million), though, due to currency exchange fluctuations, it increased in Pound Sterling (+7.5%, £856 million versus £795 million).

However, the percentage of lots sold radically changed, with a sharp reversal: it was 68% in the 2010-2011 season, followed by

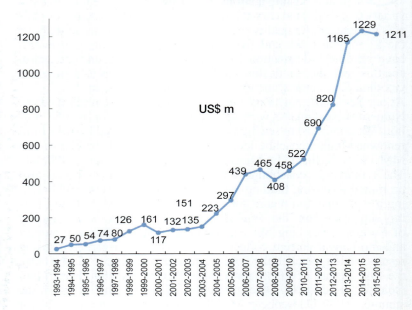

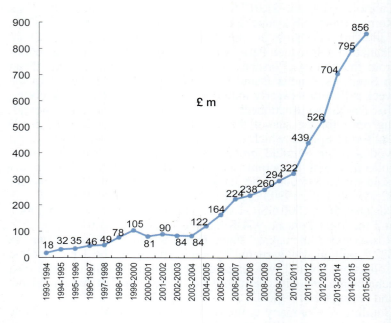

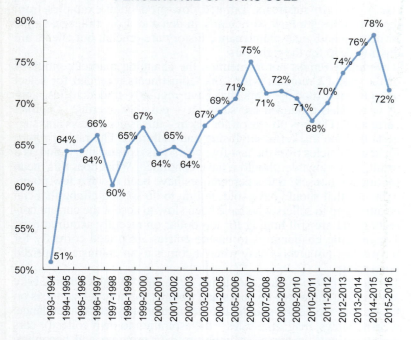

four seasons of continuous growth (70, 74, 76 and 78%), while in this last season the percentage dropped by a good six points to 72%.

This should not come as a surprise, considering the strong increase of cars offered on the market (5,643 units, + 9.5%) in respect to the 2014-2015 season (5,156 cars offered). As the underlying law of supply and demand operates in the collector car market, last season many players (whether collectors or investors) decided to take advantage of the high level of prices achieved in order to try

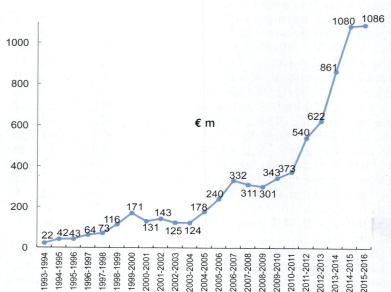

(1) Please note, as we always recall for the benefit of new readers, that we only take into consideration most of the traditional format sales organised by the most important international auction houses. We do not register data of cars for which we do not have adequate information.

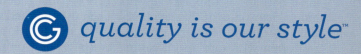

1959 FERRARI 250 GT LWB CALIFORNIA SPIDER COMPETIZIONE | SOLD $18,150,000
Pebble Beach Auctions 2016

GOODING & COMPANY

AUCTIONS & PRIVATE BROKERAGE   INFO@GOODINGCO.COM   +1.310.899.1960

NOW INVITING CONSIGNMENTS
Scottsdale Auctions   through November 1
Amelia Island Auction   through January 2
Pebble Beach Auctions   through June 1

to sell their own cars, but it seems they did not find enough buyers, or, at least, not at the price they expected.

We witnessed extraordinarily high-level cars being offered in the 2015-2016 season, most likely the highest since the start of our publication in the '90s. Flip through the pages of our Top Ten chapter and your heart will skip a beat: there has never been such a "hit parade" as important as this. It is the first time in 23 years that so many cars of this level have been offered (and sold) in the same year: iconic Ferraris such as a 335S, a 290MM, two 250 GT California with rare specifications and a SWB Competizione; a Jaguar D-Type (the one that won the 1956 Le Mans 24 Hours), an Alfa Romeo 8C 2900B Spider Touring and an 8C 2300 Monza, an Aston Martin DB4 GT Zagato, a Cobra (not just any Cobra, but the one and only prototype!) and a Bugatti Type 55 Roadster (ranking only in 12th place among the top sales despite having achieved an incredible $12,4 million!). These cars, all sold above the threshold of $10 million, contributed significantly to this year's final results and turned data into a positive outlook.

Geographical market segmentation is particularly revealing: the percentage sold at the American auctions reaches 77%, a significantly higher figure in comparison to 68% of lots sold in the United Kingdom and 65% within the continental European market. Buyers in the United States auctions are not only American and European buyers are sometimes American, as seen at Artcurial's Retromobile auction with the buyer of the Ferrari 335S; however, sales held during the month of August in Monterey (that alone represent approximately 30% of the entire season's total turnover) have an extremely important role in setting the pace for the rest of the world in the following months. For those who have never had

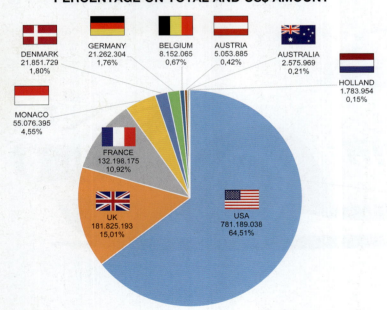

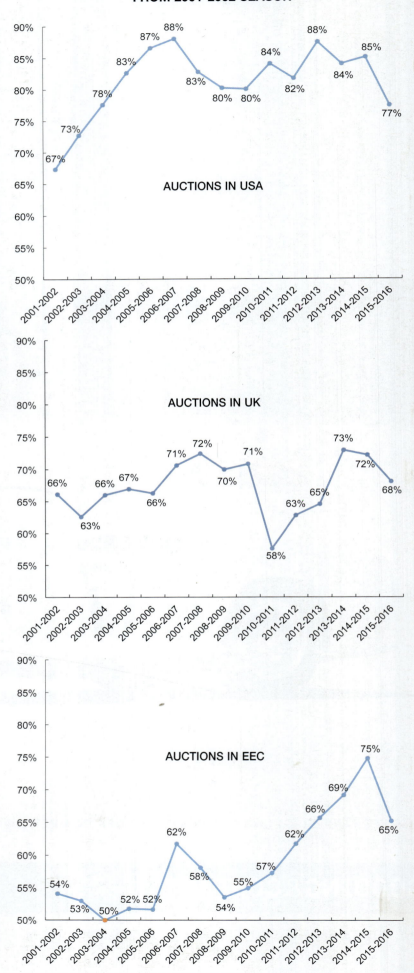

the opportunity to experience Monterey in person, it is important to note that the Monterey auctions do influence the market, but that they are not "the market": the results achieved there are not reproducible anywhere else, and represent a unique moment in the course of the year.

Thanks to the new graphs showing the percentages of cars sold since 2001-2002, divided by nation where the auctions took place, it emerges that auctions organized in the United States bring higher values. With regards to recent sales segmented by marque, the market has been pulled to a higher level mostly by one brand: Ferrari. Even in this past season, Ferrari, despite experiencing a deeper level of consolidation than other marques

(read: a decrease in values), weighted approximately 30% of the total market turnover (last year this figure was 33%), taking hold of the Top Price of the season, with four cars among the Top 6, 20 cars among the Top 35 and 45 cars among the Top 100. The percentage of Ferraris sold is significantly lower than the market average (60% versus 72%, and considerably lower than 85% from the previous season) as well as the average value (dropped to $753,000 versus $924,000 the previous season and the record $1,125,000 in 2013-2014).

The excess of supply, 812 Ferrari versus 576 (+41% year compared to last year), has strongly influenced prices. In some cases, there were simply too many examples offered. Of the seven 250 GT/L, second-series 250 GT Cabriolet and 275 GTB examples offered of each model only three found new owners; of the five Daytona Spiders offered, only one was sold; of the four 250 Berlinetta "SWB" Lusso (in steel) only one was sold; and neither the rare 275 GTS/4 NART Spider or 268SP were sold. Last year, we saw a sales rate of 100% for two of the "lower ranking" Ferrari models, the 250 GTE (ten cars offered and sold) and 330 GT 2+2 (19 cars offered, all sold). Out of curiosity, we checked the data of the same models from this season and discovered that only three original 250 GTE (all sold) and 22 examples of the 330 GT 2+2 (12 sold) were offered. This proves once more that the market does not repeat itself and it does not follow any 'scientific law'. However, we have come a long way since the 1993-1994 season, when only 65 Ferraris were offered and 14 were sold, with a sales rate of 22% and a total turnover of $876,000, equal to a mere 3.28% of the total!

Porsche, the manufacturer second in line with the greatest annual auction sales turnover, has also experienced a decrease: 66% percent sold (last season was 75%) for an average sale price of $309,000 (versus $346,000 last year). Even Lamborghini, after its dizzying spike in values experienced the last few seasons, found it difficult to continue growing at the same rate, and sold only 52% of the cars offered. On the other hand, it is natural for these marques who experienced a recent sky-high increase in prices, to be the ones that, during this phase of consolidation, suffer more than the average.

We replaced the data of the Top 100 for Manufacturing Period in order to enter general market data, and segmented this data further by manufacturing period, thus allowing a more detailed examination of these statistics, such as the number of cars offered, percentage sold and the relative revenue for each season since 1993. From this new information emerges the impact on the total turnover of cars by periods, including pre- World War II, Antique (until 1904), Veteran (1905-1918), Vintage (1919-1930) and post-Vintage (1931-1945); when combined, cars sold from these periods approximate 19% of cars sold for the season. Cars of the Classic period (1946-1964) are responsible for 41% of the total sold, post-Classic (1965-1974) equals 19%, Modern (1975-1999) adds 12% and Contemporary (built since 2000) represents 8%.

Twelve contemporary cars are represented in the overall Top 100 (two La Ferrari, four Ferrari Enzo, three McLaren P1, one Mercedes-McLaren SLR, a Pagani Huayra and one Porsche 918 Spyder), up from only five in the 2014-2015 season. This impressive growth of the contemporary segment has been cause for bewilderment and reflection. At the Bonhams auction in Monterey a La Ferrari (produced recently as one of 499 examples) achieved $3.685 million at the same time as the "former Lord Howe" Bugatti Type 51 struggled to find a new owner at $4 million. To emphasize the demand for "Instant classics", Mecum sold another example of La Ferrari for $4.7 million the following day!

Nearly half of the overall turnover is made by a few dozen cars; the 201 cars sold at auction above one million US$ are responsible for 51% of the total market turnover while the remaining 3,843 cars make up the remaining 49%. The number of cars sold above the million dollar mark have decreased for the second year in a row (from 245 in 2013-2014 and 243 last year). On the other hand, we have this year the highest number of cars sold above the threshold of $10 million.

The increase in prices of collector cars, heavily publicised by specialized and financial press, has attracted many non-specialized auction houses with an exponential number of sales, thus a further offering of cars selected by not-so-experienced consultants.

According to our usual rigorous policy, we took into account the sales promoted with a presentation of a catalogue including chassis numbers, and which had been organized by companies with a continuous and long-term presence within this field; we continue to honour auctions with a physical auction presence rather than online.

Enjoy the reading!

ADOLFO ORSI
RAFFAELE GAZZI

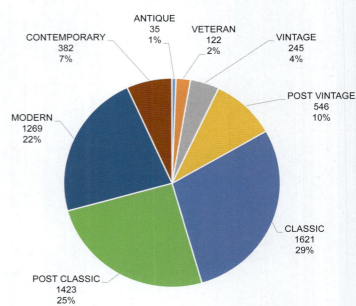

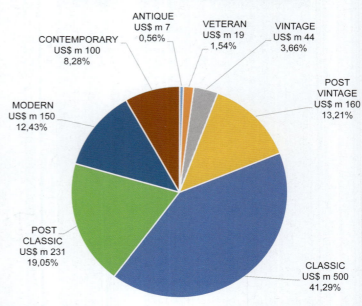

WORLD-CLASS MOTOR CARS AT BONHAMS

The Ex-Willett Brown, Vasek Polak, Fred Sebald, Richard A. Barbour, George Reilly
1956 PORSCHE 1.5-LITRE TYP 550/1500
RENNSPORT SPYDER
Sold £4,593,500 (US$6,100,000)
Goodwood Revival, September 2016

Delivered new to New York
1937 BUGATTI TYPE 57SC SPORTS TOURER
COACHWORK BY VANDEN PLAS
Sold US$8,850,000
Amelia Island, March 2016

ENQUIRIES
UK
+44 (0) 20 7468 5801
ukcars@bonhams.com

Europe
+32 (0) 476 879 471
eurocars@bonhams.com

USA
+1 212 461 6514, East Coast
+1 415 391 4000, West Coast
usacars@bonhams.com

Bonhams

bonhams.com/motorcars
Prices shown include buyer's premium. Details can be found at bonhams.com

Our database contains approximately 70,000 files regarding cars offered at the most important classic car auctions worldwide, beginning with the 1993-1994 sale season, together with a few cars offered from earlier years.

Reading each car's description (in italics), you will notice that, several times at the end of the description, there are [in brackets] references to previous offerings of the same car (auction, date and lot number and results price achieved in US$).

The following graphs give an overall view of the results achieved by a specific car in different years in an effort to provide the most meaningful data.

For a correct interpretation of the statistics, one should consider that a car offered twice at auctions in a span of several years could be in different condition with respect to the previous sale. The car could be in "better" condition, because it has been restored, or it might be "worse" because it has been damaged or not well maintained. It could also be that additional history has become known. One might also consider that the car may have been sold one or more times in different countries and customs/import taxes may have already been paid in some instances.

Last but not least, keep in mind the actual financial return to the seller. The reported price includes the buyer's commission retained by the auction house. The seller pays additional fees as well as various taxes and transportation fees. The actual sum paid to the seller is, therefore, often much lower than one might otherwise assume from the numbers reported.

1954 ALFA ROMEO 1900 C SPRINT 2° SERIE (TOURING) Chassis #AR1900C01678

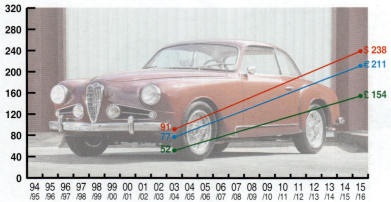

1965 ASA 1000 GT (BERTONE) Chassis #01238

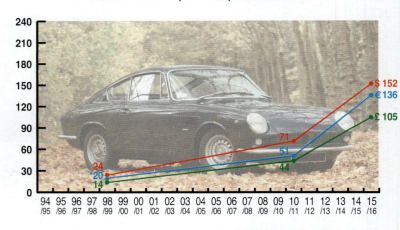

1935 ASTON MARTIN ULSTER 2/4-SEATER TOURER (BERTELLI) Chassis #D5570U

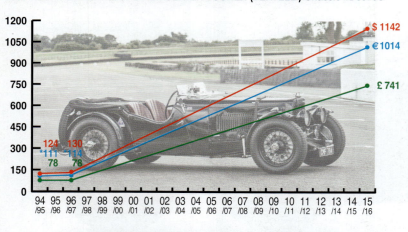

1954 ASTON MARTIN DB2/4 SPIDER (BERTONE) Chassis #LML/505

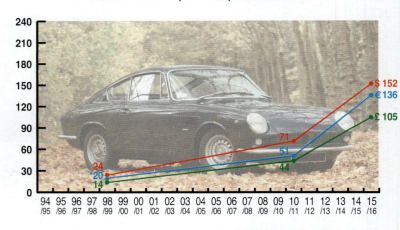

1955 ASTON MARTIN DB2/4 CABRIOLET Chassis #LML1003

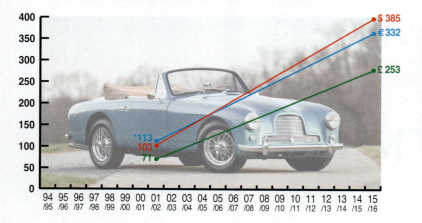

1967 AUSTIN HEALEY 3000 MkIII Chassis #HBJ8L41566

* The sale price was recorded originally in Italian Lire at the exchange rate on the day of the auction. This amount was converted later to an approximate Euro equivalent using the official value of the Lire/Euro exchange at the time of the introduction of the European Union's new currency.

CLASSIC CAR AUCTION 2015-2016 YEARBOOK

1954 BENTLEY R TYPE CONTINENTAL FASTBACK (H.J.MULLINER) Chassis #BC66LC
** Car offered but not sold. The chart shows the low estimate of the range published in the auction catalogue.

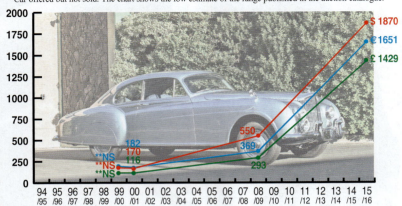

Values (thousands): $ 1870 / € 1651 / £ 1429; intermediate points 550/369/293, 182/170/116, **NS.

1960 FERRARI 250 GT CABRIOLET II SERIE (PININ FARINA) Chassis #2153GT

Values (thousands): $ 1650 / € 1513 / £ 1154; earlier points 179/167/110.

1955 JAGUAR D-TYPE Chassis #XKD501

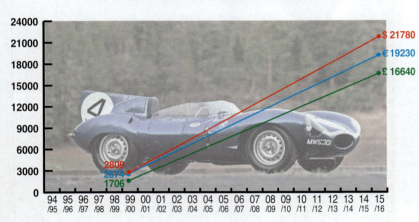

Values (thousands): $ 21780 / € 19230 / £ 16640; earlier points 2809/2674/1706.

1961 JAGUAR E-TYPE 3.8 COMPETITION ROADSTER Chassis #850007

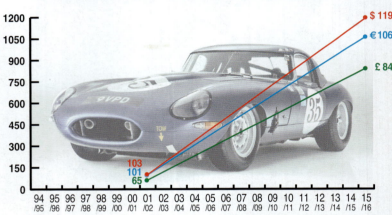

Values (thousands): $ 1191 / € 1062 / £ 840; earlier points 103/101/65.

1985 LANCIA DELTA S4 Chassis #00033

Values (thousands): $ 440 / € 388 / £ 336; earlier points 45/35/23.

1957 MASERATI A6G/54 CABRIOLET (FRUA) Chassis #2191

Values (thousands): $ 3300 / € 2914 / £ 2521; earlier points 324/289/203.

1904 MERCEDES SIMPLEX 28/32 PS REAR ENTRANCE TONNEAU Chassis #2406

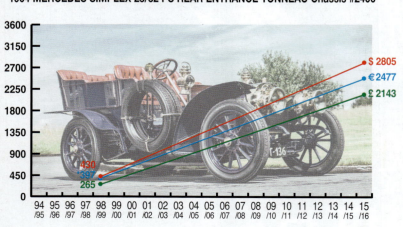

Values (thousands): $ 2805 / € 2477 / £ 2143; earlier points 430/*397/265.

1963 PORSCHE 356B 2000 GS/GT CARRERA 2 COUPÉ (REUTTER) Chassis #122561

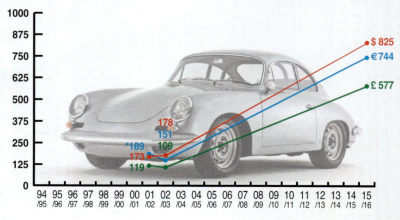

Values (thousands): $ 825 / € 744 / £ 577; earlier points 178/151/119, *189/109, 173.

20 * The sale price was recorded originally in Italian Lire at the exchange rate on the day of the auction. This amount was converted later to an approximate Euro equivalent using the official value of the Lire/Euro exchange at the time of the introduction of the European Union's new currency.

Classic Automotive Relocation Services

TRADITIONAL VALUES
MODERN THINKING

- Sea and Air Freight
- Worldwide Customs Brokerage
- Race and Rally Transportation
- International Storage
- UK and European Trucking
- UK Registration

JAPAN	LOS ANGELES	NEW YORK	EUROPE
Tel: +81 (0) 453 067 043	Tel: +1 310 695 6403	Tel: +1 516 210 6868	Tel: +44 (0) 1284 850 950
Email: info@carsjp.net	Email: info@carsusa.com	Email: info@carsusa.com	Email: info@carseurope.net
Web: www.carsjp.net	Web: www.carsusa.com	Web: www.carsusa.com	Web: www.carseurope.net

The Top 201 cars of the 2015-2016 season

This chapter is dedicated to the 201 cars which, in the sales covered in the last auction season, achieved the highest prices up to $ 1.000.000. The cars are listed in descending order according to their hammer price.

We took into consideration only the highest 100 results for the update of the usual statistics given at the end of the list, which should help one to interpret trends in the classic car market.

AUCTION RESULTS IN DESCENDING ORDER (IN US$)
2015 – 2016

No.	Year	Make	Model	Bodybuilder	Hammer price	Lot	Auction House	Date
1	1957	FERRARI	335 S	Scaglietti	35.930.639	170	Art	05-02-16
2	1956	FERRARI	290 MM	Scaglietti	28.050.000	221	RMS	10-12-15
3	1955	JAGUAR	D-Type		21.780.000	114	RMS	19-08-16
4	1939	ALFA ROMEO	8C 2900B Spider	Touring	19.800.000	234	RMS	20-08-16
5	1959	FERRARI	250 GT Spyder California lwb	Scaglietti	18.150.000	33	G&Co	20-08-16
6	1961	FERRARI	250 GT Spyder California swb	Scaglietti	17.160.000	69	G&Co	11-03-16
7	1962	ASTON MARTIN	DB4 GT	Zagato	14.300.000	215	RMS	10-12-15
8	1962	SHELBY AMERICAN	Cobra 260		13.750.000	117	RMS	19-08-16
9	1960	FERRARI	250 GT Berlinetta Competizione	P.F./Scaglietti	13.500.000	56	G&Co	20-08-16
10	1933	ALFA ROMEO	8C 2300 Monza	Brianza	11.990.000	128	G&Co	21-08-16
11	1960	FERRARI	250 GT Berlinetta Lusso	P.F./Scaglietti	11.369.635	146	H&H	14-10-15
12	1932	BUGATTI	Type 55 Roadster		10.400.000	135	G&Co	21-08-16
13	1937	MERCEDES-BENZ	540 K Spezial Roadster		9.900.000	242	RMS	29-01-16
14	1937	BUGATTI	Type 57S sports tourer	Vanden Plas	9.735.000	139	Bon	10-03-16
15	1951	FERRARI	340 America barchetta	Touring	8.261.344	232	RMS	14-05-16
16	1953	JAGUAR	C-Type		8.221.626	114	Bon	13-05-16
17	1958	FERRARI	250 GT Berlinetta TdF	P.F./Scaglietti	7.264.712	172	RMS	07-09-15
18	1950	FERRARI	166 MM/195 S Berlinetta Le Mans	Touring	6.490.000	33	G&Co	29-01-16
19	1958	FERRARI	250 GT cabriolet	Pinin Farina	5.720.000	211	RMS	10-12-15
20	1956	FERRARI	250 GT Berlinetta TdF	P.F./Scaglietti	5.720.000	232	RMS	20-08-16
21	1950	FERRARI	166 MM Berlinetta	Touring/Zagato	5.445.000	68	G&Co	20-08-16
22	1955	PORSCHE	550 Spyder	Wendler	5.335.000	34	G&Co	11-03-16
23	1955	FERRARI	750 Monza	Scaglietti	5.225.000	127	RMS	19-08-16
24	1979	PORSCHE	935 Turbo		4.840.000	60	G&Co	20-08-16
25	2014	FERRARI	LaFerrari	Ferrari Styling	4.700.000	S110	Mec	20-08-16
26	1962	FERRARI	400 Superamerica coupé	Pininfarina	4.400.000	163	RMS	12-03-16
27	1966	FORD	GT40		4.400.000	S103	Mec	20-08-16
28	1931	BUGATTI	Type 51		4.000.000	36	Bon	19-08-16
29	1933	PIERCE-ARROW	Silver Arrow		3.740.000	214	RMS	10-12-15
30	1972	MASERATI	Boomerang	Italdesign	3.714.523	11	Bon	05-09-15
31	2014	FERRARI	LaFerrari	Ferrari Styling	3.685.000	95	Bon	19-08-16
32	1967	FERRARI	330 GTC Speciale	Pininfarina	3.410.000	145	G&Co	30-01-16
33	1967	FERRARI	275 GTB4	PF/Scaglietti	3.324.757	145	H&H	14-10-15
34	2003	FERRARI	Enzo	Pininfarina	3.300.000	219	RMS	10-12-15
35	1953	FERRARI	250 Europa coupé	Vignale	3.300.000	216	RMS	10-12-15
36	1966	FORD	GT40		3.300.000	62	G&Co	11-03-16

No.	Year	Make	Model	Bodybuilder	Hammer Price	Lot	Auction House	Date
37	1957	MASERATI	A6G/54 cabriolet	Frua	3.300.000	130	G&Co	21-08-16
38	1967	FERRARI	275 GTB4	PF/Scaglietti	3.245.000	40	G&Co	20-08-16
39	1962	FERRARI	400 Superamerica coupé	Pininfarina	3.225.235	152	RMS	03-02-16
40	1997	PORSCHE	GT1 Evolution		3.145.666	261	RMS	14-05-16
41	1954	ASTON MARTIN	DB2/4 spider	Bertone	3.080.000	138	G&Co	21-08-16
42	1955	PORSCHE	550 Spyder	Wendler	3.000.015	143	RMS	03-02-16
43	1929	DUESENBERG	Model J torpedo convertible	Murphy	3.000.000	133	RMS	28-01-16
44	1973	PORSCHE	917/30 CanAm spyder		3.000.000	44	G&Co	11-03-16
45	2003	FERRARI	Enzo	Pininfarina	3.000.000	S108.1	Mec	20-08-16
46	1937	MERCEDES-BENZ	540 K cabriolet A		2.970.000	167	Bon	10-03-16
47	1966	FORD	GT40		2.900.000	125	RMS	19-08-16
48	2003	FERRARI	Enzo	Pininfarina	2.860.000	122	G&Co	30-01-16
49	1959	PORSCHE	718 RSK		2.860.000	48	G&Co	11-03-16
50	1904	MERCEDES	Simplex 28/32 PS rear entrance		2.805.000	27	Bon	19-08-16
51	1967	FERRARI	275 GTB4	PF/Scaglietti	2.750.000	123	Bon	10-03-16
52	1964	FERRARI	500 Superfast	Pininfarina	2.750.000	243	RMS	20-08-16
53	1970	PLYMOUTH	'Cuda convertible		2.675.000	F109	Mec	23-01-16
54	1930	DUESENBERG	Model J roadster	Murphy	2.664.838	14	Bon	26-09-15
55	1931	DUESENBERG	Model J convertible	Murphy	2.640.000	22	G&Co	11-03-16
56	2009	MERCEDES-BENZ	SLR McLaren Stirling Moss roadster		2.594.170	122	Bon	19-03-16
57	1984	FERRARI	GTO	PF/Scaglietti	2.585.000	148	RMS	12-03-16
58	1968	FERRARI	330 GTS	Pininfarina	2.502.500	146	G&Co	21-08-16
59	1972	LAMBORGHINI	Miura SV	Bertone	2.420.000	202	RMS	10-12-15
60	1929	DUESENBERG	Model J dual cowl phaeton	LeBaron	2.420.000	51	G&Co	29-01-16
61	1985	FERRARI	GTO	PF/Scaglietti	2.420.000	119	G&Co	21-08-16
62	1995	FERRARI	F50	Pininfarina	2.400.000	126	G&Co	30-01-16
63	1973	FERRARI	365 GTS4 Daytona spider	P.F./Scaglietti	2.365.000	229	RMS	20-08-16
64	1966	FERRARI	275 GTB	PF/Scaglietti	2.319.642*	335	Bon	04-02-16
65	1974	PORSCHE	Carrera RSR 3.0		2.310.000	36	G&Co	11-03-16
66	1995	FERRARI	F50	Pininfarina	2.310.000	64	G&Co	11-03-16
67	1971	PLYMOUTH	'Cuda convertible		2.300.000	F102	Mec	23-01-16
68	1965	SHELBY AMERICAN	Cobra 427 Competition		2.255.000	140	RMS	28-01-16
69	1971	LAMBORGHINI	Miura SV	Bertone	2.255.000	22	G&Co	20-08-16
70	1957	BMW	507 roadster		2.204.093	150	RMS	03-02-16
71	1965	FERRARI	275 GTB	PF/Scaglietti	2.117.500	145	RMS	28-01-16
72	1985	FERRARI	GTO	PF/Scaglietti	2.112.000	77	Bon	19-08-16
73	2015	McLAREN	P1		2.090.000	12	Bon	28-01-16
74	2014	McLAREN	P1		2.090.000	24	Bon	19-08-16
75	1963	FERRARI	250 GT/L	PF/Scaglietti	2.090.000	224	RMS	20-08-16
76	1930	PACKARD	Eight 734 Speedster Runabout		2.090.000	30	G&Co	20-08-16
77	1985	FERRARI	GTO	PF/Scaglietti	2.061.932	110	Bon	13-05-16
78	2014	PAGANI	Huayra		2.035.000	164	RMS	12-03-16
79	1966	FERRARI	275 GTS	PF/Scaglietti	2.033.562	243	RMS	14-05-16
80	1955	LANCIA	Aurelia B24 spider	Pinin Farina	2.007.500	35	G&Co	20-08-16
81	1971	LAMBORGHINI	Miura SV	Bertone	2.000.000	132	RMS	28-01-16
82	1968	FERRARI	330 GTS	Pininfarina	2.000.000	139	RMS	12-03-16
83	1995	FERRARI	F50	Pininfarina	1.952.500	1085	AA	25-06-16
84	1964	FERRARI	250 GT/L	PF/Scaglietti	1.880.278	162	RMS	07-09-15
85	1963	FERRARI	250 GT/L	PF/Scaglietti	1.875.000	71	G&Co	11-03-16
86	1954	BENTLEY	R Type Continental fastback	H.J.Mulliner	1.870.000	145	RMS	19-08-16
87	1934	MERCEDES-BENZ	500 K cabriolet A		1.870.000	242	RMS	20-08-16
88	2014	McLAREN	P1		1.850.000	S81	Mec	20-08-16
89	1955	CHEVROLET	Corvette V8 roadster		1.815.000	1351	B/J	29-01-16
90	1954	BENTLEY	R Type Continental fastback	H.J.Mulliner	1.815.000	147	RMS	12-03-16
91	1964	PORSCHE	356SC cabriolet	Reutter	1.760.000	206	RMS	10-12-15

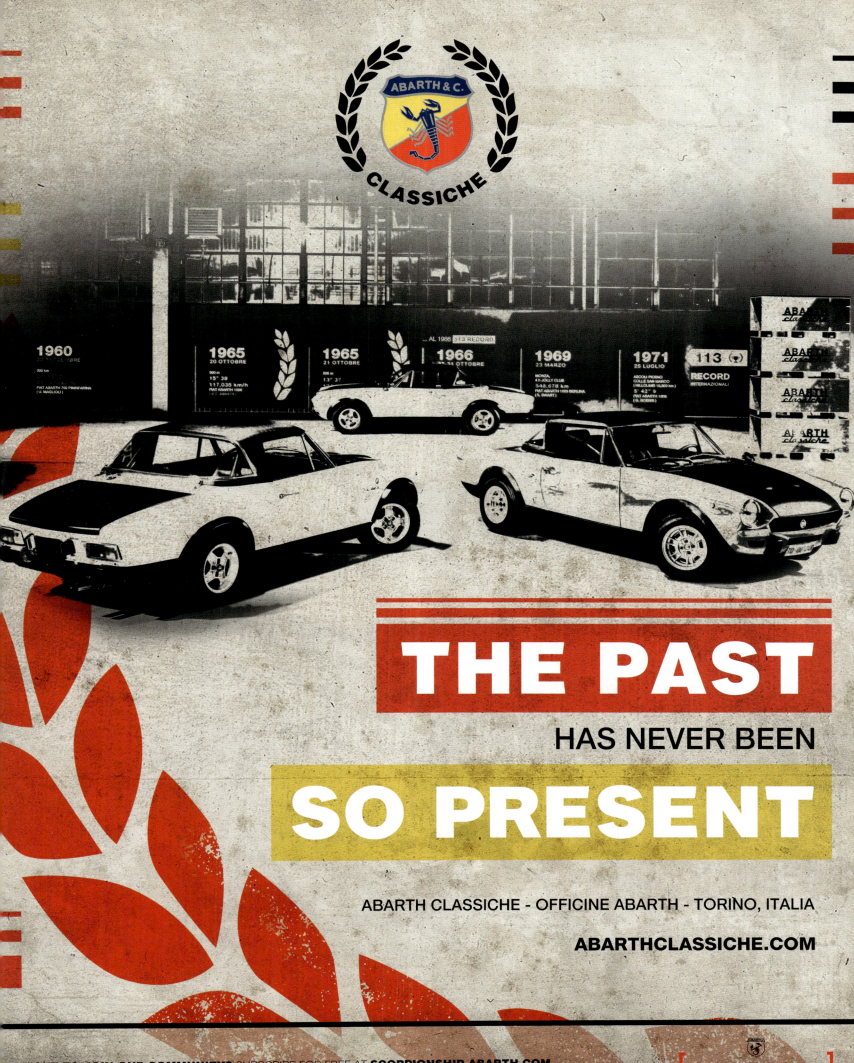

No.	Year	Make	Model	Bodybuilder	Hammer price	Lot	Auction House	Date
92	2015	PORSCHE	918 Spyder		1.760.000	1392	B/J	29-01-16
93	1965	FERRARI	275 GTS	PF/Scaglietti	1.760.000	232	RMS	29-01-16
94	1932	ROLLS-ROYCE	Phantom II Continental Berline	Figoni/Falaschi	1.760.000	125	G&Co	21-08-16
95	1965	FERRARI	275 GTB	PF/Scaglietti	1.732.500	112	RMS	19-08-16
96	2004	FERRARI	Enzo	Pininfarina	1.714.294	138	RMS	03-02-16
97	1932	BENTLEY	8l tourer	Vanden Plas	1.705.000	121	RMS	19-08-16
98	1965	ASTON MARTIN	DB5 convertible	Touring/Tickford	1.677.868	345	Bon	12-09-15
99	1961	MASERATI	5000 GT Indianapolis	Allemano	1.677.500	48	G&Co	20-08-16
100	**1963**	**ASTON MARTIN**	**DB4 cabriolet**	**Touring/Tickford**	**1.650.279**	**157**	**Art**	**05-02-16**
101	1954	SIATA	208S spider	Motto	1.650.000	227	RMS	10-12-15
102	1970	DODGE	Challenger R/T convertible		1.650.000	F111	Mec	23-01-16
103	1960	FERRARI	250 GT cabriolet II serie	Pinin Farina	1.650.000	149	RMS	28-01-16
104	1990	PORSCHE	962C		1.650.000	38	G&Co	11-03-16
105	2015	PORSCHE	918 Spyder		1.595.000	148	RMS	28-01-16
106	1962	MASERATI	5000 GT	Allemano	1.540.000	126	RMS	28-01-16
107	1958	PORSCHE	356A 1500 GS/GT Carrera	Reutter	1.540.000	46	G&Co	11-03-16
108	1929	DUESENBERG	Model J convertible	Murphy	1.540.000	155	RMS	30-07-16
109	1990	FERRARI	F40	Pininfarina	1.534.500	120	G&Co	30-01-16
110	1948	TUCKER	Model 48 Torpedo		1.525.171	266	RMS	14-05-16
111	1960	FERRARI	250 GT cabriolet II serie	Pinin Farina	1.512.500	20	G&Co	11-03-16
112	1960	FERRARI	250 GT cabriolet II serie	Pinin Farina	1.500.000	108	G&Co	21-08-16
113	1971	MASERATI	Ghibli SS Spider	Ghia	1.500.000	115	G&Co	21-08-16
114	1962	MERCEDES-BENZ	300 SL Roadster		1.485.000	21	Bon	28-01-16
115	1939	MERCEDES-BENZ	540 K cabriolet A		1.485.000	1376	B/J	29-01-16
116	1956	FERRARI	250 GT coupé	Boano	1.485.000	132	G&Co	21-08-16
117	1963	ASTON MARTIN	DB4 Vantage cabriolet	Touring/Tickford	1.470.640	209	Bon	21-05-16
118	1930	CADILLAC	Series 452 V-16 roadster	Fleetwood	1.457.500	220	RMS	20-08-16
119	1977	PORSCHE	935 Turbo		1.440.871	175	Art	09-07-16
120	1934	DELAGE	Type D8 S cabriolet	Fernandez/Darrin	1.430.000	228	RMS	10-12-15
121	1953	CADILLAC	62 coupé Ghia		1.430.000	254	RMS	29-01-16
122	2005	MASERATI	MC12		1.430.000	211	RMS	20-08-16
123	1955	MERCEDES-BENZ	300 SL gullwing		1.430.000	14	G&Co	20-08-16
124	1929	DUESENBERG	Model J convertible	Murphy	1.402.500	5142	AA	05-09-15
125	1939	SS	Jaguar 100 2.5l roadster	Van den Plas	1.402.500	231	RMS	29-01-16
126	1955	LANCIA	Aurelia B24 spider	Pinin Farina	1.402.500	44	Bon	19-08-16
127	1914	MERCEDES	28/95 PS skiff		1.401.189	28	Bon	26-09-15
128	1955	MERCEDES-BENZ	300 SL gullwing		1.398.074	224	RMS	14-05-16
129	1997	FERRARI	F50	Pininfarina	1.393.958	141	RMS	03-02-16
130	1965	SHELBY AMERICAN	Cobra 427		1.375.000*	119	RMS	19-08-16
131	1968	ASTON MARTIN	DB6 Volante Vantage		1.370.430	211	SiC	04-09-15
132	1938	BUGATTI	Type 57 cabriolet	D'Ieteren	1.347.698	17	Bon	05-09-15
133	1952	FERRARI	212 Inter cabriolet	Vignale	1.334.525	262	RMS	14-05-16
134	1964	SHELBY AMERICAN	Cobra 289		1.320.000	14	G&Co	11-03-16
135	1931	DUESENBERG	Model J Tourster	Derham	1.320.000	222	RMS	20-08-16
136	1957	MERCEDES-BENZ	300 SL Roadster		1.320.000	228	RMS	20-08-16
137	1988	PORSCHE	959		1.320.000	19	G&Co	20-08-16
138	1992	FERRARI	F40	Pininfarina	1.290.555	168	RMS	07-09-15
139	1955	MERCEDES-BENZ	300 SL gullwing		1.285.721	151	RMS	03-02-16
140	1958	MERCEDES-BENZ	300 SL Roadster		1.265.000	239	RMS	29-01-16
141	1955	MERCEDES-BENZ	300 SL gullwing		1.265.000	161	RMS	12-03-16
142	1990	FERRARI	F40	Pininfarina	1.265.000	239	RMS	20-08-16
143	1930	DUESENBERG	Model J town cabriolet	Murphy	1.254.000	64	Bon	19-08-16
144	1988	PORSCHE	959		1.250.000	1100	AA	25-06-16
145	1960	MERCEDES-BENZ	300 SL Roadster		1.237.500	153	G&Co	21-08-16
146	1955	MERCEDES-BENZ	300 SL gullwing		1.219.081	16	Bon	20-03-16

No.	Year	Make	Model	Bodybuilder	Hammer price	Lot	Auction House	Date
147	1952	CUNNINGHAM	C-3 coupé	Vignale	1.210.000	229	RMS	29-01-16
148	1932	PACKARD	Twin Six 905 roadster		1.210.000	118	RMS	12-03-16
149	1931	MARMON	V-16 convertible	LeBaron	1.210.000	117	G&Co	21-08-16
150	1975	LAMBORGHINI	Countach LP400	Bertone	1.201.751	148	Art	05-02-16
151	1925	BUGATTI	Type 35		1.200.618	118	Bon	13-05-16
152	1991	BENETTON	B191/191B		1.200.618*	106	Bon	13-05-16
153	1965	ASTON MARTIN	DB5 Vantage coupé	Touring/Tickford	1.196.541	170	RMS	07-09-15
154	1961	JAGUAR	E-Type 3.8 Competition roadster		1.191.120	96	H&H	20-04-16
155	1937	LAGONDA	LG45 Rapide tourer		1.189.168	021	Bon	06-12-15
156	2011	FERRARI	SA Aperta	Ferrari & PF	1.182.500	138	RMS	28-01-16
157	1964	ASTON MARTIN	DB5 convertible	Touring/Tickford	1.176.949	232	Bon	21-05-16
158	1965	ASTON MARTIN	DB5 Vantage coupé	Touring/Tickford	1.176.949	206	Bon	21-05-16
159	1965	BENTLEY	Continental S3 Flying Spur	Mulliner,Park Ward	1.176.929	366	Bon	12-09-15
160	1971	FERRARI	365 GTB4 Daytona	PF/Scaglietti	1.155.000	62	Bon	28-01-16
161	1955	MERCEDES-BENZ	300 SL gullwing		1.155.000	117	RMS	28-01-16
162	1959	MERCEDES-BENZ	300 SL Roadster		1.155.000	131	G&Co	30-01-16
163	1963	SHELBY AMERICAN	Cobra 289		1.155.000	179	RMS	12-03-16
164	1989	FERRARI	F40	Pininfarina	1.155.000	90	Bon	19-08-16
165	1955	MERCEDES-BENZ	300 SL gullwing		1.155.000	7200	R&S	20-08-16
166	1963	SHELBY AMERICAN	Cobra 289		1.149.632	339	Dor	17-10-15
167	1935	ASTON MARTIN	Ulster 2/4-seater tourer	Bertelli	1.142.382	365	Bon	12-09-15
168	1935	MERCEDES-BENZ	500 K cabriolet C/spezial roadster		1.134.705	16	Bon	26-09-15
169	1986	FERRARI	Testarossa Spider	Pininfarina	1.133.732	116	Art	05-02-16
170	1989	FERRARI	F40	Pininfarina	1.132.659	145	RMS	03-02-16
171	1988	PORSCHE	959		1.120.000	56	G&Co	11-03-16
172	1914	ROLLS-ROYCE	Silver Ghost skiff	Schebera/Shapiro	1.117.513	20	Bon	26-09-15
173	1937	MAYBACH	SW38 roadster		1.117.513	23	Bon	26-09-15
174	1953	FERRARI	212 Inter coupé	Vignale	1.100.000	227	RMS	29-01-16
175	1931	STUTZ	Model DV-32 convertible victoria	Rollston	1.100.000	132	RMS	12-03-16
176	1967	SHELBY AMERICAN	Cobra 427		1.100.000	F124	Mec	20-05-16
177	1994	PORSCHE	Turbo 3.6 S slantnose coupé		1.100.000	45	G&Co	20-08-16
178	1927	BENTLEY	6½l tourer		1.074.531	8	Bon	26-09-15
179	1956	MERCEDES-BENZ	300 Sc roadster		1.072.500	220	RMS	10-12-15
180	1964	SHELBY AMERICAN	Cobra 289		1.072.500	219	RMS	29-01-16
181	1938	MAYBACH	SW38 roadster	Spohn	1.072.500	148	RMS	19-08-16
182	1937	MERCEDES-BENZ	540 K cabriolet C		1.072.500	150	G&Co	21-08-16
183	1972	FERRARI	365 GTB4 Daytona	PF/Scaglietti	1.068.223	169	Art	05-02-16
184	1929	BENTLEY	4½l sports saloon	H.J.Mulliner	1.059.647	171	Bon	05-09-15
185	1961	MERCEDES-BENZ	300 SL Roadster		1.055.635	164	Art	09-07-16
186	1995	BUGATTI AUTOMOBILI	EB110 SS		1.054.870	212	Art	05-02-16
187	2011	FERRARI	SA Aperta	Ferrari & PF	1.050.000	S82	Mec	20-08-16
188	1954	MERCEDES-BENZ	300 SL gullwing		1.045.000	128	RMS	19-08-16
189	1995	BUGATTI AUTOMOBILI	EB110 SS		1.041.517	211	Art	05-02-16
190	1959	SCARAB	F1		1.038.739	330	Bon	12-09-15
191	1955	BENTLEY	R Type Continental fastback	H.J.Mulliner	1.017.500	137	G&Co	30-01-16
192	1994	PORSCHE	Turbo 3.6 S slantnose coupé		1.017.500	45	G&Co	11-03-16
193	1914	MARMON	Model 41 speedster		1.017.500	54	G&Co	20-08-16
194	1988	PORSCHE	959		1.016.781	253	RMS	14-05-16
195	1956	FIAT	642 car transporter	Bartoletti	1.012.828	333	Bon	12-09-15
196	2011	FERRARI	SA Aperta	Ferrari & PF	1.012.638	39	Bon	09-10-15
197	1948	ALFA ROMEO	6C 2500 SS cabriolet	Stabilimenti Farina	1.012.000	29	G&Co	29-01-16
198	1929	BENTLEY	4½l tourer	Vanden Plas	1.011.134	006	Bon	06-12-15
199	1932	MASERATI	8C 3000		1.001.000	175	Bon	10-03-16
200	1964	SHELBY AMERICAN	Cobra 289		1.000.000	F163	Mec	20-05-16
201	2006	BUGATTI	Veyron 16.4		1.000.000	S91	Mec	20-08-16

STATISTICS FOR MAKES AND COUNTRIES
(of the Top 100 year by year)

Makes	2015/16	14/15	13/14	12/13	11/12	10/11	09/10	08/09	07/08	06/07	05/06	04/05	03/04	02/03	01/02	00/01	99/00	98/99	97/98	96/97	95/96	94/95	93/94
Ferrari	45	52	48	33	37	37	25	31	33	22	21	25	22	19	26	31	45	28	17	26	21	11	6
Porsche	9	6	5	3	9	3	1	2	2	2	3	2	1	4	=	6	5	3	6	=	3	=	=
Aston Martin	4	4	5	3	3	5	8	=	3	5	1	2	3	5	1	1	2	1	3	1	3	2	3
Duesenberg	4	2	2	9	5	6	10	10	8	8	9	5	7	1	9	6	3	2	2	2	=	3	=
Mercedes-Benz	4	4	7	9	10	8	8	4	10	5	6	9	11	17	13	7	7	8	12	11	11	8	12
Bentley	3	1	1	4	4	1	5	2	3	3	4	5	6	5	4	1	3	2	8	11	7	16	8
Bugatti	3	2	4	3	2	3	6	10	2	6	3	2	6	4	7	7	4	4	7	6	9	3	3
Ford (USA)	3	=	3	5	=	1	=	2	2	=	4	2	2	5	2	=	1	5	4	=	=	=	=
Lamborghini	3	4	1	1	1	7	1	1	2	=	=	=	1	1	=	=	=	=	1	2	1	=	=
Maserati	3	2	3	5	=	3	1	1	2	3	3	5	5	3	5	8	4	4	1	6	5	5	=
McLaren	3	3	2	=	=	1	=	1	=	1	=	=	1	1	=	=	2	2	2	=	=	=	=
Alfa Romeo	2	1	3	4	4	3	6	4	5	3	1	1	2	2	4	2	3	5	6	2	4	3	1
Jaguar	2	4	3	1	=	1	2	1	1	2	4	1	=	4	2	5	5	5	3	=	1	3	7
Plymouth	2	1	1	1	=	1	=	=	=	1	4	=	=	=	=	1	=	=	=	=	=	=	=
Shelby American	2	3	=	4	1	1	4	4	1	5	9	5	=	1	1	1	1	4	3	=	3	3	1
BMW	1	=	2	=	3	1	1	=	1	=	=	2	=	=	=	=	=	1	2	=	=	=	5
Chevrolet	1	=	3	=	=	1	1	3	1	=	5	1	=	=	=	1	=	=	1	=	=	=	=
Lancia	1	1	=	=	=	=	=	=	=	=	=	2	=	=	=	=	=	=	=	1	=	=	=
Mercedes	1	=	=	=	1	=	=	1	=	1	1	1	=	1	1	1	=	=	1	=	=	=	=
Packard	1	3	=	=	=	3	1	=	2	6	2	2	2	=	3	2	1	3	1	1	=	1	1
Pagani	1	=	=	=	=	1	=	1	=	=	=	=	=	=	=	=	=	=	=	=	=	=	=
Pierce-Arrow	1	=	=	=	1	=	=	=	=	=	=	2	=	=	2	=	=	=	=	=	1	=	=
Rolls-Royce	1	=	1	1	2	1	8	4	13	4	1	1	7	3	4	5	3	3	6	6	16	10	14
Cadillac		1	=	=	1	=	=	=	=	1	2	1	1	3	4	1	1	1	=	=	1	5	3
General Motors		1	=	=	=	=	=	=	=	=	1	=	=	=	=	=	=	=	=	=	=	=	=
Lagonda		1	=	1	=	=	1	1	=	=	=	1	=	3	=	1	=	=	=	=	1	=	3	1
OM		1	=	=	=	=	=	=	=	=	=	=	=	=	=	=	=	=	=	=	=	=	=
Pontiac		1	=	=	=	=	=	=	=	1	=	=	=	=	=	=	=	=	=	=	=	=	=
Talbot (GB)		1	=	=	=	=	=	=	=	=	=	=	=	=	=	=	=	=	=	=	=	=	=
Talbot-Lago		1	1	3	=	3	1	2	=	1	5	=	2	=	1	=	1	=	1	=	1	2	3	=	1
Delahaye			2	1	=	3	1	=	=	4	=	=	1	=	1	1	2	1	1	2	=	2	5
Commer			1	=	=	=	=	=	=	=	=	=	=	=	=	=	=	=	=	=	=	=	=
Mercer			1	=	=	=	=	=	=	=	1	=	1	1	1	=	=	1	=	=	=	1	=
Tucker			1	=	2	1	=	1	=	=	=	1	1	=	=	=	=	=	=	=	=	=	=
Chrysler				1	1	1	1	=	1	=	3	3	3	1	=	=	1	1	=	2	=	2	=
Daimler				1	1	=	=	1	=	=	=	=	=	=	=	=	=	=	=	=	=	=	=
FIAT				1	2	1	=	=	=	=	=	=	=	=	=	=	=	=	=	=	=	1	=
Horch				1	=	=	=	1	=	=	=	2	=	=	=	=	=	=	=	=	=	=	3
Isotta Fraschini				1	1	=	=	2	=	=	1	=	=	=	1	1	=	=	=	1	=	1	2
Lincoln				1	=	=	=	=	=	1	1	1	=	=	=	=	=	1	=	1	=	1	1
Maybach				1	=	=	=	=	=	=	=	=	=	=	=	=	=	1	=	=	=	=	=
Simplex				1	=	=	=	=	1	=	1	=	2	=	1	=	=	=	=	=	=	=	=
Stutz				1	=	=	=	1	=	=	1	1	1	=	1	=	=	=	3	=	=	=
Austin Healey					1	=	=	=	=	=	=	1	=	=	=	=	=	=	=	=	=	=	=
Cord					1	=	=	1	=	=	=	1	=	=	=	=	=	=	=	=	1	=	=
De Dion-Bouton					1	=	=	=	1	1	=	=	=	=	=	=	=	=	=	=	=	=	=
DeSoto					1	=	=	=	=	=	=	=	=	=	=	=	=	=	=	=	=	=	=
Itala					1	=	=	=	=	=	=	=	=	=	=	=	=	=	=	=	=	=	=
Miller					1	=	=	=	1	=	=	=	1	=	=	=	=	=	=	=	=	=	=
Oldsmobile					1	=	=	=	1	=	1	=	=	=	=	1	=	=	=	=	=	=	=
Peugeot					1	1	1	=	1	1	=	=	=	=	=	1	=	1	=	=	=	=	=
SIATA					1	=	=	=	=	=	=	1	=	=	=	1	=	=	=	=	=	=	=
SS						1	=	=	=	=	=	=	=	=	=	=	=	=	=	2	3	1	1	1
Hispano-Suiza							2	1	=	=	2	1	1	=	=	=	=	=	=	=	2	1	1	4
Voisin							2	=	=	=	=	=	=	=	=	=	=	=	=	=	=	=	=	=
Delage							1	1	2	=	=	1	=	1	=	=	=	1	=	=	=	=	2	2
Dodge							1	1	1	2	1	=	=	=	=	=	=	=	=	=	=	=	=
Lister							1	=	=	=	=	1	=	=	1	1	=	=	=	=	=	1	1	=
Lotus								1	=	1	=	=	=	=	=	=	=	=	=	1	2	=	1	=
Matra								1	=	=	=	3	=	=	=	=	=	=	1	1	1	=	=	=
Rambler								1	=	=	=	=	=	=	=	=	=	=	=	=	=	=	=	=
Sunbeam								1	=	=	=	=	=	1	=	=	=	=	=	=	=	=	=	=
Thomas								1	=	=	=	=	=	=	=	=	=	=	=	=	=	=	=	=
Marmon									1	=	=	1	=	=	=	=	=	=	=	=	=	=	=
Reo									1	=	=	=	=	=	=	=	=	=	=	=	=	=	=	=
American Napier										1	=	=	=	=	=	=	=	=	=	=	=	=	=	=
Cooper										1	=	=	=	=	1	=	=	=	=	1	=	1	=	=

Makes	2015/16	14/15	13/14	12/13	11/12	10/11	09/10	08/09	07/08	06/07	05/06	04/05	03/04	02/03	01/02	00/01	99/00	98/99	97/98	96/97	95/96	94/95	93/94
Hummer										1	=	=	=	=	=	=	=	=	=	=	=	=	=
Kurtis										1	=	=	=	=	=	=	=	=	=	=	=	=	=
Lozier										1	=	=	=	=	=	1	=	=	=	=	=	=	=
Panhard et Levassor										1	=	=	=	=	=	=	=	1	=	=	=	=	=
Pope-Hartford										1	=	=	=	=	=	1	=	=	=	=	=	=	=
Renault										1	=	=	=	=	=	=	=	=	=	=	=	=	=
Chaparral									1	1	=	=	=	=	=	=	=	=	=	=	=	=	=
Auburn									2	=	=	1	=	=	=	=	=	=	=	=	=	1	1
OSCA									2	=	=	1	=	=	=	=	=	=	=	=	=	=	=
Bizzarrini								1	1	=	=	1	=	=	1	=	=	=	=	=	=	=	=
Buick								1	=	=	=	=	=	=	=	=	=	=	=	=	1	=	=
Farman								1	=	=	=	=	=	=	=	=	=	=	=	=	=	=	=
Invicta								1	1	=	=	1	2	1	2	1	1	=	=	=	=	=	=
American Underslung								1	=	=	=	=	=	=	=	=	=	=	=	=	=	=	=
Austro Daimler								1	=	=	=	=	=	=	=	=	=	=	=	=	=	=	=
Porsche-Kremer								1	=	=	=	=	=	=	=	=	=	=	=	=	=	=	=
Mors								2	=	=	=	2	=	=	=	=	=	=	=	=	=	=	=
Abarth								1	=	=	=	=	=	=	=	=	=	=	=	=	=	=	=
Alco								1	=	=	=	=	=	=	=	=	=	=	=	=	=	=	=
Benz								1	=	=	=	=	=	=	=	=	=	=	=	=	=	=	=
Charron								1	=	=	=	=	=	=	=	=	=	=	=	=	=	=	=
Eagle								1	=	=	=	=	=	=	=	=	=	=	=	=	=	=	=
Martini								1	=	=	=	=	=	=	=	=	=	=	=	=	=	=	=
Nardi Danese								1	=	=	=	=	=	=	=	=	=	=	=	=	=	=	=
Ghia									2	=	=	=	=	=	=	=	=	=	=	=	=	=	=
ERA									1	=	=	1	=	=	=	=	=	=	=	=	=	=	=
Mercury									1	=	=	=	=	=	=	=	=	=	=	=	=	=	=
Prost									1	=	=	=	=	=	=	=	=	=	=	=	=	=	=
Saleen									1	=	=	=	=	=	=	=	=	=	=	=	=	=	=
Watson									1	=	=	=	=	=	=	=	=	=	=	=	=	=	=
Frazer-Nash										1	=	1	=	=	1	1	2						
BRM										1	=	=	=	=	1	1							
Du Pont										3	=	=	=	=	=	=							
HWM										1	=	1	=	=	=								
Lola										1	1	=	=	=	=								
MG										1	=	1	=	=	=								
Vanwall										1	=	=	=	=	=								
Minerva											1	=	=	=	=								
Tyrrell											1	=	=	=	=								
Connaught												1	=	=	=								
Gordini												1	=	=	=								
Stevens-Duryea												1	=	=	=								
Vauxhall													3	1	=								
Spyker													1	=	=								
Cisitalia													1	=									
Columbia													1	=									
Locomobile													1	1									
Rochette													1	=									
Amilcar														2									
Alphi														1									
Audi														1									
Chenard-Walcker														1									
Darracq														1									
De Dietrich														1									
Guyot														1									
Star													1										
Wanderer														1									

Countries	2015/16	14/15	13/14	12/13	11/12	10/11	09/10	08/09	07/08	06/07	05/06	04/05	03/04	02/03	01/02	00/01	99/00	98/99	97/98	96/97	95/96	94/95	93/94
Italy	55	61	55	45	47	53	33	40	42	28	26	36	32	27	39	43	52	38	26	37	32	22	11
Germany	15	10	14	14	23	12	10	8	13	8	10	14	13	25	14	14	13	11	20	14	14	8	22
USA	14	12	11	23	15	15	18	25	20	32	34	25	23	16	22	18	7	17	8	10	2	18	6
Great Britain	13	14	11	11	11	10	25	12	20	17	19	17	21	23	14	17	19	25	34	26	38	43	39
France	3	3	9	7	4	10	14	15	5	15	11	8	10	8	11	8	9	9	11	13	13	9	22
Austria														1	=	=	=	=	=	=	=	=	=
Switzerland														1	=	=	=	=	=	=	=	=	=
Belgium																		1	=	=	=	=	=
Holland																					1	=	=

STATISTICS FOR PERIOD OF MANUFACTURING FROM 1993
(PERCENTAGE OF SALE, CARS OFFERED, TURNOVER)

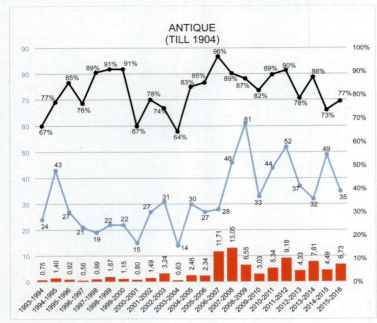

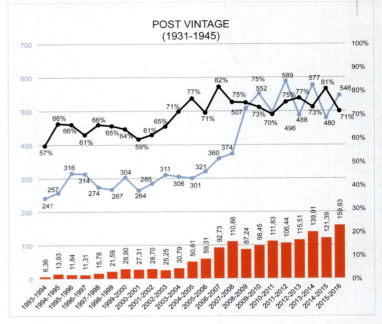

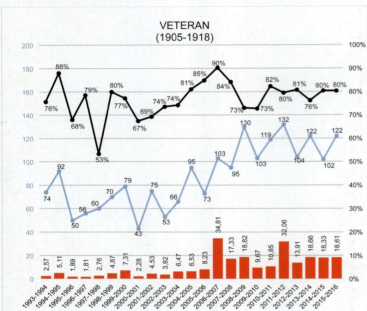

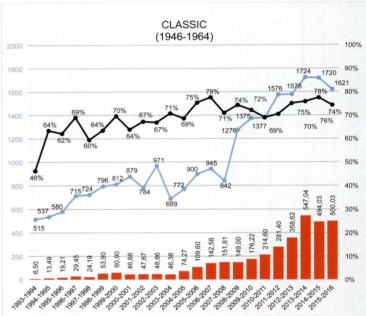

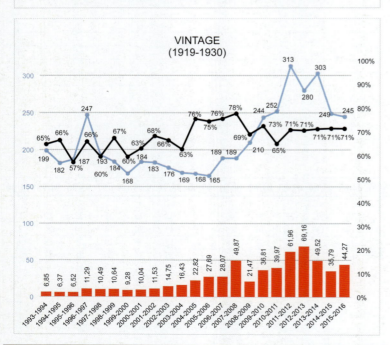

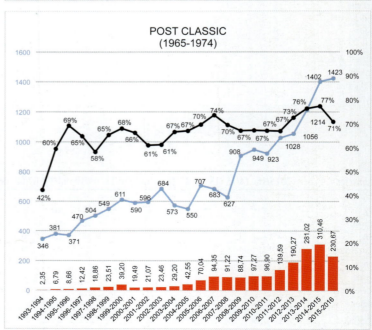

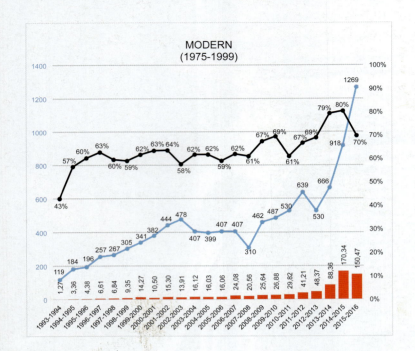
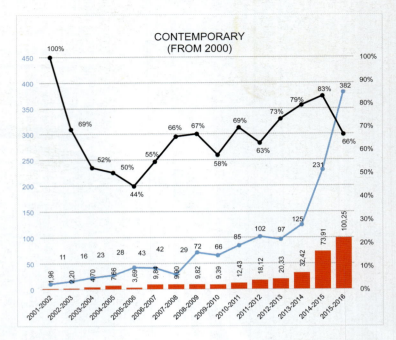

HAMMER PRICES

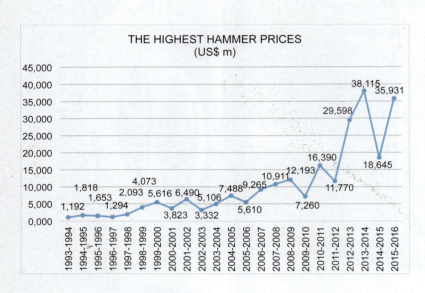
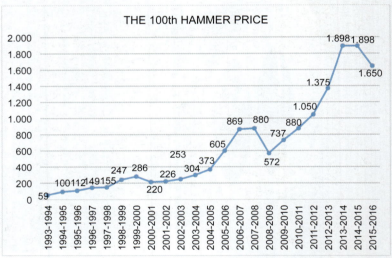
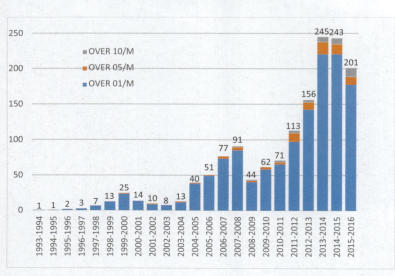
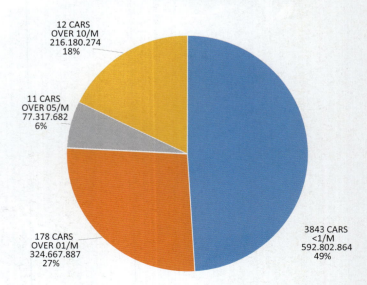

STATISTICS FOR MAKE

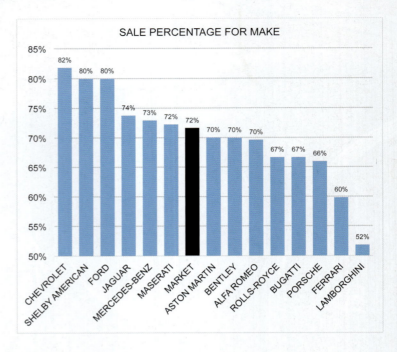

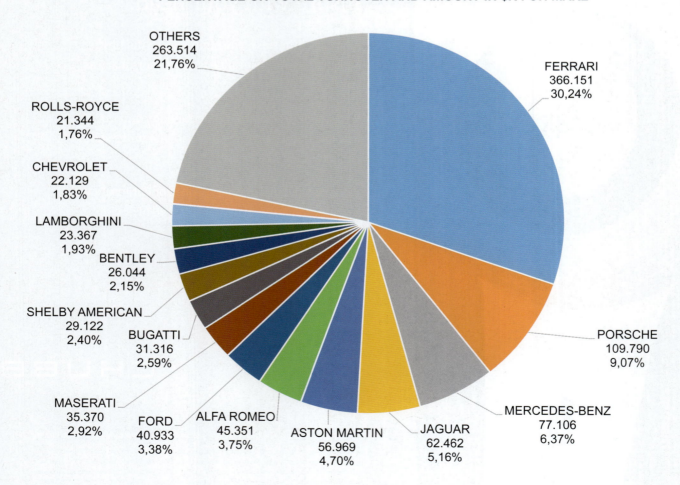

MOTORCARS OF RARITY
AND QUALITY WITHOUT COMPROMISE.
BECAUSE TRUST MATTERS.

OPUS
THE COLLECTION

WWW.OPUSCLASSICS.COM

STATISTICS FOR MAKE FROM 1993-1994
(NUMBER OF CARS OFFERED AND SOLD, PERCENTAGES, TURNOVER AND AVERAGE VALUE)

Season	Make	Cars offered	sold	% Sale	Total US$	% Turn.	Avg value US$	Cars offered	sold	% Sale	Total US$	% Turn.	Avg value US$	Cars offered	sold	% Sale	Total US$	% Turn.	Avg value US$
1993-1994	ALFA ROMEO / ASTON MARTIN / BENTLEY	47	11	23%	146.002	0,55%	13.273	76	26	34%	1.008.312	3,78%	38.781	85	44	52%	3.082.572	11,55%	70.058
1994-1995		57	29	51%	2.926.035	5,80%	100.898	48	27	56%	1.419.125	2,81%	52.560	100	57	57%	5.440.384	10,78%	95.445
1995-1996		46	33	72%	2.839.923	5,30%	86.058	80	44	55%	2.419.300	4,52%	54.984	121	69	57%	3.783.230	7,07%	54.829
1996-1997		51	29	57%	1.922.844	2,60%	66.305	82	54	66%	2.881.315	3,89%	53.358	124	84	68%	6.275.445	8,47%	74.708
1997-1998		123	80	65%	6.400.059	7,99%	80.001	101	55	54%	4.460.571	5,57%	81.101	110	58	53%	5.216.491	6,51%	89.940
1998-1999		81	48	59%	7.849.035	6,24%	163.522	71	45	63%	3.171.074	2,52%	70.468	118	68	58%	3.984.259	3,17%	58.592
1999-2000		84	48	57%	8.868.686	5,50%	184.764	115	80	70%	5.200.996	3,22%	65.012	103	61	59%	3.985.014	2,47%	65.328
2000-2001		83	45	54%	2.765.741	2,36%	61.461	118	64	54%	3.948.280	3,37%	61.692	127	74	58%	4.615.602	3,94%	62.373
2001-2002		63	31	49%	4.749.422	3,59%	153.207	130	84	65%	5.445.380	4,12%	64.826	94	56	60%	4.118.799	3,11%	73.550
2002-2003		52	32	62%	2.103.152	1,55%	65.724	88	54	61%	4.699.984	3,47%	87.037	149	86	58%	6.367.080	4,70%	74.036
2003-2004		48	29	60%	1.842.324	1,22%	63.528	92	59	64%	7.135.904	4,73%	120.948	101	63	62%	12.483.773	8,27%	198.155
2004-2005		61	40	66%	5.682.657	2,55%	142.066	123	89	72%	11.819.575	5,30%	132.804	117	82	70%	7.384.094	3,31%	90.050
2005-2006		81	46	57%	2.796.365	0,94%	60.791	94	60	64%	10.259.578	3,45%	170.993	98	67	68%	13.278.631	4,47%	198.189
2006-2007		67	43	64%	8.204.221	1,87%	190.796	107	75	70%	14.713.859	3,35%	196.185	86	60	70%	12.963.436	2,95%	216.057
2007-2008		62	35	56%	12.979.053	2,79%	370.830	98	72	73%	16.803.400	3,62%	233.381	80	52	65%	12.488.352	2,69%	240.161
2008-2009		78	34	44%	8.686.567	2,13%	255.487	139	100	72%	16.613.555	4,07%	166.136	119	84	71%	10.589.499	2,59%	126.065
2009-2010		72	42	58%	14.078.349	3,07%	335.199	176	129	73%	26.121.774	5,70%	202.494	158	116	73%	12.678.371	2,77%	109.296
2010-2011		72	47	65%	7.533.676	1,44%	160.291	235	175	74%	40.993.426	7,86%	234.248	165	93	56%	19.067.235	3,65%	205.024
2011-2012		88	57	65%	14.050.533	2,04%	246.501	188	131	70%	37.020.628	5,37%	282.600	184	129	70%	42.734.606	6,19%	331.276
2012-2013		122	86	70%	19.595.264	2,39%	227.852	161	124	77%	38.263.820	4,66%	308.579	144	105	73%	27.703.352	3,38%	263.841
2013-2014		188	152	81%	39.852.877	3,42%	262.190	165	138	84%	58.530.422	5,03%	424.133	143	94	66%	18.579.097	1,60%	197.650
2014-2015		135	97	72%	13.847.387	1,13%	142.757	188	145	77%	60.929.969	4,96%	420.207	137	91	66%	24.969.541	2,03%	274.391
2015-2016		168	117	70%	45.351.396	3,75%	387.619	187	131	70%	56.968.873	4,70%	434.877	150	105	70%	26.043.521	2,15%	248.034
1993-1994	BUGATTI / CHEVROLET / FERRARI	9	5	56%	452.027	1,69%	90.405	11	6	55%	80.349	0,30%	13.392	65	14	22%	876.118	3,28%	62.580
1994-1995		13	7	54%	968.779	1,92%	138.397	15	13	87%	201.662	0,40%	15.512	79	46	58%	4.554.304	9,03%	99.007
1995-1996		20	12	60%	2.126.224	3,97%	177.185	13	10	77%	207.087	0,39%	20.709	100	63	63%	8.328.518	15,55%	132.199
1996-1997		19	12	63%	2.395.408	3,23%	199.617	19	14	74%	478.400	0,65%	34.171	144	87	60%	14.758.354	19,92%	169.636
1997-1998		19	14	74%	2.483.931	3,10%	177.424	12	7	58%	304.307	0,38%	43.472	133	76	57%	8.528.812	10,65%	112.221
1998-1999		23	13	57%	3.893.666	3,10%	299.513	28	19	68%	939.587	0,75%	49.452	226	136	60%	31.914.731	25,38%	234.667
1999-2000		28	13	46%	3.620.530	2,24%	278.502	48	32	67%	2.289.562	1,42%	71.549	277	199	72%	52.233.656	32,37%	262.481
2000-2001		27	19	70%	7.766.789	6,63%	408.778	45	36	80%	1.415.971	1,21%	39.333	253	158	62%	29.476.643	25,16%	186.561
2001-2002		27	12	44%	3.708.893	2,80%	309.074	56	39	70%	2.516.493	1,90%	64.525	253	149	59%	29.998.519	22,68%	201.332
2002-2003		24	8	33%	4.515.102	3,33%	564.388	111	91	82%	3.883.260	2,87%	42.673	250	138	55%	19.026.366	14,04%	137.872
2003-2004		16	7	44%	4.350.427	2,88%	621.490	82	57	70%	4.646.966	3,08%	81.526	263	175	67%	30.335.209	20,11%	173.344
2004-2005		14	8	57%	5.154.382	2,31%	644.298	52	38	73%	4.102.450	1,84%	107.959	232	129	56%	41.400.760	18,57%	320.936
2005-2006		17	12	71%	8.990.195	3,03%	749.183	107	91	85%	14.827.488	4,99%	162.939	250	156	62%	43.155.315	14,53%	276.637
2006-2007		17	14	82%	7.376.359	1,68%	526.883	117	91	78%	12.572.283	2,86%	138.157	261	165	63%	94.917.161	21,60%	575.256
2007-2008		43	29	67%	29.328.333	6,31%	1.011.322	70	50	71%	10.551.819	2,27%	211.036	315	206	65%	114.997.709	24,74%	558.241
2008-2009		31	18	58%	13.977.189	3,42%	776.511	234	187	80%	21.990.297	5,39%	117.595	304	189	62%	80.515.862	19,73%	426.010
2009-2010		21	15	71%	7.546.605	1,65%	503.107	157	120	76%	12.696.077	2,77%	105.801	248	179	72%	93.695.185	20,44%	523.437
2010-2011		23	20	87%	11.716.884	2,25%	585.844	152	122	80%	14.544.568	2,79%	119.218	287	185	64%	116.180.316	22,27%	628.002
2011-2012		23	15	65%	8.535.341	1,24%	569.023	121	88	73%	11.522.448	1,67%	130.937	278	207	74%	152.242.948	22,06%	735.473
2012-2013		31	26	84%	27.177.485	3,31%	1.045.288	133	105	79%	16.329.278	1,99%	155.517	333	253	76%	225.038.835	27,43%	889.482
2013-2014		23	19	83%	20.681.615	1,78%	1.088.506	149	118	79%	32.776.758	2,81%	277.769	420	333	79%	388.052.856	33,32%	1.165.324
2014-2015		23	18	78%	16.542.095	1,35%	919.005	185	151	82%	23.264.275	1,89%	154.068	576	451	78%	416.878.614	33,92%	924.343
2015-2016		27	18	67%	35.369.469	2,92%	1.964.971	176	144	82%	22.128.966	1,83%	153.673	812	486	60%	366.151.396	30,24%	753.398
1993-1994	FORD / JAGUAR / LAMBORGHINI	34	19	56%	285.328	1,07%	15.017	134	60	45%	2.142.185	8,03%	35.703	9	3	33%	98.656	0,37%	32.885
1994-1995		41	30	73%	634.391	1,26%	21.146	147	80	54%	2.428.611	4,81%	30.358	15	9	60%	403.488	0,80%	44.832
1995-1996		24	17	71%	210.810	0,39%	12.401	143	89	62%	2.582.455	4,82%	29.016	19	13	68%	922.034	1,72%	70.926
1996-1997		25	16	64%	942.824	1,27%	58.927	188	127	68%	5.046.269	6,81%	39.734	29	13	45%	1.483.928	2,00%	114.148
1997-1998		38	28	74%	1.296.468	1,62%	46.302	156	94	60%	4.496.584	5,61%	47.836	33	14	42%	997.056	1,25%	71.218
1998-1999		53	39	74%	2.865.967	2,28%	73.486	164	111	68%	7.566.548	6,02%	68.167	28	17	61%	1.117.927	0,89%	65.760
1999-2000		46	30	65%	1.371.297	0,85%	45.710	153	113	74%	10.222.156	6,33%	90.462	47	21	45%	1.356.657	0,84%	64.603
2000-2001		49	39	80%	1.248.584	1,07%	32.015	239	163	68%	6.921.557	5,91%	42.464	32	12	38%	472.639	0,40%	39.387
2001-2002		70	56	80%	3.562.602	2,69%	63.618	239	157	66%	9.071.743	6,86%	57.782	28	18	64%	1.549.683	1,17%	86.094
2002-2003		89	66	74%	4.412.631	3,26%	66.858	264	150	57%	9.950.638	7,34%	66.338	36	25	69%	2.132.468	1,57%	85.299
2003-2004		55	41	75%	1.980.531	1,31%	48.306	212	134	63%	6.418.753	4,25%	47.901	20	10	50%	849.928	0,56%	84.993
2004-2005		77	57	74%	6.585.867	2,95%	115.542	210	144	69%	13.106.030	5,88%	91.014	19	13	68%	845.992	0,38%	65.076
2005-2006		128	109	85%	14.585.799	4,91%	133.815	231	150	65%	14.530.452	4,89%	96.870	34	22	65%	2.905.002	0,98%	132.046
2006-2007		129	114	88%	14.726.738	3,35%	129.182	196	138	70%	10.397.184	2,37%	75.342	26	19	73%	4.478.726	1,02%	235.722
2007-2008		92	75	82%	11.339.053	2,44%	151.187	153	106	69%	17.279.213	3,72%	163.011	36	28	78%	7.651.470	1,65%	273.267
2008-2009		230	199	87%	20.757.195	5,09%	104.308	238	172	72%	14.074.286	3,45%	81.827	50	26	52%	4.665.931	1,14%	179.459
2009-2010		177	137	77%	14.176.505	3,09%	103.478	280	188	67%	19.167.672	4,18%	101.956	46	31	67%	6.753.446	1,47%	217.853
2010-2011		172	143	83%	10.853.345	2,08%	75.898	306	179	58%	14.840.791	2,84%	82.909	41	32	78%	13.047.522	2,50%	407.735
2011-2012		200	158	79%	37.109.379	5,38%	234.869	377	241	64%	21.926.146	3,18%	90.980	36	19	53%	6.296.807	0,91%	331.411
2012-2013		166	125	75%	15.904.304	1,94%	127.234	315	201	64%	22.089.768	2,69%	109.899	53	39	74%	12.633.136	1,54%	323.927
2013-2014		151	128	85%	35.624.357	3,06%	278.315	392	284	72%	46.168.134	3,96%	162.564	57	49	86%	25.273.514	2,17%	515.786
2014-2015		258	230	89%	34.214.916	2,78%	148.761	374	301	80%	59.959.346	4,88%	199.200	91	73	80%	33.378.527	2,72%	457.240
2015-2016		230	184	80%	40.933.380	3,38%	222.464	328	242	74%	62.462.142	5,16%	258.108	110	57	52%	23.367.262	1,93%	409.952

Season		Cars offered	sold	% Sale	Total US$	% Turn.	Avg value US$		Cars offered	sold	% Sale	Total US$	% Turn.	Avg value US$		Cars offered	sold	% Sale	Total US$	% Turn.	Avg value US$
1993-1994	**MASERATI**	28	11	39%	203.643	0,76%	18.513	**MERCEDES BENZ**	73	33	45%	1.487.778	5,57%	45.084	**PORSCHE**	28	12	43%	249.320	0,93%	20.777
1994-1995		34	26	76%	2.298.227	4,56%	88.393		87	51	59%	2.118.601	4,20%	41.541		28	13	46%	323.341	0,64%	24.872
1995-1996		33	23	70%	2.196.980	4,10%	95.521		109	61	56%	4.060.725	7,58%	66.569		32	23	72%	1.262.196	2,36%	54.878
1996-1997		44	33	75%	3.633.429	4,90%	110.104		129	94	73%	5.172.707	6,98%	55.029		22	16	73%	385.380	0,52%	24.086
1997-1998		48	25	52%	2.278.829	2,85%	91.153		96	54	56%	3.607.195	4,50%	66.800		55	40	73%	4.805.674	6,00%	120.142
1998-1999		56	29	52%	3.979.110	3,16%	137.211		147	101	69%	11.776.653	9,37%	116.601		74	49	66%	4.641.709	3,69%	94.729
1999-2000		49	33	67%	5.483.546	3,40%	166.168		154	104	68%	10.696.867	6,63%	102.854		81	53	65%	5.318.587	3,30%	100.351
2000-2001		81	55	68%	5.352.932	4,57%	97.326		126	94	75%	10.763.394	9,19%	114.504		84	53	63%	2.753.513	2,35%	51.953
2001-2002		51	32	63%	3.215.069	2,43%	100.471		144	97	67%	14.213.631	10,75%	146.532		82	41	50%	2.005.539	1,52%	48.916
2002-2003		76	48	63%	3.962.999	2,92%	82.562		195	123	63%	19.222.539	14,19%	156.281		89	56	63%	3.953.332	2,92%	70.595
2003-2004		46	32	70%	2.700.539	1,79%	84.392		117	78	67%	8.485.603	5,62%	108.790		88	52	59%	4.129.879	2,74%	79.421
2004-2005		48	25	52%	5.332.416	2,39%	213.297		140	95	68%	22.526.510	10,10%	237.121		77	44	57%	6.263.538	2,81%	142.353
2005-2006		53	34	64%	7.831.878	2,64%	230.349		138	104	75%	22.841.443	7,69%	219.629		128	90	70%	8.328.277	2,80%	92.536
2006-2007		50	37	74%	7.875.414	1,79%	212.849		100	74	74%	18.741.995	4,26%	253.270		119	80	67%	10.926.743	2,49%	136.584
2007-2008		56	36	64%	6.355.611	1,37%	176.545		115	85	74%	42.904.160	9,23%	504.755		93	60	65%	10.477.940	2,25%	174.632
2008-2009		75	44	59%	5.132.233	1,26%	116.642		106	79	75%	13.230.515	3,24%	167.475		123	70	57%	7.731.738	1,89%	110.453
2009-2010		59	35	59%	10.832.616	2,36%	309.503		201	144	72%	32.453.536	7,08%	225.372		153	95	62%	16.048.908	3,50%	168.936
2010-2011		49	29	59%	3.716.910	0,71%	128.169		211	152	72%	59.079.547	11,32%	388.681		157	90	57%	15.353.831	2,94%	170.598
2011-2012		70	45	64%	10.359.009	1,50%	230.200		220	153	70%	57.454.250	8,33%	375.518		283	180	64%	51.855.843	7,52%	288.088
2012-2013		67	42	63%	23.050.704	2,81%	548.826		213	171	80%	102.083.509	12,44%	596.980		229	165	72%	36.650.662	4,47%	222.125
2013-2014		79	62	78%	25.876.341	2,22%	417.360		367	293	80%	102.753.424	8,82%	350.694		261	193	74%	59.306.282	5,09%	307.286
2014-2015		88	76	86%	26.629.444	2,17%	350.387		307	235	77%	86.143.173	7,01%	366.567		404	306	76%	106.029.499	8,63%	346.502
2015-2016		155	112	72%	35.369.745	2,92%	315.801		355	259	73%	77.105.895	6,37%	297.706		538	355	66%	109.789.960	9,07%	309.267
1993-1994	**ROLLS-ROYCE**	131	66	50%	2.819.764	10,57%	42.724	**SHELBY AMERICAN**	1	1	100%	118.542	0,44%	118.542	**TOTAL MARKET**	1521	775	51%	26.688.102	-	34.436
1994-1995		123	78	63%	7.130.221	14,13%	91.413		6	3	50%	561.910	1,11%	187.303		1677	1077	64%	50.452.574	-	46.845
1995-1996		155	97	63%	4.991.771	9,32%	51.462		4	3	75%	550.752	1,03%	183.584		1734	1114	64%	53.543.789	-	48.064
1996-1997		197	115	58%	5.545.837	7,49%	48.225		3	1	33%	222.500	0,30%	222.500		2083	1378	66%	74.091.707	-	53.768
1997-1998		134	70	52%	4.877.119	6,09%	69.673		11	5	45%	906.585	1,13%	181.317		2044	1230	60%	80.081.651	-	65.107
1998-1999		160	105	66%	6.931.916	5,51%	66.018		9	8	89%	1.784.073	1,42%	223.009		2193	1419	65%	125.725.161	-	88.601
1999-2000		135	82	61%	5.179.341	3,21%	63.163		5	1	20%	4.400.000	2,73%	4.400.000		2339	1569	67%	161.379.319	-	102.855
2000-2001		144	101	70%	6.801.376	5,81%	67.340		7	6	86%	1.118.479	0,95%	186.413		2359	1508	64%	117.134.292	-	77.675
2001-2002		159	101	64%	7.003.406	5,30%	69.341		9	4	44%	694.155	0,52%	173.539		2406	1558	65%	132.250.335	-	84.885
2002-2003		181	111	61%	6.651.513	4,91%	59.924		6	3	50%	513.849	0,38%	171.283		2728	1737	64%	135.493.459	-	78.004
2003-2004		177	135	76%	9.823.837	6,51%	72.769		10	6	60%	2.207.660	1,46%	367.943		2252	1516	67%	150.865.076	-	99.515
2004-2005		121	74	61%	4.292.507	1,93%	58.007		8	8	100%	5.213.300	2,34%	651.663		2347	1619	69%	222.937.471	-	137.701
2005-2006		143	97	68%	8.528.181	2,87%	87.919		21	19	90%	12.513.410	4,21%	658.601		2645	1867	71%	297.003.663	-	159.081
2006-2007		148	105	71%	29.202.051	6,65%	278.115		18	16	89%	15.650.527	3,56%	978.158		2763	2074	75%	439.456.579	-	211.888
2007-2008		109	81	74%	23.734.878	5,11%	293.023		12	10	83%	7.475.848	1,61%	747.585		2515	1792	71%	464.780.590	-	259.364
2008-2009		174	119	68%	14.062.161	3,45%	118.169		21	13	62%	17.618.500	4,32%	1.355.269		3634	2599	72%	408.142.058	-	157.038
2009-2010		192	134	70%	23.238.337	5,07%	173.420		27	17	63%	10.354.486	2,26%	609.087		3812	2693	71%	458.360.655	-	170.204
2010-2011		218	133	61%	19.931.432	3,82%	149.860		16	10	63%	5.894.770	1,13%	589.477		3827	2601	68%	521.740.498	-	200.592
2011-2012		205	125	61%	27.196.237	3,94%	217.570		15	13	87%	10.095.290	1,46%	776.561		4432	3107	70%	689.990.876	-	222.076
2012-2013		175	111	63%	19.634.010	2,39%	176.883		20	17	85%	17.464.128	2,13%	1.027.302		4170	3074	74%	820.492.634	-	266.914
2013-2014		248	173	70%	28.094.975	2,41%	162.399		17	11	65%	9.715.841	0,83%	883.258		4763	3622	76%	1.164.737.544	-	321.573
2014-2015		177	130	73%	19.327.965	1,57%	148.677		23	21	91%	27.296.762	2,22%	1.299.846		5156	4036	78%	1.229.091.228	-	304.532
2015-2016		177	118	67%	21.343.759	1,76%	180.879		20	16	80%	29.259.940	2,42%	1.828.746		5644	4044	72%	1.210.968.707	-	299.448

Average price achieved
($, £, € k)

The average price is obtained adding all the results, with the exception of the highest and lowest.

The race-prepared and spider-conversion examples have been also excluded.

MERCEDES-BENZ 300 SL "GULLWING"

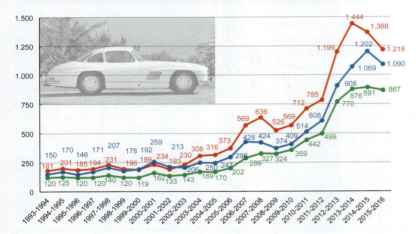

MERCEDES-BENZ 300 SL ROADSTER

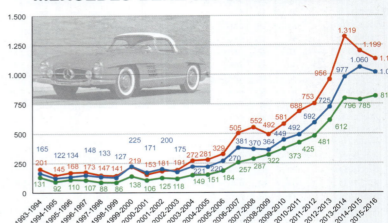

ASTON MARTIN DB 4

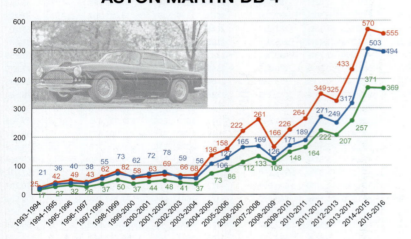

FERRARI 365 GTB/4 "DAYTONA"

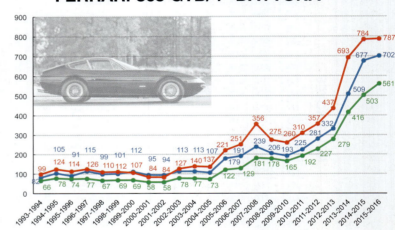

JAGUAR E-TYPE 3.8 ROADSTER

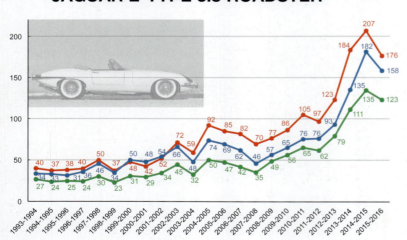

FERRARI DINO 246 GT

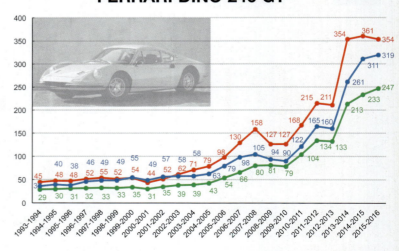

P.S.: The sale price was recorded originally in Italian Lire at the exchange rate on the day of the auction. This amount was converted later to an approximate Euro equivalent using the official value of the Lire/Euro exchange at the time of the introduction of the new currency of the European Union.

FOUR DOORS. FOUR SEATS. SHARE IN THE LUXURY OF ASTON MARTIN.

A STRIKING LOOK. INTENSE PERFORMANCE. ELEGANT LUXURY. PEERLESS CRAFTSMANSHIP.

The Rapide S is a compelling evolution of the world's most beautiful four-door sports car. Powered by our 6.0-litre, 560 PS V12 engine – it's the most potent and dynamic Rapide to date.

Stylish, spacious and hand-crafted from the finest materials the Rapide S is a car to share, delivering an unforgettable experience for you and your passengers.

Discover the Aston Martin Rapide S at **www.astonmartin.com**

Official government fuel consumption figures in mpg (litres per 100km) for the Aston Martin Rapide S: urban 14.5 (19.5); extra-urban 31.0 (9.1); combined 21.9 (12.9). CO_2 emissions 300g/km. The mpg/fuel economy figures quoted are sourced from official regulated test results obtained through laboratory testing. They are for comparability purposes only and may not reflect your real driving experience, which may vary depending on factors including road conditions, weather, vehicle load, and driving style.

The 2015-2016 season "TOP TEN"

This chapter is dedicated to the 10 cars that achieved the highest hammer prices; the cars are listed in descending order according to their hammer price in US Dollars. The descriptions and photos have been taken from the relative auction house catalogue. Of course, the Top 10s are also listed in the auction results chapter, indicated as such.

1 1957 Ferrari 335 S

Driven byt the greatest drivers, including a World Champion; Second in the 1957 Mille Miglia; Winner of the 1958 Cuba Grand Prix; In Pierre Bardinon's collection since 1970

Body: Scaglietti
Chassis: 0674
Engine: 0674

Artcurial, 5.2.2016, Paris (F)		Lot 170
Estimate	EUR	28.000.000-32.000.000
Hammer price	USD	35.930.639
	GBP	24.689.885
	EUR	32.075.200

Chassis 0674 left the Ferrari workshops at the start of 1957. Bodied as a barchetta by Scaglietti and given a four-cam 3.8-litre V12 Tipo 140 engine, this was one of the Ferrari factory 315 S. The car's first race was the Sebring 12 Hours, on 23 March, in the hands of Peter Collins and Maurice Trintignant...it finished the race 6th. After this "trial run", attention turned to the Mille Miglia in May. The car was given to Wolfgang von Trips to complete the Ferrari team...These machines dominated the event and victory was handed to Piero Taruffi...Just behind him came von Trips, whose car, number 532, performed perfectly....

Immediately after the race, the engine of chassis 0674 was increased from 3800cc to 4100cc and the car was entered for the Le Mans 24 Hours, driven by Mike Hawthorn and Luigi Musso. Hawthorn took the lead at the start, ahead of the Maseratis and Jaguars, and on the 30th lap broke the record for the average lap speed on the 24H Le Mans circuit, the first time anyone had exceeded 200km/h (203.15 km/h). Unfortunately an engine problem forced the team to retire in the 5th hour.

On 11 August, the factory sent the car to Sweden for the Swedish Grand Prix (the Kristianstad 6 Hours), driven once more by Hawthorn and Musso...They had to deal with a fire breaking out in their car, but nevertheless finished the race in fourth position.

The Ferrari then went back to the factory where it was modified at the front, in the style of the 250 Testa Rossa "ponton fender", to help cool the brakes more effectively for the hot South America climate of the Venezuelan Grand Prix on 3 November. The 335 S, chassis 0674, remained in the hands of Hawthorn and Musso. The result of this race would decide the World Title, a battle between Ferrari and Maserati, and this battle was fiercely contested. Maserati suffered a run of bad luck, however, with all three cars retiring in difficult circumstances. This left the way clear for their Maranello rival, who finished 1-2-3-4! The Constructors' World Championship Title was theirs and the second place of Hawthorn-Musso in chassis 0674 had played a major part.

Returning to the factory at Maranello, the Ferrari received a new engine - the 335 S Tipo 141, internal number 2 - and in January 1958 was sold to Luigi Chinetti...On 24 February the car took part in the Cuban Grand Prix, in Havana, sporting the NART livery...driven by Masten Gregory and Stirling Moss who won the race.

Chinetti then rented the car to Mike Garber, who entered chassis 0674 for various raced in the US during the 1958 season, driven by Gaston Andrey and Lance Reventlow. There were some excellent results including a victory in the Road America 500 and on the circuits at Thompson and Watkins Glen. The last recorded race entry was on 7 December, during the Bahamas Speed Week in Nassau, where 0674 was forced to retire. In 1960 the Ferrari was sold to Robert N. Dusek, an architect living in Solebury, Pennsylvania.

Ten years later, in 1970, Dusek sold the car to Pierre Bardinon, one of the most knowledgeable Ferrari collectors in the world.

In September 1981, Pierre Bardinon entrusted the car to the Fantuzzi workshop in Modena, to be restored to its original configuration with its first front nose. The "ponton fender" front section that was transformed to run in South America will be delivered to the new owner, as it was restored and kept alongside the car in Pierre Bardinon's museum.

Apart from trips out on the private circuit, this stunning Ferrari has not been seen much in recent years, although it did appear in the splendid exhibition "Homage to Ferrari" organized in 1987 by the Cartier Foundation in Jouy-en-Josas. Ten years later, in 1997, it participated in events organized in Rome and Maranello to celebrate the marque's 50th Anniversary...

2 1956 Ferrari 290 MM

Body: Scaglietti
Chassis: 0626
Engine: 0626

RM Auctions Sotheby's, 10.12.2015 New York (USA)		Lot 221
Estimate	EUR	28.000.000-32.000.000
Hammer price	USD	28.050.000
	GBP	18.543.855
	EUR	25.632.090

...The 1956 Mille Miglia was held on April 29th and was the third round of the World Sportscar Chanpionship. For this event, Juan Manuel Fangio was allocated chassis numebr 0626...The race was intense from the onset, with the weather immediately deteriorating to torrential rain throughout Italy. The closed cars had a distinct advantage, but the Ferraris were still supremely competitive and would take the top five places with Fangio bringing home 0626 in 4th place overall... The next outing for it was at the 2nd International ADAC 1000 KM at the Nürburgring, held at the end of May, where it was driven by Phil Hill, Ken Wharton, Olivier Gendebien and the Marquis Alfonso de Portago. This spectacular roster of drivers finished 3rd overall...

In July de Portago once again took the wheel and finished 9th overall at the 5th International Grand Prix of Rouen-Les Essarts in France.

Wolfgang von Trips...convinced Enzo Ferrari to allow him to get behind the wheel of chassis 0626 at the Swedish GP at Kristianstad, the final race of the World Championship. He was partnered with Peter Collins, and the pair did not fail to impress with a 2nd place finish, which helped Ferrari secure the 1956 World Sportcar Championship.

For the opening round of the 1957 season, the IV Mil Kilometros Ciudad de Buenos Aires, 0626 was entered in Works livery for Masten Gregory, who was partnered by Eugenio Castellotti and Luigi Musso. These three great drivers raced chassis 0626 to a famous championship victory...

In spring 1957, chassis 0626 was sold through Luigi Chinetti to Temple Buell in New York, who had the car repainted blue and white...Under Buell's ownership, this continued to compete around the world, including a 2nd place finish in both the VI Portuguese Grand Prix and RACB Grand Prix of Spa-Francorchamps, as well as earning respectable finishes at the Nassau Tourist Trophy and the Cuban Grand Prix...Throughout this season, the car was driven by Gregory, Joakim Bonnier, Paul O'Shea and Manfredo Lippman.

In March 1958, Temple Buell returned the car to Chinetti Motors, who sold it to J. Robert Williams...Chassis 0626 then passed to James Flynn and continued to be raced up until 1964, maintaining her almost unique record of never being crashed and as such maintaining her level of incredible originality. In 1968, repainted red, the 290 MM was sold to Bob Dusek...In 1970 it was purchased by Pierre Bardinon for his Collection Mas du Clos in Aubusson, France.

Bardinon owned this magnificent car for 34 years before it passed to the present custodian, who is one of the world's most renowned and discerning collectors of Ferrari and its history...For the past 12 years, chassis 0626 has been regularly maintained, benefiting from a recent engine rebuild. The provision of a removable passenger screen has also allowed her to comfortably compete in the Mille Miglia Storica, and she has run at various historic events...

The owner has had the car Ferrari Classiche certified to further confirm its stunning originality...

CONCORSO D'ELEGANZA VILLA D'ESTE

dal
1929

DAYS OF ELEGANCE

26th – 28th May 2017 / Cernobbio, Lake Como (Italy)

Find more detailed information: www.concorsodeleganzavilladeste.com

3 1955 Jaguar D-Type

Chassis: XKD 501
Engine: E 2036-9

Legendary overall winner of the 1956 24 Hours of Le Mans, raced by Ecurie Ecosse

RM Auctions Sotheby's, 19.8.2016 Monterey (USA)		Lot 114
Estimate	EUR	20.000.000-25.000.000
Hammer price	USD	21.780.000
	GBP	16.639.920
	EUR	19.229.562

...Chassis number XKD 501 was the first D-Type produced for a private team, sold to the Scottish racing team Ecurie Ecosse...It was liveried in the team's signature colors with the St. Andrew Cross emblazoned on the front fenders. It was initially entrusted to Jimmy Stewart...who unfortunately crashed the D-Type twice during practice in May 1955. Each time, the car was returned to the factory for repairs.

...XKD 501 appeared at the Leinster Trophy on 9 July, where Desmond Titterington took the car to 9th overall, and 1st in class. Ecosse driver Ninian Sanderson assumed driving duties at the British GP on 17 July, claiming 6th place.

Titterington returned to action in early August, finishing 1st and 2nd at the races at Charterhall, and then enjoyed two 1st place finishes at Snetterton a week later. Sanderson rotated in for a 1st and 2nd place at Crimond, and the two drivers teamed up for a 2nd place finish during the nine-hour race at Goodwood on 20 August. Another 2nd place by Titterington at Aintree on 3 September completed the 1955 season.

During 1956, rules chamges mandated the implementation of full-width windscreens, and XKD 501 was so equipped while receiving the engine from XKD 561 (engine no. 2036-9)...

The 24 Hours of Le Mans was held in late July...The Scottish entry, this car, again guided by the team of Sanderson and Flockhart. It was here that XKD 501 turned in its greatest performance...By the race's final lap, with just 14 cars remaining in the field, the D-Type had a seven-lap lead on Trintignant and Gendebien's Ferrari 625 LM spider, and a narrow lead over Moss in the Aston. Swaters' D-Type held at 4th place, and this is the order in which the cars finished, with XKD 501 claiming its definitive victory at the 24 Hours of Le Mans. XKD 501 completed 2,507.19 miles at an average speed of 104.47 mph, and a maximum speed of 156.868 mph on the Mulsanne Straight, good enough for 9th in the Index of Performace rankings...

Following the amazing finish at La Sarthe, XKD 501 returned to action in Britain, with a 2nd place at Aintree and 3rd at the Goodwood Trophy Race...

In 1957, Jaguar retired from factory racing altogether and sold its latest longnose D-Types, with several cars acquired by the Ecurie Ecosse. As these 3.8-liter D-Types became the team's focus, XKD 501 was only occasionally entered in various races, beginning with the Mille Miglia on 12 May, where the car retired early with Flockhart driving.

...The car was essentially retired after June 1957, and it soon passed to Ecurie Ecosse financier Major Thomson of Peebles, Scotland...In October 1970, it was sold to Sir Michael Nairn and over the following few years was sympathetically restored with emphasis on retaining its purity and originality to its 1956 Le Mans specifications...The engine head and block were returned to Jaguar to be rebuilt...Sir Nairn then used the car rather frequently, including presentation at the 1996 Goodwood Festival of Speed and the Silverstone Classic.

In 1999, XKD 501 was purchased by the consignor, one of America's most respected collectors of exceptional sports and racing cars...

4 1939 Alfa Romeo 8C 2900B Spider

One of approximately 12 extant Touring Spiders; from the collection of Sam & Emily Mann

Body: Carrozzeria Touring
Chassis: 412041
Engine: 422042

RM Auctions Sotheby's, 20.8.2016 Monterey (USA)		Lot 234
Estimate	EUR	20.000.000-25.000.000
Hammer price	USD	19.800.000
	GBP	15.127.200
	EUR	17.481.420

...Simon Moore's latest research indicates that the known history of this car starts in 1949...An amateur driver in Sao Paulo called Mario Tavares Leite imported an 8C 2900B to Brazil from Italy. The poor photo in that paper shows a Touring Spider. He raced his new acquisition at Interlagos and won a race there on 31 July 1949...He won again at Interlagos on 20 April 1950 after which the car disappeared. In an article on Brazilian racer Camillo Christofaro in a now-defunct Brazilian magazine, *Motor*, for 3 September 1986, he states: *"In 1958...Camillo took an Alfa Romeo touring car, shortened its chassis, put a Corvette engine in it..."*. It seems probable that this was the single-seater Mecanica National car raced by Christofaro after he had bought both a Tipo 308 and the 8C 2900B from his uncle, Chico Landi. The chassis was part of a hoard of parts that came from Brazil in late 1972, which was acquired by David Llewelyn.

Meanwhile, in Argentina, another long chassis 8C 2900B, also with Touring Spider coachwork, was acquired by Carlos Menditeguy. In 1953, the car was sold to a Buenos Aires racer, German Pesce, and his partner, Iantorno. The two men modified the car by removing the body and installing cycle-fendered racing coachwork, and the complete original body was set aside save for the radiator grille and sorround, which were incorporated into the new racing body. The original Touring coachwork was sold to Juan Giacchio... who retained it until his passing in 1986, and at that time it was offered by his widow to Ed Jurist of the Vintage Car Store. Hector Mendizabal confirmed that it was from an 8C 2900B Lungo chassis, the color a light silver blue with red leather - and it was missing the grille. Correspondence from both individuals during that period indicated an association with chassis 412041.

In 1983 David Black acquired the modified 8C 2900 rolling chassis from David Llewellyn; the frame had its engine bearers (and thus the chassis number) cut away to accomodate the Corvette V-8, although a correct frame number, 432042, in the proper Alfa Romeo typeface, was still present...Following Black's death, the car passed to Juan Bruijn in 1993. Guido Haschke of Switzerland subsequently acquired the rolling chassis and, at the same time, acquired the original Touring Spider body from Italian Count Vittorio Zanon di Valgiurata...

The following year, 1994, Sam Mann was alerted to the availability of the project and contacted Alfa Romeo restorer Tony Merrick to inspect the car and advise as to its authenticity...Merrick found the components to be authentic, and with his advice, Sam opted to purchase the car and engage Merrick to perform the restoration. Through the sleuthing of Moore and Merrick, a complete original 8C 2900B engine, no.422042, was acquired, thus securing the last of the necessary components for a proper and authentic restoration...During the restoration, the original body number, 2027, was located on numerous panels...When Merrick placed the body on the re-lengthened chassis, he found that the holes on the top of the frame lined up exactly with the holes in the inner fender liner panels...To summarize, since no hard evidence exists to confirm the true sequence of events, it remains possible that the Menditeguy Alfa traveled to Brazil from Argentina in the mid- to late-1950s, sans Touring body, where it was then further modified and raced with the Chevrolet V-8, only to be reunited with its original coachwork some four decades later...

Mr. Merrick had completed the restoration of the chassis, drivetrain, and body by late 1997...The Manns have spent over 12,000 miles behind the wheel between 1999 and 2013...

Prix Spécial - Chantilly Arts & Elegance 2016

Bristol 401 Touring - 1 of 8 produced - complete restoration

TOURING SUPERLEGGERA - MILANO
CERTIFIED RESTORATION OF CLASSIC CARS TO ORIGINAL SPECIFICATIONS

info@touringsuperleggera.eu

5 1959 Ferrari 250 GT Spyder California lwb

One of only nine alloy-bodied lwb California Spyders; covered headlights, disc brakes, and full competition specifications

Body: Scaglietti
Chassis: 1603GT
Engine: 1603GT

Gooding & Company, 20.8.2016 Pebble Beach (USA)		Lot 33
Estimate	USD	18.000.000-20.000.000
Hammer price	USD	18.150.000
	GBP	13.866.600
	EUR	16.024.635

...Completed on November 23, 1959, 1603 GT is among the last lwb Spyder Californias produced. As such, it is built on the highly developed 508D chassis... According to Ferrari historian Marcel Massini, this California is also the very first example to be equipped from new with Dunlop disc brakes...It was specified with a competition gearbox, a limited-slip differential, and an oversized 136-liter fuel tank, fed through a competition-style external fuel filler...It was also equipped with the outside-plug Tipo 168 engine...(internal no.22F) factory-equipped with Testa Rossa-type cylinder heads. featuring high-lift Tipo 130 camshafts and 9.8:1 compression...Breathing through three Weber 40DCL6 carburetors topped with velocity stacks and an Abarth competition exhaust, this engine developed between 275 and 280 genuine horsepower - approximately 50hp more than a standard lwb Spyder California. Once the potent chassis was completed, 1603GT was sent to Carrozzeria Scaglietti in Modena, where it received lightweight aluminium coachwork. finished in the ultra-desirable covered-headlamp arrangemet.

The Ferrari was then shipped to Luigi Chinetti Motors and immediately sold to George Reed of Homewood, Illinois...who was an active competitor in major events... As soon as the California arrived in Reed's hands, it was transported to Nassau for the Bahamas Speed Week...

After Nassau, 1603GT went through extensive testing and preparation in anticipation of its next appearance at the 12 Hours of Sebring in March 1960...where Reed and his co-driver Alan Connell achieved an incredible result with the Ferrari 5th overall and 3rd in class...

Between 1961 and 1964, 1603GT regularly contested SCCA races in the Midwest, battling with the Corvettes, Cobra and swb Berlinettas that made up the B Production grids of the day. After the 1964 season, Reed retired 1603GT from service and sold it to a resident of Kenosha, Wisconsin. By the end of the decade the car had been sold to Ed Zwintscher, who kept the aging Ferrari in static storage, where it sat undisturbed for many years in as-raced condition.

In 1984, Brian Brunkhorst acquired 1603GT and sent it to Wayne Obry's Motion Products Inc....In his care, the body and chassis were fully restored with great effort to save as much of the original aluminium coachwork as possible. At this time, the engine and gearbox were sent to Rick Bunkfeldt at Vintage Restoration Services Inc. for a complete rebuild. The completed car was then finished in dark blue with a tan interior.

In the early 1990s, the car was sold to Michael Mak, who traded it to Dennis Machul for another significant Ferrari in 2000. The following year, Todd Morici acquired 1603GT, and he campaigned it in several major vintage races before refinishing the car is its original Sebring livery. During his ownership, 1603GT was certified by Ferrari Classiche Department...

The current owner acquired 1603GT in 2010 and immediately commissioned Bob Smith Coachworks, Texas, to perform a selective cosmetic restoration, completed in January 2011...

6 1961 Ferrari 250 GT Spyder California swb

One of only 27 covered-headlight swb Spyder California; delivered new in Milan; just three Italian owners from new

Body: Scaglietti
Chassis: 2871 GT
Engine: 2871

Gooding & Company, 11.3.2016 Amelia Island (USA)		Lot 69
Estimate	USD	15.000.000-17.000.000
Hammer price	USD	17.160.000
	GBP	12.005.136
	EUR	15.473.172

...The Ferrari 250 GT chassis 2871 GT is among the most desirable Spyder California as it is a swb version featuring the highly attractive covered-headlight treatment that Scaglietti applied to just 37 examples. Originally fnished in the classic colour scheme of *Rosso Cina* (China red) with black leather upholstery, 2871 GT was equipped with features typical of the late-production swb models: a Tipo 168/61 engine, three Weber 40 DCL 6 carburetors, Abarth exhaust system, Veglia instruments, Miletto shock absorbers, and Borrani RW3591 wire wheels wearing Pirelli Cinturato tires. Completed on September 2, 1961 2871 GT was the 22nd swb Spyder California built. It was delivered new to Gianfranco Frattini, who paid Lire 5.500.000 for the new Ferrari. Well-known in design circles, Gianfranco Frattini was born in Padua on May 15, 1926, and graduated from the Politecnico di Milano in 1953. After working under his teacher and mentor, the famed industrial designer Giò Ponti, Frattini established his own design firm in Milan. In 1956, Frattini co-founded the Associazione per il Disegno Industriale, and throughout his decades-long career focused on interior designs, particularly furniture and lighting...

Early on in Frattini's ownership, 2871 GT made a cameo appearance in Vittorio De Sica's Academy Award-winning feature film *Yesterday, Today, Tomorrow*, the 1963 comedy which starred Marcello Mastroianni and Sophia Loren...

Remarkably, Gianfranco Frattini retained possession of 2871 GT until June 1978, when it was sold to Terzo Dalia...a talented craftsman specializing in highly accurate and realistic scale models of Ferrari engines and components, who retained the Spyder California for seven years. During his ownership, 2871 GT participated in two historic events hosted by the Automobile Club d'Italia in Modena - the Raid Ferrari d'Epoca in 1981 and Ferrari days in 1983.

The current owner acquired 2871 GT from sig. Dalia in December 1985, and it has been a part of his prominent Italy-based stable of important sports and racing cars ever since. As presented today, this important Ferrari remains in well-maintained and largely unrestored condition throughout...

Unlike the vast majority of 250 Ferraris, this swb Spyder California has not been fully restored from the ground up; instead, it has always been exercised and maintained in good working order. As a result, this car retains a refreshing, authentic character. Even today, it retains its original engine and rear end, confirmed by their respective internal numbers, which match the factory assembly sheets...It is offered with an original tool roll (partially complete), the original steering wheel, shift knob, front and rear bumpers, and a report compiled by Ferrari historian Marcel Massini, which includes a detailed history, copies of the Automobile Club d'Italia registration records, and period photos...

SERVING THE HISTORIC & CLASSIC CAR INDUSTRY

JSWL

- RESTORATION
- RECREATIONS
- ENGINE BUILDING
- COMPETITION PREPARATION
- RACE SUPPORT
- ACQUISITION INSPECTION

 Follow us on Facebook

Phone: +44 (0)2392 254488
Email: info@jswl.co.uk   Website: www.jswl.co.uk
Pipers Wood Industrial Park, Waterlooville, Hampshire, PO7 7XU, United Kingdom

JSWL, Triple M and Southshore Coachworks are members of JSW Group

7 1962 Aston Martin DB4GT

The 14th of just 19 DB4GTs tailor made by Zagato; the only example delivered new to Australia; successful period racing career; award winner at numerous European and American concours events

Body: Zagato
Chassis: DB4GT/0186/R
Engine: 370/186/GT

RM Auctions Sotheby's, 10.12.2015 New York (USA)		Lot 215
Estimate	USD	15.000.000-17.000.000
Hammer price	USD	14.300.000
	GBP	9.453.730
	EUR	13.067.340

Chassis DB4GT/0186/R was completed on December 19, 1961, and then shipped to Australia shortly thereafter. Laurie O'Neill would be the first lucky owner. A successful businessman...in his spare time his preferred hobby was racing...

The DB4GT Zagato would be O.Neill's weapon of choice for the 1962 season, and the Aston would bring him great success. With Doug Whiteford behind the wheel, the car was undefeated in its first two outings at Calder and Lonford on February 25 and March 3, respectively. On March 5 in Longford, Whiteford drove 0186/R to another 1st overall in the South Pacific GT Championship and a 4th-place finish in the Sports Car Championship on the same day. Whiteford and 0186/R notched one more 4th overall in the GT Scratch Race but failed to finish at the Sprts Car Trophy race the following weekend due to tire issues. This would prove to be the car's worst finish for the 1962 season.

The Zagato would finish in no less than 3rd place over the next five events while driven by Laurie O'Neill himself and Ian Georghegan. They ended the season on a high note, finishing 1st in class in the GT Scratch Race at Katoomba on October 28, 1962.

That year would mark the end of the DB4GT Zagato's racing career, as O'Neill sold the car prior to the 1963 season. For the next 30 years, it would remain in Australia with only two subsequent owners. Colin Hyams acquired the car immediately following O'Neill's ownership in 1963, and it is believed that it was shown at the 1967 Melbourne Motor Show during his ownership. Hyams then sold the car to Alex Copland in 1968, and it would remain with Copland in static storage for over 20 years.

In 1993 the Aston Martin was acquired by G.K. Speirs of Aberdeen, Scotland...There they performed a minor restoration so the car could be entered into vintage racing events. During this time the Aston Martin was frequently campaigned at such events as the 1997 Goodwood Festival of Speed and the Goodwood Revival in 1998 and 1999...

Purchased by Peter Read from Speirs, he decided that 0186/R was deserving of a complete restoration to concours standard. The process took two years from disassembly to completion, with work divided between Aston Martin specialist Richard S. Williams in England and Carrozzeria Zagato's own facilities in Italy...

Following completion in 2002, chassis 0186/R hit the concours circuit, where it immediately accrued an enviable record of accolades...At the Louis Vuitton Concours at the Hurlingham Club in June 2002, the DB4GT Zagato not only won its class but was also named Best of Show...At the Bagatelle Concours d'Elegance later that month it also won its class. Further Best in Class honors were also earned at Villa d'Este, Pebble Beach, and the Neillo Concours in 2007, as well as at the Presidio of San Francisco Concours and the Carmel-By-The-Sea Concours in 2009...

Not just a concours queen, 0186/R has also been driven respectfully on several tours, where it performed marvelously and without issue...

8 1962 Shelby American Cobra 260

The legendary and very first Shelby; offered from the Carroll Hall Shelby Trust

Chassis: CSX 2000
Engine: XHP-260-1

RM Auctions Sotheby's, 20.8.2016 Monterey (USA)		Lot 234
Estimate		Priceless!
Hammer price	USD	13.750.000
	GBP	10.505.000
	EUR	12.139.875

...The very first Cobra arrived in the United States, without a motor, in February 1962. This very first car, CSX 2000, was personally picked up at the Los Angeles airport by Carroll Shelby and his colleague Dean Moon before being brought back to Moon's shop, where they installed the now-available and larger-displacement 260-cubic inch V-8 with a Ford gearbox in a matter of hours. And with that, CSX 2000 was complete, running and driving.

...The entire company's finances rested in this prortotype and the securing of a successful deal for Shelby American that involved A.C. Cars and Ford. Amazingly, one of the car's earliest functions was as a press car for the motoring trade, particularly with prominent magazines, and in cities around the country to drump up interest and sales for the fledgling company. Time after time, however, what the public failed to realize was that every image of a Shelby Cobra in seemingly different colors was in fact the very same car - CSX 2000, repainted repeatedly in a stunt of Shelby's own invention...The colors red, then blue, finally yellow all followed for its official unveiling at the New York Auto Show, but regardless of the livery, Shelby's genius, publicity-savvy approach was generally the same. Journalists were generally treated to a tour of Moon's shop, followed by an impressive demonstration of a Weber-carbureted 260 V-8 on the dyno and concluding with a high-speed test drive through those famous oil derricks...

In fact, CSX 2000 was also the only Cobra in existence for the first five months. The stakes were high. Should CSX 2000 have been written off due a breakdown in testing or an accident by a careless journalist (or even at the hands of Carroll himself), the company would have suffered a monumental setback, one that it might not have recovered from. In the years that followed, CSX 2000 has remained an irreplaceable part of the Shelby organization...The car was first relegated to storage, likely un-driven, for about 10 years, and it was used by employees at the Carroll Shelby School of High Performance Driving...

As one analyzes the car, from front to back, it is also immediately clear that this is the only Cobra to be produced by Shelby with inboard rear disc brakes. It has the first set of hand-built and welded tubular headers, and the motor is cooled by an AC radiator. The trunk lid is longer than on production Cobras and in fact, the trunk itself is upholstered. Other telltale AC signs are the Ace bumpers, the Ace dashboard, and the hinges, which are flat, as compared to the rounder style. Also of note is the gas filler cap, which is the only one in this location, as well as the black foot boxes and the steel hand-made scatter shield over the bellhousing for the four-speed transmission. Finally, it is particularly fascinating to see the completely original upholstery and the chips in the paint, where one can see the multiple paintjobs used to promote the car during its early days...

9 1960 Ferrari 250 GT Berlinetta Competizione swb

Driven by Hugus and Pabst to 7th overall at the 1960 24 Hours of Le Mans; retains original alloy coachwork and matching-numbers engine and gearbox; certified by Ferrari Classiche

Body: Pinin Farina/Scaglietti
Chassis: 1759GT
Engine: 1759GT

Gooding & Company, 20.8.2016 Pebble Beach (USA)		Lot 56
Estimate	USD	15.000.000-18.000.000
Hammer price	USD	13.500.000
	GBP	10.314.000
	EUR	11.919.150

...The 250 GT sbw Berlinetta chassis no. 1759 GT is the sixth example built and among the very first competition cars completed for the 1960 model year, which are now referred to simply as the Comp/60s.

As noted on Ferrari build sheets for 1759 GT, this car was purpose-built to compete in the 24 Hours of Le Mans...It was equipped with the latest Tipo 168 outside-plug V-12 engine, featuring Testa Rossa cylinder heads, Weber 40DCL6 carburetors, velocity stacks, and 9.9:1 compression - possibly the highest ratio ever specified on a 250 GT Ferrari. It may have also been the first Ferrari fitted with the famous SNAP exhaust extractors.

...On June 18, 1960 Ferrari sold 1759 GT to US distributor Luigi Chinetti Motors in New York, who sold the car to Dr. Harvey Schur...It was then registered on Italian export license plates "EE 02016"" and final preparations were made for its racing debut...Chassis 1759 GT, which wore no. 19, was decorated with NART insignias, a white and blue noseband, and bold white stripes running diagonally along the passenger's side...Ed Hugus and Augie Pabst drove 1759 GT...Seventh overall and fourth in the GT category was their final placing... Following its impressive performance at Le Mans, 1759 GT was exported to the US and prepared for Dr. Schur, who requested that Chinetti Motors change the instruments from kilometers to miles per hour.

In 1962, Gilbert Horton traded in his alloy-bodied lwb Spyder California for 1759 GT...Early in his ownership, Mr. Horton entered the swb Berlinetta in the 1962 Black Otter Hillclimb in Billings...

In 1967, he sold 1759 GT to California resident Mark Slotkin, who, three years later, sold the car to Ferrari enthusiasts Charles Betz and Fred Peters...In 1973, they sold the swb Berlinetta to Philippe Bronner...who throughout the 1970s participated in a variety of vintage races with it...

In 1980 Bronner sold the competition Ferrari to Peter Giddings, who enjoyed the car for three years before selling it to Tom Mudd...who had Kent White begin a restoration of the Ferrari, which involved disassembling the car and stripping the coachwork to bare metal. The project never progressed beyond this stage, however, and in 2002 Mr. Mudd sold 1759 GT.

That October, the Ferrari was sent to GTO Engineering in England, where a comprehensive restoration was undertaken...

Since the initial restoration was completed in 2005, 1759 GT has been selectively displayed at concours... and campaigned in vintage races. For track use, a later 250-series spare engine was installed in an effort to preserve the original unit. The current owner has recently returned the car to GTO Engineering to have the original, matching-numbers engine reinstalled and prepare the car for use on the road rather than the track. Today 1759 GT is finished in its original Le Mans livery...

PASSIONE ITALIA

SULLE STRADE DEL BELPAESE

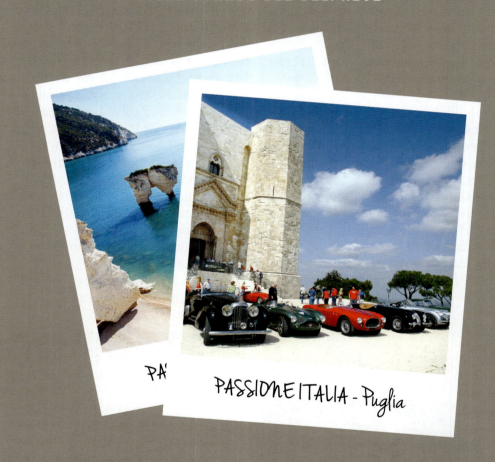

PASSIONE ITALIA - Puglia

September 20th – 24th, 2017
Basilicata – Puglia

MORE INFO

www.passione-italia.ch
info@passione-italia.ch

10 1933 Alfa Romeo 8C 2300 Monza

Owned and raced by prominent Italian drivers between 1933 and 1950; winner of the 1947 Sport Nazionale Championship with Renato Balestrero

Body: Carrozzeria Brianza
Chassis: 2311218
Engine: 2311218

Gooding & Company, 21.8.2016 Pebble Beach (USA)		Lot 128
Estimate	USD	12.000.000-15.000.000
Hammer price	USD	11.990.000
	GBP	9.160.360
	EUR	10.585.971

...Chassis 2311218 is a genuine factory-built, third-series Monza, bodied by the Milanese coachbuilder Brianza and sold new in Italy. According to Simon Moore's definitive book, *The Legendary 2.3*, this Monza was first registered in Genova on August 10, 1933, and remained in the Ligurian region for the next 17 years. During this period, it was owned by a succession of prominent Italian racing drivers, the first being Cesare Sanguinetti...In March 1934 he sold the car to Luigi Beccaria...The Monza's first definitive competition outing took place at the Klausen Hillclimb that August, where the car's third owner, Attilio Battilana, placed 7th in the sports car class...

In June 1935, the Monza's first owner, Sanguinetti, re-acquired it from Battilana...It is believed that the 2.3 continued to race in various European events, given that Sanguinetti and all of its previous Genovese owners were active throughout this period, often sharing cars...

Following WWII, the Alfa Romeo returned to the racetrack in the hands of Renato Balestrero...Throughout 1947, he campaigned it in sports car races...To comply with postwar regulations, the prewar Monza was fitted with a passenger door and a spare tire precariously mounted over the exhaust pipe.

...Following the brilliant 1947 racing season, the Monza was sold to Giovanni Ughetti, who drove it to a 1st in Class finish at the 1948 Catania-Etna Hillclimb, the Alfa's final race in Italy. In fall 1950, the Monza was shipped by boat from Naples, Italy, to Caracas, Venezuela.

Robert Ford, an engineer with an American oil-field service company, discovered it there two years later...The Monza arrived in the US in 1954, had its engine rebuilt by former Indianapolis race mechanic Marcel Periat, and was then kept at Mr. Ford's home in Ross, California...

In 1982, Peter Giddings acquired the Monza and commissioned a complete restoration...Italian car authority John de Boer was consulted...He carefully recorded all of the important component numbers including engine (2311218), frame (2131217), gearbox (2141115), steering box (2151160), front axle (2161162), rear axle (2181159) crankcase (2221162), and supercharger (2101081)...

Once the restoration was completed in 1985, The Monza embarked on its third era of racing...Over the next decade, Mr. Giddings drove the car with incredible success at venues as diverse as Monterey, Portland, Westwood, Las Vegas, Australia, New Zealand, and even La Carrera Panamericana...

In 1996, Mr. Giddings sold the Monza to Tom Hollfelder...During his 14-year ownership, the Monza continued to participate in important events including the Mille Miglia Storica, Colorado Grand and Monterey Historic Races...

Since acquiring the car in 2010, the current owner has enjoyed the Monza on the road, participating in European and US tours. Today, it remains in superb mechanical order and the well-maintained 1980s restoration possesses an inviting, consistent patina.

Brianza bodywork finished in red paint...Engine currently displacing nearly 2.9 liters...

AUTHENTIC RESTORATION
RESEARCH & HISTORICAL DOCUMENTATION

The Von Richthofen Alfa

1948 Mille Miglia at Firenze check point

Finished 3rd in class & 22nd overall. Pinin Farina custom built this very rare mid-war Alfa Romeo for the Red Baron's 1st cousin Field Marshal Wolfram von Richthofen. Documented provenance includes Mille Miglia Certificate and historic photographs. Authentically restored for race & concours.

YOUR SERVICE COMPANY SINCE 1968

Styling. Engineering. Packaging. Modelling. Prototyping. Testing. Validation. Showcars. **Ultra-Low Series Production.** Industrial Design.

www.italdesign.it

The 2015-2016 season case

First introduced with the 2009-2010 edition, this year's case study is dedicated to the ex-Janis Joplin 1964 Porsche 356SC cabriolet offered by RM Sotheby's at their 10 December 2015 sale in New York (lot 206).

1964 Porsche 356SC cabriolet
Body: Reutter
Chassis: 160371

Estimate	USD	400.000-600.000
Hammer price	USD	1.760.000
	GBP	1.163.536
	EUR	1.608.288

To say that this car is no mere Porsche is stating the obvious. It all but strikes you over the head with its presence, a rolling ensemble of flowing colors and emerging shapes that drifted out of pen, smoke, Southern Comfort, and the spirit of the age. It is an embodiment of its owner and her ethos.

Janis Joplin never needed status; she needed honesty, sincerity, and a hell of a lot of emotion, and those qualities spilled out of her in gravel tones and settled on these Stuttgart curves. She was her Porsche, and her Porsche is Janis Joplin.

The genesis of her Porsche was a similar psychedelically liveried car that Janis had seen on the streets of San Francisco in 1968...She picked up a four-year-old Porsche 356 SC cabriolet from Beverly Hills dealer Estes-Zipper. She then handed it over to her band's jack-of-all-trades "roadie", Dave Richards... He covered the car's grey paint - an ideal canvas - in candy apple red from nose to tail. He then set to work on the new finish, inch by inch, his brushes etching out what he referred to as "The History of the Universe". Portraits of the Big Brother and the Holding Company band members flowed up the left side; Janis's astrological sign, Capricorn, appeared on the right rear quarter-panel. The verdant green valley of Northern California, containing a brown road that twists beneath mountains, appears on the right door, while the front hood contains "The Eye of God", overseeing all else. Not a square inch of the Porsche's bodywork was left untouched.

Janis and her cabriolet then became a familiar sight around the Bay Area and indeed over much of California. It was no stage prop; it was Janis's daily driver, and where she went, the Porsche went too, with her own hands on the wheel, her hair blowing in the wind, and her feathered dresses rustling in a blur of color...

On the evening of October 4, 1970 Janis parked her Porsche outside her hotel in Hollywood. Janis died that night, tragically young, at only 27 years old.

Janis's attorney, Bob Gordon, commandeered the car from the ensuing presse spectacle outside the hotel and garaged it safely away. It was returned to the Joplin family...

The surviving Joplin siblings then shared use of the car for a number of years before having it restored in Denver in its original dolphin grey finish.

By the early 1990s, the car's importance as an artifact of its owner and her era had become more clear, and the Joplin family commissioned Richard's original artwork to be duplicated on a new finish, with work performed by artists Jana Mitchell and Amber Owen of the Denver Center Theater Company. Working from stacks of period photographs, they recreated each of the artist's original brush strokes, in essence retelling the history of the universe. With the work completed, it was loaned in 1995 to the Rock and Roll Hall of Fame and Museum in Cleveland, Ohio...where Janis' Porsche has remained on display for the past 20 years.

...Recently recommissioned...Janis Joplin's Porsche is offered today by her siblings, Michael and Laura, its sole owners since 1973...

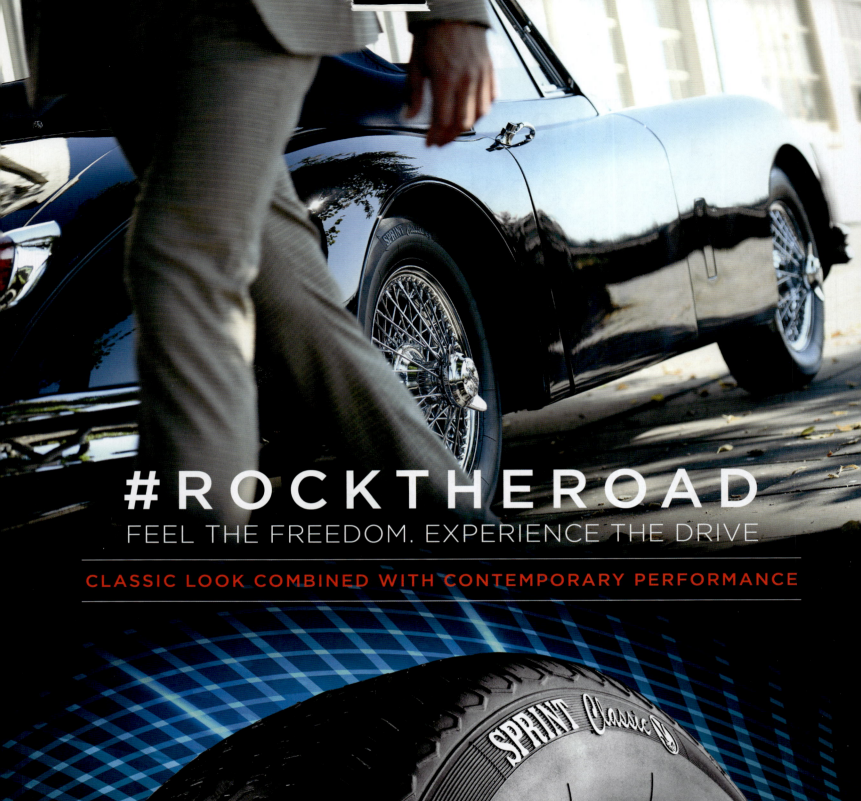

#ROCKTHEROAD
FEEL THE FREEDOM. EXPERIENCE THE DRIVE

CLASSIC LOOK COMBINED WITH CONTEMPORARY PERFORMANCE

VREDESTEIN
YOUR PERFORMANCE TYRES SINCE 1909

The 2015-2016 auction season results

This chapter lists, in alphabetical make order, the cars that were offered at auctions, covered by Historica Selecta, from 1st September 2015 to 31st August 2016.
5.644 cars (of 324 different makes) are listed in order of the model, presentation, year, and the date when they were auctioned.
From the first edition for the 1993-1994 season (Catalogo Bolaffi then Classic Car Auction Yearbook) forward, the technical data (year, chassis no., etc.), car condition, history, estimate and photos have been taken from the relative auction house catalogues, and the reported hammer prices are those communicated by the auction houses in their official lists. For this reason the authors cannot take any responsibility for mistakes and/or omissions.
The authors have not quoted most of the cars:
– listed in auction house sale catalogues without the indication of the chassis number or other identification number;
– of little historical interest because they were recently ceased to be produced or were replicas assembled with parts of various provenance.

N.B. The exchange rate is referred to as that of the day of the auction
The hammer prices include the buyer commission

Legenda

C	: central driver seat	F	: illustrated car
L	: left hand drive	SEASON CASE	: see chapter
M	: single-seater	TOP TEN	: see chapter
R	: right hand drive		
LWB	: long wheelbase	AUD	: Australian Dollar
SWB	: short wheelbase	DKK	: Danish Krone
		EUR	: Euro
NA	: not available	GBP	: Pounds Sterling
NQ	: not quoted	USD	: US Dollar
UC	: unmarked chassis		
NR	: no reserve	*	: hammer price of the "no reserve" cars
NS	: not sold	P	: price of the post auction sales
UD	: sold for an undisclosed sum		
WD	: withdrawn	Refer Dpt.	: refer Department

List of the covered sales and auction house abbreviations

Agu - Aguttes (F)
* Lyon — November 7, 2015
* Lyon — March 12, 2016
* Lyon — July 2, 2016

Art - Artcurial (F)
Hong Kong (HK) — October 6, 2015
Paris — November 1, 2015
Paris — February 5-6, 2016
Le Mans — July 9, 2016

AA - Auctions America (USA)
* Auburn, IN — September 2-6, 2015
* Hilton Head, SC — October 31, 2015
* Fort Lauderdale, FL — April 1-3, 2016
* Auburn, IN — May 5-7, 2016
* Santa Monica, CA — June 25-26, 2016

Aut - Automobilia Auktion (D)
Ladenburg — November 14, 2015
Ladenburg — May 20, 2016

B/J - Barrett-Jackson (USA)
* Las Vegas, NE — September 24-29, 2015
* Scottsdale, AZ — January 23-31, 2016
* Palm Beach, FL — April 8-10, 2016
* Uncasville, CT — June 23-25, 2016

Bon - Bonhams (GB)
Beaulieu — September 5, 2015
Chateau de Chantilly (F) — September 5, 2015
Goodwood — September 12, 2015
Ebeltoft (DK) — September 26, 2015
Philadelphia, PA (USA) — October 5, 2015
Zoute (B) — October 9, 2015
London — October 30, 2015
London — December 6, 2015
London — December 10, 2015
London — December 16, 2015
Scottsdale, AZ (USA) — January 28, 2016
Paris (F) — February 4, 2016
Amelia Island, FL (USA) — March 10, 2016
Stuttgart (D) — March 19, 2016
Goodwood — March 20, 2016
Monaco (MC) — May 13, 2016
Newport Pagnell — May 21, 2016
Greenwich, CT (USA) — June 5, 2016
Goodwood — June 24, 2016
Carmel, CA (USA) — August 19, 2016

Che - Cheffins (GB)
Cambridge — October 17, 2015
Cambridge — April 16, 2016
Cambridge — July 16, 2016

Coy - Coys (GB)
Castle Hedingham — September 6, 2015
Frankfurt (D) — September 26, 2015
Ascot — October 10, 2015
London — December 1, 2015
Birmingham Autosport — January 16, 2016
Maastricht (H) — January 16, 2016
London — March 8, 2016
Essen (D) — April 9, 2016
Ascot — April 16, 2016
Monaco (MC) — May 14, 2016
Blenheim Palace — July 2, 2016
Schloss Dyck (D) — August 6, 2016

Dor - Dorotheum (A)
* Salzburg — October 17, 2015
* Wien — June 18, 2016

G&Co. - Gooding & Company (USA)
Scottsdale, AZ — January 29-30, 2016
Amelia Island, FL — March 11, 2016
Pebble Beach, CA — August 20-21, 2016

H&H - H&H (GB)
Duxford — October 13-14, 2015
* Chateau Impney — December 9, 2015
* Donington Park — February 24, 2016
Duxford — April 20, 2016
* Donington Park — May 18, 2016
* Chateau Impney — July 10, 2016
* Donington Park — July 28, 2016

His - Historics at Brooklands (GB)
Weybridge — November 28, 2015
Brooklands — March 12, 2016
Brooklands — June 11, 2016
Brooklands — August 20, 2016

Mec - Mecum (USA)
* Dallas, TX — September 16-19, 2015
* Chicago, IL — October 8-10, 2015
* Anaheim, CA — November 12-14, 2015
* Austin, TX — December 11-12, 2015
* Kissimmee, FL — January 15-24, 2016
* Kansas City, KS — March 11-13, 2016
* Houston, TX — April 14-16, 2016
* Indianapolis, IN — May 17-22, 2016
* Portland, OR — June 17-18, 2016
* Denver, CO — July 8-9, 2016
* Harrisburg, PA — July 21-23, 2016
* Monterey, CA — August 18-20, 2016

Ose - Osenat (F)
Lyon — November 8, 2015
Fontainebleau — March 20, 2016
Fontainebleau — June 19, 2016

RMS - RM Sotheby's (USA)
London (UK) — September 7, 2015
Hershey, PA — October 8-9, 2015
New York, NY — December 10, 2015
Phoenix, AZ — January 28-29, 2016
Paris (F) — February 3, 2016
Amelia Island, FL — March 12, 2016
Monaco (MC) — May 14, 2016
Plymouth, MI — July 30, 2016
Monterey, CA — August 19-20, 2016

R&S - Russo & Steele (USA)
* Scottsdale, AZ — January 27-31, 2016
* Newport Beach, CA — June 10-12, 2016
* Monterey, CA — August 18-20, 2016

SiC - Silverstone Auctions (GB)
Salon Privé, Woodstock — September 4, 2015
* Silverstone — October 25, 2015
* Birmingham — November 14-15, 2015
* Stoneleigh Park, Coventry — February 26-27, 2016
* Birmingham — March 6, 2016
* Silverstone — May 20, 2016
* Aarhus (DK) — May 28-29, 2016
* Silverstone — July 28, 2016
* Silverstone — July 30-31, 2016

TBr - Theodore Bruce (AUS)
Melbourne — October 25, 2015

TFA - The Finest Automobile Auctions (USA)
* Hershey, PA — June 11, 2016

* Partially covered sales

PS: The cars offered by Russo & Steele are listed with the consignment number and not with the lot number

F1: 1958 Abarth 750 coupé (Zagato)

F2: 1959 Abarth 2200 coupé (Allemano)

ABARTH (I) (1949-1981)

Year	Model (Bodybuilder)	Chassis no.	Steering	Estimate	£	$	€	Date	Place	Lot	Auc. H.
1958	750 coupé (Zagato)	100584247	L	55-70.000 GBP	61.600	94.014	84.349	07-09-15	London	108	RMS F1
	"Double bubble" body finished in light metallic grey with black interior; reimported into Europe from the USA at unspecified date and fully restored in Belgium. From the Fendt Collection.										
1958	750 coupé (Zagato)	100565298	L	34-40.000 EUR	23.202*	33.674*	30.800*	03-02-16	Paris	162	RMS
	Restoration project.										
1958	750 coupé (Zagato)	462534	L	45-55.000 EUR	41.289*	60.088*	53.640*	05-02-16	Paris	215	Art
	Red with black interior; sold new to the USA, the car was raced in the 1950s and 1960s. Imported into France in 2012, it is described as in largely original condition.										
1957	750 coupé (Zagato)	260452	L	NA		NS		11-06-16	Newport Beach	6064	R&S
	Red with black interior (see lot 335 Bonhams 25.02.06 $55,299).										
1960	750 Sestriere coupé (Zagato)	757464	L	75-85.000 USD		NS		11-06-16	Hershey	137	TFA
	Silver with black interior; for over 50 years in the same family ownership, the car is described as in original condition and running order. 44,000 miles on the odometer. Currently fitted with a period correct Fiat 600 engine not stripped to check the internals (see lot 186 Bonhams 16.01.14 $53,900).										
1959	750 spider (Allemano)	476565	L	75-95.000 EUR		NS		09-07-16	Le Mans	194	Art
	Grey with black stripe; the car was raced in the USA in the 1960s and subsequently stored for nearly 30 years. Recently restored to its 1965 configuration; engine bored out to 850cc.										
1959	2200 coupé (Allemano)	112044528	L	180-200.000 EUR	88.588*	128.572*	117.600*	03-02-16	Paris	127	RMS F2
	Red with black leather interior; restored in Germany between 2002 and 2011.										
1961	1000 Bialbero coupé	1040293	L	225-275.000 USD	235.312*	308.000*	271.933*	19-08-16	Monterey	146	RMS F3
	Red; first raced as a factory competition car, in late 1961 it was sold to the USA where it was raced at some events. In the 1970s and 1980s it was raced at historic events and between 2003 and 2005 it was fully restored.										
1960	1000 Bialbero Aerodinamica (Pinin Farina)	E1351	M	Refer Dpt.		NS		21-08-16	Pebble Beach	148	G&Co
	Streamlined record car which set eight International Class G records at Monza track in 1960 driven by Giancarlo Baghetti, Mario Poltronieri, Alfonso Thiele, and Umberto Maglioli. Nicknamed "The Princess", it was subsequently exhibited at the 1960 Turin Motor Show and then remained in the Pininfarina Collection until 1970 when it was purchased by the current owner. Described as in original condition, virtually untouched since 1960. It comes with Italian ASI homologation.										
1966	1000 TC berlina	100DS2096251	L	50-70.000 GBP		NS		20-03-16	Goodwood	88	Bon
	Abarth chassis 2101687. Light blue and white; restored in the UK in 2009-10 and fitted with an Abarth A112 engine. Raced at historic events.										
1970	695 SS	23694270869	L	8-12.000 EUR	34.251	48.209	42.426	09-04-16	Essen	121	Coy
	White with red interior; restored in Italy in 1997. Imported into the UK in 2000. Registered in the RIA (Italian Abarth Register).										
1966	OT 1300 "Periscopio" (Sibona-Basano)	137C044	L	500-600.000 USD	353.998	506.000	456.260	11-03-16	Amelia Island	60	G&Co
	Delivered new to Abarth Corse Deutschland and raced in the 1966 season; acquired in 1967 by Peter Kaus, restored and displayed at the Rosso Bianco Collection until 1987; owned by Japanese collector Shiro Kosaka from 1987 to 2008; imported into the USA in 2008, mechanically fully restored and used at historic events.										
1969	850 Grand Prix/1300 Scorpione	104N1411387261	L	45-55.000 GBP		NS		07-09-15	London	109	RMS
	Built as standard 104N model and sold in Italy, in 1971 the car was fitted with a 1300 engine and the suspension were modified. Following an accident at a hill climb, also the front end was modified and the body was repainted in green and orange. Discovered in France in 1999 and subsequently restored in Italy. From the Fendt Collection.										

F3: 1961 Abarth 1000 Bialbero coupé

F4: 1974 Abarth SE027 Sport Prototipo (Pininfarina)

Year	Model	(Bodybuilder)	Chassis no.	Steering	Estimate	Hammer price £	$	€	Sale Date	Place	Lot	Auc. H.
1974	SE027 Sport Prototipo	(Pininfarina)	SE027001	R	175-250.000 GBP	168.000	256.402	230.042	07-09-15	London	127	RMS

Yellow and red; first of the three examples built, the car was exhibited at the Pininfarina stand at the 1974 Geneva Motor Show. Fitted with the 280bhp 2-litre 4-cylinder engine, it was never raced in period. Sold in Italy in 1976, it was later exported to the USA and reimported into Italy at unspecified date. **F4**

Year	Model		Chassis no.	Steering	Estimate	£	$	€	Date	Place	Lot	Auc. H.
1980	Formula Fiat-Abarth		SE0330035	M	18-20.000 GBP		NS		16-01-16	Birmingham	311	Coy

White; brakes recently overhauled. Formerly in the Gianni Giudici's collection.

AC (GB) (1908-)

Year	Model	Chassis no.	Steering	Estimate	£	$	€	Date	Place	Lot	Auc. H.
1922	12/40hp boattail sports	7350	R	37-42.000 GBP	52.640	68.895	60.826	20-08-16	Brooklands	284	His

Polished aluminium body with blue leather interior; reimported into the UK from Canada in 1995. Engine rebuilt many years ago (see lot 22 H & H 3.6.98 $28,330).

| 1933 | Ace 16/66 sports | L30 | R | 80-90.000 EUR | | NS | | 08-11-15 | Lyon | 250 | Ose |

Red with black wings; engine rebuilt circa 12 years ago. Built with coupé body, the car was fitted in 1938 at the factory with the present open body.

| 1958 | Ace Bristol | BEX406 | R | 180-220.000 GBP | | NS | | 04-09-15 | Woodstock | 231 | SiC |

Red with black interior; sold new to Canada, the car was reimported into the UK in 1990 and converted to right-hand drive. Engine and gearbox rebuilt in 2009 (see lot 82 H&H 10.6.09 $ 196,996).

| 1959 | Ace Bristol | BEX1090 | L | 250-300.000 EUR | 222.925 | 339.431 | 304.750 | 05-09-15 | Chantilly | 8 | Bon |

Blue with black interior; fully restored in the USA in the 2000s (see lots 135 RM 20.1.11 $ 217,250 and 170 Bonhams 16.8.13 $ 286,000).

| 1957 | Ace Bristol | BEX387 | L | 200-250.000 GBP | 214.300 | 330.515 | 293.334 | 12-09-15 | Goodwood | 335 | Bon |

Red with black interior; bought new by American racing driver Pierre Mion, the car won the 1959 SCCA E Production Championship. In the late 1980s it was imported into Spain where it remained until now. In good cosmetical condition and running order. **F5**

| 1956 | Ace Bristol | BEX222 | R | 130-160.000 GBP | | NS | | 12-09-15 | Goodwood | 378 | Bon |

Silver with red interior; built in left-hand drive form and fitted with a Bristol engine, the car was sold new to the USA and reimported into the UK in 1988 now fitted with a 6-cylinder Bristol engine not of the correct type for an AC. In the 1990s the car was restored, converted to right-hand drive and fitted with the present 1959 Bristol engine no.100D21038 (see lots 185 Brooks 26.10.93 NS, 326 Bonhams 12.7.13 $ 213,665 and 406 Artcurial 7.2.14 NS).

| 1956 | Ace 289 | BEX235 | L | NA | | NS | | 14-10-15 | Duxford | 33 | H&H |

Red with brown interior; fitted with Bristol engine, the car was sold new to Venezuela. Later it was imported into the USA and probably in the 1970s it was fitted with the present Ford 289 V8 engine. Reimported into the UK; interior redone in recent years (see lot 45 H&H 9.12.09 $ 175,984).

| 1959 | Ace Bristol | BEX1127 | L | 150-250.000 EUR | 247.736 | 360.525 | 321.840 | 05-02-16 | Paris | 155 | Art |

Red with black hardtop and original beige leather interior; body repainted at unspecified date. From 1973 to 2015 in the same ownership. The car requires recommissioning prior to use.

| 1960 | Ace Bristol | BEX1054 | L | 350-400.000 USD | 346.302* | 495.000* | 446.342* | 12-03-16 | Amelia Island | 128 | RMS |

Green with green leather interior; sold new to the USA. A few miles covered since a recent restoration.

| 1956 | Ace Bristol | BEX222 | R | 80-120.000 GBP | 109.020 | 157.937 | 140.025 | 20-03-16 | Goodwood | 58 | Bon |

See lot 378 Bonhams 12.9.15.

| 1962 | Ace Bristol | BE1199 | R | NA | 134.400 | 190.579 | 169.908 | 20-04-16 | Duxford | 18 | H&H |

Green with black interior; owned by the current vendor in 1964, 1966 and again since 2010. Fitted in 1966 following an accident with the present Cobra body; engine replaced with the present 100D2 unit probably in the late 1980s; restored in 2000-01.

| 1957 | Ace Bristol | BEX281 | L | 250-300.000 EUR | 226.429 | 326.255 | 287.500 | 13-05-16 | Monaco | 131 | Bon |

Metallic blue with dark blue leather interior; first restored in the late 1980s and between 2007 and 2008 again. Used at some historic events, including the Mille Miglia in Italy and the Argentinian Mille Miglia.

| 1958 | Ace Bristol | BEX406 | R | NA | 249.750 | 328.671 | 295.754 | 30-07-16 | Silverstone | 525 | SiC |

See lot 231 Silverstone Auctions 4.9.15.

| 1956 | Ace Bristol | BE172 | R | 325-375.000 USD | 235.312 | 308.000 | 271.933 | 20-08-16 | Pebble Beach | 74 | G&Co |

Silver with black interior; in single UK ownership from 1960 to 2011: mechanicals overhauled prior to be imported into the USA in 2011 (see lot 210 Bonhams 16.9.11 $222,955).

| 1960 | Aceca Bristol | BE771 | L | NA | 115.597 | 176.000 | 158.030 | 05-09-15 | Auburn | 5068 | AA |

Dark red with tan interior; restored. Converted to left-hand drive (see lots 435 Bonhams 5.2.15 $ 153,522 and S6 Mecum 15.8.15 NS).

| 1960 | Aceca Bristol | BEX766 | L | 225-275.000 USD | | NS | | 28-01-16 | Phoenix | 130 | RMS |

Grey with grey leather interior; sold new to the USA, restored in 2002-2003 (see lot 142 RM 21.1.10 $ 137,500).

| 1958 | Aceca Bristol | BEX678 | L | 200-240.000 USD | 146.216 | 209.000 | 188.455 | 12-03-16 | Amelia Island | 158 | RMS |

Black with red leather interior; sold new to the USA, at unspecified date the car was sent back to the UK and fully restored by the factory to its original specification (see lot 139 RM 9.10.14 $ 214,500). **F6**

F5: 1957 AC Ace Bristol

F6: 1958 AC Aceca Bristol

Where the world's greatest cars come to be sold - 14 QUEENS GATE PLACE MEWS, LONDON SW7 5BQ T: +44 (0)20 7584 3503 W: WWW.FISKENS.COM

SINCE UNVEILING THE 2016 RETROMOBILE COLLECTION AND DESPITE THE CONTRARY MARKETPLACE, Fiskens are proud to have achieved a number of world-record-breaking sales. Sales that have ranged from Ferraris with significant Le Mans history to original bodied WO Bentleys. Fiskens seek more of the worlds greatest cars to launch its new state-of-the-art central London mews showroom

With no two negotiations ever being the same, Fiskens's diverse knowledge and experience means there has never been a better time to consign - and all for one single commission. For a confidential discussion please call Gregor, Rory or Robert

FISKENS
FINE HISTORIC AUTOMOBILES

Year	Model	(Bodybuilder)	Chassis no.	Steering	Estimate	Hammer price £	$	€	Date	Place	Lot	Auc. H.
1958	Aceca Bristol		BEX670	L	250-300.000 USD	205.898*	269.500*	237.942*	20-08-16	Monterey	235	RMS

Grey with navy blue leather interior; sold new to Canada, in 2013 the car was imported into the USA where it received a concours-quality restoration.

AC CAR GROUP (GB)

Year	Model	(Bodybuilder)	Chassis no.	Steering	Estimate	£	$	€	Date	Place	Lot	Auc. H.
1996	Ace Brooklands		62053	R	27-32.000 GBP	28.500	41.049	36.315	11-06-16	Brooklands	229	His

Red with tan leather interior; one owner and 6,015 miles covered.

ADLER (D) (1900-1939)

Year	Model	(Bodybuilder)	Chassis no.	Steering	Estimate	£	$	€	Date	Place	Lot	Auc. H.
1914	35/80hp phaeton		46514	R	130-160.000 EUR		NS		04-02-16	Paris	400	Bon

Green with black wings; described as in original condition. Used by the German military during WWI. For many years at the Jean Tua Transport Museum in Geneva. Believed the only survivor of four examples built.

AERO (CS) (1929-1947)

Year	Model	(Bodybuilder)	Chassis no.	Steering	Estimate	£	$	€	Date	Place	Lot	Auc. H.
1935	Type 30 roadster		35329	L	25-35.000 EUR		NS		17-10-15	Salzburg	328	Dor

Red with black leather interior; since 1985 in the current ownership. Body restored in the mid-1990s, engine restored in 2005.

ALBION (GB) (1901-1913)

Year	Model	(Bodybuilder)	Chassis no.	Steering	Estimate	£	$	€	Date	Place	Lot	Auc. H.
1901	A1 8hp dogcart		CCC195	R	110-140.000 GBP	147.100	232.948	204.822	30-10-15	London	103	Bon F7

Since the 1960s in the same family ownership. Last driven at the London-Brighton Run in 2002. In good running order.

ALFA ROMEO (I) (1910-)

Year	Model	(Bodybuilder)	Chassis no.	Steering	Estimate	£	$	€	Date	Place	Lot	Auc. H.
1931	6C 1750 GT berlina (Touring)		10914592	R	120-150.000 GBP	109.166	168.367	149.426	12-09-15	Goodwood	337	Bon F8

Dark red with black roof and beige cloth interior; sold new in Italy, the car was owned from the late 1960s to the late 1980s by the Alfa Romeo historian Luigi Fusi. Acquired in 2004 by the current owner and imported into the UK, the car received a full mechanical restoration. Engine rebuilt around a new block (original included in the lot); new modified clutch (original with the car); gearbox rebuilt.

| 1929 | 6C 1750 Turismo cabriolet (J.Young) | | 0411875 | R | 180-220.000 GBP | 168.000 | 252.857 | 238.997 | 28-11-15 | Weybridge | 280 | His |

Dark blue with grey leather interior; acquired in 1984 by the current owner, later the car received a full restoration completed in 2011. A number of improvements carried out to the mechanicals.

| 1929 | 6C 1750 SS cabriolet | | 0312905 | R | 1.350-1.550.000 EUR | | NS | | 05-02-16 | Paris | 187 | Art |

Delivered to the UK Alfa Romeo importer FW Stiles in rolling chassis form and then bodied by Carlton Carriage, the car was bought new by JD Benjafield who raced it in 1929 and 1930. Later the car received a new body and was acquired by Ben Plunket who raced it at several events in 1934. Imported into Ireland, it was restored at unspecified date and fitted again with a new body. In the late 1990s it was restored by Paul Grist whose restoration gave it the appearance of an original, unrestored but regularly maintained car.

| 1929 | 6C 1750 SS spider (Zagato) | | 0312861 | R | 1.800-2.400.000 EUR | | NS | | 13-05-16 | Monaco | 119 | Bon |

Red with brown leather interior; supercharged engine. Always well maintained, the car is described as in very good mechanical condition. First owner Achille Varzi.

| 1930 | 6C 1750 GS spider | | 8513048 | R | 900-1.200.000 EUR | | NS | | 14-05-16 | Monaco | 223 | RMS |

Driven by Prof. Mario Ferraguti, the car raced three editions of the Mille Miglia, in 1931 with the supercharged engine in its original form and in 1933 and 1936 with the engine modified to run on alternative fuel supplied by an apparatus known as gasogeno. At unspecified date the engine was returned to its original specification and the car was fitted with the present, more modern body finished in dark red with red interior. From the Count Agusta collection.

| 1933 | 8C 2300 Monza (Brianza) | | 2311218 | R | 12-15.000.000 USD | 9.160.360 | 11.990.000 | 10.585.971 | 21-08-16 | Pebble Beach | 128 | G&Co TOP TEN |

The car was sold new in Italy where it had several owners and was raced until 1948. In 1950 it was sold to Venezuela and in 1954 it was imported into the USA where it remained in single ownership until 1982 when it was bought by Peter Giddings, who had it restored and raced it at numerous historic events until 1996 when it was acquired by Tom Hollfelder who in turn resold it to the current owner in 2010. Described as in very good mechanical condtion (see lot 117 Gooding & Company 15.8.10 $6,710,000).

| 1937 | 6C 2300B MM Berlinetta | | 815025 | R | 750-1.100.000 EUR | | NS | | 04-02-16 | Paris | 374 | Bon |

Red with biscuit interior; restored between 2009 and 2011. According to historical research commissioned by the owner, chassis no.815025 with cabriolet body was registered in 1938 in Switzerland where it remained until 1958 when it was exported to South America. The car may either have lost its bodywork along the way or indeed been converted to Berlinetta form. It is known to have been restored or rebuilt in the early 2000s and wore an authentic Touring coackwork badge. Currently fitted with engine no.823040 bought in the USA (see lot 224 RM 18.8.12 NS).

| 1939 | 8C 2900B Spider (Touring) | | 412041 | R | 20-25.000.000 USD | 15.127.200 | 19.800.000 | 17.481.420 | 20-08-16 | Monterey | 234 | RMS TOP TEN |

The car was imported after WWII in South America where the original body, no.2027, was replaced with a racing cycle-fendered body and the chassis was shortened to accept a Chevrolet V8 engine. In 1993 the rolling chassis was bought by Swiss Guido Haschke who at the same time acquired also the original body from Count Vittorio Zanon in Italy. In 1994 Sam and Emily Mann purchased the rolling chassis and body and had the car restored in UK by Tony Merrick, who returned the chassis to its original lenght and fitted it with the present original 8C 2900B engine no.422042.

| 1947 | 6C 2500 S cabriolet (Pinin Farina) | | 915325 | R | 450-650.000 USD | | NS | | 21-08-16 | Pebble Beach | 109 | G&Co |

Dark blue with red leather interior; sold new to Belgium, the car was purchased in 2007 by the current, third owner. Fully restored in Germany between 2010 and 2014.

F7: 1901 Albion A1 8hp dogcart

F8: 1931 Alfa Romeo 6C 1750 GT berlina (Touring)

LUKAS HÜNI AG

Established some 40 years ago, we handle with excellence and a passion for detail all aspects of collecting historic automobiles. Our services include:

- buying and selling historic motorcars, both on our own account and for clients
- looking after our collector clients and their collections all around the world
- repair work and full restorations, using only the leading specialists and restorers
- maintenance, storage in our Zurich facilities, and transport world-wide

We concentrate in the high end of pre-war and Fifties/Sixties automobiles and specialise in the models that were market leaders and successful in their day. Our preferred marques include Bugatti, Alfa Romeo, Aston Martin, Bentley, Rolls-Royce, Lancia, Ferrari and Maserati.

New cars are available on request.

Talbot Lago T26 Grand Sport Short Chassis Barchetta by Motto 1950.

We always have a selection of outstanding automobiles in stock which are either in excellent original condition or restored to perfection. We look forward to talking to you about our current stock, or the car that you are looking for.

If you wish to sell an important car, we would be happy to discuss your car and your requirements.

Visits to our showroom are by appointment only.

Lindenstrasse 26 · CH-8008 Zürich · Switzerland · Tel (+41)44-384 84 00 · Fax (+41)44-380 74 11 · cars@lukashuniag.ch

Year	Model	(Bodybuilder)	Chassis no.	Steering	Estimate	Hammer price £	$	€	Sale Date	Place	Lot	Auc. H.
1948	6C 2500 SS cabriolet	(Stabilimenti Farina)	915670	R	800-1.000.000 USD	708.096	1.012.000	926.688	29-01-16	Scottsdale	29	G&Co F9

Described as a one-off exhibited by Stabilimenti Farina at the 1948 Turin Motor Show. Sold new in Italy, the car was imported into the USA in 1979. In 1997 it was reimported into Europe and fully restored. Since 2011 in the current German ownership. Finished in light grey with maroon and grey interior.

Year	Model	(Bodybuilder)	Chassis no.	Steering	Estimate	£	$	€	Date	Place	Lot	Auc. H.
1951	6C 2500 SS Villa d'Este	(Touring)	915910	R	750-900.000 EUR		NS		03-02-16	Paris	148	RMS

Dark blue; sold new in Italy, the car was discovered in the late 1990s. Acquired in 2008 by the current owner and subsequently fully restored in Germany and Italy.

| 1947 | 6C 2500 SS coupé | (Touring) | 915539 | R | 600-900.000 USD | | NS | | 11-03-16 | Amelia Island | 29 | G&Co |

Light grey with blue interior; sold new to Portugal, the car remained in single ownership until 2006 when it was acquired by the current vendor. Fully restored between 2007 and 2010.

| 1949 | 6C 2500 SS cabriolet | (Pinin Farina) | 915766 | R | 550-800.000 EUR | | NS | | 14-05-16 | Monaco | 268 | RMS |

The car was purchased new by Prince Ali Salman Aga Khan who had it registered in Italy and retained it until 1953. After some ownership changes in Italy it was imported into the USA and was reimported into Italy in 1991. Since 2004 in the current ownership. Fully restored over a four year period and finished in black with scarlet leather interior.

| 1951 | 6C 2500 SS cabriolet | (Pinin Farina) | 915922 | R | 700-850.000 USD | 474.826 | 621.500 | 548.722 | 20-08-16 | Pebble Beach | 31 | G&Co |

Burgundy with tan interior; stored for many years, in 1998 the car was bought in 1998 by the previous owner and restored. In 2009 it was purchased by the current owner who restored the mechanicals, in 2010 drove the car at the historical Mille Miglia and while in Italy had the body restored again and finished in the present livery.

| 1953 | 1900 C Sprint | (Pinin Farina) | AR1900C01630 | L | 240-320.000 GBP | | NS | | 12-09-15 | Goodwood | 375 | Bon |

Grey with grey cloth interior; restored in the mid-1980s and subsequently stored. Acquired in late 2014 by the current owner, it has been recently recommissioned and the interior have been retrimmed. In very good overall condition.

| 1953 | 1900 C Sprint Supergioiello | (Ghia) | AR1900C01549 | L | 490-580.000 EUR | | NS | | 14-05-16 | Monaco | 277 | RMS |

Sold new to Spain, the car was raced at several events until 1961, including the 1955 Monte Carlo Rally. In more recent years it was fully restored in Italy by Cognolato.

| 1954 | 1900 C Sprint | (Pinin Farina) | AR190001647 | L | 450-550.000 USD | 315.150 | 412.500 | 364.196 | 20-08-16 | Pebble Beach | 3 | G&Co |

Dark blue with grey leather interior; sold new in Italy, from 1966 to 2015 the car was in the ownership of an Alfa Romeo dealer and was last road used in 1966. Recent cosmetic and mechanical restoration works.

| 1954 | 1900 C Sprint 2ª serie | (Touring) | AR1900C01678 | L | 180-220.000 GBP | 154.166 | 237.770 | 211.022 | 12-09-15 | Goodwood | 339 | Bon |

Dark red with beige interior; restored prior to its acquisition by the current owner in 2004, the car is described as still in very good overall condition (see lot 431 Coys 15.5.04 $ 90,737).

| 1954 | 1900 C Sprint 2ª serie | (Touring) | 01822 | L | 180-220.000 GBP | 168.000 | 253.092 | 238.762 | 01-12-15 | London | 344 | Coy |

Burgundy with tobacco interior; sold new in Italy, the car was exported to the USA in 1978 and reimported into Europe in 1999. In good overall condition (see lots Brooks 72 15.8.98 £ 61,900 and 162 6.3.00 $ 61,480, Bonhams 228 26.5.03 $ 55,019 and Artcurial 15.2.04 $ 80,110).

| 1955 | 1900 C Sprint 2ª serie | (Boano) | AR1900C01846 | L | Refer Dpt. | 692.703* | 990.000* | 906.543* | 29-01-16 | Scottsdale | 46 | G&Co F10 |

Originally finished in yellow with black roof, the car was sold new in Italy; in the 1980s it was bought by Mario Righini who in 2013 resold it to the current owner. Imported into the USA, it was subsequently restored and finished in the present red livery with black interior. One-off displayed by Carrozzeria Boano at the 1955 Turin Motor Show.

| 1955 | 1900 C Sprint 2ª serie | (Zagato) | AR1900C01909 | L | 1.400-1.800.000 USD | | NS | | 29-01-16 | Phoenix | 245 | RMS |

Dark blue with tobacco leather interior; fully restored between 2008 and 2011 and fitted with Alfa Romeo 1900 C Super Sprint engine no.1308.10480. Originally finished in ivory, the car was sold new to Venezuela where it was raced under the banner of the Scuderia Madunina of Milan, Italy. In 1993 it was reimported into Europe and later exported to the USA where it was acquired in the early 2000s by the current owner.

| 1959 | 1900 C Super Sprint coupé | (Ghia Aigle) | AR1900C10439 | L | 160-220.000 EUR | | NS | | 05-09-15 | Chantilly | 6 | Bon |

Two-tone grey with black interior; in good overall condition. Recent mechanical works (see lot 12 Bonhams 25.5.13 NS).

| 1957 | 1900 C Super Sprint | (Touring) | AR1900C10410 | L | 200-240.000 EUR | | NS | | 05-02-16 | Paris | 195 | Art |

Red with red and light grey interior; sold new to Switzerland, the car has had three owners. The engine was overhauled in 2010. In 2012 it was acquired by the current owner and was restored between 2014 and 2015.

| 1957 | 1900 C Super Sprint | (Touring) | AR1900C10596 | L | 325-375.000 USD | 211.629 | 302.500 | 272.764 | 12-03-16 | Amelia Island | 124 | RMS |

Red with silver roof and beige leather interior; fully restored in 2013 (see lot 159 Bonhams 16.1.14 $ 222,200).

| 1956 | 1900 C Super Sprint | (Touring) | AR1900C10066 | L | 250-275.000 EUR | 201.818 | 265.474 | 237.965 | 06-08-16 | Schloss Dyck | 135 | Coy |

Grey with red roof; sold new to Switzerland and later imported into Belgium. Restored.

| 1959 | 1900 C Super Sprint | (Ghia Aigle) | AR1900C10439 | L | 150-180.000 USD | 126.060 | 165.000 | 145.679 | 19-08-16 | Carmel | 43 | Bon |

See lot 6 Bonhams 5.9.15.

| 1957 | Giulietta Sprint Veloce | (Bertone) | AR1493E03808 | L | 100-130.000 GBP | 89.600 | 136.748 | 122.689 | 07-09-15 | London | 161 | RMS F11 |

Red with black interior; "Alleggerita" version sold new to racing driver Edoardo Lualdi Gabardi, the car has had a long race career in period and has been driven at several historic events, including the Mille Miglia Storica, in more recent years. Engine rebuilt in 2001.

| 1961 | Giulietta Sprint Veloce | (Bertone) | 159755 | L | 65-85.000 EUR | | NS | | 01-11-15 | Paris | 150 | Art |

Blue with grey and blue interior; restored in 1990, engine overhauled in 2003 (see lot 40 Artcurial 20.10.13 $ 79,037).

| 1957 | Giulietta Sprint | (Bertone) | AR149304862 | L | 85-125.000 EUR | 69.547 | 103.095 | 92.000 | 04-02-16 | Paris | 378 | Bon |

Black; sold new to the USA, the car was imported into the Netherlands 28 years ago and restored. Not driven after its restoration, it has been recently recommissioned and is described as in very good condition.

F9: 1948 Alfa Romeo 6C 2500 SS cabriolet (Stabilimenti Farina)

F10: 1955 Alfa Romeo 1900 C Sprint 2a serie (Boano)

Dino Cognolato

ALFA ROMEO Giulietta Sprint Speciale Prototipo

ALFA ROMEO 256 Spider Touring

ALFA ROMEO 8C 2300 Monza

ALFA ROMEO 2900 Corsa

ALFA ROMEO 256 Berlinetta Touring

Professional restorations
Full size drawings for original bodyworks
Manufacture of prototypes

DINO COGNOLATO & C. S.N.C.
CARROZZERIA NOVA RINASCENTE
Via Noalese, 66 - 35010 Vigonza (PD) -Italy-
tel +39 049 8095482   fax +39 049 8096298
novarinascente@cognolato.it

Year	Model	(Bodybuilder)	Chassis no.	Steering	Estimate	Hammer price £	$	€	Sale Date	Place	Lot	Auc. H.

F11: 1957 Alfa Romeo Giulietta Sprint Veloce (Bertone)

F12: 1960 Alfa Romeo Giulietta Spider Veloce (Pinin Farina)

Year	Model (Bodybuilder)	Chassis no.	Steering	Estimate	£	$	€	Date	Place	Lot	Auc. H.
1956	Giulietta Sprint (Bertone)	AR149301583	L	25-35.000 EUR	34.867*	50.741*	45.296*	05-02-16	Paris	165	Art

Sold new to Ireland, the car was raced at the 1956 Tulip Rally. Discovered in 2013 in the ownership of the family of its second owner, it is in "barn find" condition and apparently complete.

| 1956 | Giulietta Sprint (Bertone) | AR149301913 | L | 28-32.000 GBP | 33.040 | 47.221 | 42.579 | 12-03-16 | Brooklands | 221 | His |

Grey with grey and blue interior; fitted with a rebuilt engine and 5-speed gearbox of the series 101.

| 1962 | Giulietta Sprint (Bertone) | AR350459 | L | 28-34.000 GBP | 39.100 | 56.644 | 50.220 | 20-03-16 | Goodwood | 71 | Bon |

White with blue interior; currently fitted with a 1600 engine and 5-speed gearbox.

| 1964 | Giulietta Sprint (Bertone) | AR385432 | L | 30-35.000 EUR | 22.834 | 32.139 | 28.284 | 09-04-16 | Essen | 138 | Coy |

Blue; prepared for historic racing.

| 1961 | Giulietta Sprint (Bertone) | AR159206 | L | 58-65.000 EUR | 45.667 | 64.278 | 56.568 | 09-04-16 | Essen | 173 | Coy |

Yellow with red interior; fully restored in 2015.

| 1962 | Giulietta Sprint (Bertone) | 170016 | L | 38-42.000 EUR | NS | | | 14-05-16 | Monaco | 136 | Coy |

Red; garaged for the last 16 years since the present vendor bought it in 2000.

| 1963 | Giulietta berlina | AR225114 | L | 25-40.000 USD | 19.986 | 28.600 | 25.016 | 02-04-16 | Ft.Lauderdale | 721 | AA |

Light blue with black interior; older restoration.

| 1957 | Giulietta TI berlina | AR146801020 | L | 25-35.000 EUR | 22.354* | 29.030* | 26.224* | 09-07-16 | Le Mans | 127 | Art |

Light blue; sold new to Sweden, the car was raced until the late 1960s. Stored for many years, it was fully restored between 1996 and 2010.

| 1956 | Giulietta Spider (Pinin Farina) | 149500861 | L | 80-100.000 USD | 35.374* | 50.600* | 46.405* | 28-01-16 | Scottsdale | 71 | Bon |

White with red leatherette interior; acquired three years ago by the current owner and subsequently restored.

| 1959 | Giulietta Spider (Pinin Farina) | AR149505821 | L | 70-90.000 EUR | NS | | | 04-02-16 | Paris | 386 | Bon |

Dark blue with beige interior; restored in Italy between 2013 and 2014.

| 1962 | Giulietta Spider (Pininfarina) | AR370395 | L | 75-100.000 USD | 37.314* | 52.800* | 48.629* | 10-03-16 | Amelia Island | 114 | Bon |

Red with white interior; acquired in 2008 by the current owner and subsequently restored.

| 1961 | Giulietta Spider (Pininfarina) | AR149506495 | L | 60-80.000 USD | 44.583 | 63.800 | 55.806 | 02-04-16 | Ft.Lauderdale | 460 | AA |

Grey with red interior; restored.

| 1962 | Giulietta Spider Veloce (Pininfarina) | AR171861 | L | 75-110.000 USD | 57.651 | 82.500 | 72.163 | 02-04-16 | Ft.Lauderdale | 503 | AA |

Red with black interior; restored.

| 1959 | Giulietta Spider Veloce (Pinin Farina) | AR149506301 | L | 50-60.000 EUR | NS | | | 09-07-16 | Le Mans | 128 | Art |

Prepared for historic racing. It participated in the 1963 San Remo Rally (see Artcurial lots 72 14.2.10 NS and 145 11.11.12 $43,857).

| 1960 | Giulietta Spider Veloce (Pinin Farina) | AR149511640 | L | 80-120.000 EUR | 98.561 | 127.996 | 115.624 | 09-07-16 | Le Mans | 205 | Art F12 |

Light blue with anthracite leather interior; full restoration completed in late 2015.

| 1957 | Giulietta Spider (Pinin Farina) | AR149501529 | L | 80-110.000 USD | NS | | | 19-08-16 | Monterey | F152 | Mec |

White with black interior; sold new to the USA. Restored.

| 1958 | Giulietta Spider (Pinin Farina) | AR149503368 | L | 70-90.000 USD | 54.626* | 71.500* | 63.127* | 20-08-16 | Pebble Beach | 25 | G&Co |

Red with black interior; restored. Recent mechanical works (see lots 553 Auctions America 22.3.13 $55,000, 174 Bonhams 16.1.14 NS, and 3 Gooding & Company 16.8.14 $59,400).

F13: 1961 Alfa Romeo Giulietta Sprint Speciale (Bertone)

F14: 1961 Alfa Romeo 2000 Spider (Touring)

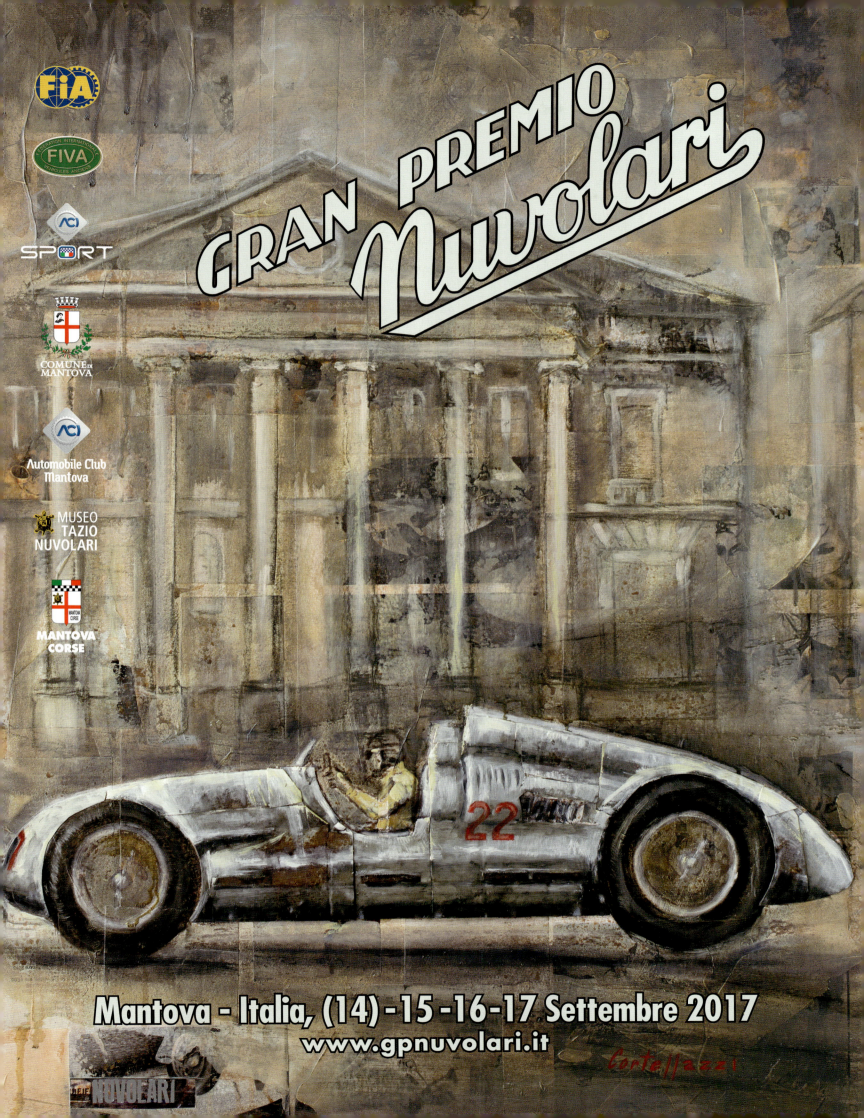

Year	Model	(Bodybuilder)	Chassis no.	Steering	Estimate	Hammer price £	$	€	Date	Place	Lot	Auc. H.
1958	Giulietta Spider Veloce	(Pinin Farina)	AR149504663	L	140-180.000 USD	113.454*	148.500*	131.111*	21-08-16	Pebble Beach	158	G&Co

Black with red interior; sold new to the USA, the car remained later unused for many years. A few years ago it was purchased by an Alfa Romeo enthusiast and subjected to a full restoration completed in 2015.

1961	Giulietta Sprint Speciale	(Bertone)	AR0012000850	L	105-120.000 EUR		NS		01-11-15	Paris	151	Art

White; raced in the 1960s in Sweden. Later it was driven at historic races. Recently it has been restored and returned to its original specification.

| 1961 | Giulietta Sprint Speciale | (Bertone) | AR1012000379 | L | 150-180.000 USD | 80.746* | 115.500* | 105.925* | 28-01-16 | Scottsdale | 73 | Bon F13 |

Red; sold new to the USA, the car was exported to Japan in 1991. Reimported into the USA in early 2013 and subsequently restored (see lots 811 Auctions America 1.8.13 NS and S15 Mecum 15.8.15 NS).

| 1960 | Giulietta Sprint Speciale | (Bertone) | AR10120000366 | L | 80-120.000 EUR | | NS | | 19-06-16 | Fontainebleau | 346 | Ose |

Black with red and beige interior; body repainted in 2007 (see lot 153 Bonhams 7.2.09 $52,975).

| 1961 | Giulietta Sprint Speciale | (Bertone) | AR1012000320 | L | 140-180.000 USD | 80.220* | 105.000* | 92.705* | 19-08-16 | Monterey | F93 | Mec |

Red with white and red interior; 150 miles covered since the restoration (see lot S138 Mecum 16.8.14 $130,000).

| 1961 | Giulietta SZ coda tonda | (Zagato) | AR101260037 | L | 450-650.000 EUR | | NS | | 04-02-16 | Paris | 322 | Bon |

Red with white stripe on the nose and black interior; raced in the USA in the 1960s. Restored in the late 1980s and subsequently driven at several historic events. Since 2013 in the current ownership, it is described as in good overall condition and presented in road trim.

| 1962 | Giulietta SZ coda tronca | (Zagato) | Ar1012600207 | L | 600-800.000 EUR | | NS | | 04-02-16 | Paris | 321 | Bon |

Red with black interior; sold new in Italy, the car was imported in 1993 into Japan from Switzerland. Since 2014 in the current ownership. Currently fitted with an Alfa Romeo 1750 engine, it comes with also the 1,290cc Type 750 Veloce engine no.AR0012000634, which is understood to be the original.

| 1962 | Giulietta SZ coda tronca | (Zagato) | AR1012600183 | L | 580-720.000 EUR | | NS | | 05-02-16 | Paris | 194 | Art |

White with red stripe; sold new to Switzerland, the car was raced in the 1960s. Later it was fitted with an Alfa Romeo Giulietta 1300 engine and used on the road. In 2003 it was acquired by the current owner and it is currently fitted with a correct series 120 engine no.00827.

| 1961 | 2000 Spider | (Touring) | AR1020402771 | L | 90-120.000 EUR | 71.552 | 109.757 | 96.600 | 09-10-15 | Zoute | 28 | Bon F14 |

Red with black leather inetrior; sold new in Italy, the car was exported in 1981 to the USA where it was restored between 2004 and 2008. Currently registered in the Netherlands (see lot 7007 Russo & Steele 12.8.10 $ 60,500).

| 1959 | 2000 Spider | (Touring) | AR1020400169 | L | 45-55.000 EUR | 47.570 | 66.956 | 58.925 | 09-04-16 | Essen | 176 | Coy |

White with red interior; showing 27,000 miles on the odometer and with the same owner since 1960, the car was driven until 1971 and stored in a garage in Texas until being purchased by the current owner.

| 1960 | 2000 Spider | (Touring) | AR1020401801 | L | 55-75.000 USD | 40.055* | 54.900* | 49.608* | 25-06-16 | Santa Monica | 1092 | AA |

White; body restored and engine rebuilt at unspecified date.

| 1962 | Ondine | | R1084957 | L | 7-9.000 GBP | 6.000 | 7.969 | 7.157 | 02-07-16 | Woodstock | 241 | Coy |

Restoration to be ultimate.

| 1965 | 2600 Berlina | | AR801478 | L | 9-11.000 GBP | 10.080 | 15.209 | 13.901 | 09-12-15 | Chateau Impney | 93 | H&H F15 |

Graphite grey with beige interior; in good overall condition. The car remained for 23 years with its first owner and was repainted in the 1990s.

| 1963 | 2600 Spider | (Touring) | AR191872 | R | 50-60.000 GBP | 40.000 | 56.720 | 50.264 | 16-04-16 | Ascot | 108 | Coy |

Red with black interior; in good working order.

| 1964 | 2600 Spider | (Touring) | AR852009 | R | 50-60.000 GBP | 82.688 | 120.460 | 107.370 | 20-05-16 | Silverstone | 304 | SiC |

Red with black hardtop; recent recommissioning. Engine, gearbox and brakes rebuilt over the years (see lot 278 Historics 7.3.15 $ 105,410).

| 1963 | 2600 Spider | (Touring) | AR191768 | L | 80-120.000 EUR | 107.706 | 139.872 | 126.352 | 09-07-16 | Le Mans | 195 | Art |

Black with red interior; fully restored at unspecified date.

| 1965 | 2600 Sprint | (Bertone) | AR824626 | L | 30-40.000 EUR | 47.941 | 75.917 | 66.752 | 01-11-15 | Paris | 118 | Art F16 |

Dark blue with original dark beige leather interior; restored in the 2000s.

| 1963 | 2600 Sprint | (Bertone) | 821999 | L | 35-45.000 EUR | | NS | | 08-11-15 | Lyon | 248 | Ose |

White with original leather interior; restored some years ago (see lot 326 Osenat 15.3.15 NS).

| 1965 | 2600 Sprint | (Bertone) | AR854316 | R | 18-23.000 GBP | | NS | | 09-12-15 | Chateau Impney | 91 | H&H |

Blue with beige interior; sold new to the UK, in the 1970s the car was exported to the USA where it was restored in the 1990s. Recently reimported.

| 1967 | 2600 Sprint | (Bertone) | 826326 | L | 25-35.000 EUR | 13.909* | 20.619* | 18.400* | 04-02-16 | Paris | 428 | Bon |

Since 1982 in the same family ownership; paintwork and interior redone in 2002. In running condition.

| 1964 | 2600 Sprint | (Bertone) | AR820935 | L | 25-35.000 EUR | 23.988 | 31.554 | 28.284 | 06-08-16 | Schloss Dyck | 158 | Coy |

Dark blue with beige interior; 52,224 miles on the odometer.

| 1965 | 2600 SZ | (Zagato) | AR856034 | L | 100-130.000 GBP | 97.820 | 134.053 | 121.131 | 24-06-16 | Goodwood | 256 | Bon F17 |

Red with black vinyl interior; prepared for historic rallying at unspecified date. Recently repainted (see lot 118 Coys 28.10.06 $59,864).

F15: 1965 Alfa Romeo 2600 Berlina

F16: 1965 Alfa Romeo 2600 Sprint (Bertone)

Year	Model	(Bodybuilder)	Chassis no.	Steering	Estimate	Hammer Price £	Hammer Price $	Hammer Price €	Sale Date	Sale Place	Lot	Auc. H.

F17: 1965 Alfa Romeo 2600 SZ (Zagato)

F18: 1961 Alfa Romeo Romeo 2 minibus

Year	Model (Bodybuilder)	Chassis no.	Steering	Estimate	£	$	€	Date	Place	Lot	Auc. H.
1961	**Romeo 2 minibus**	AR186154	L	60-90.000 EUR	47.814	70.878	63.250	04-02-16	Paris	350	Bon F18
Maroon; restored two years ago. 1,300cc engine.											
1964	**Giulia TI Super berlina**	AR595469	L	70-90.000 GBP		NS		12-09-15	Goodwood	346	Bon
Accepted as one of the cars prepared by Autodelta for the 1965 Sebring 3 Hours; driven by Teodoro Zeccoli, the car placed 6th overall and 3rd in class. In 1982 it was restored for static display purposes and remained unused for over 20 years. In 2008 it was acquired by the current owner and imported into Japan. Fitted with a 1,850cc "Super Talladega" engine giving over 200 bhp.											
1964	**Giulia TI Super berlina**	AR595469	L	40-50.000 GBP	40.250	60.878	55.630	10-12-15	London	367	Bon F19
See lot 346 Bonhams 12.9.15.											
1966	**Giulia Super berlina**	AR337918	L	50-60.000 USD	23.090*	33.000*	30.218*	29-01-16	Phoenix	203	RMS
Restored to Italian Polizia Squadra Volante specification. Used in several Italian movies (see lot 3 RM 5.2.14 $ 37,920).											
1965	**Giulia Super berlina**	AR305301	L	23-28.000 GBP		NS		02-07-16	Woodstock	208	Coy
Red; prepared for historic racing in the early 1990s.											
1963	**Giulia Sprint (Bertone)**	AR354273	L	80-100.000 USD	58.828*	77.000*	67.983*	20-08-16	Pebble Beach	21	G&Co
Dark blue; sold new to the USA. Recently restored.											
1965	**Giulia Spider (Pininfarina)**	AR390590	L	33-38.000 GBP		NS		16-01-16	Birmingham	306	Coy
White with black interior; in the 1990s the car was reimported into Italy from USA and prepared for historic racing. Engine overhauled in 2011.											
1963	**Giulia Spider (Pininfarina)**	AR375424	L	NQ		NS		20-08-16	Monterey	7077	R&S
Red with black interior; recently restored.											
1964	**Giulia Sprint GT (Bertone)**	AR605298	L	35-45.000 EUR	31.598	45.528	40.120	14-05-16	Monaco	161	Coy
Red; prepared for historic racing. Ready to use.											
1965	**Giulia Sprint GT (Bertone)**	AR616007	L	60-80.000 USD	42.020*	55.000*	48.560*	20-08-16	Pebble Beach	23	G&Co
Blue; sold new to the USA. Restored in 2015.											
1963	**Giulia Sprint Speciale (Bertone)**	AR10121380576	L	100-125.000 GBP	100.000	154.230	136.880	12-09-15	Goodwood	325	Bon F20
Dark blue with grey/blue cloth interior; since 1968 for 46 years circa in the same family ownership. Four years ago circa the body was repainted and the engine was overhauled.											
1964	**Giulia Sprint Speciale (Bertone)**	AR10121381303	L	110-130.000 EUR	86.298	130.971	117.452	26-09-15	Frankfurt	128	Coy
Dark blue with cognac leather interior; acquired in 2002 by the current owner and subsequently fully restored in Switzerland.											
1964	**Giulia Sprint Speciale (Bertone)**	AR380732	R	85-100.000 GBP	94.760	142.756	134.673	01-12-15	London	326	Coy
Blue; driven at historic rallies, offered with FIVA Identity Card. When new the car was exhibited at the 1964 Earl's Court Motor Show and was tested by the magazine "Motor" in March 1965.											
1967	**Giulia Sprint Speciale (Bertone)**	AR381227	L	NA		NS		12-12-15	Austin	S158	Mec
White; recently detailed.											
1965	**Giulia Sprint Speciale (Bertone)**	AR381060	L	120-160.000 EUR	100.930	146.881	131.120	05-02-16	Paris	196	Art
Red; since 2004 in the current ownership. Engine overhauled in 2011. Swiss papers.											
1964	**Giulia Sprint Speciale (Bertone)**	AR10121381303	L	90-110.000 EUR	86.785	122.152	107.500	09-04-16	Essen	136	Coy
See lot 128 Coys 26.9.15.											
1962	**Giulia Sprint Speciale (Bertone)**	AR380343	L	75-115.000 EUR	67.929	97.877	86.250	13-05-16	Monaco	139	Bon
Grey with grey and blue interior; restored in 2010.											
1963	**Giulia Sprint Speciale (Bertone)**	AR1012138303	L	125-145.000 EUR	88.209	127.098	112.000	14-05-16	Monaco	229	RMS
Red with red and white interior; restoration recently completed. Currently fitted with engine no.AR00121 00384.											
1963	**Giulia Sprint Speciale (Bertone)**	352819	R	80-100.000 GBP	89.600	129.051	114.168	11-06-16	Brooklands	257	His
Red with red and cream leather interior retrimmed about 10 years ago.											
1964	**Giulia Sprint Speciale (Bertone)**	AR381302	L	100-150.000 EUR	101.610	131.954	119.200	09-07-16	Le Mans	129	Art
Blue with brown leather interior; full restoration completed in 2013 in Austria.											
1965	**Giulia TZ (Zagato)**	AR10511750087	L	950-1.200.000 EUR		NS		03-02-16	Paris	149	RMS
Red; the car was sold new to Switzerland to Karl Foitek who later resold it to Peter Schetty. Acquired by Bernard Fortmann, it was sent back to Autodelta in Italy and race-prepared. In 1968 it was damaged in an accident in practice at the Mugello circuit and then repaired by Autodelta. In the years it has had several owners and at unspecified date it was fitted with the present engine coming from chassis 750066 (see lot 153 RM 16.8.02 NS).											
1965	**Giulia TZ (Zagato)**	AR10511750039	L	950-1.200.000 EUR		NS		14-05-16	Monaco	276	RMS
Sold new in Italy, the car was raced until 1974. Sold to the USA, it was restored and in 1983 it was acquired by the current Dutch owner and reimported into Europe. Little used in the past 10 years; finished in red with yellow nose.											
1965	**Giulia GTA (Bertone)**	AR613115	L	475-550.000 USD	307.868	440.000	402.908	30-01-16	Scottsdale	129	G&Co
White and red with black interior; sold to Germany to Herbert Schultze, the car was raced in German Touring Car events from 1965 to 1971. Subsequently imported into the USA, it was prepared for historic events and used in the 1980s and 1990s. Recently restored to its original racing livery.											

Year	Model	(Bodybuilder)	Chassis no.	Steering	Estimate	Hammer price £	$	€	Date	Sale Place	Lot	Auc. H.

F19: 1964 Alfa Romeo Giulia TI Super berlina

F20: 1963 Alfa Romeo Giulia Sprint Speciale (Bertone)

1965 Giulia GTA (Bertone) — AR613311 — L — 150-200.000 EUR — **339.491** — **494.053** — **441.040** — 05-02-16 — Paris — 124 — **Art**
Originally finished in white with black interior, the car was sold new to France. In single ownership from 1975 to 2014, it is described as in original condition except for the paintwork redone in red at unspecified date (see lot 505 Artcurial 7.2.14 $ 203,871). **F21**

1965 Giulia GTA (Bertone) — AR163565 — L — 275-325.000 USD — **200.086** — **286.000** — **257.886** — 12-03-16 — Amelia Island — 173 — **RMS**
Road version finished in red, the car was sold in Italy and remained with its first owner until 1992. Sold to Belgium, it was restored and remained in the same ownership until 2004. Further works have been carried between 2006 and 2015 in Switzerland and UK.

1965 Giulia GTA (Bertone) — AR752638 — R — 175-225.000 GBP — **175.100** — **239.957** — **216.826** — 24-06-16 — Goodwood — 225 — **Bon**
Red; sold new to the UK, the car was raced in period. In 1999 it was bought by the previous owner, restored and prepared for historic racing. In 2007 it was purchased by the vendor, imported into Italy, mechanically overhauled and raced at numerous historic events (see lot 655 Bonhams 3.12.07 $150,643).

1967 Giulia GT Veloce (Bertone) — AR299602 — R — 30-40.000 GBP — **32.063** — **48.813** — **45.350** — 14-11-15 — Birmingham — 318 — **SiC**
Black; recently restored.

1968 Giulia GT Veloce (Bertone) — 251700 — L — 30-50.000 EUR — **21.734*** — **32.217*** — **28.750*** — 04-02-16 — Paris — 307 — **Bon**
Green with caramel interior; the car has covered 1,500 kms since the restoration carried out in 2007. Engine and gearbox overhauled in more recent years.

1968 Gran Sport Quattroruote (Zagato) — 393035 — L — 125-175.000 USD — **88.512*** — **126.500*** — **115.836*** — 29-01-16 — Phoenix — 269 — **RMS**
Red with black leather interior; restored in the USA. **F22**

1975 Giulia 1300 Super berlina — AR0034776 — L — 12-15.000 GBP — **NS** — — — 16-04-16 — Ascot — 136 — **Coy**
Magenta with biscuit interior; in good overall condition.

1975 Giulia 1300 Super berlina — AR0034776 — L — 12-15.000 GBP — **5.500** — **7.305** — **6.560** — 02-07-16 — Woodstock — 145 — **Coy**
See lot 136 Coys 16.4.16.

1968 Giulia GT 1300 Junior (Bertone) — AR129559 — L — 20-25.000 GBP — **NS** — — — 10-10-15 — Ascot — 103 — **Coy**
Dark blue with grey cloth interior; described as in very good overall condition, the car has had just one owner and has covered 88,000 kms.

1968 Giulia GT 1300 Junior (Bertone) — AR129559 — L — 18-22.000 GBP — **17.000 P** — **24.364 P** — **22.323 P** — 16-01-16 — Birmingham — 307 — **Coy**
See lot 103 Coys 10.10.15.

1968 Giulia GT 1300 Junior (Bertone) — AR1216282 — L — 19-26.000 GBP — **21.840** — **31.214** — **28.145** — 12-03-16 — Brooklands — 134 — **His**
Red with original black vinyl interior; body repainted some years ago.

1967 Giulia GT 1300 Junior (Bertone) — AR1211799 — L — 22-25.000 GBP — **23.520** — **33.615** — **30.310** — 12-03-16 — Brooklands — 206 — **His**
Pine green with brown interior; described as in very good overall condition.

1968 Giulia GT 1300 Junior (Bertone) — AR1213731 — L — 25-32.000 EUR — **NS** — — — 09-04-16 — Essen — 213 — **Coy**
Yellow; restored in 2015.

1966 Giulia GT 1300 Junior (Bertone) — AR1237090 — L — 30-35.000 EUR — **31.760** — **45.376** — **40.320** — 19-06-16 — Fontainebleau — 347 — **Ose**
Red with black interior; restored some years ago.

1975 Giulia GTA 1300 Junior (Bertone) — AR776131 — L — 150-200.000 USD — **106.691** — **154.000** — **138.061** — 05-06-16 — Greenwhich — 21 — **Bon**
Street version finished in white with black vinyl interior; described as in highly original, unrestored condition, the car has covered 64,000 kms. **F23**

1968 Giulia GTA 1300 Junior (Bertone) — AR775774 — L — 98-110.000 GBP — **NS** — — — 11-06-16 — Brooklands — 275 — **His**
Red; sold new in Italy, the car was imported into the UK in the mid-1980s and subsequently raced. Body repainted some years ago. Engine recently refreshed (see lot 235 Coys 14.1.06 NS).

F21: 1965 Alfa Romeo Giulia GTA (Bertone)

F22: 1968 Alfa Romeo Gran Sport Quattroruote (Zagato)

Year	Model	(Bodybuilder)	Chassis no.	Steering	Estimate	Hammer Price £	$	€	Date	Place	Lot	Auc. H.

F23: 1975 Alfa Romeo Giulia GTA 1300 Junior (Bertone)

F24: 1971 Alfa Romeo 1750 berlina

Year	Model (Bodybuilder)	Chassis no.	Steering	Estimate	£	$	€	Date	Place	Lot	Auc. H.
1970	**Giulia GTA 1300 Junior (Bertone)**	AR775979	L	250-325.000 USD	195.393	255.750	225.802	19-08-16	Carmel	49	Bon
	Red with white side stripe; sold new to Austria, the car was raced in the 1970s. Restored in recent years, it is described as ready for both race and street use.										
1968	**Giulia Spider 1300 Junior (Pininfarina)**	1695044	R	8-10.000 GBP	13.560	20.459	18.701	09-12-15	Chateau Impney	11	H&H
	White; fitted with an early 1970s 1750 engine.										
1968	**Giulia Spider 1300 Junior (Pininfarina)**	AR1695017	R	24-32.000 GBP		NS		12-03-16	Brooklands	138	His
	Light metallic grey with black interior recently retrimmed; in good overall condition.										
1971	**1750 berlina**	AR1783377	L	15-25.000 EUR	21.103*	30.711*	27.416*	05-02-16	Paris	109	Art **F24**
	Grey; described as in very good original condition. 27,000 kms on the odometer.										
1969	**1750 GT Veloce (Bertone)**	AR1453189	R	16-19.000 GBP		NS		09-12-15	Chateau Impney	33	H&H
	Dark green; sold new to Japan and recently imported into the UK.										
1968	**1750 Spider Veloce (Pininfarina)**	1470116	R	9-13.000 GBP	20.160	30.343	28.680	28-11-15	Weybridge	203	His
	Red with black interior; damaged and restored in 2001, the car received further works in 2004/05.										
1969	**1750 Spider Veloce (Pininfarina)**	AR1480224	L	18-20.000 GBP	15.820	23.869	21.817	09-12-15	Chateau Impney	118	H&H
	White with black interior; US market version.										
1967	**1750 Spider Veloce (Pininfarina)**	AR148256	L	25-35.000 USD	19.814*	28.600*	25.640*	05-06-16	Greenwhich	22	Bon
	Cream with red interior; in good overall condition.										
1969	**1750 Spider Veloce (Pininfarina)**	AR1470540	L	30-35.000 GBP	32.000	42.502	38.170	02-07-16	Woodstock	119	Coy
	Red; acquired in 2002 by the current owner and subsequently restored.										
1971	**Giulia 1300 Junior Zagato**	1800921	L	12-18.000 GBP	29.120	41.618	37.527	12-03-16	Brooklands	119	His
	Red; restoration completed in 2010. Currently fitted with a 2-litre engine, the car is offered with also the original 1300 engine and gearbox.										
1973	**2000 Berlina**	AR2355063	L	15-20.000 USD	6.918	9.900	8.660	02-04-16	Ft.Lauderdale	751	AA
	Black with medium brown interior.										
1973	**2000 berlina**	2349616	L	14-18.000 EUR		NS		19-06-16	Fontainebleau	375	Ose
	Body repainted in metallic grey about 12 years ago; two owners.										
1974	**2000 GT Veloce (Bertone)**	AR2445491	L	30-40.000 EUR	24.702	37.892	33.350	09-10-15	Zoute	45	Bon **F25**
	Red with beige vinyl interior; the car has covered 10,000 kms circa since some restoration works carried out in 1996.										
1984	**2000 GT Veloce (Bertone)**	65457	L	NA	6.944	9.660	8.797	24-02-16	Donington Park	41	H&H
	Silver with black interior; imported into the UK from Italy in 2014. Body repainted at unspecified date.										
1972	**2000 GT Veloce (Bertone)**	AR3020190	L	32-38.000 USD	17.470	25.000	21.868	02-04-16	Ft.Lauderdale	795	AA
	Red with brown interior.										
1972	**2000 GT Veloce (Bertone)**	AR2422952	L	50-65.000 EUR	39.008	54.905	48.319	09-04-16	Essen	212	Coy
	In good original condition; the car raced three editions of the Targa Florio: 1975 19th overall and 3rd in class, 1976 5th overall and 1st in class, 1977 9th overall and 1st in class.										
1972	**2000 GT Veloce (Bertone)**	2411354	R	NA	24.640	34.940	31.150	20-04-16	Duxford	100	H&H
	Red with black interior; restored in the early 1990s.										
1973	**2000 GT Veloce (Bertone)**	AR2442032	L	30-40.000 EUR	32.191	42.758	38.400	02-07-16	Lyon	331	Agu
	Light metallic grey with black interior; body restored in Italy in 2007, engine rebuilt in the Netherlands in 2011.										
1972	**2000 GT Veloce (Bertone)**	2411152	R	25-30.000 GBP	22.550	29.951	26.898	02-07-16	Woodstock	157	Coy
	Blue with beige interior; paintwork and interior redone. 45,000 miles on the odometer.										
1972	**2000 GT Veloce (Bertone)**	AR12422952	L	42-48.000 EUR	40.644	52.782	47.680	09-07-16	Le Mans	186	Art
	See lot 212 Coys 9.04.16 $54,905.										
1975	**2000 Spider Veloce (Pininfarina)**	2471058	R	NA	12.995	19.988	17.517	14-10-15	Duxford	34	H&H
	Red with black interior; in good overall condition.										
1973	**2000 Spider Veloce (Pininfarina)**	AR3041888	L	25-35.000 USD	13.993*	19.800*	18.236*	10-03-16	Amelia Island	140	Bon
	Yellow with black interior; one owner until 2013. In original condition except for the paintwork redone in the original colour; 19,000 miles covered (see Bonhams lots 157 16.8.13 $ 24,750 and 9 14.8.15 $ 31,900).										**F26**
1972	**2000 Spider Veloce (Pininfarina)**	AR2472421	R	10-12.000 GBP		NS		11-06-16	Brooklands	206	His
	Red with black leather interior; recently imported into the UK from South Africa.										

Year	Model	(Bodybuilder)	Chassis no.	Steering	Estimate	Hammer price £	$	€	Date	Place	Lot	Auc. H.

F25: 1974 Alfa Romeo 2000 GT Veloce (Bertone)

F26: 1973 Alfa Romeo 2000 Spider Veloce (Pininfarina)

Year	Model	(Bodybuilder)	Chassis no.	Steering	Estimate	£	$	€	Date	Place	Lot	Auc. H.
1972	**Montreal (Bertone)**		AR1426463	L	50-70.000 EUR	40.035	61.412	54.050	09-10-15	Zoute	47	Bon
White with black cloth interior; sold in Italy. Some restoration works carried out in 1985. Subsequently the car remained unused and was recommissioned in January 2015.												
1972	**Montreal (Bertone)**		AR1427227	L	60-80.000 EUR		NS		01-11-15	Paris	120	Art
Red with black interior; body recently repainted. In good working order.												
1972	**Montreal (Bertone)**		105641426693	L	34-38.000 GBP		NS		14-11-15	Birmingham	607	SiC
Red; never fully restored. For 22 years in the current ownership. The original injection system was replaced by carburettors.												
1975	**Montreal (Bertone)**		10564	L	40-45.000 EUR		NS		16-01-16	Maastricht	416	Coy
Red with tan interior; in original condition.												
1972	**Montreal (Bertone)**		1426759	L	60-80.000 USD	53.831*	77.000*	70.617*	28-01-16	Scottsdale	7	Bon F27
Described as in largely original condition, the car has had three owner since 1973 and has covered less than 59,000 kms.												
1971	**Montreal (Bertone)**		AR1425803	L	140-180.000 USD	76.956*	110.000*	99.187*	11-03-16	Amelia Island	17	G&Co
Red; described as in very good overall condition. Imported into the USA in 1985 (see lot 115 Gooding 18.1.14 $ 176,000).												
1972	**Montreal (Bertone)**		AR142815	L	50-70.000 EUR		NS		20-03-16	Fontainebleau	340	Ose
Blue with blue cloth interior; in good condition.												
1975	**Montreal (Bertone)**		1440137	R	16-20.000 GBP	35.840	51.620	45.667	11-06-16	Brooklands	217	His
Restoration started several years ago to be completed.												
1974	**Montreal (Bertone)**		1428474	L	40-55.000 EUR	35.328	50.474	44.850	18-06-16	Wien	428	Dor
Red with light brown cloth interior; since 1982 in the current ownership. Described as in good mechanical order.												
1972	**Montreal (Bertone)**		105641426693	L	40-45.000 GBP	34.000	45.159	40.555	02-07-16	Woodstock	233	Coy
See lot 607 Silverstone Auctions 14.11.15.												
1976	**Montreal (Bertone)**		AR1440171	R	30-40.000 GBP	42.000	56.120	50.434	16-07-16	Cambridge	1257	Che
Body repainted in red in 1986 circa, interior retrimmed in cream leather in more recent years. Since 2000 in the current ownership.												
1971	**Montreal (Bertone)**		AR1425545	L	70-90.000 USD	40.339*	52.800*	46.617*	19-08-16	Carmel	101	Bon
Black with black interior; in good overall condition. Sold new to Belgium and later imported into the USA.												
1974	**Montreal (Bertone)**		AR1428175	L	80-100.000 USD	88.242*	115.500*	101.975*	19-08-16	Carmel	2	Bon
Orange with black interior; body repainted, mechanicals refurbished.												
1974	**Giulia GT 1600 Junior (Bertone)**		AR2205708	R	15-19.000 GBP	15.680	20.522	18.118	20-08-16	Brooklands	257	His
Grey with black interior; restored in 2011 (see lot 619 Silverstone Auctions 15.11.13 $26,793).												
1980	**Giulia Spider 1600 (Pininfarina)**		AR115350004094	L	12-16.000 GBP		NS		10-12-15	London	381	Bon
Metallic bronze with beige vinyl interior; in good overall condition.												
1972	**Giulia 1600 Coupé Zagato**		AR3060043	L	50-70.000 EUR	56.888*	82.787*	73.904*	05-02-16	Paris	120	Art F28
French blue with original tan interior; body repainted in 2010. Described as in very good driving order (see lot 26 Artcurial 20.10.13 $ 60,925).												
1979	**Alfasud Sprint Veloce**		5051459	R	NA	16.875	23.585	21.430	26-02-16	Coventry	708	SiC
Yellow; 968 miles covered. Believed to be a one owner car.												

F27: 1972 Alfa Romeo Montreal (Bertone)

F28: 1972 Alfa Romeo Giulia 1600 Coupé Zagato

Year	Model (Bodybuilder)	Chassis no.	Steering	Estimate	Hammer price £	$	€	Date	Place	Lot	Auc. H.

F29: 1987 Alfa Romeo 75 Turbo Evoluzione

F30: 1990 Alfa Romeo SZ (Zagato)

Year	Model (Bodybuilder)	Chassis no.	Steering	Estimate	£	$	€	Date	Place	Lot	Auc. H.
1982	**Alfasud 1.5 Ti**	5152273	R	6-7.000 GBP		NS		18-05-16	Donington Park	6	H&H
Grey-green with beige interior; one owner and 42,000 miles on the odometer. Stored from 2005 to 2015 and recently recommissioned.											
1978	**Alfetta GTV 2000**	0005272	R	7-12.000 GBP	8.960	11.727	10.353	20-08-16	Brooklands	231	His
Silver; since 1990 in the current ownership, restored between 2011 and 2012.											
1982	**GTV 6**	3002104	R	12-14.000 GBP	10.170	14.803	13.124	18-05-16	Donington Park	62	H&H
Red with grey interior; described as in good original condition. Gearbox overhauled in 2011.											
1985	**GTV 6**	00017387	L	9-14.000 EUR	12.229	17.472	15.525	18-06-16	Wien	427	Dor
Opal metallic with light brown cloth interior; in good driving order.											
1991	**Spider 2.0 (Pininfarina)**	6014789	L	9-12.000 GBP		NS		10-10-15	Ascot	168	Coy
Black with beige interior; in good condition.											
1984	**Spider 2.0 (Pininfarina)**	2479530	R	8-10.000 GBP	7.280	10.405	9.382	12-03-16	Brooklands	251	His
Red with beige leather interior; in good overall condition.											
1990	**Spider 2.0 (Pininfarina)**	6007012	R	9-12.000 GBP	12.208	17.448	15.732	12-03-16	Brooklands	252	His
Silver; until 2015 with its first owner. Described as in very good overall condition.											
1991	**Spider 2.0 (Pininfarina)**	7001182	R	8-10.000 GBP		NS		18-05-16	Donington Park	42	H&H
Yellow with black interior; in good overall condition. With hardtop.											
1984	**33 Stradale Continuation**	75002	L	Refer Dpt.	371.769	535.671	472.040	14-05-16	Monaco	138	Coy
Red with tan interior; one of probably six Continuation examples built by Giovanni Giordanengo, the offered car is based on front and rear sections of 33 Stradale chassis #02 bought by Giordanengo in 1984 from Autodelta (via Marcello Gambi). Purchased in the early 2000s by the current vendor the car was subsequently mechanically completed using original Tipo 33 parts, as the crankcase, cylinder heads and 6-speed gearbox. Offered with an Alfa Romeo Montreal engine also.											
1987	**75 V6 3.0 Group N**	3001257	L	22-27.000 GBP		NS		16-01-16	Birmingham	309	Coy
White; eligible for Group N racing. Raced at some hillclimbs in the last few years. Italian papers.											
1987	**75 Turbo Evoluzione**	59378	L	19-27.000 GBP	21.000	27.485	24.266	20-08-16	Brooklands	266	His F29
Red with grey interior; 46,000 kms covered.											
1994	**155 D2 Super Turismo**	0005467	L	110-130.000 EUR		NS		09-04-16	Essen	160	Coy
Finished in the official Alfa Romeo red livery.											
1990	**SZ (Zagato)**	3000122	L	50-70.000 GBP	67.200*	102.561*	92.017*	07-09-15	London	138	RMS F30
Red with beige interior; two owners and 349 kms covered.											
1991	**SZ (Zagato)**	300470	L	55-65.000 EUR		NS		07-11-15	Lyon	259	Agu
Red with tan interior; in good overall condition. Just over 47,000 kms covered.											
1991	**SZ (Zagato)**	000058	L	25-30.000 GBP	28.750	43.484	39.735	10-12-15	London	360	Bon
Purchased in 2005 with light-to-medium frontal damage and subsequently repaired; in good mechanical order.											
1991	**SZ (Zagato)**	3000338	L	60-70.000 GBP	59.740	81.868	73.976	24-06-16	Goodwood	214	Bon
Red with beige interior; one owner and about 4,000 miles covered.											
1993	**R.Z. (Zagato)**	3002117	L	50-70.000 GBP	47.600*	72.647*	65.179*	07-09-15	London	137	RMS
Yellow with black interior; just under 21,000 kms covered.											
1993	**R.Z. (Zagato)**	3002164	L	75-85.000 EUR	42.340*	61.007*	53.760*	14-05-16	Monaco	283	RMS
Yellow with black interior; 12,000 km percorsi (see lot 256 Historics 30.8.14 $ 49,215).											
2002	**GTV Cup (Pininfarina)**	004460	R	8-12.000 GBP	8.400	12.005	10.825	12-03-16	Brooklands	135	His
Red; recent cosmetic restoration. 3-litre V6 engine.											
2008	**8C Competizione**	39694	L	250-300.000 USD	232.742*	319.000*	288.248*	25-06-16	Santa Monica	2029	AA
Metallic red; less than 3,300 miles on the odometer. From the Riverside International Automotive Museum Collection.											
2008	**8C Competizione**	39129	L	300-400.000 USD	233.020	305.000	269.285	20-08-16	Monterey	S83	Mec F31
Metallic red with red interior; one owner and 505 miles covered. From the Modern Speed Collection.											

ALL AMERICAN RACERS (USA) (1965-)

1966	**Indy Eagle**	201	M	600-800.000 USD	735.350	962.500	849.791	20-08-16	Monterey	214	RMS

Driven by Dan Gurney at the 1966 Indy 500. Raced until 1972, the car raced again at Indianapolis in 1967, 1970, 1971, and 1972 with different drivers. Restored at unspecified date, in 2008 it was purchased by Doug Magnon who commissioned a mechanical restoration. Subsequently it was campaigned at several historic events. Engine recently rebuilt. From the Riverside International Automotive Museum Collection (see lot 225 RM 14.6.08 $528,000).

F32

Year	Model	(Bodybuilder)	Chassis no.	Steering	Estimate	Hammer price £	$	€	Date	Sale Place	Lot	Auc. H.

F31: 2008 Alfa Romeo 8C Competizione

F32: 1966 All American Racers Indy Eagle

1969	**Indy Eagle Santa Ana**		704	M	175-225.000 USD	75.636*	99.000*	87.407*	20-08-16	Monterey	213	**RMS**

Driven by Denis Hulme at the 1969 Indy 500. Subsequently the car was driven by Swede Savage at some events of the 1969 season. In 1970 it was entered for Indy as the car of Bud Morley, who failed to complete his driver's test. The car was restored many years later and fitted again with a est.850bhp 159cu.in. turbocharged V8 engine. In 2007 it was bought by Doug Magnon for the Riverside International Automotive Museum Collection. Engine recently rebuilt.

| 1969 | **Eagle Mk 5 F5000** | | 510 | M | 125-175.000 USD | 151.272* | 198.000* | 174.814* | 20-08-16 | Monterey | 212 | **RMS** |

Driven by Tony Adamowicz, the car won the 1969 Formula 5000 Championship. Subsequently stored, it was acquired in the 2000s by Doug Magnon, who had it restored and fitted again with a Traco Chevrolet engine. In 2009 the car won the Historic Formula 5000 Championship driven again by Tony Adamowicz, now into his 70s. From the Riverside International Automotive Museum Collection.

ALLARD (GB) *(1937-1959)*

1949	**L tourer**		792	R	40-50.000 USD	34.060	51.700	46.013	05-10-15	Philadelphia	256	**Bon**

Imported into the USA in 1974 and stored since. It requires recommissioning or restoration prior to use. 221 Ford V8 engine.

| 1948 | **L tourer** | | L743 | R | 50-60.000 USD | 34.203* | 52.250* | 46.429* | 08-10-15 | Hershey | 175 | **RMS** F33 |

Burgundy with new grey leather interior; in good driving order. 221 Ford V8 engine with 3-speed manual gearbox.

| 1948 | **L tourer** | | 71L632 | R | 25-30.000 GBP | 28.320 | 40.240 | 36.490 | 08-03-16 | London | 132 | **Coy** |

Black with red interior; restored in the late 1980s (see lot 566 Sotheby's 18.7.94 $ 20,687).

| 1948 | **M cabriolet** | | 625 | R | 50-70.000 USD | | NS | | 10-03-16 | Amelia Island | 149 | **Bon** |

Burgundy with burgundy leather interior; restored in the late 1980s. In good condition. Ford 221 V8 engine (see lot 306 Christie's 13.9.97 NS).

| 1951 | **P1 2-door saloon** | | P2245 | R | NA | | NS | | 20-04-16 | Duxford | 22 | **H&H** |

Blue with red interior; Mercury V8 engine overhauled in 2010, body repainted in 2011.

| 1951 | **P1 2-door saloon** | | 91P1996 | R | 50-60.000 USD | 31.626 | 45.650 | 40.925 | 05-06-16 | Greenwhich | 49 | **Bon** |

Red; restored at unspecified date. Recently serviced.

| 1951 | **J2 competition** | | 99J2121 | R | 325-375.000 USD | | NS | | 19-08-16 | Carmel | 8 | **Bon** |

British racing green with cork leather interior; first restored in the UK in 1963, fitted in 1968 in the USA with a Cobra 289 engine and Ford transmission, restored again in 2008 and fitted with a 1965 Cobra 289 engine (see lot 6 Gooding & Company 08.3.13 $330,000).

| 1951 | **K2 two-seater** | | K2029 | L | 90-120.000 USD | 66.076* | 93.500* | 86.114* | 10-03-16 | Amelia Island | 199 | **Bon** F34 |

Red with tan interior; described as in good overall condition. Sold new to the USA. 331 Cadillac V8 engine (see lot 149 RM 10.3.12 $ 104,500).

| 1950 | **K2 two-seater** | | 91K2108 | R | 80-120.000 EUR | 76.207 | 98.966 | 89.400 | 09-07-16 | Le Mans | 112 | **Art** |

Dark red with red interior; imported into Italy from Australia in 2003 and driven at several historic events. V8 Mercury engine (see Coys lots 239 30.4.10 NS, 159 23.5.10 NS, and 143 2.10.10 $134,479).

| 1952 | **K2 two-seater** | | 91K3017 | L | 150-200.000 USD | 105.050* | 137.500* | 121.399* | 19-08-16 | Monterey | 101 | **RMS** |

Dark blue with dark blue leather interior; restored some 25 years ago. Original Chrysler 331 Hemi engine; currently fitted with a 4-speed Muncie gearbox (the original 3-speed Ford/Lincoln unit is included with the sale).

| 1952 | **J2X competition** | | 3062 | L | 475-550.000 USD | 315.565 | 451.000 | 412.981 | 29-01-16 | Scottsdale | 25 | **G&Co** |

Red with black interior; acquired in 1969 by the previous owner who retained it for more than 40 years. Specially built Cadillac 331 V8 engine with six Stromberg carburettors.

F33: 1948 Allard L tourer

F34: 1951 Allard K2 two-seater

Year	Model	(Bodybuilder)	Chassis no.	Steering	Estimate	Hammer price £	$	€	Date	Place	Lot	Auc. H.

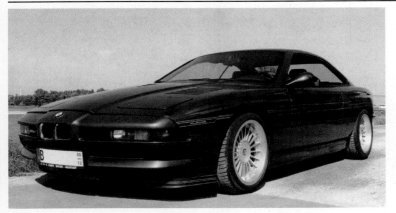

F35: 1994 Alpina B12 5.7 Coupé

F36: 1972 Alpine A110 1600S

ALPINA (D)

Year	Model		Chassis no.	Steering	Estimate	£	$	€	Date	Place	Lot	Auc. H.
1991	Z1 RLE		260055	L	75-95.000 EUR	**81.751**	117.792	103.800	14-05-16	Monaco	197	Coy
	*Black with grey interior; 11,500 kms covered.*
1994	B12 5.7 Coupé		200030	L	48-60.000 EUR	**54.806**	83.176	74.591	26-09-15	Frankfurt	141	Coy F35
	*Blue; described as in good original condition. Shift-Tronic transmission.*
2003	Z8 Roadster		62184	L	225-300.000 USD	**176.872**	253.000	232.026	28-01-16	Scottsdale	18	Bon
	*Silver with red and black leather interior; in very good original condition. Two owners and less than 17,000 miles covered.*
2003	Z8 Roadster		50075	L	220-280.000 GBP	**247.900**	339.722	306.975	24-06-16	Goodwood	216	Bon
	*Blue with blue and cream interior; one owner and 9,500 kms covered.*

ALPINE (F) (1955-1980)

Year	Model		Chassis no.	Steering	Estimate	£	$	€	Date	Place	Lot	Auc. H.
1974	A110 1300		BA0664	L	38-45.000 GBP	**36.800**	53.312	47.266	20-03-16	Goodwood	51	Bon
	*Built in Spain, the car remained with its first owner until 2005. In 2006 it was prepared for historic rallying and finished in the present Tour de Corse red, blue and white livery (see lot 225 Silverstone Auctions 23.2.13 $ 55,684).*
1973	A110 1600SC		20019	L	60-75.000 EUR	**57.699**	87.347	80.400	08-11-15	Lyon	231	Ose
	*Blue with black interior; since 1995 in the current ownership. Paintwork redone over 25 years ago.*
1972	A110 1600S		17810	L	90-130.000 EUR	**71.286**	105.673	94.300	04-02-16	Paris	317	Bon
	*Metallic blue with largely original black interior; sold new to Italy with roll cage, 5-speed Type 353-20 gearbox and large-capacity fuel tank. Described as in good overall condition; 83,000 kms on the odometer (see lot 131 Bonhams 30.4.10 NS).* F36
1970	A110 1600S Groupe 4		16693	L	90-140.000 EUR	**89.919**	130.857	116.816	05-02-16	Paris	163	Art
	*Blue; the car was bought new by driver Jean Saurel who raced it at several rallies in 1970 and 1971. Saurel discovered the car in the early 2000s in Corsica, acquired it again and prepared it for historic rallying. Used until 2011, it has been restarted in 2015.*
1971	A110 1600 S		17379	L	80-120.000 EUR	**67.929**	97.877	86.250	13-05-16	Monaco	125	Bon
	*Blue with black leather interior; described as in very good overall condition. Last serviced in July 2014. With Italian ASI homologation.*
1974	A110 1800 Groupe 4		18393	L	240-280.000 EUR		NS		14-05-16	Monaco	263	RMS
	*Works car, it did its race debut at the 1974 Tour de Corse, fitted with a 1,860cc Mignotet engine and driven by Jean-Pierre Nicolas to a 2nd overall place. In 1975 it was raced at the Monte Carlo Rally also and at the season end it was retired from competition. After some owners in Europe, in 1993 it was sold to Japan. Reimported into Europe in 2010, it has been recently restored and fitted with a 1,796cc engine.*
1970	A110 1600 S		17088	L	80-120.000 EUR	**81.288**	105.564	95.360	09-07-16	Le Mans	145	Art
	*Blue; acquired in 1997 by the current owner and prepared for historic events.*
1974	A310 V6		NQ	L	200-300.000 EUR		NS		05-02-16	Paris	162	Art
	*The car raced the 1977 Le Mans 24 Hours and was entered at the 1978 edition when it did not make the start. Still owned by Bernard Decure, who prepared it for the Le Mans race and later restored it to the red and blue "Poisson Dieppois" livery of Le Mans 1977.*

F37: 1937 Alvis 4.3 litre cabriolet

F38: 1966 Alvis TF21 cabriolet

Year	Model	(Bodybuilder)	Chassis no.	Steering	Estimate	Hammer price £	Hammer price $	Hammer price €	Date	Place	Lot	Auc. H.

ALVIS (GB) (1920-1967)

1936 Silver Eagle cabriolet (Cross/Ellis) — 13520 — R — 40-50.000 GBP — NS — — — 05-09-15 Beaulieu 143 Bon
Green with black wings; fitted at unspecified date with a 2.5-litre Speed Twenty engine. Several mechanical works carried out in recent years (see lots 587 Bonhams 8.9.12 NS and 4 H&H 5.12. 12 NS).

1932 Firefly tourer (Cross/Ellis) — 10250 — R — NA — 28.880 — 44.420 — 38.930 — 14-10-15 Duxford 129 H&H
Green and black with red interior; built with Carbodies saloon body, the car was fitted with the present, original body prior to the 1980s. Restored several years ago.

1933 Firefly tourer (Cross/Ellis) — 10778 — R — 38-45.000 GBP — NS — — — 09-12-15 Chateau Impney 130 H&H
White and black with brown interior; restored in 1993-94, the car is described as in very good overall condition.

1933 Firefly tourer (Cross/Ellis) — 15642 — R — 27-32.000 GBP — NS — — — 02-07-16 Woodstock 161 Coy
British racing green with green interior; restored in the 1990s.

1934 Speed 20 SC cabriolet (Brainsby Woollard) — 11959 — R — 85-105.000 EUR — NS — — — 07-11-15 Lyon 267 Agu
Red with beige leather interior; restored in the 1970s, the car received further works in the 2000s (see lots 118 Coys 31.7.99 NS and 22 H&H 16.10.13 NS).

1936 Speed 20 cabriolet (Vanden Plas) — 13031 — R — 80-100.000 GBP — 74.000 — 98.287 — 88.267 — 02-07-16 Woodstock 168 Coy
Dark blue; body repainted in 2007. The engine has covered 14,000 miles since the rebuild.

1934 Speed 20 SB tourer (Cross/Ellis) — 11337 — R — 150-200.000 USD — 126.060 — 165.000 — 145.679 — 19-08-16 Carmel 15 Bon
Finished in green, the car was sold new in the UK and remained with its first owner until 1961 when it was imported into the USA. Occasionally raced at historic events in the 1970s; restored in New Zealand in the 2000s (see lot 118 Gooding & Company 18.8.13 $170,500).

1937 4.3 litre cabriolet — 14315 — R — 900-1.100.000 DKK — 90.620 — 137.540 — 123.372 — 26-09-15 Ebeltoft 21 Bon **F37**
Metallic aubergine with grey leather interior; fully restored in the early 2000s and fitted with the present Vanden Plas style new body. From the Frederiksen Collection (see lot 74 H&H 20.7.11 NS).

1948 TA14 cabriolet (Carbodies) — TA1422787 — R — 18-22.000 GBP — 16.240 — 24.443 — 23.103 — 28-11-15 Weybridge 289 His
Black with original biscuit leather interior; stored from 1982 to 2002 and subsequently restored.

1952 TA21 cabriolet (Tickford) — WA7874508 — R — 55-65.000 USD — NS — — — 05-10-15 Philadelphia 236 Bon
Burgundy and white with burgundy leather interior; restored at unspecified date. From the Evergreen Collection.

1963 TD21 coupé (Graber/Park Ward) — 26937 — R — 40-45.000 GBP — 39.375 — 59.956 — 53.830 — 04-09-15 Woodstock 261 SiC
Metallic blue with beige leather interior; since 1996 in the same family ownership. Several restoration works carried out over the years.

1961 TD21 coupé (Park Ward) — 89361 — R — 16-22.000 GBP — 20.720 — 29.843 — 26.401 — 11-06-16 Brooklands 246 His
Burgundy with beige leather interior; recently reimported into the UK and cosmetically restored.

1964 TE21 cabriolet (Park Ward) — 27207 — R — NA — NS — — — 20-04-16 Duxford 56 H&H
Maroon with burnt orange leather interior; restoration started in the USA and recently completed in the UK.

1964 TE21 cabriolet (Park Ward) — 27207 — R — 90-100.000 GBP — 57.000 — 75.707 — 67.990 — 02-07-16 Woodstock 144 Coy
See lot 56 H & H 20.4.16.

1966 TF21 cabriolet — 27419 — R — 70-90.000 EUR — 68.488 — 108.453 — 95.360 — 01-11-15 Paris 125 Art **F38**
Dark blue with grey leather interior; acquired in 1998 by the current owner and subsequently restored. Automatic transmission.

AMC (USA) (1958-1986)

1967 Rambler Rebel SST convertible — A7KA77H171649 — L — 35-40.000 USD — 15.242* — 22.000* — 19.723* — 05-06-16 Greenwhich 85 Bon **F39**
Red with black stripes and black interior; restored some years ago. Automatic transmission. From the Evergreen Collection.

1968 AMX fastback — A8C397X283695 — L — 30-50.000 USD — 18.448 — 26.400 — 23.092 — 02-04-16 Ft.Lauderdale 199 AA
Red with white stripes and black interior; restored. 390 engine with 4-speed manual gearbox.

1969 Rambler Hurst S/C — A9M097X223645 — L — 65-90.000 USD — 37.752 — 55.000 — 49.022 — 20-05-16 Indianapolis F183 Mec
Red, white and blue with black interior; restored to concours condition. 315bhp 390 engine with 4-speed manual gearbox. From the Jeffrey Cohen Collection.

1978 Pacer — A8C667C390251 — L — 8-12.000 EUR — 13.453 — 19.490 — 17.280 — 20-03-16 Fontainebleau 329 Ose
Maroon with red interior; in good overall condition.

AMERICAN (USA) (1906-1914)

1908 Fifty roadster — 1427 — R — 1.400-1.750.000 USD — NS — — — 20-08-16 Monterey 231 RMS
From the late 1940s the car has been part of the collections of Cameron Peck, John Wallerich and Richard Clyne prior to be purchased by Sam and Emily Mann for their collection. Original coachwork finished in white; recently fitted with six new wooden wheels, in good running and driving order (see lot 152 Bonhams 12.3.15 $1,738,000).

F39: 1967 AMC Rambler Rebel SST convertible

F40: 1927 Amilcar CGSS

Year	Model	(Bodybuilder)	Chassis no.	Steering	Estimate	Hammer price £	$	€	Date	Place	Lot	Auc. H.

AMERICAN BANTAM (USA) (1938-1941)

| 1938 | Model 60 roadster | | 6140638 | L | 15-25.000 USD | 18.002* | 27.500* | 24.437* | 08-10-15 | Hershey | 180 | RMS |

Red and white; restored several years ago (see lot 738 Auctions America 22.3.13 $ 30,250).

AMILCAR (F) (1921-1939)

| 1922 | CC spider | | 868 | R | 15-20.000 EUR | 11.343 | 16.206 | 14.400 | 19-06-16 | Fontainebleau | 307 | Ose |

Light blue with blue wings; in good condition.

| 1927 | CGSS | | 18481 | R | 50-70.000 EUR | 34.867* | 50.741* | 45.296* | 05-02-16 | Paris | 182 | Art F40 |

Red; restored in the early 1960s. Since 1963 in the current ownership, the car is unused from 30 years and requires recommissioning prior to use.

| 1926 | G cabriolet | | 71292 | R | 40-60.000 EUR | 25.192 | 36.106 | 33.082 | 16-01-16 | Maastricht | 408 | Coy |

Weymann style body finished in black; the car comes with Italian ASI homologation.

| 1927 | C6 | | 11032 | R | 250-300.000 GBP | | NS | | 12-09-15 | Goodwood | 348 | Bon |

Blue with red interior; the car was acquired in 1982 by the late Robert Graves and subsequently it was fully restored, extensively re-engineered and improved. Engine giving approximately 150 bhp. Raced extensively in the 1990s in VSCC events. Offered from the Graves family.

| 1927 | C6 | | 11037 | R | 350-450.000 GBP | | NS | | 12-09-15 | Goodwood | 349 | Bon |

Red with brown interior; acquired in rolling chassis form by the late Robert Graves, the car was subsequently fully restored, extensively re-engineered and improved. Engine giving approximately 150bhp. Probably only raced once at one Brooklands Reunion. Offered from the Graves family.

| 1929 | M2 berline | | 27620 | R | 2-3.000 EUR | 8.184 | 11.856 | 10.512 | 20-03-16 | Fontainebleau | 302 | Ose |

Yellow and black; for restoration. For 38 years in the Jacques Blomet collection.

| 1939 | Compound G38 roadster | | R1024 | L | 12-15.000 EUR | 15.880 | 22.688 | 20.160 | 19-06-16 | Fontainebleau | 315 | Ose |

For about 50 years in the same family ownership, the car was repainted, exhibited in the family collection and never used. It requires some restoration works.

AMPHICAR (D) (1961-1968)

| 1967 | Modell 770 | | 106522695 | L | NA | 23.011 | 36.000 | 31.529 | 19-09-15 | Dallas | S170 | Mec |

Light green with white/apricot interior; believed to be 15,834 original miles.

| 1965 | Modell 770 | | 106521822 | L | NA | 52.552 | 80.000 | 74.328 | 13-11-15 | Anaheim | S151 | Mec |

Red with white interior; restored (see lot S204 Mecum 25.1.14 NS).

| 1962 | Modell 770 | | 103911022008 | L | 28-32.000 GBP | 25.300 | 38.266 | 34.967 | 10-12-15 | London | 349 | Bon |

White; described as in good working order.

| 1965 | Modell 770 | | 101221 | L | 60-80.000 USD | 65.366* | 93.500* | 85.749* | 28-01-16 | Phoenix | 105 | RMS F41 |

Green with apricot and white interior; 1,076 miles covered since the restoration. From the Craig McCaw Collection (see lot 163 RM 10.3.12 $ 63,250).

| 1963 | Modell 770 | | 100549 | L | NA | 46.886* | 66.000* | 58.080* | 09-04-16 | Palm Beach | 485 | B/J |

Red with white interior; restored.

| 1966 | Modell 770 | | 106522222 | L | 40-50.000 EUR | | NS | | 09-04-16 | Essen | 223 | Coy |

Ivory with red interior; for several years on display in an Italian museum.

| 1965 | Modell 770 | | 100251 | L | 60-80.000 USD | 47.249 | 68.200 | 61.141 | 05-06-16 | Greenwhich | 102 | Bon |

White with white and red interior; restored in 2008 (see lot 306 Bonhams 2.6.13 $ 59,400).

APAL (B)

| 1962 | GT | | 40172003 | L | 80-100.000 USD | 61.521* | 88.000* | 80.705* | 28-01-16 | Phoenix | 104 | RMS |

Red with black interior; sold new to Germany and later imported into the USA. Restored in recent years. 1600 Porsche engine.

ARMSTRONG (USA) (1896)

| 1896 | Phaeton | | NQ | R | 175-275.000 USD | 341.619 | 483.400 | 445.211 | 10-03-16 | Amelia Island | 152 | Bon F42 |

Only example built, the car was designed by Harry Dey who created a car that was equal parts electric and gasoline automobile. He used an electric dynamo as the flywheel of the opposed-twin gasoline engine. This design allowed the engine to charge its storage batteries for ignition and lighting but could also rotate the engine for starting. The car remained at the factory until 1963 when it was bought by a long-time employer who resold it in 1995. Later it was imported into the UK where it was fully restored and returned to road use (see lot 152 RM 9.10.14 NS).

F41: 1965 Amphicar Modell 770

F42: 1896 Armstrong Phaeton

Year	Model	(Bodybuilder)	Chassis no.	Steering	Estimate	Hammer price £	$	€	Date	Place	Lot	Auc. H.

F43: 1929 Armstrong-Siddeley 30hp MkII shooting brake

F44: 1955 Arnolt MG TD coupé (Bertone)

ARMSTRONG-SIDDELEY (GB) *(1919-1960)*

1929	**30hp MkII shooting brake**		12567	R	60-80.000 GBP	**63.100**	**96.082**	**86.264**	05-09-15	Beaulieu	110	Bon F43

Ordered new by HRH The Duke of York, later King George VI, who retained it until 1932; since 1936 in the same titled family ownership; used until 1939 and returned on the road in the mid-1960s; engine rebuilt in the early 1990s. Unused for many years, it requires recommissioning prior to use.

| 1932 | **20hp saloon** | | 45252 | R | NA | **17.080** | **24.219** | **21.593** | 20-04-16 | Duxford | 8 | H&H |

Green and black with black leather interior; described as in good original condition.

| 1955 | **Sapphire** | | 344882 | R | NQ | **5.400*** | **7.867*** | **7.012*** | 20-05-16 | Silverstone | 362 | SiC |

The car requires recommissioning prior to use.

| 1958 | **Star Sapphire saloon** | | 320022 | R | 6-8.000 GBP | **4.830*** | **7.355*** | **6.603*** | 05-09-15 | Beaulieu | 187 | Bon |

Two-tone body; restored in the early 1990s.

| 1959 | **Star Sapphire** | | 330529 | R | NA | **10.640** | **14.801** | **13.479** | 24-02-16 | Donington Park | 101 | H&H |

Dark green and light grey with original green leather interior; in the same family ownership for 23 years. Automatic transmission.

ARNOLT (USA) *(1953-1963)*

| 1955 | **MG TD coupé (Bertone)** | | 26873 | L | 20-30.000 USD | **26.088*** | **39.600*** | **35.244*** | 05-10-15 | Philadelphia | 213 | Bon F44 |

Emerald green with grey leather interior; unused from nearly two decades.

| 1957 | **Bristol Bolide roadster (Bertone)** | | 404X3074 | L | 325-375.000 USD | **200.086** | **286.000** | **257.886** | 12-03-16 | Amelia Island | 169 | RMS F45 |

Dark blue and orange with black interior; sold new to the USA, the car has had a long race career and in 1977 it was fitted with a Chevrolet V8 engine. In 2009 it was acquired by the current owner who had it fully restored and fitted again with its original Bristol engine.

| 1954 | **Bristol Bolide DeLuxe roadster (Bertone)** | | 404X3075 | L | 450-550.000 USD | **340.362** | **445.500** | **393.332** | 19-08-16 | Monterey | 126 | RMS |

Red with cream stripe; raced at some events until 1966 and subsequently stored for nearly five decades. Bought by the current owner, the car received subsequently a concours-quality restoration completed in 2015. Engine rebuilt on a new recreation block stamped with the original engine number.

ARROWS (GB) *(1978-)*

| 1985 | **A8** | | A86 | M | 150-180.000 EUR | | **NS** | | 14-05-16 | Monaco | 140 | Coy |

Barclay livery; BMW engine rebuilt but not yet driven.

| 1987 | **A10** | | A103 | M | 100-120.000 GBP | | **NS** | | 28-07-16 | Silverstone | 116 | SiC |

Driven by Derek Warwick during the 1987 Formula 1 season. Bought in 2002 by the current owner and subsequently prepared for historic events. Partial engine rebuild in 2016.

ASA (I) *(1962-1967)*

| 1965 | **1000 GT (Bertone)** | | 01126 | L | 90-130.000 EUR | **99.105** | **146.911** | **131.100** | 04-02-16 | Paris | 357 | Bon |

Light metallic grey with black interior; three owners since new. Fully restored to concours condition between 2008 and 2014.

F45: 1957 Arnolt Bristol Bolide roadster (Bertone)

F46: 1965 Asa 1000 GT (Bertone)

Year	Model	(Bodybuilder)	Chassis no.	Steering	Estimate	Hammer price £	$	€	Date	Place	Lot	Auc. H.

F47: 1931 Aston Martin International 1.5l tourer

F48: 1935 Aston Martin Ulster 2/4-seater tourer (Bertelli)

| 1965 | 1000 GT (Bertone) | | 01238 | L | 100-130.000 EUR | 104.600 | 152.222 | 135.888 | 05-02-16 | Paris | 122 | Art |

Dark blue with black interior; engine rebuilt in 2006, several restoration works carried out between 2012 and 2015 (see lots 49 Poulain 14.12.98 $ 24,003 and 152 Artcurial 7.11.10 $ 71,426). **F46**

ASTON MARTIN (GB) (1922-)

| 1931 | International 1.5l tourer | | A1100 | R | 200-275.000 USD | 183.615 | 280.500 | 249.252 | 08-10-15 | Hershey | 153 | RMS |

Green with green interior; imported into the USA in the 1950s. Recently restored (see lot 138 RM 21.1.10 $ 154,000). **F47**

| 1930 | International 1.5l sports tourer | | S50 | R | 150-170.000 GBP | NS | | | 24-06-16 | Goodwood | 284 | Bon |

Light blue with dark blue interior; with the same owner from 1952 to 1991 and used until 1956, the car was fully restored between 1992 and 1995 (see lot 566 Bonhams 7.7.06 NS).

| 1933 | Le Mans | | L3328L | R | 400-450.000 EUR | NS | | | 04-02-16 | Paris | 334 | Bon |

Black with red interior; restored in 2013 in Switzerland.

| 1935 | Ulster 2/4-seater tourer (Bertelli) | | D5570U | R | 700-900.000 GBP | 740.700 | 1.142.382 | 1.013.870 | 12-09-15 | Goodwood | 365 | Bon |

Black with red interior; one of four Ulsters ordered with the 4 seater body, the car has had a long pre- and post-war race career. In 1936 the engine was fitted with supercharger. In 1952 it was acquired by Bill Burton who last raced it in 1975. Restored between the late 1980s and 1993; acquired in 2002 by the current owner and restored again in 2003; in 2007 the engine was rebuilt and later also the gearbox (see Brooks lots 242 19.3.95 $ 123,838 and 874 20.6.97 $ 129,925). **F48**

| 1934 | 1.5l Mk II 2/4 seater (Bertelli) | | C4406S | R | 450-500.000 USD | NS | | | 30-01-16 | Scottsdale | 133 | G&Co |

Red with black interior; older restoration. Imported in 1956 into the USA; in single ownership from 1988 for more than 25 years.

| 1934 | 1.5l Mk II tourer | | G3297L | R | 80-120.000 GBP | 85.500* | 123.864* | 109.816* | 20-03-16 | Goodwood | 54 | Bon |

White with tan leather interior; built with saloon body, the car was fitted with the present tourer body probably in the 1960s. Later it remained for 35 years with the same owner and was used at numerous historical events.

| 1934 | 1.5l Mk tourer | | G3297L | R | 190-220.000 EUR | 130.641 | 171.847 | 154.040 | 06-08-16 | Schloss Dyck | 150 | Coy |

See lot 54 Bonhams 20.3.16.

| 1949 | DB2 prototype coupé | | LMA249 | R | 600-900.000 GBP | 679.100 | 930.639 | 840.930 | 24-06-16 | Goodwood | 241 | Bon |

One of the development prototypes fitted with the four cylinder engine; Works car at the 1949 Le Mans and Spa 24 Hours races. Sold subsequently to private hands, it was raced until 1957. Cylinder block replaced in the 1950s. In 1965 it was purchased by Christopher Angell, in whose family it remained since. Last used in 1971 probably; for restoration. **F49**

| 1951 | DB2 coupé | | LML5035 | R | 350-450.000 EUR | NS | | | 05-09-15 | Chantilly | 14 | Bon |

Olive green with beige leather interior; sold new to France, the car raced the 1952 Lyon Charbonnieres Rally. In 1982 it was acquired by Jean-Louis Herbert who retained it for 29 years and had it restored in 1999. Described as still in excellent overall condition (see lot 58 H&H 4.12.13 NS).

| 1950 | DB2 Vantage coupé | | LML5019 | R | 300-350.000 GBP | 302.400 | 461.523 | 414.076 | 07-09-15 | London | 167 | RMS |

First Vantage built, the car was sold new to the USA to racing driver Bill Spear and did its race debut at the 1950 Sebring 6 Hours where it placed 14th overall and 2nd in class. Later it was raced at several racing events in period and in more recent years at historic events, including the 2009 Mille Miglia (see lot 270 RM 1.5.10 $ 387,733). **F50**

| 1955 | DB2/4 coupé | | LML938 | L | 190-260.000 EUR | 178.879 | 274.392 | 241.500 | 09-10-15 | Zoute | 21 | Bon |

Dark green with green leather interior; restored in 2000 circa, the car is described as in very good driving order.

| 1955 | DB2/4 coupé | | LML933 | R | 125-150.000 GBP | 125.000 | 188.313 | 177.650 | 01-12-15 | London | 323 | Coy |

Silver with blue leather interior; restored in recent years. The engine has covered less than 500 miles since the rebuild (see lots 332 Coys 8.3.11 NS and 305 Bonhams 13.9.14 NS).

| 1954 | DB2/4 coupé | | LML656 | R | NA | 207.200 | 293.810 | 261.942 | 20-04-16 | Duxford | 80 | H&H |

Metallic grey with red interior; used until 1969, the car was acquired in 2011 by the current owner and subsequently fully restored (see lot 36 H&H 13.4.11 $ 118,251).

F49: 1949 Aston Martin DB2 prototype coupé

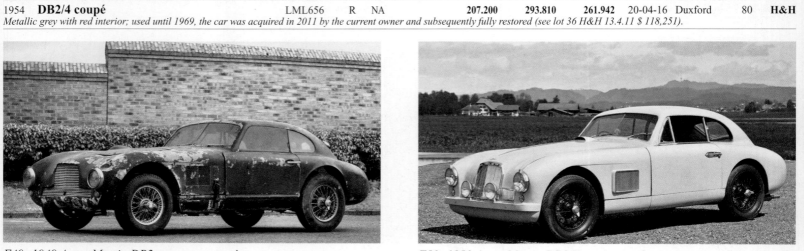

F50: 1950 Aston Martin DB2 Vantage coupé

-THE-
HOUTKAMP COLLECTION

Fine Historic Automobiles
Amsterdam

A passionate family company with a long track record in retailing the most significant historical road and race cars as well as Mille Miglia eligible cars.

If you share the same passion, please do not hesitate to contact us!

John H. Houtkamp *Rutger H. Houtkamp*
+31 6 53 94 45 49 *+31 6 25 09 81 50*

Visit us online for current and expected cars
www.houtkamp.nl
info@houtkamp.nl

Year	Model	(Bodybuilder)	Chassis no.	Steering	Estimate	Hammer price £	$	€	Sale Date	Place	Lot	Auc. H.

F51: 1954 Aston Martin DB2/4 coupé

F52: 1955 Aston Martin DB2/4 cabriolet

Year	Model	(Bodybuilder)	Chassis no.	Steering	Estimate	£	$	€	Date	Place	Lot	Auc. H.
1955	DB2/4 coupé		LML1004	R	135-165.000 GBP	151.875	221.252	197.210	20-05-16	Silverstone	320	SiC
	Aston Martin racing green; purchased by the current owner in 1976, used for two years and then stored from 1978 to 2008 when a full restoration was started and completed at unspecified date.											
1954	DB2/4 coupé		LML662	R	30-50.000 GBP	59.740	87.029	77.572	21-05-16	Newp.Pagnell	201	Bon
	For restoration; in the same family ownership for 46 years and stored since 1975.											
1954	DB2/4 coupé		LML790	R	150-180.000 GBP	158.300	230.611	205.553	21-05-16	Newp.Pagnell	245	Bon F51
	Green with beige leather interior; fully restored between 2005 and 2013.											
1954	DB2/4 cabriolet		LML818	R	220-270.000 GBP	NS			07-09-15	London	156	RMS
	Imperial crimson with beige leather interior; originally sold to racing driver Hermano Da Silva Ramos who, although unconfirmed, may have raced it at some events (see Coys lots 153 30.11.06 NS and 231 27.5.07 $ 154,260).											
1955	DB2/4 cabriolet		LML1003	L	375-475.000 USD	276.844	396.000	363.172	28-01-16	Scottsdale	49	Bon F52
	Blue with blue leather interior; sold new to the USA, the car was restored between the late 1990s-early 2000s. From the BHA Automobile Museum (see lot 70 RM 17.8.01 $ 102,850).											
1954	DB2/4 cabriolet		LML816	R	200-250.000 GBP	NS			21-05-16	Newp.Pagnell	208	Bon
	Green with beige leather interior; recent mechanical rebuild.											
1953	DB2/4 cabriolet		LML558	R	240-280.000 GBP	326.300	475.354	423.701	21-05-16	Newp.Pagnell	222	Bon
	Sea green with pale beige interior; from 1953 to 1955 the car remained in the factory ownership and was used as demonstrator, for magazine advertising and also at some races driven by Angela Abecassis, David Brown's daughter. Between 1953 and 1954 it was fitted with a 3-litre engine. Later sold to private hands, it was first restored in the late 1980s, raced at historic events between 1999 and 2003 and restored again between 2004 and 2006 (see lot 309 Bonhams 17.5.08 $ 292,100).											
1955	DB2/4 cabriolet		LML1009	R	200-220.000 GBP	NS			21-05-16	Newp.Pagnell	239	Bon
	For restoration (see lot 206 Bonhams 19.5.12 $ 179,534).											
1954	DB2/4 spider (Bertone)		LML505	L	3.000-4.000.000 USD	2.353.120	3.080.000	2.719.332	21-08-16	Pebble Beach	138	G&Co
	Blue with blue interior; designed by Franco Scaglione and built in just three examples by Bertone. Exhibited by Stanley Arnolt at the 1954 New York Motor Show where it was bought by its first owner. First restored in the 1970s; sold in 1984 to Switzerland and restored again; purchased by Carlos Monteverde in 1996; purchased in 2003 circa by the current owner and subsequently restored to concours condition (see lot 121 Christie's 16.5.96 $ 275,117).											F53
1953	DB3S		DB3S5	R	6.000-7.000.000 GBP	NS			21-05-16	Newp.Pagnell	244	Bon
	Built with glassfibre body for personal use of David Brown, in 1954 the car was delivered to the factory's Competition Department, fitted with an aluminium body and raced as a Works car at several events. At the end of the 1955 season it was acquired by Roy Salvadori and raced during the 1956 season as Works entrant also. Subsequently it had some other owners and was raced until the late 1950s. In 2007 it was purchased by the current owner and in 2014 it was fully restored by Aston Martin Works.											F54
1957	DB2/4 MkII coupé		AM3001202	R	240-270.000 GBP	258.000	392.857	352.712	04-09-15	Woodstock	243	SiC
	Dark green with silver roof and beige interior; restored in 2012. The car was driven by Stirling Moss at the 2012 Ennstal Classic Alpine Rally and completed the 2013 Mille Miglia Storica (see lot 565 Bonhams 6.12.10 $ 82,859).											
1957	DB2/4 MkII cabriolet (Tickford)		AM3001265	L	450-550.000 USD	NS			21-08-16	Pebble Beach	112	G&Co
	Black with black interior; sold new to France, the car was imported into the USA in the late 1980s. In good overall condition.											
1958	DB MkIII coupé (Tickford)		AM30031690	R	160-200.000 GBP	186.300	287.330	255.007	12-09-15	Goodwood	323	Bon
	Dark green with green leather interior; from 1971 for 40 years in the same family ownership, from 2012 to 2014 in the ownership of actor Orlando Bloom (see lots Coys 176 16.7.11 NS and 140 8.10.11 NS, and Bonhams 240 17.5.14 $ 256,673).											
1958	DB MkIII coupé		AM30031781	R	130-160.000 GBP	NS			10-10-15	Ascot	139	Coy
	Red with light grey leather interior; restored in the late 1980s. Since 2000 in the current ownership (see lots 48 H&H 28.7.99 $ 35,817, 115 Brooks 13.5.00 NS and 17 H&H 4.10.00 $ 29,936).											

F53: 1954 Aston Martin DB2/4 spider (Bertone)

F54: 1953 Aston Martin DB3S

F55: 1959 Aston Martin DB MkIII coupé (Tickford)

F56: 1959 Aston Martin DB MkIII coupé

Year	Model (Bodybuilder)	Chassis no.	Steering	Estimate	Hammer price £	$	€	Date	Place	Lot	Auc. H.
1958	**DB MkIII coupé**	AM30031696	R	NA	212.800	327.308	286.854	14-10-15	Duxford	44	H&H
	Silver with burgundy interior; described as in very good overall condition. Engine recently overhauled (see lots 332 Bonhams 9.5.09 $ 134,894 and 242 Artcurial 4.2.11 $ 149,510).										
1958	**DB MkIII coupé**	AM30031781	R	100-115.000 GBP	130.000 P	186.316 P	170.703 P	16-01-16	Birmingham	323	Coy
	See lot 139 Coys 10.10.15.										
1957	**DB MkIII coupé**	AM30031358	L	240-300.000 EUR	211.035	307.114	274.160	05-02-16	Paris	154	Art
	Gold with beige leather interior; original engine rebuilt in 2014 (see lot 18 RM 5.2.14 $ 280,611).										
1958	**DB MkIII coupé**	AM30031433	R	NA	208.125	290.876	264.298	26-02-16	Coventry	733	SiC
	Dark blue; since 1960 in the same family ownership, the car was fully restored in the 2000s.										
1959	**DB MkIII coupé (Tickford)**	AM30031848	R	220-260.000 GBP	371.100	540.618	481.873	21-05-16	Newp.Pagnell	212	Bon **F55**
	For circa 45 years in the current ownership; 50,056 miles covered since new. Special Series engine rebuilt at the factory in 1970.										
1959	**DB MkIII coupé**	AM30001789	R	150-190.000 GBP	191.900	279.560	249.182	21-05-16	Newp.Pagnell	218	Bon **F56**
	Light grey with black leather interior; restored in the UK in 2008 (see lot 214 Bonhams 14.9.13 $ 232,845).										
1958	**DB MkIII coupé**	AM30031756	R	170-210.000 GBP		NS		21-05-16	Newp.Pagnell	231	Bon
	Metallic marron with beige leather interior; restored in the 1990s. Engine, gearbox and clutch restored in more recent years.										
1958	**DB MkIII coupé**	AM30031378	L	310-350.000 EUR		NS		09-07-16	Le Mans	162	Art
	Dark grey with red interior; sold new to the USA, the car remained with its first owner until 1996 when it was imported into Belgium and later fully restored.										
1958	**DB MkIII cabriolet (Tickford)**	AM30031492	L	350-450.000 GBP	443.900	646.674	576.404	21-05-16	Newp.Pagnell	236	Bon **F57**
	Dark blue with black leather interior; sold new to the USA, the car was purchased by the current owner in 1990. 4,000 miles covered since the restoration completed in the early 2000s. Swiss papers.										
1963	**DB4 Vantage coupé (Touring/Tickford)**	DB41197R	R	675-775.000 GBP		NS		04-09-15	Woodstock	222	SiC
	Dark green with red leather interior; acquired in 2004 by the current owner. Subsequently the mechanicals were rebuilt. The original Borg Warner automatic transmission was replaced and is included in the sale (see lot 667 Bonhams 6.12.04 $ 99,044).										
1960	**DB4 coupé (Touring/Tickford)**	DB4361R	R	380-420.000 GBP		NS		04-09-15	Woodstock	246	SiC
	Red with black interior retrimmed about 20 years ago; at unspecified date the engine was upgraded to Vantage specification and the original drum brakes were replaced by discs. The car was sold new to Australia where it remained until 2014.										
1960	**DB4 coupé (Touring/Tickford)**	DB4416L	L	325-425.000 GBP	330.000	503.646	451.869	07-09-15	London	130	RMS
	Light grey with red leather; acquired by the current owner in 1989 in California and subsequently restored.										
1963	**DB4 coupé (Touring/Tickford)**	DB41046R	L	480-550.000 EUR	393.803	623.604	548.320	01-11-15	Paris	124	Art **F58**
	Silver with new black leather interior; described as in very good overall condition. Sold new in the UK, the car was imported into France and converted to left-hand drive.										
1961	**DB4 coupé (Touring/Tickford)**	DB4529R	R	330-380.000 GBP		NS		06-12-15	London	020	Bon
	Silver with dark blue leather interior; original engine replaced by factory in 1970. The car was restored between 1999 and 2001 and received further works in 2013-14 (see lots 272 RM 29.10.08 $ 158,865 and 339 Bonhams 21.5.11 $ 252,423).										
1962	**DB4 coupé (Touring/Tickford)**	DB4905R	L	525-625.000 USD	307.868	440.000	402.908	29-01-16	Phoenix	234	RMS
	Dark blue with white gold leather interior; built in right-hand drive form and sold new in the UK, the car was later exported to Northern Europe and converted to left-hand drive. In 2006 it was sold to the USA where it received several works including body repainting. Last serviced in September 2015.										

F57: 1958 Aston Martin DB MkIII cabriolet (Tickford)

F58: 1963 Aston Martin DB4 coupé (Touring/Tickford)

Year	Model	(Bodybuilder)	Chassis no.	Steering	Estimate	Hammer price £	Hammer price $	Hammer price €	Date	Place	Lot	Auc. H.
1961	**DB4 coupé**	(Touring/Tickford)	DB4829L	L	450-650.000 EUR	460.752	683.006	609.500	04-02-16	Paris	315	**Bon**
	Originally finished in black with dark grey leather interior, the car was sold new to Spain. In 1981 it was acquired by the current owner who kept it garaged until 2013 when a long restoration was started and recently completed. Body restored in Spain and finished in silver; engine rebuilt in the UK.											
1961	**DB4 coupé**	(Touring/Tickford)	DB4679L	L	450-550.000 EUR	412.894	600.875	536.400	05-02-16	Paris	156	**Art**
	Dark green with black leather interior; sold new to France, probably the car has had just three owners. 13,000 kms on the odometer. In 1962 the engine was upgraded with three carburettors as in the Vantage model. Originally dark blue the leather interior were dyed black at unspecified date.											
1960	**DB4 coupé**	(Touring/Tickford)	DB4415R	R	NA		UD		20-04-16	Duxford	81	**H&H**
	Metallic sage with black leather interior; from the late 1980s to 2014 in an European collection. The car has covered 500 miles since the mechanicals overhaul and body repainting. Sold for an undisclosed sum.											
1960	**DB4 coupé**	(Touring/Tickford)	DB4323R	R	350-385.000 GBP	337.500	491.670	438.244	21-05-16	Newp.Pagnell	210	**Bon**
	Engine rebuilt and interior retrimmed in red leather in 1989; several mechanical works carried out between 2007 and 2012. Since 1992 in the current ownership; in good driving order.											
1961	**DB4 coupé**	(Touring/Tickford)	DB4566L	L	550-600.000 GBP	NS			21-05-16	Newp.Pagnell	214	**Bon**
	Originally finished in white, the car was sold new to the USA. Restored in recent times, it is currently finished in black with black interior. Should the car remain in the EU, local import taxes of 5% will be applied to the hammer price.											
1959	**DB4 coupé**	(Touring/Tickford)	DB4147R	R	370-430.000 GBP	NS			21-05-16	Newp.Pagnell	223	**Bon**
	Grey with red interior; body replaced in April 1960 following an accident with a Series 2 body. Purchased in 1976 by the current owner, it remained unused for 29 years until 2014 when it was subjected to a full restoration completed in 2015.											
1959	**DB4 coupé**	(Touring/Tickford)	DB4144L	L	590-640.000 GBP	NS			21-05-16	Newp.Pagnell	240	**Bon**
	Grey; sold new to the USA. Engine rebuilt at unspecified date. In good overall condition, it requires just some attention (see lot 326 Bonhams 21.5.11 $ 413,130).											
1959	**DB4 coupé**	(Touring/Tickford)	DB4147R	R	300-350.000 GBP	NS			24-06-16	Goodwood	267	**Bon**
	See lot 223 Bonhams 21.5.16.											
1960	**DB4 coupé**	(Touring/Tickford)	DB4245L	L	700-850.000 USD	NS			19-08-16	Carmel	47	**Bon**
	Red with mushroom leather interior; in the 1990s restored to concours condition. Recently the car has been cosmetically refreshed and the engine has been rebuilt (see lots 138 RM 23.6.11 $339,969 and 214 Bonhams 9.5.15 $761,865).											
1962	**DB4 GT**	(Zagato)	DB4GT0186R	R	15-17.000.000 USD	9.453.730	14.300.000	13.067.340	10-12-15	New York	215	**RMS** **TOP TEN**
	The 14th of 19 examples built, the car was sold new to Australia where it was raced at several events of the 1962 season. Following two other Australian ownerships, in 1993 it was acquired by G.K. Speirs and reimported into the UK where it received a minor restoration and was subsequently raced at historic events. Purchased by Peter Read, the car was subjected to a concours-quality restoration completed in 2002.											
1963	**DB4 cabriolet**	(Touring/Tickford)	DB4C1100L	L	1.250-1.500.000 EUR	1.133.996	1.650.279	1.473.200	05-02-16	Paris	157	**Art** **F59**
	Dark blue with tan leather interior; sold new to the USA, the car was imported into France in 1991 and later restored. Described as in excellent overall condition.											
1963	**DB4 Vantage cabriolet**	(Touring/Tickford)	DB4C1166R	R	1.100-1.400.000 GBP	1.009.500	1.470.640	1.310.836	21-05-16	Newp.Pagnell	209	**Bon**
	Blue with blue leather interior; always well maintained over the years, the car is described as in very good overall condition. Two owners since 1984.											
1962	**DB4 Vantage cabriolet**	(Touring/Tickford)	DB4C1085R	R	Refer Dpt.	NS			21-05-16	Newp.Pagnell	252	**Bon**
	Red with cream interior; exhibited at the Aston Martin stand at the 1962 Earls Court Motor Show, the car was sold new in the UK and exported to the USA probably in the early 2000s.											
1965	**DB5 Vantage coupé**	(Touring/Tickford)	DB52016R	R	700-900.000 GBP	784.000	1.196.541	1.073.531	07-09-15	London	170	**RMS** **F60**
	Silver with black leather interior; full restoration completed in 2002. Described as in very good overall condition.											
1964	**DB5 coupé**	(Touring/Tickford)	DB51579R	R	400-450.000 GBP	516.700	782.232	717.490	06-12-15	London	004	**Bon**
	Light blue with blue leather interior; since 1993 in the Gordon Willey collection, the car is unused from some time and requires recommissioning prior to use.											
1964	**DB5 coupé**	(Touring/Tickford)	DB51759R	L	800-1.100.000 USD	545.997	781.000	716.255	28-01-16	Scottsdale	108	**Bon**
	Built in right-hand drive form and finished in red, the car was sold new in the UK. Later it was exported to the USA and in 1994 it was imported into Canada where it was restored and converted to left-hand drive. During the restoration the engine was enlarged to 4.2-litre and the original ZF gearbox (included with the sale) was replaced with the present Toyota Supra unit. In 2013 it was restored again and finished in the present silver livery.											
1963	**DB5 coupé**	(Touring/Tickford)	DB51301L	L	1.100-1.300.000 EUR	NS			03-02-16	Paris	144	**RMS**
	First series example built, the car was sold new to Germany. In 1969 the original engine was replaced at the factory by the present unit no.400-2667 and in the mid-1970s the car was imported into the USA where it was first restored. In 2003 the car was restored again and the engine was rebuilt to 4.2-litre specification (see lots 87 Christie's 19.8.01 $ 138,000 and 561 RM 15.8. 09 $ 341,000).											
1965	**DB5 Vantage coupé**	(Touring/Tickford)	DB52084R	R	450-550.000 GBP	807.900	1.176.949	1.049.058	21-05-16	Newp.Pagnell	206	**Bon**
	Green with black leather interior; since 1973 in the current ownership, the car is in original condition. Mechanically in good condition, it requires some attention to the paintwork. Off the road since 2006.											
1965	**DB5 coupé**	(Touring/Tickford)	DB52264R	R	Refer Dpt.	NS			21-05-16	Newp.Pagnell	234	**Bon**
	Aston Martin racing green with black interior; restored in recent times. Automatic transmission (see lot 1769 Sotheby's 5.12.94 $ 34,071).											
1963	**DB5 coupé**	(Touring/Tickford)	DB51336L	L	Refer Dpt.	NS			21-05-16	Newp.Pagnell	247	**Bon**
	Red with white gold interior (see lot 74 Christie's 11.9.13 NS).											

F59: 1963 Aston Martin DB4 cabriolet (Touring/Tickford)

F60: 1965 Aston Martin DB5 Vantage coupé (Touring/Tickford)

Year	Model (Bodybuilder)	Chassis No.	Steering	Estimate	Hammer price £	Hammer price $	Hammer price €	Date	Place	Lot	Auc. H.
1963	DB5 coupé (Touring/Tickford)	DB51308R	R	550-650.000 GBP		NS		24-06-16	Goodwood	259	Bon
Dark green with gold white leather interior; bought in 1994 by the second owner and subsequently restored. Engine enlarged to 4.2-litre.											
1965	DB5 convertible (Touring/Tickford)	DB5C2119R	L	1.000-1.200.000 GBP	1.087.900	1.677.868	1.489.118	12-09-15	Goodwood	345	Bon **F61**
Light green with sand leather interior; the car was acquired in 1989 by a previous owner in a state of partial restoration. Subsequently the engine was rebuilt and the body was repainted in 1993. In 2005 it was acquired by the current owner and restored again.											
1964	DB5 convertible (Touring/Tickford)	DB5C1287R	R	750-850.000 GBP	807.900	1.176.949	1.049.058	21-05-16	Newp.Pagnell	232	Bon
Dark red with light grey leather interior; since 1973 in the current ownership, the car received a long restoration completed in 2015. The replacement cylinder block has been stamped with the original's number.											
1969	DB6 Vantage coupé	DB63585R	R	150-200.000 GBP	163.900	249.571	224.068	05-09-15	Beaulieu	145	Bon
For restoration; working engine. Since 1975 in the current ownership.											
1967	DB6 Vantage coupé	DB63029R	R	250-300.000 GBP	303.900	468.705	415.978	12-09-15	Goodwood	369	Bon
Green with black interior; since new in the same family ownership. 29,658 miles on the odometer. Restored between 1990 and 1992.											
1966	DB6 coupé	DB62398L	L	525-625.000 USD	346.055	495.000	453.965	28-01-16	Phoenix	153	RMS **F62**
Dark green with tan leather interior; body repainted in 2004, engine rebuilt in 2007 to 4.2-litre specification and fitted with a modern Tremec 5-speed gearbox (the original ZF unit is included in the sale), interior recently retrimmed.											
1966	DB6 coupé	DB62590R	L	400-475.000 EUR	295.294	428.574	392.000	03-02-16	Paris	118	RMS
Red with black interior; sold new to the UK, the car was imported in the early 1980s in Canada where in 1985 it was converted to left-hand drive. Restored between 2005 and 2006. Recently serviced (see lot 246 RM 14.3.09 $ 121,000).											
1968	DB6 coupé	DB63342	R	300-350.000 GBP		NS		16-04-16	Ascot	115A	Coy
Light blue with blue leather interior; restoration completed in 2015. Automatic transmission (see lot 285 Historics 7.3.15 $ 290,727).											
1968	DB6 coupé	DB63471R	R	195-250.000 GBP		NS		21-05-16	Newp.Pagnell	205	Bon
Silver with red leather interior; sold new to South Africa and reimported into the UK in the early 1990s. Since 1994 in the current ownership; restored between 1994 and 1995. Automatic transmission (see lot 12 Coys 25.10.93 NS).											
1968	DB6 coupé	DB63368R	R	200-250.000 GBP	197.500	287.718	256.454	21-05-16	Newp.Pagnell	220	Bon
Dark grey with magnolia leather interior; body repainted in recent years. Automatic transmission.											
1966	DB6 Vantage coupé	DB62594R	R	165-185.000 GBP	191.900	279.560	249.182	21-05-16	Newp.Pagnell	224	Bon
Unused for 25 years; for restoration. Automatic transmission.											
1970	DB6 coupé	DB6MK24198R	R	190-230.000 GBP	203.100	295.876	263.725	21-05-16	Newp.Pagnell	230	Bon
Red; since 1979 in the current ownership. Webasto sunroof. Automatic transmission.											
1966	DB6 coupé	DB62739R	R	200-220.000 GBP		NS		21-05-16	Newp.Pagnell	238	Bon
For restoration; automatic transmission (see lot 34 Bonhams 21.3.15 NS).											
1967	DB6 coupé	DB63030R	L	450-500.000 GBP		NS		21-05-16	Newp.Pagnell	243	Bon
At unspecified date the car was converted to left-hand drive and the automatic transmission was replaced with a manual unit. Not taxed since 2009, it requires recommissioning prior to use.											
1967	DB6 coupé	DB64015R	R	200-220.000 GBP		NS		21-05-16	Newp.Pagnell	246	Bon
Automatic transmission; engine replaced at unspecified date (see lot 370 Bonhams 27.6.14 NS).											
1967	DB6 coupé	DB63151R	L	200-220.000 GBP		NS		21-05-16	Newp.Pagnell	251	Bon
Converted to left-hand drive at date unknown; partially restored.											
1967	DB6 Vantage coupé	DB62866R	R	250-290.000 GBP		NS		11-06-16	Brooklands	276	His
Recently reimported into the UK from Australia and serviced.											
1968	DB6 coupé	DB63471R	R	175-205.000 GBP	186.300	255.306	230.695	24-06-16	Goodwood	238	Bon
See lot 205 Bonhams 21.5.16.											
1968	DB6 coupé	DB63342	R	260-300.000 GBP	220.000	292.204	262.416	02-07-16	Woodstock	134	Coy
See lot 115A Coys 16.4.16.											
1967	DB6 coupé	DB63205R	R	280-325.000 GBP	215.000	285.563	256.452	02-07-16	Woodstock	164	Coy
Blue with tan interior; purchased in 2006 by the current owner and restored.											
1967	DB6 Vantage coupé	DB62974R	L	300-400.000 USD	260.524	341.000	301.069	19-08-16	Carmel	85	Bon
Grey with black leather interior; sold new in the UK, later the car was imported into the USA where it was restored and converted to left-hand drive.											
1966	DB6 coupé	DB62409LIN	L	450-525.000 USD	336.160	440.000	388.476	19-08-16	Monterey	147	RMS
Aston Martin green with green leather interior; sold new to the USA. Restored in 1991 and sold to Japan in 1992, the car has been later reimported into the USA and refreshed in 2016.											

F61: 1965 Aston Martin DB5 convertible (Touring/Tickford)

F62: 1966 Aston Martin DB6 coupé

Year	Model (Bodybuilder)	Chassis no.	Steering	Estimate	Hammer Price £	$	€	Date	Place	Lot	Auc. H.
1968	**DB6 Volante Vantage**	DBVC3698R	R	825-925.000 GBP	900.000	1.370.430	1.230.390	04-09-15	Woodstock	211	SiC **F63**
	Sage green with tan leather interior; acquired in 2013 by the current owner and subsequently subjected to a major service. Described as in very good overall condition.										
1968	**DB6 Volante**	DBVC3707R	R	600-700.000 GBP	617.500	899.574	801.824	21-05-16	Newp.Pagnell	219	Bon
	Pewter with magnolia leather interior; in very good overall condition. Several restoration works to the body and mechanicals carried out in the 2000s. ZF automatic transmission replaced in 2004.										
1968	**DB6 Volante**	DBVC3708R	R	750-800.000 GBP		NS		21-05-16	Newp.Pagnell	241	Bon
	Red with cream leather interior; rebuilt in 1981 following an accident to Mark 2 specification using new body panels, between 2001 and 2002 body repainted and engine rebuilt to Vantage specification and increased to 4.2-litre. Automatic transmission (see lot 227 Coys 25.5.08 $ 357,822).										
1969	**DB6 Volante**	DBVC3705R	R	Refer Dpt.		NS		21-05-16	Newp.Pagnell	248	Bon
	Red with natural leather interior; the car requires some works to the body and interior (see lot 325 Bonhams 17.5.08 $ 452,771).										
1970	**DBS Vantage**	DBS5352L	L	120-160.000 EUR	143.824	227.751	200.256	01-11-15	Paris	122	Art **F64**
	Silver with dark green leather interior; since 1990 in the current ownership. Mechanicals overhauled in the 1990s. Little used since 2005, it requires recommissioning prior to use.										
1968	**DBS**	DBS5162R	R	50-60.000 GBP	51.750	75.389	67.197	20-05-16	Silverstone	328	SiC
	Stored since 1986; for restoration. Automatic transmission.										
1971	**DBS**	DBS5764R	R	100-140.000 GBP	96.700	140.873	125.565	21-05-16	Newp.Pagnell	242	Bon
	Red with original black leather interior; engine rebuilt and increased to 4.2-litre in 1993, body repainted in 1994. Described as in good overall condition.										
1971	**DBS Vantage**	DBS5701R	R	75-95.000 GBP	70.310	92.528	83.261	30-07-16	Silverstone	520	SiC
	Purple with cream interior; in driving condition. Several works carried out over the years. Manual gearbox.										
1971	**DBS V8 (Ogle Design)**	DBSV810380R	R	NA	88.140	135.568	118.813	14-10-15	Duxford	89	H&H
	First of the three Sotheby Specials built, the car was fitted with a sperimental fuel-injected V8 engine (dated 1967) and 5-speed manual gearbox. Exhibited at the 1972 Montreal and Geneva Motor Shows, the car was subsequently partially stripped for parts and stored. Since the mid-1970s in the current ownership it requires full restoration.										
1971	**DBS V8**	DBSV810201LC	L	90-120.000 EUR	130.126	206.061	181.184	01-11-15	Paris	123	Art
	Dark blue with tan leather interior; since 1989 in the current ownership. Body repainted and gearbox rebuilt in the early 1990s; engine rebuilt in 1996.										
1970	**DBS V8**	DBSV810016R	R	65-75.000 GBP	84.375	128.453	119.340	14-11-15	Birmingham	613	SiC
	Metallic beige; bought in 1975 by the previous owner, the car was stored from 1987 to May 2015 when it was recommissioned and subsequently acquired by the present owner. Body repainted in the 1980s; automatic transmission.										
1969	**DBS V8**	DBSV810149RC	R	75-90.000 GBP	107.020	161.226	152.097	01-12-15	London	338	Coy
	Described as in very good overall condition; paintwork and interior redone; engine overhauled.										
1971	**DBS V8**	DBSV810329CC	R	34-38.000 GBP	85.880	129.576	118.437	09-12-15	Chateau Impney	10	H&H
	In the same family ownership since 1988 and off the road since 2002; unwarranted 48,000 miles on the odometer.										
1972	**DBS V8**	DBSV810002RCA	R	60-70.000 GBP	68.625	99.973	89.110	20-05-16	Silverstone	350	SiC
	Blue with beige leather interior; restored many years ago, it requires further attention. Automatic transmission.										
1972	**DBS V8**	DBSV810331RC	R	110-140.000 GBP	113.500	165.347	147.380	21-05-16	Newp.Pagnell	204	Bon
	Blue with fawn leather interior; restored. Engine rebuilt. Automatic transmission.										
1971	**DBS V8**	DBSV810165RCA	R	90-110.000 GBP	74.750	99.283	89.162	02-07-16	Woodstock	214	Coy
	Burgundy with cream leather interior; in good condition. Automatic transmission.										
1973	**AM V8 series 2**	V810653RCA	R	NA	78.750	110.061	100.005	26-02-16	Coventry	735	SiC
	Metallic anthracite grey with magnolia leather interior; in good working order. Automatic transmission.										
1972	**AM V8 series 2**	V810568RCA	R	100-120.000 GBP		NS		21-05-16	Newp.Pagnell	211	Bon
	Dark metallic blue with fawn interior; purchased in 2005 by the current owner and restored between 2007 and 2015. Automatic transmission (see lot 681 Bonhams 26.4.04 $ 10,269).										
1972	**AM V8 series 2**	DBSV810569LCA	L	100-120.000 GBP		NS		21-05-16	Newp.Pagnell	217	Bon
	Silver with black leather interior; several mechanical works carried out between 2001 and 2003. Stored from 2003 to 2014 and subsequently recommissioned (see lot 224 Bonhams 11.5.02 NS).										
1972	**AM V8 series 2**	V810500RCA	R	75-95.000 GBP		NS		21-05-16	Newp.Pagnell	250	Bon
	Red; restored in 2002-03. In running condition.										
1974	**AM V8 series 3**	V811198RCAC	R	60-80.000 GBP		NS		05-09-15	Beaulieu	166	Bon
	Blue with blue leather interior; restored over the last 10 years. Automatic transmission; electric sunroof.										
1973	**AM V8 series 3**	V811006RCA	R	NA	72.800	111.974	98.134	14-10-15	Duxford	66	H&H
	For restoration; yellow with black interior. The car was used by the factory as a development car for the new Series 3. Since 1987 in the current ownership.										
1974	**AM V8 series 3**	V811289RCA	R	75-90.000 GBP	97.000	139.020	127.371	16-01-16	Birmingham	315	Coy
	Green with black interior; described as in very good overall condition. For 36 years in the same family ownership; 37,182 miles covered.										

F63: 1968 Aston Martin DB6 Volante Vantage

F64: 1970 Aston Martin DBS Vantage

Year	Model (Bodybuilder)	Chassis no.	Steering	Estimate	Hammer price £	$	€	Date	Sale Place	Lot	Auc. H.

F65: 1974 Aston Martin AM V8 series 3

F66: 1974 Aston Martin Lagonda

Year	Model	Chassis no.	Steering	Estimate	£	$	€	Date	Place	Lot	Auc. H.
1974	**AM V8 series 3**	V811149LCA	L	50-80.000 EUR	95.628	141.756	126.500	04-02-16	Paris	306	Bon F65
1978	**AM V8 series 3**	V811973RCAS	R	NA	47.250	66.892	60.981	06-03-16	Birmingham	313	SiC
1973	**AM V8 series 3**	V811059RCA	R	60-70.000 GBP	63.960	90.881	82.412	08-03-16	London	122	Coy
1973	**AM V8 series 3**	V811038RCA	R	NA	51.520	73.055	65.132	20-04-16	Duxford	13	H&H
1978	**AM V8 series 3**	V811790RCAS	R	80-100.000 GBP	81.563	118.821	105.910	20-05-16	Silverstone	312	SiC
1977	**AM V8 series 3**	V811774RCAS	R	50-70.000 GBP	66.460	96.819	86.298	21-05-16	Newp.Pagnell	202	Bon
1973	**AM V8 series 3**	V811050RCA	R	38-48.000 GBP	58.240	83.883	74.209	11-06-16	Brooklands	294	His
1977	**AM V8 series 3**	V811656RCAS	L	60-80.000 EUR	78.239	101.605	91.784	09-07-16	Le Mans	161	Art
1977	**AM V8 series 3**	V811568RCAC	R	70-90.000 GBP		NS		20-08-16	Brooklands	307	His
1974	**Lagonda**	L12003RCAC	R	400-500.000 GBP	427.100	646.587	593.071	06-12-15	London	028	Bon F66
1979	**AM V8 Vantage series 4**	V8VOR12186	R	200-250.000 GBP	197.500	287.718	256.454	21-05-16	Newp.Pagnell	225	Bon F67
1981	**AM V8 series 4**	V8SOR12280	R	80-100.000 GBP		NS		21-05-16	Newp.Pagnell	229	Bon
1980	**AM V8 series 4**	V8SOR12233	R	95-110.000 GBP	99.000	130.284	117.236	30-07-16	Silverstone	932	SiC
1984	**AM V8 Volante**	15343	L	130-170.000 EUR	69.801	105.935	95.000	26-09-15	Frankfurt	117	Coy
1986	**AM V8 Volante**	15486	L	140-180.000 EUR	118.997	188.437	165.688	01-11-15	Paris	165	Art
1979	**AM V8 Volante**	V8COR15075	R	100-115.000 GBP	151.875	231.215	214.812	14-11-15	Birmingham	624	SiC

1974 AM V8 series 3 — White with black leather interior; described as in good original condition, only the body requires some attention. 66,221 kms on the odometer.

1978 AM V8 series 3 — For restoration.

1973 AM V8 series 3 — Described as in very good original condition; engine rebuilt in New Zealand.

1973 AM V8 series 3 — Stalled restoration project.

1978 AM V8 series 3 — Dark green with fawn interior; in good overall condition. For 20 years in the same family ownership.

1977 AM V8 series 3 — Restored between 2009 and 2011; the original automatic transmission was replaced with a manual unit.

1973 AM V8 series 3 — Light blue with blue interior; recently recommissioned following three years in storage.

1977 AM V8 series 3 — Green with fawn interior; built in right-hand drive form and later converted to left-hand drive. Interior restored in 2015. Manual gearbox.

1977 AM V8 series 3 — Red with parchment leather interior; automatic transmission.

1974 Lagonda — Cumberland grey with wildberry leather interior; the car was exhibited at the 1974 Earls Court Motor Show. At unspecified date it was fitted with the present 480bhp 7.0-litre R S Williams engine. Several restoration works were carried out in the early 2000s. Bought in 2010 by Aston Martin Lagond Ltd, the car has covered 10 miles in the past five years and has been recommissioned at the factory for the sale (see lot 332 Bonhams 22.5.10 $ 483,865).

1979 AM V8 Vantage series 4 — Silver with grey leather interior; described as in very good overall condition.

1981 AM V8 series 4 — Green with tan leather interior; 30,000 miles covered since the restoration carried out in 2006. Automatic transmission.

1980 AM V8 series 4 — Grey with cream leather interior; restored by the previous owner (see lot 142 Silverstone Auctions 28.3.15 $130,528).

1984 AM V8 Volante — White with brown leather interior; 23,700 miles covered. Automatic transmission.

1986 AM V8 Volante — Black with beige interior; body restored in the early 2000s, engine upgraded to X-Pack specification in 2009.

1979 AM V8 Volante — Blue with fawn interior; acquired in 2010 by the current owner, the car received subsequently some restoration works. The original automatic transmission (included with the sale) was replaced with a 6-speed DB7 gearbox.

F67: 1979 Aston Martin AM V8 Vantage series 4

F68: 1982 Aston Martin AM V8 Volante

Year	Model (Bodybuilder)	Chassis No.	Steering	Estimate	Hammer Price £	Hammer Price $	Hammer Price €	Date	Sale Place	Lot	Auc. H.
1982	**AM V8 Volante**	15261	L	125-150.000 USD	92.281	132.000	121.057	28-01-16	Scottsdale	79	Bon
	Metallic burgundy with original beige leather interior; single ownership for over 30 years. Less than 29,000 miles covered. Manual gearbox.										
1984	**AM V8 Volante**	15343	L	150-180.000 EUR	106.060	157.220	140.300	04-02-16	Paris	363	Bon
	See lot 117 Coys 26.9.15.										
1982	**AM V8 Volante**	15260	L	160-200.000 USD	149.255	211.200	194.515	10-03-16	Amelia Island	112	Bon F68
	British racing green with natural leather interior; in recent years the engine was overhauled and the interior were redone. Manual gearbox.										
1981	**AM V8 Volante**	V8COR15167	R	60-80.000 GBP	130.300	188.766	167.357	20-03-16	Goodwood	10	Bon
	Metallic green with cream leather interior; 25,700 miles covered. Since 1983 in the Kingsley Curtis Collection.										
1985	**AM V8 Volante**	15378	L	100-120.000 USD	69.880	100.000	87.470	02-04-16	Ft.Lauderdale	723	AA
	Red with black interior; described as in very good original condition. Automatic transmission.										
1986	**AM V8 Volante**	15486	L	120-140.000 GBP	137.250	199.946	178.219	20-05-16	Silverstone	323	SiC
	See lot 165 Artcurial 1.11.15.										
1986	**AM V8 Volante**	15454	R	200-240.000 GBP		NS		21-05-16	Newp.Pagnell	233	Bon
	Green with magnolia leather interior; the original automatic transmission was replaced in 1989 with a manual unit. Body repainted at date unknown. Last serviced in April 2013.										
1980	**AM V8 Volante**	V8COL15186	L	95-125.000 EUR	86.368	112.161	101.320	09-07-16	Le Mans	160	Art
	Imperial burgundy with beige leather interior; since 1999 in the current ownership. Clutch replaced in 2003, engine overhauled in 2007, body repainted in 2014-15. Manual gearbox (see lot 30 Poulain 3.5.99 NS).										
1980	**AM V8 Volante**	V8COL15191	L	180-220.000 USD	176.484	231.000	203.950	19-08-16	Carmel	103	Bon
	Silver with black leather interior; 40,000 miles on the odometer. Manual gearbox.										
1987	**AM V8 Vantage**	12564	L	500-575.000 USD	315.565	451.000	412.981	29-01-16	Phoenix	257	RMS F69
	One of 137 Series III examples built with the 432bhp 580X (X-Pack) engine, the car was originally finished in red with magnolia interior, right-hand drive and 5-speed manual gearbox. Sold new in Scotland, it was later imported into Norway where it was repainted in the present Balmoral green livery and was converted to left-hand drive form. Just over 61,000 miles covered; recently serviced in the USA.										
1985	**AM V8 Vantage**	12466	R	200-250.000 GBP		NS		21-05-16	Newp.Pagnell	235	Bon
	Silver with blue interior; the car was used by the factory for development work (identified as Development Project number DP2035) and fitted with a X-Pack engine and automatic transmission. In early 1988 it was sold to private hands and in late 1988 the automatic transmission was replaced by the factory with a manual unit. Since 2002 in the current ownership.										
1982	**AM V8 Vantage**	V8VOL12332	L	450-525.000 USD	273.130	357.500	315.637	19-08-16	Monterey	106	RMS
	Grey with tobacco leather interior; in the same family ownership from new to 2015. Restoration recently completed (see lot 206 RM 16.1.15 $132,000).										
1982	**Lagonda**	LOOL13167	L	45-60.000 EUR	35.956	56.938	50.064	01-11-15	Paris	121	Art
	Green with magnolia leather interior.										
1989	**Lagonda**	13601	L	90-120.000 USD	84.591*	121.000*	110.969*	28-01-16	Scottsdale	6	Bon F70
	Metallic red with magnolia leather interior; described as in very good overall condition, the car has had three owners and has covered less than 36,000 miles.										
1985	**Lagonda**	13466	L	NA	73.125	103.523	94.375	06-03-16	Birmingham	342	SiC
	Dark grey with grey interior; displayed at the 1986 New York Motor Show and then sold in the USA. Later it was reimported into Europe and recommissioned in the UK. 31,000 miles on the odometer.										
1986	**Lagonda shooting brake**	13511	L	200-240.000 GBP		NS		21-05-16	Newp.Pagnell	237	Bon
	Dark blue with grey leather interior; conversion carried out in Switzerland by Roos Engineering between 1996 and 2000. German and Swiss papers.										
1984	**Lagonda**	13347	L	38-48.000 EUR	39.232	52.112	46.800	02-07-16	Lyon	341	Agu
	White with grey interior; described as in fair overall condition. Since 1996 in the current ownership.										
1985	**Lagonda**	13466	L	85-125.000 USD		NS		30-07-16	Plymouth	146	RMS
	See lot 342 Silverstone Auctions 6.3.16.										
1983	**Lagonda**	13268	L	60-80.000 USD	68.913*	90.200*	79.638*	19-08-16	Carmel	6	Bon
	Black with black interior; in highly original condition. Two owners; 7,567 miles covered.										
1987	**Vantage Volante**	15595	R	220-260.000 GBP	225.500	328.508	292.812	21-05-16	Newp.Pagnell	221	Bon F71
	Medium grey with light grey leather interior; body repaired in 2002 and repainted, 432bhp X-Pack engine rebuilt in 2003. 72,740 miles covered since new (see lots 232 Bonhams 18.5.13 $ 145,605 and 336 Silverstone Auctions 22.2.14 $ 280,040).										
1988	**Vantage Volante**	15702	L	800-1.200.000 EUR		NS		09-07-16	Le Mans	165	Art
	Red with tan leather interior; one owner and 1,550 kms covered. X-Pack; manual gearbox.										
1991	**Virage**	50222	L	60-80.000 USD	34.605*	49.500*	45.396*	28-01-16	Scottsdale	107	Bon
	Dark metallic green with black leather interior; manual gearbox.										

F69: 1987 Aston Martin AM V8 Vantage

F70: 1989 Aston Martin Lagonda

Year	Model	(Bodybuilder)	Chassis no.	Steering	Estimate	Hammer price £	$	€	Date	Sale Place	Lot	Auc. H.

F71: 1987 Aston Martin Vantage Volante

F72: 1993 Aston Martin Virage Volante

Year	Model	Chassis no.	Steering	Estimate	£	$	€	Date	Place	Lot	Auc. H.
1990	**Virage**	50007	R	30-40.000 USD	28.763*	40.700*	37.485*	10-03-16	Amelia Island	110	Bon

Dark metallic green with parchment leather interior; since 1992 in the current ownership. In good overall condition; less than 40,000 miles covered.

| 1991 | **Virage** | 50274 | R | 48-55.000 GBP | | NS | | 11-06-16 | Brooklands | 319 | His |

British racing green with red leather interior; recently serviced. Automatic transmission.

| 1990 | **Virage** | 50148 | R | 35-42.000 GBP | | NS | | 30-07-16 | Silverstone | 555 | SiC |

Blue with red leather interior; 34,000 miles covered. Manual gearbox.

| 1993 | **Virage Volante** | 60083 | R | 80-120.000 GBP | 141.500 | 206.137 | 183.738 | 21-05-16 | Newp.Pagnell | 203 | Bon **F72** |

Red with black leather interior; one owner and circa 26,000 miles covered. Converted to 6.3 specification by the factory in 1995.

| 1996 | **Virage Volante** | 60099 | R | 55-75.000 GBP | 63.100 | 91.924 | 81.935 | 21-05-16 | Newp.Pagnell | 253 | Bon |

Blue with parchment interior; in good overall condition. Converted in 1996 by Aston Martin Works to "wide body" specification. 32,000 miles covered (see lot 215 Bonhams 12.5.07 NS).

| 1994 | **Virage Volante** | 60110 | R | 85-110.000 GBP | | NS | | 11-06-16 | Brooklands | 313 | His |

British racing green with magnolia leather interior; 6.3-litre engine rebuilt in 2015. Automatic transmission.

| 1995 | **Vantage** | 70027 | R | 100-120.000 GBP | 130.300 | 197.079 | 180.088 | 10-12-15 | London | 386 | Bon |

Anthracite grey with beige leather interior; 24,200 miles on the odometer. Automatic transmission.

| 2000 | **Vantage V600 Le Mans** | 70259 | R | 320-420.000 GBP | 449.500 | 654.832 | 583.676 | 21-05-16 | Newp.Pagnell | 215 | Bon |

Green; one owner and 2,637 miles covered. One of the 40 Le Mans examples built and one of four built to 600bhp and 6-speed manual gearbox.

| 1988 | **Vantage prototype** | 2055/1 | R | 200-250.000 GBP | | NS | | 21-05-16 | Newp.Pagnell | 216 | Bon |

One of the five development prototypes of the model and one of three surviving; 21,523 miles covered.

| 1994 | **DB7 coupé** | 100146 | R | 45-55.000 GBP | 50.400 | 72.032 | 64.950 | 12-03-16 | Brooklands | 224 | His |

Green with parchment interior; 3,300 miles covered.

| 1998 | **DB7 Volante** | 202246 | R | 22-30.000 GBP | 28.000 | 40.018 | 36.084 | 12-03-16 | Brooklands | 157 | His |

Royal blue with cream leather interior; last serviced in January 2016.

| 1997 | **DB7 Volante** | 201518 | R | 32-38.000 GBP | 32.200 | 42.143 | 37.207 | 20-08-16 | Brooklands | 269 | His |

Purple with cream leather interior; 13,895 miles covered. Last serviced in January 2016.

| 1996 | **V8 Sportsman** | 79008 | L | 350-550.000 EUR | | NS | | 05-09-15 | Chantilly | 26 | Bon |

One of two examples converted by factory to shooting brake form between September 1996 and December 1997. Green with green leather interior; 27,600 kms covered. From the Alain Dominique Perrin collection.

| 1997 | **V8 Coupé** | 79041 | R | 55-75.000 GBP | 70.940 | 103.345 | 92.116 | 21-05-16 | Newp.Pagnell | 249 | Bon **F73** |

Dark green with parchment leather interior; in good overall condition. Recently serviced.

| 2000 | **DB7 V12 Vantage** | 300932 | R | 40-45.000 GBP | | NS | | 04-09-15 | Woodstock | 258 | SiC |

Dark green with magnolia leather interior; 12,850 miles covered.

| 2001 | **DB7 V12 Vantage** | 302605 | R | 20-24.000 GBP | 23.730 | 35.804 | 32.726 | 09-12-15 | Chateau Impney | 25 | H&H |

Dark metallic blue with blue and tan leather interior; last serviced 400 miles ago. Manual gearbox.

| 2003 | **DB7 V12 Vantage Volante** | 404139 | R | 40-50.000 GBP | 61.875 | 94.217 | 84.589 | 04-09-15 | Woodstock | 224 | SiC **F74** |

Silver with parchment leather interior; one owner and just over 8,500 miles covered. Last serviced in August 2015.

F73: 1997 Aston Martin V8 Coupé

F74: 2003 Aston Martin DB7 V12 Vantage Volante

Year	Model	(Bodybuilder)	Chassis No.	Steering	Estimate	Hammer Price £	Hammer Price $	Hammer Price €	Date	Place	Lot	Auc. H.
2001	DB7 V12 Vantage Volante		402366	L	42-52.000 EUR	39.108	55.894	50.400	12-03-16	Lyon	339	Agu
Dark blue with magnolia and blue interior; 51,000 kms covered. Manual gearbox.												
2002	DB7 V12 Vantage Volante		402542	R	28-32.000 GBP	36.800*	53.312*	47.266*	20-03-16	Goodwood	95	Bon
Silver with black leather interior; in good overall condition. Circa 39,000 miles covered.												
2001	DB7 V12 Vantage Volante		401899	R	20-24.000 GBP	22.120	32.198	28.546	18-05-16	Donington Park	103	H&H
Black with parchment interior; three owners and 82,000 recorded miles.												
2000	DB7 V12 Vantage Volante		400544	R	35-45.000 GBP		NS		30-07-16	Silverstone	916	SiC
Silver with blue leather interior; last serviced in May 2016 at 31,954 miles. 6-speed manual gearbox.												
2003	V12 Vanquish coupé		500754	R	65-75.000 GBP	77.625	118.176	109.793	14-11-15	Birmingham	323	SiC
Green with parchment leather interior; in very good overall condition. Upgraded in 2004 with a Sports Dynamic Pack. Last serviced in November 2014 at 18,046 miles.												
2005	V12 Vanquish S coupé		501561	R	NQ	82.440*	124.196*	117.164*	01-12-15	London	308	Coy
Titanium grey with dark grey leather interior; 16,000 miles covered.												
2005	V12 Vanquish S coupé		501616	L	55-65.000 USD	69.980*	100.100*	91.802*	28-01-16	Scottsdale	74	Bon
Sold new to the USA; less than 3,000 miles covered.												
2001	V12 Vanquish coupé		500120	R	NA	61.313	85.691	77.861	26-02-16	Coventry	728	SiC
Silver with black and ivory interior; mechanical refreshed and body repainted between 2014 and 2015.												
2002	V12 Vanquish coupé		500268	L	50-60.000 GBP	49.960	70.988	64.373	08-03-16	London	110	Coy
Blue with grey and tan interior; 21,100 miles covered.												
2003	V12 Vanquish coupé		500063	R	50-55.000 GBP	61.980	89.790	79.607	20-03-16	Goodwood	70	Bon
Silver with tan leather interior; circa 50,000 miles covered. Engine rebuilt in 2015 to S specification.												
2003	V12 Vanquish coupé		01008	R	50-60.000 GBP	59.625	86.862	77.423	20-05-16	Silverstone	314	SiC
Silver; 65,545 miles on the odometer. Several works carried out in 2014.												
2007	V12 Vanquish S coupé		502483	L	90-110.000 GBP	82.140	119.662	106.659	21-05-16	Newp.Pagnell	226	Bon F75
Black with black leather interior; sold new to Japan, the car has covered 27,046 kms. Should the car remain in EU, local import taxes of 20% will be applied to the hammer price.												
2002	V12 Vanquish coupé		500252	R	69-76.000 GBP	76.720	110.500	97.757	11-06-16	Brooklands	231	His
Silver with black and ivory interior; 28,726 miles covered. Described as in very good overall condition (see lot 313 Silverstone Auctions 22.2.15 $ 91,673).												
2002	V12 Vanquish coupé		500390	L	NA	38.562	50.500	45.849	23-07-16	Harrisburg	T248	Mec
Silver with tan interior; believed to be 5,000 miles.												
2003	DB AR1 Roadster (Zagato)		800051	L	275-325.000 USD	192.418	275.000	251.818	29-01-16	Scottsdale	43	G&Co
Light blue with white leather interior; less than 2,500 miles covered. Recently serviced.												
2003	DB AR1 Roadster (Zagato)		800089	L	250-300.000 USD	253.955	363.000	327.317	12-03-16	Amelia Island	146	RMS
Two owners and less than 700 miles covered (see lot 138 Gooding 23.1.10 $ 170,500).												
2003	DB AR1 Roadster (Zagato)		800015	L	180-230.000 EUR	264.627	381.293	336.000	14-05-16	Monaco	242	RMS F76
Black with red interior; one owner and less than 24,300 kms covered. Swiss papers.												
2003	DB9 coupé		01517	R	30-40.000 GBP	33.750	49.167	43.824	20-05-16	Silverstone	310	SiC
Sage with sand interior; 30,000 miles covered. Last serviced in April 2015.												
2005	DB9 coupé		02411	R	29-34.000 GBP	35.840	46.907	41.413	20-08-16	Brooklands	259	His
Titanium grey with black leather interior; last serviced in December 2015.												
2006	DB9 Volante		05706	R	45-55.000 GBP	54.000	82.210	76.378	14-11-15	Birmingham	635	SiC
Red with cream leather interior; in very good overall condition, the car has had three owners. Last serviced in April 2015 at 9,296 miles.												
2005	DB9 Volante		03712	R	45-55.000 GBP	49.500	65.142	58.618	30-07-16	Silverstone	910	SiC
Black with black leather interior; 12,800 miles covered.												
2007	V8 Vantage		04337	L	45-60.000 EUR		NS		20-03-16	Fontainebleau	367	Ose
Two owners and 68,900 kms covered.												
2011	DBS Volante		12532	L	140-160.000 USD	106.960	140.000	123.606	19-08-16	Monterey	F146	Mec
Silver with blue leather interior; one owner and 5,126 miles covered.												
2011	One-77		17725	L	1.750-2.250.000 EUR		NS		13-05-16	Monaco	130	Bon
Bronze pearl metallic with ivory and chocolate interior; one owner and 850 kms covered. Numer 25 of 77 examples built.												

F75: 2007 Aston Martin V12 Vanquish S coupé

F76: 2003 Aston Martin DB AR1 Roadster (Zagato)

Year	Model	(Bodybuilder)	Chassis no.	Steering	Estimate	Hammer price £	$	€	Date	Place	Lot	Auc. H.
2016	Vulcan		11	L	2.300-3.300.000 USD		NS		20-08-16	Monterey	S99	Mec

Dark blue and black; one of 24 examples built. Only track use. 820bhp 7-litre V-10 engine.

AUBURN (USA) *(1903-1936)*

Year	Model	(Bodybuilder)	Chassis no.	Steering	Estimate	£	$	€	Date	Place	Lot	Auc. H.
1931	8-98 phaeton sedan		GU74969	L	110-130.000 USD	61.479	89.100	77.971	07-05-16	Auburn	776	AA
	Blue with blue soft-top; restored many years ago.											
1931	8-98A Custom convertible		GU51336	L	120-140.000 USD	58.344	85.000	75.761	20-05-16	Indianapolis	F195	Mec
	Turquoise with turquoise interior; in good overall condition.											
1932	12-160 convertible sedan		BB1856A	L	NQ		NS		20-08-16	Monterey	7003	R&S
	Silver and maroon; the car has covered 800 miles since the restoration completed in 2001 (see lot 3108 Auctions America 2.8.14 NS).											
1932	8-100A Custom cabriolet		6212F	L	120-140.000 USD	72.006	110.000	97.746	08-10-15	Hershey	159	RMS
	Ivory with red accents and tan leather interior; restored several years ago.											
1932	8-100A boattail speedster		8761	L	275-350.000 USD		NS		29-01-16	Scottsdale	31	G&Co
	Black with black leather interior; full restoration completed in 2008.											
1933	12-161 convertible		400	L	100-150.000 EUR	108.668	161.086	143.750	04-02-16	Paris	419	Bon
	Red and beige with beige leather interior; restored at unspecified date (see lot 231 Bonhams 23.1.10 NS).											
1933	12-161A Salon phaeton (Limousine Body Co.)		2156H	L	200-240.000 USD		NS		19-08-16	Carmel	104	Bon
	Two-tone red with light brown interior; restored in the 1980s. Recently serviced.											
1934	12-165 Salon convertible		1091F	L	2.300-3.600.000 DKK	220.886	335.254	300.719	26-09-15	Ebeltoft	11	Bon
	Black and silver with black leather interior; fully restored at unspecified date. From the Frederiksen Collection.											
1933	12-165 Salon phaeton		1094H	L	1.800-2.300.000 DKK	164.249	249.291	223.612	26-09-15	Ebeltoft	40	Bon F77
	Navy blue with blue leather interior; an older restoration, the car is described as still in very good overall condition. From the Frederiksen Collection.											
1934	1250 Salon speedster		1122E	L	275-350.000 USD	219.168	313.500	287.511	28-01-16	Phoenix	122	RMS
	Black; car rebuilt in the 1970s on an original Salon chassis, original engine and an original Auburn speedster body. During the restoration the chassis number 1122A was modified to 1122E, with "E" being the correct suffix for a factory speedster (see lot 159 RM 8.3.14 $ 286,000).											
1934	1250 Twelve Salon phaeton		12501064H	L	375-450.000 USD		NS		12-03-16	Amelia Island	195	RMS
	Red with tan interior; the car remained in the same family ownership from new to 1979 and was last used in the mid-1950s. It was subsequently restored by its second owner who retained it for 10 years. Described as still in good overall condition.											
1935	8-851 SC convertible		33705F	L	NA	92.116	140.250	125.930	05-09-15	Auburn	5140	AA
	Maroon with maroon interior; restored (see lots 268 RM 19.1.07 $ 121,000 and 35 Gooding 21.1.11 $ 99,000).											
1935	8-851 SC speedster		32924E	L	450-550.000 USD	500.214	715.000	644.716	12-03-16	Amelia Island	134	RMS F78
	Cigarette cream with brown leather interior; an older restoration, the car is described as still in good overall condition (see lot 8 H&H 3.10.05 $ 315,873).											
1935	8-851 SC boattail speedster		32069E	L	725-875.000 USD	408.740	535.000	472.352	20-08-16	Monterey	S117	Mec
	Pale yellow with red interior; in the same family ownership from 1949 to late 2013, the car was restored in the early 1950s and used until 1962. Bought in early 2014 by the current owner and returned to running condition (see lot 142 Bonhams 16.1.14 $467,500).											
1935	8-851 SC boattail speedster		33151E	L	900-1.200.000 USD	756.360	990.000	874.071	21-08-16	Pebble Beach	137	G&Co
	Silver with black leather interior; the car was discovered in Mississippi in 1960 and subsequently recommissioned. In recent years it was purchased by the current owner and fully restored (see lot 118 RM 19.8.11 $231,000).											
1936	8-852 SC phaeton sedan		34614H	L	90-110.000 USD	62.617	90.750	79.415	07-05-16	Auburn	779	AA
	Burgundy with tan leather interior; an older restoration, the car is described as still in good overall condition.											

AUDI (D) *(1910-)*

Year	Model	(Bodybuilder)	Chassis no.	Steering	Estimate	£	$	€	Date	Place	Lot	Auc. H.
1984	Quattro		900940	R	NA	27.517	39.019	34.787	20-04-16	Duxford	27	H&H
	Red with brown interior; bought in 2011 by the current owner and subsequently restored. First owner Nigel Mansell.											
1981	Quattro		85CA900146	L	120-150.000 GBP		NS		24-06-16	Goodwood	229	Bon
	First used as a press test by Volkswagen/Audi Group (UK) and later assigned to David Sutton Motorsport's official Audi Rally Team where it was prepared as a reconnaissance car. Sold in 1985, it was used as a private entry in international events. Bought in 1995 by the current owner; engine rebuilt; in early 2016 returned to 1981 body specification (see lot 878 Brooks 26.10.95 NS).											
1983	Quattro		900942	L	35-45.000 EUR	31.984	42.072	37.712	06-08-16	Schloss Dyck	178	Coy F79
	Brown; in good overall condition.											

F77: 1933 Auburn 12-165 Salon phaeton

F78: 1935 Auburn 8-851 SC speedster

Year	Model (Bodybuilder)	Chassis No.	Steering	Estimate	Hammer Price £	Hammer Price $	Hammer Price €	Date	Place	Lot	Auc. H.
\multicolumn{12}{l}{## AUSTIN (GB) *(1906-)*}
1919	20hp coupé Blue and black; engine rebuilt in 2008.	P48757	R	12-15.000 GBP		NS		08-03-16	London	145	Coy
1927	Seven coupé (Maythorn) Blue and black; sold new to the USA to the Pulitzer family. Restoration completed in 1987. Four owners.	36828	R	15-25.000 USD	18.002*	27.500*	24.437*	08-10-15	Hershey	152	RMS F80
1931	Seven saloon Brown with black wings and green/grey interior; restored in the 1970s. Since 1969 in the present, second ownership.	143052	R	10-12.000 GBP		NS		09-12-15	Chateau Impney	81	H&H
1934	Seven saloon Black and blue; it requires some attention prior to use. In single ownership from 1968 to 2015.	192468B96176	R	5-7.000 GBP	5.600	8.004	7.217	12-03-16	Brooklands	232	His
1928	Seven "Chummy" tourer Red with black wings; restored in 1988. Engine and gearbox rebuilt in the late 1990s. From the Kingsley Curtis Collection.	69290	R	8-10.000 GBP	9.775*	14.161*	12.555*	20-03-16	Goodwood	8	Bon
1931	Seven tourer Red with black wings and interior; in good cosmetic condition. Since 1934 in Italy and since 1965 in the Quattroruote Collection.	124313	R	15-20.000 EUR		NS		14-05-16	Monaco	133	RMS
1928	Seven saloon Brown with beige interior; until the early 1960s with its first owner. Restored between the 1990s and early 2000s.	73829	R	11-13.000 GBP	10.360	15.080	13.370	18-05-16	Donington Park	28	H&H
NQ	Seven tourer Body repainted many years ago; mechanical condition unknown.	M55402	R	2-3.000 GBP	9.500	12.694	11.408	16-07-16	Cambridge	1251	Che
1932	Seven 2-door saloon Blue; mechanical condition unknown. It requires some restoration works.	155052	R	2-3.000 GBP	4.800	6.414	5.764	16-07-16	Cambridge	1252	Che
1919	Twenty coupé Body in original condition, finished in blue with black wings; engine rebuilt in 2008.	P48757	R	12-15.000 GBP	16.756	23.760	21.056	16-04-16	Ascot	123	Coy
1939	12/4 taxicab (Strachan) Blue; restored.	81695	R	20-24.000 GBP	24.640	35.215	31.754	12-03-16	Brooklands	194	His
1955	A30 two-door saloon Black with red interior; restored a few years ago.	2A79048	L	10-12.000 EUR	8.969	12.993	11.520	20-03-16	Fontainebleau	322	Ose
1952	A90 Atlantic Blue; restored.	BE2123307	R	20-26.000 GBP	41.440	59.686	52.803	11-06-16	Brooklands	219	His F81
1950	A135 Princess saloon (Vanden Plas) Black and burgundy with burgundy cloth interior; restored some years ago.	VDM416202	L	35-40.000 EUR		NS		20-03-16	Fontainebleau	328	Ose
1954	A40 Somerset saloon Grey with light brown interior; restored. 39,787 miles covered since new.	GS4880248	R	7-10.000 GBP	11.760	17.700	16.730	28-11-15	Weybridge	208	His
1961	Metropolitan convertible Blue and white with matching vinyl interior; restored in the 1980s.	E90261	L	17-20.000 USD	12.574*	18.150*	16.271*	05-06-16	Greenwhich	12	Bon
1955	A50 Cambridge saloon Black with red leather interior; restored some four years ago.	HSS78280	R	NQ	6.160*	8.062*	7.118*	20-08-16	Brooklands	288	His
1961	A55 Cambridge Grey with red interior; in good overall condition. 20,952 recorded miles.	AHS8171293	R	725-8.000 GBP		NS		28-07-16	Donington Park	34	H&H
1981	Mini 95L pick-up Blue; 6,780 miles covered. Only example built in the mid-1990s by British Motor Heritage. 1,275cc fuel-injected engine. From the collection of Michael Standring.	XLU10010758779	R	NQ	11.200*	16.857*	15.933*	28-11-15	Weybridge	252	His
1986	Mini Mayfair/John Cooper protot. Red with white roof; on request of Austin Rover Japan the car was fitted by John Cooper with a MG Metro engine and shipped to Japan. Back to the UK in 1987, it was fitted by Cooper with a 1275cc engine and proposed in 1988 to Austin Rover which in 1989 re-established the "Mini Cooper". In very good overall condition, the car is offered from the collection of Michael Standring of Wood & Pickett.	SAXXL2S1N20310810	R	17-22.000 GBP	19.040	28.657	27.086	28-11-15	Weybridge	253	His
1963	Mini Van Grey; restored between 2000 and 2003 and finished in the Wood & Pickett livery. From the collection of Michael Standring.	AAV7325997	R	NQ	11.200*	16.857*	15.933*	28-11-15	Weybridge	256	His
1961	Mini Countryman Green; restored in the 1990s. Engine (1,000cc) and gearbox replaced.	MAW4L72058	L	30-50.000 EUR	46.795*	68.099*	60.792*	05-02-16	Paris	150	Art F82

F79: 1983 Audi Quattro

F80: 1927 Austin Seven coupé (Maythorn)

Year	Model	(Bodybuilder)	Chassis no.	Steering	Estimate	Hammer price £	$	€	Date	Place	Lot	Auc. H.
1966	**Mini**		AA257867603A	R	11-15.000 GBP	9.500	12.618	11.332	02-07-16	Woodstock	129	**Coy**
Ivory with red interior; described as in very good overall condition.												
1978	**Mini Clubman 1275 GT**		XE2D2463968A	R	130-160.000 GBP		NS		02-07-16	Woodstock	198	**Coy**
In 1978 with financial backing from British Leyland and Patrick Motors, the racing driver Richard Longman modified and prepared the car to enter it in the British Touring Car Championship. The car won its class in 11 of 12 races in 1978 and in 10 of 12 races in 1979, and won the Championship in both the years. Subsequently it went into storage and did not race for the next 30 years.												
1963	**Mini Cooper**		CA2S7L365453	L	25-35.000 USD	24.006*	34.650*	31.064*	05-06-16	Greenwhich	25	**Bon**
Red with white roof; fully restored. One of the two cars prepared for the 1963 New York Motor Show.												
1965	**Mini Cooper S**		CA2S7800244	L	42-52.000 EUR	28.899	41.419	37.950	16-01-16	Maastricht	456	**Coy**
Red with black roof; described as in very good overall condition.												
1966	**Mini Cooper S**		4A2S4L892687	L	40-60.000 EUR	32.114*	46.735*	41.720*	05-02-16	Paris	149	**Art**
Green with white roof and green and grey interior; several restoration works carried out between 1993 and 2008.												
1970	**1800 saloon MkII**		AHSAD38722A	R	3.5-4.000 GBP		NS		17-10-15	Cambridge	2502	**Che**
Black with red leather interior; just one owner.												

AUSTIN-HEALEY (GB) (1953-1970)

Year	Model	(Bodybuilder)	Chassis no.	Steering	Estimate	Hammer price £	$	€	Date	Place	Lot	Auc. H.
1955	**100**		BN1223802	R	50-60.000 GBP	59.740	92.137	81.772	12-09-15	Goodwood	303	**Bon**
Light blue and ivory; fitted with the Le Mans kit at unspecified date. Restored 15-20 years ago; engine rebuilt in 2010.												
1955	**100**		BN1L222891	L	40-50.000 EUR	33.586	50.844	46.800	07-11-15	Lyon	253	**Agu**
Red with black and red interior; in good driving order. Body repainted some years ago (see lot 206 Bonhams 23.1.10 NS).												
1954	**100**		BN1156396	R	40-45.000 GBP		NS		09-12-15	Chateau Impney	79	**H&H**
Green with green interior; restored and fitted with a 5-speed gearbox. For over 40 years in the same family ownership.												
1956	**100 (coupé conversion)**		BN2L231178	L	50-70.000 USD	46.180*	66.000*	60.436*	29-01-16	Scottsdale	44	**G&Co**
Red; conversion carried out in the USA in the 1960s. Restored between 2008 and 2009.												
1955	**100**		BN1L224877	L	85-95.000 USD	61.494	88.000	76.974	02-04-16	Ft.Lauderdale	231	**AA**
Ice blue with blue interior; fully restored.												
1954	**100**		BN1L149903	L	65-80.000 EUR		NS		09-04-16	Essen	126	**Coy**
Two-tone body; the car won the historic 1992 Carrera PanAmericana.												
1956	**100**		BN2L228737	L	NA	45.838	65.000	57.603	16-04-16	Houston	S171	**Mec**
Silver with black interior; restored.												
1954	**100**		BN1220983	R	37-44.000 GBP	47.040	67.752	59.938	11-06-16	Brooklands	255	**His**
British racing green; reimported into the UK from Australia in 2012 and subsequently fully restored.												
1954	**100**		BN1L49903	L	65-80.000 EUR	65.159	85.710	76.829	06-08-16	Schloss Dyck	175	**Coy**
See lot 126 Coys 9.4.16.												
1955	**100**		BN1L227294	L	110-140.000 USD	68.913*	90.200*	79.638*	19-08-16	Carmel	14	**Bon**
Black with black leather interior; the car has covered 3,000 miles since the restoration. Engine rebuilt to Le Mans specification.												
1953	**100**		BN1L140217	L	70-90.000 USD	47.903*	62.700*	55.358*	19-08-16	Carmel	97	**Bon**
Sold new to the USA, the car remained with its second owner for nearly six decades and was restored between 2011 and 2014 (see lot 267 Bonhams 31.5.15 $57,200).												
1954	**100**		BN1L151422	L	125-150.000 USD	109.252*	143.000*	126.255*	20-08-16	Pebble Beach	29	**G&Co**
Light green; bought in 2013 by the current owner and subsequently restored to Le Mans specification.												
1956	**100**		BN2L231033	L	50-75.000 USD	26.052*	34.100*	30.107*	21-08-16	Pebble Beach	101	**G&Co**
Stored since 1962; for restoration.												
1953	**100/100S coupé**		BN1142615	R	Refer Dpt.	639.900	968.745	888.565	06-12-15	London	014	**Bon**
Red with white leather interior; originally finished in red with black roof, the car is one of two 100s built in coupé form. Included in the Special Test Car development program, in 1955 it was fitted with Dunlop disc brakes, 100S mechanicals and other innovative modifications of which many found their way into production. It remained the Donald Healey personal car until 1962 when it was sold to its first private owner. In 1972 it was acquired by the current, second owner Arthur Carter. Described as in good overall condition.												**F83**
1956	**100M Le Mans**		BN2L231253	L	125-175.000 USD	142.267*	203.500*	186.630*	28-01-16	Phoenix	108	**RMS**
Red and black with red interior; fully restored.												
1956	**100M Le Mans**		BN2L233008	L	160-200.000 EUR	84.370*	122.450*	112.000*	03-02-16	Paris	146	**RMS**
Black and red with red and black interior; described as in very good overall condition (see lots RM 2274 21.4.07 $ 231,000 and 140 20.1.11 $ 107,250, RM/Sotheby's 2.5.15 $ 170,500 and 1098 Auctions America 18.7.15 NS).												

F81: 1952 Austin A90 Atlantic

F82: 1961 Austin Mini Countryman

Year	Model	(Bodybuilder)	Chassis No.	Steering	Estimate	Hammer Price £	$	€	Sale Date	Place	Lot	Auc. H.
1956	**100M Le Mans**		BN2L230740	L	160-200.000 USD	153.912*	220.000*	198.374*	12-03-16	Amelia Island	175	RMS **F84**
{Black and red with red interior; sold new to the USA, the car has covered approximately 2,500 miles since a full restoration completed in 2009.}
| 1956 | **100M** | | BN1L150648 | L | 90-110.000 EUR | 109.978 | 158.463 | 139.640 | 14-05-16 | Monaco | 111 | Coy |
{Ivory and blue; for over 40 years in storage and recently restored.}
| 1958 | **100-Six** | | BN6L1393 | L | 50-60.000 EUR | | NS | | 08-11-15 | Lyon | 215 | Ose |
{Green and white; restored some years ago.}
| 1957 | **100-Six** | | BN4042832 | R | 42-48.000 GBP | 41.063 | 62.514 | 58.080 | 14-11-15 | Birmingham | 615 | SiC |
{Black and red; body repainted three years ago.}
| 1959 | **100-Six** | | BN4LS75477 | R | 26-30.000 GBP | 29.120 | 43.829 | 41.426 | 28-11-15 | Weybridge | 249 | His |
{Light ivory and red; sold new to the USA, the car was reimported into the UK in 1990, restored and converted to right-hand drive. Engine upgraded to 3000 specification (see lot 123 Coys 11.7.15 $ 36,620).}
| 1959 | **100-Six** | | BN6974 | R | 150-200.000 GBP | 158.300 | 229.329 | 203.321 | 20-03-16 | Goodwood | 33 | Bon **F85** |
{Red with white hardtop; acquired by Don Grimshaw, the car was raced in period at several rallies, among them the 1962 and 1965 editions of the Monte Carlo Rally and the 1965 East African Safari. In 1977 it was bought by Arthur Carter in whose collection it remained for nearly 30 years. It incorporates many "works only" modifications indicating at the very least it was worked on the BMC's Competitions Department. Among other features it has a 3-litre XSP engine and four wheel race brakes. Restored in 2005-06 (see Coys lots 355 5.12.07 NS and 222 25.5.08 NS).}
| 1958 | **100-Six** | | BN6L3718 | R | 35-40.000 GBP | 45.425 | 65.807 | 58.344 | 20-03-16 | Goodwood | 49 | Bon |
{Healey blue and ivory; restored between 2006 and 2009 and converted to right-hand drive.}
| 1958 | **Sprite "Frogeye"** | | AN57946 | R | NA | 14.672 | 22.567 | 19.778 | 14-10-15 | Duxford | 17 | H&H |
{White with red interior; the car has covered 1,100 miles since the restoration.}
| 1959 | **Sprite "Frogeye"** | | AN5L16468 | L | 40-60.000 USD | 42.332* | 60.500* | 55.400* | 29-01-16 | Phoenix | 275 | RMS **F86** |
{Bought in 1963 by Donna Mae Mims, the car was repainted in pink livery and race-prepared. That same year she won the SCCA H/Production One-Liter Class Championship. Raced until 1987, the car was restored in the 2000s. Currently fitted with an engine and gearbox more enjoyable to drive on the street, it is offered with also the competition-spec units. From the Craig McCaw Collection (see lot 24 Gooding 17.1.14 $ 48,400).}
| 1959 | **Sprite "Frogeye"** | | AN514896 | R | 2.5-3.500 GBP | 10.580* | 15.327* | 13.589* | 20-03-16 | Goodwood | 2 | Bon |
{Red; for restoration. Since 1980 circa in the Kingsley Curtis Collection.}
| 1959 | **Sprite "Frogeye"** | | AN511884 | R | NA | 23.520 | 33.351 | 29.734 | 20-04-16 | Duxford | 88 | H&H |
{Iris blue with royal blue vinyl interior; 27 miles covered since the restoration completed in 2012. For 30 years in the current ownership.}
| 1958 | **Sprite "Frogeye"** | | AN51389 | R | 15-18.000 GBP | 15.980 | 21.030 | 18.924 | 30-07-16 | Silverstone | 506 | SiC |
{Blue with dark blue interior; restored. 1275cc A-Series rebuilt engine.}
| 1959 | **Speedwell Sprite GT** | (Williams/Pritchard) | AN530370 | R | 70-90.000 USD | | NS | | 05-10-15 | Philadelphia | 262 | Bon |
{Sold new to racer Dan Margulies, the car was raced in the 1960s. Imported into the USA in the 1970s, it was subsequently raced at historic events. Restored in the 2000s, it is described as in ready to race condition. 90bhp 1,293cc engine.}
| 1960 | **3000** | | HBN7L9613 | L | 32-36.000 GBP | | NS | | 28-11-15 | Weybridge | 223 | His |
{White with black interior; recently reimported from the USA, the car is described as in good overall condition.}
| 1959 | **3000** | | HBN71342 | R | 140-200.000 GBP | 191.900 | 290.517 | 266.472 | 06-12-15 | London | 015 | Bon |
{Red with old English white hardtop; Works car for the 1959 and 1960 seasons, it was driven among others by Jack Sears, Pat Moss and John Gott, who in late 1960 bought it for personal use. Retired as a Works driver from rallying, he prepared the car for Modsport racing and used it until September 1972 when he had a fatal accident at the Lydden Hill circuit. About one year later the damaged car and the original Works engine, which had been put aside by Gott, were acquired by Arthur Carter who subsequently had the car restored to Modsport racing specification.}
| 1959 | **3000** | | HBN7L12119 | L | 40-45.000 EUR | 28.937 P | 41.473 P | 38.000 P | 16-01-16 | Maastricht | 410 | Coy |
{Red with grey interior; restored.}
| 1960 | **3000** | | HBN7L1780 | L | 80-100.000 USD | 46.174* | 66.000* | 59.512* | 12-03-16 | Amelia Island | 190 | RMS |
{Silver with red leather interior; the car has covered 217 miles since the restoration completed in 2009 (see lot S67 Mecum 16.8.12 $ 72,500).}
| 1961 | **3000** | | HBN713708 | R | 250-300.000 EUR | 317.552 | 457.551 | 403.200 | 14-05-16 | Monaco | 231 | RMS **F87** |
{Red with white hardtop; ex-Works car for the first part of the 1961 season, it did its debut at the Acropolis Rally. During that year the car was purchased by Rauno Aaltonen who imported it into Finland and retained it until 1965. Since then it is in the same family ownership; restored in 1995, it was driven at some historic events until 1997. Original engine.}
| 1962 | **3000 MkII** | | HBJ7L21019 | L | 30-38.000 GBP | 35.400 | 54.300 | 47.790 | 10-10-15 | Ascot | 127 | Coy |
{Red and ivory; restored about 25 years ago and recently refurbished.}
| 1962 | **3000 MkII** | | HBT7L17267 | L | 45-55.000 EUR | | NS | | 16-01-16 | Maastricht | 426 | Coy |
{Healey blue with dark blue leather interior; restored (see lot 306 Bonhams 5.2.15 $ 47,237).}
| 1961 | **3000 MkII** | | HBN7L16207 | L | 80-120.000 USD | 49.217* | 70.400* | 64.564* | 28-01-16 | Scottsdale | 87 | Bon |
{Green and ivory with ivory hardtop; acquired in 1987 by the current Australian owner and subsequently restored.}

F83: 1953 Austin-Healey 100/100S coupé

F84: 1956 Austin-Healey 100M Le Mans

Year	Model	(Bodybuilder)	Chassis no.	Steering	Estimate	Hammer price £	$	€	Date	Sale Place	Lot	Auc. H.

F85: 1958 Austin-Healey 100-Six

F86: 1959 Austin-Healey Sprite "Frogeye"

Year	Model	Chassis no.	Steering	Estimate	£	$	€	Date	Place	Lot	Auc. H.
1962	3000 MkII	HBT7L17689	L	NA	68.501	97.900	89.647	30-01-16	Scottsdale	5105	R&S

Healey blue and ivory with blue leather interior; 200 miles covered since the restoration.

| 1963 | 3000 MkII | BHJ7L24275 | L | 45-55.000 EUR | 40.238 | 53.448 | 48.000 | 02-07-16 | Lyon | 353 | Agu |

White with black interior; restored in the USA in 1988.

| 1961 | 3000 MkII | HBT7L17943 | L | 40-50.000 EUR | 35.111 | 46.186 | 41.400 | 06-08-16 | Schloss Dyck | 126 | Coy |

Old English white with red leather interior; described as in very good overall condition, the car has had one owner and has covered 79,000 miles (see Coys lots 407 2.12.14 NS and 144 10.1.15 NS).

| 1965 | 3000 MkIII | HBJ8L32329 | L | 50-65.000 USD | 32.274* | 49.500* | 43.570* | 09-10-15 | Hershey | 286 | RMS |

British racing green; acquired in 2013 by the current, second owner, the car received subsequently several mechanical and cosmetic works.

| 1965 | 3000 MkIII | HBJ8L26649 | L | 47-53.000 EUR | 43.059 | 65.184 | 60.000 | 07-11-15 | Lyon | 278 | Agu |

Blue and ivory with dark blue interior; restored at unspecified date.

| 1966 | 3000 MkIII | HBJ8L39239 | R | 42-48.000 GBP | | NS | | 14-11-15 | Birmingham | 605 | SiC |

White with black hardtop; sold new to the USA, the car was reimported into the UK in 2006. Restored on a new chassis and converted to right-hand drive.

| 1965 | 3000 MkIII | HBJ8L27876 | L | 35-40.000 GBP | | NS | | 09-12-15 | Chateau Impney | 151 | H&H |

Old English white with original red vinyl interior; body repainted. Recently reimported into the UK.

| 1967 | 3000 MkIII | HBJ8L39725 | L | 60-80.000 USD | 46.141* | 66.000* | 60.529* | 28-01-16 | Scottsdale | 113 | Bon |

British racing green with original black interior; since 1974 in the current ownership. Engine rebuilt in 1985; body restored and repainted in 1994.

| 1966 | 3000 MkIII | HBJ8L35652 | L | NA | 68.501* | 97.900* | 89.647* | 29-01-16 | Scottsdale | 1405 | B/J |

Metallic ice green with tan interior; fully restored.

| 1967 | 3000 MkIII | HBJ8L35053 | L | 70-90.000 USD | 41.562* | 59.400* | 54.393* | 29-01-16 | Scottsdale | 36 | G&Co |

Healey blue and Old English white; restored between 2007 and 2010 (see lot 14 Gooding 9.3.12 $ 59,400).

| 1965 | 3000 MkIII | HBJ8L33909 | L | 60-90.000 EUR | | NS | | 04-02-16 | Paris | 339 | Bon |

Red and ivory with black interior; described as in very good overall condition.

| 1967 | 3000 MkIII | HBJ8L41566 | L | 75-100.000 USD | 53.639* | 75.900* | 69.904* | 10-03-16 | Amelia Island | 127 | Bon |

Metallic gold with red interior; full restoration completed in 2004 (see RM lots 235 13.8.04 $ 82,500 and 132 20.1.11 $ 85,250).

| 1967 | 3000 MkIII | HBJ841372 | R | 60-80.000 GBP | 91.100 | 131.977 | 117.009 | 20-03-16 | Goodwood | 31 | Bon F88 |

Red; never restored, the car is described as in very good original condition. One owner and circa 31,000 miles covered.

| 1964 | 3000 MkIII | HBJ8L25720 | L | 60-80.000 USD | 31.661 | 45.700 | 40.970 | 05-06-16 | Greenwhich | 30 | Bon |

Red with original black interior; described as in very good running order. Body repainted many years ago.

| 1964 | 3000 MkIII | HBJ8L27652 | L | 45-50.000 EUR | 56.714 | 81.029 | 72.000 | 19-06-16 | Fontainebleau | 343 | Ose |

Dark green and white; restored at unspecified date.

| 1966 | 3000 MkIII | HBJ8L35323 | L | 60-75.000 USD | 45.968 | 60.500 | 54.438 | 30-07-16 | Plymouth | 147 | RMS |

British racing green with biscuit leather interior; restored to concours condition.

F87: 1961 Austin-Healey 3000

F88: 1967 Austin-Healey 3000 MkIII

Year	Model	(Bodybuilder)	Chassis no.	Steering	Estimate	Hammer Price £	$	€	Date	Place	Lot	Auc. H.

AUTOBIANCHI (I) (1955-1996)

Year	Model	Chassis no.	Steering	Estimate	£	$	€	Date	Place	Lot	Auc. H.
1959	Bianchina Trasformabile	110B017491	L	8-12.000 USD	6.884*	10.450*	9.301*	05-10-15	Philadelphia	275	Bon
In original condition; for restoration. Since nearly new in the Alexis du Pont collection.											
1961	Bianchina Trasformabile	026726	L	15-20.000 GBP	26.621	40.834	35.938	10-10-15	Ascot	147	Coy F89
Light blue with blue and white interior.											
1968	Bianchina Cabriolet	110FB5009027	L	14-18.000 EUR	13.698*	21.691*	19.072*	01-11-15	Paris	101	Art
Light green with black interior; restored and fitted with a Fiat 126 engine.											
1958	Bianchina Trasformabile	001085	L	16-20.000 GBP	20.060	30.220	28.509	01-12-15	London	302	Coy
Red and white with red and white interior; described as in good original working order.											
1964	Bianchina Cabriolet	110B122005703	L	20-30.000 EUR	21.092*	30.612*	28.000*	03-02-16	Paris	102	RMS F90
Green with tan interior; recently restored. Sold new to France.											
1966	Bianchina Panoramica	98501	L	15-20.000 EUR	11.928*	17.359*	15.496*	05-02-16	Paris	190	Art
White with black roof; paintwork and interior redone, engine overhauled.											
1959	Bianchina Trasformabile	009662	L	17-22.000 GBP	14.160	20.120	18.245	08-03-16	London	141	Coy
Burgundy with tan interior; restored in the 1980s in Italy.											
1960	Bianchina Trasformabile	110B020309	L	50-70.000 USD		NS		10-03-16	Amelia Island	178	Bon
Light blue with tan and cream interior; restored. For 22 years in the Willem van Huystee Collection.											
1965	Bianchina Panoramica	110F3082800	L	6-9.000 GBP	5.175*	7.497*	6.647*	20-03-16	Goodwood	20	Bon
Described as in good original condition; engine rebuilt.											
1959	Bianchina Trasformabile	009662	L	17-22.000 GBP		NS		16-04-16	Ascot	143	Coy
See lot 141 Coys 8.3.16.											
1962	Bianchina Cabriolet	110B122003542	L	25-30.000 EUR	19.516	28.120	24.780	14-05-16	Monaco	181	Coy
Red with red and white interior; restoration completed in 2016 in Italy.											
1958	Bianchina Trasformabile	110B010511	L	22-28.000 EUR	17.642*	25.420*	22.400*	14-05-16	Monaco	226	RMS
Grey and white; restored (see lot 284 Coys 27.10.07 $ 33,937).											
1962	Bianchina Cabriolet	006397	L	13-15.000 EUR		NS		28-05-16	Aarhus	149	SiC
Red with grey interior; in good running order.											
1970	Bianchina Cabriolet	9329	L	10-12.000 EUR	18.716	26.740	23.760	19-06-16	Fontainebleau	345	Ose
Green with light brown interior; restored.											
1967	Bianchina Panoramica	120B142281	L	35-40.000 USD		NS		25-06-16	Santa Monica	1135	AA
Blue; described as in original condition except for the paintwork redone in 2015.											
1962	Bianchina Cabriolet	110B122003542	L	20-25.000 GBP	18.000	23.908	21.470	02-07-16	Woodstock	235	Coy
See lot 181 Coys 14.5.16.											
1958	Bianchina Trasformabile	110N013578	L	35-45.000 USD	27.581*	36.300*	32.663*	30-07-16	Plymouth	173	RMS
Red with red and white vinyl interior; restored.											
1959	Bianchina Trasformabile	110B022919	L	40-50.000 USD	40.339*	52.800*	46.617*	19-08-16	Carmel	99	Bon
Mint green with tan and cream interior; restored a few years ago (see lot 68 RM 17.1.14 $33,000).											

AUTOKRAFT (GB) (1980-1996)

Year	Model	Chassis no.	Steering	Estimate	£	$	€	Date	Place	Lot	Auc. H.
1995	AC Cobra MkIV	17511	R	90-110.000 GBP		NS		04-09-15	Woodstock	215	SiC
Red with black leather interior; 3,300 miles covered. 5.0-litre Ford V8 engine with automatic transmission (see lot 747 Brooks 2.12.98 NS).											
1987	AC Cobra MkIV	17194	L	120-140.000 GBP	61.600*	94.014*	84.349*	07-09-15	London	118	RMS
Black with leather interior; 225bhp 5-liter Ford V8 engine with 5-speed manual gearbox.											
1995	AC Cobra MkIV	17511	R	85-95.000 GBP	82.140	118.996	105.501	20-03-16	Goodwood	65	Bon
See lot 215 Silverstone Auctions 4.9.15.											
1987	AC Cobra MkIV	17230	L	130-160.000 USD		NS		05-06-16	Greenwhich	65	Bon
Black with tan interior; low mileage and original condition. 302 Ford Cobra V8 engine with 5-speed manual gearbox.											

F89: 1961 Autobianchi Bianchina Trasformabile

F90: 1964 Autobianchi Bianchina Cabriolet

Year	Model	(Bodybuilder)	Chassis no.	Steering	Estimate	Hammer price £	$	€	Date	Place	Lot	Auc. H.

F91: 1953 Bandini 750 Sport

F92: 1900 Bardon Type A tonneau

1982 AC Cobra MkIV AK02 L 70-110.000 EUR 76.092 108.714 96.600 18-06-16 Wien 432 Dor
Red with black leather interior; sold new to the USA and imported into Austria 2013. Ford 351 V8 engine.

AUTOVIA (GB) *(1937-1939)*

1939 V8 special 2-seater 63143 R 40-46.000 GBP NS 11-06-16 Brooklands 261 His
Red; discovered in pieces in 1976 and later restored (see lots H&H 72 23.7.97 $ 15,893, and Coys 577 10.12.13 $ 108,908 and 134 3.11.14 NS).

BANDINI (I) *(1946-1992)*

1953 750 Sport 153 L 115-140.000 GBP NS 07-09-15 London 113 RMS
Red with black interior; sold new to the USA to cartoonist and racer Alex Raymond, the car, fitted with the Crosley engine, was raced in the 1950s in SCCA events. Fully restored in the USA in the 2000s. Offered with FIVA Identity Card. From the Fendt Collection.

1953 750 Sport (Motto) 003 L 375-425.000 EUR NS 09-07-16 Le Mans 193 Art
Red; Crosley engine with Bandini twin-cam head. Raced in period in Italy and subsequently exported to the USA. Restored at unspecified date and reimported into Italy in the early 2000s.

1953 750 Sport 156 L 100-150.000 USD 85.721* 112.200* 99.061* 19-08-16 Carmel 29 Bon **F91**
Red; it is believed the car was sold new to the USA and raced in period. In 1992 it was bought by the late Raymond Milo and later restored in Italy. 750 Crosley engine.

BARDON (F) *(1899-1906)*

1900 Type A tonneau 5 R 80-90.000 EUR 71.714* 104.082* 95.200* 03-02-16 Paris 112 RMS **F92**
Blue with blue interior; restored in Switzerland. New body. Dated 1900 by the Veteran Car Club of Great Britain.

BELSIZE (GB) *(1897-1925)*

1909 14/16hp Roi des Belges tourer G78(engine) R 45-55.000 GBP 36.386 55.405 49.743 05-09-15 Beaulieu 131 Bon **F93**
Pale yellow with black wings and burgundy interior; restored in the late 1980s (see lot 432 Bonhams 20.6.15 NS).

BENETTON (I) *(1985-2001)*

1991 B191/191B B191B06 M 220-280.000 EUR 833.260* 1.200.618* 1.058.000* 13-05-16 Monaco 106 Bon **F94**
Driven by Nelson Piquet during the 1991 F1 season, the car was modified to "B" specification for the 1992 season and driven by Martin Brundle and later by Michael Schumacher. Described as "on the button" (see lot 28 Bonhams 30.11.14 NS).

BENTLEY (GB) *(1919-)*

1928 3/4.5l tourer HT1649 R NA UD 14-10-15 Duxford 141 H&H
Black with dark green leather interior; built with Vanden Plas saloon body, in the 1960s the car was fitted with the present Vanden Plas style body. In the 1990s the engine was converted to the present specification. The old FIVA Identity Card which accompanies the car states the following (among other): "The chassis, gearbox and suspension are as original. The wheels have been reduced 1 inch in diameter to 20 inches and the brakes have been converted to hydraulic operation. The engine retains its original numbered crankcase but has been enlarged to 4398cc".

F93: 1909 Belsize 14/16hp Roi des Belges tourer

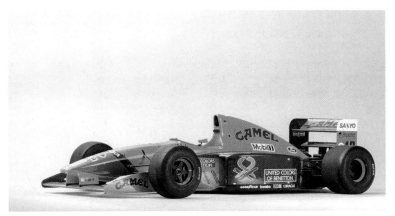

F94: 1991 Benetton B191/191B

Year	Model	(Bodybuilder)	Chassis no.	Steering	Estimate	Hammer Price £	Hammer Price $	Hammer Price €	Date	Place	Lot	Auc. H.
1926	3l light tourer	(Vanden Plas)	HP393	R	190-220.000 GBP	281.500	425.769	389.061	10-12-15	London	351	Bon F95

Green with black wings; described as in very good overall condition. Engine rebuilt in 1990; since 1993 in the current ownership. One of two or three light tourer examples known in existence.

| 1924 | 3l Speed Model tourer | | 717 | R | 450-525.000 USD | | NS | | 10-03-16 | Amelia Island | 177 | Bon |

Light grey with dark grey wings and burgundy interior; sold new in the UK, the car was imported into the USA in 1998. Approximately 10 years ago the car received some restoration works and the engine was rebuilt. According to recent research by marque historian Dr. Clare Hay the body could be the original one built by H.J.Mulliner. The present engine, 1923 unit no.403, was fitted at unspecified date. From the Willem van Huystee Collection (see lot 49 Coys 2.3.98 $ 99,087).

| 1923 | 3l Tourist Trophy Replica tourer | (Park Ward) | 160 | R | 240-280.000 GBP | | NS | | 20-03-16 | Goodwood | 15 | Bon |

Black with red interior; numerous mechanical works carried out in the 1920s and 1930s, original engine no.157 replaced in the 1960s with the present, later unit no.DE1206 rebuilt to Speed Model specification. Body repainted in 1992, engine rebuilt again in 2012. Since 1967 in the Kingsley Curtis Collection.

| 1925 | 3l/4,5l tourer | | 916 | R | NA | | NS | | 20-04-16 | Duxford | 101 | H&H |

Black with red interior; since 1987 in the current ownership. Fitted decades ago with the present Vanden Plas style tourer body. Probably in the early 1990s the engine was enlarged to 4.5-litre specification using a new block.

| 1924 | 3l/4,5l tourer | | 735 | R | 320-370.000 GBP | 284.850 | 378.338 | 339.769 | 02-07-16 | Woodstock | 201 | Coy |

British racing green with brown leather interior; the car was sold new to Archie J. Ballantine, son of the distiller George Ballantine. It was discovered in 1998 in "kit of parts"; the chassis had been shortened. Subsequently the car was imported into Australia and restored over a number of years. The engine was upgraded to 4.5-litre specification, including a new cylinder block and Phoenix crankshaft and rods. The B-Type gearbox was rebuilt with new gears. The body is new and built in Vanden Plas style. The car has covered less than 2,000 miles since the restoration.

| 1927 | 3l Speed Model tourer | (Vanden Plas) | AX1668 | R | 650-800.000 USD | 516.846 | 676.500 | 597.282 | 20-08-16 | Pebble Beach | 27 | G&Co |

Green with green interior; sold new to Argentina, the car was raced at the 1927 Grand Prix Sport at the Autodromo de San Martin. In 1970 it was imported into the USA, where it was restored between the late 1990s-early 2000s. Driven at the 2007 Mille Miglia Retrospective. Recently serviced.

| 1926 | 3l/4,5l tourer | | 911 | R | 600-750.000 USD | 521.048 | 682.000 | 602.138 | 20-08-16 | Monterey | 233 | RMS |

Built with Freestone & Webb coupé body, in 2003 the car was purchased by Brian Hussey who subsequently had it fully restored and fitted with the present Vanden Plas style tourer body. The chassis was shortened and the engine was built upon a "Blower"-specification 4.5-litre block. Since 2012 in the Sam and Emily Mann Collection (see lots Bonhams 25 25.3.07 $387,418, TSAC 163 6.10.07 NS, and RM 149 27.10.10 $460,766 and 376 12.5.12 $529,151).

| 1927 | 6½l tourer | | WK2658 | R | 4.600-6.000.000 DKK | 707.969 | 1.074.531 | 963.844 | 26-09-15 | Ebeltoft | 8 | Bon F96 |

Sold new to Australia, the car was first bodied with a taper-tail 2-seater body, in the early 1930 it was rebodied as a close-coupled 4-seater coupé, and in the 1940s it received the present 4-seater tourer body. In the early 1970s the car was imported into the USA and later it was acquired by the Frederiksen Collection.

| 1926 | 6½l tourer | | WK2661 | R | 825-950.000 EUR | | NS | | 05-02-16 | Paris | 197 | Art |

Blue with grey leather interior; delivered new with Mulliner saloon body, the car was fitted in the 1960s with the present Vanden Plas style tourer body. Since 1993 in the current ownership; body restored in 2007; engine rebuilt in 2010.

| 1929 | 6½l Speed Six tourer project | (Barker) | RC2898 | R | 100-200.000 GBP | 205.340 | 297.476 | 263.739 | 20-03-16 | Goodwood | 85 | Bon |

Restoration to be completed. The heart of this project is the engine no.LB2340S originally fitted to Speed Six chassis no.LB2334, the chassis is a replacement item purchased from Julian Ghosh in 1990, the bulkhead is a genuine Speed Six component, the body was originally fitted to chassis FA2513.

| 1929 | 4½l sports saloon | (H.J.Mulliner) | PB3527 | R | 150-250.000 GBP | 695.900 | 1.059.647 | 951.365 | 05-09-15 | Beaulieu | 171 | Bon F97 |

Since 1935 in the same family ownership, the car was parked in their garage in 1985 and is in original condition. The engine is seized but shows no signs of frost damage. For restoration.

| 1929 | 4½l tourer | (Cadogan) | DS3570 | R | 400-500.000 GBP | 420.000 | 641.004 | 575.106 | 07-09-15 | London | 146 | RMS |

Dark green with red interior; original body modernised in the late 1930s and restored in recent years. With a detailed report of Dr Clare Hay (see lot 359 Bonhams 22.6.07 $ 288,567).

| 1929 | 4½l tourer | (Vanden Plas) | MR3399 | R | 400-500.000 GBP | 667.900 | 1.011.134 | 927.446 | 06-12-15 | London | 006 | Bon F98 |

Maroon with brown leather interior; described as in highly original condition, since 1996 the car is the Gordon Willey collection and requires recommissioning prior to use (lot 52 Christie's 19.2.96 $ 275,089).

| 1928 | 4½l tourer | | PM3252 | R | 700-900.000 USD | 596.409 | 852.500 | 768.699 | 12-03-16 | Amelia Island | 145 | RMS |

Dark green with green leather interior; built with Broom coupé body, the car has had several UK owners prior to be imported into Zimbabwe in 1982. Back to the UK in 1999, it was restored and fitted with the present Vanden Plas style tourer body. Subsequently it was imported into the USA (see lot 157 Gooding 21.8.11 $ 770,000).

| 1929 | 4½l tourer | | DS3551 | R | 250-300.000 GBP | 320.700 | 464.598 | 411.907 | 20-03-16 | Goodwood | 87 | Bon |

Built with Gurney Nutting coupé body; current chassis to correct specification but no markings can be seen to the front cross-member (it is likely the unnumbered frame fitted by Bentley Motors during accident repair work in 1931); engine no.DS3551 (as the chassis) to correct 1929 specification; earlier Type C gearbox no.6003. The present body was fitted in the early 1960s probably; the car is in the same family ownership since 1969, is not used for 30 years and requires recommissioning prior to use.

| 1931 | 8l tourer | (Swallow) | YF5013 | R | 1.000-1.250.000 USD | | NS | | 12-03-16 | Amelia Island | 171 | RMS |

British racing green; bodied in France in saloon form by Saoutchik, the car was subsequently sold in the UK and in 1935 it was fitted with a Hooper tourer body. In the mid-1950s it was imported into the USA and in 1962 it was acquired by Norris Allen who had it restored. The chassis was shortened to the measures of the Speed Six team cars and fitted with the present new 4-seater tourer body built in the UK. According to the research of Dr. Clare Hay, the engine, front and rear axles and shortened frame are original.

| 1932 | 8l tourer | (Vanden Plas) | YX5118 | R | 2.500-3.000.000 USD | 1.302.620 | 1.705.000 | 1.505.345 | 19-08-16 | Monterey | 121 | RMS F99 |

Built with Mayfair tourer body, in 1935 circa the car was bought by its second owner who had it rebodied in 1938 with the present Vanden Plas Le Mans-style tourer body. In 1967 the car passed to its third owner and in 1968 it was acquired by Hans Dieter Holterbosch who retained it for 45 years and had it restored in the UK. Several years ago it was acquired by the current, fifth owner. Described as in very good running order.

| 1932 | 4l saloon | (Thrupp/Maberly) | VA4085 | R | 150-200.000 GBP | | NS | | 01-12-15 | London | 328 | Coy |

Black and blue with black interior; the car was acquired in 1962 by the previous owner who drove it until 1969. Subsequently stored for 30 years, it was bought by the current owner and fully restored over a 12 years period. The engine is yet to be fully run in (see lot 240 Bonhams 14.9.13 NS).

| 1932 | 4l saloon | (Thrupp/Maberly) | VA4085 | R | 130-160.000 GBP | 142.400 | 201.923 | 178.940 | 16-04-16 | Ascot | 141 | Coy F100 |

See lot 328 Coys 1.12.15.

| 1934 | 3½l cabriolet | (Thrupp/Maberly) | B185AE | R | 60-80.000 GBP | 93.000 | 141.611 | 127.140 | 04-09-15 | Woodstock | 225 | SiC |

In the same family ownership since 1965, the car has been stored for 50 years. Complete except for the soft top, it requires full restoration.

| 1934 | 3½l cabriolet | (J.Young) | B193AE | R | 120-150.000 GBP | 124.700 | 192.325 | 170.689 | 12-09-15 | Goodwood | 359 | Bon F101 |

White and beige with beige interior; over the past ten years maintained and improved as and when necessary. From the late James Crickmay's collection.

| 1933 | 3½l saloon | (Park Ward) | B15AE | R | 100-150.000 GBP | | NS | | 12-09-15 | Goodwood | 381 | Bon |

Light grey with blue side stripe and grey interior; in the 1990s the engine was rebuilt and the body was restored. When new the car was used as a demonstrator by the factory and was driven also by W O Bentley and Malcolm Campbell (see lot 70 H&H 13.9.06 $ 66,523).

| 1935 | 3½l sports saloon | (Mann Egerton) | B35DK | R | 25-32.000 GBP | 42.550 | 64.357 | 58.808 | 10-12-15 | London | 302 | Bon |

Black; several works carried out in the 1990s. It requires recommissioning prior to use. From the Gordon Willey Collection.

| 1934 | 3½l cabriolet | (Thrupp/Maberly) | B75BL | R | 200-225.000 USD | | NS | | 28-01-16 | Scottsdale | 52 | Bon |

Black with brown interior; restored in the UK at unspecified date and refreshed in recent years in the USA (see lot 126 RM/Sotheby's 14.3.15 $ 231,000).

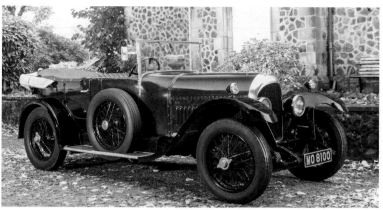
F95: 1926 Bentley 3l light tourer (Vanden Plas)

F96: 1927 Bentley 6½l tourer

F97: 1929 Bentley 4½l sports saloon (H.J.Mulliner)

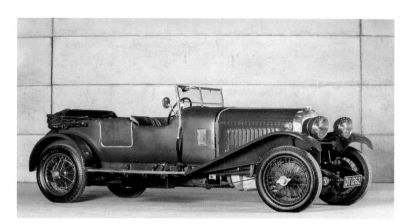
F98: 1929 Bentley 4½l tourer (Vanden Plas)

F99: 1932 Bentley 8l tourer (Vanden Plas)

F100: 1932 Bentley 4l saloon (Thrupp/Maberly)

F101: 1934 Bentley 3½l cabriolet (J.Young)

F102: 1935 Bentley 3½l saloon (Park Ward)

Year	Model	(Bodybuilder)	Chassis no.	Steering	Estimate	Hammer price £	Hammer price $	Hammer price €	Date	Place	Lot	Auc. H.
1935	3½l saloon	(Park Ward)	B117DK	R	90-120.000 USD	64.522	91.300	84.087	10-03-16	Amelia Island	176	Bon F102

Royal blue and old English white with brown interior; in good driving order. From the Willem van Huystee Collection.

| 1934 | 3½l tourer | | B120AH | R | 50-70.000 GBP | 51.750 | 70.918 | 64.082 | 24-06-16 | Goodwood | 235 | Bon |

Built with Thrupp & Maberly saloon body, the car was fitted with the present body probably in the 1940s. Described as in good working order (see lot 26 H & H 21.2.06 $39,260).

| 1935 | 3½l Owen Sedanca | (Gurney Nutting) | B130FB | R | 175-195.000 GBP | | NS | | 02-07-16 | Woodstock | 211 | Coy |

Light green with cream leather interior; described as in very good overall condition. Built with Rippon saloon body, at unspecified date the car was fitted with the present body, built in 1934 and originally fitted to chassis B99BN.

| 1939 | 4¼l cabriolet | (Vanden Plas) | B105MX | R | 200-300.000 EUR | | NS | | 05-09-15 | Chantilly | 12 | Bon |

Two-tone green with red leather interior; restored in the 1980s. Acquired in 2011 by the current owner, the car received subsequently further cosmetic and mechanical works (see lot 325 Bonhams 5.2.11 $ 329,189).

| 1937 | 4¼l saloon | (Hooper) | B44LS | R | 50-60.000 GBP | | NS | | 05-09-15 | Beaulieu | 129 | Bon |

Since 1967 in the same family ownership in Germany; described as in good original condition, in working order but little used since 2004.

| 1937 | 4¼l two-door saloon | (Hooper) | B188LS | R | 15-20.000 GBP | 13.800* | 21.013* | 18.866* | 05-09-15 | Beaulieu | 170 | Bon |

Restoration project.

| 1937 | 4¼l "Aerofoil" coupé | (Gurney Nutting) | B90KT | R | 300-400.000 EUR | 252.368 | 384.261 | 345.000 | 05-09-15 | Chantilly | 19 | Bon F103 |

Black and white with blue leather interior; one of four examples built with Aerofoil aerodynamic body. Restored in the UK in the 1990s and again in 2006-07 in Belgium (see lot 83 Christie's 24.7.00 NS).

| 1937 | 4¼l cabriolet | (J.Young) | B14KT | R | 275-350.000 EUR | | NS | | 05-09-15 | Chantilly | 22 | Bon |

Dark red with champagne leather interior; one of four examples with parallel door on both the sides. Sold new in the UK, the car was exported in the 1950s to Nigeria and in 1968 to South Africa. In 2000 it was reimported into the UK and subsequently fully restored (see lot 70 Coys 30.4.02 NS).

| 1937 | 4¼l saloon | (Park Ward) | BK47KU | R | 195-260.000 AUD | | NS | | 24-10-15 | Melbourne | 25 | TBr |

Two-tone brown with tan leather interior; restored many years ago, the car is described as in good driving order.

| 1936 | 4¼l coupé | (Gurney Nutting) | B25HM | R | 180-220.000 GBP | 201.600 | 304.174 | 278.027 | 09-12-15 | Chateau Impney | 129 | H&H |

Dark blue with grey interior; body repainted in 1951. Since 1974 in the current ownership; overhauled in 2003; recently serviced.

| 1939 | 4¼l brougham saloon | (Freestone/Webb) | B66LS | R | 35-40.000 GBP | 47.150 | 71.314 | 65.166 | 10-12-15 | London | 301 | Bon |

Black and red; mechanicals restored between 1978 and 1980. Little used over the last 12 years, it requires recommissioning prior to use. From the Gordon Willey Collection (see lot 615 Sotheby's 11.6.94 NS).

| 1939 | 4¼l cabriolet | (H.J.Mulliner) | B95LE | R | 140-170.000 GBP | 253.500 | 383.419 | 350.362 | 10-12-15 | London | 304 | Bon F104 |

Maroon with burgundy interior; several works carried out between 2012 and 2015. From the Gordon Willey Collection.

| 1936 | 4¼l sedanca coupé | (Gurney Nutting) | B171HM | R | 90-110.000 GBP | 119.100 | 180.139 | 164.608 | 10-12-15 | London | 306 | Bon |

Black with black interior; several restoration works carried out in the 1990s. From the Gordon Willey Collection.

| 1938 | 4¼l coupé | (H.J.Mulliner) | B83LE | R | 60-80.000 GBP | 96.700 | 146.259 | 133.649 | 10-12-15 | London | 307 | Bon |

Black with tan interior; some works carried out in 1993 and 2015. It requires recommissioning prior to use. From the Gordon Willey Collection.

| 1939 | 4¼l cabriolet | | B137MX | R | 200-250.000 EUR | | NS | | 04-02-16 | Paris | 424 | Bon |

Built with Park Ward saloon body, the car was restored in 2007-08 and fitted with the present, new Vanden Plas style body.

| 1937 | 4¼l tourer | (Thrupp/Maberly) | B39KU | R | 140-180.000 USD | 122.436 | 173.250 | 159.563 | 10-03-16 | Amelia Island | 122 | Bon |

Two-tone green with brown leather interior; in fine overall condition. Since 1995 in the Wade Carter Collection.

| 1936 | 4¼l tourer | | B200GA | R | 150-180.000 GBP | | NS | | 24-06-16 | Goodwood | 224 | Bon |

Dark green; probably restored in the 1970s and fitted with the present Vanden Plas style body. Recently serviced. (see lot 527 Bonhams 7.12.09 $160,603).

| 1937 | 4¼l cabriolet | (H.J.Mulliner) | B79KU | R | 180-240.000 GBP | | NS | | 24-06-16 | Goodwood | 246 | Bon |

Black with beige interior; restored in the USA in 1979-80. Purchased in 2010 by the current owner, subsequently the car received further works. Exhibited at the Mulliner stand at the 1937 London Motor Show (see lots RM 209 28.10.09 $233,433, and Coys 117 14.8.10 NS and 125 2.10.10 $287,436).

| 1936 | 4¼l tourer | (Vanden Plas) | B138GA | R | 600-800.000 USD | 504.240 | 660.000 | 582.714 | 19-08-16 | Carmel | 81 | Bon |

Maroon with black wings and maroon leather interior; used at some racing events between the late 1940s - early 1950s. Restored between the late 1980s - early 1990s, the car received further works in the 2000s.

| 1939 | 4¼l coupé | (Park Ward) | B30MR | R | 750-900.000 USD | 588.280 | 770.000 | 679.833 | 20-08-16 | Monterey | 241 | RMS F105 |

One-off nicknamed "Honeymoon Express", the car was displayed at the Park Ward stand at the 1938 London Motor Show. In the 1960s it was purchased by Maurice Richmond who imported it into the USA in 1967 and retained it until 2002. Between 2006 and 2011 the car received a concours-quality restoration in the UK (see lot 141 RM 4.2.15 $769,171).

| 1939 | Mk V cabriolet | (Saoutchik) | B14AW | R | 850-1.200.000 USD | | NS | | 11-06-16 | Hershey | 129 | TFA |

Blue with beige interior; described as the only Mk V cabriolet built, originally the car was delivered to Binder in France to be bodied in coupé form. The work was not completed for the war outbreak and in 1940 the car was delivered to Saoutchick who fitted it with the present body. In the early 1950s it was reimported into the UK and in the mid-1960s it was imported into the USA. In 1995 circa it was purchased by Charles Howard, who reimported it again in the UK and had it restored. In 2003 the car was imported in the USA again.

F103: 1937 Bentley 4¼l "Aerofoil" coupé (Gurney Nutting)

F104: 1939 Bentley 4¼l cabriolet (H.J.Mulliner)

Year	Model (Bodybuilder)	Chassis no.	Steering	Estimate	Hammer price £	$	€	Date	Sale Place	Lot	Auc. H.

F105: 1939 Bentley 4¼l coupé (Park Ward)

F106: 1949 Bentley Mk VI estate car (Rippon)

1951 Mk VI standard saloon — B68MD — R — 13.5-14.500 GBP — 11.760 — 17.743 — 16.218 — 09-12-15 — Chateau Impney — 56 — H&H
Black and cream with new beige leather interior; restored in the 1990s.

1947 Mk VI saloon (Vanden Plas) — B294BH — R — 40-50.000 GBP — 23.000 — 34.788 — 31.788 — 10-12-15 — London — 336 — Bon
Two-tone grey; bought in 2005 by the current owner. Several works to the body, mechanicals and interior carried out between 2008 and 2014.

1949 Mk VI saloon (H.J.Mulliner) — B3EW — R — 7-10.000 GBP — 10.925* — 16.524* — 15.099* — 10-12-15 — London — 385 — Bon
Restoration project.

1949 Mk VI estate car (Rippon) — B91FU — R — 160-190.000 USD — 84.664* — 121.000* — 110.800* — 29-01-16 — Phoenix — 261 — RM S F106
Blue with wooden panels and tan leather interior; imported into the USA in the late 1980s and later restored. From the Craig McCaw Collection (see lot 3 Christie's 15.6.96 $ 59,700).

1947 Mk VI cabriolet (Park Ward) — B282CF — R — 60-80.000 GBP — NS — — — 05-09-15 — Beaulieu — 157 — Bon
Burgundy with magnolia leather interior; cosmetically restored in the early 1990s (see lot 744 Coys 7.12.10 $ 127,992).

1948 Mk VI cabriolet (J.Young) — B267DZ — R — 120-150.000 USD — 89.205 — 127.600 — 117.022 — 28-01-16 — Scottsdale — 13 — Bon
Black with caramel interior; imported into the USA in 1970 and recently restored (see lot 144 RM 8.9.14 NS).

1952 Mk VI cabriolet (Park Ward) — B135LNY — L — 100-125.000 USD — 72.580 — 95.000 — 83.876 — 20-08-16 — Monterey — S5 — Mec
Two-tone brown with grey leather interior; extensive repairs carried out in the USA at unspecified date.

1950 Mk VI coupé (Park Ward) — B279FU — R — 60-75.000 EUR — NS — — — 26-09-15 — Frankfurt — 125 — Coy
Gold with beige interior (see lot 135 Coys 18.1.14 NS).

1953 R Type standard saloon — B125TO — R — 20-24.000 GBP — 20.160 — 30.417 — 27.803 — 09-12-15 — Chateau Impney — 73 — H&H
Dark blue with beige interior; 49,412 miles on the odometer.

1954 R Type standard saloon — B51ZX — R — 24-28.000 GBP — NS — — — 10-12-15 — London — 345 — Bon
Black and silver with light grey leather interior; engine overhauled in 2010.

1952 R Type standard saloon — B68SR — R — 80-100.000 EUR — 37.048* — 53.381* — 47.040* — 14-05-16 — Monaco — 239 — RMS F107
The car was used by drivers Couper, Tabor and Fillingham at the 1953 Monte Carlo Rally, where they received the cup for winning the Concours de Confort. Described as in largely original condition; only the paintwork was redone to its original colour in the early 1990s (see lot 348 Bonhams 19.1.12 NS).

1953 R Type standard saloon — B119TO — R — 12-14.000 GBP — 11.800 — 15.673 — 14.075 — 02-07-16 — Woodstock — 229 — Coy
Two-tone grey; in running order. Biscuit leather interior in need of retrim.

1955 R Type standard saloon — B206ZY — R — 15-20.000 GBP — 29.680 — 38.845 — 34.295 — 20-08-16 — Brooklands — 310 — His
Grey with light grey interior; recently restored.

1954 R Type Continental fastback (H.J.Mulliner) — BC58D — R — 900-1.100.000 GBP — NS — — — 04-09-15 — Woodstock — 227 — SiC
Burgundy with beige leather interior; several restoration works carried out over the last two years. Original 4.9-litre engine.

1953 R Type Continental fastback (H.J.Mulliner) — BC32C — R — 850-1.100.000 GBP — NS — — — 12-09-15 — Goodwood — 354 — Bon
Dark green with green leather interior; sold new to France, the car was later exported to the USA and in 1979 it was acquired by the current owner and imported into the UK. Fully restored between 1990 and 1994. Recommissioned in 2014, including a gearbox overhaul. In 1957 the car had been fitted at the factory with the 4.9-litre engine.

1955 R Type Continental fastback (H.J.Mulliner) — BC67LD — L — 1.300-1.600.000 USD — 711.945 — 1.017.500 — 931.725 — 30-01-16 — Scottsdale — 137 — G&Co
Black with original brown leather interior; sold new to France and imported into the USA probably in the 2000s. Body repainted at unspecified date. 4.9-litre engine with automatic transmission (see lot 208 RM/Sotheby's 2.5.15 $ 1,127,500).

F107: 1952 Bentley R Type standard saloon

F108: 1954 Bentley R Type Continental fastback (H.J.Mulliner)

Year	Model	(Bodybuilder)	Chassis no.	Steering	Estimate	Hammer Price £	$	€	Sale Date	Place	Lot	Auc. H.
1954	R Type Continental fastback	(H.J.Mulliner)	BC2LD	L	1.200-1.400.000 USD	1.269.774	1.815.000	1.636.586	12-03-16	Amelia Island	147	RMS F108

Maroon with putty leather interior; 4.9-litre engine. Sold new to the USA, in 1995 the car was reimported into the UK where it was restored prior to be sold again to the USA. In 2009 the restoration was upgraded to concours standards.

1954	R Type Continental fastback	(H.J.Mulliner)	BC14D	R	750-950.000 EUR		NS		14-05-16	Monaco	257	RMS

Dark green with green leather interior; described as in very good overall condition. 4.9-litre engine. From the collection of Luca Bassani Antivari.

1954	R Type Continental fastback	(H.J.Mulliner)	BC66LC	L	1.300-1.700.000 USD	1.428.680	1.870.000	1.651.023	19-08-16	Monterey	145	RMS

Silver blue with light blue leather interior; sold new to the USA, in 2008 the car was acquired by the current, fifth owner and subsequently subjected to a concours-quality restoration. Automatic transmission (see RM lots 240 5.8.00 NS, 49 10.3.01 $170,500, and 479 16.8.08 $550,000).

1958	S1 saloon		B49FD	R	12-15.000 GBP	17.825	27.142	24.369	05-09-15	Beaulieu	168	Bon

Black; since 1969 in the current ownership, it was last used regularly in the 1970s. It starts and runs but needs recommissioning.

1955	S1 saloon	(Hooper)	B460AN	R	26-30.000 GBP	26.621	40.834	35.938	10-10-15	Ascot	152	Coy

Silver blue; sold new in the UK, the car was exported to the USA in 1970 and reimported into the UK in 2008 (see lots Gooding 156 19.8.07 $ 46,200, Artcurial 60 8.2.09 NS and 26 13.7.09 $ 49,446, and Coys 308 12.7.14 NS).

1956	S1 saloon	(J.Young)	B470AN	R	NA	40.320	62.016	54.351	14-10-15	Duxford	125	H&H

Blue with stone interior; car restored several years ago, interior retrimmed in the 2000s (see lot 43 H&H 21.6.14 $ 51,523).

1956	S1 saloon		B135DE	R	NA	26.880	41.344	36.234	14-10-15	Duxford	59	H&H

Dark blue with blue leather interior; body repainted and interior re-connolised in recent times. Gearbox replaced.

1955	S1 saloon	(H.J.Mulliner)	B216AN	R	150-200.000 EUR		NS		01-11-15	Paris	130	Art

Dark metallic grey with red leather interior; in good overall condition, the car has seen little use in the last years and requires servicing prior to use (see Lots Artcurial 62 8.2.09 NS and 6 13.7.09 NS, and Bonhams 154 30.4.10 NS).

1956	S1 saloon	(J.Young)	B470AN	R	35-40.000 GBP	36.960	55.765	50.972	09-12-15	Chateau Impney	131	H&H

See lot 125 H&H 14.10.15.

1958	S1 saloon		B476FA	R	22-26.000 GBP	13.570	20.525	18.755	10-12-15	London	327	Bon

Recent works including the automatic transmission overhaul.

1959	S1 saloon		B57LGD	L	40-50.000 EUR	44.294*	64.286*	58.800*	03-02-16	Paris	111	RMS F109

Tudor grey with light grey interior; since new in the same family ownership. Engine replaced in 1971; body repainted some time ago.

1955	S1 saloon	(Hooper)	B50AN	R	28-34.000 GBP	32.200	46.648	41.358	20-03-16	Goodwood	79	Bon

Two-tone blue; restored in 1995, the car was acquired in 1996 by the current, second owner. Exhibited at the Hooper stand at the 1955 Earls Court Motor Show.

1958	S1 saloon lwb		ALB24	R	NA		NS		20-04-16	Duxford	65	H&H

Black with burgundy leather interior; recently restored. Automatic transmission.

1957	S1 saloon		B488EG	L	28-35.000 EUR		NS		14-05-16	Monaco	185	Coy

Metallic burgundy and sand with beige leather interior; restored in 2015. Front end updated with S3 twin headlamp.

1956	S1 saloon		B134LBA	R	34-40.000 EUR	25.313	37.078	33.200	28-05-16	Aarhus	224	SiC

White with white leather interior; in good overall condition.

1957	S1 (cabriolet/conversion)		B134FA	L	210-240.000 EUR		NS		06-08-16	Schloss Dyck	113	Coy

Conversion carried out at unspecified date; car restored between 2014 and 2016.

1958	S1 cabriolet	(H.J.Mulliner)	B212LFA	L	7.200-9.200.000 DKK		NS		26-09-15	Ebeltoft	6	Bon

Blue with blue interior; an older restoration, it is described as in good overall condition. First owner John D. Rockefeller Jr. From the Frederiksen Collection.

1956	Continental S1 fastback	(H.J.Mulliner)	BC94AF	R	NA		NS		20-04-16	Duxford	86	H&H

Dark blue with original champagne leather interior; since 1984 in the current ownership. Body repainted in the early 1980s; engine overhauled 5,000 miles ago in 1987.

1957	Continental S1 fastback	(H.J.Mulliner)	BC47CH	R	200-300.000 GBP	234.460	321.304	290.332	24-06-16	Goodwood	280	Bon

Blue with grey leather interior; the body requires some repairs and repainting. Automatic transmission (see Bonhams lots 1000 23.9.06 $161,000 and 265 23.1.10 NS).

1957	Continental S1 coupé	(Park Ward)	BC59BG	R	250-300.000 USD	161.631	231.000	211.527	30-01-16	Scottsdale	104	G&Co

Since 1986 in the same family ownership; recently serviced. Sliding sunroof; automatic transmission.

1958	Continental S1 Flying Spur	(H.J.Mulliner)	BC45DJ	R	90-100.000 GBP	186.300	281.779	257.485	10-12-15	London	303	Bon

Dark blue with tan leather interior; several works carried out between 2012 and 2015 including a body repainting. The original manual gearbox was replaced with an automatic unit by factory in 1961. The car requires recommissioning prior to use. From the Gordon Willey Collection.

1958	Continental S1 Flying Spur	(H.J.Mulliner)	BC2FM	R	160-200.000 USD	130.844*	187.000*	171.236*	29-01-16	Phoenix	222	RMS

Black with tan leather interior; cosmetically restored several years ago. Imported into the USA in 2012. From the Craig McCaw Collection.

F109: 1959 Bentley S1 saloon

F110: 1959 Bentley Continental S2 saloon (Hooper)

Year	Model (Bodybuilder)	Chassis No.	Steering	Estimate	Hammer price £	Hammer price $	Hammer price €	Date	Place	Lot	Auc. H.
1961	S2 saloon	B373DV	R	25-30.000 GBP	30.000	39.264	34.665	20-08-16	Brooklands	308	His
	Dark green and Tudor grey; restored between 2000 and 2001. Further works to the body carried out in 2015 (see lot 17 H & H 5.6.96 $12,159).										
1959	Continental S2 saloon (Hooper)	BC1AR	R	100-120.000 GBP	102.300	157.777	140.028	12-09-15	Goodwood	360	Bon F110
	Silver with red interior; restored in the 1980s. Recently serviced. From the late James Crickmay's collection (see lot 630 Bonhams 28.4.03 NS).										
1960	Continental S2 saloon (J.Young)	BC35AR	R	175-225.000 USD	57.717*	82.500*	74.390*	11-03-16	Amelia Island	65	G&Co
	Garnet with tan leather interior; imported into the USA in 2008 and subsequently restored.										
1962	Continental S2 cabriolet (Mulliner,Park Ward)	BC131LCZ	L	175-200.000 EUR	145.536	230.462	202.640	01-11-15	Paris	128	Art
	Black with magnolia leather interior; described as in very good overall condition. Three owners (see lot 124 Bonhams 26.9.09 $ 215,942).										
1962	Continental S2 cabriolet (Mulliner,Park Ward)	BC77BY	R	180-225.000 USD		NS		25-06-16	Santa Monica	1069	AA
	Restored within the past two years.										
1962	Continental S2 coupé (Mulliner,Park Ward)	BC71CZ	R	240-295.000 GBP	220.000	292.204	262.416	02-07-16	Woodstock	142	Coy
	Pewter with original green leather interior; body restored.										
1961	Continental S2 Flying Spur (Mulliner,Park Ward)	BC90LBY	L	200-250.000 EUR		NS		05-09-15	Chantilly	9	Bon
	Burgundy with tan leather interior; sold new to the USA where it was restored in 2000 circa. Acquired in 2008 by the current owner, it received subsequently further works.										
1961	Continental S2 Flying Spur (Mulliner,Park Ward)	BC48CZ	R	110-130.000 GBP		NS		06-12-15	London	003	Bon
	Tudor grey with light grey leather interior; body repainted in recent years. 45,394 miles on the odometer. From 1992 to 2007 it was part of the Bernie Ecclestone collection (see lots 219 RM 31.10.07 $ 91,164, 635 Bonhams 1.12.08 $ 56,632 and 277 Historics 29.8.15 NS).										
1962	Continental S2 Flying Spur (Mulliner,Park Ward)	BC59LCZ	L	200-300.000 USD	157.647	225.500	206.806	28-01-16	Scottsdale	5	Bon
	Two-tone grey with red leather interior; restored between 2012 and 2014. Sold new to the USA.										
1962	Continental S2 Flying Spur (Mulliner,Park Ward)	BC73CZ	L	100-130.000 GBP		NS		20-03-16	Goodwood	42	Bon
	Red with beige leather interior; paintwork and interior redone in 2011-12 (see lot 350 Bonhams 19.4.10 $ 76,961).										
1959	Continental S2 Flying Spur (H.J.Mulliner)	BC12LAR	L	160-200.000 EUR	144.915	208.803	184.000	13-05-16	Monaco	138	Bon
	Dark grey with beige leather interior; the car was sold new to the USA, where it was restored at unspecified date. Reimported into Europe in 2003; engine rebuilt in 2010 (see lot 267 Artcurial 10.6.13 $ 230,472).										
1965	S3 saloon	B378HN	R	NA	19.040	26.487	24.120	24-02-16	Donington Park	64	H&H
	Grey with blue interior; since 1987 in the current ownership. Overhauled brakes.										
1963	S3 saloon	B370LCN	L	20-26.000 GBP	22.400	32.014	28.867	12-03-16	Brooklands	217	His
	Black and dark blue with light tan interior; reimported into the UK from the USA in 2010. Recently checked.										
1963	S3 saloon	B4LCN	L	95-125.000 EUR		NS		14-05-16	Monaco	282	RMS
	Sand and black pearl; restored in Italy in recent years.										
1962	Continental S3 cabriolet (Mulliner,Park Ward)	BC4LXA	L	150-200.000 EUR	130.390	198.535	178.250	05-09-15	Chantilly	25	Bon
	Marine blue with beige leather interior; exhibited at the 1962 Paris Motor Show, the car was subsequently sold new to the USA. Restored at unspecified date. From the Alain Dominique Perrin collection.										
1962	Continental S3 cabriolet (Mulliner,Park Ward)	BC30LXA	L	330-370.000 EUR		NS		26-09-15	Frankfurt	135	Coy
	Black; fully restored.										
1962	Continental S3 cabriolet (Mulliner,Park Ward)	BC30LXA	L	250-300.000 EUR	178.908	265.208	236.666	04-02-16	Paris	381	Bon F111
	See lot 135 Coys 26.9.15.										
1966	Continental S3 cabriolet (Mulliner,Park Ward)	BC62XE	R	120-160.000 USD	153.736	220.000	192.434	02-04-16	Ft.Lauderdale	485	AA
	White with red leather interior; just over 30,000 miles on the odometer. Since 1972 in the current ownership.										
1965	Continental S3 cabriolet (Mulliner,Park Ward)	BC24XE	R	NA	184.800	262.046	233.624	20-04-16	Duxford	24	H&H
	Blue with cream interior; body and interior restored between 2002 and 2004, engine overhauled in 2005. Stored from 2007 to 2012 and subsequently overhauled.										
1963	Continental S3 cabriolet (Mulliner,Park Ward)	BC56LXA	L	150-200.000 EUR	172.736	224.322	202.640	09-07-16	Le Mans	159	Art
	Black with red leather interior; some mechanical works carried out in recent years (see lots 13 Artcurial 15.12.03 $122,146, 242 Bonhams 15.5.04 NS, and 35 Artcurial 13.12.04 $102,745).										
1965	Continental S3 Flying Spur (Mulliner,Park Ward)	BC68XE	R	400-600.000 GBP	763.100	1.176.929	1.044.531	12-09-15	Goodwood	366	Bon F112
	Dark blue with beige leather interior; first owner the Rolling Stones lead guitarist Keith Richards who renamed the car "Blue Lena" in honour of the American singer Lena Horne. Richards retained the car until 1978 and subsequently it has had just two other owners prior to the current one who acquired it in 2006 and later had it fully restored (see lot 156 Christie's 7.9.96 NS).										
1963	Continental S3 Flying Spur (Mulliner,Park Ward)	BC92LXB	R	NA	174.720	247.753	220.881	20-04-16	Duxford	85	H&H
	Blue with white leather interior; reimported into the UK from the USA in 1972 and converted to right-hand drive. Since 1987 in the current ownership; body restored and repainted in 2009-10.										
1968	T saloon	RUE448F	R	NQ	13.440*	20.229*	19.120*	28-11-15	Weybridge	248	His
	Dark green; body repainted.										

F111: 1962 Bentley Continental S3 cabriolet (Mulliner,Park Ward)

F112: 1965 Bentley Continental S3 Flying Spur (Mulliner,Park Ward)

Year	Model (Bodybuilder)	Chassis No.	Steering	Estimate	Hammer Price £	$	€	Date	Place	Lot	Auc. H.
1979	T2 shooting brake (Panelcraft)	SBH37727	R	45-55.000 GBP		NS		01-12-15	London	318	Coy
	Dark green with vinyl roof and beige interior; since 1989 in the same family ownership. Stored for 10 years circa, the car has been recently recommissioned and the body has been repainted.										
1978	T2 saloon	SBH35120	R	15-18.000 GBP	11.500*	16.660*	14.771*	20-03-16	Goodwood	21	Bon
	Black with dark green leather interior; in good working order.										
1968	T cabriolet (Mulliner,Park Ward)	CBH4006	R	77.5-85.000 AUD		NS		24-10-15	Melbourne	42	TBr
	Blue with champagne leather interior; described as in largely original condition.										
1990	Mulsanne S	31932	R	20-30.000 GBP	29.813	45.387	42.168	14-11-15	Birmingham	623	SiC
	Beige and burgundy with parchment leather interior; in the same family ownership until 2012. 9,146 miles covered since new.										
1990	Continental cabriolet (Mulliner,Park Ward)	30100	R	40-50.000 GBP	67.020	102.051	91.623	05-09-15	Beaulieu	120	Bon F113
	Black with red interior; described as in very good overall condition. Body repainted in 2013.										
1990	Continental cabriolet (Mulliner,Park Ward)	30140	L	50-70.000 GBP	48.300	73.054	66.755	10-12-15	London	332	Bon
	Dark blue with light grey interior; in good overall condition.										
1994	Turbo R	54719	R	16-20.000 GBP	17.825	27.142	24.369	05-09-15	Beaulieu	189	Bon
	Racing green; 27,500 miles covered.										
1997	Turbo R	59416	L	22-28.000 EUR	18.946	28.681	26.400	08-11-15	Lyon	220	Ose
	Black with tan interior; in good overall condition.										
1997	Turbo R lwb	60202	R	5-7.000 GBP	18.400*	26.656*	23.633*	20-03-16	Goodwood	96	Bon
	Maroon with cream leather interior; 33,750 miles covered.										
1997	Turbo RT	66254	R	19-22.000 GBP		NS		30-07-16	Silverstone	918	SiC
	Ocean mica metallic with magnolia leather interior; showing some 47,300 miles.										
1995	Continental R	5350	L	50-70.000 EUR		NS		26-09-15	Frankfurt	107	Coy
	Burgundy with cream and red interior; sold new to Dubai, the car was reimported into the UK in 2010. Just under 19,000 kms covered.										
1999	Continental SC	65010	R	45-55.000 GBP	108.000	164.419	152.755	14-11-15	Birmingham	629	SiC
	Royal ebony with sandstone leather interior; in very good overall condition. Last serviced in April 2014 at 53,870 miles.										
1993	Continental R	52033	R	25-29.000 GBP	30.240	45.514	43.019	28-11-15	Weybridge	293	His
	British racing green with magnolia leather interior; 62,163 miles on the odometer (see lots 40 H&H 21.6.14 $ 41,028 and 276 Historics 29.11.14 NS).										
1997	Continental T	53404	L	90-120.000 EUR		NS		04-02-16	Paris	425	Bon
	Dark metallic green with beige leather interior; one owner and about 47,000 kms covered. Last serviced 500 kms ago.										
1995	Continental R	5350	L	45-55.000 EUR	46.467	66.953	59.000	14-05-16	Monaco	115	Coy
	See lot 107 Coys 26.9.15.										
1996	Continental R	53152	R	55-65.000 GBP		NS		18-05-16	Donington Park	59	H&H
	Silver with black interior; described as in very good overall condition. One of 10 special examples commissioned in 1996 by Jack Barclay to Mulliner, Park Ward.										
1993	Continental R	42644	R	28-32.000 GBP	25.200	36.681	32.521	18-05-16	Donington Park	71	H&H
	Black with magnolia interior; described as in very good overall condition.										
1993	Continental	52033	R	28-35.000 GBP	31.920	45.974	40.672	11-06-16	Brooklands	245	His
	See lot 293 Historics 28.11.15.										
1998	Continental T	67003	R	48-56.000 GBP	59.360	85.496	75.637	11-06-16	Brooklands	305	His F114
	Black; described as in very good overall condition.										
2001	Continental R420 Mulliner	63524	L	100-125.000 USD		NS		25-06-16	Santa Monica	1087	AA
	Black with black leather interior; one of 18 examples built in 2001.										
1993	Continental R	42678	L	35-45.000 EUR	36.579*	47.504*	42.912*	09-07-16	Le Mans	154	Art
	White with biscuit leather interior; 23,880 miles on the odometer. Last serviced in April 2016.										
2002	Continental R Le Mans	01761	L	120-145.000 USD	68.760	90.000	79.461	19-08-16	Monterey	F20	Mec
	Silver with light grey leather interior; 16,000 miles covered.										
1993	Continental R	42650	R	30-35.000 GBP	32.200	42.143	37.207	20-08-16	Brooklands	337	His
	Silver with ivory leather interior; described as in very good overall condition. 68,049 miles covered (see lot 265 Historics 29.8.15 $53,434).										
1996	Brooklands	58245	R	10-14.000 GBP	11.200	14.659	12.942	20-08-16	Brooklands	328	His
	Silver with grey leather interior; last serviced in 2015.										

F113: 1990 Bentley Continental cabriolet (Mulliner,Park Ward)

F114: 1998 Bentley Continental T

Year	Model	(Bodybuilder)	Chassis no.	Steering	Estimate	Hammer price £	$	€	Date	Place	Lot	Auc. H.
2007	**Azure**	(Pininfarina)	12302	L	NA	68.866*	104.500*	93.716*	26-09-15	Las Vegas	693	B/J
Red with cotswold interior; just over 18,000 original miles.												
1997	**Azure**	(Pininfarina)	61543	R	70-80.000 GBP	73.125	111.326	103.428	14-11-15	Birmingham	345	SiC
Royal blue with saddle leather interior; stored from 2009 to 2015, the car was serviced in August 2015 at 17,361 miles.												
1998	**Azure**	(Pininfarina)	6166	R	NA	66.000	93.436	85.180	06-03-16	Birmingham	352	SiC
Blue with cream leather interior; last serviced in December 2015 at 14,100 miles.												
1998	**Azure**	(Pininfarina)	61622	L	50-60.000 USD		NS		10-03-16	Amelia Island	108	Bon
British racing green with magnolia leather interior; in good driving order. From the Italian Vintage Cars Collection (see lot 731 Bonhams 18.9.11 NS).												
1998	**Azure**	(Pininfarina)	61606	L	50-70.000 EUR	74.491	106.464	96.000	12-03-16	Lyon	325	Agu
Dark blue with cream interior; described as in very good overall condition. 45,000 kms covered (see Artcurial lots 26 16.11.08 NS and 43 13.7.09 $ 115,375).												
2000	**Azure**	(Pininfarina)	62005	L	NA	35.946*	50.600*	44.528*	09-04-16	Palm Beach	135	B/J
White with cream interior; 32,840 actual miles.												
1998	**Azure**	(Pininfarina)	61686	R	35-40.000 GBP	44.070	64.148	56.872	18-05-16	Donington Park	25	H&H
Black with biscuit interior; described as in very good overall condition. 47,000 miles on the odometer.												
2000	**Azure**	(Pininfarina)	62033	L	68-76.000 GBP		NS		11-06-16	Brooklands	292	His
Silver with light grey leather interior; described as in very good overall condition (see lot 213 RM 3.10.12 $ 101,750).												
2001	**Azure**	(Pininfarina)	62538	L	40-60.000 EUR	53.316*	70.819*	63.600*	02-07-16	Lyon	352	Agu
Black with tan interior; sold new to the USA and later imported into France. Little used in the last years it requires servicing prior to use.												
2000	**Azure**	(Pininfarina)	62090	R	60-70.000 GBP	62.980	83.650	75.123	02-07-16	Woodstock	122	Coy
Three owners and 35,000 miles covered.												
2000	**Arnage Red Label**		05131	R	NA	17.640	27.132	23.779	14-10-15	Duxford	57	H&H
Red with cream interior; circa 62,000 miles covered.												
2008	**Arnage T Mulliner**		13534	R	58-64.000 GBP	60.000	90.306	85.356	28-11-15	Weybridge	266	His
Black with parchment leather interior; 16,452 miles covered.												
1999	**Arnage Green Label**		02198	R	18-24.000 GBP	25.200	37.929	35.850	28-11-15	Weybridge	274	His
Dark blue with beige leather interior; in very good overall condition. 35,000 miles on the odometer.												
2003	**Arnage Red Label**		09186	R	15-18.000 GBP	24.295	36.656	33.505	09-12-15	Chateau Impney	19	H&H
Black; 13,000 kms covered.												
2003	**Arnage T**		09419	R	28-34.000 GBP	31.920	45.620	41.135	12-03-16	Brooklands	191	His
Light metallic blue with blue leather interior; described as in very good overall condition.												
1998	**Arnage Green Label**		01344	R	12-15.000 GBP	16.240	23.390	20.693	11-06-16	Brooklands	225	His
Recently serviced.												
2007	**Arnage T Mulliner**		12255	R	32-37.000 GBP	48.720	70.171	62.079	11-06-16	Brooklands	293	His
Black with parchment leather interior; 32,000 miles covered.												
2000	**Arnage Red Label**		05454	R	12-16.000 GBP	15.904	20.815	18.377	20-08-16	Brooklands	279	His
Green with cream leather interior; in good overall condition.												
2016	**Continental GT V8 S convertible**		58251	R	NQ	250.000*	342.600*	309.575*	24-06-16	Goodwood	244	Bon F115
Unique design by Sir Peter Blake. Hand built by Bentley's Mulliner division. New and unregistered. All proceeds to the Care2Save charity.												

BENZ (D) *(1885-1926)*

Year	Model		Chassis no.	Steering	Estimate	£	$	€	Date	Place	Lot	Auc. H.
1914	**8/20 PS tourer**		15996(engine)	L	80-120.000 EUR	30.873*	44.484*	39.200*	14-05-16	Monaco	112	RMS F116
Red with black wings and black interior; restored at unspecified date. Since 1962 in the Quattroruote Collection.												

BERLIET (F) *(1895-1939)*

Year	Model		Chassis no.	Steering	Estimate	£	$	€	Date	Place	Lot	Auc. H.
1926	**7cv Type VI torpedo**		5077	R	11-13.000 EUR	7.535	11.407	10.500	08-11-15	Lyon	202	Ose
Since 1977 in the current ownership; restored in 2013.												

F115: 2016 Bentley Continental GT V8 S convertible

F116: 1914 Benz 8/20 PS tourer

Year	Model	(Bodybuilder)	Chassis no.	Steering	Estimate	Hammer price £	Hammer price $	Hammer price €	Date	Place	Lot	Auc. H.

BERTONE (I) (1921-2012)

1984 X1/9 VS 7151709 R NA 11.813 16.724 15.246 06-03-16 Birmingham 350 SiC
Red and dark grey with black leather interior; in good overall condition. 19,400 miles covered.

BIZZARRINI (I) (1965-1969)

1966 5300 GT Strada (Sports Cars/Giugiaro) IA30248 L 495-700.000 GBP NS   07-09-15 London 110 RMS
Black with black interior; aluminium body. Raced at some events in Italy and France in the 1960s and 1970s. The original engine was replaced at unspecified date with the present 350 bhp 327 Chevrolet unit. Restored in Germany between 2008 and 2010. From the Fendt Collection.

1978 P538 "Lavost" B04 L 750-950.000 USD NS   20-08-16 Monterey S111 Mec
Red; commissioned by French Jacques Lavost, the car is one of the examples built by Bizzarrini after the closing of the factory, using the same components as the originals. Chevrolet 327 V8 engine rebuilt in 2013. ASI homologated (see lot S186 Mecum 16.8.14 NS).

BLACKHAWK (USA) (1929-1930)

1930 Model L-6 2-door speedster L64DA40L L 90-120.000 USD NS   05-10-15 Philadelphia 217 Bon
Restored many years ago, the car is described as in good running order.

BMW (D) (1929-)

1936 315/328 roadster 69850 L 290-330.000 EUR NS   16-01-16 Maastricht 437 Coy
Car rebuilt within the last five years using an original BMW 315 chassis, original front and rear axles from a 328, a BMW engine with Bristol cylinder head and Volvo 4-speed gearbox. Roadster type new body finished in red with black interior.

1935 315 sports cabriolet 44635 L 60-90.000 EUR 48.916 69.887 62.100 18-06-16 Wien 434 Dor
Cream with black leather interior; built with 4-seater cabriolet body, the car was rebodied after WWII. Since 1985 in the current ownership; restored at unspecified date.

1936 319 cabriolet (Reutter) 56716 L 60-90.000 EUR 61.598 88.006 78.200 18-06-16 Wien 421 Dor
Two-tone grey with grey leather interior; last registered in 1959, the car was discovered in the early 2000s and subsequently restored. Currently fitted with a 315 engine.

1936 319 cabriolet (Drauz) 86421 L 60-70.000 GBP NS   10-07-16 Chateau Impney 72 H&H
Grey and blue with black leatherette interior; restored in the 1990s, the car is described as in good overall condition.

1941 327 coupé 87282 L 150-170.000 EUR NS   26-09-15 Frankfurt 110 Coy
Black and cream with dark red interior; restored (see lot 525 Coys 12.10.13 $ 201,591).

1938 327 cabriolet 73246 L 140-170.000 EUR 100.267 152.171 136.464 26-09-15 Frankfurt 144 Coy
Dark green and black; acquired in 1990 by the current owner and subsequently restored. In the 1950s the car was fitted with a 501 engine (the original unit is included with the sale). Also it was fitted during the restoration with a 5-speed Volvo gearbox. F117

1939 327/28 cabriolet 74497 L NA NS   14-10-15 Duxford 56 H&H
Cream with black interior; acquired in 1990 by the current owner, and subsequently restored.

1937 327/28 cabriolet 74582 L 350-450.000 USD NS   10-03-16 Amelia Island 185 Bon
Two-tone blue with blue interior; discovered in the USA in the 1980s and subsequently subjected to a long restoration recently completed.

1940 327 cabriolet 87220 L 120-160.000 EUR 157.495* 204.529* 184.760* 09-07-16 Le Mans 122 Art
Black and red with red interior; bought in 1999 by the current owner and subsequently restored. 8,857 kms covered since the restoration.

1938 327 cabriolet 229523 L 140-160.000 EUR NS   06-08-16 Schloss Dyck 153 Coy
Two-tone blue with blue interior; in very good overall condition. For 25 years in the current ownership.

1937 328 cabriolet 85043 L 220-270.000 GBP 326.300 503.252 446.639 12-09-15 Goodwood 328 Bon
Since 1968 in the same ownership, the car requires full restoration.

1938 328 roadster 85378 L 550-650.000 GBP 539.100 831.454 737.920 12-09-15 Goodwood 368 Bon
White with dark red interior; in the same ownership in Sweden from 1965 to 2013, the car was fully restored between 2009 and 2011. Currently fitted with a Volvo gearbox, it is offered with several spare sparts, including two gearboxes. F118

1939 328 roadster 85351 L 700-900.000 USD 420.200* 550.000* 485.595* 19-08-16 Monterey 123 RMS
Silver; the car has been driven at numerous historical events in the past 30 years. Since 1996 in the current ownership, it is documented with service and restoration invoices dating to 1998. Fitted with a proper period BMW engine in 328 configuration and with a Volvo synchromesh gearbox (a period-correct BMW gearbox is included with the sale).

1938 320 cabriolet (Autenrieth) 93644 L 75-95.000 EUR NS   04-02-16 Paris 371 Bon
Dark red and black with red interior; since 1989 in the current ownership. Engine rebuilt some years ago; body repainted in recent times. The gearbox has covered 130 kms since the rebuild.

F117: 1938 BMW 327 cabriolet

F118: 1938 BMW 328 roadster

Year	Model (Bodybuilder)	Chassis No.	Steering	Estimate	Hammer price £	Hammer price $	Hammer price €	Sale Date	Sale Place	Lot	Auc. H.
1938	320 coupé	93343	L	NA	39.072*	55.000*	48.400*	09-04-16	Palm Beach	138	B/J
Red and black with red leather interior; an older restoration.											
1956	501 saloon	46866	L	35-40.000 EUR		NS		28-05-16	Aarhus	127	SiC
Blue; restored in the 1990s probably.											
1955	502 cabriolet	61001	L	140-160.000 EUR		NS		06-08-16	Schloss Dyck	116	Coy
Silver with cream leather interior; fully restored.											
1959	507 roadster	70205	L	2.300-2.600.000 USD		NS		10-12-15	New York	210	RMS
Black with red leather interior; restored in the USA in the late 1980s, the car is described as still in very good overall condition.											
1957	507 roadster	70131	L	1.900-2.200.000 EUR	1.518.653	2.204.093	2.016.000	03-02-16	Paris	150	RMS F119
White with red interior; sold new to Switzerland, the car remained for 43 years from 1969 in the same ownership. Original engine replaced in the 1960s by the present unit supplied by BMW Munich. In original condition except for the paintwork redone in the 1970s. Last serviced in March 2015.											
1957	507 roadster	70044	L	2.400-2.700.000 USD		NS		20-08-16	Monterey	226	RMS
Light green with original red leather interior and black hardtop; sold new in Germany, the car remained in single ownership from 1963 to 2014 when it was acquired by the current, fourth owner. Described as in largely original condition except for the paintwork redone twice in the car's early life. The front brakes have been recently replaced and the original ones are included with the sale. 73,000 kms on the odometer.											
1955	Isetta 250	408585	L	15-20.000 GBP		NS		16-04-16	Ascot	131	Coy
Yellow; recently restored.											
1961	Isetta 300	590666	L	20-30.000 EUR	28.028	40.604	36.000	20-03-16	Fontainebleau	319	Ose
White and red; restored.											
1958	Limousine 600	122850	L	40-60.000 USD	17.303*	24.750*	22.698*	28-01-16	Phoenix	175	RMS
Blue with white roof; restored in the 2000s. From the Craig McCaw Collection (see lot 105 RM 13.3.10 $ 74,250).											
1959	Limousine 600	131144	L	30-40.000 EUR		NS		09-04-16	Essen	214	Coy
Grey; for 26 years on display in a museum in Italy.											
1958	Limousine 600	132907	L	NQ	26.893	35.200	31.078	20-08-16	Monterey	7079	R&S
Yellow with white roof; restored.											
1962	700 2-door saloon	00801895	L	7-9.000 EUR	7.705*	12.201*	10.728*	01-11-15	Paris	160	Art F120
White; since 2009 with the present, third owner who subsequently subjected the car to several mechanicals works.											
1963	700 Sport coupé	810083	R	12-15.000 GBP		NS		28-11-15	Weybridge	213	His
White; an older restoration, the car is described as in very good working order.											
1965	3200 CS (Bertone)	76466	L	50-70.000 EUR	38.331	58.798	51.750	09-10-15	Zoute	48	Bon F121
Silver with original dark red leather interior; restored in Spain in 2014-15.											
1965	3200 CS (Bertone)	76533	L	60-70.000 GBP		NS		24-06-16	Goodwood	272	Bon
Blue with light brown interior; fully restored in 1991-92.											
1969	1800 saloon	1907035	L	6.5-8.500 EUR	6.889	10.429	9.600	07-11-15	Lyon	249	Agu
Black with habana leather interior; in good overall condition. Three owners.											
1968	2000 CS (Karmann)	1108579	L	20-25.000 EUR	15.799	22.764	20.060	14-05-16	Monaco	164	Coy
White; cosmetic restoration. Leather interior.											
1973	2002 cabriolet	2791175	R	8-9.000 GBP	7.345	11.082	10.129	09-12-15	Chateau Impney	7	H&H
Yellow; restored several years ago.											
1973	2002 Ti	1653598	R	38-45.000 GBP	44.360	63.577	58.249	16-01-16	Birmingham	344	Coy
Blue with yellow stripe; prepared for historic racing to Group 2 specification.											
1971	2002 cabriolet	2790182	L	30-40.000 EUR	47.712*	69.434*	61.984*	05-02-16	Paris	110	Art F122
Light grey with original blue interior; body repainted in 2014. Engine replaced.											
1970	2002 Tii	16538442	R	NA	32.060	44.807	40.713	26-02-16	Coventry	113	SiC
Prepared for historic racing to Group 2 specification.											
1974	2002 Touring	03462285	L	10-15.000 EUR	11.343	16.206	14.400	19-06-16	Fontainebleau	362	Ose
Silver; described as in very good condition. Body recently repainted.											
1973	2002 Touring	3441243	R	8-10.000 GBP	4.928	6.450	5.694	20-08-16	Brooklands	225	His
Maroon with tan interior; in good overall condition. One owner and 69,000 miles covered.											

F119: 1957 BMW 507 roadster

F120: 1962 BMW 700 2-door saloon

Year	Model	(Bodybuilder)	Chassis no.	Steering	Estimate	Hammer price £	$	€	Date	Sale Place	Lot	Auc. H.

F121: 1965 BMW 3200 CS (Bertone)

F122: 1971 BMW 2002 cabriolet

Year	Model	Chassis no.	Steering	Estimate	£	$	€	Date	Place	Lot	Auc. H.
1974	**2002 Turbo**	4290165	L	60-80.000 EUR	39.120*	57.991*	51.750*	04-02-16	Paris	390	**Bon** F123
	Silver; registered in Spain.										
1977	**2002 Turbo**	4290203	L	65-75.000 EUR	51.667	72.723	64.000	09-04-16	Essen	142	Coy
	Silver with black interior; in good condition (see lot 361 Bonhams 20.4.09 $ 40,227).										
1974	**2002 Turbo**	4290927	L	85-105.000 EUR		NS		02-07-16	Lyon	339	Agu
	White; described as in very good overall condition. Engine rebuilt in 2011.										
1974	**2002 Turbo**	4290233	L	NQ	88.242	115.500	101.975	20-08-16	Monterey	7045	R&S
	White; purchased in December 2014 by the current owner and subsequently restored.										
1972	**3.0 CSI**	2261598	L	NA	22.494	34.500	30.367	09-10-15	Chicago	F117.1	Mec
	Blue with black interior; body repainted.										
1972	**3.0 CSA**	2231128	R	42-47.000 GBP	45.000	68.508	63.648	14-11-15	Birmingham	341	SiC
	Metallic blue; in very good overall condition. 10,925 on the odometer. Recently serviced.										
1974	**3.0 CSI**	4340282	L	28-33.000 EUR	25.192	36.106	33.082	16-01-16	Maastricht	423	Coy
	Metallic blue; in good condition.										
1975	**3.0 CS**	430722	L	28-35.000 EUR	24.736	34.817	30.641	09-04-16	Essen	113	Coy
	Blue with blue interior; described as in very good mechanical condition. Gearbox recently rebuilt.										
1975	**3.0 CSI**	2265967	R	43-48.000 GBP		NS		02-07-16	Woodstock	238	Coy
	Fjord metallic with blue interior; described as in good overall condition. Manual gearbox.										
1972	**3.0 CS**	2240219	L	15-25.000 EUR	21.989	28.924	25.927	06-08-16	Schloss Dyck	120	Coy
	White with red interior.										
1973	**3.0 CSL Group 2**	2275236	L	220-260.000 EUR	179.780	284.689	250.320	01-11-15	Paris	164	**Art** F124
	Finished in orange, it is one of three cars prepared in period by Heidegger. Mechanicals restored for the 2015 Tour Auto. Offered with FIA Techical Passport.										
1973	**3.0 CSL**	2275449	L	275-350.000 USD	238.393	341.000	312.731	28-01-16	Scottsdale	25	Bon
	Silver with black interior; fitted with the "Batmobile" aerodynamic package. Sold new to France, the car was also part of a German collection. Described as in very good overall condition, the car is still fitted with the original engine and gearbox and has less than 40,000 kms on the odometer.										
1972	**3.0 CSL**	2275051	L	110-125.000 EUR	83.705	117.817	103.685	09-04-16	Essen	158	Coy
	Metallic fjordblau; until 2003 with its first owner. Decribed as in very good overall condition. Body repainted to the original colour.										
1972	**3.0 CSL**	2285033	R	100-150.000 GBP	102.300	140.192	126.678	24-06-16	Goodwood	227	Bon
	Red with black interior; restored in the mid-1980s.										
1980	**M1 (Italdesign)**	301080	L	450-650.000 EUR	344.981	529.185	465.750	09-10-15	Zoute	22	Bon
	Orange with black leather and cloth interior; described as in good overall condition, the car has covered 62,443 kms. Since 1994 in the current ownership.										
1981	**M1 (Italdesign)**	301426	L	800-1.000.000 USD		NS		10-12-15	New York	217	RMS
	White with black-chequered cloth interior; the car remained unsold at a Pennsylvania BMW dealership until 2015. In original condition; 682 kms covered; recently serviced.										

F123: 1974 BMW 2002 Turbo

F124: 1973 BMW 3.0 CSL Group 2

Year	Model	(Bodybuilder)	Chassis no.	Steering	Estimate	Hammer price £	Hammer price $	Hammer price €	Date	Place	Lot	Auc. H.
1980	M1	(Italdesign)	4301096	L	525-625.000 USD		NS		28-01-16	Scottsdale	98	Bon
	*Orange with original black interior; 36,000 kms on the odometer. Sold new in Germany, the car was later exported to Mexico where it remained for many years prior to be imported into the USA (see Mecum lots S194 16.8.14 NS and S65 15.8.15 NS).*											
1978	M1	(Italdesign)	4301011	L	400-500.000 USD	209.730	300.000	275.130	28-01-16	Phoenix	131	RMS
	*Dark metallic blue with black leather interior; BMW press vehicle when new, the car has resided in California since 1981. In single ownership for 25 years. Original engine replaced at unspecified date (see lot 443 RM 6.2.09 NS).*											
1980	M1	(Italdesign)	4301006	L	575-650.000 USD		NS		30-01-16	Scottsdale	149	G&Co
	*Orange; sold new to the USA to racing driver Alf Gebhardt. In largely original condition; 21,000 kms covered; three owners.*											
1981	M1	(Italdesign)	4301393	L	500-600.000 USD		NS		02-04-16	Ft.Lauderdale	525	AA
	*Dark blue with black leather and cloth interior; one owner. 13,500 kms on the odometer.*											
1978	M1	(Italdesign)	4301013	L	550-650.000 EUR		NS		09-04-16	Essen	125	Coy
	*Red with black/grey interior; first registered to BMW themselves.*											
1981	M1	(Italdesign)	4301413	L	180-220.000 GBP	303.900	416.465	376.319	24-06-16	Goodwood	245	Bon
	*White; since 1987 in the current ownership. 3,049 miles on the odometer.*											
1981	M1	(Italdesign)	301348	L	450-600.000 USD	441.210	577.500	509.875	19-08-16	Monterey	149	RMS F125
	*Orange with leather and cloth interior; the car remained in the ownership of an Italian BMW dealer until 1984 when it was sold to Japan. Described as in very good original condition, it has covered 12,838 miles.*											
1986	M635 CSI		1053019	L	45-65.000 EUR	49.405	75.785	66.700	09-10-15	Zoute	4	Bon F126
	*Silver with black leather interior; in very good original condition. Three owners and 75,000 kms covered.*											
1983	635 CSI		1185941	R	40-45.000 AUD	16.988	26.168	23.609	24-10-15	Melbourne	16	TBr
	*Restored between 2000 and 2006 as a JPS tribute car to the mid-1980s Australian Touring Car Championship car driven by Denny Hulme among others.*											
1989	635 CSI		188545	R	8-11.000 GBP	8.176	12.306	11.631	28-11-15	Weybridge	234	His
	*Graphite grey with grey leather interior; described as in very good overall condition.*											
1985	M635 CSI		760069	R	20-25.000 GBP	27.600	41.745	38.146	10-12-15	London	317	Bon
	*White; recommissioned and serviced in 2014.*											
1985	M635 CSI		1051218	L	40-60.000 EUR	32.114*	46.735*	41.720*	05-02-16	Paris	114	Art
	*Grey with black interior; described as in good overall condition. Two owners.*											
1987	M635 CSI		2560534	L	30-40.000 USD	14.770*	20.900*	19.249*	10-03-16	Amelia Island	117	Bon
	*Red; two owners. In good overall condition.*											
1985	M635 CSI		1052229	L	35-45.000 USD	17.102*	24.200*	22.288*	10-03-16	Amelia Island	200	Bon
	*Blue with blue leather interior; in good overall condition.*											
1985	M635 CSI		760168	R	16-20.000 GBP	15.300	21.867	19.717	12-03-16	Brooklands	161	His
	*Blue with black leather interior; in good driving order. Manual gearbox.*											
1987	M635 CSI		1053187	L	35-45.000 EUR	40.644*	52.782*	47.680*	09-07-16	Le Mans	104	Art
	*Red; described as in good overall condition. One owner and 132,102 kms covered.*											
1989	325i cabriolet		8862129	L	NA	13.675*	19.250*	16.940*	09-04-16	Palm Beach	638	B/J
	*Blue; automatic transmission.*											
1988	M6		561631	L	85-100.000 USD	68.760	90.000	79.461	19-08-16	Monterey	F67	Mec
	*Red with natural leather interior; in original condition. 25,000 miles covered.*											
1992	M3 Sport Evolution		79303	L	75-125.000 EUR	64.207	101.675	89.400	01-11-15	Paris	163	Art F127
	*Black; since new in the same family ownership. The car requires servicing prior to use. Never raced.*											
1999	M3 Evolution cabriolet		EX67101	R	NA	21.938*	33.398*	31.029*	14-11-15	Birmingham	604	SiC
	*Red with grey leather interior; one owner and 30,000 miles covered.*											
1989	M3		40794	L	NA	42.750	59.747	54.288	26-02-16	Coventry	406	SiC
	*Red with anthracite and black interior; described as in very good working order. Body repainted several years ago.*											
1987	M3		90573	L	40-55.000 GBP	39.880	56.550	50.113	16-04-16	Ascot	109	Coy
	*Black; described as in very good overall condition.*											
1987	M3		691681	L	35-45.000 EUR	34.982	46.015	41.247	06-08-16	Schloss Dyck	137	Coy
	*Silver; 65,500 kms on the odometer.*											

F125: 1981 BMW M1 (Italdesign)

F126: 1986 BMW M635 CSI

Year	Model (Bodybuilder)	Chassis no.	Steering	Estimate	Hammer price £	$	€	Sale Date	Place	Lot	Auc. H.
1990	**M3 Sport Evolution**	79052	L	65-80.000 GBP	78.400	102.610	90.591	20-08-16	Brooklands	283	His
Black; sold new to Italy and imported into the UK in 2005. Top-end engine rebuild in 2010.												
1986	**M5**	10184485	L	50-60.000 EUR	36.153	50.887	44.783	09-04-16	Essen	115	Coy
Black with grey interior; restored. For 29 years in single ownership.												
1986	**M5**	1018409	L	55-65.000 EUR	37.741	55.282	49.500	28-05-16	Aarhus	228	SiC
White with black leather interior; recommissioned in recent years.												
1988	**M5**	791970	L	50-75.000 USD	36.978*	48.400*	42.732*	19-08-16	Carmel	59	Bon
Black with tan interior; mechanicals overhauled in 2014. Less than 85,000 miles covered since new.												
1990	**Z1**	05313	L	NA	35.840	50.821	45.309	20-04-16	Duxford	76	H&H
Metallic blue with cream leather and cloth interior; sold new to Oman and imported into the UK in 2001. Recently serviced.												
1989	**Z1**	01387	L	35-55.000 EUR	75.175	108.317	95.450	13-05-16	Monaco	104	Bon **F128**
Red with black interior; one owner and approximately 2,800 kms covered.												
1990	**Z1**	03134	L	50-100.000 USD	77.737*	101.750*	89.835*	19-08-16	Carmel	67	Bon
Red; the car remained in the ownership of an Italian BMW dealer for over 20 years and subsequently it was bought by the present, second owner. 35 kms covered.												
1991	**850i**	13160	L	80-90.000 EUR	66.905	97.999	87.750	28-05-16	Aarhus	112	SiC
One owner and 1,759 kms covered. Manual gearbox. Last serviced in June 2015.												
1991	**850i**	12556	L	11-16.000 EUR	12.575	16.703	15.000	02-07-16	Lyon	327	Agu
Metallic red with grey leather interior; two owners. Body repainted in 2003.												
1999	**Z3M coupé**	29610	R	25-28.000 GBP		NS		14-11-15	Birmingham	642	SiC
Blue with blue and black leather interior; 45,000 miles covered.												
2003	**Z3 M coupé**	69227	R	44-52.000 GBP	51.520	74.204	65.647	11-06-16	Brooklands	291	His
Titanium grey with red and black leather interior; one onwer and less than 11,000 miles covered.												
2002	**Z8**	61329	L	NA		NS		31-10-15	Hilton Head	147	AA
Titanium grey with black leather interior; 543 miles covered. With hardtop.												
2000	**Z8**	77434	L	150-200.000 EUR	201.613	319.263	280.720	01-11-15	Paris	139	Art **F129**
Grey with red leather interior; 27,500 kms covered.												
2001	**Z8**	79219	L	100-130.000 GBP	127.240	191.687	180.833	01-12-15	London	329	Coy
Silver with red and black leather interior; sold new to the UK. Since 2005 in the same family ownership.												
2000	**Z8**	77771	L	130-160.000 GBP	147.400	211.254	193.551	16-01-16	Birmingham	326	Coy
Silver with black interior; 17,000 miles covered.												
2002	**Z8**	61329	L	275-325.000 USD	184.562*	264.000*	242.114*	28-01-16	Phoenix	164	RMS
See lot 147 Auctions America 31.10.15.												
2002	**Z8**	79499	L	180-220.000 EUR	147.788	219.077	195.500	04-02-16	Paris	351	Bon
Black with red and black interior; just less than 33,500 miles covered. With hardtop.												
2002	**Z8**	61368	L	175-225.000 USD	132.153	187.000	172.227	10-03-16	Amelia Island	148	Bon
Silver with black and red leather interior; in excellent overall condition. Less than 12,000 miles covered. With hardtop.												
2001	**Z8**	60971	L	220-240.000 USD	149.893	214.500	187.623	02-04-16	Ft.Lauderdale	542	AA
Black with tan leather interior; just over 7,000 miles covered. With hardtop.												
2001	**Z8**	61046	L	NA	132.845	187.000	164.560	09-04-16	Palm Beach	432	B/J
Silver with black interior; 20,000 actual miles.												
2003	**Z8**	77674	L	175-225.000 EUR	144.915	208.803	184.000	13-05-16	Monaco	122	Bon
In good overall condition; circa 23,000 kms covered.												
2001	**Z8**	60797	L	120-140.000 GBP		NS		20-05-16	Silverstone	319	SiC
Titanium grey with black leather interior; 39,900 miles on the odometer. Last serviced in May 2014.												
2000	**Z8**	60073	L	200-250.000 USD	138.442	189.750	171.458	25-06-16	Santa Monica	1105	AA
Sold new to Pennsylvania, the car remained for many years with the owner of the dealership.												
2002	**Z8**	61275	L	125-175.000 USD	105.308	138.600	124.712	30-07-16	Plymouth	126	RMS
Tungsten grey with black leather interior; 23,385 miles covered. With hardtop.												

F127: 1992 BMW M3 Sport Evolution

F128: 1989 BMW Z1

Year	Model	(Bodybuilder)	Chassis no.	Steering	Estimate	Hammer price £	Hammer price $	Hammer price €	Sale Date	Sale Place	Lot	Auc. H.
2002	Z8		61661	L	180-220.000 USD	138.666	181.500	160.246	19-08-16	Carmel	113	Bon
Titanium grey with red and black interior; one owner and 8,500 miles covered. Recently serviced.												
2002	Z8		61881	L	200-240.000 USD		NS		20-08-16	Monterey	S154	Mec
Silver with black leather interior; 12,645 miles covered.												

BOCAR (USA)

Year	Model	(Bodybuilder)	Chassis no.	Steering	Estimate	£	$	€	Date	Place	Lot	Auc. H.
1959	XP-5		003	L	500-700.000 USD	315.150	412.500	364.196	19-08-16	Monterey	153	RMS
Meister Brauser III blue and black livery; fitted with the 283 Chevrolet Corvette engine, the car was raced at SCCA events and was driven by Augie Pabst and Harry Heuer. In single ownership from 1970 to 2014. Restored in 2014.												F130

BRISCOE (USA) (1914-1821)

Year	Model	(Bodybuilder)	Chassis no.	Steering	Estimate	£	$	€	Date	Place	Lot	Auc. H.
1917	Model B 4-24 touring		23990	L	18-24.000 USD	18.842*	28.600*	25.454*	05-10-15	Philadelphia	225	Bon
Red with black fenders; from the Evergreen Collection.												F131

BRISTOL (GB) (1947-)

Year	Model	(Bodybuilder)	Chassis no.	Steering	Estimate	£	$	€	Date	Place	Lot	Auc. H.
1948	400 coupé		4001368	R	55-60.000 GBP	55.200	79.968	70.899	20-03-16	Goodwood	80	Bon
Restored in Australia in the late 1990s and later reimported into the UK.												
1947	400 cabriolet	(Pinin Farina)	4001102	R	300-400.000 EUR	176.418	254.195	224.000	14-05-16	Monaco	249	RMS
Only example built, the car was exhibited at the 1947 Geneva Motor Show. It was fitted with the first prototype Frazer Nash-specification Bristol sports engine, number FNS 1001, and rallied until 1949. Fully restored between 1989 and 1999.												F132
1950	402 cabriolet		402718	R	30-50.000 GBP	104.540	159.183	142.917	05-09-15	Beaulieu	111	Bon
For restoration; in the same family ownership since 1969.												
1959	406 coupé		407113	R	NQ	5.900*	8.888*	8.385*	01-12-15	London	303	Coy
Prototype of a model never gone into production, the car is fitted with a Armstrong-Siddeley Star Sapphire 6-cylinder engine and DG Borg Warner automatic transmission. For restoration.												
1964	408		7043	R	10-12.000 AUD	5.840	8.995	8.116	24-10-15	Melbourne	6	TBr
Restoration project.												
1965	408		4087211	R	35-45.000 GBP		NS		11-06-16	Brooklands	264	His
Dark blue with black interior; in good overall condition. Sunroof; automatic transmission.												
1972	411		7640206	R	32-36.000 GBP	30.380	39.980	35.976	30-07-16	Silverstone	545	SiC
Light metallic blue; restored several years ago. Recent mechanical works (see lot 38 H & H 21.6.14 $36,257).												

BSA (GB) (1907-1939)

Year	Model	(Bodybuilder)	Chassis no.	Steering	Estimate	£	$	€	Date	Place	Lot	Auc. H.
1933	Three Wheeler		WRG213A	R	NA	7.280	10.127	9.222	24-02-16	Donington Park	30	H&H
For restoration; two-cylinder Hotchkiss engine.												

BUCKMOBILE (USA) (1903-1905)

Year	Model	(Bodybuilder)	Chassis no.	Steering	Estimate	£	$	€	Date	Place	Lot	Auc. H.
1904	15hp runabout		244	R	40-60.000 USD	30.760*	44.000*	40.352*	28-01-16	Scottsdale	54	Bon
Wooden body and leather interior; bought in 2012 by the current owner, the car received subsequently some restoration works (see lot 413 Bonhams 8.10.12 $ 46,000).												F133

BUGATTI (F) (1909-1956)

Year	Model	(Bodybuilder)	Chassis no.	Steering	Estimate	£	$	€	Date	Place	Lot	Auc. H.
1920	Type 23/13		981	R	360-420.000 EUR	275.263	400.584	357.600	05-02-16	Paris	183	Art
Black with black interior; probably sold new in France, the car reappeared in the early 1960s in the USA. Later it was part of the Ben Moser Collection and in the late 1980s of the Hayashi Collection in Japan. In the mid-1990s it was reimported into the USA where probably the chassis was shortened to the Type 13 specification and fitted with the present, new, Brescia style body. According to the historian David Sewell's research the chassis, engine and gearbox are original. UK papers (see lots 108 Gooding 19.8.12 $ 379,500 and 108 RM 8.9.14 NS).												F134
1925	Type 30 torpedo		4409	R	400-500.000 EUR		NS		26-09-15	Frankfurt	139	Coy
Red with black interior; sold new to Germany, the car was rediscovered after WWII in the Dresden area. Acquired in 1983 by the current owner, it received a long restoration completed in the late 1990s. It still bears its original body, engine, gearbox and rear axle.												
1925	Type 30 torpedo		4409	R	300-350.000 GBP		NS		01-12-15	London	325	Coy
See lot 139 Coys 26.9.15.												
1925	Type 30 torpedo		4725	R	500-650.000 USD		NS		12-03-16	Amelia Island	157	RMS
Yellow with black wings and brown leather interior; unknown coachbuilder. The car remained in the same family ownership from new to 1960. Later it was refinished in the present livery and fitted with the present engine no.418. For two decades in the current ownership, it is described as still in good overall condition.												
1925	Type 35		4450	R	1.000-1.500.000 EUR	833.260	1.200.618	1.058.000	13-05-16	Monaco	118	Bon
Light blue with yellow stripe on the bonnet; bought new by Glen Kidston, the car had a long race career with several owners over the years. In 1938 it was acquired by Lyndon Duckett, who fitted it with an Anzani R1 engine and later imported it into Australia. Driven in the years at several races and historic events, since 1964 the car is with the current owner who fully restored it between 2006 and 2008. Also numerous original parts were used during the restoration and the car is currently fitted again with a Bugatti engine, no.75C.												F135
1927	Type 38A Grand Sport		38470	R	400-600.000 USD	305.448	440.000	389.224	11-06-16	Hershey	127	TFA
Maroon with tan leather interior; sold new to the UK, the car was raced at several events and in the early 1930s the chassis was shortened and the car fitted with the not supercharged engine no.209 from chassis 38275. After some ownership changes, the car was exported to the USA where in 1991 it was acquired by the JWR Collection and fully restored. The chassis was returned to its correct long-wheelbase form and fitted with a new body, and the engine was fitted with an original Bugatti supercharger.												
1928	Type 40 boattail roadster		40532	R	150-200.000 EUR	132.313*	190.646*	168.000*	14-05-16	Monaco	222	RMS
The car was restored in Italy around 1964 when the body was modified to its present specification and finished in blue; from the Count Agusta Collection. The engine is believed to be a replacement and restamped 40532.												
1929	Type 40A roadster		40748	R	425-500.000 USD	260.325	375.000	331.725	11-06-16	Hershey	144	TFA
Two-tone grey with grey leather interior; sold new in France, the car was imported into the USA after WWII. Since 1961 in the same family ownership; restored to concours condition in 2004; engine rebuilt in 2015.												

F129: 2000 BMW Z8

F130: 1959 Bocar XP-5

F131: 1917 Briscoe Model B 4-24 touring

F132: 1947 Bristol 400 cabriolet (Pinin Farina)

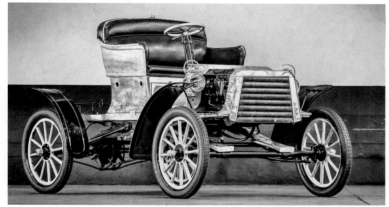
F133: 1904 Buckmobile 15hp runabout

F134: 1920 Bugatti Type 23/13

F135: 1925 Bugatti Type 35

F136: 1931 Bugatti Type 49 roadster (Gangloff)

Year	Model	(Bodybuilder)	Chassis No.	Steering	Estimate	Hammer Price £	Hammer Price $	Hammer Price €	Sale Date	Sale Place	Lot	Auc. H.
1927	Type 52		127	R	25-35.000 EUR	53.393	80.828	74.400	07-11-15	Lyon	245	Agu
	French blue; since the 1930s in the same family ownership. Repainted and retrimmed in the 1970s.											
1931	Type 49 roadster	(Gangloff)	49431	R	900-1.100.000 USD	595.983	852.500	781.828	28-01-16	Phoenix	128	RMS
	Red with black wings and black interior; in driving order. Registered new in France, the car was acquired in 1967 circa by Jess Pourret who reported the car to Bugatti historian Hugh Conway as chassis 49431 with engine 275. Later the car was owned by Michel Seydoux who resold it through Edgar Bensoussan. At some point the car gained the serial number tag 49122 but according to recent historical research by Kees Jansen it is actually 49431 with engine 275, transmission 277, rear axle 277 and Gangloff body 393.											F136
1931	Type 49 Grand Sport tourer	(Compton)	49119	R	550-750.000 USD	673.461	962.500	881.361	30-01-16	Scottsdale	143	G&Co
	Blue with largely original brown leather interior; displayed at the Bugatti stand at the 1931 Olympia Motor Show in London, in January 1932 the car was delivered to its first owner who retained it until 1973. Bought by the Stratford upon Avon Motor Museum, the car remained on display until 1975 when it was acquired by the current, third owner and imported into the USA. Body repainted at unspecified date.											F137
1931	Type 51		51121	R	Refer Dpt.	3.056.000	4.000.000	3.531.600	19-08-16	Carmel	36	Bon
	The car was acquired new by Lord Howe who raced it until late 1934 and had it driven also by Brian Lewis and Piero Taruffi. From 1935 to 1939 it had some owners and was entered at several races. In 1954 the car was acquired by A.M. Mackay and later rebuilt by Bugatti specialist Geoffrey St. John. In 1983 Mackay sold it to the present owner who imported it into the USA. Unused for many years, the car has been recently checked and made to run again, but it requires a through recommissioning prior to be used or campaigned properly.											F138
1932	Type 55 Roadster		55213	R	10-14.000.000 USD	7.945.606	10.400.000	9.182.160	21-08-16	Pebble Beach	135	G&Co
	The car was entered by the factory at the 1932 Mille Miglia for Achille Varzi and Count Luigi Castelbarco. Little is known of the car until 1946 when it was owned by Georges Metz, Orleans. In 1951 it was purchased by Jean-Baptiste Altieri, Paris, who resold it in 1983 to Nicolas Seydoux, Paris. In 2008 it was bought by Peter Livanos, Switzerland, who had it restored by Laurent Rondoni and finished in the present black and blue livery. The car is currently fitted with engine and gearbox built by Rondoni (the original units are included with the sale).											F139
1938	Type 57 cabriolet	(D'Ieteren)	57589	R	1.400-1.700.000 EUR	885.115	1.347.698	1.210.000	05-09-15	Chantilly	17	Bon
	Black and burgundy with ostrich leather interior; sold in rolling chassis form to Belgium where it was bodied by D'Ieteren with the present one-off body. After WWII it resurfaced in France where it was also owned by painter André Derain. In the late 1950s it was exported to the USA; in the late 1990s it was restored in France and subsequently it was exhibited at Retromobile in 2000 and 2001. Offered with Swiss Permis de Circulation and a copy of the old French Carte Grise.											F140
1937	Type 57S sports tourer	(Vanden Plas)	57541	R	Refer Dpt.	6.879.725	9.735.000	8.965.935	10-03-16	Amelia Island	139	Bon
	Car delivered new to George Rand, New York Bugatti agent, who raced it at the Roosevelt Raceway. Back to the UK it was displayed at the Bugatti stand at the 1938 London Motor Show. After WWII it was bought by Jack Robinson and exported to Trinidad. At this time it had been already fitted with a Type 35B supercharger and the crankshaft, crankcase and cylinder block had been replaced. In 1985 it was bought by Peter Agg who had it restored and repainted light blue. The engine was rebuilt and fitted with a Type 57 supercharger. Since 1995 in the current ownership.											F141
1939	Type 57 cabriolet	(Gangloff)	57731	R	500-600.000 EUR	520.433*	749.876*	660.800*	14-05-16	Monaco	139	RMS
	Black and cream; an older restoration, the car is described as still in good overall condition. Displayed at the 1939 Geneva Motor Show, the car was later used as a demonstrator by the factory and used by racing driver Jean-Pierre Wimille. Sold later to private hands, it remained in France until 1964 when it was acquired by the Quattroruote Collection.											
1938	Type 57C Atalante		57766	R	2.200-2.500.000 USD		NS		10-12-15	New York	203	RMS
	Black and blue with brown interior; built with Stelvio body, in the early 1940s the car was fitted with the present Atalante body coming from #57733. In 1947 it was bought by Al Garthwaite who later sold it to Samuel Scher from whom it passed to John W. Strauss. The latter used it until the early 1960s when the car was stored in a garage where it remained until 2007 when it was sold by the Strauss estate. Restored to concours condition in recent years (see lots 39 Christie's 3.6.07 $ 852,500, 221 RM 29.10.08 $ 1,059,102 and 25 Gooding 18.1.13 $ 2,035,000).											
1936	Type 57 Stelvio		57406	R	900-1.200.000 USD		NS		12-03-16	Amelia Island	129	RMS
	Dark blue and black with light grey leather interior; sold new in France, the car was acquired in 1974 by Alec Ulmann and imported into the USA. Sold by Ulmann's widow in 1988, it was subsequently restored. For 20 years in the current ownership, it is described as still in good overall condition.											
1937	Type 57 Ventoux		57547	R	250-350.000 EUR	447.082	580.599	524.480	09-07-16	Le Mans	125	Art
	Black with light brown interior; not used in the last three years, the car requires recommissioning prior to use. Body repainted in 1952.											
1946	Type 73C		73C004	M	270-320.000 GBP		NS		24-06-16	Goodwood	251	Bon
	Chassis purchased (together with 005) in the early 1960s by Bart Loyens from Molsheim. In 1985 it passed to the current owner, John Barton. New engine block (the original frost-damaged unit stamped "4" included with the sale). The complete car was first track tested in 2014 and is described as in ready to race condition. Offered with a VSCC Blue Form (1985).											
1950	Type 101C coupé	(Antem)	101504	R	1.500-1.800.000 EUR		NS		05-09-15	Chantilly	23	Bon
	Black and red with matching interior; sold new in France, the car was exported in 1959 to the USA where it has had several owners, among them Gene Cesari, Bill Harrah, Nicholas Cage and John O'Quinn. Following O'Quinn's untimely death in 2009, it was acquired by the current owner and imported into Belgium. Described as in largely original condition, except for the paintwork originally green, the car has covered less then 14,000 kms since new (see RM lots 63 9.3.02 NS, 2254 21.4.07 $ 990,000, 254 1.5.10 NS and 234 20.8.11 $ 616,00).											

BUGATTI (F) (1998-)

Year	Model	(Bodybuilder)	Chassis No.	Steering	Estimate	£	$	€	Date	Place	Lot	Auc. H.
2006	Veyron 16.4		795023	L	1.200-1.500.000 USD	764.000	1.000.000	882.900	20-08-16	Monterey	S91	Mec
	Two-tone metallic grey with grey leather interior; one owner and 3,839 miles covered. From the Modern Speed Collection.											F142
2012	Veyron 16.4 Grand Sport		795054	L	1.700-2.100.000 USD		NS		19-08-16	Monterey	120	RMS
	Pearl with cognac leather interior; first used by Bugatti for promotional purpose, the car has had subsequently one owner and has covered just under 1,100 miles. Recently serviced.											

BUGATTI AUTOMOBILI (I) (1987-1996)

Year	Model	(Bodybuilder)	Chassis No.	Steering	Estimate	£	$	€	Date	Place	Lot	Auc. H.
1995	EB110 SS		39038	L	600-770.000 GBP	627.200	957.233	858.825	07-09-15	London	171	RMS
	Yellow with red interior; sold new to Japan, the car was later reimported into Europe. Two owners and 10,100 kms covered. Last serviced in late 2014.											
1995	EB110 SS		39017	L	800-1.200.000 EUR	715.683	1.041.517	929.760	05-02-16	Paris	211	Art
	Silver; 1,373 kms covered. The car was bought new by Gildo Pallanca Pastor who drove it in March 1995 to set the World ice speed record at 315 km/h, ultimately homologated by the FIA at 296 km/h. Retained by Pastor until 2015, it is described as in very good overall condition and is offered with a spare engine.											
1995	EB110 SS		39044	L	800-1.200.000 EUR	724.858	1.054.870	941.680	05-02-16	Paris	212	Art
	Silver; bought new by Gildo Pallanca Pastor, the car was race-prepared and entered at some IMSA events in the USA. Subsequently it was prepared for the 1995 Le Mans 24 Hours but it did not start the race for an accident in qualifying. Repaired with a new carbofibre chassis, it was road registered and remained with Pastor until 2015.											F143
1999	EB112		39003	L	Refer Dpt.		NS		05-02-16	Paris	213	Art
	One of the two cars completed in 1998 by Gildo Pallanca Pastor at his Monaco Racing Team workshop, after the factory closing. Body designed by Giorgetto Giugiaro; fitted with the Bugatti 6-litre aspirated engine. Retained by Pastor until 2015, it is described as in excellent overall condition.											

BUICK (USA) (1903-)

Year	Model	(Bodybuilder)	Chassis No.	Steering	Estimate	£	$	€	Date	Place	Lot	Auc. H.
1910	Model 16 toy tonneau		1367(engine)	R	50-60.000 USD	44.930*	68.200*	60.698*	05-10-15	Philadelphia	251	Bon
	Red with black leather interior; restored, the car is described as in good driving order. From the collection of Jim Hearn.											F144

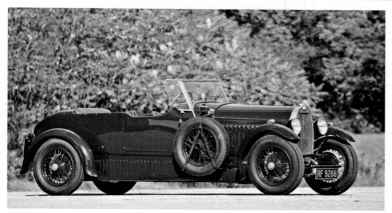
F137: 1931 Bugatti Type 49 Grand Sport tourer (Compton)

F138: 1931 Bugatti Type 51

F139: 1932 Bugatti Type 55 Roadster

F140: 1938 Bugatti Type 57 cabriolet (D'Ieteren)

F141: 1937 Bugatti Type 57S sports tourer (Vanden Plas)

F142: 2006 Bugatti Veyron 16.4

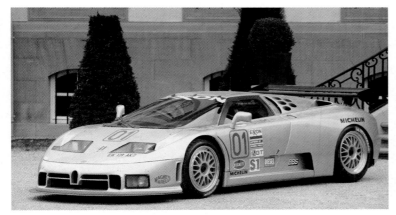
F143: 1995 Bugatti Automobili EB110 SS

F144: 1910 Buick Model 16 toy tonneau

Year	Model	(Bodybuilder)	Chassis no.	Steering	Estimate	Hammer Price £	Hammer Price $	Hammer Price €	Date	Place	Lot	Auc. H.
1912	Model 35 touring		1368	R	35-50.000 USD		NS		25-06-16	Santa Monica	1126	AA
	Black with black interior; restored.											
1915	Model C36 roadster		115826	L	20-25.000 USD	12.601*	19.250*	17.106*	08-10-15	Hershey	191	RMS
	Cream with red wheels; since new in two family ownership. Restored in the 1960s, the car remained later in storage for many years and has been recently returned to the road.											
1917	Model D34 roadster		23183	L	20-25 000 USD	7.971*	12.100*	10.769*	05-10-15	Philadelphia	208	Bon
	Red with black fenders and black leather interior; fully restored.											
1919	Model H49 touring		516274	L	35-45.000 USD		NS		02-04-16	Ft.Lauderdale	741	AA
	Green with black interior; restored approximately 13 years ago.											
1925	Standard Series 20 touring		100832	R	10-12.000 GBP	14.672	21.357	18.934	18-05-16	Donington Park	83	H&H
	Blue with brown interior; restored in New Zealand in the mid-1990s.											
1935	Series 60 convertible		2982831	L	NA	73.119*	104.500*	95.691*	29-01-16	Scottsdale	1373	B/J
	Yellow with red wheels; restored.											
1934	Series 60 convertible		83120428	L	75-95.000 USD	54.416	77.000	70.917	10-03-16	Amelia Island	188	Bon
	Red with black interior; since 1972 in the same family ownership. Restored between the early 2000s-2006.											
1931	Series 90 roadster		2584845	L	130-170.000 USD	107.754*	154.000*	141.018*	29-01-16	Phoenix	256	RMS F145
	Black with red leather interior; restored at unspecified date, the car is described as still in very good overall condition (see RM lots 229 4.8.07 $ 148,500 and 138 13.3.10 $ 154,000).											
1931	Series 90 Special Sedan		187413	L	45-55.000 USD	30.740*	44.550*	38.986*	07-05-16	Auburn	864	AA
	Blue with black roof and fenders and light tan interior; restored.											
1937	Special series 40 convertible		3080729	L	90-110.000 USD	55.848	80.000	74.016	23-01-16	Kissimmee	F223	Mec
	Black with tan leather interior; restored.											
1936	Special series 40 convertible		43010701	L	NA	29.669	42.500	39.321	23-01-16	Kissimmee	W167	Mec
	Dark green.											
1936	Century series 60 coupé	(Fisher)	2858318	L	NA	31.296	48.000	42.250	09-10-15	Chicago	S87	Mec
	Blue with original tan interior; restored.											
1936	Roadmaster 80 convertible sedan		2948988	L	90-120.000 USD	53.790*	82.500*	72.617*	09-10-15	Hershey	263	RMS
	Green with tan leather interior; the car has covered a few miles since a full restoration.											
1941	Super series 50 business coupé		14023283	L	20-30.000 USD	7.921*	12.100*	10.752*	08-10-15	Hershey	125	RMS
	Two-tone grey with grey cloth interior; older cosmetic restoration. From the Richard Roy estate.											
1940	Super series 50 Estate Wagon		13687615	L	275-325.000 USD		NS		11-03-16	Amelia Island	10	G&Co
	Maroon with black roof and wooden panels; acquired 25 years ago by the current owner and later restored to concours condition.											
1941	Super series 50 convertible		1496047	L	75-90.000 USD		NS		20-05-16	Indianapolis	F208.1	Mec
	Black with red interior; restored.											
1941	Super series 50 convertible		14194310	R	70-110.000 EUR		NS		09-07-16	Le Mans	171	Art
	Yellow with red leather interior; since 1989 in the current ownership. Restored.											
1941	Roadmaster series 70 convertible		13977054	L	100-150.000 USD		NS		10-03-16	Amelia Island	159	Bon
	Cream with red leather interior; restored between the late 1990s-early 2000s.											
1941	Roadmaster series 70 convertible		13940312	L	125-150.000 USD	63.149	92.000	82.000	20-05-16	Indianapolis	S153	Mec
	Metallic grey with maroon leather interior; restored.											
1941	Special series 40A convertible		14093459	L	60-80.000 USD	32.274*	49.500*	43.570*	09-10-15	Hershey	222	RMS
	Light yellow with red interior; described as in very good overall condition (see lot 680 Auctions America 28.3.15 $ 58,300).											
1941	Special series 40A sport coupé		14170203	L	NA	13.962	20.000	18.504	23-01-16	Kissimmee	L70	Mec
	Maroon with tan interior; until 1989 with its first owner. Believed to be 12,800 original miles.											
1948	Super series 50 convertible		15016672	L	50-65.000 USD	45.968	60.500	54.438	30-07-16	Plymouth	138	RMS
	Two-tone green; restored.											
1948	Roadmaster series 70 sedan		41060COLO	L	NA	23.090*	33.000*	30.218*	29-01-16	Scottsdale	930	B/J
	Red and maroon with red interior; restored. Automatic transmission.											
1948	Roadmaster series 70 estate wagon	(Hercules)	14929364	L	85-105.000 USD	63.498*	90.750*	83.100*	29-01-16	Phoenix	274	RMS F146
	Green with wooden panels and leather and cloth interior; described as in largely original condition, only the paintwork was redone in the mid-1980s. From 1969 to 1982 it was in the Harrah Collection. 33,215 miles on the odometer.											

F145: 1931 Buick Series 90 roadster

F146: 1948 Buick Roadmaster series 70 estate wagon (Hercules)

Year	Model (Bodybuilder)	Chassis No.	Steering	Estimate	Hammer Price £	Hammer Price $	Hammer Price €	Date	Place	Lot	Auc. H.
1947	Roadmaster series 70 estate wagon (Hercules)	14794589	L	60-80.000 USD	45.968	60.500	54.438	30-07-16	Plymouth	121	RMS
	Deep metallic maroon with wooden panels and red leather and grey cloth interior; full restoration completed in 2009 (see lot 120 RM 18.1.13 $82,500).										
1953	Roadmaster series 70 estate wagon	16760302	L	NA		NS		12-03-16	Kansas City	S133	Mec
	Maroon with tan interior; restored 10 years ago. Rebuilt 188bhp 322 engine with automatic transmission.										
1953	Roadmaster series 70 estate wagon	V1781517	L	100-125.000 USD	65.007	89.100	80.511	25-06-16	Santa Monica	1124	AA
	Blue with wooden panels and red interior; restored. Automatic transmission.										
1953	Roadmaster Skylark convertible	V1224897	L	NA	83.130	127.500	112.226	09-10-15	Chicago	S131	Mec
	Red with red and white interior.										
1953	Roadmaster Skylark convertible	16754774	L	NA	123.147*	176.000*	161.163*	29-01-16	Scottsdale	1365	B/J
	Blue with blue and white interior; restoration completed in 2013 (see lots 1299 Barrett-Jackson 18.1.14 $ 187,000 and F190 Mecum 16.5.15 NS).										
1953	Roadmaster Skylark convertible	168228663	L	125-150.000 USD	76.967*	110.000*	100.727*	29-01-16	Phoenix	225	RMS
	White with red and white interior; restored in 1993. Recently serviced (see lot 560 Auctions America 14.3.14 $ 154,000).										
1954	Roadmaster Skylark convertible	V5811917	L	140-160.000 USD		NS		19-08-16	Monterey	F120	Mec
	Red with black and white leather interior; described as in very good overall condition. Since new in the same family ownership.										
1954	Skylark Sport convertible	7A1068854	L	NA	97.535*	148.500*	133.338*	05-09-15	Auburn	5139	AA
	Yellow with black and cream interior; fully restored in 1991. Automatic transmission.										
1954	Skylark Sport convertible	7A1064548	L	NA	68.975	105.000	97.556	13-11-15	Anaheim	S153	Mec
	Light green with two-tone green interior; recently restored. Automatic transmission.										
1954	Skylark Sport convertible	7A1074081	L	150-200.000 USD	125.658	180.000	166.536	23-01-16	Kissimmee	S130	Mec F147
	Yellow with yellow and black interior; restoration completed in 2003. Automatic transmission (see lot 6114 Russo & Steele 19.1.06 $ 181,500).										
1954	Skylark Sport convertible	7A1068854	L	175-200.000 USD	97.832	140.000	122.458	02-04-16	Ft.Lauderdale	544	AA
	See lot 5139 Auctions America 5.9.15.										
1957	Century Caballero estate wagon	6D2016949	L	NA	36.124	55.000	49.385	05-09-15	Auburn	5059	AA
	Red and white with white and red interior; with its first owner until 2012 and subsequently restored. 300bhp 364 engine with automatic transmission (see lots 47 Gooding 16.8.14 $ 280,000 and 146 RM-Sotheby's 25.7.15 NS).										
1957	Century series 60 convertible	6D3044270	L	90-110.000 USD	38.964	51.000	45.028	19-08-16	Monterey	F149	Mec
	Red and beige with matching interior; fully restored.										
1957	Roadmaster series 70 convertible	7D4016970	L	NA		NS		19-09-15	Dallas	S20.1	Mec
	Black and red with black interior; 300bhp 364 engine with automatic transmission.										
1957	Roadmaster series 70 convertible	7D4021740	L	80-100.000 USD	103.891*	148.500*	133.902*	12-03-16	Amelia Island	184	RMS F148
	Black and red with red interior; restored some years ago. From the Richard & Linda Kughn Collection (see lots 44 Worldwide Group 3.5.08 $ 214,500 and 302 RM 21.1.11 $ 121.000).										
1957	Roadmaster series 70 Riviera coupé	7D4025319	L	25-35.000 USD	16.129*	23.375*	20.455*	07-05-16	Auburn	754	AA
	Two-tone body with vinyl and cloth interior; from the Wayne Carini Collection.										
1957	Roadmaster series 70 convertible	7D4016970	L	130-150.000 USD	82.368	120.000	106.956	20-05-16	Indianapolis	S137	Mec
	See lot S20.1 Mecum 19.09.15.										
1958	Limited series 700 convertible	8E1041138	L	140-160.000 USD		NS		25-06-16	Santa Monica	1081	AA
	Black with red leather interior; 10 miles covered since the restoration.										
1960	Electra 225 convertible	8G1049515	L	NA	59.036	93.500	82.205	31-10-15	Hilton Head	153	AA
	Pearl beige with two-tone beige interior; restored. 325bhp 401 engine with automatic transmission (see lot 607 Auctions America 14.3.14 $ 90,200).										
1960	Electra 225 convertible	8G1074925	L	60-70.000 USD	37.950	55.000	48.131	07-05-16	Auburn	842	AA
	Red with leather interior; restored. Automatic transmission.										
1965	Riviera Gran Sport	494475H930646	L	50-60.000 USD	84.664*	121.000*	110.800*	29-01-16	Scottsdale	30	G&Co
	Maroon; fully restored several years ago.										
1963	Riviera sport coupé	7J105700	L	30-40.000 EUR	16.874*	24.490*	22.400*	03-02-16	Paris	117	RMS
	Burgundy; in the same family ownership since new. In original condition. 53,528 miles on the odometer.										
1970	Gran Sport GS convertible	446670H191432	L	150-200.000 USD		NS		23-01-16	Kissimmee	F133	Mec
	Blue with white interior; body repainted. 455 Stage 1 engine with 3-speed manual gearbox.										
1970	Gran Sport GS convertible	446670H292998	L	NA		NS		16-04-16	Houston	S119	Mec
	Blue with white interior; restored in 2008. 455 Stage 1 engine with automatic transmission.										

F147: 1954 Buick Skylark Sport convertible

F148: 1957 Buick Roadmaster series 70 convertible

Year	Model	(Bodybuilder)	Chassis no.	Steering	Estimate	Hammer price £	$	€	Date	Place	Lot	Auc. H.
1970	Gran Sport GS convertible		446670H270577	L	200-250.000 USD	126.984	185.000	164.891	20-05-16	Indianapolis	F146	Mec F149
Blue with white and black interior; restored some years ago to concours condition. 455 Stage 1 engine with 4-speed manuale gearbox. From the Mike Guarise Collection.												
1970	GSX hardtop		446370H255253	L	NA	88.550	115.000	103.880	09-07-16	Denver	S36	Mec
Yellow with black interior; 360bhp 455 engine with automatic transmission.												
1972	Gran Sport hardtop		1G37U2H172627	L	NA	40.023*	57.200*	52.378*	29-01-16	Scottsdale	1022	B/J
Gold with black vinyl roof and black interior; 455 engine with 4-speed manual gearbox.												
1987	GNX		1G4GJ117XHP447978	L	NA	73.350	112.500	99.023	09-10-15	Chicago	S105.1	Mec
Black with black and grey interior; just one owner and 16 actual miles. Automatic transmission.												
1987	GNX		1G4GJ1171HP445942	L	NA	88.512*	126.500*	115.836*	29-01-16	Scottsdale	1281	B/J
Black with grey interior; 294 actual miles. Automatic transmission.												
1987	GNX		1G4GJ1174HP451735	L	NA	83.614*	117.700*	103.576*	09-04-16	Palm Beach	397	B/J
Black with black interior; 1,200 miles covered.												

CADILLAC (USA) (1903-)

Year	Model	(Bodybuilder)	Chassis no.	Steering	Estimate	£	$	€	Date	Place	Lot	Auc. H.
1914	Model 30 speedster		91132(engine)	R	40-60.000 USD	30.603*	46.750*	41.542*	08-10-15	Hershey	129	RMS
Pale yellow with brown interior; fitted at date unknown with the present body. It requires a thorough mechanical service. From the Richard Roy estate.												
1912	Model 30 touring		43397	R	80-120.000 USD	35.860*	55.000*	48.411*	09-10-15	Hershey	264	RMS F150
Black and green with black interior; for over 50 years in the same family ownership, the car has been recently exhumed from storage. It requires servicing prior to use.												
1918	Type 57 touring		57G247(ENGINE)	L	NA	48.993	70.000	62.195	18-06-16	Portland	S119	Mec
Burgundy with original black leather interior.												
1918	Type 59 touring		V59686	L	20-30.000 USD		NS		05-10-15	Philadelphia	266	Bon
Described as in largely original condition.												
1924	V-63A touring (Fisher)		63C1026(engine)	L	40-60.000 USD	21.516*	33.000*	29.047*	09-10-15	Hershey	273	RMS
Maroon with black fenders and black leather interior; in good, largely original condition.												
1928	Series 314 convertible		309994(engine)	L	40-60.000 USD	35.509	53.900	47.971	05-10-15	Philadelphia	259	Bon
Green with black fenders; discovered a little over 10 years ago, the car received subsequently several restoration works.												
1928	Series 314 convertible		309994(engine)	L	40-60.000 USD		NS		05-06-16	Greenwhich	60	Bon
See lot 259 Bonhams 5.10.15.												
1929	Series 341B Imperial sedan (Fisher)		330530	L	60-80.000 USD	46.804*	71.500*	63.535*	08-10-15	Hershey	158	RMS
Black and blue; fully restored.												
1930	Series 452 V-16 sedan (Fleetwood)		700375	L	60-70.000 GBP	65.340	99.493	89.326	05-09-15	Beaulieu	159	Bon
For 20 years in the current ownership; chassis, engine transmission and electrics already restored, paint and interior to be redone (see lot 152 Christie's 7.9.96 NS).												
1934	Series 452 V-16 convertible sedan (Fleetwood)		5100040(engine)	L	3.000-4.000.000 DKK	283.188	429.813	385.538	26-09-15	Ebeltoft	22	Bon
Black with black interior; concours quality restoration completed in 2009. From the Frederiksen Collection (see lot 142 Gooding 19.8.12 $ 550,000).												
1931	Series 452 V-16 town brougham		703164	L	1.600-2.000.000 DKK	158.585	240.695	215.901	26-09-15	Ebeltoft	43	Bon
Built with standard town car body, between the mid-1960s/late 1980s the car was fitted with the present new body replica of one of the six town car brougham built in period by Fleetwood of which just three, as the one offered, with faux cane work on the rear body panels. From the Frederiksen Collection.												
1930	Series 452 V-16 coupé (Fleetwood)		701540(engine)	L	450-600.000 USD	207.988*	319.000*	280.784*	09-10-15	Hershey	261	RMS F151
Black and metallic pewter with light brown leather interior; restoration completed in 2013.												
1930	Series 452 V-16 roadster		702201(engine)	L	350-450.000 USD		NS		09-10-15	Hershey	269	RMS
Salmon and brown with salmon leather interior; restored after the mid-1990s and fitted with the present, new, Fleetwood style roadster body.												
1930	Series 452 V-16 double phaeton		700665	L	200-250.000 EUR	173.869	257.738	230.000	04-02-16	Paris	418	Bon
Black with red leather interior; rebodied in Fleetwood style (see lot 230 Bonhams 23.1.10 NS).												
1930	Series 452 V-16 sport phaeton (Fleetwood)		702425(engine)	L	600-750.000 USD	525.250	687.500	606.994	19-08-16	Monterey	130	RMS
Pewter and black with black leather interior; restored many years ago, the car is described as still in very good overall condition (see lot 32 Christie's 12.2.02 $371,784).												
1930	Series 452 V-16 roadster (Fleetwood)		701432(engine)	L	950-1.200.000 USD	1.113.530	1.457.500	1.286.827	20-08-16	Monterey	220	RMS F152
The car was part of the Briggs Cunningham collection from 1959 to 1986 and subsequently of the Miles Collier Collection. In the early 2000s it was acquired by the current owner and later fully restored to its original specification by RM Auto Restoration.												

F149: 1970 Buick Gran Sport GS convertible

F150: 1912 Cadillac Model 30 touring

Year	Model	(Bodybuilder)	Chassis no.	Steering	Estimate	Hammer price £	$	€	Date	Place	Lot	Auc. H.

F151: 1930 Cadillac Series 452 V-16 coupé (Fleetwood)

F152: 1930 Cadillac Series 452 V-16 roadster (Fleetwood)

Year	Model (Bodybuilder)	Chassis no.	Steer	Estimate	£	$	€	Date	Place	Lot	Auc. H.
1931	Series 355A convertible	804225	L	NA		NS		05-09-15	Auburn	5150	AA
	Deep maroon with black fenders and maroon leather interior; restored approximately 20 years ago.										
1931	Series 355A convertible	801187	L	NA	88.512*	126.500*	115.836*	29-01-16	Scottsdale	1335	B/J
	Maroon with black fenders and black leather interior; restored (see lot 231 Bonhams 31.5.15 $ 101,200).										
1931	Series 370 V-12 roadster (Fleetwood)	101039	L	1.000-1.300.000 DKK	141.594	214.906	192.769	26-09-15	Ebeltoft	37	Bon F153
	Silver and black with black leather interior; first restored in 1982 and in the mid-1990s again. From the Frederiksen Collection (see lots 129 RM 31.7.03 NS and E678 Auctions America 2.9.10 $ 130,900).										
1931	Series 370A V-12 coupé	1000451(engine)	L	NA		NS		14-10-15	Duxford	64	H&H
	For restoration; it comes with a spare V12 engine.										
1932	Series 370B V-12 town sedan (Fisher)	1301468(engine)	L	50-60.000 USD	59.983*	85.800*	78.687*	28-01-16	Scottsdale	57	Bon
	Brown and cream with brown interior; restored in the 1980s, the car is described as in good running order.										
1934	Series 370D V-12 coupé (Fleetwood)	4100270	L	NA	230.901	330.000	302.181	29-01-16	Scottsdale	1377	B/J
	Dark blue.										
1931	Series 370 V-12 phaeton	1004488	L	NA	115.451*	165.000*	151.091*	29-01-16	Scottsdale	1931	B/J
	Yellow and green with tan interior; restored in 2005.										
1931	Series 370A V-12 phaeton (Fisher)	1004917(engine)	L	175-225.000 USD	119.282	170.500	153.740	12-03-16	Amelia Island	151	RMS F154
	Maroon and cream with brown interior; restored in the late 1990s. From the Richard & Linda Kughn Collection.										
1931	Series 370A V-12 phaeton (Fisher)	1004710(engine)	L	160-200.000 USD	96.195*	137.500*	123.984*	12-03-16	Amelia Island	177	RMS
	Two-tone brown with tan leatherette interior; restored in the early 1980s.										
1934	Series 370 V-12 town sedan (Fleetwood)	4100102	L	60-75.000 USD	36.053	52.250	45.724	07-05-16	Auburn	747	AA
	Maroon with tan cloth interior; restored some years ago.										
1932	Series 370B V-12 convertible (Fisher)	1300524(engine)	L	130-150.000 USD		NS		19-08-16	Monterey	F131	Mec
	Blue with grey interior; restored at unspecified date.										
1931	Series 370A V-12 phaeton (Fisher)	1004917(engine)	L	210-250.000 USD	152.800	200.000	176.580	20-08-16	Monterey	S49	Mec
	See lot 151 RM/Sotheby's 12.3.16.										
1931	Series 370 V-12 convertible (Fleetwood)	1000319(engine)	L	NQ	113.454	148.500	131.111	20-08-16	Monterey	7002	R&S
	Grey and burgundy; restoration completed in 1997.										
1937	Series 90 V-16 limousine (Fleetwood)	5130347	L	150-200.000 USD	72.006	110.000	97.746	08-10-15	Hershey	172	RMS
	Black with original leather interior to the front compartment and cloth to the rear; in good driving order. Exported to the UK early in its life and reimported into the USA in 1994.										
1938	Series 90 V-16 convertible (Fleetwood)	5270250(engine)	L	350-450.000 USD	227.403	325.000	297.603	29-01-16	Phoenix	260	RMS F155
	Red with light brown leather interior; in good overall condition. Body refinished some time ago.										
1939	Series 90 V-16 sedan (Fleetwood)	5290133(engine)	L	NA	69.270	99.000	90.654	30-01-16	Scottsdale	5154	R&S
	Full restoration completed in August 2015.										

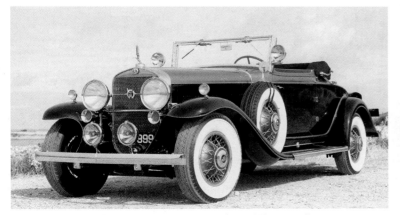

F153: 1931 Cadillac Series 370 V-12 roadster (Fleetwood)

F154: 1931 Cadillac Series 370A V-12 phaeton (Fisher)

Year	Model	(Bodybuilder)	Chassis no.	Steering	Estimate	Hammer price £	Hammer price $	Hammer price €	Date	Place	Lot	Auc. H.
1936	Series 70 convertible		3111479	L	NA		NS		13-11-15	Anaheim	S138	Mec
	Green with tan interior; restored.											
1936	Series 70 convertible	(Fleetwood)	3111479	L	130-150.000 USD	90.948	132.500	118.097	20-05-16	Indianapolis	F116	Mec
	See lot S138 Mecum 13.11.15.											
1936	Series 75 convertible sedan		3112867	L	NA		NS		26-09-15	Las Vegas	705	B/J
	Light brown with beige leather interior; concours quality restoration. From 1957 to 2008 in the same family ownership.											
1938	Series 75 formal sedan	(Fleetwood)	3271513(engine)	L	50-60.000 USD	19.723*	30.250*	26.626*	09-10-15	Hershey	265	RMS
	Black with black vinyl roof and leather and cloth interior; described as in working order.											
1939	Series 75 convertible sedan	(Fleetwood)	29836	L	100-120.000 USD		NS		28-01-16	Scottsdale	92	Bon
	Green; acquired in 2011 by the current owner and subsequently restored.											
1936	Series 75 convertible sedan		3112867	L	NA	76.967*	110.000*	100.727*	29-01-16	Scottsdale	1410	B/J
	See lot 705 Barrett-Jackson 26.9.15.											
1939	Series 75 Imperial sedan		3291984	L	30-40.000 EUR	23.785*	33.479*	29.463*	09-04-16	Essen	188	Coy
	Black with black leather interior to the front compartment and beige cloth to the rear; from the Brundza Collection (see lot 154 Coys 10.1.15 NS).											
1939	Series 75 convertible	(Fleetwood)	3290731	L	80-120.000 USD	72.398	104.500	93.684	05-06-16	Greenwhich	105	Bon
	Blue with light brown interior; engine rebuilt several years ago, body repainted and interior retrimmed in recent years.											
1940	Series 75 convertible	(Fleetwood)	33200481	L	90-130.000 USD	54.626*	71.500*	63.127*	19-08-16	Carmel	45	Bon
	Maroon with tan leather interior; in good overall condition, the car was restored in the 1990s.											
1939	Series 75 convertible	(Fleetwood)	3291095	L	250-300.000 USD	159.676	209.000	184.526	20-08-16	Pebble Beach	8	G&Co
	Dark blue with tan leather interior; restored to concours condition about 10 yeasrs ago.											
1942	Series 60 Special town car	(Derham)	12924	L	80-120.000 USD	55.801*	79.750*	73.027*	29-01-16	Phoenix	272	RMS
	Maroon with brown leather interior to the front compartment and tan cloth to the rear; acquired in 1974 by the current owner and subsequently restored.											
1938	Series 60 Special Opera coupé		8271176	L	50-75.000 USD	30.560*	40.000*	35.316*	19-08-16	Monterey	F135	Mec
	Maroon with beige interior; restoration completed in 2016.											
1941	Series 61 coupé		5354616(engine)	L	50-70.000 USD	27.002*	41.250*	36.655*	08-10-15	Hershey	169	RMS
	Maroon with tan cloth interior; restored. Engine rebuilt in 2015.											
1941	Series 62 convertible		8353409(engine)	L	30-40.000 USD	21.602*	33.000*	29.324*	08-10-15	Hershey	151	RMS
	Stored for many years, the car was discovered in 2014 and recommissioned for road use. Paintwork to be redone. Automatic transmission.											
1941	Series 62 coupé		5344883	L	30-40.000 USD	30.481*	46.750*	41.149*	09-10-15	Hershey	219	RMS
	Two-tone blue with blue cloth interior; in original condition. 12,976 actual miles. From the estate of Jim Miller.											
1941	Series 62 convertible		8348245	L	80-90.000 USD	55.904	80.000	69.976	02-04-16	Ft.Lauderdale	718	AA
	Green with tan interior; restored at unspecified date. 3-speed manual gearbox.											
1941	Series 62 convertible		8357578	L	70-100.000 EUR	54.351	77.653	69.000	18-06-16	Wien	423	Dor
	Black with black leather interior; acquired in 1996 by the current owner and subsequently restored.											
1942	Series 67 Imperial sedan	(Fisher)	9380014	L	30-45.000 USD	12.537*	16.500*	14.847*	30-07-16	Plymouth	118	RMS
	Black; in original condition. Three owners since new.											
1949	61 club coupé		496150666	L	NA	36.115*	49.500*	44.728*	24-06-16	Uncasville	718	B/J
	Silver with green interior; for many years on display in a museum. Just over 33,000 original miles.											
1947	62 convertible		8438510	L	100-120.000 USD	57.376	88.000	77.458	09-10-15	Hershey	226	RMS
	Cream with light brown leather interior; fully restored. 3-speed manual gearbox.											
1947	62 convertible		8456799	L	65-75.000 USD	57.376*	88.000*	77.458*	09-10-15	Hershey	276	RMS
	Maroon with burgundy interior; 250 miles covered since the restoration completed in 1995. Since 1981 in the current ownership.											
1947	62 convertible		8425259	L	60-80.000 EUR	58.214	92.185	81.056	01-11-15	Paris	171	Art
	Black; in very good original condition. 20,000 kms covered. Sold new to France, the car remained in the same family ownership for 57 years until 2004.											
1948	62 cabriolet	(Saoutchik)	486234577	L	1.000-1.500.000 USD	693.330	907.500	801.232	21-08-16	Pebble Beach	140	G&Co
	One of two examples bodied by Saoutchik; exhibited at the 1949 Paris Motor Show; imported into California in 1950; fully restored in the early 1990s; acquired in 2002 by the current owner.											
1951	75 Fleetwood limousine		517557236	L	90-120.000 GBP	85.500	123.864	109.816	20-03-16	Goodwood	72	Bon
	The car was formerly used by President Juan Peron and his wife Evita; for long time on display at the Eva Peron Museum, it requires recommissioning prior to use. UE taxes paid (see lot 149 Silverstone Auctions 4.9.14 NS).											

F155: 1938 Cadillac Series 90 V-16 convertible (Fleetwood)

F156: 1953 Cadillac 62 coupé Ghia

Year	Model	(Bodybuilder)	Chassis no.	Steering	Estimate	Hammer price £	Hammer price $	Hammer price €	Date	Place	Lot	Auc. H.
1953	62 coupé Ghia		536253053	L	1.500-1.800.000 USD	1.000.571	1.430.000	1.309.451	29-01-16	Phoenix	254	RMS F156
	Black with tan leather interior; one of two examples built by Carrozzeria Ghia on a Luigi Segre design. Built on the 62 convertible chassis fitted with the 210bhp 331 engine with automatic transmission. Bought about 20 years ago by the current owner and subsequently restored.
1953	62 convertible		536273698	L	65-95.000 USD	39.989	57.200	52.458	28-01-16	Scottsdale	82	Bon
	Black with original red interior; stored from 1963 to 2008, subsequently the car received some restoration works (see Bonhams lots 34 11.10.13 NS and 95 14.8.15 NS).
1955	62 Coupé de Ville		5562103879	L	NA	20.011*	28.600*	26.189*	29-01-16	Scottsdale	926	B/J
	White with green roof and green and white interior; rebuilt engine and automatic transmission.
1953	62 Coupé de Ville		5362106790	L	18-25.000 EUR		NS		09-04-16	Essen	191	Coy
	Turquoise with light green cloth interior; from the Brundza Collection (see lot 171 Coys 10.1.15 NS).
1955	62 Coupé de Ville		5562124273	L	30-40.000 USD	14.626*	19.250*	17.321*	30-07-16	Plymouth	113	RMS
	Beige with white roof; since 1971 in the same family ownership. Engine rebuilt in 1989, paintwork redone in 1991, interior recently retrimmed.
1953	62 Eldorado convertible		536219617	L	175-225.000 USD	139.620	200.000	185.040	23-01-16	Kissimmee	S189	Mec F157
	Red with red and white leather interior; 100 miles covered since a full restoration (see lot S137 Mecum 15.11.14 $ 210,000).
1953	62 Eldorado convertible		536234856	L	NA	180.872*	258.500*	236.708*	29-01-16	Scottsdale	1366	B/J
	Azure blue with azure blue interior; recent five year restoration (see lot 215 RM/Sotheby's 2.5.15 $ 291,500).
1953	62 Eldorado convertible		536236409	L	160-180.000 USD		NS		25-06-16	Santa Monica	1109	AA
	Red with red interior; restored (see lot S125 Mecum 28.2.15 $135,000).
1955	62 sedan		556273250(engine)	L	30-40.000 EUR		NS		14-05-16	Monaco	113	RMS
	Black with cloth interior; in original condition. Purchased new by Editoriale Domus, publishers of Quattroruote, and since 1964 on display at the Quattroruote Collection.
1956	62 Biarritz convertible		5662048649	L	190-220.000 USD	184.483	264.000	230.921	02-04-16	Ft.Lauderdale	496	AA F158
	Blue with blue and white leather interior; recently restored.
1956	62 Biarritz convertible		5662108293	L	175-225.000 USD	163.345	233.750	204.461	02-04-16	Ft.Lauderdale	527	AA
	White with red and white leather interior; restored between 2001 and 2002.
1961	62 convertible		61F066001	L	50-65.000 USD	46.618*	71.500*	62.934*	09-10-15	Hershey	221	RMS
	Blue with blue interior; in original condition. 16,070 original miles. From the estate of Jim Miller.
1959	62 convertible		59F031170	L	120-150.000 USD	80.282	115.000	106.398	23-01-16	Kissimmee	S143	Mec
	Black with red leather interior; 390 engine with automatic transmission.
1959	62 convertible		59F118989	L	125-175.000 USD	88.398	126.500	110.650	02-04-16	Ft.Lauderdale	550	AA
	Red with red and white interior.
1959	62 convertible		59F119099	L	50-70.000 GBP	61.980	84.937	76.750	24-06-16	Goodwood	242	Bon
	Blue with blue interior; since 1988 in the current, second ownership. 189 miles covered since the restoration carried out from 1994 to 2000.
1958	62 sedan		58K078147	L	NA	27.490	39.600	35.030	11-06-16	Newport Beach	6110	R&S
	Beige with beige and black interior; described as in good original condition, the car has covered 11,750 miles.
1958	62 Coupé de Ville		58J091308	L	80-100.000 USD	51.952	68.000	60.037	19-08-16	Monterey	F142	Mec
	Mauve with white roof and white leather and mauve cloth interior; restored.
1957	Eldorado Biarritz convertible		5762067663	L	115-130.000 USD	59.292	90.000	80.100	05-10-15	Philadelphia	239	Bon
	Red with original red leather interior; restored. From the Evergreen Collection.
1957	Eldorado Biarritz convertible		5762095559	L	200-275.000 USD	143.440*	220.000*	193.644*	09-10-15	Hershey	231	RMS
	Light green with green leather interior; concours quality restoration carried out at unspecified date (see lot 40 Worldwide Group 18.2.11 $ 247,500).
1958	Eldorado Biarritz convertible		58E023213	L	200-275.000 USD	143.440*	220.000*	193.644*	09-10-15	Hershey	247	RMS
	Silver with black leather interior; fully restored in recent years.
1959	Eldorado Biarritz convertible		59E096470	L	175-225.000 USD	121.924*	187.000*	164.597*	09-10-15	Hershey	252	RMS
	Metallic sand with white leather interior; in the early 1990s restored to concours condition (see lot 114 RM 13.3.04 $ 115,500).
1959	Eldorado Biarritz convertible		59E038331	L	195-225.000 USD	101.225	145.000	134.154	23-01-16	Kissimmee	F126	Mec
	Sand with original sand leather interior; engine rebuilt.
1960	Eldorado Biarritz convertible		60E073629	L	NA	153.934*	220.000*	201.454*	29-01-16	Scottsdale	1334	B/J
	Heather with white interior; 161 miles covered since the restoration completed less than four years ago.
1960	Eldorado Biarritz convertible		60E042833	L	NA	115.451*	165.000*	151.091*	29-01-16	Scottsdale	1411	B/J
	Heather with white interior; restored.

F157: 1953 Cadillac 62 Eldorado convertible

F158: 1956 Cadillac 62 Biarritz convertible

Year	Model	(Bodybuilder)	Chassis no.	Steering	Estimate	Hammer price £	Hammer price $	Hammer price €	Date	Place	Lot	Auc. H.
1959	Eldorado Biarritz convertible		59E050647	L	300-375.000 USD	273.233	390.500	357.581	29-01-16	Phoenix	263	RMS F159
Ebony with white leather interior; the car has covered 22 miles since a full, concours-quality restoration.												
1958	Eldorado Biarritz convertible		58E047525	L	175-225.000 USD	126.996*	181.500*	166.200*	30-01-16	Scottsdale	144	G&Co
Bronze; restored in 2008 (see lot 103 Gooding 19.1.13 $ 192,500).												
1957	Eldorado Biarritz convertible		5762002756	L	NA	107.754	154.000	141.018	30-01-16	Scottsdale	5103	R&S
Black with red leather interior; the car has covered less than 200 miles since a restoration completed in 2014.												
1958	Eldorado Biarritz convertible		58E054995	L	140-180.000 USD	88.499*	126.500*	114.065*	12-03-16	Amelia Island	135	RMS
Black with red leather interior; restored in 1991. From the Richard & Linda Kughn Collection (see lot 239 RM 22.1.10 $ 140,250).												
1960	Eldorado Biarritz convertible		60E109555	L	175-200.000 USD	103.772	148.500	129.893	02-04-16	Ft.Lauderdale	515	AA
White with red interior; restored.												
1958	Eldorado Biarritz convertible		58E007317	L	NA	74.453	107.250	94.873	11-06-16	Newport Beach	6039	R&S
Light metallic blue with blue interior; restored.												
1958	Eldorado Brougham		58P007550	L	NA	76.399	121.000	106.383	31-10-15	Hilton Head	157	AA F160
Grey with blue cloth and leather interior; restored in 2009. Four owners and 49,000 original miles.												
1958	Eldorado Brougham		58P060521	L	NA	86.203*	123.200*	112.814*	29-01-16	Scottsdale	1258.1	B/J
Blue with blue interior; recent cosmetic restoration.												
1957	Eldorado Brougham		5770146813	L	90-100.000 USD		NS		07-05-16	Auburn	808	AA
Light green with green interior; restored.												
1957	Eldorado Brougham		5770087865	L	90-120.000 USD	60.192	82.500	74.547	25-06-16	Santa Monica	1079	AA
Body refinished in black in recent years.												
1958	Eldorado Brougham		58P021440	L	200-250.000 USD	226.908	297.000	262.221	20-08-16	Monterey	216	RMS
Grey with blue and white interior; concours-quality restoration carried out between 2010 and 2012. From the Skip Barber Collection.												
1960	62 DeVille coupé		60G058043	L	NA	20.212	31.000	27.286	09-10-15	Chicago	S15	Mec
White with green interior; 46,700 original miles. In the same family ownership from 1961 to 2014.												
1967	62 DeVille convertible		F7277284	L	40-60.000 USD	38.478*	55.000*	49.594*	12-03-16	Amelia Island	113	RMS
White with maroon leather interior; less than 300 miles covered since the restoration.												
1970	DeVille 2-door hardtop	(Fisher)	J0332324	L	30-40.000 USD	26.052*	34.100*	30.107*	19-08-16	Carmel	68	Bon
Light metallic blue with white roof and white leather interior; in good overall condition.												
1966	Eldorado convertible		E6263446	L	NA	48.900	75.000	66.015	09-10-15	Chicago	F140	Mec
Black with black interior.												
1976	Eldorado convertible		6L67S6Q193983	L	50-70.000 USD	36.559*	52.250*	47.845*	29-01-16	Phoenix	206	RMS F161
White with white leather interior; single ownership for over 40 years. 250 miles covered.												
1993	Fleetwood Brougham sedan		1G6DW5477MR708187	L	10-20.000 EUR	13.040*	19.330*	17.250*	04-02-16	Paris	429	Bon
Blue with blue interior; 10,000 kms covered (see lot 38 Christie's 8.2.03 $ 32,960).												

CAGIVA (I)

Year	Model	(Bodybuilder)	Chassis no.	Steering	Estimate	£	$	€	Date	Place	Lot	Auc. H.
1993	Moke		200024	L	10-15.000 EUR	39.694*	57.194*	50.400*	14-05-16	Monaco	284	RMS F162
White with white leather interior; one owner and 1,833 kms covered.												

CAMERON (USA) (1903-1920)

Year	Model	(Bodybuilder)	Chassis no.	Steering	Estimate	£	$	€	Date	Place	Lot	Auc. H.
1910	Four 24hp runabout		1151	R	35-50.000 USD	36.003*	55.000*	48.873*	08-10-15	Hershey	190	RMS
Dark green with cream chassis and wheels; acquired 10 years ago by the current owner and subsequently restored.												

CAR-NATION (USA) (1912-19159

Year	Model	(Bodybuilder)	Chassis no.	Steering	Estimate	£	$	€	Date	Place	Lot	Auc. H.
1913	Cyclecar Roadster		649	L	35-40.000 USD	16.766*	24.200*	21.695*	05-06-16	Greenwhich	71	Bon
Green with black fenders and black leatherette interior: discovered in 1954, restored and used at some historic events in the late 1950s. For many years on display in a museum. One of two known surviving examples. From the Evergreen Collection.												F163

F159: 1959 Cadillac Eldorado Biarritz convertible

F160: 1958 Cadillac Eldorado Brougham

F161: 1976 Cadillac Eldorado convertible

F162: 1993 Cagiva Moke

CASE (USA) *(1911-1927)*

Year	Model	Chassis no.	Steering	Estimate	£	$	€	Date	Place	Lot	Auc. H.
1913	**Model O touring**	22117	R	NA	57.076	86.900	78.028	05-09-15	Auburn	7054	AA

Dark green with green leather interior; restoration completed in 2014.

CD (F) *(1962-1966)*

1962	**66 coach**	108	L	85-125.000 EUR		NS		09-07-16	Le Mans	148	Art

Blue; first example built, the car was exhibited at the 1962 Paris Motor Show. Acquired in 1995 by the current owner and subsequently restored.

CHALMERS (USA) *(1908-1923)*

1917	**Model Six-30 roadster**	13792	L	18-24.000 USD	9.421*	14.300*	12.727*	05-10-15	Philadelphia	224	Bon

Blue with black fenders and black interior; from the Evergreen Collection (see lot 319 RM 7.10.10 $ 17,600).

CHANDLER (USA) *(1914-1929)*

1928	**Six sedan**	47480	L	NA	9.099	13.000	11.551	18-06-16	Portland	S45	Mec

Maroon with tan cloth interior; engine overhauled in 2012.

CHAPARRAL (USA) *(1961-1970)*

1961	**Mark 1 Prototype**	001	R	900-1.400.000 USD		NS		19-08-16	Monterey	111	RMS

First example built, the car was raced by Jim Hall until March 1963. Original chassis, bodywork and fuel tanks; currently fitted with an est. 400bhp 327 Chevrolet engine with 4-speed gearbox. From the Jack Boxstrom Collection.

CHEETAH (USA)

1964	**GT coupé**	BTC003	L	300-500.000 USD		NS		19-08-16	Carmel	26	Bon

Raced in period. In 1972 the new owner modified the car for road use and stamped his own "serial number", BTC003, into the frame in order to register it for road use. In 1989 it was bought by the current owner, fitted with a new body and raced at historic events for 21 years. In 2012 the car was fitted again with its original body and finished in the 1965 green livery. Rochester fuel-injection unit restored; in ready to race condition.

CHEVROLET (USA) *(1911-)*

1932	**Confederate BA DeLuxe sedan**	32569T14838	L	20-30.000 EUR		NS		20-03-16	Fontainebleau	316	Ose

Tow-tone body with cloth interior; restored a few years ago.

1934	**Master coupé**	1DA0526718	L	35-50.000 USD	20.943	30.000	27.756	23-01-16	Kissimmee	S95.1	Mec

Black with brown cloth interior; restored.
F164

F163: 1913 Car-Nation Cyclecar Roadster

F164: 1934 Chevrolet Master coupé

Year	Model	(Bodybuilder)	Chassis No.	Steering	Estimate	Hammer Price £	Hammer Price $	Hammer Price €	Date	Place	Lot	Auc. H.
1941	**Special Deluxe convertible**		5AH0441154	L	50-60.000 USD	27.002*	41.250*	36.655*	08-10-15	Hershey	171	**RMS**
Black with new brown leather interior; in good overall condition.												
1952	**Styleline DeLuxe 2-door sedan**		9KK141617	L	NA	14.104	20.000	17.724	16-04-16	Houston	T209	**Mec**
Two-tone blue with grey interior; believed to be 29,000 miles. Automatic transmission.												
1954	**Bel Air Six hardtop**		C54N056295	L	40-45.000 USD		NS		02-04-16	Ft.Lauderdale	147	**AA**
Blue and white with white and blue vinyl and cloth interior; described as in original condition. Automatic transmission.												
1953	**Corvette roadster**		E53F001065	L	NA	239.616	379.500	333.656	31-10-15	Hilton Head	168	**AA**
Since 1998 in the current ownership; restored. Automatic transmission (see lot 1 Christie's 17.10.98 $ 81,700).												
1953	**Corvette roadster**		E53F001027	L	300-400.000 USD	244.335	350.000	323.820	23-01-16	Kissimmee	F183	**Mec** **F165**
White with red interior; restored in 1996. 3,796 miles covered since new. Automatic transmission (see lot F74 Mecum 14.8.15 NS).												
1954	**Corvette roadster**		E54S002886	L	NA	66.320	95.000	87.894	23-01-16	Kissimmee	F45.1	**Mec**
Blue with beige interior; 5 miles covered since a full restoration. Automatic transmission.												
1953	**Corvette roadster**		E53F001072	L	300-350.000 USD	139.620	200.000	185.040	23-01-16	Kissimmee	S225	**Mec**
White with red interior; restored. Automatic transmission (see lot S120.1 Mecum 1.8.15 NS).												
1954	**Corvette roadster**		E54S002031	L	55-65.000 USD	49.986*	71.500*	65.573*	28-01-16	Scottsdale	109	**Bon**
White with red interior; recently restored. Automatic transmission.												
1954	**Corvette roadster**		E54S004622	L	60-80.000 USD	57.676*	82.500*	75.661*	28-01-16	Scottsdale	47	**Bon**
White with red vinyl interior; acquired in 1996 by the current owner and subjected to a full restoration completed in 1999. Automatic transmission. From the BHA Automobile Museum.												
1953	**Corvette roadster**		E53F001300	L	NA	373.290*	533.500*	488.526*	29-01-16	Scottsdale	1359	**B/J**
White with red interior; last 1953 Corvette built at the plant in Flint, Missouri. Fully restored in the 2000s. Automatic transmission.												
1953	**Corvette roadster**		E53F001214	L	180-220.000 USD		NS		02-04-16	Ft.Lauderdale	507	**AA**
White with red interior; restored in the 1990s. Automatic transmission.												
1954	**Corvette roadster**		E54S003460	L	80-120.000 EUR		NS		09-07-16	Le Mans	113	**Art**
Red with black interior and red hardtop; imported already restored into Italy from Hawaii a few years ago. Engine rebuilt.												
1954	**Corvette roadster**		E54S001289	L	NA	78.269	102.500	93.060	23-07-16	Harrisburg	S149	**Mec**
Red with red interior; restored. Automatic transmission.												
1954	**Corvette roadster**		E54S004625	L	60-80.000 USD	44.296*	58.300*	52.458*	30-07-16	Plymouth	149	**RMS**
White with red interior; for 20 years in the current ownership, engine rebuilt four years ago, automatic transmission.												
1953	**Corvette roadster**		E53F1228	L	150-200.000 USD	103.140	135.000	119.192	19-08-16	Monterey	F87	**Mec**
White with red interior.												
1957	**Model 150 2-door sedan**		VA57A124372	L	NA	143.928*	205.700*	188.359*	29-01-16	Scottsdale	1357	**B/J** **F166**
Black and white with black interior; one of the six cars prepared by factory for the NASCAR races, it was driven during the 1957 season by Jack Smith. 283 fuel-injected engine with manual gearbox.												
1955	**Corvette V8 roadster**		VE55S001001	L	NA	1.269.956	1.815.000	1.661.996	29-01-16	Scottsdale	1351	**B/J**
White with red interior; fully restored, automatic transmission, first Corvette equipped with the V8 engine. Sold as a package with lots 1352: 1956 Corvette #E56S001001, red and white with red interior, fully restored, 3-speed manual gearbox, first Corvette equipped with the 265 V8 dual 4-barrell configuration; and 1353: 1957 Corvette #E57S100001, green and beige with beige and green interior, fully restored, automatic transmission, first Corvette equipped with the 283 engine.												
1955	**Corvette V8 roadster**		VE55S001250	L	NA	76.967*	110.000	100.727*	29-01-16	Scottsdale	1355	**B/J**
Red with white and red interior; restored. Automatic transmission.												
1956	**Corvette V8 roadster**		E56S001947	L	80-100.000 EUR	79.388*	114.388*	100.800*	14-05-16	Monaco	281	**RMS**
Blue with silver coves and red interior; restored in the USA in 2012 and subsequently imported into Germany. 225bhp 265 engine with 3-speed manual gearbox.												
1956	**Corvette V8 roadster**		E56S003714	L	NA	69.489	100.100	88.548	11-06-16	Newport Beach	6067	**R&S**
Black with silver coves and red interior; an older restoration, the car is described as still in very good overall condition. With hardtop. 240bhp engine with 3-speed manual gearbox.												
1955	**Corvette V8 roadster**		VE55S001176	L	175-225.000 USD	93.590*	122.500*	108.155*	20-08-16	Monterey	S146	**Mec** **F167**
Blue with dark beige leather interior; restored in 2008. Automatic transmission.												
1960	**Bel Air sedan**		01619N203843	L	14-16.000 GBP	11.500	17.394	15.894	10-12-15	London	362	**Bon**
White with aquamarine interior; restored at date unknown. 283 engine with automatic transmission.												
1962	**Bel Air hardtop**		21537L117241	L	90-100.000 USD	62.829	90.000	83.268	23-01-16	Kissimmee	F135	**Mec**
Red with red interior; restored. 409bhp 409 engine with 4-speed manual gearbox.												

F165: 1953 Chevrolet Corvette roadster

F166: 1957 Chevrolet Model 150 2-door sedan

Year	Model	(Bodybuilder)	Chassis no.	Steering	Estimate	Hammer price £	$	€	Date	Place	Lot	Auc. H.

F167: 1955 Chevrolet Corvette V8 roadster

F168: 1955 Chevrolet Bel Air Nomad

Year	Model	Chassis no.	Steering	Estimate	£	$	€	Date	Place	Lot	Auc. H.
1962	**Bel Air hardtop**	21637S211106	L	NA	64.652*	92.400*	84.611*	29-01-16	Scottsdale	1302	B/J
	Red with red interior; restored. 409bhp 409 engine with 4-speed manual gearbox.										
1955	**Bel Air Nomad**	VC550061437	L	NA	52.356*	73.700*	64.856*	09-04-16	Palm Beach	405	B/J F168
	Turquoise and ivory with matching interior; restored. 265 engine with automatic transmission.										
1957	**Bel Air sport coupé**	VC57N151774	L	NA	46.886*	66.000*	58.080*	09-04-16	Palm Beach	493	B/J
	Black with black and silver interior; body repainted. 270bhp 283 engine with 3-speed manual gearbox.										
1960	**Bel Air Nomad**	01835L125354	L	NQ	34.320	50.000	44.565	20-05-16	Indianapolis	S270	Mec
	Turquoise with black interior; 280bhp 348 engine with automatic transmission.										
1962	**Bel Air hardtop**	21637S120438	L	NA	76.989	110.000	97.735	18-06-16	Portland	S111	Mec
	Red with red interior; fully restored. 409 engine pro-built by Lamar Walden with 540bhp and 4-speed Borg Warner T-10 manual gearbox.										
1957	**Bel Air convertible**	VC57L187632	L	NA		NS		31-10-15	Hilton Head	158	AA
	Cream with cream interior; restoration completed in 2011. 283 fuel-injected engine with automatic transmission (see lot 525 Auctions America 4.3.11 $ 126,500).										
1956	**Bel Air convertible**	VC56T060712	L	125-150.000 USD	90.753	130.000	120.276	23-01-16	Kissimmee	F125	Mec
	Two-tone blue with matching interior; concours-quality restoration completed in 2015. 225bhp 265 engine with automatic transmission.										
1957	**Bel Air convertible**	VC57L162969	L	NA	76.791	110.000	101.772	23-01-16	Kissimmee	T171	Mec
	Turquoise with turquoise and white interior; 171 miles covered since a concours restoration completed in 2008. 220bhp 283 engine with automatic transmission.										
1957	**Bel Air convertible**	VC57K138880	L	100-125.000 USD	123.042*	176.000*	161.410*	28-01-16	Phoenix	169	RMS F169
	Red with red and silver vinyl interior; the car has covered 50 miles since a full restoration. 283bhp 283 fuel-injected engine with 3-speed manual gearbox.										
1957	**Bel Air convertible**	VC57F179252	L	90-100.000 USD	45.771	65.500	57.293	02-04-16	Ft.Lauderdale	428	AA
	Red with red and silver interior; restored. 283 engine with automatic transmission.										
1957	**Bel Air convertible**	VC57L173489	L	120-150.000 USD		NS		30-07-16	Plymouth	137	RMS
	Blue with matching interior; less than 1,000 miles covered since the restoration carried out several years ago. Mechanical freshening in 2015. 250bhp 283 fuel-injected engine with automatic transmission.										
1957	**Bel Air convertible**	VC57J253226	L	125-150.000 USD	84.040	110.000	97.119	19-08-16	Monterey	F147	Mec
	Red with red and silver interior; for 38 years in the current ownership. Recently restored. 283bhp 283 fuel-injected engine with 3-speed manual gearbox.										
1957	**Cameo pick up**	V3A57J110624	L	40-50.000 USD	30.317*	42.900*	39.511*	10-03-16	Amelia Island	201	Bon
	Blue and white with matching interior; restored. 165bhp 265 engine with 3-speed manual gearbox.										
1956	**Corvette convertible**	E56S002253	L	50-65.000 USD	43.204*	66.000*	58.648*	08-10-15	Hershey	174	RMS
	Black with silver coves and red interior; fully restored at unspecified date. 225bhp 265 engine with 3-speed manual gearbox.										
1957	**Corvette convertible**	E57S106183	L	80-90.000 EUR		NS		16-01-16	Maastricht	442	Coy
	Red with white coves and red interior; imported into the Netherlands in 1997 and subsequently restored. 270bhp 283 engine with manuale gearbox.										
1957	**Corvette convertible**	E57S102001	L	NA	130.844*	187.000*	171.236*	29-01-16	Scottsdale	1354	B/J F170
	Black with silver coves and red interior; restored. 283bhp 283 fuel-injected engine with 3-speed manual gearbox.										

F169: 1957 Chevrolet Bel Air convertible

F170: 1957 Chevrolet Corvette convertible

Year	Model	(Bodybuilder)	Chassis no.	Steering	Estimate	Hammer Price £	Hammer Price $	Hammer Price €	Date	Place	Lot	Auc. H.
1957	Corvette convertible		E57S104701	L	160-200.000 USD	84.664*	121.000*	110.800*	29-01-16	Scottsdale	14	G&Co
	Arctic blue; fully restored in the 2000s. 270bhp 283 engine with 4-speed manual gearbox.											
1958	Bel Air Impala convertible		F58A118235	L	NA		NS		18-06-16	Portland	S118.1	Mec
	Red with red, black, and silver interior; rebuilt 348 engine with automatic transmission.											
1958	Bel Air Impala convertible		58B226126	L	NQ	82.359	107.800	95.177	20-08-16	Monterey	7128	R&S
	Restoration completed in 2000.											
1958	Bel Air Impala sport coupé		F58S170267	L	70-90.000 USD	50.853	73.700	64.495	07-05-16	Auburn	809	AA
	Red with three-tone red interior; fully restored. Two owners. Three-speed column-shift manual gearbox.											
1961	Corvette convertible		10867S105021	L	NA	74.980	115.000	101.223	09-10-15	Chicago	S161	Mec
	Red with red interior; fully restored. Believed to be 27,741 actual miles.											
1958	Corvette convertible		J58S102800	L	35-55.000 EUR	36.657*	58.048*	51.040*	01-11-15	Paris	109	Art
	Light blue with grey coves and black vinyl interior; restored at date unknown.											
1959	Corvette convertible		J59S100243	L	NA		NS		29-01-16	Scottsdale	1389	B/J
	Purple with black interior; 283 fuel-injected engine with 4-speed manual gearbox. The car won the 1959 SCCA B/Production National Championship driven by Jim Jeffords and was raced also in the 1960s. In 1974 it was acquired by Chip Miller, from whose Collection it is offered.											
1959	Corvette convertible		J59S102243	L	NA	103.905	148.500	135.981	30-01-16	Scottsdale	5229	R&S
	Sapphire and white with turquoise interior; recently restored. 270bhp 283 engine with 4-speed manual gearbox.											
1961	Corvette convertible		10867S109208	L	85-105.000 USD	76.956*	110.000*	99.187*	12-03-16	Amelia Island	197	RMS
	Red with white coves and red vinyl interior; the car was stored for 33 years following a full restoration. Returned to the road in 2015. 230bhp 283 engine with 4-speed manual gearbox.											
1958	Corvette convertible		J58S105724	L	NA	97.318	138.000	122.296	16-04-16	Houston	S101	Mec F171
	Black with silver coves and red interior; restored. With hardtop. 290bhp fuel-injected 283 engine with 4-speed manual gearbox.											
1960	Corvette convertible		00867S102799	L	60-90.000 EUR	44.104*	63.549*	56.000*	14-05-16	Monaco	233	RMS
	White with red interior; 4-speed manual gearbox.											
1962	Corvette convertible		20867S104396	L	135-165.000 USD	77.046*	105.600*	95.420*	25-06-16	Santa Monica	1077	AA
	White with black interior; restored. 327 fuel-injected engine with 4-speed manual gearbox.											
1962	Corvette convertible		20867S105371	L	60-80.000 EUR	54.322	72.155	64.800	02-07-16	Lyon	336	Agu
	Cream with red leatherette interior; mechanicals restored over the last two years.											
1958	Corvette convertible		J58S105724	L	145-170.000 USD	127.970	167.500	147.886	19-08-16	Monterey	F89	Mec
	See lot S101 Mecum 16.4.16.											
1965	Corvair Corsa convertible		107675W116143	L	16-20.000 EUR	23.543	34.108	30.240	20-03-16	Fontainebleau	375	Ose
	Red; described as in very good overall condition. Rebuilt engine.											
1966	Corvair Corsa convertible		107676L107092	L	35-45.000 USD	21.907	31.350	27.422	02-04-16	Ft.Lauderdale	446	AA F172
	Beige with black interior; 180bhp 164 supercharged engine with 4-speed manual gearbox.											
1965	Corvair Corsa convertible		107675L105155	L	25-35.000 USD	18.216*	26.400*	23.103*	07-05-16	Auburn	765	AA
	275 miles covered since the restoration carried out in 2007; 180bhp 164 supercharged engine with 4-speed manual gearbox.											
1964	Impala Super Sport hardtop		41447Y11952	L	35-45.000 USD	21.740	33.000	29.370	05-10-15	Philadelphia	246	Bon
	Dark metallic blue with blue interior; in original condition except for the paintwork redone in 1982. With its first owner until 2006 when it was acquired by the vendor. 340bhp 409 engine with 4-speed manual gearbox.											
1964	Impala SS convertible		41467S163943	L	NA	37.490	57.500	50.612	09-10-15	Chicago	S71	Mec
	Tan with tan interior; 340bhp 409 engine with 4-speed manual gearbox.											
1959	Impala convertible		F59L121770	L	130-160.000 USD	73.301	105.000	97.146	23-01-16	Kissimmee	S140.1	Mec
	Red with red interior; the car has covered 269 miles since the restoration completed in 2015. 348 engine with 4-speed manual gearbox.											
1959	Impala convertible		F59J145285	L	90-120.000 USD	73.119*	104.500*	95.691*	29-01-16	Phoenix	207	RMS F173
	Black with red vinyl interior; 5 miles covered since a full restoration. 320bhp 348 Turbo Thrust engine with automatic transmission.											
1965	Impala convertible		516667019671	L	20-30.000 EUR	22.603*	33.506*	29.900*	04-02-16	Paris	411	Bon
	White with red interior; described as in largely original condition. 327 engine with manual gearbox.											
1959	Impala convertible		F59J145285	L	160-180.000 USD		NS		25-06-16	Santa Monica	2083	AA
	See lot 207 RM/Sotheby's 29.1.16.											
1962	Impala SS convertible		21867L177970	L	50-75.000 USD	50.042	65.500	57.830	20-08-16	Monterey	S188	Mec
	Cream with gold interior; 409 engine with 4-speed manual gearbox.											

F171: 1958 Chevrolet Corvette convertible

F172: 1966 Chevrolet Corvair Corsa convertible

Year	Model	(Bodybuilder)	Chassis no.	Steering	Estimate	Hammer price £	Hammer price $	Hammer price €	Sale Date	Sale Place	Lot	Auc. H.
1966	**Nova Super Sport hardtop**		118376W150156	L	NA	54.186	82.500	74.077	05-09-15	Auburn	5089	AA F174
	Blue with black interior; 17,000 original miles. 350bhp 327 L79 engine with 4-speed manual gearbox.											
1966	**Nova SS hardtop**		118376N108617	L	NA	37.509*	52.800*	46.464*	09-04-16	Palm Beach	146	B/J
	Red with red interior; a few miles covered since a full restoration. 350bhp 327 L79 engine with 4-speed manual gearbox.											
1966	**Corvette Sting Ray convertible**		194676S113111	L	NA	93.922	143.000	128.400	05-09-15	Auburn	5106	AA
	Silver pearl metallic; 425bhp 427 engine with 4-speed manual gearbox. With hardtop.											
1967	**Corvette Sting Ray convertible**		194677S112888	L	NA	83.364*	126.500*	113.445*	26-09-15	Las Vegas	687	B/J
	Blue with original black interior; restored. Since 1989 in the same ownership. 435bhp 427 engine with 4-speed manual gearbox.											
1967	**Corvette Sting Ray convertible**		194677S102264	L	NA	85.397	130.000	120.783	13-11-15	Anaheim	S133.1	Mec
	Yellow with black interior; fully restored. 400bhp 427 engine with 4-speed manual gearbox.											
1967	**Corvette Sting Ray convertible**		194677S114905	L	NA		NS		13-11-15	Anaheim	S99	Mec
	Green with white stinger and dark green vinyl interior; concours-quality restoration completed in 2010. 435bhp 427 engine with 4-speed manual gearbox.											
1967	**Corvette Sting Ray convertible**		194677S118843	L	225-275.000 USD	136.130	195.000	180.414	23-01-16	Kissimmee	S113	Mec F175
	Blue with black stinger, blue interior and black vinyl-covered hardtop; with its second owner for over 30 years since 1981, the car is described as in highly original condition and has covered 15,050 miles. 435bhp 427 engine with 4-speed manual gearbox (see lot F198 Mecum 6.9.14 $ 210,000).											
1966	**Corvette Sting Ray convertible**		194676S123488	L	NA	111.696	160.000	148.032	23-01-16	Kissimmee	S76	Mec
	Light green with green interior; fully restored. 425bhp 427 engine with 4-speed manual gearbox.											
1966	**Corvette Sting Ray convertible**		194676S119861	L	75-100.000 USD	36.912*	52.800*	48.423*	28-01-16	Scottsdale	110	Bon
	Maroon with black interior; restored at unspecified date. 350bhp 327 L79 engine with 4-speed manual gearbox.											
1967	**Corvette Sting Ray convertible**		194677S114905	L	NA	128.535*	183.700*	168.214*	29-01-16	Scottsdale	1310	B/J
	See lot S99 Mecum 13.11.15.											
1965	**Corvette Sting Ray convertible**		194675S103388	L	140-180.000 USD	92.360*	132.000*	120.872*	29-01-16	Scottsdale	38	G&Co
	Red; the car has covered 1,000 miles since a full restoration carried out between 2001 and 2003. 375bhp 327 fuel-injected engine with 4-speed manual gearbox.											
1967	**Corvette Sting Ray convertible**		194677S121302	L	175-225.000 USD	92.360*	132.000*	120.872*	30-01-16	Scottsdale	113	G&Co
	Red; in original condition. Approximately 42,000 on the odometer. For 44 years with its first owner. 435bhp 427 L71 engine with 4-speed manual gearbox.											
1967	**Corvette Sting Ray convertible**		194677S107007	L	NA	76.967	110.000	100.727	30-01-16	Scottsdale	5042	R&S
	Red with black interior; restored in 2012. 435bhp 427 engine.											
1967	**Corvette Sting Ray convertible**		194677S106613	L	NA	94.285	134.750	123.391	30-01-16	Scottsdale	5241	R&S
	Blue with blue interior; restored to concours condition. 400bhp 427 engine with automatic transmission.											
1966	**Corvette Sting Ray convertible**		194676S100291	L	28-34.000 GBP	48.160	68.830	62.064	12-03-16	Brooklands	245	His
	Blue with black original interior; restored in 2014.											
1967	**Corvette Sting Ray convertible**		194677S118476	L	NA	128.938*	181.500*	159.720*	09-04-16	Palm Beach	375	B/J
	White with red leather interior; restored. 400bhp 427 engine with 4-speed manual gearbox.											
1967	**Corvette Sting Ray convertible**		194677S118405	L	NA	88.150	125.000	110.775	16-04-16	Houston	F144	Mec
	Silver with black leather interior; restored. 435bhp 427 engine with 4-speed manual gearbox.											
1967	**Corvette Sting Ray convertible**		194677S122843	L	NA	82.861	117.500	104.129	16-04-16	Houston	F213	Mec
	Yellow with black interior; concours-quality restoration. 390bhp 427 engine with 4-speed manual gearbox.											
1967	**Corvette Sting Ray convertible**		194677S115681	L	NA	111.984	160.000	142.160	18-06-16	Portland	S122	Mec
	Maroon with black vinyl interior; restored. 435bhp 427 L71 engine with 4-speed manual gearbox.											
1967	**Corvette Sting Ray convertible**		194677S121397	L	NA	112.358*	154.000*	139.154*	24-06-16	Uncasville	667	B/J
	Maroon with white interior; 435bhp 427 L89 engine with 4-speed manual gearbox.											
1967	**Corvette Sting Ray convertible**		194677S101603	L	NA	96.250	125.000	112.913	09-07-16	Denver	S110	Mec
	Yellow with black singer and black leather interior; 400bhp 427 L36 engine with 4-speed manual gearbox. 4-wheel disc brakes J56 option. With hardtop.											
1965	**Corvette Sting Ray convertible**		194675S123365	L	NA	55.440	72.000	65.038	09-07-16	Denver	S184	Mec
	Yellow with black interior; 300bhp 327 engine with 4-speed manual gearbox.											
1967	**Corvette Sting Ray convertible**		194677S104841	L	NA	122.176	160.000	145.264	23-07-16	Harrisburg	S140	Mec
	Silver pearl with teal blue interior; restored in 2015. 400bhp 427 engine with 4-speed manual gearbox.											
1967	**Corvette Sting Ray convertible**		194677S104512	L	160-180.000 USD	180.686	236.500	208.806	20-08-16	Pebble Beach	53	G&Co
	Blue with blue leather interior; fully restored. 435bhp 427 L71 engine with 4-speed manual gearbox (see lot 80 RM 18.1.02 $95,700).											

F173: 1959 Chevrolet Impala convertible

F174: 1966 Chevrolet Nova Super Sport hardtop

Year	Model	(Bodybuilder)	Chassis no.	Steering	Estimate	Hammer Price £	Hammer Price $	Hammer Price €	Date	Place	Lot	Auc. H.
1963	**Corvette Sting Ray coupé**		30837S103110	L	75-95.000 GBP	72.800*	111.107*	99.685*	07-09-15	London	104	**RMS**
	Silver blue with black vinyl interior; restored. 250 bhp 327 engine with 4-speed manual gearbox (see lot 180 RM 8.9.14 $ 126,224).											
1963	**Corvette Sting Ray coupé**		30837S108862	L	NA	92.684	145.000	126.991	19-09-15	Dallas	S92	**Mec**
	Red with black interior; fully restored. 360bhp L84 327 fuel-injected engine with 4-speed manual gearbox.											
1965	**Corvette Sting Ray coupé**		194375S123442	L	NA	112.360	170.500	152.904	26-09-15	Las Vegas	721	**B/J**
	Blue with original blue leather interior; restored. 425bhp 396 engine with 4-speed manual gearbox.											
1963	**Corvette Sting Ray coupé**		30837S107148	L	80-120.000 USD	50.204	77.000	67.775	09-10-15	Hershey	285	**RMS**
	Red with red interior; restored three years ago. 340bhp 327 engine with 4-speed manual gearbox.											
1963	**Corvette Sting Ray coupé**		30837S112333	L	NA	85.761	130.000	118.716	12-12-15	Austin	S112.1	**Mec**
	Silver with black interior; restored about 10 years ago. 360bhp 327 engine with 4-speed manual gearbox.											
1964	**Corvette Sting Ray coupé**		40837S107999	L	450-500.000 USD		NS		23-01-16	Kissimmee	F131	**Mec**
	Red with white and red interior; raced at SCCA events in 1964 and 1965. Restored to its original specification. 327 fuel-injected engine with 4-speed manual gearbox.											
1967	**Corvette Sting Ray coupé**		194377S105531	L	175-200.000 USD	115.187	165.000	152.658	23-01-16	Kissimmee	F141 **F176**	**Mec**
	Blue with dark blue vinyl interior; stored from 1973 to 2014, the car is in original, unrestored condition and has covered 33,666 miles. 435bhp 427 L71 engine with 4-speed manual gearbox.											
1963	**Corvette Sting Ray coupé**		30837S103363	L	NA	58.640	84.000	77.717	23-01-16	Kissimmee	F82	**Mec**
	Silver with blue interior; last owner since 1970. 300bhp 327 engine with automatic transmission.											
1964	**Corvette Sting Ray coupé**		40837S104574	L	275-325.000 USD		NS		23-01-16	Kissimmee	S208	**Mec**
	White with black interior; 36-gallon fuel tank. In very good overall condition. 375bhp 327 engine with 4-speed manual gearbox (see Mecum lots S117 10.4.15 $ 220,000 and S69 16.5.15 NS).											
1963	**Corvette Sting Ray coupé**		30837S104422	L	160-220.000 USD	99.971*	143.000*	131.145*	28-01-16	Scottsdale	29	**Bon**
	Silver with black vinyl interior; in very good overall condition. Body repainted in recent years. Less than 40,000 miles on the odometer. 360bhp 327 fuel-injected engine with 4-speed manual gearbox.											
1966	**Corvette Sting Ray coupé**		194376S109547	L	70-90.000 USD	33.067*	47.300*	43.379*	28-01-16	Scottsdale	78	**Bon**
	Maroon with black vinyl interior; 425bhp 427 engine with 4-speed manual gearbox.											
1963	**Corvette Sting Ray coupé**		194377S119280	L	NA	92.360*	132.000*	120.872*	29-01-16	Scottsdale	1103	**B/J**
	Marine blue with black interior; in original condition. Until 2002 with its first owner; 33,880 original miles. 350bhp 327 L79 engine with 4-speed manual gearbox.											
1963	**Corvette Sting Ray coupé**		30837S103163	L	NA	100.057*	143.000*	130.945*	29-01-16	Scottsdale	1304	**B/J**
	White with blue interior; 360bhp 327 fuel-injected engine with 4-speed manual gearbox.											
1967	**Corvette Sting Ray coupé**		194377S111356	L	NA		NS		29-01-16	Scottsdale	1371	**B/J**
	Black with black leather interior; described as in very good original condition. 40,275 original miles. 435bhp 427 engine with 4-speed manual gearbox.											
1967	**Corvette Sting Ray coupé**		194377S117137	L	NA	48.972	70.000	63.119	12-03-16	Kansas City	S136	**Mec**
	Maroon with black interior; 390bhp 427 engine with automatic transmission.											
1966	**Corvette Sting Ray coupé**		194376S102264	L	120-140.000 USD	51.502	73.700	64.465	02-04-16	Ft.Lauderdale	437	**AA**
	Blue with blue interior; restored in 2003. 450bhp 427 L72 engine with 4-speed manual gearbox (see lot 71 Gooding 7.8.14 $ 107,250).											
1965	**Corvette Sting Ray coupé**		194375S121413	L	NA	91.428*	128.700*	113.256*	09-04-16	Palm Beach	445	**B/J**
	Red with white interior; fully restored. 425bhp 396 L78 engine with 4-speed manual gearbox.											
1963	**Corvette Sting Ray coupé**		30837S119168	L	NA	78.277	111.000	98.368	16-04-16	Houston	S123	**Mec**
	Silver blue with blue interior; restored. 300bhp 327 engine with 4-speed manual gearbox.											
1967	**Corvette Sting Ray coupé**		194377S106706	L	85-95.000 USD	54.870	79.200	71.003	05-06-16	Greenwhich	50	**Bon**
	Black with saddle vinyl interior; restored. 390bhp 427 engine with 4-speed manual gearbox.											
1966	**Corvette Sting Ray coupé**		194376S124595	L	NA	66.491	95.000	84.408	18-06-16	Portland	S131	**Mec**
	Blue with black leather interior; fully restored. Side mount exhaust. 425bhp 427 engine with 4-speed manual gearbox.											
1963	**Corvette Sting Ray coupé**		30837S101022	L	NA	107.800	140.000	126.462	09-07-16	Denver	S128	**Mec**
	Black with tan leather interior; 100 miles covered since the restoration carried out in 2010. 360bhp 327 fuel-injected engine with 4-speed manual gearbox.											
1967	**Corvette Sting Ray coupé**		194377S102167	L	NA	95.450	125.000	113.488	23-07-16	Harrisburg	F258	**Mec**
	Green with tan interior; restored. 435bhp 427 engine with 4-speed manual gearbox.											
1963	**Corvette Sting Ray coupé**		30837S103175	L	NA	91.632	120.000	108.948	23-07-16	Harrisburg	S157.1	**Mec**
	Blue with blue interior; restored. One owner. 340bhp 327 engine with 4-speed manual gearbox.											
1967	**Corvette Sting Ray coupé**		194377S100848	L	65-80.000 USD	39.919*	52.250*	46.132*	19-08-16	Carmel	88	**Bon**
	Silver with black vinyl interior; restored. 300bhp 327 engine with 4-speed manual gearbox.											

F175: 1967 Chevrolet Corvette Sting Ray convertible

F176: 1967 Chevrolet Corvette Sting Ray coupé

Year	Model	(Bodybuilder)	Chassis no.	Steering	Estimate	Hammer price £	Hammer price $	Hammer price €	Date	Place	Lot	Auc. H.
1963	**Corvette Sting Ray coupé**		30837S117322	L	150-160.000 USD	106.960	140.000	123.606	19-08-16	Monterey	F157	Mec
	Black with black interior; one owner until 2016. 43,777 miles on the odometer. Air conditioning and automatic transmission.											
1967	**Corvette Sting Ray coupé**		194377S119262	L	175-225.000 USD	118.420	155.000	136.850	19-08-16	Monterey	F30	Mec
	Green with white stinger and saddle leather interior; 14,875 miles covered. 435bhp 427 L71 engine with 4-speed manual gearbox.											
1963	**Corvette Sting Ray coupé**		30837S101490	L	NQ	109.252	143.000	126.255	20-08-16	Monterey	7024	R&S
	Red; restoration completed in 2016. 360bhp 327 fuel-injected engine with 4-speed manual gearbox.											
1963	**Corvette Sting Ray Z06 coupé**		30837S108848	L	600-750.000 USD	495.651	710.000	656.892	23-01-16	Kissimmee	S160	Mec **F177**
	Silver with red interior; raced in period, the car was fully restored between 1979 and 1984. 360bhp 327 fuel-injected engine with 4-speed manual gearbox. For 35 years in the collection of the previous owner, Vance Shappley (see lot S150.1 Mecum 25.1.14 $ 475,000).											
1963	**Corvette Sting Ray Z06 coupé**		30837S109268	L	250-300.000 USD	176.270	252.500	233.613	23-01-16	Kissimmee	S204	Mec
	Blue with saddle interior; raced at numerous events until the 1970s, the car was damaged in an accident and remained unrepaired with the same owner from 1974 to 2011. Full restoration completed in 2013 (see lot F117 Mecum 14.8.15 NS).											
1963	**Corvette Sting Ray Z06 coupé**		30837S113873	L	375-450.000 USD		NS		29-01-16	Scottsdale	45	G&Co
	Silver with black interior; restored between 2008 and 2010.											
1963	**Corvette Sting Ray Z06 coupé**		30837S108672	L	NA		NS		16-04-16	Houston	S116	Mec
	Silver with black interior; restored at unspecified date. 36-gallon fuel tank.											
1963	**Corvette Sting Ray Z06 coupé**		30837S114581	L	225-300.000 USD	144.144	210.000	187.173	20-05-16	Indianapolis	F134	Mec
	Red with black interior; fully restored at unspecified date. From the Joe McMurrey Collection (see lot F110 Mecum 13.08.10 $159,000).											
1963	**Corvette Sting Ray Z06 coupé**		30837S109301	L	NA		NS		24-06-16	Uncasville	703	B/J
	Silver with black interior; full restoration completed in 2009.											
1963	**Corvette Sting Ray Z06 coupé**		30837S118890	L	325-375.000 USD	175.720	230.000	203.067	19-08-16	Monterey	F150	Mec
	Red with black interior; restored in the early '80 and subsequently placed in storage until very recently. 36 gallon big tank.											
1965	**Chevelle two-door sedan**		138375K167816	L	NA		NS		13-11-15	Anaheim	S116	Mec
	Black with red interior; recently restored. Z16 Performance Package. 396 engine with 4-speed manual gearbox.											
1966	**Chevelle 300 DL two-door sedan**		133116K123322	L	NA	22.387	32.000	28.854	12-03-16	Kansas City	F134	Mec
	Blue with blue interior; restored. 425bhp 427 engine with 4-speed manual gearbox.											
1965	**Impala Super Sport convertible**		166675J198399	L	NA	44.774	64.000	57.709	12-03-16	Kansas City	S135	Mec
	Black with black interior; 843 miles covered since the restoration. 340bhp 409 engine with 4-speed manual gearbox.											
1967	**Caprice two-door hardtop**		166477F126658	L	NA	19.261*	26.400*	23.855*	24-06-16	Uncasville	67	B/J
	Red with black interior; restored. 325bhp 396 engine with automatic transmission.											
1970	**Chevelle SS convertible**		136670B134303	L	275-325.000 USD	160.563	230.000	212.796	23-01-16	Kissimmee	F130	Mec **F178**
	Red with white stripes and parchment and black interior; fully restored at unspecified date. Two owners and 44,000 miles. 450bhp 454 LS6 engine with automatic transmission (see lot 1320 Barrett-Jackson 17.1.06 $ 513,000).											
1970	**Chevelle SS convertible**		136670B138594	L	NA	123.147*	176.000*	161.163*	29-01-16	Scottsdale	1417	B/J
	Green with black interior; for 26 years in the current ownership, the car is described as in good original condition. 454 LS6 engine with 4-speed manual gearbox.											
1970	**Chevelle SS convertible**		136670B152004	L	200-250.000 USD		NS		02-04-16	Ft.Lauderdale	553	AA
	Red with black interior; fully restored. 450bhp 454 LS6 engine with automatic transmission.											
1967	**Chevelle SS convertible**		138677B128624	L	NA	57.045*	80.300*	70.664*	09-04-16	Palm Beach	502	B/J
	Blue with black interior; 325bhp 396 engine with 4-speed manual gearbox.											
1970	**Chevelle SS convertible**		136670L177486	L	NA	80.178	105.000	95.330	23-07-16	Harrisburg	S112	Mec
	Blue with white stripes and ivory interior; restored. 350bhp 396 engine with 4-speed manual gearbox.											
1970	**Chevelle SS coupé**		136370B133770	L	NA	89.488	140.000	122.612	19-09-15	Dallas	S111	Mec
	Black cherry with white stripes and ivory interior; concours quality restoration. 450bhp 454 LS6 engine with 4-speed manual gearbox.											
1969	**Chevelle SS DeLuxe coupé**		134279B383899	L	NA	45.145	71.500	62.863	31-10-15	Hilton Head	120	AA
	Orange with black interior; restored. 375bhp 396 L78 engine with 4-speed manual gearbox.											
1970	**Chevelle SS coupé**		136370R242793	L	NA	57.725*	82.500*	75.545*	29-01-16	Scottsdale	1134	B/J
	Black cherry with black interior; restored. 454 LS5 engine with 4-speed manual gearbox.											
1967	**Chevelle SS coupé**		138177S207482	L	100-125.000 USD	43.102*	61.600*	56.407*	29-01-16	Scottsdale	12	G&Co
	Red with red vinyl interior; restored between 2007 and 2008. Optioned with the J52 front disc brake package. 325bhp 396 engine with 4-speed manual gearbox.											

F177: 1963 Chevrolet Corvette Sting Ray Z06 coupé

F178: 1970 Chevrolet Chevelle SS convertible

Year	Model	(Bodybuilder)	Chassis no.	Steering	Estimate	Hammer price £	Hammer price $	Hammer price €	Date	Place	Lot	Auc. H.
1970	**Chevelle SS coupé**		136370L172047	L	NA	119.884	170.000	150.654	16-04-16	Houston	S105	Mec
	*Yellow with bonnet black stripes and black cloth interior; concours-quality restoration. 450bhp 454 LS6 engine with 4-speed manual gearbox.*
1969	**Chevelle SS Yenko coupé**		136379B406668	L	300-350.000 usd		NS		20-05-16	Indianapolis	F172	Mec
	*Yellow with black interior; 425bhp 427 L72 engine with 4-speed manual gearbox. Formerly in the Otis Chandler Collection.*
1970	**Chevelle SS coupé**		136370L187160	L	NA		NS		09-07-16	Denver	S36.1	Mec
	*Yellow with black vinyl top and black interior; restored. 450bhp 454 LS6 engine with automatic transmission.*
1970	**Chevelle SS coupé**		136370K179597	L	NA	80.178	105.000	95.330	23-07-16	Harrisburg	S112.1	Mec
	*Black with black interior; in original condition, 33,610 original miles. 450bhp 454 engine with automatic transmission (see lot F194 Mecum 23.1.15 $135,000).*
1969	**Camaro Yenko coupé**		194379N613759	L	275-325.000 usd	209.430	300.000	277.560	23-01-16	Kissimmee	F157	Mec
	*Orange with black roof and black interior; restored in the early 2000s and recently refreshed. 425bhp 427 L72 engine with 4-speed manual gearbox.*
1969	**Camaro Yenko coupé**		124379N579576	L	275-325.000 usd	230.373	330.000	305.316	23-01-16	Kissimmee	F163	Mec
	*Green with black stripes and black interior; recently restored. 425bhp 427 engine with 4-speed manual gearbox.*
1969	**Camaro Yenko coupé**		124379N578842	L	NA	230.901*	330.000*	302.181*	29-01-16	Scottsdale	1390	B/J
	*Yellow with black side stripe and black interior; acquired in 2012 and subsequently restored.*
1968	**Camaro Trans AM coupé**		9908H046	L	900-1.200.000 usd	692.604	990.000	892.683	12-03-16	Amelia Island	180	RMS
	*One of two examples prepared by the Penske team for the 1968 season, the car was driven among others by Mark Donahue and Sam Posey. Sold to Europe in mid-1969, it has had a long race career until 1987. Reimported into the USA in the late 1980s, it was subjected to a five year restoration and finished in the blue Sunoco livery of the 1968 season. Fitted with an est.420bhp 302 Traco-Chevrolet engine, the car has been subsequently raced at numerous historic events.* **F179**
1967	**Camaro Yenko Super SS coupé**		124377N241474	L	350-380.000 usd		NS		02-04-16	Ft.Lauderdale	555	AA
	*Blue with white nose stripe and black interior; restored. Approximately 450bhp 427 L72 engine with 4-speed manual gearbox (see lots 428 Barrett-Jackson 18.1.02 $ 118,800 and 146 Gooding 17.1.15 $ 357,500).*
1969	**Camaro Yenko coupé**		124379N664141	L	300-350.000 usd	154.440	225.000	200.543	20-05-16	Indianapolis	S154	Mec
	*Yellow with black roof and black interior; restored. 425bhp 427 engine with automatic transmission (see lot X34 Mecum 14.10.05 $204,750).*
1969	**Camaro Yenko coupé**		124379N614804	L	275-325.000 usd	178.464	260.000	231.738	20-05-16	Indianapolis	S200	Mec
	*Blue with black interior; concours-quality restoration completed in 2007. 425bhp 427 L72 engine with 4-speed manual gearbox.*
1969	**Camaro Yenko SC coupé**		124379N615226	L	300-350.000 usd	213.920	280.000	247.212	19-08-16	Monterey	F115	Mec
	*Yellow with black roof and black interior; fully restored. 11,800 miles on the odometer. 427 L72 engine original to the car.*
1969	**Camaro RS/SS convertible**		124679N639597	L	50-60.000 usd		NS		30-07-16	Plymouth	162	RMS
	*Indy 500 Pace Car Edition; in good overall condition. Automatic transmission.*
1970	**Camaro Z/28 coupé**		124870N534345	L	NA	44.010	67.500	59.414	09-10-15	Chicago	S97	Mec
	*Green with green interior; in the same ownership since 1975. Body repainted in 1980. Believed to be under 27,000 miles. 360bhp 350 engine with 4-speed manual gearbox.*
1969	**Camaro Z/28 coupé**		124379N688403	L	NA	54.701*	77.000*	67.760*	09-04-16	Palm Beach	436	B/J
	*Yellow with black roof and black and yellow interior; restored. 4-speed manual gearbox.*
1969	**Camaro Z/28 coupé**		124379N583968	L	NA	104.333*	143.000*	129.215*	24-06-16	Uncasville	671	B/J
	*Green with white stripes, black vinyl roof and black interior; restored. Manual gearbox. Recently serviced.*
1969	**Camaro Z/28 coupé**		124379L526864	L	60-80.000 usd	43.701*	57.200*	50.502*	19-08-16	Carmel	1	Bon
	*Gold with black stripes, black roof and black interior; restored. Manual gearbox.*
1969	**Camaro Z/28 coupé**		124379N636361	L	120-150.000 usd	76.400*	100.000*	88.290*	19-08-16	Monterey	F95	Mec
	*Dark green with white stripes and white and black interior; restored.*
1969	**Camaro ZL-1**		124379N609510	L	800-1.000.000 usd		NS		23-01-16	Kissimmee	F107	Mec
	*Blue with black interior; raced at some drag racing events in the 1970s, the car was restored to its original specification in the late 1980s and restored again in 2000. 430bhp 427 engine with 4-speed manual gearbox (see lot X20 Mecum 14.10.05 $ 840,000).*
1969	**Camaro ZL-1**		124379N610168	L	900-1.200.000 usd		NS		23-01-16	Kissimmee	S90.1	Mec
	*Orange with black interior; raced for several years in period. Restored in 2004. 430bhp 427 engine with 4-speed manual gearbox.*
1969	**Camaro ZL-1**		124379N634918	L	380-420.000 usd	282.490	404.250	353.597	02-04-16	Ft.Lauderdale	510	AA
	*White with black interior; fully restored. Engine rebuilt using a correct ZL1 replacement block. 4-speed manual gearbox. Raced in period.* **F180**
1969	**Camaro ZL-1**		344678M360554	L	550-750.000 usd		NS		20-05-16	Indianapolis	S208	Mec
	*Blue with black interior; raced in the early 1970s. First restored in 1988 and in 2000 again to concours condition. 4-speed manual gearbox.*
1969	**Nova SS coupé**		114279W399689	L	80-100.000 usd	49.565	71.000	65.689	23-01-16	Kissimmee	T235	Mec
	*White with blue interior; restored. 375bhp 396 L78 engine with automatico transmission.*

F179: 1968 Chevrolet Camaro Trans AM coupé

F180: 1969 Chevrolet Camaro ZL-1

Year	Model	(Bodybuilder)	Chassis no.	Steering	Estimate	Hammer price £	Hammer price $	Hammer price €	Date	Place	Lot	Auc. H.
1968	**Corvette convertible**		194678S423668	L	NA	36.846	56.100	50.372	05-09-15	Auburn	5153	AA
	Red with black interior; restored. 435bhp 427 engine with 4-speed manual gearbox.											
1968	**Corvette coupé**		194378S415053	L	NA	217.470*	330.000*	295.944*	26-09-15	Las Vegas	738	B/J **F181**
	Red with red interior; for 38 years in the current ownership. Body repainted, engine rebuilt. 24,760 actual miles. 430bhp 427 L88 engine with 4-speed manual gearbox.											
1969	**Corvette Stingray convertible**		194679S723530	L	NA	404.077*	577.500*	528.817*	29-01-16	Scottsdale	1369	B/J **F182**
	Blue with blue interior; stored for 25 years, the car was fully restored between 2012 and 2013. 430bhp 427 L88 engine with 4-speed manual gearbox (see Mecum lots S163 25.1.14 NS and S82 15. 8.15 $ 750,000).											
1969	**Corvette Stingray convertible**		194679S710546	L	175-225.000 USD	69.270*	99.000*	90.654*	29-01-16	Scottsdale	18	G&Co
	Gold with black interior; for 45 years with its first owner, the car is described as in very good original condition. 435bhp 427 engine with automatic transmission.											
1969	**Corvette Stingray convertible**		194679S710164	L	600-800.000 USD		NS		20-05-16	Indianapolis	S149	Mec
	Green with dark green interior; raced in period as a drag car. Restored between 1986 and 1988. 430bhp 427 L88 engine with 4-speed manual gearbox (see lot S165.1 Mecum 25.01.14 $510,000).											
1969	**Corvette Stingray convertible**		194679S710170	L	650-750.000 USD		NS		25-06-16	Santa Monica	1111	AA
	Burgundy with black interior; hardtop covered in black vinyl, side exhaust. Show condition restoration. 430bhp 427 L88 engine with manual gearbox.											
1970	**Corvette Stingray ZR1 convertible**		194670S404021	L	NQ	121.858	159.500	140.823	20-08-16	Monterey	7011	R&S
	White; LT1 engine with 4-speed manual gearbox (see lot S81 Mecum 15.8.15 NS).											
1971	**Corvette Stingray coupé**		194371S100419	R	45-50.000 AUD	26.013	40.070	36.151	24-10-15	Melbourne	9	TBr
	Dark green; the car was imported into Australia in 1987 and subsequently converted to right-hand drive. Restored between the late 1990s and 2003; 454 engine rebuilt to LS6 specification.											
1970	**Corvette Stingray coupé**		194370S409324	L	30-45.000 EUR	39.380*	62.360*	54.832*	01-11-15	Paris	172	Art
	Red with red interior; in original condition. 40,670 miles covered. LS5 454 engine.											
1968	**Corvette Stingray coupé**		194378S417431	L	700-900.000 USD		NS		23-01-16	Kissimmee	S140	Mec
	Silver with original black leather interior; restored in 1987. 430bhp 427 engine with 4-speed manual gearbox.											
1972	**Corvette Stingray coupé**		1Z37L2S514454	L	NA	134.692*	192.500*	176.272*	29-01-16	Scottsdale	1332	B/J
	Green with saddle leather interior; fully restored. 16,300 miles covered. ZR1 package. 255bhp 350 LT1 engine with 4-speed manual gearbox.											
1969	**Corvette Stingray coupé**		194379S728007	L	700-800.000 USD		NS		30-01-16	Scottsdale	147	G&Co
	Black with black interior; restored in the early 2000s. Just over 2,000 miles covered since new. 427 L88 engine with 4-speed manual gearbox (see lot S87 Mecum 15.8.15 NS).											
1969	**Corvette Stingray coupé**		194379S714904	L	NA		NS		30-01-16	Scottsdale	5074	R&S
	Gold with saddle vinyl interior; in original condition, never restored, the car has covered approximately 2,600 miles since new. 427 L88 engine with 4-speed manual gearbox (see lot 1271 Barrett-Jackson 17.1.06 $ 334,800).											
1969	**Corvette Stingray coupé**		194379S720677	L	NA	455.854	624.800	564.569	24-06-16	Uncasville	688	B/J
	Silver with black leather interior; fully restored. 427 L88 engine with 4-speed manual gearbox. Side exhausts.											
1970	**Nova V-8 Yenko Deuce coupé**		114270W352754	L	NA		NS		18-06-16	Portland	S150	Mec
	Silver with black interior; restored. One of 175 examples modified by Don Yenko. 360bhp LT1 350 engine with 4-speed manual gearbox.											
1978	**Corvette coupé Silver Anniversary**		1Z87L85427	L	20-30.000 EUR	17.387*	25.774*	23.000*	04-02-16	Paris	432	Bon
	One owner and 22,246 kms covered.											
1978	**Corvette coupé Silver Anniversary**		906163	L	35-45.000 EUR	28.985	38.127	34.176	06-08-16	Schloss Dyck	115	Coy
	Indianapolis Pace Car limited edition; 198 miles covered.											

CHEVRON (GB) *(1966-1978)*

Year	Model	(Bodybuilder)	Chassis no.	Steering	Estimate	£	$	€	Date	Place	Lot	Auc. H.
1977	**B36**		367705	R	190-230.000 EUR	132.313	190.646	168.000	14-05-16	Monaco	247	RMS **F183**
	Yellow with black stripes; fitted with the 1,975cc Cosworth BDG engine, the car was sold new to the USA and raced until 1980. Imported into Switzerland in the 2000s and later fully restored.											

CHRYSLER (USA) *(1923-)*

Year	Model	(Bodybuilder)	Chassis no.	Steering	Estimate	£	$	€	Date	Place	Lot	Auc. H.
1926	**Series F-58 coach**		F00830(engine)	L	12-17.000 USD	10.441*	15.950*	14.173*	08-10-15	Hershey	147	RMS
	Restored many years ago; from the estate of Richard Roy.											
1927	**Model G-70 roadster**		PR580R	L	24-28.000 EUR		NS		28-05-16	Aarhus	210	SiC
	Maroon with black fenders and maroon interior; restored.											
1926	**Model G-70 roadster**		H126321(engine)	L	45-55.000 USD	24.387*	35.200*	31.557*	05-06-16	Greenwhich	75	Bon
	Yellow and green with black fenders and brown leather interior; restored in the 1970s probably. From the Evergreen Collection.											

F181: 1968 Chevrolet Corvette coupé

F182: 1969 Chevrolet Corvette Stingray convertible

Year	Model (Bodybuilder)	Chassis no.	Steering	Estimate	Hammer price £	$	€	Date	Place	Lot	Auc. H.

F183: 1977 Chevron B36

F184: 1931 Chrysler Imperial CG convertible

Year	Model (Bodybuilder)	Chassis no.	Steering	Estimate	£	$	€	Date	Place	Lot	Auc. H.
1926	**Model G-70 coupé**	CP446295	L	13-15.000 GBP		NS		28-07-16	Donington Park	49	**H&H**
	Blue with black fenders; restored many years ago.										
1928	**Series 80 L Imperial touralette (Locke)**	L2653(engine)	L	350-400.000 USD		NS		10-03-16	Amelia Island	162	**Bon**
	Black with cream fenders and cane work on the body rear part; restored several decades ago.										
1929	**Series 75 roadster**	R302359(engine)	L	50-75.000 USD	21.602*	33.000*	29.324*	08-10-15	Hershey	135	**RMS**
	Maroon and black with brown interior; restored in the 1970s. In need of recommissioning. From the Richard Roy estate.										
1929	**Series 75 roadster**	CY282E	L	40-60.000 USD	16.561*	25.300*	22.482*	08-10-15	Hershey	142	**RMS**
	Green with red vinyl interior; paintwork and interior redone in the 1950s. Unused for over 60 years. Acquired in 1949 by Richard Roy from whose estate it is offered.										
1929	**Series 75 tonneau phaeton**	CE7H	L	75-100.000 USD	32.403*	49.500*	43.986*	08-10-15	Hershey	146	**RMS**
	Two-tone green; restored many years ago, the car is described as still in good overall condition. From the estate of Richard Roy.										
1929	**Series 75 roadster**	R291011	L	10-15.000 GBP	20.700	31.309	28.609	10-12-15	London	355	**Bon**
	Yellow with black fenders; last used in 2011, it requires recommissioning prior to use.										
1929	**Series 75 roadster**	CY7L	L	130-170.000 EUR	101.244*	146.940*	134.400*	03-02-16	Paris	108	**RMS**
	Ivory and black; restored to the 1929 Mille Miglia 5-Litre class-winning car specification. Between 2012 and 2015 it was driven at the Le Mans Classic, Grand Prix Nuvolari and Mille Miglia Storica.										
1931	**Imperial CG convertible**	7802566	L	250-300.000 USD	126.011*	192.500*	171.056*	08-10-15	Hershey	166	**RMS** F184
	Light grey and light green with tan interior; 12,378 miles covered since the restoration.										
1931	**Imperial CG roadster (LeBaron)**	6005318	L	450-600.000 USD		NS		28-01-16	Scottsdale	39	**Bon**
	Black with red leather interior; restored many years ago. Formerly in the Harrah Collection.										
1932	**Six Series CI coupé**	C13748	L	NA	16.493	25.000	22.830	12-12-15	Austin	S67.1	**Mec**
	Light blue and white with light blue and white interior.										
1931	**Imperial CL dual cowl phaeton (LeBaron)**	CL1002	L	3.600-4.300.000 DKK	279.223	423.795	380.140	26-09-15	Ebeltoft	19	**Bon** F185
	Black with red leather interior; first restored in 1970 circa and again in the 1980s. From the Frederiksen Collection (see lots 311 Brooks 6.10.00 NS and 72 RM 4.8.01 NS).										
1933	**Imperial CL dual cowl phaeton (LeBaron)**	7803639	L	750-950.000 USD		NS		10-03-16	Amelia Island	180	**Bon**
	Grey and burgundy with burgundy interior; bought new by Marjorie Merryweather Post, the car was fitted with the present body coming from a 1931 Imperial CG also in the ownership of Mrs Post. In 1956 it was acquired by Bruce R. Thomas who had it restored. Approximately 10 years ago the car was acquired by the current owner who had it restored again.										
1936	**Imperial Airflow sedan**	7015285	L	100-125.000 USD	114.752	176.000	154.915	09-10-15	Hershey	277	**RMS** F186
	Metallic beige with tan cloth interior; following an over 50 year period on display in a motor museum, the car received a concours-quality restoration between 2013 and 2014.										
1937	**Imperial Airflow sedan**	C172000	L	NQ	24.710	36.000	32.087	20-05-16	Indianapolis	S32	**Mec**
	Two-tone maroon with grey interior; restored.										
1936	**Imperial Airflow sedan**	7019207	L	40-50.000 USD	30.497	41.800	37.770	25-06-16	Santa Monica	1128	**AA**
	Restored many years ago.										
1941	**New Yorker convertible**	3541040	L	65-75.000 USD	35.056*	50.600*	45.363*	05-06-16	Greenwhich	78	**Bon**
	Green with beige and tan interior; an older restoration. From the Evergreen Collection.										

F185: 1931 Chrysler Imperial CL dual cowl phaeton (LeBaron)

F186: 1936 Chrysler Imperial Airflow sedan

Year	Model	(Bodybuilder)	Chassis No.	Steering	Estimate	Hammer Price £	Hammer Price $	Hammer Price €	Date	Place	Lot	Auc. H.
1942	Windsor club coupé		70507040	L	40-60.000 USD	32.274*	49.500*	43.570*	09-10-15	Hershey	275	RMS
Dark blue with blue cloth interior; restored.												
1947	New Yorker coupé		7044044	L	NQ	14.707	19.250	16.996	20-08-16	Monterey	7149	R&S
Restored; semi-automatic transmission.												
1947	Town and Country convertible		C3939896	L	NA	101.147	154.000	138.277	05-09-15	Auburn	5119	AA
Blue with wooden panels and blue and tan interior (see lot 52 Worldwide Group 5.9.09 $ 264,000).												
1948	Town and Country convertible		7407193	L	750-1.000.000 DKK	92.886	140.979	126.456	26-09-15	Ebeltoft	12	Bon
Blue with wooden panels and leather and cloth interior; described as in very good running condition. Wooden parts restored in 2013. From the Frederiksen Collection (see lot 372 Bonhams 5.2.15 $ 164,000).												
1947	Town and Country 6-cylinder sedan		71002156	L	140-160.000 USD	97.208	148.500	131.957	08-10-15	Hershey	168	RMS F187
Red with wooden panels and leather and cloth interior; restored in 2013 to concours condition.												
1947	Town and Country convertible		7404990	L	140-180.000 USD		NS		08-10-15	Hershey	176	RMS
Yellow with original wooden panels; in good driving order. Body repainted (see lot 687 America Auctions 28.3.15 NS).												
1948	Town and Country convertible		7406169	L	NA		NS		31-10-15	Hilton Head	130	AA
Green with wooden panels and green and tan interior.												
1946	Town and Country convertible		C392903	L	NA		NS		12-12-15	Austin	S95	Mec
Burgundy with burgundy interior; one owner until 2014. Recent mechanical works. Semi-automatic transmission.												
1947	Town and Country convertible		740387	L	200-250.000 USD	119.197	170.500	156.366	28-01-16	Phoenix	113	RMS
Sand with wooden panels; restored at unspecified date.												
1948	Town and Country convertible		7407812	L	90-110.000 USD	73.119*	104.500*	95.691*	30-01-16	Scottsdale	138	G&Co
Beige with wooden panels and original brown leather and tan cloth interior; in largely original condition.												
1948	Town and Country convertible		7407588	L	120-150.000 USD	92.347*	132.000*	119.024*	11-03-16	Amelia Island	49	G&Co
Dark blue with wooden panels and tartan cloth interior; restoration completed in 2008.												
1946	Town and Country convertible		C3912569	L	NA	76.243*	104.500*	94.426*	24-06-16	Uncasville	715	B/J
Burgundy with wooden panels and birgundy and tan interior; restored several years ago.												
1951	Windsor DeLuxe convertible		709384494	L	35-40.000 EUR		NS		08-11-15	Lyon	221	Ose
Red with red and white interior; some works carried out in France in recent years.												
1951	Imperial convertible		7746661	L	90-100.000 USD	48.300	70.000	61.257	07-05-16	Auburn	856	AA
Light grey with blue interior; restored. Automatic transmission.												
1953	New Yorker Town & Country station wagon		76561406	L	NA	24.629*	35.200*	32.233*	29-01-16	Scottsdale	973	B/J
Beige with brown roof, mahogany panels at the back and brown leather interior; restored. 331 Hemi engine with automatic transmission.												
1953	Special	(Ghia)	7232631	L	700-900.000 USD		NS		10-12-15	New York	213	RMS
Two-tone metallic green; sold new to Switzerland, the car was reimported into the USA in the early 1970s. In 1982 it was bought by Fran Roxas who restored it and resold it to Joe Bortz who retained the car for 20 years circa. Described as still in good overall condition (see RM lots 90 28.1.05 $ 354,750 and 275 24.7.10 $ 858,000).												
1959	300E hardtop		M591100137	L	140-160.000 USD	58.640	84.000	77.717	23-01-16	Kissimmee	F122	Mec F188
Black with tan interior; less than 100 miles covered since a full restoration completed in 2014.												
1955	C-300 coupé		3N552067	L	NA	32.326*	46.200*	42.305*	29-01-16	Scottsdale	975.1	B/J
Red with black roof and red interior; automatic transmission.												
1957	300C hardtop		3N572091	L	NA	30.476*	42.900*	37.752*	09-04-16	Palm Beach	706	B/J
Red with tan leather interior; restored.												
1961	300G hardtop		8413120342	L	NA		NS		24-06-16	Uncasville	641	B/J
Red with tan interior; the car has covered 10 miles since a concours-quality restoration. 3-speed manual gearbox (see lot 5064 Barrett-Jackson 17.1.15 $220,000).												
1960	300 F GT Special		8403110398	L	250-325.000 USD	336.160	440.000	388.476	20-08-16	Pebble Beach	73	G&Co
Black; one of six examples built at the factory with 400-plus bhp engine; 1960 Daytona Beach Flying Mile Record in its class at 144.9mph driven by Gregg Ziegler; in single ownership from late 1960 to 2008; in original condition; 11,400 miles covered (see lots 6013 Russo & Steele 20.1.10 NS, 47 Worldwide 18.2.11 NS, and 19 Gooding & Company 08.3.13 $236,500).												
1961	300G convertible		8413114498	L	NA	60.034*	85.800*	78.567*	29-01-16	Scottsdale	1121	B/J
Maroon with tan interior; restored. Automatic transmission.												
1958	300D convertible		LC41242	L	120-150.000 USD	33.542	48.000	41.986	02-04-16	Ft.Lauderdale	486	AA
Black with beige leather interior.												

F187: 1947 Chrysler Town and Country 6-cylinder sedan

F188: 1959 Chrysler 300E hardtop

Year	Model	(Bodybuilder)	Chassis no.	Steering	Estimate	£	$	€	Date	Place	Lot	Auc. H.

F189: 1949 Cisitalia 202 cabriolet (Stabilimenti Farina)

F190: 1953 Cisitalia 505 DF coupé (Ghia)

Year	Model (Bodybuilder)	Chassis no.	St	Estimate	£	$	€	Date	Place	Lot	Auc. H.
1962	300H convertible	8423121259	L	NA		NS		18-06-16	Portland	F216	Mec
	Red with tan interior; restored.										
1955	New Yorker DeLuxe convertible	N5510413	L	55-65.000 USD		NS		25-06-16	Santa Monica	1062	AA
	Black with maroon side stripe and black interior; restored.										
1962	New Yorker sedan	8323156802	L	20-30.000 USD	13.372*	17.600*	15.836*	30-07-16	Plymouth	170	RMS
	Black with red vinyl interior; described as in good original condition. 26,593 miles covered.										
1986	LeBaron Town & Country convertible	1C3BC55E7GG109742	L	9-15.000 USD	3.044	4.620	4.112	05-10-15	Philadelphia	241	Bon
	Black with faux-wood side panels; in original condition. Supercharged engine. From the Evergreen Collection.										

CISITALIA (I) (1946-1965)

Year	Model (Bodybuilder)	Chassis no.	St	Estimate	£	$	€	Date	Place	Lot	Auc. H.
1948	202 CMM (Vignale)	002CMM	L	2.000-3.000.000 USD		NS		21-08-16	Pebble Beach	123	G&Co
	One of two examples (known as Coupé Aerodinamicos) built by Vignale on a Giovanni Savonuzzi design; fitted with the engine enlarged to 1,220cc, it was a Works entry for Piero Taruffi at the 1948 Mille Miglia. Later it was sold to Argentina where it was raced until 1954. Restored in Uruguay in the 1970s, in 1981 it was sold to Japan where it received further restoration works. Between 1988 and 1993 it was driven at three editions of the historic Mille Miglia.										
1949	202 cabriolet (Stabilimenti Farina)	062SC	R	240-280.000 EUR	220.210	320.467	286.080	05-02-16	Paris	180	Art F189
	Apple green with beige interior; restored in Italy at unspecified date. First owner the movie producer Carlo Ponti.										
1953	505 DF coupé (Ghia)	00209	L	130-150.000 GBP	145.600	222.215	199.370	07-09-15	London	111	RMS F190
	One of 10 examples built and one of two known survivors. Sold new to Switzerland; mechanicals restored in Germany between 2005 and 2007; further restoration works carried out later in the USA. In concours condition. From the Fendt Collection.										

CITROËN (F) (1919-)

Year	Model (Bodybuilder)	Chassis no.	St	Estimate	£	$	€	Date	Place	Lot	Auc. H.
1928	B14 G faux cabriolet	330442	L	15-18.000 EUR		NS		19-06-16	Fontainebleau	308	Ose
	Green with black wings; restored in the 1980s probably.										
1932	C4 G torpedo	108538	L	20-30.000 EUR	32.114*	46.735*	41.720*	06-02-16	Paris	312	Art
	Green with black wings and red leather interior; restored. Since 1971 in the André Trigano Collection.										
1931	C4 G coach	105315	L	20-30.000 EUR	21.103*	30.711*	27.416*	06-02-16	Paris	340	Art
	Black and red; restored. From the André Trigano Collection.										
1929	P19 chenillette half-track	19483	L	40-60.000 EUR	27.526*	40.058*	35.760*	06-02-16	Paris	316	Art F191
	Sand; restored. 6-cylinder 2.5-litre engine. From the André Trigano Collection.										
1934	8A Rosalie berline	818537	L	10-15.000 EUR	9.175*	13.353*	11.920*	06-02-16	Paris	305	Art
	Dark green with black wings; fully restored. From the André Trigano Collection.										
1935	7C coupé	66561	L	100-150.000 EUR	82.579*	120.175*	107.280*	06-02-16	Paris	311	Art F192
	Black with red leather interior; fully restored at unspecified date. From the André Trigano Collection.										
1936	11 UA Rosalie limousine	285287	L	12-16.000 EUR	9.634*	14.020*	12.516*	06-02-16	Paris	313	Art
	Black with beige cloth interior; restored. From the André Trigano Collection.										

F191: 1929 Citroën P19 chenillette half-track

F192: 1935 Citroën 7C coupé

Year	Model	(Bodybuilder)	Chassis No.	Steering	Estimate	Hammer Price £	$	€	Date	Place	Lot	Auc. H.
1954	11B berline		273164	L	11.5-14.500 EUR	14.014	20.302	18.000	20-03-16	Fontainebleau	333	Ose
	Black; since 1988 in the current ownership. Body repainted in 2000 circa; engine rebuilt.											
1953	11BL légère berline		626577	L	15-20.000 EUR	15.598*	22.700*	20.264*	06-02-16	Paris	342	Art
	Black with grey cloth interior; restored. From the André Trigano Collection.											
1937	11BL berline		367169	L	20-25.000 EUR		NS		14-05-16	Monaco	121	RMS
	Black; in good cosmetic condition. From the Quattroruote Collection.											
1952	11BL légère berline		598493	L	10-12.000 EUR	10.776	15.395	13.680	19-06-16	Fontainebleau	305	Ose
	Black with grey cloth interior; paintwork redone.											
1937	11 BN cabriolet		123786	L	150-200.000 EUR	126.184	192.131	172.500	05-09-15	Chantilly	24	Bon
	Black/burgundy with beige leather interior; offered with sundry invoices and Controle Technique (issued June 2015). From the collection of Alain Dominique Perrin, in whose family ownership the car arrived in 1955.											
1938	11 BL cabriolet		407483	L	150-180.000 EUR		NS		04-02-16	Paris	393	Bon
	Burgundy with burgundy leather interior; since 1999 in the current ownership. Restoration completed in 2005.											
1939	11 BL cabriolet		437937	L	80-100.000 EUR	64.228*	93.469*	83.440*	06-02-16	Paris	310	Art
	Ivory with dark red interior; acquired already restored in 1985 by the current owner, the car is described as still in good overall condition.											
1939	11 B cabriolet		149701	L	140-200.000 EUR	128.456*	186.939*	166.880*	06-02-16	Paris	332	Art F193
	Black with red leather interior; fully restored. Since 1978 in the André Trigano Collection.											
1937	11 BL cabriolet		384595	L	70-90.000 EUR	96.529*	125.357*	113.240*	09-07-16	Le Mans	121	Art
	Black with red interior; restored at unspecified date, the car is described as in good overall condition.											
1952	Light Fifteen saloon		9521175	R	12-15.000 GBP	11.500	17.511	15.722	05-09-15	Beaulieu	112	Bon
	Black with red interior; stored for many years, the car was recommissioned in 2014.											
1939	Light Fifteen cabriolet		103631	R	65-75.000 EUR	55.646	88.118	77.480	01-11-15	Paris	176	Art
	White with blue interior; restored in the early 2000s.											
1955	Light Fifteen		9550254	R	8-12.000 GBP	6.720	9.679	8.563	11-06-16	Brooklands	204	His
	Red with original dark burgundy leather interior; body repainted in the early 1970s, engine restored in 1992 and recently overhauled (see lot 506 Sotheby's 7.7.97 $ 10,069).											
1939	15 Six cabriolet		680959	L	650-1.100.000 EUR		NS		14-05-16	Monaco	264	RMS
	First of four examples built at the factory, the car was sold new to Mrs Anna Michelin. In 1954 it was imported into the USA where remained in the same family ownership until the early 1990s. In 1997 it was purchased by a Dutch collector, who had it restored and fitted again with its original engine discovered in France. Restored again by the current owner and refinished in its original dark green livery.											
1953	15 Six D Familiale		723240	L	16-20.000 GBP	16.800	25.286	23.900	28-11-15	Weybridge	218	His
	Black; following a 23 years storage period, in 1995 the car was acquired by the present owner and recommissioned for road use. Body repainted in 2012.											
1949	15 Six D berline		690855	L	25-35.000 EUR	29.361*	42.729*	38.144*	06-02-16	Paris	304	Art F194
	Nera; engine rebuilt, gearbox overhauled. 23,635 kms on the odometer. Probably the car has had two owners and since 1988 is in the André Trigano Collection.											
1954	15 Six D limousine familiale		724203	L	20-30.000 EUR	18.810*	27.373*	24.436*	06-02-16	Paris	317	Art
	Black; restored. From the André Trigano Collection.											
1952	15 Six D		720303	L	30-35.000 EUR	44.844	64.967	57.600	20-03-16	Fontainebleau	320	Ose
	Black with grey cloth interior; fully restored some years ago, the car is described as in very good overall condition.											
1950	15 Six D berline		694832	L	30-40.000 EUR		NS		19-06-16	Fontainebleau	325	Ose
	Described as in very good running order; engine rebuilt.											
1955	15 Six H		727677	L	25-30.000 EUR	18.085	27.377	25.200	08-11-15	Lyon	222	Ose
	Black; in good original condition except for the paintwork redone over 20 years ago. Just one owner.											
1991	2CV 6		372304	L	3-6.000 EUR	7.705*	12.201*	10.728*	01-11-15	Paris	106	Art
	Yellow with blue interior; one owner and 10,000 kms covered.											
1959	2CV AZ		1072346	L	5-10.000 EUR	7.320	11.081	10.200	07-11-15	Lyon	286	Agu
	Grey/blue; fully restored between 2011 and 2013.											
1974	2CV6		AZA9103167	L	20-30.000 USD	34.605*	49.500*	45.396*	28-01-16	Phoenix	103	RMS
	Yellow and black; fully restored. From the Craig McCaw Collection.											
1962	2CV Sahara 4X4		0332	L	85-125.000 EUR		NS		04-02-16	Paris	382	Bon
	Partially restored some 10 years ago; described as in good condition.											

F193: 1939 Citroën 11 B cabriolet

F194: 1949 Citroën 15 Six D berline

Year	Model (Bodybuilder)	Chassis no.	Steering	Estimate	Hammer price £	Hammer price $	Hammer price €	Sale Date	Sale Place	Lot	Auc. H.
1990	2CV6 Charleston	371037	L	20-40.000 EUR	29.361*	42.729*	38.144*	06-02-16	Paris	335	Art
	Two-tone grey; in very good overall condition. One owner and 2,900 kms covered.										
1964	2CV AK fourgonnette	9017234	L	8-12.000 EUR	9.634*	14.020*	12.516*	06-02-16	Paris	336	Art
	Grey; until 2013 with its first owner. Body repainted.										
1961	2CV Sahara	05100197	L	60-90.000 EUR	133.044	193.615	172.840	06-02-16	Paris	348	Art F195
	Since new in the same family ownership; in original condition; 11,367 kms on the odometer. Unused for many years it requires recommissioning prior to use.										
1956	2CV AZ	315836	L	8-12.000 EUR	14.014	20.302	18.000	20-03-16	Fontainebleau	331	Ose
	Grey; restored (see Osenat lots 332 20.3.11 $ 12,717 and 311 12.10.12 $ 15,661).										
1969	2CV AK350 Van	91952B1	L	16-21.000 EUR		NS		09-04-16	Essen	228	Coy
	Grey-rose; restored in recent years.										
1962	2CV Sahara	0233	L	95-105.000 USD	59.562	85.800	75.899	11-06-16	Hershey	108	TFA
	Grey with burgundy interior; in running condition. Restored by the current owner.										
1963	2CV Sahara	0617	L	70-90.000 EUR	68.078	88.409	79.864	09-07-16	Le Mans	147	Art
	Green; restoration completed in 2008.										
1957	DS 19	29854	L	17-20.000 GBP	20.700	29.988	26.587	20-03-16	Goodwood	81	Bon
	Bought in 1989 by the current owner and restored.										
1964	DS 19	4413414	L	22-26.000 EUR		NS		14-05-16	Monaco	116	RMS
	Blue with grey roof; in original condition. Since 1983 in the Quattroruote Collection.										
1973	DS 20	4532928	R	12-15.000 GBP		NS		05-09-15	Beaulieu	114	Bon
	Some works to the bodywork carried out in the 1990s; recommissioned in 2014. The original 2.1-litre and 5-speed gearbox were replaced with a 2-litre engine and a 4-speed gearbox. The original units are available if required.										
1967	DS 21 Pallas	4479847	L	40-60.000 EUR	20.864*	30.929*	27.600*	04-02-16	Paris	397	Bon
	Palladium grey with original black leather interior; described as in very good, largely original condition. Manual gearbox.										
1969	DS 21 Prestige	4495453	L	30-50.000 EUR	26.609*	38.723*	34.568*	06-02-16	Paris	331	Art
	Black with tan leather interior; body repainted, engine overhauled. From the André Trigano Collection.										
1966	DS 21	4469031	L	15-20.000 EUR	15.696	22.738	20.160	20-03-16	Fontainebleau	332	Ose
	Black with gery roof and red interior; 90,600 kms covered (see lot 358 Osenat 15.3.15 $ 19,791).										
1972	DS 21	04FD0889	L	14-18.000 GBP		NS		02-07-16	Woodstock	156	Coy
	Cream with black roof and brown interior; restored in 2010.										
1974	DS 23 Pallas	01F68592	R	300-400.000 DKK	23.788	36.104	32.385	26-09-15	Ebeltoft	1	Bon
	Blue; body repainted in the 2000s. From the Frederiksen Collection.										
1972	DS 23ie Pallas	00FG5277	L	35-45.000 EUR	18.834*	29.825*	26.224*	01-11-15	Paris	175	Art
	Metallic brown with original tobacco leather interior; with its first owner until the late 2012. Engine replaced in 1986; body repainted in 2007.										
1974	DS 23ie Pallas	02FG2990	L	50-80.000 EUR	48.630*	70.770*	63.176*	06-02-16	Paris	333	Art F196
	Sand with tan interior; 9,900 kms covered since the restoration completed in 2008. With sunroof.										
1972	DS 23ie Pallas	00FG0528	L	25-35.000 EUR	45.966	66.591	59.040	20-03-16	Fontainebleau	324	Ose
	Black with original black leather interior; restored a few years ago.										
1973	DS 23ie Pallas	00FG7053	R	16-20.000 GBP		NS		18-05-16	Donington Park	86	H&H
	Grey with black leather interior; 50,500 recorded miles. Interior retrimmed in 2016.										
1973	DS 23 Pallas	06730012547DS4153	R	14-17.000 GBP	16.520	21.621	19.089	20-08-16	Brooklands	260	His
	White with maroon leather interior; in good overall condition. Interior redone in 2015.										
1968	ID 21 break	3561005	L	40-60.000 EUR	55.053*	80.117*	71.520*	06-02-16	Paris	319	Art F197
	Dark blue and white with brown interior; restored in Italy.										
1972	D Super 5	4546046	R	NA	16.594	23.492	21.416	06-03-16	Birmingham	314	SiC
	Restored in 2014.										
1961	DS 19 cabriolet (Chapron)	4200224	L	170-230.000 EUR	168.245	256.174	230.000	05-09-15	Chantilly	7	Bon
	Forest green with red leather interior; sold new to Portugal where it remained until 2012. Body restored in 2003, mechanicals restored in 2013, interior retrimmed in 2014.										
1967	DS 21 cabriolet	DS21M4473040	L	120-180.000 EUR	127.771	195.995	172.500	09-10-15	Zoute	40	Bon
	Dark blue with light brown leather interior; restored in the 2000s. Since 2006 in the current ownership (see lot 110 Christie's 8.7.06 $ 180,170).										

F195: 1961 Citroën 2CV Sahara

F196: 1974 Citroën DS 23ie Pallas

Year	Model	(Bodybuilder)	Chassis no.	Steering	Estimate	Hammer price £	Hammer price $	Hammer price €	Date	Place	Lot	Auc. H.
1967	DS 21 Le Caddy cabriolet	(Chapron)	437016	L	250-350.000 EUR	199.949	296.399	264.500	04-02-16	Paris	356	Bon F198
Originally finished in royal red and black with beige leather interior, the car was exhibited by Henri Chapron at the 1967 Paris Motor Show. Over the years it has had several owners and the body colour was changed several times. In 2007 it was acquired by the current owner who had it fully restored between 2009 and 2012 and finished in the present dark blue livery.
1963	DS 19 cabriolet		4272038	L	120-150.000 EUR	123.322	178.659	158.400	20-03-16	Fontainebleau	352	Ose
Dark red with original black leather interior; body repainted in the 1970s. Since new in the same family ownership.
1964	Ami 6 berline		9325334	L	6-10.000 EUR	11.469*	16.691*	14.900*	06-02-16	Paris	302	Art
Light blue with white roof and red cloth interior; in very good overall condition.
1973	Ami Super		01JF3169	L	5-10.000 EUR	9.175*	13.353*	11.920*	06-02-16	Paris	326	Art
Beige with cloth and leatherette interior; in original condition. 36,535 kms on the odometer. From the André Trigano Collection.
1967	Ami 6 berline		9456436	L	12-18.000 EUR		NS		19-06-16	Fontainebleau	327	Ose
White with red cloth interior; restored four years ago.
1980	Mehari 4X4		OOCE0519	L	20-30.000 EUR	21.295	32.666	28.750	09-10-15	Zoute	3	Bon
Green; restored in 2011.
1980	Mehari 4X4		00CE0445	L	20-30.000 EUR	38.537*	56.082*	50.064*	06-02-16	Paris	307	Art F199
Beige; 1,705 kms covered. Since new in the André Trigano Collection.
1979	Mehari		10CA5345	L	9-11.000 EUR	11.174	15.970	14.400	12-03-16	Lyon	349	Agu
White with white and yellow interior; bought in 2007 by the current owner and subsequently restored.
1981	Mehari 4x4		0325	L	45-55.000 EUR		NS		14-05-16	Monaco	193	Coy
Yellow; described as in very good overall condition.
1971	M35	(Heuliez)	0417	L	15-20.000 EUR	16.333*	23.768*	21.218*	06-02-16	Paris	325	Art
One of the 257 examples built with the Wankel engine; in original condition. Since 1980 in the André Trigano Collection.
1973	SM		00SD0338	L	350-450.000 DKK	37.381	56.735	50.891	26-09-15	Ebeltoft	2	Bon
Blue with tobacco leather interior; restored in the USA. From the Frederiksen Collection.
1973	SM Mylord cabriolet		00SC1326	L	250-300.000 EUR		NS		26-09-15	Frankfurt	157	Coy
The car was built on a standard SM chassis using original parts and drawings from the Carrosserie Chapron. Completed over a 30 years period. The car is registered within the Chapron Register bearing no. 7670.
1974	SM		009503	L	20-25.000 GBP	22.876	35.089	30.883	10-10-15	Ascot	134	Coy
Metallic gold with brown leather interior; unrestored.
1972	SM		00SB9355	L	NA		NS		31-10-15	Hilton Head	166	AA
Blue/green with tan leather interior; in good overall condition.
1970	SM		00SB0150	L	15-20.000 EUR	15.071	22.814	21.000	08-11-15	Lyon	225	Ose
Light blue; in good working order. Two owners.
1972	SM		00SC0732	L	42-48.000 GBP	51.188	77.929	72.400	14-11-15	Birmingham	317	SiC
Champagne with black leather interior; restored in 2014. Engine rebuilt.
1972	SM		00SB54920	L	30-36.000 GBP		NS		28-11-15	Weybridge	229	His
Blue with brown leather interior; sold new to Italy where it remained in the same family ownership until its recent import into the UK.
1972	SM		00SB9711	L	40-60.000 GBP	24.833	37.560	34.322	10-12-15	London	329	Bon
Metallic beige with beige velour interior; for 40 years in the same family ownership. Engine rebuilt in 2006 and bored out to 3 litres; body repainted.
1974	SM		009503	L	25-30.000 EUR	21.940	31.444	28.811	16-01-16	Maastricht	449	Coy
See lot 134 Coys 10.10.15.
1971	SM		00SB3320	L	65-85.000 EUR	56.507	83.765	74.750	04-02-16	Paris	349	Bon F200
Beige with brown interior; concours-quality restoration carried out in 2012.
1971	SM		00SB3623	L	19-24.000 GBP	23.520	33.615	30.310	12-03-16	Brooklands	159	His
Metallic beige with orange interior; described as in very good overall condition. 37,371 kms on the odometer.
1972	SM		00SB8453	L	15-20.000 EUR	21.301	30.859	27.360	20-03-16	Fontainebleau	345	Ose
Grey with black leather interior; in good original condition. Since 1984 in the current ownership.
1971	SM		00SB1157	L	28-42.000 EUR	26.270	37.532	33.350	18-06-16	Wien	411	Dor
Gold with brown leather interior; body repainted many years ago.

F197: 1968 Citroën ID 21 break

F198: 1967 Citroën DS 21 Le Caddy cabriolet (Chapron)

Year	Model	(Bodybuilder)	Chassis no.	Steering	Estimate	Hammer price £	$	€	Date	Place	Lot	Auc. H.

F199: 1980 Citroën Mehari 4X4

F200: 1971 Citroën SM

Year	Model	Chassis no.	Steering	Estimate	£	$	€	Date	Place	Lot	Auc. H.
1971	**SM**	00SB0835	L	20-30.000 EUR	**28.167**	37.414	33.600	02-07-16	Lyon	367	Agu

Blue with grey interior; restored about 10 years ago. Engine replaced by the factory in 1986.

| 1973 | **SM** | 00SC2891 | L | 50-85.000 USD | **27.353** | 36.000 | 32.393 | 30-07-16 | Plymouth | 144 | RMS |

Pearl grey with black interior; European-specification model. Manual gearbox.

| 1975 | **SM** | 00SC3040 | R | 40-50.000 GBP | **41.630** | 54.785 | 49.298 | 30-07-16 | Silverstone | 518 | SiC |

Grey with black leather interior; the car received some restoration works between the late 2015 - early 2016 (see lots 110 Coys 11.3.14 NS and 247 Silverstone Auctions 20.9.14 NS).

| 1985 | **Visa Mille Pistes** | VR9860 | L | 20-30.000 EUR | **19.995*** | 29.640* | 26.450* | 04-02-16 | Paris | 337 | Bon |

White; road going version. Some 29,000 kms covered since new (see lot 170 Bonhams 10.5.08 $ 33,776).

| 1984 | **Visa Mille Pistes** | VR9873 | L | 30-50.000 EUR | **29.361*** | 42.729* | 38.144* | 06-02-16 | Paris | 323 | Art |

Ehite; two owners and 2,500 kms covered.

| 1986 | **BX 4TC Groupe B** | XL3002 | L | 40-60.000 EUR | **47.712*** | 69.434* | 61.984* | 06-02-16 | Paris | 322 | Art |

White; described as in very good original condition. 45,745 kms on the odometer. Not road registered. From the André Trigano Collection.

CLEMENT & CIE. (F) (1895-1903)

| 1903 | **12/16hp rear-entrance tonnau** | 4281 | R | 400-500.000 GBP | **415.900** | 658.619 | 579.099 | 30-10-15 | London | 110 | Bon |

Red with black wings and black interior; in the same ownership from the early 1930s to 1968, the car was driven in 1934 at its first London-Brighton Run. Since 1977 in the current ownership, it received some mechanical works in the 1980s and was restored in the USA about 10 years ago.

F201

CLEMENT-BAYARD (F) (1903-1922)

| 1904 | **9/11hp AC2K rear-entrance tonneau** | 6022 | R | 140-160.000 GBP | | NS | | 30-10-15 | London | 111 | Bon |

White with black interior; in the same family ownership from the 1930s to 2009, the car remained on display from 1960 for circa 50 years at the Swiss National Transport Museum in Lucerne. Acquired in 2010 by the current owner, later it received a full mechanical restoration and the body was repainted.

| 1912 | **Type AC4A torpedo** | 13280 | R | 20-30.000 EUR | **19.995** | 29.640 | 26.450 | 04-02-16 | Paris | 395 | Bon |

Red with black wings and black interior; single ownership since 1958. Restored in the 1960s.

CLEVELAND (USA) (1919-1926)

| 1919 | **Model 40 roadster** | 3813 | L | 15-25.000 USD | **5.073*** | 7.700* | 6.853* | 05-10-15 | Philadelphia | 226 | Bon |

Toffee and cream; restored at unspecified date. From the Evergreen Collection.

CLYNO (GB) (1922-1930)

| 1926 | **10.8hp royal tourer** | 13940 | R | 12-15.000 GBP | **12.650** | 19.262 | 17.294 | 05-09-15 | Beaulieu | 182 | Bon |

Royal blue with black leather interior; restored.

F201: 1903 Clement & Cie. 12/16hp rear-entrance tonnau

F202: 1904 Columbia Mk XLIII rear-entrance tonneau

Year	Model	(Bodybuilder)	Chassis no.	Steering	Estimate	£	$	€	Date	Place	Lot	Auc. H.

COLUMBIA (USA) (1897-1913)

| 1904 | Mk XLIII rear-entrance tonneau | | 4220 | R | 90-110.000 GBP | 79.500 | 125.896 | 110.696 | 30-10-15 | London | 109 | Bon F202 |

Dark green with brown leather interior; cosmetically restored in the early 1960s. Since 2004 in the current ownership, it is described as in good running order (see lot 222 Bonhams11.10.02 NS).

COLUMBUS ELECTRIC (USA) (1903-1915)

| 1903 | Folding top runabout | | 3174(voltmeter) | R | 100-150.000 USD | | NS | | 09-10-15 | Hershey | 236 | RMS |

Black with maroon velour interior; in very good, largely original condition and very good driving order. New batteries. From the Harold Coker collection.

CONNAUGHT (GB) (1948-1959)

| 1948 | L2 | | 1356 | R | 80-120.000 GBP | 79.125 | 102.752 | 92.822 | 10-07-16 | Chateau Impney | 66 | H&H |

British racing green with black interior; first example built, it was owned and raced by Kenneth McAlpine until 1951. Later the car was imported into Australia; in 1989 it was reimported into the UK and restored (see Brooks lots 843 20.6.97 NS and 966 23.6.00 $65,220, and Bonhams 515 11.7.03 $56,425).

| 1952 | A-Type Formula 2 | | AX | M | 80-120.000 GBP | 85.500 | 129.438 | 118.725 | 06-12-15 | London | 016 | Bon F203 |

Car assembled in the early 1960s by Jack and John Horton using an original 7-feet 1-inch wheelbase chassis and an engine built with original spares previously acquired by the Hortons as they owned already an AL10 long wheelbase Connaught A-Type. The completed car was subsequently bought by Dan Margulies who raced it at historic events until the late 1960s. Later it was acquired by Arthur Carter, who had it restored in 1983. To be recommissioned prior to use; with FIA Technical Passport (see lot 60 H&H 6.6.01 NS).

COOPER (GB) (1947-1971)

| 1951 | Mark V | | MKV1951 | M | 28-38.000 GBP | 33.600 | 48.394 | 42.813 | 11-06-16 | Brooklands | 249 | His F204 |

Bought new by Ken Wharton who raced it during the 1951 season. Recommissioned in the early 1990s and used at some historic events. 500cc Jap engine with Norton gearbox (see lot 444 Coys 12.03.13 $ 61,790).

| 1952 | Mark VI Formula 3 | | MK62152 | M | 15-20.000 USD | 17.392* | 26.400* | 23.496* | 05-10-15 | Philadelphia | 272 | Bon |

Fitted with a 500cc Norton engine, the car was bought new by Alexis du Pont who raced it at several events in the USA. Currently fitted with a Triumph engine. From the Alexis du Pont collection.

| 1954 | Mark VIII | | MK4254 | M | 25-28.000 GBP | 26.450 | 40.794 | 36.205 | 12-09-15 | Goodwood | 304 | Bon |

The car has had a long race career in period and has been raced at numerous historic events in more recent years. Restored in 2005-06; Jap engine.

| 1958 | Mark XII Formula 3 | | MKXII158 | M | 20-30.000 USD | 17.392* | 26.400* | 23.496* | 05-10-15 | Philadelphia | 273 | Bon |

Fitted with a 500 Norton Manx engine, the car was bought new by Alexis du Pont and raced until 1960. In original condition; from the Alexis du Pont collection.

| 1968 | T86B BRM | | F1168 | M | Refer Dpt. | | NS | | 14-05-16 | Monaco | 130 | Coy |

Ex-Works car driven at some 1968 GPs by Brian Redman and Lucien Bianchi. In recent years driven at historic events. Described as in ready to race condition (see lot 253 Coys 30.4.10 NS).

CORD (USA) (1929-1937)

| 1930 | L-29 phaeton sedan | | FD3007A | L | NA | 90.310 | 137.500 | 123.461 | 05-09-15 | Auburn | 5141 | AA |

White with tan leather interior; restored many years ago. Since 1973 in the current ownership.

| 1930 | L-29 cabriolet | | 2928423 | L | 150-175.000 USD | 96.126 | 137.500 | 126.101 | 28-01-16 | Phoenix | 159 | RMS |

Pewter grey with black moldings and grey leather interior; restored in the 1970s. Original engine replaced many years ago with a 1929 unit.

| 1930 | L-29 cabriolet | | 2928140 | L | 200-250.000 USD | 142.369 | 203.500 | 183.496 | 12-03-16 | Amelia Island | 115 | RMS F205 |

Dark blue with light blue moldings and pale blue interior; the car remained in the same ownership from 1939 to 1982 when it was acquired by the successive owner who restored it and retained it until 2009. Recently mechanically and aesthetically freshened (see lot 387 RM 14.8.09 $ 187,000).

| 1930 | L-29 cabriolet | | 2927648 | L | 150-200.000 USD | 142.083 | 187.000 | 168.263 | 30-07-16 | Plymouth | 140 | RMS |

Cream with blue accents; fully restored in the 1970s. From the estate of Wendell Gates II, who had acquired it in 1946.

| 1936 | 810 Sportsman | | 2533F | L | 160-180.000 USD | 100.043* | 143.000* | 128.943* | 11-03-16 | Amelia Island | 13 | G&Co |

Cream with black leather interior; discovered in 1971 and restored. For 44 years with the previous owner. Original engine replaced with the present unit no.1879 (see lot 236 RM 16.1.15 $ 159,500).

| 1936 | 810 Sportsman | | 8102260F | L | 160-220.000 USD | 107.738* | 154.000* | 138.862* | 12-03-16 | Amelia Island | 182 | RMS |

Tan with dark red leather interior; an older restoration, the car is described as in good overall condition (see lots 20 Christie's 15.6.96 $ 39,100 and 290 RM 29.10.08 NS).

| 1937 | 810 sedan | | 1577A | R | 28-35.000 GBP | 42.550 | 61.642 | 54.651 | 20-03-16 | Goodwood | 91 | Bon |

Red; bought already restored in South Africa by the father of the current owner and imported into the UK. On museum display since 1977 and never used, the car requires recommissioning prior to use.

F203: 1952 Connaught A-Type Formula 2

F204: 1951 Cooper Mark V

Year	Model	(Bodybuilder)	Chassis no.	Steering	Estimate	Hammer price £	$	€	Date	Sale Place	Lot	Auc. H.

F205: 1930 Cord L-29 cabriolet

F206: 1937 Cord 812 SC Phaeton

Year	Model	Chassis no.	Steering	Estimate	£	$	€	Date	Place	Lot	Auc. H.
1937	812 Sportsman	8121113F	L	NA		NS		05-09-15	Auburn	5129	AA

Green with dark green leather interior; restored at unspecified date (see lot S729 Russo & Steele 17.1.15 $ 151,250).

| 1937 | 812 SC Sportsman | 31631F | L | 1.000-2.000.000 DKK | | NS | | 26-09-15 | Ebeltoft | 30 | Bon |

Maroon with tan interior; according to previous owner Jules Heumann (who acquired it in 2011) the car was built over a 30 year period by Henry Portz using original Cord parts. Engine replaced in 2013. From the Frederiksen Collection.

| 1937 | 812 SC Phaeton | 32465H | L | 150-175.000 USD | 115.210* | 176.000* | 156.394* | 08-10-15 | Hershey | 179 | RMS F206 |

Black with red leather interior; restored in the late 1960s. Body repainted in more recent years.

| 1937 | 812 SC Phaeton | 32269H | L | 225-250.000 USD | 146.112* | 209.000* | 191.674* | 28-01-16 | Phoenix | 125 | RMS |

Dark blue with red leather interior; restored several years ago. In the same ownership from 1967 to 2013 (see lot 226 RM 17.8.13 $ 225,500).

| 1937 | 812 Custom Beverly | 81210180S | L | 100-125.000 USD | 100.294 | 132.000 | 118.774 | 30-07-16 | Plymouth | 130 | RMS |

Blue with blue cloth interior; restored several years ago.

| 1937 | 812 SC Phaeton | 32462H | L | 275-325.000 USD | 205.898 | 269.500 | 237.942 | 20-08-16 | Pebble Beach | 52 | G&Co |

Ivory with red leather interior; full restoration completed in 2006 (see lots 183 RM 11.3.06 $209,000 and 24 Gooding & Company 12.3.10 $258,500).

COSTIN-NATHAN (GB)

| 1966 | Prototype | NQ | R | 25-30.000 GBP | 80.230 | 104.187 | 94.118 | 10-07-16 | Chateau Impney | 61 | H&H F207 |

White and blue with black interior; unused for 45 years, the car requires a full restoration. First example built, the car was raced in 1966 by Roger Nathan fitted with a 1-litre Hillman Imp engine and spider body built by Williams & Pritchard. In 1967 the car was sold and raced with a GT body and a Ford 1.6-litre Twin-Cam engine.

CREANCHE (F) (1899-1906)

| 1900 | Type A voiturette | 73 | R | 70-80.000 EUR | 37.966* | 55.102* | 50.400* | 03-02-16 | Paris | 113 | RMS F208 |

White with red interior; restored in Switzerland, new body built in 1972. One of two known survivors of the marque. Dated 1900 by the Veteran Car Club of Great Britain.

CROSLEY (USA) (1939-1952)

| 1942 | 2-cylinder convertible | CB423347 | L | NA | 9.424* | 14.300* | 12.824* | 26-09-15 | Las Vegas | 322 | B/J |

Yellow with red interior; restored.

| 1949 | Series CD Hot Shot roadster | VC20014 | L | NA | 6.252* | 8.800* | 7.744* | 09-04-16 | Palm Beach | 29 | B/J |

White with black interior; 400 miles covered since the restoration.

| 1950 | Series CD Hot Shot roadster | WN5400193351 | L | 20-25.000 USD | 8.383* | 12.100* | 10.848* | 05-06-16 | Greenwhich | 80 | Bon |

Red with tan vinyl interior; restored some years ago. From the Evergreen Collection.

| 1950 | Series CD woody wagon | CD202069 | L | NA | 9.163 | 12.000 | 10.895 | 23-07-16 | Harrisburg | T243 | Mec |

Green with tan interior; restored.

F207: 1966 Costin-Nathan Prototype

F208: 1900 Creanche Type A voiturette

Year	Model	(Bodybuilder)	Chassis no.	Steering	Estimate	Hammer price £	Hammer price $	Hammer price €	Date	Place	Lot	Auc. H.

CUNNINGHAM (USA) (1950-1957)

| 1952 | C-3 coupé | (Vignale) | 5208 | L | 900-1.100.000 USD | 846.637 | 1.210.000 | 1.107.997 | 29-01-16 | Phoenix | 229 | RMS F209 |

Silver and two-tone blue livery; raced at some events until 1956. The car spent many years in the Petersen Automotive Museum in Los Angeles before to be acquired by the current owner and was subsequently restored to concours condition by RM Auto Restoration. 220bhp Chrysler Hemi 331 engine with 3-speed manual gearbox (ved. lotto 509 Auctions America 1.8.13 $ 407,000).

| 1952 | C-3 roadster | | 5236 | L | 275-325.000 USD | 194.343 | 275.000 | 253.275 | 10-03-16 | Amelia Island | 197 | Bon |

White with blue stripes; one of 14 C-3 chassis built but never fitted with a coachwork, it was sold new in Indiana and later it went to Wisconsin where it remained for several decades prior to be discovered by the current owner. Subsequently it has been restored and fitted with the present new body in the C-2R style. The car is currently fitted with a 331 ci Chrysler Fire Power V8 engine and T-10 4-speed manual gearbox (the original engine block is included with the sale).

DAIMLER (GB) (1896-1983)

| 1935 | LQ20 limousine | (Windovers) | 40958 | R | 20-25.000 EUR | 10.466* | 14.731* | 12.964* | 09-04-16 | Essen | 184 | Coy |

Black and maroon with black leather interior to the front compartment and grey cloth to the rear; 18,341 miles on the odometer. From the Brundza Collection (see lot 150 Coys 10.1.15 $ 25,123).

| 1936 | Light 20 | | 42531 | R | 24-28.000 GBP | NS | | | 11-06-16 | Brooklands | 247 | His |

Black and blue; in largely original condition. Two owners and 79,920 miles covered. Sunroof.

| 1939 | DB18 cabriolet | (Carlton Carriage) | 49531 | R | 230-260.000 GBP | 206.000 | 273.609 | 245.717 | 02-07-16 | Woodstock | 167 | Coy F210 |

Black and silver with green leather interior; fully restored in Germany. The car remained in the factory's ownership until 1950 and was loaned to Winston Churchill for his political campaigns both in 1944 and 1949 (see lots 509 Bonhams/Brooks 26.7.01 $9,839, 39 Historics 4.12.10 NS, and 142 RM 8.9.14 NS).

| 1950 | DB18 Special Sports | (Barker) | 53820 | R | 28-35.000 USD | 12.320* | 18.700* | 16.643* | 05-10-15 | Philadelphia | 235 | Bon |

Body repainted about 20 years ago; in need of refurbishment. From the Evergreen Collection.

| 1951 | DB18 Special Sports | (Barker) | DB59756 | R | 34-48.000 EUR | 32.955 | 50.893 | 44.800 | 17-10-15 | Salzburg | 335 | Dor |

Cream and blue with grey leather interior; car restored in 1987, engine overhauled in 1999, some mechanical works carried out in 2014.

| 1950 | DB18 Special Sports | (Barker) | D53855 | R | 23-26.000 GBP | NS | | | 09-12-15 | Chateau Impney | 34 | H&H |

Two-tone green with dark green leather interior; in good running order.

| 1964 | SP250 | | 104368 | R | 50-60.000 GBP | 82.410 | 127.101 | 112.803 | 12-09-15 | Goodwood | 311 | Bon F211 |

Black; ex-Metropolitan Police. Acquired in 2005 by the previous owner and subsequently fully restored. Since 2014 in the Chris Evans collection (see lot 275 Historics 30.8.14 $ 83,573).

| 1961 | SP250 | | 100523 | L | 35-50.000 EUR | 25.683 | 40.670 | 35.760 | 01-11-15 | Paris | 133 | Art |

Red with black interior; body repainted about 15 years ago, interior retrimmed in more recent years. Since October 1961 in the same family ownership.

| 1960 | SP250 | | 100637 | R | 26-30.000 GBP | 27.200 | 40.939 | 38.695 | 28-11-15 | Weybridge | 308 | His |

Ivory with tan interior; engine rebuilt at unspecified date, body repainted in 1989 (see lot 132 Coys 11.3.14 NS).

| 1962 | SP250 | | 103893 | R | 28-32.000 GBP | 29.120 | 42.387 | 37.579 | 18-05-16 | Donington Park | 111 | H&H |

Green with green interior; restored at unspecified date.

| 1960 | SP250 | | 874 | R | 22-26.000 GBP | NS | | | 28-07-16 | Donington Park | 118 | H&H |

The car requires some attention to the paintwork; with hardtop.

| 1962 | M-Major | | 37109 | R | NA | 5.712 | 7.946 | 7.236 | 24-02-16 | Donington Park | 50 | H&H |

Burgundy and silver with red leather interior; recently restored.

| 1963 | 2.5l V8 | | 1A2911BW | R | NQ | 26.438* | 40.249* | 37.394* | 14-11-15 | Birmingham | 626 | SiC |

Opalescent green; fully restored. Rebuilt engine and gearbox.

| 1964 | 2.5l V8 Vicarage convertible | | 1A7045BW | R | 100-130.000 GBP | NS | | | 24-06-16 | Goodwood | 250 | Bon |

Black with red leather interior; conversion completed by Vicarage in 2004 for Prince Faisal of Saudi Arabia. Interior retrimmed in more recent years (see lot 375 Bonhams 22.6.07 $145,781).

| 1966 | 2.5l V8 | | P1A12390BW | R | 10-12.000 GBP | 15.120 | 19.909 | 17.952 | 28-07-16 | Donington Park | 39 | H&H |

White; cosmetically restored in Australia in 1984 and reimported into the UK in 1992.

| 1966 | 2.5l V8 | | 1A11217BW | R | 12-15.000 GBP | 19.600 | 25.652 | 22.648 | 20-08-16 | Brooklands | 309 | His |

Light blue with blue leather interior; in good overall condition. Automatic transmission.

| 1969 | Sovereign | | 1A33301BW | R | 6-8.000 GBP | 11.312 | 17.068 | 15.600 | 09-12-15 | Chateau Impney | 47 | H&H |

Light blue with dark blue interior; restored between 1989 and 2003. Since 1983 in the current ownership.

| 1969 | V8 250 | | P1K4615BW | R | 25-30.000 GBP | 31.500 | 41.454 | 37.302 | 30-07-16 | Silverstone | 902 | SiC |

Old English white with red leather interior; fully restored between 1999 and 2001. Power steering and automatic transmission.

| 1969 | Sovereign | | 1A34658BW | R | 5-7.500 GBP | 4.928 | 7.417 | 7.011 | 28-11-15 | Weybridge | 319 | His |

Blue with blue interior; in good driving order.

F209: 1952 Cunningham C-3 coupé (Vignale)

F210: 1939 Daimler DB18 cabriolet (Carlton Carriage)

Year	Model	(Bodybuilder)	Chassis no.	Steering	Estimate	Hammer price £	$	€	Date	Place	Lot	Auc. H.

F211: 1964 Daimler SP250

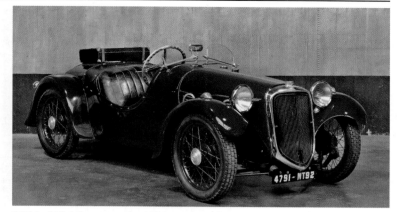

F212: 1934 Darmont Type V-Junior roadster

1984	DS420 Limousine	(Windovers)	20055	L	15-20.000 EUR	15.222*	21.426*	18.856*	09-04-16	Essen	194	Coy

Black with cream leather interior; from the Brundza Collection.

1981	Sovereign 4.2		DCALP3C330673	R	NA	33	47	42	20-04-16	Duxford	43	H&H

Beige; recent restoration works. The car was used in the TV series "Minder" and has covered 43,990 miles.

1977	Sovereign 4.2 coupé		2H1986BW	R	7-8.000 GBP	13.552	19.726	17.489	18-05-16	Donington Park	43	H&H

Silver with black leather interior; in good overall condition. 33,500 miles covered (see lot 10 H&H 1.10.10 $ 11,312).

1977	Sovereign coupé		2H2498BW	R	14-18.000 GBP	14.560	20.971	18.552	11-06-16	Brooklands	220	His

Green with tan leather interior; since 1990 with the present, third owner.

1988	Double Six saloon		479386	L	NQ	14.625*	22.269*	19.994*	04-09-15	Woodstock	203	SiC

Metallic blue with light grey leather interior; body repainted in 1996. Just one owner and 3,297 kms covered.

1988	Double Six saloon		480391	R	2-3.000 GBP	3.650	5.637	4.962	17-10-15	Cambridge	2500	Che

Red with beige leather interior; in good overall condition. Since 1993 in the current ownership; last used in 2011.

DALLARA (I) (1978-)

1992	392 Formula 3		F392033	M	15-20.000 GBP		NS		28-07-16	Silverstone	126	SiC

Unused for several years, the car requires some recommissioning prior to use; 2-litre Alfa Romeo Novamotor engine (see lot 155 Coys 10.1.15 NS).

DARMONT (F) (1921-1940)

1934	Type V-Junior roadster		60051	R	20-30.000 EUR	13.909*	20.619*	18.400*	04-02-16	Paris	398	Bon F212

Red with black interior; restored several years ago (see Artcurial lots 2 13.2.05 $ 22,360 and 191 6.2.15 $ 25,229).

DARRACQ (F) (1896-1920)

1904	8hp two-seater		6363	R	35-50.000 GBP	74.300	117.661	103.455	30-10-15	London	102	Bon F213

Since 1954 in the same family ownership. Last driven at the London-Brighton Run in 1996. Stored and not run for circa 15 years, it requires recommissioning prior to use.

DE DION-BOUTON (F) (1883-1948)

1899	Type D 3hp vis-a-vis		947(engine)	R	65-95.000 EUR		NS		04-02-16	Paris	316	Bon

One of three examples of the model known to survive; since 1985 in the current ownership; for 30 years on static display.

1901	Type G 4.5hp vis-a-vis		1405	R	40-60.000 EUR	37.031	56.058	51.600	08-11-15	Lyon	205	Ose F214

In the same family ownership since the end of WWI, the car was dismantled at that time and the engine used for production of cider. In 1982 a long restoration was started using the original parts and those collected over the years by the family.

1901	Type G 4.5hp vis-a-vis		1671(6060 engine)	R	60-70.000 GBP		NS		10-12-15	London	340	Bon

Red with tan upholstery; restored in the 1970s. Several mechanical works carried out in recent years. It was driven at the London-Brighton Run in the 1980s and from 2000 to 2011 (see lot 727 Brooks 27.4.00 $ 33,455).

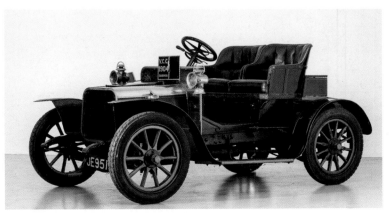

F213: 1904 Darracq 8hp two-seater

F214: 1901 De Dion-Bouton Type G 4.5hp vis-a-vis

Year	Model	(Bodybuilder)	Chassis no.	Steering	Estimate	Hammer price			Sale		Lot	Auc. H.
						£	$	€	Date	Place		
1902	Type K1 8hp rolling chassis		5166C(engine)	R	40-50.000 EUR	35.284*	50.839*	44.800*	14-05-16	Monaco	123	RMS
Restored; from the Quattroruote Collection.												
1923	Type IT 10hp torpedo		12616	R	30-40.000 EUR	22.686	32.412	28.800	19-06-16	Fontainebleau	309	Ose
Restored in the 1980s; engine rebuilt in 2013.												

DE LOREAN (GB) *(1976-1982)*

Year	Model	(Bodybuilder)	Chassis no.	Steering	Estimate	£	$	€	Date	Place	Lot	Auc. H.
1981	DMC 12 (Italdesign)		5866	L	NA	29.120	41.292	36.814	20-04-16	Duxford	5	H&H
Recently reimported from the USA, the car received some mechanical works. 9,300 miles covered since new.												

DE TOMASO (I) *(1961-2004)*

Year	Model	(Bodybuilder)	Chassis no.	Steering	Estimate	£	$	€	Date	Place	Lot	Auc. H.
1968	Vallelunga (Ghia)		807DTO126	L	320-360.000 EUR		NS		13-05-16	Monaco	116	Bon
Yellow with black interior; in 2004 restored to concours condition. The car was sold new to Switzerland where it remained until two years ago.												
1969	Mangusta (Ghia)		8MA518	L	170-210.000 GBP	201.600	307.682	276.051	07-09-15	London	164	RMS
Sold new in Italy, later the car was exported to the USA where it was restored in 1998. Reimported into Europe in 2008, it received further restoration works in 2010 and 2011 (see lot 210 Coys 25.10.08 NS).												F215
1969	Mangusta (Ghia)		8MA856	L	300-350.000 USD	196.347*	297.000*	271.399*	10-12-15	New York	231	RMS
Orange; the car received a five year full restoration and is described as in show condition.												
1971	Mangusta (Ghia)		8MA1266	L	200-300.000 EUR	252.324	367.202	327.800	05-02-16	Paris	147	Art
Orange with black leather interior; restored in the late 1990s. In 2004 it was acquired by the current owner who later had the engine rebuilt, enlarged to 5.7-litre and upgraded to 430bhp.												
1971	Pantera (Ghia)		01365	L	90-110.000 GBP		NS		04-09-15	Woodstock	210	SiC
Red with black interior; sold new to Hawaii, the car has had two owners until 2014. Restored at unspecified date. In 1972 used in an episode of the television series "Hawaii 5-0".												
1973	Pantera (Ghia)		05517	L	NA	80.282	115.000	106.398	23-01-16	Kissimmee	F87	Mec
Blue with black interior; 3,000 original miles. Original owner until June 2013.												
1987	Pantera GT5-S (Ghia)		11022	L	225-250.000 USD	153.582	220.000	203.544	23-01-16	Kissimmee	S108	Mec F216
Black with tan leather interior; 11,700 kms covered. In single ownership from 1997 to 2015.												
1974	Pantera (Ghia)		06428	L	100-125.000 USD	69.270*	99.000*	90.654*	29-01-16	Phoenix	210	RMS
White with black interior; restored in Canada at unspecified date.												
1971	Pantera (Ghia)		01992	L	110-130.000 USD	79.292	112.200	103.336	10-03-16	Amelia Island	155	Bon
Lime green with black interior; less than 12,000 miles covered. Body repainted.												
1973	Pantera L (Ghia)		04987	L	50-70.000 USD	36.338	52.000	45.484	02-04-16	Ft.Lauderdale	216	AA
Red with black interior; described as in original condition.												
1972	Pantera (Ghia)		03682	L	85-95.000 USD		NS		02-04-16	Ft.Lauderdale	543	AA
Red with black interior; restoration completed in 2015.												
1974	Pantera (Ghia)		07241	L	85-100.000 EUR		NS		09-04-16	Essen	154	Coy
Yellow; described as in excellent overall condition, the car has covered approximately 24,000 miles. Sold new to the USA, it remained in the same ownership until 2014 when it was acquired by the current, second owner and imported into Germany.												
1974	Pantera (Ghia)		06857	L	95-105.000 EUR		NS		09-04-16	Essen	216	Coy
Orange; body repainted (see lot 160 Coys 18.4.15 $ 81,100).												
1974	Pantera L (Ghia)		06836	L	125-150.000 USD	70.699	103.000	91.804	20-05-16	Indianapolis	S100	Mec
Red with black interior; in original condition, 7,600 actual miles. Ford 351 Cleveland engine. For 35 years in the current, second ownership (see Mecum lots S156 9.7.13 $ 84,350 and S88.1 Mecum 4.12.14 NS).												
1974	Pantera GTS (Ghia)		07005	L	130-175.000 USD	80.652	117.500	104.728	20-05-16	Indianapolis	S99	Mec
Burgundy with black interior; 763 original miles. Ford 351 Cleveland engine (see Mecum lots S136 25.1.14 NS and S130.1 04.12.14 NS).												
1974	Pantera (Ghia)		07350	L	NA	69.990	100.000	88.850	18-06-16	Portland	S165.1	Mec
Red with black interior; in original condition. Two owners and 10,926 miles covered. 351 Cleveland engine.												
1974	Pantera (Ghia)		07241	L	65-85.000 GBP	65.772	87.358	78.453	02-07-16	Woodstock	139	Coy
See lot 154 Coys 9.4.16.												
1973	Pantera GTS (Ghia)		07010	L	75-95.000 EUR	75.191	97.646	88.208	09-07-16	Le Mans	142	Art
Yellow and black with black interior; mechanicals recently overhauled. 351 Cleveland Ford engine.												

F215: 1969 De Tomaso Mangusta (Ghia)

F216: 1987 De Tomaso Pantera GT5-S (Ghia)

Year	Model	(Bodybuilder)	Chassis no.	Steering	Estimate	£	$	€	Date	Place	Lot	Auc. H.
1971	**Pantera**	(Ghia)	02113	L	NA	38.500	50.000	45.165	09-07-16	Denver	S171	**Mec**
	Blue with black interior; restored in 2015. Ford 351 Cleveland engine.											
1972	**Pantera**	(Ghia)	03055	L	75-85.000 EUR		NS		06-08-16	Schloss Dyck	155	**Coy**
	Red with black interior; described as in good original condition.											
1974	**Pantera**	(Ghia)	07241	L	80-100.000 EUR	87.935	115.671	103.685	06-08-16	Schloss Dyck	176	**Coy**
	See lot 139 Coys 2.7.16.											
1974	**Pantera GTS**	(Ghia)	07226	L	100-130.000 USD	77.737*	101.750*	89.835*	19-08-16	Carmel	23	**Bon**
	Less than 28,000 miles on the odometer, body repainted, original interior.											
1974	**Pantera**	(Ghia)	07350	L	130-150.000 USD		NS		19-08-16	Monterey	F136	**Mec**
	See lot S165.1 Mecum 18.6.16.											

DEHO (F) *(1946-1948)*

1948	**Simca 8 sport**		894718	L	80-85.000 EUR		NS		09-04-16	Essen	151	**Coy**
	Red with brown interior; 1200 engine restored.											

DELAGE (F) *(1905-1953)*

1924	**Type DI shooting brake** (Carross. Castraise)	18613	R	45-75.000 USD		NS		11-06-16	Hershey	107	**TFA**
	Yellow with black wings and black interior; restored many years ago. Mechanicals refreshed in 2013-14 (see lot 59 BCA 10.06.97 $17,085).											
1929	**Type DM spider** (Guillaume Busson)	28055	R	180-190.000 EUR		NS		26-09-15	Frankfurt	143	**Coy**
	Burgundy; restored in recent years and until today on display at the Automobile Museum Stainz. Argentinian documents; EEC taxes paid (see lot 132 Coys 18.1.14 NS).											
1934	**Type D8 S cabriolet** (Fernandez/Darrin)	38229	R	1.300-1.600.000 USD	945.373	1.430.000	1.306.734	10-12-15	New York	228	**RMS** F217
	Lilac with polished aluminium hood sweep panel and lilac leather interior; fully restored in the USA between 1986 and 1991, the car is described as still in very good overall condition.											
1930	**Type D8 C cabriolet** (Chapron)	34738	R	300-350.000 USD	123.130*	176.000*	158.699*	12-03-16	Amelia Island	183	**RMS**
	Grey and dark blue with grey leather interior; sold new to Scotland, the car was imported into the USA in 1966. In 1973 it was acquired by the current owner and fully restored between 1992 and 1994.											
1932	**Type D8 N pick up**	32988	R	20-30.000 EUR	57.849	82.649	73.440	19-06-16	Fontainebleau	306	**Ose**
	Built with Chapron saloon body, the car was converted to pick up in the 1950s probably. Unused for 15 years ago; mechanicals complete.											
1935	**Type D8-85 limousine**	40087	R	50-60.000 EUR	52.177	74.546	66.240	19-06-16	Fontainebleau	321	**Ose**
	Restored in 1978 and subsequently little used.											
1936	**Type D6-70 Mylord cabriolet** (Figoni/Falaschi)	50714	R	125-150.000 GBP		NS		07-09-15	London	107	**RMS**
	White and burgundy with red interior; restored at unspecified date. Used at some historic events (see lot 409 Artcurial 7.2.14 NS).											
1936	**Type D8-100 coupé chauffeur** (Franay)	50770	R	350-400.000 USD		NS		10-03-16	Amelia Island	181	**Bon**
	Originally finished in white, probably it is the car displayed at the Franay stand at the 1936 Paris Motor Show and subsequently sold in France where it remained until the mid-1950s. Imported into the USA, it was probably first restored in the 1970s and finished in grey. In more recent years it has been restored again and finished in the present black livery with black leather interior to the front compartment and grey cloth to the rear.											
1936	**Type D8-100 cabriolet** (De Villars)	51597	R	200-250.000 EUR	296.142	429.026	380.376	20-03-16	Fontainebleau	335	**Ose** F218
	For 47 years in the current ownership; engine requiring recommissioning prior to use. According to the marque historian Daniel Cabart, even if badged as a D8-100 the car is actually a D8-120 example.											
1947	**Type D6 3L Competition**	880003	R	1.200-1.400.000 EUR		NS		09-07-16	Le Mans	126	**Art**
	Between 1947 and 1951 the car was raced at several events, among others the Spa and Le Mans 24 Hours races, and was driven by several racers, among them Philippe Etancelin and Maurice Trintignant. From 1951 to 1981 it was owned by Charles Pozzi who sold it to Claude Afchaing who retained it until 2002. Still fitted with its original body finished in France blue; recently refreshed (see lot 362 Bonhams 6.2.14 $1,474,329).											

DELAHAYE (F) *(1894-1954)*

1938	**Type 134 G coach**	48223	R	20-30.000 EUR	30.270	43.853	38.880	20-03-16	Fontainebleau	334	**Ose**
	Cream and maroon with light brown interior; restored about 20 years ago.											
1937	**Type 135 Competition**	46580	R	350-450.000 GBP		NS		01-12-15	London	315	**Coy**
	Blue with black interior; discovered in Argentina in the late 1960s by collector Roberto "Gallego" Rodriguez who had it restored and retained it until 2003 when it was bought by the current owner. The car was used at several historic events in South America. With FIVA Identity Card. Offered with the original Cotal gearbox ready to be fitted. European taxes to be paid.											

F217: 1934 Delage Type D8 S cabriolet (Fernandez/Darrin)

F218: 1936 Delage Type D8-100 cabriolet (De Villars)

F219: 1949 Delahaye Type 135 M Malmaison cabriolet (Pourtout)

F220: 1937 Delahaye Type 135 MS cabriolet (Chapron)

Year	Model (Bodybuilder)	Chassis no.	Steering	Estimate	Hammer Price £	Hammer Price $	Hammer Price €	Date	Place	Lot	Auc. H.
1937	Type 135 Competition	46580	R	Refer Dpt.	183.191	263.954	232.600	14-05-16	Monaco	118	Coy
	See lot 315 Coys 1.12.15.										
1949	Type 135 M cabriolet (Guilloré)	801221	R	450-600.000 USD	315.565	451.000	412.981	29-01-16	Phoenix	264	RMS
	Formerly in the Brooks Stevens collection, in the early 1980s the car was bought by Richard Adatto who restored it in the present two-tone livery, exhibited it at the 1984 Pebble Beach Concours d'Elegance, and retained it until the early 1990s. Described as still in good overall condition.										
1946	Type 135 M coach (Guilloré)	800410	R	150-200.000 USD		NS		10-03-16	Amelia Island	194	Bon
	Two-tone grey with red leather interior; since 1960 in the present ownership. Restored in the early 1990s.										
1949	Type 135 M Malmaison cabriolet (Pourtout)	801199	R	500-800.000 USD	346.302	495.000	446.342	12-03-16	Amelia Island	127	RMS F219
	Dark blue with tan leather interior; sold new in France, the car was imported into the USA many years later. Restored at unspecified date, it is described as still in good overall condition. One of three examples known to survive.										
1950	Type 135 M Atlas cabriolet (Guilloré)	801636	R	350-450.000 USD	213.814	308.000	272.457	11-06-16	Hershey	128	TFA
	Dark blue with blue interior; described as in highly original condition (see Bonhams lots 40 14.08.15 $363,000 and 140 16.01.14 NS).										
1939	Type 135 M cabriolet (Chapron)	60188	R	250-300.000 EUR	306.258	437.556	388.800	19-06-16	Fontainebleau	322	Ose
	Two-tone blue; acquired in 1988 by the current owner and subsequently restored.										
1949	Type 135 M cabriolet (Guilloré)	801242	R	100-200.000 EUR	91.449	118.759	107.280	09-07-16	Le Mans	124	Art
	Light blue with light brown interior; in original, unrestored condition and little used in the last years, the car requires recommissioning prior to use.										
1937	Type 135 MS cabriolet (Chapron)	48482	R	NA		NS		05-09-15	Auburn	7072	AA
	Two-tone blue with blue leather interior; restored at unspecified date (see lot 5100 Barrett-Jackson 17.1.15 $ 385,000).										
1949	Type 135 MS coupé (Ghia)	800514	R	180-260.000 USD	123.868	180.263	160.920	05-02-16	Paris	134	Art
	Metallic blue with light grey leather interior; first owner the Shah of Iran who retained it until 1957. Later it was imported into the USA where it was restored and was part of the Blackhawk Collection and of the John O'Quinn Collection. Since 2010 in the current European ownership, it is described as in very good overall condition (see lots 446 Hershey Auctions 8.10. 04 $ 94,600 and 290 RM 1.5.10 $ 149,128).										
1937	Type 135 MS cabriolet (Chapron)	48482	R	475-550.000 USD	307.061	434.500	400.175	10-03-16	Amelia Island	146	Bon F220
	See lot 7072 Auctions America 5.9.15.										
1949	Type 148 L coupé (Antem)	801278	R	200-280.000 EUR	213.380	277.104	250.320	09-07-16	Le Mans	150	Art
	Metallic grey; body built in 1949 for the 1935 Delahaye 135 Competition chassis 46094. In 1979 the body was dismantled from its chassis and fitted in the late 1980s to the present chassis, originally fitted with a Letourneur et Marchand saloon body. The car is currently fitted with a Type 135 M 3.5-litre with three carburettors (see lot 20 Poulain/Sotheby's 19.6.01 $40,486).										
1953	Type 235 coupé (Saoutchik)	818039	R	NA		NS		29-01-16	Scottsdale	1379.1	B/J
	Plum with cream interior.										
1952	Type 235 coupé (Chapron)	818040	R	300-400.000 EUR	229.386	333.820	298.000	05-02-16	Paris	130	Art F221
	One of three examples built; exhibited at the Delahaye stand at the 1952 Paris Motor Show. Described as in good preserved condition. Cotal electromagnetic gearbox.										

DELAUNAY-BELLEVILLE (F) (1904-1948)

Year	Model (Bodybuilder)	Chassis no.	Steering	Estimate	£	$	€	Date	Place	Lot	Auc. H.
1913	Type O6 torpedo (Rothschild)	6563	R	500-700.000 USD	343.800	450.000	397.305	19-08-16	Carmel	10	Bon F222
	Blue with black wings and black leather interior; in the same family ownership from 1913 to 2012. Restored in the late 1980s (see lot 322 Artcurial 3.2.12 $620,836).										

F221: 1952 Delahaye Type 235 coupé (Chapron)

F222: 1913 Delaunay-Belleville Type O6 torpedo (Rothschild)

| MOULD MAKING | FRAMEWORK MAKING | MECHANICS | CAR BODY CONSTRUCTION | SADDLERY | CAR PAINTING |

René Große Restaurierungen GmbH & Co.KG | Waldstraße 34 | 14789 Wusterwitz | GERMANY
FON +49 3 38 39 711 85 | FAX +49 3 38 39 714 08 | E-MAIL kontakt@rene-grosse.com

Year	Model	(Bodybuilder)	Chassis no.	Steering	Estimate	Hammer price £	Hammer price $	Hammer price €	Sale Date	Sale Place	Lot	Auc. H.
DELIN (B)												
1901	4hp voiturette		4	R	58-70.000 GBP		NS		01-12-15	London	336	Coy
Maroon; described as in very good condition. Entered at several London-Brighton Run editions.												
1901	4hp voiturette		4	R	58-70.000 GBP	64.520	91.676	83.134	08-03-16	London	109	Coy **F223**
See lot 336 Coys 1.12.15.												
DELLOW (GB) *(1949-1957)*												
1955	Mark IIB		399B552	R	12-16.000 GBP	21.280	27.851	24.589	20-08-16	Brooklands	338	His
Two owners and 59,000 miles covered. Never raced; described as in original condition.												
DESOTO (USA) *(1929-1961)*												
1932	Series SC DeLuxe convertible		SC20504(engine)	L	45-55.000 USD	25.911*	37.400*	33.529*	05-06-16	Greenwhich	76	Bon
Yellow with brown fenders and brown interior; restored in the early 1980s probably. From the Evergreen Collection.												
1935	Airflow sedan		9603496	L	NA	24.629*	35.200*	32.233*	29-01-16	Scottsdale	1147	B/J
Brown and cream; restored.												
1949	S-13 Custom convertible		50013751	L	40-60.000 USD	50.021*	71.500*	64.472*	12-03-16	Amelia Island	192	RMS
Grey with blue leatherette and cloth interior; an older restoration. From the Richard & Linda Kughn Collection.												
1959	Firedome convertible		M431110592	L	NA	92.360*	132.000*	120.872*	29-01-16	Scottsdale	1450	B/J
Coral with grey interior; restored in the early 2000s (see lot 634 Barrett-Jackson 16.1.03 $ 48,060).												
1956	Fireflite convertible		50384411	L	NA	130.844*	187.000*	171.236*	29-01-16	Scottsdale	1315.1	B/J
Pink-grey; restored.												
1957	Adventurer convertible		50418679	L	NA	115.451*	165.000*	151.091*	29-01-16	Scottsdale	1380	B/J
Black; automatic transmission.												
1958	Adventurer convertible		LS37760	L	NA	184.721*	264.000*	241.745*	29-01-16	Scottsdale	1381	B/J **F224**
White with tan and white interior; automatic transmission.												
1959	Adventurer convertible		M491100249	L	NA	153.934*	220.000*	201.454*	29-01-16	Scottsdale	1382	B/J
Black with tan, black and white interior; automatic transmission.												
1959	Firesweep convertible		M412109913	L	NA	37.074	58.000	50.796	19-09-15	Dallas	F196.1	Mec
White and green with largely original two-tone green interior (see lot S236 Mecum 1.8.15 $ 57,000).												
1959	Firesweep convertible		M412110778	L	65-95.000 USD	89.232	130.000	115.869	20-05-16	Indianapolis	S189	Mec
Red with red and white interior; used until 1964, then stored for 50 years and subsequently restored. 3,270 original miles.												
DETROIT ELECTRIC (USA) *(1907-1939)*												
1919	Model 75 Brougham		12022	L	40-50.000 USD	19.723*	30.250*	26.626*	09-10-15	Hershey	224	RMS **F225**
Blue with black fenders; it requires several restoration works.												
1920	Model 82 brougham		12578	L	60-80.000 USD	50.147*	66.000*	59.387*	30-07-16	Plymouth	119	RMS
Beige and brown with brown interior; restored at unspecified date (see lot 245 RM 7.10.11 $44,000).												
DFP (F) *(1906-1935)*												
1913	10/12hp Special two-seater	(Harrison)	M2217	R	45-65.000 GBP	46.000	66.640	59.082	20-03-16	Goodwood	30	Bon
Burgundy with black interior; the car was sold new by the DFP dealership of Walter Owen Bentley and his brother Horace. Discovered in the early 1950s, it was bought by the Montagu Motor Museum and restored. Engine rebuilt in more recent years.												
DKW (D) *(1928-1966)*												
1955	F91 cabriolet	(Karmann)	66043390	L	39-46.000 EUR	38.056	53.565	47.140	09-04-16	Essen	155	Coy **F226**
Yellow; until 1971 with its first owner, later the car remained stored from 1974 to 2012 when it was acquired by the current vendor and received some cosmetic restoration works.												

F223: 1901 Delin 4hp voiturette

F224: 1958 Desoto Adventurer convertible

F225: 1919 Detroit Electric Model 75 Brougham

F226: 1955 DKW F91 cabriolet (Karmann)

DODGE (USA) *(1914-)*

Year	Model	(Bodybuilder)	Chassis no.	Steering	Estimate	£	$	€	Date	Place	Lot	Auc. H.
1926	**Series 116 touring**		10768	R	9-11.000 GBP	17.854	23.185	20.945	10-07-16	Chateau Impney	6	H&H
Red and black with black interior; described as in very good mechanical order. The car has been driven at the 2010 Peking to Paris and at 2016 Paris to Wien.												
1931	**Series DC roadster**		E142RW	R	10-15.000 GBP	12.650	19.133	17.484	10-12-15	London	354	Bon
Grey with blue fenders; purchased by its late owner just after WWII and in regular use until relatively recently. Cylinder head replaced in 1999; body repainted.												
1934	**Series DR convertible**		3737492	L	32-36.000 EUR		NS		28-05-16	Aarhus	140	SiC
Two-tone red; circa 2,000 kms covered since a long restoration carried out between 1975 and 1990.												
1953	**Coronet convertible**		47001579	L	NA	17.148	24.500	21.768	18-06-16	Portland	S30.1	Mec
Black with red interior; 140bhp 241 Red Ram Hemi engine with 3-speed transmission.												
1959	**Coronet Lancer V8 hardtop**		H314103840	L	NA	45.516	69.300	62.224	05-09-15	Auburn	4089	AA **F227**
Two-tone pink with pink and black interior; restored in 1991. Automatic transmission.												
1956	**Suburban 2-door**		98177938	L	NA	29.247*	41.800*	38.276*	29-01-16	Scottsdale	974	B/J
Turquoise and ivory; 315 D-500 engine with automatic transmission. Built in Canada.												
1958	**Custom Royal Lancer coupé**		LD3L3040	L	40-60.000 USD	43.032*	66.000*	58.093*	09-10-15	Hershey	220	RMS
Black and beige; in original condition. 22,462 actual miles. From the estate of Jim Miller.												
1960	**Polara D500 2-door hardtop**		6307101191	L	NA	57.798	88.000	79.015	05-09-15	Auburn	5122	AA
Light blue with blue vinyl and cloth interior; fully restored. 330bhp 383 engine with automatic transmission (see lot 215 RM 1.12.12 $ 85,800).												
1963	**Polara convertible**		6332117130	L	120-140.000 USD	80.282	115.000	106.398	23-01-16	Kissimmee	F150	Mec **F228**
Pale blue with midium blue interior; 1,400 miles covered since the restoration carried out in 2006. 415bhp 426 engine with 3-speed manual gearbox.												
1963	**Polara 500 2-door hardtop**		6432118960	L	150-200.000 USD	69.810	100.000	92.520	23-01-16	Kissimmee	F132	Mec
Ivory with original white and tan interior; cosmetically and mechanically refreshed in the 1990s. Believed to be 36,416 miles. 415bhp 426 engine with automatic transmission.												
1964	**330 Series Lightweight**		6142229092	L	NA		NS		20-05-16	Indianapolis	F250.1	Mec
Red with original red interior; stored from 1966 to 2006 and subsequently restored. 425bhp 426 Hemi engine with automatic transmission.												
1963	**330 Series Lightweight hardtop**		6132174418	L	135-165.000 USD		NS		19-08-16	Monterey	F106	Mec
White with red interior; described as in as-raced condition. One of 34 examples built. 426 Max Wedge engine with automatic transmission.												
1969	**Charger Daytona hardtop**		XX29L9B390013	L	NA	131.036	205.000	179.539	19-09-15	Dallas	S97	Mec
Red with black interior; restored. 375bhp 440 engine with 4-speed manual gearbox.												
1969	**Charger Daytona hardtop**		XX29J9B386573	L	700-900.000 USD	383.955	550.000	508.860	23-01-16	Kissimmee	F103	Mec **F229**
Red with black stripe and black interior; 425bhp 426 Hemi engine with 4-speed manual gearbox (see lot S100 Mecum 10.4.15 NS).												
1969	**Charger Daytona hardtop**		XX29L9B379751	L	250-325.000 USD	188.487	270.000	249.804	23-01-16	Kissimmee	F155	Mec
Red with white tail stripe and black interior; restored in the 2000s. 375bhp 440 engine with automatic transmission.												
1969	**Charger 500 hardtop**		XX29J9B164183	L	75-100.000 USD	108.206	155.000	143.406	23-01-16	Kissimmee	F198	Mec
Red with white interior; 425bhp 426 Hemi engine with 4-speed manual gearbox.												

F227: 1959 Dodge Coronet Lancer V8 hardtop

F228: 1963 Dodge Polara convertible

Year	Model	(Bodybuilder)	Chassis no.	Steering	Estimate	Hammer price £	$	€	Date	Place	Lot	Auc. H.

F229: 1969 Dodge Charger Daytona hardtop

F230: 1969 Dodge Coronet R/T convertible

Year	Model	Chassis no.	Steering	Estimate	£	$	€	Date	Place	Lot	Auc. H.
1967	**Charger hardtop**	XP29J72149176	L	NA	27.924	40.000	37.008	23-01-16	Kissimmee	T163	Mec

Black with black vinyl interior; restored. Believed to be 25,321 original miles. 426 Hemi engine with 4-speed manual gearbox.

| 1969 | **Charger Super Bee hardtop** | WM23M9A291999 | L | NA | 53.877* | 77.000* | 70.509* | 29-01-16 | Scottsdale | 1023 | B/J |

Orange with black vinyl roof and original black interior; body repainted. 390bhp 440 Six-Pack engine with automatic transmission.

| 1968 | **Charger R/T hardtop** | XS29J8B216221 | L | NA | 169.327 | 242.000 | 221.599 | 30-01-16 | Scottsdale | 5092 | R&S |

Turquoise; restored. Hemi engine with manual gearbox.

| 1969 | **Charger Daytona hardtop** | XX29L9B355142 | L | NA | 111.602 | 159.500 | 146.054 | 30-01-16 | Scottsdale | 5132 | R&S |

Red; restored. 440 Magnum engine with automatic transmission.

| 1969 | **Coronet R/T convertible** | WS27J9G278020 | L | 600-800.000 USD | 436.313 | 625.000 | 578.250 | 23-01-16 | Kissimmee | F105 | Mec F230 |

Metallic green with white interior; 18,403 miles. 425bhp 426 Hemi engine with 4-speed manual gearbox.

| 1967 | **Coronet R/T convertible** | WS27J77190997 | L | 225-275.000 USD | 139.620 | 200.000 | 185.040 | 23-01-16 | Kissimmee | F108 | Mec |

Dark metallic green with white interior; fully restored. 425bhp 426 Hemi engine with 4-speed manual gearbox.

| 1969 | **Coronet Super Bee hardtop** | WM21M9A301771 | L | 160-185.000 USD | 97.734 | 140.000 | 129.528 | 23-01-16 | Kissimmee | F162 | Mec |

Butterscotch with black bonnet and black interior; until 2005 with its first owner, the car is in original condition and has covered 23,000 miles. 440 Six Pack engine with automatic transmission (see lot S119 Mecum 27.6.15 NS).

| 1970 | **Coronet Super Bee hardtop** | WM23V0G122703 | L | NA | 45.474 | 65.000 | 58.611 | 12-03-16 | Kansas City | S179 | Mec |

Black with black interior; restored eight years ago. 390bhp 440 engine with 4-speed manual gearbox.

| 1968 | **Dart Super Stock hardtop** | L023M8B297862 | L | 225-275.000 USD | 209.430 | 300.000 | 277.560 | 23-01-16 | Kissimmee | F101 | Mec |

Yellow with black interior; described as in original condition and never raced. 3,786 miles. 425bhp 426 Hemi engine with Hurst automatic transmission.

| 1970 | **Challenger R/T convertible** | JS27R0B209728 | L | 2.000-2.500.000 USD | 1.151.865 | 1.650.000 | 1.526.580 | 23-01-16 | Kissimmee | F111 | Mec F231 |

Green with black stripe and black vinyl interior; 1,140 miles covered since the restoration. One of nine Challenger convertibles built with the 425bhp 426 Hemi engine of which just four with the automatic transmission.

| 1970 | **Challenger R/T convertible** | JS27V0B100021 | L | 500-750.000 USD | 314.145 | 450.000 | 416.340 | 23-01-16 | Kissimmee | F114 | Mec |

Red with white side stripe and white and black vinyl interior; restored in 2004. 390bhp 440 Six Pack engine with 4-speed manual gearbox.

| 1970 | **Challenger R/T convertible** | JS27V0B111163 | L | 180-220.000 USD | 118.677 | 170.000 | 157.284 | 23-01-16 | Kissimmee | F148 | Mec |

Orange with black stripes and black interior; restored in the 1990s. Body repainted in 2013. 390bhp 440 Six Pack engine with 4-speed manual gearbox.

| 1970 | **Challenger R/T hardtop** | JS23R0B339366 | L | 250-325.000 USD | 202.449 | 290.000 | 268.308 | 23-01-16 | Kissimmee | F158 | Mec |

Plum with black roof and black vinyl interior; fully restored. 425bhp 426 Hemi engine with 4-speed manual gearbox.

| 1971 | **Challenger R/T hardtop** | JS23R1B242313 | L | 525-575.000 USD | NS | | | 23-01-16 | Kissimmee | S129 | Mec |

Black with black interior; raced at some drag stripes in the 1980s. Engine rebuilt in 2003. 425bhp 426 Hemi engine with 4-speed manual gearbox (see lots 173 RM 18.1.13 NS and S147 Mecum 17. 8.13 NS).

| 1970 | **Challenger R/T hardtop** | JS23V0B212630 | L | NA | 100.057* | 143.000* | 130.945* | 29-01-16 | Scottsdale | 1424 | B/J |

Red with black roof and black interior; restored to concours condition. 440 Six Pack engine with 4-speed manual gearbox.

| 1970 | **Challenger R/T SE convertible** | JB27V0B203932 | L | NQ | NS | | | 20-08-16 | Monterey | 7057 | R&S |

Orange with black interior; restored. 440 Six Pack engine with 4-speed manual gearbox.

F231: 1970 Dodge Challenger R/T convertible

F232: 1994 Dodge Viper RT/10

Year	Model	(Bodybuilder)	Chassis no.	Steering	Estimate	Hammer price £	$	€	Date	Place	Lot	Auc. H.

F233: 1961 Dolphin America

F234: 1958 Dual-Ghia Convertible

Year	Model	(Bodybuilder)	Chassis no.	Steering	Estimate	£	$	€	Date	Place	Lot	Auc. H.
1986	Shelby Omni GLHS		1B3BZ18E9GD251155	L	40-60.000 USD	21.010*	27.500*	24.280*	19-08-16	Monterey	118	RMS

Carroll Shelby's personal car; 7,733 miles covered. Proceeds to benefit the Carroll Hall Shelby Trust.

1994	Viper RT/10		102296	L	50-75.000 USD	31.574*	46.000*	41.000*	20-05-16	Indianapolis	S81	Mec

Red with black interior; 507 original miles.

| 1994 | Viper RT/10 | | 200381 | L | 200-300.000 EUR | 182.897 | 237.518 | 214.560 | 09-07-16 | Le Mans | 180 | Art |

Yellow; one of two examples prepared by Luigi Cimarosti in Belgium for the 1994 Le Mans 24 Hours, where it placed 19th overall. Slightly modified, the car was raced until 1996 at some BPR Series events. Bought in 2003 by the current owner and overhauled. **F232**

| 2002 | Viper GTS | | 100998 | L | NA | 40.490 | 58.000 | 53.662 | 23-01-16 | Kissimmee | K15 | Mec |

Red with white stripes and black interior; one owner and 265 miles covered.

| 1998 | Viper GTS-R | | 401030 | L | 95-115.000 USD | 61.120 | 80.000 | 70.632 | 19-08-16 | Monterey | F144 | Mec |

White with blue stripes and black and blue interior; 9,953 miles covered.

| 2006 | Viper SRT10 Coupé | | 100875 | L | 60-80.000 USD | 43.461* | 57.200* | 51.469* | 30-07-16 | Plymouth | 125 | RMS |

Yellow with black stripes; less than 2,600 miles covered.

DOLPHIN (USA) (1960-1961)

| 1961 | America | | 0261 | L | 50-65.000 GBP | 53.760 | 80.914 | 76.479 | 28-11-15 | Weybridge | 294 | His |

The parts of the car, including the chassis, were bought in 1964 at the closing of Dolphin by Charles Thompson who in the 1980s resold them to Phil Binks. He had the car fully restored in the early 2000s and fitted with a 105E Ford engine and Hewland 5-speed gearbox. Raced at historic events in the USA; engine rebuilt in 2010; car recently imported into the UK. **F233**

DORT (USA) (1915-1924)

| 1923 | Six sport touring | | 100329 | L | 20-30.000 USD | 12.320* | 18.700* | 16.643* | 05-10-15 | Philadelphia | 228 | Bon |

Dark green with black fenders; restored many years ago. Formerly in the Harrah and Nethercutt collections. From the Evergreen Collection (see lot 110 Gooding 22.1.11 $ 15,400).

DUAL-GHIA (USA) (1956-1958)

| 1958 | Convertible | | 195 | L | 385-425.000 USD | 253.991 | 363.000 | 332.399 | 29-01-16 | Scottsdale | 37 | G&Co |

Maroon with maroon and cream interior; restored in recent years. Engine rebuilt (see lot 119 RM 15.8.14 $ 385,000).

| 1958 | Convertible | | 191 | L | 250-350.000 USD | 281.534 | 368.500 | 325.349 | 19-08-16 | Carmel | 107 | Bon |

Restored at unspecified date, the car is described as in very good overall condition. Interior retrimmed in recent years (see lots 63 Worldwide 1.11.08 $ 319,000, 254 RM 14.3.09 $ 209,000, 79 Gooding & Company 9.3.12 $ 214,500, 230 RM 16.1.15 NS and 488 Auctions America 28.3.15 $ 225,500). **F234**

DUESENBERG (USA) (1920-1937)

| 1923 | Model A sport phaeton | | 977 | L | 225-275.000 USD | 244.820 | 374.000 | 332.336 | 08-10-15 | Hershey | 161 | RMS |

Dark green with green leather interior; since 1948 in the same family ownership. Acquired in rolling chassis form, the car was subsequently fitted with the present Cadillac body of the 1920s, which was adapted to the chassis. Cosmetically restored in 1974, the car received a full restoration between 1989 and 2009 and was subsequently exhibited at Concours d'Elegance events.

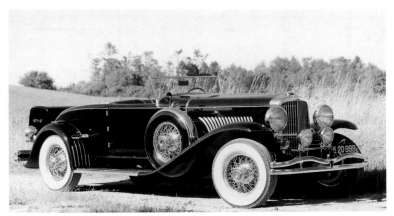

F235: 1930 Duesenberg Model J roadster (Murphy)

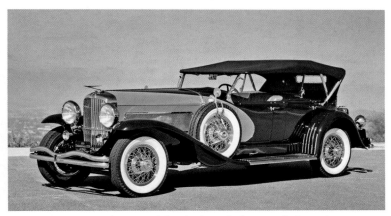

F236: 1929 Duesenberg Model J dual cowl phaeton (LeBaron)

Year	Model	(Bodybuilder)	Chassis no.	Steering	Estimate	Hammer price £	Hammer price $	Hammer price €	Date	Place	Lot	Auc. H.
1929	Model J convertible	(Murphy)	2168	L	NA	921.162	1.402.500	1.259.305	05-09-15	Auburn	5142	AA

Silver grey with green leather interior; engine J-147. Built with LeBaron body, probably in 1930 the car was fitted with the present body coming from car chassis 2177, engine no.J-121. The engine was first repaired in the 1950s using parts from engines J-245 and J-524, and repaired again in 2000 circa. Acquired in 2007 by the current owner, the car received subsequently a concours-quality restoration (see lots 239 RM 21.1.00 NS, 245 RM 5.8.00 $ 550,000, 319 Brooks 6.10.00 $ 530,500 and 55 H&H 24.5.06 $ 621,093).

| 1930 | Model J roadster | (Murphy) | 2346 | L | 17-21.000.000 DKK | 1.755.763 | 2.664.838 | 2.390.333 | 26-09-15 | Ebeltoft | 14 | Bon |

Black with black interior; J-330 engine. Described as in very good overall condition; sympathetic restoration carried out in the 1950s. Unbroken chain of ownership since new; body, chassis, engine and mechanical components never been apart. From the Frederiksen Collection. **F235**

| 1929 | Model J torpedo convertible | (Murphy) | 2199 | L | 3.000-3.500.000 USD | 2.097.300 | 3.000.000 | 2.751.300 | 28-01-16 | Phoenix | 133 | RMS |

Two-tone red with tan leather interior; after some ownership changes, in 1951 the car was acquired by William Coverdale who fitted it with the present J-414 engine and retained it until 1985. Restored in the early 1990s; in the current ownership for over two decades.

| 1929 | Model J dual cowl phaeton | (LeBaron) | 2151 | L | 1.800-2.400.000 USD | 1.693.274 | 2.420.000 | 2.215.994 | 29-01-16 | Scottsdale | 51 | G&Co |

Dark blue with red leather interior; engine J-129. First owner John Duval Dodge. In the Richard Kughn collection for 30 years from 1977, the car was subsequently fully restored to concours condition between 2009 and 2010 (see lot 143 Gooding 18.1.14 $ 2,090,000). **F236**

| 1934 | Model J town car | (Murphy) | 2531 | L | 1.200-1.400.000 USD | | NS | | 29-01-16 | Phoenix | 236 | RMS |

Black with black leather interior to the front compartment and grey cloth to the rear; original engine J-295. Until 1947 with its first owner; in single ownership from 1956 for 25 years and first restored; later part of the Richard and Linda Kughn collection; acquired in 1990 circa by the current owner and restored again.

| 1931 | Model J convertible | (Murphy) | 2388 | L | 2.500-3.000.000 USD | 1.846.944 | 2.640.000 | 2.380.488 | 11-03-16 | Amelia Island | 22 | G&Co |

Black with black interior; original engine J-357. The car has had just five owners and is described as in largely original condition. Recently acquired by the current owner, it received a major service and cosmetic freshening (see lot 22 RM 16.1.14 $ 2,200,000).

| 1929 | Model J convertible | (Murphy) | 2551 | L | 1.250-1.650.000 USD | 1.170.092 | 1.540.000 | 1.385.692 | 30-07-16 | Plymouth | 155 | RMS |

Maroon; engine J-119. Paintwork and interior redone in recent years. Recent service. In 1934 the present body was fitted to car chassis 2144 and engine J-119, previously fitted with a Derham saloon body. In the late 1940s the car was bought by Melvin Clemans, who had it rebuilt with frame no.2551 and firewall no.2577, and retained it until 1963. At unspecified date it was acquired by Eric Bardeen who used it for several years. Offered today by Mr Bardeen to benefit the operations of Hillsdale College, Michigan.

| 1930 | Model J town cabriolet | (Murphy) | 2401 | L | 900-1.200.000 USD | 958.056 | 1.254.000 | 1.107.157 | 19-08-16 | Carmel | 64 | Bon |

Charcoal and burgundy with black roof and leather interior to the front compartment and cloth to the rear; J-381 engine. Restored several years ago (see lots 440 Hershey Auctions 5.10.05 NS and 5004 Barrett-Jackson 20.1.12 $ 1,045,000).

| 1933 | Model J convertible | (Bohman/Schwartz) | 2421 | L | 3.500-4.500.000 USD | | NS | | 20-08-16 | Monterey | S114 | Mec |

Ivory with red interior; engine J-386. Built with LeBaron convertible berline body, not long thereafter the car was fitted with the present body. Described as in very good overall condition. Formerly in the Harrah, Blackhawk and Imperial Palace collections.

| 1930 | Model J torpedo phaeton | | 2276 | L | 1.100-1.300.000 USD | | NS | | 20-08-16 | Monterey | S147 | Mec |

Black with black leather interior; built with Judkins limousine body. In 1937 the car was purchased by Pacific Auto Rental in Hollywood and subsequently used in several films. Sold by Pacific Auto in 1985, it was restored by Fran Roxas who modified the body to the present Walker LaGrande-style configuration (see lots Bonhams 425 6.6.10 NS, 451 19.8.11 NS and 321 23.2.13 $ 698,500, and Mecum S154 17.8.13 $ 950,000, S180 7.9.13 NS, S186 25.1.14 NS, and B2 12.4.14 NS).

| 1932 | Model J phaeton | | 2480 | L | 700-800.000 USD | 458.400 | 600.000 | 529.740 | 20-08-16 | Monterey | S45 | Mec |

Two-tone red with tan interior; engine J-463. Built with Rollston limousine body, the car was later fitted with a Dietrich convertible body. Between 1946 and 1956 it was damaged in a garage fire and in the 1970s it was restored and fitted with the present, new LaGrande-style phaeton body. Engine rebuilt to SJ specification (see Mecum lots S92.1 10.4.15 $ 500,000 and S124 15.8.15 NS).

| 1931 | Model J Tourster | (Derham) | 2468 | L | 1.300-1.600.000 USD | 1.008.480 | 1.320.000 | 1.165.428 | 20-08-16 | Monterey | 222 | RMS |

Pale green with tan leather interior; engine J-451. Over the years the car has had several owners and was part also of the collections of Cameron Peck e Joseph Murphy. Restored many years ago between the late 1950s - early 1970s. Since 2001 in the current ownership, it is described as in good driving order (see lots 26 P.R.Group 27.11.99 NS, and 240 RM 11.3.00 $ 726,000). **F237**

EDSEL (USA) *(1957-1959)*

| 1959 | Corsair convertible | | W9UR712456 | L | 55-65.000 USD | 16.004* | 23.100* | 20.709* | 05-06-16 | Greenwhich | 83 | Bon |

White with white and turquoise interior; in running condition. 303bhp 361 Super Express engine with automatic transmission. From the Evergreen Collection.

EISERT (USA)

| 1964 | Harrison Special Indy Car | | 001 | M | 350-450.000 USD | 183.360 | 240.000 | 211.896 | 19-08-16 | Monterey | F151 | Mec |

Only example built, the car is fitted with a "small block" Chevrolet Corvette engine de-stroked to 302CI, and 4-speed Colotti gearbox. Raced in the 1960s, the car failed to qualify for the Indy 500 in 1965, 1966 and 1968. Restored to the red "Arciero Bros." livery of 1966 Indy. Driven at several historic events. **F238**

EL MOROCCO (USA) *(1956-1957)*

| 1957 | El Morocco convertible | | VC57F216422 | L | NA | 126.996* | 181.500* | 166.200* | 29-01-16 | Scottsdale | 1356 | B/J |

Black with red interior; acquired in 1990 by the current owner and restored in 1992. Chevrolet 283 V8 engine with automatic transmission. **F239**

F237: 1931 Duesenberg Model J Tourster (Derham)

F238: 1964 Eisert Harrison Special Indy Car

Year	Model	(Bodybuilder)	Chassis no.	Steering	Estimate	Hammer price £	$	€	Date	Place	Lot	Auc. H.

ELVA (GB) *(1955-1973)*

| 1959 | **Mark III** | | 10054 | R | 110-130.000 GBP | **102.600** | **147.046** | **134.724** | 16-01-16 | Birmingham | 325 | **Coy** |

Unpainted aluminium body; the car was sold new to the USA where it had a long race career. Reimported into the UK six years ago and subsequently restored, it has been raced at several club events. 1450cc Coventry Climax OHC FWB engine. **F240**

| 1959 | **Mark III** | | 10054 | R | 75-85.000 GBP | **87.360** | **125.825** | **111.314** | 11-06-16 | Brooklands | 252 | **His** |

See lot 325 Coys 16.1.16.

EMW (DDR) *(1945-1955)*

| 1953 | **327 cabriolet** | | 87596 | L | 80-100.000 GBP | **85.500** | **129.319** | **118.170** | 10-12-15 | London | 331 | **Bon** |

Two-tone grey with blue leather interior; recently restored in the UK. Engine overhauled. Formerly in the collection of the Federation Hellenique Des Vehicules D'Epoque Automobile Museum in Nafplias (see Coys lots 114 14.6.14 $ 60,903 and 131 18.4.15 NS).

| 1952 | **327 cabriolet** | | 87528 | L | 90-120.000 GBP | | **NS** | | 24-06-16 | Goodwood | 276 | **Bon** |

Two-tone blue with grey leather interior; sold new to Switzerland, the car is currently registered in the Netherlands as a BMW 327/2. Engine modified to 328 specification.

ESSEX (USA) *(1917-1939)*

| 1930 | **Super Six sedan** | | 1230298 | R | NA | **32.102*** | **44.000*** | **39.758*** | 24-06-16 | Uncasville | 442.1 | **B/J** |

Maroon with red interior; reimported into the USA in 1975 and restored in 1996-97.

| 1930 | **Super Six sedan** | | 1005724 | R | 7-10.000 GBP | **3.410*** | **4.529*** | **4.067*** | 02-07-16 | Woodstock | 125 | **Coy** |

Blue and black; from the 1960s in the current ownership. For restoration.

| 1929 | **Challenger town sedan** | | 1113047(engine) | L | 5-10.000 USD | **4.680*** | **7.150*** | **6.353*** | 08-10-15 | Hershey | 123 | **RMS** |

In original condition, unused for many years. From the Richard Roy estate.

EURORACING (I)

| 1982 | **Formula 3** | | 1012 | M | 65-75.000 GBP | | **NS** | | 16-01-16 | Birmingham | 363 | **Coy** |

Built in 1981 as March 813 chassis 4, the car won the 1981 European Formula 3 Championship driven by Mauro Baldi. Sold in 1982 to Paolo Pavanello's Euroracing, it was rebuilt as Euroracing 101 for the 1982 European Championship which it won again driven by Oscar Larrauri. Restored in 2015; rebuilt Alfa Romeo engine.

FACEL VEGA (F) *(1954-1964)*

| 1954 | **FV Prototype** | | FV540002 | L | 350-550.000 EUR | **385.368** | **560.817** | **500.640** | 05-02-16 | Paris | 133 | **Art** |

Black with black leather interior; built on a shorter wheelbase than the series examples, the car was originally finished in blue-grey with blue roof and was displayed at the 1954 Paris Motor Show. Used as a base for the development of the future models and modified over the years, the car remained in the factory ownership until 1962 when it passed to Jean Daninos himself who retained it until 1976. Since 1998 in the current, fifth ownership. Original DeSoto Firedome 276 engine with Pont-a-Mousson 4-speed manual gearbox. **F241**

| 1957 | **FV4** | | FV457NY8 | L | 130-190.000 EUR | **174.333** | **253.703** | **226.480** | 05-02-16 | Paris | 132 | **Art** |

Dark maroon with light brown leather interior; the car was sold new to the USA where it received a concours-quality restoration between 2006 and 2010. In 2011 it was reimported into Europe (see lots 59 Gooding 20.8.11 $ 143,000 and 255 Bonhams 2.2.12 $ 203,284).

| 1958 | **FV4** | | FVSNY277 | L | 175-200.000 EUR | **165.158** | **240.350** | **214.560** | 05-02-16 | Paris | 214 | **Art** |

Finished in yellow with black interior, the car was sold new to the USA. In the late 1990 it was imported into the UK where it was restored to the present dark blue livery with red interior.

| 1955 | **FV** | | 55050 | L | NQ | **138.666** | **181.500** | **160.246** | 20-08-16 | Monterey | 7183 | **R&S** |

White with black roof; sold new to the USA. Restored in 1994-95. Automatic transmission (see lots Bonhams 448 17.8.07 $102,960, and Gooding & Company 11 22.1.10 $137,500 and 144 18.1.14 $203,500).

| 1959 | **HK500** | | HKZ1 | L | 100-120.000 EUR | | **NS** | | 26-09-15 | Frankfurt | 131 | **Coy** |

Complete, for restoration; first owner actress Ava Gardner.

| 1961 | **HK500** | | CC7 | L | 140-180.000 EUR | **108.668** | **161.086** | **143.750** | 04-02-16 | Paris | 310 | **Bon** |

Green with tan interior; for 50 years in the same family ownership. In original condition; 79,850 kms covered; sunroof.

| 1960 | **HK500** | | BE8 | L | 100-150.000 EUR | **82.579** | **120.175** | **107.280** | 05-02-16 | Paris | 128 | **Art** |

Silver with black roof and tan interior; body repainted, original interior. Mechanicals overhauled about 10 years ago. Manual gearbox. Since 1978 in the André Trigano Collection.

| 1959 | **HK500** | | HK1BN2 | R | NA | | **NS** | | 06-03-16 | Birmingham | 348 | **SiC** |

Stored for 35 years; for restoration.

F239: 1957 El Morocco El Morocco convertible

F240: 1959 Elva Mark III

Year	Model	(Bodybuilder)	Chassis no.	Steering	Estimate	Hammer price £	$	€	Date	Place	Lot	Auc. H.

F241: 1954 Facel Vega FV Prototype

F242: 1959 Facel Vega Excellence

Year	Model	(Bodybuilder)	Chassis no.	Steering	Estimate	£	$	€	Date	Place	Lot	Auc. H.
1961	**HK500**		HKC2	L	130-160.000 EUR		NS		14-05-16	Monaco	216	**RMS**

Blue; sold new to the USA, the car was reimported into Europe in the 1980s and was recently restored.

| 1959 | **HK500** | | HKBC2 | R | 175-225.000 USD | | NS | | 19-08-16 | Carmel | 93 | **Bon** |

Creamy yellow with oxblood leather interior; restored in the 1990s. 383 Hemi engine with 4-speed Pont-a-Mousson manual gearbox (see lot 136 RM 8.9.14 NS).

| 1962 | **Facel II** | | HK2A114 | R | 60-70.000 GBP | **57.500** | **86.969** | **79.471** | 10-12-15 | London | 343 | **Bon** |

Restoration project.

| 1962 | **Facel II** | | HK2A141 | L | 275-325.000 USD | **196.266** | **280.500** | **256.854** | 29-01-16 | Scottsdale | 53 | **G&Co** |

Tudor grey with black interior; sold new in France, the car was imported into the USA in 1970 circa. In single ownership from 1985 to 2015. In the early 1980s the car was restored, the engine was rebuilt and the transmission was replaced (see lot 153 Bonhams 15.1.15 $ 253,000).

| 1963 | **Facel II** | | HK2B171 | L | 220-280.000 EUR | **177.176** | **257.144** | **235.200** | 03-02-16 | Paris | 140 | **RMS** |

Metallic blue with tan leather interior; in original condition, the car is in the same family ownership since new and has covered 20,601 miles. Displayed at the 1963 Geneva Motor Show.

| 1959 | **Excellence** | | EX18004 | L | 160-180.000 EUR | **129.168** | **181.808** | **160.000** | 09-04-16 | Essen | 146 | **Coy** |

Black with red leather interior; in good original condition. One owner and 46,000 kms covered. **F242**

FAURE (F)

| 1941 | **Type PFA** | | NQ | L | 15-25.000 EUR | **15.598*** | **22.700*** | **20.264*** | 05-02-16 | Paris | 178 | **Art** |

For restoration; electric car since new in the same family ownership. Stored after WWII; without batteries.

FERRARI (I) (1946-)

| 1950 | **166 MM/195 S Berlinetta Le Mans (Touring)** | | 0060M | R | 5.750-6.500.000 USD | **4.541.053** | **6.490.000** | **5.942.893** | 29-01-16 | Scottsdale | 33 | **G&Co** |

French blue with black interior; still under factory ownership, the car was raced at some events and subsequently displayed by Luigi Chinetti at the 1950 Paris Motor Show. Bought by Briggs Cunningham, it was fitted at the factory with the 2.3-litre 195 S engine and then exported to the USA where it was raced until late 1952. After several ownership changes, it was fully restored between 1999 and 2001 (see lot 31 Gooding 21.8.05 NS).

| 1950 | **166 MM Berlinetta (Touring/Zagato)** | | 0046M | R | 6.000-8.000.000 USD | **4.159.980** | **5.445.000** | **4.807.391** | 20-08-16 | Pebble Beach | 68 | **G&Co** |

Built with Touring Barchetta body, the car was driven at the 1950 and 1951 MM by Nuccio Bertone. In 1952 it was bought by Emilio Giletti who raced it at several events and won the 2-Litre Class Italian Champion Title. In 1953 it passed to Luigi Bosisio who had it converted to coupé form by Zagato who left much of the Touring body intact. Sold in 1955 to the USA and fitted with a V8 Chevrolet engine; bought, together with the original engine, in 1966 by the previous owner who retained it until 2007. Described as in unrestored condition; fitted again with its original rebuilt engine. **F243**

| 1950 | **195 Inter berlinetta (Touring)** | | 0081S | R | NA | | NS | | 29-01-16 | Scottsdale | 1395 | **B/J** |

Dark blue with camel interior; restored (see lots 590 RM 18.8.07 $ 429,000 and 26 Gooding 20.8.11 $ 990,000).

| 1951 | **340 America barchetta (Touring)** | | 0116A | R | 7.500-9.000.000 EUR | **5.733.582** | **8.261.344** | **7.280.000** | 14-05-16 | Monaco | 232 | **RMS** |

Sold new to France to Pierre Louis-Dreyfus, the car raced the Le Mans 24 Hours in 1951 driven by Louis-Dreyfus and Louis Chiron and the 1952 edition driven by Louis-Dreyfus and René Dreyfus. After some ownership changes, in 1964 it was acquired by Pierre Bardinon who had it restored in Modena. In 1974 it was bought by Giuseppe Medici and imported in Italy and in 1982 it was bought by Ennio Gianaroli and imported in Belgium. Restored again in recent years by its current Italian owner to the Le Mans 1951 specification and finished in red with black interior. **F244**

F243: 1950 Ferrari 166 MM Berlinetta (Touring/Zagato)

F244: 1951 Ferrari 340 America barchetta (Touring)

OUR PASSION PRODUCES RESULTS

1956 Ferrari 290 MM by Scaglietti Sold for $28,050,000 at New York 2015

When it comes to the presentation of important and historic Ferraris at auction, RM Sotheby's is the clear market leader, having successfully sold more examples than any other auction house.

CONSIGN TODAY

RM AUCTIONS | Sotheby's

www.rmsothebys.com

CORPORATE +1 519 352 4575   CALIFORNIA +1 310 559 4575   EUROPE +44 (0) 20 7851 7070

Year	Model	(Bodybuilder)	Chassis no.	Steering	Estimate	Hammer price £	Hammer price $	Hammer price €	Sale Date	Sale Place	Lot	Auc. H.

F245: 1953 Ferrari 212 Inter coupé (Vignale)

F246: 1952 Ferrari 212 Inter cabriolet (Vignale)

Year	Model (Bodybuilder)	Chassis	Steer	Estimate	£	$	€	Date	Place	Lot	Auc.
1953	212 Inter coupé (Vignale)	0257EU	R	2.000-2.400.000 USD		NS		10-12-15	New York	225	RMS

Black with green roof and green leather interior; exhibited at the 1954 San Remo Concours d'Elegance, the car was subsequently sold to the USA. In 1979 it was reimported into Europe and in 2009 it was sold again to the USA where it was fully restored to concours condition and fitted again with its original engine no.0257EU. Certified by Ferrari Classiche (see lots 582 RM 18.8. 07 $ 495,000 and 128 Gooding 18.1.14 $ 1,787,500).

| 1953 | 212 Inter coupé (Vignale) | 0285EU | L | 1.800-2.200.000 USD | 769.670 | 1.100.000 | 1.007.270 | 29-01-16 | Phoenix | 227 | RMS |

Red with black roof; sold new to the USA, since 1994 the car is in the current ownership. Described as in largely original condition, never fully restored (see lot 426 Bonhams 19.8.11 NS). **F245**

| 1952 | 212 Inter cabriolet (Vignale) | 0227EL | L | 1.250-1.500.000 EUR | 926.194 | 1.334.525 | 1.176.000 | 14-05-16 | Monaco | 262 | RMS |

Black with red leather interior; sold new in Europe, the car was imported into the USA in the late 1950s. Between 1979 and 1980 it was restored and refinished in dark metallic grey. In 1985 it was reimported into Europe and in 1987 it was purchased by the current Dutch owner. In 2009 the body was repainted to its original colour. **F246**

| 1952 | 212 Europa coupé (Pinin Farina) | 0263EU | L | 1.300-1.600.000 USD | | NS | | 19-08-16 | Monterey | 131 | RMS |

Two-tone blue with light blue interior; exhibited at the 1953 Geneva and Turin Motor Shows, the car was subsequently sold to France. In the early 1960s it was imported into the USA. After some ownership changes, it was acquired by Wayne Obry, who restored it to concours condition between 1991 and 1993. Several years ago it was acquired by the current owner.

| 1953 | 250 Europa coupé (Vignale) | 0313EU | L | 3.800-4.500.000 USD | 2.181.630 | 3.300.000 | 3.015.540 | 10-12-15 | New York | 216 | RMS |

One of four 250 Europas bodied by Vignale on a Michelotti design, the car was shipped to Luigi Chinetti in the USA and exhibited at the 1954 New York Motor Show. In 1960 circa it was fitted with a Chevrolet V8 engine and some years later it was taken off the road. Discovered in 2003 and imported into Switzerland, the car received a full restoration completed in 2011. Currently fitted with Ferrari engine no.0331EU. Certified by Ferrari Classiche (see lot 160 Bonhams 16.8.13 $ 2,805,000). **F247**

| 1955 | 500 Mondial (Scaglietti) | 0424MD | R | 5.000-6.500.000 USD | | NS | | 10-12-15 | New York | 224 | RMS |

Blue; described as in original condition. Sold to French Yves Dupont, this 2nd series Mondial was numbered #0424MD instead of #0564MD to avoid tax and import duties in France. In late 1955 it was returned to Maranello to be refurbished and never collected back. Retained by factory, in 1965 it was repainted red over the blue livery and put on display at the Autodromo Monza Museum. Sold again by factory in 1975; red paint removed in the 2000s; used at numerous historic events; certified by Ferrari Classiche (see lot 63 - #0564MD - Christie's 30.11.98 NS).

| 1955 | 750 Monza (Scaglietti) | 0510M | R | 4.000-5.000.000 USD | 3.991.900 | 5.225.000 | 4.613.153 | 19-08-16 | Monterey | 127 | RMS |

Bought new by Allen Guiberson, Dallas, the car did its race debut at the 1955 Sebring 12 Hours where it placed second overall driven by Phil Hill and Carroll Shelby. Subsequently it was raced at other events and driven by both Hill and Shelby until March 1956. Acquired by Jim Hall, the car was raced until March 1958. Stored for nearly 40 years, in the mid-1990 it was restored to the present white and red livery and subsequently exhibited at some historical events. From the Jim Hall Collection. **F248**

| 1958 | 250 GT/250 Testa Rossa recreation | 0803GT | R | 500-600.000 GBP | 527.900 | 799.188 | 733.042 | 06-12-15 | London | 027 | Bon |

White with blue stripes and light blue interior; the car was built in the mid-1990s by DK Engineering using a 250 GT Ellena chassis and mechanicals. Raced at historic events in 1996. Engine rebuilt in 2007. Formerly part of the collection of Chris Evans who had it repainted in the present livery.

| 1956 | 250 GT coupé (Boano) | 0609GT | L | 1.500-1.800.000 USD | | NS | | 28-01-16 | Scottsdale | 44 | Bon |

Alloy body finished in white ivory with red roof and red interior; sold new in Italy, the car has had in the years several owners in Europe and received some restoration works between the late 1980s-early 1990s. In late 2012 it was acquired by German Mario Bernardi who restored the mechanicals in 2013 and resold the car to the current owner who imported it into the USA.

| 1956 | 250 GT coupé (Boano) | 0613GT | L | 1.500-2.000.000 USD | 1.134.540 | 1.485.000 | 1.311.107 | 21-08-16 | Pebble Beach | 132 | G&Co |

Alloy body finished in red with black roof and tan interior; sold new to the USA, the car was raced at some events in 1958 and 1959. Imported into the UK, it was restored in the mid-1980s and then sold to Japan. Reimported into the USA in 2002, it was subsequently refreshed and the engine was rebuilt. Certified by Ferrari Classiche.

| 1958 | 250 GT Berlinetta TdF (P.F./Scaglietti) | 0897GT | L | 4.500-5.500.000 GBP | 4.760.000 | 7.264.712 | 6.517.868 | 07-09-15 | London | 172 | RMS |

Red with black interior; sold in Italy, the car was raced at some events in 1959 and subsequently exported to the USA. At some point the original engine was removed and in the early 1970s the car was restored and fitted with engine no.1555GT from a 250 GT coupé. In 1989 the car was restored again in California and then it was acquired by Swiss Engelbert E. Stieger, who also sourced and purchased the original engine no.0897GT. In 1995 the car was acquired by German Matthias Fitch. Recently the original engine was rebuilt and re-fitted to the car. **F249**

F247: 1953 Ferrari 250 Europa coupé (Vignale)

F248: 1955 Ferrari 750 Monza (Scaglietti)

sport auto modena
MECHANICAL RESTORATION OF CLASSIC CARS

Founded in the 1960s, sport auto modena is one of the repair shops with the most established tradition and experience on Maranello racing cars.

sport auto modena di Diena e Silingardi
Via Toscanini 90 41122 MODENA - ITALIA
Tel. +39 059 364317 Fax +39 059 371180
info@sportautomodena.191.it

art and photos By Massimo Trenti

Year	Model	(Bodybuilder)	Chassis no.	Steering	Estimate	Hammer price £	$	€	Date	Place	Lot	Auc. H.

F249: 1958 Ferrari 250 GT Berlinetta TdF (P.F./Scaglietti)

F250: 1958 Ferrari 250 GT cabriolet (Pinin Farina)

1957 250 GT Berlinetta TdF (P.F./Scaglietti)   0619GT   L   Refer Dpt.   NS   12-03-16   Amelia Island   174   **RMS**
Built with chassis no.0805GT, the car was renumbered 0619GT and sold to French private racer Pierre Noblet (previously owner of TdF chassis 0619GT) who raced it and resold it at the end of the 1960 season. Damaged in a road accident in France in 1968 circa, the car was acquired unrepaired in 1975 by the current owner, Wayne Sparling, a former NART technician living in Florida. Subjected to a full restoration completed in the early 2000s and finished in its original grey livery, the car has been subsequently driven at numerous historic events.

1956 250 GT Berlinetta TdF (P.F./Scaglietti)   0507GT   L   7.000-9.000.000 USD   **4.370.080**   **5.720.000**   **5.050.188**   20-08-16   Monterey   232   **RMS**
Silver grey with blue leather interior; sold new in Italy, the car was raced until 1959, and was entered also at the 1956 Mille Miglia and 1959 Tour de France. In 1968 it was bought by Danish Claus Ahlefeld who retained it for 32 years. Since 2000 is part of the Sam and Emily Mann Collection and has been restored to its original configuration (see lot 168 Brooks 27.5.00 $738,038).

1956 290 MM   0626   R   28-32.000.000 USD   **18.543.855**   **28.050.000**   **25.632.090**   10-12-15   New York   221   **RMS**
Red with blue and yellow nose stripes; Works car, it did the race debut at the 1956MM driven by Manuel Fangio. Used by tha factory until early 1957 it was driven among others by Phil Hill, Alfonso de Portago, Wolfgang von Trips, Masten Gregory and Luigi Musso. Sold in April 1957 to the USA to Temple Buell, later it had also other owners and was raced until 1964 maintaining the almost unique record of never being crashed. In 1970 it was bought by Pierre Bardinon who in 2004 resold it to the current owner. Certified by Ferrari Classiche.   **TOP TEN**

1958 250 GT cabriolet (Pinin Farina)   0791GT   L   6.000-7.500.000 USD   **3.781.492**   **5.720.000**   **5.226.936**   10-12-15   New York   211   **RMS**
White with dark blue leather interior; sold new to the USA, in 1969 the car was fitted with an outside-plug replacement engine. In 1971 it was bought by Robert Donner Jr. who had it restored in 1975 and retained it for 40 years. Bought by the current, fifth owner, it has been restored again by DK Engineering in Europe and fitted with a type 128-C engine supplied by Ferrari. Certified by Ferrari Classiche (see lot 39 Gooding 17.1.14 $ 6,160,000).   **F250**

1957 335 S (Scaglietti)   0674   R   28-32.000.000 EUR   **24.689.885**   **35.930.639**   **32.075.200**   05-02-16   Paris   170   **Art**
Works car built with the 315 engine with which it raced in 1957 the Sebring 12 Hours and the Mille Miglia. Fitted with the 335 engine it raced the Le Mans 24 Hours, Swedish GP and Venezuela GP for which it was fitted with a 250TR style nose. Sold to Luigi Chinetti in 1958, it raced the Cuba GP and other events until the season end. Driven among others by Collins, Trintignant, von Trips, Hawthorn, Musso, Moss, and Gregory. In 1970 it was acquired by Pierre Bardinon who had it restored in 1981 to its original configuration by Fantuzzi, in Modena.   **TOP TEN F251**

1962 250 GT cabriolet II serie (Pininfarina)   3803GT   L   1.000-1.200.000 GBP   NS   06-12-15   London   023   **Bon**
Silver with silver hardtop and black leather interior; sold new in Italy, the car was originally finished in white with blue interior. In 1995 the engine was rebuilt in France and in 1996 the car was registered in the UK. In 2001 it was acquired by the current owner who had the engine rebuilt in December 2014 (see lot 745 Sotheby's 11.12.95 $ 123,769).

1960 250 GT cabriolet II serie (Pinin Farina)   2153GT   L   1.800-2.100.000 USD   **1.153.515**   **1.650.000**   **1.513.215**   28-01-16   Phoenix   149   **RMS**
Dark blue with natural leather interior; sold new to Belgium, the car was imported into the USA probably in the late 1960s. Between 2013 and 2015 it was fully restored to its original colour specification (see lot 700 Barrett-Jackson 16.1.03 $ 178,200).   **F252**

1960 250 GT cabriolet II serie (Pinin Farina)   1967GT   L   1.800-2.200.000 USD   NS   29-01-16   Scottsdale   41   **G&Co**
Light blue with tan interior; sold new to the USA, the car was first restored in the early 1990s. In 2011 it was acquired by the current owner, who in 2013 commissioned further restoration works.

1960 250 GT cabriolet II serie (Pinin Farina)   1939GT   L   2.000-2.300.000 USD   NS   30-01-16   Scottsdale   124   **G&Co**
Dark blue with white leather interior; originally finished in shell grey with black interior, the car was sold new in Italy. In the early 1970s it was imported into the USA and dismantled for restoration. In 1987 it was acquired, still unrestored, by Richard Cole who commissioned a restoration completed in 2000. Since 2013 in the Tony Shooshani Collection (see lot 127 RM 16. 8.13 $ 1,292,500).

1960 250 GT cabriolet II serie (Pinin Farina)   1925GT   L   1.400-1.800.000 EUR   NS   05-02-16   Paris   200   **Art**
The car was ordered by the Prince Moulay Abdallah, younger brother of the King of Morocco and was finished in dark blue with white leather interior and stainless steel hardtop. Back to France, in 1966 it was fitted with the present engine no.3903. Later the interior were retrimmed in black leather. Since 1985 in the collection of Adrien Maeght.

1960 250 GT cabriolet II serie (Pinin Farina)   1695GT   L   1.500-1.800.000 USD   **1.058.145**   **1.512.500**   **1.363.821**   11-03-16   Amelia Island   20   **G&Co**
Originally finished in dark green with brown leather interior, the car was displayed at the 1960 Geneva Motor Show. In 1963 it was imported in Sweden where it was repainted in red. Subsequently it has had several owners in the USA, in Switzerland and Sweden again, in France and in 2002 it was reimported into the USA. In 2000 the body was repainted in the present dark grey livery (see lots 23 TSAC 25.5.90 NS and 402 Brooks 18.12.99 $ 120,376).

F251: 1957 Ferrari 335 S (Scaglietti)

F252: 1960 Ferrari 250 GT cabriolet II serie (Pinin Farina)

ARTCURIAL
// Motorcars

1957 Ferrari 335 Sport Scaglietti - Chassis 0674
Pierre Bardinon Collection
Sold 32,1 M€ / 24,7 M£ / 35,7 M$ including premium at Retromobile 2016
World auction record for a collectors' car in € and £

YOUR CAR COULD BE OUR NEXT RECORD

artcurial.com/motorcars

Contact :
+33 (0)1 42 99 20 73
motorcars@artcurial.com

Year	Model	(Bodybuilder)	Chassis no.	Steering	Estimate	Hammer price £	$	€	Date	Place	Lot	Auc. H.
1960	250 GT cabriolet II serie	(Pinin Farina)	2143GT	L	1.500-2.000.000 USD	1.146.000	1.500.000	1.324.350	21-08-16	Pebble Beach	108	G&Co

Shell grey with red interior; sold new in Italy, the car was subsequently imported into the USA where since 1963 it is in the same family ownership. Restored in the 1990s, it is described as still in very good overall condition. With hardtop.

| 1959 | 250 GT Spyder California lwb | (Scaglietti) | 1603GT | L | 18-20.000.000 USD | 13.866.600 | 18.150.000 | 16.024.635 | 20-08-16 | Pebble Beach | 33 | G&Co TOP TEN |

One of nine alloy body examples, the car was built with covered headlamp, disc brakes and competition specifications as the gearbox and 136-liter fuel tank. Bought by George Reed it was raced until 1964. In the 1980s the engine and gearbox were rebuilt and the body was restored and refinished in dark blue. In the 2000s it was raced at historic events, repainted in the original silver livery and certified by Ferrari Classiche. In 2010 it was bought by the current owner and cosmetically restored (see lot 46 Gooding & Company 14.8.10 $7,260,000).

| 1958 | 250 GT Spyder California lwb | (Scaglietti) | 1055GT | L | 12-14.000.000 USD | NS | | | 20-08-16 | Monterey | 221 | RMS |

Covered headlamp version originally finished in red with black leather interior, the car was sold new to the USA. First restored in the mid-1970s and between 1992 and 1994 again. In 1998 it was reimported into Europe where the engine was rebuilt. In 2001 circa it was imported again in the USA and in 2014 it was bought by the current owner, who had it refinished in the present dark blue livery with blue interior. Also the engine was rebuilt again. Certified by Ferrari Classiche (see lots 130 Christie's 6.5.91 WD, and 112 RM 17.1.14 $8,800,000).

| 1959 | 250 GT Coupé | (Pinin Farina) | 1649GT | L | 450-550.000 EUR | 437.437 | 666.052 | 598.000 | 05-09-15 | Chantilly | 15 | Bon F253 |

Silver grey with black interior; 410 Superamerica-style air outlets in the front wings. Sold new in Italy, in 1962 the car was exported to Switzerland where it was restored between 2002 and 2005. Currently registered in Germany.

| 1960 | 250 GT Coupé | (Pinin Farina) | 1989GT | L | 480-620.000 EUR | 420.763 | 649.792 | 572.000 | 17-10-15 | Salzburg | 338 | Dor |

Silver grey with black interior; sold new in Italy, the car was imported into the USA in 1963. Following some ownership changes, in 2011 it was acquired by the current owner and imported into Germany, where it has been fully restored, except for the interior already replaced at unspecified date.

| 1960 | 250 GT Coupé | (Pinin Farina) | 1749GT | L | 400-475.000 EUR | 345.915 | 502.043 | 459.200 | 03-02-16 | Paris | 137 | RMS |

Black with beige interior; sold new in Italy, later the car was exported to the USA. Back to Italy, it was restored in the 1990s (see lot 62 Brooks 7.9.98 $ 79,149).

| 1958 | 250 GT Coupé | (Pinin Farina) | 1023GT | L | 480-560.000 EUR | 403.718 | 587.522 | 524.480 | 05-02-16 | Paris | 199 | Art |

Grey with red leather interior; sold new in Europe, the car was later exported to the USA and reimported into Europe 10 years ago. At unspecified date it was fitted with the present engine no.3563 and was fitted with four disc brakes. Restored to its original colours (see lot 251 Artcurial 10.6.13 $ 445,051).

| 1960 | 250 GT Coupé | (Pinin Farina) | 1743GT | L | 800-1.000.000 USD | 705.936 | 924.000 | 815.800 | 20-08-16 | Pebble Beach | 64 | G&Co |

Silver with red leather interior; ordered new by Swiss racing driver Willy Daetwyler with a competition-spec Tipo 128 F engine, limited-slip differential, servo-assisted brakes and Borrani wire wheels. The car was delivered to Daetwyler in California, where it remained since. Bought in 2011 by the current owner and subsequenly fully restored.

| 1959 | 250 GT Coupé | (Pinin Farina) | 1447GT | L | 700-800.000 USD | 504.240 | 660.000 | 582.714 | 21-08-16 | Pebble Beach | 129 | G&Co |

Grey with black interior; the car was sold new to the USA where it has had several owners. Restored in the mid-1990s, it is described as still in very good overall condition.

| 1961 | 250 GT Spyder California swb | (Scaglietti) | 2871GT | L | 15-17.000.000 USD | 12.005.136 | 17.160.000 | 15.473.172 | 11-03-16 | Amelia Island | 69 | G&Co TOP TEN |

Covered-headlamp version finished in red with black leather interior; the car remained in Italy since new and was acquired in 1985 by the current third owner. Described as in well-maintained and largely unrestored condition throughout. Used in the 1963 movie "Yesterday, Today, Tomorrow" starring Sophia Loren and Marcello Mastroianni.

| 1960 | 250 GT Berlinetta Lusso | (P.F./Scaglietti) | 1995GT | R | NA | 7.392.000 | 11.369.635 | 9.964.416 | 14-10-15 | Duxford | 146 | H&H F254 |

Red with red interior; sold new to the UK, the car was fitted with a semi-competition engine giving 252bhp. Following some ownership changes, in 1976 it was acquired by the late Richard Colton who retained it for nearly 40 years up to the time of his passing in March 2015. Never restored, it received regular maintainance works in the years. The body was slightly modified to Competizione specification with the removal of the front and rear bumpers, the provision of front brake cooling ducts and the 16"x5.5" Borrani wheels were replaced with 15"x6.5" items.

| 1963 | 250 GT Berlinetta Lusso | (PF/Scaglietti) | 4065GT | L | 9-12.000.000 EUR | NS | | | 05-02-16 | Paris | 138 | Art |

Dark blue with black leather interior; the car was sold new to the USA where in the 1970s it was repainted red. In 1982 it was acquired by the current owner who imported it into France and in 2000 registered it in Switzerland. In 2001 the car was restored to its original colours. Described as in very good overall condition.

| 1961 | 250 GT Berlinetta Lusso | (PF/Scaglietti) | 2917GT | L | Refer Dpt. | NS | | | 09-07-16 | Le Mans | 118 | Art |

Originally finished in light blue with natural leather interior, the car was exhibited at the 1961 Paris Motor Show. In 1967 and 1968 it was raced by its fourth owner at some hillclimbs in France. In late 1969 it was purchased by the present, sixth owner. Currently finished in red with black leather interior; engine rebuilt in 1985 by Sport Auto in Modena.

| 1962 | 250 GT Berlinetta Lusso | (PF/Scaglietti) | 3359GT | L | 10-12.000.000 USD | NS | | | 21-08-16 | Pebble Beach | 121 | G&Co |

Silver with red leather interior; sold new in Italy, the car has had in the years several owners in the UK, USA, France and Switzerland. Raced at some events in the UK in 1973 and 1974; driven at five editions of the historic Tour de France between 1999 and 2005; fully restored in Italy between 2010 and 2011; exhibited at the 2012 Villa d'Este Concours d'Elegance; reimported into the USA in 2015. Certified by Ferrari Classiche.

| 1960 | 250 GT Berlinetta Competizione | (P.F./Scaglietti) | 1759GT | L | 15-18.000.000 USD | 10.314.000 | 13.500.000 | 11.919.150 | 20-08-16 | Pebble Beach | 56 | G&Co TOP TEN |

Red with white stripes on the front and rear right fenders and black interior; purchased new by Harvey Schur of Scarsdale, New York, the car did its race debut at the 1960 Le Mans 24 Hours where driven by Pabst/Hugus it placed 7th overall and 4th in class. Imported into the USA, it was raced at one hillclimb event in 1962. In the 1970s and 1980s it was raced at historic events. Restored between 2002 and 2005. Original rebuilt engine. Certified by Ferrari Classiche (see lot 85 Gooding & Company 17.1.09 NS).

| 1962 | 400 Superamerica coupé | (Pininfarina) | 3931SA | L | 3.000-3.300.000 EUR | 2.222.235 | 3.225.235 | 2.950.000 | 03-02-16 | Paris | 152 | RMS |

Second series on the long-wheelbase chassis, the car was finished in grey with black leather interior and displayed at the 1962 London Motor Show. Subsequently it was delived to the USA to Luigi Chinetti who exhibited it at the Chicago Motor Show. It was restored in the early 1980s and soon after sold to Japan were it was part of the collection of Yoshijuki Hayashi and later of Yoshiho Matsuda. In the early 2000s it was reimported into the USA before returning to Europe (see lot 162 RM 16.8.02 $ 363,000).

F253: 1959 Ferrari 250 GT Coupé (Pinin Farina)

F254: 1960 Ferrari 250 GT Berlinetta Lusso (P.F./Scaglietti)

  OFFICIAL FERRARI & FERRARI CLASSICHE DEALER
Niki Hasler AG

Niki Hasler AG
Hardstrasse 15 - 4052 Basel
Switzerland
Tel: 0041 61 375 92 92
Fax: 0041 61 375 92 99
niki.hasler@nikihasler.ch
www.ferrari-basel.ch

Year	Model (Bodybuilder)	Chassis no.	Steering	Estimate	Hammer price £	$	€	Date	Place	Lot	Auc. H.

F255: 1962 Ferrari 400 Superamerica coupé (Pininfarina)

F256: 1962 Ferrari 250 GTE 2+2 (Pininfarina)

Year	Model (Bodybuilder)	Chassis no.	Steering	Estimate	£	$	€	Date	Place	Lot	Auc. H.
1962	400 Superamerica coupé (Pininfarina)	3949SA	L	2.700-3.300.000 USD	3.078.240	4.400.000	3.967.480	12-03-16	Amelia Island	163	RMS

Covered-headlamp aerodynamic coupé built on the long-wheelbase chassis, the car was exhibited at the 1962 Turin Motor Show. Originally finished in red with black interior it was sold new to the USA to Erwin Goldschmidt in whose family it remained until 2003. In 2012 it was acquired by the current owner who had it fully restored and finished in the present metallic blue livery with tan leather interior. The original engine and gearbox were rebuilt (see lots 168 Barrett-Jackson 22.6.03 $ 432,000 and 34 Gooding 18.8.12 $ 2,365,000). **F255**

| 1962 | 250 GTE 2+2 (Pininfarina) | 3823GT | L | 300-350.000 GBP | 331.875 | 505.346 | 453.706 | 04-09-15 | Woodstock | 226 | SiC |

Light blue with beige leather interior; exhibited at the 1962 Paris Motor Show, the car was sold new to France. Engine rebuilt in the 2000s. Acquired in 2013 by the current owner. Paintwork and interior redone subsequently (see lot 47 Artcurial 20.10.13 $ 286,513). **F256**

| 1963 | 250 GTE/250 GT swb recreation | 3493GT | L | 500-600.000 GBP | 606.300 | 935.096 | 829.903 | 12-09-15 | Goodwood | 316 | Bon |

Cream with amaranth stripes and amaranth interior; conversion carried out in the Netherlands and completed in 2012. From the Chris Evans collection.

| 1961 | 250 GTE 2+2 (Pininfarina) | 2369GT | L | 450-550.000 USD | 309.420 | 405.000 | 357.575 | 21-08-16 | Pebble Beach | 155 | G&Co |

Originally finished in silver with red interior, the car was sold new in Italy. In the 1970s it was imported into the USA and in the 1990s it was restored and finished in the present red livery with tan interior.

| 1963 | 330 America (Pininfarina) | 5069 | L | 290-350.000 EUR | 339.644 | 489.383 | 431.250 | 13-05-16 | Monaco | 127 | Bon |

Red with black interior; sold new to the USA, the car was reimported into Europe in 1995. First restored in Canada in 1989, the car was restored again in the late 1990s.

| 1964 | 250 GT/L (PF/Scaglietti) | 5885 | L | 1.100-1.400.000 GBP | **1.232.000** | 1.880.278 | 1.686.978 | 07-09-15 | London | 162 | RMS |

Silver grey with black leather interior; sold new to Switzerland, the car has had several European owners over the years. Body restored in 1988; engine rebuilt in 2009.

| 1963 | 250 GT/L (PF/Scaglietti) | 4851 | L | 1.400-1.800.000 GBP | NS | | | 12-09-15 | Goodwood | 314 | Bon |

Metallic grey with black leather interior; sold new to the USA where the car was restored in 2006. In 2011 it was imported into the UK. Certified by Ferrari Classiche. From the Chris Evans collection.

| 1964 | 250 GT/L (PF/Scaglietti) | 5537 | L | 2.200-2.500.000 USD | NS | | | 30-01-16 | Scottsdale | 127 | G&Co |

Dark blue with tan interior; the history of the car is known since 1980 circa whne it was in the ownership of Carl Walston, California, who retained it for over 20 years. Restored in recent years. From the Toni Shooshani Collection (see lot 131 RM 16.8.13 $ 1,386,000).

| 1963 | 250 GT/L (PF/Scaglietti) | 4365 | L | 1.900-2.400.000 USD | **1.311.750** | 1.875.000 | 1.690.688 | 11-03-16 | Amelia Island | 71 | G&Co |

Originally finished in smoke grey, the car was sold new in Italy. In 1966 it was acquired by the current, second owner who commissioned Scaglietti to retrim the interior in tan leather and subsequently imported the car into the USA. Currently finished in dark blue, the car was restored and the engine rebuilt between 1991 and 1993. **F257**

| 1964 | 250 GT/L (PF/Scaglietti) | 5851 | L | 1.600-1.900.000 EUR | NS | | | 13-05-16 | Monaco | 124 | Bon |

Dark metallic blue with burgundy leather interior; restored in the early 1990s. Body repainted in the late 1990s. Certified by Ferrari Classiche.

| 1964 | 250 GT/L (PF/Scaglietti) | 5681 | L | 1.550-1.800.000 EUR | NS | | | 14-05-16 | Monaco | 248 | RMS |

Brown with beige leather interior; sold new to France, the car was reimported into Italy in the early 1980s and subsequently refinished in the present livery. Since 1999 in the current ownership, it is described as in good overall condition (see lot 35 Artcurial 28.6.08 NS).

| 1963 | 250 GT/L (PF/Scaglietti) | 4415 | L | 2.000-2.500.000 USD | **1.596.760** | 2.090.000 | 1.845.261 | 20-08-16 | Monterey | 224 | RMS |

Sold new to the USA, from 1964 to 2001 the car remained with the same owner who in 1990 had it restored and repainted in red. In 2003 the car was restored again and refinished in black. In 2011 it was bought by the current owner who had it restored again and finished in the present iron grey livery with burgundy interior. Certified by Ferrari Classiche (see lot 106 Gooding & Company 17.8.08 $627,000).

| 1962 | 268 SP (Fantuzzi) | 0798 | R | Refer Dpt. | NS | | | 20-08-16 | Monterey | 240 | RMS |

One of two cars fitted with the 2.6-litre 8-cylinder engine; factory entry at the 1962 Le Mans 24 Hours for Giancarlo Baghetti and Ludovico Scarfiotti: in late 1962 sold to the USA to Scuderia NART; bought in 1964 by John O'Brien and raced at the 1964 SCCA Class D Modified Championship; raced in the USA until 1966; bought in 1969 by Pierre Bardinon and restored in the early 1970s by Fantuzzi in Modena; acquired from Bardinon by the current owner in 1996; used at numerous historic events; certified by Ferrari Classiche. **F258**

F257: 1963 Ferrari 250 GT/L (PF/Scaglietti)

F258: 1962 Ferrari 268 SP (Fantuzzi)

MODENA
WWW.CREMONINICLASSIC.IT

1986 ★ 2016
30
of Knowledge and Passion for Restoration

1960 Ferrari 250 GT SWB Scaglietti Berlinetta Competizione

Year	Model	(Bodybuilder)	Chassis no.	Steering	Estimate	Hammer Price £	Hammer Price $	Hammer Price €	Sale Date	Sale Place	Lot	Auc. H.

F259: 1964 Ferrari 330 GT 2+2 (Pininfarina)

F260: 1967 Ferrari 330 GT 2+2 (Pininfarina)

Year	Model (Bodybuilder)	Chassis no.	Steering	Estimate	£	$	€	Date	Place	Lot	Auc. H.
1964	330 GT 2+2 (Pininfarina)	6129	R	190-220.000 GBP	196.875	299.782	269.148	04-09-15	Woodstock	213	SiC

Metallic blue with light grey leather interior; several restoration works carried out in the 2000s, gearbox overhauled in 2007, brakes rebuilt in 2009. First series (see lots 335 Brooks 8.5. 96 NS and 73 Christie's 7.6.04 $ 47,512). **F259**

1964	330 GT 2+2 (Pininfarina)	5669	L	185-225.000 GBP		NS		04-09-15	Woodstock	237	SiC

Red with beige leather interior; restored between 1992 and 1993. First series.

1966	330 GT 2+2 (Pininfarina)	8319	L	175-225.000 GBP	156.800*	239.308*	214.706*	07-09-15	London	119	RMS

Dark blue with red leather interior believed to be original; sold new to Spain, the car was reimported into Italy in the mid-1980s. Restored at unspecified date. Second series with single headlamp.

1964	330 GT 2+2 (Pininfarina)	5421	L	140-160.000 GBP	140.000	213.668	191.702	07-09-15	London	149	RMS

Originally finished in dark grey with black interior, the car was sold new to Germany. Body repainted in the present red livery at unspecified date. First series with twin headlamp.

1967	330 GT 2+2 (Pininfarina)	9033	L	350-380.000 EUR		NS		26-09-15	Frankfurt	158	Coy

Red with beige interior; restored in Germany in 2014. Second series with single headlamp (see lots Bonhams 202 17.12.05 $ 49,690 and 249 20.5.06 $ 57,260, Coys 223 18.5.09 $ 97,427 and Bonhams 163 20.5.11 NS).

1965	330 GT 2+2 (Pininfarina)	7515	L	350-450.000 USD		NS		28-01-16	Phoenix	167	RMS

Red with red interior; 28,119 miles on the odometer. Body repainted in the 1980s; several mechanical works carried out in 2015. First series with twin headlamp.

1966	330 GT 2+2 (Pininfarina)	8325	L	375-425.000 USD	203.963	291.500	266.927	30-01-16	Scottsdale	135	G&Co

Dark blue with grey interior; restored many years ago. Second series with single headlamp.

1965	330 GT 2+2	6537	L	NA	157.782	225.500	206.490	30-01-16	Scottsdale	5073	R&S

The car was bought new by John W. Mecom Jr who sent back it to Italy for a new front-end design with covered single headlamps and an angular frontal treatment with large split radiator-grille openings. After some ownership changes and a long-term storage, the car was restored in recent years and finished in blue.

1965	330 GT 2+2 (Pininfarina)	7113	L	310-340.000 EUR		NS		05-02-16	Paris	201	Art

Silver with red leather interior; restored at unspecified date. First series with twin headlamp (see lot 350 Bonhams 26.6.15 $ 287,000).

1964	330 GT 2+2 (Pininfarina)	5409	L	350-400.000 EUR		NS		05-02-16	Paris	223	Art

Light metallic brown with biscuit leather interior; sold new to the USA, in the mid-1970s the car was repainted in metallic grey and fitted with a sunroof. In 2009 it was reimported into Europe and restored subsequently to its original colour. First series with twin headlamp.

1964	330 GT 2+2 (Pininfarina)	5421	L	210-240.000 EUR	167.605	239.544	216.000	12-03-16	Lyon	324	Agu

See lot 253 RM-Sotheby's 7.9.15.

1964	330 GT 2+2 (Pininfarina)	5721	L	220-250.000 EUR		NS		12-03-16	Lyon	334	Agu

Grey with black interior; in fair overall condition. Recently serviced (see lot 744 Barrett-Jacksin 18.1.02 $ 38,880).

1967	330 GT 2+2 (Pininfarina)	7399	L	280-300.000 EUR	246.311	346.691	305.105	09-04-16	Essen	129	Coy

Silver with black leather interior; body recently repainted. Last serviced in 2015. Second series with single headlamp.

1967	330 GT 2+2 (Pininfarina)	9033	L	250-300.000 EUR		NS		14-05-16	Monaco	199	Coy

See lot 158 Coys 26.9.15.

1964	330 GT 2+2 (Pininfarina)	5779	L	280-350.000 EUR	283.572	405.144	360.000	19-06-16	Fontainebleau	336	Ose

Blue with black leather interior; described as in good overall condition. Engine rebuilt 10,000 kms ago; recently serviced. First series with twin headlamp (see lots Osenat 252 12.12.10 NS and 324 20.3.11 $59,346, and Chevau-Légerè 26 25.9.11 NS).

1967	330 GT 2+2 (Pininfarina)	7901	L	NA	240.768	330.000	298.188	24-06-16	Uncasville	665.1	B/J

Black with red interior; fully restored. Second series with single headlamp.

1965	330 GT 2+2 (Pininfarina)	7399	L	180-205.000 GBP		NS		24-06-16	Goodwood	260	Bon

See lot 129 Coys 9.4.16.

1966	330 GT 2+2 (Pininfarina)	8485	L	325-375.000 USD		NS		30-07-16	Plymouth	150	RMS

Blue with cream interior; sold new in Italy, the car was imported into the USA in the early 1970s. 30,000 miles covered since the restoration. Second series with single headlamp (see RM lots 27 16.8.02 WD, 133 15.8.03 $51,500, and 233 13.8.04 $60,500).

1965	330 GT 2+2 (Pininfarina)	5933	L	220-240.000 EUR	198.971	261.729	234.608	06-08-16	Schloss Dyck	127	Coy

Light metallic gold with black leather interior; described as in very good overall condition. Engine rebuilt at unspecified date. First series with twin headlamp.

1965	330 GT 2+2 (Pininfarina)	7857	L	275-325.000 USD	189.090	247.500	218.518	20-08-16	Pebble Beach	77	G&Co

Red with black interior; restored in the 1990s. Second series with single headlamp.

1966	330 GT 2+2 (Pininfarina)	7883	L	450-550.000 USD		NS		20-08-16	Monterey	S150.1	Mec

Silver with blue interior; restoration completed in 2016. Second series with single headlamp.

1967	330 GT 2+2 (Pininfarina)	8787	L	350-450.000 USD	563.068	737.000	650.697	20-08-16	Monterey	217	RMS

Silver with black leather interior; recent concours-quality restoration. In single ownership from 1970 to 2013. Second series with single headlamp (see lot 142 Gooding & Company 18.8.13 $176,000). **F260**

discrete private treaty sales

Paul Russell and Company
Passionately Dedicated to the Preservation of Fine Automobiles since 1978

Alex Finigan (+1) 978.768.6092
Alex@PaulRussell.com

PaulRussell.com   Essex, MA USA

Brian Morrison (+1) 978.768.6143
Brian@PaulRussell.com

Year	Model	(Bodybuilder)	Chassis no.	Steering	Estimate	Hammer price £	$	€	Date	Place	Lot	Auc. H.

F261: 1964 Ferrari 500 Superfast (Pininfarina)

F262: 1965 Ferrari 275 GTB (PF/Scaglietti)

1964 500 Superfast (Pininfarina) — 5985SA — L — 2.800-3.400.000 USD — **2.101.000** — 2.750.000 — 2.427.975 — 20-08-16 — Monterey — 243 — **RMS** — F261
Dark blue with orange leather interior; exhibited by Chinetti Motors at the 1964 Chicago Motor Show and then sold to Hans Dieter Holterbosch. After some ownership changes, the car was purchased in 1966 by John L. Brady, who retained it for 47 years. Engine rebuilt in the 1990s; body repainted in recent years. 14,075 miles covered since new.

1966 275 GTB (PF/Scaglietti) — 08221 — R — 2.600-2.900.000 GBP — NS — 12-09-15 — Goodwood — 318 — **Bon**
"Long nose" version with alloy body and 6-carburettors engine; finished in red with black interior, the car was sold new to the UK. Restored in the mid-1980s. Body recently repainted in pale green. Certified by Ferrari Classiche. From the Chris Evans collection (see lot 75 Christie's 7.6.04 $ 383,678).

1965 275 GTB (PF/Scaglietti) — 07053 — L — 2.400-2.800.000 USD — **1.480.344** — 2.117.500 — 1.941.959 — 28-01-16 — Phoenix — 145 — **RMS** — F262
Originally finished in dark blue with black interior, the car was sold new to the USA. After some ownership changes, it remained with the same owner from 1977 to 2012 and subsequently it was restored and finished in the present light blue livery. Certified by Ferrari Classiche.

1966 275 GTB (PF/Scaglietti) — 08869 — L — 2.600-3.000.000 USD — NS — 29-01-16 — Scottsdale — 49 — **G&Co**
"Long nose" version finished in red with black interior; sold new in Italy, the car was imported into the USA in 1977 and driven at track events in the 1980s and 1990s. Restored between the late 1990s - 2001, it is described as in very good overall condition.

1966 275 GTB (PF/Scaglietti) — 08973 — L — 2.500-3.500.000 EUR — **1.564.817*** — 2.319.642* — 2.070.000* — 04-02-16 — Paris — 335 — **Bon** — F263
"Long nose" version originally finished in silver with black leather interior, the car was sold new in Italy. In the 1970s it was imported into Canada and later into the USA where it was restored between 1989 and 1991 and finished in the present dark blue with tan interior. In 2009 it was acquired by the current Swiss owner who in 2014 had the engine and gearbox overhauled. Certification by Ferrari Classiche in progress.

1966 275 GTB (PF/Scaglietti) — 08647 — R — 1.600-1.900.000 GBP — NS — 24-06-16 — Goodwood — 228 — **Bon**
"Long nose" body finished in red with black interior; six-carburettor engine. Restored in 1991. Acquired in 2004 by the current owner, the car has covered circa 1,300 miles since the engine rebuild carried out in 2009.

1965 275 GTB (PF/Scaglietti) — 07093 — L — 2.000-2.400.000 USD — **1.323.630** — 1.732.500 — 1.529.624 — 19-08-16 — Monterey — 112 — **RMS**
Silver grey with red leather interior; sold new in Italy, the car was imported into the USA in 1970. Fully restored in 2005. Certified by Ferrari Classiche. From the Jack Boxstrom Collection.

1966 275 GTB (PF/Scaglietti) — 08603 — L — 2.600-2.800.000 USD — NS — 20-08-16 — Monterey — S123 — **Mec**
"Long nose" version finished in red with black leather interior; sold new to the USA. Engine rebuilt in the late 1970s; body repainted in 1994 to its original colour; described as in very good overall condition (see lot 115 RM 15.1.15 $ 2,750,000).

1965 275 GTS (PF/Scaglietti) — 07935 — L — 1.600-2.000.000 USD — **1.231.472** — 1.760.000 — 1.611.632 — 29-01-16 — Phoenix — 232 — **RMS**
Silver with red interior; sold new to Austria, the car was later reimported into Italy and exported to the USA in the early 1990s. Restored many years ago, it was acquired some 10 years ago by the current owner and it received recently some mechanical works and new upholstery.

1965 275 GTS (PF/Scaglietti) — 07521 — L — 1.500-2.000.000 EUR — NS — 13-05-16 — Monaco — 120 — **Bon**
Red with beige leather interior; sold new to the USA, in 1988 the car was reimported into Europe. Acquired in 2008 by the current owner, it was restored between 2013 and 2015. Certified by Ferrari Classiche.

1966 275 GTS (PF/Scaglietti) — 07805 — L — 1.650-1.850.000 EUR — **1.411.343** — 2.033.562 — 1.792.000 — 14-05-16 — Monaco — 243 — **RMS** — F264
White with blue interior; described as in very good original condition. Three owners and less than 24,000 original miles. Certified by Ferrari Classiche (see lot 227 RM 16.8.14 $ 1,760,000).

1965 275 GTS (PF/Scaglietti) — 07331 — L — 1.500-1.750.000 USD — NS — 19-08-16 — Monterey — 144 — **RMS**
Finished in dark green with orange interior, the car was sold new to the USA. Between 1995 and 2000 it was restored and refinished in the present red livery with tan interior. In 2013 it was purchased by the current owner who subsequently had the engine rebuilt (see lot 237 RM 17.8.13 $ 990,000).

F263: 1966 Ferrari 275 GTB (PF/Scaglietti)

F264: 1966 Ferrari 275 GTS (PF/Scaglietti)

Classic cars for sale and professional restoration

FERRARI 365 GTB/4 DAYTONA – 1971
Classiche Ferrari

FERRARI 308 GTS – 1979
Classiche Ferrari

PORSCHE 914-6 – 1970
Full restoration

FERRARI 550 BARCHETTA – 2001
Classiche Ferrari

SHOWROOM

Exposure and sales: CHAMBÉRY - FRANCE +33 (0)4 79 88 66 36
Workshop and restoration: ANNEMASSE - FRANCE +33 (0)4 50 84 21 80

Info@jeanlainvintage.com - www.jeanlainvintage.com - Join us on

Year	Model	(Bodybuilder)	Chassis no.	Steering	Estimate	Hammer price £	$	€	Date	Place	Lot	Auc. H.

F265: 1967 Ferrari 275 GTB4 (PF/Scaglietti)

F266: 1968 Ferrari 275 GTS4 NART Spider (PF/Scaglietti)

Year	Model (Bodybuilder)	Chassis	Steer	Estimate	£	$	€	Date	Place	Lot	Auc.
1967	**275 GTB4** (PF/Scaglietti)	10177	R	NA	2.161.600	3.324.757	2.913.837	14-10-15	Duxford	145	**H&H**

Silver with blue interior; sold new in the UK, the car was acquired in 1974 by the late Richard Colton who retained it for over 40 years, up to the time of his passing in March 2015. Over the years the car received several works, the engine was rebuilt in 1974, the body was repainted in 1979. The windscreen is a replacement unit as the window door glasses. The original Borrani wire wheels were replaced with alloy wheels. Never restored and described as "well used", it requires servicing prior to use. **F265**

| 1967 | **275 GTB4** (PF/Scaglietti) | 10717 | L | 2.800-3.500.000 USD | | NS | | 23-01-16 | Kissimmee | S119 | **Mec** |

Grey with original saddle leather interior; described as in original condition except for the paintwork redone in the early 1970s. In single ownership from 1970 to October 2015. It is believed to have covered less than 15,000 kms since new.

| 1967 | **275 GTB4** (PF/Scaglietti) | 10325 | L | 2.700-3.200.000 USD | 1.943.425 | 2.750.000 | 2.532.750 | 10-03-16 | Amelia Island | 123 | **Bon** |

Silver with black interior; the car was sold new to Barnett Joseph Sumski who first registered it on Italian EE plate and imported it into the USA in 1968. Since 1971 circa in the Wade Carter Collection, its third owner. Described as in good overall condition.

| 1967 | **275 GTB4** (PF/Scaglietti) | 10413 | L | 2.900-3.200.000 USD | | NS | | 05-06-16 | Greenwhich | 101 | **Bon** |

Dark green with black leather interior; sold new in Italy, the car was imported into the USA in the early 1970s and was acquired by the current, third owner in the mid-1970s. Several restoration works carried out between the mid-1980s-mid 1990s. Interior retrimmed in 2002. Last serviced in March 2016.

| 1967 | **275 GTB4** (PF/Scaglietti) | 10497 | L | 3.200-3.600.000 USD | 2.479.180 | 3.245.000 | 2.865.011 | 20-08-16 | Pebble Beach | 40 | **G&Co** |

Nocciola (copper metallic gold) with original black leather interior; sold new to the USA, the car remained in single ownership from 1975 to 2003. In 2008 it was bought by the current owner who had later the body repainted in the original colour. Last serviced in late 2015; 28,000 believed original miles (see lot 56 Gooding & Company 16.8.08 $1,430,000).

| 1967 | **275 GTB4** (PF/Scaglietti) | 10717 | L | 3.250-3.750.000 USD | | NS | | 20-08-16 | Monterey | S115 | **Mec** |

See lot S119 Mecum 23.1.16.

| 1968 | **275 GTS4 NART Spider** (PF/Scaglietti) | 11057 | L | 19-23.000.000 EUR | | NS | | 14-05-16 | Monaco | 254 | **RMS** |

Originally finished in dark grey with black interior, the car was sold new to Spain. In 1982 it was imported in the UK and refinished in red. From 1983 to 1995 it was owned by Albert Obrist who had it restored in Italy and repainted in dark metallic grey. Subsequently the car was owned by Chris Cox, Carlos Monteverde, Bernard Carl (who had it repainted in the current dark metallic red livery) and Lord Irvine Laidlaw (who had it retrimmed in its current beige). Certified by Ferrari Classiche. **F266**

| 1967 | **330 GTC** (Pininfarina) | 10927 | L | NA | 402.833 | 638.000 | 560.930 | 31-10-15 | Hilton Head | 161 | **AA** |

Red with dark beige interior; sold new in Italy and later imported into the USA. Body repainted at unspecified date.

| 1967 | **330 GTC** (Pininfarina) | 11089 | L | 450-550.000 GBP | 449.500 | 680.498 | 624.176 | 06-12-15 | London | 025 | **Bon** |

Silver with original black leather interior; sold new in Italy, the car was imported into Switzerland in the early 1970s. It remained in the same ownership from 1977 to 2006 when it was sold to Germany. Restored in 2011; currently registered in the UK (see lot 18 Automobilia Ladenburg 22.5.10 NS). **F267**

| 1967 | **330 GTC** (Pininfarina) | 9955 | L | 650-750.000 USD | | NS | | 23-01-16 | Kissimmee | T206 | **Mec** |

Red with tan interior; restored in the late 1990s. 45,798 miles covered since new. Interior retrimmed in 2013. The engine has covered 500 miles since the rebuild.

| 1966 | **330 GTC** (Pininfarina) | 09895 | L | 750-850.000 USD | | NS | | 30-01-16 | Scottsdale | 114 | **G&Co** |

Silver with black leather interior; in good overall condition. Body repainted many years ago; engine rebuilt in 2011.

| 1967 | **330 GTC Speciale** (Pininfarina) | 10107 | L | 3.400-4.000.000 USD | 2.385.977 | 3.410.000 | 3.122.537 | 30-01-16 | Scottsdale | 145 | **G&Co** |

Originally finished in silver with black leather interior and Campagnolo alloy wheels, the car was sold new in Italy to Maria Maddalena Da Lisca, wife of Pietro Barilla. In the early 1970s it was imported into the USA where it was repainted in dark blue and fitted with Borrani wire wheels. Between 1987 and 1988 it received some restoration works and the body was repainted in the present black livery. One of four examples built; since 1994 in the current ownership; less than 57,500 kms on the odometer. **F268**

| 1968 | **330 GTC** (Pininfarina) | 11589 | L | 400-500.000 EUR | 412.894* | 600.875* | 536.400* | 05-02-16 | Paris | 137 | **Art** |

Red with black leather interior; since 1993 in the current ownership. Engine rebuilt between 2012 and 2014. Certified by Ferrari Classiche.

F267: 1967 Ferrari 330 GTC (Pininfarina)

F268: 1967 Ferrari 330 GTC Speciale (Pininfarina)

CARROZZERIA
AutoSport
BACCHELLI & VILLA

- Restorations
- Bodywork painting
- Repairs
- Prototypes

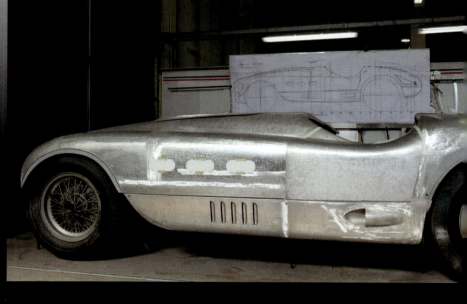

RESTORATION... BETWEEN history AND PASSION

Carrozzeria Autosport srl
Via 1° Maggio, 3 - 41030 Bastiglia (MO)
Tel. +39 059.90.40.72 - Fax +39 059.90.47.54
info@autosport.it - www.autosport.it

Year	Model	(Bodybuilder)	Chassis No.	Steering	Estimate	Hammer price £	$	€	Date	Place	Lot	Auc. H.
1968	330 GTC	(Pininfarina)	11427	L	NA		NS		09-04-16	Palm Beach	408	B/J
	*Red with black interior; sold new in Italy, in 1972 the car was imported into the USA and later resold to Switzerland. Reimported into the USA, it received recently a full service (see lots 164 RM 8.9.14 $ 631,120, and 251 RM-Sotheby's 14.8.15 $ 715,000).*
1968	330 GTC	(Pininfarina)	11137	L	600-700.000 EUR	580.558	817.153	719.135	09-04-16	Essen	180	Coy
	*Ruby red; acquired 10 years ago by the current owner and subsequently partially restored, cosmetically and mechanically as necessary (see lots Coys 60 26.7.97 $ 77,407, Bonhams 128 5.9.03 NS, and Coys 240 15.1.05 NS and 318 14.5.05 NS).*
1968	330 GTC	(Pininfarina)	11265	L	550-650.000 EUR	513.975	740.570	652.600	14-05-16	Monaco	188A	Coy
	*Silver with black interior; until 2014 in the Maranello Collection (see lot 201 Bonhams 13.09.14 NS).*
1968	330 GTC	(Pininfarina)	10903	L	550-650.000 EUR	379.299	546.520	481.600	14-05-16	Monaco	227	RMS
	*Yellow with black interior; purchased in 1993 by the current owner and restored at that time. Certified by Ferrari Classiche. Swiss papers.*
1969	330 GTC	(Pininfarina)	11313	L	625-725.000 USD		NS		25-06-16	Santa Monica	2069	AA
	*Silver with black leather interior; well cared for (see lot 113 Sotheby's 9.9.97 $60,700).*
1968	330 GTC	(Pininfarina)	11543	L	625-675.000 USD	420.200	550.000	485.595	20-08-16	Pebble Beach	61	G&Co
	*Blue with original black leather interior; sold new in Italy, the car was later imported into the USA. In 1975 it was purchased by William J. Carpenter, who used it until the late 1990s and retained it until 2015 when it was bought by the current owner. In as-found condition; 54,000 kms on the odometer.*
1968	330 GTS	(Pininfarina)	10817	L	2.300-2.600.000 USD	1.399.200	2.000.000	1.803.400	12-03-16	Amelia Island	139	RMS F269
	*Originally finished in silver with red leather interior, the car was sold new to the USA. At unspecified date it was restored and finished in the present yellow livery with tan interior (see lot 109 Gooding 17.1.15 $ 2,420,000).*
1967	330 GTS	(Pininfarina)	9781	L	2.100-2.400.000 EUR		NS		14-05-16	Monaco	256	RMS
	*Hazelnut with black interior; the car was sold new to the USA where probably in the 1980s it was refinished in yellow. First restored in the late 1990s, it has been recently restored again to its original hazelnut livery (see lots 5353 Russo & Steele 23.1.04 $ 260,000 and 230 RM-Sotheby's 14.8.15 sold for an undisclosed sum).*
1967	330 GTS	(Pininfarina)	10375	L	1.700-1.900.000 EUR		NS		09-07-16	Le Mans	166	Art
	*Red with black interior; sold new to the USA, the car was restored in 1994 and 2006 again. Certified by Ferrari Classiche (see lots 134 RM 20.1.06 $357,500 and 2113 Auctions America 18.7.15 $1,622,500).*
1968	330 GTS	(Pininfarina)	10913	L	2.700-3.000.000 USD	1.911.910	2.502.500	2.209.457	21-08-16	Pebble Beach	146	G&Co
	*Silver with dark red leather interior; the car was sold new to the USA to William Harrah who in 1969 had it converted to Targa form. In 1973 it was purchased by Robert Donner Jr. and after his death it passed to Mark Haddaway who had it restored in its original configuration and later resold it to the current owner. 27,000 miles on the odometer (see lot S101 Mecum 15.8.15 NS).*
1970	365 GT 2+2	(Pininfarina)	13535	R	145-165.000 GBP	185.625	282.651	253.768	04-09-15	Woodstock	235	SiC
	*Blu; acquired in 2009 by the current owner and subsequently restored (see lots 116 Christie's 24.3.03 NS, 215 Bonhams 30.7.05 $ 51,445 and 232 18.9.09 $ 63,524).*
1968	365 GT 2+2	(Pininfarina)	11583	R	160-180.000 GBP		NS		07-09-15	London	165	RMS
	*Originally finished in light blue with beige interior, the car was sold new to the UK. Following some ownership changes, in 2006 it was acquired by the present owner. Currently finished in red with black interior (see Sotheby's lots 284 22.5.93 NS and 318 7.12.98 NS).*
1970	365 GT 2+2	(Pininfarina)	13773	L	270-320.000 EUR		NS		09-10-15	Zoute	9	Bon
	*Gold with black leather interior; fully restored in Italy. Certified by Ferrari Classiche.*
1967	365 GT 2+2	(Pininfarina)	11471	L	NA		NS		23-01-16	Kissimmee	S85.1	Mec
	*Red with beige interior; redone paintwork and interior.*
1968	365 GT 2+2	(Pininfarina)	11781	L	275-325.000 USD		NS		28-01-16	Scottsdale	35	Bon
	*Dark metallic red with black leather interior; sold new to the USA. Recently serviced.*
1970	365 GT 2+2	(Pininfarina)	13109	L	350-425.000 USD	216.907	310.000	283.867	29-01-16	Scottsdale	9	G&Co
	*Silver meatllic with original black leather interior; less than 28,000 covered since new. Body repainted in the early 2000s. Recently serviced (see lot 12 Gooding 16.1.15 $ 375,000).*
1968	365 GT 2+2	(Pininfarina)	11853	L	300-375.000 USD		NS		29-01-16	Phoenix	244	RMS
	*Yellow with black interior; sold new in Italy, in the mid-1970s the car was imported into the USA. At unspecified date it was restored, including the engine rebuild (see lot 112 RM 18.1.13 $ 148,500).*
1970	365 GT 2+2	(Pininfarina)	13583	L	375-425.000 USD		NS		11-03-16	Amelia Island	50	G&Co
	*Green with black interior; imported into the USA in the 2000s when the engine was rebuilt. Body and interior restored between 2015 and 2016 (see lot 272 RM 19.1.07 $ 74,250).*
1970	365 GT 2+2	(Pininfarina)	13471	L	240-280.000 USD	165.266	236.500	206.867	02-04-16	Ft.Lauderdale	508	AA
	*Black with black interior; restored in the early 1990s. Transmission rebuilt in more recent years. Certified by Ferrari Classiche.*
1968	365 GT 2+2	(Pininfarina)	11783	L	230-270.000 USD	170.775	247.500	216.587	07-05-16	Auburn	833	AA F270
	*Red with tan leather interior; in good overall condition. Imported into the USA in 1979. In 2009 gearbox rebuilt and clutch replaced.*
1970	365 GT 2+2	(Pininfarina)	12793	L	235-250.000 USD		NS		25-06-16	Santa Monica	1106	AA
	*Red; body repainted many years ago. Recently serviced.*

F269: 1968 Ferrari 330 GTS (Pininfarina)

F270: 1968 Ferrari 365 GT 2+2 (Pininfarina)

CELEBRATING **30** YEARS

My customers and I have shared passion and enthusiasm for the world's most exciting and beautiful cars for 30 years. Our clients appreciate our expertise, discretion and dependability in buying and selling their classic automobiles. Please feel free to contact us and trust in our experience and global network.

Yours, Axel Schuette

AXEL SCHUETTE FINE CARS

best cars. best expertise. best service. since 1987

Aston Martin DB4GT Zagato, Le Mans 1961, sold by **AXEL SCHUETTE** FINE CARS

BENTLEY // BMW // FERRARI // LAMBORGHINI // MASERATI // MERCEDES-BENZ // PORSCHE

AXEL SCHUETTE FINE CARS • Germany • Fon +49 5202 72000 • www.axelschuette.de • info@axelschuette.de

Year	Model (Bodybuilder)	Chassis No.	Steering	Estimate	Hammer Price £	$	€	Sale Date	Place	Lot	Auc. H.
1969	365 GT 2+2 (Pininfarina)	11827	L	240-280.000 EUR		NS		09-07-16	Le Mans	141	Art
Dark blue with original tobacco leather interior; in good overall condition.											
1968	365 GT 2+2 (Pininfarina)	11781	L	225-275.000 USD	155.474	203.500	179.670	19-08-16	Carmel	56	Bon
See lot 35 Bonhams 28.1.16.											
1970	365 GT 2+2 (Pininfarina)	13109	L	NQ	264.726	346.500	305.925	20-08-16	Monterey	7016	R&S
See lot 9 Gooding & Company 29.1.16.											
1967	365 GT 2+2 (Pininfarina)	12167	L	NQ		NS		20-08-16	Monterey	7031	R&S
Red with black interior; 48,017 kms covered.											
1968	Dino 206 GT (PF/Scaglietti)	00186	L	325-375.000 GBP	347.200*	529.897*	475.421*	07-09-15	London	129	RMS
Red with black interior; sold new in Italy, the car remained in single ownership from 1982 to 2014. At some point the original engine, no.046, was removed from the car due to a dropped valve and replaced with a correct Fiat Dino 2 litre engine. The original unit is included in the sale.											
1969	Dino 206 GT (PF/Scaglietti)	00404	L	700-850.000 USD	509.047	770.000	703.626	10-12-15	New York	209	RMS
Red with black interior; for many years in a Japanese collection, the car was restored at unspecified date. Confirmed by the factory to be the very first car built on the longer L-series chassis used for the new Dino 246 GT. Certified by Ferrari Classiche.											
1969	Dino 206 GT (PF/Scaglietti)	00378	L	700-800.000 USD		NS		30-01-16	Scottsdale	125	G&Co
Red with original black interior; sold new in Italy, the car was exported to the USA in the early 1970s. From 1979 circa to 2013 it remained with the same owner who had the body repainted and the engine rebuilt. Since 2014 in the Tony Shooshani Collection (see lot 70 Gooding 7.3.14 $ 638,000).											
1968	Dino 206 GT (PF/Scaglietti)	00294	L	400-450.000 EUR	441.045	635.488	560.000	14-05-16	Monaco	252	RMS F271
Red; described as in largely original condition, except for the paintwork redone at unspecified date. In Italy since new, the car is in the same family ownership since 1981.											
1968	Dino 206 GT (PF/Scaglietti)	00222	L	700-900.000 USD	588.280	770.000	679.833	20-08-16	Pebble Beach	24	G&Co
Red with black interior; sold new in Italy, in 1976 the car was purchased by Richard LeBlond of Phoenix, Arizona, who in the late 1980s dismantled it for a restoration never started. In 2007 the dismantled car was bought by the current owner and subsequently received a six-year full restoration.											
1968	Dino 206 GT (PF/Scaglietti)	00298	L	700-825.000 USD	525.250	687.500	606.994	20-08-16	Monterey	245	RMS
Red with black interior; acquired in 1978 by the current owner and subsequently subjected to a long restoration. 250 miles covered since the completion.											
1972	Dino 246 GT (PF/Scaglietti)	05470	R	285-325.000 GBP		NS		04-09-15	Woodstock	233	SiC
Red with original beige leather interior; just one owner and 23,301 miles covered. Approximately 20 years ago the original metallic blue colour of the body was changed to the present red.											
1972	Dino 246 GT (PF/Scaglietti)	03292	R	250-300.000 GBP		NS		12-09-15	Goodwood	373	Bon
Red with black interior; sold new to the UK, the car was exported to the USA in the 1980s and reimported into the UK in 2011 circa. Mechanically refreshed in the USA; last serviced in July 2014 (see RM lots 234 26.10.11 $ 143,118 and 128 8.9.14 $ 324,576).											
1971	Dino 246 GT (PF/Scaglietti)	01706	L	325-385.000 EUR	228.155	346.262	310.521	26-09-15	Frankfurt	155	Coy
Yellow with black interior; since 1974 in the current ownership, the car was fully restored at unspecified date and is described as in excellent overall condition.											
1973	Dino 246 GT (PF/Scaglietti)	03552	R	525-575.000 AUD	229.343	353.273	318.719	24-10-15	Melbourne	37	TBr
Silver with original black interior; body recently repainted. Recently serviced (see lots Coys 85 30.7.94 NS and 40 20.10.94 $ 48,833, Brooks 798 12.6.98 $ 55,379, and Coys 111 20.4.05 NS and 214 27.2.07 NS).											
1972	Dino 246 GT/GTS (spider/conversion)	03128	L	NA		NS		31-10-15	Hilton Head	141	AA
Conversion carried out at unspecified date (see RM lots 292 8.3.08 $ 155,750 and 336 14.8.09 $ 159,500).											
1974	Dino 246 GT (PF/Scaglietti)	07204	R	230-264.000 GBP	235.200	354.329	334.266	01-12-15	London	315A	Coy
Red with tan interior; since 1979 in the same family ownership. Restored at unspecified date.											
1974	Dino 246 GT (PF/Scaglietti)	07204	R	230-265.000 GBP	227.000 P	325.336 P	298.074 P	16-01-16	Birmingham	316	Coy
See lot 315A Coys 1.12.15.											
1972	Dino 246 GT (PF/Scaglietti)	03152	L	325-375.000 USD		NS		28-01-16	Scottsdale	100	Bon
Metallic iron grey with black interior with red inserts; sold new to the USA. Restored in recent years.											
1972	Dino 246 GT (PF/Scaglietti)	03314	L	350-400.000 USD	235.597	337.000	309.063	28-01-16	Scottsdale	17	Bon
Originally finished in French blue, the car was sold new to the USA. At unspecified date the mechanicals were restored and the body repainted in the present red livery. Low mileage.											
1970	Dino 246 GT (PF/Scaglietti)	01040	L	375-425.000 USD	276.844	396.000	363.172	28-01-16	Phoenix	127	RMS F272
Yellow with black interior; the car was sold new in Italy where it was restored in recent years (see lot 167 RM 4.2.15 $ 397,405).											
1973	Dino 246 GT (PF/Scaglietti)	05690	L	450-525.000 USD		NS		29-01-16	Scottsdale	15	G&Co
Yellow with original black interior; sold new to Canada, the car has had three owners. Just over 38,700 miles on the odometer. Body repainted many years ago to its original colour.											
1973	Dino 246 GT (PF/Scaglietti)	03580	L	400-500.000 USD		NS		29-01-16	Phoenix	247	RMS
Metallic brown with sand interior; sold new to the USA. Recent concours-quality restoration.											

F271: 1968 Ferrari Dino 206 GT (PF/Scaglietti)

F272: 1970 Ferrari Dino 246 GT (PF/Scaglietti)

Year	Model	(Bodybuilder)	Chassis no.	Steering	Estimate	Hammer Price £	$	€	Date	Place	Lot	Auc. H.
1971	**Dino 246 GT**	(PF/Scaglietti)	01448	L	280-330.000 EUR	275.263	400.584	357.600	05-02-16	Paris	108	**Art**

Red with black interior; since 1984 in the same ownership. Interior redone in 2002, body restored in 2008, engine and gearbox overhauled in 2009.

| 1973 | **Dino 246 GT** | (PF/Scaglietti) | 06658 | L | 300-350.000 EUR | 275.263 | 400.584 | 357.600 | 05-02-16 | Paris | 219 | **Art** |

Silver with original black interior; restored. Since 1978 in the ownership of French driver Patrick Perrier.

| 1971 | **Dino 246 GT** | (PF/Scaglietti) | 02188 | L | 220-240.000 GBP | | NS | | 08-03-16 | London | 124 | **Coy** |

Red with black interior; sold new in Italy. Recently registered in the UK.

| 1975 | **Dino 246 GT** | (PF/Scaglietti) | 06620 | L | 290-310.000 EUR | | NS | | 12-03-16 | Lyon | 332 | **Agu** |

Red with original beige interior; body repainted.

| 1972 | **Dino 246 GT** | (PF/Scaglietti) | 03138 | R | NA | | NS | | 20-04-16 | Duxford | 89 | **H&H** |

Dark blue with blue interior; in good overall condition. Body repainted many years ago. For over 30 years in the current ownership.

| 1973 | **Dino 246 GT** | (PF/Scaglietti) | 06580 | L | 250-350.000 EUR | 226.429 | 326.255 | 287.500 | 13-05-16 | Monaco | 126 | **Bon** |

Red with black leather interior; acquired in 1991 by the current owner and subsequently restored (se elot 23 Bonhams 10.10.14 NS).

| 1972 | **Dino 246 GT** | (PF/Scaglietti) | 03712 | L | NQ | 212.784 | 310.000 | 276.303 | 20-05-16 | Indianapolis | F243 | **Mec** |

Yellow with tan interior; the engine has covered 250 miles since the rebuild (see lot 427 RM 16.08.08 $154,000).

| 1970 | **Dino 246 GT** | (PF/Scaglietti) | 01118 | L | 180-240.000 GBP | 191.900 | 262.980 | 237.630 | 24-06-16 | Goodwood | 223 | **Bon** |

Dark grey with tan interior; purchased in 1998 by the current owner and restored over the last three years.

| 1972 | **Dino 246 GT** | (PF/Scaglietti) | 03478 | R | 180-220.000 GBP | 281.500 | 385.768 | 348.581 | 24-06-16 | Goodwood | 268 | **Bon** |

White with black leather interior; recently restored. 36,825 miles covered (see Coys lots 327 3.3.08 $147,669 and 413 4.12.08 $87,780).

| 1973 | **Dino 246 GT** | (PF/Scaglietti) | 02940 | R | 250-300.000 GBP | 260.000 | 345.332 | 310.128 | 02-07-16 | Woodstock | 194 | **Coy** |

Red; acquired in 2004 by the current owner and restored in 2014-15 (see Coys lots 84 22.7.00 $61,878 and 71 30.4.02 NS).

| 1972 | **Dino 246 GT** | (PF/Scaglietti) | 04372 | L | 220-280.000 EUR | | NS | | 09-07-16 | Le Mans | 117 | **Art** |

Red with beige interior; since 1992 in the same family ownership. Several works carried out in 2014.

| 1973 | **Dino 246 GT** | (PF/Scaglietti) | 06686 | L | 400-500.000 USD | 243.716 | 319.000 | 281.645 | 20-08-16 | Pebble Beach | 71 | **G&Co** |

Originally finished in yellow with black vinyl interior; sold new to the USA; imported into the USA in 1975; in single ownership from 1976 to 2016 when it was bought by the current vendor; refinished in the present black livery at uspecified date; requiring mechanical attention before road use.

| 1972 | **Dino 246 GT** | (PF/Scaglietti) | 03542 | L | 375-425.000 USD | 327.756 | 429.000 | 378.764 | 21-08-16 | Pebble Beach | 134 | **G&Co** |

Red with black interior; described as in highly original condition, the car has covered less than 7,000 miles. Five owners.

| 1974 | **Dino 246 GTS** | (PF/Scaglietti) | 08252 | L | 400-500.000 USD | | NS | | 23-01-16 | Kissimmee | T200.1 | **Mec** |

Yellow with tan interior; 26,751 kms covered. Body repainted in 2001.

| 1974 | **Dino 246 GTS** | (PF/Scaglietti) | 08454 | L | 425-500.000 USD | 277.081 | 396.000 | 362.617 | 29-01-16 | Phoenix | 214 | **RMS** |

Medium metallic green with tan interior with black inserts; sold new to the USA. In 2014 the car received a cosmetic restoration and subsequently the engine was rebuilt. Approximately 8,700 miles on the odometer.   **F273**

| 1974 | **Dino 246 GTS** | (PF/Scaglietti) | 08236 | L | 275-350.000 USD | 157.782* | 225.500* | 206.490* | 30-01-16 | Scottsdale | 142 | **G&Co** |

White with red interior; sold new to the USA, the car is unused from the mid-1980s and requires full restoration.

| 1973 | **Dino 246 GTS** | (PF/Scaglietti) | 04870 | L | NA | 261.688 | 374.000 | 342.472 | 30-01-16 | Scottsdale | 5161 | **R&S** |

Red; recent cosmetic restoration (see lots Russo & Steele S648 16.8.13 $ 247,500, Bonhams 150 15.1.15 NS, and Russo & Steele 3404 6.6.15 $ 340,000 and S666 15.8.15 NS).

| 1974 | **Dino 246 GTS** | (PF/Scaglietti) | 06458 | L | 325-375.000 USD | 216.691 | 297.000 | 268.369 | 25-06-16 | Santa Monica | 2096 | **AA** |

Yellow with black interior; restored (see lot S644 Russo & Steele 15.8.08 NS).

| 1972 | **Dino 246 GTS** | (PF/Scaglietti) | 03792 | L | 375-425.000 USD | 252.120 | 330.000 | 291.357 | 20-08-16 | Monterey | S98 | **Mec** |

Red with black interior; in the same family ownership from 1972 to 2016, the car is described as in very good original condition with just 13,600 miles on the odometer.

| 1974 | **Dino 246 GTS** | (PF/Scaglietti) | 07906 | L | 350-425.000 USD | | NS | | 21-08-16 | Pebble Beach | 159 | **G&Co** |

Silver with original blue interior; sold new to the USA. Body repainted approximately 20 years ago; just over 30,000 miles on the odometer.

| 1969 | **365 GTC** | (Pininfarina) | 12367 | L | 550-700.000 GBP | | NS | | 07-09-15 | London | 128 | **RMS** |

Originally finished in blue with black leather interior, the car was sold new in Italy. Later it was exported to the USA where the body was repainted in the present red livery. Acquired 15 years ago by the current owner, it was subsequently imported into the UK where the engine was rebuilt.

| 1969 | **365 GTC** | (Pininfarina) | 12487 | L | 800-950.000 USD | | NS | | 25-06-16 | Santa Monica | 1099 | **AA** |

Red with black interior; engine and gearbox rebuilt in 2015.

| 1969 | **365 GTC** | (Pininfarina) | 12141 | L | 750-850.000 USD | 521.048 | 682.000 | 602.138 | 20-08-16 | Monterey | 244 | **RMS** |

Red with light brown leather interior; sold new in Italy, the car was imported in 1975 into the USA, where it was restored in the 2000s. In more recent years the car was sent to Italy where it received further works to the mechanicals and body.   **F274**

F273: 1974 Ferrari Dino 246 GTS (PF/Scaglietti)

F274: 1969 Ferrari 365 GTC (Pininfarina)

For more than 30 years JD CLASSICS has built up
A WORLD CLASS REPUTATION for restoring, racing
and retailing the most significant road and race cars.

Ferrari 250 GT Berlinetta SWB

jdclassics@jdclassics.com   www.jdclassics.com

WYCKE HILL BUSINESS PARK, WYCKE HILL, MALDON, ESSEX, CM9 6UZ, U.K.   +44 (0)1621 879579

MAYFAIR SHOWROOM, 26-28 MOUNT ROW, MAYFAIR, LONDON, W1K 3SQ, U.K.   +44 (0) 207 125 1400

Year	Model	(Bodybuilder)	Chassis No.	Steering	Estimate	Hammer Price £	Hammer Price $	Hammer Price €	Date	Place	Lot	Auc. H.
1972	365 GTB4 Daytona	(PF/Scaglietti)	16447	L	500-550.000 GBP		NS		04-09-15	Woodstock	232	SiC
{*Metallic grey with black leather interior; body repainted in 2011, gearbox rebuilt in 2014 (see Gooding lots 39 9.3.12 $ 330,000 and 130 17.1.15 $ 698,500).*}												
1971	365 GTB4 Daytona	(PF/Scaglietti)	14475	L	750-950.000 EUR	613.300	940.774	828.000	09-10-15	Zoute	35	Bon
{*Blue with beige leather interior; sold new to Canada, the car was later imported into Belgium. Engine and gearbox rebuilt in 2001; mechanicals and body restored in 2006; engine rebuilt again in 2010 (see lot 258 Bonhams 18.12.01 NS).*}												
1973	365 GTB4 Daytona	(PF/Scaglietti)	16951	L	800-1.000.000 USD	559.952	847.000	773.989	10-12-15	New York	201	RMS
{*Black with red leather interior with black inserts; sold new to the USA, the car was restored in 1986 and in 2004 again and is described as in concours condition. The original engine was replaced with the present, European specification unit, no.B1934. Certified by Ferrari Classiche.*}												
1973	365 GTB4 Daytona	(PF/Scaglietti)	16701	L	700-850.000 USD		NS		23-01-16	Kissimmee	S170	Mec
{*Light metallic blue with black interior; US specification example. Described as in original condition except for the paintwork redone at unspecified date. 17,360 believed-accurate miles; recently serviced.*}												
1973	365 GTB4 Daytona	(PF/Scaglietti)	16109	L	750-900.000 USD		NS		23-01-16	Kissimmee	T203	Mec
{*Yellow with black interior; restored in the 1990s. 48,760 miles covered since new. Since 1999 in the current ownership.*}												
1971	365 GTB4 Daytona	(PF/Scaglietti)	14219	L	1.000-1.200.000 USD	807.461	1.155.000	1.059.251	28-01-16	Scottsdale	62	Bon F275
{*Red with tan leather interior with black inserts; sold new to the USA, the car remained until 1998 with its first owner. Restored between 2006 and 2007. Just over 8,000 miles covered since new. Ferrari Classiche Certification in progress.*}												
1972	365 GTB4 Daytona	(PF/Scaglietti)	15437	L	750-875.000 USD	496.361	710.000	651.141	28-01-16	Phoenix	163	RMS
{*Originally finished in red with beige leather interior, the car was sold new to the USA. In 1995 it was sold to Japan where the body was repainted in the present black livery. In 2005 it was reimported into the USA, where the engine was rebuilt and the interior were retrimmed in tan leather with black inserts.*}												
1972	365 GTB4 Daytona	(PF/Scaglietti)	15279	L	950-1.100.000 USD		NS		29-01-16	Scottsdale	55	G&Co
{*Yellow with black leather interior; sold new to the USA. Concours-quality restoration completed in 2008. Approximately 44,500 miles covered since new. Certified by Ferrari Classiche.*}												
1971	365 GTB4 Daytona	(PF/Scaglietti)	14819	L	700-800.000 USD	481.044	687.500	629.544	29-01-16	Phoenix	220	RMS
{*Yellow with black interior; sold new to the USA. Several restoration works carried out in the early 2000s. Certified by Ferrari Classiche (see lots 169 Barrett-Jackson 22.6.03 $ 145,800, 29 Gooding 22.1.10 $ 291,500, and 126 RM 27.4.13 $ 407,000).*}												
1971	365 GTB4 Daytona	(PF/Scaglietti)	14093	L	700-900.000 EUR		NS		03-02-16	Paris	125	RMS
{*Yellow with black leather interior; at unspecified date the car was fully restored in Italy to its original colours.*}												
1972	365 GTB4 Daytona	(PF/Scaglietti)	15375	L	750-900.000 EUR	734.034	1.068.223	953.600	05-02-16	Paris	169	Art
{*Silver with black leather interior; sold new to France. Fully restored. Certified by Ferrari Classiche.*}												
1971	365 GTB4 Daytona	(spider/conversion)	14185	L	675-800.000 EUR		NS		05-02-16	Paris	174	Art
{*Black with beige leather interior; sold new to the USA, the car remained in the same family ownership from 1972 to 2014. Conversion carried out by Straman in the 1980s. UK registered.*}												
1971	365 GTB4 Daytona	(PF/Scaglietti)	14345	L	850-950.000 USD		NS		11-03-16	Amelia Island	58	G&Co
{*Red with tan interior; sold new in Italy, later the car was imported into Switzerland. In 2006 it was restored in the Netherlands and in 2008 it was acquired by the current owner and imported into the USA. Certified by Ferrari Classiche (see lot 336 RM 18.5.08 $ 426,195).*}												
1972	365 GTB4 Daytona	(PF/Scaglietti)	15271	L	750-825.000 USD	423.258*	605.000*	545.529*	12-03-16	Amelia Island	160	RMS F276
{*Red with black leather interior; less than 32,000 miles covered. Cosmetic restoration carried out in 2002; engine rebuilt at 26,000 miles with upgraded internals giving 409bhp.*}												
1971	365 GTB4 Daytona	(PF/Scaglietti)	14769	L	675-725.000 USD	453.521	649.000	567.680	02-04-16	Ft.Lauderdale	504	AA
{*Red with black leather interior; 76,000 miles on the odometer (see lots 153 RM 15.1.15 $ 715,000 and F188 Mecum 16.5.15 $ 775,000).*}												
1973	365 GTB4 Daytona	(PF/Scaglietti)	16853	L	Refer Dpt.	619.825	893.088	787.000	14-05-16	Monaco	133A	Coy
{*Yellow with black interior; restored in the early 2000s.*}												
1972	365 GTB4 Daytona	(PF/Scaglietti)	15381	R	580-640.000 GBP		NS		24-06-16	Goodwood	247	Bon
{*Light metallic blue with beige leather interior; 27,907 miles covered. From 1974 for more than 30 years in the same ownership. In 2012 circa mechanicals overhauled and body repainted. Certified by Ferrari Classiche (see Bonhams lots 353 3.7.09 NS and 442 1.7.11 NS).*}												
1970	365 GTB4 Daytona	(PF/Scaglietti)	13183	L	750-850.000 USD	437.760	600.000	542.160	25-06-16	Santa Monica	2080	AA
{*Red with black interior; sold new in Italy, the car was imported into the USA in the late 1970s. Restored many years ago and recently refreshed.*}												
1973	365 GTB4 Daytona	(P.F./Scaglietti)	16811	L	625-675.000 USD		NS		30-07-16	Plymouth	145	RMS
{*Originally finished in silver with black interior, the car was sold new in Italy. Imported into the USA in 1977. Currently finished in rubin red with beige interior with black inserts; in good overall condition.*}												
1972	365 GTB4 Daytona	(P.F./Scaglietti)	15677	L	700-800.000 EUR		NS		06-08-16	Schloss Dyck	147	Coy
{*Light metallic blue; the car has covered 500 kms since a full restoration carried out between 2009 and 2014. Sold new to the USA and reimported into Europe in 1978.*}												
1971	365 GTB4 Daytona	(P.F./Scaglietti)	14203	L	600-750.000 USD		NS		19-08-16	Carmel	33	Bon
{*Dino yellow and largely original black leather interior; body repainted many years ago. Mechanicals refurbished in 2014. 52,000 miles on the odometer.*} | | | | | | | | | | | | |

F275: 1971 Ferrari 365 GTB4 Daytona (PF/Scaglietti)

F276: 1972 Ferrari 365 GTB4 Daytona (PF/Scaglietti)

Year	Model	(Bodybuilder)	Chassis no.	Steering	Estimate	Hammer Price £	Hammer Price $	Hammer Price €	Date	Place	Lot	Auc. H.
1973	365 GTB4 Daytona	(P.F./Scaglietti)	16109	L	650-800.000 USD		NS		19-08-16	Monterey	F141	Mec

See lot T203 Mecum 23.1.16.

1972	365 GTB4 Daytona	(P.F./Scaglietti)	15305	L	800-900.000 USD	567.270	742.500	655.553	19-08-16	Monterey	113	RMS

Red with black leather interior; since 1976 with the present, second owner. 4,838 miles on the odometer. Certified by Ferrari Classiche.

1972	365 GTB4 Daytona	(P.F./Scaglietti)	15273	L	800-1.000.000 USD	630.300*	825.000*	728.393*	20-08-16	Pebble Beach	55	G&Co

Red with black leather interior; in largely original condition, just over 12,000 miles covered. In single ownership from 1975 to 2016.

1972	365 GTB4 Daytona shooting brake	(Panther Westwinds)	15275	L	750-1.000.000 USD		NS		20-08-16	Pebble Beach	69	G&Co

One-off designed by Luigi Chinetti Jr. in the early 1970s; finished in black with tan leather interior; bought in 2013 by the current owner and subsequently restored (see lots 281 Bonhams 19.12.03 NS, 227 Bonhams 17.12.05 $260,877, 250 Coys 10.5.08 NS, 345 Bonhams 15.8.08 NS, and 66 Bonhams 11.10.10 $300,039).

1971	365 GTB4 Daytona	(PF/Scaglietti)	14189	L	750-850.000 USD	588.280	770.000	679.833	20-08-16	Monterey	223	RMS

Black with beige leather interior with black inserts; described as in highly original condition, the car has had three owners and has covered 22,216 miles. Last serviced in March 2016. Certified by Ferrari Classiche.

1969	365 GTB4 Daytona	(PF/Scaglietti)	12525	L	750-850.000 USD	546.260	715.000	631.274	21-08-16	Pebble Beach	126	G&Co

Silver with black interior; sold new in Italy, the car was imported in 1979 into the USA where it remained in single ownership until late 2012. Described as in original, unrestored condition; mechanicals freshened.

1973	365 GTS4 Daytona spider	(PF/Scaglietti)	17013	L	2.000-2.400.000 GBP		NS		07-09-15	London	144	RMS

Dark brown with original tan leather interior with black inserts; largely original paintwork. 3,805 miles covered. Sold new to the USA where it has had several owners. Certified by Ferrari Classiche in 2009 (see RM lots 145 20.3.99 NS, 83 9.3.02 NS and 170 13.3.04 NS).

1971	365 GTS4 Daytona spider	(PF/Scaglietti)	14543	L	2.300-2.600.000 GBP		NS		12-09-15	Goodwood	321	Bon

Originally finished in white with black interior, the car was sold new to the USA to William Harrah who resold it in 1976 to Jack Frost who retained it until 2006. Certified by Ferrari Classiche in 2009. Restored in 2011 and refinished in black with red leather interior. From the Chris Evans collection (see lots 214 RM 17.5.09 NS, 344 RM 14.8.10 $ 990,000 and 119 Silverstone Auctions 4.9.14 $ 3,734,280).

1973	365 GTS4 Daytona spider	(PF/Scaglietti)	15369	L	2.500-3.000.000 USD		NS		12-03-16	Amelia Island	166	RMS

Yellow with black interior; sold new to Lebanon, the car was imported into the USA in 1978. In 1994 it was involved in an accident and the rear half of the body sustained fire damage. That same year it was repaired using original and NOS parts and in 1995 it was sold to the UK. Later it was reimported into the USA and recently the body was repainted, the interior retrimmed and the mechanicals serviced. Certified by Ferrari Classiche (see lots 115 Coys 26.7.97 NS and 419 Brooks 28.8.99 $ 354,500).

1972	365 GTS4 Daytona spider	(PF/Scaglietti)	15535	L	2.400-2.800.000 EUR		NS		14-05-16	Monaco	265	RMS

Red with black leather interior; sold new to Lebanon, later the car had several owners in Canada and in Europe, and was restored in Italy between the late 1990s - early 2000s. Since 2005 in the current ownership. Certified by Ferrari Classiche (see lots Poulain 150 29.4.96 $ 388,408, Brooks 164 19.12.98 NS, and Bonhams 270 18.12.01 $ 402,433 and 255 18.12.04 NS).

1973	365 GTS4 Daytona spider	(PF/Scaglietti)	16847	L	2.150-2.600.000 USD	1.806.860	2.365.000	2.088.059	20-08-16	Monterey	229	RMS

Originally finished in silver with black interior, the car was sold new to the USA. At unspecified date the body was refinished in the present red livery and the interior were retrimmed in tan leather. For 15 years in the current ownership, it was recently subjected to a two year restoration. **F277**

1974	365 GT4 BB	(Pininfarina)	17967	R	300-375.000 GBP	336.000	512.803	460.085	07-09-15	London	131	RMS

Red with black door sills and beige interior; sold new to the UK. Offered with its registration numer, BB 365. Recently serviced. Certified by Ferrari Classiche (see Coys lots 48 8.9.93 NS and 101 26.7.97 NS). **F278**

1977	365 GT4 BB	(Pininfarina)	21689	R	200-250.000 GBP	231.100	356.426	316.330	12-09-15	Goodwood	355	Bon

Yellow with black leather interior; the car was sold by its first owner in 1981 to the current owner, who in 1985 resold it to a friend and reacquired it from the friend in 2010. Recommissioned in 2011, it remained subsequently unused and was recently serviced.

1973	365 GT4 BB	(Pininfarina)	17941	R	600-650.000 AUD		NS		24-10-15	Melbourne	45	TBr

Red with tan and black interior; sold new to Australia, the car was involved early in its life in an accident and was subsequently repaired using a new body, supplied by the factory, of the new model 512 BB. Again restored between 2008 and 2010.

1974	365 GT4 BB	(Pininfarina)	18035	L	400-450.000 EUR		NS		01-11-15	Paris	142	Art

Red and black with beige leather interior; in very good original condition, the car has covered less than 40,000 kms. Stored for some time, it requires recommissioning prior to use.

1975	365 GT4 BB	(Pininfarina)	18419	L	500-600.000 USD	346.352	495.000	453.272	30-01-16	Scottsdale	139	G&Co

Red with beige leather interior; sold new in Italy, the car was imported in 1978 into the USA where it remained in the same ownership until 2011. Described as in largely original condition except fro the paintwork redone in its original colour. Approximately 35,000 kms on the odometer. Recently serviced. Certified by Ferrari Classiche (see lot 200 RM 12.3.11 $ 220,000).

1974	365 GT4 BB	(Pininfarina)	17709	L	400-500.000 EUR	301.320	437.320	400.000	03-02-16	Paris	109	RMS

Red with beige leather interior; sold new in Italy. Since 2003 in the current ownership. Less than 33,000 kms covered.

1976	365 GT4 BB	(Pininfarina)	19153	R	NA		NS		06-03-16	Birmingham	345	SiC

Red with black interior; imported into the UK from Australia. Body repainted; recommissioned for road use.

1974	365 GT4 BB	(Pininfarina)	18001	L	380-450.000 EUR		NS		14-05-16	Monaco	214	RMS

Originally finished in yellow with black leather interior, the car was sold new to France. In 1981 it was imported into the USA where it remained from 1984 for nearly 30 years with the same owner who had it repainted in the present black livery. Less than 9,000 kms covered since new (see lot 54 Gooding 13.3.15 $ 401,500).

F277: 1973 Ferrari 365 GTS4 Daytona spider (PF/Scaglietti)

F278: 1974 Ferrari 365 GT4 BB (Pininfarina)

Year	Model	(Bodybuilder)	Chassis No.	Steering	Estimate	Hammer Price £	$	€	Date	Place	Lot	Auc. H.
1974	365 GT4 BB	(Pininfarina)	18153	R	350-400.000 EUR		NS		09-07-16	Le Mans	201	Art

Red with black interior; restored between 2013 and 2014 (see lot 191 Brooks 30.4.92 $120,545).

| 1975 | 365 GT4 BB | (Pininfarina) | 18635 | L | 525-575.000 USD | | NS | | 21-08-16 | Pebble Beach | 149 | G&Co |

Blue with black leather interior; sold new to Japan where it remained with its first owner until 2011. Imported into the USA in 2015 and recently purchased by the current, fourth owner. In original condition; less than 7,800 kms covered; certified by Ferrari Classiche.

| 1972 | 365 GTC4 | (Pininfarina) | 15181 | L | NA | 206.892 | 315.000 | 282.839 | 05-09-15 | Auburn | 5127 | AA |

Originally finished in blue with blue interior, the car was sold new to the USA. In 1990 circa the body was repainted in the present red livery and the interior retrimmed in black. Described as in good overall condition.

| 1972 | 365 GTC4 | (Pininfarina) | 16095 | L | 320-380.000 EUR | | NS | | 01-11-15 | Paris | 117 | Art |

Red with black leather interior; recently restored. Certified by Ferrari Classiche.

| 1971 | 365 GTC4 | (Pininfarina) | 14891 | L | 350-400.000 USD | | NS | | 28-01-16 | Phoenix | 120 | RMS |

Originally finished in silver with black interior, the car was sold new to the USA. In 2011 it was imported in Germany where it was restored and finished in the present light metallic blue livery. In 2013 it was reimported into the USA where the interior were reupholstered in blue leather. Recently serviced.

| 1972 | 365 GTC4 | (Pininfarina) | 15761 | L | 300-375.000 USD | | NS | | 29-01-16 | Phoenix | 268 | RMS |

Red with tan interior; paintwork and interior redone some time ago. Clutch rebuilt in 2009 (see lot 31 Artcurial 30.9.07 NS).

| 1972 | 365 GTC4 | (Pininfarina) | 15365 | L | 350-400.000 USD | | NS | | 30-01-16 | Scottsdale | 151 | G&Co |

Dark red with beige leather interior; three owners and 39,000 miles covered. Mechanicals restored some years ago; body repainted in 2015.

| 1972 | 365 GTC4 | (Pininfarina) | 15615 | L | 250-300.000 EUR | | NS | | 04-02-16 | Paris | 364 | Bon |

Silver with black leather interior; sold new to the USA and later reimported into Europe. Described as in very good overall condition.

| 1972 | 365 GTC4 | (Pininfarina) | 15211 | L | 325-375.000 USD | 238.564 | 341.000 | 307.480 | 12-03-16 | Amelia Island | 193 | RMS F279 |

Red with black interior; sold new to the USA, later the car was sold to Switzerland where it was restored. Subsequently it was reimported into the USA (see RM lots 68 17.8.01 $ 55,000, 222 20.8.11 $ 170,500 and 159 18.1.13 $ 176,000).

| 1971 | 365 GTC4 | (Pininfarina) | 14733 | L | 280-320.000 EUR | | NS | | 19-06-16 | Fontainebleau | 337 | Ose |

Red with beige leather interior; restored in Germany in the 1990s and subsequently little used.

| 1971 | 365 GTC4 | (Pininfarina) | 14419 | L | 400-475.000 USD | | NS | | 25-06-16 | Santa Monica | 1096 | AA |

Dark blue with red leather interior; full restoration completed in 20166. Owned by Pininfarina SpA until 1973 for Sergio Pininfarina personal use.

| 1971 | 365 GTC4 | (Pininfarina) | 15331 | L | 325-375.000 USD | 202.646 | 277.750 | 250.975 | 25-06-16 | Santa Monica | 2073 | AA |

Silver with black leather interior; body repainted and mechanicals overhauled.

| 1971 | 365 GTC4 | (Pininfarina) | 14179 | L | 425-475.000 EUR | | NS | | 09-07-16 | Le Mans | 144 | Art |

Ivory with dark blue leather interior; the car was exhibited at the 1971 Geneva Motor Show. In the same ownership from 1986 to 2015. Body repainted.

| 1972 | 365 GTC4 | (Pininfarina) | 15609 | L | 300-400.000 USD | | NS | | 19-08-16 | Monterey | F136.1 | Mec |

Grey with beige interior; in original condition. Three owners; 18,826 miles covered; last serviced in 2014.

| 1971 | 365 GTC4 | (Pininfarina) | 14419 | L | 425-475.000 USD | | NS | | 20-08-16 | Monterey | S136 | Mec |

See lot 1096 Auctions America 25.6.16.

| 1972 | 365 GTC4 | (Pininfarina) | 14971 | L | NQ | | NS | | 20-08-16 | Monterey | 7151 | R&S |

Red with tan interior; less than 39,000 original miles. Body repainted three years ago.

| 1975 | 365 GT4 2+2 | (Pininfarina) | 17795 | L | 65-85.000 EUR | | NS | | 26-09-15 | Frankfurt | 147 | Coy |

Silver with black leather interior; body repainted. Clutch replaced in 2015. Three owners (see lot 341 Coys 10.3.15 $ 95,506).

| 1973 | 365 GT4 2+2 | (Pininfarina) | 17229 | L | 90-120.000 EUR | | NS | | 09-10-15 | Zoute | 32 | Bon |

Bronze with beige leather interior; described as partially restored.

| 1976 | 365 GT4 2+2/barchetta | | 19235 | L | 250-300.000 GBP | | NS | | 10-10-15 | Ascot | 114 | Coy |

Red; body in the style of the Ferrari sports cars of the 1950s, built by Carrozzeria Daddario, Turin, in the 1980s.

| 1973 | 365 GT4 2+2 | (Pininfarina) | 17175 | R | NQ | 30.938* | 47.100* | 43.759* | 14-11-15 | Birmingham | 322 | SiC |

Red with tan interior; in good working order. Formerly owned by boxer Sir Henry Cooper.

| 1974 | 365 GT4 2+2 | (Pininfarina) | 18037 | L | NA | 41.886 | 60.000 | 55.512 | 23-01-16 | Kissimmee | K2 | Mec F280 |

Red; clutch and interior replaced in 2005, body repainted in 2015. Equipped with a late 1970s 400 block (see lot F24 Mecum 14.8.15 NS).

| 1976 | 365 GT4 2+2 | (Pininfarina) | 18815 | R | 50-55.000 GBP | 59.063 | 86.043 | 76.693 | 20-05-16 | Silverstone | 354 | SiC |

Light metallic grey; fully restored between 1993 and 1996. Last serviced in December 2015 (see lots 504 Bonhams 7.7.06 $ 15,235, 141 Coys 30.11.06 NS, and 351 Silverstone Auctions 22.2.14 $ 68,092).

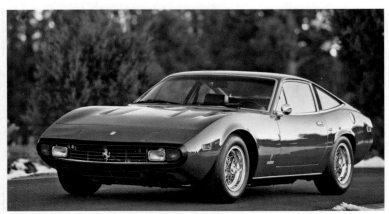

F279: 1972 Ferrari 365 GTC4 (Pininfarina)

F280: 1974 Ferrari 365 GT4 2+2 (Pininfarina)

Year	Model	(Bodybuilder)	Chassis no.	Steering	Estimate	Hammer price £	Hammer price $	Hammer price €	Date	Place	Lot	Auc. H.
1976	365 GT4 2+2	(Pininfarina)	18815	R	48-55.000 GBP		NS		30-07-16	Silverstone	957	SiC
	See lot 354 Silverstone Auctions 20.5.16.											
1973	365 GT4 2+2	(Pininfarina)	17261	L	55-70.000 EUR		NS		06-08-16	Schloss Dyck	145	Coy
	Light blue with black interior; in good overall condition. In 2003 the car was used in a film on the Enzo Ferrari life.											
1976	365 GT4 2+2	(Pininfarina)	19179	L	NQ		NS		20-08-16	Monterey	7160	R&S
	Red with black interior; body repainted in 1982.											
1979	308 GT4	(Bertone)	15046	R	35-45.000 GBP	50.400*	76.920*	69.013*	07-09-15	London	136	RMS
	Silver with blue leather and cloth interior; last serviced in 2014.											
1977	308 GT4	(Bertone)	13588	L	65-85.000 EUR	53.078*	84.051*	73.904*	01-11-15	Paris	114	Art **F281**
	Dark metallic grey with black leather interior; recently restored.											
1979	308 GT4	(Bertone)	14970	L	100-130.000 USD		NS		23-01-16	Kissimmee	S244	Mec
	Red with black leather interior; believed to be 28,750 miles.											
1976	308 GT4	(Bertone)	12314	R	NA	33.469	47.382	43.195	06-03-16	Birmingham	309	SiC
	Green with tan interior; restored between 1994 and 1996. The body and paintwork require some attention.											
1981	308 GT4	(Bertone)	15584	L	60-70.000 EUR		NS		09-04-16	Essen	206	Coy
	Metallic maroon with beige leather interior; described as in very good overall condition.											
1975	308 GT4	(Bertone)	07996	L	70-80.000 EUR		NS		28-05-16	Aarhus	238	SiC
	Red with black cloth interior; unwarranted 12,309 kms on the odometer.											
1976	308 GT4	(Bertone)	12736	L	55-65.000 EUR		NS		09-07-16	Le Mans	134	Art
	Yellow with original black leather interior; several mechanical works carried out in the 2000s (see lot 39 Poulain 28.6.99 NS).											
1979	308 GT4	(Bertone)	14816	R	35-40.000 GBP	45.563	59.961	53.956	30-07-16	Silverstone	934	SiC
	Red; recently serviced.											
1976	208 GT4	(Bertone)	11378	L	35-40.000 GBP	47.250	62.181	55.953	30-07-16	Silverstone	530	SiC
	Light blue; fully restored in Italy.											
1979	308 GTB	(PF/Scaglietti)	26815	R	60-70.000 GBP	84.375	128.478	115.349	04-09-15	Woodstock	212	SiC
	Red with black interior; restoration completed in 2014. 28,870 miles covered since new (see lot 143 Silverstone Auctions 4.9.14 $ 105,616).											
1981	308 GTBi	(PF/Scaglietti)	34807	L	70-80.000 EUR	56.242	85.356	76.546	26-09-15	Frankfurt	115	Coy
	Red with tan interior; 49,000 miles covered. Recently serviced.											
1976	308 GTB	(PF/Scaglietti)	19611	R	135-150.000 GBP		NS		10-10-15	Ascot	122	Coy
	Fibreglass body finished in red; car sold new to the UK and described as in very good overall condition.											
1978	308 GTB	(PF/Scaglietti)	24721	L	NA	64.245	101.750	89.459	31-10-15	Hilton Head	139	AA
	Black with black interior; 27,000 miles on the odometer (see lot F135 Mecum 14.8.15 NS).											
1979	308 GTB	(PF/Scaglietti)	28199	L	150-190.000 EUR		NS		01-11-15	Paris	115	Art
	Gold with tan leather interior; restored in 2015.											
1976	308 GTB	(PF/Scaglietti)	19161	L	180-220.000 EUR		NS		01-11-15	Paris	119	Art
	Red with black interior; since 1987 in the current ownership. 91,092 kms covered. Fiberglass body.											
1981	308 GTBi	(PF/Scaglietti)	34807	L	45-55.000 GBP	45.900	69.878	64.921	14-11-15	Birmingham	633A	SiC
	See lot 115 Coys 26.9.15.											
1976	308 GTB	(PF/Scaglietti)	19357	R	100-120.000 GBP	102.300	154.729	141.389	10-12-15	London	368	Bon **F282**
	Glass-fibre body finished in silver with blue interior; since 1991 in the Shikoku Automobile Museum in Japan and never used. 62,238 kms on the odometer.											
1984	308 GTB 4V	(PF/Scaglietti)	49461	L	100-140.000 USD	53.831*	77.000*	70.617*	28-01-16	Scottsdale	20	Bon
	Red with tan interior; restored in recent years.											
1976	308 GTB	(PF/Scaglietti)	19681	L	300-350.000 USD	250.143	357.500	327.363	30-01-16	Scottsdale	112	G&Co
	Fiberglass body finished in red with tan leather interior; restored in Italy between 2013 and 2014. Certified by Ferrari Classiche.											
1979	308 GTB	(PF/Scaglietti)	27175	L	140-160.000 EUR	84.370	122.450	112.000	03-02-16	Paris	157	RMS
	Blue with beige leather interior; two owners. Last serviced in March 2015.											
1976	308 GTB	(PF/Scaglietti)	19069	L	180-220.000 EUR	105.833	156.884	140.000	04-02-16	Paris	369	Bon
	Fiberglass body fineshed in silver with black interior; recently serviced. Body repainted.											

F281: 1977 Ferrari 308 GT4 (Bertone)

F282: 1976 Ferrari 308 GTB (PF/Scaglietti)

Year	Model	(Bodybuilder)	Chassis No.	Steering	Estimate	Hammer Price £	$	€	Date	Place	Lot	Auc. H.
1982	308 GTBi	(PF/Scaglietti)	39835	L	NA		NS		26-02-16	Coventry	436	SiC
	Blue; engine rebuilt in 2009 circa. 19,000 miles on the odometer.											
1978	308 GTB	(PF/Scaglietti)	24721	L	100-130.000 USD		NS		10-03-16	Amelia Island	137	Bon
	See lot 139 Auctions America 31.10.15.											
1976	308 GTB	(PF/Scaglietti)	19145	L	275-325.000 USD	165.455	236.500	213.252	11-03-16	Amelia Island	5	G&Co
	Fiberglass body finished in red with black interior; sold new in Italy, in 1985 the car was imported into the USA where it remained for 25 years in the same ownership. Paintwork and interior believed original. Comprehensive service between November 2015 and January 2016.											
1981	308 GTBi	(PF/Scaglietti)	36245	L	75-85.000 EUR	60.990	87.167	78.600	12-03-16	Lyon	341	Agu
	Red with beige interior; body repainted two years ago. In single ownership from 1984 to 2015.											
1976	308 GTB	(PF/Scaglietti)	19069	L	110-130.000 GBP	113.500	164.427	145.779	20-03-16	Goodwood	59	Bon
	See lot 369 Bonhams 4.2.16.											
1981	308 GTB	(PF/Scaglietti)	34883	L	60-70.000 USD	44.199	63.250	55.325	02-04-16	Ft.Lauderdale	759	AA
	Red with black interior.											
1976	308 GTB	(PF/Scaglietti)	19611	R	125-145.000 GBP		NS		16-04-16	Ascot	132	Coy
	See lot 122 Coys 10.10.15.											
1984	308 GTB 4V	(PF/Scaglietti)	49461	L	NA		NS		16-04-16	Houston	F134	Mec
	See lot 20 Bonhams 28.1.16.											
1979	308 GTB	(PF/Scaglietti)	26303	R	60-70.000 GBP		NS		20-05-16	Silverstone	355	SiC
	Red; body repainted many years ago, engine upgraded to 300bhp in 1991 and rebuilt in 2007. The car requires some attention to the paintwork and interior.											
1975	308 GTB	(PF/Scaglietti)	19715	L	180-210.000 EUR		NS		28-05-16	Aarhus	216	SiC
	Fiberglass body finished in red with black leather interior; 42,000 kms on the odometer. Recently serviced.											
1983	308 GTB 4V	(PF/Scaglietti)	41797	L	80-115.000 USD	51.440	74.250	66.565	05-06-16	Greenwhich	64	Bon
	Red with tan interior; described as in very good overall condition. Engine-out service in the winter of 2015.											
1979	308 GTB	(PF/Scaglietti)	30461	L	150-175.000 USD		NS		11-06-16	Hershey	112	TFA
	Red with black interior; in original condition. 23,000 miles covered. Last serviced in May 2015 (see lot 103 Bonhams 14.08.15 $126,500).											
1976	308 GTB	(PF/Scaglietti)	20077	R	120-160.000 GBP		NS		24-06-16	Goodwood	212	Bon
	Glassfibre body finished in silver with black interior; sold new to Australia and imported into the UK in 2015. Described as in very good overall condition.											
1976	308 GTB	(PF/Scaglietti)	19665	R	140-180.000 GBP		NS		24-06-16	Goodwood	271	Bon
	Fiberglass body finished in red with black interior; approximately 45,000 miles covered. Recently serviced; body repainted.											
1977	308 GTB	(PF/Scaglietti)	22683	L	80-100.000 USD	54.173*	74.250*	67.092*	25-06-16	Santa Monica	2031	AA
	Red with tan interior; believed to be in original condition, the car shows less than 12,000 miles. From the Riverside International Automotive Museum Collection.											
1977	308 GTB	(PF/Scaglietti)	21043	L	155-195.000 EUR	131.076	170.221	153.768	09-07-16	Le Mans	115	Art
	Fiberglass body finished in red with black interior; 47,940 kms on the odometer. Mechanicals overhauled in 2016.											
1978	308 GTB	(PF/Scaglietti)	23533	R	110-130.000 GBP		NS		30-07-16	Silverstone	927	SiC
	Red; in good overall condition. Approximately 23,500 miles covered. Last serviced in December 2015.											
1981	308 GTS	(PF/Scaglietti)	35067	L	NA	35.402	53.900	48.397	05-09-15	Auburn	3135	AA
	Red with tan interior; 42,000 miles on the odometer.											
1979	308 GTS	(PF/Scaglietti)	30237	L	NA	49.129*	74.800*	67.163*	05-09-15	Auburn	4110	AA
	Red with tan leather interior; one owner and 24,101 miles on the odometer.											
1983	308 GTS 4V	(PF/Scaglietti)	43205	L	NA		NS		05-09-15	Auburn	5143	AA
	Red with black interior; 17,400 miles.											
1981	308 GTSi	(PF/Scaglietti)	36295	L	40-50.000 USD	21.740	33.000	29.370	05-10-15	Philadelphia	211	Bon
	Red with black interior retrimmed in 2012; recently serviced.											
1983	308 GTS 4V	(PF/Scaglietti)	46057	L	NA	75.040	115.419	101.154	14-10-15	Duxford	26	H&H
	Red with tan leather interior; recent cosmetic restoration. 77,000 kms covered.											
1984	308 GTS 4V	(PF/Scaglietti)	49867	L	80-90.000 EUR	60.283	91.258	84.000	07-11-15	Lyon	273	Agu
	Red with biscuit leather interior; sold new to the USA, the car was later imported into France. Body repainted in 2015.											
1979	308 GTS	(PF/Scaglietti)	30583	L	NA	106.746	162.500	150.979	13-11-15	Anaheim	S125	Mec
	Black; two owners and 1,909 miles covered. Stored since 1981. New water pump and timing belts.											
1982	308 GTSi	(PF/Scaglietti)	42501	R	60-70.000 GBP		NS		14-11-15	Birmingham	308	SiC
	Red with black leather interior; described as in very good overall condition. Since 1989 in the current ownership. Last serviced in August 2015 at 68,603 miles.											
1983	308 GTS 4V	(PF/Scaglietti)	45435	R	68-80.000 GBP	71.680	107.886	101.972	28-11-15	Weybridge	243	His
	Red with black interior; acquired in 2008 by the current owner and subsequently restored.											
1980	308 GTS	(PF/Scaglietti)	30309	R	64-70.000 GBP		NS		28-11-15	Weybridge	301	His
	Red with cream interior; body repainted in 1989 from white to red.											
1985	308 GTS 4v	(PF/Scaglietti)	53017	L	NA	37.697	54.000	49.961	23-01-16	Kissimmee	F277.1	Mec
	Red with tan interior; recently serviced.											
1985	308 GTS	(PF/Scaglietti)	57063	L	NA	32.811	47.000	43.484	23-01-16	Kissimmee	F52	Mec
	Red with black leather interior; described as in highly original condition. Recently serviced.											
1980	308 GTS	(PF/Scaglietti)	29869	L	90-120.000 USD	69.810	100.000	92.520	23-01-16	Kissimmee	T213	Mec
	Silver with red interior; 8,865 miles covered.											
1980	308 GTSi	(PF/Scaglietti)	32621	L	90-110.000 USD	42.296*	60.500*	55.485*	28-01-16	Scottsdale	4	Bon
	Light gold with original brown interior; less than 43,000 miles on the odometer. Body repainted several years ago.											

Year	Model	(Bodybuilder)	Chassis no.	Steering	Estimate	Hammer price £	$	€	Date	Place	Lot	Auc. H.
1984	308 GTS	(PF/Scaglietti)	51989	L	NA		NS		30-01-16	Scottsdale	5529	R&S
Red with black leather interior; recent cosmetic refurbishment (see Russo & Steele lots 3307 6.6.15 $ 67,100 and S648 15.8.15 $ 72,600).												
1982	308 GTSi	(PF/Scaglietti)	41139	L	50-70.000 EUR	41.289*	60.088*	53.640*	05-02-16	Paris	102	Art
Red with original black leather interior; body repainted.												
1985	308 GTS 4V	(PF/Scaglietti)	58519	L	95-145.000 EUR	100.930*	146.881*	131.120*	05-02-16	Paris	168	Art F283
Red; sold to Switzerland, the car has had just one owner and has covered 7,500 kms. Recently serviced.												
1979	308 GTS	(PF/Scaglietti)	26835	L	160-180.000 USD	130.825*	187.000*	168.618*	11-03-16	Amelia Island	21	G&Co
Red; since 1993 with the present, second owner. Approximately 5,800 kms covered. Body repainted in 2005. Last serviced in March 2015.												
1982	308 GTSi	(PF/Scaglietti)	38685	L	50-60.000 USD	38.050	54.450	47.627	02-04-16	Ft.Lauderdale	423	AA
Red with tan interior; 2016 cosmetic restoration. Recently serviced (see lot 333 Barrett-Jackson 19.3.04 $ 32,400).												
1981	308 GTSi	(PF/Scaglietti)	37145	L	65-75.000 USD	44.583	63.800	55.806	02-04-16	Ft.Lauderdale	461	AA
Silver with black interior; recently serviced.												
1983	308 GTS 4V	(PF/Scaglietti)	47181	L	75-85.000 USD	47.658	68.200	59.655	02-04-16	Ft.Lauderdale	513	AA
Red with cream leather interior; described as in very good overall condition.												
1979	308 GTS	(PF/Scaglietti)	27297	L	NA	59.389*	83.600*	73.568*	09-04-16	Palm Beach	421	B/J
Red with cream leather interior; recent engine-out service.												
1985	308 GTS	(PF/Scaglietti)	57399	L	55-65.000 EUR	49.377	69.500	61.163	09-04-16	Essen	120	Coy
Red with black leather interior; last serviced in 2015.												
1981	308 GTSi	(PF/Scaglietti)	36379	L	50-60.000 GBP	51.750	75.389	67.197	20-05-16	Silverstone	309	SiC
Black with tan interior; body repainted in the past. 10,561 kms on the odometer. Recently recommissioned in the UK (see lot 265 Artcurial 5.7.14 $ 64,788).												
1978	308 GTS	(PF/Scaglietti)	25377	L	80-90.000 EUR		NS		28-05-16	Aarhus	131	SiC
Red; in good running order. The paintwork requires some attention.												
1980	308 GTS	(PF/Scaglietti)	33951	L	75-85.000 EUR		NS		28-05-16	Aarhus	227	SiC
Red; 49,000 miles on the odometer. In single ownership from 1989 to 2015.												
1981	308 GTS	(PF/Scaglietti)	30653	R	90-110.000 GBP		NS		11-06-16	Brooklands	296	His
Silver with blue leather interior; engine and gearbox rebuilt 8,000 miles ago in 2010.												
1982	308 GTSi	(PF/Scaglietti)	41079	L	NA	44.141*	60.500*	54.668*	24-06-16	Uncasville	624.1	B/J
Yellow with black interior; less than 42,000 miles.												
1985	308 GTS 4V	(PF/Scaglietti)	54307	L	NA	48.956*	67.100*	60.632*	24-06-16	Uncasville	725	B/J
Red with tan interior; 55,000 original miles.												
1979	308 GTS	(PF/Scaglietti)	28725	L	70-80.000 USD	46.548	63.800	57.650	25-06-16	Santa Monica	2052	AA
Yellow with black interior.												
1984	308 GTS 4V	(PF/Scaglietti)	50209	L	60-80.000 EUR	57.918	75.214	67.944	09-07-16	Le Mans	106	Art
Red with magnolia leather interior; last serviced in April 2016 at 64,000 kms.												
1979	308 GTS	(PF/Scaglietti)	28469	L	90-110.000 EUR		NS		09-07-16	Le Mans	138	Art
Grey with red interior; body repainted 10 years ago. Recently interior retrimmed and engine overhauled (see lots Poulain 36 2.4.90 $92,302, Poulain/Sotheby's 8 17.6.02 NS, and Artcurial 37 12.6.06 $26,211 and 12 16.11.08 $26,908).												
1981	308 GTSi	(PF/Scaglietti)	37199	L	120-145.000 USD	117.656*	154.000*	135.967*	19-08-16	Carmel	21	Bon
Red with tan leather interior; in original condition. Two owners and 3,112 kms covered. Last serviced in January 2015.												
1977	308 GTS	(PF/Scaglietti)	23173	L	70-90.000 USD	42.020*	55.000*	48.560*	19-08-16	Carmel	82	Bon
Silver and black with black interior; described as in good overall condition. Less than 40,000 miles on the odometer.												
1979	308 GTS	(PF/Scaglietti)	28725	L	70-90.000 USD		NS		19-08-16	Monterey	F172	Mec
See lot 2052 Auctions America 25.6.16.												
1981	308 GTSi	(PF/Scaglietti)	36913	L	90-130.000 USD		NS		19-08-16	Monterey	F186	Mec
Red with tan leather interior; 7,900 miles covered. Recently serviced.												
1984	308 GTS 4V	(PF/Scaglietti)	49625	L	70-90.000 USD	42.784	56.000	49.442	20-08-16	Monterey	S173	Mec
Red with tan interior; last serviced in 2016.												
1981	400i	(Pininfarina)	30849	R	NA	18.480	28.424	24.911	14-10-15	Duxford	6	H&H F284
Red with magnolia leather interior; 60,000 miles covered. Last serviced in 2014.												

F283: 1985 Ferrari 308 GTS 4V (PF/Scaglietti)

F284: 1981 Ferrari 400i (Pininfarina)

Year	Model (Bodybuilder)	Chassis No.	Steering	Estimate	Hammer Price £	Hammer Price $	Hammer Price €	Sale Date	Sale Place	Lot	Auc. H.
1978	400 (Pininfarina)	23455	L	80-90.000 EUR		NS		07-11-15	Lyon	281	Agu
Metallic brown with biscuit interior; described as in very good overall condition. Automatic transmission.											
1983	400i (Pininfarina)	46653	L	60-70.000 EUR	55.229	79.156	72.527	16-01-16	Maastricht	443	Coy
Dark blue with tan interior; in very good overall condition. First owner King Hussein of Jordan.											
1982	400i (Pininfarina)	40871	R	24-28.000 GBP	28.000	40.018	36.084	12-03-16	Brooklands	176	His
Light blue with beige leather interior; in good driving order. Since 1994 in the current ownership. Automatic transmission.											
1978	400 GT (Pininfarina)	24743	L	55-85.000 EUR	50.728	72.476	64.400	18-06-16	Wien	431	Dor
Metallic blue with original beige leather interior; automatic transmission (see lot 174 Brooks 19.12.98 $20,071).											
1984	400i GT (Pininfarina)	50811	L	30-40.000 GBP	49.450*	67.766*	61.234*	24-06-16	Goodwood	211	Bon
Silver with original tan leather interior; acquired in 1994 by the current owner and imported into the UK in 2015. 29.976 miles on the odometer. Manual gearbox.											
1982	400i (Pininfarina)	42007	L	45-65.000 EUR	41.244	54.784	49.200	02-07-16	Lyon	333	Agu
Blue with cream interior; described as in very good overall condition. Automatic transmission.											
1984	400i (Pininfarina)	47359	R	23-30.000 GBP		NS		10-07-16	Chateau Impney	46	H&H
Metallic blue with tobacco interior; since 1993 in the current ownership. 53,400 miles on the odometer.											
1983	400i (Pininfarina)	44251	R	30-35.000 GBP	30.940	40.717	36.639	30-07-16	Silverstone	542	SiC
Dark green with cream interior; restored several years ago. Automatic transmission (see lot 37 H & H 17.4.13 $18,947).											
1979	512 BB (Pininfarina)	27863	R	300-350.000 GBP		NS		04-09-15	Woodstock	242	SiC
Blue with tan interior; 15,660 miles on the odometer. Restoration works carried out in 2015.											
1982	512 BBi (Pininfarina)	40421	L	190-240.000 GBP	212.800	324.775	291.387	07-09-15	London	147	RMS
White with cream leather interior; 13,500 kms covered. Last serviced in March 2014. Certified by Ferrari Classiche.											
1979	512 BB (Pininfarina)	27321	L	385-440.000 EUR		NS		09-10-15	Zoute	17	Bon
Metallic blue with cream leather interior; sold new to Germany. Restored in France at unspecified date. Last serviced in 2014.											
1984	512 BBi (Pininfarina)	47413	L	NA	227.462	360.250	316.732	31-10-15	Hilton Head	183	AA
Red with black interior; believed to be two owners and 3,600 miles since new. Engine-out service in June 2013.											
1982	512 BBi (Pininfarina)	43487	L	300-350.000 EUR	231.145	366.029	321.840	01-11-15	Paris	141	Art
Red with beige leather interior; 8,561 kms covered. It requires servicing prior to use.											
1978	512 BB (Pininfarina)	22901	L	350-400.000 EUR	273.950	433.812	381.440	01-11-15	Paris	143	Art F285
Red and black with beige interior; in good original condition. For 20 years in the current ownership.											
1984	512 BBi (Pininfarina)	48417	L	350-400.000 EUR		NS		07-11-15	Lyon	269	Agu
Red with black leather interior; 16,500 miles on the odometer. Mechanicals overhauled in 2014.											
1982	512 BBi (Pininfarina)	42841	L	210-250.000 GBP	205.000	308.833	291.346	01-12-15	London	324	Coy
Black with black leather interior; restoration completed in 2014.											
1982	512 BBi (Pininfarina)	44753	R	150-200.000 GBP	186.300	281.779	257.485	10-12-15	London	326	Bon
Red with black interior; 29,835 kms on the odometer. Offered for sale by a Japanese collector.											
1978	512 BB (Pininfarina)	24445	L	275-325.000 USD	176.872*	253.000*	232.026*	28-01-16	Scottsdale	26	Bon
Red with black leather interior; in very good overall condition. Last serviced in 2014.											
1984	512 BBi (Pininfarina)	50591	L	400-450.000 USD	253.773	363.000	332.907	28-01-16	Phoenix	151	RMS
Red with tan leather interior; described as in largely original condition, the car has covered just over 24,000 kms. Last serviced in November 2015.											
1980	512 BB (Pininfarina)	31641	L	325-375.000 USD	242.446	346.500	317.290	29-01-16	Scottsdale	57	G&Co
Black with tan leather interior; imported into the USA in 1981. 30,000-mile engine-out service carried out in 2013.											
1983	512 BBi (Pininfarina)	45405	L	400-475.000 USD		NS		29-01-16	Phoenix	226	RMS
Black with black interior; described as in very good original condition. 12,000 kms covered since new.											
1984	512 BBi (Pininfarina)	47859	L	325-400.000 USD	192.418	275.000	251.818	29-01-16	Phoenix	262	RMS
Red with tan leather interior; described as in original condition. 17,400 miles covered. Recently serviced.											
1984	512 BBi (Pininfarina)	51725	L	400-475.000 USD	307.868	440.000	402.908	30-01-16	Scottsdale	121	G&Co
Metallic grey with burgundy leather interior; sold new to the USA to racing driver A.J. Foyt who retained it until 1992. Approximately 28,000 miles on the odometer; restored in recent years. From the Tony Shooshani Collection (see lot 986 Barrett-Jackson 19.1.07 $ 82,500).											
1977	512 BB (Pininfarina)	23125	L	400-450.000 EUR		NS		03-02-16	Paris	131	RMS
Red with black interior; last serviced in 2015. Certified by Ferrari Classiche (see lots 128 Sotheby's 9.9.97 NS and 107 Artcurial 6.2.15 $ 382,055).											
1983	512 BBi (Pininfarina)	46511	L	260-320.000 EUR		NS		04-02-16	Paris	325	Bon
Red with black interior; last serviced, including the clutch replacement, in April 2015 in the Netherlands.											
1980	512 BB (Pininfarina)	31971	L	350-450.000 EUR		NS		05-02-16	Paris	117	Art
Red with black interior; since 2003 in the current ownership. 23,560 kms covered. It requires recommissioning prior to use.											
1977	512 BB (Pininfarina)	20509	L	390-440.000 EUR		NS		05-02-16	Paris	218	Art
Silver with black interior; restoration recently completed at the factory. 33,000 kms covered since new. Certified by Ferrari Classiche.											
1984	512 BBi (Pininfarina)	52631	L	375-450.000 USD		NS		10-03-16	Amelia Island	143	Bon
Red with beige interior; in largely original condition. Believed to be a three owners and less than 8,000 original miles car.											
1984	512 BBi (Pininfarina)	47867	L	300-350.000 USD	207.781	297.000	267.805	11-03-16	Amelia Island	12	G&Co
Red with tan interior; two owners, low mileage, recent service.											
1980	512 BB (Pininfarina)	33715	L	275-325.000 USD	207.781*	297.000*	267.805*	12-03-16	Amelia Island	123	RMS
Red with original black leather interior; sold new to the USA. Less than 45,000 kms covered. Body repainted.											
1983	512 BBi (Pininfarina)	44231	L	300-310.000 USD		NS		02-04-16	Ft.Lauderdale	569	AA
Red with tan leather interior; described as in very good original condition (see RM lots 94 2.8.03 $ 71,500 and 139 10.3.12 $ 112,750).											

Year	Model	(Bodybuilder)	Chassis no.	Steering	Estimate	£	$	€	Date	Place	Lot	Auc. H.
1983	512 BBi	(Pininfarina)	44991	L	NA		NS		09-04-16	Palm Beach	383	B/J
	Red with black interior; for 31 years until 2016 in single ownership. 65,773 kms covered; 60,000 kms service carried out in 1998 prior to a long-term storage.											
1983	512 BBi	(Pininfarina)	47239	L	290-320.000 EUR	237.278	333.976	293.915	09-04-16	Essen	196	Coy
	Red; described as in excellent overall condition, the car has covered 30,000 kms.											
1982	512 BBi	(Pininfarina)	42511	L	290-340.000 EUR		NS		13-05-16	Monaco	140	Bon
	Medium metallic grey with cream interior; described as in good overall condition, the car received some restoration works in Germany and Italy.											
1981	512 BB	(Pininfarina)	37589	L	320-380.000 EUR		NS		14-05-16	Monaco	240	RMS
	Red with tan interior; in good original condition. 48,500 kms on the odometer.											
1982	512 BBi	(Pininfarina)	42513	L	325-375.000 EUR		NS		14-05-16	Monaco	260	RMS
	Red with black interior; recent engine-out service.											
1982	512 BBi	(Pininfarina)	43029	L	350-400.000 EUR		NS		28-05-16	Aarhus	219	SiC
	Red with tan interior; 6,729 kms on the odometer. Certified by Ferrari Classiche.											
1979	512 BB	(Pininfarina)	27699	L	NA		NS		24-06-16	Uncasville	664	B/J
	Red with tan interior.											
1984	512 BBi	(Pininfarina)	47859	L	NA		NS		24-06-16	Uncasville	684	B/J
	See lot 262 RM/Sotheby's 29.1.16.											
1979	512 BB	(Pininfarina)	28443	R	250-300.000 GBP		NS		24-06-16	Goodwood	252	Bon
	Red with black interior; one owner and 21,738 miles covered. Restored in 2015; engine rebuilt.											
1984	512 BBi	(Pininfarina)	52631	L	325-350.000 USD	224.717	308.000	278.309	25-06-16	Santa Monica	1102	AA
	See lot 143 Bonhams 10.3.16.											
1978	512 BB	(Pininfarina)	23025	L	320-350.000 USD		NS		25-06-16	Santa Monica	2090	AA
	Red with black interior; less than 16,000 miles on the odometer. Two owners. Engine-out service in 2015.											
1982	512 BBi	(Pininfarina)	42511	L	230-260.000 GBP	204.000	270.953	243.331	02-07-16	Woodstock	209	Coy
	See lot 140 Bonhams 13.5.16.											
1979	512 BB	(Pininfarina)	28297	L	240-280.000 EUR		NS		09-07-16	Le Mans	208	Art
	Red with black interior; in good overall condition. 48,900 kms covered. Since 1989 in the current ownership (see lot 67 Artcurial 22.6.15 NS).											
1982	512 BBi	(Pininfarina)	42511	L	240-280.000 EUR	232.187	305.421	273.773	06-08-16	Schloss Dyck	139	Coy
	See lot 209 Coys 2.7.16.											
1984	512 BBi	(Pininfarina)	48253	L	375-450.000 USD		NS		19-08-16	Monterey	150	RMS
	Black with black leather and grey cloth interior; sold new to the USA. Acquired in 1999 by the current owner and subsequently fully restored.											
1984	512 BBi	(Pininfarina)	49257	L	375-450.000 USD	239.514	313.500	276.789	20-08-16	Pebble Beach	5	G&Co
	Silver with black leather interior; in the early 2000s restored to concours condition. Three owners.											
1981	512 BB	(Pininfarina)	36777	L	375-450.000 USD		NS		20-08-16	Monterey	S125	Mec
	Black with tan leather interior; 2,456 kms covered. Sold new to the USA, the car remained in the same family ownership until 2015.											
1984	512 BBi	(Pininfarina)	50475	L	240-280.000 USD	214.302*	280.500*	247.653*	20-08-16	Monterey	215	RMS
	Red with black leather interior; described as in very good original condition. 3,669 miles on the odometer. From the Riverside International Automotive Museum Collection.											
1988	208 GTS Turbo	(PF/Scaglietti)	76855	L	60-80.000 EUR	63.885	97.997	86.250	09-10-15	Zoute	44	Bon F286
	Red with black leather interior; 2-liter version for the Italian market. The car has covered 74,500 kms and was last serviced in April 2013. It comes with Italian ASI homologation.											
1988	208 GTS Turbo	(PF/Scaglietti)	81307	L	NA		NS		14-11-15	Birmingham	617	SiC
	Blue with blue leather interior; first owner Prince Jefri of the Brunei Royal Family. 2,671 kms covered.											
1987	208 GTS Turbo	(PF/Scaglietti)	75441	L	65-85.000 EUR		NS		02-07-16	Lyon	335	Agu
	Red with black interior; just over 50,000 kms covered. Recently serviced.											
1989	Mondial T	(PF/Scaglietti)	80187	L	25-30.000 EUR	17.224	26.074	24.000	08-11-15	Lyon	249	Ose
	Red; less than 28,000 kms on the odometer.											
1987	Mondial 4V	(PF/Scaglietti)	72899	L	20-25.000 GBP	25.760	38.867	35.526	09-12-15	Chateau Impney	22	H&H
	Light metallic grey; recently serviced.											
1983	Mondial 4V	(PF/Scaglietti)	48643	L	35-45.000 EUR	25.311*	36.735*	33.600*	03-02-16	Paris	128	RMS F287
	Red with leather and cloth interior; two owners. Just over 38,000 kms on the odometer. Recently serviced.											

F285: 1978 Ferrari 512 BB (Pininfarina)

F286: 1988 Ferrari 208 GTS Turbo (PF/Scaglietti)

CLASSIC CAR AUCTION 2015-2016 YEARBOOK

Year	Model (Bodybuilder)	Chassis no.	Steering	Estimate	Hammer price £	$	€	Date	Place	Lot	Auc. H.
1985	Mondial 4V (PF/Scaglietti)	45233	L	NA		NS		26-02-16	Coventry	716	SiC
	Grey with beige interior; 56,000 kms covered. Recently serviced.										
1988	Mondial 3.2 (PF/Scaglietti)	76134	R	NA	29.600	41.905	38.202	06-03-16	Birmingham	330	SiC
	Red with cream interior; last serviced in January 2015 at 37,109 miles (see H&H lots 70 28.7.04 $ 28,267 and 18 5.12.12 NS).										
1986	Mondial 3.2 (PF/Scaglietti)	60749	L	42-52.000 EUR		NS		12-03-16	Lyon	316	Agu
	White with red interior; major service in 2014.										
1982	Mondial 8 (PF/Scaglietti)	38123	L	24-28.000 GBP	24.295	35.364	31.353	18-05-16	Donington Park	66	H&H
	Red with black interior; 29,711 miles on the odometer.										
1983	Mondial 4V (PF/Scaglietti)	45193	L	30-40.000 EUR	27.161	36.077	32.400	02-07-16	Lyon	366	Agu
	Blue with cream interior; in good overall condition. Last serviced in April 2016.										
1982	Mondial 4V (PF/Scaglietti)	43179	R	21-26.000 GBP	20.833	27.431	24.735	28-07-16	Donington Park	73	H&H
	Red; recently serviced.										
1981	Mondial (PF/Scaglietti)	38275	L	NQ	16.880*	22.214*	19.989*	30-07-16	Silverstone	523	SiC
	Red; in working order, the car requires some restoration works.										
1984	Mondial cabriolet (PF/Scaglietti)	52753	L	NA		NS		23-01-16	Kissimmee	F80	Mec
	Red with black leather interior; 48,000 actual miles. Recently serviced.										
1989	Mondial T cabriolet (PF/Scaglietti)	81920	L	NA	23.443*	33.000*	29.040*	09-04-16	Palm Beach	86.1	B/J
	Red with tan interior; 26,000 miles on the odometer.										
1986	Mondial 3.2 cabriolet (PF/Scaglietti)	65495	L	NA	35.165*	49.500*	43.560*	09-04-16	Palm Beach	88	B/J
	Red with tan interior; 26,440 miles on the odometer. Last serviced at 20,071 miles.										
1986	Mondial cabriolet (PF/Scaglietti)	62933	L	50-75.000 USD	37.066	54.000	48.130	20-05-16	Indianapolis	T196	Mec F288
	Red with beige interior; believed to be 7,937 original miles.										
1985	Mondial 4V cabriolet (PF/Scaglietti)	56173	L	25-35.000 USD	34.109*	46.750*	42.243*	25-06-16	Santa Monica	1067	AA
	Black with tan interior; approximately 11,000 miles on the odometer.										
1984	Mondial cabriolet (PF/Scaglietti)	85458	R	45-55.000 GBP	40.000	53.128	47.712	02-07-16	Woodstock	193	Coy
	Red; 20,600 miles covered. Cambelt service at 20,129 miles.										
1989	Mondial cabriolet (PF/Scaglietti)	82384	L	NA	32.340	42.000	37.939	09-07-16	Denver	S39	Mec
	Blue with camel interior; 22,707 actual miles.										
1985	GTO (PF/Scaglietti)	55669	L	2.000-2.400.000 USD		NS		29-01-16	Scottsdale	19	G&Co
	Red with black interior; sold new to the USA, the car is described as in very good overall condition. Last major service (including new timing belts) in 2013. Certified by Ferrari Classiche (see lot 7 Gooding 17.8.13 $ 1,512,500).										
1985	GTO (PF/Scaglietti)	58335	L	2.400-2.800.000 USD		NS		29-01-16	Phoenix	240	RMS
	Red with black leather interior; fitted with factory air conditioning and power windows. Sold new to the USA, the car has covered 14,975 kms. Complete service in 2011. Certified by Ferrari Classiche.										
1984	GTO (PF/Scaglietti)	55237	L	2.300-2.600.000 USD	1.808.466	2.585.000	2.330.895	12-03-16	Amelia Island	148	RMS F289
	Red with black central interior with red inserts; sold new to Japanese collector Yoshiho Matsuda who retianed it until 2010. Some years later it was imported into the USA. 10,911 kms on the odometer (see lot 158 RM 15.1.15 $ 2,750,000).										
1985	GTO (PF/Scaglietti)	55171	L	1.300-1.700.000 EUR	1.431.033	2.061.932	1.817.000	13-05-16	Monaco	110	Bon
	Red with black and red interior; described as in very good overall condition. One owner, 49,285 kms covered, recommissioned in 2015, certified by Ferrari Classiche.										
1985	GTO (PF/Scaglietti)	56651	L	1.800-2.200.000 USD	1.613.568	2.112.000	1.864.685	19-08-16	Carmel	77	Bon
	Red with red and black interior; one owner and 7,500 kms covered. In original condition. Major service carried out a few months ago.										
1985	GTO (PF/Scaglietti)	57485	L	2.000-3.000.000 USD		NS		20-08-16	Monterey	S105.1	Mec
	Red with black interior; sold new to the USA. In original condition. 11,980 kms covered.										
1985	GTO (PF/Scaglietti)	57481	L	2.250-2.750.000 USD	1.848.880	2.420.000	2.136.618	21-08-16	Pebble Beach	119	G&Co
	Red with black and red interior; sold new to collector Robert Rubin, the car was purchased in 2002 by the current, third owner. Described as in very good original condition, it has covered 12,775 kms. Last serviced in July 2016.										
1988	Testarossa (Pininfarina)	76899	L	NA	74.054	112.750	101.238	05-09-15	Auburn	4140	AA
	Black with tan leather interior; 19,516 actual miles. 1,025 miles covered since an engine-out service.										
1991	Testarossa (Pininfarina)	90218	L	160-190.000 GBP	151.200*	230.761*	207.038*	07-09-15	London	114	RMS
	Finished in yellow with black interior, the car was delivered new to Denmark where it remained at the dealership for 17 years before to be delivered to his first and sole owner, who had it repainted in the present red livery. 400 kms covered.										

F287: 1983 Ferrari Mondial 4V (PF/Scaglietti)

F288: 1986 Ferrari Mondial cabriolet (PF/Scaglietti)

Year	Model	(Bodybuilder)	Chassis No.	Steering	Estimate	Hammer Price £	$	€	Date	Place	Lot	Auc. H.
1985	Testarossa	(Pininfarina)	58959	L	120-160.000 GBP	109.200*	166.661*	149.528*	07-09-15	London	176	RMS

Red with cream interior; just under 73,000 kms covered. Sold to its second owner in 2011.

| 1988 | Testarossa | (Pininfarina) | 78344 | L | 75-85.000 GBP | | NS | | 12-09-15 | Goodwood | 306 | Bon |

Red with tan interior; 71,400 kms on the odometer. Last serviced in January 2015.

| 1985 | Testarossa | (Pininfarina) | 58267 | L | 100-120.000 GBP | 102.300 | 157.777 | 140.028 | 12-09-15 | Goodwood | 367 | Bon |

Red with tan leather interior; sold new to the USA to actor Tom Selleck. Imported into Finland in 2009. Circa 18,000 miles covered. Last serviced in June 2015.

| 1988 | Testarossa | (Pininfarina) | 74641 | L | NA | 92.045 | 144.000 | 126.115 | 19-09-15 | Dallas | S59 | Mec |

Yellow with black interior; believed to be 7,878 original miles. Recently serviced (see lot 2090 Auctions America 18.7.15 NS).

| 1986 | Testarossa | (Pininfarina) | 62173 | L | 110-130.000 EUR | 80.921 | 124.130 | 109.250 | 09-10-15 | Zoute | 11 | Bon |

Red with cream interior; sold new to the USA, the car was reimported into Europe in recent years and is described as in very good overall condition (see Bonhams lots 224 13.9.14 $ 102,222 and 118 24.5.15 NS).

| 1990 | Testarossa | (Pininfarina) | 89974 | L | NA | 67.200 | 103.360 | 90.586 | 14-10-15 | Duxford | 96 | H&H |

Red with black interior; recently imported from Japan. 70,445 kms covered. EU taxes to be paid.

| 1992 | Testarossa | (Pininfarina) | 91915 | L | 90-140.000 EUR | 80.916 | 124.960 | 110.000 | 17-10-15 | Salzburg | 336 | Dor |

Red with black interior; 46,317 kms on the odometer. Recently serviced.

| 1991 | Testarossa | (Pininfarina) | 87938 | L | 120-140.000 EUR | 95.883 | 151.834 | 133.504 | 01-11-15 | Paris | 145 | Art |

Red; recently imported from Japan. Three owners and 22,500 kms covered.

| 1991 | Testarossa | (Pininfarina) | 88493 | L | 90-110.000 EUR | 77.506 | 117.331 | 108.000 | 07-11-15 | Lyon | 264 | Agu |

Red with black leather interior; described as in very good overall condition. Last serviced in January 2015.

| 1986 | Testarossa | (Pininfarina) | 63801 | L | 155-175.000 EUR | | NS | | 07-11-15 | Lyon | 271 | Agu |

Red with black interior; body repainted. Recently serviced.

| 1991 | Testarossa | (Pininfarina) | 89819 | L | NA | | NS | | 13-11-15 | Anaheim | S67.1 | Mec |

Silver with blue interior; believed to be 15,334 original miles.

| 1989 | Testarossa | (Pininfarina) | 82010 | L | 75-85.000 GBP | 75.375 | 114.751 | 106.610 | 14-11-15 | Birmingham | 141 | SiC |

Red; 47,000 kms on the odometer. Originally white, the body was repainted in recent years.

| 1987 | Testarossa | (Pininfarina) | 68791 | L | 74-86.000 GBP | 84.000 | 126.428 | 119.498 | 28-11-15 | Weybridge | 272 | His |

Black with light tan interior; 51,430 kms on the odometer. Last serviced in July 2015.

| 1990 | Testarossa | (Pininfarina) | 87232 | L | 60-70.000 GBP | 65.500 | 98.584 | 93.180 | 28-11-15 | Weybridge | 300 | His |

Red with tan leather interior; 61,017 miles covered. Engine-out service in August 2012 at 60,686 miles in the USA.

| 1991 | Testarossa | (Pininfarina) | 87139 | L | 400-500.000 USD | 210.891* | 319.000* | 291.502* | 10-12-15 | New York | 204 | RMS F290 |

Black with black leather interior; sold new to Canada, the car has had just one owner and has covered 296 kms. Maintained at regular intervals; last serviced in October 2014.

| 1986 | Testarossa | (Pininfarina) | 63631 | L | Refer Dpt. | | NS | | 23-01-16 | Kissimmee | S180 | Mec |

White with tan interior; 16,124 actual miles. Used in the TV series "Miami Vice" and subsequently stored from 1990 to 2015. Recently serviced. Certified by Ferrari Classiche (see lot S56 Mecum 15.8.15 NS).

| 1986 | Testarossa | (Pininfarina) | 60807 | L | NA | 87.263 | 125.000 | 115.650 | 23-01-16 | Kissimmee | T87.1 | Mec |

Red with black interior; 29,075 miles.

| 1990 | Testarossa | (Pininfarina) | 85998 | L | NA | | NS | | 23-01-16 | Kissimmee | W147.1 | Mec |

Yellow with black interior; believed to be 23,634 miles. Recently serviced.

| 1989 | Testarossa | (Pininfarina) | 83189 | L | 90-130.000 USD | 90.743* | 129.800* | 119.040* | 28-01-16 | Scottsdale | 23 | Bon |

Red; sold new to Switzerland and imported into Canada in 2006. Less than 43,000 kms covered. Last serviced in Novembre 2015.

| 1991 | Testarossa | (Pininfarina) | 87482 | L | 200-250.000 USD | 107.661* | 154.000* | 141.233* | 28-01-16 | Phoenix | 110 | RMS |

Silver with red leather interior with black insert; ex-personal car of the Ferrari Canada importer Luigi Della Grotta, who never registered it and retained it until his passing away in 2012. Bought by the current owner from the Della Grotta estate, the car was road registered in 2015 and has covered 4,900 miles since new. Last serviced in March 2015.

| 1985 | Testarossa | (Pininfarina) | 58071 | L | 175-225.000 USD | 123.147* | 176.000* | 161.163* | 29-01-16 | Scottsdale | 8 | G&Co |

Metallic plum; less than 4,400 covered since new. Recent engine-out service.

| 1988 | Testarossa | (Pininfarina) | 76440 | L | NA | 86.588 | 123.750 | 113.318 | 30-01-16 | Scottsdale | 5078 | R&S |

White with tan interior; sold new to the USA. Major service in June 2015 at 22,846 miles.

| 1988 | Testarossa | (Pininfarina) | 73399 | L | NA | 126.996 | 181.500 | 166.200 | 30-01-16 | Scottsdale | 5392 | R&S |

Red with cream leather interior; described as in very good overall condition, the car has covered 4,621 miles.

F289: 1984 Ferrari GTO (PF/Scaglietti)

F290: 1991 Ferrari Testarossa (Pininfarina)

Year	Model	(Bodybuilder)	Chassis No.	Steering	Estimate	Hammer Price £	Hammer Price $	Hammer Price €	Sale Date	Sale Place	Lot	Auc. H.
1989	Testarossa	(Pininfarina)	80637	L	200-220.000 EUR	143.428	208.164	190.400	03-02-16	Paris	105	RMS
Red with black interior; 960 kms covered.												
1989	Testarossa	(Pininfarina)	82548	L	120-160.000 EUR	94.916	137.756	126.000	03-02-16	Paris	155	RMS
Black with black interior; acquired new by the current owner's company and then transferred into his name in 2001.												
1987	Testarossa	(Pininfarina)	68793	L	135-175.000 EUR		NS		04-02-16	Paris	309	Bon
Red with black interior; restored in Italy in 2012. Approximately 55,000 kms covered since new. Certified by Ferrari Classiche.												
1985	Testarossa	(Pininfarina)	57535	L	135-185.000 EUR	113.015	167.530	149.500	04-02-16	Paris	361	Bon
Red with tan leather interior; sold new to the USA and recently reimported into Europe. Last serviced in April 2014.												
1990	Testarossa	(Pininfarina)	84596	L	130-160.000 EUR		NS		04-02-16	Paris	417	Bon
Red with cream leather interior; 22,000 miles covered. Recently serviced.												
1986	Testarossa	(Pininfarina)	65133	L	130-170.000 EUR	119.280	173.586	154.960	05-02-16	Paris	112	Art
Silver with black interior; described as in very good overall condition. Two owners.												
1986	Testarossa Spider	(Pininfarina)	62897	L	680-900.000 EUR	779.049	1.133.732	1.012.080	05-02-16	Paris	116	Art
Silver with blue leather interior; one-off built at the factory for Avv. Giovanni Agnelli. Since 1991 in the present, second ownership. 23,000 kms covered. Fitted with a Valeo automatic transmission system.												F291
1989	Testarossa	(Pininfarina)	79068	L	100-150.000 EUR	82.579	120.175	107.280	05-02-16	Paris	167	Art
White with red leather interior; 51,177 kms on the odometer. Last serviced in November 2015.												
1989	Testarossa	(Pininfarina)	81583	L	NA		NS		26-02-16	Coventry	439	SiC
Red with biscuit interior; the present engine, fitted to the car in 2001, has covered 34,000 kms.												
1991	Testarossa	(Pininfarina)	91799	L	NA		NS		26-02-16	Coventry	713	SiC
Red with tan interior; 4,608 kms covered. Recently serviced.												
1988	Testarossa	(Pininfarina)	78092	L	75-90.000 GBP	93.640	133.053	120.655	08-03-16	London	125	Coy
Red with black interior; 66,000 kms covered.												
1986	Testarossa	(Pininfarina)	65247	L	180-240.000 USD	108.832*	154.000*	141.834*	10-03-16	Amelia Island	130	Bon
Silver with tan interior; in very good, largely original condition. Recently serviced; gearbox rebuilt.												
1991	Testarossa	(Pininfarina)	86474	L	175-225.000 USD	119.282*	170.500*	153.740*	11-03-16	Amelia Island	28	G&Co
Red with beige leather interior; in highly original condition. Two owners and less than 8,500 miles covered.												
1991	Testarossa	(Pininfarina)	90524	L	110-120.000 EUR	88.458	126.426	114.000	12-03-16	Lyon	322	Agu
Red with black interior; 55,000 kms covered. Timing belts replaced in 2015.												
1987	Testarossa	(Pininfarina)	78890	R	74-86.000 GBP	108.640	155.268	140.004	12-03-16	Brooklands	225	His
Red with tan leather interior; 35,407 miles covered. Last serviced in January 2016.												
1986	Testarossa	(Pininfarina)	61421	L	130-170.000 USD	126.977*	181.500*	163.659*	12-03-16	Amelia Island	152	RMS
Red; in largely original condition. 40,000 kms on the odometer.												
1990	Testarossa	(Pininfarina)	84451	L	95-125.000 GBP	102.300	148.202	131.394	20-03-16	Goodwood	69	Bon
Blue with cream leather interior; 22,508 kms covered. Recently serviced.												
1987	Testarossa	(Pininfarina)	65571	L	120-150.000 EUR		NS		20-03-16	Fontainebleau	350	Ose
Red with beige leather interior; major service in 2013.												
1991	Testarossa	(Pininfarina)	88381	L	75-90.000 USD	60.726	86.900	76.011	02-04-16	Ft.Lauderdale	753	AA
Black with black leather interior.												
1990	Testarossa	(Pininfarina)	83434	L	NA	61.734*	86.900*	76.472*	09-04-16	Palm Beach	384	B/J
Red with tan interior; 54,500 actual miles. Differential and transmission rebuilt.												
1987	Testarossa	(Pininfarina)	70385	L	NA	134.408	189.200	166.496	09-04-16	Palm Beach	419	B/J
Red with tan interior; 37,980 actual miles. Major service in October 2014.												
1992	Testarossa	(Pininfarina)	85920	L	115-120.000 EUR		NS		09-04-16	Essen	119	Coy
Black with tan leather interior; described as in very good overall condition. 73,000 kms covered.												
1989	Testarossa	(Pininfarina)	79616	L	90-110.000 EUR	78.285	110.188	96.971	09-04-16	Essen	171	Coy
Red with black leather interior; two owners and 31,000 kms covered. Recently serviced.												
1989	Testarossa	(Pininfarina)	79507	L	160-180.000 USD		NS		07-05-16	Auburn	839	AA
Red with tan leather interior; 16,534 original miles. Major service less than 2,000 miles ago (see lot S152 Mecum 15.8.15 $ 122,500).												
1987	Testarossa	(Pininfarina)	72207	L	110-130.000 EUR		NS		13-05-16	Monaco	142	Bon
Silver with original red leather interior; body repainted. Some 30,000 miles covered. Last serviced in 2015.												
1990	Testarossa	(Pininfarina)	83643	L	85-100.000 USD		NS		20-05-16	Indianapolis	F170	Mec
Red with original black leather interior.												
1987	Testarossa	(Pininfarina)	70623	R	100-120.000 GBP	120.375	175.362	156.307	20-05-16	Silverstone	307	SiC
Red; 12,425 miles. Extensive work and detailing carried out in 2015.												
1991	Testarossa	(Pininfarina)	89839	L	110-120.000 EUR		NS		28-05-16	Aarhus	147	SiC
Red; 52,200 kms covered. Last serviced in January 2016.												
1986	Testarossa	(Pininfarina)	64581	L	120-130.000 EUR		NS		28-05-16	Aarhus	222	SiC
Red; described as in very good overall condition. Body repainted in 2015.												
1991	Testarossa	(Pininfarina)	91089	L	110-120.000 EUR		NS		28-05-16	Aarhus	231	SiC
Red; 74,500 kms on the odometer. Engine recently rebuilt.												
1986	Testarossa	(Pininfarina)	63017	L	170-200.000 USD	120.409	173.800	155.812	05-06-16	Greenwhich	43	Bon
Red with tan interior; less than 3,800 miles covered. Recent engine-out service.												
1989	Testarossa	(Pininfarina)	78923	L	95-110.000 GBP		NS		11-06-16	Brooklands	277	His
Black with black interior; recently recommissioned in the UK.												

Year	Model (Bodybuilder)	Chassis No.	Steering	Estimate	Hammer Price £	Hammer Price $	Hammer Price €	Date	Place	Lot	Auc. H.
1991	Testarossa (Pininfarina) *See lot 713 Silverstone Auctions 26.2.16.*	91799	L	120-140.000 GBP	159.040	229.065	202.649	11-06-16	Brooklands	312	His
1989	Testarossa (Pininfarina) *Red with tan interior; less than 12,000 miles covered. Recent engine-out service.*	77482	L	NA	112.634	162.250	143.526	11-06-16	Newport Beach	6091	R&S
1987	Testarossa (Pininfarina) *See lot 350 Osenat 20.3.16 NS.*	65571	L	90-120.000 EUR		NS		19-06-16	Fontainebleau	339	Ose
1990	Testarossa (Pininfarina) *See lot W1471 Mecum 23.1.16.*	85998	L	NA		NS		24-06-16	Uncasville	638.1	B/J
1988	Testarossa (Pininfarina) *Red with tan interior; 21,000 actual miles. Recently serviced. 512 TR front bumper.*	76119	L	NA	104.333*	143.000*	129.215*	24-06-16	Uncasville	649	B/J
1989	Testarossa (Pininfarina) *Silver with red interior; 23,584 original miles.*	79168	L	NA	74.638*	102.300*	92.438*	24-06-16	Uncasville	655	B/J
1986	Testarossa (Pininfarina) *Red with tan interior; two owners. Recent engine-out service.*	65813	L	180-220.000 USD		NS		25-06-16	Santa Monica	1051	AA
1991	Testarossa (Pininfarina) *See lot S67.1 Mecum 13.11.15.*	89819	L	140-160.000 USD		NS		25-06-16	Santa Monica	1072	AA
1989	Testarossa (Pininfarina) *Red with beige interior; three owners and 18,300 kms covered.*	79184	L	100-120.000 EUR	93.554	124.267	111.600	02-07-16	Lyon	340	Agu
1990	Testarossa (Pininfarina) *Red with black interior; the car requires servicing prior to use.*	83920	L	90-110.000 EUR		NS		02-07-16	Lyon	348	Agu
1989	Testarossa (Pininfarina) *Red with black interior; 12,000 miles on the odometer.*	81675	L	60-70.000 GBP	69.080	91.752	82.399	02-07-16	Woodstock	131	Coy
1988	Testarossa (Pininfarina) *See lot 125 Coys 8.3.16.*	78092	L	70-90.000 GBP	79.900	106.123	95.305	02-07-16	Woodstock	225	Coy
1987	Testarossa (spider/conversion) *Yellow with black interior; conversion carried out by Lorenz & Rankl at unspecified date. 20,630 kms covered since new.*	81586	L	170-230.000 EUR		NS		09-07-16	Le Mans	200	Art
1990	Testarossa (Pininfarina) *Red with tan interior; since 1999 in the current ownership. 38,315 miles covered; engine-out service in 2013; body repainted in 2016.*	84383	R	120-140.000 GBP	106.400	138.171	124.818	10-07-16	Chateau Impney	49	H&H
1986	Testarossa (Pininfarina) *Red with beige leather interior; bought in 2011 by the present, second owner. Less than 20,000 miles covered. Engine out service in February 2013. Certified by Ferrari Classiche.*	66067	L	150-175.000 USD	91.176	120.000	107.976	30-07-16	Plymouth	124	RMS
1987	Testarossa (Pininfarina) *Red with black interior; last serviced in April 2016 (see lots 28 Artcurial 13.7.09 $71,755, 97 Artcurial 14.2.10 NS, 46 Chevau-Légerè 3.2.11 NS, and 111A Silverstone Auctions 17.11.12 NS).*	68157	L	85-105.000 GBP		NS		30-07-16	Silverstone	502	SiC
1988	Testarossa (Pininfarina) *Red with biscuit leather interior; sold new to the USA. Last serviced in May-June 2016 at 4,390 miles.*	76213	L	140-180.000 USD	99.167*	129.800*	114.600*	19-08-16	Carmel	58	Bon
1990	Testarossa (Pininfarina) *Yellow with black interior; 18,237 kms on the odometer.*	87014	L	175-200.000 USD		NS		19-08-16	Monterey	F111	Mec
1986	Testarossa (Pininfarina) *Red with ivory leather interior; two owners and 15,600 miles covered. Last serviced in July 2015.*	65189	L	160-180.000 USD	101.230	132.500	116.984	19-08-16	Monterey	F56	Mec
1990	Testarossa (Pininfarina) *Red with red and tan interior; approximately 4,500 miles covered. Major service in July 2015.*	84044	L	225-275.000 USD	126.060*	165.000*	145.679*	20-08-16	Pebble Beach	17	G&Co
1989	Testarossa (Pininfarina) *Red with black leather interior; sold new to Japan and later imported into the UK. 15,811 kms covered.*	78749	L	73-83.000 GBP		NS		20-08-16	Brooklands	350	His
1985	Testarossa (Pininfarina) *Red with tan interior; 21,118 miles covered. Recently serviced.*	57779	L	155-175.000 USD		NS		20-08-16	Monterey	S155	Mec
1988	Testarossa (Pininfarina) *Black with black leather interior; 9,536 miles covered.*	78728	L	180-225.000 USD		NS		20-08-16	Monterey	S54	Mec
1987	Testarossa (Pininfarina) *Black with tan leather interior; 22,968 miles covered. Recently serviced.*	71287	L	160-185.000 USD	91.680	120.000	105.948	20-08-16	Monterey	S67	Mec

F291: 1986 Ferrari Testarossa Spider (Pininfarina)

F292: 1989 Ferrari 328 GTB (PF/Scaglietti)

Year	Model (Bodybuilder)	Chassis no.	Steering	Estimate	Hammer Price £	Hammer Price $	Hammer Price €	Sale Date	Sale Place	Lot	Auc. H.
1991	Testarossa (Pininfarina) *White; low mileage.*	89632	L	NQ		NS		20-08-16	Monterey	7020	R&S
1986	Testarossa (Pininfarina) *See lot 43 Bonhams 5.6.16.*	63017	L	NQ		NS		20-08-16	Monterey	7060	R&S
1989	328 GTB (PF/Scaglietti) *Red with cream leather interior; since 1996 in the current ownership, the car has covered 91,500 miles.*	81879	R	NA	68.320	105.083	92.095	14-10-15	Duxford	108	H&H F292
1988	328 GTB (PF/Scaglietti) *Red with black leather interior; several mechanical works carried out in 2013 and 2014. 48,000 kms covered.*	78163	L	95-105.000 EUR	73.200	110.813	102.000	07-11-15	Lyon	275	Agu
1986	328 GTB (PF/Scaglietti) *Red with black interior; in good overall condition. Recently imported into the UK from Japan.*	63397	L	49-59.000 GBP		NS		09-12-15	Chateau Impney	92	H&H
1989	328 GTB (PF/Scaglietti) *Red with black leather interior; sold new to Sweden and inported into the USA in 2015. Last serviced in September 2015.*	80998	L	140-180.000 USD	115.451*	165.000*	151.091*	29-01-16	Scottsdale	32	G&Co
1986	328 GTB (PF/Scaglietti) *Prepared for historic racing to Group 4 specification. Raced at numerous events of the Ferrari Challenge and Pirelli Ferrari Formula Classic. Engine rebuilt in January 2016.*	62161	L	NA	58.500	81.760	74.289	26-02-16	Coventry	109	SiC
1987	328 GTB (PF/Scaglietti) *Red with beige leather interior; 39,570 kms covered. Last serviced in late 2015.*	73997	L	75-95.000 EUR	76.207	98.966	89.400	09-07-16	Le Mans	207	Art
1989	328 GTB (PF/Scaglietti) *Red with tan leather interior; 22,300 recorded miles.*	82566	L	125-150.000 USD	88.242*	115.500*	101.975*	20-08-16	Pebble Beach	1	G&Co
1989	328 GTS (PF/Scaglietti) *Red with tan interior; little used in the last years, the car has been recently recommissioned. Formerly in the Mohamed Al-Fayed's collection (see lots 90 Christie's 7.6.04 $ 64,789 and 806 Silverstone Auctions 25.7.15 NS).*	79938	R	110-130.000 GBP	137.250	208.991	187.634	04-09-15	Woodstock	239	SiC
1987	328 GTS (PF/Scaglietti) *Red with tan interior.*	70511	L	NA	44.071	67.100	60.249	05-09-15	Auburn	5071	AA
1989	328 GTS (PF/Scaglietti) *Black with beige leather interior; just one owner and 556 miles covered. Stored fo 25 years, the car has been recently recommissioned.*	81188	R	170-200.000 GBP	190.400	290.588	260.715	07-09-15	London	154	RMS F293
1989	328 GTS (PF/Scaglietti) *Red with black interior; 15,518 miles covered. Until 1991 owned by Nigel Mansell. From the Chris Evans collection.*	82947	R	100-130.000 GBP	130.300	200.962	178.355	12-09-15	Goodwood	312	Bon
1987	328 GTS (PF/Scaglietti) *Red with tan leather interior; less than 26,000 miles covered.*	69769	L	95-115.000 USD		NS		05-10-15	Philadelphia	245	Bon
1989	328 GTS (PF/Scaglietti) *Red with black interior; in very good overall condition.*	81294	L	75-95.000 EUR	64.207	101.675	89.400	01-11-15	Paris	116	Art
1986	328 GTS (PF/Scaglietti) *Red with tan interior; last serviced in January 2015.*	61551	L	NA		NS		13-11-15	Anaheim	F168.1	Mec
1986	328 GTS (PF/Scaglietti) *Red with tan interior; recently imported into the UK from the USA. Last cambelt service in April 2013 at 43,191 miles.*	61285	L	58-64.000 GBP	54.320	81.757	77.276	28-11-15	Weybridge	267	His
1986	328 GTS (PF/Scaglietti) *Red; 47,000 miles covered. European taxes to be paid.*	60157	L	60-70.000 GBP	57.120	86.051	81.179	01-12-15	London	351	Coy
1988	328 GTS/196SP Evocation *Red with blue cloth interior; car commissioned by guitarist Chris Rea and based on a 328 GTS chassis and engine. Aluminium body.*	78231	R	65-75.000 GBP		NS		16-01-16	Birmingham	341	Coy
1987	328 GTS (PF/Scaglietti) *See lot 245 Bonhams 5.10.15.*	69769	L	85-110.000 USD	44.603*	63.800*	58.511*	28-01-16	Scottsdale	105	Bon
1988	328 GTS (PF/Scaglietti) *Red with brown leather interior; 10,250 miles since new. Recently serviced.*	78733	L	120-160.000 USD	69.211*	99.000*	90.793*	28-01-16	Phoenix	141	RMS
1988	328 GTS (PF/Scaglietti) *Red with ivory leather interior; just over 15,000 miles covered. From the Tony Shooshani Collection.*	74921	L	125-150.000 USD	76.967*	110.000*	100.727*	30-01-16	Scottsdale	123	G&Co
1988	328 GTS (PF/Scaglietti) *Red with black interior; three owners and 6,000 kms covered. Recently serviced. Certified by Ferrari Classiche.*	75926	L	135-165.000 EUR	105.462	153.062	140.000	03-02-16	Paris	134	RMS
1987	328 GTS (PF/Scaglietti) *White with black leather interior; 25,000 kms covered. Recently serviced. Swiss papers.*	72001	L	75-85.000 EUR	69.733*	101.481*	90.592*	05-02-16	Paris	172	Art
1988	328 GTS (PF/Scaglietti) *White with red interior; last serviced in March 2015 at 51,119 kms.*	75893	L	NA		NS		26-02-16	Coventry	413	SiC
1986	328 GTS (PF/Scaglietti) *Red with tan interior; 2,918 miles covered. Last serviced in January 2016.*	61039	L	175-225.000 USD	134.673*	192.500*	173.577*	11-03-16	Amelia Island	70	G&Co
1988	328 GTS (PF/Scaglietti) *Red with black leather and alcantara interior; imported into the UK from Japan in 2015. 48,659 kms on the odometer. Recently serviced.*	69301	L	58-65.000 GBP	58.240	83.237	75.054	12-03-16	Brooklands	247	His
1988	328 GTS (PF/Scaglietti) *Red with tan interior; just over 13,000 miles covered. Last serviced in March 2014. Certified by Ferrari Classiche.*	78015	L	120-160.000 USD	126.977*	181.500*	163.659*	12-03-16	Amelia Island	109	RMS
1987	328 GTS (PF/Scaglietti) *Red; mechanicals overhauled in 2015.*	72953	L	85-95.000 EUR	95.295	138.055	122.400	20-03-16	Fontainebleau	356	Ose
1986	328 GTS (PF/Scaglietti) *Red with tan interior; in good overall condition. 46,000 original kms. Recently serviced.*	64895	L	75-85.000 USD	49.964	71.500	62.541	02-04-16	Ft.Lauderdale	432	AA
1986	328 GTS (PF/Scaglietti) *Red with tan leather interior; described as in good original condition.*	62129	L	60-75.000 USD	45.352	64.900	56.768	02-04-16	Ft.Lauderdale	563	AA

Year	Model	(Bodybuilder)	Chassis no.	Steering	Estimate	Hammer price £	Hammer price $	Hammer price €	Date	Place	Lot	Auc. H.
1986	328 GTS	(PF/Scaglietti)	62773	L	60-70.000 EUR	58.411	82.215	72.353	09-04-16	Essen	118	Coy
	Silver with black interior; in good overall condition. Last serviced in 2015.											
1989	328 GTS	(PF/Scaglietti)	82726	L	NA		NS		16-04-16	Houston	S168	Mec
	Red with tan interior; believed to be 15,256 actual miles.											
1988	328 GTS	(PF/Scaglietti)	78405	L	NA	50.400	71.467	63.716	20-04-16	Duxford	52	H&H
	Red with tan interior; recently imported into the UK. 37,780 miles on the odometer. Recently serviced.											
1986	328 GTS	(PF/Scaglietti)	60333	L	45-65.000 USD	41.184	60.000	53.478	20-05-16	Indianapolis	T218.1	Mec
	Red with cream interior; 29,000 miles covered. Last serviced at 28,000 miles.											
1987	328 GTS	(PF/Scaglietti)	72953	L	80-100.000 EUR		NS		19-06-16	Fontainebleau	338	Ose
	See lot 356 Osenat 20.3.16.											
1986	328 GTS	(PF/Scaglietti)	64263	L	NA	65.810*	90.200*	81.505*	24-06-16	Uncasville	647	B/J
	Red with beige interior; in very good overall condition.											
1988	328 GTS	(PF/Scaglietti)	78740	L	NA	44.141	60.500	54.668	24-06-16	Uncasville	758	B/J
	Red with tan interior; last serviced in August 2015.											
1989	328 GTS	(PF/Scaglietti)	82624	R	120-160.000 GBP	119.100	163.215	147.482	24-06-16	Goodwood	230	Bon
	Red; 5,550 miles covered. Recently serviced.											
1986	328 GTS	(PF/Scaglietti)	60087	L	120-140.000 USD		NS		25-06-16	Santa Monica	2082	AA
	Red with tan leather interior; one owner.											
1988	328 GTS	(PF/Scaglietti)	75109	L	120-160.000 USD		NS		25-06-16	Santa Monica	2095	AA
	Red with tan leather interior; engine-out service one year ago.											
1986	328 GTS	(PF/Scaglietti)	62665	L	85-105.000 EUR	76.453	101.551	91.200	02-07-16	Lyon	346	Agu
	Red with black interior; 24,800 kms on the odometer. Last serviced in January 2015.											
1986	328 GTS	(PF/Scaglietti)	78314	L	50-60.000 GBP	69.000	91.646	82.303	02-07-16	Woodstock	133	Coy
	Red with black leather interior; in good overall condition.											
1988	328 GTS	(PF/Scaglietti)	77152	L	100-140.000 USD	75.980	100.000	89.980	30-07-16	Plymouth	111	RMS
	Red with tan interior; sold new to Canada, original condition, two owners, 17,171 actual kms. Last serviced in May 2016.											
1985	328 GTS	(PF/Scaglietti)	66595	L	45-55.000 GBP	55.130	72.551	65.285	30-07-16	Silverstone	552	SiC
	Red; recently serviced.											
1989	328 GTS	(PF/Scaglietti)	80262	L	220-250.000 USD	145.160	190.000	167.751	19-08-16	Monterey	F103	Mec
	Red with beige interior; one owner and 2,135 miles covered. Last serviced in February 2016.											
1988	328 GTS	(PF/Scaglietti)	78015	L	120-160.000 USD	75.636*	99.000*	87.407*	19-08-16	Monterey	103	RMS
	See lot 109 RM/Sotheby's 12.3.16.											
1988	328 GTS	(PF/Scaglietti)	78555	L	125-145.000 USD		NS		20-08-16	Monterey	S179	Mec
	Red with tan interior; 14,950 miles covered.											
1987	328 GTS	(PF/Scaglietti)	69387	L	NQ	48.323	63.250	55.843	20-08-16	Monterey	7158	R&S
	Black with parchment interior; 35,000 miles covered.											
1989	328 GTS	(PF/Scaglietti)	81887	L	180-220.000 USD	126.060*	165.000*	145.679*	21-08-16	Pebble Beach	136	G&Co
	Red; described as in very good original condition. About 18,000 recorded miles. Recently serviced.											
1986	412 (Pininfarina)		63377	L	NA	45.145	71.500	62.863	31-10-15	Hilton Head	187	AA
	Red with beige leather interior; recently serviced. Manual gearbox.											
1987	412 (Pininfarina)		71141	L	20-30.000 EUR	42.805*	67.783*	59.600*	01-11-15	Paris	105	Art
	Grey with black leather interior; one owner and 51,050 kms covered. Unused in the past rhree years, the car requires servicing prior to use. Automatic transmission.											
1989	412 GT (Pininfarina)		78593	R	30-36.000 GBP	42.560	64.057	60.546	28-11-15	Weybridge	265	His
	In good overall condition; engine replaced in 2012 (see lot 031 Bonhams 21.3.15 $ 51,243).											
1986	412 (Pininfarina)		61165	L	45-50.000 GBP		NS		16-01-16	Birmingham	353	Coy
	Blue with cream interior; sold new to Germany. Body repainted. Automatic transmission. 19.977 miles on the odometer.											
1989	412 (Pininfarina)		79592	L	70-100.000 EUR	68.816*	100.146*	89.400*	05-02-16	Paris	111	Art F294
	Grey with red leather interior; two owners and 52,500 kms covered. Manual gearbox.											
1987	412 (Pininfarina)		61165	L	NA	50.625	71.670	65.337	06-03-16	Birmingham	347	SiC
	See lot 353 Coys 16.1.16.											

F293: 1989 Ferrari 328 GTS (PF/Scaglietti)

F294: 1989 Ferrari 412 (Pininfarina)

Year	Model	(Bodybuilder)	Chassis no.	Steering	Estimate	Hammer price £	Hammer price $	Hammer price €	Date	Place	Lot	Auc. H.
1986	412	(Pininfarina)	66685	L	55-70.000 EUR	52.319	75.795	67.200	20-03-16	Fontainebleau	369	Ose
	*Red; in good driving order.*
1986	412	(Pininfarina)	75417	L	NA	28.208	40.000	35.448	16-04-16	Houston	S145.1	Mec
	*Blue with cream interior; automatic transmission.*
1986	412	(Pininfarina)	63025	L	65-85.000 EUR	50.805	65.977	59.600	09-07-16	Le Mans	206	Art
	*Silver with black leather interior; just over 38,400 kms covered. Engine rebuilt in 2008, gearbox rebuilt in 2011. Last serviced in December 2015.*
1992	F40	(Pininfarina)	93256	L	780-900.000 GBP	845.600	1.290.555	1.157.880	07-09-15	London	168	RMS
	*Red with red interior; just one owner and less than 4,000 kms covered. In September 2011 replaced clutch, cam belts, fuel tanks and tyres; last serviced in preparation for sale.*
1993	F40	(Pininfarina)	93779	L	720-780.000 GBP		NS		12-09-15	Goodwood	329	Bon
	*Red with red interior; 12,835 kms covered. Cam belts replaced in 2013, fuel cells in 2014. Certified by Ferrari Classiche.*
1991	F40	(Pininfarina)	91573	L	NA		NS		14-10-15	Duxford	127	H&H
	*Red with tan leather interior; sold new to the UK. Since 2002 in the current ownership. Regularly maintained; last serviced in March 2015 at 18,799 miles. Certified by Ferrari Classiche.*
1990	F40	(Pininfarina)	86554	L	1.300-1.600.000 USD	1.073.690	1.534.500	1.405.142	30-01-16	Scottsdale	120	G&Co F295
	*Red with red interior; sold new to the USA, the car is described as in very good original condition and has covered 3,720 miles. Certified by Ferrari Classiche. Since 2013 in the Tony Shooshani Collection.*
1989	F40	(Pininfarina)	80161	L	1.000-1.200.000 EUR	780.419	1.132.659	1.036.000	03-02-16	Paris	145	RMS
	*Red with red interior; delivered new to Stefano Casiraghi, the car was acquired in 1989 by the current owner. Just over 4,000 kms covered since new. Recently serviced.*
1990	F40	(Pininfarina)	87784	L	950-1.100.000 EUR		NS		04-02-16	Paris	336	Bon
	*Red with red interior; since 2013 in the current ownership. 14,704 miles covered. Major service in mid-2013. Certified by Ferrari Clasiche.*
1989	F40	(Pininfarina)	80727	L	Refer Dpt.		NS		05-06-16	Greenwhich	10	Bon
	*Red with red interior; less than 9,000 kms covered. Recently serviced. European-specification car (see lot S77 Mecum 15.8.15 $ 1,150,000).*
1990	F40	(Pininfarina)	84557	L	1.100-1.300.000 EUR		NS		09-07-16	Le Mans	209	Art
	*Red with red interior; in original condition. 6,769 kms covered. Two owners. Last serviced in March 2016. Certified by Ferrari Classiche.*
1989	F40	(Pininfarina)	79763	L	1.000-1.200.000 USD	882.420	1.155.000	1.019.750	19-08-16	Carmel	90	Bon
	*Red with red interior; sold new in Italy, the car was later imported into Germany and then into Japan. Less than 4,500 kms covered. Serviced in April 2013 at 3,500 kms.*
1990	F40	(Pininfarina)	85788	L	2.000-2.300.000 USD		NS		20-08-16	Monterey	S116.1	Mec
	*Red with red interior; 557 miles covered. Recently serviced. Certified by Ferrari Classiche.*
1990	F40	(Pininfarina)	87123	L	1.200-1.400.000 USD	966.460	1.265.000	1.116.869	20-08-16	Monterey	239	RMS
	*Red with red cloth interior; described as in very good original condition, the car has covered 2,400 kms. Recently serviced in Denmark.*
1989	348 tb	(Pininfarina)	79908	L	75-95.000 EUR		NS		26-09-15	Frankfurt	152	Coy
	*Red; one of the pre-production examples, the car was exhibited at the 1989 Geneva Motor Show. 8,000 kms covered (see lot 158 Coys 8.8.15 NS).*
1991	348 tb	(Pininfarina)	88630	L	65-75.000 EUR	48.226	73.006	67.200	07-11-15	Lyon	255	Agu
	*Red with black leather interior; since 1996 in the current, second ownership. 19,400 kms covered; last serviced in September 2015.*
1992	348 tb	(Pininfarina)	93985	L	25-30.000 GBP	31.860	47.997	45.279	01-12-15	London	340	Coy
	*Red with black interior; 48,000 miles covered. European taxes to be paid.*
1990	348 tb	(Pininfarina)	83911	L	35-45.000 GBP	33.600	50.696	46.338	09-12-15	Chateau Impney	53	H&H
	*Red; 28,800 kms covered.*
1990	348 tb	(Pininfarina)	82135	L	130-150.000 EUR		NS		28-05-16	Aarhus	130	SiC
	*Red with tan interior; 2,500 kms covered. Engine overhauled in 2015.*
1993	348 tb	(Pininfarina)	92832	R	NA	50.630	66.629	59.956	30-07-16	Silverstone	507	SiC
	*Red; last serviced in February 2016 at 61,056 miles.*
1990	348 tb	(Pininfarina)	82135	L	105-125.000 GBP		NS		30-07-16	Silverstone	519	SiC
	*See lot 130 Silverstone Auctions 28.5.16.*
1990	348 ts	(Pininfarina)	87190	L	NA	36.512	56.000	49.291	09-10-15	Chicago	S198	Mec
	*Red with tan interior; last serviced in April 2015.*
1991	348 ts	(Pininfarina)	89643	L	33-40.000 GBP	48.280	74.057	65.178	10-10-15	Ascot	143	Coy
	*Red with black interior; described as in good overall condition.*
1992	348 ts	(Pininfarina)	95429	L	NA		NS		14-10-15	Duxford	29	H&H
	*Red with black interior; 54,009 kms covered.*

F295: 1990 Ferrari F40 (Pininfarina)

F296: 1994 Ferrari 348 Serie Speciale (Pininfarina)

Year	Model (Bodybuilder)	Chassis no.	Steering	Estimate	Hammer price £	$	€	Date	Place	Lot	Auc. H.
1992	348 ts (Pininfarina)	90810	L	NA	23.648	36.000	33.448	13-11-15	Anaheim	F192	Mec
	Yellwo with black interior; upgraded exhaust.										
1990	348 ts (Pininfarina)	87190	L	NA	37.697	54.000	49.961	23-01-16	Kissimmee	S14	Mec
	See lot S198 Mecum 9.10.15.										
1990	348 ts (spider/conversion)	87079	L	NA	46.180*	66.000*	60.436*	29-01-16	Scottsdale	971	B/J
	Red with tan interior; conversion carried out by Straman in California. 2,998 actual miles.										
1996	348 ts (Pininfarina)	96717	L	NA	44.444	62.115	56.439	26-02-16	Coventry	721	SiC
	Red with black leather interior; last serviced in December 2015 at 23,633 kms.										
1993	348 ts (Pininfarina)	96142	L	60-70.000 EUR		NS		14-05-16	Monaco	119	Coy
	White with black interior; 41,000 kms on the odometer										
1991	348 ts (Pininfarina)	88054	L	NA	56.179*	77.000*	69.577*	24-06-16	Uncasville	704	B/J
	Red with cream leather interior; 12,500 actual miles. Recently serviced.										
1994	348 Serie Speciale (Pininfarina)	94421	R	50-60.000 GBP	70.000 P	99.463 P	90.195 P	08-03-16	London	129	Coy F296
	Red with cream interior; described as in very good overall condition.										
1994	348 Spider (Pininfarina)	98316	L	45-65.000 EUR	59.593	85.171	76.800	12-03-16	Lyon	331	Agu F297
	Dark metallic blue with dark blue leather interior; timing belts replaced in April 2014 (see lot 40 Artcurial 13.7.09 $ 65,928).										
1994	348 GTS (Pininfarina)	90913	L	60-85.000 EUR	50.495	76.634	68.724	26-09-15	Frankfurt	103	Coy
	Red with black leather interior; described as in very good original condition. 40,438 kms covered.										
1992	512 TR (Pininfarina)	91947	L	NA	188.564	295.000	258.361	19-09-15	Dallas	S222	Mec
	Red with tan interior; one owner. Believed to be 3,200 original miles.										
1994	512 TR (Pininfarina)	99273	L	140-170.000 EUR	86.871	131.841	118.232	26-09-15	Frankfurt	168	Coy
	Red; 24,000 kms covered.										
1993	512 TR (Pininfarina)	97042	L	190-240.000 EUR		NS		09-10-15	Zoute	33	Bon
	Red with black leather interior; described as in very good overall condition, the car has covered 44,000 kms.										
1996	512 TR (Pininfarina)	96804	L	NA	128.800	198.107	173.622	14-10-15	Duxford	116	H&H
	Silver with red leather interior; 32,078 kms covered. Sold new to Japan and recently imported into the UK; EU taxes to be paid.										
1992	512 TR (Pininfarina)	91449	L	NA		NS		13-11-15	Anaheim	S169.1	Mec
	Red with beige interior; recently serviced.										
1993	512 TR (Pininfarina)	97388	R	110-130.000 GBP	185.625	282.596	262.548	14-11-15	Birmingham	313	SiC
	Red with black leather interior; in very good overall condition. Last serviced in October 2015 at 21,656 miles.										
1992	512 TR (Pininfarina)	94054	L	100-115.000 GBP		NS		14-11-15	Birmingham	627	SiC
	Red with black leather interior; recently imported into the UK from Japan. 54,300 kms covered.										
1993	512 TR (Pininfarina)	96191	L	275-325.000 USD	169.182	242.000	221.938	28-01-16	Phoenix	165	RMS
	Red with white interior; 11,608 miles covered. Last serviced in 2013 at 11,473 miles.										
1992	512 TR (Pininfarina)	92146	L	NA	250.143*	357.500*	327.363*	29-01-16	Scottsdale	1396.1	B/J F298
	Yellow with black interior; one owner and 901 miles covered. Last serviced in May 2015 (see lots 44 Christie's 17.6.00 NS and S120 Mecum 15.8.15 NS).										
1992	512 TR (Pininfarina)	93141	L	200-250.000 EUR		NS		04-02-16	Paris	377	Bon
	Red with black interior; 15,920 kms covered. Engine recently overhauled in the UK.										
1993	512 TR (Pininfarina)	97363	L	140-180.000 EUR	99.974	148.199	132.250	04-02-16	Paris	415	Bon
	Red with black interior; 59,633 kms covered. Last serviced in 2015.										
1995	512 TR (Pininfarina)	96310	L	190-230.000 EUR		NS		05-02-16	Paris	119	Art
	Red with beige leather interior; less than 30,000 kms covered. Last serviced in September 2015.										
1992	512 TR (Pininfarina)	93206	L	150-170.000 GBP		NS		08-03-16	London	127	Coy
	Red with black leather interior; 8,000 kms covered.										
1992	512 TR (Pininfarina)	92300	L	140-160.000 EUR	111.737	159.696	144.000	12-03-16	Lyon	337	Agu
	Red with black interior; in very good overall condition, 65,000 kms covered.										
1994	512 TR (Pininfarina)	97656	L	110-140.000 GBP	113.500	164.427	145.779	20-03-16	Goodwood	52	Bon
	Red with beige leather interior; 18,966 kms covered. Last serviced in February 2016.										

F297: 1994 Ferrari 348 Spider (Pininfarina)

F298: 1992 Ferrari 512 TR (Pininfarina)

Year	Model	(Bodybuilder)	Chassis No.	Steering	Estimate	Hammer Price £	$	€	Date	Place	Lot	Auc. H.
1992	512 TR	(Pininfarina)	94660	L	155-160.000 EUR		NS		09-04-16	Essen	112	Coy
Red with black leather interior; described as in very good overall condition, the car has covered 70,000 kms (see Coys lots 102 18.1.14 NS and 134 9.5.14 NS).												
1994	512 TR	(Pininfarina)	99319	L	180-220.000 EUR		NS		13-05-16	Monaco	132	Bon
Blue with beige interior; circa 40,000 kms covered. Cam belt change circa 18 months ago. Swiss papers.												
1993	512 TR	(Pininfarina)	96993	L	135-165.000 EUR		NS		14-05-16	Monaco	270	RMS
Dark blue with red leather interior; for 10 years in the current ownership. 37,250 kms covered. Last serviced 150 kms ago.												
1992	512 TR	(Pininfarina)	94054	L	125-135.000 EUR		NS		28-05-16	Aarhus	113	SiC
See lot 627 Silverstone Auctions 14.11.15.												
1994	512 TR	(Pininfarina)	98789	L	130-140.000 EUR		NS		28-05-16	Aarhus	234	SiC
Red with cream leather interior; last serviced in May 2015 at 50,769 kms.												
1994	512 TR	(Pininfarina)	97271	L	325-375.000 USD		NS		11-06-16	Hershey	142	TFA
Red with black interior; sold new to Canada. Three owners and less than 30,000 kms on the odometer.												
1992	512 TR	(Pininfarina)	92637	L	200-250.000 USD	146.467	200.750	181.398	25-06-16	Santa Monica	1084	AA
White with tan interior; paintwork and interior recently restored. Recent service (see lot S637 Russo & Steele 15.8.15 $195,250).												
1992	512 TR	(Pininfarina)	95107	L	90-110.000 EUR	75.447	100.215	90.000	02-07-16	Lyon	357	Agu
Metallic black with beige interior; three owners and 96,500 kms covered. Last serviced in June 2014.												
1993	512 TR	(Pininfarina)	95878	L	90-100.000 GBP	72.000	95.630	85.882	02-07-16	Woodstock	138	Coy
Red with black leather interior; 12,000 miles on the odometer.												
1992	512 TR	(Pininfarina)	91741	L	NA		NS		09-07-16	Denver	S129.1	Mec
Black with red interior; 21,000 actual miles. Certified by Ferrari Classiche.												
1994	512 TR	(Pininfarina)	94901	R	155-175.000 GBP	162.000	213.192	191.840	30-07-16	Silverstone	938	SiC
Blue with cream leather interior; last serviced in June 2016 at 16,775 miles.												
1993	512 TR	(Pininfarina)	97205	L	80-100.000 EUR	70.228	92.378	82.806	06-08-16	Schloss Dyck	164	Coy
Black; three owners and 63,000 kms covered.												
1992	512 TR	(Pininfarina)	93534	L	140-160.000 EUR		NS		06-08-16	Schloss Dyck	177	Coy
Red with black interior; 39,000 kms covered.												
1991	512 TR	(Pininfarina)	90791	L	250-325.000 USD	172.282*	225.500*	199.094*	19-08-16	Carmel	16	Bon
Red with black leather interior; less than 6,000 miles covered. Engine-out service in 2014.												
1993	512 TR	(Pininfarina)	97313	L	88-108.000 GBP		NS		20-08-16	Brooklands	325	His
Red with black leather interior; sold new in Italy, the car was exported to Japan in 1995 and in 2015 it was imported into the UK. Recently serviced.												
1992	512 TR	(Pininfarina)	91640	L	250-275.000 USD	156.620	205.000	180.995	20-08-16	Monterey	S128	Mec
Black with black leather interior; sold new to the USA. 12,000 miles covered.												
1993	512 TR	(Pininfarina)	95268	L	NQ		NS		20-08-16	Monterey	7203	R&S
White.												
1995	456 GT	(Pininfarina)	102254	L	35-40.000 GBP	39.375	59.956	53.830	04-09-15	Woodstock	253	SiC
Black with black interior; in good overall condition. 50,000 kms covered.												
1994	456 GT	(Pininfarina)	99134	L	70-90.000 EUR	59.626	91.464	80.500	09-10-15	Zoute	49	Bon F299
Red with black interior; one registered owner and 12,000 kms covered. Manual gearbox.												
1997	456 GTA	(Pininfarina)	108367	L	NA	27.058	41.500	36.528	09-10-15	Chicago	F216	Mec
Black with tan interior; believed to be 19,400 original miles. Automatic transmission (see lot S23 Mecum 17.5.14 $ 45,000).												
1997	456 GTA	(Pininfarina)	108323	R	40-45.000 GBP	42.750	65.083	60.466	14-11-15	Birmingham	310	SiC
Grey with red leather interior; last serviced in September 2015 at 27,519 miles.												
1999	456M GTA	(Pininfarina)	113248	R	32-35.000 GBP	37.125	56.519	52.510	14-11-15	Birmingham	338	SiC
Grey; in very good overall condition. Recently serviced at 44,942 miles. Automatic transmission.												
2002	456M GTA	(Pininfarina)	128477	L	45-55.000 GBP	52.200	74.813	68.544	16-01-16	Birmingham	351	Coy
Blue with tan interior; recently serviced.												
1999	456M GTA	(Pininfarina)	114626	L	55-65.000 EUR	52.668	75.486	69.164	16-01-16	Maastricht	415	Coy
Yellow with black leather interior; 25,750 miles covered.												
1997	456 GTA	(Pininfarina)	106383	L	NA	36.944*	52.800*	48.349*	29-01-16	Scottsdale	1224	B/J
Blue with tan interior; 22,735 actual miles. Automatic transmission.												
1999	456M GTA	(Pininfarina)	114510	L	60-80.000 EUR	46.403*	67.347*	61.600*	03-02-16	Paris	103	RMS
Silver with green leather interior; one owner and 45,000 kms on the odometer. Recently serviced. Automatic transmission.												
1999	456M GTA	(Pininfarina)	114798	R	NA	50.625	70.754	64.289	26-02-16	Coventry	724	SiC
Dark blue with black leather interior; last serviced in September 2015 at 33,819 miles. Automatic transmission.												
1997	456 GTA	(Pininfarina)	108323	R	48-58.000 GBP	48.840	69.397	62.930	08-03-16	London	126	Coy
See lot 310 Silverstone Auctions 14.11.15.												
1998	456M GTA	(Pininfarina)	113158	R	35-40.000 GBP	38.080	54.424	49.074	12-03-16	Brooklands	188	His
Metallic blue with tan leather interior; last serviced in January 2016. Automatic transmission.												
1996	456 GT	(Pininfarina)	99606	L	45-55.000 EUR	51.298	72.204	63.543	09-04-16	Essen	162	Coy
Gunmetal grey with black interior; 33,000 kms covered. Manual gearbox.												
1995	456 GT	(Pininfarina)	101900	L	65-75.000 EUR	62.345	89.831	79.160	14-05-16	Monaco	160	Coy
Blue with blue leather interior; one owner and 16,000 kms covered. Last serviced in March 2016.												
2001	456M GTA	(Pininfarina)	121965	R	50-60.000 GBP	45.000	65.556	58.433	20-05-16	Silverstone	360	SiC
Metallic grey; 24,900 miles covered. Last serviced in August 2015.												

Year	Model	(Bodybuilder)	Chassis no.	Steering	Estimate	Hammer price £	$	€	Date	Place	Lot	Auc. H.
2003	456M	(Pininfarina)	130508	L	64-74.000 EUR	68.621	100.512	90.000	28-05-16	Aarhus	128	SiC
	Titanium grey; 11,900 kms on the odometer. Manual gearbox (see lot 425 Bonhams 6.2.14 $ 86,908).											
1999	456M GTA	(Pininfarina)	117687	L	50-60.000 EUR	40.318	59.056	52.880	28-05-16	Aarhus	236	SiC
	Metallic silver blue with dark blue leather interior; last serviced in August 2015 at 94,000 kms.											
2000	456M GTA	(Pininfarina)	118256	L	45-65.000 USD	32.102	44.000	39.758	25-06-16	Santa Monica	1103	AA
	Blue with tan interior; automatic transmission.											
1997	456 GTA	(Pininfarina)	108187	R	60-65.000 GBP	61.312	80.687	72.606	30-07-16	Silverstone	912	SiC
	Titanium grey with blue leather interior; 6,686 miles covered. Recently serviced.											
2002	456M GTA	(Pininfarina)	128477	L	45-50.000 GBP	48.375	63.662	57.286	30-07-16	Silverstone	926	SiC
	See lot 351 Coys 16.1.16.											
1996	F512M	(Pininfarina)	105381	L	250-285.000 EUR		NS		26-09-15	Frankfurt	127	Coy
	Red with black leather interior; 31,942 kms covered.											
1996	F512M	(Pininfarina)	104668	L	170-220.000 GBP	168.000	253.092	238.762	01-12-15	London	332A	Coy
	Red with black interior; sold new to Germany, in 1997 the car was exported to Japan. In 2014 it was imported into the UK where it received a service at 24,900 kms (see lot 440 Coys 2.12.14 $ 238,680).											
1995	F512M	(Pininfarina)	100154	L	400-475.000 USD	253.773	363.000	332.907	28-01-16	Phoenix	121	RMS F300
	Yellow with black leather interior; 23,900 miles covered. Last serviced in March 2015.											
1996	F512M	(Pininfarina)	104354	L	220-260.000 EUR	156.482	231.964	207.000	04-02-16	Paris	421	Bon
	Red with black interior; sold new to Japan. 41,708 kms covered. To be registered within EU.											
1995	F512M	(Pininfarina)	101097	L	NA		NS		26-02-16	Coventry	736	SiC
	Red with black leather interior; recently serviced.											
1995	F512M	(Pininfarina)	103477	L	400-500.000 EUR		NS		14-05-16	Monaco	234	RMS
	Red with black interior; sold new to Japan, the car has covered 3,951 kms and is in original condition.											
1996	F512M	(Pininfarina)	105381	L	220-260.000 EUR		NS		09-07-16	Le Mans	116	Art
	See lot 127 Coys 26.9.15.											
1997	F355 Berlinetta	(Pininfarina)	108005	L	50-60.000 GBP		NS		04-09-15	Woodstock	257	SiC
	Titanium grey with burgundy leather interior; one owner and approximately 50,000 miles covered.											
1995	F355 Berlinetta	(Pininfarina)	101962	L	NA	46.480	71.491	62.655	14-10-15	Duxford	106	H&H
	Red with black interior; sold new in Italy and recently imported into the UK. 91,673 kms covered.											
1995	F355 Berlinetta	(Pininfarina)	103344	L	NA	39.414	60.000	55.746	13-11-15	Anaheim	F123.1	Mec
	Black with beige interior; recently serviced (see lots 716 Barrett-Jackson 22.1.04 $ 78,840 and S611 Russo & Steele 14.8.09 $ 44,000).											
1999	F355 Berlinetta	(Pininfarina)	114851	L	NA	103.500*	157.568*	146.390*	14-11-15	Birmingham	611	SiC
	Titanium grey with burgundy leather interior; in very good original condition. Last serviced in March 2015 at 8,793 kms. F1 gearbox.											
1999	F355 Berlinetta	(Pininfarina)	114864	L	50-60.000 GBP		NS		01-12-15	London	310	Coy
	Red with black interior; 31,000 miles covered. F1 gearbox. European taxes to be paid.											
1999	F355 Berlinetta	(Pininfarina)	114851	L	NA	85.000	118.796	107.942	26-02-16	Coventry	433	SiC
	See lot 611 Silverstone Auctions 14.11.15.											
1998	F355 Berlinetta	(Pininfarina)	111553	L	NA		NS		06-03-16	Birmingham	318	SiC
	Red with black interior; last serviced in December 2014 at 54,870 kms. F1 gearbox.											
1997	F355 Berlinetta	(Pininfarina)	108999	L	NQ		NS		20-05-16	Indianapolis	F261.1	Mec
	Black with grey interior; just under 26,000 miles. Major service in September 2014.											
1998	F355 Berlinetta	(Pininfarina)	111553	L	55-65.000 GBP		NS		02-07-16	Woodstock	217	Coy
	See lot 318 Silverstone Auctions 6.3.16.											
1999	F355 Berlinetta	(Pininfarina)	114864	L	40-50.000 GBP		NS		02-07-16	Woodstock	219	Coy
	See lot 310 Coys 1.12.15.											
1995	F355 Berlinetta	(Pininfarina)	101647	L	52-57.000 GBP		NS		30-07-16	Silverstone	535	SiC
	Silver with burgundy interior; 55,256 kms covered at March 2016. Manual gearbox.											
1996	F355 Berlinetta	(Pininfarina)	112927	L	70-80.000 GBP		NS		20-08-16	Brooklands	323	His
	Grey with black interior; sold new to Switzerland and later imported into the UK. Last serviced in late 2015.											

F299: 1994 Ferrari 456 GT (Pininfarina)

F300: 1995 Ferrari F512M (Pininfarina)

Year	Model (Bodybuilder)	Chassis No.	Steering	Estimate	Hammer price £	Hammer price $	Hammer price €	Date	Place	Lot	Auc. H.
1998	F355 Berlinetta (Pininfarina)	111176	L	NQ		NS		20-08-16	Monterey	7133	R&S
	Yellow with black interior; engine-out service in 2014 at 13,600 miles. F1 gearbox.										
1997	F355 Berlinetta (Pininfarina)	108999	L	NQ	66.392	86.900	76.724	20-08-16	Monterey	7164	R&S
	See lot F261.1 Mecum 20.5.16.										
1995	F355 Berlinetta (Pininfarina)	99948	L	NQ		NS		20-08-16	Monterey	7251	R&S
	Black with black interior.										
1995	F355 GTS (Pininfarina)	100920	L	NQ		WD		04-09-15	Woodstock	220	SiC
	Red with black interior; last serviced in October 2014 (see lot 363 Silverstone Auctions 23.5.15 $ 109,089).										
1996	F355 GTS (Pininfarina)	104897	L	NA	46.724	74.000	65.061	31-10-15	Hilton Head	182	AA
	Black with black interior; approximately 21,000 miles on the odometer. Recently serviced.										
1998	F355 GTS (Pininfarina)	111633	L	60-80.000 EUR	50.510	79.984	70.328	01-11-15	Paris	140	Art
	Titanium grey with red leather interior; last serviced in 2013 at 64,000 kms. F1 gearbox.										
1997	F355 GTS (Pininfarina)	110208	L	90-115.000 USD	57.156	82.500	73.961	05-06-16	Greenwhich	55	Bon
	Red with tan leather interior; 21,400 miles covered. Recent engine-out service. 6-speed manual gearbox.										
1994	F355 GTS (Pininfarina)	100582	L	70-90.000 GBP		NS		24-06-16	Goodwood	257	Bon
	Yellow with black interior; about 37,000 kms covered. Recently serviced.										
1996	F355 GTS (Pininfarina)	100953	L	55-75.000 EUR	56.901	73.894	66.752	09-07-16	Le Mans	135	Art
	Red; body probably repainted. Engine-out service in 2013.										
1996	F355 GTS (Pininfarina)	105291	L	45-55.000 GBP		NS		30-07-16	Silverstone	544	SiC
	Black with black leather interior; 33,567 miles on the odometer. Manual gearbox.										
1999	F355 Spider (Pininfarina)	115326	L	NA	43.494*	66.000*	59.189*	26-09-15	Las Vegas	450	B/J
	Red with black leather interior; F1 gearbox, less than 29,000 miles on the odometer, clutch replaced in 2011, recently serviced (see lot S126 Mecum 6.6.15 NS).										
1997	F355 Spider (Pininfarina)	108607	L	43-50.000 GBP		NS		14-11-15	Birmingham	643	SiC
	Black with biscuit leather interior; imported into the UK in 1998. Last serviced in February 2015.										
1997	F355 Spider (Pininfarina)	106813	L	54-60.000 GBP		NS		28-11-15	Weybridge	292	His
	Red with grey leather interior; 40,380 kms covered (see lot 94 Barrett-Jackson/Coys 17.5.02 NS).										
1999	F355 Spider (Pininfarina)	114444	L	NA	24.434	35.000	32.382	23-01-16	Kissimmee	G165.1	Mec
	Silver with black interior; F1 gearbox.										
1996	F355 Spider (Pininfarina)	105369	L	NA	36.301	52.000	48.110	23-01-16	Kissimmee	W148.1	Mec
	Red with tan interior; belived to be 14,485 actual miles.										
1996	F355 Spider (Pininfarina)	106114	L	120-140.000 USD	84.664*	121.000*	110.800*	29-01-16	Scottsdale	2	G&Co
	British racing green with beige leather interior; less than 6,000 miles covered. Last serviced in 2014 at 4,600 miles.										
1996	F355 Spider (Pininfarina)	104590	R	NA	79.875	111.633	101.433	26-02-16	Coventry	409	SiC
	Red with black interior; in very good overall condition. 27,135 miles covered.										
1995	F355 Spider (Pininfarina)	103773	L	60-80.000 USD	56.114	80.300	70.238	02-04-16	Ft.Lauderdale	493	AA
	Silver with red interior; driven sparingly.										
1999	F355 Spider Serie Fiorano (Pininfarina)	116556	L	200-250.000 USD	147.971	211.750	185.218	02-04-16	Ft.Lauderdale	529	AA F301
	Red with beige interior; 6-speed manual gearbox. One of 104 examples built.										
1997	F355 Spider (Pininfarina)	108607	L	65-75.000 EUR		NS		09-04-16	Essen	178	Coy
	See lot 643 Silverstone Auctions 14.11.15.										
1998	F355 Spider (Pininfarina)	109753	L	65-75.000 USD	37.950*	55.000*	48.131*	07-05-16	Auburn	834	AA
	Yellow with black interior (see lot 5059 Auctions America 8.5.14 $ 63,800).										
1998	F355 Spider (Pininfarina)	111189	R	80-95.000 GBP	86.625	126.195	112.483	20-05-16	Silverstone	337	SiC
	Red with cream leather interior; 25,820 miles covered. Last serviced in october 2014 at 25,400 miles (see lot 144 Silverstone Auctions 28.3.15 $ 107,100).										
1999	F355 Spider (Pininfarina)	115918	L	52-58.000 GBP		NS		11-06-16	Brooklands	321	His
	Yellow with black leather interior; last serviced less than 2,000 kms ago at 78,452 kms. F1 gearbox.										
1997	F355 Spider (Pininfarina)	106713	L	NA	39.325	53.900	48.704	24-06-16	Uncasville	747	B/J
	Metallic blue with tan interior (see lot 153 Barrett-Jackson 18.4.15 $55,000).										

F301: 1999 Ferrari F355 Spider Serie Fiorano (Pininfarina)

F302: 1996 Ferrari F355 Challenge (Pininfarina)

Year	Model	(Bodybuilder)	Chassis no.	Steering	Estimate	Hammer price £	$	€	Date	Place	Lot	Auc. H.
1997	F355 Spider	(Pininfarina)	105723	L	70-90.000 EUR	64.381	85.517	76.800	02-07-16	Lyon	338	Agu

Dark blue with tan leather interior; just over 66,000 kms covered. 6-speed manual gearbox.

| 1996 | F355 Challenge | (Pininfarina) | 104532 | L | 125-165.000 EUR | 135.796 | 197.621 | 176.416 | 05-02-16 | Paris | 173 | Art F302 |

Yellow with red interior; raced at the France Ferrari Challenge from 1998 to 2000 and subsequently at other events until 2008. Restored and road registered. 17,000 kms on the odometer.

| 1995 | F50 | (Pininfarina) | 99999 | L | 2.500-2.900.000 USD | 1.679.280 | 2.400.000 | 2.197.680 | 30-01-16 | Scottsdale | 126 | G&Co |

Red; car used by Ferrari for promotional purpose and displayed at the 1995 Geneva and Tokyo Motor Shows. In 1998 it was sold to Jacques Swaters who retained it until 2005. In 2007 it was imported into the USA. Less than 1,100 miles covered. Certified by Ferrari Classiche. From the Tony Shooshani Collection (see RM lots 246 21.1.11 $ 742,500 and 213 17.8.13 $ 1,677,500).

| 1997 | F50 | (Pininfarina) | 106825 | L | 1.250-1.500.000 EUR | 960.458 | 1.393.958 | 1.275.000 | 03-02-16 | Paris | 141 | RMS |

Red with black interior with red inserts; sold new in Italy, the car was later resold to France. Less than 30,000 kms covered. Certified by Ferrari Classiche.

| 1995 | F50 | (Pininfarina) | 104021 | L | 2.400-2.800.000 USD | 1.616.076 | 2.310.000 | 2.082.927 | 11-03-16 | Amelia Island | 64 | G&Co F303 |

Red with black and red interior; approximately 5,300 miles covered. Serviced in 2014. Ferrari Classiche certified.

| 1995 | F50 | (Pininfarina) | 104794 | L | 1.800-2.100.000 USD | 1.424.544 | 1.952.500 | 1.764.279 | 25-06-16 | Santa Monica | 1085 | AA |

Red with black and red interior; 13,000 miles covered. Three owners. Last serviced in April 2016. Certified by Ferrari Classiche.

| 1999 | 550 Maranello | (Pininfarina) | 114144 | R | 65-75.000 GBP | 110.250 | 167.878 | 150.723 | 04-09-15 | Woodstock | 245 | SiC |

Silver with burgundy leather interior; approximately 43,800 miles covered.

| 1999 | 550 Maranello | (Pininfarina) | 116980 | L | 100-140.000 EUR | NS | | | 09-10-15 | Zoute | 36 | Bon |

Dark blue with beige leather interior; two owners and 48,500 kms covered. Last serviced in July 2015.

| 1998 | 550 Maranello | (Pininfarina) | 110242 | R | NA | 150.080 | 230.838 | 202.308 | 14-10-15 | Duxford | 142 | H&H |

Green with tan leather interior; two owners and 29,000 miles covered. Last serviced in July 2014.

| 1999 | 550 Maranello | (Pininfarina) | 114367 | L | NA | NS | | | 13-11-15 | Anaheim | S124.1 | Mec |

Blue with cream interior; believed to be 23,389 original miles. Last serviced in October 2015.

| 2000 | 550 Maranello | (Pininfarina) | 120147 | L | 230-260.000 GBP | NS | | | 28-11-15 | Weybridge | 242 | His |

Red with black leather interior; in very good original condition. One of the 33 examples of the World Speed Record edition.

| 1998 | 550 Maranello | (Pininfarina) | 113260 | R | 48-56.000 GBP | 73.920 | 111.257 | 105.159 | 28-11-15 | Weybridge | 304 | His |

Silver with red leather interior; 28,000 miles covered. Recently serviced.

| 1997 | 550 Maranello | (Pininfarina) | 108287 | L | NA | NS | | | 30-01-16 | Scottsdale | 5520 | R&S |

Black with black interior; 30,000 original miles. Last serviced less than 200 miles ago.

| 1999 | 550 Maranello | (Pininfarina) | 111048 | L | 130-160.000 EUR | NS | | | 04-02-16 | Paris | 355 | Bon |

Red with tan leather interior; sold new to Japan and imported into the UK in 2015. 14.800 kms covered. Recently serviced.

| 2001 | 550 Maranello | (Pininfarina) | 122067 | L | 100-150.000 EUR | 91.281 | 135.312 | 120.750 | 04-02-16 | Paris | 389 | Bon |

Red with black leather interior; 13,300 kms covered. Last serviced in June 2015.

| 1999 | 550 Maranello | (Pininfarina) | 115480 | L | NA | 110.250 | 154.085 | 140.006 | 26-02-16 | Coventry | 710 | SiC |

Gunmetal grey with beige leather interior; 21,000 miles covered.

| 1997 | 550 Maranello | (Pininfarina) | 107162 | L | 80-90.000 EUR | 58.852 | 82.836 | 72.900 | 09-04-16 | Essen | 137 | Coy |

Silver; cambelt service in 2016.

| 1998 | 550 Maranello | (Pininfarina) | 110849 | L | 100-140.000 EUR | 92.619 | 133.452 | 117.600 | 14-05-16 | Monaco | 278 | RMS F304 |

Titanium grey with burgundy leather interior; 31,600 kms on the odometer. Recently serviced.

| 1998 | 550 Maranello | (Pininfarina) | 105811 | L | 165-195.000 EUR | NS | | | 28-05-16 | Aarhus | 225 | SiC |

Red with tan interior; one owner and 9,600 kms covered.

| 1997 | 550 Maranello | (Pininfarina) | 109701 | L | NA | NS | | | 11-06-16 | Newport Beach | 6255 | R&S |

Red with beige interior.

| 2000 | 550 Maranello | (Pininfarina) | 120150 | L | 210-225.000 USD | NS | | | 11-06-16 | Hershey | 138 | TFA |

Blue with saddle interior.

| 1998 | 550 Maranello | (Pininfarina) | 111736 | L | 100-120.000 EUR | NS | | | 19-06-16 | Fontainebleau | 340 | Ose |

Titanium grey with Cartier leather interior; less than 58,000 kms covered (see lots 18 Artcurial 5.4.04 NS and 380 Osenat 20.3.11 $57,933).

| 1999 | 550 Maranello | (Pininfarina) | 114351 | L | 85-100.000 GBP | николаNS | | | 24-06-16 | Goodwood | 253 | Bon |

Red with black interior; 28,500 kms on the odometer. Recently serviced.

| 1997 | 550 Maranello | (Pininfarina) | 107263 | L | 85-95.000 GBP | 74.000 | 98.287 | 88.267 | 02-07-16 | Woodstock | 206 | Coy |

Red with beige leather interior; 15,000 miles on the odometer.

F303: 1995 Ferrari F50 (Pininfarina)

F304: 1998 Ferrari 550 Maranello (Pininfarina)

Year	Model (Bodybuilder)	Chassis No.	Steering	Estimate	Hammer Price £	Hammer Price $	Hammer Price €	Date	Place	Lot	Auc. H.
2000	550 Maranello (Pininfarina)	120634	R	120-150.000 GBP		NS		30-07-16	Silverstone	511	SiC
Silver with black leather interior; 36,600 miles covered.											
1999	550 Maranello (Pininfarina)	114351	L	85-95.000 GBP		NS		30-07-16	Silverstone	922	SiC
See lot 253 Bonhams 24.6.16.											
1998	550 Maranello (Pininfarina)	112768	L	240-260.000 USD	214.302*	280.500*	247.653*	20-08-16	Pebble Beach	59	G&Co
Titanium grey with dark blue leather interior; two owners and 5,800 miles covered.											
1997	550 Maranello (Pininfarina)	109664	L	140-160.000 USD	91.680	120.000	105.948	20-08-16	Monterey	S113	Mec
Black with black leather interior; recently serviced (see lot 176 Auctions America 14.3.14 $53,000).											
1998	550 Maranello (Pininfarina)	110686		180-200.000 USD	80.220	105.000	92.705	20-08-16	Monterey	S26	Mec
Red with beige leather interior; 9,173 miles covered.											
2000	550 Maranello (Pininfarina)	118498	L	NQ	148.751	194.700	171.901	20-08-16	Monterey	7064	R&S
One owner and 3,781 miles covered. Last serviced in April 2016.											
2000	360 Modena (Pininfarina)	121588	L	NA		NS		05-09-15	Auburn	5067	AA
Yellow with black interior (see lot 708 Auctions America 28.3.15 NS).											
2002	360 Modena (Pininfarina)	130267	L	NA	51.468*	78.100*	70.040*	26-09-15	Las Vegas	751	B/J
Black with black interior; 26,160 original miles. F1 gearbox. Last serviced in May 2015.											
2003	360 Modena (Pininfarina)	132590	L	NA		NS		14-10-15	Duxford	121	H&H
Black with black interior; two owners and 35,300 kms covered. Last serviced in May 2015.											
2001	360 Modena (Pininfarina)	125007	L	NA	42.560	65.462	57.371	14-10-15	Duxford	53	H&H
Grey with beige interior; 58,000 kms covered. The car received some cosmetic Challemge Stradale modifications.											
1999	360 Modena (Pininfarina)	117405	R	50-60.000 GBP	51.750	78.784	73.195	14-11-15	Birmingham	622	SiC
Grey with black leather interior; last serviced in October 2014 at 17,718 miles. F1 gearbox (see lot 281 Historics 30.8.14 $ 75,216).											
2000	360 Modena (Pininfarina)	119959	L	40-50.000 EUR	40.970	58.555	52.800	12-03-16	Lyon	343	Agu
Titanium grey with red interior; 62,000 kms covered. Last serviced in 2014. F1 gearbox.											
1999	360 Modena (Pininfarina)	118405	L	NA	31.029	44.000	38.993	16-04-16	Houston	F196	Mec
Burgundy with tan interior; serviced in 2013 at 32,728 miles. F1 gearbox.											
1999	360 Modena (Pininfarina)	117390	L	NA	49.364	70.000	62.034	16-04-16	Houston	S103.1	Mec
Red with tan interior; F1 gearbox.											
2002	360 Modena (Pininfarina)	125719	L	NA		NS		11-06-16	Newport Beach	6257	R&S
Black; recently serviced.											
2003	360 Modena (Pininfarina)	120075	L	40-50.000 GBP	41.000	54.456	48.905	02-07-16	Woodstock	200	Coy
Silver with blue interior; 12,620 miles covered. F1 gearbox.											
2003	360 Spider (Pininfarina)	134564	L	NA	76.704	120.000	105.096	19-09-15	Dallas	S105.1	Mec F305
Blue with tan interior; under 2,900 actual miles. F1 gearbox. Last serviced in August 2015 (see lot F159 Mecum 16.8.12 $ 105,000).											
2004	360 Spider (Pininfarina)	136010	L	NA	47.119*	71.500*	64.121*	26-09-15	Las Vegas	692	B/J
Matt black with tan interior; F1 gearbox. Clutch replaced; recently serviced.											
2004	360 Spider (Pininfarina)	138825	R	68-74.000 GBP		NS		14-11-15	Birmingham	614	SiC
Red with cream interior; unused for the last five years, recently the car received some overhaul works.											
2005	360 Spider (Pininfarina)	139473	R	150-170.000 GBP		NS		28-11-15	Weybridge	246	His
Red with black interior; 81 miles covered. Last serviced in August 2015.											
2003	360 Spider (Pininfarina)	134564	L	NA		NS		23-01-16	Kissimmee	L88	Mec
See lot S105.1 Mecum 19.9.15.											
2005	360 Spider (Pininfarina)	140035	L	120-150.000 USD		NS		23-01-16	Kissimmee	S115	Mec
Black with black interior; 12,966 miles covered. F1 gearbox (see lot S114 Mecum 24.1.15 $ 100,000).											
2004	360 Spider (Pininfarina)	136281	L	NA	80.815*	115.500*	105.763*	29-01-16	Scottsdale	1046	B/J
Black with black leather interior; 4,700 actual miles. F1 gearbox.											
2001	360 Spider (Pininfarina)	124968	L	NA	61.574*	88.000*	80.582*	29-01-16	Scottsdale	1125.1	B/J
Titanium grey with black interior; less than 18,000 original miles. Last serviced in November 2015. F1 gearbox.											

F305: 2003 Ferrari 360 Spider (Pininfarina)

F306: 2004 Ferrari 360 Challenge Stradale (Pininfarina)

Year	Model (Bodybuilder)	Chassis No.	Steering	Estimate	Hammer Price £	Hammer Price $	Hammer Price €	Date	Place	Lot	Auc. H.
2003	360 Spider (Pininfarina)	130476	L	110-130.000 USD		NS		02-04-16	Ft.Lauderdale	778	AA
	Metallic grey; 20,581 miles.										
2001	360 Spider (Pininfarina)	126212	L	NA		NS		16-04-16	Houston	F151.1	Mec
	Red with tan interior; 26,000 miles.										
2000	360 Spider (Pininfarina)	122397	L	NA	58.179	82.500	73.112	16-04-16	Houston	S106.1	Mec
	Silver with red and black interior; one owner and 4,000 miles. Last serviced in 2016.										
2003	360 Spider (Pininfarina)	134564	L	NA		NS		16-04-16	Houston	S113	Mec
	See lot L88 Mecum 23.1.16.										
2002	360 Spider (Pininfarina)	130030	L	60-70.000 EUR	39.457	57.794	51.750	28-05-16	Aarhus	233	SiC
	Yellow with black interior; in good overall condition. F1 gearbox.										
2001	360 Spider (Pininfarina)	124971	L	70-90.000 USD	55.377*	75.900*	68.583*	25-06-16	Santa Monica	2028	AA
	Light blue with black leather interior; F1 gearbox. From the Riverside International Automotive Museum Collection.										
2001	360 Spider (Pininfarina)	124958	L	125-150.000 EUR	110.856	143.962	130.047	09-07-16	Le Mans	137	Art
	Blue with blue and saddle leather interior; 41,650 kms on the odometer. F1 gearbox. Recently serviced. Presented when new by Giovanni Agnelli to Jean Todt.										
2001	360 Spider (Pininfarina)	125427	L	NA		NS		09-07-16	Denver	S150.1	Mec
	Red with black interior; 20,000 actual miles. 6-speed manual gearbox.										
2004	360 Challenge Stradale (Pininfarina)	138735	L	170-200.000 EUR	130.350	206.415	181.496	01-11-15	Paris	146	Art F306
	Yellow with white stripe; just over 26,000 kms covered. Last serviced in 2014.										
2004	360 Challenge Stradale (Pininfarina)	139046	L	275-325.000 USD	203.963	291.500	266.927	30-01-16	Scottsdale	153	G&Co
	Black with red interior; 3,100 miles covered. Last serviced in December 2015.										
2003	360 Challenge Stradale (Pininfarina)	134636	L	160-180.000 GBP		NS		08-03-16	London	128	Coy
	Red with white stripes; last serviced in the early 2015.										
2004	360 Challenge Stradale (Pininfarina)	139600	L	225-275.000 USD	176.999*	253.000*	228.130*	11-03-16	Amelia Island	74	G&Co
	Red with white stripe and red alcantara interior; approximately 9,000 miles covered. Recent major service.										
2004	360 Challenge Stradale (Pininfarina)	138791	L	140-160.000 GBP		NS		20-05-16	Silverstone	343	SiC
	Blue with tan interior; 5,781 on the odometer.										
2004	360 Challenge Stradale (Pininfarina)	138521	L	170-190.000 EUR		NS		02-07-16	Lyon	354	Agu
	Red with black and red interior; just over 49,000 kms covered. Last serviced in April 2015.										
2001	550 Barchetta Pininfarina	124242	L	280-360.000 EUR		NS		05-09-15	Chantilly	5	Bon
	Gunmetal grey with tan interior; just one owner and 7,800 kms covered. Last serviced in September 2013 (see lot 8 Bonhams 11.9.10 NS).										
2001	550 Barchetta Pininfarina	124112	L	NA		NS		13-11-15	Anaheim	S141.1	Mec
	Red with black interior; last serviced in September 2015.										
2002	550 Barchetta Pininfarina	124120	L	240-280.000 GBP	247.900	375.296	344.234	06-12-15	London	029	Bon
	Silver with black leather interior; sold new to France, the car is currently registered in the UK. 15,900 kms covered. Recently serviced.										
2002	550 Barchetta Pininfarina	124274	L	450-550.000 EUR	341.437	506.137	451.666	04-02-16	Paris	342	Bon
	Dark green with tan leather interior; registered in Italy. 395 kms covered.										
2001	550 Barchetta Pininfarina	124118	L	375-425.000 EUR	396.940	571.939	504.000	14-05-16	Monaco	246	RMS F307
	Grey with black interior; 771 kms covered. Recently serviced. 6-speed manual gearbox.										
2001	550 Barchetta Pininfarina	124146	L	230-260.000 GBP		NS		11-06-16	Brooklands	279	His
	Yellow with grey interior; 35,921 kms covered.										
2002	550 Barchetta Pininfarina	124262	L	270-320.000 GBP	270.300	370.419	334.712	24-06-16	Goodwood	234	Bon
	Red with black interior; 1,200 kms covered. Fitted with the Fiorano Handling Pack.										
2001	550 Barchetta Pininfarina	124113	L	450-600.000 USD		NS		19-08-16	Monterey	132	RMS
	Red with beige interior; US-specification example. 3,344 miles covered. Certified by Ferrari Classiche.										
2001	550 Barchetta Pininfarina	124150	L	475-575.000 USD	248.300	325.000	286.943	20-08-16	Pebble Beach	7	G&Co
	Titanium grey with burgundy leather interior; first owner Greg Garrison. Bought in 2013 by the current, third owner. Low mileage. Certified by Ferrari Classiche.										
2003	Enzo (Pininfarina)	135440	L	3.000-3.500.000 USD	2.181.630	3.300.000	3.015.540	10-12-15	New York	219	RMS F308
	Red with black leather interior; two owners and 560 miles covered. Last serviced in September 2015.										
2003	Enzo (Pininfarina)	132049	L	2.400-2.800.000 USD	2.001.142	2.860.000	2.618.902	30-01-16	Scottsdale	122	G&Co
	Red with red leather interior; sold new to the USA, the car has had three owners and has covered approximately 2,700 miles. From the Tony Shooshani Collection.										

F307: 2001 Ferrari 550 Barchetta Pininfarina

F308: 2003 Ferrari Enzo (Pininfarina)

Year	Model (Bodybuilder)	Chassis No.	Steering	Estimate	Hammer Price £	$	€	Date	Place	Lot	Auc. H.
2004	Enzo (Pininfarina)	135564	L	1.500-2.000.000 EUR	1.181.174	1.714.294	1.568.000	03-02-16	Paris	138	RMS
	Originally finished in red with black interior, the car was sold new to the UK. In 2006 it was imported into the USA where it remained damaged in an accident. Returned to Europe, it was repaired and finished in the present black livery with red interior. Certified by Ferrari Classiche.										
2003	Enzo (Pininfarina)	128800	L	2.500-3.500.000 USD	2.292.000	3.000.000	2.648.700	20-08-16	Monterey	S108.1	Mec
	Red with black interior; sold new to the USA. One owner and 2,050 miles covered. Certified by Ferrari Classiche.										
2003	Enzo (Pininfarina)	133927	L	2.500-3.500.000 USD		NS		20-08-16	Monterey	S127.1	Mec
	Black; US specification example. Last serviced in July 2016. Ferrari Classiche certification in progress.										
2001	575M Maranello (Pininfarina)	123761	L	90-120.000 GBP	72.800*	111.107*	99.685*	07-09-15	London	153	RMS
	Red with beige interior; experimental pre-series example sold directly by factory to its first and sole owner. F1 gearbox; 12,543 kms covered.										
2002	575M Maranello (Pininfarina)	128695	L	NA	60.435	92.000	85.477	13-11-15	Anaheim	S166.1	Mec
	Red with tan interior; 35,000 miles covered (see lot S4 Mecum 15.8.15 NS).										
2003	575M Maranello (Pininfarina)	130437	R	65-75.000 GBP	70.313	107.045	99.451	14-11-15	Birmingham	324	SiC
	Silver with dark blue leather interior; sold new to New Zealand, the car was recently imported into the UK. Last serviced in July 2015.										
2005	575M Maranello (Pininfarina)	139933	L	250-300.000 USD		NS		23-01-16	Kissimmee	S146	Mec
	Red with black leather interior; 2,130 miles. F1 gearbox.										
2002	575M Maranello (Pininfarina)	129697	L	300-400.000 EUR	260.803	386.607	345.000	04-02-16	Paris	331	Bon
	Blue with cream interior; one owner and 1,927 kns covered. Manual gearbox. Last serviced in May 2015.										
2003	575M Maranello (Pininfarina)	134307	L	50-70.000 EUR	63.783	91.160	82.200	12-03-16	Lyon	318	Agu
	Silver with black interior; last serviced in February 2016. 107,000 kms covered.										
2002	575M Maranello (Pininfarina)	127464	L	400-475.000 USD	323.215	462.000	416.585	12-03-16	Amelia Island	137 F309	RMS
	Dark blue with saddle interior; 4,511 miles covered. Six-speed manual gearbox.										
2002	575M Maranello (Pininfarina)	127063	L	200-250.000 EUR		NS		14-05-16	Monaco	220	RMS
	Silver with dark blue leather interior; 590 kms covered. F1 gearbox.										
2005	575M Maranello (Pininfarina)	141040	L	225-255.000 EUR		NS		28-05-16	Aarhus	229	SiC
	Red with red interior; one owner and 3,299 kms covered.										
2002	575M Maranello (Pininfarina)	130074	L	70-90.000 USD	85.353	123.200	110.449	05-06-16	Greenwhich	38	Bon
	Black with beige leather interior; three owners and less than 17,000 miles covered. Transmission rebuilt in 2012.										
2003	575M Maranello (Pininfarina)	123764	L	75-85.000 GBP		NS		11-06-16	Brooklands	299	His
	Black with red leather interior; described as in very good overall condition. F1 gearbox.										
2003	575M Maranello (Pininfarina)	133205	L	295-350.000 USD	183.963	265.000	234.419	11-06-16	Hershey	111	TFA
	Titanium grey with black interior; 27,705 miles on the odometer. Last serviced in August 2015. 6-speed manual gearbox.										
2002	575M Maranello (Pininfarina)	128656	L	100-120.000 EUR	86.513	114.913	103.200	02-07-16	Lyon	359	Agu
	Black with black interior; just over 15,000 kms covered. Last serviced in late 2015.										
2004	575M Maranello (Pininfarina)	137847	L	80-90.000 GBP	56.000	74.379	66.797	02-07-16	Woodstock	136	Coy
	Black with tan interior.										
2004	575M Maranello (Pininfarina)	139114	L	85-95.000 GBP		NS		02-07-16	Woodstock	231	Coy
	Silver with beige leather interior; 16,300 miles covered. Fitted with the Fiorano Handling Package.										
2003	575M Maranello (Pininfarina)	128299	L	175-225.000 EUR		NS		09-07-16	Le Mans	136	Art
	Red with black leather interior; 50,175 kms on the odometer. Fitted with the Fiorano Handling Package. Manual gearbox.										
2005	575M Maranello (Pininfarina)	141040	L	160-180.000 GBP		NS		30-07-16	Silverstone	534	SiC
	See lot 229 Silverstone Auctions 28.5.16.										
2004	575M Maranello (Pininfarina)	135174	L	380-425.000 USD		NS		20-08-16	Monterey	S118	Mec
	Red with tan interior; 18,250 miles covered. 6-speed manual gearbox.										
2002	575M Maranello (Pininfarina)	129981	L	350-370.000 USD		NS		20-08-16	Monterey	S122	Mec
	Titanium grey with dark blue leather interior; 18,400 miles covered. 6-speed manual gearbox. Recently serviced.										
2002	575M Maranello (Pininfarina)	129467	L	275-300.000 USD		NS		20-08-16	Monterey	S71.1	Mec
	Red with black leather interior; 246 kms on the odometer. Fitted with the Fiorano Handling Package.										
2002	575M Maranello (Pininfarina)	129443	L	140-180.000 USD	134.464*	176.000*	155.390*	21-08-16	Pebble Beach	127	G&Co
	Black with saddle leather interior; less than 6,700 kms covered. Recently serviced.										

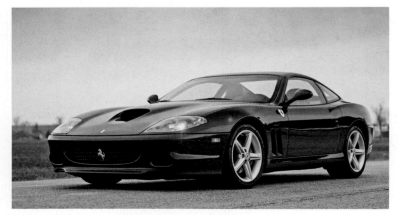

F309: 2002 Ferrari 575M Maranello (Pininfarina)

F310: 2005 Ferrari 612 Scaglietti (Pininfarina)

Year	Model (Bodybuilder)	Chassis no.	Steering	Estimate	Hammer Price £	Hammer Price $	Hammer Price €	Date	Place	Lot	Auc. H.
2005	612 Scaglietti (Pininfarina)	143296	L	80-100.000 GBP	117.600	179.481	161.030	07-09-15	London	134	RMS F310
	Gunmetal grey with red leather interior; two owners and 8,500 kms covered. 6-speed manual gearbox.										
2005	612 Scaglietti (Pininfarina)	141131	L	55-65.000 GBP	56.250	85.635	79.560	14-11-15	Birmingham	334	SiC
	Medium grey with tan leather interior; last serviced in June 2015 at 70,383 kms.										
2005	612 Scaglietti (Pininfarina)	140176	L	NA	61.574*	88.000*	80.582*	29-01-16	Scottsdale	1433	B/J
	Silver with black interior; 22,468 actual miles. Recently serviced.										
2005	612 Scaglietti (Pininfarina)	143297	L	NA		NS		26-02-16	Coventry	741	SiC
	Black with biscuit interior; in very good driving order.										
2005	612 Scaglietti (Pininfarina)	143297	L	68-74.000 EUR	50.611	74.133	66.380	28-05-16	Aarhus	141	SiC
	See lot 141 Silverstone Auctions 26.2.16.										
2007	F430 (Pininfarina)	157152	L	NA		NS		13-11-15	Anaheim	F158	Mec
	Red with tan interior; recently serviced. F1 gearbox (see lot 1087 Auctions America 18.7.15 $ 93,000).										
2008	F430 (Pininfarina)	160343	L	225-275.000 USD	152.800	200.000	176.580	20-08-16	Monterey	S134	Mec
	Dark grey with saddle leather interior; one owner and 5,574 miles covered. Recently serviced.										
2008	F430 Spider (Pininfarina)	159468	L	NA		NS		19-09-15	Dallas	S104	Mec
	Red with tan interior; 11,760 original miles.										
2005	F430 Spider (Pininfarina)	142806	L	NA	71.720	110.000	96.822	09-10-15	Chicago	F168.1	Mec
	Blue with tan leather interior; 31,250 actual miles.										
2006	F430 Spider (Pininfarina)	148800	R	NA	73.920	113.696	99.644	14-10-15	Duxford	42	H&H
	Black with black interior; 23,600 miles covered. F1 gearbox.										
2008	F430 Spider (Pininfarina)	159327	L	NA	95.251	145.000	134.720	13-11-15	Anaheim	F188	Mec
	Black with black interior; 3,300 miles covered. Last serviced at 2,700 miles.										
2009	F430 Spider (Pininfarina)	166206	L	215-240.000 USD		NS		23-01-16	Kissimmee	S251	Mec
	Red with tan interior; 4,262 actual miles.										
2007	F430 Spider (Pininfarina)	152545	L	375-450.000 USD	250.143*	357.500*	327.363*	29-01-16	Phoenix	235	RMS
	Yellow with tan leather interior with alligator upholstery accents; 420 miles covered. 6-speed manual gearbox. Car outfitted with numerous additional options.										
2007	F430 Spider (Pininfarina)	151183	L	120-135.000 USD	78.790	112.750	98.622	02-04-16	Ft.Lauderdale	548	AA
	Blue with tan leather interior; F1 gearbox.										
2005	F430 Spider (Pininfarina)	144085	L	NA	73.308	105.600	93.414	11-06-16	Newport Beach	6123	R&S
	Yellow with black interior; recently serviced. F1 gearbox.										
2007	F430 Spider (Pininfarina)	152034	L	90-120.000 USD	108.346*	148.500*	134.185*	25-06-16	Santa Monica	2125	AA
	Grey with burgundy leather interior; F1 gearbox. From the Riverside International Automotive Museum Collection.										
2009	F430 Scuderia (Pininfarina)	167377	L	200-230.000 GBP	225.000	342.608	307.598	04-09-15	Woodstock	229	SiC F311
	Medium grey with red interior; never road registered. 85 kms covered (see lot 322 Silverstone Auctions 23.5.15 $ 387,090).										
2009	F430 Scuderia (Pininfarina)	169983	L	180-220.000 GBP		NS		14-11-15	Birmingham	628	SiC
	Medium grey with black and red interior; just over 400 kms covered. Last serviced in April 2015.										
2008	F430 Scuderia (Pininfarina)	163908	R	NA	177.750	248.423	225.725	26-02-16	Coventry	426	SiC
	Silver with black interior; just over 7,500 miles covered.										
2009	F430 Scuderia (Pininfarina)	167922	L	240-260.000 EUR		NS		14-05-16	Monaco	180	Coy
	White; 8,900 kms covered.										
2009	F430 Scuderia (Pininfarina)	164871	L	120-150.000 GBP	131.630	173.225	155.876	30-07-16	Silverstone	512	SiC
	Red; 28,338 kms covered. Recently serviced (see lot 370 Silverstone Auctions 23.5.15 $202,343).										
2009	F430 Scuderia Spider 16M (Pininfarina)	168698	R	300-320.000 GBP		NS		16-04-16	Ascot	127	Coy
	Red with black interior; 7,500 miles covered. Last serviced in 2015. Certified by Ferrari Classiche.										
2009	F430 Scuderia Spider 16M (Pininfarina)	168684	L	185-225.000 GBP		NS		11-06-16	Brooklands	297	His
	White with deep red leather interior; last serviced in March 2016 (see lot 256 Historics 6.6.15 $ 326,244).										
2009	F430 Scuderia Spider 16M (Pininfarina)	166772	L	NQ	271.220	355.000	313.430	20-08-16	Monterey	7181	R&S F312
	Black with Italian tri-colour stripe and grey interior.										

F311: 2009 Ferrari F430 Scuderia (Pininfarina)

F312: 2009 Ferrari F430 Scuderia Spider 16M (Pininfarina)

Year	Model	(Bodybuilder)	Chassis no.	Steering	Estimate	Hammer price £	Hammer price $	Hammer price €	Date	Place	Lot	Auc. H.
2005	Superamerica	(Pininfarina)	145743	L	370-430.000 GBP	611.900	926.355	849.684	06-12-15	London	019	Bon F313
	Grey with burgundy leather interior; sold new in Italy, the car is currently registered in the UK. 6-speed manual gearbox.											
2005	Superamerica	(Pininfarina)	144839	L	650-750.000 USD	477.195	682.000	624.507	29-01-16	Phoenix	218	RMS
	Medium metallic grey with natural leather interior; two owners and less than 3,700 miles covered. 6-speed manual gearbox.											
2005	Superamerica	(Pininfarina)	143339	L	NA		NS		30-01-16	Scottsdale	5247	R&S
	Dark green with cream interior; approximately 10,500 miles covered.											
2005	Superamerica	(Pininfarina)	144858	L	300-400.000 EUR	252.109	373.720	333.500	04-02-16	Paris	326	Bon
	Red with black leather interior; one owner and some 23,000 kms covered. Last serviced in January 2015.											
2006	Superamerica	(Pininfarina)	146055	L	NA		NS		26-02-16	Coventry	429	SiC
	White with red leather interior; sold new to Switzerland, the car has had one owner and has covered 17,461 kms.											
2005	Superamerica	(Pininfarina)	143329	L	310-360.000 EUR		NS		14-05-16	Monaco	153	Coy
	Red with light brown interior; described as in very good overall condition, the car has had just one owner (see lot 213 Coys 20.5.06 NS).											
2006	Superamerica	(Pininfarina)	145745	L	375-425.000 EUR	379.299	546.520	481.600	14-05-16	Monaco	258	RMS
	Red with beige leather interior; 221 kms covered.											
2005	Superamerica	(Pininfarina)	144847	L	700-900.000 USD		NS		05-06-16	Greenwhich	54	Bon
	Red with beige leather interior; one owner and 11,800 miles covered. 6-speed manual gearbox.											
2005	Superamerica	(Pininfarina)	144238	L	385-425.000 USD	280.896	385.000	347.886	25-06-16	Santa Monica	2072	AA
	Red with tan leather interior; 7,500 miles on the odometer. Fitted with the Fiorano Handling Package.											
2005	Superamerica	(Pininfarina)	143087	L	400-450.000 USD		NS		20-08-16	Monterey	S138	Mec
	Titanium grey with saddle leather interior; two owners and 7,952 miles covered.											
2005	Superamerica	(Pininfarina)	145102	L	390-425.000 USD	259.760	340.000	300.186	20-08-16	Monterey	S61	Mec
	Red with black leather interior; 11,455 miles covered.											
2005	Superamerica	(Pininfarina)	142022	L	375-425.000 USD	252.120	330.000	291.357	20-08-16	Monterey	248	RMS
	Red with saddle leather interior; first owner Roger Penske. Bought two years ago by the present, third owner. 4,479 miles covered since new. Certified by Ferrari Classiche.											
2005	Superamerica	(Pininfarina)	143339	L	NQ		NS		20-08-16	Monterey	7084	R&S
	See lot 5247 Russo & Steele 30.1.16.											
2007	599 GTB Fiorano	(Pininfarina)	150858	L	NA	118.252	185.000	162.023	19-09-15	Dallas	S83.1	Mec
	Black with black interior; recently serviced.											
2012	599 GTB Fiorano	(Pininfarina)	187669	L	240-280.000 GBP		NS		28-11-15	Weybridge	278	His
	Red with black interior; one of the 40 exaples of the Alonso Edition.											
2009	599 GTB Fiorano	(Pininfarina)	165719	L	235-255.000 USD	136.130	195.000	180.414	23-01-16	Kissimmee	S102	Mec F314
	White with black stripes; 9,246 miles covered. 635bhp engine modified by Vorsteiner, California; F1 gearbox.											
2007	599 GTB Fiorano	(Pininfarina)	150620	L	NA		NS		30-01-16	Scottsdale	5742	R&S
	Red with black interior; recently serviced.											
2007	599 GTB Fiorano	(Pininfarina)	153692	L	70-80.000 GBP	66.000	87.661	78.725	02-07-16	Woodstock	166	Coy
	Red with black interior; in very good overall condition.											
2009	599 GTB Fiorano	(Pininfarina)	165611	L	85-95.000 GBP	78.750	103.635	93.256	30-07-16	Silverstone	541	SiC
	White with red leather interior; 22,000 kms covered. Recently serviced.											
2007	599 GTB Fiorano	(Pininfarina)	150620	L	550-650.000 USD		NS		20-08-16	Monterey	S106	Mec
	See lot 5742 Russo & Steele 30.1.16.											
2010	Ferrari California	(Pininfarina)	170395	L	400-600.000 EUR	302.789	440.642	393.360	05-02-16	Paris	118	Art F315
	Red; 33,100 kms covered. Last serviced in July 2015. Manual gearbox.											
2010	Ferrari California	(Pininfarina)	173698	R	90-105.000 GBP		NS		12-03-16	Brooklands	174	His
	Black with sand leather interior; recently serviced. 19,000 miles on the odometer.											
2011	599 GTO	(Ferrari & PF)	183219	L	750-900.000 USD	538.307	770.000	706.167	28-01-16	Phoenix	156	RMS
	White; one owner and approximately 1,500 miles covered.											
2010	599 GTO	(Ferrari & PF)	173538	L	400-600.000 EUR	321.657	476.815	425.500	04-02-16	Paris	365	Bon
	Red; one owner and 40,700 kms covered. Certified by Ferrari Classiche.											

F313: 2005 Ferrari Superamerica (Pininfarina)

F314: 2009 Ferrari 599 GTB Fiorano (Pininfarina)

Year	Model (Bodybuilder)	Chassis no.	Steering	Estimate	Hammer price £	$	€	Date	Sale Place	Lot	Auc. H.

F315: 2010 Ferrari Ferrari California (Pininfarina)

F316: 2011 Ferrari 599 GTO (Ferrari & PF)

Year	Model (Bodybuilder)	Chassis no.	Steering	Estimate	£	$	€	Date	Place	Lot	Auc. H.
2011	**599 GTO (Ferrari & PF)**	179533	L	650-750.000 USD	**480.975**	687.500	619.919	12-03-16	Amelia Island	181	RMS **F316**
	Rosso fuoco (fire red) with grey stripe and alcantara interior; two owners and less than 7,200 kms covered. Certified by Ferrari Classiche.										
2011	**599 GTO (Ferrari & PF)**	NQ	L	700-1.000.000 EUR		NS		14-05-16	Monaco	275	RMS
	Red with dull grey roof and black interior; one owner and 180 kms covered. Swiss papers.										
2011	**599 GTO (Ferrari & PF)**	176093	L	750-900.000 USD	**519.520**	680.000	600.372	20-08-16	Monterey	S84	Mec
	Pearl white with red stripe and red leather and alcantara interior; 1,965 miles covered. From the Modern Speed Collection.										
2015	**458 Italia (Pininfarina)**	206300	L	NA		NS		16-04-16	Houston	S1221	Mec
	Red with tan interior; two owners and 5,900 miles covered.										
2013	**458 Aperta (Pininfarina)**	192012	L	260-300.000 USD		NS		20-05-16	Indianapolis	S140	Mec
	Metallic black with black and orange interior; 13,491 actual miles.										
2012	**458 Aperta (Pininfarina)**	188745	L	NA		NS		24-06-16	Uncasville	682	B/J
	Red with tan leather and alcantare interior; 1,550 actual miles.										
2013	**458 Challenge (Pininfarina)**	179358	L	250-350.000 USD		NS		23-01-16	Kissimmee	T199	Mec
	Yellow; the car was raced in Europe by German Rinaldi Racing. Approximately 6,400 kms of running time on the engine and transmission. Non-street legal race car.										
2011	**458 Challenge (Pininfarina)**	179489	L	180-220.000 USD		NS		19-08-16	Monterey	F137	Mec
	Red; raced at the North America Ferrari Challenge. 4,400 miles covered.										
2011	**458 Challenge (Pininfarina)**	179225	L	200-240.000 USD	**142.868***	187.000*	165.102*	20-08-16	Pebble Beach	15	G&Co
	Red; campaigned by a Ferrari Challenge Series veteran. Upgraded with 2014 Challenge Evo Aero kit. Fitted with a new 4.5-litre engine in October 2012.										
2014	**458 Challenge (Pininfarina)**	201323	L	200-400.000 USD		NS		20-08-16	Monterey	S158.1	Mec
	White with red interior; never raced. 30 kms covered.										
2011	**SA Aperta (Ferrari & PF)**	182506	L	800-1.200.000 EUR	**660.149**	1.012.638	891.250	09-10-15	Zoute	39	Bon **F317**
	Red with black leather interior; sold new to Japan, the car was acquired in 2014 by the current, second owner and imported into Switzerland. 4,786 kms covered; last serviced in September 2015. With Ferrari Classiche documents.										
2011	**SA Aperta (Ferrari & PF)**	182788	L	1.100-1.500.000 USD	**826.686**	1.182.500	1.084.471	28-01-16	Phoenix	138	RMS
	Red with black interior; 1,200 miles covered. With hardtop. Certified by Ferrari Classiche.										
2011	**SA Aperta (Ferrari & PF)**	182259	L	1.250-1.500.000 USD	**802.200**	1.050.000	927.045	20-08-16	Monterey	S82	Mec
	Red with white stripe on the bonnet and red leather and alcantara interior; one owner and 870 miles covered. From the Modern Speed Collection.										
2013	**F12 Berlinetta (Ferrari & PF)**	194271	L	NA		NS		24-06-16	Uncasville	653	B/J
	Red with tan interior; less than 3,600 miles covered.										
2014	**458 Speciale (Ferrari & PF)**	201984	L	180-220.000 GBP		NS		01-12-15	London	334	Coy
	Black; 2,079 miles covered (see lot 122 Coys 11.7.14 $ 350,374).										
2014	**LaFerrari (Ferrari Styling Center)**	206526	L	3.600-4.200.000 USD	**2.815.340**	3.685.000	3.253.487	19-08-16	Carmel	95	Bon
	Red with black and red interior; sold new to the USA. 230 miles covered.										
2014	**LaFerrari (Ferrari Styling Center)**	207195	L	3.900-4.500.000 USD	**3.590.800**	4.700.000	4.149.630	20-08-16	Monterey	S110	Mec **F318**
	Black with black leather and alcantara interior; 211 miles covered.										

F317: 2011 Ferrari SA Aperta (Ferrari & PF)

F318: 2014 Ferrari LaFerrari (Ferrari Styling Center)

Year	Model	(Bodybuilder)	Chassis No.	Steering	Estimate	Hammer Price £	$	€	Date	Place	Lot	Auc. H.

FERVES (I) (1966-1971)

1973 Ranger — FVS0557 — L — 16-26.000 GBP — 29.120* — 44.443* — 39.874* — 07-09-15 — London — 123 — RMS **F319**
Green with white vinyl interior with green and yellow stripes; Fiat 500 engine. Formerly owned by designer Philippe Stark.

FIAT (I) (1899-)

1911 Landaulet — A1463 — R — 80-100.000 AUD — — NS — — 24-10-15 — Melbourne — 28 — TBr
Red with black wings and leather interior to the front compartment and cloth to the rear; probably sold new to Australia, the car was rediscovered many years ago in a farm. Restored over a number of years; new body. 20hp Tipo 2 engine with 4-speed gearbox.

1927 509 torpedo — 210313 — R — 10-15.000 GBP — 13.800 — 21.013 — 18.866 — 05-09-15 — Beaulieu — 181 — Bon
White with black wings; engine rebuilt at unspecified date. Offered with several spare parts, among them an engine (dismantled) and a gearbox.

1926 509A torpedo — 239477 — R — 20-26.000 EUR — 16.195 — 23.211 — 21.267 — 16-01-16 — Maastricht — 445 — Coy
Red with black interior; in good overall condition.

1927 509A spider — 109A132498 — R — 40-60.000 EUR — 15.752* — 22.696* — 20.000* — 14-05-16 — Monaco — 122 — RMS **F320**
Red with black wings; paintwork and interior to be refreshed. Since 1959 or 1960 in the Quattroruote Collection.

1927 509 spider (Brandone) — 31008832 — R — 170-180.000 EUR — — NS — — 06-08-16 — Schloss Dyck — 140 — Coy
Red; restored. One of two cars modified by the Ortelli garage in Cannes in 1927 to SM specification; unblown engine. Type "Monza Spinto" body. French papers; with FIVA passport.

1927 503 berlina — 4222003 — R — 18-22.000 EUR — 22.988 — 33.672 — 30.150 — 28-05-16 — Aarhus — 246 — SiC
Red and black with black interior; body restored in the 1980s, engine overhauled in the 2000s.

1930 525N spider — 201727 — L — 60-80.000 EUR — 55.572* — 80.071* — 70.560* — 14-05-16 — Monaco — 132 — RMS **F321**
Blue; described as in original condition except for the paintwork redone some years ago. Since 1966 in the Quattroruote Collection.

1934 508 Balilla berlina 2 porte — 6CVF6831 — L — 6-8.000 EUR — — NS — — 08-11-15 — Lyon — 203 — Ose
Yellow with black wings; stored for some time, the car was acquired at unspecified date by the current owner and returned to working order. In original condition; only lacking the rear seat.

1934 508 Balilla berlina 2 porte — 6CVF6831 — L — 4-6.000 EUR — 3.924 — 5.685 — 5.040 — 20-03-16 — Fontainebleau — 314 — Ose
See lot 203 Osenat 8.11.15.

1932 508 Balilla berlina 2 porte — 002248 — L — 15-20.000 EUR — 6.616* — 9.532* — 8.400* — 14-05-16 — Monaco — 127 — RMS
Described as in original condition; since 1984 in the Quattroruote Collection.

1935 508 S Balilla spider Sport — 070269 — R — NA — — NS — — 14-10-15 — Duxford — 124 — H&H
Green with green interior; sold new to the UK, the car was raced at some events in the 1930s. In 1966 it was acquired by the current owner in need of restoration and fitted with a Ford 10 engine allied to the original gearbox. Over the years the wings and floor were rebuilt and the car was fitted with the present 1,089cc Fiat 508C engine.

1935 508 S Balilla spider Camerano — 12217 — L — 50-80.000 EUR — 50.450 — 73.088 — 64.800 — 20-03-16 — Fontainebleau — 305 — Ose **F322**
The car was modified in France by Victor and René Camerano and was raced at numerous events between 1935 and 1949. In the 1960s and 1970s it was driven at historical events (see lot 327 Osenat 14.6.15 NS).

1935 508 S Balilla spider Sport — 071328 — L — 70-90.000 GBP — 48.300* — 66.190* — 59.810* — 24-06-16 — Goodwood — 206 — Bon
Red with tan interior; bought in 2011 by the current owner and subsequently fully restored (see lot 609 Silverstone Auctions 26.7.14 NS).

1937 1500 barchetta — 019373 — L — 80-120.000 EUR — 69.547 — 103.095 — 92.000 — 04-02-16 — Paris — 414 — Bon
Old English white with red interior; built with saloon body, in more recent years the car was fitted with the present aluminium barchetta body. Italian papers.

1937 1500 barchetta — 019373 — L — 80-85.000 EUR — 63.831 — 89.844 — 79.067 — 09-04-16 — Essen — 117 — Coy
See lot 414 Bonhams 4.2.16. Red with tan interior.

1937 1500 barchetta — 012942 — L — 110-125.000 EUR — 89.125 — 125.446 — 110.399 — 09-04-16 — Essen — 220 — Coy
White with red interior; restored in the 2000s. Rebodied some 30 years ago with the present Zagato-style body. The engine was fitted with supercharger probably in the 1950s. Offered with Fiat Historic Register certification no.326315 (see car chassis no.12941 offered by Coys on 21.5.07 lot 261 NS, 11.8.07 lot 233 NS, and 10.5.08 lot 278 NS).

1937 1500 berlina — 016433 — L — 35-45.000 EUR — 31.503* — 45.392* — 40.000* — 14-05-16 — Monaco — 135 — RMS **F323**
Described as in very good original cosmetic condition; leather interior. Mechanicals in need of recommissioning prior to use. Since 1960 in the Quattroruote Collections.

1937 500A Topolino — 028474 — R — 20-25.000 GBP — 14.160 — 20.079 — 17.793 — 16-04-16 — Ascot — 119 — Coy
Dark red with black wings and red interior; restored. Since 1992 in the current ownership.

1948 500A Topolino — 126372 — L — 18-22.000 USD — 15.749* — 22.825* — 19.974* — 07-05-16 — Auburn — 512 — AA
Navy blue with red interior.

1939 508C Nuova Balilla convertibile (Viotti) — 508C241939 — L — 28-34.000 EUR — 26.639 — 37.496 — 32.998 — 09-04-16 — Essen — 103 — Coy
Green with green leather interior; bodily and mechanically restored approximately 10 years ago.

F319: 1973 Ferves Ranger

F320: 1927 Fiat 509A spider

Year	Model	(Bodybuilder)	Chassis no.	Steering	Estimate	£	$	€	Date	Place	Lot	Auc. H.

F321: 1930 Fiat 525N spider

F322: 1935 Fiat 508 S Balilla spider Camerano

Year	Model	(Bodybuilder)	Chassis no.	Steering	Estimate	£	$	€	Date	Place	Lot	Auc. H.
1948	**1100 S Mille Miglia spider**		1100S500177	L	100-130.000 GBP	137.200	209.395	187.868	07-09-15	London	112	RMS

Red with black interior; originally a coupé, the car was fitted probably in the 1950s with the present body. Discovered in Germany in the early 1960s and restored in the 2000s: the engine and chassis in Italy and the body in Germany. Offered with FIVA Identity Card the car participated in the 2014 Mille Miglia Storica. From the Fendt Collection. **F324**

1951	**500C Topolino**		299155	L	10-14.000 EUR		NS		14-05-16	Monaco	120	RMS

Purchased in 1991 by the Quattroruote Collection from its original owner and subsequently restored.

1953	**500C Belvedere**		443805	L	10-16.000 EUR	12.358	19.085	16.800	17-10-15	Salzburg	305	Dor

Green with brown interior; described as in very good overall condition (see lots 268 Historics 24.11.12 NS and 372 Bonhams 28.4.14 $ 20,342).

1951	**500C Giardiniera**		304000	L	35-40.000 USD		NS		25-06-16	Santa Monica	1036	AA

Dark green with wooden panels and brown interior.

1953	**500C Belvedere**		446167	L	9-12.000 GBP	8.000	10.626	9.542	02-07-16	Woodstock	253	Coy

Two-tone grey with brown interior; in good overall condition (see lot 222 Coys 11.7.15 NS).

1962	**Campagnola**		1101A015724	L	15-20.000 EUR	9.703*	13.981*	12.320*	14-05-16	Monaco	118	RMS

White; civilian model in original condition. 10,447 kms on the odometer. Since new in the Quattroruote Collection.

1953	**8V Elaborata**	(Zagato)	106000022	L	Refer Dpt.		NS		28-01-16	Scottsdale	60	Bon

Smoke grey with red interior; sold new in Italy, the car was raced in period in Italy and France. In 1998 it was imported into the USA where it was restored between 1999 and 2001 The nose was modified to a more typical Zagato appearance replacing the original wider grille radiator; the original 4-speed gearbox (included with the sale) was replaced with the present 5-speed unit. In 2011 it was acquired by the current owner and restored again to concours condition (see lot 127 Gooding 21.8.11 $ 1,127,500).

1955	**1100/103 TV trasformabile**		000243	L	60-70.000 EUR		NS		09-04-16	Essen	208	Coy

Metallic red with beige interior; with Italian ASI homologation.

1960	**600D**		832620	L	6-9.000 GBP		NS		12-03-16	Brooklands	213	His

Pistachio green; restored at unspecified date. Full lenght fabric roof. In single ownership from 1965 to 2015.

1956	**600**		100116364	L	15-20.000 EUR	9.703*	13.981*	12.320*	14-05-16	Monaco	115	RMS

Blue; in good, probably restored condition. Since 1984 in the Quattroruote Collection.

1963	**600D**		100D1548289	L	18-22.000 USD	10.669*	15.400*	13.806*	05-06-16	Greenwhich	19	Bon

White with grey interior; restored.

1961	**600 Jolly**	(Ghia)	297597	L	70-90.000 USD	92.444*	121.000*	106.831*	20-08-16	Pebble Beach	80	G&Co

Light blue with wicker seats; recently restored.

1966	**600 Multipla**		100D108129535	L	8-12.000 GBP	22.137*	34.142*	30.301*	12-09-15	Goodwood	301	Bon

Blue; stored for 12 years, the car has been recently recommissioned. 24,000 kms on the odometer. Fitted in 2000 circa with a Fiat 900cc engine.

1957	**600 Multipla**		100108043042	L	40-50.000 USD	32.274*	49.500*	43.570*	09-10-15	Hershey	257	RMS

White and light green; restored in recent years (see lot 221 RM 16.8.14 $ 231,000 - included in the lot also a Ghia bodied Fiat 600 Jolly).

1957	**600 Multipla Mirafiori**		100108027591	L	150-200.000 USD	100.057*	143.000*	130.945*	29-01-16	Scottsdale	34	G&Co

Believed to be the sole survivor of five examples built, the car was retained by the factory until 1965 when it was sold to a Fiat employer who retained it for 30 years. Currently fitted with a 750cc 600D engine. Finished in aquamarine with tan interior; restored in the 1990s; panoramic plexiglas roof.

F323: 1937 Fiat 1500 berlina

F324: 1948 Fiat 1100 S Mille Miglia spider

Year	Model (Bodybuilder)	Chassis no.	Steering	Estimate	Hammer price £	$	€	Date	Place	Lot	Auc. H.
1965	**600 Multipla** Blue with white roof; restored.	100D108126736	L	30-50.000 EUR	33.519*	48.297*	42.560*	14-05-16	Monaco	209	RMS
1959	**600 Multipla** Red and white with red interior; restored in 1995-96. Interior retrimmed in 2013. Engine replaced in 2015 with a period correct unit.	100108061372	L	25-35.000 USD	21.338*	30.800*	27.612*	05-06-16	Greenwhich	11	Bon
1959	**600 Multipla** Red and cream with matching interior; recent restoration.	100108059556	L	20-25.000 GBP	15.000	19.923	17.892	02-07-16	Woodstock	250	Coy
1958	**600 Multipla** Two-tone body; described as in good original condition. 51,393 kms on the odometer.	43112	L	14-20.000 EUR	20.322*	26.391*	23.840*	09-07-16	Paris	197	Art
1956	**642 car transporter (Bartoletti)** Discovered in Arizona by Don Orosco and fully restored in the 2000s; fitted with a turbocharged Bedford engine as replacement of the original Fiat unit. The transporter was owned by Lance Reventlow for Scarab, Carroll Shelby for Cobra, Alan Mann Racing in the UK, David Piper, Steve McQueen's Solar Production for the movie "Le Mans", and Anthony Bamford's JCB (see lot 234 RM 18.8.12 $ 990,000 - presented as a Fiat 306/2 chassis no.001625).	NQ	R	575-750.000 GBP	656.700	1.012.828	898.891	12-09-15	Goodwood	333	Bon F325
1959	**Nuova 500 Trasformabile** Blue; restored between 2003 and 2005. Body repainted in 2013. Fitted in 2015 with a later 499cc engine (the 479cc unit is included with the sale).	079825	L	18-24.000 GBP	15.525	22.491	19.940	20-03-16	Goodwood	92	Bon F326
1965	**500 F** Blue with red interior; restored in France.	100F2857695	L	10-14.000 GBP	17.920*	27.350*	24.538*	07-09-15	London	126	RMS
1963	**500 D** White with white and blue interior.	491589	L	10-15.000 EUR	10.728	16.282	14.601	26-09-15	Frankfurt	102	Coy
1965	**500 D** Dark blue with red interior; in good overall condition.	110D820275	L	8-12.000 GBP		NS		10-10-15	Ascot	107	Coy
1967	**500 Giardiniera** Beige with red interior; in good working order.	198608	L	6-8.000 EUR	7.277*	11.523*	10.132*	01-11-15	Paris	102	Art
1978	**500 F** Beige with beige vinyl interior; restored in 2013.	0955950	L	7-12.000 EUR	11.129*	17.624*	15.496*	01-11-15	Paris	113	Art
1970	**500 L** Blue with red interior; restored in 2015. Two owners.	2442840	L	8-12.000 GBP	8.280*	12.524*	11.444*	10-12-15	London	334	Bon
1961	**500 My Car (Francis Lombardi)** Dark red with red interior; restored.	2738573	L	10-15.000 EUR	12.332	17.866	15.840	20-03-16	Fontainebleau	321	Ose
1963	**500 Giardiniera** Ivory; restored.	120085514	L	12-15.000 EUR		NS		14-05-16	Monaco	195	Coy
1962	**500 Trasformabile** Light green; restored in 2015.	341038	L	16-20.000 EUR	14.870	21.425	18.880	14-05-16	Monaco	200	Coy
1960	**500 Mare (Holiday)** Conversion made at unspecified date from a 500 Giardiniera. Described as in very good overall condition.	120307585	L	20-30.000 EUR	41.458*	59.736*	52.640*	14-05-16	Monaco	285	RMS
1973	**500 My Car (Francis Lombardi)** Red; in good overall condition.	2097894	L	12-15.000 EUR		NS		19-06-16	Fontainebleau	376	Ose
1959	**500 Jolly (Ghia)** Red with wicker seats; recently restored.	110147301	L	NA	69.270*	99.000*	90.654*	29-01-16	Scottsdale	1083	B/J
1971	**500 Jolly (Ghia)** Red with wicker seats; restored in 2014.	5045627	L	20-30.000 EUR	28.077*	40.456*	35.650*	13-05-16	Monaco	102	Bon
1959	**1200 Trasformabile** White; restored in Italy 30 years ago circa. Since 1982 in the Italian Vintage Cars Collection.	103G115004228	L	40-50.000 USD	27.208*	38.500*	35.459*	10-03-16	Amelia Island	107	Bon F327
1962	**1500 S cabriolet (Pininfarina)** Light blue with black interior; described as in original condition.	118S006573	L	20-30.000 USD	19.986	28.600	25.016	02-04-16	Ft.Lauderdale	233	AA
1965	**2300 S coupé (Ghia)** In the late 1980s the car was prepared for historic racing also using many original Abarth parts. Raced until 1992, it was subsequently stored for 22 years and recommissioned in 2014.	114BS117899	L	30-40.000 GBP		NS		20-03-16	Goodwood	60	Bon
1962	**2300 S coupé (Ghia)** White with black interior; restored, the car is described as in good overall condition.	114BS083967	L	24-28.000 GBP		NS		10-07-16	Chateau Impney	12	H&H
1965	**2300 S coupé (Ghia)** See lot 60 Bonhams 20.3.16.	114BS117899	L	37-42.000 GBP		NS		10-07-16	Chateau Impney	56	H&H

F325: 1956 Fiat 642 car transporter (Bartoletti)

F326: 1959 Fiat Nuova 500 Trasformabile

Year	Model (Bodybuilder)	Chassis no.	Steering	Estimate	Hammer price £	$	€	Date	Sale Place	Lot	Auc. H.
1965	**1500 cabriolet (Pininfarina)** Red; restored at unspecified date.	118K047086	L	35-45.000 USD	22.472	30.800	27.831	25-06-16	Santa Monica	1035	AA
1964	**1500 cabriolet (Pininfarina)** Red with black interior and black hardtop.	031255	L	23-28.000 GBP	15.000	19.923	17.892	02-07-16	Woodstock	244	Coy
1962	**1600 S coupé (Pininfarina)** White; in good overall condition.	022203	L	45-55.000 EUR	33.456	48.206	42.480	14-05-16	Monaco	150	Coy
1962	**1600 S coupé (Pininfarina)** See lot 150 Coys 14.5.16.	022203	L	36-40.000 GBP		NS		02-07-16	Woodstock	234	Coy
1968	**850 Special berlina** Beige with beige interior; restoration completed in 2016. One owner until 2014. Offered with a 1967 Franza Gardena caravan.	0992443	L	18-22.000 EUR	13.011	18.747	16.520	14-05-16	Monaco	147	Coy
1967	**850 spider (Bertone)** Red with black interior; body repainted in the mid-1990s. Since 1987 in the current ownership.	0017164	L	11-16.000 EUR	13.182	20.357	17.920	17-10-15	Salzburg	304	Dor
1975	**124 Abarth Rally (Pininfarina)** The car remained in the factory's ownership until 1977 when it was sold to Italian driver Vanni Tacchini who raced it until 1978. Stored for 30 years, it was recommissioned in 2009 and subsequently driven by Tacchini himself at several historic rallies until 2012. Circa 2,600 kms covered since the recommissioning.	0092696	L	140-180.000 EUR	118.231	175.262	156.400	04-02-16	Paris	358	Bon F328
1969	**125 Samantha coupé (Vignale)** Turquoise green with light beige interior; restoration completed in 2012. Currently fitted with a 2000cc Fiat engine (the original 1600cc unit is included in the sale) (see lot 259 Historics 6.6.15 NS).	0226401	R	19-25.000 GBP		NS		09-12-15	Chateau Impney	133	H&H
1967	**Dino spider (Pininfarina)** Red with tan interior; engine rebuilt in recent years.	135AS0000438	L	140-160.000 USD		NS		28-01-16	Scottsdale	10	Bon
1967	**Dino spider (Pininfarina)** Blue; sold new in Italy and currently registered in the UK. Described as in good overall condition; with hardtop.	135AS000696	L	90-140.000 EUR		NS		04-02-16	Paris	362	Bon
1967	**Dino spider (Pininfarina)** Red with original black interior; equipped from new as a hardtop only spider - never having had a soft top. Recent cosmetic restoration.	135AS0000076	L	135-155.000 USD		NS		10-03-16	Amelia Island	156	Bon
1967	**Dino spider (Pininfarina)** Blue with brown interior; from the Riverside International Automotive Museum Collection.	135AS000619	L	70-90.000 USD	89.887*	123.200*	111.324*	25-06-16	Santa Monica	2020	AA F329
1970	**Dino 2400 spider (Pininfarina)** Silver with red interior; restored several years ago, the car is described as still in very good overall condition.	135BS0001254	L	150-200.000 EUR		NS		04-02-16	Paris	323	Bon
1969	**Dino 2400 coupé (Bertone)** Red with tan leather interior; imported into the UK in 1990 and later restored (see lot 61 H&H 15.4.15 NS).	135BC0003725	L	38-45.000 GBP	43.680	61.938	55.220	20-04-16	Duxford	40	H&H
1974	**Dino 2400 coupé (Bertone)** Silver with blue cloth interior; in good overall condition.	0005466	L	40-50.000 GBP	36.000	47.815	42.941	02-07-16	Woodstock	195	Coy F330
1978	**130 coupé (Pininfarina)** Grey; described as in good overall condition. 17,000 miles on the odometer.	00004378	R	NA	22.500	31.446	28.573	26-02-16	Coventry	738	SiC

F327: 1959 Fiat 1200 Trasformabile   F328: 1975 Fiat 124 Abarth Rally (Pininfarina)

F329: 1967 Fiat Dino spider (Pininfarina)   F330: 1974 Fiat Dino 2400 coupé (Bertone)

Year	Model	(Bodybuilder)	Chassis no.	Steering	Estimate	Hammer Price £	Hammer Price $	Hammer Price €	Date	Place	Lot	Auc. H.
1973	130 coupé	(Pininfarina)	130BC0002591	L	40-60.000 USD	20.778*	29.700*	26.780*	11-03-16	Amelia Island	3	G&Co
	Blue; restored many years ago. Interior believed original. Clutch recently replaced.
1974	130 coupé	(Pininfarina)	130BC0003706	L	13-17.000 GBP		NS		16-04-16	Ascot	142	Coy
	Silver with orange velour interior; recent mechanical works. In the same ownership from 1976 to 2015.
1972	130 coupé	(Pininfarina)	130BC0001878	L	15-20.000 EUR		NS		14-05-16	Monaco	130	RMS
	Dark grey with red cloth interior; automatic transmission. Since 1983 in the Quattroruote Collection.
1973	130 coupé	(Pininfarina)	0003014	L	13-15.000 GBP	11.500	15.274	13.717	02-07-16	Woodstock	197	Coy
	Dark grey; manual gearbox.
1974	130 coupé	(Pininfarina)	130BC0003706	L	10-12.000 GBP	8.680	11.360	10.030	20-08-16	Brooklands	334	His
	See lot 142 Coys 16.4.16.
1976	131 Abarth Gruppo 4		2040414	L	180-220.000 EUR		NS		09-07-16	Le Mans	181	Art
	The car was prepared in 1976 by the Jolly Club team for driver Ciro Nappi and was raced at the Giro d'Italia, Monza 6 Hours and some hillclimbs. Restored and adapted to current FIA HCV standards. Alitalia livery.
1983	126 Abarth replica		8362973	R	10-15.000 GBP	14.375	22.171	19.677	12-09-15	Goodwood	310	Bon
	Bright orange with black vinyl interior; fully restored in recent years, engine rebuilt to Abarth specification. From the Chris Evans collection.
1979	Spider 2000	(Pininfarina)	124CS20157834	L	7-10.000 GBP	8.400	12.643	11.950	28-11-15	Weybridge	226	His
	Azure blue with biscuit interior; recently cosmetically restored.
1979	Spider 2000	(Pininfarina)	124CS20149247	L	8-10.000 EUR	8.563	12.053	10.607	09-04-16	Essen	174	Coy
	Metallic grey/green with beige interior; restored circa 10 years ago.
1983	Spider 2000	(Pininfarina)	ZFA124CS008182259	L	15-20.000 EUR	6.616*	9.532*	8.400*	14-05-16	Monaco	124	RMS
	US market specification; in original condition, 25,291 miles covered. Since new in the Quattroruote Collection.
1980	Spider 2000	(Pininfarina)	124CS000169099	L	NQ	11.345	14.850	13.111	20-08-16	Monterey	7028	R&S
	White with red interior; 29,000 miles covered.
2005	Barchetta		57621	L	6-9.000 GBP	8.400	12.005	10.825	12-03-16	Brooklands	108	His
	Blue; in very good overall condition. 22,277 miles covered.
1999	Barchetta		44605	L	NQ	6.720*	9.679*	8.563*	11-06-16	Brooklands	213	His
	Silver with black interior; in good overall condition.

FLANDERS (USA) (1911-1914)

Year	Model		Chassis no.	Steering	Estimate	£	$	€	Date	Place	Lot	Auc. H.
1912	Model S 20 runabout		68500(engine)	R	20-25.000 USD	21.338*	30.800*	27.612*	05-06-16	Greenwhich	69	Bon
	Blue; formerly in the Harrah Collection, the car comes from the Evergreen Collection.

FLINT (USA) (1902-1904)

Year	Model		Chassis no.	Steering	Estimate	£	$	€	Date	Place	Lot	Auc. H.
1902	8hp Roadster		NQ	R	22-25.000 GBP	26.450	40.275	36.160	05-09-15	Beaulieu	109	Bon
	Red with black interior; for restoration. The carburettor, ignition systen and wings are missing. The car comes with a 1904 USA licensing receipt (see lot 26 H&H 1.10.10 $ 34.806).

FMR (D) (1957-1964)

Year	Model		Chassis no.	Steering	Estimate	£	$	€	Date	Place	Lot	Auc. H.
1957	Messerschmitt KR 200 cabriolet		63575	C	50-70.000 EUR	42.185*	61.225*	56.000*	03-02-16	Paris	116	RMS F331
	Red and cream with aubergine interior; restored.
1958	Messerschmitt KR 200 cabriolet		68619	C	40-60.000 USD	19.052*	27.500*	24.654*	05-06-16	Greenwhich	32	Bon
	Red with black vinyl interior; restored in the 1990s.
1959	Messerschmitt KR 200 cabriolet		71703	C	28-33.000 EUR		NS		02-07-16	Lyon	364	Agu
	Dark grey with maroon interior; bought in 2009 by the current owner and subsequently restored.
1959	Messerschmitt KR 200		72056	C	40-50.000 USD	50.147*	66.000*	59.387*	30-07-16	Plymouth	168	RMS
	Turquoise; 25 miles covered since the restoration.
1957	Messerschmitt KR 200		65101	C	30-40.000 EUR	25.987	34.183	30.641	06-08-16	Schloss Dyck	138	Coy
	White with red interior; restored in 2009. 23,708 kms covered since new.
1959	Messerschmitt KR 200		71951	C	33-38.000 EUR	25.987	34.183	30.641	06-08-16	Schloss Dyck	182	Coy
	Silver and red with red interior; restored.

FORD (CDN)

Year	Model	(Bodybuilder)	Chassis no.	Steering	Estimate	£	$	€	Date	Place	Lot	Auc. H.
1918	Model T runabout	(Queensland)	C163463(engine)	R	8-12.000 USD	2.899*	4.400*	3.916*	05-10-15	Philadelphia	227	Bon
	Red with black fenders; one of three surviving examples bodied in Australia. From the Evergreen Collection.
1914	Model T touring		C6769	R	25-35.000 USD	15.218	23.100	20.559	05-10-15	Philadelphia	247	Bon
	Black; fully restored.

FORD (F) (1916-1954)

Year	Model	(Bodybuilder)	Chassis no.	Steering	Estimate	£	$	€	Date	Place	Lot	Auc. H.
1952	Comète	(Facel/Stabilimenti Farina)	766	L	60-80.000 EUR	38.445*	55.948*	49.945*	05-02-16	Paris	127	Art F332
	Black with brown interior; recently restored. From the André Trigano Collection.

FORD (GB) (1911-)

Year	Model		Chassis no.	Steering	Estimate	£	$	€	Date	Place	Lot	Auc. H.
1953	Prefect saloon		C699122	R	3-4.000 GBP	2.070*	3.152*	2.830*	05-09-15	Beaulieu	184	Bon
	Grey with red interior.

Year	Model	(Bodybuilder)	Chassis no.	Steering	Estimate	Hammer price £	Hammer price $	Hammer price €	Date	Place	Lot	Auc. H.
1958	**Zephyr MkII saloon**		2060L132201	R	16-18.000 GBP		NS		16-01-16	Birmingham	310	Coy
In the 1990s prepared for historic rallying. Recently recommissioned.												
1955	**Zephyr saloon**		EOTTA126798	R	8-10.000 GBP		NS		12-03-16	Brooklands	130	His
A running example requiring some restoration works.												
1961	**Consul Classic station wagon**		109E18717	R	NA	8.680	12.308	10.973	20-04-16	Duxford	1	H&H
Built with saloon body, the car formed part of a small butch of 17 examples sold to the Ford dealer in Nairobi, where all the cars were converted to station wagon for police use. Back to the UK in 1964, it was restored in the late 1970s and fitted with a later 1,500cc engine. For restoration.												
1960	**Anglia 105E**		105E115195	R	NA	22.500	31.446	28.573	26-02-16	Coventry	130	SiC
Dark blue with silver roof; prepared for historic racing. 1,650cc engine.												
1964	**Anglia 105E**		nr	R	3-5.000 GBP	6.900*	9.996*	8.862*	20-03-16	Goodwood	18	Bon
Blue; two owners. Used until 1989 and recommissioned in 2014. Since 1980 in the Kingsley Curtis Collection.												
1966	**Cortina DeLuxe**		BB7F509609	R	55-65.000 GBP		NS		28-07-16	Silverstone	121	SiC
Car acquired in 2013 by the current owner and prepared for historic racing to Cortina Lutus MkI specification. It won the CTCRC Class Championship in 2014 and 2015. 183bhp engine; ready to use.												
1963	**Cortina GT 4-door saloon**		142546	R	24-28.000 GBP	26.280	34.395	30.367	20-08-16	Brooklands	316	His
Dark green; described as in very good original condition, the car has had two owners and has covered 19,244 miles.												
1966	**Cortina Lotus**		BAT44362065	R	45-55.000 GBP	50.625	77.072	71.604	14-11-15	Birmingham	319	SiC
White with green side stripe; fully restored. In 1977, due to an accident, the car was re-shelled with an ex-experimental 125E Lotus shell sourced directly from Ford.												
1970	**Cortina Lotus MkII**		BA91KT17534	R	28-35.000 GBP		NS		10-12-15	London	366	Bon
Alan Mann Racing red and gold livery; believed restored recently (see lot 148 Coys 8.8.15 NS).												
1965	**Cortina Lotus**		BA74FT54434	L	35-45.000 EUR		NS		16-01-16	Maastricht	441	Coy
White with green side stripe; restored and prepared for rally/race use.												
1966	**Cortina Lotus**		BA74FY59122	R	44-52.000 GBP	44.800	64.028	57.734	12-03-16	Brooklands	197	His
White with green side stripe and original black interior; never raced, the car is described as in very good overall condition.												
1966	**Cortina Lotus**		BA74FL59042	R	48-54.000 GBP	50.400	72.032	64.950	12-03-16	Brooklands	210	His F333
White with green side stripe; described as in very good overall condition, the car has covered 9,826 miles since the restoration carried out 15 years ago (see lot 238 Historics 7.3.15 $ 71,407).												
1966	**Cortina Lotus**		BA74FY59122	R	45-55.000 GBP		NS		02-07-16	Woodstock	154	Coy
See lot 197 Historics 12.3.16.												
1985	**Escort RS Turbo**		30754	R	NA	60.188*	91.630*	85.130*	14-11-15	Birmingham	608	SiC
White; described as in very good original condition, the car has had just one owner and has covered 5,568 miles.												
1973	**Escort RS2000**		BFATNC00158	R	36-40.000 GBP		NS		28-11-15	Weybridge	245	His
Two-tone blue with black interior; restoration completed in 2006.												
1977	**Escort MkII Group 4**		BBATTC69901	L	90-110.000 GBP		NS		16-01-16	Birmingham	342	Coy
Ex-Works car from 1977 to 1979, it was driven by Waldegard, Nicolas and Brookes. Sold to private hands, it has had subsequently a long race career. Restored to 1977 Group 4 specification.												
1972	**Escort Mexico**		BFATMK00275	R	NA	43.875	61.320	55.717	26-02-16	Coventry	717	SiC
Blue; fully restored in the 2000s using a new Mk1 Type 49 shell in storage since 1975. 500 miles covered isnce the restoration.												
1968	**Escort Twin-Cam**		BB49HT35068	R	75-85.000 EUR	60.524	86.502	78.000	12-03-16	Lyon	320	Agu
Yellow with black bonnet and dark green roof; ex-Works car built to Group 2 specification, it was raced during the 1969 season and was driven, among others, by Hannu Mikkola, Ove Anderssonand Roger Clark. Sold to private hands, it was raced for some years. Stored for 30 years, it was acquired 12 years ago by the current owner who had the mechanicals restored.												
1974	**Escort RS2000**		BFATPU00032	R	30-35.000 GBP	36.000	52.445	46.746	20-05-16	Silverstone	305	SiC
Silver with black interior; some restoration works carried out in the 2000s.												
1968	**Escort Twin-Cam**		501635	L	15-19.000 GBP	17.080	24.600	21.763	11-06-16	Brooklands	328	His
White with black interior; restored at unspecified date.												
1978	**Escort RS2000**		CXATUR63333	R	18-23.000 GBP		NS		02-07-16	Woodstock	248	Coy
White with black cloth interior; described as in good overall condition.												
1972	**Escort RS1600**		BFATMB03731	R	45-55.000 GBP	52.880	69.590	62.620	30-07-16	Silverstone	515	SiC
Green; 3,490 miles covered since the restoration (see lot 312 Silverstone Auctions 22.2.15 $74,377).												
1974	**Capri RS3100**		BBECND10799	R	45-50.000 GBP	48.375	73.646	68.422	14-11-15	Birmingham	315	SiC
Road version, the car received a long restoration and has completed only running-in mileage since completion. The rebuilt engine gives 180bhp.												

F331: 1957 FMR Messerschmitt KR 200 cabriolet

F332: 1952 Ford Comète (Facel/Stabilimenti Farina)

Year	Model (Bodybuilder)	Chassis no.	Steering	Estimate	Hammer price £	Hammer price $	Hammer price €	Date	Place	Lot	Auc. H.
1986	Capri 2.8	34626	R	10-12.000 GBP		NS		10-12-15	London	315	Bon
	Red; restored between 2012 and 2014. Engine rebuilt.										
1979	Capri Group 1	CC13	R	NA	65.250	91.193	82.861	26-02-16	Coventry	115	SiC
	Originally prepared by CC Racing to Group 1 specification for the 1979 Spa 24 Hours and subsequently raced at other events. Unused for 20 years, it was recommissioned between 2014 and 2015 and is described as in ready to race condition.										
1987	Capri 280 Brooklands	11676	R	NA	54.000	75.470	68.575	26-02-16	Coventry	422	SiC
	Green with grey leather interior; described as in very good original condition. Two owners and 936 miles covered.										
1973	Capri RS3100	BBECND07339	R	NA	49.500	70.077	63.885	06-03-16	Birmingham	337	SiC
	Red; restored some years ago.										
1977	Capri 2.0 S	GAECST04460	R	NA	52.083	73.854	65.843	20-04-16	Duxford	44	H&H
	White with black vinyl roof and black interior; recent restoration works. Used in the TV series "Minder".										
1974	Capri RS3100	BBECND26249	R	44-48.000 GBP		NS		20-05-16	Silverstone	346	SiC
	Red; restored in 2001 by the current owner.										
1987	Capri 2.8i	91542	R	8-9.000 GBP	12.992	17.107	15.425	28-07-16	Donington Park	62	H&H
	Restored in 2006.										
1973	Capri 1.6 XL	BBECNA15706	R	11-12.000 GBP	9.708	12.783	11.526	28-07-16	Donington Park	80	H&H
	In original condition. 17,133 recorded miles.										
1974	Capri RS3100	BBECND26249	R	38-42.000 GBP	51.750	68.103	61.282	30-07-16	Silverstone	536	SiC
	See lot 346 Silverstone Auctions 20.5.16.										
1974	Granada GXL saloon	BAGFPT52583	R	8-12.000 GBP		NS		12-03-16	Brooklands	200	His
	White with black roof and black interior; restored. 20,616 miles on the odometer. 3-litre V6 engine.										
1986	RS200 (Ghia/Tickford)	00135	L	NA	121.000	186.110	163.108	14-10-15	Duxford	78	H&H
	White with red interior; sold new to the USA, the car was later reimported into the UK and refreshed. 11,400 miles covered; 350bhp engine.										
1986	RS200 (Ghia/Tickford)	00169	L	475-600.000 USD		NS		10-12-15	New York	230	RMS
	White; 1,960 kms covered since new. Currently titled in the USA.										
1985	RS200 Evolution (Ghia/Tickford)	00070	L	475-675.000 USD	365.541	522.500	471.138	12-03-16	Amelia Island	121	RMS F334
	White with red interior; one of 24 examples built. Delivered by factory with 600bhp. 430 kms covered.										
1987	RS200 (Ghia/Tickford)	00112	R	100-130.000 GBP	147.100	213.104	188.935	20-03-16	Goodwood	68	Bon
	White with red interior; one owner and 6,173 kms covered. Stored since 1994, it requires recommissioning prior to use. Up-rated 350bhp engine.										
1987	Sierra RS Cosworth hatchback	19084	R	NA	33.900	52.142	45.697	14-10-15	Duxford	5	H&H
	Blue with cloth interior; 57,000 miles on the odometer. Since 1987 in the current ownership, the car was stored from 2002 to 2014, and has been recently recommissioned.										
1987	Sierra RS500 Cosworth hatchback	38798	R	70-80.000 GBP	90.000	137.016	127.296	14-11-15	Birmingham	618	SiC
	White; approximately 14,000 miles covered.										
1987	Sierra RS500 Cosworth hatchback	38984	R	52-62.000 GBP		NS		18-05-16	Donington Park	70	H&H
	Blue with grey interior; previously modified but restored back to standard specification between 2013 and 2015.										
1987	Sierra RS500 Cosworth hatchback	39018	R	50-60.000 GBP	51.750	75.389	67.197	20-05-16	Silverstone	348	SiC
	Black with grey interior; 250 miles covered since the restoration. Fitted with a refurbished engine.										
1987	Sierra RS500 Cosworth hatchback	39030	R	60-70.000 GBP	75.380	99.200	89.265	30-07-16	Silverstone	522	SiC
	Black with grey cloth interior; two owners and 19,640 miles covered. Recently serviced.										
1993	Sapphire RS Cosworth	98109	R	27-29.000 GBP	35.438	53.951	50.124	14-11-15	Birmingham	639	SiC
	Dark green with black leather interior; 20,006 miles on the odometer.										
1988	Sapphire RS Cosworth	60245	R	16-18.000 GBP		NS		09-12-15	Chateau Impney	29	H&H
	Metallic grey.										
1993	Escort RS Cosworth Group N	96981	R	45-55.000 GBP	46.200	66.214	60.665	16-01-16	Birmingham	355	Coy
	Built by Mike Little Preparations (MLP) on behalf of Ford to Group N specification, the car was entered into the 1993 World Rally Championship under the management of Marlboro Team Ford. Restored in 2010 and used for demonstration purposes.										
1995	Escort RS Cosworth Lux	90317	R	NA	52.875	73.898	67.146	26-02-16	Coventry	418	SiC
	Blue with black leather Recaro seats; in excellent overall condition. 5,300 miles covered.										
1992	Escort RS Cosworth	95122	R	28-35.000 GBP	67.580	97.903	86.800	20-03-16	Goodwood	17	Bon
	White; 2,494 miles covered. Recommissioned in 2015. Since new in the Kingsley Curtis Collection.										

F333: 1966 Ford Cortina Lotus

F334: 1985 Ford RS200 Evolution (Ghia/Tickford)

Year	Model	(Bodybuilder)	Chassis no.	Steering	Estimate	Hammer price £	$	€	Date	Place	Lot	Auc. H.
1995	**Escort RS Cosworth**		90125	R	39-43.000 GBP		NS		11-06-16	Brooklands	253	His
	Metallic green with dark grey leather interior; 20,500 on the odometer.											

FORD (USA) *(1903-)*

Year	Model	(Bodybuilder)	Chassis no.	Steering	Estimate	£	$	€	Date	Place	Lot	Auc. H.
1906	**Model N runabout**		3643	R	25-35.000 EUR		NS		04-02-16	Paris	391	Bon
	White with black interior; for 15 years in the current ownership.											
1906	**Model N runabout**		2475	R	20-25.000 USD	9.229	12.650	11.431	25-06-16	Santa Monica	2051	AA
	Red with black interior; stored for the last 40 years.											
1921	**Model T touring**		3879923	L	7-9.000 GBP	6.440	9.806	8.804	05-09-15	Beaulieu	177	Bon
	Black; in working order. Since 1983 in the current ownership.											
1925	**Model T touring**		11654854	L	NA	8.699*	13.200*	11.838*	26-09-15	Las Vegas	20	B/J
	Black with black interior; restored.											
1926	**Model T coupé**		13349288	L	NA	9.095	13.000	11.722	12-03-16	Kansas City	F77	Mec
	Black with grey interior.											
1920	**Model T runabout**		1635438	L	20-25.000 EUR		NS		20-03-16	Fontainebleau	315	Ose
	In good overall condition.											
1915	**Model T runabout**		714840	L	25-30.000 USD	12.955*	18.700*	16.765*	05-06-16	Greenwhich	73	Bon F335
	Black with black interior; restored. From the Evergreen Collection.											
1917	**Model T coupé**		C129142	L	10-12.000 GBP	11.200	14.747	13.298	28-07-16	Donington Park	54	H&H
	Black; built in Canada.											
1929	**Model A fordor sedan (Briggs)**		A847958(engine)	L	15-20.000 USD	6.481*	9.900*	8.797*	08-10-15	Hershey	139	RMS
	Brown and black; in unrestored condition. It requires recommissioning prior to use. From the estate of Richard Roy.											
1931	**Model A coupé**		A4366814	L	20-30.000 USD	13.627*	20.900*	18.396*	09-10-15	Hershey	214	RMS
	Maroon and black with beige interior; since 2012 in the AACA Museum, the car requires servicing prior to use.											
1931	**Model A DeLuxe phaeton**		A4201822	L	13-18.000 GBP	33.600	50.571	47.799	28-11-15	Weybridge	237	His
	Blue with black fenders; restored many years ago to concours condition, the car is described as still in very good overall condition.											
1929	**Model A roadster**		A2653771	L	NA	18.849	27.000	24.980	23-01-16	Kissimmee	K80	Mec
	Brown with black fenders and black interior; fully restored.											
1930	**Model A Tudor sedan**		A306228217	L	13-18.000 GBP	19.320	27.612	24.898	12-03-16	Brooklands	169	His
	Cream and maroon with black fenders; for 28 years in the current ownership. Restored 23 years ago.											
1931	**Model A roadster**		CAT1101	L	NA	20.988	30.000	27.051	12-03-16	Kansas City	F180.1	Mec
	Maroon with black fenders and brown leather interior; restored.											
1931	**Model A DeLuxe roadster**		11375	L	23-28.000 EUR		NS		20-03-16	Fontainebleau	304	Ose
	Described as in good working order (see lot 476 Osenat 19.6.11 $ 28,968).											
1930	**Model A convertible**		3176624	L	15-20.000 EUR	17.938	25.987	23.040	20-03-16	Fontainebleau	306	Ose
	Two-tone green; in good working order (see Osenat lots 310 15.3.15 NS and 306 14.6.15 NS).											
1930	**Model A coupé**		AZ275165	L	NA	14.847*	20.350*	18.388*	24-06-16	Uncasville	51	B/J
	Two-tone grey with tan interior; restored several years ago.											
1928	**Model A open cab pickup**		A444386	L	25-35.000 USD	20.895*	27.500*	24.745*	30-07-16	Plymouth	112	RMS
	Green with black fenders; restored at unspecified date, it is described as in very good overall condition (see RM lots 34 4.8.01 $27,500, 56 23.1.04 $20,900 and 207 1.8.09 $20,900).											
1932	**Model B roadster**		B5077225	L	NA	47.684	72.600	65.188	05-09-15	Auburn	5115	AA
	Green with black fenders and brown leather interior; recently restored.											
1932	**Model B roadster**		B500623	L	NQ	37.752	55.000	49.022	20-05-16	Indianapolis	S90	Mec
	Blue with brown interior; restored.											
1932	**Model 18 V8 DeLuxe roadster**		C18D1493	L	60-75.000 USD	38.396	55.000	50.886	23-01-16	Kissimmee	S104	Mec
	Blue with black fenders and brown interior; 1,357 miles covered since the restoration.											
1932	**Model 18 V8 speedster**		1814449	L	1.200-1.400.000 USD	538.692	770.000	694.309	12-03-16	Amelia Island	162	RMS F336
	Dark grey with dark grey-brown leather interior; the first of three one-off speedsters built in the 1930s for Edsel Ford. When the second one was underway, the offered car was sold to an Indianapolis mechanic who in turn resold it to a young GM designer. Believed to be lost for almost 50 years, it was discovered when in the ownership of a body man in Connecticut by the current owner, who bought and restored it to its original specification. After restoration completion, the Speedster was shown at the 2013 Amelia Island Concours d'Elegance.											

F335: 1915 Ford Model T runabout

F336: 1932 Ford Model 18 V8 speedster

Year	Model	(Bodybuilder)	Chassis no.	Steering	Estimate	Hammer Price £	Hammer Price $	Hammer Price €	Sale Date	Sale Place	Lot	Auc. H.
1932	Model 18 V8 roadster		B1131935	L	NA	42.312	60.000	53.172	16-04-16	Houston	S158	Mec
Maroon and black; 30 miles covered since the restoration.												
1932	Model 18 V8 roadster		1874786	L	90-110.000 USD		NS		30-07-16	Plymouth	133	RMS
Blue with black fenders and brown leather interior; older restoration.												
1933	Model 40 V8 DeLuxe roadster		5422885322	L	50-60.000 EUR		NS		20-03-16	Fontainebleau	326	Ose
Dark blue with red leather interior; restored a few years ago.												
1934	Model 40 V8 DeLuxe roadster		18876605	L	65-75.000 USD	53.130	77.000	67.383	07-05-16	Auburn	473	AA
Green with green interior; restored 22 years ago.												
1936	Model 68 DeLuxe convertible		181623811	L	35-45.000 USD	30.122*	46.200*	40.665*	09-10-15	Hershey	216	RMS
Beige with brown interior; since 2001 in the AACA Museum, the car was used in the movie "The Good Shepard", directed by Robert De Niro and starring Matt Damon. It requires servicing prior to use.												
1936	Model 68 DeLuxe roadster		182465388	L	65-75.000 USD	48.411	74.250	65.355	09-10-15	Hershey	278	RMS
Black with brown leatherette interior; restored about 20 years ago. In good driving order.												
1936	Model 68 coupé		182628689	L	NA	40.128*	55.000*	49.698*	24-06-16	Uncasville	366	B/J
Black with tan interior; emerged from a long-term storage, the car is described as ready to use.												
1937	Model 78 station wagon		18F3763718	R	50-60.000 EUR	44.986	64.474	59.075	16-01-16	Maastricht	453	Coy
Black with wooden panles; restored first in the USA and again in Germany where it is registered since 2002 (see lots Brooks 793 2.12.98 NS, 720 18.6.99 $ 33,051 and 436 26.10.99 $ 33,368, and Coys 432 2.12.14 NS and 232 16.5.15 NS).												
1937	Model 78 DeLuxe roadster		183556313	L	60-80.000 USD	41.789	55.000	49.489	30-07-16	Plymouth	157	RMS
Maroon with light brown interior; restored several years ago and freshened around 2008.												
1938	Model 81A DeLuxe convertible		184517683	L	35-45.000 USD	26.186	37.950	33.210	07-05-16	Auburn	846	AA
Red with tan leather interior; restored.												
1939	Model 91A DeLuxe station wagon		1814801771	L	120-160.000 USD	65.422*	93.500*	85.618*	29-01-16	Phoenix	228	RMS F337
Black with wooden panels and tan interior; paintwork and interior redone in the early 1980s. From the Craig McCaw Collection.												
1939	Model 91A DeLuxe convertible		185039262	L	50-75.000 USD	41.256	54.000	47.677	20-08-16	Monterey	S36	Mec
In good overall condition; gearbox rebuilt.												
1940	Model 01A coupé		185498891	L	65-85.000 USD	37.818*	49.500*	43.704*	19-08-16	Carmel	46	Bon
Midnight blue; the car has covered 662 miles since a full restoration.												
1941	Super DeLuxe station wagon		99A315781	L	90-120.000 USD	47.249*	68.200*	61.141*	05-06-16	Greenwhich	68	Bon
Tan with wooden panels and dark red interior; restored in the early 2000s.												
1942	Super DeLuxe station wagon		186808429	L	NA	34.363	49.500	43.788	11-06-16	Newport Beach	6132	R&S
Maroon with wooden panels and brown interior; restored.												
1942	Super DeLuxe station wagon		186771494	L	60-75.000 USD	45.968*	60.500*	54.438*	30-07-16	Plymouth	165	RMS
Black with wooden panels and brown interior; in good overall condition (see RM lots 142 12.8.10 $79,750, and 105 19.1.12 $68,750).												
1944	GPW		212461	L	16-20.000 GBP	33.350	51.436	45.649	12-09-15	Goodwood	302	Bon
Acquired by the previous owner in the late 1960s directly from the British Army and fully restored over a period of many years.												
1942	GPW		47887	L	15-20.000 EUR	12.790*	18.429*	16.240*	14-05-16	Monaco	136	RMS
In good overall condition; since 1983 in the Quattroruote Collection.												
1947	Super DeLuxe sportsman convertible		1849644	L	160-200.000 USD	96.822	148.500	130.710	09-10-15	Hershey	229	RMS
Red with wooden panels and maroon interior (see lot 683 Auctions America 28.3.15 NS).												
1947	Super DeLuxe sportsman convertible		799A2011953	L	250-300.000 USD	181.922	260.000	238.082	30-01-16	Scottsdale	116	G&Co
Black with wooden panels and red interior; restored, the car is described as in concours condition. In the same ownership from 1951 to 2006.												
1947	Super DeLuxe sportsman convertible		799A1934335	L	175-225.000 USD	107.738*	154.000*	138.862*	12-03-16	Amelia Island	140	RMS F338
Dark green with wooden panels and red leather interior; restored several years ago. Interior recently replaced (see lot 165 RM 16.1.09 $ 162,250).												
1947	Super DeLuxe convertible		799A1594294	L	60-75.000 USD		NS		20-08-16	Monterey	S21	Mec
Black with tan interior; in good overall condition.												
1948	Model 89A Super DeLuxe convertible		899A2201066	L	50-60.000 USD	28.802*	44.000*	39.098*	08-10-15	Hershey	177	RMS
Yellow with leather and cloth interior; restored several years ago (see lot 736 RM 26.3.10 $ 88,000).												
1951	Custom DeLuxe convertible		B1AT146666	L	30-40.000 USD	25.102*	38.500*	33.888*	09-10-15	Hershey	227	RMS
Black with red interior; restored.												
1950	Custom DeLuxe station wagon		B0CS135462	L	60-80.000 USD	31.342*	41.250*	37.117*	30-07-16	Plymouth	156	RMS
Light green with wooden panels; restored at unspecified date (see lot 137 RM 15.11.14 $57,750).												
1953	Crestline Victoria hardtop		B3FV232187	L	NA	13.854	21.000	19.177	12-12-15	Austin	F143	Mec
Ivory and red; recently restored. Automatic transmission.												
1954	Crestline Skyliner hardtop		U4DF136874	L	35-40.000 USD	24.668	35.750	31.285	07-05-16	Auburn	476	AA
Metallic blue with white roof and two-tone vinyl interior; restored. Upgraded 312 Y-block V8 engine; 3-speed manual gearbox with overdrive (see lot 129 RM 15.11.14 $ 35,750).												
1957	Thunderbird convertible		F7FH330742	L	NA	143.820	225.000	197.055	19-09-15	Dallas	S114	Mec
Blue with two-tone blue interior; concours quality restoration. 300bhp 312 supercharged engine with 3-speed manual gearbox with overdrive.												
1956	Thunderbird convertible		P6FH359496	L	35-40.000 USD	28.688*	44.000*	38.729*	09-10-15	Hershey	218	RMS
Coral with black and white interior; in original condition. 47,293 miles on the odometer. 225bhp 292 engine with automatic transmission. From the estate of Jim Miller.												
1957	Thunderbird convertible		F7FH394793	L	NA		NS		31-10-15	Hilton Head	155	AA
Black; fully restored. 312 supercharged engine with automatic transmission (see lots 247 RM 10.10.14 $ 137,500 and 478 Auctions America 28.3.15 NS).												
1957	Thunderbird convertible		F7FH331499	L	NA	121.527	185.000	171.884	13-11-15	Anaheim	S121.1	Mec F339
Bronze with bronze interior; restored. 300bhp 312 supercharged engine with 3-speed manual gearbox with overdrive (see lot 2124 Auctions America 18.7.15 $ 142,500).												

Year	Model (Bodybuilder)	Chassis no.	Steering	Estimate	Hammer price £	Hammer price $	Hammer price €	Date	Place	Lot	Auc. H.
1966	**Thunderbird convertible**	6Y85Z113571	L	NA	47.954	73.000	67.824	13-11-15	Anaheim	S226	**Mec**
	Red with white interior; restoration completed in 2014. 390 engine with automatic transmission. Used in the movie "Thelma & Louise".										
1957	**Thunderbird convertible**	D7FH334663	L	60-80.000 USD	26.915*	38.500*	35.308*	28-01-16	Scottsdale	1	**Bon**
	Black with turquoise and white interior; restored in the 2000s. 245bhp 312 engine with automatic transmission.										
1957	**Thunderbird convertible**	D7FH260754	L	37-42.000 EUR	31.659	45.247	40.800	12-03-16	Lyon	314	**Agu**
	White with white and black interior; in good overall condition. 245bhp 312 engine with manual gearbox.										
1965	**Thunderbird convertible**	5Y857Z162416	L	25-30.000 EUR	23.543	34.108	30.240	20-03-16	Fontainebleau	378	**Ose**
	In good overall condition; 300bhp 390 engine.										
1957	**Thunderbird convertible**	F7FH333817	M	NA	137.533	193.600	170.368	09-04-16	Palm Beach	386	**B/J**
	Red with red interior; restored at unspecified. 300bhp 312 supercharged engine with automatic transmission (see lot 314 RM 11.11.06 $ 319,000).										
1955	**Thunderbird convertible**	P5FH201109	L	28-35.000 GBP		NS		11-06-16	Brooklands	284	**His**
	Light blue with light blue and white interior; restored. 198bhp 292 engine with 3-speed manual gearbox.										
1966	**Thunderbird convertible**	6Y85Q120795	L	20-25.000 GBP	22.400	32.263	28.542	11-06-16	Brooklands	287	**His**
	Metallic ice blue with black leather interior; restored in Europe at unspecified date. 428 engine (see lot 296 Historics 3.7.15 $ 34,003).										
1966	**Thunderbird convertible**	6Y85Z131806	L	25-35.000 USD	18.805*	24.750*	22.270*	30-07-16	Plymouth	108	**RMS**
	Burgundy; in good overall condition. Fitted with the "roadster tonneau" for the rear seat.										
1960	**Thunderbird convertible**	0Y73Y112964	L	60-80.000 USD	41.789	55.000	49.489	30-07-16	Plymouth	117	**RMS**
	Black with tan leather interior; restored about 10 years ago. 300bhp 352 engine with automatic transmission (see lot 220 RM 13.11.10 $79,750).										
1956	**Fairlane Crown Victoria**	M6RW139728	L	30-40.000 USD	37.950	55.000	48.131	07-05-16	Auburn	732	**AA**
	Green and white with light green vinyl and medium green cloth interior; restored. 3-speed manual gearbox.										
1955	**Fairlane Crown Victoria Skyliner**	U5GF165121	L	80-100.000 USD		NS		30-07-16	Plymouth	134	**RMS**
	White and rose with matching vinyl interior; restored. Automatic transmission.										
1957	**Station Wagon Country Sedan**	D7LX183461	L	NA	48.489*	69.300*	63.458*	29-01-16	Scottsdale	1165	**B/J**
	White and green with white and green interior; restoration completed in 2011. 3-speed manual gearbox.										
1957	**Fairlane 500 Skyliner retractable hardtop**	F7FW387795	L	NA		NS		09-04-16	Palm Beach	387	**B/J**
	Red with red and white interior; at unspecified date restored to concours condition. 300bhp 312 supercharged engine with automatic transmission (see lot 328 RM 11.11.06 $ 258,500).										
1959	**Fairlane 500 Skyliner retractable hardtop**	H9RW170979	L	70-90.000 USD	35.526	46.500	41.055	19-08-16	Monterey	F72	**Mec**
	Blue and white with matching interior; restored. 352 engine with automatic transmission.										
1957	**Fairlane 500 Sunliner convertible**	D7EC155495	L	90-110.000 USD	75.395	108.000	99.922	23-01-16	Kissimmee	S103	**Mec**
	Brown and pink with matching interior; fully restored. 312 engine with automatic transmission.										
1957	**Ranchero**	C7KF131745	L	NA	70.520	100.000	88.620	16-04-16	Houston	S110	**Mec**
	Red and white with matching interior; restored. 292 engine with automatic transmission.										
1965	**Thunderbird hardtop**	5Y83Z140758	L	20-25.000 EUR		NS		20-03-16	Fontainebleau	368	**Ose**
	Imported into France in 2014 and subsequently subjected to some restoration works.										
1959	**Galaxie Sunliner convertible**	C9FC129826	L	24-28.000 USD	22.770*	33.000*	28.878*	07-05-16	Auburn	859	**AA**
	Red and white with red, black and white interior; restored. Automatic transmission.										
1963	**Galaxie 500 Lightweight hardtop**	3N66R140734	L	NA	102.272	160.000	140.128	19-09-15	Dallas	S120.1	**Mec** **F340**
	White with red interior; fully restored about 20 years ago. 425bhp 427 engine with 4-speed manual gearbox.										
1964	**Galaxie 500 XL convertible**	4Z69R101919	L	NA	97.478	152.500	133.560	19-09-15	Dallas	S162	**Mec**
	Red with red interior; restored. 425bhp 427 engine with 4-speed manual gearbox.										
1964	**Galaxie 500 convertible**	4E65R215889	L	NA	91.086	142.500	124.802	19-09-15	Dallas	S163	**Mec**
	White with red interior; restored. 427 engine with 4-speed manual gearbox.										
1963	**Galaxie 500 hardtop**	3G66R161859	L	NA	35.208	54.000	47.531	09-10-15	Chicago	S75.1	**Mec**
	White with black interior; restored. 425bhp 427 rebuilt engine with 4-speed manual gearbox.										
1964	**Galaxie 500XL convertible**	4Z69R123308	L	120-150.000 USD	85.517	122.500	113.337	23-01-16	Kissimmee	S118	**Mec**
	Red with white interior; full restoration completed in 2014. 425bhp 427 engine with 4-speed manual gearbox.										
1963	**Galaxie 500 XL hardtop**	3A68R194502	L	NA	45.411*	64.900*	59.429*	29-01-16	Scottsdale	1076	**B/J**
	Black with black interior; restored. The 427 engine and 4-speed manual gearbox have been rebuilt.										

F337: 1939 Ford Model 91A DeLuxe station wagon

F338: 1947 Ford Super DeLuxe sportsman convertible

F339: 1957 Ford Thunderbird convertible

F340: 1963 Ford Galaxie 500 Lightweight hardtop

Year	Model (Bodybuilder)	Chassis no.	Steering	Estimate	Hammer price £	$	€	Date	Place	Lot	Auc. H.
1963	**Galaxie 500 XL hardtop**	3J68R182240	L	NA	119.350	155.000	140.012	09-07-16	Denver	S37	Mec
	Black with black interior; fully restored. 425bhp 427 engine with 4-speed manual gearbox.										
1963	**Thunderbird sports roadster**	3Y89M106102	L	200-250.000 USD	86.588*	123.750*	113.318*	29-01-16	Scottsdale	28	G&Co
	Red with black leather interior; restored to concours condition. 340bhp 390 engine with automatic transmission (see lot 9011 Russo & Steele 19.1.11 $ 70,000).										
1962	**Thunderbird sports roadster**	2Y85Z106867	L	NA	96.307*	132.000*	119.275*	24-06-16	Uncasville	757	B/J F341
	Red with white leather interior; 3,600 miles covered since the restoration. 390 Tri-Power engine with automatic transmission.										
1965	**Mustang convertible**	5F08C765557	L	25-30.000 EUR	17.224	26.074	24.000	07-11-15	Lyon	252	Agu
	White with blue and white interior; restored at unspecified date. 3-speed manual gearbox.										
1967	**Mustang GT convertible**	7R03S200188	L	70-90.000 USD	52.358	75.000	69.390	23-01-16	Kissimmee	F232	Mec
	White with red interior; 390 engine with 4-speed manual gearbox.										
1971	**Mustang convertible**	1F03F100966	R	28-32.000 GBP	NS			12-03-16	Brooklands	242	His
	Dark blue with black interior; built in right-hand form for a managing director of Ford UK. Restored in 1997 (see lot 288 Historics 29.11.14 $ 42,806).										
1966	**Mustang GT convertible**	6F08A166757	L	NA	21.688	31.000	27.953	12-03-16	Kansas City	S188	Mec
	Red with red interior; restored in 2015. 3-speed manual gearbox.										
1965	**Mustang GT convertible**	5F08A797904	L	55-75.000 USD	38.050	54.450	47.627	02-04-16	Ft.Lauderdale	226	AA
	Silver smoke grey with red interior; three year restoration. 4-speed manual gearbox.										
1965	**Mustang hardtop**	5T07C158055	L	20-28.000 EUR	NS			08-11-15	Lyon	223	Ose
	Pale yellow with black interior; automatic transmission. Unused for several years, the car has been recently recommissioned.										
1968	**Mustang hardtop**	8F01R179900	L	NA	35.260	50.000	44.310	16-04-16	Houston	S93.1	Mec
	Gold with black roof and gold interior; 428 Cobra Jet engine with automatic transmission.										
1966	**GT40**	GT40P1065	L	3.200-3.600.000 USD	2.308.680	3.300.000	2.975.610	11-03-16	Amelia Island	62	G&Co
	Road version finished in blue with black interior, the car was used by the factory for promotional purposes. In late 1967 it was sold to its first private owner. After several ownership changes in the USA and UK, in 2010 it was acquired by the current owner. First restored between 1982 and 1984, in 2009 it was restored again to its original livery. Just over 3,200 covered (see lots Christie's 66 19.8.01 NS and 53 18.8.02 $ 436,500, RM 244 31.10.07 $ 2,005,599 and 443 16.8.08 $ 1,465,000, and Gooding 54 14.8.10 $ 1,650,000).										
1966	**GT40**	P1057	R	3.250-3.750.000 USD	2.215.600	2.900.000	2.560.410	19-08-16	Monterey	125	RMS
	Road version originally finished in dark green, the car was sold new to the USA. After some ownership changes, it was acquired by Robert Ash who restored it between 1987 and 1990 circa to the present red livery with white side stripes. For 25 years in the current ownership; engine rebuilt in 2015.										
1966	**GT40**	P1061	R	3.750-4.250.000 USD	NS			19-08-16	Monterey	141	RMS
	Road version retained by the factory for promotional purpose until late 1967. Subsequently the car has had some owners in the USA, UK and Australia. In the mid-1980s it was prepared for historic racing and finished in the present dark green with yellow stripe and nose livery. Since 1992 in the Jim Click Ford Performance Collection. 302 engine bored out to 351c.i.										
1966	**GT40**	P1028	L	4.000-5.000.000 USD	3.361.600	4.400.000	3.884.760	20-08-16	Monterey	S103	Mec F342
	Silver with black leather interior; first road version example delivered to North America, the car was used by Ford North America for promotional purpose until 1967 when it was sold to its first private owner. In 1975 it was purchased by the Schroeder family in whose ownership it remained for nearly 40 years. Subsequently it has been fully restored and refinished in its original silver livery.										

F341: 1962 Ford Thunderbird sports roadster

F342: 1966 Ford GT40

Year	Model	(Bodybuilder)	Chassis no.	Steering	Estimate	Hammer price £	$	€	Date	Place	Lot	Auc. H.
1968	**Mustang fastback**		8F02S111348	L	NA	48.272	69.000	62.217	12-03-16	Kansas City	S199	Mec
	Gold with gold interior; recently restored. 320bhp 390 engine with 4-speed manual gearbox.
1968	**Mustang Lightweight fastback**		8F02R135031	L	175-225.000 USD	96.096	140.000	124.782	20-05-16	Indianapolis	F180.1	Mec
	White with black interior; fully restored. 428 Cobra Jet engine with 4-speed manual gearbox. One of 50 examples built; Factory sponsored drag car driven by Dave Lyall. From the Jeffrey Cohen Collection.
1966	**Fairlane 500 GTA convertible**		6H44S105815	L	NA	32.919	51.500	45.104	19-09-15	Dallas	S91.1	Mec
	Silver metallic with red vinyl interior; fully restored. 335bhp 390 engine with automatic transmission.
1966	**Fairlane 500 XL hardtop**		6A43R249537	L	NA	181.225	275.000	246.620	26-09-15	Las Vegas	743	B/J **F343**
	White with black interior; 23 miles covered since the restoration. One of 57 examples built. 427 engine with 4-speed manual gearbox.
1968	**Mustang Shelby GT350 fastback**		8T02J14934501144	L	NA	72.490*	110.000*	98.648*	26-09-15	Las Vegas	722	B/J
	Red with white stripes and black interior; less than 600 miles covered since the restoration. The original automatic transmission was replaced with a 4-speed manual gearbox.
1966	**Mustang Shelby GT350 fastback**		SFM6S1513	L	255-295.000 AUD	133.548	205.713	185.591	24-10-15	Melbourne	10	TBr
	Red with white stripes and black interior; fully restored in the USA in 2011 and subsequently imported into Australia. Described as in concours condition.
1965	**Mustang Shelby GT350 fastback**		SFM5S342	L	325-375.000 USD		NS		28-01-16	Phoenix	129	RMS
	White with blue stripes; restored in the 2000s, the car was later acquired by the current owner who had it upgraded for use in vintage rallies fitting a new 313bhp 289 engine, a 5-speed manual gearbox and upgraded power brakes. All the replaced original parts are offered with the car, including the original engine.
1968	**Mustang Shelby GT350H fastback**		8T02J149278	L	NA	115.451*	165.000*	151.091*	29-01-16	Scottsdale	1457.1	B/J
	Blue with black interior; 200 miles covered since the restoration. Automatic transmission.
1966	**Mustang Shelby GT350 fastback**		SFM6S1747	L	NA	134.692	192.500	176.272	30-01-16	Scottsdale	5158	R&S
	Blue with white stripes; restored. 4-speed manual gearbox.
1966	**Mustang Shelby GT350 fastback**		SFM6S748	L	180-200.000 EUR	134.991	195.919	179.200	03-02-16	Paris	142	RMS
	White with blue stripes; sold new to the UK, the car was raced at minor events. In 1977 it was imported into Germany, modified to GT350R specification and raced for 11 years. In the late 1980s it was restored and prepared for historic racing. Described as in ready to race condition.
1966	**Mustang Shelby GT350 fastback**		SFM6S1509	L	200-250.000 EUR		NS		04-02-16	Paris	388	Bon
	White with blue stripes; fitted with a 423bhp Roxwell Racing engine, the car is offered with a spare Paxton supercharged engine. Described as in good overall condition.
1966	**Mustang Shelby GT350 fastback**		SFM6M1509	L	100-130.000 GBP		NS		20-03-16	Goodwood	43	Bon
	See lot 388 Bonhams 4.2.16.
1965	**Mustang Shelby GT350 fastback**		SFM5S472	L	350-450.000 USD	219.842	314.600	275.181	02-04-16	Ft.Lauderdale	495	AA
	White with blue stripes and original black interior; body repainted some time ago. The engine has covered a few miles since the rebuild (see lot 163 RM 18.1.13 $ 172,500).
1966	**Mustang Shelby GT350 fastback**		SFM6S364	L	170-190.000 USD		NS		02-04-16	Ft.Lauderdale	551	AA
	White with blue stripes and black interior; restored in 1991 and fitted with the present 4-speed manual gearbox as replacement of the original automatic transmission (see lot 568 Auctions America 4.3.11 $ 147,400).
1966	**Mustang Shelby GT350 fastback**		SFM6S462	L	200-225.000 USD		NS		07-05-16	Auburn	817	AA
	White with blue stripes and black interior; restored at unspecified date. Cambio manuale.
1965	**Mustang Shelby GT350 fastback**		SFM5S041	L	350-450.000 USD	343.200	500.000	445.650	20-05-16	Indianapolis	F125	Mec **F344**
	White with blue stripes and black interior; restored to concours condition in the early 1990s. From the Joe McMurrey Collection.
1967	**Mustang Shelby GT350 fastback**		67200F2A02148	L	275-350.000 USD	195.624	285.000	254.021	20-05-16	Indianapolis	F127	Mec
	Dark blue with black interior; restored in 1996. 390bhp 289 engine with Paxton supercharger. From the Joe McMurrey Collection.
1966	**Mustang Shelby GT350 fastback**		SFM6S163	L	80-120.000 USD	110.502*	159.500*	142.992*	05-06-16	Greenwich	95	Bon
	Used when new as racer/demonstrator by Harr Ford dealership in Worcester, Massachusetts. A "barn find" in original condition, stored since 1976; one owner car.
1965	**Mustang Shelby GT350 fastback**		SFM5S377	L	NA	213.470	305.000	270.993	18-06-16	Portland	S86	Mec
	White with blue stripes and blue interior; restored many years ago. For 38 years in the current ownership. Original engine and 4-speed manual gearbox.
1965	**Mustang Shelby GT350 fastback**		SFM5S391	L	340-380.000 USD		NS		25-06-16	Santa Monica	1080	AA
	White with blue stripes; at unspecified date the car was fitted with a Boss 302 engine and Ford Top Loader 4-speed manual gearbox. Restored.
1968	**Mustang Shelby GT350 fastback**		8T02J149447	L	NA	83.996	110.000	99.869	23-07-16	Harrisburg	F132	Mec
	Metallic gold with black interior; restored. Manual gearbox.
1966	**Mustang Shelby GT350 fastback**		SFM6S2157	L	140-160.000 USD	92.444*	121.000*	106.831*	19-08-16	Carmel	17	Bon
	Green with white stripes; the car has covered 1,000 miles since the restoration carried out in 2013. Manual gearbox.
1967	**Mustang Shelby GT350 fastback**		67200F5A01493	L	100-150.000 USD	84.040*	110.000*	97.119*	19-08-16	Carmel	25	Bon
	Green with black interior; since 1976 in the current, third ownership. Restored in 2012. Manual gearbox.

F343: 1966 Ford Fairlane 500 XL hardtop

F344: 1965 Ford Mustang Shelby GT350 fastback

Year	Model	(Bodybuilder)	Chassis no.	Steering	Estimate	Hammer Price £	$	€	Date	Place	Lot	Auc. H.
1965	**Mustang Shelby GT350R fastback**		SFM5R108	L	850-950.000 USD	567.270	742.500	655.553	19-08-16	Monterey	124	RMS

White with red, white and green stripes; the car was raced until 1972 and won the 1966 SCCA Southwest Division and 1967 B-Production Class championships. In 1967 it won its class at the Sebring 12 Hours. Stored for 10 years, in the 1980s the car was restored and subsequently raced at historic races in the USA and Europe (see lots Gooding & Company 80 20.8.06 $748,000 and 39 21.1.11 NS, and RM/Sotheby's 212 2.5.15 $770,000).

Year	Model	(Bodybuilder)	Chassis no.	Steering	Estimate	£	$	€	Date	Place	Lot	Auc. H.
1966	**Mustang Shelby GT350 fastback**		SFM6S2363	L	350-450.000 USD	168.080*	220.000*	194.238*	19-08-16	Monterey	136	RMS

Road version originally finished in blue, the car was race-prepared in 1969 by Don Roberts and won the 1970 SCCA B-Production Southern Pacific Division Championship. In the early 1980s it was prepared for historic racing and used until 1990. In 2002 it was bought by Jim Click and raced again. Engine rebuilt in 2015. White, black and red livery. From the Jim Click Ford Performance Collection.

1965	**Mustang Shelby GT350 fastback**		SFM5S277	L	475-575.000 USD	439.300	575.000	507.668	20-08-16	Monterey	S97	Mec

White with blue stripes and black interior; the car remained unused from 1968 to 1976 when it was bought by the second owner, who repainted it and drove it until 1980. In early 2015 it was purchased by the current, third owner and returned to the road. Original engine rebuilt; 27,000 miles covered since new.

1965	**Mustang Shelby GT350 fastback**		SFM5S199	L	NQ		NS		20-08-16	Monterey	7010	R&S

White with blue stripes; restored (see lot S79 Mecum 15.8.15 NS).

1968	**Mustang Shelby GT350 convertible**		8T03J192402	L	120-140.000 USD		NS		20-08-16	Monterey	S131	Mec

Blue with black interior; restored in 1992-93. 302 engine with 4-speed manual gearbox.

1967	**Mustang Shelby GT500 fastback**		67400F2A01926	L	90-120.000 GBP	126.000	192.301	172.532	07-09-15	London	175	RMS

Blue with black interior; restored. The engine was rebuilt and enlarged to 462 cu.in. giving 437 bhp; 4-speed manual gearbox.

1967	**Mustang Shelby GT500 fastback**		67400F5A01509	L	NA	121.448	190.000	166.402	19-09-15	Dallas	S93	Mec

Dark green with white stripes and black interior; restored. 428 CI Police Interceptor with 4-speed manual gearbox.

1968	**Mustang Shelby GT500KR fastback**		8T02R215943	L	NA		NS		12-12-15	Austin	S39	Mec

White with black interior; restored. Automatic transmission.

1967	**Mustang Shelby GT500 fastback**		67400F7A01538	L	120-160.000 USD	136.130	195.000	180.414	23-01-16	Kissimmee	S114	Mec

Lime gold with white stripes and black interior; since 1990 in the current ownership. Restored in 2009. 355bhp 428 engine with 4-speed manual gearbox

1968	**Mustang Shelby GT500KR fastback**		8T02R21092103794	L	175-225.000 USD	101.225	145.000	134.154	23-01-16	Kissimmee	S145	Mec

Dark green with black interior; restored at unspecified date. 428 Cobra Jet engine with automatic transmission (see lot S95 Mecum 6.6.2015 $ 165,000).

1967	**Mustang Shelby GT500 fastback**		67402F4A01487	L	NA	100.057*	143.000*	130.945*	29-01-16	Scottsdale	1287	B/J

White with black interior; less than 50,000 actual miles. 4-speed manual gearbox (see lot F175.1 Mecum 16.5.15 $ 141,000).

1967	**Mustang Shelby GT500 E fastback**		AZ324165	L	NA	200.114*	286.000*	261.890*	29-01-16	Scottsdale	1301	B/J

Black with grey stripes; described as one of the 35 Super Snake examples, built by Unique Performance, authorized and serialized by Carroll Shelby. Supercharged 427 engine with 5-speed manual gearbox.

1968	**Mustang Shelby GT500KR fastback**		8T02R21325203977	L	NA	73.119*	104.500*	95.691*	29-01-16	Scottsdale	1438	B/J

Pale yellow with black interior; automatic transmission (see lot 514 Barrett-Jackson 19.1.13 $ 108,900).

1968	**Mustang Shelby GT500KR fastback**		8T02R21589804128	L	NA	146.916	210.000	189.357	12-03-16	Kansas City	S106	Mec F345

Black with black interior; recently restored. 428 Cobra Jet engine with 4-speed manual gearbox.

1967	**Mustang Shelby GT500 fastback**		67400F4A01094	L	NA	118.932	170.000	153.289	12-03-16	Kansas City	S120.1	Mec

White with blue stripes and black interior; currently fitted with a 427 engine with 4-speed manual gearbox, the car is offered with its original, rebuilt 428 engine also.

1967	**Mustang Shelby GT500 fastback**		67400FA02878	L	150-175.000 USD	117.224	167.750	146.731	02-04-16	Ft.Lauderdale	474	AA

Lime gold with black interior; described as in original condition. 58,000 miles on the odometer. 428 Interceptor engine with 4-speed manual gearbox.

1967	**Mustang Shelby GT500 fastback**		67410F5A01997	L	NA	109.306	155.000	137.361	16-04-16	Houston	S91	Mec

Green with black interior; believed to be 37,332 miles. Automatic transmission.

1968	**Mustang Shelby GT500 fastback**		8T02S126866	L	110-125.000 USD	110.055	159.500	139.578	07-05-16	Auburn	813	AA

Black with black interior; restored in 2003. Automatic transmission.

1967	**Mustang Shelby GT500 fastback**		67400F2A01923	L	190-210.000 USD	116.688	170.000	151.521	20-05-16	Indianapolis	S132	Mec

Blue with black interior; restored to concours condition in 2010. 355bhp 428 Police Interceptor engine with 4-speed manual gearbox.

1967	**Mustang Shelby GT500 fastback**		67410F4A01867	L	NA	110.725	159.500	141.094	11-06-16	Newport Beach	6141	R&S

White with blue stripes; 428 engine with 4-speed manual gearbox.

1967	**Mustang Shelby GT500 fastback**		67412F0A02402	L	NA	61.600	80.000	72.264	09-07-16	Denver	S173	Mec

Blue with black interior; unrestored. Since 1988 in the current ownership. 428 engine with automatic transmission.

1967	**Mustang Shelby GT500 fastback**		67400F4A01122	L	NQ	118.496	155.100	136.938	20-08-16	Monterey	7243	R&S

White with white stripes.

F345: 1968 Ford Mustang Shelby GT500KR fastback

F346: 1968 Ford Mustang Shelby GT500KR convertible

Year	Model	(Bodybuilder)	Chassis no.	Steering	Estimate	Hammer price £	$	€	Sale Date	Place	Lot	Auc. H.
1967	Thunderbird Landau 4-door sedan		7Y84Z135101	L	NA	10.006*	14.300*	13.095*	29-01-16	Scottsdale	1206	B/J
{Black with black interior; the paintwork, vinyl roof and interior have been redone.}

| 1968 | Mustang Shelby GT500 convertible | | 8T03S149495 | L | NA | 73.940* | 112.200* | 100.621* | 26-09-15 | Las Vegas | 731 | B/J |

Red with black interior; automatic transmission.

| 1968 | Mustang Shelby GT500 convertible | | 8T03S17798402442 | L | NA | | NS | | 09-10-15 | Chicago | S130.1 | Mec |

Blue with black interior; 360bhp 428 Police Interceptor engine with automatic transmission.

| 1969 | Mustang Shelby GT500 convertible | | 9F03R480072 | L | NA | 80.470 | 122.500 | 113.815 | 13-11-15 | Anaheim | S100.1 | Mec |

Silver with white interior; restored about 20 years ago. Automatic transmission.

| 1968 | Mustang Shelby GT500 convertible | | 8T03S116053 | L | NA | 72.259 | 110.000 | 102.201 | 13-11-15 | Anaheim | S86.1 | Mec |

White with black interior; restored. Manual gearbox (see lot 6174 Russo & Steele 19.1.06 $ 203,500).

| 1968 | Mustang Shelby GT500 convertible | | 8T03S116039 | L | NA | 115.451* | 165.000* | 151.091* | 29-01-16 | Scottsdale | 1413 | B/J |

Blue with black interior; restored. 420bhp 428 Police Interceptor engine with automatic transmission.

| 1968 | Mustang Shelby GT500KR convertible | | 8T03R215917 | L | NA | 150.086* | 214.500* | 196.418* | 29-01-16 | Scottsdale | 1429 | B/J |

White with black interior; 200 miles covered since the restoration. 4-speed manual gearbox.

| 1968 | Mustang Shelby GT500 convertible | | 8T03R210288 | L | 140-160.000 USD | 101.850 | 145.750 | 127.488 | 02-04-16 | Ft.Lauderdale | 518 | AA |

Lime gold with black interior; recent concours-quality restoration. Manual gearbox.

| 1968 | Mustang Shelby GT500KR convertible | | 8T03R21037803762 | L | 80-120.000 EUR | 108.686 | 156.602 | 138.000 | 13-05-16 | Monaco | 109 | Bon F346 |

Yellow with black interior; restored in 2014. Manual gearbox. Swiss papers.

| 1968 | Mustang Shelby GT500KR convertible | | 8T03R210167 | L | 175-225.000 USD | 123.552 | 180.000 | 160.434 | 20-05-16 | Indianapolis | F126 | Mec |

Yellow with black interior; body repainted. Rebuilt 428 Cobra Jet engine with 4-speed manual gearbox. From the Joe McMurrey Collection.

| 1969 | Mustang Shelby GT500 convertible | | 9F03R482546 | L | 175-225.000 USD | 101.244 | 147.500 | 131.467 | 20-05-16 | Indianapolis | S109 | Mec |

Green with black vinyl interior; restored. 30,225 miles on the odometer. Automatic transmission.

| 1968 | Mustang Shelby GT500 convertible | | 8T03S17798402442 | L | NA | 83.988 | 120.000 | 106.620 | 18-06-16 | Portland | S114 | Mec |

See lot S130.1 Mecum 9.10.15.

| 1968 | Mustang Shelby GT500KR convertible | | 8T03R206130 | L | NA | 148.474* | 203.500* | 183.883* | 24-06-16 | Uncasville | 668 | B/J |

Green with black interior; concours-quality restoration. Manual gearbox.

| 1972 | LTD hardtop | | 2B62S189697 | L | 12-16.000 GBP | 11.760 | 16.807 | 15.155 | 12-03-16 | Brooklands | 209 | His |

Green with black roof and black interior; described as in very good overall condition.

| 1970 | LTD hardtop sedan | | 0J66N144614 | L | 10-15.000 USD | 14.208* | 18.700* | 16.826* | 30-07-16 | Plymouth | 105 | RMS |

Light metallic green with white vinyl roof and cloth and vinyl interior; in largely original condition. One owner until 2012; less than 25,000 miles covered. 360bhp Thunder Jet engine with automatic transmission.

| 1970 | Mustang Mach 1 | | 0T05R117586 | L | NA | 86.988* | 132.000* | 118.378* | 26-09-15 | Las Vegas | 7002 | B/J F347 |

Blu with original white interior; 428 Super Cobra Jet engine with 4-speed manual gearbox.

| 1970 | Mustang Mach 1 | | 0T05R109357 | L | NA | 53.436 | 81.000 | 73.969 | 12-12-15 | Austin | S40 | Mec |

Orange with red interior; concours-quality restoration. 428 Cobra Jet engine with 4-speed manual gearbox.

| 1969 | Mustang Mach 1 | | 9T02R180319 | L | NA | 61.574* | 88.000* | 80.582* | 29-01-16 | Scottsdale | 1033 | B/J |

Maroon with white interior; fully restored in 2015. 428 Super Cobra Jet engine with 4-speed manual gearbox.

| 1969 | Mustang Mach 1 | | 9F02R173596 | L | 85-95.000 EUR | | NS | | 09-04-16 | Essen | 153 | Coy |

Metallic black jade; repainted body, rebuilt 428 Super Cobra Jet engine and 4-speed manual gearbox.

| 1970 | Mustang Boss 302 | | 0T02G125945 | L | NA | 46.394* | 70.400* | 63.135* | 26-09-15 | Las Vegas | 672 | B/J |

Orange with black interior; restoration completed in 2014. 4-speed manual gearbox.

| 1970 | Mustang Boss 302 | | 0F02G137299 | L | NA | 50.701 | 80.300 | 70.600 | 31-10-15 | Hilton Head | 173 | AA |

White with black interior; restored. Manual gearbox.

| 1970 | Mustang Boss 302 | | 0F02G187619 | L | NA | 76.967* | 110.000* | 100.727* | 29-01-16 | Scottsdale | 1132.1 | B/J |

Red with white interior; engine recently rebuilt. Manual gearbox.

| 1970 | Mustang Boss 302 | | 0F0ZG206317 | L | NA | 62.343 | 89.100 | 81.589 | 30-01-16 | Scottsdale | 5547 | R&S |

Described as in original condition except for the paintwork redone in 1991; less than 11,000 original miles.

| 1970 | Mustang Boss 302 | | 0F2G204666 | L | 90-125.000 USD | 58.064 | 76.000 | 67.100 | 19-08-16 | Monterey | F156 | Mec |

Red with black stripes on the bonnet and black interior; described as in original, urestored condition, the car has had one owner and has covered 44,205 miles. 4-speed manual gearbox.

| 1969 | Mustang Boss 302 Trans Am | | 9F02M148628 | L | 1.000-1.300.000 USD | | NS | | 19-08-16 | Monterey | 138 | RMS |

One of three cars built by Kar Kraft and prepared by Shelby for the 1969 Trans Am season. Raced until October 1971, it was driven by Peter Revson, Horst Kwech, Dan Gurney, George Follmer, Parnelli Jones, and Jerry Thompson. Restored in the late 1980s and subsequently raced at historic events. Since 2003 in the Jim Click Ford Performance Collection.

| 1970 | Mustang Boss 302 Trans Am | | BME3 | L | 1.000-1.300.000 USD | | NS | | 19-08-16 | Monterey | 139 | RMS |

Back-up car of the Bud Moore Engineering for the 1971 Trans Am season, it was never used and sold in 1972 to Morris Davis. Fitted with a 351 engine it was raced at IMSA GT events from 1973 to 1975. Restored in the early 1990s and raced at historic events. From the Jim Click Ford Performance Collection.

| 1969 | Mustang Boss 429 | | 9F02Z198774 | L | NA | 159.800 | 250.000 | 218.950 | 19-09-15 | Dallas | S105 | Mec |

Red with black interior; Kar Kraft no.1886. Fully restored.

| 1969 | Mustang Boss 429 | | 9F02Z159821 | L | NA | | NS | | 09-10-15 | Chicago | F169 | Mec |

Red with black interior; Kar Kraft no.1333.

| 1970 | Mustang Boss 429 | | 0F02Z119436 | L | NA | | NS | | 09-10-15 | Chicago | S147 | Mec |

Blue with black interior; Kar Kraft no.2218. Believed to be 32,837 actual miles.

| 1969 | Mustang Boss 429 | | 9F02Z173035 | L | NA | 111.673 | 170.000 | 157.947 | 13-11-15 | Anaheim | S127 | Mec |

White with black interior; Kar Kraft no.1639. Restored. Jon Kaase Engines Boss Nine engine (the original 429 CI unit is included in the sale).

| 1969 | Mustang Boss 429 | | 9F02Z173034 | L | 250-275.000 EUR | | NS | | 16-01-16 | Maastricht | 430 | Coy |

White with black interior; restored.

Year	Model	(Bodybuilder)	Chassis no.	Steering	Estimate	Hammer price £	Hammer price $	Hammer price €	Date	Place	Lot	Auc. H.
1969	**Mustang Boss 429**		9F02Z172933	L	375-425.000 USD		NS		23-01-16	Kissimmee	F159	**Mec**
Red with black interior; Kar Kraft no.1633. Concours-quality restoration.												
1970	**Mustang Boss 429**		0F02Z119436	L	175-225.000 USD	125.658	180.000	166.536	23-01-16	Kissimmee	F188	**Mec**
See lot S147 Mecum 9.10.15.												
1969	**Mustang Boss 429**		9F02Z158672	L	195-225.000 USD	139.620	200.000	185.040	23-01-16	Kissimmee	F208	**Mec**
Black with black interior; Kar Kraft no.1317. 1,650 miles covered since the restoration carried out in the early 1990s.												
1969	**Mustang Boss 429**		9F02Z172921	L	250-350.000 USD	178.016	255.000	235.926	23-01-16	Kissimmee	S174	**Mec**
Jade black with black vinyl interior; Kar Kraft no.1607. 33,175 original miles. Body repainted in 1988. 429 engine with 4-speed manual gearbox.												
1970	**Mustang Boss 429**		0F02Z142204	L	NA	207.811*	297.000*	271.963*	29-01-16	Scottsdale	1339.1	**B/J**
Coral red with black interior; restoration completed in 2013 (see lot S111 Mecum 6.6.15 NS).												
1969	**Mustang Boss 429**		0F02Z195403	L	NA	246.294*	352.000*	322.326*	29-01-16	Scottsdale	1360	**B/J**
Maroon with black interior; stored for 33 years, the car has been recently restored.												
1970	**Mustang Boss 429**		9F02Z127597	L	NA	200.114*	286.000*	261.890*	29-01-16	Scottsdale	1400.2	**B/J**
Green with black interior; described as in very good overall condition. Restored (see lot 168 RM 13.3.10 $ 154,000).												
1969	**Mustang Boss 429**		9F02Z198892	L	NA		NS		30-01-16	Scottsdale	5075	**R&S**
Red with black vinyl interior; Kar Kraft no. 2029. Recently restored.												
1969	**Mustang Boss 429**		9F02Z159752	L	NA	390.720	550.000	484.000	09-04-16	Palm Beach	423 F348	**B/J**
Black with black interior; Kar Kraft no.1371. The car received some restoration works (see lot 2518 Barrett-Jackson 17.1.15 $ 550,000).												
1970	**Mustang Boss 429**		0F02Z140991	L	NA	190.404	270.000	239.274	16-04-16	Houston	S93	**Mec**
Green with black interior; Kar Kraft no.2446. Restoration completed in 2010 (see lot S28 Mecum 1.8.15 NS).												
1970	**Mustang Boss 429**		0F02Z104685	L	250-275.000 USD	164.703	238.700	208.886	07-05-16	Auburn	811	**AA**
Blue with white vinyl interior; in good original condition. Two owners and 16,700 original miles.												
1969	**Mustang Boss 429**		9F02Z195417	L	250-300.000 USD	178.464	260.000	231.738	20-05-16	Indianapolis	F117	**Mec**
Black with black interior; Kar Kraft no.1808. 11,458 actual miles.												
1970	**Mustang Boss 429**		0F02Z120978	L	275-325.000 USD	164.736	240.000	213.912	20-05-16	Indianapolis	S108	**Mec**
Green with black interior; Kar Kraft no.2240. 48,750 miles. Concours-quality restoration.												
1970	**Mustang Boss 429**		0F02Z123173	L	400-500.000 USD		NS		20-05-16	Indianapolis	S168	**Mec**
Pastel blue with white interior; Kar Kraft no.2290. Concours-quality restoration completed in 2014 (see lot 228 RM 20.01.12 $170,500).												
1969	**Mustang Boss 429**		9F02Z173035	L	NA	167.976	240.000	213.240	18-06-16	Portland	S102	**Mec**
See lot S127 Mecum 13.11.15.												
1969	**Mustang Boss 429**		9F02Z198754	L	NA	252.806	346.500	313.097	24-06-16	Uncasville	669	**B/J**
White with black interior; fully restored. Two owners.												
1969	**Mustang Boss 429**		9F02Z198892	L	250-275.000 USD	160.512	220.000	198.792	25-06-16	Santa Monica	1098	**AA**
See lot 5075 Russo & Steele 30.1.16.												
1970	**Mustang Boss 429**		0F02Z108692	L	NA	167.992	220.000	199.738	23-07-16	Harrisburg	S124	**Mec**
Blue with white interior; Kar Kraft no.2161. For 15 years in the current ownership. Manual gearbox.												
1970	**Mustang Boss 429**		0F2Z124194	L	375-425.000 USD	275.040	360.000	317.844	19-08-16	Monterey	F121	**Mec**
Green with black interior; Kar Kraft no.2286. Restored (see lot 1283.1 Barrett-Jackson 18.1.10 $275,000).												
1970	**Mustang Boss 429**		0F2Z124556	L	265-315.000 USD	156.620*	205.000*	180.995*	19-08-16	Monterey	F99	**Mec**
Black with black interior; Kar Kraft no.2299. Restored in 2011.												
1970	**Torino GT convertible**		OH37M164510	L	NA	18.537	29.000	25.398	19-09-15	Dallas	F108.1	**Mec**
White with black interior; 351 engine with automatic transmission.												
1970	**Torino hardtop**		0A38J139687	L	NA	43.980	63.000	58.288	23-01-16	Kissimmee	T196	**Mec**
Yellow with black bonnet and black interior; 34,294 miles covered. 429 Super Cobra Jet engine with 4-speed manual gearbox.												
1971	**Mustang Boss 351**		1F02R151027	L	55-70.000 USD	72.072	105.000	93.587	20-05-16	Indianapolis	F157	**Mec**
Blue with black interior; fully restored. 18,000 miles covered (see lot 1239 Barrett-Jackson 18.01.14 $66,000).												
1972	**Gran Torino hardtop**		2H38H158303	L	16-20.000 GBP		NS		28-11-15	Weybridge	307	**His**
Two-tone brown with brown interior; in good overall condition. Recently imported into the UK.												
2005	**GT**		400962	L	NA	175.201*	266.750*	239.515*	05-09-15	Auburn	5091	**AA**
Red with white stripes and black leather interior; approximately 2,900 miles covered.												

F347: 1970 Ford Mustang Mach 1

F348: 1969 Ford Mustang Boss 429

Year	Model	(Bodybuilder)	Chassis no.	Steering	Estimate	Hammer Price £	Hammer Price $	Hammer Price €	Date	Place	Lot	Auc. H.
2005	GT		401266	L	150-200.000 GBP	326.300	503.252	446.639	12-09-15	Goodwood	383	Bon
Black with black interior; two owners and approximately 800 miles covered.												
2005	GT		401094	L	300-400.000 EUR	276.837	424.655	373.750	09-10-15	Zoute	34	Bon
Blue with white stripes and black interior; European market version. Until 2014 with its first owner; approximately 29,000 kms covered.												
2005	GT		400859	L	NA		NS		09-10-15	Chicago	S145	Mec
Blue with black interior; 1,100 miles covered.												
2005	GT		400140	L	NA	149.960	230.000	202.446	09-10-15	Chicago	S177.1	Mec
Red with black interior; one owner and 6,941 miles covered (see lot T224 Mecum 16.5.14 NS).												
2005	GT		401051	R	450-500.000 AUD		NS		24-10-15	Melbourne	43	TBr
Red with white stripes and black interior; two owners and 3,700 miles covered. Imported into Australia in 2011 and converted to right-hand drive.												
2005	GT		400329	L	NA	177.363	270.000	250.857	13-11-15	Anaheim	S135.1	Mec
Red with black interior.												
2006	GT		400489	L	NA	290.268	440.000	401.808	12-12-15	Austin	S100	Mec
Heritage Edition blue with orange stripes; 573 miles covered.												
2006	GT		401518	L	NA		NS		12-12-15	Austin	S143.1	Mec
Red with white stripes and black interior; one owner and 1,457 miles covered.												
2005	GT		401528	L	400-450.000 USD		NS		23-01-16	Kissimmee	S133	Mec
White with blue stripes and ebony interior; 100 miles covered (see lot F192.1 Mecum 6.9.14 $ 280,000).												
2005	GT		401512	L	375-425.000 USD	244.335	350.000	323.820	23-01-16	Kissimmee	S227	Mec
Red with white stripes and black interior; one owner and 18 miles covered.												
2006	GT		401862	L	320-360.000 USD	216.721	310.000	284.301	28-01-16	Scottsdale	84	Bon
Dark metallic blue with white stripes; less than 300 miles covered.												
2005	GT		401041	L	300-325.000 USD	215.323	308.000	282.467	28-01-16	Phoenix	112	RMS
Silver with black interior; 1,114 miles covered (see lot 2103 Auctions America 18.7.15 $ 288,750).												
2006	GT		401469	L	NA	365.593*	522.500*	478.453*	29-01-16	Scottsdale	1370	B/J
Heritage Edition blue with orange stripes and black interior; 5,718 miles covered (see Mecum lots S155.1 15.11.14 $ 375,000 and F191 16.5.15 NS).												
2006	GT		401627	L	NA	230.901*	330.000*	302.181*	29-01-16	Scottsdale	1434	B/J
Red; 1,966 miles covered.												
2006	GT		401172	L	300-350.000 USD	223.204	319.000	292.108	29-01-16	Scottsdale	5	G&Co
Tungsten grey with white stripes and black leather interior; less than 1,000 miles covered.												
2006	GT		401952	L	325-375.000 USD		NS		10-03-16	Amelia Island	164	Bon
Red with white stripes and black interior; one owner until early 2016 and just over 100 miles covered.												
2006	GT		400362	L	NA		NS		12-03-16	Kansas City	S119.1	Mec
Tungsten grey with black interior; 7,600 actual miles.												
2005	GT		400395	L	320-380.000 USD		NS		12-03-16	Amelia Island	187	RMS
Red with white stripes; two owners and less than 300 miles covered (see lot 253 RM-Sotheby's 14.8.15 $ 363,000).												
2005	GT		400334	L	200-250.000 GBP	225.500	326.682	289.632	20-03-16	Goodwood	26	Bon
Black with silver stripes and black interior; two owners and 5,061 miles covered.												
2005	GT		401956	L	300-325.000 USD	222.917	319.000	279.029	02-04-16	Ft.Lauderdale	541	AA
Black with black interior; approximately 2,500 miles covered.												
2006	GT		401948	L	NA	293.040*	412.500*	363.000*	09-04-16	Palm Beach	426	B/J
Heritage Edition blue with orange stripes and black interior; 3,050 miles covered.												
2006	GT		401786	L	NA	299.710	425.000	376.635	16-04-16	Houston	S111.1	Mec
Heritage Edition blue with orange stripes and black interior; 1,265 actual miles.												
2005	GT		400839	L	260-300.000 USD		NS		20-05-16	Indianapolis	S114	Mec
Red with white stripes and black interior; two owners and 2,185 original miles.												
2005	GT		401323	L	290-320.000 USD	183.592	265.000	237.573	05-06-16	Greenwhich	39	Bon
Red with white stripes and black interior; one owner and 113 miles covered.												
2006	GT		401543	L	NA	203.123	292.600	258.834	11-06-16	Newport Beach	6004	R&S
Black with grey stripes and black interior; 2,500 miles covered.												

F349: 2004 Ford GT

F350: 1929 Franklin Model 135 faux cabriolet

Year	Model	(Bodybuilder)	Chassis no.	Steering	Estimate	Hammer price £	$	€	Date	Place	Lot	Auc. H.
2006	GT		401971	L	NA	190.905	275.000	243.265	11-06-16	Newport Beach	6092	R&S

Red with white stripes and black interior; 2,850 miles covered.

2004	GT prototype		400004	L	NA		NS		24-06-16	Uncasville	654	B/J

Black with black interior; CP-1 (Confirmation Protype 1) has been the first fully functional GT prototype built. It remained at the factory until 2008 when it was sold with a chip in the engine to limit the top speed to 5 mph. For display only; sold on bill of sale; not street legal.

2006	GT		400029	L	250-300.000 USD	222.710*	305.250*	275.824*	25-06-16	Santa Monica	2116	AA

Tungsten with black interior; less than 2,000 miles covered. From the Riverside International Automotive Museum Collection.

2006	GT		400822	L	400-450.000 EUR		NS		09-07-16	Le Mans	210	Art

Heritage Edition blue with orange stripes and black interior; 5,000 miles on the odometer. Imported into Austria from the USA in 2007.

2005	GT		401201	L	NA		NS		23-07-16	Harrisburg	S110.1	Mec

White with blue stripes and black interior; one owner and 1,259 miles covered.

2006	GT		400284	L	375-425.000 USD		NS		30-07-16	Plymouth	163	RMS

Heritage Edition blue with orange stripes; 9,700 miles covered.

2005	GT		400107	L	200-230.000 GBP	213.750	281.295	253.123	30-07-16	Silverstone	531	SiC

Red with white stripes; 10,080 miles covered.

2006	GT		401505	L	300-350.000 USD	175.720*	230.000*	203.067*	19-08-16	Monterey	F90	Mec

Yellow with black interior; two owners and 7,250 miles on the odometer.

2006	GT		400611	L	300-350.000 USD	202.460*	265.000*	233.969*	19-08-16	Monterey	F91	Mec

Black; 1,700 miles covered since new.

2005	GT		400788	L	250-300.000 USD	181.450*	237.500*	209.689*	19-08-16	Monterey	F92	Mec

Red with black interior; one owner and 4,500 miles covered.

2006	GT		402009	L	325-360.000 USD	259.760	340.000	300.186	20-08-16	Monterey	S57	Mec

Red with white stripes; 6 miles covered.

2004	GT		PB21	L	NQ	638.704	836.000	738.104	20-08-16	Monterey	7012	R&S

Blue with white stripes; one of the pre-production examples, it was used for mileage accumulation and electrical prove-out. Subsequently it was fitted with a prototype small-diameter pulley for greater supercharger boost. Later this part was offered separately for sale by Ford Racing.

F349

2006	GT		401676	L	300-350.000 USD	220.605	288.750	254.937	21-08-16	Pebble Beach	106	G&Co

Black with silver stripes; 1,720 miles covered.

FRANKLIN (USA) (1902-1934)

1929	Model 135 faux cabriolet		35185899L14	L	70-110.000 USD	46.116	70.000	62.300	05-10-15	Philadelphia	232	Bon

White with blue fenders and blue interior; restored. From the Evergreen Collection (see RM lots 207 11.3.06 $ 34,100 and 203 5.8.06 $ 37,400).

F350

FRAZER (USA) (1947-1951)

1951	Manhattan convertible sedan		F516B001050	L	60-80.000 USD		NS		25-06-16	Santa Monica	1058	AA

Green; 230 miles covered since the restoration. Automatic transmission.

FRAZER-NASH (GB) (1924-1957)

1932	TT Replica (Compton)		2050	R	250-300.000 GBP	326.300	493.986	453.100	06-12-15	London	010	Bon

Red with black interior; acquired in 1966 by the current owner, the car received a long restoration started in 1996. 1929 Meadows 4ED engine from a Lea Francis rebuilt in 2006. Ex-Works car for the 1932 and 1933 seasons, in 1934 it was exported to South Africa where it had a long race career also after WWII.

F351

1932	Colmore sports (Elkington)		10246	R	180-220.000 GBP		NS		05-09-15	Beaulieu	132	Bon

Black with red interior; upgraded by the factory in 1934 with a Gough engine and a 4-speed bevel box. Restored in the late 1960s. Since 1981 in the same family ownership. Little used in the last 20 years but always maintained.

1938	BMW 328 roadster		85HF260217	R	550-650.000 GBP	617.500	934.833	857.461	06-12-15	London	007	Bon

Silver with red leather interior; first owner the racing driver Billy Cotton. Restored by Bristol Cars between 1991 and 1992, since 1993 the car is part of the Gordon Willey collection. Unused from some time, it requires recommissioning prior to use.

1955	Le Mans Coupé		421200206	R	380-420.000 GBP	337.500	510.941	468.653	06-12-15	London	008	Bon

British racing green with beige interior; the car was acquired in 1993 by Gordon Willey and subsequently subjected to a full restoration completed in 1995. Unused from several years, it is currently not running.

F352

F351: 1932 Frazer-Nash TT Replica (Compton)

F352: 1955 Frazer-Nash Le Mans Coupé

Year	Model	(Bodybuilder)	Chassis no.	Steering	Estimate	Hammer price £	Hammer price $	Hammer price €	Date	Place	Lot	Auc. H.

FRICK (USA)

1957 Special GT Coupé (Vignale) — FCC1003 — L — 180-220.000 USD — NS — 05-06-16 Greenwhich — 57 — Bon
Red with black roof and grey leather interior; one-off engineered by Bill Frick and bodied by Vignale on a Michelotti design. 270bhp 331 Cadillac engine modified by Frick and 4-speed General Motors T-10 manual gearbox. Since 1989 in the current ownership.

FRISSBEE (USA)

1981 GB-2 Can-Am — 2 — C — 145-175.000 USD — NS — 10-03-16 Amelia Island — 135 — Bon
One of two examples built on the chassis designed by Trevor Harris and fitted with a 5-litre Chevrolet engine. The car was raced at the Can-Am Chanpionship and was driven, among others, by Danny Sullivan who won the 1981 Las Vegas round. Restored in the late 1990s and raced at historic events.

GAZ (RUS) (1932-)

1983 M14 Chaika — 372 — L — 20-25.000 EUR — 13.320* — 18.748* — 16.499* — 09-04-16 Essen — 193 — Coy
Black with gold and beige interior; from the Brundza Collection.

GHIA (I) (1926-)

1963 L6.4 coupé — 0313 — L — 250-330.000 EUR — 185.613 — 269.389 — 246.400 — 03-02-16 Paris — 123 — RMS — **F353**
Metallic maroon with tan leather interior; the car was sold new to South Africa where it was restored in the mid-1990s. Later imported into the USA, it is currently registered in Europe (see RM lots 258 19.4.08 $ 275,000 and 146 27.10.10 $ 230,383).

1962 L6.4 coupé — 0319 — L — 350-425.000 USD — 441.210 — 577.500 — 509.875 — 19-08-16 Monterey — 152 — RMS
Metallic red with red leather interior; sold new in Italy, the car was imported into the USA in the 1980s. Fully restored in recent years.

1965 Fiat 1500 GT — 1160389867 — L — 65-95.000 EUR — 52.087 — 73.314 — 64.520 — 09-04-16 Essen — 197 — Coy
Red; fully restored.

1967 450 SS convertibile — 4016 — L — NQ — NS — 20-08-16 Monterey — 7088 — R&S
Yellow with black interior; restored approximately 10 years ago. Rebuilt engine and automatic transmission.

GINETTA (GB) (1957-)

1964 G4 — GAN3278 — R — NQ — 16.095* — 24.688* — 21.728* — 10-10-15 Ascot — 102 — Coy
Red with green stripe; restored. Engine rebuilt.

1967 G12 — G123 — R — 45-55.000 GBP — 46.600 — 66.787 — 61.190 — 16-01-16 Birmingham — 318 — Coy — **F354**
Red with blue stripe; damaged in a race accident in 1967 and not repaired, the car was acquired in 2012 by the current owner and subsequently restored and fitted with a Gathercole Lotus/Ford 1600cc engine and a rebuilt Hewland Mk9 gearbox. Raced in 2013 and 2014; engine overhauled in early 2015.

1972 G15 — B411041346HSO — R — 15-20.000 GBP — 12.000 — 15.938 — 14.314 — 02-07-16 Woodstock — 153 — Coy
Orange with black interior; in good overall condition.

GLAS (D) (1951-1969)

1957 Goggomobil T-250 — 0146583 — L — NA — 14.498* — 22.000* — 19.730* — 26-09-15 Las Vegas — 323 — B/J
Light blue with grey cloth interior; restored (see lot 295 RM 15.2.13 $ 25,875).

1959 Goggomobil TS-250 coupé — 02132084 — L — NA — 14.498* — 22.000* — 19.730* — 26-09-15 Las Vegas — 324 — B/J
Red and white with grey interior; in good overall condition (see lot 407.1 Barrett-Jackson 20.1.12 $ 27,500).

1959 Goggomobil TS-250 coupé — 02132084 — L — 30-35.000 USD — 19.225* — 27.500* — 25.220* — 28-01-16 Scottsdale — 86 — Bon
See lot 324 Barrett-Jackson 26.9.15.

1960 Goggomobil TS-400 Isard coupé — 02156611 — L — 35-45.000 USD — 18.387* — 24.200* — 21.775* — 30-07-16 Plymouth — 152 — RMS
Red with white roof and red interior; restored.

GORDON KEEBLE (GB) (1959-1971)

1964 GK1 (Bertone) — C36F10047 — R — 70-80.000 GBP — 73.480 — 104.195 — 92.335 — 16-04-16 Ascot — 116 — Coy — **F355**
Light blue with black interior; restored in the early 2000s. Manual gearbox.

F353: 1963 Ghia L6.4 coupé

F354: 1967 Ginetta G12

F355: 1964 Gordon Keeble GK1 (Bertone)

F356: 1939 Graham Model 97 Supercharged cabriolet (Pourtout)

GRAHAM (USA) *(1930-1941)*

Year	Model	Chassis no.	Steering	Estimate	£	$	€	Date	Place	Lot	Auc. H.
1938	**Special Model 96 sedan**	226966	L	25-35.000 EUR	26.907	38.980	34.560	20-03-16	Fontainebleau	317	Ose
	Black with grey cloth interior; restored a few years ago.										
1939	**Model 97 Supercharged cabriolet (Pourtout)**	501450	L	150-200.000 EUR	128.456	186.939	166.880	05-02-16	Paris	192	Art **F356**
	White; acquired in 1983 by the current owner and subsequently restored. From the early 1950s to 1970 the car was in the ownership of Francoise Sagan's family.										
1941	**Custom Hollywood sedan**	900053	L	45-55.000 USD	29.979	42.900	37.525	02-04-16	Ft.Lauderdale	784	AA
	Blue with beige interior.										
1941	**Custom Hollywood Supercharged sedan**	710851	L	NA	24.929	39.000	34.156	19-09-15	Dallas	F100	Mec
	White with tan interior.										

GROSSER WERKMEISTER (DDR)

Year	Model	Chassis no.	Steering	Estimate	£	$	€	Date	Place	Lot	Auc. H.
1952	**Sports**	6250052	L	Refer Dpt.		NS		09-04-16	Essen	148	Coy
	One-off racing car built by Georg Werkmeister. BMW 328 engine and other 328 mechanical parts, 2-seater sports body. The car was raced until 1954 in the German Democratic Republic in sports and Formula 2 events. Later the car was fitted with an EMW engine. In 2004 the car was fully restored and fitted with a period correct BMW 328 engine. New body built to original specification. With FIA and FIVA papers. Driven at several historic events.										
1952	**Sports**	6250052	L	Refer Dpt.	440.000	584.408	524.832	02-07-16	Woodstock	210	Coy **F357**
	See lot 148 Coys 9.4.16.										

HARTNETT (AUS) *(1950-1955)*

Year	Model	Chassis no.	Steering	Estimate	£	$	€	Date	Place	Lot	Auc. H.
1951	**Pacific 4-seater tourer**	11	R	50-55.000 AUD	50.434	77.687	70.089	24-10-15	Melbourne	20	TBr **F358**
	Believed to be the only example on the road today of four known survivors of the marque. Since new in the same family ownership, the car is in good overall condition and has covered 17,115 miles. 592cc 2-cylinder engine.										

HE (GB)

Year	Model	Chassis no.	Steering	Estimate	£	$	€	Date	Place	Lot	Auc. H.
1929	**16/60hp Six Sports tourer**	HEC6035	R	80-100.000 GBP	98.940	135.587	122.517	24-06-16	Goodwood	240	Bon **F359**
	Believed to be the only survivor of three Six Sports short chassis examples built; acquired in 1990 by the current owner. Engine rebuilt, bored out to 2.5-litre and fitted with a new cylinder head; original HE Six gearbox rebuilt. Described as in good mechanical order.										

HEALEY (GB) *(1946-1971)*

Year	Model	Chassis no.	Steering	Estimate	£	$	€	Date	Place	Lot	Auc. H.
1949	**2.4l Elliott saloon**	B1797	R	30-35.000 GBP	32.200	49.662	44.075	12-09-15	Goodwood	327	Bon **F360**
	Grey with beige interior; in good overall condition, the car was restored in 1999.										

F357: 1952 Grosser Werkmeister Sport

F358: 1951 Hartnett Pacific 4-seater tourer

Year	Model	(Bodybuilder)	Chassis no.	Steering	Estimate	Hammer Price £	$	€	Date	Place	Lot	Auc. H.

HEINE-VELOX (USA) (1921-1923)

Year	Model	(Bodybuilder)	Chassis no.	Steering	Estimate	£	$	€	Date	Place	Lot	Auc. H.
1921	V12 limousine		0005	L	NA	69.270*	99.000*	90.654*	29-01-16	Scottsdale	1397	B/J F361

Red with tan interior; fully restored. On display at the Shangai Automotive Museum in China from 2006 to 2015.

HEINKEL (D) (1955-1958)

Year	Model	Chassis no.	Steering	Estimate	£	$	€	Date	Place	Lot	Auc. H.
1958	Kabine	1534397	L	5-6.000 GBP	8.064	12.167	11.121	09-12-15	Chateau Impney	8	H&H

Believed to be one owner car and 7,000 miles covered; it requires recommissioning prior to use.

| 1957 | Kabine 150 | 483145 | L | 11-15.000 GBP | 8.450 | 11.223 | 10.079 | 02-07-16 | Woodstock | 189 | Coy |

Blue; restored eight years ago.

| 1957 | Kabine 150 | 483145 | L | 11-14.000 EUR | 11.994 | 15.777 | 14.142 | 06-08-16 | Schloss Dyck | 102 | Coy |

See lot 189 Coys 2.7.16.

HILLMAN (GB) (1907-1978)

Year	Model	(Bodybuilder)	Chassis no.	Steering	Estimate	£	$	€	Date	Place	Lot	Auc. H.
1926	14hp saloon		E575	R	NA	19.040	29.285	25.666	14-10-15	Duxford	18	H&H

Blue with black interior; in usable condition. Body probably built by Charlesworth.

| 1934 | Aero Minx saloon | | AM205 | R | 25-30.000 EUR | | NS | | 28-05-16 | Aarhus | 132 | SiC |

Coffee and cream with beige leather interior; restored at unspecified date (see lot 800 Bonhams 3.12.01 $ 14,721).

| 1960 | Minx MkIIIA cabriolet | | B1037859HLCX | L | 7-10.000 USD | 5.073* | 7.700* | 6.853* | 05-10-15 | Philadelphia | 240 | Bon |

Black with red interior; 57,000 miles covered. From the Evergreen Collection.

| 1967 | Super Imp | | B442027539H50 | R | 6.5-7.500 GBP | 8.960 | 13.519 | 12.357 | 09-12-15 | Chateau Impney | 62 | H&H F362 |

White with black interior; unwarranted 34,000 miles on the odometer.

HISPANO-SUIZA (F) (1911-1938)

Year	Model	(Bodybuilder)	Chassis no.	Steering	Estimate	£	$	€	Date	Place	Lot	Auc. H.
1930	H6b coupé chauffeur	(Binder)	12306	R	220-280.000 EUR		NS		14-05-16	Monaco	134	RMS

Two-tone brown with leather interior to the front compartment and cloth to the rear; an older restoration, it requires some attention to the rear of the body. Purchased in 1962 in the USA by the Quattroruote Collection.

| 1930 | H6c cabriolet de ville | (Kellner) | 12401 | R | 3.000-4.300.000 DKK | 294.515 | 447.005 | 400.959 | 26-09-15 | Ebeltoft | 18 | Bon |

Burgundy and black; body modified by Hibbard & Darrin in period. Body repainted at unspecified date; mechanicals restored in the 2000s. From the Frederiksen Collection.

| 1935 | K6 cabriolet | (Fernandez/Darrin) | 16014 | R | 600-800.000 USD | 607.518 | 869.000 | 796.960 | 28-01-16 | Scottsdale | 55 | Bon F363 |

Two-tone red with tan interior; restored.

HOLDEN (AUS) (1948-)

Year	Model	Chassis no.	Steering	Estimate	£	$	€	Date	Place	Lot	Auc. H.
1965	HD station wagon	M29484	R	35-40.000 AUD		NS		24-10-15	Melbourne	36	TBr

White; described as in good original condition and with just one previous owner.

| 1969 | HT Belmont van | HT18821AS | R | 40-45.000 AUD | | NS | | 24-10-15 | Melbourne | 18 | TBr |

White; restored.

| 1974 | Torana SLR 5000 | ALH000378M | R | 295-365.000 AUD | 130.952 | 201.715 | 181.985 | 24-10-15 | Melbourne | 33 | TBr |

Red and white; prepared at the factory for the Marlboro-Holden Dealer Team, the car raced at the 1974 Australian Touring Car Championship driven by Colin Bond and Peter Brock. Replaced by the new model Torana L34, it was delivered to Wayne Negus who raced it for some years at the Production Touring Car series. Restored to its original specification.

HOLSMAN (USA) (1903-1910)

Year	Model	Chassis no.	Steering	Estimate	£	$	€	Date	Place	Lot	Auc. H.
1908	Highwheeler Modek 11-K surrey	2651V	R	30-50.000 USD	18.002*	27.500*	24.437*	08-10-15	Hershey	133	RMS

Restored in the mid-1960s and last used in the late 1960s; mechanicals in need of recommissioning. Twin-cylinder engine. From the Richard Roy estate.

| 1908 | Highwheeler runabout | 2478V | R | 25-35.000 USD | 25.202* | 38.500* | 34.211* | 08-10-15 | Hershey | 188 | RMS F364 |

Black with black interior; acquired 20 years ago circa by the current, third owner and subsequently restored.

HONDA (J) (1948-)

Year	Model	Chassis no.	Steering	Estimate	£	$	€	Date	Place	Lot	Auc. H.
1968	S800 coupé	1055549	L	20-30.000 EUR	28.865	41.255	37.200	12-03-16	Lyon	345	Agu

Dark grey with red interior; acquired 10 years ago by the current owner and subsequently restored.

| 1992 | NSX | 004878 | R | 50-55.000 GBP | 53.438 | 81.354 | 75.583 | 14-11-15 | Birmingham | 336 | SiC |

Silver; in very good overall condition. 9,575 kms covered. Recently imported into the UK from Japan. Recently serviced.

| 1991 | NSX | 001112 | L | NA | 31.006 | 47.000 | 42.920 | 12-12-15 | Austin | F182 | Mec |

Black with black interior; believed to be 17,000 original miles and two-owner car.

| 2001 | NSX | 200005 | R | NA | 69.750 | 97.483 | 88.576 | 26-02-16 | Coventry | 434 | SiC |

Blue with black leather interior; last serviced in December 2015 at 32,973 miles.

| 2005 | NSX | 200015 | R | 80-100.000 GBP | | NS | | 20-05-16 | Silverstone | 330 | SiC |

Pearl white with red leather interior; two owners and 48,000 miles covered.

| 1993 | NSX | 005295 | R | 25-30.000 GBP | 25.313 | 33.312 | 29.976 | 30-07-16 | Silverstone | 921 | SiC |

Silver with black roof and black leather interior; unwarranted 79,000 kms covered. Last serviced in April 2015.

| 1991 | NSX | 000144 | R | 27-35.000 GBP | 42.560 | 55.703 | 49.178 | 20-08-16 | Brooklands | 341 | His F365 |

Red with black roof and black leather interior; described as in very good overall condition.

F359: 1929 HE 16/60hp Six Sports tourer

F360: 1949 Healey 2.4l Elliott saloon

F361: 1921 Heine-Velox V12 limousine

F362: 1967 Hillman Super Imp

F363: 1935 Hispano-Suiza K6 cabriolet (Fernandez/Darrin)

F364: 1908 Holsman Highwheeler runabout

F365: 1991 Honda NSX

F366: 1937 Horch 853 sport cabriolet

Year	Model	(Bodybuilder)	Chassis no.	Steering	Estimate	Hammer price £	Hammer price $	Hammer price €	Date	Place	Lot	Auc. H.

HORCH (D) (1899-1940)

| 1937 | 853 sport cabriolet | | 853163 | L | 2.200-2.800.000 DKK | 345.489 | 524.371 | 470.356 | 26-09-15 | Ebeltoft | 10 | Bon F366 |

Black and silver with black leather interior; rediscovered in Russia in the 1990s and subsequently fully restored. From the Frederiksen Collection.

HRG (GB) (1935-1965)

| 1939 | 1100 | | S59 | R | 58-66.000 GBP | | NS | | 20-03-16 | Goodwood | 27 | Bon |

Red; built with pre-War components, the car was first registered in 1946 and sold to Uruguay where it has had a long race career. Reimported into Europe in the 1980s without its chassis plate, the car was restored in the UK in the early 2000s. The original frost-damaged engine block was replaced but is included with the sale. The original gearbox was replaced with the present 1938 unit.

| 1938 | Le Mans | | W73 | R | 30-40.000 GBP | 68.700 | 103.909 | 94.950 | 10-12-15 | London | 382 | Bon |

Only example built, the car was raced at some events after WWII. In late 1949 the original body was replaced with the present one. In the 1950s the HRG 1.5-litre engine was damaged by intense cold and was replaced by a Ford Consul engine and gearbox. Since 1965 in the current ownership; for restoration.

| 1949 | Maserati sports | | 491 | R | 60-70.000 GBP | 84.380 | 130.139 | 115.499 | 12-09-15 | Goodwood | 377 | Bon F367 |

Dark blue; the car was commissioned to HRG by John Gilbert and was built on an extended version of their standard 1500 chassis. Gilbert supplied the pre-war Maserati 8-cylinder engine originally fitted to. The car has had a long race career and over the years it has been fitted with Singer, Ford and Jaguar engines. Currently fitted with a 2.4-litre Jaguar unit. Restored in 2014.

| 1956 | 1500 roadster | (St. Leonards) | WS231 | R | 150-200.000 USD | 100.043* | 143.000* | 128.943* | 12-03-16 | Amelia Island | 189 | RMS |

Black with burgundy leather interior; restoration completed in 2015. The car is currently fitted with a 1,798cc BMC engine, and the original Singer unit is included with the sale.

HUDSON (USA) (1909-1957)

| 1913 | Model 37 touring | | 36570 | R | 35-45.000 GBP | | NS | | 10-12-15 | London | 348 | Bon |

Blue with black wings and black interior; restored many years ago. Body repainted 10 years ago (see lot 342 Sotheby's 4.9.93 $ 22,968).

| 1917 | Super Six phaeton | | J5137 | L | 30-40.000 USD | 17.281* | 26.400* | 23.459* | 08-10-15 | Hershey | 134 | RMS |

Blue and black with black interior; restored many years ago, the car requires recommissioning prior to use. From the Richard Roy estate.

| 1918 | Super Six limousine | | 70M272 | L | NA | 18.058 | 28.600 | 25.145 | 31-10-15 | Hilton Head | 129 | AA |

Burgundy with black fenders and tan interior; in single ownership for over 40 years. Paintwork and interior redone at unspecified date.

| 1930 | Great Eight saloon | (Johnson & Smith) | 898162 | R | 13-16.000 GBP | | NS | | 28-11-15 | Weybridge | 228 | His |

Dark blue with black fenders; sold new to New Zealand where it was bodied. Restored several years ago, the car is described as in good working order (see lot 283 Historics 9.3.13 $ 17,674).

| 1931 | Greater Eight roadster | | 916483 | L | 125-150.000 USD | 69.963 | 99.000 | 91.179 | 10-03-16 | Amelia Island | 160 | Bon F368 |

Three-tone body with tan interior; restored some time ago.

| 1936 | Custom 8 Series 65 business coupé | | NQ | L | 50-70.000 USD | 27.985* | 39.600* | 36.472* | 10-03-16 | Amelia Island | 158 | Bon |

Tan with tan cloth interior; restored many years ago.

| 1936 | DeLuxe Eight Stratton saloon | (Coachcraft) | 643679 | R | 40-60.000 USD | 28.453* | 40.700* | 37.326* | 28-01-16 | Scottsdale | 64 | Bon |

Dark green and black with beige and brown interior; in good overall condition.

| 1950 | Commodore 8 convertible brougham | | 50482033 | L | 60-75.000 USD | 41.928 | 60.000 | 52.482 | 02-04-16 | Ft.Lauderdale | 442 | AA |

Yellow with dark red interior; in good overall condition. Column-shift manual gearbox (see lots 166 RM 26.7.14 $ 82,500 and 2144 Auctions America 8.5.15 NS).

| 1951 | Hornet convertible brougham | | 7A71472 | L | 1.000-1.300.000 DKK | 113.275 | 171.925 | 154.215 | 26-09-15 | Ebeltoft | 17 | Bon F369 |

Gold; restored, the car is described as in excellent overall condition. From the Frederiksen Collection.

| 1953 | Hornet club coupé | | 228933 | L | NA | | NS | | 14-10-15 | Duxford | 63 | H&H |

Dark metallic green with cream roof and grey-green cloth interior; described as in very good overall condition. Automatic transmission.

| 1953 | Hornet convertible | | 7C229279 | L | 80-120.000 USD | 130.844* | 187.000* | 171.236* | 29-01-16 | Scottsdale | 6 | G&Co |

Black with red interior; restoration completed in 2009. Engine fitted with the Twin H-Power intake (see lot S96.1 Mecum 22.11.13 $ 160,500).

| 1951 | Hornet convertible brougham | | 7A122578 | L | 140-180.000 USD | 147.070* | 192.500* | 169.958* | 19-08-16 | Carmel | 37 | Bon |

Grey with maroon leather interior; recent full restoration. 308 6-cylinder engine with automatic transmission.

HUMBER (GB) (1901-1976)

| 1920 | 15.9hp saloon | | M4658 | R | NA | | NS | | 14-10-15 | Duxford | 36 | H&H |

Blue and black with grey cloth interior; described as in largely original condition. Apparently just 25,000 miles covered since new.

| 1927 | 9/20hp tourer | | 4708 | R | 10-12.000 GBP | 9.200 | 13.915 | 12.715 | 10-12-15 | London | 347 | Bon |

Green with black wings; in running order except for the electrical system.

F367: 1949 HRG Maserati sports

F368: 1931 Hudson Greater Eight roadster

Year	Model	(Bodybuilder)	Chassis no.	Steering	Estimate	Hammer price £	$	€	Date	Sale Place	Lot	Auc. H.

F369: 1951 Hudson Hornet convertible brougham

F370: 1952 HWM F2

1957	**Hawk MkVIA saloon**		A5463345ODHSO	R	10-15.000 GBP		NS		10-12-15	London	314	Bon

Black with tan leather interior; in good working order (see lot 403 Bonhams 1.7.11 $ 16,569).

| 1957 | **Hawk MkVIa saloon** | | A5463345ODHSO | R | 10-15.000 GBP | 13.440 | 17.590 | 15.530 | 20-08-16 | Brooklands | 256 | His |

See lot 314 Bonhams 10.12.15.

| 1963 | **Super Snipe estate** | | B8203721BWHUO | R | 15-18.000 GBP | 17.250 | 26.605 | 23.612 | 12-09-15 | Goodwood | 326 | Bon |

Black with grey roof; regularly maintained.

HUPMOBILE (USA) (1909-1940)

| 1927 | **Model E coupé** | | E26391 | L | NA | 17.515 | 26.940 | 23.610 | 14-10-15 | Duxford | 46 | H&H |

Yellow and black with black interior; the car requires servicing prior to use. Interior restored.

HUPP (USA)

| 1932 | **Comet** | | 4 | L | 450-600.000 USD | | NS | | 19-08-16 | Monterey | F107 | Mec |

Fitted with a Hupmobile Eight engine, the car was prepared and raced by Russ Snowberger at the 1932 Indy 500 where it placed 5th. Many years later, the car was restored by Russ Snowberger's son, John, around the original Hupp engine and was driven at the Brickyard in the parade before the race.

HWM (GB) (1949-1956)

| 1952 | **F2** | | 52107 | M | 160-200.000 GBP | 169.500 | 232.283 | 209.892 | 24-06-16 | Goodwood | 231 | Bon **F370** |

Built with unsupercharged 2-litre 4-cylinder Alta engine for Formula 2 racing, in 1954 the car was fitted with the present supercharged Alta engine for the free-Formula "Tasman" racing in New Zealand, where it was raced until the early 1960s. Prepared for historic racing (see lots 126 Coys 26.7.97 $ 146,291 and 328 Bonhams 12.7.13 $ 239,033).

IMPERIAL (USA) (1954-1975)

| 1955 | **Imperial Newport hardtop** | | C5512061 | L | NA | 43.684 | 67.000 | 58.973 | 09-10-15 | Chicago | F87 | Mec **F371** |

Black with cream and gold interior; restoration completed in 2013 (see lot 267 RM 22.1.10 $ 52,250).

| 1956 | **Imperial 2-door hardtop** | | 6561468 | L | NA | 35.405 | 50.600 | 46.334 | 30-01-16 | Scottsdale | 5174 | R&S |

Green and white; recently restored.

| 1960 | **Crown Imperial convertible** | | 9204106018 | L | 120-140.000 USD | 66.924 | 97.500 | 86.902 | 20-05-16 | Indianapolis | S230 | Mec **F372** |

Mauve with mauve leather interior; recent restoration.

| 1962 | **Crown Imperial convertible** | | 9223176860 | L | 55-65.000 USD | 28.959* | 41.800* | 37.474* | 05-06-16 | Greenwich | 84 | Bon |

White with white interior; some cosmetic and mechanical works carried out over the past nine years. From the Evergreen Collection.

INNOCENTI (I) (1961-1996)

| 1974 | **Mini 1000** | | 953404 | L | 6-8.000 EUR | 3.717 | 5.356 | 4.720 | 14-05-16 | Monaco | 176 | Coy |

Red with white roof and red and white interior; restored.

F371: 1955 Imperial Imperial Newport hardtop

F372: 1960 Imperial Crown Imperial convertible

Year	Model	(Bodybuilder)	Chassis no.	Steering	Estimate	Hammer price £	Hammer price $	Hammer price €	Date	Place	Lot	Auc. H.
1969	**Mini Traveller**		157860	L	14-18.000 GBP	**9.300**	**12.352**	**11.093**	02-07-16	Woodstock	199	Coy
Metallic burgundy; restored a few years ago.												

INTERMECCANICA (I) *(1959-1975)*

Year	Model	(Bodybuilder)	Chassis no.	Steering	Estimate	£	$	€	Date	Place	Lot	Auc. H.
1964	**Apollo coupé**		1029104A	L	100-120.000 GBP		NS		11-06-16	Brooklands	272	His
Red with black interior; in good overall condition.												
1963	**Apollo coupé**		1027104A	L	NQ	**86.141**	**112.750**	**99.547**	20-08-16	Monterey	7087	R&S
Red with black interior; restored. Automatic transmission.												
1968	**Torino convertibile**		50050	L	NA	**104.760**	**159.500**	**143.215**	05-09-15	Auburn	5125	AA **F373**
Yellow with black interior; since 1983 in the current ownership. Period correct 225bhp 289 engine (not original to the car) with manual gearbox.												
1970	**Italia Spyder**		59248314	L	NA	**58.720**	**93.000**	**81.766**	31-10-15	Hilton Head	200	AA
Black with original black interior; the engine has covered 1,000 miles since the rebuild. For 30 years in the same family ownership.												
1968	**Italia Spyder**		50049	L	160-200.000 USD	**84.591***	**121.000***	**110.969***	28-01-16	Phoenix	173	RMS
Dark blue with tan leather interior; since 1978 in the same family ownership. Restored (see lot 181 RM/Sotheby's 14.3.15 $ 181,500).												
1971	**Italia Spyder**		50385414	L	110-160.000 USD	**92.347***	**132.000***	**119.024***	12-03-16	Amelia Island	196	RMS
Red with black interior; imported into the USA in the late 1970s. Recently restored; 351 Ford Windsor V8 engine rebuilt and ugraded to 400bhp circa.												
1971	**Italia Spyder**		50408141	L	110-130.000 USD	**74.638**	**102.300**	**92.438**	25-06-16	Santa Monica	1074	AA
White; manual gearbox.												

INTERNATIONAL (USA) *(1907-1980)*

Year	Model	(Bodybuilder)	Chassis no.	Steering	Estimate	£	$	€	Date	Place	Lot	Auc. H.
1908	**Highwheeler A runabout**		1547	R	40-50.000 USD	**49.278**	**74.800**	**66.572**	05-10-15	Philadelphia	248	Bon
Well-preserved example; in working order.												

INVICTA (GB) *(1925-1950)*

Year	Model	(Bodybuilder)	Chassis no.	Steering	Estimate	£	$	€	Date	Place	Lot	Auc. H.
1934	**4.5l S-Type tourer**	(Carbodies)	S165	R	500-600.000 GBP	**561.500**	**850.055**	**779.699**	06-12-15	London	005	Bon **F374**
British racing green with brown leather interior; sold new to India, the car was imported into the mid-1960s in Germany where it was restored. Since 1999 in the Gordon Willey collection, the car requires recommissioning prior to use (see lot 650 Brooks 14.4.99 $ 228,490).												
1934	**12/45 1.5l tourer**		L239	R	70-90.000 EUR	**44.294***	**64.286***	**58.800***	03-02-16	Paris	121	RMS
Originally with saloon body, the car was fitted with the present tourer body probably in the late 1980s (see lot 721 Brooks 2.8.96 $ 29,205).												
1934	**12/45 1.5l tourer**		L239	R	85-95.000 EUR		NS		06-08-16	Schloss Dyck	148	Coy
See lot 121 RM/Sotheby's 3.2.16.												

ISO (I) *(1953-1979)*

Year	Model	(Bodybuilder)	Chassis no.	Steering	Estimate	£	$	€	Date	Place	Lot	Auc. H.
1967	**Rivolta GT IR300**	(Bertone)	410389	L	85-125.000 EUR	**69.547**	**103.095**	**92.000**	04-02-16	Paris	416	Bon **F375**
Light metallic blue with black vinyl interior; restored two years ago in Italy.												
1963	**Rivolta GT**	(Bertone)	340079	L	NA	**25.875**	**36.631**	**33.394**	06-03-16	Birmingham	327	SiC
For restoration.												
1965	**Grifo A3/C**	(Sports Cars/Giugiaro)	B0213	L	1.300-1.600.000 USD		NS		28-01-16	Scottsdale	42	Bon
Aluminium body finished in red with black interior; delivered new to Auto Becker in Germany, the car soon passed to Swiss driver Pierre De Siebenthal who retained it until 1993 when sold it to Italy to Salvatore Diomante. The latter started a long restoration completed in 2013 when the car was acquired by the current owner and showed at the Pebble Beach Concours d'Elegance (see lot S162 Mecum 16.8.14 NS).												
1967	**Grifo GL**	(Bertone)	GL730147	L	375-450.000 USD	**281.534**	**368.500**	**325.349**	19-08-16	Carmel	13	Bon **F376**
Silver with black leather interior; sold new to Switzerland, the car was part also of the Peter Monteverdi's collection. Imported into Germany in the 1990s; acquired in 2004 by the present owner; currently fitted with a Tremec 5-speed gearbox and Borrani wire wheels.												
1968	**Grifo 7l**	(Bertone)	7L850226D	R	225-275.000 GBP		NS		04-09-15	Woodstock	238	SiC
Red with black leather interior; exhibited at the 1968 Earls Court Show. The car is currently fitted with a 454 Chevrolet V8 engine and Tremec TKO600 5-speed gearbox (see lot 255 Historics 6.6.15 NS).												
1970	**Grifo 7l**	(Bertone)	7L020316	L	270-300.000 EUR		NS		26-09-15	Frankfurt	142	Coy
Metallic green with beige leather interior; restored between 2002 and 2004.												

F373: 1968 Intermeccanica Torino convertibile

F374: 1934 Invicta 4.5l S-Type tourer (Carbodies)

Year	Model	(Bodybuilder)	Chassis no.	Steering	Estimate	Hammer price £	$	€	Date	Sale Place	Lot	Auc. H.

F375: 1967 Iso Rivolta GT IR300 (Bertone)

F376: 1967 Iso Grifo GL (Bertone)

1969	**Grifo 7l** (Bertone)		7L950297	L	625-725.000 USD	**521.048**	**682.000**	**602.138**	21-08-16	Pebble Beach	152	**G&Co**

Metallic blue with cream leather interior; concours-quality restoration carried out in the USA in the 1990s.

1972	**Grifo** (Bertone)		250391	L	300-400.000 USD	**277.042***	**396.000***	**357.073***	11-03-16	Amelia Island	26	**G&Co**

Metallic silver fox with red Cartier leather interior; acquired in 2012 by the current owner and subsequently restored in Italy.

1973	**Grifo** (Bertone)		FAGL310395	L	300-350.000 EUR		**NS**		13-05-16	Monaco	128	**Bon**

Red with camel leather interior; restored in the USA between 2005 and 2007. Ford 351 Cleveland engine with automatic transmission.

1972	**Grifo** (Bertone)		GL220369	L	550-650.000 USD	**390.786**	**511.500**	**451.603**	20-08-16	Pebble Beach	66	**G&Co**

Red with black leather interior; purchased in 1974 by the current owner, the car is in original condition and has covered about 24,000 kms. Little used since 1979 and recommissioned in 2015.

1973	**Fidia** (Ghia)		B310179D	R	70-80.000 GBP	**52.000**	**69.066**	**62.026**	02-07-16	Woodstock	158	**Coy**

Metallic blue with champagne leather interior; 51,500 miles covered. Ford V8 engine; gearbox upgraded to the later Ford Automatic Over Drive (AOD) unit (see lot 162 Historics 6.6.15 NS). **F377**

1972	**Lele** (Bertone)		EA500179	L	90-110.000 EUR		**NS**		26-09-15	Frankfurt	169	**Coy**

White pearl; described as in very good original condition. In the same family ownership from new to 2014. 39,000 kms covered.

1975	**Lele** (Bertone)		5002640	R	45-55.000 GBP		**NS**		16-04-16	Ascot	111	**Coy**

Red with tan interior; recently recommissioned.

ISOTTA FRASCHINI (I) (1900-1949)

1929	**Tipo 8A landaulette** (Castagna)		1390	R	3.800-4.600.000 DKK	**345.489**	**524.371**	**470.356**	26-09-15	Ebeltoft	32	**Bon**

Blue with black wings and leather and cloth interior; an older restoration, it is described as still in good overall condition. From the Frederiksen Collection (see lot 237 Bonhams 31.8.07 $ 603,448). An old registration document inspected in the 1980s indicated the car was a Tipo 8A 1349 and quoted chassis and engine number as 1390. It appears the chassis no. is incorrectly quoted and it is most likely to be 1349. Sadly, this old registration was not passed on to the current owner. A Tipo 8A tourer no.1390 survives in a private collection in Europe. **F378**

1924	**Tipo 8A torpedo** (LeBaron)		489	R	NA		**NS**		29-01-16	Scottsdale	1384	**B/J**

Black and red with black interior; in single ownership for 40 years. Several mechanical works carried out in 2014.

1926	**Tipo 8A torpedo**		146	R	200-300.000 EUR	**169.522**	**251.295**	**224.250**	04-02-16	Paris	408	**Bon**

Two-tone green; restored at unspecified date (see lots Bonhams 243 23.1.10 NS and Coys 332 10.3.15 NS).

1929	**Tipo 8A cabriolet** (Franay)		1402	R	600-700.000 USD		**NS**		10-03-16	Amelia Island	165	**Bon**

Black with red interior; restored at unspecified date.

JACKSON (USA) (1903-1923)

1913	**Sultanic touring**		15603	R	30-40.000 USD	**19.723***	**30.250***	**26.626***	09-10-15	Hershey	272	**RMS**

Described as in largely original condition except for the paintwork redone many years ago. 2,396 miles on the odometer. Recently recommissioned for road use.

F377: 1973 Iso Fidia (Ghia)

F378: 1929 Isotta Fraschini Tipo 8A landaulette (Castagna)

Year	Model	(Bodybuilder)	Chassis no.	Steering	Estimate	Hammer price £	$	€	Date	Place	Lot	Auc. H.

JAGUAR (GB) *(1945-)*

Year	Model	Chassis no.	Steering	Estimate	£	$	€	Date	Place	Lot	Auc. H.
1948	2.5l saloon	NQ	R	70-80.000 AUD	34.508	53.155	47.955	24-10-15	Melbourne	26	TBr
	Black and burgundy; restored. Four owners since new.										
1947	3.5l saloon	612044	R	32-38.000 GBP		NS		20-03-16	Goodwood	78	Bon
	Black and green with grey leather interior; restored in the 1980s. In working order (see lot 1635 Cheffins 25.4.15 NS).										
1948	3.5l cabriolet	617141	R	90-110.000 GBP	98.940	149.785	137.388	06-12-15	London	018	Bon **F379**
	Ivory with red leather interior; restored between 1990 and 1992. Body repainted in the early 2000s, fitted in 2002 with a Getrag 5-speed gearbox, engine rebuilt in 2006.										
1950	Mk V 3.5l saloon	627681	L	NA		NS		14-10-15	Duxford	61	H&H
	Light grey with red interior; the car has covered 5,180 since the restoration carried out 15 years ago in the USA.										
1951	Mk V 3.5l cabriolet	647465	L	90-110.000 USD	61.205	93.500	83.084	08-10-15	Hershey	181	RMS
	Red with beige leather interior; fully restored at unspecified date (see lot 8 Gooding 13.3.15 $ 94,600).										
1951	Mk V 3.5l cabriolet	640139	R	39-46.000 GBP	41.500	62.462	59.038	28-11-15	Weybridge	240	His
	Green with green leather interior; sold new to the USA where it was restored in 1991/92. Reimported into the UK in 2007.										
1949	XK 120 alloy roadster	670061	R	325-375.000 GBP		NS		12-09-15	Goodwood	315	Bon
	Silver with blue interior. Built in left-hand form, the car was sold new to the USA. Converted to right-hand drive at unspecified date. Recommissioned in the mid-2000s in the USA. Reimported into the UK in 2014. From the Chris Evans collection (see lots 264 Brooks 18.6.94 NS and 141 RM 8.3.14 $ 495,000).										
1949	XK 120 alloy roadster	660005	R	400-450.000 AUD	299.657	461.582	416.433	24-10-15	Melbourne	35	TBr
	Ivory with blue interior; sold new to Australia, the car was taken off the road in 1969 by its then owner. Upon his death some 46 years later, it has now been discovered. Original chassis, body, engine, gearbox, steering wheel and wheels.										
1949	XK 120 alloy roadster	670047	L	350-450.000 USD	284.778*	407.000*	372.690*	29-01-16	Phoenix	252	RMS **F380**
	Black and cream with red leather interior; bought new by Brooks Stevens, the car was raced in period and remained in his family ownership until 1996. Described as in original condition, including large parte of the paint, it is currently fitted with a 3.8-litre Jaguar E-Type engine, but the original unit, in working order, is included in the sale. From the Craig McCaw Collection (see lot 22 Christie's 29.8.99 $ 79,500).										
1950	XK 120 alloy roadster	670123	L	365-500.000 EUR	202.881	292.324	257.600	14-05-16	Monaco	218	RMS
	Pastel blue; sold new to the USA, the car was raced at some events in period. From 1976 for 33 years it was part of the collection of Walter Hill who had it restored in the early 1990s. In 2013 it was acquired by the current German owner from the Arturo Keller Collection (see lot 55 Gooding 21.8.05 $ 192,500).										
1949	XK 120 alloy roadster	670056	L	380-480.000 USD	302.544	396.000	349.628	19-08-16	Carmel	42	Bon
	Light metallic grey with red leather interior; sold new to the USA, in the late 1960s the car was reimported into Europe where it was fully restored between 2006 and 2007 (see lot 78 Christie's 11.2.06 $237,305).										
1950	XK 120 alloy roadster	670132	L	400-475.000 USD	294.140	385.000	339.917	19-08-16	Monterey	135	RMS
	Black with two-tone biscuit leather interior; retained by the first owner until 1978, restored by the second one after 10 years of use, acquired in 2014 by the current, third owner.										
1951	XK 120 roadster	671372	L	75-90.000 GBP	92.250	140.469	126.115	04-09-15	Woodstock	217	SiC
	White with red interior; restoration completed in 2004. Sold new to the USA and later imported into Denmark.										
1951	XK120 roadster "LT1" recreation	671751	R	80-100.000 GBP	81.200	123.927	111.187	07-09-15	London	105	RMS
	British racing green; recreation of one of the three cars built by the factory for the 1951 Le Mans 24 Hours, which they never raced. Built on an original left-hand drive chassis; new aluminium body; engine rebuilt to C-Type specification (see lot 226 Bonhams 13.9.14 $ 133,067).										
1952	XK 120 roadster	S671957	L	100-130.000 GBP	89.600*	136.748*	122.689*	07-09-15	London	133	RMS
	Pastel green with green leather interior; sold new to the USA, the car has been always well-maintained and has covered less than 15,000 miles. In original condition; recent major service (see Gooding lots 44 20.1.12 $ 154,000 and 119 17.8.14 $ 181,500).										
1954	XK 120 SE roadster	S674964	L	70-80.000 GBP	83.260	128.412	113.966	12-09-15	Goodwood	307	Bon
	Pastel blue; sold new to the USA, the car was later reimported into Europe. 200 miles covered since a full restoration completed in 2009.										
1950	XK 120 roadster	660059	R	130-160.000 GBP	158.300	244.146	216.681	12-09-15	Goodwood	336	Bon
	Opalescent bronze with biscuit and tan interior; sold new to Australia. First restored in 1995; restored again in 2005 by JD Classics; reimported into the UK in 2007 (see lot 218 Bonhams 9. 8.08 $ 214,359).										
1950	XK 120 roadster	660498	R	90-120.000 GBP	96.700	149.140	132.363	12-09-15	Goodwood	350	Bon
	Dark grey with red and biscuit interior; on display in a private museum from 1967 to 1999 when it was acquired by the current owner. Engine rebuilt in 1999, body repainted in 2006. Upgraded at unspecified date with Jaguar disc brakes. 30,350 miles covered since new.										
1954	XK 120 SE roadster	S675342	L	100-120.000 EUR	85.181	130.663	115.000	09-10-15	Zoute	41	Bon
	Red with black leather interior; restored in 2005 in the USA. Currently registered in the UK.										

F379: 1948 Jaguar 3.5l cabriolet

F380: 1949 Jaguar XK 120 alloy roadster

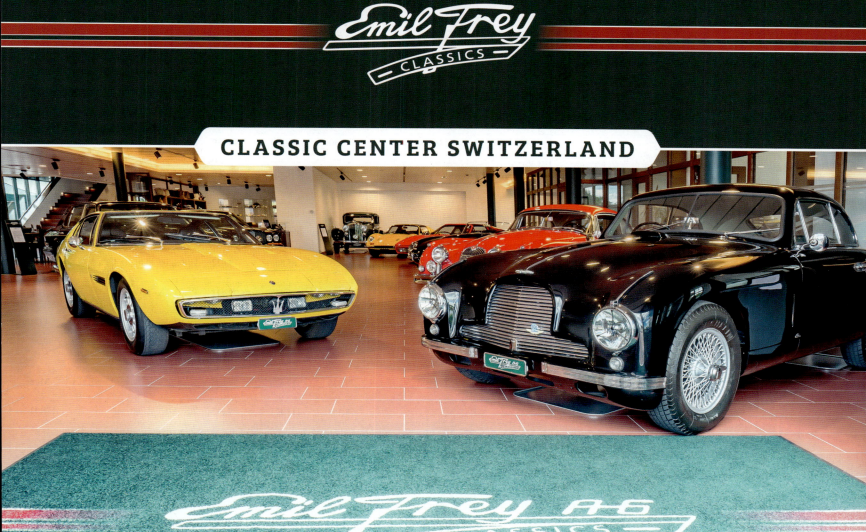

WHERE FASCINATION TAKES HOLD

As a leading international center of excellence for classic cars, we offer a full range of services for car enthusiasts, advising them every step of the way.

We are located halfway between Zurich and Berne in a fully renovated 19th-century factory, a unique setting that is filled with ambiance.

OUR SERVICES INCLUDE
- Purchase and sale of classic cars
- Service, maintenance and complete restorations to the highest quality standards
- Roos Engineering Ltd Aston Martin and Lagonda Heritage Specialist
- State-of-the-art classic car storage facilities
- Logistics & transport in Switzerland and abroad
- Expertise in the FIVA Vehicle ID Card
- Museum with over 70 cars from the Emil Frey Collection
- Café-Bar and shop
- Unique event space for up to 550 people
- Driving instruction in our Driving Center Safenwil

Experts for your passion

Year	Model	(Bodybuilder)	Chassis no.	Steering	Estimate	Hammer price £	Hammer price $	Hammer price €	Date	Place	Lot	Auc. H.
1953	XK 120 roadster		661123	R	220-260.000 AUD	104.998	161.735	145.916	24-10-15	Melbourne	39	TBr
	Sold new in the UK, the car was later exported to the USA and in 1989 it was imported into Australia. Between 1996 and 2008 it received a full, concours-quality restoration and was finished in cream.											
1954	XK 120 roadster		S674706	L	110-140.000 EUR		NS		08-11-15	Lyon	241	Ose
	Light blue with blue and white interior; restored.											
1954	XK 120 SE roadster		S674330	L	69-79.000 GBP		NS		28-11-15	Weybridge	283	His
	British racing green with burgundy leather interior; reimported into the UK from the USA in 2014 and subsequently restored (see lot 266 Historics 7.3.15 $ 69,069).											
1950	XK 120 roadster		676083	L	50-60.000 GBP	60.040	86.049	78.839	16-01-16	Birmingham	346	Coy
	Gunmetal grey with red interior; restored in the past.											
1954	XK 120 roadster		676091	L	90-120.000 EUR	71.714	104.082	95.200	03-02-16	Paris	153	RMS
	Black with tan leather interior, recently retrimmed in Italy by Interni Auto Maieli.											
1954	XK 120 roadster		S676151	L	100-150.000 EUR		NS		05-02-16	Paris	125	Art
	Silver with blue interior; the car has covered 100 kms since the restoration. With hardtop.											
1954	XK 120 roadster		S676423	L	100-150.000 EUR	85.719*	124.745*	111.360*	05-02-16	Paris	126	Art
	Pale green with tan interior; the car has covered less than 100 kms since the restoration.											
1950	XK 120 M roadster		S672788	L	70-90.000 USD	60.635*	85.800*	79.022*	10-03-16	Amelia Island	121	Bon
	White with beige leather interior; restored in the 1990s. Recently serviced. From the Wade Carter Collection.											
1954	XK 120 roadster		S674330	L	55-65.000 GBP	60.480	86.438	77.941	12-03-16	Brooklands	181	His
	See lot 283 Historics 28.11.15.											
1954	XK 120 roadster		674779	L	100-120.000 EUR		NS		20-03-16	Fontainebleau	349	Ose
	Black with brown interior; since 1983 in the current ownership. Mechanicals overhauled in 1984.											
1954	XK 120 roadster		675924	L	125-135.000 EUR		NS		09-04-16	Essen	165	Coy
	British racing green with cognac leather interior; restored. Since 1991 in the current ownership.											
1954	XK 120 SE roadster		S676188	L	NA	79.335	112.500	99.698	16-04-16	Houston	S113.1	Mec
	White with red interior; restored.											
1950	XK 120 roadster		660240	R	NA	78.400	111.171	99.113	20-04-16	Duxford	15	H&H
	Red with beige and red interior; raced by amateur racing drivers at several events in period. Restored between 1988 and 1995; engine replaced during the restoration; gearbox replaced with the present 5-speed unit in more recent years; body repainted in 2011 (see lots Brooks 477 23.7.98 NS, Coys 27 4.3.02 NS, 232 22.7.02 NS, and 165 5.12.02 $ 40,625, and H&H 62 19.4.12 NS, and 35 26.2.13 $ 105,181).											
1953	XK 120 roadster		667035	R	NA	90.720	128.641	114.688	20-04-16	Duxford	94	H&H
	Blue with grey interior; restored approximately 20 years ago. Fitted with a 5-speed gearbox (the original 4-speed unit is included with the sale).											
1953	XK 120 SE roadster		S675382	R	95-110.000 GBP		NS		11-06-16	Brooklands	256	His
	Silver with red interior; reimported into the UK from the USA in 2011 and later restored, converted to right-hand drive, and fitted with 5-speed gearbox and 4-wheel disc brakes (see lots 293 Historics 18.02.12 NS and 128 Coys 21.4.12 NS).											
1950	XK 120 roadster		670268	L	120-160.000 EUR	103.642	134.593	121.584	09-07-16	Le Mans	157	Art
	Green with green leather interior; bought in 2011 by the current owner and subsequently restored.											
1952	XK 120 SE roadster		S672983	L	90-110.000 EUR		NS		06-08-16	Schloss Dyck	134	Coy
	Silver with red interior; in good overall condition. Mechanicals overhauled.											
1954	XK 120 SE roadster		S674322	L	140-180.000 USD	92.444*	121.000*	106.831*	20-08-16	Pebble Beach	46	G&Co
	Red with black leather interior; restored in the mid-1990s and fitted with a 5-speed gearbox and front disc barkes. The original parts are included with the sale.											
1953	XK 120 coupé		680421	L	85-95.000 EUR	57.832	87.770	78.710	26-09-15	Frankfurt	137	Coy
	Light metallic green with beige leather interior; fully restored at unspecified date (see lots 129 Artcurial 11.11.12 NS, and Coys 625 4.12.12 $ 89,563 and 137 18.1.14 NS).											
1954	XK 120 coupé		669108	R	NA	112.000	172.267	150.976	14-10-15	Duxford	143	H&H
	Green with green interior; sold new to Miss P.M. Burt, the car was raced in the 1950s. Later acquired by the late Richard Colton, the car was fully restored between 1996 and 1997 and prepared for historic racing. 3.8-litre engine and 5-speed Getrag gearbox.											F381
1952	XK 120 coupé		679351	L	NA	128.800	198.107	173.622	14-10-15	Duxford	75	H&H
	Gunmetal grey with red interior; reimported into the UK from the USA in the late 1990s and subsequently restored and prepared for historic racing by John May. E-Type 3.8 engine and E-Type 4.2 gearbox.											
1952	XK 120 coupé		679445	R	78-90.000 GBP		NS		28-11-15	Weybridge	273	His
	Champagne with red leather interior; reimported into the UK from the USA in the late 1990s, the car was subsequently restored, converted to right-hand drive and prepared for historic rallying. 4.2-litre engine (see lots Coys 8 2.3.98 $ 25,185 and 81 25.7.97 $ 28,103, and Bonhams 363 17.9.10 NS).											

F381: 1954 Jaguar XK 120 coupé

F382: 1953 Jaguar C-Type

INTERNATIONAL VALUERS AND AUCTIONEERS

COYS
FOUNDED 1919

• MOTOR CARS • MOTORCYCLES • SPORTING GUNS • AUTOMOBILIA •
• AERONAUTICA • RARE MECHANICAL COMPONENTS •
• MASCOTS & BADGES • PRECISION TOYS & MODELS •
• BOOKS & LITERATURE • 19TH & 20TH CENTURY POSTERS & MOTORING ART •
•• FINE CLOCKS & WATCHES • FORMULA 1 • NAUTICAL •

UNITED KINGDOM • MONACO • FRANCE • ITALY • HOLLAND • BELGIUM • GERMANY • USA
OFFICES AND CONSULTANTS WORLDWIDE

COYS LONDON
Manor Court, Lower
Mortlake Road, Richmond,
TW9 2LL, United Kingdom
Tel. +44 (0) 208 614 7888
Fax +44 (0) 208 614 7889
auctions@coys.co.uk
www.coys.co.uk

COYS EUROPE
Michael Haag
Elisabethstr. 4,
D-68165 Mannheim,
Germany
Tel: +49 (0) 621 412004
Fax: +49 (0) 621 415551
coyseurope@web.de

COYS FRANCE
Jacques Morabito
34, avenue des Champs-
Élysées
75008 Paris
+33 (0)1 4076 5798
+33 (0)6 0203 6792
jacques.morabito@coys.co.uk

COYS ITALIA
Giuliano Fazi
+39 335 148 8303
giuliano.fazi@coys.co.uk

Year	Model	(Bodybuilder)	Chassis No.	Steering	Estimate	Hammer Price £	Hammer Price $	Hammer Price €	Date	Place	Lot	Auc. H.
1952	XK 120 coupé		679870	R	66-72.000 GBP	75.040	107.247	96.704	12-03-16	Brooklands	241	His
	Black; reimported into the UK in 2013 and subsequently restored. 50 miles covered since. Fitted with disc brakes all-round and 5-speed gearbox.											
1954	XK 120 coupé		681467	L	60-80.000 EUR	76.236	110.444	97.920	20-03-16	Fontainebleau	359	Ose
	Black with red interior; described as in good overall condition.											
1953	XK 120 coupé		680421	L	85-95.000 EUR	76.547	100.691	90.257	06-08-16	Schloss Dyck	105	Coy
	See lot 137 Coys 26.9.15.											
1953	XK 120 cabriolet		677643	R	80-120.000 GBP	NS			20-03-16	Goodwood	82	Bon
	Pastel green with green leather interior; restored in 2012 circa and fitted with 5-speed gearbox and disc brakes (see lot 44 Historics 2.6.10 NS).											
1953	XK 120 cabriolet		677580	L	80-100.000 EUR	79.400	113.440	100.800	19-06-16	Fontainebleau	332	Ose
	Green; reimported from the USA into Europe in 2000 and subsequently restored.											
1953	XK 120 cabriolet		667149	R	125-150.000 GBP	NS			02-07-16	Woodstock	175	Coy
	Grey with red interior; two owners. Recent restoration (see lot 352 Historics 22.10.11 $44,520).											
1954	XK 120 cabriolet		667106	R	30-38.000 GBP	53.350	69.824	61.646	20-08-16	Brooklands	291	His
	Light blue with light blue and white interior; for 27 years in the current ownership, the car is unused since 2001 and requires recommissioning prior to use.											
1953	C-Type		XKC011	R	4.000-5.000.000 EUR	5.706.017	8.221.626	7.245.000	13-05-16	Monaco	114	Bon F382
	British racing green with black leather interior; originally chassis no.XKC047 restamped XKC011 by Jaguar Cars Ltd in 1954. Engine no.E1066-9. Sold to the Ecurie Francorchamps, in 1953 the car raced the Le Mans 24 Hours (placing 9th overall), Spa 24 Hours and Nürburgring 1000Km. Back to the factory, in 1955 it was sold to Dunlop and used for tests. Subsequently it had other three owners and was raced until the early 1960s. Since 1963 in the ownership of the Guy Griffiths family, it is described as one of the most original C-Type extant.											
1953	Mk VII		737189BW	L	12-18.000 EUR	NS			08-11-15	Lyon	226	Ose
	Black and white with original grey interior; for over 20 years in the current ownership.											
1952	Mk VII		713431	R	55-75.000 GBP	NS			20-03-16	Goodwood	34	Bon
	Light grey with original red leather interior; restored in New Zealand between 1997 and 2004 and reimported into the UK in 2014. Currently fitted with a 5-speed manual gearbox (the original Moss unit is included with the sale).											
1953	Mk VII		737189BW	L	12-18.000 EUR	15.135	21.926	19.440	20-03-16	Fontainebleau	373	Ose F383
	See lot 226 Osenat 8.11.15.											
1955	XK 140 coupé		804065	R	45-50.000 GBP	46.000	70.044	62.887	05-09-15	Beaulieu	144	Bon
	Maroon with biscuit leather interior; for 45 years with the last owner, the car is in good original condition and has 74,718 miles on the odometer.											
1955	XK 140 SE coupé		S814978	L	70-90.000 EUR	42.185*	61.225*	56.000*	03-02-16	Paris	130	RMS F384
	Dark blue with black leather interior; some mechanical works carried out in 2014 (see lot 214 RM 9.9.13 $ 79,042).											
1957	XK 140 SE coupé		S815870DN	L	70-100.000 EUR	NS			04-02-16	Paris	409	Bon
	Cream with red leather interior; interior retrimmed in 2011, body repainted in 2013.											
1955	XK 140 coupé		S804248	R	NA	50.400	71.467	63.716	20-04-16	Duxford	25	H&H
	White with red interior; some restoration works carried out at unspecified date.											
1956	XK 140 MC coupé		S815928	R	NA	86.240	122.288	109.025	20-04-16	Duxford	58	H&H
	Black with red leather interior; fully restored and converted to right-hand drive. 5-speed gearbox; XK 150 brakes.											
1956	XK 140 SE coupé		S815931	L	85-105.000 EUR	NS			19-06-16	Fontainebleau	333	Ose
	Light blue with red interior; fully restored.											
1955	XK 140 SE cabriolet		A818030	L	150-180.000 EUR	NS			03-02-16	Paris	160	RMS
	Pastel blue with red leather interior; in original condition. Two owners (see lot 157 Coys 8.8.15 NS).											
1954	XK 140 SE cabriolet		S817079	L	90-110.000 EUR	NS			04-02-16	Paris	387	Bon
	Ivory with dark green interior; described as in good overall condition.											
1955	XK 140 cabriolet		807335	R	120-150.000 GBP	NS			20-03-16	Goodwood	77	Bon
	Grey with red leather interior; restored between 1992 and 1997. In 2010 body repainted and engine fitted with a Ford 5-speed gearbox. Engine rebuilt in 2013.											
1955	XK 140 cabriolet		807261DN	R	130-160.000 GBP	124.700	170.889	154.416	24-06-16	Goodwood	263	Bon
	Dark green with beige interior; fully restored between 2006 and 2010 and fitted with a 5-speed gearbox.											
1955	XK 140 SE cabriolet		807093	R	90-100.000 GBP	105.915	140.676	126.335	02-07-16	Woodstock	181	Coy
	Old English white with tobacco leather interior; restored at unspecified date.											
1955	XK 140 MC cabriolet		S817884DN	L	100-140.000 USD	142.083	187.000	168.263	30-07-16	Plymouth	142	RMS
	British racing green with sage green leather interior; concours-quality restoration carried out between 1998 and 2000. Currently fitted with a 5-speed Borg-Warner T-5 gearbox (the original unit is included with the sale).											

F383: 1953 Jaguar Mk VII

F384: 1955 Jaguar XK 140 SE coupé

Year	Model	(Bodybuilder)	Chassis no.	Steering	Estimate	Hammer Price £	$	€	Date	Place	Lot	Auc. H.
1955	XK 140MC roadster		S810907	L	NA	**119.209**	**181.500**	**162.969**	05-09-15	Auburn	4147	AA **F385**
Red with tan interior; recently restored.												
1954	XK 140 SE roadster		S812916DN	L	70-90.000 GBP	**67.800**	**104.568**	**92.805**	12-09-15	Goodwood	370	Bon
Red with tan leather interior; sold new to the USA, the car was reimported into the UK approximately 11 years ago. Restored in 2012; engine rebuilt.												
1955	XK 140 MC roadster		S810834	L	NA	**90.290**	**143.000**	**125.726**	31-10-15	Hilton Head	186	AA
Red with biscuit and red leather interior; 900 miles covered since a full restoration.												
1956	XK 140 SE roadster		S811629DN	L	120-140.000 EUR		NS		08-11-15	Lyon	235	Ose
Grey with grey interior; restored. Currently fitted with a Getrag gearbox; the original Moss unit is included in the sale.												
1955	XK 140 SE roadster		A810835DN	L	110-140.000 USD	**83.053***	**118.800***	**108.951***	28-01-16	Scottsdale	33	Bon
Green with green leather interior; acquired in 2008 by the previous owner and subsequently restored.												
1955	XK 140 MC roadster		S810516	L	140-180.000 USD	**96.209***	**137.500***	**125.909***	29-01-16	Scottsdale	10	G&Co
Old English white with red interior; recent concours-quality restoration. Fitted with a 5-speed Borg-Warner manual gearbox.												
1956	XK 140 SE roadster		S812692	L	120-150.000 EUR		NS		04-02-16	Paris	383	Bon
Pastel blue with red interior; never restored, the car received new interior and several mechanical works in 2014.												
1956	XK 140 roadster		813052	L	NA		NS		26-02-16	Coventry	407	SiC
Dark green; the car was sold new to the USA where it was restored prior to be reimported into the UK in 2014.												
1957	XK 140 roadster		810906DN	L	100-130.000 EUR		NS		09-04-16	Essen	122	Coy
Red with black leather interior; described as in good overall condition, over the last 25 years the car has been used at numerous classic rallies.												
1957	XK 140 SE roadster		S812855	L	120-140.000 EUR	**113.559**	**149.377**	**133.898**	06-08-16	Schloss Dyck	130	Coy
Grey with red leather interior; a few years ago the paintwork and interior were redone and the engine was overhauled.												
1955	D-Type		XKD501	R	20-25.000.000 USD	**16.639.920**	**21.780.000**	**19.229.562**	19-08-16	Monterey	114	RMS **TOP TEN**
Bought new by the Ecurie Ecosse and finished in the traditional blue livery; raced at several events until 1957, the car won the 1956 Le Mans 24 Hours driven by Ron Flockhart and Ninian Sanderson. It remained in the ownership of Major Thomson (financier of the Ecurie Ecosse) until 1970 when it was acquired by Sir Michael Nairn, who later had it restored and retained it until 1999 when it was purchased by the current owner (see lot 219 Christie's 1.11.99 $ 2,809,496).												
1959	2.4		S91578	R	16-19.000 GBP	**13.833**	**20.871**	**19.077**	09-12-15	Chateau Impney	116	H&H
Ivory with burgundy interior; engine overhauled in 2014.												
1958	2.4		909550	R	19-24.000 GBP	**18.500**	**24.359**	**21.965**	28-07-16	Donington Park	98	H&H
Restored in recent years.												
1958	3.4		S986312BW	L	NA	**21.641**	**31.000**	**28.681**	23-01-16	Kissimmee	K192	Mec
Black with saddle interior; unrestored. 16,600 miles. Automatic transmission.												
1958	3.4		S975178DN	R	NQ	**32.480***	**42.766***	**38.564***	28-07-16	Donington Park	88	H&H
Grey; repainted many years ago (see lot 203 Coys 25.5.08 $24,476).												
1957	Mk VIII		781095	R	30-40.000 EUR	**27.395***	**43.381***	**38.144***	01-11-15	Paris	126	Art **F386**
Two-tone grey with burgundy leather interior; restored in the 1980s.												
1957	Mk VIII		762369BW	R	23-26.000 GBP	**27.600**	**41.745**	**38.146**	10-12-15	London	323	Bon
Dark blue and ivory with magnolia interior; restored between 2008 and 2015. Automatic transmission.												
1958	XK 150 coupé		S835746DN	R	45-55.000 GBP		NS		05-09-15	Beaulieu	174	Bon
Metallic grey; sold new to the USA with a 3.4-litre engine, converted to right-hand drive at date unknown, imported into the UK from Australia. Currently fitted with MkIX 3.8-litre engine and all-synchromesh gearbox.												
1958	XK 150 SE coupé		824314	R	55-65.000 GBP		NS		12-09-15	Goodwood	319	Bon
White with red interior; restored in the 1980s. From the Chris Evans collection (see lot 269 Historics 24.11.12 $ 71,411).												
1959	XK 150 S coupé		T825056DN	R	NA		NS		14-10-15	Duxford	14	H&H
Red with black interior; reced from the 1960s to the 1990s, the car has been recently restored (see lot 160 Coys 26.10.13 $ 120,643).												
1960	XK 150 S coupé		T836345DN	L	70-80.000 EUR	**90.424**	**136.886**	**126.000**	07-11-15	Lyon	256	Agu
Pearl grey with red leather interior; described as in very good overall condition. Body repainted in 2000. 3.4-litre engine.												
1959	XK 150 coupé		S825026DN	R	30-35.000 GBP	**37.950**	**57.399**	**52.451**	10-12-15	London	369	Bon
Restored in 1980-81.												
1958	XK 150 coupé		S835229	L	NA	**37.697**	**54.000**	**49.961**	23-01-16	Kissimmee	K9	Mec
Blue with new red leather interior.												

F385: 1955 Jaguar XK 140MC roadster

F386: 1957 Jaguar Mk VIII

Year	Model	(Bodybuilder)	Chassis no.	Steering	Estimate	Hammer Price £	$	€	Date	Place	Lot	Auc. H.
1959	XK 150 SE coupé		S834046BW	R	NA	41.625	58.929	53.721	06-03-16	Birmingham	338	SiC
Dark green; built in left-hand form with automatic transmission, the car was reimported from the USA into the UK in 2012. Later it was restored, converted to right-hand drive and fitted with a Moss 4-speed manual gearbox. 3.4-litre engine (see Bonhams lots 354 29.4.13 NS and 160 15.6.13 $ 43,119, and Historics 252 8.3.14 NS).												
1960	XK 150 coupé		S825235DN	R	65-75.000 GBP	NS			08-03-16	London	115	Coy
Gunmetal grey with red interior; several restoration works carried out over the years. Body repainted in 2013 (see lot 278 Historics 29.8.15 $ 106,868).												
1959	XK 150 coupé		S834891BW	L	65-85.000 EUR	72.872	105.571	93.600	20-03-16	Fontainebleau	365	Ose
Old English white with red interior; paintwork and interior redone circa 20 years ago. Fitted in 2000 with a 3.8-litre engine and 5-speed Getrag gearbox (the original units are included with the sale).												
1960	XK 150 coupé		S836733DN	L	65-75.000 EUR	NS			14-05-16	Monaco	125	Coy
Blue; described as in original condition. It comes with Italian ASI homologation.												
1957	XK 150 coupé		S834209	L	110-140.000 USD	63.030*	82.500*	72.839*	19-08-16	Carmel	40	Bon F387
Silver with red leather interior; bought in 2013 by the current owner and subsequently fully restored.												
1958	XK 150 coupé		S835438DN	R	36-44.000 GBP	39.620	51.855	45.781	20-08-16	Brooklands	273	His
Dark green with original red interior; reimported from the USA and converted to right-hand drive. Body repainted in 2012 (see lot 236 Historics 29.11.14 $55,910).												
1960	XK 150 cabriolet		S838700DN	L	120-150.000 EUR	94.217	143.457	128.800	05-09-15	Chantilly	28	Bon
Blue with grey leather interior; 3.8-litre engine and gearbox overhauled, interior restored, body repainted in 2007/08. From the Alain Dominique Perrin collection.												
1958	XK 150 cabriolet		S837926	L	60-80.000 GBP	61.600*	94.014*	84.349*	07-09-15	London	102	RMS
Black with tan leather interior; in the 1990s restored and fitted with a 3.8-litre engine.												
1958	XK 150 SE cabriolet		S837694BW	L	120-140.000 EUR	79.310	120.365	107.941	26-09-15	Frankfurt	124	Coy
Red with beige leather interior; restored in 2013 and fitted with power steering and power brakes. 3.4-litre engine.												
1959	XK 150 SE cabriolet		S827443	R	NA	90.720	139.536	122.291	14-10-15	Duxford	55	H&H
Red with black interior; restored in recent years. 3.4-liter engine.												
1959	XK 150 cabriolet		S838545DN	R	70-85.000 GBP	95.200	143.286	135.432	28-11-15	Weybridge	277	His
Dark blue with beige interior; fully restored in the 1990s and fitted with a 3.8-litre engine, 5-speed Getrag gearbox, Koni shock-absorbers, four-pot front disc brakes and power steering.												
1960	XK 150 cabriolet		S838656DN	L	100-150.000 GBP	427.100	646.587	593.071	06-12-15	London	026	Bon F388
Dark blue with black leather interior; sold new to the USA, the car was discovered in Nevada in original condition after completing 40,000 miles since new. In 2009 it was reimported into the UK and subjected to a concours-quality restoration. 3.8-litre engine with manual gearbox with overdrive.												
1960	XK 150 S cabriolet		T827610	R	150-180.000 GBP	168.000	253.478	231.689	09-12-15	Chateau Impney	89	H&H
British racing green with original green interior; engine overhauled in 2012.												
1959	XK 150 S cabriolet		T827334DN	R	70-90.000 GBP	85.500	129.319	118.170	10-12-15	London	365	Bon
Old English white with red leather interior; restored at unspecified date. Further restoration works carried out from 2013 to date. 3.4-litre engine (see lot 585 Bonhams 8.9.12 $ 113,135).												
1960	XK 150 cabriolet		S838432DN	L	175-225.000 USD	107.754*	154.000*	141.018*	29-01-16	Phoenix	221	RMS
Blue with tan interior; restored. The original 4-speed manual gearbox (included in the sale) was replaced with a 5-speed unit.												
1960	XK 150 cabriolet		S838745BW	L	NA	69.750	97.483	88.576	26-02-16	Coventry	711	SiC
Blue with dark blue leather interior; sold new to the USA, later the car was reimported into the UK and restored 15 years ago circa. 3.8-litre engine. 5-speed gearbox.												
1958	XK 150 cabriolet		S837510DN	L	60-80.000 USD	40.423*	57.200*	52.681*	10-03-16	Amelia Island	186	Bon
Silver with red interior; restored in the USA in 2001. Currently fitted with a later 3.8-litre engine (see RM lots 38 12.3.05 $ 62,700, 150 20.8.05 $ 57,750 and 152 20.1.11 $ 68,750).												
1960	XK 150 SE cabriolet		S838862DN	L	90-110.000 GBP	NS			12-03-16	Brooklands	182	His
Reimported from the USA and recently restored. 3.8-litre engine (see lot 280 Historics 31.8.13 NS).												
1959	XK 150 cabriolet		S827284	R	100-120.000 GBP	85.800	121.664	107.816	16-04-16	Ascot	118	Coy
Ivory with red leather interior; restored. 39,838 miles covered since new.												
1960	XK 150 S cabriolet		T838705DN	L	300-350.000 EUR	220.522	317.744	280.000	14-05-16	Monaco	259	RMS
Black with red leather interior; fully restored in Belgium in 2003. 3.8-litre engine (see lots 18 Gooding 22.1.06 $ 159,500 and 162 RM 20.1.11 $ 255,000).												
1960	XK 150 SE cabriolet		S827581DN	R	75-95.000 GBP	NS			24-06-16	Goodwood	282	Bon
Green with light brown interior; restored in the 1980s. Since 1976 in the same family ownership. 3.4-litre engine.												
1959	XK 150 cabriolet		S827284	R	80-90.000 GBP	57.700	76.637	68.825	02-07-16	Woodstock	172	Coy
See lot 118 Coys 16.4.16.												
1960	XK 150 cabriolet		S838864DN	L	150-180.000 USD	92.444*	121.000*	106.831*	19-08-16	Carmel	50	Bon
Built with the 3.8-litre engine, the car has been upgraded with fuel injection system, 5-speed gearbox, upgraded clutch, air conditioning and E-Type seats with burgundy leather. The original Moss 4-speed gearbox is included with the sale.												

F387: 1957 Jaguar XK 150 coupé

F388: 1960 Jaguar XK 150 cabriolet

Year	Model	(Bodybuilder)	Chassis no.	Steering	Estimate	Hammer Price £	Hammer Price $	Hammer Price €	Date	Place	Lot	Auc. H.
1959	**XK 150 S cabriolet**		T827370DN	R	96-116.000 GBP	**120.960**	**158.312**	**139.769**	20-08-16	Brooklands	293	**His**
Maroon with biscuit leather interior; restored in Germany in the 1990s. Last serviced in early 2016. 3.4-litre engine.												
1960	**XK 150 cabriolet**		S838709	L	NQ	**58.828**	**77.000**	**67.983**	20-08-16	Monterey	7237	**R&S**
White; 3.8-litre engine.												
1958	**XK 150 S roadster**		T831517	L	90-110.000 GBP		**NS**		04-09-15	Woodstock	262	**SiC**
Old English white with dark blue leather interior; in good overall condition.												
1958	**XK 150 roadster**		S830831	L	55-65.000 USD	**37.683**	**57.200**	**50.908**	05-10-15	Philadelphia	212	**Bon**
Dark red with black leather interior; in highly original condition. Unused from time, it requires recommissioning prior to use.												
1958	**XK 150 S roadster**		T831803DN	L	110-160.000 EUR	**85.181**	**130.663**	**115.000**	09-10-15	Zoute	46	**Bon**
Old English white with red leather interior; sold new to the USA, the car was acquired in 1998 by the current owner and imported into Spain. Some cosmetic restoration works carried out in the early 1990s (see lot 263 Bonhams 13.9.14 NS).												
1959	**XK 150 S roadster**		T832064	L	140-180.000 EUR	**103.342**	**156.442**	**144.000**	07-11-15	Lyon	268	**Agu**
Pearl white with red leather interior; sold new to the USA, the car was later imported into France. Restored many years ago. 3.4-litre engine (see lot 26 Poulain/Sotheby's 18.12.00 NS).												
1958	**XK 150 S roadster**		S830783DN	L	110-130.000 GBP		**NS**		28-11-15	Weybridge	279	**His**
British racing green with tan leather interior; reimported into the UK in 2014 from the USA where it had been restored. 3.4-litre engine rebuilt in the UK.												
1958	**XK 150 S roadster**		T831740DN	L	70-90.000 GBP	**92.520**	**139.381**	**131.489**	01-12-15	London	313	**Coy**
Red with black interior; in good overall condition. 3.4-litre engine.												
1958	**XK 150 S roadster**		T831825DN	L	275-350.000 USD		**NS**		11-03-16	Amelia Island	73	**G&Co**
Cream with red leather interior; concours-quality restoration completed in 2012. 3.4-litre engine.												
1960	**XK 150 S roadster**		T831703DN	L	90-120.000 EUR	**98.658**	**142.927**	**126.720**	20-03-16	Fontainebleau	338	**Ose**
White; since 1963 in the same family ownership. Never restored; 3.4-litre engine rebuilt in 2008.												
1958	**XK 150 S roadster**		S830505DN	L	130-140.000 EUR		**NS**		09-04-16	Essen	157	**Coy**
Old English white with red leather interior; restored in 2008. 3.4-litre engine.												
1958	**XK 150 S roadster**		S830725DN	L	175-225.000 EUR	**181.143**	**261.004**	**230.000**	13-05-16	Monaco	107	**Bon** **F389**
Grey with dark blue interior; sold new to the USA and reimported into Europe in 2000. Restored between 2003 and 2008; recent mechanical works. 3.4-litre engine.												
1958	**XK 150 S roadster**		S830505DN	L	125-145.000 EUR	**106.449**	**153.380**	**135.160**	14-05-16	Monaco	191	**Coy**
See lot 157 Coys 9.4.16.												
1957	**XK 150 SE roadster**		S831179	L	40-60.000 USD	**26.673***	**38.500***	**34.515***	05-06-16	Greenwhich	5A	**Bon**
Restoration project; 3.4-litre engine.												
1958	**XK 150 S roadster**		S830505DN	L	100-115.000 GBP		**NS**		02-07-16	Woodstock	184	**Coy**
See lot 191 Coys 14.5.16.												
1958	**XK 150 S roadster**		T831629DN	L	155-185.000 EUR		**NS**		09-07-16	Le Mans	158	**Art**
Red with black leather interior; fully restored between 1999 and 2001, the car remained with its first owner until 2009. 3.4-litre engine.												
1958	**XK 150 roadster**		S830744	L	155-170.000 EUR		**NS**		06-08-16	Schloss Dyck	149	**Coy**
Black with red leather interior; recently restored.												
1958	**XK 150 roadster**		S830365DN	L	140-180.000 USD	**121.858***	**159.500***	**140.823***	19-08-16	Carmel	106	**Bon**
Black with grey leather interior; acquired 23 years ago by the current owner and fully restored between 2004 and 2014.												
1960	**Mk IX**		775853BW	R	14-16.000 GBP		**NS**		10-12-15	London	309	**Bon**
Two-tone grey with original red leather interior; for 20 years in the current ownership, the car received some restoration works.												
1960	**Mk IX**		79201BW	L	NA	**34.905**	**50.000**	**46.260**	23-01-16	Kissimmee	K20	**Mec** **F390**
Red and grey with grey interior; restored. Automatic transmission.												
1959	**Mk IX**		771021BW	R	18-22.000 GBP		**NS**		08-03-16	London	143	**Coy**
Two-tone body; some restoration works carried out recently.												
1966	**Mk II 2.4**		120304DN	R	15-18.000 GBP	**14.833**	**19.262**	**17.401**	10-07-16	Chateau Impney	58	**H&H**
Silver with red interior; described as in good, highly original condition.												
1967	**Mk II 3.4**		181435DN	L	20-24.000 GBP		**NS**		05-09-15	Beaulieu	129A	**Bon**
Opalescent grey with black leather interior; described as in good working order (see lot 208 Coys 20.5.06 $ 35,291).												
1961	**Mk II 3.4**		178304DN	L	30-35.000 EUR	**25.835**	**39.110**	**36.000**	08-11-15	Lyon	247	**Ose**
Gunmetal grey with tan leather interior; interior retrimmed in 2008, paintwork redone in 2011, automatic transmission rebuilt in 2015.												

F389: 1958 Jaguar XK 150 S roadster

F390: 1960 Jaguar Mk IX

Year	Model	(Bodybuilder)	Chassis no.	Steering	Estimate	Hammer Price £	Hammer Price $	Hammer Price €	Sale Date	Sale Place	Lot	Auc. H.
1960	Mk II 3.4		175483DN	L	35-45.000 USD	23.070*	33.000*	30.264*	28-01-16	Scottsdale	53	Bon
British racing green with saddle leather interior; paintwork and interior recently redone.											
1961	Mk II 3.4		153371	L	22-26.000 EUR	20.931	29.461	25.927	09-04-16	Essen	131	Coy
Dark blue with light grey interior; restored in the early 2000s.											
1961	Mk II 3.4		156356	R	18-22.000 GBP		NS		20-08-16	Brooklands	335	His
Pearl grey with red interior; in good overall condition. Since 1988 in the current ownership.											
1962	Mk II 3.8		112113DN	R	18-25.000 GBP	19.876	30.488	26.833	10-10-15	Ascot	105	Coy
Gunmetal grey with red interior; described as in very good overall condition. Fitted with Cooper Craft disc brakes and power steering.											
1963	Mk II 3.8		206215	R	24-28.000 GBP	28.750	43.484	39.735	10-12-15	London	372	Bon
British racing green with cream interior; restored and fitted with XJ40 electric seats and Moss 4-speed manual gearbox as replacement of the original automatic transmission.											
1960	Mk II Vicarage		200445BW	L	50-70.000 EUR	53.217*	77.446*	69.136*	05-02-16	Paris	153	Art F391
One of the cars modified by Vicarage, it was sold to Germany. Among other features it presents modern air-conditioning, power steering, power windows, sunroof and electrically adjustable XJ seats.											
1964	Mk II 3.8		223412DN	L	35-45.000 EUR	30.728	43.916	39.600	12-03-16	Lyon	344	Agu
Metallic grey with blue interior; several restoration works carried out in 2015.											
1961	Mk II 3.8		P217188BW	R	25-30.000 GBP	23.600	33.465	29.656	16-04-16	Ascot	139	Coy
Red with red leather interior; restored in 2010.											
1963	Mk II 3.8		219324BW	L	20-30.000 GBP	18.400*	25.215*	22.785*	24-06-16	Goodwood	201	Bon
White with red interior; reimported into the UK from the USA in 2015. Restored in 2007; automatic transmission.											
1962	Mk II 3.8		207440	R	NA	47.810	62.918	56.617	30-07-16	Silverstone	532	SiC
Opalescent blue with grey-blue leather interior; fully restored in 2012 (see lot 475 Silverstone Auctions 27.7.13 $62,871).											
1963	Mk X		351935BW	L	25-30.000 EUR		NS		20-03-16	Fontainebleau	325	Ose
Black with grey leather interior; fully restored.											
1964	Mk X		353522DN	L	15-20.000 EUR		NS		02-07-16	Lyon	363	Agu
Maroon with beige leather interior; described as in good overall condition.											
1966	Mk X 4.2		1D76047BW	L	15-25.000 EUR		NS		09-04-16	Essen	221	Coy
Beige with light brown interior; body repainted some years ago.											
1964	E-Type 3.8 coupé		890183	L	100-120.000 GBP	113.500	172.826	155.166	05-09-15	Beaulieu	153	Bon
Red with red interior; sold new to the USA, the car remained with its first owner for 45 years. Reimported into the UK, it was restored in 2010/11.											
1964	E-Type 3.8 coupé		861330	R	80-100.000 GBP		NS		05-09-15	Beaulieu	163	Bon
Red with black leather interior; body restored in the early 1990s, engine rebuilt in 1997 when the original cylinder block was replaced with one from a 3.8-litre Jaguar MkII.											
1962	E-Type 3.8 coupé		886827	L	130-160.000 EUR		NS		05-09-15	Chantilly	3	Bon
Gunmetal grey with red leather interior; the car has covered 250 kms since a full restoration carried out in 2013-14.											
1961	E-Type 3.8 coupé		860083	R	50-60.000 GBP	96.700	149.140	132.363	12-09-15	Goodwood	305	Bon
Red; for restoration.											
1962	E-Type 3.8 coupé		860472	R	110-140.000 GBP		NS		12-09-15	Goodwood	351	Bon
Opalescent silver grey with red leather interior; until 2001 with its first owner. Full restoration recently completed (see lot 52 H&H 30.10.13 $ 69,009)											
1963	E-Type 3.8 coupé		888169	L	180-220.000 GBP	180.700	278.694	247.342	12-09-15	Goodwood	363	Bon
Fully restored in 2014 as a "continuation" of the semi-lightweight E-type driven by Maurice Charles and John Coundley at the 1962 Le Mans 24 Hours. Race engine built in 2013. Offered with FIA Historic Technical Passport papers.											
1964	E-Type 3.8 coupé		861701	R	NA	68.320	105.083	92.095	14-10-15	Duxford	19	H&H
Red with red interior; restored in the 1980s, since 1991 in the current ownership.											
1962	E-Type 3.8 coupé		860472	R	NA	125.440	192.939	169.093	14-10-15	Duxford	77	H&H
See lot 351 Bonhams 12.9.15.											
1962	E-Type 3.8 coupé		885451	L	80-100.000 EUR	65.063	103.030	90.592	01-11-15	Paris	168	Art
Grey-blue with black leather interior; restored some years ago. Further mechanical works carried out in more recent years.											
1963	E-Type 3.8 coupé		889318	L	62-72.000 GBP	85.120	128.114	121.092	28-11-15	Weybridge	295	His
Golden sand with beige interior; restoration completed in Australia in 2014. Car imported into the UK in 2015.											
1962	E-Type 3.8 coupé		860657	R	100-120.000 GBP		NS		10-12-15	London	371	Bon
White with blue stripes; prepared for historic racing. 340bhp engine built by Rob Beere.											
1963	E-Type 3.8 coupé		888701	L	100-150.000 EUR	114.753	170.107	151.800	04-02-16	Paris	426	Bon F392
British racing green with tan leather interior; sold new to the USA, the car was later imported into Italy and fully restored between 2008 and 2015. Currently fitted with a Hewland 5-speed gearbox (the original Moss unit is included with the sale).											
1963	E-Type 3.8 coupé		861107	R	NQ	61.160*	86.902*	78.805*	08-03-16	London	113	Coy
For restoration; stored in 1969. Raced at some events between 1967 and 1969.											
1961	E-Type 3.8 coupé		860029	R	125-175.000 EUR	110.261	158.872	140.000	14-05-16	Monaco	274	RMS
Opalescent dark blue with dark blue interior; restored in the USA in the 1990s, reimported into the UK in 2010, interior retrimmed between 2012 and 2013, engine rebuilt in 2015.											
1963	E-Type 3.8 coupé		861292	R	60-80.000 GBP	74.300	101.821	92.006	24-06-16	Goodwood	207	Bon
Since new in the same family ownership; described as in highly original condition. Recently recommissioned.											
1963	E-Type 3.8 coupé		889478	L	130-160.000 EUR	116.691	154.999	139.200	02-07-16	Lyon	344	Agu
Cream with black leather interior; the car has covered 30 kms since a full restoration.											
1963	E-Type 3.8 coupé		889653	L	70-80.000 GBP		NS		02-07-16	Woodstock	182	Coy
White with black interior; restored within the last 10 years.											
1961	E-Type 3.8 coupé		860088	R	120-140.000 GBP		NS		10-07-16	Chateau Impney	71	H&H
Red with beige interior; since 1986 in the current ownership. Restoration started decades ago and not yet completed.											

Year	Model	(Bodybuilder)	Chassis no.	Steering	Estimate	Hammer price £	Hammer price $	Hammer price €	Date	Place	Lot	Auc. H.
1963	E-Type 3.8 coupé		888677	L	150-200.000 USD	86.141*	112.750*	99.547*	19-08-16	Carmel	35	Bon
Green with biscuit leather interior; recent full restoration.												
1964	E-Type 3.8 roadster		879744	L	NA	104.760	159.500	143.215	05-09-15	Auburn	4143	AA
British racing green with tan interior; recently restored.												
1963	E-Type 3.8 roadster		878567	L	NA		NS		05-09-15	Auburn	5124	AA
Red with tan interior; full restoration recently completed.												
1962	E-Type 3.8 roadster		877073	L	140-180.000 EUR	138.802	211.344	189.750	05-09-15	Chantilly	4	Bon
Gunmetal grey with beige leather interior; reimported into Europe from the USA in 2014 and subsequently fully restored.												
1964	E-Type 3.8 roadster		880117	L	NA		NS		26-09-15	Las Vegas	694	B/J
Cream with black leather interior; restored (see lot 117 Bonhams 12.3.15 $ 128,700).												
1962	E-Type 3.8 roadster		875939	L	160-200.000 EUR	84.496	128.237	115.000	26-09-15	Frankfurt	126	Coy
Cream with black interior; recently restored.												
1964	E-Type 3.8 roadster		880249	L	100-125.000 EUR		NS		26-09-15	Frankfurt	130	Coy
Finished in golden sand with beige interior, the car was sold new to the USA where it remained for 45 years in the same family ownership. 28,000 miles covered (see Bonhams lots 445 3.6.12 $ 46,800 and 494 17.8.12 $ 51,750).												
1962	E-Type 3.8 roadster		877020	L	100-125.000 USD	101.455	154.000	137.060	05-10-15	Philadelphia	157	Bon
Black with black interior; acquired in 1963 by the current, second owner. 72,000 miles covered. Interior retrimmed at unspecified date.												
1961	E-Type 3.8 roadster		875353	L	190-260.000 EUR	208.692	320.124	281.750	09-10-15	Zoute	8	Bon
Gunmetal grey with red leather interior; sold new to Belgium to Ado Blaton, father-in-law of Jacky Ickx. The car has covered 10,000 kms since a full restoration carried out in 2012. Last serviced in June 2015. Four owners since new.												
1962	E-Type 3.8 roadster		877200	L	NA	85.120	130.923	114.742	14-10-15	Duxford	54	H&H
Silver with black leather interior; reimported into the UK from the USA in 2014 and subsequently restored (see Coys lots 119 18.4.15 NS and 158 11.7.15 NS).												
1961	E-Type 3.8 roadster		876327	L	100-150.000 EUR	85.609	135.566	119.200	01-11-15	Paris	127	Art
Old English white with red leather interior; bought in 1990 by the current owner and subsequently restored.												
1962	E-Type 3.8 roadster		878021	R	115-125.000 EUR		NS		07-11-15	Lyon	270	Agu
White with dark blue interior; for over 30 years in the same ownership, the car was restored in the late 1980s. Later it was stored for over 20 years and has been recently recommissioned. With hardtop.												
1962	E-Type 3.8 roadster		850608	R	75-90.000 GBP	100.800	151.855	143.257	01-12-15	London	333	Coy
Old English white with biscuit leather interior; reimported into the UK from Switzerland in 2015. Described as in very good mechanical order. Getrag 5-speed gearbox.												
1962	E-Type 3.8 roadster		850375	R	100-120.000 GBP		NS		09-12-15	Chateau Impney	138	H&H
Red with biscuit interior; concours-quality restoration carried out in 2007 in Australia.												
1963	E-Type 3.8 roadster		879718	L	180-240.000 USD	96.126*	137.500*	126.101*	28-01-16	Phoenix	136	RMS
Primrose yellow with brown leather interior; restoration completed in 1999 (see Bonhams lots 345 23.2.13 $ 96,800 and 126 15.1.15 $ 112,750).												
1961	E-Type 3.8 roadster		875169	L	NA	307.868	440.000	402.908	29-01-16	Scottsdale	1368.1	B/J
Gunmetal grey with red leather interior; recent show-condition restoration.												
1961	E-Type 3.8 roadster		875657	L	275-350.000 USD	181.922	260.000	238.082	29-01-16	Scottsdale	7	G&Co
Bronze with pumpkin leather interior; concours-quality restoration completed in 2013. Fitted with larger front disc brakes and 5-speed manual gearbox (the original 4-speed unit is included with the sale).												
1962	E-Type 3.8 roadster		877396	L	240-280.000 USD	207.811*	297.000*	271.963*	29-01-16	Phoenix	237	RMS
Black with crimson leather interior; since 1982 in the current ownership, the car has covered 10 miles since a full restoration to concours condition. With hardtop.												
1962	E-Type 3.8 roadster		876520	L	200-250.000 USD	111.602*	159.500*	146.054*	29-01-16	Phoenix	241	RMS
Opalescent bronze with black interior; at unspecified date the body was repainted and the engine and gearbox were rebuilt.												
1964	E-Type 3.8 roadster		880239	L	150-250.000 USD		NS		10-03-16	Amelia Island	134	Bon
Dark metallic blue with red interior; full restoration recently completed. With hardtop.												
1962	E-Type 3.8 roadster		876540	L	250-280.000 USD	142.369	203.500	183.496	11-03-16	Amelia Island	23	G&Co
White with red interior; since 1962 in the same family ownership. Restored in the 1980s. Less than 77,000 miles covered since new.												
1963	E-Type 3.8 roadster		879574	L	80-120.000 GBP	75.420	109.261	96.869	20-03-16	Goodwood	45	Bon
Originally finished in opalescent golden sand with tan interior, the car was sold new to the USA. Body restored between 1990 and 1994, interior retrimmed in 1990, mechanicals overhauled in 2012.												

F391: 1960 Jaguar Mk II Vicarage

F392: 1963 Jaguar E-Type 3.8 coupé

CLASSIC CAR AUCTION 2015-2016 YEARBOOK

Year	Model (Bodybuilder)	Chassis No.	Steering	Estimate	Hammer Price £	$	€	Date	Place	Lot	Auc. H.
1964	E-Type 3.8 roadster	880753	L	150-200.000 USD	96.085	137.500	120.271	02-04-16	Ft.Lauderdale	533	AA
	Red with red interior; paintowrk and interior redone in the mid-1990s. Currently fitted with a 5-speed manual gearbox (see lot 335 Bonhams 1.6.14 $ 129,800).										
1964	E-Type 3.8 roadster	881815	L	90-100.000 EUR	66.755	96.186	84.760	14-05-16	Monaco	151	Coy
	Ivory with green leather interior; sold new to the USA, the car was later imported into Finland where it was restored during 2013 and 2014.										
1962	E-Type 3.8 roadster	881149	L	150-160.000 EUR	NS			14-05-16	Monaco	162	Coy
	Red with beige interior; in good overall condition. Mechanicals overhauled in Italy. Italian ASI homologated.										
1964	E-Type 3.8 roadster	880359	L	90-120.000 USD	71.636	103.400	92.698	05-06-16	Greenwhich	56	Bon
	Opalescent grey with red interior; one owner and just over 40,000 miles on the odometer. Used until 1990 when it was put in storage, the car has been recently recommissioned and returned to the road. In original condition except for the paintwork redone prior to 1990.										
1962	E-Type 3.8 roadster	879997	L	150-175.000 USD	NS			05-06-16	Greenwhich	9	Bon
	Primrose yellow with red leather interior; restored several years ago.										
1963	E-Type 3.8 roadster	879578	L	130-150.000 GBP	130.000	187.239	165.646	11-06-16	Brooklands	270	His
	British racing green with tan leather interior; the car received a concours-quality restoration many years ago and is described as still in very good overall condition.										
1961	E-Type 3.8 roadster	850028	R	200-250.000 GBP	225.500	309.025	279.237	24-06-16	Goodwood	220	Bon F393
	Red with red leather interior; since 1980 in the current ownership, the car was restored in the mid-1980s and has covered 11,236 miles since. 4.2 gearbox.										
1962	E-Type 3.8 roadster	878238	L	100-140.000 GBP	NS			24-06-16	Goodwood	226	Bon
	Dark opalescent blue with blue interior; sold new to the USA, the car was acquired in 1997 by the current owner and reimported into the UK. 11,498 miles covered since new. In highly original condition; only the gearbox was replaced with a 4.2-litre unit (the original Moss gearbox is included with the sale).										
1963	E-Type 3.8 roadster	879574	L	85-100.000 GBP	73.000	96.959	87.074	02-07-16	Woodstock	174	Coy
	See lot 45 Bonhams 20.3.16.										
1962	E-Type 3.8 roadster	850439	R	120-140.000 GBP	NS			02-07-16	Woodstock	178	Coy
	Gunmetal grey; restored some years ago, the car is described as in very good overall condition.										
1961	E-Type 3.8 roadster	850062	R	140-170.000 GBP	140.630	185.069	166.534	30-07-16	Silverstone	528	SiC
	Red with black interior; first restored in the 1970s and in the 1990s again. Body recently repainted.										
1963	E-Type 3.8 roadster	879628	L	180-220.000 USD	100.848*	132.000*	116.543*	19-08-16	Carmel	53	Bon
	Red with tan interior; fully restored in the late 1990s. The engine was rebuilt (now giving 290bhp) and fitted with a 5-speed gearbox, the clutch was replaced and the brakes were upgraded (see lots 420 RM 18.8.00 $74,800 and 34 Gooding & Company 20.8.06 $85,800).										
1963	E-Type 3.8 roadster	876751	L	185-235.000 USD	NS			19-08-16	Monterey	F104	Mec
	British racing green with tan leather interior; 18,716 miles on the odometer.										
1964	E-Type 3.8 roadster	881503	R	100-120.000 GBP	116.000	151.821	134.038	20-08-16	Brooklands	342	His
	Cream with red interior; restored and converted to right-hand drive.										
1962	E-Type 3.8 roadster	876479	L	250-325.000 USD	151.272	198.000	174.814	21-08-16	Pebble Beach	104	G&Co
	Black with red leather interior; recently repainted. With hardtop.										
1961	E-Type 3.8 Competition roadster	850007	R	NA	840.000	1.191.120	1.061.928	20-04-16	Duxford	96	H&H F394
	Blue with blue interior; described as one of the seven Project Specification ZP 537/24 competition examples built by the factory, the car was sold new to John Coombs and raced in period. Acquired in 2002 by the current owner in dilapidated state, it was subsequently fully restored and raced at several historic events. It is accompanied by numerous original components which were not utilised in its restoration (see lot 240 Coys 22.7.02 $ 102,753).										
1964	E-Type 4.2 coupé	1E23492	R	55-65.000 GBP	60.750	92.504	83.051	04-09-15	Woodstock	248	SiC
	Red with black interior; cylinder block replaced early in its life. Body repainted; Series II bonnet.										
1966	E-Type 4.2 coupé	1E32907	L	35-45.000 GBP	70.000*	106.834*	95.851*	07-09-15	London	132	RMS
	Black with red interior; two Swiss owners and 60,000 miles covered since new.										
1965	E-Type 4.2 coupé	1E31772	L	130-160.000 EUR	110.735	169.862	149.500	09-10-15	Zoute	20	Bon
	Metallic silver blue with blue leather interior; the car has covered 250 kms since a full restoration carried out between 2014 and 2015.										
1967	E-Type 4.2 coupé	1E33649	L	80-120.000 EUR	68.144	104.530	92.000	09-10-15	Zoute	26	Bon
	Since 1981 in the ownership of the former Jaguar importer for Belgium. Partially restored in 1987, the car is described as a highly original example.										
1967	E-Type 4.2 coupé	1E34184	L	55-65.000 GBP	NS			10-10-15	Ascot	133	Coy
	Red with black interior; 41,000 miles covered. Body repainted at unspecified date; in 2014 carried out several mechanical works including an engine rebuild.										
1967	E-Type 4.2 coupé	1E33293	L	60-80.000 EUR	85.609*	135.566*	119.200*	01-11-15	Paris	129	Art
	Silver metallic with original blue leather interior; for 19 years in the current ownership. Body restored many years ago; gearbox rebuilt.										
1965	E-Type 4.2 coupé	1E20730	R	45-55.000 GBP	54.880	82.803	75.685	09-12-15	Chateau Impney	46	H&H
	Red; restored.										

F393: 1961 Jaguar E-Type 3.8 roadster

F394: 1961 Jaguar E-Type 3.8 Competition roadster

Year	Model (Bodybuilder)	Chassis No.	Steering	Estimate	Hammer price £	Hammer price $	Hammer price €	Sale Date	Place	Lot	Auc. H.
1965	E-Type 4.2 coupé	1E30738	L	40-60.000 USD	37.297*	53.350*	48.927*	28-01-16	Scottsdale	9	Bon
	Black; last used in 1976. For restoration. Working engine.										
1967	E-Type 4.2 coupé	1E33956	L	150-200.000 USD	75.043*	107.250*	98.209*	29-01-16	Scottsdale	24	G&Co
	Old English white with red leather interior; recently restored. The engine has been rebuilt, upgraded to 360bhp and fitted with a Medatronics JT5 5-speed manual gearbox (the original unit is included with the sale).										
1966	E-Type 4.2 coupé	1E32607	L	130-160.000 EUR		NS		04-02-16	Paris	311	Bon
	Cream with blue leather interior; fully restored between 2014 and 2015 in the Netherlands.										
1966	E-Type 4.2 coupé	1E33199	L	100-150.000 EUR	69.547	103.095	92.000	04-02-16	Paris	420	Bon
	British racing green with light brown leather interior; bought in 2001 in dismantled form and subjected to a full restoration completed in 2015.										
1965	E-Type 4.2 coupé	1E30680	L	100-140.000 USD	111.586*	159.500*	143.821*	12-03-16	Amelia Island	150	RMS F395
	Dark blue with beige leather interior; restored in the 2000s. Engine-out service in 2014 (see lots Bonhams 314 17.1.14 $ 111,150, and RM 90 17.1.14 NS and 163 15.8.14 $ 159,500).										
1967	E-Type 4.2 coupé 2+2	1E50821	R	NA	50.400	71.467	63.716	20-04-16	Duxford	45	H&H
	Red with black leather interior; body restored by the previous owner (see lot 109 H&H 29.7.15 $ 64,804).										
1968	E-Type 4.2 coupé	1E21726	R	39-49.000 GBP	41.440	59.686	52.803	11-06-16	Brooklands	263	His
	Red with black leather interior; described as in very good mechanical order. Body recently repainted.										
1967	E-Type 4.2 coupé 2+2	1E7777B	R	30-40.000 GBP	39.200	56.460	49.949	11-06-16	Brooklands	274	His
	Red with tan interior; reimported into the UK from the USA in 1990 and subsequently restored and converted to right-hand drive.										
1965	E-Type 4.2 coupé	1E20402	R	75-85.000 GBP	124.880	164.342	147.883	30-07-16	Silverstone	527	SiC
	Opalescent silver blue with blue interior; stored since 1989 circa for 20 years and subsequently restored. Fitted with a 5-speed gearbox (the original 4-speed unit is included with the sale). 647 miles covered since the restoration.										
1966	E-Type 4.2 coupé 2+2	1E50531	R	60-70.000 GBP	61.600	80.622	71.179	20-08-16	Brooklands	347	His
	Red with biscuit leather interior; recently restored.										
1965	E-Type 4.2 roadster	1E10552	L	120-160.000 EUR	94.217	143.457	128.800	05-09-15	Chantilly	29	Bon
	Metallic grey with burgundy leather interior; fully restored. From the Alain Dominique Perrin collection.										
1965	E-Type 4.2 roadster	1E12273	L	70-90.000 GBP	84.000*	128.201*	115.021*	07-09-15	London	117	RMS
	Red with black leather interior; imported into Italy from the USA in the late 1980s and subsequently restored.										
1965	E-Type 4.2 roadster	1E12172	L	140-180.000 EUR	149.066	228.660	201.250	09-10-15	Zoute	29	Bon
	Dark opalescent green with green leather interior; sold new to the USA in 2014 the car was imported into the Netherlands and fully restored. Engine rebuilt.										
1967	E-Type 4.2 roadster	1E15675	L	60-70.000 GBP		NS		10-10-15	Ascot	149	Coy
	White; described as in good overall condition (see lot 238 RM 14.3.09 $ 66,000).										
1967	E-Type 4.2 roadster	1E13621	L	NA		NS		31-10-15	Hilton Head	145	AA
	Primrose yellow with black leather interior; restored and fitted with a 5-speed manual gearbox.										
1968	E-Type 4.2 roadster	1E18116	L	80-100.000 EUR	73.200	110.813	102.000	08-11-15	Lyon	240	Ose
	Cream with habana interior; fully restored.										
1966	E-Type 4.2 roadster	1E13510	R	130-160.000 GBP		NS		28-11-15	Weybridge	299	His
	Primrose yellow with black leather interior; sold new to the USA, in 2012 the car was reimported into the UK, restored and converted to right-hand drive.										
1967	E-Type 4.2 roadster	1E1909	R	75-95.000 GBP	120.520	181.563	171.283	01-12-15	London	345	Coy
	Opalescent blue with new dark blue interior; in good overall condition. The engine has covered about 7,000 miles since the rebuild.										
1965	E-Type 4.2 roadster	1E10804	L	250-325.000 USD	196.347*	297.000*	271.399*	10-12-15	New York	207	RMS F396
	Opalescent grey; the car was sold new to the USA and in 1987 with 23,000 miles recorded it was dismantled for a restoration never started. After many years in storage, it was acquired by the current owner who commissioned a concours-quality restoration.										
1968	E-Type 4.2 roadster	1E17108	L	90-120.000 USD	63.828*	91.300*	83.731*	28-01-16	Scottsdale	69	Bon
	Red with black leather interior; body repainted and some mechanical works carried out in the 2000s. Less than 28,000 miles on the odometer.										
1967	E-Type 4.2 roadster	1E13274	L	220-250.000 USD		NS		28-01-16	Scottsdale	80	Bon
	White with black interior; in the 2000s the body was repainted and the mechanicals received some restoration works (see Mecum lots S167 24.1.15 $ 192,500 and F129 14.8.15 NS).										
1966	E-Type 4.2 roadster	1E12582	L	225-275.000 USD	269.385*	385.000*	352.545*	29-01-16	Scottsdale	50	G&Co
	Primrose yellow with black leather interior; sold new to the USA, the car was used by its first owner until 1973 when it was put in storage where it remained for over 40 years prior to be acquired by the current, second owner. In original condition, it has covered 7,500 original miles and requires mechanical recommissioning prior to use.										
1966	E-Type 4.2 roadster	1E13041	L	275-325.000 USD	153.934*	220.000*	201.454*	30-01-16	Scottsdale	132	G&Co
	Black with red leather interior; recently restored and fitted with a 5-speed Tremec gearbox (the original 4-speed unit is included with the sale). With hardtop.										

F395: 1965 Jaguar E-Type 4.2 coupé

F396: 1965 Jaguar E-Type 4.2 roadster

Year	Model	(Bodybuilder)	Chassis no.	Steering	Estimate	Hammer Price £	$	€	Date	Place	Lot	Auc. H.
1965	E-Type 4.2 roadster		1E10934	L	250-300.000 USD	134.692*	192.500*	176.272*	30-01-16	Scottsdale	156	G&Co
Black with black interior; full restoration completed in 2015.													
1967	E-Type 4.2 roadster		1E14561	L	200-250.000 USD		NS		10-03-16	Amelia Island	154	Bon
Black with black leather interior; described as in original condition and believed to be a 18,700 original mile car. Only the black soft top was replaced in 1985.													
1967	E-Type 4.2 roadster		1E15563	L	80-100.000 GBP		NS		20-03-16	Goodwood	47	Bon
Primrose yellow with black interior; restored in the USA in the early 1990s. Reimported into the UK in recent years and subjected to several mechanical works.													
1968	E-Type 4.2 roadster		1E18333	L	NA	105.400	149.457	133.247	20-04-16	Duxford	11	H&H
Opalescent maroon with cinnamon leather interior; recent cosmetic restoration.													
1967	E-Type 4.2 roadster		1E15099	L	230-280.000 EUR		NS		13-05-16	Monaco	136	Bon
Black with black interior; described as in highly original condition, the car has covered 51,900 miles. Sold new to the USA, it was reimported into the UK in 2013 (see lot 211 RM 17.8.13 $ 253,000).													
1967	E-Type 4.2 roadster		1E14936	L	160-190.000 EUR	105.851*	152.517*	134.400*	14-05-16	Monaco	235	RMS
Opalescent silver blue with dark blue interior; restored in the USA in the late 1980s probably, in recent years the car was reimported into Europe and mechanically restored. Body repainted in early 2016.													
1966	E-Type 4.2 roadster		1E13646	L	60-70.000 GBP	44.000	58.441	52.483	02-07-16	Woodstock	176	Coy
Metallic grey with black interior; described as in good driving order.													
1965	E-Type 4.2 roadster		1E10525	L	140-180.000 USD	121.188	159.500	143.518	30-07-16	Plymouth	159	RMS
Silver blue; 800 miles covered since the restoration.													
1967	E-Type 4.2 roadster		1E14600	L	290-320.000 USD	168.080	220.000	194.238	19-08-16	Carmel	74	Bon
Metallic golden sand with black leather interior; sold new to the USA to singer Diana Ross. Subjected to a recent full restoration and subsequently exhibited at the 2015 Salon Privé Concours d'Elegance.													
1965	E-Type 4.2 roadster		1E10520	L	250-325.000 USD	193.292*	253.000*	223.374*	19-08-16	Monterey	122	RMS
Opalescent dark green with green leather interior; sold new to the USA, the car remained later unused for 30 years prior to be fully restored. 26,685 believed original miles on the odometer.													
1966	E-Type 4.2 roadster		1E13101	L	200-250.000 USD	193.292	253.000	223.374	20-08-16	Pebble Beach	12	G&Co
Dark blue with biscuit leather interior; restored in the early 2000s (see lot 421 RM 15.8.03 $101,201).													
1967	E-Type 4.2 roadster		1E15251	L	225-260.000 USD	168.080	220.000	194.238	20-08-16	Monterey	S160	Mec
Opalescent silver-blue with dark blue leather interior; 100 miles covered since a full restoration (see lot 255 RM/Sotheby's 14.8.15 $198,000).													
1967	E-Type 4.2 roadster		1E13757	L	300-350.000 USD		NS		20-08-16	Monterey	S73	Mec
Black with black leather interior; concours-quality restoration completed in 2016. First owner the American singer and songwriter Bobby Darin.													
1965	S-Type 3.8		1B5363DN	R	NA		NS		26-02-16	Coventry	125	SiC
White with blue stripes; prepared for historic racing in the early 1980s. Acquired in 1991 by the current owner and restored in 1995. Last raced in April 2010.													
1967	S-Type 3.8		1B87998DN	L	10-12.000 EUR		NS		20-03-16	Fontainebleau	364	Ose
Burgundy with magnolia interior; stored for some years, it requires recommissioning prior to use.													
1968	420		P1F7709BW	R	8-12.000 GBP		NS		28-11-15	Weybridge	316	His
Old English white with original blue leather interior; 76,083 miles on the odometer. In the same family ownership until it was recently purchased by the vendor. Stored in 1981, it has been recently recommissioned and the body has been repainted.													
1968	340		1J50819DN	R	20-25.000 GBP	20.700	31.309	28.609	10-12-15	London	328	Bon
Purchased by the current, third owner in 1983 and subsequently fully restored.													
1968	340		PJ51888BW	R	15-20.000 GBP	32.480	46.781	41.386	11-06-16	Brooklands	322	His
Blue with red leather interior; restored in 2012 and fitted with power steering and 5-speed manual gearbox as replacement of the original automatic transmission.													
1969	E-Type 4.2 coupé series II 2+2		1R35240BW	R	26-30.000 GBP	42.560	64.215	58.694	09-12-15	Chateau Impney	77	H&H F397
Blue with cream leather interior; engine overhauled 5,000 miles ago. Automatic transmission.													
1969	E-Type 4.2 coupé series II		1R25711	L	12-16.000 GBP	18.400	27.830	25.431	10-12-15	London	378	Bon
Restoration project.													
1969	E-Type 4.2 coupé series II		1R26061	L	60-70.000 GBP		NS		20-03-16	Goodwood	67	Bon
Restored in Canada in 2010 and fitted with a 5-speed gearbox.													
1969	E-Type 4.2 coupé series II		1R41931BW	L	40-50.000 EUR	32.348	45.530	40.069	09-04-16	Essen	110	Coy
Black with tan leather interior; reimported into Europe from the USA in 2000, the car received subsequently some mechanical works.													
1969	E-Type 4.2 coupé series II		1R26459	L	45-55.000 GBP	40.320	58.690	52.033	18-05-16	Donington Park	57	H&H
Red with black leather interior; reimported into the UK from the USA and restored in 2002 (see lots 69 RM 18.1.02 $ 17,600 and 91 Bonhams 6.9.02 $ 23,441).													
1968	E-Type 4.2 coupé series II		1R25175	L	55-75.000 EUR	54.351	77.653	69.000	18-06-16	Wien	410	Dor
Red with brown leather interior; the car was sold new to the USA where it was restored in the mid-1990s and subsequently reimported into Europe.													
1970	E-Type 4.2 coupé series II		1R20965	R	80-95.000 GBP	118.130	155.459	139.890	30-07-16	Silverstone	533	SiC
Primrose yellow with black leather interior; stored in 1989. Recent full restoration. 38,600 miles covered since new.													
1969	E-Type 4.2 coupé series II		1R26912	L	65-75.000 USD	46.222*	60.500*	53.415*	19-08-16	Carmel	80	Bon
Red with black interior; restored in the 2010. Engine replaced in the 1980s.													
1969	E-Type 4.2 roadster series II		1R11841	L	120-150.000 EUR		NS		26-09-15	Frankfurt	133	Coy
Red with black interior; recently restored.													
1970	E-Type 4.2 roadster series II		IE3288129	L	38-40.000 GBP		NS		10-10-15	Ascot	118	Coy
White with black interior; restored in 2007.													
1968	E-Type 4.2 roadster series II		IR27509	L	70-80.000 GBP		NS		10-10-15	Ascot	128	Coy
Red with black interior; in the same ownership from 1971 to 2013. Stored since 1978, it has been recently restored. Engine rebuilt (see lot 163 Coys 11.7.15 NS).													
1969	E-Type Lightweight roadster evocation		1R41065	R	NA	151.299	232.713	203.951	14-10-15	Duxford	144	H&H
Green with green interior; the car was commissioned by the late Richard Colton to Bryan Wingfield who used as donor car a E-Type 4.2 roadster series II. 282bhp 3.8-litre engine, built by Dave Butcher, and Getrag 5-speed gearbox. Completed in 1992, the car was raced at numerous historic events.													

Year	Model	(Bodybuilder)	Chassis no.	Steering	Estimate	£	$	€	Date	Place	Lot	Auc. H.
1970	E-Type 4.2 roadster series II		1R1615	R	65-73.000 GBP	61.600	92.714	87.632	28-11-15	Weybridge	244	His
\multicolumn{13}{l}{Red with beige leather interior; restored in 1989. Engine rebuilt in 2010.}
1969	E-Type 4.2 roadster series II		1R9512	L	75-100.000 USD	53.831*	77.000*	70.617*	28-01-16	Phoenix	106	RMS
\multicolumn{13}{l}{Light blue with black interior; recently serviced.}
1969	E-Type 4.2 roadster series II		1R11841	L	80-120.000 EUR	65.201*	96.652*	86.250*	04-02-16	Paris	318	Bon
\multicolumn{13}{l}{See lot 133 Coys 26.9.15.}
1968	E-Type 4.2 roadster series II		1R7953	R	NA	41.625	58.929	53.721	06-03-16	Birmingham	308	SiC
\multicolumn{13}{l}{Reimported into the UK from the USA in the 1990s, converted to right-hand drive and then stored for 20 years, the car was mechanically restored in 2015. Paintwork to be redone; without interior and soft top.}
1970	E-Type 4.2 roadster series II		1R11811	L	75-95.000 EUR	76.236	110.444	97.920	20-03-16	Fontainebleau	376	Ose
\multicolumn{13}{l}{Red; described as in good overall condition.}
1969	E-Type 4.2 roadster series II		1R1201	R	NA	70.560	100.054	89.202	20-04-16	Duxford	64	H&H
\multicolumn{13}{l}{Red with black leather interior; body restored in 2001. Recently serviced (see lot 310 Silverstone Auctions 23.5.15 $ 91,494).}
1969	E-Type 4.2 roadster series II		1R7140	L	80-100.000 EUR	68.519	98.728	87.000	14-05-16	Monaco	167	Coy
\multicolumn{13}{l}{Light yellow with black interior; sold new to the USA, the car remained with its first owner until 2015. Stored in 1985, it has covered 45,000 miles. Reimported into the UK and recommissioned.}
1969	E-Type 4.2 roadster series II		1R8404	L	100-130.000 USD	67.232*	88.000*	77.695*	19-08-16	Carmel	91	Bon
\multicolumn{13}{l}{Black with red interior; recently restored.}
1972	E-Type V12 5.3 coupé		VC1572912	R	12-16.000 GBP	25.200	37.929	35.850	28-11-15	Weybridge	210	His
\multicolumn{13}{l}{Old English white with black leather interior; sold new to the USA, the car was reimported into the UK in 1990 and was converted to right-hand drive in the late 1990s. Unused since 2000, it requires some restoration works.}
1972	E-Type V12 5.3 coupé		1S50890	R	24-28.000 GBP	41.245	54.307	48.970	28-07-16	Donington Park	70	H&H
\multicolumn{13}{l}{48,030 recorded miles; since 1982 in the current ownership (see lot 176 Christie's 26.6.06 NS).}
1971	E-Type V12 5.3 coupé		1S50652	R	22-28.000 GBP	31.900	41.751	36.860	20-08-16	Brooklands	280	His
\multicolumn{13}{l}{White with black interior; in good overall condition. Manual gearbox.}
1974	E-Type V12 5.3 roadster		1S2335	R	110-130.000 GBP	112.000	170.542	153.115	04-09-15	Woodstock	219	SiC
\multicolumn{13}{l}{Dark blue with red leather interior; paintwork and interior redone in 2013. 43,177 miles covered.}
1974	E-Type V12 5.3 roadster		1S2267	R	95-115.000 GBP		NS		04-09-15	Woodstock	252	SiC
\multicolumn{13}{l}{Blue with original cinnamon leather interior; 19,500 miles covered. Body repainted in 2009.}
1972	E-Type V12 5.3 roadster		1S20537BW	R	55-65.000 GBP	58.620	89.261	80.139	05-09-15	Beaulieu	148	Bon
\multicolumn{13}{l}{Silver with red interior; sold new to the USA, the car was re-imported into the UK 25 years ago and converted to right hand drive. Body restored in 2005; several mechanical works carried out in more recent years (see Bonhams lots 422 22.11.05 NS and 391 22.6.07 $ 63,155).}
1973	E-Type V12 5.3 roadster		1S2121BW	R	50-70.000 GBP	44.500	68.632	60.912	12-09-15	Goodwood	341	Bon
\multicolumn{13}{l}{White with black interior; three owners and 25,100 miles covered. Overhauled in 2003 and little used in the following years. Automatic transmission; with hardtop.}
1973	E-Type V12 5.3 roadster		UD1S23037	L	63-73.000 EUR	53.934	85.407	75.096	01-11-15	Paris	170	Art
\multicolumn{13}{l}{Mustard with light brown interior; sold new to the USA where it remained in the same family ownership until 2015, the car was recently imported into Holland. 50,364 miles covered.}
1972	E-Type V12 5.3 roadster		1S1630	R	70-80.000 GBP	70.313	107.045	99.451	14-11-15	Birmingham	340	SiC
\multicolumn{13}{l}{Red; body repainted in 2007, engine rebuilt in 2015.}
1974	E-Type V12 5.3 roadster		1S2595	R	60-70.000 GBP	73.125	111.326	103.428	14-11-15	Birmingham	621	SiC
\multicolumn{13}{l}{Red with black interior; in good overall condition. Interior retrimmed in 1993. Manual gearbox.}
1973	E-Type V12 5.3 roadster		1S1836	R	60-80.000 GBP		NS		01-12-15	London	348	Coy
\multicolumn{13}{l}{Blue with biscuit interior; described as in very good overall condition. Manual gearbox.}
1974	E-Type V12 5.3 roadster		UE1S25261	L	125-175.000 USD	65.366*	93.500*	85.749*	28-01-16	Phoenix	166	RMS
\multicolumn{13}{l}{Old English white with red leather interior; in the early 1990s restored to concours condition. Recently serviced (see lot 178 Bonhams 16.1.14 $ 121,000).}
1974	E-Type V12 5.3 roadster		UE1S23762BW	L	45-65.000 EUR	58.662	83.840	75.600	12-03-16	Lyon	327	Agu
\multicolumn{13}{l}{Red with tan interior; in good overall condition. Last serviced in 2016. Automatic transmission (see lot 232 Coys 3.10.09 $ 40,415}
1972	E-Type V12 5.3 roadster		UC1S20621	L	70-100.000 USD	65.413*	93.500*	84.309*	12-03-16	Amelia Island	119	RMS
\multicolumn{13}{l}{Light blue with original dark blue interior; recent mechanical and cosmetic restoration.}
1973	E-Type V12 5.3 roadster		1S1500	R	60-90.000 GBP	96.700	140.089	124.201	20-03-16	Goodwood	41	Bon
\multicolumn{13}{l}{Red with black leather interior; several restoration works carried out in 2008.}

F398

F397: 1969 Jaguar E-Type 4.2 coupé series II 2+2

F398: 1973 Jaguar E-Type V12 5.3 roadster

Year	Model (Bodybuilder)	Chassis no.	Steering	Estimate	Hammer price £	$	€	Sale Date	Place	Lot	Auc. H.
1974	E-Type V12 5.3 roadster	UES257415	L	65-75.000 EUR		NS		09-04-16	Essen	168	Coy
	Red; restored in the 1990s. Since 1993 in the current ownership.										
1975	E-Type V12 5.3 roadster	1S2572	R	65-75.000 GBP	77.625	113.084	100.796	20-05-16	Silverstone	313	SiC
	Silver; 12,000 miles covered since the restoration carried out between 2002 and 2004. Engine overhauled in 2013.										
1972	E-Type V12 5.3 roadster	1S20236BW	L	90-110.000 EUR	96.414	137.749	122.400	19-06-16	Fontainebleau	334	Ose
	Light blue with navy blue interior; sold new to the USA. Three owners and 27,800 miles covered.										
1972	E-Type V12 5.3 roadster	1S1512	R	65-75.000 GBP	78.220	107.193	96.860	24-06-16	Goodwood	289	Bon
	Red with black interior; unrestored. 35,000 miles covered.										
1974	E-Type V12 5.3 roadster	UE1S23843BW	L	60-75.000 USD	68.072*	89.100*	78.666*	19-08-16	Carmel	61	Bon
	British racing green with cinnamon interior; sold new to the USA, since 2007 in the current ownership, less than 21,000 miles covered since new.										
1973	E-Type V12 5.3 roadster	UD1S23025BW	L	80-100.000 USD	57.300	75.000	66.218	19-08-16	Monterey	F52	Mec
	White with red leather interior; 24,400 miles covered. Automatic transmission.										
1978	XJ6 4.2 saloon	JAALL3BC104569	R	15-18.000 GBP		NS		20-05-16	Silverstone	366	SiC
	Blue with cream leather interior; in original condition. 20,215 miles covered. Automatic transmission.										
1971	XJ6 2.8 saloon	1G55484DN	L	10-15.000 EUR	10.864	14.431	12.960	02-07-16	Lyon	369	Agu
	Beige with tan interior; in good overall condition. Manual gearbox.										
1976	XJ12C	2G1008BW	R	NA	69.440	106.806	93.605	14-10-15	Duxford	13	H&H F399
	Metallic green with tan leather interior; pre-production vehicle, it is unused since many years and requires restoration.										
1977	XJ12C	2G51159BW	L	9-15.000 EUR	10.710	16.540	14.560	17-10-15	Salzburg	303	Dor
	White with black roof and blue leather interior; some restoration works carried out in the 1980s. Since 1998 in the current ownership.										
1977	XJ12C	2G14753W	R	17-22.000 GBP		NS		28-11-15	Weybridge	286	His
	Blue with dark blue leather interior; restored at unspecified date.										
1975	XJ12C	2G1073BW	R	NA	26.880	38.116	33.982	20-04-16	Duxford	63	H&H
	Blue with black vinyl roof and dark blue interior; recently serviced following a period in storage.										
1977	XJ12C	2G1475BW	R	18-25.000 GBP	15.500	20.587	18.488	02-07-16	Woodstock	179	Coy
	Blue with blue leather interior; one owner since 1990.										
1988	XJ-S V12 HE Eventer (Lynx)	148813	R	25-30.000 GBP	39.100	59.139	54.040	10-12-15	London	308	Bon
	Red; in good overall condition, the car received some works to the body and mechanicals in 2014 and 2015 (see lot 337 Silverstone Auctions 26.7.14 $ 71,307).										
1981	XJ-S coupé	104871	L	5-10.000 EUR	6.984*	9.981*	9.000*	12-03-16	Lyon	310	Agu
	Light blue with black interior; in good overall condition. Gearbox restored in recent years. Since 1995 in the current ownership.										
1987	XJ-S HE Eventer (Lynx)	141792	R	70-90.000 GBP	84.380	115.634	104.488	24-06-16	Goodwood	283	Bon F400
	Metallic blue; one-off with interior designed by Paolo Gucci. Exhibited by Gucci himself at the 1990 Geneva Motor Show. Bought in 2014 by the current owner and subsequently restored (see lot 308 Bonhams 7.12.14 $ 66,378).										
1989	XJ-S HE coupé	152419	R	7-9.000 GBP		NS		02-07-16	Woodstock	187	Coy
	Metallic black; body repainted in recent times.										
1985	XJ-SC V12 HE cabriolet	125005	R	NA	18.480	28.424	24.911	14-10-15	Duxford	72	H&H
	Cobalt blue; described as in original condition. 14,200 miles on the odometer.										
1988	XJ-SC V12 HE cabriolet	148831	L	16-21.000 EUR	16.295	23.289	21.000	12-03-16	Lyon	346	Agu
	Dark grey with white leather interior; in good overall condition.										
1989	XJ-SC V12 HE cabriolet	8161401	L	15-20.000 EUR	17.938	25.987	23.040	20-03-16	Fontainebleau	346	Ose
	Dark blue with Cartier red leather interior; serviced in January 2015.										
1986	XJ-SC V12 HE cabriolet	135019	R	10-12.000 GBP	8.800	12.809	11.356	18-05-16	Donington Park	45	H&H
	Red with cream interior; 31,960 miles on the odometer.										
1993	XJ-SC V12 HE cabriolet	180963	L	18-26.000 EUR	25.364	36.238	32.200	18-06-16	Wien	444	Dor
	Dark red with beige leather interior; in good overall condition. Since 1995 in the current ownership; 46,204 kms on the odometer.										
1985	XJ-SC V12 HE cabriolet	125360	R	10-15.000 GBP	11.800	15.444	13.635	20-08-16	Brooklands	346	His
	Sage green; 47,454 miles covered. Last serviced 1,000 miles ago.										
1989	XJ-S V12 HE convertible	161950	R	7-9.000 GBP	8.560	13.130	11.556	10-10-15	Ascot	162	Coy
	Red with charcoal interior; in good overall condition.										

F399: 1976 Jaguar XJ12C

F400: 1987 Jaguar XJ-S HE Eventer (Lynx)

Year	Model	(Bodybuilder)	Chassis No.	Steering	Estimate	Hammer price £	$	€	Date	Place	Lot	Auc. H.
1988	XJ-S V12 HE convertible		151777	R	9-12.000 GBP	10.080	15.171	14.340	28-11-15	Weybridge	264	His
White with barley leather interior; in good overall condition (see lot 207 Historics 6.6.15 NS).												
1988	XJ-S V12 HE convertible		149573	R	NQ	12.880*	19.433*	17.763*	09-12-15	Chateau Impney	27	H&H
First registered to Jaguar Cars; since 1996 in the current, third ownership; 49,900 miles on the odometer.												
1988	XJ-S V12 HE convertible		147386	R	18-24.000 GBP	18.400	27.830	25.431	10-12-15	London	379	Bon
Brown with brown leather interior; restored in 2012-13.												
1994	XJ-S V12 HE convertible		195141	R	10-14.000 GBP	11.200	16.131	14.271	11-06-16	Brooklands	216	His
Blue with barley leather interior; in good overall condition.												
1990	XJ-S V12 HE convertible		171857	R	11-15.000 GBP	9.870	13.109	11.773	02-07-16	Woodstock	180	Coy
Sage green; described as in very good overall condition. For 20 years in the current ownership.												
1988	XJ-S V12 HE convertible		153633	R	22-25.000 GBP	23.060	30.347	27.308	30-07-16	Silverstone	559	SiC
Metallic ice blue with cream leather interior; described as in very good original condition, the car has covered 18,568 miles.												
1989	XJR-S coupé		156079	R	8-11.000 GBP	14.560	21.914	20.713	28-11-15	Weybridge	317	His
Red with magnolia leather interior; in good overall condition. 32,300 miles covered.												
1994	XJ-S 4.0 coupé		196604	L	10-15.000 EUR	13.453	19.490	17.280	20-03-16	Fontainebleau	361	Ose
Engine in good working order.												
1991	XJ-S 4.0 coupé		180468	R	8-10.000 GBP	7.840	10.323	9.308	28-07-16	Donington Park	32	H&H
Light metallic grey; 67,000 recorded miles.												
1992	XJ220		220874	L	280-420.000 EUR	323.686	496.519	437.000	09-10-15	Zoute	27	Bon **F401**
Burgundy with beige leather interior; registered in 1997, the car has covered 1,080 kms. Since new in the collection of the former Jaguar importer for Belgium.												
1991	XJ220		220693	R	300-350.000 GBP	315.000	479.556	445.536	14-11-15	Birmingham	333	SiC
Metallic green; sold new to the Bruney Royal Family, the car was reimported into the UK in 2002. Body repainted in 2007; 5,782 miles on the odometer; last serviced in August 2015 (see lot 344 Silverstone Auctions 16.11.14 $ 386,100).												
1994	XJ220		220619	L	425-500.000 USD	269.385	385.000	352.545	29-01-16	Phoenix	238	RMS
Silver with grey interior; in very good overall condition, the car has covered less than 6,900 kms. Clutch replaced.												
1992	XJ220		220869	L	270-350.000 EUR	226.029	335.059	299.000	04-02-16	Paris	333	Bon
Dark green with smoke grey leather interior; in original condition. Two owners and 9,500 kms covered.												
1994	XJ220		220640	L	NA	275.625	385.214	350.016	26-02-16	Coventry	730	SiC
Green with sand interior; described as in very good overall condition (see lots Coys 414 4.12.08 $ 178,486, and Silverstone Auctions 626 26.7.14 $ 318,440 and 354 23.5.15 NS).												
1994	XJ220		220628	L	225-275.000 USD	260.832*	357.500*	323.037*	25-06-16	Santa Monica	2039	AA
Green with tan interior; less than 8,700 kms on the odometer. From the Riverside International Automotive Museum Collection.												
1993	XJ220		220857	L	250-325.000 USD	289.938	379.500	335.061	20-08-16	Monterey	218	RMS
Silver with smoke grey leather interior; in good overall condition. Sold new to Japan, in 2003 the car was imported into the USA. Since 2012 it is in Canada.												
1993	XJ220		220667	L	NQ	332.340	435.000	384.062	20-08-16	Monterey	7100	R&S
Red; sold new to Canada and leater imported into the USA. 871 kms covered.												
2000	XKR convertible		07022	R	10-12.000 GBP		NS		28-07-16	Donington Park	18	H&H
Blue with cream leather interior; 93,300 recorded miles.												

JENSEN (GB) *(1935-1976)*

Year	Model	(Bodybuilder)	Chassis No.	Steering	Estimate	£	$	€	Date	Place	Lot	Auc. H.
1936	Ford V8 tourer		183192631	L	250-300.000 USD	173.176	247.500	226.636	29-01-16	Phoenix	265	RMS **F402**
One of three examples built in left-hand drive form for the US market. Fully restored between 2007 and 2013.												
1939	S-Type tourer		S244544	R	70-80.000 GBP	63.650	84.540	75.922	02-07-16	Woodstock	220	Coy
Cream with original grey leather interior; two owners since new. Raced at some club events in period (see Coys lots 126 3.3.03 NS and 753 4.12.03 NS).												
1959	541R		3674319	R	37-42.000 GBP	35.000	45.451	41.059	10-07-16	Chateau Impney	53	H&H
Grey and burgundy with red interior; restored at unspecified date, the car is described as in good overall condition.												
1964	C-V8		1042087	R	20-28.000 GBP	38.200	57.548	54.290	01-12-15	London	317	Coy
Dark metallic blue with red leather interior; the car has covered approximately 6,000 miles since a restoration completed in 2011. Gearbox recently overhauled. Webasto sunroof (see lot 9 H&H 17.4.13 $ 44,398).												

F401: 1992 Jaguar XJ220

F402: 1936 Jensen Ford V8 tourer

Year	Model	(Bodybuilder)	Chassis No.	Steering	Estimate	Hammer Price £	$	€	Date	Place	Lot	Auc. H.
1967	Interceptor		1172642	L	42-54.000 GBP	51.520	77.543	73.292	28-11-15	Weybridge	241	His
	Red with beige roof and tan interior; described as in very good driving order. Formerly owned for 20 years by author Harold Robbins.											
1968	Interceptor		1153077	R	40-50.000 GBP	42.560	60.827	54.847	12-03-16	Brooklands	243	His
	Blue; first restored in the early 1990s and in recent times again.											
1968	Interceptor		1152774	R	35-40.000 GBP		NS		30-07-16	Silverstone	524	SiC
	Light blue; restored between 2014 and 2015.											
1969	Interceptor		1153336	R	24-32.000 GBP	39.200	51.305	45.296	20-08-16	Brooklands	275	His
	Gunmetal grey with oxblood vinyl roof and oxblood leather interior; restoration completed in 2016.											
1969	Interceptor FF		119167	R	56-62.000 GBP	58.500	88.048	83.222	28-11-15	Weybridge	271	His
	White with black leather interior; in very good overall condition. Several works carried out between 2005 and 2010.											
1969	Interceptor FF		119165	R	78-86.000 GBP		NS		12-03-16	Brooklands	244	His
	Blue with silver roof and black interior; some mechanical works carried out over the last three years.											
1971	Interceptor MkII		1234165	R	25-30.000 GBP		NS		28-11-15	Weybridge	225	His
	Red; several restoration works carried out between 1993 and 2014.											
1973	Interceptor MkIII		1368165	R	19-24.000 GBP		NS		16-04-16	Ascot	133	Coy
	Silver with red leather interior; described as in good original condition.											
1975	Interceptor MkIII cabriolet		9919	R	45-55.000 GBP	72.563	110.470	102.633	14-11-15	Birmingham	325	SiC
	Metallic red with magnolia leather interior; fully restored about three years ago. Engine and gearbox rebuilt (see lot 515 Brooks 2.4.97 $ 26,483).											
1975	Interceptor MkIII cabriolet		23111623	L	57.5-62.500 USD	41.509	59.400	51.957	02-04-16	Ft.Lauderdale	707	AA
	Red with tan interior (see lot 244 Bonhams 31.5.15 $ 53,900).											
1976	Interceptor MkIII cabriolet		23401848	R	45-55.000 GBP	46.000	63.038	56.962	24-06-16	Goodwood	215	Bon
	Black with black interior; circa 50,600 miles covered. First owner the Led Zeppelin drummer, John Bonham (see lot 331 Sotheby's 4.9.93 NS).											
1976	Interceptor MkIII cabriolet		23111925	L	45-55.000 GBP		NS		02-07-16	Woodstock	254	Coy
	Green with ivory interior; 62,000 miles on the odometer. Interior retrimmed.											

JOWETT (GB) (1906-1953)

Year	Model	(Bodybuilder)	Chassis No.	Steering	Estimate	£	$	€	Date	Place	Lot	Auc. H.
1928	7hp Sports Racer		823147	R	40-50.000 USD	23.624*	34.100*	30.571*	05-06-16	Greenwhich	74	Bon
	Light green with green interior; first restored in the 1970s and fitted with the present new body. Restored again in more recent years. From the Evergreen Collection (see lot 116 RM 9.10.14 $ 38,500).											
1948	Javelin		D8PA1203	R	8-11.000 GBP		NS		12-03-16	Brooklands	125	His
	Beige with tan interior; in good overall condition.											
1952	Jupiter cabriolet		E2SA694R	R	24-28.000 GBP	21.938	33.398	31.029	14-11-15	Birmingham	320	SiC
	Red; restored at unspecified date.											

KAISER (USA) (1946-1955)

Year	Model	(Bodybuilder)	Chassis No.	Steering	Estimate	£	$	€	Date	Place	Lot	Auc. H.
1951	DeLuxe sedan		K512017015	L	NA	10.225	15.500	14.155	12-12-15	Austin	F147	Mec
	Light green with green interior; restored.											
1953	Darrin 161		161001001	L	200-250.000 USD	138.422	198.000	181.586	28-01-16	Scottsdale	95	Bon
	Champagne with red vinyl interior; first production car built, it was exhibited at the 1953 Los Angeles Motor Show. In the same family ownership from 1956 for several decades, it was first restored in 1973. Restored again in more recent years (see lot S97 Mecum 15.8.15 NS).											F403
1954	Darrin 161		161001390	L	140-180.000 USD	123.147*	176.000*	161.163*	29-01-16	Phoenix	209	RMS
	Yellow with cream interior; fully restored over the past four years. Engine fitted with a McCulloch supercharger. With a black hardtop.											
1954	Darrin 161		161001031	L	100-120.000 EUR	50.622	73.470	67.200	03-02-16	Paris	133	RMS
	Champagne with red interior; recently restored.											
1954	Darrin 161		161001429	L	130-160.000 USD	97.171*	137.500*	126.638*	10-03-16	Amelia Island	131	Bon
	White with red interior; in the same family ownership until 1978. Restored in 2007-08; cosmetically restored again in 2013 (see lot 71 Worldwide Group 1.11.08 $ 75,900).											
1954	Darrin 161		161001371	L	130-160.000 USD	83.829*	121.000*	108.477*	05-06-16	Greenwhich	45	Bon
	White with red leather interior; restored several years ago.											

F403: 1953 Kaiser Darrin 161

F404: 1962 Kurtis Aguila

Year	Model	(Bodybuilder)	Chassis no.	Steering	Estimate	Hammer price £	Hammer price $	Hammer price €	Date	Place	Lot	Auc. H.
1954	Special club sedan		K545012312	L	NA	10.821	15.500	14.341	23-01-16	Kissimmee	G131.1	Mec

Ivory with green roof and bamboo interior; 3-speed manual gearbox with overdrive.

KELSEY (USA) (1902-1911)

Year	Model	(Bodybuilder)	Chassis no.	Steering	Estimate	£	$	€	Date	Place	Lot	Auc. H.
1911	Motorette		290	R	50-65.000 USD	26.895*	41.250*	36.308*	09-10-15	Hershey	223	RMS

Black with black interior; restored in the 1990s (see lot 163 Bonhams 12.13.15 NS).

KRIT (USA) (1910-1915)

Year	Model	(Bodybuilder)	Chassis no.	Steering	Estimate	£	$	€	Date	Place	Lot	Auc. H.
1912	Four Model A Roadster		231926(engine)	R	20-25.000 USD	16.766*	24.200*	21.695*	05-06-16	Greenwhich	70	Bon

Yellow with black interior; older restoration. From the Evergreen collection.

KURTIS (USA) (1938-1962)

Year	Model	(Bodybuilder)	Chassis no.	Steering	Estimate	£	$	€	Date	Place	Lot	Auc. H.
1962	Aguila		62S1	L	450-600.000 USD	296.281	423.500	381.870	12-03-16	Amelia Island	143	RMS

Black with red stripe and red interior; the car was commissioned by motorcycle racer Herb Stelter who fitted it with a 350bhp 327 Chevrolet Corvette engine. Raced at some events until 1965. Restored in the early 1990s and driven at historic events, in more recent years it was repainted and the mechanicals were refreshed (see lot 198 RM 16.1.09 $ 165,000). **F404**

LA BUIRE (F) (1902-1930)

Year	Model	(Bodybuilder)	Chassis no.	Steering	Estimate	£	$	€	Date	Place	Lot	Auc. H.
1924	Type 12A berline	(Hollingdrake)	1604	R	19-22.000 GBP	9.200	13.328	11.816	20-03-16	Goodwood	12	Bon

Black and yellow; restoration commenced around 2007 to be completed. From the Kingsley Curtis Collection.

LAGONDA (GB) (1908-1974)

Year	Model	(Bodybuilder)	Chassis no.	Steering	Estimate	£	$	€	Date	Place	Lot	Auc. H.
1928	2-litre Speed Model tourer		OH9090	R	NA	73.920	104.819	93.450	20-04-16	Duxford	87	H&H

Black with red interior; restored in 1990 circa. In 1960 circa a previous owner fitted the car with the present tourer body and with a low chassis front axle.

| 1928 | 2-litre Speed Model tourer | | 8942 | R | 70-90.000 GBP | | NS | | 24-06-16 | Goodwood | 279 | Bon |

Grey with red leather interior; described as in very good overall condition. Since 1949 in the same family ownership. In recent times the engine has been rebuilt and the interior retrimmed (see lot 29 H & H 4.12.13 $60,984).

| 1927 | 2-litre tourer | | SM8787 | R | 95-115.000 EUR | | NS | | 06-08-16 | Schloss Dyck | 122 | Coy |

Black with green leather interior; two owners since 1947. Recently serviced.

| 1933 | 3-litre saloon | | Z10271 | R | 10-20.000 GBP | 29.900* | 45.529* | 40.876* | 05-09-15 | Beaulieu | 122 | Bon |

Restoration project; since 1964 in the current ownership.

| 1933 | 3-litre tourer | | Z10462 | R | 90-110.000 GBP | 87.360 | 131.809 | 120.478 | 09-12-15 | Chateau Impney | 110 | H&H |

Green with red interior; built with saloon body, the car was fitted with the present, new body probably in the 1960s. Since 1971 in the same family ownership. At unspecified date it was fitted with the present Meadows 4.5-litre engine.

| 1936 | Rapier | (Ranalah) | R11477 | R | NA | 26.880 | 41.344 | 36.234 | 14-10-15 | Duxford | 103 | H&H |

Car on restoration: body to be restored, chassis and mechanicals, including engine, already restored.

| 1934 | M45 sports | | Z10606 | R | 70-90.000 GBP | | NS | | 05-09-15 | Beaulieu | 126 | Bon |

Dark green with polished aluminium bonnet and wings, red wire wheels and red interior; built with saloon body, probably in the early 1970s the car was fully restored in the style of a Fox & Nichol team car. Since 1976 in the same family ownership; recommissioned in 2015.

| 1935 | M45A tourer | | Z11408 | R | NA | | NS | | 20-04-16 | Duxford | 95 | H&H |

Green with black interior; described as in good working order. Built with saloon body, probably in the 1970s the car was fitted with the present, Le Mans style tourer body.

| 1937 | LG45 saloon | | 12192G10 | R | NA | | NS | | 14-10-15 | Duxford | 25 | H&H |

Maroon and red with burgundy leather interior; engine overhauled in 1979, body repainted many years ago, interior redone in recent years.

| 1937 | LG45 Rapide tourer | | 12173R | R | 500-700.000 GBP | 785.500 | 1.189.168 | 1.090.745 | 06-12-15 | London | 021 | Bon **F405** |

Grey with largely original blue leather interior; since new in the same family ownership. The car has been regularly serviced over the years and the engine has been rebuilt in recent times.

| 1937 | LG45 saloon | | 12257G10 | R | 85-115.000 GBP | 83.260 | 120.619 | 106.939 | 20-03-16 | Goodwood | 32 | Bon |

Black and grey; an older restoration, the car is described as in very good overall condition.

| 1939 | LG6 Rapide cabriolet | | 12372 | R | 3.400-4.200.000 DKK | 538.056 | 816.644 | 732.521 | 26-09-15 | Ebeltoft | 31 | Bon |

Blue with cognac leather interior; the car was exhibited at the 1940 New York Motor Show and subsequently was acquired by its first owner who retained it until 1961 when it was bought by the second one who resold it in 2006 to Skip Barber. The latter fully restored the car and displayed it at the 2008 Pebble Beach Concours d'Elegance. From the Frederiksen Collection.

F405: 1937 Lagonda LG45 Rapide tourer

F406: 1954 Lagonda DB 3l cabriolet

Year	Model	(Bodybuilder)	Chassis no.	Steering	Estimate	Hammer Price £	$	€	Date	Place	Lot	Auc. H.
1939	LG6 saloon		12339	R	55-65.000 GBP	77.660	117.461	107.334	10-12-15	London	325	Bon

Burgundy with tan leather interior; acquised about 20 years ago by the current owner and subsequently fully restored.

| 1937 | LG6 Rapide tourer | | 12312 | R | 700-850.000 USD | 469.096 | 671.000 | 615.374 | 28-01-16 | Phoenix | 147 | RMS |

Believed to be the car exhibited at the 1938 New York and London Motor Shows, it was sold in the UK in 1940 and imported into the USA in 1957. In the same ownership from late 1957 to 1998, it was restored in the late 1960s. Bought in 2010 by the current owner, it was subsequently restored again and finished in the present dark aubergine livery with red leather interior.

| 1938 | LG6 limousine de ville | (Thrupp/Maberly) | E3048 | R | 80-120.000 USD | 36.580* | 52.800* | 47.335* | 05-06-16 | Greenwhich | 59 | Bon |

Black with leather interior to the front compartment and cloth to the rear; one-off body fitted to a long chassis. Probably when new the car was retained by the factory and in 1949 it was imported into the USA. Described as in original condition; engine rebuilt many years ago.

| 1939 | V12 sedanca de ville | (Hooper) | 18021 | R | NA | | NS | | 14-10-15 | Duxford | 41 | H&H |

Black and maroon with leather interior to the front compartment and cloth to the rear; car delivered after WWII. Since 1973 in the current ownership. Stored from the mid-1970s to 2006 and subsequently restored.

| 1938 | V12 cabriolet | (J.Young) | 14036 | R | 140-170.000 GBP | 152.700 | 230.959 | 211.047 | 10-12-15 | London | 305 | Bon |

Green with green interior; stored from 1950 to 1984, the car was subsequently restored. Acquired in 1994 by Gordon Willey for his collection, the car received further restoration works to the body including a repainting.

| 1939 | V12 cabriolet | | 14113 | R | 450-550.000 USD | 324.163 | 458.700 | 422.463 | 10-03-16 | Amelia Island | 170 | Bon |

Originally finished in black with buff leather interior, the car was sold new to the USA. In the mid-1990s it was acquired by the current owner already restored to its present red livery with tan interior.

| 1957 | DB 3l saloon | | LB2901209 | R | NA | 21.280 | 30.175 | 26.902 | 20-04-16 | Duxford | 2 | H&H |

Black with blue interior; for 56 years in the current ownership, the car was stored for over 20 years and requires several works prior to use.

| 1954 | DB 3l cabriolet | | LB29031 | R | NA | 339.000 | 480.702 | 428.564 | 20-04-16 | Duxford | 31 | H&H F406 |

Edinburgh green with original grey leather interior; first owner HRH Prince Philip, the Duke of Edinburgh, who retained it until 1961. Acquired in 1977 by the current, third owner; body restored and repainted in 1990; engine overhauled 10 years ago.

| 1955 | DB 3l cabriolet | (Tickford) | LB290189 | R | 25-35.000 GBP | 89.420 | 130.267 | 116.112 | 21-05-16 | Newp.Pagnell | 207 | Bon |

Red with blue leather interior; for restoration. The car remained in the factory's ownership until 1956 and from 1955 to 1956 it had been on loan to Juan Manuel Fangio.

| 1963 | Rapide | (Touring/Tickford) | LR146R | R | 350-400.000 GBP | | NS | | 06-12-15 | London | 024 | Bon |

Blue with beige leather interior; in 1970 the car was fitted at the factory with a ZF 5-speed gerabox and in 1974 the body was repainted in black. In 2006 it was acquired by Aston Martin Lagonda Ltd and subsequently subjected to a full restoration recently completed. The engine was converted to 4.2-litre capacity by R S Williams (see lot 134 Bonhams 13.6.06 $ 43,628).

LAMBORGHINI (I) (1963-)

| 1966 | 350 GT (Touring) | | 0148 | L | NA | | NS | | 30-01-16 | Scottsdale | 5199 | R&S |

Black with tan leather interior; restored at unspecified date, the car is described as in concours condition (see Russo & Steele lots 7003 12.8.10 NS and S740 18.1.14 $ 742,630).

| 1966 | 350 GT (Touring) | | 0409 | L | 680-780.000 EUR | | NS | | 05-02-16 | Paris | 144 | Art F407 |

Dark grey with tobacco leather interior; the car has covered about 2,000 kms since the restoration completed in 2013 in Italy.

| 1965 | 350 GT (Touring) | | 0343 | L | 650-750.000 USD | | NS | | 11-03-16 | Amelia Island | 16 | G&Co |

Originally finished in silver with tobacco interior, the car was sold new to Spain where it remained for over 40 years and was repainted at some point to the present dark metallic green livery. In 2009 it was sold to Japanese collector Isao Noritake. In 2015 it was bought by the current owner, imported into the USA and serviced. 97,195 kms on the odometer.

| 1966 | 350 GT (Touring) | | 0391 | L | 700-850.000 EUR | | NS | | 14-05-16 | Monaco | 230 | RMS |

Silver grey with black interior; sold new in Italy. In recent years the car was fully restored in the Netherlands. Original engine no.0364.

| 1966 | 350 GT (Touring) | | 0316 | L | 750-950.000 USD | 554.664 | 726.000 | 640.985 | 21-08-16 | Pebble Beach | 124 | G&Co |

Light metallic blue with black leather interior; sold new to the USA, the car remained in the same family ownership from 1966 to 2013. Described as in original, unrestored condition it has covered less than 10,000 miles. Mechanicals freshened in 2014.

| 1968 | Miura (Bertone) | | 3315 | L | 750-900.000 USD | 603.560 | 790.000 | 697.491 | 20-08-16 | Monterey | S77 | Mec F408 |

Red with black interior; since 1985 in the same family ownership. In original condition except for the paintwork redone at unspecified date. 45,590 kms covered. Engine rebuilt in 1997.

| 1971 | Miura S (Bertone) | | 4782 | L | 1.300-1.500.000 USD | | NS | | 29-01-16 | Phoenix | 250 | RMS |

White with blue and white interior; sold new in Italy, the car was damaged in an accident in 1972 circa. Returned to the factory for repairs, it remained unrepaired until 1983 when it was bought by Japanese collector Isao Noritake, who had it repaired to its original specification and retained it for 32 years in his museum in Japan. 3,788 kms covered since new.

| 1970 | Miura S (Bertone) | | 4239 | L | 900-1.100.000 EUR | | NS | | 05-02-16 | Paris | 202 | Art |

Red with original black leatherette interior; originally finished in green, the car was sold new in Italy and later imported into France. Since 1980 in the current ownership, it is described as in largely original condition, except for the paintwork.

F407: 1966 Lamborghini 350 GT (Touring)

F408: 1968 Lamborghini Miura (Bertone)

THE FIRST MIURA SV PRESENTED DURING 1971 GENEVA MOTOR SHOW

APRIL '15
BEGINNING OF RESTORATION

FEBRUARY '16
FINISHED RESTORATION

MARCH '16
PRESENTED AT AMELIA ISLAND CONCOURS D'ELEGANCE

MAY '16
WINS THE AWARD AT CONCORSO DI ELEGANZA VILLA D'ESTE

JUNE '16
WINS AWARD AT GOODWOOD CONCOURS D'ELEGANCE

AUGUST '16
2° PLACE AT PEBBLE BEACH CONCOURS D'ELEGANCE

SEPTEMBER '16
WINS AWARD AT SALON PRIVÉ CONCOURS

**ARCHIVE
CERTIFICATION
RESTORATION CENTER
HERITAGE SPARE PARTS**

Lamborghini PoloStorico   Via Modena, 12   I-40019 Sant'Agata Bolognese   polostorico@lamborghini.com   www.lamborghini.com

Year	Model	(Bodybuilder)	Chassis no.	Steering	Estimate	Hammer price £	$	€	Sale Date	Place	Lot	Auc. H.

F409: 1972 Lamborghini Miura SV (Bertone) *F410: 1973 Lamborghini Espada 400 GT (Bertone)*

Year	Model	(Bodybuilder)	Chassis	St.	Estimate	£	$	€	Date	Place	Lot	Auc.
1972	**Miura SV (Bertone)**		5014	L	2.400-2.800.000 USD	1.599.862	2.420.000	2.211.396	10-12-15	New York	202	**RMS** F409

Yellow with black leather interior; sold new in Italy, the car was later exported to Japan. Following the current owner purchase, the car has been subjected to a full restoration in Italy. Described as in concours condition.

1971	**Miura SV (Bertone)**		4912	L	2.000-2.400.000 USD	1.398.200	2.000.000	1.834.200	28-01-16	Phoenix	132	**RMS**

Originally finished in blue with blue leather interior, the car was sold new to the USA. In 1992 it was sold to Japan where it remained for 20 years prior to be reimported into the USA. Restored many years ago in the present yellow livery with beige interior.

1971	**Miura SV (Bertone)**		4920	L	2.200-2.600.000 USD	1.722.820	2.255.000	1.990.940	20-08-16	Pebble Beach	22	**G&Co**

Red with tan leather interior; sold new in Italy, in 1978 circa the car was purchased by Claudio Zampolli who imported it into the USA, later returned it back to Italy for the restoration after which reimported it into the USA where he sold it in 1995. Since 2005 in the current ownership, the car is described as in very good overall condition.

1972	**Miura SV (Bertone)**		3673	L	1.900-2.200.000 USD	NS			20-08-16	Monterey	237	**RMS**

Red with black interior; the car was sold new to South Africa and remained until 1990 with its first owner. Described as in largely original condition with regard to the body and interior, it received a full mechanical restoration. 25,000 miles on the odometer.(see lot 158 Bonhams/Brooks 20.1.01 NS).

1968	**400 GT 2+2 (Touring)**		1183	L	575-650.000 USD	400.901	577.500	510.857	11-06-16	Hershey	133	**TFA**

Burgundy with beige interior; the car was imported into the USA in the early 1970s probably. Between 2009 and 2015 it was cosmetically and mechanically restored.

1968	**400 GT 2+2 (Touring)**		1294	L	300-400.000 USD	298.342*	390.500*	344.772*	20-08-16	Pebble Beach	2	**G&Co**

Amaranth with mustard leather interior; in the same family ownership since 1976 when it was last road-registered. In original condition and not currently running, it requires recommissioning prior to use.

1971	**Espada 400 GT (Bertone)**		8023	L	150-200.000 EUR	NS			05-02-16	Paris	113	**Art**

Silver with beige interior; body and interior restored. Since 1993 in the current ownership.

1969	**Espada 400 GT (Bertone)**		7216	L	280-340.000 EUR	NS			05-02-16	Paris	146	**Art**

White with original leather interior; clutch and shock absorbers replaced in 2009 at 9,064 ms, body restored in 2013.

1973	**Espada 400 GT (Bertone)**		9060	L	140-180.000 USD	69.260*	99.000*	89.268*	11-03-16	Amelia Island	63	**G&Co**

Red; described as in very good overall condition.

1973	**Espada 400 GT (Bertone)**		9448	L	95-110.000 USD	68.413	97.900	85.633	02-04-16	Ft.Lauderdale	209	**AA**

Silver with original black interior; body restored. Recently serviced (see lots 2006 Auctions America 2.8.14 $ 132,000 and 259 RM 16.1.15 $ 110,000).

1973	**Espada 400 GT (Bertone)**		8852	L	110-140.000 EUR	90.572	130.502	115.000	13-05-16	Monaco	141	**Bon** F410

Dark metallic red with tan interior; sold new to the USA, the car was reimported into Europe in 2011. Mechanicals overhauled in Germany in 2012; last serviced in 2014 (see lot 109 RM 19.8.11 $ 55,000).

1969	**Espada 400 GT (Bertone)**		7533	L	130-160.000 EUR	112.610	148.128	132.779	06-08-16	Schloss Dyck	151	**Coy**

Silver with dark red leather interior; described as in very good overall condition.

1969	**Islero 400 GTS 2+2 (Marazzi)**		6432	R	300-350.000 GBP	NS			12-09-15	Goodwood	340	**Bon**

Silver with burgundy leather interior; restored in the mid-1980s, the car was subsequently stored for about 20 years and was recommissioned in 2008. Used in the 1971 movie "The Man Who Haunted Himself" starring Roger Moore (see lot 194 RM 27.10.10 $ 168,357).

1969	**Islero 400 GTS 2+2 (Marazzi)**		6453	L	170-210.000 EUR	169.745	247.027	220.520	05-02-16	Paris	143	**Art** F411

Red with leather and cloth interior; mechanicals restored at unspecified date.

F411: 1969 Lamborghini Islero 400 GTS 2+2 (Marazzi) *F412: 1974 Lamborghini Urraco P250 (Bertone)*

Year	Model	(Bodybuilder)	Chassis no.	Steering	Estimate	Hammer Price £	Hammer Price $	Hammer Price €	Date	Place	Lot	Auc. H.
1969	Islero 400 GTS 2+2	(Marazzi)	6531	L	450-500.000 USD		NS		20-08-16	Monterey	S107	Mec
	Red with tan leather interior; sold new to Switzerland, the car was imported in 1998 into the USA and cosmetically restored. Mechanicals rebuilt in 2009 (see lot 319 RM/Sotheby's 15.8.15 $ 401,500).											
1971	Jarama 400 GT 2+2	(Bertone)	10160	L	240-260.000 EUR		NS		05-02-16	Paris	204	Art
	Dark green; the car has covered 200 kms since the restoration.											
1972	Jarama 400 GT 2+2	(Bertone)	10258	L	150-175.000 USD		NS		20-08-16	Monterey	S158	Mec
	Blue with black interior; recently serviced.											
1975	Urraco P250	(Bertone)	15980	L	NA		NS		23-01-16	Kissimmee	T72.1	Mec
	Yellow with black interior; 6,495 actual miles.											
1975	Urraco P300	(Bertone)	20168	L	NA		NS		26-02-16	Coventry	424	SiC
	Silver with black leather interior; sold new to Canada, the car was imported into the UK in 2014 and subsequently overhauled. Body repainted in more recent times.											
1974	Urraco P250	(Bertone)	15618	L	80-90.000 EUR	69.836	99.810	90.000	12-03-16	Lyon	321	Agu F412
	Black with black and white interior; for 25 years in the current ownership, the car was fully restored in the 2000s.											
1981	Countach LP400S	(Bertone)	1121296	L	245-315.000 GBP	263.200	401.696	360.400	07-09-15	London	141	RMS
	Red with beige leather interior; in very good, largely original condition. Three owners. Swiss papers.											
1975	Countach LP400	(Bertone)	1120110	L	1.200-1.500.000 EUR	825.788	1.201.751	1.072.800	05-02-16	Paris	148	Art F413
	Black with black leather interior; sold new in Italy, the car was imported in 1977 into the USA were it was restored between 2006 and 2007. Subsequently it was reimported into Europe.											
1976	Countach LP400	(Bertone)	1120154	L	1.200-1.500.000 USD		NS		21-08-16	Pebble Beach	113	G&Co
	Blue with blue and white interior; sold new to Canada and later imported into the USA. Restored at unspecified date (see lots 532 RM 15.8.09 NS and 23 Gooding & Company 12.3.10 $330,000).											
1981	Countach S LP400	(Bertone)	1121316	L	900-1.100.000 USD	636.309	962.500	879.533	10-12-15	New York	226	RMS
	Metallic green with khaki leather interior; sold new to a Saudi sheikh, the car was later imported into Switzerland and then it was bought by the current, third owner and imported into the USA. 6,031 kms covered. Fully restored in Italy while in the Swiss ownership.											
1981	Countach S LP400	(Bertone)	1121358	L	380-450.000 EUR		NS		03-02-16	Paris	107	RMS
	Originally finished in white, the car was sold new to Switzerland. Later it was imported into the USA where it was restored and refinished in the current yellow livery with black leather interior.											
1981	Countach S LP400	(Bertone)	1320	R	NA	213.750	298.737	271.441	26-02-16	Coventry	414	SiC
	Yellow with oatmeal interior; in good overall condition. Body repainted in 1998 (see lot 162 Coys 5.12.02 NS).											
1978	Countach S LP400	(Bertone)	1121028	L	350-550.000 EUR	396.940*	571.939*	504.000*	14-05-16	Monaco	219	RMS
	Originally finished in dark metallic blue with white leather interior, at unspecified date the body was repainted in the present red livery and the interior were retrimmed in black. Purchased in 2001 by the current owner and stored since, the car received recently some minor recommissioning.											
1985	Countach 5000 S	(Bertone)	12743	L	NA		NS		19-09-15	Dallas	S110.1	Mec
	Red with black interior; restored. Recently serviced.											
1984	Countach 5000 S	(Bertone)	12675	L	400-500.000 EUR		NS		26-09-15	Frankfurt	146	Coy
	White with white leather interior; 51,800 kms covered including 1,500 kms since 1990. Engine rebuilt at unspecified date. One registered owner.											
1984	Countach 5000 S	(Bertone)	12675	L	230-340.000 GBP		NS		01-12-15	London	321	Coy
	See lot 146 Coys 26.9.15.											
1987	Countach 5000 4V	(Bertone)	12146	L	NQ		NS		23-01-16	Kissimmee	S25.1	Mec
	Black with black interior; unrestored. Believed to be 28,000 original miles. Recent engine-out service.											
1988	Countach 5000 4V	(Bertone)	12269	L	350-500.000 USD	207.633	297.000	272.379	28-01-16	Scottsdale	66	Bon F414
	White with black interior; in largely original condition. Less than 35,000 kms covered. Last serviced in October 2015.											
1988	Countach 5000 4V	(Bertone)	12340	L	375-425.000 USD		NS		28-01-16	Phoenix	135	RMS
	White with red interior; described as in very good overall condition, the car has covered 13,759 kms.											
1984	Countach 5000 S	(Bertone)	12675	L	275-295.000 GBP	253.800	360.624	327.021	08-03-16	London	112	Coy
	See lot 321 Coys 1.12.15.											
1987	Countach 5000 4V	(Bertone)	12140	L	375-425.000 EUR	299.226	421.170	370.650	09-04-16	Essen	147	Coy
	Black with black leather interior; in good original condition. 21,000 kms on the odometer.											
1985	Countach 5000 4V	(Bertone)	12880	L	320-380.000 GBP		NS		16-04-16	Ascot	121	Coy
	Red with black interior; restored. 37,629 kms covered since new (see lot 459 Coys 14.7.07 $ 94,455).											
1983	Countach 5000 S	(Bertone)	12566	R	275-325.000 GBP	281.250	409.725	365.203	20-05-16	Silverstone	349	SiC
	White with white leather interior; finished in red, the car was sold new to Saudi Arabia. In 1988 it was imported into the UK and refinished in red. 1,847 kms covered since the restoration carried out between 2010 and 2011.											

F413: 1975 Lamborghini Countach LP400 (Bertone)

F414: 1988 Lamborghini Countach 5000 4V (Bertone)

Year	Model	(Bodybuilder)	Chassis no.	Steering	Estimate	Hammer price £	$	€	Date	Place	Lot	Auc. H.
1983	Countach 5000 S	(Bertone)	12588	L	Refer Dpt.		NS		19-06-16	Fontainebleau	341	Ose
	Red with white interior; described as in very good driving order.											
1987	Countach 5000 4V	(Bertone)	12159	L	350-425.000 USD		NS		25-06-16	Santa Monica	2048	AA
	Pearl white with red leather interior; recently serviced. The original US bumpers replaced with the European ones.											
1988	Countach 5000 4V	(Bertone)	12332	L	375-425.000 USD		NS		19-08-16	Monterey	F138	Mec
	Black with black interior; for 27 years with its first owner. 15,640 kms covered. Last serviced in 2013.											
1986	Countach 5000 4V	(Bertone)	12886	L	550-650.000 USD		NS		20-08-16	Monterey	S78	Mec
	Red with tan interior; in very good original condition. 19,389 kms covered. Since 1988 in the current ownership.											
1988	Countach 5000 4V	(Bertone)	12315	L	NQ	245.817	321.750	284.073	20-08-16	Monterey	7202	R&S
	Red with cream interior.											
1989	Countach 25°	(Bertone)	12672	L	NA		NS		26-09-15	Las Vegas	449	B/J
	Red with tan interior; in very good overall condition. Two owners and 17,412 actual miles.											
1989	Countach 25°	(Bertone)	12820	L	330-400.000 EUR		NS		09-10-15	Zoute	38	Bon
	Blue with beige interior; 34,000 kms on the odometer. Clutch rebuilt 3,000 kms ago.											
1989	Countach 25°	(Bertone)	12499	L	NA	217.044	343.750	302.225	31-10-15	Hilton Head	176	AA F415
	White with black leather interior; described as in very good overall condition. 10,900 kms covered.											
1989	Countach 25°	(Bertone)	12694	L	NA		NS		12-12-15	Austin	S132	Mec
	Black with tan interior; one owner. Last serviced in 2015.											
1989	Countach 25°	(Bertone)	12651	L	350-450.000 USD		NS		23-01-16	Kissimmee	T212	Mec
	Red with ivory interior; 10,565 kms covered. Extensive engine service in 2014 (see Mecum lots S169 24.1.15 $ 350,000 and S60 15.8.15 NS).											
1990	Countach 25°	(Bertone)	12886	L	NA		NS		30-01-16	Scottsdale	5523	R&S
	Red; less than 29,000 kms covered.											
1990	Countach 25°	(Bertone)	12923	L	450-550.000 USD		NS		10-03-16	Amelia Island	125	Bon
	Red with black interior; less than 2,700 kms on the odometer. Imported into the USA in 2014 (see lot 119 RM 8.9.14 $ 360,640).											
1989	Countach 25°	(Bertone)	12681	R	250-300.000 GBP	241.875	352.364	314.075	20-05-16	Silverstone	344	SiC
	Red with white leather interior; restored in 2003, the car was used until 2004 when it entered long-term storage. 13,000 covered since new. Last serviced in May 2014.											
1989	Countach 25°	(Bertone)	12699	L	300-375.000 USD		NS		05-06-16	Greenwhich	24	Bon
	Red with black interior; described as in very good overall condition. Just over 10,000 kms on the odometer.											
1989	Countach 25°	(Bertone)	12470	L	325-375.000 USD	212.678	291.500	263.399	25-06-16	Santa Monica	2071	AA
	Red with tan interior; in good overall condition. Just over 5,300 kms covered.											
1990	Countach 25°	(Bertone)	12031	L	370-390.000 GBP	365.000	484.793	435.372	02-07-16	Woodstock	162	Coy
	Red with black interior; in the same ownership until 2015. 625 kms covered.											
1989	Countach 25°	(Bertone)	12499	L	275-350.000 USD	176.484	231.000	203.950	19-08-16	Monterey	107	RMS
	See lot 176 Auctions America 31.10.15.											
1976	Silhouette	(Bertone)	40002	L	275-325.000 USD	99.320*	130.000*	114.777*	20-08-16	Monterey	S92	Mec F416
	White; one of two prototypes built, the car was exhibited at the 1976 Turin Motor Show (see lots 50 Poulain 13.12.99 WD and 207 Brooks 6.3.00 NS).											
1984	Jalpa 3500	(Bertone)	12087	L	NA	80.815	115.500	105.763	30-01-16	Scottsdale	5408	R&S
	Paintwork and interior redone; for nearly 30 years in the same family ownership.											
1982	Jalpa 3500	(Bertone)	12067	L	NA	78.750	110.061	100.005	26-02-16	Coventry	421	SiC
	Black; probably used new by Patrick Mimran (at the time owner of the Lamborghini factory) and sold in 1983 in Italy. In the years it has had owners in Germany and USA, and in 2015 it was imported into the UK.											
1988	Jalpa 3500	(Bertone)	12376	L	60-70.000 GBP	58.500	85.223	75.962	20-05-16	Silverstone	316	SiC
	Black with black leather interior; body repainted in the past. In recent time it was imported into the UK and serviced (see lots 786 Auctions America 22.3.13 $ 47,300 and 247 Bonhams 31.5.15 $ 94,600).											
1998	Diablo SV	(Gandini)	12872	R	140-160.000 GBP	185.000	281.700	252.914	04-09-15	Woodstock	223	SiC
	Dark blue with leather and alcantara interior; 50,285 kms covered. Last serviced in August 2015.											
1993	Diablo	(Gandini)	12837	L	100-130.000 GBP	115.740	178.506	158.425	12-09-15	Goodwood	380	Bon
	Red with black interior; 23,259 kms covered. In very good overall condition.											
1996	Diablo	(Gandini)	12454	L	NA		NS		19-09-15	Dallas	F211.1	Mec
	Yellow with caramel interior; believed to be 25,380 kms.											

F415: 1989 Lamborghini Countach 25° (Bertone)

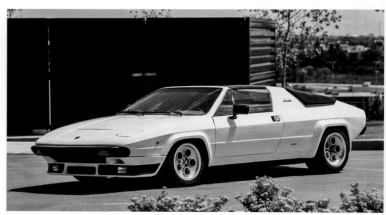

F416: 1976 Lamborghini Silhouette (Bertone)

Year	Model (Bodybuilder)	Chassis no.	Steering	Estimate	Hammer price £	Hammer price $	Hammer price €	Date	Place	Lot	Auc. H.
1994	**Diablo (Gandini)**	12255	L	95-110.000 GBP		NS		01-12-15	London	314	**Coy**
	Metallic black with black interior; 52,000 kms covered. European taxes to be paid.										
1998	**Diablo SV (Gandini)**	12920	R	180-225.000 GBP		NS		16-01-16	Birmingham	317	**Coy**
	Yellow with black interior; 16,947 miles covered. Since 2004 in the current ownership.										
1998	**Diablo SV (Gandini)**	12906	L	250-300.000 EUR		NS		04-02-16	Paris	366	**Bon**
	Yellow with black interior; two owners and 40,042 kms covered.										
1993	**Diablo VT (Gandini)**	12958	L	200-250.000 EUR		NS		04-02-16	Paris	373	**Bon**
	Grey with tan leather interior; in very good overall condition. 15,200 kms covered.										
1999	**Diablo VT Roadster (Gandini)**	12183	L	250-300.000 EUR		NS		05-02-16	Paris	203	**Art**
	Purple with blue and cream interior; in very good overall condition. 25,412 kms on the odometer.										
1991	**Diablo (Gandini)**	12446	L	180-240.000 EUR	**155.982**	**226.997**	**202.640**	05-02-16	Paris	210	**Art**
	Yellow; 5,474 kms on the odometer. First owner Keke Rosberg who retained it until 2015.										
1999	**Diablo SV (Gandini)**	12330	R	NA	**174.375**	**246.863**	**225.048**	06-03-16	Birmingham	321	**SiC**
	Orange red with black and grey leather and alcantara interior; described as in very good overall condition.										
1994	**Diablo (Gandini)**	12368	L	140-160.000 EUR	**124.773**	**178.327**	**160.800**	12-03-16	Lyon	326	**Agu**
	Red with beige interior; gearbox, clutch and brakes redone in 2013. 44,400 kms covered.										
1991	**Diablo (Gandini)**	12526	L	100-115.000 GBP	**98.560**	**140.862**	**127.014**	12-03-16	Brooklands	183	**His**
	Yellow with blue leather interior; sold new to the USA and imported into the UK in 2003. Recently serviced.										
1991	**Diablo (Gandini)**	12159	L	NA	**99.243**	**139.700**	**122.936**	09-04-16	Palm Beach	391	**B/J**
	Black with black leather interior.										
1998	**Diablo VT Roadster (Gandini)**	12925	L	NA		NS		09-04-16	Palm Beach	430	**B/J**
	Red with black leather interior; last serviced in July 2015.										
1997	**Diablo VT Roadster (Gandini)**	12610	L	NA	**114.595**	**162.500**	**144.008**	16-04-16	Houston	S121.1	**Mec**
	Red with white leather interior; 25,352 actual miles. Recently serviced.										
2001	**Diablo GT (Gandini)**	12555	L	620-680.000 EUR	**551.464**	**794.587**	**700.200**	14-05-16	Monaco	170	**Coy**
	Black with black and yellow interior; described as in very good original condition. 6,700 kms on the odometer. One of 80 examples built.										
1995	**Diablo SE30 Jota (Gandini)**	12132	L	490-550.000 EUR	**529.254**	**762.586**	**672.000**	14-05-16	Monaco	241	**RMS**
	Metallic blue/violet with white and blue leather interior; car no.132 of the 150 Special Edition examples built to commemorate Lamborghini's 30th anniversary. Fitted at the factory with the Jota package; 595bhp. Sold new to Japan and currently registered in Germany. 6,731 kms covered; recent engine-out service.										**F417**
1991	**Diablo (Gandini)**	12184	L	90-110.000 GBP	**79.000**	**115.087**	**102.582**	20-05-16	Silverstone	318	**SiC**
	Red with black and yellow interior; 46,285 kms on the odometer. Recently imported into the UK and serviced.										
1994	**Diablo VT (Gandini)**	12195	R	160-190.000 GBP		NS		11-06-16	Brooklands	295	**His**
	Red with cream leather interior; one owner and 13,380 kms covered. Gearbox rebuilt in 2001; recently serviced.										
1998	**Diablo SV Monterey (Gandini)**	12017	L	NA	**172.550**	**236.500**	**213.701**	24-06-16	Uncasville	662	**B/J**
	Red; 11,000 kms covered (see lot S174 Mecum 25.1.14 $120,000).										
1992	**Diablo (Gandini)**	12576	L	NA	**128.410**	**176.000**	**159.034**	24-06-16	Uncasville	692	**B/J**
	White with white interior; 52,740 actual kms.										
1992	**Diablo (Gandini)**	12779	L	100-120.000 GBP	**102.300**	**140.192**	**126.678**	24-06-16	Goodwood	232	**Bon**
	Silver with black interior; in very good overall condition. Since 1999 in the current ownership; 34,851 miles on the odometer.										
1994	**Diablo (Gandini)**	12711	L	85-95.000 GBP		NS		02-07-16	Woodstock	151	**Coy**
	Red with black interior; described as in very good overall condition.										
2001	**Diablo GT (Gandini)**	24	L	475-525.000 GBP	**510.226**	**677.682**	**608.598**	02-07-16	Woodstock	191	**Coy**
	Metallic grey; example n. 24 of the 80 built. 1,100 miles covered.										
1998	**Diablo SV (Gandini)**	12955	L	235-265.000 USD		NS		19-08-16	Monterey	F126	**Mec**
	Black with black leather interior; 32,768 kms covered.										
1999	**Diablo VT Roadster (Gandini)**	12197	L	325-375.000 USD	**231.110***	**302.500***	**267.077***	19-08-16	Monterey	104	**RMS**
	Red with cream leather interior; two owners and less than 6,300 miles covered. Last serviced in February 2016.										
1995	**Diablo VT (Gandini)**	12298	R	130-150.000 GBP		NS		20-08-16	Brooklands	326	**His**
	Turquoise with leather and alcantara interior; 11,064 miles covered. Last serviced in April 2014 at 10,402 miles.										

F417: 1995 Lamborghini Diablo SE30 Jota (Gandini)

F418: 2007 Lamborghini Murciélago LP640-4 coupé

Year	Model	(Bodybuilder)	Chassis no.	Steering	Estimate	Hammer Price £	Hammer Price $	Hammer Price €	Date	Place	Lot	Auc. H.
2005	**Murciélago Roadster**		01482	L	100-120.000 GBP		NS		04-09-15	Woodstock	254	SiC
Yellow with black and yellow leather interior; last serviced in May 2015.											
2002	**Murciélago coupé**		12026	L	120-160.000 GBP	95.200*	145.294*	130.357*	07-09-15	London	152	RMS
Pre-production example used by factory for test, development and early promotion. In February 2002 on the Circuito di Nardò it set world record speed for production car for one hour, 100 kms and 100 miles. In that same 2002 it was sold to its first private owner. 117,500 kms covered since new.											
2005	**Murciélago coupé**		01650	L	130-160.000 EUR		NS		26-09-15	Frankfurt	166	Coy
Yellow; two owners and 55,000 kms covered. LP580 model aesthetically updated to LP640 model. Recently serviced.											
2007	**Murciélago LP640-4 coupé**		02595	L	275-325.000 USD	207.633	297.000	272.379	28-01-16	Phoenix	111	RMS **F418**
Gold with black leather interior; less than 6,000 miles covered. 6-speed manual gearbox. Recent service and clutch replacement.											
2005	**Murciélago Roadster**		01543	L	200-250.000 USD		NS		10-03-16	Amelia Island	195	Bon
Yellow with black interior; sold new to the USA. Just over 6,000 miles covered. 6-speed manual gearbox.											
2007	**Murciélago LP640 Roadster**		02609	L	190-225.000 EUR		NS		09-04-16	Essen	166	Coy
Black with black interior; 26,800 kms covered.											
2002	**Murciélago LP620 coupé**		12084	L	130-145.000 EUR	90.068	131.928	118.130	28-05-16	Aarhus	215	SiC
Yellow; 19,675 kms covered. Manual gearbox.											
2005	**Murciélago Roadster**		01482	L	95-110.000 GBP		NS		11-06-16	Brooklands	300	His
Yellow with yellow and black interior; 39,000 kms on the odometer. Last serviced 1,000 kms ago (see lot 254 Silverstone Auctions 9.4.15 NS).											
2002	**Murciélago coupé**		12053	L	120-140.000 EUR	111.662	148.318	133.200	02-07-16	Lyon	356	Agu
Black with black interior; less than 34,000 kms covered. Engine-out service in November 2015.											
2006	**Gallardo**		03899	L	115-140.000 USD	69.810	100.000	92.520	23-01-16	Kissimmee	S165	Mec
Grey with grey and black interior; modified by Titan Motorsports to Superleggera specification. 580bhp engine.											
2007	**Gallardo Spider**		05471	L	90-120.000 USD	84.591*	121.000*	110.969*	28-01-16	Scottsdale	76	Bon
Metallic blue with tan interior; one owner and 1,200 miles covered.											
2007	**Gallardo Spider**		05264	L	90-100.000 USD	73.793	105.600	92.368	02-04-16	Ft.Lauderdale	205	AA
Yellow with yellow and black leather interior; just over 1,300 actual miles.											
2004	**Gallardo**		01895	R	35-45.000 GBP	58.240	83.883	74.209	11-06-16	Brooklands	240	His
Black with black leather interior; recently serviced.											
2006	**Gallardo Spider**		03707	L	NA	73.836*	101.200*	91.444*	24-06-16	Uncasville	638.2	B/J
Silver with red and white leather interior; 8,356 actual miles.											
2006	**Concept S**		LA00001	L	2.400-3.000.000 USD		NS		10-12-15	New York	212	RMS
White with black interior; concept designed by Luc Donckerwolke and first presented as a non-running design study at the 2005 Geneva Motor Show. This model remains at the Lamborghini museum and this fully operable Concept S was built on the Gallardo platform with the 512bhp 5-litre 10-cylinder engine. One-off exhibited at the 2006 Concorso Italiano in California, the car was acquired by the current and only owner and has covered 180 miles.											
2008	**Reventòn**		03148	L	1.200-1.600.000 USD		NS		19-08-16	Carmel	60	Bon
One of 20 examples built; four previous owners and less than 1,000 miles covered. Last serviced in 2015.											
2015	**Aventador**		03155	L	NA		NS		16-04-16	Houston	S159.1	Mec
Black with cream interior; 14,000 miles.											

LANCIA (I) *(1906-)*

Year	Model	(Bodybuilder)	Chassis no.	Steering	Estimate	Hammer Price £	Hammer Price $	Hammer Price €	Date	Place	Lot	Auc. H.
1925	**Lambda 4ª serie torpedo**		12968	R	100-130.000 GBP	107.000	165.026	146.462	12-09-15	Goodwood	338	Bon
Dark blue; sold new to the UK. Restored in 2000-01. Currently fitted with a Volvo 4-speed manual gearbox (the original 3-speed unit is included with the sale) (see lots 377 Brooks 21.10.97 NS and 71 Christie's 24.7.00 $ 42,784).												**F419**
1926	**Lambda 6ª serie torpedo**		14656	R	100-150.000 USD	53.877*	77.000*	70.509*	29-01-16	Phoenix	208	RMS
Blue with black interior; restored in Italy at unspecified date, in 2005 the car was sold to Japan and in more recent years it was imported into the USA (see lot 219 Bonhams 15.8.14 NS).											
1929	**Lambda 8ª serie torpedo**		19955	R	180-200.000 EUR		NS		09-04-16	Essen	130	Coy
Dark red; sold new to the UK, the car remained in single ownership from 1953 to 1999 when it was bought by the current owner as a short chassis with its original engine, gearbox and back axle and non-original bodywork. Subsequently fully restored, the car was fitted with the present, new body built to the style of the three spyders which Casaro built for Lancia for the 1928 Mille Miglia. Currently fitted with a new engine built on a 3-litre block produced in Australia (the original unit is included with the sale).											
1922	**Lambda 1ª serie torpedo**		10081	R	160-220.000 EUR		NS		14-05-16	Monaco	128	RMS
Red with black wings and interior; restored over 50 years ago. In the Sword Collection in Scotland until 1962 when it was acquired by the Quattroruote Collection.											

F419: 1925 Lancia Lambda 4ª serie torpedo

F420: 1933 Lancia Artena faux cabriolet (Stabilimenti Farina)

CHRISTOPH GROHE
FINE CLASSIC CARS

The fine classic car bears witness to an artisanal skill and lifestyle of a bygone era. It is also a dynamic sculpture endowed with competition-bred mechanics or exceptional coachwork.

With a certain passion, I personally select the cars on offer, the criteria being quality and rarity. Some are presented in original condition, others have been the subject of a professional restoration.

I am located in Switzerland near Geneva. Any visitor is welcome upon prior appointment.

LANCIA LAMBDA TORPEDO, 1st SERIE 1923

LANCIA LAMBDA BERLINA, 8th SERIE 1929

LANCIA AURELIA B24, SPIDER 1955

LANCIA APPIA GTZ, ZAGATO 1957

CHRISTOPH GROHE SA
RTE D'ALLAMAN 10
CH-1173 FÉCHY
SWITZERLAND

TEL +41 21 807 35 65
FAX +41 21 807 34 23

INFO@CHRISTOPHGROHE.COM
WWW.CHRISTOPHGROHE.COM

Year	Model (Bodybuilder)	Chassis no.	Steering	Estimate	Hammer price £	Hammer price $	Hammer price €	Date	Place	Lot	Auc. H.
1933	Artena faux cabriolet (Stabilimenti Farina)	283677	R	50-90.000 EUR	43.467	64.435	57.500	04-02-16	Paris	406	Bon F420
	Black; described as in good working order. From new for 77 years in the same family ownership in Italy.										
1932	Artena berlina	281848	R	20-30.000 EUR	24.104	34.920	30.960	20-03-16	Fontainebleau	312	Ose
	Recommissioned in the mid-2000s (see lot 448 Osenat 16.12.05 $ 31,156).										
1932	Astura cabriolet (Pinin Farina)	301550	R	NA		NS		14-10-15	Duxford	138	H&H
	Blue with blue and grey interior; recent full restoration. Sold new to Scotland.										
1931	Astura cabriolet (Pinin Farina)	301550	R	130-170.000 EUR	108.213	155.922	137.400	14-05-16	Monaco	187	Coy
	See lot 138 H & H 14.10.15.										
1939	Astura cabriolet (Pinin Farina)	301550	R	90-110.000 GBP	90.850	120.667	108.366	02-07-16	Woodstock	203	Coy F421
	See lot 187 Coys 14.5.16.										
1934	Augusta	3110278	R	40-50.000 EUR		NS		09-04-16	Essen	124	Coy
	Blue with cloth interior; restored in 2010.										
1938	Aprilia cabriolet (Worblaufen)	392179	R	65-80.000 GBP		NS		01-12-15	London	350	Coy
	Two-tone blue; for the last 50 years in an Italian collection. It comes with Italian ASI homologation.										
1948	Aprilia cabriolet (Langenthal)	5391096	R	68-78.000 EUR	53.522	76.709	70.285	16-01-16	Maastricht	429	Coy
	Light blue with blue leather interior; sold new to Switzerland, the car was imported into the Netherlands in recent years. Described as in very good overall condition.										
1949	Aprilia berlina	43827130	R	60-80.000 USD	26.915*	38.500*	35.308*	28-01-16	Scottsdale	112	Bon
	Silver with beige cloth interior; sold new to the UK, the car was imported into the USA in 2012 and subsequently restored (see lot 305 RM 12.5.12 $ 40,592).										
1939	Aprilia berlina Lusso	1011152	R	45-55.000 EUR		NS		09-04-16	Essen	227	Coy
	Light grey; restored in 2012. The car's original chassis numer was 3811314, but this was officially re-stamped in Italy in 1953 to 1011152.										
1940	Aprilia cabriolet (Stabilimenti Farina)	43910853	R	120-180.000 EUR	104.157	150.077	132.250	13-05-16	Monaco	115	Bon F422
	Ivory and burgundy with beige leather interior; restored in Italy between 2006 and 2012.										
1952	Ardea	25023374	R	10-12.000 GBP	13.440	19.358	17.125	11-06-16	Brooklands	262	His F423
	Grey with grey cloth interior; restored at unspecified date and imported into the UK in 2016.										
1947	Ardea Furgoncino	5502021	R	10-12.000 GBP	8.960	11.727	10.353	20-08-16	Brooklands	301	His
	Light van finished in dark grey with black wings; restoration to be completed.										
1951	Aurelia B52 coupé (Bertone)	B521074	R	175-245.000 EUR	126.184	192.131	172.500	05-09-15	Chantilly	20	Bon F424
	Black with beige cloth interior; one-off exhibited at the Bertone stand at the 1951 Turin Motor Show. Discovered in Belgium and believed never restored, it is said to drive perfectly. Circa 3,700 kms covered since new.										
1954	Aurelia B20 4ª serie (Pinin Farina)	B203411	R	85-100.000 GBP	95.625	145.608	130.729	04-09-15	Woodstock	214	SiC
	Light blue with oatmeal cloth interior; restored in the late 1990s.										
1958	Aurelia B20 4ª serie (Pinin Farina)	B20S1686	L	130-180.000 EUR		NS		09-10-15	Zoute	30	Bon
	Light brown with dark beige cloth interior; recently restored. Floor gear shift.										
1953	Aurelia B20 3ª serie (Pinin Farina)	2632	R	100-150.000 EUR	89.008	137.456	121.000	17-10-15	Salzburg	310	Dor
	Dark red with brown interior; in 2005 the car was acquired by the current owner and subsequently the body was repainted and the brakes were overhauled.										
1957	Aurelia B20 6ª serie (Pinin Farina)	B20S1499	L	100-130.000 EUR		NS		16-01-16	Maastricht	424	Coy
	White with grey and blue interior; in driving order (see lot 159 Coys 8.8.15 NS).										
1952	Aurelia B20 2ª serie (Pinin Farina)	B201569	R	135-175.000 EUR	108.668	161.086	143.750	04-02-16	Paris	422	Bon
	Amaranth with grey cloth interior; reimported in Italy from the USA some time ago. Restored 10 years ago.										
1952	Aurelia B20 2ª serie (Pinin Farina)	B201532	R	115-135.000 EUR	114.693	166.910	149.000	05-02-16	Paris	222	Art F425
	White with beige cloth interior; in good overall condition.										
1955	Aurelia B20 4ª serie (Pinin Farina)	3418	L	125-150.000 EUR		NS		14-05-16	Monaco	127	Coy
	Amaranth; it comes with Italian ASI homologation.										
1952	Aurelia B20 2ª serie (Pinin Farina)	B202065	R	100-130.000 USD	83.829	121.000	108.477	05-06-16	Greenwhich	104	Bon
	Red with pale yellow roof; prepared for historic racing in the USA in the late 1980s, the car was raced at some historic events in Italy and track events in the USA. Last raced about 10 years ago. Recently serviced.										
1953	Aurelia B20 3ª serie (Pinin Farina)	B202389	R	90-110.000 GBP		NS		10-07-16	Chateau Impney	55	H&H
	Green with beige cloth interior; imported into the UK in 1965. Since 1987 in the current ownership. Restored from 1989 to 1991. 4ª Series engine.										
1959	Appia 1ª serie Giardinetta (Riva)	80S2762	L	35-45.000 EUR	25.995	36.589	32.200	09-04-16	Essen	101	Coy
	Beige and blue with cloth interior; restored in 2015.										
1953	Appia 1ª serie berlina	C104343	R	13-15.000 EUR		NS		09-04-16	Essen	163	Coy
	Dark green with cloth interior; for many years on display in a museum.										
1955	Appia 1ª serie berlina	C108906	L	12-16.000 EUR		NS		14-05-16	Monaco	137	RMS
	Blue with cloth interior; described as in good overall condition. For 50 years in the Quattroruote Collection.										
1962	Appia 3ª serie berlina	8080796088	L	NQ	5.040*	6.596*	5.824*	20-08-16	Brooklands	321	His
	Dark blue with grey-blue interior; restored some years ago.										
1955	Aurelia B24 spider (Pinin Farina)	B24S1131	L	900-1.100.000 USD	615.736	880.000	805.816	29-01-16	Phoenix	249	RMS F426
	Dark blue with red leather interior; fully restored in the 1990s. During the works the engine was fitted with a period-correct Nardi twin-carburettor set-up. Fitted with Borrani center-lock wire wheels and Nardi steering wheel. From the Craig McCaw Collection (see RM lots 570 18.8.07 $ 550,000 and 135 18.1.13 $ 825,000).										
1955	Aurelia B24 spider (Pinin Farina)	B24S1002	L	900-1.300.000 EUR		NS		04-02-16	Paris	347	Bon
	Light grey with red leather interior; the car was displayed at the 1955 Brussels Motor Show and probably at the Geneva Motor Show too and was sold to Belgium in late 1955. In the 1960s the engine block was damaged by freeze and in the 1970s the car was restored for the first time and the engine was rebuilt on a B20 4th series block. In 1998 the car was acquired by the current owner and later restored to Brussels 1955 specification. Less than 10,000 kms covered since the restoration; last serviced in 2013 (see Coys lots 46 15.12.93 NS e 114 25.7.98 $ 95,281).										
1955	Aurelia B24 spider (Pinin Farina)	B24S1094	L	1.200-1.500.000 USD	1.071.510	1.402.500	1.238.267	19-08-16	Carmel	44	Bon
	Originally finished in pale green pastel with dark green vinyl interior, the car was sold new to the USA. In the 1980s circa the body was refinished in the present red livery and in the 2000s the interior were reupholstered in blue. Five owners and less than 63,000 miles covered since new.										

F421: 1939 Lancia Astura cabriolet (Pinin Farina)

F422: 1940 Lancia Aprilia cabriolet (Stabilimenti Farina)

F423: 1952 Lancia Ardea

F424: 1951 Lancia Aurelia B52 coupé (Bertone)

F425: 1952 Lancia Aurelia B20 2a serie (Pinin Farina)

F426: 1955 Lancia Aurelia B24 spider (Pinin Farina)

F427: 1957 Lancia Aurelia B24 convertibile (Pinin Farina)

F428: 1958 Lancia Appia Coupé (Pinin Farina)

Year	Model	(Bodybuilder)	Chassis no.	Steering	Estimate	Hammer price £	Hammer price $	Hammer price €	Date	Place	Lot	Auc. H.
1955	**Aurelia B24 spider**	(Pinin Farina)	B24S1077	L	1.650-1.950.000 USD	**1.533.730**	**2.007.500**	**1.772.422**	20-08-16	Pebble Beach	35	G&Co
	Dark blue with brown leather interior and dark blue hardtop; sold new in Italy. Bought in 1985 by Jean Sage who had it restored and retained it until 1998. Cosmetically restored in the USA in 2012. Further restoration works carried out by Paul Russell and Company in 2014 (see lot 117 Gooding & Company 18.1.14 $ 1,815,000).
1957	**Aurelia B24 convertibile**	(Pinin Farina)	B24S1478	L	225-250.000 GBP	**246.400**	**376.056**	**337.396**	07-09-15	London	140	RMS F427
1956	**Aurelia B24 convertibile**	(Pinin Farina)	B24S1186	L	280-320.000 EUR	**210.924**	**306.124**	**280.000**	03-02-16	Paris	122	RMS
1958	**Aurelia B24 convertibile**	(Pinin Farina)	B24S1676	L	290-350.000 EUR	**255.806**	**368.583**	**324.800**	14-05-16	Monaco	225	RMS
1958	**Appia Coupé**	(Pinin Farina)	812012020	L	35-55.000 EUR	**42.590**	**65.332**	**57.500**	09-10-15	Zoute	5	Bon F428
1961	**Flaminia Gran Turismo**	(Touring)	824001732	L	42-55.000 GBP	**50.400**	**72.591**	**64.220**	11-06-16	Brooklands	267	His
1966	**Flaminia 3C GT**	(Touring)	824103330	L	110-140.000 USD	**73.406**	**105.000**	**96.296**	28-01-16	Scottsdale	72	Bon F429
1963	**Flaminia 3C GT**	(Touring)	824103542	L	40-70.000 EUR	**32.515***	**42.225***	**38.144***	09-07-16	Le Mans	140	Art
1965	**Flaminia 3C 2.8 GTL**	(Touring)	8261401098	L	60-80.000 EUR	**76.207**	**98.966**	**89.400**	09-07-16	Le Mans	192	Art
1962	**Flaminia Convertibile**	(Touring)	824142197	L	120-140.000 EUR	**115.270**	**166.089**	**146.360**	14-05-16	Monaco	137	Coy
1964	**Flaminia 3C 2.8 Convertibile**	(Touring)	8261341123	L	200-250.000 EUR	**147.788**	**219.077**	**195.500**	04-02-16	Paris	346	Bon F430
1958	**Flaminia Sport**	(Zagato)	824001057	L	490-580.000 EUR		NS		14-05-16	Monaco	211	RMS
1959	**Flaminia Sport**	(Zagato)	824001061	L	750-1.000.000 USD		NS		21-08-16	Pebble Beach	110	G&Co
1960	**Flaminia 3C 2.8 Sport**	(Zagato)	824032067	L	200-250.000 EUR		NS		05-02-16	Paris	158	Art
1962	**Superjolly open-top bus**		2163293	L	45-60.000 EUR	**39.962**	**57.580**	**50.740**	14-05-16	Monaco	113	Coy F431
1969	**Flavia 1.8 Coupé**	(Pininfarina)	81533116483	R	NA		NS		20-04-16	Duxford	6	H&H
1964	**Flavia Coupé**	(Pininfarina)	008172	L	22-26.000 EUR	**23.253**	**33.222**	**29.520**	19-06-16	Fontainebleau	378	Ose
1967	**Flavia 1.8 Coupé**	(Pininfarina)	815331016074	R	14-16.000 GBP	**21.000**	**27.651**	**24.933**	28-07-16	Donington Park	74	H&H
1965	**Flavia Sport 1.8**	(Zagato)	815532001403	L	45-55.000 GBP	**33.600***	**51.280***	**46.008***	07-09-15	London	120	RMS F432
1965	**Flavia Sport 1.8**	(Zagato)	815533001500	R	NA		NS		26-02-16	Coventry	108	SiC
1965	**Flavia Sport 1.8**	(Zagato)	815532001388	L	85-95.000 EUR	**64.109**	**92.373**	**81.400**	14-05-16	Monaco	169	Coy
1968	**Fulvia berlina**		818210016433	L	4-6.000 EUR	**3.806***	**5.357***	**4.714***	09-04-16	Essen	218	Coy
1972	**Fulvia Coupé 1.3 S**		818630032017	L	11-13.000 GBP		NS		28-11-15	Weybridge	315	His

Descriptions:
- 1957 Aurelia B24 convertibile: Red with black interior; the car remained until 1985 with its first owner and was subsequently restored. In recent years it received a mechanical overhaul and the clutch and brakes were replaced (see lot 399 Artcurial 8.2.13 $ 374,432).
- 1956 Aurelia B24 convertibile: Originally finished in light blue with brown interior, the car is currently presented in metallic grey with black interior. Recently serviced.
- 1958 Aurelia B24 convertibile: Originally finished in red with black leather interior, the car was sold new to the USA where it was still in the 1990s. Subsequently it was reimported into Europe and restored to its present livery, dark blue with orange leather interior.
- 1958 Appia Coupé: Dark blue with white roof and white interior; partially restored, the car is described as in very good overall condition. Three owners.
- 1961 Flaminia Gran Turismo: Gunmetal grey with burgundy leather interior; restored in Italy eight years ago. Imported into the UK and recommissioned for road use in 2015.
- 1966 Flaminia 3C GT: White with grey roof and beige interior; body repainted in the late 1990s, mechanicals and interior restored in more recent years.
- 1963 Flaminia 3C GT: Complete; for restoration.
- 1965 Flaminia 3C 2.8 GTL: White with red leather interior; in good overall condition.
- 1962 Flaminia Convertibile: White; some restoration works carried out many years ago. Described as in very good mechanical order.
- 1964 Flaminia 3C 2.8 Convertibile: Metallic silver grey with black interior; one owner until 2004. In 2015 the car was partially dismantled, extensively serviced and repainted (see Poulain/Sotheby's lots 21 6.5.02 NS and 45 17.6.02 $ 32,674).
- 1958 Flaminia Sport: Black with light grey leather interior; recent full restoration.
- 1959 Flaminia Sport: White with dark red interior; for 35 years from 1977 to 2012 with the previous owner in California, the car has been subsequently fully restored in Costa Rica.
- 1960 Flaminia 3C 2.8 Sport: For restoration; unused from the 1970s, the car has had just one owner. Sold without registration.
- 1962 Superjolly open-top bus: White and blue; special vehicle never registered and used by Lancia during factory visits by VIPs. In 1978 the seats were modified for the visit of Pope Paolo VI. Restored; sold on bill of sale.
- 1969 Flavia 1.8 Coupé: Blue with red interior; described as in good overall condition. 37,000 miles on the odometer.
- 1964 Flavia Coupé: Described as in very good overall condition.
- 1967 Flavia 1.8 Coupé: Burgundy; restored. Since 1977 in the current ownership.
- 1965 Flavia Sport 1.8: Red; prepared for historic racing by Carlo Facetti in the early 1990s but never raced. Recent recommissioning work to the mechanicals.
- 1965 Flavia Sport 1.8: Red; prepared in 2002 for historic racing in 2002. Engine rebuilt in more recent years. In ready to race condition.
- 1965 Flavia Sport 1.8: Red with black interior; restored. One owner until 2014.
- 1968 Fulvia berlina: Dark blue with dark red interior; to be recommissioned prior to use.
- 1972 Fulvia Coupé 1.3 S: Longchamp bronze; described as in good original condition. 52,000 kms on the odometer.

F429: 1966 Lancia Flaminia 3C GT (Touring)

F430: 1964 Lancia Flaminia 3C 2.8 Convertibile (Touring)

F431: 1962 Lancia Superjolly open-top bus

F432: 1965 Lancia Flavia Sport 1.8 (Zagato)

Year	Model (Bodybuilder)	Chassis no.	Steering	Estimate	£	$	€	Date	Place	Lot	Auc. H.
1973	**Fulvia Coupé 1.3 S**	81863142774	R	8-10.000 GBP	10.080	15.209	13.901	09-12-15	Chateau Impney	12	H&H
	Grey-blue with original interior; restored seven years ago. One owner and 72,300 miles on the odometer.										
1975	**Fulvia Coupé 1.3**	818630064180	L	8-12.000 GBP	9.440	13.529	12.396	16-01-16	Birmingham	358	Coy
	White with black interior; in good overall condition.										
1968	**Fulvia Coupé Rallye 1.3 HF**	001352	L	32-37.000 GBP	37.640	53.946	49.425	16-01-16	Birmingham	304	Coy
	Red with black vinyl interior; in good overall condition. It comes with Italian ASI homologation.										
1970	**Fulvia Coupé Rallye 1.6 HF**	818540001645	L	60-80.000 GBP	50.400*	76.920*	69.013*	07-09-15	London	135	RMS F433
	Red with black interior; never raced. 33.724 kms on the odometer.										
1973	**Fulvia Coupé Rallye 1.6 HF**	818540002272	L	150-180.000 EUR		NS		09-07-16	Le Mans	213	Art
	One of the Works cars for the 1973 World Rally Championship, it raced the Monte Carlo and San Remo rallies among others. In 1974 it was sold to Jolly Club team. Raced until the late 1970s. Restored in recent years to 1973 Monte Carlo specification (see lot 389 RM 12.5.12 NS).										
1969	**Fulvia Sport 1.3 S (Zagato)**	001594	L	20-25.000 GBP	25.960	37.206	34.088	16-01-16	Birmingham	334	Coy
	White with blue stripes; prepared for historic racing (see lot 166 Coys 8.8.15 NS).										
1972	**Fulvia Sport 1.3 S (Zagato)**	818651002886	R	13-18.000 GBP	17.700	25.150	22.806	08-03-16	London	116	Coy
	Red with black interior.										
1970	**Fulvia Sport 1.3 S (Zagato)**	818363002710	R	18-22.000 GBP	31.050	44.982	39.881	20-03-16	Goodwood	63	Bon F434
	In good overall condition; body recently repainted. Since 2005 in the current ownership (see lots 311 Sotheby's 7.12.98 NS, and 71 Coys 10.10.01 NS).										
1971	**Fulvia Sport 1.3 (Zagato)**	818362002365	L	30-35.000 EUR	24.736	34.817	30.641	09-04-16	Essen	123	Coy
	Red with black interior; in good overall condition.										
1972	**Fulvia Sport 1600 (Zagato)**	818750001054	L	50-60.000 EUR	39.032	56.241	49.560	14-05-16	Monaco	182	Coy
	Red with black interior; restored.										
1973	**Fulvia Sport (Zagato)**	81875001552	L	30-35.000 GBP		NS		11-06-16	Brooklands	241	His
	Red with black interior; recently restored.										
1972	**Fulvia Sport 1.3 S (Zagato)**	8186512877	R	25-30.000 GBP	18.000	23.908	21.470	02-07-16	Woodstock	150	Coy
	Lobster with black interior; restored.										
1970	**Fulvia Sport 1.3 S (Zagato)**	818363002603	R	15-20.000 GBP	18.592	24.144	21.810	10-07-16	Chateau Impney	23	H&H
	Red with black interior; since 2000 in the current ownership, the car received some restoration works in 2013.										
1971	**Fulvia Sport 1.3 (Zagato)**	818362002365	L	30-35.000 EUR	27.986	36.813	32.998	06-08-16	Schloss Dyck	112	Coy
	See lot 123 Coys 9.4.16.										
1975	**Stratos (Bertone)**	001976	L	270-320.000 GBP	308.000	470.070	421.744	07-09-15	London	157	RMS F435
	Road version finished in blue; sold in Italy. Since 1994 in the current ownership.										
1974	**Stratos Gruppo 4 (Bertone)**	001619	L	370-470.000 EUR	279.160	431.112	379.500	17-10-15	Salzburg	337	Dor
	Blue with black interior; the car was bought new in 1978 by its first owner who had it prepared to Group 4 specification and raced it at several Italian rallies. In 1984 it was sold to Germany and in 2009 it was acquired by the current, fourth owner who had the mechanicals and chassis overhauled. In unrestored condition.										

F433: 1970 Lancia Fulvia Coupé Rallye 1.6 HF

F434: 1970 Lancia Fulvia Sport 1.3 S (Zagato)

Year	Model (Bodybuilder)	Chassis No.	Steering	Estimate	Hammer Price £	$	€	Sale Date	Place	Lot	Auc. H.
1975	**Stratos (Bertone)**	01834	L	350-450.000 EUR		NS		04-02-16	Paris	359	Bon
	Orange with tan cloth interior; road version sold new in Italy, the car is described as in largely original condition. Currently with its third owner, it has been recently serviced in the UK.										
1976	**Stratos (Bertone)**	829ARO001735	L	350-450.000 EUR		NS		05-02-16	Paris	166	Art
	Road version finished in red with alcantara interior; described as in very good working order, the car was driven at the 2015 Tour Auto. Never raced in period (see lot 7 Artcurial 22.7.13 $ 411,915).										
1979	**Beta 2.0 berlina**	828CB1029133	R	NQ	4.704*	6.775*	5.994*	11-06-16	Brooklands	203	His
	Silver with blue cloth; two owners and 29,000 miles covered. Automatic transmission.										
1982	**Montecarlo (Pininfarina)**	137AS0005742	R	NA	15.525	21.979	20.037	06-03-16	Birmingham	312	SiC
	Red with grey interior; in good original condition. 23,800 covered. Since 1984 in the current, third ownership.										
1976	**Montecarlo (Pininfarina)**	137AS0001922	L	12-18.000 EUR	12.682	18.119	16.100	18-06-16	Wien	437	Dor
	Light metallic blue with brown leather interior; body repainted in the 2000s.										
1992	**Delta Integrale Evoluzione**	568688	L	NA	29.680	45.651	40.009	14-10-15	Duxford	107	H&H
	Metallic red with grey alcantara interior; sold new in Italy, the car was imported into the UK in 1998. Described as in very good overall condition; 88,000 kms covered; recently serviced.										
1994	**Delta Integrale Evoluzione 2**	585635	L	45-55.000 GBP	45.480	68.516	64.636	01-12-15	London	349	Coy
	Red with beige alcantara interior; restoration completed in recent times.										
1992	**Delta Integrale Evoluzione**	580642	L	120-150.000 EUR	101.244	146.940	134.400	03-02-16	Paris	136	RMS **F436**
	Special edition Martini 6; just one Italian owner and less than 28,000 kms covered.										
1992	**Delta Integrale Evoluzione**	567553	L	NA	106.875	149.369	135.721	26-02-16	Coventry	722	SiC
	Martini livery with grey alcantara interior; one owner and 50 kms covered (see lot 325 Silverstone Auctions 22.2.15 NS).										
1992	**Delta Integrale Evoluzione**	058052	L	48-60.000 GBP	92.960	132.858	119.798	12-03-16	Brooklands	228	His
	Martini 6 special edition; it is believed the car was first owned by Giovanni Agnelli and it was especially finished with some unique features as a blue-printed engine, competition suspension set-up, electric rear wing and some body badging Abarth not Lancia. Clutch recently replaced.										
1993	**Delta Integrale Evoluzione 2**	583191	L	30-40.000 GBP	33.040	46.851	41.518	16-04-16	Ascot	112	Coy
	Red with beige interior; in very good overall condition.										
1994	**Delta Integrale Evoluzione 2**	584838	L	70-75.000 EUR		NS		14-05-16	Monaco	142	Coy
	Red with beige alcantara interior; one owner and approximately 38,000 kms covered. In original condition. Recently serviced.										
1991	**Delta Integrale Evoluzione**	539662	L	370-390.000 EUR	203.479	293.187	258.360	14-05-16	Monaco	152	Coy
	Martini livery; when new the car was retained by the factory and used as test-car. The body was updated in 1992 to Evoluzione 2 specification. Later it was sold to Jolly Autosport and raced until 2000 at some World and Italian Rally Championship events. Meticulous maintenance.										
1992	**Delta Integrale Evoluzione**	567529	L	30-35.000 GBP		NS		11-06-16	Brooklands	226	His
	Dark metallic green with grey alcantara interior; recently imported into the UK, the car received some works to the mechanicals and paintwork.										
1992	**Delta Integrale Evoluzione**	562931	L	45-55.000 GBP		NS		02-07-16	Woodstock	124	Coy
	Metallic red with green alcantara interior; restored in 2011, engine rebuilt in 2015 (see lot 363 Bonhams 9.12.13 $21,288).										
1994	**Delta Integrale Evoluzione 2**	585635	L	45-55.000 GBP		NS		02-07-16	Woodstock	146	Coy
	See lot 349 Coys 1.12.15.										
1993	**Delta Integrale Evoluzione 2**	583021	L	35-40.000 GBP	28.000	37.190	33.398	02-07-16	Woodstock	247	Coy
	Blue with beige interior; repainted in 2015. Recent mechanical overhaul.										
1993	**Delta Integrale Evoluzione**	568612	L	40-60.000 EUR	43.692*	56.740*	51.256*	09-07-16	Le Mans	131	Art
	Described as in good overall condition; 74,000 kms covered.										
1992	**Delta Integrale Evoluzione**	567462	L	85-120.000 EUR		NS		09-07-16	Le Mans	187	Art
	Martini edition; since 2006 in the current ownership. 53,330 kms covered. Last serviced in January 2016.										
1993	**Delta Integrale Evoluzione 2**	588158	L	65-75.000 EUR	55.668	73.227	65.639	06-08-16	Schloss Dyck	168	Coy
	Red; the car was sold new to Japan where it has had just one owner. 60,000 kms covered.										
1980	**037 prototype (Pininfarina)**	SE037001	L	320-400.000 EUR		NS		13-05-16	Monaco	134	Bon
	Red with black roof; first development prototype built, the car was modified in the early 1981 by Pininfarina following test at the wind tunnel and was first road tested in November 1981. Once its development duties has ended, it was acquired by its creator, Sergio Limone. Restored between 2013 and 2014, it has been used by the current owner at some historic events.										
1982	**037 (Pininfarina)**	000063	L	335-355.000 EUR		NS		14-05-16	Monaco	255	RMS
	Road version finished in red with black interior; described as in largely original condition. Less than 33,000 kms covered. Recently serviced.										

F435: 1975 Lancia Stratos (Bertone)

F436: 1992 Lancia Delta Integrale Evoluzione

Year	Model	(Bodybuilder)	Chassis no.	Steering	Estimate	Hammer price £	Hammer price $	Hammer price €	Sale Date	Place	Lot	Auc. H.
1984	037 Gruppo B	(Pininfarina)	0410	L	450-650.000 EUR		NS		09-07-16	Le Mans	133	Art

The car was driven in 1984 by Vudafieri/Pirollo for the Jolly Club-Totip team at several Italian rallies of the Italian, European and World championships. In 1986 it raced the Safari Rally in Kenya driven by Preston/Lyall. Later it passed to the Tre Gazzelle team and was raced until 1987. Restored in 1987 to the Safary Rally Martini livery. Since 1989 in the current ownership (see lot 15 Poulain 10.10.98 NS).

Year	Model	(Bodybuilder)	Chassis no.	Steering	Estimate	£	$	€	Date	Place	Lot	Auc. H.
1986	Delta S4		0090	L	350-400.000 EUR		NS		09-04-16	Essen	132	Coy

Stradale version used in period as a recce car by the Grifone Esso team who built the car to Group B specification in the 1986 season. Totally restored by an Italian collector in 2015 to Lancia Martini livery. Described as in excellent overall condition.

| 1984 | Delta S4 Prototype | | SE038003 | L | 300-400.000 EUR | | NS | | 09-07-16 | Le Mans | 132 | Art |

Red; prototype of the road version, the car was used for tests on road and track and remained in the factory ownership until 1989 when it was sold without registration to the present owner. Restored at unspecified date.

| 1985 | Delta S4 | | 00033 | L | 475-550.000 USD | 336.160 | 440.000 | 388.476 | 20-08-16 | Pebble Beach | 63 | G&Co |

Road version finished in red with beige alcantara interior; restored. Recently serviced (see lot 44 Christie's 19.4.05 $44,866).

| 1988 | Thema 8.32 | | 834000000126332 | L | 12-17.000 EUR | 10.911 | 16.559 | 14.850 | 26-09-15 | Frankfurt | 114 | Coy |

Red with black interior; in original condition.

| 1991 | Thema 8.32 | | 260990 | L | 8-12.000 EUR | 8.380 | 11.977 | 10.800 | 12-03-16 | Lyon | 311 | Agu |

Brown with tan interior; unusd from 2007 to 2015 when it was serviced. Brakes restored.

| 1993 | Hyena (Zagato) | | 015 | L | 220-260.000 EUR | | NS | | 05-02-16 | Paris | 217 | Art |

Green; 7,000 kms covered. One of 24 examples built.

LASALLE (USA) (1927-1940)

| 1929 | Series 328 convertible | | 415702 | L | 85-95.000 USD | 80.711 | 115.500 | 101.028 | 02-04-16 | Ft.Lauderdale | 462 | AA |

Red with black wings and tan interior; in good overall condition (see lot 1369 Barrett-Jackson 18.1.14 $ 110,000).

| 1930 | Series 340 phaeton | (Fleetwood) | 605131(engine) | L | 125-150.000 USD | 54.005* | 82.500* | 73.310* | 08-10-15 | Hershey | 143 | RMS |

Maroon and black with black leather interior; in good driving order. While this is not the original body to this chassis, it may well be an original Fleetwood body. From the estate of Richard Roy.

| 1930 | Series 340 touring | (Fleetwood) | 604401(engine) | L | 70-100.000 USD | 54.005* | 82.500* | 73.310* | 08-10-15 | Hershey | 182 | RMS |

Two-tone green; originally a right-hand drive model, the car was sold to Argentina. Restored many years ago and converted to left-hand drive.

| 1935 | Series 35-50 convertible | | 2207498 | L | 140-160.000 USD | 83.338 | 126.500 | 112.585 | 05-10-15 | Philadelphia | 218 | Bon F437 |

Cream with brown leather interior; subjected to a long restoration started 20 years ago and completed three years ago.

| 1937 | Series 37-50 convertible | | 2254636 | L | 65-75.000 USD | | NS | | 07-05-16 | Auburn | 780 | AA |

Grey with black leather interior; soft-top and interior redone.

| 1940 | Series 40-52 convertible | | 4330807 | L | 160-200.000 USD | 138.666* | 181.500* | 160.246* | 20-08-16 | Pebble Beach | 43 | G&Co |

Dark green with tan interior; fully restored (see lot 239 RM 5.8.00 $82,500).

LEA-FRANCIS (GB) (1903-1960)

| 1929 | P Type roadster (Cross/Ellis) | | 13953 | R | 14-18.000 GBP | 21.275 | 32.395 | 29.085 | 05-09-15 | Beaulieu | 134 | Bon |

British racing green with black wings; for 28 years in the current ownership. In 1980 the car was restored and the engine was modified.

| 1928 | S Type Hyper Sports | | 14005 | R | 160-220.000 GBP | 158.300 | 216.934 | 196.023 | 24-06-16 | Goodwood | 222 | Bon F438 |

One of the Works team cars at the 1928 Ards TT, the car was raced until the late 1930s. Bought by the previous owner in 1956 and used until 1959-60. Discovered in 1993 and subsequently restored.

| 1951 | Fourteen station wagon | | 8926 | R | 22-28.000 GBP | 22.000 | 31.196 | 27.645 | 16-04-16 | Cambridge | 1499 | Che |

Grey with black roof and wooden panels; restored.

| 1950 | 2.5l (Westland) | | 5110 | R | 35-42.000 GBP | 33.600 | 48.394 | 42.813 | 11-06-16 | Brooklands | 258 | His |

Blue; bought just restored in 2011 by the current owner.

LEON BOLLEE (F) (1895-1933)

| 1897 | Voiturette | | 891 | C | 70-90.000 USD | 82.478* | 126.500* | 111.345* | 09-10-15 | Hershey | 256 | RMS |

Black; restored. Formerly in the Harrah and Blackhawk collections; since 2000 in the current ownership.

F437: 1935 Lasalle Series 35-50 convertible

F438: 1928 Lea-Francis S Type Hyper Sports

Year	Model	(Bodybuilder)	Chassis no.	Steering	Estimate	Hammer price £	$	€	Date	Place	Lot	Auc. H.

LIGIER (F) (1969-)

1972 JS2 — 24887203 — L — 100-150.000 EUR — 110.105* — 160.233* — 143.040* — 05-02-16 — Paris — 161 — Art **F439**
Road versione modified to the specification of the cars which raced the 1973 Le Mans 24 Hours.

LINCOLN (USA) (1920-)

1924 Model L LeBaron convertible (Murray) — 18183 — L — 350-550.000 DKK — 30.584 — 46.420 — 41.638 — 26-09-15 — Ebeltoft — 47 — Bon
Dark green and black; fully restored. From the Frederiksen Collection.

1929 Model L town sedan — 58529 — L — 40-50.000 EUR — — NS — — 09-04-16 — Essen — 172 — Coy
Black; offered with Italian ASI certificate.

1930 Model L convertible roadster (LeBaron) — 64277 — L — 80-100.000 USD — — NS — — 30-07-16 — Plymouth — 127 — RMS
Grey with black fenders and brown leather interior; restored (see lots 189 RM 16.1.09 NS and S45.1 Mecum 7.10.11 $62,500).

1930 Model L roadster (LeBaron) — 64754 — L — 150-180.000 USD — 50.424* — 66.000* — 58.271* — 19-08-16 — Carmel — 19 — Bon
Two-tone green with green leather interior; restored in the 1970s and recently refreshed. Believed to have covered 25,448 miles since new.

1931 Model K V8 (Judkins) — 69100 — L — 40-50.000 USD — 28.842* — 41.800* — 36.579* — 07-05-16 — Auburn — 872 — AA
Black with beige cloth interior.

1934 Model KB V12 convertible sedan (Dietrich) — KB3444 — L — 1.600-2.000.000 DKK — 164.249 — 249.291 — 223.612 — 26-09-15 — Ebeltoft — 41 — Bon
Blue with blue interior; the car was restored in the mid-1990s and the engine was enlarged to 455 cu.in. giving 220bhp. In 2006 circa the body was repainted again. From the Frederiksen Collection (see lot 129 Gooding 18.8.13 $ 275,000).

1932 Model KB V12 dual cowl phaeton — KB1367 — L — 300-350.000 USD — 207.988 — 319.000 — 280.784 — 09-10-15 — Hershey — 260 — RMS **F440**
Brown with brown leather interior; at unspecified date, the car was fully restored including the recreation of its original Brunn coachwork. Currently fitted with a 1935 gearbox. Described as in concours condition (see RM lots 262 8.3.08 NS and 253 20.1.12 $ 269,500).

1932 Model KB V12 coupé (Judkins) — KB1635 — L — 225-275.000 USD — — NS — — 28-01-16 — Scottsdale — 36 — Bon
Dark tan with black fenders; restoration completed about seven years ago.

1934 Model KB V12 convertible sedan (Dietrich) — KB3434 — L — 275-350.000 USD — 146.237* — 209.000* — 191.381* — 30-01-16 — Scottsdale — 111 — G&Co
Dark blue with brown interior; restored in the 2000s (see lots S639 Russo & Steele 16.8.12 NS, 132 RM 27.7.13 $ 275,000 and 24 Gooding 15.8.15 $ 275,000).

1932 Model KB V12 sport phaeton — KB830 — L — NA — — NS — — 09-04-16 — Palm Beach — 412 — B/J
Red and maroon with tan interior; restored and fitted with the present, new, Brunn style body (see lots Auctions America 588 22.3.13 $ 275,000 and S52 Mecum 15.8.15 $ 230,000).

1932 Model KB V12 sedan — KB1291 — L — 75-95.000 USD — 52.690 — 75.900 — 67.141 — 11-06-16 — Hershey — 106 — TFA
Two-tone blue with tan interior; restored some years ago. The chassis was replaced with a period correct 1932 KB 145 in. chassis. Engine recently rebuilt.

1932 Model KB V12 coupé (Judkins) — KB1635 — L — 200-235.000 USD — 137.452 — 198.000 — 175.151 — 11-06-16 — Hershey — 126 — TFA
See lot 36 Bonhams 28.01.16.

1932 Model KB V12 Berline (Judkins) — KB758 — L — 250-310.000 USD — — NS — — 21-08-16 — Pebble Beach — 145 — G&Co
Two-tone brown; described as in largely original, unrestored condition. Three owners and less than 75,000 miles covered.

1933 Model KA V12 2-door Victoria — KA1136 — L — 35-45.000 USD — 21.632 — 31.350 — 27.434 — 07-05-16 — Auburn — 745 — AA
Black with tan cloth interior.

1935 Series K V12 sedan — 3965 — L — 20-30.000 EUR — 17.994* — 25.790* — 23.630* — 16-01-16 — Maastricht — 448A — Coy
Black with cloth interior; restored many years ago (see lot 133 Coys 10.1.15 $ 37,685).

1938 Series K V12 roadster (LeBaron) — K9059 — L — 50-70.000 USD — 86.129* — 123.200* — 112.987* — 28-01-16 — Scottsdale — 45 — Bon
Early history unknown; restored at unspecified date.

1937 Series K V12 sedan (Judkins) — K8375 — L — NA — 46.180* — 66.000* — 60.436* — 29-01-16 — Scottsdale — 1338 — B/J
Black and green with fawn interior; restored.

1935 Series K V12 convertible (LeBaron) — K3722 — L — NA — 103.905* — 148.500* — 135.981* — 29-01-16 — Scottsdale — 1398.1 — B/J
Silver with grey interior; several restoration works carried out in recent years (see lots 312 Bonhams 12.9.10 NS and 77 Gooding 11.3.11 NS).

1935 Series K V12 roadster (LeBaron) — K3948 — L — 175-225.000 USD — — NS — — 02-04-16 — Ft.Lauderdale — 755 — AA
Yellow with tan leather interior; restored at unspecified date.

1939 Zephyr convertible — H84568 — L — NA — 39.936 — 63.250 — 55.609 — 31-10-15 — Hilton Head — 126 — AA
Black with burgundy interior; restored many years ago and recently refreshed.

F439: 1972 Ligier JS2

F440: 1932 Lincoln Model KB V12 dual cowl phaeton

Year	Model	(Bodybuilder)	Chassis no.	Steering	Estimate	Hammer price £	Hammer price $	Hammer price €	Date	Place	Lot	Auc. H.
1938	Zephyr convertible sedan		H53942	L	125-175.000 USD	46.141*	66.000*	60.529*	28-01-16	Phoenix	157	RMS
	Black with brown leather interior; the car has covered 100 miles since the restoration carried out some years ago (see lot 811 RM 10.6.12 $ 132,000).											
1940	Zephyr coupé		H95145	L	130-160.000 USD	61.574*	88.000*	80.582*	30-01-16	Scottsdale	154	G&Co
	Beige with brown interior; recently restored.											
1941	Zephyr coupé		H120055	L	250-300.000 USD	150.064	214.500	193.415	11-03-16	Amelia Island	52	G&Co
	Black with cloth interior; restored many years ago. In 2012 the paintwork and interior were replaced.											
1938	Zephyr convertible sedan		H52241	L	NA	50.794*	71.500*	62.920*	09-04-16	Palm Beach	413	B/J
	Black with tan interior; 20 miles covered since a full restoration.											
1937	Zephyr coupé		H66822	L	125-175.000 USD		NS		19-08-16	Carmel	63	Bon
	Deep red with tan cloth interior; body recently repainted.											
1942	Continental convertible		26H5676	L	130-150.000 USD		NS		20-08-16	Monterey	S41	Mec
	Blue with blue leather interior; restored.											
1946	V12 Continental convertible		H150723	L	115-130.000 USD		NS		05-10-15	Philadelphia	233	Bon
	Red with tan leather interior; full restoration completed about 10 years ago. From the Evergreen Collection (see lot 231 RM 5.8.06 $ 103,400).											
1948	V12 Continental convertible		8H181010	L	NA	32.430*	45.650*	40.172*	09-04-16	Palm Beach	708	B/J
	Grey with red interior; restored in 2000.											
1946	V12 Continental convertible		H144078	L	60-80.000 USD	37.950	55.000	48.131	07-05-16	Auburn	849	AA
	Yellow with red leather interior; concours-quality restoration.											
1950	Cosmopolitan limousine	(Henney)	50LP623TH	L	150-175.000 USD		NS		20-05-16	Indianapolis	S139	Mec
	Black with leather interior to the front compartment and cloth to the rear; one of nine examples built for President Harry S. Truman. Lengthened chassis; 152bhp 337 engine with automatic transmission.											
1955	Capri convertible		55WA25734H	L	75-110.000 USD	36.234	55.000	48.950	05-10-15	Philadelphia	237	Bon F441
	Light coral with light coral and white interior; in good overall condition. From the Evergreen Collection.											
1955	Capri convertible		55LA7631H	L	50-60.000 USD		NS		30-07-16	Plymouth	109	RMS
	Red with red and white leather interior; restored. Power steering, power brakes, and automatic transmission.											
1956	Continental MkII coupé		C56B2094	L	80-120.000 USD	44.603*	63.800*	58.511*	28-01-16	Scottsdale	89	Bon
	White with original white interior; described as in very good overall condition. Less than 21,000 miles on the odometer.											
1956	Continental MkII coupé		C5681015	L	NA	30.800	40.000	36.132	09-07-16	Denver	S151.1	Mec
	Red with grey leather interior; restored in 1983. Unused for the past 15 years.											
1956	Continental MkII coupé		C56C2466	L	70-90.000 USD	37.818*	49.500*	43.704*	19-08-16	Carmel	3	Bon
	Bought in 1989 by the current, second owner and restored in the late 2000s.											
1956	Continental MkII coupé		C56A1713	L	190-240.000 USD	252.120*	330.000*	291.357*	20-08-16	Pebble Beach	37	G&Co
	Light blue with medium blue and white leather interior; acquired in 2007 by the current owner and restored to concours condition.											
1956	Premiere convertible		56WA24105L	L	90-120.000 USD	48.063*	68.750*	63.051*	28-01-16	Phoenix	168	RMS
	Turquoise with turquoise and white interior; recent full restoration.											
1956	Premiere coupé		56WA39943L	L	30-40.000 USD	18.975*	27.500*	24.065*	07-05-16	Auburn	529	AA
	Red with red and black interior; restored several years ago.											
1960	Continental MkV convertible		OY85H405253	L	70-90.000 USD	42.326*	60.500*	54.553*	12-03-16	Amelia Island	112	RMS
	Red with red leather interior; an older restoration. From the Richard & Linda Kughn Collection.											
1964	Continental convertible sedan		4Y86N431544	L	NA	40.631	64.350	56.577	31-10-15	Hilton Head	119	AA
	Black with white interior; restored.											
1965	Continental convertible sedan		5Y86N410101	L	NA	48.872	70.400	62.276	11-06-16	Newport Beach	6055	R&S
	Black with black leather interior; fully restored.											
1961	Continental convertible sedan		1Y86H420678	L	100-125.000 USD		NS		20-08-16	Monterey	S39	Mec
	White with black and white interior; restored many years ago. When new the car was loaned by Ford Company to the White House for First Lady Jacqueline Kennedy's personal use (see lot 646 Barrett-Jackson 16.1.03 $40,500).											

LISTER (GB) (1953-)

Year	Model	(Bodybuilder)	Chassis no.	Steering	Estimate	Hammer price £	Hammer price $	Hammer price €	Date	Place	Lot	Auc. H.
1989	XJ-S convertible		146261	R	25-30.000 GBP	26.450	40.006	36.557	10-12-15	London	388	Bon F442
	Red with cream leather interior; in good overall condition. 68,000 miles on the odometer (see lot 385 Bonhams 16.11.11 NS).											

F441: 1955 Lincoln Capri convertible

F442: 1989 Lister XJ-S convertible

Year	Model	(Bodybuilder)	Chassis no.	Steering	Estimate	Hammer Price £	Hammer Price $	Hammer Price €	Sale Date	Sale Place	Lot	Auc. H.

F443: 1913 Locomobile Model 48 M baby tonneau

F444: 1913 Lorraine-Dietrich Type SLF limousine

Year	Model	Chassis no.	Steering	Estimate	£	$	€	Date	Place	Lot	Auc. H.
1990	XJ-S 6.0 coupé	174048	L	60-80.000 EUR	46.467	66.953	59.000	14-05-16	Monaco	120	Coy
	Black with cream interior; in original condition. Circa 10,000 kms covered. One owner for 25 years.										
1989	XJ-S convertible	146261	R	26-34.000 GBP	32.480	42.510	37.531	20-08-16	Brooklands	314	His
	See lot 388 Bonhams 10.12.15 $40,006.										

LOCOMOBILE (USA) (1899-1929)

Year	Model	Chassis no.	Steering	Estimate	£	$	€	Date	Place	Lot	Auc. H.
1910	Model 40 Type I demi-tonneau	2376	R	450-600.000 USD		NS		20-05-16	Indianapolis	S188	Mec
	Black; in the early 2000s restored to concours condition (see Mecum lots S136 17.8.13 NS, S207 16.8.14 NS, and S159.1 4.12.14 NS).										
1913	Model 48 M baby tonneau	6410(engine)	R	300-400.000 USD	158.413*	242.000*	215.041*	08-10-15	Hershey	154	RMS F443
	White with black leather interior; restoration completed in 1995. In storage for the last years, the car requires servicing prior to use.										
1927	Model 90 Sportif	33464	L	NA		NS		11-06-16	Newport Beach	6081	R&S
	Dark green with light brown interior (see lot S161 Mecum 16.08.14 NS).										

LORRAINE-DIETRICH (F) (1905-1930)

Year	Model	Chassis no.	Steering	Estimate	£	$	€	Date	Place	Lot	Auc. H.
1913	Type SLF limousine	16629	R	15-25.000 EUR	48.208	69.840	61.920	20-03-16	Fontainebleau	307	Ose F444
	Two-tone body with cloth interior; in need of recommissioning prior to use. For 52 years in the current ownership.										
1925	B 3/6 Le Mans torpedo	122892	R	600-1.000.000 EUR		NS		05-09-15	Chantilly	21	Bon
	French blue; ex-Works car placed third overall at the 1925 Le Mans 24 Hours driven by Stalter and Brisson. It was subsequently driven by private owners until 1935. In 1949 it was transformed into a harvester by the then owner who kept all the mechanical components removed in the process. In 1976 it was acquired by the current owner who bought also the original parts and started a full restoration completed in 1997.										

LOTUS (GB) (1948-)

Year	Model	Chassis no.	Steering	Estimate	£	$	€	Date	Place	Lot	Auc. H.
1963	Super Seven S2	SB1801	R	20-25.000 EUR		NS		08-11-15	Lyon	230	Ose
	Green; sold new to France in kit form. Bought in 1998 by the current owner and subsequently prepared for racing.										
1971	Seven S4	543077GT	R	11-15.000 GBP	12.320	18.543	17.526	28-11-15	Weybridge	263	His
	Red with black interior; restored. Engine rebuilt.										
1966	Super Seven	5B2151	R	25-30.000 GBP	30.680	43.971	40.286	16-01-16	Birmingham	314	Coy F445
	Green with yellow nose and red interior; restored in 1991/92 when it was acquired by the present owner. Ford 1600 engine.										
1965	Seven S2	SB1887	R	NA		NS		20-04-16	Duxford	20	H&H
	Silver and yellow with black interior; Cosworth 1500 twin-cam engine. 25 years ago prepared for historic racing (see lot 309 Historics 1.6.13 $ 26,450).										
1962	Super Seven S2	SB1558	R	38-46.000 EUR	32.983	43.386	38.890	06-08-16	Schloss Dyck	103	Coy
	Dark green; described as in very good overall condition. 120 E engine.										
1961	Elite S2	EB1461649	R	55-65.000 GBP	57.500	88.682	78.706	12-09-15	Goodwood	379	Bon F446
	Blue with grey roof; the car was stripped in 1969 for repairs never started. In 1997 it was rediscovered and subsequently fully restored.										

F445: 1966 Lotus Super Seven

F446: 1961 Lotus Elite S2

HALL & HALL

Hall and Hall specialise in the sale and purchase of the World's finest competition cars
We also offer a race preparation and restoration service of the highest standard.
Please enquire...

Illustrations show cars we have previously sold

Sales
Mobile: +44 (0)7973 338752
E-mail: historiccars@gmail.com
www.hallandhall.net

Rick Hall
Tel no: 01778 392562
Mobile: 07710 971277
E-mail: info@hallandhall.net

Year	Model	(Bodybuilder)	Chassis No.	Steering	Estimate	Hammer Price £	$	€	Date	Place	Lot	Auc. H.
1959	Elite		1110	R	65-95.000 EUR	46.849	71.865	63.250	09-10-15	Zoute	24	Bon
	Yellow with black interior; full restoration completed in the UK in 1990. Described as still in good overall condition (see lot 93 Christie's 11.6.02 $ 65,392).
1960	Elite		1412	R	50-60.000 GBP		NS		01-12-15	London	337	Coy
	Red with white roof; restored in the 1990s (see lot 318 Coys 10.3.15 $ 87,070).
1961	Elite S2 Super 95		1864	R	75-90.000 GBP		NS		06-12-15	London	012	Bon
	Yellow with silver roof and grey interior; sold new in the UK, in the mid-1970s the car was exported to the USA where it was restored in the early 2000s. In 2007 circa it was reimported into the UK. Several mechanical works carried out in 2013 by the current owner.
1959	Elite		1105	R	NA	56.000	79.408	70.795	20-04-16	Duxford	82	H&H
	Silver with black leather interior; two owners since new. Restored in 2006. The engine has covered 200 miles since the rebuild.
1962	Elite		EB2121707	R	48-56.000 GBP		NS		11-06-16	Brooklands	301	His
	Yellow with black interior; engine recently rebuilt. For 26 years in the current ownership.
1958	Elite		MYH1009P	R	75-100.000 GBP		WD		30-07-16	Silverstone	509	SiC
	Light green; stored for many years, the car has been recently restored and prepared for historic racing. Exhibited at the Lotus stand at the 1958 Earls Court Motor Show, the car was acquired new by Jazz Legend Chris Barber and raced from 1958 to 1963. Driven also by Sir John Whitmore; class winner at the 1963 Goodwood Tourist Trophy.
1962	Elite S2		1765	R	30-40.000 GBP	44.800	58.634	51.766	20-08-16	Brooklands	290	His
	Green with black vinyl interior; since 1970 in the same family ownership. Unused from 2006 for 10 years.
1960	18 F.Junior		754	M	55-65.000 GBP	50.000 P	71.660 P	65.655 P	16-01-16	Birmingham	336	Coy
	Green; bought new by Ken Tyrell, the car was driven at the time by John Surtees and Henry Taylor and then sold to the USA. Restored in 1998, it was reimported into the UK in 2006 and restored again. In 2008 it won the British Formula Junior Championship. Ford 105E engine with Renault Dauphine gearbox with Hewland gears (see lots 236 Coys 15.1.11 NS and 326 Silverstone Auctions 26.7.14 NS). F447
1962	23		23S12	R	NQ		NS		20-08-16	Monterey	7068	R&S
	Red; for 38 years in the current ownership. Raced in period and more recently in vintage events.
1971	Elan Sprint roadster		0399G	R	35-40.000 GBP		NS		04-09-15	Woodstock	206	SiC
	Red and white Gold Leaf Team Lotus livery with black interior; bought in 2006 by the current owner and subsequently fully restored. A genuine Lotus replacement chassis had been fitted in 1983.
1967	Elan S3 roadster		457637	R	20-25.000 GBP	22.671	34.775	30.606	10-10-15	Ascot	124	Coy
	Dark green and white; engine rebuilt.
1965	Elan S2 roadster		264143	L	60-70.000 GBP		NS		10-10-15	Ascot	129	Coy
	White with black interior; the car was sold new to Nassau and raced in the 1960s. It remained with its first owner until 1988 and was later reimported into the UK where it was restored between 2009 and 2011. Raced at historic events, it is described as being "on the button" (see lot 129 Coys 8.10.11 NS).
1966	Elan S2 roadster		455897	R	45-50.000 GBP	50.625	77.072	71.604	14-11-15	Birmingham	312	SiC
	White with black interior; stored since 2005, the car requires some works prior to use. First owner actor Peter Sellers.
1972	Elan Sprint roadster		72050688G	R	30-35.000 GBP	34.313	52.238	48.532	14-11-15	Birmingham	346	SiC
	Orange and white with black interior; in good overall condition.
1964	Elan S2 roadster		CHN0263915	R	24-30.000 GBP	27.440	41.300	39.036	28-11-15	Weybridge	220	His
	Red with black interior; restored 8,000 miles ago.
1968	Elan S4 roadster		458017	R	22-230.000 GBP	25.960	39.109	36.894	01-12-15	London	311	Coy
	Red and white with black interior; engine rebuilt to Sprint specification.
1965	Elan S2 roadster		264143	L	50-60.000 GBP		NS		16-01-16	Birmingham	330	Coy
	See lot 129 Coys 10.10.15.
1965	Elan roadster		4530	L	55-75.000 USD		NS		28-01-16	Scottsdale	58	Bon
	Yellow with black interior; long restoration completed in 2015. With hardtop.
1969	Elan SE roadster		459764	L	70-90.000 USD	38.484*	55.000*	50.364*	30-01-16	Scottsdale	107	G&Co
	Yellow; since 1972 in the current ownership. Fully restored between 2014 and 2015.
1970	Elan S4		0095E	R	NA	29.250	40.880	37.145	26-02-16	Coventry	123	SiC
	Prepared for historic racing with several 26R components.
1965	Elan S2 roadster		264530	L	55-75.000 USD	42.755*	60.500*	55.721*	10-03-16	Amelia Island	168	Bon
	See lot 58 Bonhams 28.1.16.
1969	Elan S4 roadster		459196	R	18-24.000 GBP	27.600	39.984	35.449	20-03-16	Goodwood	98	Bon
	Dark green; the car has covered 350 miles since the restoration carried out 19 years ago.
1969	Elan S4 roadster		459196	R	27-32.000 GBP		NS		02-07-16	Woodstock	137	Coy
	See lot 98 Bonhams 20.3.16.

F447: 1960 Lotus 18 F.Junior

F448: 1968 Lotus 56 Indianapolis

Year	Model	(Bodybuilder)	Chassis no.	Steering	Estimate	Hammer price £	$	€	Date	Place	Lot	Auc. H.
1974	**Europa Special**		73101303Q	L	32-38.000 EUR		NS		02-07-16	Lyon	362	Agu

Black with original sand leatherette interior; until 2015 with its first owner. Recently restored.

| 1966 | **47 GT Group 4** | | 47GT10 | R | 125-165.000 EUR | | NS | | 09-07-16 | Le Mans | 188 | Art |

Gold Leaf Team Lotus livery; sold new to Nick Moor Racing. Engine and gearbox overhauled in 2002. Bought in 2011 by the current owner and used at some historic events (see lots Bonhams 365 15.8.08 NS and 20 18.8.11 $ 139,000, and Coys 316 7.12.11 $ 117,000).

| 1968 | **56 Indianapolis** | | 563 | M | 900-1.200.000 USD | | NS | | 19-08-16 | Monterey | 134 | RMS |

One of the three Lotus cars with turbine engine raced at the 1968 Indy 500 Miles and sponsored by STP. Driven by Graham Hill, this car lost a wheel after 110 laps and was forced to retire. Never raced again, it was displayed at the STP headquarters for several years before being given to NASCAR legend Richard Petty, in whose collection it remained for 15 years. Bought by the current owner, it was restored under the supervision of Clive Chapman, son of Colin, and Vince Granatelli, son of Andy.   **F448**

| 1969 | **Plus 2** | | 501070 | R | 12-14.000 GBP | | NS | | 18-05-16 | Donington Park | 24 | H&H |

Red with black vinyl interior; older restoration.

| 1972 | **Plus 2 130/5** | | 72101001L | R | 28-35.000 GBP | 72.800 | 104.854 | 92.762 | 11-06-16 | Brooklands | 320 | His |

Blue; described as in good overall condition. First example built with the 5-speed gearbox, the car was first registered to Lotus Cars Ltd and delivered to Ronnie Peterson.

| 1969 | **Plus 2** | | 502402 | R | 12-14.000 GBP | 11.480 | 15.116 | 13.630 | 28-07-16 | Donington Park | 68 | H&H |

White; restoration completed in 2015.

| 1986 | **Esprit Turbo** (Italdesign) | | 12181 | R | 15-17.000 GBP | | NS | | 09-12-15 | Chateau Impney | 72 | H&H |

Red with beige interior; for 22 years in the current ownership. Last serviced in 2013.

| 1989 | **Esprit** (Italdesign) | | 13633 | R | 10-15.000 GBP | 12.980* | 18.603* | 17.044* | 16-01-16 | Birmingham | 332 | Coy |

Blue with taupe leather interior; in good overall condition.

| 1983 | **Esprit Turbo** (Italdesign) | | 60363 | L | 35-45.000 USD | 32.298* | 46.200* | 42.370* | 28-01-16 | Scottsdale | 16 | Bon |

Silver with red leather interior; described as in good original condition, the car has covered just over 32,000 miles.

| 1989 | **Esprit Turbo** (Italdesign) | | 13555 | R | 16-22.000 GBP | 15.120 | 21.610 | 19.485 | 12-03-16 | Brooklands | 142 | His |

Pearl white with blue interior; recently recommissioned.

| 1979 | **Esprit** (Italdesign) | | 78100495G | R | 30-40.000 GBP | 35.440 | 46.639 | 41.968 | 30-07-16 | Silverstone | 513 | SiC |

John Player Special black and gold livery; described as in good driving order. Used by the factory at the October 1978 Motor Show and subsequently in their promotions.

| 1979 | **Elite** | | 79051512A | R | NQ | 8.400* | 12.005* | 10.825* | 12-03-16 | Brooklands | 163 | His |

Stored for some time, in 2012 the car was acquired by the current owner and recommissioned. Automatic transmission.

LOZIER (USA) (1901-1918)

| 1911 | **Model 51 touring** | | 3574 | R | 900-1.100.000 USD | 692.703 | 990.000 | 906.543 | 29-01-16 | Phoenix | 230 | RMS |

Olive green with black leather interior; the car was presented in 1934 by its first owner to the Henry Ford Museum where it remained until 1968 when it was acquired by Ken Pearson who fully restored it. Described as still in very good overall condition. From the Craig McCaw Collection, its fourth owner (see lot 129 RM 9.3.13 $ 1,100,000).   **F449**

LYNX (GB)

| 1979 | **Jaguar D-Type replica** | | 850567 | R | NA | 157.500 | 220.122 | 200.009 | 26-02-16 | Coventry | 420 | SiC |

Ecurie Ecosse blue; built in 1979, the car is based on a 1962 Jaguar E-Type 3.8. Body repainted and engine rebuilt (on a 4.2-litre block) in the 1990s. 10,357 miles covered; recently serviced.

| 1989 | **Jaguar D-Type replica** | | 1E76306 | R | 250-300.000 USD | 155.474 | 203.500 | 179.670 | 19-08-16 | Carmel | 94 | Bon |

Car based on a 1966 Jaguar E-Type 4.2 2+2 coupé chassis and fitted with many original Jaguar parts.

| 2015 | **Jaguar XKSS replica** | | P1R431038W | L | 220-250.000 GBP | 247.500 | 376.868 | 338.357 | 04-09-15 | Woodstock | 255 | SiC |

Black with red interior; replica completed in 2015 and based on a 1969 Jaguar E-Type. 4.2-litre 6-cylinder engine with 5-speed Getrag gearbox.

| 1988 | **Jaguar XKSS replica** | | 1E50912 | R | 325-375.000 GBP | 359.900 | 555.074 | 492.631 | 12-09-15 | Goodwood | 320 | Bon |

Dark green with green leather interior; 3.8-litre Jaguar engine. Sold new to the USA, the car was reimported into the UK in 2011. Body repainted in 2013. From the Chris Evans collection (see lot 244 Bonhams 13.9.14 $ 622,955).

MARCH (GB) (1969-)

| 1971 | **711** | | 7112 | M | 550-650.000 EUR | | NS | | 14-05-16 | Monaco | 228 | RMS |

The car was driven at some 1971 Formula 1 Grand Prix by Ronnie Peterson and during that same season by Niki Lauda at the Austrian Grand Prix. In 1973 it was acquired by the current owner who had it restored in 1996 in the UK and subsequently drove it at several historic races.

| 1976 | **763** | | 16 | M | 50-60.000 EUR | 39.032 | 56.241 | 49.560 | 14-05-16 | Monaco | 126 | Coy |

Yellow; described as in ready to race condition (see lot 111 Coys 9.5.14 NS).

F449: 1911 Lozier Model 51 touring

F450: 1931 Marmon V-16 convertible sedan (LeBaron)

Year	Model	(Bodybuilder)	Chassis no.	Steering	Estimate	Hammer Price £	$	€	Date	Place	Lot	Auc. H.
1985	**85B F3000**		85B05	M	80-120.000 EUR		NS		04-02-16	Paris	384	**Bon**

Marlboro livery; one of the cars used by the French Team Oreca, it was driven by Michel Ferté in the 1985 Formula 3000 Championship. Subsequently it has had several owners and in 2011 it was imported into Australia and raced at several historic events. Chassis rebuilt in 2012-13; engine and gearbox recently rebuilt; last raced in June 2015.

MARCOS (GB) (1959-)

Year	Model	(Bodybuilder)	Chassis no.	Steering	Estimate	£	$	€	Date	Place	Lot	Auc. H.
1970	**Type 3L**		3M5720	R	12-15.000 GBP		NS		09-12-15	Chateau Impney	63	**H&H**

Red with black interior; internal roll cage and 3-point harnesses.

MARMON (USA) (1902-1933)

Year	Model	(Bodybuilder)	Chassis no.	Steering	Estimate	£	$	€	Date	Place	Lot	Auc. H.
1914	**Model 41 speedster**		30781	L	1.000-1.500.000 USD	777.370	1.017.500	898.351	20-08-16	Pebble Beach	54	**G&Co**

White with black interior; discovered in 1947. Fully restored in the late 1990s. Formerly in the collection of James Melton, Brooks Stevens and Sam and Emily Mann (see lot 32 Gooding & Company 20.8.06 $616,000).

| 1924 | **Model 34C speedster** | | B25001 | L | 125-175.000 USD | 132.682 | 203.500 | 179.121 | 09-10-15 | Hershey | 234 | **RMS** |

Light green with black fenders and brown interior; full concours-quality restoration.

| 1922 | **Model 34B touring** | | 1220135 | L | 175-225.000 USD | 121.858* | 159.500* | 140.823* | 20-08-16 | Pebble Beach | 6 | **G&Co** |

Grey with grey leather interior; concours-quality restoration completed in 2005 circa.

| 1927 | **E-75 Series 7-seater speedster (Wilson)** | | 10RL21 | R | 85-90.000 AUD | 39.817 | 61.332 | 55.333 | 24-10-15 | Melbourne | 40 | **TBr** |

Two-tone grey; described as in very good overall order.

| 1933 | **V-16 sedan (LeBaron)** | | 16140933 | L | 125-175.000 USD | | NS | | 08-10-15 | Hershey | 156 | **RMS** |

Black; in the same family ownership from 1958 for over 56 years, the car remained all the time in a family barn in Texas. Described as in original condition; 32,250 miles on the odometer.

| 1931 | **V-16 convertible sedan (LeBaron)** | | 16145593 | L | 600-750.000 USD | 442.497 | 632.500 | 570.325 | 12-03-16 | Amelia Island | 144 | **RMS** |

Black with orange moldings, dark red interior and black cloth top; the car was restored in the 1960s probably and in 1972 it was acquired by Briggs Cunningham who fitted it with the present engine no.16860. Bought by S. Ray Miller, it was subjected to a full concours-quality restoration between 1988 and 1989. Engine recently rebuilt.
F450

| 1931 | **V-16 convertible (LeBaron)** | | 16144652 | L | 1.200-1.500.000 USD | 924.440 | 1.210.000 | 1.068.309 | 21-08-16 | Pebble Beach | 117 | **G&Co** |

Green with olive green leather interior; first restored at unspecified date, in 2002 the car was purchased by the current owner and subsequently fully restored.

MARTINI (F) (1963-1990)

| 1973 | **Mk 11 Formula Renault** | | MK1131 | M | 20-30.000 EUR | | NS | | 09-07-16 | Le Mans | 184 | **Art** |

Described as the car which helped René Arnoux to win the 1973 French Formula Renault Championship. Restored in the 2000s and fitted with R12 Gordini engine and gearbox.

| 1976 | **Mk19** | | MK19001 | M | 60-80.000 EUR | | NS | | 09-07-16 | Le Mans | 179 | **Art** |

Blue; the car was raced by Patrick Tambay at the 1976 Formula 2 European Championship, where he placed third. At the time fitted with the Renaul V6 engine, the car is currently fitted with a rebuilt BMW M12/7 engine.

MASERATI (I) (1914-)

| 1932 | **8C 3000** | | 3004(engine) | R | Refer Dpt. | 707.407 | 1.001.000 | 921.921 | 10-03-16 | Amelia Island | 175 | **Bon** |

Car built in the UK by Peter Shaw using a newly built chassis, the original crankcase no.3004, original rear axle no.3004 and an earlier original Maserati gearbox no.26. New body with original aero screen, oil tank and water filler cap. Fitted with lights and cycle wings, it was road registered and driven at the 1987 Mille Miglia Storica. In 1999 it was acquired by the current owner, Willem van Huystee, who had the engine rebuilt. Driven at several historic events. Recently inspected by a FIVA representative, it will be granted a technical passport.
F451

| 1949 | **A6 1500 (Pinin Farina)** | | 078 | L | 675-700.000 USD | | NS | | 11-06-16 | Hershey | 130 | **TFA** |

Dark blue with red leather interior; sold new in Italy, in 1963 the car was imported into the USA where it remained in the same ownership for 40 years. In 2003 it was reimported into Italy and fully restored. In 2013 it was purchased by the present American owner. Currently fitted with a 5-speed gearbox (the original 4-speed unit is included with the sale).

| 1948 | **A6 1500 (Pinin Farina)** | | 060 | L | 800-1.100.000 USD | 651.310 | 852.500 | 752.672 | 20-08-16 | Pebble Beach | 50 | **G&Co** |

Light metallic blue with leather and cloth interior; built with the three carburettor engine, when new the car was raced at some events in Italy. Driven by Franco Bordoni it won the class at the 1949 Coppa Inter-Europa at Monza. In 1951 it was imported into the USA and following some ownership changes in 1998 it was bought by the current owner of Houston, Texas, and shipped to Italy for a full restoration. Currently fitted with engine no.085, it is offered with also the original engine no.060.
F452

| 1951 | **A6G 2000 coupé (Pinin Farina)** | | 2020 | L | 400-500.000 USD | | NS | | 20-08-16 | Monterey | 207 | **RMS** |

Light blue with tan interior; sold new in Italy, in 1960 the car was imported into the UK where it remained for 10 years circa prior to be imported into the USA. In 2000 it was acquired by John Bookout who had it restored in 2001. Purchased by Doug Magnon circa five years later, it has been restored again to concours condition in recent years. From the Riverside International Automotive Museum Collection.

F451: 1932 Maserati 8C 3000

F452: 1948 Maserati A6 1500 (Pinin Farina)

MASERATI
CLASSICHE

The Importance of Origins

MASERATI CLASSICHE OPENS THE DOORS TO THE MASERATI HISTORICAL ARCHIVE

As of today, you will have the possibility to receive historical documents of your Trident-branded classic vehicle simply requesting them. The Vehicle's sales orders, technical characteristics, historical and aesthetic features and the Vehicle's technical and test documents are just a few examples of the items you may request. For information and orders: maserati.classiche@maserati.com

WWW.MASERATI.COM – MASERATI PASSION/MASERATI CLASSIC section

Timeless Emotions

Year	Model (Bodybuilder)	Chassis No.	Steering	Estimate	Hammer price £	Hammer price $	Hammer price €	Date	Place	Lot	Auc. H.
1957	A6G/54 cabriolet (Frua)	2191	L	Refer Dpt.	2.521.200	3.300.000	2.913.570	21-08-16	Pebble Beach	130	G&Co

Originally finished in ivory with red stripe on the bonnet and red leather interior, the car was sold new to the USA. In the mid-1980s it was bought by Frank Mandarano who restored it and refinished it in red with black stripe. In 1992 the car was acquired by Alfredo Brener who had it restored again and refinished in ivory with black stripe and black interior, and had the engine rebuilt. For the last 13 years in the current ownership (see lot 451 RM 15.8.03 $ 324,500). **F453**

Year	Model	Chassis No.	St.	Estimate	£	$	€	Date	Place	Lot	Auc. H.
1960	3500 GT (Touring)	AM101902	R	200-240.000 GBP		NS		07-09-15	London	122	RMS

Grey with red roof and red interior; restored in the UK probably in the late 1980s. In more recent years the car was cosmetically restored again (see lot 857 Brooks 26.10.95 NS).

| 1960 | 3500 GT (Touring) | AM101962 | L | 90-120.000 GBP | 100.060 | 154.323 | 136.962 | 12-09-15 | Goodwood | 362 | Bon |

For restoration; the bumpers are missing.

| 1961 | 3500 GT (Touring) | AM1011730 | L | 200-250.000 GBP | 197.500 | 304.604 | 270.338 | 12-09-15 | Goodwood | 382 | Bon |

Dark blue with dark red leather interior; sold new in Italy, the car was acquired in 1984 by the current, second owner. The mechanicals were overhauled in 2004 and the car has covered 7,445 kms since. **F454**

| 1960 | 3500 GT (Touring) | AM1011018 | L | 200-250.000 EUR | | NS | | 08-11-15 | Lyon | 232 | Ose |

Dark blue with grey interior; restoration completed some years ago. The original fuel-injection system was replaced by Weber carburettors (see lot 995 Brooks 6.12.99 $ 36,648).

| 1961 | 3500 GT (Touring) | AM1011232 | L | 175-200.000 GBP | 170.240 | 256.467 | 241.945 | 01-12-15 | London | 331 | Coy |

Red; restoration completed in 2015. Sold new to Switzerland; stored for over 30 years; currently registered in Belgium.

| 1963 | 3500 GT (Touring) | AM1012638 | L | NA | | NS | | 23-01-16 | Kissimmee | S88.1 | Mec |

Orange with mustard interior; stored for 30 years, mechanically reconditioned.

| 1963 | 3500 GT (Touring) | AM1012640 | L | 260-300.000 EUR | | NS | | 04-02-16 | Paris | 320 | Bon |

Red with tan interior; restored many years ago, in the early 2000s the car received several mechanical works and the body was repainted in the present red livery. The original Lucas fuel-injection system was replaced with Weber carburettors (see lots 27 RM 10.3.01 $ 27,500 and 454 Bonhams 19.8.11 $ 183,000).

| 1960 | 3500 GT (Touring) | AM101740 | R | 180-220.000 GBP | 135.900 | 196.878 | 174.550 | 20-03-16 | Goodwood | 14 | Bon |

Metallic grey with red leather interior; body repainted in 1979. 44,000 miles on the odometer, but only 2,500 miles covered since 1972. In running order, it requires further recommissioning works. Since 1965 in the Kingsley Curtis Collection.

| 1964 | 3500 GT (Touring) | AM1012808 | L | 100-120.000 GBP | 96.700 | 140.089 | 124.201 | 20-03-16 | Goodwood | 66 | Bon |

Grey with black leather interior; sold new in Italy, the car was imported in 1965 into the UK. Not used since 2012, it requires recommissioning prior to use.

| 1963 | 3500 GT (Touring) | AM1012638 | L | 200-240.000 USD | 130.676 | 187.000 | 163.569 | 02-04-16 | Ft.Lauderdale | 530 | AA |

See lot S88.1 Mecum 23.1.16.

| 1962 | 3500 GT (Touring) | AM1011978 | L | 175-200.000 USD | 116.217 | 167.750 | 150.388 | 05-06-16 | Greenwhich | 66 | Bon |

Metallic grey with black leather interior; described as in highly original condition and very good mechanical order.

| 1960 | 3500 GT (Touring) | AM1011132 | R | 180-220.000 GBP | 236.700 | 324.374 | 293.106 | 24-06-16 | Goodwood | 221 | Bon |

Black with red leather interior; sold new to Switzerland, the car was purchased in 2008 by the current owner and imported into the UK. Mechanicals and interior restored in 2008, body restored in 2015-16.

| 1963 | 3500 GT (Touring) | AM1012716 | L | 170-220.000 GBP | | NS | | 24-06-16 | Goodwood | 254 | Bon |

Red with beige interior; sold new in Italy and imported into the USA in the 1970s. Restoration completed in 2003. Mechanicals restored between 2010 and 2014. Non-original engine re-stamped with the original's number; injection system replaced with three Weber carburettors (see lots 332 Bonhams 6.5.06 NS and 152 RM 8.9.14 $ 234,416).

| 1960 | 3500 GT (Touring) | AM1011018 | L | 150-180.000 EUR | 142.846 | 189.740 | 170.400 | 02-07-16 | Lyon | 347 | Agu |

See lot 232 Osenat 8.11.15 NS.

| 1963 | 3500 GT (Touring) | AM1012576 | L | 240-280.000 EUR | 228.622 | 296.897 | 268.200 | 09-07-16 | Le Mans | 199 | Art |

Metallic grey with black interior; full restoration completed in 2015.

| 1961 | 3500 GT (Touring) | AM1011754 | L | 350-450.000 USD | 315.150 | 412.500 | 364.196 | 19-08-16 | Carmel | 66 | Bon |

Grey with maroon leather interior; stored for many years, the car was acquired almost a decade ago by the current owner and subsequently subjected to a seven-year full restoration.

| 1962 | 3500 GT (Touring) | AM1012102 | L | 400-500.000 USD | 437.008 | 572.000 | 505.019 | 20-08-16 | Pebble Beach | 51 | G&Co |

Metallic gold with white leather interior; purchased new by Eddie Fisher as a gift for Elizabeth Taylor. Later the car passed to Anthony Quinn and following some ownership changes in 1999 it was bought by the current owner of Houston, Texas. Fully restored in the USA and Italy.

| 1961 | 3500 GT (Touring) | AM1011802 | L | 240-280.000 USD | 193.292* | 253.000* | 223.374* | 20-08-16 | Monterey | 206 | RMS |

Black with black leather interior; restored many years ago. From the Riverside International Automotive Museum Collection.

| 1963 | 3500 GTI (Touring) | AM1012590 | L | 250-300.000 USD | 176.484* | 231.000* | 203.950* | 20-08-16 | Monterey | 208 | RMS |

Light grey with blue leather interior; sold new in Italy and subsequently imported into the USA. Restored at unspecified date. From the Riverside International Automotive Museum Collection.

| 1960 | 3500 GT (Touring) | AM101930 | L | 250-325.000 USD | 197.494 | 258.500 | 228.230 | 21-08-16 | Pebble Beach | 157 | G&Co |

White with original black leather interior; sold new in Italy, the car was imported into the USA in 1979 and subsequently restored. Described as still in very good overall condition (see lot 130 Gooding & Company 21.8.11 $ 148,500).

F453: 1957 Maserati A6G/54 cabriolet (Frua)

F454: 1961 Maserati 3500 GT (Touring)

PETER WIESNER
Sports & Classic Cars

la passione della vita

Phone: +43 (0)664 2017878

Mail: peterwiesner@aon.at

Year	Model	(Bodybuilder)	Chassis No.	Steering	Estimate	Hammer Price £	Hammer Price $	Hammer Price €	Date	Place	Lot	Auc. H.
1960	3500 GT Spider	(Vignale)	AM101775	L	900-1.200.000 USD		NS		20-08-16	Pebble Beach	47	G&Co
	Pre-production example sold new in Italy, after some ownership changes it was bought by collector Luigi Chilò in 1983 and subsequently fully restored. Since 2003 it is part of an important Maserati collection in the USA. Body repainted in the original green livery between 2015 and 2016.											
1959	3500 GT Spider	(Vignale)	AM101505	L	1.500-2.000.000 USD		NS		28-01-16	Phoenix	139	RMS
	One of the development prototypes of the new model, the car was finished in grey with red interior and exhibited at the Maserati stand at the 1959 Turin Motor Show. Sold new to the USA, the car was reimported into Italy in the 1980s, restored and finished in the present red livery with beige interior. Later reimported into the USA, since 2002 it is in the current ownership.											
1962	3500 GT Spider	(Vignale)	AM1011385	L	525-575.000 USD	330.958	473.000	433.126	30-01-16	Scottsdale	118	G&Co
	Originally finished in grey with natural leather interior, the car was sold new in Italy. In 1967 circa it was exported to the UK and in the 1970s it was imported into the USA. Repainted at date unknown in the present red livery, the car was stored many years ago and requires restoration. Currently fitted with engine no. AM101.01725 from a 3500 GTI Sebring.											
1960	3500 GT Spider	(Vignale)	AM101879	L	500-700.000 EUR	422.069	614.228	548.320	05-02-16	Paris	136	Art
	Silver with red leather interior; sold new in Italy, in the mid-1960s the car was imported into Sweden. Unused from the late 1960s, it requires full restoration. With hardtop.											
1960	3500 GT Spider	(Vignale)	AM101925	L	800-1.000.000 EUR	621.896	880.000	810.480	10-03-16	Amelia Island	133	Bon
	Originally finished in white with red leather interior, the car was sold new to Switzerland. After some ownership changes, in 2010 it was bought by Peter Wiesner, Austria, who had it fully restored in Italy and finished in the present grey livery with maroon interior. Since 2011 in the current ownership. Currently fitted with a 5-speed gearbox, it is offered with the original 4-speed unit also. F455											
1960	3500 GT Spider	(Vignale)	AM1011415	L	750-850.000 EUR	655.109	943.927	831.800	14-05-16	Monaco	166	Coy
	Grey with red interior; described as in very good overall condition, the car was restored in 2005. The original Lucas injection system was replaced with carburettors.											
1960	3500 GT Spider	(Vignale)	AM101971	L	900-1.100.000 USD	649.400	850.000	750.465	20-08-16	Monterey	219	RMS
	Green with tan leather interior; described as in very good overall condition, never fully restored. With hardtop. For over 30 years in the current ownership.											
1962	5000 GT	(Allemano)	AM103040	L	1.500-2.000.000 USD	1.076.614	1.540.000	1.412.334	28-01-16	Phoenix	126	RMS
	Dark blue with red leather interior; sold new to Switzerland, the car was imported into the USA in the 1970s. Later the paintwork and interior were replaced, the engine was rebuilt and the car was exhibited at the 1997 Pebble Beach Concours d'Elegance where it won its class. Described as still in very good overall condition.											
1961	5000 GT Indianapolis	(Allemano)	AM103014	L	1.500-2.000.000 USD	1.281.610	1.677.500	1.481.065	20-08-16	Pebble Beach	48	G&Co
	First of the 22 examples built with Allemano body and the only one carrying the name Indianapolis. Finished in grey with red leather interior, the car was sold new to the USA. In 1991 it was purchased by Lord Brocket in the UK, and in 1996 by the current owner in Houston, Texas. Reunited with its original engine, the car was fully restored between 1999 and 2006. From June 2014 to January 2015 it was on display at the Museo Enzo Ferrari in Modena, for the historical show dedicated to the 100th anniversary of the Maserati. F456											
1966	Sebring 3700 GTI	(Vignale)	AM10110275	L	265-315.000 EUR	200.174	307.058	270.250	09-10-15	Zoute	15	Bon
	Maroon with black leather interior; sold new in Italy, the car was exported in 2000 to Belgium. 12,000 kms covered since the engine rebuild in 1997.											
1965	Sebring 3700 GTI	(Vignale)	AM10110021	L	NA	150.021	237.600	208.898	31-10-15	Hilton Head	164	AA
	Red with white leather interior; acquired 12 years ago by the current owner and imported into the USA. Body repainted.											
1965	Sebring 3700 GTI	(Vignale)	AM10110011	R	140-160.000 GBP	194.440	292.924	276.338	01-12-15	London	342	Coy
	Light metallic grey with black leather interior; described as in original condition except for the paintwork redone at unspecified date. 72,000 miles on the odometer. From 1980 circa for 35 years in the same German ownership.											
1967	Sebring 3700 GTI	(Vignale)	AM101S10567	L	120-180.000 EUR	173.869	257.738	230.000	04-02-16	Paris	312	Bon
	Silver with blue leather interior; in original, unrestored condition. Three owners; Swiss papers.											
1963	Sebring 3500 GTI	(Vignale)	AM10101535	L	200-250.000 EUR	252.324	367.202	327.800	05-02-16	Paris	198	Art F457
	Amaranth with beige leather interior; acquired in 2003 by the current owner and fully restored between 2011 and 2015 in the UK by Bill McGrath Ltd. Described as in concours condition.											
1963	Sebring 3500 GTI	(Vignale)	AM10101549	L	275-350.000 USD	227.020	324.500	292.602	12-03-16	Amelia Island	116	RMS
	Amaranth red with black leather interior; sold new in Italy, the car was exported in 1965 to the USA where it was acquired by Buick engineer Joe Turlay who retained it for 20 years. In the early 2000s it was restored to its original specification (see lot 978 Barrett-Jackson 10.10.13 NS).											
1962	Sebring 3500 GTI	(Vignale)	AM10101557	R	180-200.000 GBP	196.875	286.808	255.642	20-05-16	Silverstone	339	SiC
	Red with beige leather interior; restored in the 1990s (see lots Brooks 760 12.6.98 $ 38,484, H&H 76 8.10.03 $ 32,185, and Bonhams 342 19.4.10 $ 64,210).											
1966	Sebring 3700 GTI	(Vignale)	AM101210425	L	160-180.000 GBP		NS		24-06-16	Goodwood	248	Bon
	Silver with blue leather interior; restored in the late 1990s.											
1967	Sebring 3500 GTI	(Vignale)	AM10101483	L	20-30.000 USD	35.313*	48.400*	43.734*	25-06-16	Santa Monica	2015	AA
	Restoration project; from the Riverside International Automotive Museum Collection.											
1966	Sebring 3500 GTI	(Vignale)	AM10110135	L	40-60.000 USD	90.288*	123.750*	111.821*	25-06-16	Santa Monica	2025	AA
	Mechanicals and interior restoration to be finished; body repainted in blue. From the Riverside International Automotive Museum Collection.											
1963	Sebring 3500 GTI	(Vignale)	AM10101765	L	200-230.000 EUR	179.042	235.513	211.109	06-08-16	Schloss Dyck	109	Coy
	Dark blue with burgundy leather interior; restored at unspecified date.											
1963	Sebring 3500 GTI	(Vignale)	AM10101563	L	350-425.000 USD		NS		21-08-16	Pebble Beach	118	G&Co
	Light grey with black leather interior; sold new in Italy, the car was imported into the USA in the late 1970s. In single ownership from 1983 to 2005; body repainted several years ago; interior retrimmed in recent years. The original fuel-injection system (included in the sale) was replaced with three Weber carburettors.											

F455: 1960 Maserati 3500 GT Spider (Vignale)

F456: 1961 Maserati 5000 GT Indianapolis (Allemano)

F457: 1963 Maserati Sebring 3500 GTI (Vignale)

F458: 1966 Maserati Quattroporte (Frua)

Year	Model (Bodybuilder)	Chassis no.	Steering	Estimate	Hammer £	Price $	€	Date	Place	Lot	Auc. H.
1966	**Quattroporte (Frua)**	AM1071476	L	50-70.000 EUR	51.517	78.185	70.115	26-09-15	Frankfurt	164	Coy
	Dark grey with beige leather interior; described as in very good overall condition. Mechanicals restored in Germany between 2009 and 2010.										
1966	**Quattroporte (Frua)**	AM1071026	L	85-95.000 EUR	70.154	98.744	86.900	09-04-16	Essen	114	Coy F458
	Dark blue with mustard leather interior; first owner the Prince Karim Aga Khan. In 2003 the car was reimported into Italy where it remained in single ownership since.										
1967	**Quattroporte (Frua)**	AM1071208	L	8-10.000 USD	12.038*	16.500*	14.909*	25-06-16	Santa Monica	2014	AA
	For restoration; from the Riverside International Automotive Museum Collection.										
1968	**Mistral 4.0 coupé (Frua)**	AM109A11608	L	125-175.000 GBP		NS		07-09-15	London	151	RMS
	Light metallic blue with dark red leather interior, restored in the 1990s. The car was delivered new to Italian driver Umberto Maglioli in Venezuela. Subsequently it was imported into the USA, later it moved to Australia and in 2011 it was imported into the UK. Recent mechanical works; gearbox rebuilt. The body requires some attention (see lots 445 Coys 30.9.04 NS and 38 Bonhams 19.11.06 $ 28,944).										
1966	**Mistral 4.0 coupé (Frua)**	AM109A1686	L	160-180.000 EUR	136.975	216.906	190.720	01-11-15	Paris	152	Art
	Silver with beige leather interior; restored at unspecified date.										
1969	**Mistral 4.0 coupé (Frua)**	AM109A11742	L	150-200.000 USD	138.422	198.000	181.586	28-01-16	Scottsdale	59	Bon
	Silver with blue leather interior; the car was sold new in Italy where it remained until early 2015. Described as in very good overall condition (see lot 128 RM 4.2.15 $ 198,703).										
1965	**Mistral 3.7 coupé (Frua)**	AM109528	L	220-250.000 EUR	164.521	238.777	218.400	03-02-16	Paris	120	RMS F459
	Metallic grey; described as in very good overall condition.										
1968	**Mistral (spider/conversion)**	AM1093A1289	L	50-80.000 EUR	52.161*	77.321*	69.000*	04-02-16	Paris	427	Bon
	Built with coupé body, the car was sold new to the USA. In 1988 it was imported into the UK where a restoration with conversion to spider form was started and then stopped in 1991. In partially restored and incomplete condition; several mechanicals parts are also missing.										
1967	**Mistral 4.0 coupé (Frua)**	AM109A11174	L	30-40.000 GBP	53.320	75.762	68.703	08-03-16	London	136	Coy
	For restoration; injection system replaced at unspecified date with three carburettors.										
1966	**Mistral 3.7 coupé (Frua)**	AM109704	L	190-210.000 EUR	176.917	252.852	228.000	12-03-16	Lyon	323	Agu
	Light green with black interior; the car has covered less than 3,000 kms since the restoration carried out in the 2000s. The original fuel-injection system was replaced with three Weber carburettors.										
1967	**Mistral 4.0 coupé (Frua)**	AM109A11172	L	165-185.000 EUR		NS		12-03-16	Lyon	330	Agu
	Cream with black interior; for restoration.										
1967	**Mistral 4.0 coupé (Frua)**	AM1091118	L	110-140.000 USD	132.422	181.500	164.003	25-06-16	Santa Monica	2026	AA
	Red with dark red interior; from the Riverside International Automotive Museum Collection.										
1964	**Mistral 3.7 Spider (Frua)**	AM109S035	R	475-575.000 GBP	526.400	803.392	720.800	07-09-15	London	124	RMS F460
	Silver Auteuil with black leather interior; the car was exhibited at the 1964 Earls Court Motor Show where it was acquired by actress Diana Dors. In 1976 it was exported to Australia, where it was restored at unspecified date, probably in the early 2000s.										
1966	**Mistral 3.5 Spider (Frua)**	AM109S067	R	400-500.000 GBP		NS		06-12-15	London	009	Bon
	Red with magnolia leather interior; believed to be one of the 1966 Turin Motor Show cars, it was sold new to the UK where it was restored in the mid-1990s. Since 2005 in the current ownership; body restored and repainted in 2012; recently serviced (see lot 271 Coys 3.3.05 $ 68,797).										

F459: 1965 Maserati Mistral 3.7 coupé (Frua)

F460: 1964 Maserati Mistral 3.7 Spider (Frua)

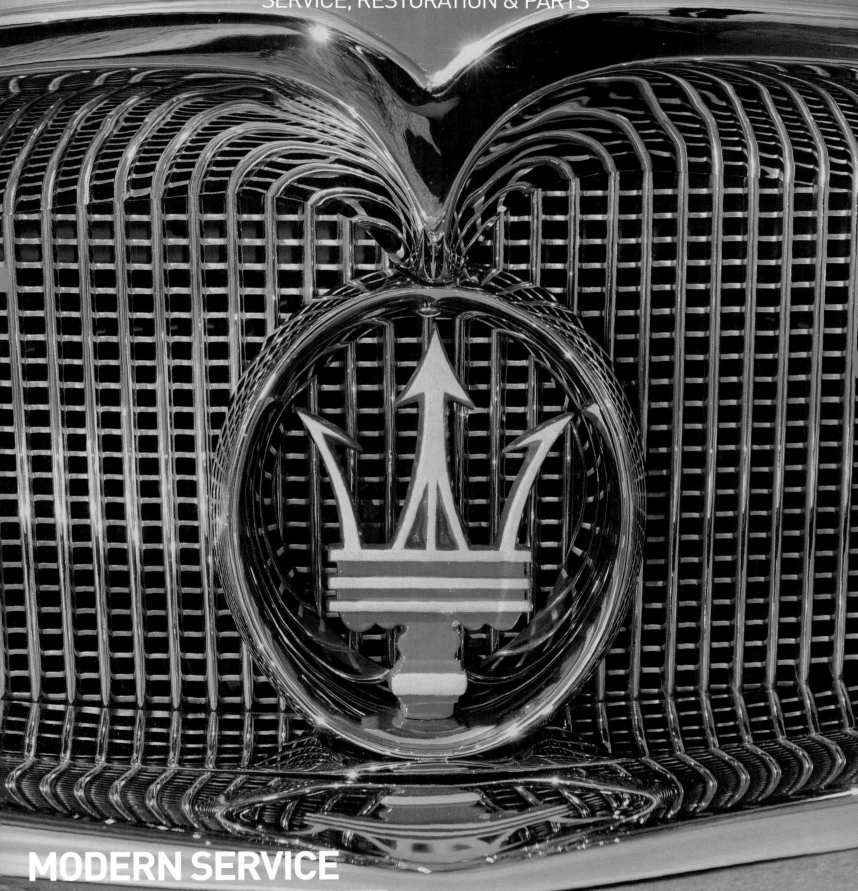

Year	Model	(Bodybuilder)	Chassis no.	Steering	Estimate	Hammer Price £	$	€	Date	Place	Lot	Auc. H.
1965	**Mistral 3500 Spider**	(Frua)	AM109S085	L	550-600.000 EUR		NS		05-02-16	Paris	159	**Art**

Red with beige leather interior; sold new to Germany, later the car was imported into the USA where it was restored and subsequently sold to Sweden in the late 1980s. Recently recommissioned.

1965	**Mistral 3.5 Spider**	(Frua)	AM109S099	L	400-500.000 USD	315.150	412.500	364.196	20-08-16	Monterey	209	**RMS**

Black with mustard leather interior; sold new to the UK, the car was subsequently imported into the USA where it was converted to left-hand drive. In single ownership from 1973 to 2003 when it was bought by Doug Magnon. Injection system replaced with three Weber carburettors at unspecified date. Never fully restored. With hardtop. From the Riverside International Automotive Museum Collection.

1968	**Mexico 4.7**	(Frua)	1121103	L	550-750.000 EUR	454.262	691.670	621.000	05-09-15	Chantilly	16	**Bon**

One-off finished in light green with burgundy leather interior; exhibited at the Frua stand at the 1968 Geneva Motor Show, the car returned to the factory in December 1969 and was sold in March 1970 to Spain, where it remained in the same ownership from 1980 to 2013. Imported into Belgium, it was restored and in September 2014 it was exhibited at both the Salon Privé and the Chantilly Concours d'Elegance events and at the Maserati Concours d'Elegance, organized by the factory for the centennial celebration, where it received the Best of Show award. **F461**

1969	**Mexico 4.2**	(Vignale)	AM112520	L	90-140.000 EUR	81.329	128.788	113.240	01-11-15	Paris	148	**Art**

Red with light brown leather interior; since 1976 in the current ownership. Restored in the mid-1980s; gearbox replaced in the 1990s. **F462**

1970	**Mexico 4.2**	(Vignale)	AM112900	L	85-120.000 EUR		NS		09-07-16	Le Mans	196	**Art**

Grey with light beige leather interior; described as in good overall condition.

1967	**Mexico 4.7**	(Vignale)	AM1121162	L	150-200.000 USD	79.838*	104.500*	92.263*	19-08-16	Carmel	7	**Bon**

Dark metallic red with tan leather interior; both cosmetic and mechanical refurbishments carried out over the years. Recently serviced.

1968	**Mexico 4.7**	(Vignale)	AM1121216	L	90-120.000 USD	75.636*	99.000*	87.407*	20-08-16	Monterey	202	**RMS**

White with original red leather interior; sold new in Italy and later imported into the USA. Restored in the 1990s. From the Riverside International Automotive Museum Collection.

1969	**Ghibli coupé**	(Ghia)	AM1151052	L	250-290.000 EUR	214.024	338.915	298.000	01-11-15	Paris	147	**Art**

Rubin red with black leather interior; restored in 2005. Body repainted in more recent years.

1968	**Ghibli coupé**	(Ghia)	AM115538	L	320-360.000 USD	192.253	275.000	252.203	28-01-16	Scottsdale	41	**Bon**

Dark blue with red leather interior; discovered in 2006 and subsequently fully restored. Described as in concours condition. Currently fitted with engine no.115.720 fitted during the restoration.

1967	**Ghibli coupé**	(Ghia)	AM115532	L	200-250.000 USD	134.692*	192.500*	176.272*	29-01-16	Phoenix	223	**RMS**

Black with light grey leather interior; restored in 2000 in the USA.

1969	**Ghibli coupé**	(Ghia)	AM1150752	L	210-250.000 EUR		NS		03-02-16	Paris	106	**RMS**

Red with black interior; sold new to the USA, the car was later reimported into Europe and restored in Switzerland at unspecified date (see Brooks lots 175 15.3.99 NS and 217 6.3.00 $ 34,489).

1968	**Ghibli coupé**	(Ghia)	AM115388	L	250-280.000 EUR		NS		05-02-16	Paris	220	**Art**

Silver with red interior; in good overall condition. Engine rebuilt between 2011 and 2015 (see lots 37 Poulain 13.12.93 NS and 28 Artcurial 16.11.08 NS).

1969	**Ghibli coupé**	(Ghia)	AM1151160	L	325-375.000 USD	223.172	319.000	287.642	12-03-16	Amelia Island	178	**RMS**

Dark metallic green with white leather interior; fully restored in recent years. Engine rebuilt.

1967	**Ghibli coupé**	(Ghia)	AM115182	L	150-180.000 EUR		NS		20-03-16	Fontainebleau	361	**Ose**

Red; to be overhauled prior to use. The interior require some attention. Automatic transmission.

1967	**Ghibli coupé**	(Ghia)	AM115010	L	320-380.000 EUR		NS		13-05-16	Monaco	112	**Bon**

Metallic copper with original white leather interior; first Ghibli delivered in Europe. Restored to original specification. The car won the Ghibli class at the official concours d'elegance celebrating the marque's 100 years in Turin in 2014.

1970	**Ghibli coupé**	(Ghia)	AM1151504	L	230-280.000 EUR	243.872	348.424	309.600	19-06-16	Fontainebleau	335	**Ose**

Red with cream interior; paintwork and interior redone some years ago, mechanicals overhauled. Two owners (see lots 7 Worldwide 2.9.10 $53,900 and 348 Osenat 17.3.13 $98,668).

1967	**Ghibli coupé**	(Ghia)	AM115532	L	225-275.000 USD	134.464*	176.000*	155.390*	19-08-16	Carmel	83	**Bon**

See lot 223 RM/Sotheby's 29.1.16.

1968	**Ghibli coupé**	(Ghia)	AM115758	L	160-200.000 USD	100.848*	132.000*	116.543*	20-08-16	Monterey	205	**RMS**

Red with white leather interior; in largely original condition. Imported into the USA in the 2000s. From the Riverside International Automotive Museum Collection (see lot 253 Bonhams 15.5.04 $ 21,987).

1970	**Ghibli SS coupé**	(Ghia)	AM115491786	L	325-400.000 USD	230.703	330.000	302.643	28-01-16	Phoenix	137	**RMS**

Beige with parchment leather interior; until 2009 with its first owner. Paintwork and interior redone by the second one prior to resell it to the current vendor. 82.000 kms covered since new. Fully serviced and ready to use (see lot 111 Gooding 17.8.14 $ 264,000). **F463**

1970	**Ghibli SS coupé**	(Ghia)	AM115492034	L	300-350.000 EUR	178.215	264.181	235.750	04-02-16	Paris	344	**Bon**

Red with beige leather interior; body repainted at unspecified date, interior retrimmed in 2000.

1971	**Ghibli SS coupé**	(Ghia)	AM115492098	L	280-340.000 EUR	206.447	300.438	268.200	05-02-16	Paris	135	**Art**

Rubin red with beige leather interior; restored in the late 1990s (see lot 26 Artcurial 18.6.07 $ 83,039).

1971	**Ghibli SS coupé**	(Ghia)	AM115492434	L	340-365.000 EUR		NS		09-04-16	Essen	149	**Coy**

Metallic green with tan interior; 71,000 kms covered.

F461: 1968 Maserati Mexico 4.7 (Frua)

F462: 1969 Maserati Mexico 4.2 (Vignale)

1958 Porsche 718 RSK

1933 Maserati 8CM

1954 Lancia D24

1954 Aston Martin DB2-4 Drophead

EGON ZWEIMÜLLER GMBH
WWW.ZWEIMUELLERCARS.COM – TEL. +43 (0)7223 - 821 480

Year	Model	(Bodybuilder)	Chassis no.	Steering	Estimate	Hammer Price £	$	€	Date	Place	Lot	Auc. H.
1970	Ghibli SS coupé	(Ghia)	AM115491854	R	210-240.000 GBP		NS		24-06-16	Goodwood	237	Bon

Red with tan leather interior; sold new to Australia, the car was imported in 1990 into the UK where it was restored between 1994 and 1995. Engine rebuilt in 1996 and in 2004 again (see lots 92 H & H 21.11.7 $110,948 and 569 Bonhams 11.7.08 NS).

| 1969 | Ghibli SS Spider | (Ghia) | AM115S1005 | L | 900-1.200.000 USD | | NS | | 20-08-16 | Monterey | S121 | Mec |

Yellow with black leather interior; sold new to the USA, the car was reimported into Europe in 2008 circa and subsequently restored. Produced prior to the completion of the homologation process, it does not bear the number "49" in the chassis number (see lot 328 Artcurial 7.2.14 $1,017,398).

| 1971 | Ghibli SS Spider | (Ghia) | AM115S491237 | L | 1.750-2.250.000 USD | 1.146.000 | 1.500.000 | 1.324.350 | 21-08-16 | Pebble Beach | 115 | G&Co |

Light metallic blue with ivory leather interior; sold new to the USA. The car has covered 200 miles since a concours-quality restoration completed in 2014.

| 1973 | Indy 4.9 | (Vignale) | AM116491854 | L | 75-115.000 EUR | 59.626 | 91.464 | 80.500 | 09-10-15 | Zoute | 14 | Bon F464 |

Metallic red with beige interior; sold new in Italy and later exported to Holland. Paintwork and interior redone in 2010. In very good overall condition.

| 1970 | Indy 4.2 | (Vignale) | AM116512 | R | NA | | NS | | 26-02-16 | Coventry | 438 | SiC |

Light blue with cream interior; restored and converted to right hand drive at unspecified date (see lot 240 Bonhams 6.12.09 NS).

| 1973 | Indy 4.9 | (Vignale) | AM116491854 | L | 65-85.000 GBP | | NS | | 20-03-16 | Goodwood | 75 | Bon |

See lot 14 Bonhams 9.10.15.

| 1971 | Indy 4.2 | (Vignale) | AM116948 | L | 70-90.000 EUR | 78.478 | 113.692 | 100.800 | 20-03-16 | Fontainebleau | 357 | Ose |

Red with beige interior; body restored approximately 10 years ago, new interior, mechanicals overhauled in 2015.

| 1971 | Indy 4.2 | (Vignale) | AM116504 | L | 65-85.000 USD | 41.235 | 59.400 | 52.545 | 11-06-16 | Hershey | 147 | TFA |

Blue with black interior; restored some 12 years ago (see lots 237 Osenat 04.06.08 $32,230, 28 Chevau-Légerè 25.9.11 NS, and 271 Artcurial 11.02.14 $71,657).

| 1973 | Indy 4.9 | (Vignale) | AM116492028 | L | 75-100.000 USD | 62.600* | 85.800* | 77.529* | 25-06-16 | Santa Monica | 2023 | AA |

Dark blue with white leather interior; from the Riverside International Automotive Museum Collection.

| 1970 | Indy 4.2 | (Vignale) | AM116444 | L | 65-85.000 EUR | | NS | | 02-07-16 | Lyon | 337 | Agu |

Red with white leather interior; some restoration works carried out in the past.

| 1970 | Indy 4.9 | (Vignale) | AM11647706 | L | 75-100.000 USD | 50.424* | 66.000* | 58.271* | 20-08-16 | Monterey | 201 | RMS |

Light blue with black leather interior; built with the 4.7-liter engine, many years ago the car was upgraded with the present 4.9-liter unit. Body repainted; front seats reupholstered. From the Riverside International Automotive Museum Collection.

| 1971 | Tipo 121 Quattroporte | (Frua) | AM121002 | L | 175-225.000 USD | 67.232* | 88.000* | 77.695* | 20-08-16 | Monterey | 210 | RMS |

First ot two examples built, the car was exhibited at the Frua stand at the 1971 Paris Motor Show, then at the 1972 Geneva Motor Show, and later at the Barcelona Motor Show in 1973 and 1974. Sold in Spain, it was restored in 1980 and finished in the present dark blue livery with beige leather interior. In 2000 it was purchased by Alfredo Brener and imported into the USA. From the Riverside International Automotive Museum Collection. **F465**

| 1973 | Bora 4.7 | (Italdesign) | AM117422 | L | 250-300.000 EUR | 170.361 | 261.326 | 230.000 | 09-10-15 | Zoute | 16 | Bon F466 |

Light blue with black leather interior; sold new to France, in 1990 the car was exported to Japan where it remained for 14 years before to be reimported into Europe. Less than 40,000 kms covered since new. Recently serviced.

| 1973 | Bora 4.9 | (Italdesign) | AM11749562 | L | 180-220.000 USD | 130.844* | 187.000* | 171.236* | 29-01-16 | Scottsdale | 26 | G&Co |

Black with original red leather interior; sold new to the USA. Several mechanical works carried out in the 2000s.

| 1974 | Bora 4.9 | (Italdesign) | AM11749US0720 | L | 220-260.000 EUR | | NS | | 03-02-16 | Paris | 135 | RMS |

Gold with tan interior; several mechanical works carried out in recent years.

| 1973 | Bora 4.7 | (Italdesign) | AM117278 | L | 220-270.000 EUR | 139.095 | 206.190 | 184.000 | 04-02-16 | Paris | 345 | Bon |

Yellow with original black leather interior; engine overhauled in the 1980s, body repainted in 2002 (see lot 123 Coys 11.8.12 NS).

| 1973 | Bora 4.9 | (Italdesign) | AM11749534 | L | 180-220.000 USD | 132.153 | 187.000 | 172.227 | 10-03-16 | Amelia Island | 115 | Bon |

Medium metallic blue with black interior; originally finished in red, the car was sold new to the USA. Restored between 2008 and 2009.

| 1973 | Bora 4.9 | (Italdesign) | AM11749568 | L | 225-275.000 USD | 119.282* | 170.500* | 153.740* | 11-03-16 | Amelia Island | 55 | G&Co |

Red; in highly original condition. Less than 2,700 miles on the odometer. Several works carried out in late 2013.

| 1973 | Bora 4.9 | (Italdesign) | AM11749536 | L | 150-160.000 EUR | 120.563 | 173.715 | 153.080 | 14-05-16 | Monaco | 117 | Coy |

Black with black leather interior; body recently repainted. Reimported into Europe from the USA and fitted with European bumpers.

| 1975 | Bora 4.7 | (Italdesign) | AM117466 | L | 190-240.000 EUR | 158.776 | 228.776 | 201.600 | 14-05-16 | Monaco | 212 | RMS |

Black with tan leather interior; sold new in Italy, where it was restored prior to be exported to Germany in 2003.

| 1973 | Bora 4.9 | (Italdesign) | AM11749680 | L | 160-200.000 USD | 111.264 | 160.600 | 143.978 | 05-06-16 | Greenwhich | 27 | Bon |

Originally finished in maroon with mustard interior, the car was sold new to the USA. Described as in good overall condition, it is currently finished in red with tan interior.

| 1973 | Bora 4.9 | (Italdesign) | AM11749562 | L | 170-200.000 EUR | | NS | | 06-08-16 | Schloss Dyck | 125 | Coy |

See lot 26 Gooding & Company 29.1.16.

F463: 1970 Maserati Ghibli SS coupé (Ghia)

F464: 1973 Maserati Indy 4.9 (Vignale)

Year	Model (Bodybuilder)	Chassis no.	Steering	Estimate	Hammer price £	$	€	Date	Sale Place	Lot	Auc. H.

F465: 1971 Maserati Tipo 121 Quattroporte (Frua)

F466: 1973 Maserati Bora 4.7 (Italdesign)

Year	Model (Bodybuilder)	Chassis no.	Steering	Estimate	£	$	€	Date	Place	Lot	Auc. H.
1973	**Bora 4.9** (Italdesign)	AM11749620	L	140-180.000 USD	96.646*	126.500*	111.687*	20-08-16	Monterey	204	RMS

Red with white leather interior; sold new to the USA. From the Riverside International Automotive Museum Collection.

| 1972 | **Bora** (Italdesign) | AM117256 | L | NQ | | NS | | 20-08-16 | Monterey | 7161 | R&S |

Red with black leather interior; in good overall condition. European specification.

| 1972 | **Boomerang** (Italdesign) | 081 | L | Refer Dpt. | 2.439.553 | 3.714.523 | 3.335.000 | 05-09-15 | Chantilly | 11 | Bon |

Non-functional concept car on a Bora rolling chassis exhibited at the 1971 Turin Motor Show and subsequently at the 1972 Geneva Motor Show as a fully operational vehicle. Sold to Spain, in 1980 it was imported into Germany where later it was restored. In the early 2000s the restoration was refreshed and the car was recommissioned for road use. Exhibited at numerous historic events, since 2005 it is in the current ownership (see Christie's lots 116 22.5.90 NS, 40 12.2.02 $ 631,748 and 119 12.2.05 $ 1,004,297). **F467**

| 1978 | **Khamsin** (Bertone) | AM120US1238 | L | 150-200.000 EUR | 128.456 | 186.939 | 166.880 | 05-02-16 | Paris | 145 | Art |

Red with dark grey leather interior; sold new to the USA, the car was reimported into Europe in 1989. Described as in very good overall condition, it has covered less than 25,000 miles (see Coys lots 215 22.7.06 $ 35,727 and 117 24.3.12 $ 61,868). **F468**

| 1978 | **Khamsin** (Bertone) | AM120US1242 | L | 250-300.000 EUR | | NS | | 05-02-16 | Paris | 160 | Art |

Gold with beige leather interior; sold new to the USA, from 2004 to 2007 the car was owned by Marc Sonnery founder of the Maserati Khamsin Register. Later it was imported into Holland where the body was repainted.

| 1979 | **Khamsin** (Bertone) | AM120371 | R | 95-105.000 GBP | | NS | | 08-03-16 | London | 131 | Coy |

Red with tan interior; engine rebuilt in 2015 (see lot 73 H&H 4.12.02 NS).

| 1978 | **Khamsin** (Bertone) | AM120409 | R | 80-100.000 GBP | 80.000 | 115.896 | 102.752 | 20-03-16 | Goodwood | 94 | Bon |

Red with cream leather interior; between 2011 and 2014 restored in the UK by Bill McGrath Maserati (see Coys lots 445 20.11.97 NS, 206 29.9.05 NS, and 144 26.4.14 $ 129,160).

| 1979 | **Khamsin** (Bertone) | AM120371 | R | 85-95.000 GBP | | NS | | 24-06-16 | Goodwood | 274 | Bon |

See lot 131 Coys 8.3.16.

| 1975 | **Khamsin** (Bertone) | AM120146 | L | 180-240.000 EUR | | NS | | 09-07-16 | Le Mans | 198 | Art |

Black with black interior; for 27 years in the current, third ownership. 62,000 kms covered. Mechanicals restored in 2012 (see lot 263 Brooks 8.9.97 NS).

| 1975 | **Khamsin** (Bertone) | AM120US1046 | L | 100-140.000 USD | 117.656* | 154.000* | 135.967* | 20-08-16 | Monterey | 203 | RMS |

Yellow with black leather interior; US-market version later fitted with European specification bumpers. Less than 19,200 miles in the odometer. From the Riverside International Automotive Museum Collection.

| 1982 | **Merak 2.0** (Italdesign) | AM122D3384 | L | 60-90.000 EUR | 57.923 | 88.851 | 78.200 | 09-10-15 | Zoute | 12 | Bon **F469** |

Champagne with beige interior; 36,197 kms covered. Same owner for 32 years.

| 1978 | **Merak SS** (Italdesign) | AM122A503 | R | 35-40.000 GBP | 49.960 | 75.265 | 71.003 | 01-12-15 | London | 312 | Coy |

Yellow with grey interior; overhauled by McGrath Maserati in 2011.

| 1975 | **Merak** (Italdesign) | AM1221116 | L | 45-65.000 EUR | 42.207* | 61.423* | 54.832* | 05-02-16 | Paris | 216 | Art |

Yellow with black leatherette interior; restored. Engine rebuilt.

| 1976 | **Merak SS** (Italdesign) | AM122A1338 | L | 80-100.000 USD | 42.326* | 60.500* | 54.553* | 11-03-16 | Amelia Island | 79 | G&Co |

Originally finished in silver with blue leather interior, the car was sold new to France. Currently finished in red with tan interior. Recent engine-out service.

| 1975 | **Merak** (Italdesign) | AM122US2062 | L | 44-48.000 USD | 36.897 | 52.800 | 46.184 | 02-04-16 | Ft.Lauderdale | 791 | AA |

Red with tan interior; just over 38,050 actual miles.

F467: 1972 Maserati Boomerang (Italdesign)

F468: 1978 Maserati Khamsin (Bertone)

Year	Model	(Bodybuilder)	Chassis no.	Steering	Estimate	Hammer Price £	$	€	Date	Place	Lot	Auc. H.
1973	**Merak**	(Italdesign)	AM1220526	L	75-85.000 EUR	55.288	79.663	70.200	14-05-16	Monaco	128	Coy
Bronze; restored in 2011. Original interior.											
1975	**Merak**	(Italdesign)	AM122US1388	L	45-55.000 USD	36.115*	49.500*	44.728*	25-06-16	Santa Monica	2024	AA
White with black interior; from the Riverside International Automotive Museum Collection.											
1979	**Merak SS**	(Italdesign)	AM1220294	R	28-32.000 GBP	34.875	45.896	41.299	30-07-16	Silverstone	942	SiC
Red with cream leather interior; recently serviced.											
1975	**Merak**	(Italdesign)	AM1220890	L	45-50.000 EUR	33.983	44.701	40.069	06-08-16	Schloss Dyck	166	Coy
White with red leather interior; 29,000 recorded kms.											
1986	**Quattroporte III 4.9**	(Italdesign)	AM33049M005714	L	NA		NS		14-10-15	Duxford	43	H&H
Dark aquamarine blue with dark tan leather interior; described as in very good overall condition. Body repainted, engine overhauled.											
1984	**Quattroporte III 4.9**	(Italdesign)	305176	L	14-20.000 EUR	13.182	20.357	17.920	17-10-15	Salzburg	330	Dor
Metallic grey with brown leather interior; in good overall condition. Sold new to the USA; 47,968 miles on the odometer.											
1979	**Quattroporte III 4.9**	(Italdesign)	330US0142	L	3-8.000 EUR	6.287*	9.517*	8.760*	07-11-15	Lyon	248	Agu
Brown with light brown leather interior; since 1990 in the current ownership, the car is unused from many years and not in working order.											
1986	**Quattroporte III 4.9**	(Italdesign)	AM33049M005714	L	25-30.000 GBP		NS		09-12-15	Chateau Impney	104	H&H
See lot 43 H&H 14.10.15.											
1986	**Quattroporte III 4.9**	(Italdesign)	305830	L	30-40.000 USD	27.684*	39.600*	36.317*	28-01-16	Scottsdale	101	Bon F470
Black with mustard leather interior; less than 46,000 miles covered. Body repainted.											
1984	**Quattroporte III 4.9**	(Italdesign)	304330	L	25-35.000 EUR	24.342	36.083	32.200	04-02-16	Paris	348	Bon
Silver grey with cognac interior; until 2004 with its first owner. 41,000 miles on the odometer.											
1982	**Quattroporte III**	(Italdesign)	301840	L	35-45.000 USD	22.862*	33.000*	29.585*	05-06-16	Greenwhich	23	Bon
Metallic silver blue with tan leather interior; since new to early 2016 owned by Ron Tonkin, owner of the Gran Turismo Ferrari dealership in Portland, Oregon. In very good condition; just over 18,000 miles covered.											
1982	**Quattroporte III**	(Italdesign)	301646	L	4-8.000 USD	6.501*	8.910*	8.051*	25-06-16	Santa Monica	2136	AA
Black with tan interior; 135,000 miles covered. From the Riverside International Automotive Museum Collection.											
1982	**Quattroporte III**	(Italdesign)	302014	L	4-8.000 USD	6.340*	8.690*	7.852*	25-06-16	Santa Monica	2140	AA
Dark red with tan interior; less than 60,000 miles covered. From the Riverside International Automotive Museum Collection.											
1980	**Quattroporte III**	(Italdesign)	AM330US0646	L	4-8.000 USD	8.026*	11.000*	9.940*	25-06-16	Santa Monica	2142	AA
Red with tan interior; from the Riverside International Automotive Museum Collection.											
1980	**Kyalami**	(Ghia)	AM1290208	L	5-10.000 USD	22.472*	30.800*	27.831*	25-06-16	Santa Monica	2027	AA
Mostly completed car; from the Riverside International Automotive Museum Collection.											
1988	**Biturbo 2.5l**		180242	R	12-15.000 GBP		NS		16-04-16	Ascot	102	Coy
Ivory with tan interior; in good overall condition. 29,700 covered since new.											
1987	**Biturbo 2.5**		180023	R	8-12.000 GBP		NS		02-07-16	Woodstock	120	Coy
Ivory; original interior.											
1990	**Spyder 2.8**	(Zagato)	331929	L	4-8.000 USD	6.742*	9.240*	8.349*	25-06-16	Santa Monica	2137	AA F471
White with grey interior; from the Riverside International Automotive Museum Collection.											
1988	**222**		HB117119	L	60-75.000 GBP		NS		01-12-15	London	316	Coy
Red with black side stripe; driven by Nick May, the car raced the 1988 British Touring Car Championship. One owner since new.											
1988	**222**		HB117119	L	40-60.000 GBP		NS		16-01-16	Birmingham	345	Coy
See lot 316 Coys 1.12.15.											
1989	**222**		118270	L	10-12.000 GBP	6.000	7.969	7.157	02-07-16	Woodstock	245	Coy
White with black leather interior; repainted about five years ago.											
1991	**Shamal**		300122	L	45-60.000 GBP	40.715	62.453	54.965	10-10-15	Ascot	166	Coy
Since 1995 with the current Italian owner.											
1994	**Shamal**		300350	L	50-70.000 EUR	44.517	70.494	61.984	01-11-15	Paris	144	Art F472
Dark blue with light beige interior; two owners and 48,269 kms covered.											
1991	**Shamal**		300122	L	45-50.000 GBP		NS		16-01-16	Birmingham	354	Coy
See lot 166 Coys 10.10.15.											

F469: 1982 Maserati Merak 2.0 (Italdesign)

F470: 1986 Maserati Quattroporte III 4.9 (Italdesign)

Year	Model	(Bodybuilder)	Chassis no.	Steering	Estimate	Hammer price £	$	€	Date	Sale Place	Lot	Auc. H.

F471: 1990 Maserati Spyder 2.8 (Zagato)

F472: 1994 Maserati Shamal

1992 Shamal — 320011 R 75-90.000 GBP — NS — 11-06-16 Brooklands 307 **His**
Black with black leather interior; described as in good overall condition (see lot 240 Coys 1.10.09 $ 32,274).

1993 Ghibli 2.8 — 400005 R 6-10.000 GBP 7.504 10.725 9.670 12-03-16 Brooklands 179 **His**
In good overall condition; automatic transmission.

1997 Ghibli Cup — 361632 L 35-45.000 EUR NS 09-07-16 Le Mans 105 **Art**
Black with black leather interior; described as in very good original condition.

1995 Ghibli Open Cup — 361220 L 60-80.000 USD 21.010* 27.500* 24.280* 20-08-16 Pebble Beach 49 **G&Co**
White with green fenders; driven by Federico D'Amore, the car placed first in the Professional Class and second overall in the 1995 Selenia Ghibli Open Cup Championship. Upgraded with the 1996 Championship specification. Since 1997 part of an important Maserati collection in the USA, the car was never driven since and requires recommissioning prior to use. **F473**

2000 3200 GT (Italdesign) — 002659 R 16-22.000 GBP 19.600 28.012 25.259 12-03-16 Brooklands 219 **His**
Silver with oxblood leather interior; 15,462 miles. Last serviced in summer 2015. Automatic transmission.

2003 Spyder Cambiocorsa — 10255 L 25-35.000 USD 23.190* 35.200* 31.328* 05-10-15 Philadelphia 243 **Bon**
Metallic red with beige leather interior; less than 19,000 miles covered. From the Evergreen Collection.

2005 Spyder Cambiocorsa 90th Anniversary — 0019294 L 35-40.000 USD 28.090* 38.500* 34.789* 25-06-16 Santa Monica 2017 **AA**
Silver with blue leather interior; less than 20,000 miles on the odometer. From the Riverside International Automotive Museum Collection.

2006 4200 GT GranSport MC Victory — 0026086 L 55-75.000 USD 42.134* 57.750* 52.183* 25-06-16 Santa Monica 2021 **AA**
One of 180 examples built; Cambiocorsa gearbox. From the Riverside International Automotive Museum Collection.

2006 4200 Spyder Gran Sport — 24460 L NA 18.142 27.500 25.113 12-12-15 Austin F177 **Mec**
Black with black interior; 26,403 original miles.

2002 4200 Spyder Cambiocorsa — 007668 L NA 14.624* 20.900* 19.138* 29-01-16 Scottsdale 914 **B/J**
Silver with tan interior; less than 50,000 miles covered since new.

2004 MC12 — 12099 L 1.800-2.200.000 USD NS 20-08-16 Monterey S130.1 **Mec**
White and blue with blue interior; 1,200 kms covered (see lot 460 RM 19.8.06 $1,072,500).

2005 MC12 — 16977 L 1.300-1.600.000 USD 1.092.520 1.430.000 1.262.547 20-08-16 Monterey 211 **RMS**
Bought new by Doug Magnon, the car was imported into the USA under the Show and Display law. Never registered for road use and only driven on tracks during associated concours and Maserati Club events. 6,200 miles covered. From the Riverside International Automotive Museum Collection. **F474**

MATFORD (F)

1939 V8 F92 A cabriolet — 6906 L 17-22.000 EUR NS 02-07-16 Lyon 365 **Agu**
Beige with maroon leatherette interior; restored in the 1980s, subsequently the car remained unused for 20 years and requires recommissioning prior to use.

MATRA (F) (1965-1983)

1968 Jet 6 — 30142 L 45-55.000 EUR NS 19-06-16 Fontainebleau 351 **Ose**
Yellow with burgundy leather interior; restored in the early 2000s.

F473: 1995 Maserati Ghibli Open Cup

F474: 2005 Maserati MC12

Year	Model	(Bodybuilder)	Chassis No.	Steering	Estimate	Hammer Price £	Hammer Price $	Hammer Price €	Date	Place	Lot	Auc. H.

MAXWELL (USA) (1904-1925)

1913 Model 25 touring — 11968 — L — 10-14.000 USD — **10.508*** — **15.950*** — **14.196*** — 05-10-15 — Philadelphia — 267 — Bon
Red with black fenders and black interior; laid up some years ago and in recent years having been made to run (see lot 316 Bonhams 12.9.10 NS).

MAYBACH (D) (1921-1941)

1933 DS-8 Zeppelin cabriolet — 1435 — L — 20-24.000.000 DKK — NS — — — 26-09-15 — Ebeltoft — 48 — Bon
Dark blue with dark blue leather interior; built with a 7-seat tourer body, the car was given as a gift of State from the Reichsmacht on behalf of Adolf Hitler to the Maharaja of Patiala. The car was registered only after WWII and remained in India for many years. In 2001-2002 circa it was acquired by German dr.Fassbender who had it fully restored and fitted with the present 2-seater cabriolet body constructed in accordance with a period Spohn design which had never been built. From the Frederiksen Collection (see lot 154 Sotheby's 9.9.97 $ 327,334).

1937 SW38 roadster — 1834 — L — 8.5-10.000.000 DKK — **736.288** — **1.117.513** — **1.002.398** — 26-09-15 — Ebeltoft — 23 — Bon
Two-tone blue with cream leather interior; built with limousine body, the car was rediscovered in Hungary some years ago and subsequently fully restored. New body in the style of Spohn. From the Frederiksen Collection.

1938 SW38 roadster (Spohn) — 2055 — L — 1.250-1.600.000 USD — **819.390** — **1.072.500** — **946.910** — 19-08-16 — Monterey — 148 — RMS **F475**
Black with oxblood leather interior; sold new in Germany, the car was imported into the USA probably in the late 1950s. After some ownership changes, the car was restored probably in the 1980s and subsequently it was part of the Richard and Linda Kughn collection also. In 1999 it was bought by the current owner.

MAZDA (J) (1960-)

1970 Cosmo Sport L10B coupé — L10B10732 — R — 130-160.000 GBP — NS — — — 07-09-15 — London — 150 — RMS
Car recently acquired by the consignor from a collection in Japan. Carefully maintained; engine overhauled 10,000 kms ago.

1968 Cosmo Sport 110S coupé — L10A10419 — R — 65-85.000 GBP — **51.750** — **79.814** — **70.835** — 12-09-15 — Goodwood — 376 — Bon
Red with vinyl and cloth interior; body repainted in 2015 (see Bonhams lots 12.3.15 NS and 273 31.5.15 NS).

1970 Cosmo Sport L10B coupé — L10B10769 — R — 80-100.000 EUR — NS — — — 09-10-15 — Zoute — 19 — Bon
White with black interior; one of three examples imported into France in 1970. Several restoration works carried out in 2015. The engine has covered 584 kms since the rebuild.

1967 Cosmo Sport 110S coupé — L10A10260 — R — 180-200.000 USD — **73.056*** — **104.500*** — **95.837*** — 28-01-16 — Scottsdale — 40 — Bon
White with black leather, checkered cloth interior; recently restored (see lot 29 Bonhams 14.8.15 NS).

1970 Cosmo Sport L10B coupé — L10B10897 — R — 100-150.000 USD — **57.725*** — **82.500*** — **75.545*** — 29-01-16 — Phoenix — 217 — RMS
White; body repainted 20 years ago circa, original interior. Recently serviced. Two owners and 56,000 kms covered.

1970 Cosmo Sport L10B coupé — L10B10769 — R — 85-135.000 EUR — **104.321** — **154.643** — **138.000** — 04-02-16 — Paris — 360 — Bon
See lot 19 Bonhams 9.10.15.

1967 Cosmo Sport 110S coupé — L10A10394 — R — 150-200.000 USD — **79.838*** — **104.500*** — **92.263*** — 20-08-16 — Pebble Beach — 34 — G&Co
Red with black interior; restored in recent years in Japan and subsequently imported into the USA.

McLAREN (GB) (1963-)

1966 M1B — 3019 — R — 240-280.000 GBP — NS — — — 24-06-16 — Goodwood — 262 — Bon
Fitted with the V8 Chevrolet engine, the car was driven by Masten Gregory during the 1966 CanAm season. Raced in recent years at historic events, it is currently fitted with an engine built by Robert Jung, who works for Edelbrock in California.

1966 M1B — 3008 — R — 200-260.000 EUR — **184.930** — **240.157** — **216.944** — 09-07-16 — Le Mans — 143 — Art **F476**
Yellow and red; the car was raced in the UK and Sweden until the early 1970s. Engine rebuilt in 2010.

2012 MP4-12C coupé — 000465 — L — 90-120.000 GBP — **79.900** — **120.961** — **110.949** — 06-12-15 — London — 030 — Bon
Graphite grey with black alcantara and carbon interior; sold new to Saudi Arabia, the car has covered 15,000 kms circa. Manufacturer's warranty valid until 2nd March 2017.

2012 MP4-12C High Sport coupé — 001505 — L — 1.300-1.600.000 USD — NS — — — 23-01-16 — Kissimmee — S148 — Mec
One of 10 examples built of the High Sport edition; finished in the F1 Vodafone Racing Team livery. Leather and alcantara interior; 203 miles covered.

2015 P1 — 000371 — L — 1.900-2.200.000 USD — **1.461.119** — **2.090.000** — **1.916.739** — 28-01-16 — Scottsdale — 12 — Bon **F477**
White; less than 300 miles covered.

2014 P1 — 000090 — L — 1.900-2.100.000 USD — **1.596.760** — **2.090.000** — **1.845.261** — 19-08-16 — Carmel — 24 — Bon
Orange, less than 1,200 miles covered, sold new to the USA.

2014 P1 — 000002 — L — 2.500-3.000.000 USD — **1.413.400** — **1.850.000** — **1.633.365** — 20-08-16 — Monterey — S81 — Mec
Exposed carbon fiber body with green accents and black leather interior; 576 miles covered. From the Modern Speed Collection.

F475: 1938 Maybach SW38 roadster (Spohn)

F476: 1966 McLaren M1B

Since 1972

Trading the finest classic cars for more than 40 years.

Take advantage of our international experience and contact us.

HEADQUARTERS
THIESEN HAMBURG GMBH
Griegstraße 73 · 22763 Hamburg-Othmarschen
+49 (0)40/45 03 43-0 · sales@thiesen-automobile.com

CLASSIC REMISE
THIESEN BERLIN GMBH
Wiebestraße 29-38 · 10553 Berlin
+49 (0)30/34 50 20 44 · larkamp@thiesen-berlin.com

www.THIESEN-AUTOMOBILE.com

Year	Model	(Bodybuilder)	Chassis no.	Steering	Estimate	£	$	€	Date	Place	Lot	Auc. H.
						Hammer price			Sale			

F477: 2015 McLaren P1

F478: 1904 Mercedes Simplex 28/32 PS rear entrance tonneau

Year	Model	(Bodybuilder)	Chassis no.	Steering	Estimate	£	$	€	Date	Place	Lot	Auc. H.
2014	P1		000091	L	NQ		NS		20-08-16	Monterey	7182	R&S
Dark orange; last serviced in May 2016.												
2015	570S		000105	L	200-250.000 USD	156.620	205.000	180.995	20-08-16	Monterey	S66	Mec
Silver with saddle leather interior; 289 miles covered.												

McLAUGHLIN-BUICK (CND) (1923-1942)

1931	Series 90 convertible		187686	L	100-140.000 USD	50.204*	77.000*	67.775*	09-10-15	Hershey	280	RMS
Cream and burgundy; restored, the car is described as in very good overall condition.												

MECCA (USA) (1915-1916)

1916	Thirty touring		441	L	15-25.000 USD	8.696*	13.200*	11.748*	05-10-15	Philadelphia	223	Bon
Black with black interior; stored from the early 1950s until a few years ago. In running order. One of the only, if not the only, surviving examples. From the Evergreen Collection.												

MERCEDES (D) (1886-1926)

1904	Simplex 28/32 PS rear entrance tonneau		2406	R	2.500-3.000.000 USD	2.143.020	2.805.000	2.476.535	19-08-16	Carmel	27	Bon
Dark blue with dark red leather interior; built with Thrupp & Maberly body, at the WWI outbreak the car was donated to the War Department for military use. After the war it was acquired by a farmer and discovered in another farm in the 1970s. Subjected to a full restoration completed in 1983, it was fitted with the present, new body and subsequently driven at several editions of the London to Brighton Run. Restored again in more recent years (see lot 631 Brooks 14.4.99 $ 429,632).												F478
1914	28/95 PS skiff		15979	R	10-13.000.000 DKK	923.191	1.401.189	1.256.852	26-09-15	Ebeltoft	28	Bon
According to the 1993 auction catalogue, the car was ordered in 1914 by Mercedes Paris but the order was cancelled due to the WWI outbreak. Today the archives of M-B Classic state the car was sold in 1920 in rolling chassis form, with the present engine no.22781, to the USA where it was fitted with the present Sindelfingen-built body. Over the years the car has had several owners and in 2003 it was exhibited at Pebble Beach in the Preservation Class. Later it was acquired by the Frederiksen Collection (see lot 79 Sotheby's 18.8.93 $ 178,500).												F479

MERCEDES-BENZ (D) (1926-)

1928	630 K La Baule Transformable (Saoutchik)		35813	L	1.000-1.300.000 USD	680.574	973.500	892.797	28-01-16	Scottsdale	34	Bon
Two-tone blueish grey with leather and cloth interior; the car's history remains vague, but the car is believed to have been in the USA and Canada for a very long time. Restored some years ago.												F480
1926	630 K La Baule Transformable (Saoutchik)		35426	L	800-1.200.000 EUR	590.455	855.403	758.403	19-03-16	Stuttgart	112	Bon
Sold new to the USA, in the 1970s the car was acquired by collector Gerald Rolph who subsequently performed a full restoration. In 2007 it was acquired by the current owner who had it refinished in the present two-tone green livery. At some point the original engine was replaced with a period 630 unit, numbered 60616, coming from a standard 24/100/140 chassis.												
1931	260 Stuttgart roadster		83411	L	100-150.000 EUR		NS		19-03-16	Stuttgart	140	Bon
Red with black wings and black interior; restored between 1998 and 2005.												
1932	200 Stuttgart cabriolet		84557	L	70-90.000 EUR	64.464	93.390	82.800	19-03-16	Stuttgart	124	Bon
Blue and ivory with blue interior; restored many years ago (see lot 109 RM 9.9.13 $ 75,529).												
1935	170 saloon		123537	L	30-45.000 USD	18.327	26.400	23.353	11-06-16	Hershey	105	TFA
Maroon with black fenders, black vinyl roof and tan leather interior; restored some years ago (see lot 114 RM 09.09.13 $ 61,477).												

F479: 1914 Mercedes 28/95 PS skiff

F480: 1928 Mercedes-Benz 630 K La Baule Transformable (Saoutchik)

Dreams become legends.
Legends become classics.

F481: 1934 Mercedes-Benz 500 K cabriolet C

F482: 1935 Mercedes-Benz 500 K cabriolet C/spezial roadster

Year	Model	(Bodybuilder)	Chassis no.	Steering	Estimate	£	$	€	Date	Place	Lot	Auc. H.
1935	**200 cabriolet C**		119787	L	150-200.000 EUR		NS		19-03-16	Stuttgart	139	**Bon**
Blue; restored in 2011.												
1934	**500 K cabriolet C**		113658	L	400-500.000 EUR	445.849	678.861	609.500	05-09-15	Chantilly	18	**Bon**
Blue and black; the car was sold new to Switzerland and imported in the USA in the late 1950s. Reimported into Europe at date unknown. Restored.												F481
1935	**500 K cabriolet C/spezial roadster**		113688	L	6.500-9.000.000 DKK	747.615	1.134.705	1.017.819	26-09-15	Ebeltoft	16	**Bon**
Black with saddle leather interior; built with cabriolet C body, the car was acquired in 2008 by the German restorer Franz Prahl who over the next three years fitted it with the present Spezial Roadster replica body. From the Frederiksen Collection.												F482
1935	**500 K cabriolet C**		113715	L	800-1.200.000 EUR		NS		19-03-16	Stuttgart	121	**Bon**
Two-tone red with beige interior; restored.												
1936	**500 K Sport Roadster**		130857	R	3.500-4.500.000 EUR		NS		19-03-16	Stuttgart	132	**Bon**
Red with beige leather interior; restored at unspecified date. Sold new to the USA, subsequently the car has had several owners in Europe and the USA.												
1935	**500 K cabriolet**	(Saoutchik)	123696	R	6.000-7.000.000 EUR		NS		19-03-16	Stuttgart	145	**Bon**
Black and silver with beige interior; in rolling chassis form, the car was exhibited by Mercedes-Benz at the 1935 Paris Motor Show. Acquired by Charles Crocker, it was subsequently bodied by Saoutchik and then imported into the USA, where it remained in the Crocker family ownership until 1959. After some ownership changes, in 1989 the car was acquired by the current owner. Restored at unspecified date.												
1935	**500 K cabriolet C**		113715	L	550-650.000 GBP		NS		24-06-16	Goodwood	277	**Bon**
See lot 121 Bonhams 19.3.16.												
1935	**500 K cabriolet A**		113717	L	2.200-2.600.000 USD		NS		19-08-16	Carmel	57	**Bon**
Sold new to a German living in London, the car has had over the years several owners in Europe and in the USA. In 1994 it was bought by the German restorer Klaus Kienle, who resold it to a customer who subsequently commissioned a full restoration. In 2014 the car was exhibited at the Villa d'Este Concours d'Elegance.												
1934	**500 K cabriolet A**		105391	L	2.000-2.500.000 USD	1.428.680	1.870.000	1.651.023	20-08-16	Monterey	242	**RMS**
Sold new to Switzerland, in 1951 the car was purchased by Walter M. Halle who imported it into the USA. In 1971 Mr. Halle gave the car to the Crawford Auto-Aviation Museum in Cleveland, Ohio, where it remained on display until 1990 when it was bought by the current owner. Restored in the late 1990s and finished in the present red livery with light tan leather interior.												F483
1939	**170 V roadster**		416603	L	200-300.000 EUR		NS		19-03-16	Stuttgart	125	**Bon**
Black and beige with red interior; in 2011 the car was restored and the engine was replaced with the present unit no.271994.												
1939	**170 V convertible saloon**		443571	L	80-90.000 USD		NS		11-06-16	Hershey	122	**TFA**
Black with tan leather interior; described as in very good overall condition (see lot 124 RM 09.09.13 $49,182).												
1938	**170 V cabriolet B**		411635	L	55-75.000 EUR	52.540	75.064	66.700	18-06-16	Wien	426	**Dor**
Beige and black with brown cloth interior; restored in Italy at unspecified date.												
1938	**230 saloon**		431443	L	60-70.000 EUR		NS		08-11-15	Lyon	252	**Ose**
Black; restored 12 years ago.												
1940	**230 cabriolet B**		446561	L	NA	103.150*	145.200*	127.776*	09-04-16	Palm Beach	420	**B/J**
Green and beige with beige leather interior; restored between 2006 and 2009.												
1936	**230 cabriolet B**		670334	L	120-140.000 EUR	71.058	100.016	88.019	09-04-16	Essen	141	**Coy**
Two-tone grey with tan leather interior; restored (see lot 133 Coys 9.8.08 $ 220,392).												F484

F483: 1934 Mercedes-Benz 500 K cabriolet A

F484: 1936 Mercedes-Benz 230 cabriolet B

Year	Model	(Bodybuilder)	Chassis no.	Steering	Estimate	Hammer price £	$	€	Date	Place	Lot	Auc. H.

F485: 1937 Mercedes-Benz 540 K Spezial Roadster

F486: 1937 Mercedes-Benz 540 K cabriolet A

1938 230 cabriolet B — 405661 — L — NQ — NS — 20-08-16 Monterey — 7112 — R&S
Blue and cream with dark red interior; restored in Germany in the 1990s. Imported into the USA in the late 1990s.

1939 540 K cabriolet A — 54008420 — L — NA — 1.039.055 — 1.485.000 — 1.359.815 — 29-01-16 Scottsdale — 1376 — B/J
Burgundy with tan leather interior; originally built with cabriolet B body, the car was fitted with the present body at unspecified date.

1937 540 K Spezial Roadster — 130894 — L — 10-13.000.000 USD — 6.927.030 — 9.900.000 — 9.065.430 — 29-01-16 Phoenix — 242 — RMS   F485
Sold new to the USA, the car remained with its first owner until the mid-1950s circa. Restored in the 1980s in the present red livery with red leather interior, since 1989 it is in the current ownership. 10,277 miles on the odometer, a figure that is believed to be original.

1937 540 K cabriolet A — 154083 — R — Refer Dpt. — 2.098.899 — 2.970.000 — 2.735.370 — 10-03-16 Amelia Island — 167 — Bon   F486
Black with parchment leather interior; sold new to the UK to a member of the Embiricos family. In the 1980s the car was imported into the USA where it was bought by Don Williams who had it restored in the present livery.

1939 540 K cabriolet A — 408371 — L — 3.000-4.000.000 USD — NS — 12-03-16 Amelia Island — 188 — RMS
Red with tan leather interior; sold new to France, the car was later imported into the USA where it was part of the collections of James Melton, Otis Chandler and William Lyon also. First restored in the early 1970s, it was restored again in the early 1990s in the present livery. For 20 years in the current ownership.

1938 540 K roadster (Lancefield) — 169317 — R — 2.700-3.500.000 EUR — NS — 19-03-16 Stuttgart — 130 — Bon
One-off finished in red with black wings; in very good overall condition.

1939 540 K cabriolet A — 408388 — L — 2.000-2.600.000 EUR — NS — 19-03-16 Stuttgart — 141 — Bon
Black with black leather interior; an older restoration, the car is described as still in good overall condition.

1937 540 K cabriolet A — 154146 — L — Refer Dpt. — NS — 05-06-16 Greenwhich — 31 — Bon
Burgundy with beige leather interior; sold new in Germany, the car was later imported into the USA by its first owner. Following some ownership changes, in 1996 it was reimported into Germany where the engine was rebuilt. In the mid-2000s it was imported again in the USA and later subjected to a full restoration completed in 2014 (see lots 121 Coys 12.5.12 NS and 139 RM 15.1.15 NS).

1938 540 K cabriolet (Norrmalm) — 169389 — L — 950-1.300.000 USD — NS — 11-06-16 Hershey — 131 — TFA
Black with red interior; the car was sold new to Sweden where it was bodied. Until 1955 with its first owner, in 1964 it was imported into the USA. From 1991 to 2001 it was in Japan, and since 2001 is part of the JWR Collection in the USA.

1937 540 K cabriolet C — 154062 — R — 1.200-1.400.000 USD — 819.390 — 1.072.500 — 946.910 — 21-08-16 Pebble Beach — 150 — G&Co
Red with tan interior; sold new to a British customer by the Mercedes-Benz dealership in Brussels, the car was rediscovered in the USA in the mid-1970s. In the 1980s it was bought by the Imperial Palace Collection, Las Vegas, and then sold to Japan. In the early 2000s it was reimported into the USA. Described as in good driving order.

1937 320N cabriolet A — 172289 — L — 1.900-2.500.000 DKK — 356.816 — 541.564 — 485.777 — 26-09-15 Ebeltoft — 3 — Bon   F487
Silver with saddle leather interior; discovered in Russia about 15 years ago and subsequently restored. New body; with hardtop. From the Frederiksen Collection.

1938 320 cabriolet A — 420976 — L — Refer Dpt. — NS — 26-09-15 Frankfurt — 154 — Coy
Red with tan interior; fully restored at unspecified date.

1938 320 cabriolet A — 191150 — L — 600-700.000 USD — NS — 10-03-16 Amelia Island — 172 — Bon
Dark blue with grey leather interior; in 2007 the car was reimported into Germany where it was restored to concours condition before to be re-exported to the USA (see lot 252 Bonhams 15.8.14 $ 517,000).

1938 320 cabriolet B — 435053 — L — 350-450.000 EUR — NS — 19-03-16 Stuttgart — 120 — Bon
Blue with beige interior; restored in 2010. Recent works to the engine and gearbox.

1951 170 Da convertible saloon — 13013951 — L — 40-50.000 USD — 19.802* — 30.250* — 26.880* — 08-10-15 Hershey — 150 — RMS   F488
Green; one of the examples built for the German Police. Imported into the USA at unspecified date. For 30 years in the current ownership. Described as in good driving order.

1951 170 S saloon — 1360400901351 — L — 24-28.000 GBP — 25.760 — 36.816 — 33.197 — 12-03-16 Brooklands — 195 — His
Maroon with grey cloth interior; restored at unspecified date.

1951 170 S saloon — 13604019873 — L — 40-50.000 EUR — NS — 19-03-16 Stuttgart — 133 — Bon
Black with original cloth interior; partially restored. Engine replaced at unspecified date.

1954 170 SD delivery truck — 1361854503673 — L — 45-50.000 GBP — 36.800 — 53.312 — 47.266 — 20-03-16 Goodwood — 83 — Bon
Blue and white; fully restored. According to the sale catalogue the car was used for the delivery of spare parts by the Juan Manuel Fangio's Mercedes-Benz dealership in Argentina (see lot 105 Silverstone Auctions 4.9.14 NS).

1951 170 DA Kombi (Lueg) — 1361710629651 — L — 60-80.000 EUR — 54.719 — 71.979 — 64.520 — 06-08-16 Schloss Dyck — 121 — Coy
Beige with black wings and brown leather interior; recently restored.

1950 170 S cabriolet B — 13604312365 — L — 90-120.000 EUR — NS — 19-03-16 Stuttgart — 107 — Bon
Black with beige interior; restored circa 10 years ago.

1950 170 S cabriolet A — 13692210511 — L — 120-160.000 EUR — NS — 19-03-16 Stuttgart — 149 — Bon
Metallic blue with beige interior; restored in 2010.

Year	Model	(Bodybuilder)	Chassis no.	Steering	Estimate	£	$	€	Date	Place	Lot	Auc. H.

F487: 1937 Mercedes-Benz 320N cabriolet A

F488: 1951 Mercedes-Benz 170 Da convertible saloon

Year	Model	(Bodybuilder)	Chassis no.	Steering	Estimate	£	$	€	Date	Place	Lot	Auc. H.
1950	170 S cabriolet B		13604311895	L	100-120.000 EUR	74.649	98.194	88.019	06-08-16	Schloss Dyck	129	Coy
	Burgundy with cream leather interior; some restoration works carried out a few years ago.											
1953	220 saloon		1870110223453	L	60-90.000 USD	46.141*	66.000*	60.529*	28-01-16	Scottsdale	103	Bon F489
	Blue with grey fenders and grey leather interior; two registered owners and 63,000 kms covered. Subjected to a long restoration completed in 2012.											
1952	220 cabriolet A		1870120563052	L	90-130.000 EUR	109.862	157.457	144.271	16-01-16	Maastricht	428	Coy
	Cream with burgundy interior; in good condition (see lot 125 Coys 11.8.12 NS).											
1952	220 cabriolet A		1870120277952	L	105-125.000 EUR	92.219	133.600	118.450	19-03-16	Stuttgart	105	Bon
	Red with tan leather interior; cosmetically restored (see lot 103 RM 9.9.13 $ 107,146).											
1953	220 cabriolet A		1870120213453	L	130-160.000 EUR	80.580	116.738	103.500	19-03-16	Stuttgart	127	Bon
	White with red interior; body repainted in recent years.											
1952	220 cabriolet A		1870120503352	L	125-175.000 USD	96.115	126.500	113.825	30-07-16	Plymouth	141	RMS
	Ivory with navy blue leather interior; restored in the early 2000s (see lot 34 Christie's 17.8.03 $58,750).											
1952	220 cabriolet A		0598752	L	110-130.000 EUR	87.935	115.671	103.685	06-08-16	Schloss Dyck	157	Coy
	Maroon with black leather interior; described as in very good original condition. For 64 years with its first two owners.											
1952	220 cabriolet A "Rose Garden"		1870120963952	L	200-250.000 USD	142.868*	187.000*	165.102*	20-08-16	Monterey	225	RMS F490
	One of the cars painted by artist Hiro Yamagata with birds and flowers.											
1952	300 saloon		1860110183352	L	65-100.000 EUR	42.286	60.605	55.530	16-01-16	Maastricht	439	Coy
	Black with grey leather interior; described as in excellent overall condition (see lot 146 Coys 11.8.12 NS).											
1958	300 saloon		1890108501107	L	55-75.000 EUR	33.289	47.711	43.715	16-01-16	Maastricht	451	Coy
	Blue with white roof and red leather interior; restored 15 years ago.											
1956	300c station wagon	(Binz)	1860026500263	L	375-425.000 USD	342.503	489.500	448.235	29-01-16	Scottsdale	17	G&Co
	Midnight blue with red leather interior; one-off commissioned by Mrs Caroline Ryan Foulke, New York, and originally finished in medium grey. Partially restored at unspecified date, in 2010 the car was acquired by the current owner and subjected to further restoration works (see lot 40 Gooding 12.3.10 $ 242,000).											
1957	300d saloon		1890107500062	L	70-90.000 EUR		NS		19-03-16	Stuttgart	150	Bon
	Black with grey cloth interior; de-registered in 1968, the car was stored until a few years ago when it was acquired by the current, second owner and recommissioned.											
1952	300 saloon		1860110183352	L	55-70.000 EUR	41.862	58.922	51.854	09-04-16	Essen	144	Coy
	See lot 439 Coys 16.1.16.											
1962	300d saloon		18901012003041	L	70-90.000 USD		NS		30-07-16	Plymouth	167	RMS
	Black with original red leather interior; for 52 years with the previous owner, the car was bought two years ago by the current, third owner. Subsequently the body was repainted and the mechanicals were refreshed.											
1958	300d saloon		30008500158	L	NQ	37.520*	49.106*	43.354*	20-08-16	Brooklands	239	His
	Silver and maroon with cream leather interior; some restoration works carried out in the early 1990s. With power steering (see lots H & H 24 28.7.99 $30,819, Coys 184 Coys 16.7.11 NS and 114 8.10.11 NS, and Historics 276 18.2.12 NS).											
1956	300c saloon		6500189	L	NQ	34.456	45.100	39.819	20-08-16	Monterey	7155	R&S
	Described as in original condition; 61,650 miles covered; single-family car.											

F489: 1953 Mercedes-Benz 220 saloon

F490: 1952 Mercedes-Benz 220 cabriolet A "Rose Garden"

Year	Model	(Bodybuilder)	Chassis no.	Steering	Estimate	Hammer Price £	Hammer Price $	Hammer Price €	Date	Place	Lot	Auc. H.
1956	300d cabriolet		1860336500337	L	140-200.000 EUR	118.137	182.442	160.600	17-10-15	Salzburg	315	Dor
{Light grey with original red leather interior; in original condition except for the paintwork redone many years ago. Since 1966 in the its second ownership. Automatic transmission.}
| 1952 | 300d cabriolet | | 1860140115052 | L | 250-300.000 USD | | NS | | 28-01-16 | Phoenix | 154 | RMS |
{Green with green leather interior; restored many years ago. Brakes recently rebuilt (see lot 85 RM 21.9.02 $ 107,800).}
| 1955 | 300b cabriolet | | 5500515 | L | 100-150.000 EUR | 137.631* | 200.292* | 178.800* | 05-02-16 | Paris | 176 | Art F491 |
{White with red leather interior; sold new to the USA, the car remained in the same family ownership until 2013. Unused for 20 years, it was recommissioned and in 2013 imported into France (see lot 369 Artcurial 7.2.14 $ 153,712).}
| 1953 | 300d cabriolet | | 186160001553 | L | 200-300.000 EUR | 179.067 | 259.417 | 230.000 | 19-03-16 | Stuttgart | 137 | Bon |
{Red with beige interior; restored in 2015.}
| 1955 | 300 Sc coupé | | 1880145500025 | L | 600-800.000 USD | | NS | | 10-12-15 | New York | 208 | RMS |
{Black; fully restored in the USA in the 1990s, the car is described as still in very good overall condition.}
| 1956 | 300 Sc coupé | | 1880145500029 | L | 650-750.000 USD | | NS | | 28-01-16 | Scottsdale | 70 | Bon |
{Light metallic burgundy with tan leather interior; sold new to the USA and restored in the 2000s (see Gooding lots 52 17.1.14 $ 550,000 and 66 15.8.15 $ 671,000).}
| 1957 | 300 Sc coupé | | 1880147500024 | L | 450-550.000 EUR | 375.445 | 544.901 | 498.400 | 03-02-16 | Paris | 110 | RMS F492 |
{Black with cream leather interior; restored at unspecified date (see lot 116 RM 18.1.13 $ 275,000).}
| 1954 | 300 S coupé | | 1880113500356 | L | 400-500.000 USD | 303.174 | 429.000 | 395.109 | 10-03-16 | Amelia Island | 145 | Bon |
{Beige grey with light green leather interior; restored approximately 25 years ago to its original colours.}
| 1956 | 300 Sc coupé | | 1880145500029 | L | 650-700.000 USD | | NS | | 20-08-16 | Monterey | S159 | Mec |
{See lot 70 Bonhams 28.1.16.}
| 1957 | 300 Sc cabriolet | | 1880136500145 | L | 1.000-1.300.000 USD | | NS | | 29-01-16 | Phoenix | 246 | RMS |
{Black with red leather interior; recently restored in California.}
| 1957 | 300 Sc cabriolet | | 1880136500105 | L | 750-900.000 USD | 617.779 | 894.989 | 793.500 | 19-03-16 | Stuttgart | 131 | Bon F493 |
{Cream with beige leather interior; restored circa 20 years ago.}
| 1954 | 300 S cabriolet | | 1880103500280 | L | NQ | | NS | | 20-08-16 | Monterey | 7096 | R&S |
{Black with dark red leather interior; restored many years ago (see lot 125 RM 9.9.13 $439,124).}
| 1956 | 300 Sc roadster | | 1880156500069 | L | 1.200-1.400.000 USD | 709.030 | 1.072.500 | 980.050 | 10-12-15 | New York | 220 | RMS F494 |
{Dark blue with medium brown leather interior; restored in the USA at unspecified date, the car is described as in very good overall condition.}
| 1956 | 300 Sc roadster | | 1880155500016 | L | 950-1.150.000 USD | | NS | | 10-03-16 | Amelia Island | 153 | Bon |
{Originally finished in white, the car was sold new to the USA. Approximately 20 years ago, it was fully restored and finished in the present black livery with black interior.}
| 1953 | 300 S roadster | | 1880120007153 | L | 750-900.000 EUR | | NS | | 19-03-16 | Stuttgart | 111 | Bon |
{Dark green with red-brown leather interior; sold new to the USA. The car has covered less than 50 miles since a full restoration carried out by Kienle in Germany.}
| 1952 | 300 S roadster | | 1880120011852 | L | 475-525.000 USD | 353.593 | 506.000 | 442.598 | 02-04-16 | Ft.Lauderdale | 524 | AA |
{Cream with tan leather interior.}
| 1953 | 300 S roadster | | 1880120009253 | L | 520-680.000 EUR | 469.942 | 671.414 | 596.600 | 18-06-16 | Wien | 433 | Dor |
{Black with brown leather interior; since 1982 with the current, German owner. Restored circa 20 years ago.}
| 1955 | 220a saloon | | 1800105518432 | L | 35-45.000 EUR | 22.383* | 32.427* | 28.750* | 19-03-16 | Stuttgart | 102 | Bon F495 |
{Medium blue with grey interior; restored in 1992-93. Fitted with a 220 S engine.}
| 1955 | 300 SL gullwing | | 1980405500129 | L | 925-1.125.000 GBP | | NS | | 28-11-15 | Weybridge | 282 | His |
{Finished in silver with red interior, the car was sold new in Germany and shortly after resold to the USA to Harley Earl. After some ownership changes, it was restored between 1990 and 1994 and finished in the present red livery with tan interior. Later it was imported into Japan where it was on display in a museum. Currently registered in the UK; engine rebuilt 1,000 kms ago.}
| 1955 | 300 SL gullwing | | 1980405500810 | L | 1.000-1.300.000 GBP | | NS | | 06-12-15 | London | 011 | Bon |
{Silver grey with blue leather and Rudge-Withworth centre-lock steel wheels; sold new to the UK, since 1973 the car is in the current ownership. It has covered 44,000 miles and is described as in original condition except for the paintwork redone at unspecified date. Last serviced in 2011.}
| 1955 | 300 SL gullwing | | 1980405500640 | L | 5-7.000.000 USD | | NS | | 10-12-15 | New York | 223 | RMS |
{One of four series cars prepared by the factory's Racing Dpt. Upgrades include an NSL engine with revised camshaft profile, Rudge knock-off wheels, competition-type fuel-injection pump and special ventilated drum brakes. Used for training and competition by the factory, in September 1956 it was sold to Hans Hommel who entered it at the Tour de France where it placed 2nd overall driven by Stirling Moss and Georges Houel. Bought in 1966 by the current owner's father, it remained stored for 40 years and was restored between 2008 and 2011 to 1956 TdF specification.}
| 1955 | 300 SL gullwing | | 1980405500548 | L | 1.100-1.500.000 USD | 807.461 | 1.155.000 | 1.059.251 | 28-01-16 | Phoenix | 117 | RMS |
{Silver with original red leather interior; the body, originally ivory, was repainted many years ago.}

F491: 1955 Mercedes-Benz 300b cabriolet

F492: 1957 Mercedes-Benz 300 Sc coupé

F493: 1957 Mercedes-Benz 300 Sc cabriolet

F494: 1956 Mercedes-Benz 300 Sc roadster

Year	Model	(Bodybuilder)	Chassis no.	Steering	Estimate	£	$	€	Date	Place	Lot	Auc. H.
1954	**300 SL gullwing**		1980404500101	L	1.200-1.400.000 USD		NS		29-01-16	Scottsdale	13	**G&Co**

Originally finished in black with red interior, the car was sold new to the USA. Since 1989 in the same family ownership, the car was later restored and finished in the present silver livery with blue interior. Unused since the mid-1990s, it was started in December 2015 and requires recommissioning prior to road use.

| 1955 | **300 SL gullwing** | | 1980405500272 | L | 1.000-1.400.000 EUR | 885.881 | 1.285.721 | 1.176.000 | 03-02-16 | Paris | 151 | **RMS** |

White with red leather interior; sold new to the USA, in the early 1990s the car was reimported into Europe. In 1993 and 1999 it was driven at the Mille Miglia Storica. Following a period of display in the previous owner's collection, it has been recently recommissioned. **F496**

| 1955 | **300 SL gullwing** | | 1980405500587 | L | 900-1.200.000 USD | 637.443 | 902.000 | 830.742 | 10-03-16 | Amelia Island | 120 | **Bon** |

Originally finished in anthracite grey with grey leather interior, the car was sold new to the USA. Later the body was repainted in red and the interior redone in tan leather. In good driving order. Since 1999 in the Wade Carter Collection (see lot 709 Barrett-Jackson 21.1.99 $ 195,300).

| 1955 | **300 SL gullwing** | | 1980405500397 | L | 1.300-1.500.000 USD | 884.994 | 1.265.000 | 1.140.651 | 12-03-16 | Amelia Island | 161 | **RMS** |

Cream with red leather interior; sold new to the USA. In 2007 circa the car was fully restored in the USA and in 2011 it received further mechanical restoration in Germany.

| 1955 | **300 SL gullwing** | | 1980405500037 | L | 800-1.000.000 GBP | 841.500 | 1.219.081 | 1.080.823 | 20-03-16 | Goodwood | 16 | **Bon** |

Silver with blue leather and blue-checked cloth interior; sold new to the UK, the car was restored between 1997 and 2000. 60,000 miles on the odometer. Since 1967 in the Kingsley Curtis Collection.

| 1955 | **300 SL gullwing** | | 1980405500799 | L | 1.100-1.300.000 EUR | 970.299 | 1.398.074 | 1.232.000 | 14-05-16 | Monaco | 224 | **RMS** |

Silver metallic with dark blue interior; since new in the Agusta family ownership in Italy, over the years the car has been always mechanically maintained as necessary and refinished in its original combination of colour. At unspecified date it was upgraded with front disc brakes.

| 1954 | **300 SL gullwing** | | 1980404500120 | L | 1.100-1.500.000 USD | 798.380 | 1.045.000 | 922.631 | 19-08-16 | Monterey | 128 | **RMS** |

Originally finished in light metallic blue, the car was sold new to the USA to George Tilp, who in 1956 resold it to Jim Hall, who had it refinished in the present red livery with tan vinyl interior. Recently the car has been serviced and returned to running order, but will benefit from further maintenance prior to extended driving use. From the Jim Hall Collection.

| 1955 | **300 SL gullwing** | | 1980405500654 | L | 1.400-1.600.000 USD | 1.092.520 | 1.430.000 | 1.262.547 | 20-08-16 | Pebble Beach | 14 | **G&Co** |

Originally finished in white with black interior, the car was sold new to the USA. In the early 1990s it was fully restored and finished in the present blue livery with grey leather interior (see lot 151 Gooding & Company 19.8.12 $1,127,500).

| 1955 | **300 SL gullwing** | | 1980405500548 | L | NQ | 882.420 | 1.155.000 | 1.019.750 | 20-08-16 | Monterey | 7200 | **R&S** |

See lot 117 RM/Sotheby's 28.1.16.

| 1957 | **300 SL Roadster** | | 1980427500188 | L | 650-850.000 GBP | | NS | | 07-09-15 | London | 115 | **RMS** |

Dark blue with red leather interior; originally finished in ivory with black leather interior, the car was sold new to Portugal. Later it was imported into the USA and then into Italy, where it was restored in 2006.

| 1961 | **300 SL Roadster** | | 19804210002973 | L | 10-15.000.000 HKD | | NS | | 06-10-15 | Hong Kong | 200 | **Art** |

Gunmetal grey with brown leather interior; in the same family ownership in Germany from 1965 to 2013. Interior retrimmed in 1982; body repainted and engine rebuilt in 1989 circa. Recently serviced (see lot 127 Bonhams 28.3.15 $ 1,092,500).

| 1958 | **300 SL Roadster** | | 1980427500641 | L | 800-1.000.000 EUR | 594.009 | 940.638 | 827.080 | 01-11-15 | Paris | 157 | **Art** |

Metallic grey with dark green leather interior; the car was acquired in the USA in 1989 by the current owner and subseuqently it was subjected in France to a full restoration completed 25 years ago. 6,000 km circa covered since.

| 1962 | **300 SL Roadster** | | 19804210003091 | L | 1.500-1.800.000 USD | 1.038.164 | 1.485.000 | 1.361.894 | 28-01-16 | Scottsdale | 21 | **Bon** |

Red with black interior; restored in the 2000s. Recent service and cosmetic freshening. With hardtop (see lot 111 Christie's 20.8.00 NS).

F495: 1955 Mercedes-Benz 220a saloon

F496: 1955 Mercedes-Benz 300 SL gullwing

Year	Model	(Bodybuilder)	Chassis no.	Steering	Estimate	Hammer Price £	Hammer Price $	Hammer Price €	Date	Place	Lot	Auc. H.
1957	**300 SL Roadster**		1980427500128	L	1.000-1.200.000 USD	653.659	935.000	857.489	28-01-16	Phoenix	158	RMS
Silver with red leather interior; body and interior restored many years ago, engine rebuilt in more recent years. With hardtop.											
1957	**300 SL Roadster**		1980427500282	L	900-1.100.000 USD	554.162	792.000	725.234	29-01-16	Scottsdale	59	G&Co
Originally finished in graphite grey with medium grey leather interior, the car was sold new to the USA and used until 1986 when it was put in storage. At unspecified date the body was repainted in the present silver livery and the interior were retrimmed in black vinyl.											
1958	**300 SL Roadster**		1980428500154	L	1.250-1.500.000 USD	885.121	1.265.000	1.158.361	29-01-16	Phoenix	239	RMS
Anthracite grey with grey leather interior; sold new to the UK and later imported into the USA. Several mechanical works carried out in 2013; body repainted and interior retrimmed more recently (see lot S737 Russo & Steele 19.1.13 $ 727,100).											
1959	**300 SL Roadster**		198042109500070	L	1.250-1.500.000 USD	808.154	1.155.000	1.057.634	30-01-16	Scottsdale	131	G&Co F497
Medium blue with blue leather interior; sold new to the USA, the car was acquired in 1973 by Liong Liem, Connecticut, who retained it for over 40 years and had it restored between 1986 and 1992. Described as still in good overall condition. With hardtop.											
1957	**300 SL Roadster**		1980427500378	L	1.000-1.300.000 USD		NS		12-03-16	Amelia Island	138	RMS
Silver with deep red leather interior; restored in 2002. For 42 years in the current ownership.											
1961	**300 SL Roadster**		19804210002973	L	1.200-1.500.000 EUR		NS		19-03-16	Stuttgart	144	Bon
See lot 200 Artcurial 6.10.15 NS.											
1961	**300 SL Roadster**		19804210002781	L	700-1.100.000 EUR	812.877	1.055.635	953.600	09-07-16	Le Mans	164	Art
Black with beige leather interior; sold new to the USA, the car was reimported into Germany in the 1980s and fully restored. With hardtop (see lot 232 Artcurial 5.7.14 $1,515,877).											
1957	**300 SL Roadster**		1980427500251	L	1.150-1.350.000 USD		NS		19-08-16	Carmel	51	Bon
Originally finished in red, the car was sold new to the USA. Stored from the late 1990s to 2012, it has been subsequently fully restored over a two and half years period and finished in the present metallic anthracite grey livery with red leather interior.											
1961	**300 SL Roadster**		19804210002756	L	1.250-1.500.000 USD		NS		19-08-16	Monterey	133	RMS
Yellow with dark green interior; retained by the factory when new for promotional purpose, the car was sold in 1963 to its first USA private owner. Purchased in 2013 by the current owner and subsequently fully restored.											
1957	**300 SL Roadster**		1980427500089	L	1.300-1.650.000 USD	1.008.480	1.320.000	1.165.428	20-08-16	Monterey	228	RMS
Originally finished in black with red leather interior, the car was sold new to the USA. Discovered in the early 2000s, it was fully restored between 2003 and 2005 and finished in the present blue livery with parchment leather interior (see lot 172 RM 18.1.08 $742,500).											
1960	**300 SL Roadster**		19804210002507	L	1.100-1.300.000 USD	945.450	1.237.500	1.092.589	21-08-16	Pebble Beach	153	G&Co
White with blue leather interior; the car has covered less than 500 miles since the restoration completed in 2006. Sold new to the USA, it has had four owners.											
1960	**190 SL**		12104210017844	L	70-85.000 GBP	76.500	116.487	104.583	04-09-15	Woodstock	234	SiC
Silver with red interior; in good overall condition.											
1959	**190 SL**		1210407502462	L	NA	97.535	148.500	133.338	05-09-15	Auburn	5072	AA
Black; restored about 15 years ago. With an unrestored hardtop.											
1961	**190 SL**		12104010022284	L	110-150.000 GBP		NS		07-09-15	London	169	RMS
White with red interior; 800 kms covered since a full restoration. Three owners since new.											
1960	**190 SL**		12104210017217	L	110-130.000 EUR		NS		26-09-15	Frankfurt	118	Coy
White with red leather interior; recently restored.											
1960	**190 SL**		12104010016852	L	120-140.000 EUR		NS		26-09-15	Frankfurt	120	Coy
Black with black hardtop and red interior; restored (see lot 112 Coys 18.4.15 $ 142,377).											
1961	**190 SL**		12104010016740	L	85-100.000 EUR	57.997	88.020	78.935	26-09-15	Frankfurt	123	Coy
White with black interior; engine recently refreshed.											
1959	**190 SL**		121042109500718	L	60-70.000 GBP		NS		10-10-15	Ascot	150	Coy
Black with brown leather interior; described as in good original condition.											
1961	**190 SL**		12104210020516	L	70-90.000 EUR	47.085	74.561	65.560	01-11-15	Paris	154	Art
Red with beige interior; mechanicals restored in the 1980s, body and interior restored in more recent years.											
1962	**190 SL**		1210422002440	R	95-115.000 GBP	95.625	145.580	135.252	14-11-15	Birmingham	631	SiC
White with red leather interior; some restoration works carried out prior to 2004 when the car was acquired by the current owner. Interior retrimmed about 10 years ago; body repainted again in recent times. The hardtop requires some attention.											
1960	**190 SL**		019958	L	90-110.000 GBP		NS		09-12-15	Chateau Impney	70	H&H
Black with red interior; imported into the UK from the USA in 2014 and subsequently restored. With hardtop (see lot 132 Coys 19.4.15 $ 151,396).											
1959	**190 SL**		121040109501948	L	NA	69.269	105.000	95.886	12-12-15	Austin	S22	Mec
Dark grey with maroon interior; restoration completed in 2000.											
1961	**190 SL**		12104010016740	L	85-110.000 EUR	62.058	88.944	81.495	16-01-16	Maastricht	420	Coy
See lot 123 Coys 26.9.15.											
1962	**190 SL**		12104010023541	L	140-160.000 USD	80.746*	115.500*	105.925*	28-01-16	Scottsdale	19	Bon
Light grey with black leather interior; in the same family ownership from 1965 to 2012. Restored; engine replaced. With hardtop.											
1963	**190 SL**		024539	L	NA	100.057*	143.000*	130.945*	29-01-16	Scottsdale	1375.1	B/J
Black with red interior; restoration completed in 2012 (see lot 100 Bonhams 14.8.15 $ 107,800).											
1962	**190 SL**		1210421000593	L	NA	111.602*	159.500*	146.054*	29-01-16	Scottsdale	1430	B/J
Light blue with red leather interior; restored. Two-family-owned since new.											
1960	**190 SL**		12104210015076	L	50-70.000 USD	51.953*	74.250*	67.991*	29-01-16	Scottsdale	60	G&Co
Black with white hardtop and red interior; used until the mid-1990s when it was put in storage. For restoration or preservation.											
1961	**190 SL**		12104210020375	L	150-200.000 USD	115.451*	165.000*	151.091*	29-01-16	Phoenix	273	RMS F498
Grey/blue with natural leather interior; fully restored 10 years ago.											
1961	**190 SL**		12104010020825	L	120-140.000 EUR	84.370*	122.450*	112.000*	03-02-16	Paris	156	RMS
Silver with red interior; 500 kms covered since the restoration.											

Year	Model	(Bodybuilder)	Chassis no.	Steering	Estimate	Hammer price £	$	€	Date	Place	Lot	Auc. H.
1958	**190 SL**		1210408501593	L	120-160.000 EUR		NS		04-02-16	Paris	379	Bon
Blue with blue interior; restoration completed in 2010 (see lot 57 Artcurial 22.6.15 NS).											
1956	**190 SL**		1210426504019	L	75-85.000 GBP	81.320	115.548	104.781	08-03-16	London	135	Coy
Ivory with dark red interior; restored in 2013.											
1963	**190 SL**		121042109500296	L	250-350.000 USD		NS		10-03-16	Amelia Island	126	Bon
Dark grey with light green leather interior; the car has covered 200 miles circa since a full restoration.											
1958	**190 SL**		1210427503297	L	140-160.000 USD	79.292*	112.200*	103.336*	10-03-16	Amelia Island	184	Bon
Black with bamboo leather interior; recent full restoration.											
1957	**190 SL**		1210427501199	L	190-240.000 USD	134.673*	192.500*	173.577*	11-03-16	Amelia Island	57	G&Co
White with dark red interior; concours-quality restoration completed in 2015 in Germany.											
1961	**190 SL**		12104010022880	L	135-150.000 EUR	114.603	166.027	147.200	19-03-16	Stuttgart	104	Bon
Pastel blue with dark blue leather interior; fully restored in the USA and reimported into Germany three years ago.											
1958	**190 SL**		1210407503097	L	85-125.000 EUR	80.580	116.738	103.500	19-03-16	Stuttgart	128	Bon
Silver with blue interior; acquired in 2008 by the present, second owner and subsequently restored.											
1962	**190 SL**		1210421000862	L	140-165.000 USD	103.772	148.500	129.893	02-04-16	Ft.Lauderdale	482	AA
Blue with black interior; two previous long time owners. Just under 22,000 miles on the odometer.											
1960	**190 SL**		019958	L	110-130.000 EUR	88.222	124.175	109.280	09-04-16	Essen	150	Coy
See lot 70 H&H 9.12.15.											
1961	**190 SL**		12104010016740	L	95-110.000 GBP	75.000	106.350	94.245	16-04-16	Ascot	124	Coy
See lot 420 Coys 16.1.16.											
1958	**190 SL**		1210427503150	L	120-140.000 EUR	130.266	187.696	165.400	14-05-16	Monaco	116	Coy
Metallic blue with cognac leather interior; a few hundreds kms covered since a recent full restoration.											
1958	**190 SL**		1210408501593	L	110-120.000 EUR	92.336	133.044	117.240	14-05-16	Monaco	144	Coy
See lot 379 Bonhams 4.2.16.											
1958	**190 SL**		1210408500089	L	130-150.000 EUR	114.672*	165.227*	145.600*	14-05-16	Monaco	236	RMS
Black with red interior; recently restored in Germany.											
1962	**190 SL**		7501152	R	70-80.000 GBP	101.813	148.321	132.204	20-05-16	Silverstone	342	SiC
Silver with dark blue leather interior; restored in 1986, the car is described as still in good overall condition. Engine and gearbox overhauled in 1990 (see lot 375 Historics 1.6.13 $ 95,560).											
1959	**190 SL**		12104010014685	L	150-200.000 USD	133.364	192.500	172.576	05-06-16	Greenwhich	58	Bon
Black with tan leather interior; acquired in 2008 by the current owner and fully restored between 2013 and 2015. The car is offered together with a 2013 Teardrop trailer from Mini Tears of Lakehead, California, modified at the rear with 190 SL style fenders by the same restorer of the car.											
1962	**190 SL**		123104210024577	L	95-110.000 GBP	100.800	145.182	128.439	11-06-16	Brooklands	271	His
Light metallic blue with cream leather interior; fully restored.											
1960	**190 SL**		12104220017542	R	90-120.000 GBP	101.180	138.657	125.291	24-06-16	Goodwood	281	Bon
White with red leather interior and red hardtop; the car remained from 1971 to 2011 with the same owner who had it restored.											
1959	**190 SL**		121040109500769	L	150-180.000 EUR	132.787	176.378	158.400	02-07-16	Lyon	350	Agu
Black with beige interior; described as in in very good original, unrestored condition. Two owners and 77,190 kms covered.											
1957	**190 SL**		1210407501884	L	100-130.000 EUR	86.368	112.161	101.320	09-07-16	Le Mans	202	Art
Silver with red interior; restoration recently completed.											
1957	**190 SL**		1210427501407	L	140-180.000 USD	117.009	154.000	138.569	30-07-16	Plymouth	161	RMS
Grey with black interior; restoration recently completed. With hardtop.											
1961	**190 SL**		12104210020091	L	65-80.000 EUR	53.770	70.730	63.401	06-08-16	Schloss Dyck	132	Coy
White with blue interior; 31,174 miles on the odometer. Reimported in 2015 into Europe from the USA where it had remained for 59 years in the same ownership.											
1957	**190 SL**		1210407502449	L	125-150.000 USD	88.242*	115.500*	101.975*	19-08-16	Carmel	96	Bon
White with black interior; paintwork and interior redone at unspecified date. Engine recently detailed.											
1961	**190 SL**		12104210016932	L	125-150.000 USD	99.320*	130.000*	114.777*	19-08-16	Monterey	F94	Mec
Black with red leather interior; one owner until 2012. Overhauled in 2015.											
1955	**190 SL**		1210425500064	L	200-250.000 USD		WD		19-08-16	Monterey	102	RMS
Silver with light green interior; restoration supervised by Paul Bracq in France. With hardtop. Unused since the restoration.											

F497: 1957 Mercedes-Benz 300 SL Roadster

F498: 1961 Mercedes-Benz 190 SL

Year	Model	(Bodybuilder)	Chassis No.	Steering	Estimate	Hammer Price £	$	€	Date	Place	Lot	Auc. H.
1963	190 SL		1210401001346	L	80-100.000 GBP		NS		20-08-16	Brooklands	292	His
Black with red interior; restored in 2014.												
1959	220 SE saloon		128010109500879	L	NA	33.234	50.600	45.434	05-09-15	Auburn	3106	AA
Burgundy with tan leather interior; restored.												
1958	220 S saloon		180010Z8502794	R	35-45.000 GBP	39.880	57.156	52.366	16-01-16	Birmingham	331	Coy
Silver with dark blue roof; in 2008 prepared for historic racing and fitted with a later W123 2.8-litre engine.												
1959	220 S saloon		180010609506532	R	14-18.000 GBP	14.560	19.056	16.824	20-08-16	Brooklands	302	His
Black with blue velour interior; in good overall condition.												
1960	220 SE cabriolet		12803020003093	R	130-160.000 GBP		NS		04-09-15	Woodstock	240	SiC
Cream and chocolate; fully restored. Engine rebuilt and fitted with a modern BMW 6-speed gearbox. Air conditioning (see lot 472 Bonhams 9.9.06 $ 43.042).												
1958	220 S cabriolet		180030Z8518726	L	120-140.000 USD	71.720	110.000	96.822	09-10-15	Hershey	274	RMS
Light ivory with red leather interior; three owners. Car restored in the early 1990s; engine rebuilt in 2007; body repainted in 2014.												
1957	220 S cabriolet		1800307506195	R	28-38.000 GBP	47.720	73.198	64.422	10-10-15	Ascot	136	Coy
White with brown interior; since 1973 in the current ownership.												
1960	220 SE cabriolet		12803011003850	L	65-80.000 GBP		NS		28-11-15	Weybridge	268	His
Yellow with beige interior; several restoration works carried out in the USA between 1979 and 1981.												
1960	220 SE cabriolet		12803020003425	R	80-100.000 GBP	84.000	126.428	119.498	28-11-15	Weybridge	296	His
Dark blue with maroon leather interior; bought in 2004 by the current owner and subsequently restored (see lots Sotheby's 291 16.10.93 NS, and Historics 237 19.7.11 NS and 263 26.5.12 NS).												
1958	220 S cabriolet		8511829	L	NA	76.967*	110.000*	100.727*	29-01-16	Scottsdale	1400	B/J
Blue and beige; in good overall condition. For 20 years in the current ownership (see lot 170 RM 9.10.14 NS).												
1957	220 S cabriolet		1800307505670	L	70-90.000 EUR	58.197	84.311	74.750	19-03-16	Stuttgart	134	Bon
Green with tan leather interior; restored several years ago (see lot 133 RM 9.9.13 $ 75,529).												
1960	220 SE cabriolet		12803010003899	L	110-140.000 EUR	80.580	116.738	103.500	19-03-16	Stuttgart	148	Bon F499
Black and silver; restored in 2010.												
1960	220 SE cabriolet		12803010003229	L	110-120.000 USD	76.868	110.000	96.217	02-04-16	Ft.Lauderdale	724	AA
Red with black leather interior; fully restored at unspecified date.												
1959	220 SE cabriolet		128030109500977	L	NA	156.288*	220.000*	193.600*	09-04-16	Palm Beach	415	B/J
Black with red interior; the car has covered 300 miles since the restoration completed in 2002.												
1959	220 S cabriolet		180030N8517551	L	NA	62.515	88.000	77.440	09-04-16	Palm Beach	440	B/J
White with red leather interior; restored.												
1959	220 S cabriolet		180030105502262	L	55-65.000 GBP	58.000	77.036	69.182	02-07-16	Woodstock	230	Coy
Red; restoration completed in 1992 (see lot 333 Bonhams 3.12.12 $73,968).												
1959	220 S cabriolet		180030119509783	L	60-80.000 EUR	86.368*	112.161*	101.320*	09-07-16	Le Mans	120	Art
Dark blue with brown leather interior; restored in the 1990s.												
1960	220 SE cabriolet		12803010003512	L	160-200.000 USD	125.367	165.000	148.467	30-07-16	Plymouth	151	RMS
Black with tan leather interior; restored seven years ago. 15,598 miles on the odometer.												
1961	220 SE cabriolet		1280300038508	L	65-85.000 EUR	45.976	60.478	54.211	06-08-16	Schloss Dyck	136	Coy
Yellow with tan interior; restored between 1979 and 1981.												
1960	220 SE cabriolet		12803010003476	L	200-250.000 USD	201.696*	264.000*	233.086*	20-08-16	Pebble Beach	39	G&Co
An older restoration, the car was acquired in 2012 by the current owner and subsequently refreshed cosmetically and mechanically.												
1957	220 S cabriolet		180037N7509637	L	100-130.000 USD	42.020*	55.000*	48.560*	20-08-16	Pebble Beach	67	G&Co
For over 30 years in single ownership; body repainted in 1992; original interior.												
1959	220 SE coupé		128637N8500062	L	33-38.000 GBP	35.840	51.223	46.187	12-03-16	Brooklands	222	His
Silver with black roof and maroon leather interior; restored approximately 10 years ago.												
1958	220 S coupé		1800377516490	L	65-85.000 EUR	56.854	82.365	73.025	19-03-16	Stuttgart	129	Bon F500
Blue with red interior; restored. Engine replaced. Sunroof.												
1964	220 S saloon		11101220139321	R	16-20.000 GBP	18.760	26.812	24.176	12-03-16	Brooklands	212	His
Chestnut with tan interior; in good overall condition.												

F499: 1960 Mercedes-Benz 220 SE cabriolet

F500: 1958 Mercedes-Benz 220 S coupé

Year	Model	(Bodybuilder)	Chassis no.	Steering	Estimate	Hammer Price £	$	€	Date	Place	Lot	Auc. H.
1964	220 Sb saloon		11101210133157	L	10-12.000 GBP	12.656	18.422	16.333	18-05-16	Donington Park	89	H&H
\multicolumn{13}{l}{Grey with grey cloth interior; described as in good original condition.}
1965	220 SE cabriolet		11102122077522	R	9-11.000 GBP	10.080	15.209	13.901	09-12-15	Chateau Impney	20	H&H
\multicolumn{13}{l}{Light blue; 57,500 miles on the odometer.}
1966	220 SEb cabriolet		11102322078852	R	60-70.000 GBP	57.500	86.969	79.471	10-12-15	London	387	Bon F501
\multicolumn{13}{l}{Blue with original cream leather interior; until 2006 with its first owner, the car was fully restored in 2000. Automatic transmission (see Bonhams lots 564 7.7.06 NS and 574 11.7.08 $ 50,132).}
1965	220 SE cabriolet		11102310074835	L	120-160.000 EUR		NS		19-03-16	Stuttgart	126	Bon
\multicolumn{13}{l}{Light grey with red leather interior; restored in 1977 by the second owner.}
1962	220 SEb cabriolet		11102310030470	L	60-80.000 USD	53.346*	77.000*	69.031*	05-06-16	Greenwhich	17	Bon
\multicolumn{13}{l}{White with red interior; imported into the USA in 1984, the car was acquired by the current owner in 2007 and later received several restoration works. Before it left Europe, its original engine was replaced with a 250SL unit.}
1963	220 SE coupé		11102122048082	R	25-35.000 GBP		NS		10-10-15	Ascot	157	Coy
\multicolumn{13}{l}{White with black interior; some restoration works carried out 10 years ago. Automatic transmission.}
1964	220 SEb coupé		11102110028934	L	26-32.000 GBP		NS		12-03-16	Brooklands	156	His
\multicolumn{13}{l}{Cream with black roof and original maroon leather interior; restored in the 2000s and fitted with a 250 engine and manual gearbox.}
1965	220 SE coupé		11102112081319	L	40-150.000 EUR		NS		09-04-16	Essen	127	Coy
\multicolumn{13}{l}{Burgundy with white roof and tan leather interior; described as in original, unrestored condition, the car has covered 4,600 miles (see lots 210 RM 23.9.00 $ 33,000, and 119 Coys 8.8.15 NS).}
1965	220 SE coupé		11102110078070	L	50-65.000 EUR		NS		09-04-16	Essen	134	Coy
\multicolumn{13}{l}{White with blue roof and blue interior; described as in good overall condition.}
1964	300 SE saloon		11201422005805	R	35-45.000 GBP	39.880	57.156	52.366	16-01-16	Birmingham	338	Coy
\multicolumn{13}{l}{Silver with blue roof; prepared for historic racing in the late 1990s.}
1964	300 SE cabriolet		11202322005461	R	NA	80.230	123.402	108.150	14-10-15	Duxford	120	H&H
\multicolumn{13}{l}{Blue with cream interior; restored in the 2000s (see lot 29 H&H 7.12.11 $ 89,232).}
1965	300 SE cabriolet		11202310008317	L	280-320.000 EUR		NS		03-02-16	Paris	124	RMS
\multicolumn{13}{l}{White with blue leather interior; fully restored. Manual gearbox (see lot 130 Artcurial 30.10.11 $ 121,462).}
1964	300 SE cabriolet		12202312005430	L	170-230.000 EUR		NS		19-03-16	Stuttgart	109	Bon
\multicolumn{13}{l}{Blue with red leather interior; restored in 2013-14. Automatic transmission.}
1966	300 SE cabriolet		1120231006581	L	250-300.000 USD		NS		20-08-16	Monterey	S182	Mec
\multicolumn{13}{l}{Black with red leather interior; restored.}
1967	300 SE coupé		11202122009814	R	24-28.000 GBP	25.300	38.524	34.588	05-09-15	Beaulieu	179	Bon
\multicolumn{13}{l}{Two-tone metallic grey with red leather interior; recently serviced. Electric sunroof.}
1963	300 SE coupé		11202110004361	L	40-50.000 USD	29.712	45.100	40.139	05-10-15	Philadelphia	215	Bon
\multicolumn{13}{l}{Black; from 1965 to 2015 in the same family ownership and used until 2000. Mechanicals recently restored.}
1965	300 SE coupé		11202112008175	L	35-45.000 EUR	42.805*	67.783*	59.600*	01-11-15	Paris	156	Art F502
\multicolumn{13}{l}{Red with black interior retrimmed in the 1980s; body requires repainting.}
1965	300 SE coupé		11202110007926	L	80-100.000 USD	55.801*	79.750*	73.027*	30-01-16	Scottsdale	103	G&Co
\multicolumn{13}{l}{Silver with burgundy interior; restored several years ago. Manual gearbox.}
1964	300 SE coupé		11202122007233	R	NA		NS		06-03-16	Birmingham	368	SiC
\multicolumn{13}{l}{Gold; in 2001 prepared for historic rallying (see lot 374 Bonhams 17.9.10 NS).}
1964	300 SE coupé		11202112005514	L	28-32.000 EUR	18.871	27.641	24.750	28-05-16	Aarhus	122	SiC
\multicolumn{13}{l}{White with tan leather interior; restored in the 1990s.}
1965	300 SE coupé		11202110009107	L	60-80.000 USD	48.057	63.250	56.912	30-07-16	Plymouth	114	RMS
\multicolumn{13}{l}{Medium blue with cognac leather interior; in original condition. Manual gearbox.}
1966	230 SL		11304222013266	R	55-65.000 GBP	58.500	89.078	79.975	04-09-15	Woodstock	207	SiC
\multicolumn{13}{l}{White with red interior; restored. The original 230 engine was replaced at unspecified date with a 250 unit.}
1964	230 SL		11304210003289	L	50-65.000 EUR	43.130	65.456	58.700	26-09-15	Frankfurt	161	Coy
\multicolumn{13}{l}{Dark green; in good overall condition. Body repainted several years ago.}
1965	230 SL		11304210009481	L	37-42.000 GBP		NS		10-10-15	Ascot	138	Coy
\multicolumn{13}{l}{White with blue interior; described as in very good overall condition.}

F501: 1966 Mercedes-Benz 220 SEb cabriolet

F502: 1965 Mercedes-Benz 300 SE coupé

Year	Model	(Bodybuilder)	Chassis no.	Steering	Estimate	Hammer price £	$	€	Date	Place	Lot	Auc. H.
1965	230 SL		11304210010396	L	140-180.000 USD	88.436*	126.500*	116.013*	28-01-16	Scottsdale	15	Bon **F503**
Maroon with parchment interior; recently restored in Germany.												
1965	230 SL		11304210008833	L	90-120.000 USD		NS		28-01-16	Scottsdale	93	Bon
White with blue hardtop; restored.												
1964	230 SL		11304210006961	L	55-65.000 EUR	54.937	78.517	70.800	12-03-16	Lyon	319	Agu
White with red leather interior; restored in recent years.												
1966	230 SL		11304212016845	L	70-85.000 EUR	62.024	87.301	76.829	09-04-16	Essen	207	Coy
Metallic grey with blue leather interior; described as in very good overall condition.												
1966	230 SL		11304212015292	L	58-66.000 GBP	63.840	91.949	81.345	11-06-16	Brooklands	243	His
Black with ivory interior; imported into the UK from the USA in 2010. Several mechanical works carried out in 2014; body repainted in early 2016. Automatic transmission.												
1966	230 SL		11304212011004	L	50-60.000 EUR	43.977	57.848	51.854	06-08-16	Schloss Dyck	117	Coy
Ivory with black leather interior; described as in good driving order.												
1965	230 SL		11304210008833	L	90-120.000 USD	63.870*	83.600*	73.810*	19-08-16	Carmel	105	Bon
See lot 93 Bonhams 28.1.16.												
1965	600		10001212000529	L	65-75.000 EUR	59.739	90.663	81.305	26-09-15	Frankfurt	159	Coy
Dark blue with blue leather interior; restored in recent years.												
1970	600		10001222001909	R	NA	35.030	53.880	47.220	14-10-15	Duxford	118	H&H
Dark green with tan interior; paintwork and interior redone in 2014, suspension recently overhauled (see lot 51 H&H 29.7.15 NS).												
1965	600		10001212000174	L	50-80.000 EUR	57.358	90.829	79.864	01-11-15	Paris	155	Art
White with grey velour interior; mechanicals restored in 2009 (see lot 255 Artcurial 10.6.13 NS).												
1967	600		10001212000983	L	80-120.000 EUR	61.000	92.344	85.000	08-11-15	Lyon	224	Ose
Metallic blue; for over 30 years in the current ownership, the car is described as in very good working order (see lot 145 Bonhams 20.5.11 NS).												
1966	600		10001212000487	L	90-120.000 EUR	75.933	110.205	100.800	03-02-16	Paris	154	RMS
Medium metallic blue with blue leather interior (see lots 220 RM 15.8.08 $ 60,500 and 335 Bonhams 14.11.09 $ 87,750).												
1968	600		10001212001044	L	300-400.000 EUR		NS		19-03-16	Stuttgart	119	Bon
Black with red interior; full restoration completed in 2014.												
1971	600		10001212001979	L	80-110.000 EUR		NS		19-03-16	Stuttgart	153	Bon
Light ivory with parchment leather interior; recently serviced.												
1969	600		10001212001212	L	50-75.000 USD	30.360	44.000	38.504	07-05-16	Auburn	850	AA
Blue with blue interior.												
1964	600		12000105	L	120-140.000 EUR	107.223	157.056	140.630	28-05-16	Aarhus	207	SiC
Black with tan interior.												
1968	600 Pullman		10001612000753	L	180-250.000 EUR	133.736	202.965	182.015	26-09-15	Frankfurt	138	Coy **F504**
Dark blue with red leather interior; described as in very good overall condition.												
1973	600 Pullman		10001412002282	L	250-280.000 EUR		NS		26-09-15	Frankfurt	151	Coy
Dark blue with black vinyl roof and dark blue interior; sold new in Germany. Restored in the early 1990s and exported to Japan; reimported into Germany in 2014 and mechanically restored again (see lot 031 Bonhams 12.7.14 NS).												
1969	600 Pullman		10001212001430	L	NA	48.618	77.000	67.698	31-10-15	Hilton Head	184	AA
Red with black interior; described as in very good overall condition. Body originally finished in grey.												
1971	600 Pullman landaulette		10001512001879	L	1.000-1.500.000 EUR		NS		19-03-16	Stuttgart	138	Bon
Black with dark red interior; partially restored in 2012, the car is described as in very good overall condition. Engine replaced. Sold new to Senegal.												
1966	600 Pullman		10001412000603	L	260-320.000 EUR		NS		19-03-16	Stuttgart	142	Bon
Black with red leather interior; sold new to the USA to the Petersen Publishing Company, the car remained subsequently in the ownership of the Petersen family until 2004. 37,724 miles covered since new (see lots 16 Gooding 15.8.04 $ 73,700, and 190 RM 31.10.12 NS).												
1967	600 Pullman		10001212000860	L	70-100.000 EUR	36.981*	48.645*	43.604*	06-08-16	Schloss Dyck	142	Coy
Silver with black roof; described as in good overall condition.												
1967	230 S saloon		11101012099730	L	20-30.000 EUR	19.990	26.295	23.570	06-08-16	Schloss Dyck	161	Coy
Beige with beige interior; in good driving order. Automatic transmission.												
1966	250 SE cabriolet		11102322084512	R	65-75.000 GBP	67.500	102.782	92.279	04-09-15	Woodstock	209	SiC
Blue with light red interior; acquired in 2009 by the current owner and subsequently restored (see Coys lots 422 20.11.97 NS and 167 10.1.15 NS).												

F503: 1965 Mercedes-Benz 230 SL

F504: 1968 Mercedes-Benz 600 Pullman

Year	Model	(Bodybuilder)	Chassis no.	Steering	Estimate	Hammer price £	Hammer price $	Hammer price €	Sale Date	Sale Place	Lot	Auc. H.
1966	250 SE cabriolet		11102322084512	R	68-78.000 GBP	61.800	82.083	73.715	02-07-16	Woodstock	221	Coy
See lot 209 Silverstone Auctions 4.9.15.											
1970	280 SE cabriolet		11102512004293	L	NA	100.674	157.500	137.939	19-09-15	Dallas	S156	Mec
Burgundy with tan interior; 46,000 actual miles. Automatic transmission.											
1970	280 SE cabriolet		11102510003233	L	NA	72.611	115.000	101.108	31-10-15	Hilton Head	144	AA
Green with bamboo leather interior; in good overall condition. 4-speed manual gearbox.											
1969	280 SE cabriolet		11102512001849	L	100-120.000 USD	105.309	150.700	131.817	02-04-16	Ft.Lauderdale	489	AA
Light ivory with cognac leather interior; in the same family ownership since new. Some recent restoration works.											
1969	280 SE cabriolet		11102512002529	L	100-140.000 USD	100.294	132.000	118.774	30-07-16	Plymouth	120	RMS
Blue; in good overall condition. Body repainted.											
1968	280 SE coupé		108018100010357	L	25-30.000 GBP		NS		05-09-15	Beaulieu	165	Bon
Silver with cream leather interior; seats in need of re-upholstering. Manual gearbox.											
1969	280 SE coupé		11102412003812	L	70-90.000 USD	39.989*	57.200*	52.458*	28-01-16	Scottsdale	38	Bon
Ivory with beige interior; recent cosmetic restoration. Automatic transmission.											
1970	280 SE coupé		11102412003812	L	100-125.000 USD		NS		20-08-16	Monterey	S186	Mec
See lot 38 Bonhams 28.1.16.											
1970	280 SE 3.5 cabriolet		1102712000810	L	280-350.000 EUR	266.087	387.231	345.680	05-02-16	Paris	177	Art F505
Black with black leather interior; sold new to the USA, in 1991 the car was imported in Austria by its second owner who in 1993 resold it to the current vendor. Described as in very good original condition; 36,000 miles on the odometer.											
1971	280 SE 3.5 cabriolet		11102712001947	L	175-225.000 USD	188.327	269.500	235.732	02-04-16	Ft.Lauderdale	478	AA
Blue with blue interior; described as in near-original condition.											
1971	280 SE 3.5 cabriolet		11102712002921	L	350-375.000 USD		NS		25-06-16	Santa Monica	1110	AA
Silver with navy blue leather interior; restored. Two owners.											
1971	280 SE 3.5 cabriolet		11102712004031	L	150-230.000 EUR	142.254	184.736	166.880	09-07-16	Le Mans	163	Art
White with red interior; since 1986 in the same family ownership. Little used in recent years, it requires recommissioning prior to use.											
1971	280 SE 3.5 cabriolet		11102712004198	L	275-350.000 USD	222.706	291.500	257.365	19-08-16	Carmel	69	Bon
Light ivory with red leather interior; restored in the early 2000s, the car remained with its first owner until 2005 when it was acquired by the present vendor. Just over 52,000 miles covered since new.											
1971	280 SE 3.5 cabriolet		11102712003922	L	275-350.000 USD	226.908	297.000	262.221	20-08-16	Pebble Beach	11	G&Co
Black with cognac leather interior; less than 45,000 miles covered. Gifted by Frank Sinatra to her daughter Christina. Three owners.											
1970	280 SE 3.5 coupé		11102622000852	R	50-60.000 GBP	45.166	69.280	60.974	10-10-15	Ascot	121	Coy
Metallic blue with cream leather interior; restored (see lot 127 Coys 11.7.15 NS).											
1971	280 SE 3.5 coupé		11102622002529	R	40-50.000 GBP	47.376	71.306	67.397	28-11-15	Weybridge	276	His
Ivory with black interior; several works carried out within the last 12 months.											
1970	280 SE 3.5 coupé		11102612001521	L	140-180.000 USD	88.436*	126.500*	116.013*	28-01-16	Phoenix	109	RMS
Dark blue with white roof and beige interior; recent cosmetic restoration and mechanical servicing.											
1970	280 SE 3.5 coupé		11102610000302	L	175.200.000 EUR	128.664	186.736	170.800	03-02-16	Paris	147	RMS
Anthracite grey; recently restored. Electric sunroof; manual gearbox (see lot 132 Artcurial 9.7.10 $ 43,222).											
1971	280 SE 3.5 coupé		11102612001627	L	150-175.000 USD	84.652*	121.000*	109.106*	11-03-16	Amelia Island	1	G&Co
Silver with red leather interior; restored many years ago. Recently serviced. Sunroof.											
1971	280 SE 3.5 coupé		11102612004325	L	125-175.000 USD	111.586*	159.500*	143.821*	12-03-16	Amelia Island	111	RMS F506
Silver with original dark blue leather interior; 40,000 miles on the odometer. Body repainted.											
1971	280 SE 3.5 coupé		11102612002949	L	110-150.000 EUR		NS		19-03-16	Stuttgart	143	Bon
White with blue interior; restoration completed in 2015 (see lot 33 Bonhams 14.8.15 $ 99,000).											
1971	280 SE 3.5 coupé		11102610000524	L	100-120.000 USD	73.793	105.600	92.368	02-04-16	Ft.Lauderdale	487	AA
Silver grey metallic with original burgundy leather interior; imported into the USA in the 1990s. Body repainted in the mid-2000s. Manual gearbox.											
1970	280 SE 3.5 coupé		11102622002520	R	55-65.000 GBP	47.420	62.983	56.563	02-07-16	Woodstock	196	Coy
Ivory with black leather interior; engine rebuilt at unspecified date.											

F505: 1970 Mercedes-Benz 280 SE 3.5 cabriolet

F506: 1971 Mercedes-Benz 280 SE 3.5 coupé

Year	Model	(Bodybuilder)	Chassis no.	Steering	Estimate	Hammer Price £	Hammer Price $	Hammer Price €	Sale Date	Sale Place	Lot	Auc. H.
1971	280 SE 3.5 coupé		11102612003580	L	250-275.000 USD	243.716	319.000	281.645	20-08-16	Pebble Beach	26	G&Co
	White with blue roof and blue leather interior; sold new to Japan, the car was bought in early 2016 by the current, third owner and imported into the USA. In original condition; 5,100 kms covered since new.											
1972	280 SE 3.5 saloon		10805722011216	R	9-13.000 GBP	14.560	21.914	20.713	28-11-15	Weybridge	217	His
	Light metallic blue with blue interior; in good overall condition. 41,996 miles covered.											
1972	280 SE 3.5 saloon		10805722007284	R	14-18.000 GBP	16.131	23.054	20.788	12-03-16	Brooklands	258	His F507
	Silver with blue interior; in good overall condition. 44,900 miles on the odometer.											
1966	230 Universal station wagon		11000360000976	R	12-15.000 GBP		NS		12-03-16	Brooklands	264	His
	Green with tan interior; in good working order.											
1967	250 SL California		11304322001208	R	20-30.000 GBP	36.800	56.035	50.309	05-09-15	Beaulieu	164	Bon
	White; stored for the last three years, it requires recommissioning prior to use. Automatic transmission.											
1967	250 SL		WDB11304322001250	R	55-65.000 GBP	56.871	87.234	76.776	10-10-15	Ascot	130	Coy
	Dark metallic grey; several restoration works recently carried out.											
1967	250 SL		11304322003816	R	37-45.000 GBP	42.560	64.057	60.546	28-11-15	Weybridge	235	His
	White with black interior; recently serviced.											
1968	250 SL		11304310004496	L	110-130.000 USD	100.043*	143.000*	128.943*	11-03-16	Amelia Island	68	G&Co
	Full restoration completed in 2014; with hardtop. Manual gearbox.											
1967	250 SL		11304322003932	R	NA	100.000	141.800	126.420	20-04-16	Duxford	55	H&H
	Silver with dark blue interior; acquired in 1993 by the current owner and subsequently fully restored. Automatic transmission.											
1967	250 SL		113404312003581	L	38-45.000 GBP	72.600	95.019	83.889	20-08-16	Brooklands	330	His
	Fully restored; automatic transmission.											
1967	250 SL		11304310003579	L	150-160.000 USD	64.940	85.000	75.047	20-08-16	Monterey	S149	Mec
	Blue with black leather interior; 200 miles covered since the restoration completed in 2016. 5-speed manual gearbox.											
1970	280 SL		11304412019580	L	60-80.000 GBP	51.750	78.800	70.747	05-09-15	Beaulieu	152	Bon
	Red; automatic transmission. Body repainted in 2014.											
1970	280 SL		11304422012754	R	100-130.000 GBP	119.100	183.688	163.024	12-09-15	Goodwood	317	Bon
	Silver with blue leather interior; restored in 2008. Automatic transmission. From the Chris Evans collection (see lot 116 RM 8.9.14 $ 144,256).											
1968	280 SL		11304412001199	L	75-100.000 EUR		NS		26-09-15	Frankfurt	105	Coy
	Dark grey with habana interior; restored. Automatic transmission; hardtop.											
1968	280 SL		11304412001599	L	35-40.000 GBP	41.000	62.890	55.350	10-10-15	Ascot	125	Coy
	Red with black interior; automatic transmission.											
1970	280 SL		11304410002435	L	37-42.000 GBP		NS		10-10-15	Ascot	164	Coy
	Black with cream leather interior; manual gearbox.											
1970	280 SL California		NQ	R	210-240.000 AUD	110.189	169.731	153.129	24-10-15	Melbourne	41	TBr
	Silver with red leather interior; sold new to Australia where it was fully restored to concours condition between 2010 and 2013.											
1970	280 SL		11304412014916	L	29-37.000 GBP	37.520	56.471	53.376	28-11-15	Weybridge	287	His
	Black with black interior; imported into the UK from the USA in 2012. Body recently repainted (see lot 248 Coys 11.10.14 NS).											
1968	280 SL		11304410000615	L	100-130.000 USD	86.129*	123.200*	112.987*	28-01-16	Scottsdale	48	Bon
	Green with cognac interior; described as in very good overall condition. 5-speed ZF manual gearbox. From the BHA Automobile Museum.											
1969	280 SL		11304412001530	L	130-160.000 USD	69.270*	99.000*	90.654*	29-01-16	Scottsdale	20	G&Co
	Red with white hardtop and beige leather interior; restored between 2012 and 2015. Automatic transmission.											
1968	280 SL		11304412006311	L	150-180.000 USD	80.815*	115.500*	105.763*	29-01-16	Phoenix	215	RMS
	Metallic anthracite grey with dark grey interior; restoration completed in 1990. Automatic transmission.											
1969	280 SL		11304412991199	L	80-100.000 EUR	69.547*	103.095*	92.000*	04-02-16	Paris	301	Bon
	See lot 105 Coys 26.9.15.											
1970	280 SL		11804420016494	R	68-78.000 GBP	71.240	101.225	91.793	08-03-16	London	118	Coy
	Ivory with tan interior; recently repainted and serviced. 51,500 miles covered. 5-speed manual gearbox.											
1970	280 SL		11304412013778	L	125-150.000 USD	80.804*	115.500*	104.146*	11-03-16	Amelia Island	8	G&Co
	Red with cognac interior; recently restored. Automatic transmission.											

F507: 1972 Mercedes-Benz 280 SE 3.5 saloon

F508: 1968 Mercedes-Benz 280 SL

Year	Model (Bodybuilder)	Chassis no.	Steering	Estimate	Hammer price £	Hammer price $	Hammer price €	Sale Date	Sale Place	Lot	Auc. H.
1968	**280 SL**	11304410002012	L	160-220.000 USD	142.369*	203.500*	183.496*	12-03-16	Amelia Island	122	RMS **F508**
	Medium blue with cream leather interior; recent full restoration carried out in Germany. 4-speed manual gearbox.										
1969	**280 SL**	13098312006695	L	85-125.000 EUR	76.999	111.549	98.900	19-03-16	Stuttgart	106	Bon
	Light ivory with cognac interior; in very good overall condition. Automatic transmission.										
1970	**280 SL**	11304412008326	L	90-110.000 GBP	96.700	140.089	124.201	20-03-16	Goodwood	62	Bon
	Light metallic blue with blue leather interior; imported into the UK from the USA in 1992, the car has covered circa 200 miles since the restoration completed in 2015. Automatic transmission.										
1970	**280 SL**	11304410021751	L	100-120.000 EUR	123.493*	177.937*	156.800*	14-05-16	Monaco	280	RMS
	Brown with beige interior and white hardtop; recently restored in Germany. Manual gearbox.										
1968	**280 SL**	11304422006002	R	90-120.000 GBP	97.820	134.053	121.131	24-06-16	Goodwood	217	Bon
	Light blue with blue leather interior; restored in 2015. Automatic transmission.										
1969	**280 SL**	WDB113280SL011241	L	55-65.000 EUR	59.465	78.220	70.115	06-08-16	Schloss Dyck	107	Coy
	Metallic gold with tan interior; described as in largely original condition. Reimported into Europe from the USA; 47,102 miles covered.										
1969	**280 SL**	11304410009229	L	140-180.000 USD	79.838*	104.500*	92.263*	19-08-16	Carmel	38	Bon
	Silver with red leather interior; restored. Manual gearbox.										
1969	**280 SL**	11304412012652	L	80-110.000 USD	50.424*	66.000*	58.271*	19-08-16	Carmel	65	Bon
	Two-tone body with brown interior; bought new by Jane Russell, the car remained in her family ownership after her passing in 2011.										
1971	**280 SL**	11304412022135	L	250-275.000 USD	159.676	209.000	184.526	20-08-16	Pebble Beach	20	G&Co
	Blue with blue interior; described as in very good unrestored condition, the car has covered less than 18,500 miles.										
1971	**280 SL**	11304412022065	L	250-300.000 USD		NS		20-08-16	Monterey	S104	Mec
	Tobacco with tan leather interior; concours-quality restoration.										
1970	**280 SL**	11304412015336	L	175-225.000 USD	130.262*	170.500*	150.534*	21-08-16	Pebble Beach	111	G&Co
	Beige with cognac leather interior; restoration completed in 2013. Automatic transmission.										
1971	**300 SEL 6.3 saloon**	W10901872004359	L	70-85.000 EUR		NS		26-09-15	Frankfurt	156	Coy
	Fully restored.										
1971	**300 SEL 6.3 saloon**	10901812004898	L	175-250.000 USD	151.272*	198.000*	174.814*	20-08-16	Pebble Beach	41	G&Co
	Black with black leather interior; the car has covered 2,000 miles since a concours-quality restoration carried out in 2004.										
1972	**250 CE coupé**	11402222021266	L	10-13.000 GBP	10.080	14.406	12.990	12-03-16	Brooklands	127	His
	Light blue with grey interior; in good condition. Automatic transmission (see lot 212 Historics 8.3.14 $ 15,589).										
1972	**300 SEL 3.5 saloon**	10905612004409	L	50-60.000 EUR		NS		06-08-16	Schloss Dyck	169	Coy
	Grey with brown leather interior; in good overall condition. Two owners. Sunroof.										
1978	**350 SL**	10704322013666	R	8-12.000 GBP	19.470	27.904	25.566	16-01-16	Birmingham	320	Coy
	Blue with blue cloth and leather interior; described as in very good overall condition. 36,600 miles covered.										
1973	**350 SL**	10704322008832	R	8-12.000 GBP	12.320	17.608	15.877	12-03-16	Brooklands	114	His
	Light blue with blue interior; restored nine years ago and recommissioned in 2015 (see lot 12 Brooks 21.10.95 $ 7,952).										
1973	**350 SL**	10704310010982	L	30-50.000 EUR	38.499	55.775	49.450	19-03-16	Stuttgart	103	Bon **F509**
	Silver with tan interior; circa 17,500 kms covered. First owner Nicolae Ceausescu. Recently recommissioned. All the proceeds of the sale will be donated to the charity "Crosscause" which supports and educates special-needs orphans.										
1980	**450 SL**	10704422061762	R	12-16.000 GBP	19.320	27.612	24.898	12-03-16	Brooklands	133	His
	Silver with black leather interior; cosmetically restored in 2015.										
1977	**450 SL**	10704412039246	L	22-30.000 EUR	15.221*	22.050*	19.550*	19-03-16	Stuttgart	158	Bon
	Lime green with dark green hardtop and green interior; in good overall condition.										
1974	**450 SL**	10704412019263	L	18-23.000 EUR		NS		20-03-16	Fontainebleau	362	Ose
	Beige with beige interior; described as in good overall condition.										
1980	**450 SLC**	10702422031739	R	9.5-10.500 AUD	4.247	6.542	5.902	24-10-15	Melbourne	1	TBr
	Described as in very good driving order; body repainted at unspecified date. Sunroof.										
1980	**450 SLC**	10702412031126	L	18-22.000 EUR	17.011	24.645	21.850	19-03-16	Stuttgart	157	Bon **F510**
	Silver with blue cloth interior; in very good overall condition. Circa 58,000 kms covered.										
1980	**450 SLC**	10702412026711	L	30-40.000 USD	12.537*	16.500*	14.847*	30-07-16	Plymouth	116	RMS
	Silver with black interior; described as in very good overall condition.										

F509: 1973 Mercedes-Benz 350 SL

F510: 1980 Mercedes-Benz 450 SLC

Year	Model	(Bodybuilder)	Chassis No.	Steering	Estimate	Hammer Price £	Hammer Price $	Hammer Price €	Sale Date	Place	Lot	Auc. H.
1972	**280 SEL 4.5 saloon**		10806812008778	L	40-50.000 EUR	23.357	33.837	30.000	19-03-16	Stuttgart	123	**Bon**
Green with brown interior; in good original condition. Three owners (see lot 276 Bonhams 7.6.09 $ 33,930).													
1973	**280 CE coupé**		11407210004314	L	8-12.000 EUR	7.287	10.557	9.360	20-03-16	Fontainebleau	374	**Ose**
Light metallic blue with black leather interior; 85,000 kms on the odometer.													
1976	**350 SE station wagon**	(Crayford)	11602822026049	L	18-24.000 EUR	30.819	48.804	42.912	01-11-15	Paris	158	**Art F511**
One of 15 examples built; acquired in 2012 by the current owner and subsequently fully restored and converted to left-hand drive.													
1985	**280 SL**		WDB1070422A03003	R	50-60.000 GBP		NS		20-05-16	Silverstone	361	**SiC**
Red with cloth interior; in very good, unrestored overall condition. Since new in the same family ownership; 6,500 miles covered.													
1985	**280 SL**		1070422A022673	R	12-18.000 GBP	14.784	21.293	18.838	11-06-16	Brooklands	230	**His**
Light metallic green with biscuit interior; body recently repainted.													
1975	**280 SLC**		10702210001222	L	NQ	21.375*	32.548*	29.222*	04-09-15	Woodstock	202	**SiC**
White with red leather interior; just one owner and 16,500 km covered.													
1976	**450 SEL 6.9 saloon**		11603612001097	L	Refer Dpt.	67.298	102.470	92.000	05-09-15	Chantilly	27	**Bon F512**
Dark blue with brown interior; first owner the French singer and composer, Claude Francois. From the collection of its second owner, Alain Dominique Perrin.													
1975	**450 SEL 6.9 saloon**		11603612000163	L	30-40.000 EUR		NS		01-11-15	Paris	159	**Art**
Grey; 90 kms covered since 1991.													
1979	**450 SEL 6.9 saloon**		11603612006349	L	60-80.000 USD	42.332*	60.500*	55.400*	29-01-16	Phoenix	204	**RMS**
Metallic brown with brown interior; in original condition. Less than 30,000 miles covered.													
1978	**450 SEL 6.9 saloon**		11603612004168	L	30-40.000 EUR	26.860	38.913	34.500	19-03-16	Stuttgart	151	**Bon**
Dark blue with beige cloth interior; body repainted and mechanicals overhauled during the last 10 years. Two owners.													
1977	**450 SEL 6.9 saloon**		11603622002143	R	18-22.000 GBP		NS		28-07-16	Donington Park	76	**H&H**
Metallic grey with blue leather interior; in good overall condition.													
1978	**280 TE station wagon**		230931000034	L	6-8.000 EUR		NS		14-05-16	Monaco	114	**RMS**
White with blue interior; in original condition and low mileage, the car is part of the Quattroruote Collection since new.													
1983	**380 SL**		1070452A005463	R	35-45.000 AUD	15.927	24.533	22.133	24-10-15	Melbourne	3	**TBr**
Black with grey interior; described as in largely original condition.													
1985	**380 SL**		1070452A022836	R	10-15.000 GBP	18.200	27.393	25.891	28-11-15	Weybridge	259	**His**
Light metallic blue with cream leather interior; cosmetic restoration carried out in 2015.													
1985	**380 SL**		WDBBA45C4FA026795	L	60-80.000 USD	25.212*	33.000*	29.136*	19-08-16	Carmel	11	**Bon**
Silver with blue interior; for 30 years with its first owner, the car is described as in very good original condition and has covered just over 7,800 miles.													
1980	**380 SL**		1070452000093	R	14-18.000 GBP	20.720	27.118	23.942	20-08-16	Brooklands	340	**His**
Light green with green interior; in good overall condition.													
1984	**500 SL**		1070462A001706	R	22-26.000 GBP		NS		10-10-15	Ascot	145	**Coy**
Light green with tan leather interior; 66,000 miles covered.													
1986	**500 SL**		WDB1070462A052008	R	15-17.000 GBP	19.600	29.572	27.030	09-12-15	Chateau Impney	112	**H&H**
Silver with blue interior; body recently repainted.													
1986	**500 SL**		1070461A042166	L	50-80.000 EUR	49.243	71.340	63.250	19-03-16	Stuttgart	118	**Bon**
Red with black leather interior; described as in very good original condition. 53,000 kms covered.													
1984	**500 SL**		1070461A01494	L	25-35.000 USD	14.861*	21.450*	19.230*	05-06-16	Greenwich	20	**Bon**
White with blue interior; described as in good, highly original condition.													
1985	**280 SE**		WDB1260211A175447	L	NQ	15.700*	23.906*	21.463*	04-09-15	Woodstock	201	**SiC**
White with grey cloth interior; in excellent overall condition, the car has covered 57,000 kms.													
1986	**560 SEC**		WDB1260541A283204	L	NQ	26.487*	40.332*	36.210*	04-09-15	Woodstock	204	**SiC**
Light grey with blue leather interior; 38,000 kms covered.													
1989	**560 SEC 6.0 AMG**		WDB1260451A436448	L	100-150.000 USD	107.661*	154.000*	141.233*	28-01-16	Phoenix	171	**RMS F513**
Silver with black interior; one of circa 50 examples modified by AMG and fitted with the 385bhp 6.0-litre engine, the car was sold new to Japan and has covered just over 90.000 kms. Recently serviced. Currently registered in the USA.													
1989	**560 SL**		WDBBA48D5KA093145	L	70-80.000 USD	41.562*	59.400*	54.393*	29-01-16	Scottsdale	48	**G&Co**
Metallic black pearl with grey leather interior; in original condition. 15,815 miles covered.													

F511: 1976 Mercedes-Benz 350 SE station wagon (Crayford)

F512: 1976 Mercedes-Benz 450 SEL 6.9 saloon

Year	Model	(Bodybuilder)	Chassis no.	Steering	Estimate	Hammer price £	$	€	Date	Sale Place	Lot	Auc. H.

F513: 1989 Mercedes-Benz 560 SEC 6.0 AMG

F514: 1995 Mercedes-Benz 500 SL

Year	Model	Chassis no.	Steering	Estimate	£	$	€	Date	Place	Lot	Auc. H.
1989	**560 SL**	WDBBA48DK3KA101453	L	25-35.000 EUR	27.003	38.593	34.800	12-03-16	Lyon	342	Agu
	Dark grey with light grey interior; in good overall condition. Body repainted.										
1987	**560 SL**	WDBBA48D6JA076675	L	30-40.000 USD	11.766*	15.400*	13.597*	19-08-16	Carmel	98	Bon
	White with light grey leather interior; in good overall condition.										
1995	**500 SL**	WDB1290671F105298	L	25-30.000 EUR	21.488*	31.130*	27.600*	19-03-16	Stuttgart	114	Bon F514
	Silver with black leather interior; 34,554 kms covered.										
1996	**SL73 AMG**	115979	L	95-120.000 EUR	57.619	87.446	78.420	26-09-15	Frankfurt	108	Coy
	Silver with black leather interior.										
1996	**SL73 AMG**	134374	L	70-85.000 EUR	63.850	96.902	86.900	26-09-15	Frankfurt	171	Coy
	Black with black interior.										
1989	**190E 2.5-16**	2010351F6545589	L	35-45.000 EUR		NS		19-03-16	Stuttgart	117	Bon
	Dark grey with black leather interior; some mechanical works carried out in 2011-12. 204bhp RUF engine.										
1990	**190E 2.5-16 Evolution II**	2010361F738656	L	NA	292.500	408.798	371.446	26-02-16	Coventry	411	SiC
	Black with black interior; in excellent overall condition. 2,772 kms covered.										
1990	**190E 2.5-16 Evolution II**	2010336F735117	L	140-180.000 EUR	111.917	162.136	143.750	19-03-16	Stuttgart	108	Bon F515
	Black with black leather interior; 48,000 kms on the odometer. Body restored; last serviced in May 2015.										
1989	**190E 2.5-16 Evolution**	20110361F610814	L	55-75.000 EUR		NS		19-03-16	Stuttgart	135	Bon
	Black with black leather interior; in good overall condition, the car has had one owner and has covered 126,500 kms. Swiss papers.										
1989	**190E 2.5-16 Evolution**	2010361F597554	L	100-120.000 EUR		NS		28-05-16	Aarhus	226	SiC
	Black; recently serviced.										
1990	**190E 2.5-16 Evolution II**	741504	L	180-220.000 GBP		NS		20-08-16	Brooklands	289	His
	Black with black leather interior; described as in very good overall condition. 8,663 miles covered. Sold new in Germany and later exported to Japan. Currently UK registered.										
1994	**600 SEL saloon**	12098012025829	L	25-35.000 EUR	22.383	32.427	28.750	19-03-16	Stuttgart	110	Bon
	Black with black leather interior; the car is offered by the "All Time Stars" trade section within the Mercedes-Benz Museum. Example of the "Concours Edition" category, restored by the factory experts.										
2000	**CLK-GTR coupé**	000023	L	1.800-2.000.000 EUR		NS		04-02-16	Paris	352	Bon F516
	Silver with grey interior; one of 25 examples built. Sold new to Switzerland; 3,285 kms covered. Recently serviced at Mercedes-Benz Stuttgart. UE taxes to be paid (see lot 243 Bonhams 26.5.03 $ 955,435).										
2003	**Maybach 62**	000472	L	60-70.000 GBP	65.520	98.614	93.209	28-11-15	Weybridge	270	His
	Two-tone body with black leather interior; in very good overall condition.										
2007	**SLR McLaren coupé**	000675	L	200-230.000 EUR	149.816	227.369	203.900	26-09-15	Frankfurt	160	Coy
	Silver; two owners and 29,000 kms covered.										
2008	**SLR McLaren coupé**	001193	L	160-180.000 GBP	175.000	263.638	248.710	01-12-15	London	327	Coy
	Silver with red leather interior; one owner and 16,000 miles covered. Recently serviced.										

F515: 1990 Mercedes-Benz 190E 2.5-16 Evolution II

F516: 2000 Mercedes-Benz CLK-GTR coupé

Year	Model	(Bodybuilder)	Chassis no.	Steering	Estimate	Hammer price £	Hammer price $	Hammer price €	Date	Place	Lot	Auc. H.
2009	**SLR McLaren Stirling Moss roadster**		000018	L	Refer Dpt.		NS		01-12-15	London	343	Coy
White; never registered. One of 75 examples built. European taxes to be paid.												
2006	**SLR McLaren coupé**		000587	L	NA	161.627	245.000	223.734	12-12-15	Austin	S144	Mec
Silver with red interior; 10,100 original miles.												
2006	**SLR McLaren coupé**		000896	L	290-320.000 USD	186.742	267.500	247.491	23-01-16	Kissimmee	S131	Mec
Black; 1,118 miles.												
2008	**SLR McLaren roadster**		001543	L	NA	280.930*	401.500*	367.654*	29-01-16	Scottsdale	1394	B/J
Silver with red interior; 6,957 original miles. Recently serviced.												
2008	**SLR McLaren roadster**		001804	L	375-450.000 USD	277.081	396.000	362.617	29-01-16	Scottsdale	23	G&Co
Silver with black interior; one owner and less than 2,000 miles covered.												
2004	**SLR McLaren coupé**		000391	L	230-280.000 EUR	206.706	300.002	274.400	03-02-16	Paris	161	RMS F517
Silver with red leather interior; 6,500 kms covered. Delivered new to former Italian footballer Alessandro Del Piero.												
2009	**SLR McLaren roadster**		001553	L	350-400.000 EUR	269.496	399.494	356.500	04-02-16	Paris	332	Bon
Sold new to Japan and bought in July 2015 by the present, second owner. Registered in the UK. Some 13,000 kms covered.												
2008	**SLR McLaren roadster**		001702	L	NA		NS		26-02-16	Coventry	430	SiC
Black with red interior; one owner and 20,000 kms covered. Recently serviced.												
2008	**SLR McLaren roadster**		001557	L	360-425.000 USD	277.042	396.000	357.073	11-03-16	Amelia Island	7	G&Co
Black with red leather interior; less than 2,000 miles covered. Recently serviced.												
2009	**SLR McLaren Stirling Moss roadster**		199976M900032	L	2.000-2.400.000 EUR	1.790.665	2.594.170	2.300.000	19-03-16	Stuttgart	122	Bon F518
Bought directly from McLaren, the car has had one owner and has covered 7,200 kms. Swiss papers. One od 75 examples built of the limited edition "Stirling Moss".												
2006	**SLR McLaren coupé**		000457	L	275-325.000 USD	211.387	302.500	264.597	02-04-16	Ft.Lauderdale	522	AA
Black with red leather interior; less than 5,500 miles covered.												
2006	**SLR McLaren coupé**		000979	L	NA		NS		09-04-16	Palm Beach	406	B/J
Silver with red leather interior; one owner and less than 7,200 miles covered.												
2010	**SLR McLaren roadster**		001842	L	340-380.000 EUR		NS		09-04-16	Essen	205	Coy
Silver with black leather interior; 20,920 kms covered.												
2007	**SLR McLaren 722 roadster**		001373	L	330-380.000 GBP		NS		16-04-16	Ascot	138	Coy
Antimony grey with black leather and alcantara interior; 13,000 kms covered.												
2006	**SLR McLaren coupé**		000585	L	NA	144.566	205.000	181.671	16-04-16	Houston	S114	Mec
Silver with black interior; 22,000 miles.												
2009	**SLR McLaren roadster**		001855	L	NA		NS		16-04-16	Houston	S97.1	Mec
Black with grey interior; 3,200 original miles.												
2008	**SLR McLaren roadster**		001821	L	310-360.000 EUR	240.015	345.830	304.750	13-05-16	Monaco	121	Bon
Blue with copper leather interior; circa 9,700 miles covered. Sold new to Japan, the car was acquired in 2015 by the current, second owner and imported into the UK.												
2006	**SLR McLaren coupé**		000827	L	NA	156.542	225.500	199.477	11-06-16	Newport Beach	6258	R&S
Black with red interior.												
2006	**SLR McLaren coupé**		000943	L	240-275.000 USD	168.538	231.000	208.732	25-06-16	Santa Monica	1090	AA
Black with black interior; recently serviced.												
2006	**SLR McLaren coupé**		000832	L	180-225.000 USD	143.250	187.500	165.544	19-08-16	Monterey	F122	Mec
Silver with red leather interior; 21,336 miles covered.												
2006	**SLR McLaren coupé**		000826	L	400-500.000 USD	273.130	357.500	315.637	20-08-16	Pebble Beach	75	G&Co
Black with black interior; serviced in May 2016 at 344 miles.												
2005	**CLK DTM AMG**		WDB2093421F14803	L	130-160.000 GBP	225.500	347.789	308.664	12-09-15	Goodwood	309	Bon F519
Silver; one of 100 examples built. Just one owner and 8,490 miles covered.												
2005	**CLK DTM**		WDB2093421F165651	L	350-425.000 USD	310.948	407.000	359.340	20-08-16	Pebble Beach	79	G&Co
Black; one owner and just over 2,600 miles covered. Last serviced in June 2016.												
2009	**SL65 AMG Black Series coupé**		159462	R	180-210.000 GBP	203.100	294.231	260.862	20-03-16	Goodwood	57	Bon
One of 350 examples built; one owner and 3,900 miles covered. Last serviced in September 2015.												

F517: 2004 Mercedes-Benz SLR McLaren coupé

F518: 2009 Mercedes-Benz SLR McLaren Stirling Moss roadster

Year	Model	(Bodybuilder)	Chassis no.	Steering	Estimate	Hammer price £	$	€	Date	Sale Place	Lot	Auc. H.

F519: 2005 Mercedes-Benz CLK DTM AMG   F520: 2014 Mercedes-Benz SLS AMG Black Series coupé

Year	Model	Chassis no.	Steering	Estimate	£	$	€	Date	Place	Lot	Auc. H.
2013	**SLS AMG GT coupé**	009998	L	NA	129.426	185.000	166.815	12-03-16	Kansas City	S138.1	Mec
	White with black interior; 1,043 miles.										
2014	**SLS AMG Black Series coupé**	011147	L	425-550.000 USD	352.968	462.000	407.900	19-08-16	Monterey	154	RMS F520
	Yellow with black interior; sold new to the USA. 315 miles covered.										
2014	**SLS AMG Black Series coupé**	010824	L	NQ	319.352	418.000	369.052	20-08-16	Monterey	7117	R&S
	White with black interior.										

MERCER (USA) (1910-1925)

1922	**Series 5 Sporting**	5368	L	150-200.000 USD	57.605*	88.000*	78.197*	08-10-15	Hershey	138	RMS
	Blue and black with black interior; paintwork redone decades ago, front seats retrimmed in the 2000s. The car needs servicing prior to use. From the estate of Richard Roy.										
1923	**Series 6 Sporting**	20239	L	175-225.000 USD	54.005*	82.500*	73.310*	08-10-15	Hershey	144	RMS
	Light blue with black fenders and brown leather interior; restored in the late 1980s. The paintwork requires some attention. Formerly in the Harrah Collection. From the estate of Richard Roy.										
1923	**Series 6 Sporting**	20024	L	175-225.000 USD	130.732	187.000	171.498	28-01-16	Scottsdale	90	Bon F521
	Black with black interior; concours-quality restoration completed in 2014.										

MERCURY (USA) (1939-2010)

1939	**Series 99A convertible**	99A56839	L	NA	40.128*	55.000*	49.698*	24-06-16	Uncasville	428	B/J
	Burgundy with tan interior; in the same family opwnership since new.										
1941	**Series 19A coupé**	441643	L	35-40.000 USD	17.213*	26.400*	23.237*	09-10-15	Hershey	217	RMS
	Black with grey cloth interior; described as in original condition, the car has covered 37,892 miles. From new for over 50 years in the same family ownership. From the estate of Jim Miller.										
1948	**Series 89M convertible**	899A2155227	L	60-70.000 USD		NS		25-06-16	Santa Monica	1121	AA
	Maroon; restored.										
1956	**Montclair convertible**	56WA60329M	L	70-90.000 USD	44.205	67.100	59.719	05-10-15	Philadelphia	238	Bon F522
	White and red with red and white interior; restored just over a decade ago. Automatic transmission. From the Evergreen Collection (see lot 35 RM 28.1.05 $ 62,700).										
1955	**Montclair hardtop**	555L98180M	L	NA	21.641	31.000	28.681	23-01-16	Kissimmee	G210	Mec
	Black with black and white interior; restored. Automatic transmission.										
1955	**Montclair hardtop Sun Valley**	55WA47445M	L	NA	18.889	27.000	24.346	12-03-16	Kansas City	S92	Mec
	Turquoise with turquoise interior; restored. 198bhp 292 engine.										
1955	**Montclair convertible**	55SL122810M	L	70-90.000 USD	33.431*	44.000*	39.591*	30-07-16	Plymouth	129	RMS
	Red with red and white vinyl and cloth interior; restored. Automatic transmission (see RM lots 219 21.1.00 $42,900 and 142 15.11.14 $66,000).										
1957	**Monarch Lucerne convertible**	376AK57587533	L	65-75.000 USD	31.499*	45.650*	39.948*	07-05-16	Auburn	758	AA
	Three-tone red, black and white body with matching interior; automatic transmission.										
1960	**Parklane hardtop**	0W53M525039	L	14-16.000 GBP		WD		20-04-16	Duxford	60	H&H
	Black with white roof and matching interior; described as in original condition except for the paintwork redone. 310bhp 430 engine with automatic transmission.										

F521: 1923 Mercer Series 6 Sporting   F522: 1956 Mercury Montclair convertible

Year	Model	(Bodybuilder)	Chassis no.	Steering	Estimate	Hammer price £	Hammer price $	Hammer price €	Date	Place	Lot	Auc. H.
1959	Parklane 2-door hardtop		L9JC512300	L	55-65.000 USD	33.616*	44.000*	38.848*	19-08-16	Carmel	73	Bon F523

Metallic beige; in largely original condition. Body repainted in 1987; just over 45,000 miles covered.

Year	Model	(Bodybuilder)	Chassis no.	Steering	Estimate	£	$	€	Date	Place	Lot	Auc. H.
1970	Cougar Eliminator hardtop		0F91G516287	L	NA	60.804*	86.900*	79.574*	29-01-16	Scottsdale	1254	B/J

Blue with black interior; restored. Boss 302 engine with 4-speed manual gearbox.

MESSERSCHMITT (D) (1953-1956)

Year	Model	Chassis no.	Steering	Estimate	£	$	€	Date	Place	Lot	Auc. H.
1955	KR 200 cabriolet	55660	C	14-18.000 GBP	9.833	14.245	12.630	20-03-16	Goodwood	89	Bon

Red; purchased in the USA in 1994. On display in a museum in recent years, it requires recommissioning prior to use (see lot 67 Christie's 28.8.94 $ 8,050).

METZ (USA) (1898-1922)

Year	Model	Chassis no.	Steering	Estimate	£	$	€	Date	Place	Lot	Auc. H.
1914	Model 22 runabout	2480	L	25-35.000 EUR		NS		09-04-16	Essen	217	Coy

Orange with black interior; described as in good condition. With ASI homologation.

MG (GB) (1924-1980)

Year	Model	(Bodybuilder)	Chassis no.	Steering	Estimate	£	$	€	Date	Place	Lot	Auc. H.
1931	F Magna tourer		F0353	R	18-22.000 GBP	21.850	33.271	29.871	05-09-15	Beaulieu	123	Bon

Two-tone blue with white leather interior; engine rebuilt in 2004.

| 1932 | F Magna two-seater | | F0700 | R | 100-125.000 USD | 73.108* | 104.500* | 94.228* | 12-03-16 | Amelia Island | 194 | RMS |

Red with dark red interior; built with Jarvis body, in the 1960s the car was restored and fitted with the present, new F2 style body, and the engine was rebuilt and fitted with a period-correct Arnott supercharger. Restored again in the 1990s (see lot 121 RM 21.1.10 $ 121,000).

| 1932 | F Magna tourer | | F1164 | R | NA | | NS | | 20-04-16 | Duxford | 93 | H&H |

Black with red leather interior; restored 10-15 years ago, the car is described as in very good overall condition.

| 1933 | J2 Midget | (Carbodies) | 2532 | R | 22-26.000 GBP | | NS | | 10-12-15 | London | 333 | Bon |

Red; acquired in 1974 by the current owner. Fully restored between 1978 and 1984 and fitted with an engine built around a M-Type Midget cylinder block.

| 1935 | KN Magnette tourer | | KN0440 | R | 70-90.000 GBP | 88.860 | 121.774 | 110.035 | 24-06-16 | Goodwood | 236 | Bon F524 |

One of about 20 KN chassis sold by London MG agent University Motors, as the "University Special" Speed Model. Over the years the car was mechanically modified, the engine was enlarged to 1,680cc and fitted with a supercharger. Driven at numerous historic events. Engine rebuilt in 2012. (see lot 397 Bonhams 7.9.13 NS).

| 1933 | L Magna tourer | | L0489 | R | 40-50.000 GBP | 48.300 | 73.546 | 66.031 | 05-09-15 | Beaulieu | 173 | Bon |

Two-tone red with red interior; restored.

| 1933 | L Magna/Magnette K3 recreation | | L0472 | R | 100-120.000 GBP | | NS | | 10-12-15 | London | 339 | Bon |

Red with black seats; the car was built by Peter Gregory on a L Magna chassis fitted with a 2-seater sports body. Engine fitted with an original Marshall supercharger; ENV pre-selector gearbox. Raced at historic events between 2003 and 2006. With FIVA Passport.

| 1933 | L Magna roadster | | L0317 | R | 150-200.000 USD | 69.211* | 99.000* | 90.793* | 28-01-16 | Phoenix | 119 | RMS |

British racing green with dark green interior; built with four-seater tourer body, the car was fitted with the present two-seater body many years ago. Cycle-type wings.

| 1936 | NB Magnette tourer | (Carbodies) | NA0933 | R | 75-100.000 USD | 67.232* | 88.000* | 77.695* | 19-08-16 | Carmel | 109 | Bon |

Two-tone red with dark red interior; raced in the UK before WWII, the car was imported into the USA in the 1950s. Stored for many years, it received subsequently a full restoration completed in 2014.

| 1934 | PA/B Midget | | PA1711 | R | 95-120.000 GBP | 151.200 | 230.761 | 207.038 | 07-09-15 | London | 155 | RMS F525 |

British racing green; an older restoration, the car is described as still in very good overall condition. Only survivor of the three cars prepared at the factory for the 1935 Le Mans 24 Hours all-women Works team. It placed 24th overall and first of the three, driven by Joan Richmond and Eva Gordon-Simpson. Post-Le Mans the car continued to compete with the added bonus of a supercharger fitted by the factory (see lot 164 RM 27.10.10 $ 124,052).

| 1934 | PA Midget | | PA1706 | R | 23-27.000 GBP | | NS | | 16-01-16 | Birmingham | 305 | Coy |

Blue; restored between 1969 and 1970. Body repainted in the late 1990s; engine rebuilt in recent times. Since 1969 in the current ownership.

| 1934 | PA Midget | | PA0953 | R | NA | | NS | | 24-02-16 | Donington Park | 63 | H&H |

Green with brown interior; some restoration works carried out following about 50 years of storage from the 1960s.

| 1934 | PA Midget | | AWL692 | R | 20-25.000 GBP | 24.190 | 34.372 | 31.169 | 08-03-16 | London | 111 | Coy |

Blue with blue interior; restored in 1969/70. Engine rebuilt in more recent years. Since 1969 in the present ownership.

| 1935 | PA Airline coupé | (Carbodies) | PA0835 | R | 120-150.000 USD | 93.284 | 132.000 | 121.572 | 10-03-16 | Amelia Island | 198 | Bon F526 |

Red; concours-quality restoration completed in 2004.

| 1938 | SA cabriolet | (Tickford) | CHSA1513 | R | 70-80.000 USD | 51.821* | 74.800* | 67.058* | 05-06-16 | Greenwich | 53 | Bon F527 |

Burgundy with black wings and burgundy leather interior; recent restoration.

F523: 1959 Mercury Parklane 2-door hardtop

F524: 1935 MG KN Magnette tourer

Year	Model	(Bodybuilder)	Chassis no.	Steering	Estimate	Hammer Price £	$	€	Date	Sale Place	Lot	Auc. H.

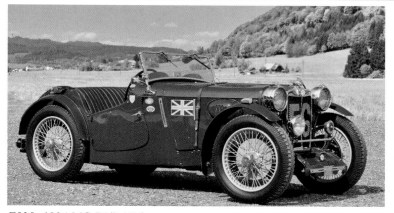

F525: 1934 MG PA/B Midget   F526: 1935 MG PA Airline coupé (Carbodies)

Year	Model	Chassis no.	Steering	Estimate	£	$	€	Date	Place	Lot	Auc. H.
1938	TA	TA1753	R	60-80.000 GBP		NS		12-09-15	Goodwood	352	Bon

Involved in a major accident in the 1960s, the car was acquired still in a dismantled state 11 years ago by the previous owner. Subsequently it was fully restored and has covered 100 miles since the restoration.

| 1937 | TA | TA1053 | R | 30-40.000 AUD | 20.705 | 31.893 | 28.773 | 24-10-15 | Melbourne | 4 | TBr |

Two-tone body; the car has covered 110 miles since the restoration.

| 1937 | TA | TA1775 | R | 35-40.000 EUR | 22.988 | 30.238 | 27.105 | 06-08-16 | Schloss Dyck | 124 | Coy |

Red; body repainted three years ago. Engine rebuilt.

| 1949 | TC | TC8109 | L | 35-45.000 USD | 39.220* | 56.100* | 51.449* | 28-01-16 | Scottsdale | 67 | Bon |

Light cream yellow with red leatherette interior; restored several years ago.

| 1947 | TC | TC3110 | R | 40-50.000 USD | 35.759* | 50.600* | 46.603* | 10-03-16 | Amelia Island | 116 | Bon |

Black with red interior; first owner the Kent County Police Department. Restored in the 2000s to the Police specification.

| 1949 | TC | TC8371 | R | 40-50.000 USD | 24.387* | 35.200* | 31.557* | 05-06-16 | Greenwhich | 40 | Bon |

Black with red interior; recent restoration.

| 1949 | TC | TC5825 | R | 45-65.000 USD | 26.893* | 35.200* | 31.078* | 19-08-16 | Carmel | 22 | Bon |

Dark red with black leather interior; restored.

| 1951 | TD | TD5486 | L | 25-35.000 EUR | | NS | | 08-11-15 | Lyon | 204 | Ose |

Black with red leather interior; reimported into Europe from the USA in 2008 and subsequently restored.

| 1951 | TD | TD8774 | L | 18-22.000 GBP | | NS | | 09-12-15 | Chateau Impney | 139 | H&H |

Black with red interior; restored. Reimported from the USA and registered in the UK.

| 1953 | TDC MkII | TDC23007EXUNA | L | 17-20.000 GBP | | NS | | 12-03-16 | Brooklands | 249 | His |

Red; described as one of the 13 TD Competition examples built in left-hand form between 1950 and 1953. In good driving order, the car is currently fitted with a 5-speed gearbox as replacement of the original 4-speed unit.

| 1951 | TD | TD5486 | L | 25-35.000 EUR | 24.042 | 34.830 | 30.880 | 20-03-16 | Fontainebleau | 313 | Ose |

See lot 204 Osenat 8.11.15.

| 1952 | TD | TD22011 | R | 14-18.000 GBP | 14.560 | 20.971 | 18.552 | 11-06-16 | Brooklands | 210 | His |

Green with green leather interior; reimported from the USA into the UK in 1990, restored and converted to right-hand drive (see lot 39 H & H 22.10.10 $24,184).

| 1953 | TD | TD28037 | L | 30-40.000 USD | 22.920* | 30.000* | 26.487* | 19-08-16 | Monterey | F98 | Mec |

Green with tan interior; restored at unspecified date.

| 1954 | TF | HDE333712 | L | 30-50.000 EUR | 17.387* | 25.774* | 23.000* | 04-02-16 | Paris | 303 | Bon F528 |

Red with black leather interior; restored (see lots 30 Bergé 17.12.12 $ 38,650 and 61 Bonhams 18.5.14 NS).

| 1955 | TF | HDA466538 | L | 15-25.000 USD | 9.526* | 13.750* | 12.327* | 05-06-16 | Greenwhich | 3 | Bon |

Black; since new in the same family ownership, the car was put in storage in the late 1980s. For restoration.

| 1955 | TF | HDA466997 | L | 35-55.000 EUR | 40.644* | 52.782* | 47.680* | 09-07-16 | Le Mans | 103 | Art |

Ivory and light green; restored between 2011 and 2015. Less than 500 kms covered since the engine rebuild.

F527: 1938 MG SA cabriolet (Tickford)   F528: 1954 MG TF

311

Year	Model	(Bodybuilder)	Chassis no.	Steering	Estimate	Hammer Price £	Hammer Price $	Hammer Price €	Sale Date	Sale Place	Lot	Auc. H.
1954	TF		HDC166389	R	24-28.000 GBP	25.760	33.918	30.585	28-07-16	Donington Park	102	H&H
	Red with beige leather interior; restored in the early 1990s. Since 1986 in the same family ownership.											
1958	MGA roadster		HDK1347564	R	22-26.000 GBP	32.063	48.813	45.350	14-11-15	Birmingham	329	SiC
	Red with black interior; fully restored in the USA between 2012 and 2013.											
1956	MGA roadster		HDA4315756	L	35-50.000 USD	29.247*	41.800*	38.276*	29-01-16	Scottsdale	1	G&Co
	Blue with navy blue leather interior; until 2010 with its first owner and subsequently restored.											
1958	MGA roadster		15GBUH38286	L	16-22.000 GBP	24.080	34.415	31.032	12-03-16	Brooklands	162	His
	Dark green with tan interior; restored in 2013.											
1956	MGA roadster		HDC1311802	R	25-28.000 GBP	21.240	30.118	26.690	16-04-16	Ascot	125	Coy
	Red with black interior; restoration completed in 2000 (see lot 76 H&H 28.7.99 $ 19,158).											
1958	MGA roadster		HDL4353459	L	15-25.000 USD	19.814*	28.600*	25.640*	05-06-16	Greenwhich	92	Bon
	Red with black interior; with its second owner from the late 1960s for over 45 years, the car is described as in original condition and believed to be only 1,500 original miles. Bought in 2015 by the current owner and returned to the road.											
1959	MGA coupé		HMA4363737	L	45-55.000 USD	35.400*	50.600*	45.626*	11-03-16	Amelia Island	61	G&Co
	British racing green with camel interior; restored between 2006 and 2007.											
1959	MGA Twin Cam roadster		YD11626	R	120-160.000 GBP		NS		07-09-15	London	121	RMS
	Green with white hardtop; prepared at the BMC Competition Department, the car was sold to South Africa where it was raced for some years. Resold to Canada, it was later reimported into the UK and subsequently sold to Switzerland (see lots 191 Brooks 26.10.93 $ 30,875 and 140 TSAC 6.10.07 NS).											
1959	MGA Twin Cam roadster		YD3971	L	40-50.000 EUR		NS		26-09-15	Frankfurt	121	Coy
	Red with black interior; sold new to the USA where it was restored in 2002. Engine rebuilt soon after the re-importation of the car into the UK in 2011.											
1959	MGA Twin Cam roadster		YD32312	L	45-65.000 EUR		NS		09-10-15	Zoute	23	Bon
	Red with black interior; restored many years ago. Engine rebuilt in recent years (see lot 316 Bonhams 6.2.14 $ 49,662).											
1959	MGA Twin Cam roadster		YD31288	L	NA		NS		31-10-15	Hilton Head	143	AA
	Black with red leather interior.											
1959	MGA Twin Cam roadster		YD31719	L	30-40.000 EUR	23.115	36.603	32.184	01-11-15	Paris	169	Art F529
	Green; fully restored in the 1990s.											
1958	MGA Twin Cam roadster		YD1528	R	NA	73.125	102.200	92.861	26-02-16	Coventry	732	SiC
	Red with black hardtop; ex-Works car, it raced the 1958 Liege-Rome-Liege placing 10th overall driven by John Gott. Described as in lovely overall condition.											
1959	MGA Twin Cam roadster		YD31878	L	NA	29.380	41.661	37.142	20-04-16	Duxford	16	H&H
	Blue with black interior; since 1960 in the current ownership, the car was fully restored between the late 1990s-early 2000s. Upgraded 1790cc MGB engine.											
1959	MGA Twin Cam roadster		YD11914	R	48-58.000 GBP	50.400	72.591	64.220	11-06-16	Brooklands	254	His
	Red with black leather interior; recent full restoration.											
1959	MGA Twin Cam roadster		YD31290	L	28-34.000 GBP	33.600	48.394	42.813	11-06-16	Brooklands	308	His
	Red with black interior; restored in Denmark 12 years ago, engine rebuilt in the UK in recent years (see lot 221 Silverstone Auctions 23.2.13 $ 45,888).											
1958	MGA Twin Cam roadster		YD3834	L	20-30.000 EUR	32.515*	42.225*	38.144*	09-07-16	Le Mans	212	Art
	Red with black interior; recently restored.											
1959	MGA 1600 roadster		GNH71075	R	15-20.000 GBP	16.675*	25.391*	22.796*	05-09-15	Beaulieu	156	Bon
	Red with black interior; body repainted in 1986; engine replaced with a rebuilt unit in 2008 (see lot 58 H&H 25.7.01 NS).											
1959	MGA 1600 roadster		GHNL69477	L	20-25.000 GBP		NS		10-10-15	Ascot	153	Coy
	Black with red leather interior; restored (see lot 228 Coys 11.7.15 NS).											
1961	MGA 1600 coupé		GHD99602	R	16-20.000 GBP	19.040	25.070	22.606	28-07-16	Donington Park	117	H&H
	Grey; engine and gearbox recently overhauled.											
1962	MGA 1600 MkII roadster		GHNL2105738	L	35-45.000 USD	24.626*	35.200*	31.740*	11-03-16	Amelia Island	2	G&Co
	Beige with saddle leatherette interior; restored in the 1980s (see lot 5 Gooding 8.3.13 $ 33,000).											
1962	MGA 1600 MkII roadster		GHNL2102918	L	25-35.000 EUR	28.167	37.414	33.600	02-07-16	Lyon	330	Agu
	Light blue with black interior; bought in 2003 by the current owner and subsequently restored.											
1962	MGA 1600 MkII roadster		GHN2102782	R	16-20.000 GBP	24.640	32.249	28.472	20-08-16	Brooklands	277	His
	Light blue with black interior; body restored and engine rebuilt at unspecified date.											
1961	MGA 1600 MkII coupé		GHDL2105452	R	NA	16.240	24.979	21.892	14-10-15	Duxford	28	H&H
	Old English white with black interior; reimported into the UK from the USA in 2007, restored and converted to right-hand drive.											

F529: 1959 MG MGA Twin Cam roadster

F530: 1965 MG MGB EX234 prototype roadster (Pininfarina)

Year	Model	(Bodybuilder)	Chassis no.	Steering	Estimate	Hammer price £	$	€	Date	Place	Lot	Auc. H.
1961	**MGA 1600 MkII coupé**		GHDL2105016	L	20-25.000 EUR		NS		09-04-16	Essen	108	Coy
Beige with original red leather interior; described as in good overall condition.													
1964	**MGB roadster**		GHN3L28684	L	20-30.000 USD	13.627*	20.900*	18.396*	09-10-15	Hershey	291	RMS
Red with black vinyl interior; restored three years ago.													
1963	**MGB roadster**		GHN313973	R	14-18.000 GBP		NS		09-12-15	Chateau Impney	99	H&H
Red; body repainted.													
1964	**MGB roadster**		GHN332967	R	15-20.000 GBP	23.000	33.320	29.541	20-03-16	Goodwood	90	Bon
Two owners; approximately 2,000 miles covered since a full restoration carried out between 2007 and 2009.													
1963	**MGB roadster**		GHN325609	R	17-22.000 GBP	17.360	22.721	20.059	20-08-16	Brooklands	278	His
Old English white with red interior; in the 1990s restored using a new body shell, engine rebuilt.													
1965	**MGB EX234 prototype roadster**	(Pininfarina)	EX234	R	35-45.000 GBP	63.100	86.472	78.137	24-06-16	Goodwood	209	Bon **F530**
Prototype designed with the 1,275cc A-Series engine and gearbox; bodied by Pininfarina, it was intended to replace both the Midget and the MGB, but it entered never the production. Sold by the factory in 1977 to MG dealer, Syd Beer. 6,400 miles covered. Offered by the Beer Family Trust.													
1962	**MGB GT**		GHD383284	R	8-10.000 GBP	8.960	12.806	11.547	12-03-16	Brooklands	153	His
British racing green with black leather interior; in good original condition. 26,530 miles covered.													
1976	**MGB MkII roadster**		GHN5399450G	R	5-8.000 GBP	14.672	20.969	18.908	12-03-16	Brooklands	237	His
White; in 2007-8 restored with a new body shell finished to some series 1 aesthetical modifications.													
1971	**MGB MkII roadster**		LHNS249519	R	12-14.000 GBP		NS		18-05-16	Donington Park	37	H&H
White with cream interior; 430 miles covered since the restoration completed in 2015.													
1977	**MGB MkII roadster**		GHN5UH425247G	L	15-20.000 EUR	18.149	25.929	23.040	19-06-16	Fontainebleau	329	Ose
White; restored some years ago.													
1972	**MGB GT MkII**		GHD5274537	R	8-12.000 GBP	12.650*	18.326*	16.248*	20-03-16	Goodwood	97	Bon
Blue; described as in very good original condition, 4,980 miles covered. Recently recommissioned.													
1968	**MGC roadster**		CGN12155G	R	17-19.000 GBP		NS		09-12-15	Chateau Impney	78	H&H
Red with black interior; recent cosmetic restoration.													
1969	**MGC roadster**		GCN1084G	R	15-18.000 GBP	19.470	27.665	25.087	08-03-16	London	106	Coy
Blue with black leather interior; restored in 1990 and unused since, the car requires light recommissioning prior to use.													
1969	**MGC roadster**		GCN1U8175G	R	20-24.000 GBP	22.400	32.263	28.542	11-06-16	Brooklands	298	His
Red; reimported into the UK from the USA in 2014 and subsequently restored and converted to right-hand drive.													
1968	**MGC roadster**		GCN11093	R	14-18.000 GBP	19.600	25.652	22.648	20-08-16	Brooklands	263	His
British racing green with black leather interior; recently restored.													
1969	**MGC GTS Sebring**		500757	R	150-250.000 EUR	110.261	158.872	140.000	14-05-16	Monaco	217	RMS **F531**
One of the four lightweight shells which remained unused at the BMC Competition Department. It was acquired by racing driver John Chatham who completed the car using original competition components and raced it in the early 1970s. The car remained in Chatham's ownership until 2004 when it was acquired by the current owner, restored and prepared for historic racing.													
1968	**MGC GT**		GCD125485	R	9-11.000 GBP	11.200	16.303	14.454	18-05-16	Donington Park	12	H&H
Black with black interior; engine overhauled in 1997, body repainted in 2009.													
1969	**MGC GT**		GCD16138G	R	17-20.000 GBP	18.000	23.688	21.316	30-07-16	Silverstone	956	SiC
Red with black leather interior; recently restored.													
1970	**Midget MkIII**		GAN592713	R	NQ	10.920*	15.728*	13.914*	11-06-16	Brooklands	325	His
Green with black interior; restored in 2003.													
1973	**MGB GT V8**		GD2D14286	R	5-7.000 GBP	14.560	21.968	20.080	09-12-15	Chateau Impney	4	H&H
Dark red; recently serviced.													
1975	**MGB GT V8**		GD2D12514G	R	14-16.000 GBP	12.995	17.111	15.429	28-07-16	Donington Park	77	H&H
Gold with black interior; recently repainted.													

MICHELOTTI (I) *(1947-1990)*

Year	Model	Chassis no.	Steering	Estimate	£	$	€	Date	Place	Lot	Auc. H.
1970	**Spiaggetta**	100GB1290331	L	60-80.000 EUR	48.515*	69.904*	61.600*	14-05-16	Monaco	221	RMS **F532**
White with wicker seats; Fiat 850 engine. From the Count Agusta Collection.												

F531: 1969 MG MGC GTS Sebring

F532: 1970 Michelotti Spiaggetta

Year	Model	(Bodybuilder)	Chassis no.	Steering	Estimate	Hammer price £	Hammer price $	Hammer price €	Sale Date	Place	Lot	Auc. H.

MILLER (USA) *(1915-1935)*

1926 91 Locomobile Junior 8 Special — 8 — M — 750-1.000.000 USD — **588.280** — **770.000** — **679.833** — 20-08-16 — Monterey — 230 — **RMS F533**
One of two specials built by Harry Miller for Cliff Durant, son of General Motors founder William Crapo Durant. The car has had a long racing career and raced four editions of the Indy 500 Miles from 1926 to 1929. From the 1940s to 1986 it was owned by Joe Gemsa and in 2008 it was bought by Sam Mann as an incomplete restoration retaining an original frame fitted with a Miller Marine engine. Subsequently it was fully restored and fitted with a correct Miller 91 engine. From the Sam and Emily Mann Collection.

MINERVA (B) *(1899-1939)*

1925 15CV Type AD sports — 41527 — R — 25-30.000 GBP — **NS** — — — 05-09-15 — Beaulieu — 172 — **Bon**
Red with tan interior; restored in the 1980s in Australia. The front of the body forward of the scuttle appears to be original, the "boat tail" rear section was fabricated during the restoration. Mechanically the car appears in good order.

MITCHELL (USA) *(1903-1923)*

1912 Model 5.6 roadster — 27027 — R — 100-150.000 USD — **NS** — — — 09-10-15 — Hershey — 245 — **RMS**
Black and white with black leather interior; cosmetically refinished some years ago.

MMC (GB) *(1897-1908)*

1904 8hp rear-entrance tonneau — 1154 — R — 40-60.000 GBP — **51.750** — **81.951** — **72.057** — 30-10-15 — London — 112 — **Bon F534**
In the same family ownership since 1955, the car was restored in 1960 circa and received further works in the 1980s. Last road registered in the 1960s, it requires recommissioning prior to use. As no number was found on the chassis, that recorded on the V5 registration document is thought to be the number stamped on the rear axle.

MONICA (F) *(1973-1975)*

1975 560 — 0104 — L — 120-140.000 EUR — **86.118** — **130.368** — **120.000** — 07-11-15 — Lyon — 265 — **Agu F535**
Light blue with blue leather interior; recently restored. The car was exhibited at the 1975 Barcelona Motor Show and sold new to Spain (see lot 40 Poulain 12.12.94 NS).

MORETTI (I) *(1945-1984)*

1955 750 Sport bialbero spider — 1601 — L — 175-225.000 GBP — **NS** — — — 07-09-15 — London — 143 — **RMS**
Red with black interior; the car was exported to Venezuela where it was raced until the late 1960s. In 1981 it was reimported into Italy by Massimo Colombo. Restored in more recent years; since the mid-2000s in the current ownership (see lot 141 Coys 10.8.13 NS).

1953 750 Sport bialbero coupé (Michelotti) — 1290 — L — 160-190.000 USD — **100.848*** — **132.000*** — **116.543*** — 19-08-16 — Monterey — 129 — **RMS F536**
Red and black with black interior; sold new to the USA, in 2005 the car was imported into the Netherlands, subsequently it was restored and in 2010 it was imported again into the USA. Engine no. 1294 rebuilt. From the Skip Barber Collection (see RM lots 288 1.5.10 $201,323 and 122 25.5.13 $173,900).

1959 Branca Formula Junior — 020 — M — 85-125.000 EUR — **38.040*** — **54.811*** — **48.300*** — 13-05-16 — Monaco — 105 — **Bon F537**
Red; one of two examples known to survice. Restored in the early 2000s, the car raced the 2008 Monaco Historic Grand Prix. Described as "on the button" (see lot 145 Bonhams 21.5.07 $ 54,112).

1972 128 coupé — 128A0800557 — L — 9-14.000 EUR — **6.341** — **9.059** — **8.050** — 18-06-16 — Wien — 402 — **Dor**
White with black leatherette interior; body recently repainted.

1978 126 Minimaxi — 5156250 — L — 12-18.000 USD — **6.988** — **10.000** — **8.747** — 02-04-16 — Ft.Lauderdale — 119 — **AA**
Light green with black interior; restored. Fiat 126 twin-cylinder engine.

MORGAN (GB) *(1910-)*

1929 Aero — 2189 — R — 18-25.000 GBP — **18.000** — **27.610** — **24.300** — 10-10-15 — Ascot — 115 — **Coy**
Dark green; for 52 years in the same family ownership. 1100 JAP engine.

1929 Aero — 1574A — R — NA — **16.800** — **25.840** — **22.646** — 14-10-15 — Duxford — 15 — **H&H**
Blue with black interior; restoration completed in 2006.

1934 Sport — N119 — R — 20-25.000 GBP — **26.450** — **40.275** — **36.160** — 05-09-15 — Beaulieu — 108 — **Bon**
Red with black interior; since 1960 in the current ownership. Restored in the 1990s and uprated with Morris Minor hydraulic front brakes. Unused in the past 10 years, it requires recommissioning prior to use.

1937 Super Sport — D1731 — R — 15-25.000 USD — **57.974*** — **88.000*** — **78.320*** — 05-10-15 — Philadelphia — 271 — **Bon F538**
In original condition; recently used. Matchless MX-2 engine. Since 1953 in the Alexis du Pont collection.

1933 Super Sport — D743 — R — 30-35.000 GBP — **33.600** — **50.696** — **46.338** — 09-12-15 — Chateau Impney — 120 — **H&H**
Orange with black interior; recent cosmetic and mechanical restoration. Raced at historic events; 70bhp 1,220cc JAP engine (see lot 19 H&H 16.10.13 $ 47,580).

1932 Super Sport — R174 — R — 35-40.000 GBP — **44.800** — **58.177** — **52.555** — 10-07-16 — Chateau Impney — 32 — **H&H**
Black with green interior; restored by the current owner. 1100cc V-twin JAP engine (see lot 1071 Bonhams 1.12.03 NS).

1938 4/4 cabriolet — 44761 — R — NA — **NS** — — — 14-10-15 — Duxford — 133 — **H&H**
Blue and black with black interior; restored in the 1980s, the car is described as in good overall condition.

1961 Plus 4 — 4755 — R — 75-85.000 GBP — **NS** — — — 16-01-16 — Birmingham — 340 — **Coy**
The car was rebuilt to Super Sport specification between 2000 and 2006. Raced at several historic events (see lot 148 Silverstone Auctions 25.2.12 NS).

1961 Plus 4 — 4796 — L — 45-60.000 USD — **28.453*** — **40.700*** — **37.326*** — 28-01-16 — Scottsdale — 63 — **Bon**
Silver with burgundy interior; sold new to the USA. Restored in recent years.

1963 4/4 — B802 — L — 55-65.000 USD — **55.369*** — **79.200*** — **72.634*** — 28-01-16 — Scottsdale — 97 — **Bon F539**
British racing green with tan leather interior; restoration completed in 2009.

1968 4/4 — B1456 — L — NA — **34.875** — **48.741** — **44.288** — 26-02-16 — Coventry — 432 — **SiC**
Red with black interior; 150 kms covered since the restoration carried out in 2014. Ford 1600 engine.

F533: 1926 Miller 91 Locomobile Junior 8 Special

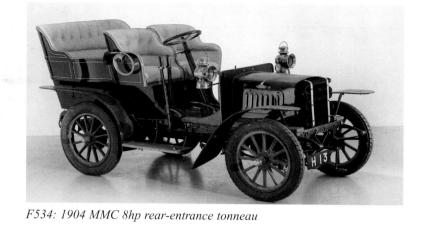
F534: 1904 MMC 8hp rear-entrance tonneau

F535: 1975 Monica 560

F536: 1953 Moretti 750 Sport bialbero coupé (Michelotti)

F537: 1959 Moretti Branca Formula Junior

F538: 1937 Morgan Super Sport

F539: 1963 Morgan 4/4

F540: 2009 Morgan Aeromax Coupé

Year	Model	(Bodybuilder)	Chassis no.	Steering	Estimate	Hammer price £	Hammer price $	Hammer price €	Date	Place	Lot	Auc. H.
1963	4/4		B1243	L	35-45.000 USD	29.721	42.900	38.460	05-06-16	Greenwhich	103	Bon
	British racing green with black interior; since 1966 in the current ownership. Body repainted and seats retrimmed.											
1976	4/4		B3808	L	35-40.000 EUR	37.432	53.479	47.520	19-06-16	Fontainebleau	372	Ose
	White with black leather interior; in good running order. Ford 1600 engine.											
2009	Aeromax Coupé		48A0100	L	150-200.000 EUR	126.184	192.131	172.500	05-09-15	Chantilly	30	Bon F540
	Burgundy with black leather interior; 6,200 kms covered. Example no.100 of 100 built. Swiss papers. From the collection of its sole owner, Alain Dominique Perrin.											

MORRIS (GB) *(1912-1983)*

Year	Model	(Bodybuilder)	Chassis no.	Steering	Estimate	£	$	€	Date	Place	Lot	Auc. H.
1913	Oxford tourer		343	R	20-25.000 GBP	33.350	50.442	46.093	10-12-15	London	380	Bon F541
	Red with black interior; since 1992 in the current ownership, the car is described as in good overall condition.											
1928	Oxford utility truck	(Parkes Body Co.)	266091	R	30-40.000 USD	45.382*	59.400*	52.444*	21-08-16	Pebble Beach	103	G&Co
	Green with wooden panels; restored at unspecified date. One of three examples built and the only known survivor.											
1925	Cowley tourer		101623	R	11-15.000 GBP	15.525	23.640	21.224	05-09-15	Beaulieu	167	Bon
	Green with black wings; since 1976 in the current ownership. Restoration completed in 1980.											
1925	Cowley tourer		33558	R	12-15.000 GBP	13.800	20.873	19.073	10-12-15	London	364	Bon
	Grey with black wings; restored in 2010.											
1934	Minor two-seater tourer		34MS45076	R	7-9.000 GBP		NS		12-03-16	Brooklands	230	His
	Dark green; it requires some attention prior to use.											
1929	Taxicab		060G	R	27-30.000 GBP		NS		14-11-15	Birmingham	637	SiC
	Red and black; bought 46 years ago by the current owner and subsequently fully restored, the car is described as in very good working order. The only known survivor of the 840 Morris-Commercial Taxicabs built.											
1948	Ten saloon		SMTN85880	R	105-11.500 GBP	10.080	13.272	11.968	28-07-16	Donington Park	108	H&H
	Until 2005 with its first owner; 33,871 recorded miles.											
1937	12/4 saloon		35TW8416	R	15-20.000 EUR		NS		16-01-16	Maastricht	448	Coy
	Dark blue and black with blue interior; restored in England at unspecified date.											
1938	Eight two-seater tourer		192504	R	12-15.000 EUR	11.582	16.964	15.190	28-05-16	Aarhus	145	SiC
	Red with black wings; restored in the 1990s.											
1938	Commercial Super Six taxicab		1861G2SW	R	20-26.000 GBP		NS		12-03-16	Brooklands	196	His
	Not used in recent years; one of three examples known to survive.											
1970	Minor 1000 Traveller		1274663	R	5-7.000 GBP	6.900*	10.507*	9.433*	05-09-15	Beaulieu	155	Bon
	Old English white with blue interior; restored. Replacement engine still under warranty.											
1968	Minor 1000 Traveller		MAW5D1227700M	L	15-20.000 EUR		NS		01-11-15	Paris	103	Art
	Old English white; restored.											
1968	Minor 1000 Traveller		MAW5D1227700M	L	8-12.000 EUR	12.846*	18.694*	16.688*	05-02-16	Paris	115	Art F542
	See lot 103 Artcurial 1.11.15.											
1960	Minor 2-door saloon		MA253878162	R	3-4.000 GBP	3.300	4.679	4.147	16-04-16	Cambridge	3309	Che
	Green; restored in the mid-1990s.											
1969	Mini Traveller		MAW61220898A	R	NQ	7.504*	11.294*	10.675*	28-11-15	Weybridge	251	His
	White; stored for the past 18 years, the car was acquired one year ago by the current, second owner and subsequently recommissioned by Wood & Pickett.											
1960	Mini		MA25415808	R	16-19.000 GBP		NS		28-11-15	Weybridge	254	His
	Light blue; restored in 2013 by Wood & Pickett. From the collection of Michael Standring.											
1959	Mini		MA2541290	R	45-55.000 GBP	42.000	55.784	50.098	02-07-16	Woodstock	227	Coy
	Light blue; one of the first press examples, the car was delivered to Autosport journalist John Bolster who drove it also at the Journalist's Race at Goodwood in 1960. Subsequently Bolster purchased the car and retained it for many years until it was bought by the present, second owner. Restored; engine and gearbox rebuilt.											
1964	Mini		KA2S4639736	R	17-20.000 GBP	16.313	21.468	19.318	30-07-16	Silverstone	913	SiC
	Grey with old English white roof; original interior. Body repainted at unspecified date.											
1965	Mini Cooper		753113	L	30-50.000 EUR		NS		14-05-16	Monaco	135	Coy
	Red with black roof: rally-raced in the 1960s and 1970s, the car was later prepared for historic rallying and used until 2009.											

F541: 1913 Morris Oxford tourer

F542: 1968 Morris Minor 1000 Traveller

Year	Model	(Bodybuilder)	Chassis No.	Steering	Estimate	Hammer price £	$	€	Date	Place	Lot	Auc. H.
1971	**Mini Cooper S**		XAD1312155A	R	16-20.000 GBP	17.920	26.971	25.493	28-11-15	Weybridge	258	His
Red with black roof; the car was restored in 2013 on an original new Leyland MkIII shell. 1,275cc rebuilt engine.											
1966	**Mini Cooper S**		850926	R	Refer Dpt.	114.240	172.103	162.358	01-12-15	London	332	Coy
Works car from 1966 to 1968 it was driven by Timo Makinen and Paddy Hopkirk. In late 1968 it was sold to private hands and it is in the current ownership for more than 30 years. Finished in red with white roof; stored for the last few years; described as in good working order.												F543
1966	**Mini Cooper S**		KA2S4896682	R	NA	28.130	39.314	35.722	26-02-16	Coventry	116	SiC
Dark blue with white roof; prepared for historic racing. 1,293cc engine.											
1969	**Mini Moke**		MAB1L1187994A	L	8-12.000 EUR	10.765	16.296	15.000	07-11-15	Lyon	283	Agu
Red with beige interior; restored at unspecified date.											
1971	**1300 GT saloon**		MA4D216291M	R	3-4.000 GBP	3.360	5.070	4.634	09-12-15	Chateau Impney	38	H&H
Red with black roof; restored, it is described as in good overall condition.											

MORS (F) *(1895-1925)*

Year	Model	(Bodybuilder)	Chassis No.	Steering	Estimate	£	$	€	Date	Place	Lot	Auc. H.
1913	**RX torpedo**		125217	R	30-40.000 EUR		NS		08-11-15	Lyon	208	Ose
Blue with black wings; for 29 years in the current ownership. Not in working order.											
1913	**RX torpedo**		125217	R	15-20.000 EUR	23.543	34.108	30.240	20-03-16	Fontainebleau	308	Ose
See lot 208 Osenat 8.11.15.											

MUNTZ (USA) *(1950-1954)*

Year	Model	(Bodybuilder)	Chassis No.	Steering	Estimate	£	$	€	Date	Place	Lot	Auc. H.
1953	**Jet convertible**		53M602	L	250-325.000 USD	143.418	205.000	184.849	11-03-16	Amelia Island	18	G&Co
Dark blue with snakeskin-pattern vinyl interior; bought in 2000 by the current owner and subsequently fully restored.											
1952	**Jet convertible**		M134	L	200-300.000 USD	126.060*	165.000*	145.679*	19-08-16	Carmel	76	Bon
Fully restored, the car is described as in excellent overall condition.												F544

NAPIER (GB) *(1900-1924)*

Year	Model	(Bodybuilder)	Chassis No.	Steering	Estimate	£	$	€	Date	Place	Lot	Auc. H.
1904	**Model D45 side-entrance tonneau**		49(engine)	R	350-400.000 GBP	326.333	516.781	454.386	30-10-15	London	108	Bon
Dark green with red interior; car assembled by the Napier Motor Company of America in Boston. Formerly part of the collections of George Waterman and Kenneth Stein who restored it to running order for the 1984 London-Brighton Run. Further restoration works carried out following its import into the UK in 2000.												F545
1912	**15hp tourer**		7759	R	5-8.000 GBP	20.930*	31.870*	28.613*	05-09-15	Beaulieu	104	Bon
Restoration project. Believed to have been in the same family ownership since the 1930s and last used in 1980. Without chassis plate or number stamping; no documents.											
1913	**30/35hp tourer**	(Cunard)	11667	R	150-180.000 USD		NS		05-10-15	Philadelphia	250	Bon
Blue with blue interior; sold new in the UK, the car was imported into the USA in the 2000s. Body repainted at unspecified date, engine rebuilt in 1986. In working order (see lots 1163 Bonhams 12.7.02 NS, 256 RM 8.3.08 NS and 137 Gooding 15.8.10 NS).											

NASH (USA) *(1917-1957)*

Year	Model	(Bodybuilder)	Chassis No.	Steering	Estimate	£	$	€	Date	Place	Lot	Auc. H.
1947	**Ambassador Suburban sedan**		454676	L	100-125.000 USD		NS		02-04-16	Ft.Lauderdale	491	AA
Blue with wooden panels and red leather interior; Best in Class at the 2001 Amelia Island Concours d'Elegance.											
1948	**Ambassador Suburban sedan**		R470808	L	80-100.000 USD	43.643*	63.250*	55.350*	07-05-16	Auburn	786	AA
Maroon with wooden panels and maroon leather interior; fully restored.												F546
1948	**Ambassador Custom convertible**		R491581	L	100-115.000 USD		NS		05-06-16	Greenwhich	79	Bon
Green with green leather interior; restored over 10 years ago, the car is described as still in very good overall condition. From the Evergreen Collection (see lot 262 RM 5.8.06 $ 104,500).											
1951	**Rambler Custom convertible**		D35913	L	22-28.000 USD	16.698*	24.200*	21.177*	07-05-16	Auburn	852	AA
Maroon with cloth interior.											
1954	**Ambassador Country Club Le Mans**		R737780	L	18-28.000 EUR	17.211	24.590	21.850	18-06-16	Wien	435	Dor
Red with black interior; imported when new into Austria. Described as in largely original condition.											
1954	**Metropolitan convertible**		E15430	L	NA	11.598*	17.600*	15.784*	26-09-15	Las Vegas	144	B/J
Pink; restoration completed in August 2015.											
1954	**Metropolitan convertible**		3960	L	30-40.000 USD	14.401*	22.000*	19.549*	08-10-15	Hershey	184	RMS
Blue; restored. Engine rebuilt.											

F543: 1966 Morris Mini Cooper S

F544: 1952 Muntz Jet convertible

Year	Model	(Bodybuilder)	Chassis no.	Steering	Estimate	Hammer price £	$	€	Sale Date	Place	Lot	Auc. H.

F545: 1904 Napier Model D45 side-entrance tonneau

F546: 1948 Nash Ambassador Suburban sedan

| 1958 | Metropolitan coupé | | E41104 | L | 25-30.000 USD | 25.102* | 38.500* | 33.888* | 09-10-15 | Hershey | 248 | RMS |

White and green with black and white vinyl interior; restored. Engine rebuilt.

NATIONAL (USA) (1900-1924)

| 1911 | Model 40 roadster | | 8307(engine) | R | 200-275.000 USD | 251.020 | 385.000 | 338.877 | 09-10-15 | Hershey | 240 | RMS F547 |

Medium blue with yellow chassis and black leather interior; discovered in the early 1950s and restored, the car was restored again in the 2000s. Sister car to the 1912 Indy 500 winner. From the Harold Coker collection.

NEWTON BENNETT (I)

| 1925 | Type S150 14hp tourer | | 2032 | R | 45-55.000 EUR | | NS | | 04-02-16 | Paris | 403 | Bon |

Black; the car has covered 400 miles since the restoration. The cars were built in Turin, Italy, by Ceirano and marketed in the UK as Newton Bennett.

NISSAN (J) (1933-)

| 1972 | Datsun 240Z | | HLS378447 | L | 22-26.000 GBP | | NS | | 12-03-16 | Brooklands | 234 | His |

Yellow with black and yellow interior; restored in 2013.

| 1972 | Datsun 240Z | | HLS3083622 | L | 18-22.000 GBP | 25.760 | 33.452 | 30.219 | 10-07-16 | Chateau Impney | 4 | H&H |

Green with black interior; restored at unspecified date. Imported into the UK from the USA in 2015.

| 1971 | Datsun 240Z | | HLS3021344 | L | 23-26.000 GBP | | NS | | 30-07-16 | Silverstone | 516 | SiC |

Red with black interior; one owner until 2014. 56,000 miles covered.

| 1972 | Fairlady ZG coupé | | HS30100011 | R | 65-85.000 USD | 41.999 | 60.500 | 53.518 | 11-06-16 | Hershey | 143 | TFA |

Maroon with black interior; imported into the USA from Japan in 2013. Body repainted to original colour.

| 1972 | Skyline 2000 GT-R | | KPGC10001443 | R | 225-275.000 USD | 142.868* | 187.000* | 165.102* | 21-08-16 | Pebble Beach | 142 | G&Co |

Beige; purchased in Japan in 2015 and subsequently restored in Costa Rica.

| 1978 | Datsun 260Z | | RS30021058 | R | 25-35.000 GBP | | NS | | 30-07-16 | Silverstone | 919 | SiC |

Metallic bronze; stored in 1995 at 8,150 miles. Running engine; mechanicals to be recommissioned.

| 1975 | Datsun 280Z | | GHLS30041804 | L | 35-45.000 USD | 34.605* | 49.500* | 45.396* | 28-01-16 | Scottsdale | 31 | Bon |

Light blue with black interior; until very recently with its first owner, the car is described as in very good original condition and has covered just over 2,000 miles.

| 1989 | Skyline GT-R | | BNR32000591 | R | 50-70.000 USD | 57.676* | 82.500* | 75.661* | 28-01-16 | Phoenix | 174 | RMS F548 |

Just one owner and less than 14,000 kms covered; routinely serviced by the Nissan dealership in Tokyo.

NSU (D) (1905-1977)

| 1971 | Prinz 4L | | OS11009098 | R | 65-8.000 GBP | 5.040 | 6.636 | 5.984 | 28-07-16 | Donington Park | 45 | H&H |

Blue with tan vinyl interior; in highly original condition, 26,800 recorded miles.

F547: 1911 National Model 40 roadster

F548: 1989 Nissan Skyline GT-R

Year	Model	(Bodybuilder)	Chassis No.	Steering	Estimate	Hammer Price £	Hammer Price $	€	Date	Place	Lot	Auc. H.
1971	**1000 C**		0611036795	R	6.5-7.500 GBP	5.916	8.926	8.159	09-12-15	Chateau Impney	32	H&H
	Blue; recent cosmetic restoration. Two owners.											

OLDSMOBILE (USA) *(1896-2004)*

Year	Model	(Bodybuilder)	Chassis No.	Steering	Estimate	£	$	€	Date	Place	Lot	Auc. H.
1904	**Model 6C curved dash runabout**		21688(engine)	R	60-80.000 USD	37.653*	57.750*	50.832*	09-10-15	Hershey	253	RMS
	Black and red with black leather interior; fully restored for the current owner.											
1904	**French Front Light Tonneau**		25816	R	70-100.000 USD	46.222	60.500	53.415	19-08-16	Carmel	100	Bon
	Red with black leather interior; discovered in the 1980s and subsequently restored. Mechanicals rebuilt in the last few years.											
1911	**Autocrat roadster**		65877	R	700-850.000 USD	455.422	698.500	614.820	09-10-15	Hershey	262	RMS
	Yellow with black seats; nicknamed "The Yellow Peril", the car was acquired new by John Henry Greenway Albert and raced at some events in 1910s. It remained with the Albert family until the early 1970s, it was first restored probably in the early 1980s and restored again in 2008 by the previous owner. Described as in very good driving order (see lots 325 Christie's 19.3.99 $ 100,000 and 260 RM 14.3.09 $ 660,000).											**F549**
1917	**Model 45 touring**		126312	L	NA	13.284*	18.700*	16.456*	09-04-16	Palm Beach	351	B/J
	Green with black interior; restored in the early 2000s. Recent mechanical works. Owned by the first two families for 81 years (see RM lots 250 13.3.04 $ 27,500, and 111 6.10.11 $ 14,850).											
1923	**Model 43-A brougham**		24365	L	25-30.000 USD	12.601*	19.250*	17.106*	08-10-15	Hershey	189	RMS
	Blue and black with blue interior; recently restored.											
1924	**Mod.30-B turtle deck speedster**	(Schutte)	129	L	60-90.000 USD	46.618*	71.500*	62.934*	09-10-15	Hershey	279	RMS
	Red with black fenders; described as in largely original condition.											
1938	**Series L Eight convertible**		L226664	L	NA	32.512	49.500	44.446	05-09-15	Auburn	7043	AA
	Cream with red interior; in good overall condition.											
1941	**Series 66 station wagon**	(Hercules)	6654477	L	125-175.000 USD	63.030*	82.500*	72.839*	21-08-16	Pebble Beach	156	G&Co
	Cream with wooden panels, brown Everflex roof and maroon interior; restoration completed four years ago circa. Automatic transmission.											
1950	**Futuramic Series 98 club sedan**		509M17236	L	NQ	26.770	39.000	34.761	20-05-16	Indianapolis	S66	Mec
	Blue with grey interior; restored.											
1949	**Futuramic Series 88 station wagon**		498M25924	L	NA	44.542*	62.700*	55.176*	09-04-16	Palm Beach	439	B/J
	Metallic green with wooden panels and brown interior; restoration completed in October 2015. Automatic transmission.											
1953	**Classic 98 convertible**		539W6350	L	70-80.000 USD	38.709	56.100	49.093	07-05-16	Auburn	853	AA
	White with white and black interior; in good overall condition.											
1953	**Fiesta 98 convertible**		539M41305	L	NA	137.271*	209.000*	187.661*	05-09-15	Auburn	5145	AA **F550**
	Black with black and ivory interior; restored. Automatic transmission.											
1957	**Series Super 88 Holiday coupé**		578C08853	L	NA	43.349	66.000	59.261	05-09-15	Auburn	5092	AA
	White with three-tone interior; fully restored. 300bhp 371 J-2 engine.											
1957	**Series Super 88 convertible**		578M9395	L	55-75.000 EUR	62.222	90.142	79.920	20-03-16	Fontainebleau	323	Ose
	Red and white with red and white interior; in good overall condition. Automatic transmission.											
1957	**Series 98 Starfire convertible**		579M26916	L	125-150.000 USD	92.360*	132.000*	120.872*	29-01-16	Phoenix	267	RMS
	Red with red interior; 15 miles covered since the restoration. 300bhp 371 J-2 engine with automatic transmission.											
1956	**Series 98 Starfire convertible**		569W2919	L	NA	58.608*	82.500*	72.600*	09-04-16	Palm Beach	435	B/J
	Black and white with black and white interior.											
1959	**Series 98 convertible**		599C07024	L	NA		NS		18-06-16	Portland	S132	Mec
	Blue and white with white, blue and grey interior; restored.											
1961	**Series 98 Starfire convertible**		616M03036	L	60-70.000 USD	65.810	90.200	81.505	25-06-16	Santa Monica	1047	AA
	Black with red interior; restored. Automatic transmission.											
1963	**Starfire convertible**		636M02224	L	NA	20.288	29.000	26.149	12-03-16	Kansas City	S173	Mec
	Blue with white interior; 394 engine with automatic transmission.											
1966	**Toronado**		396876M502641	L	NA	14.585	23.100	20.310	31-10-15	Hilton Head	108	AA
	Red with red interior; transmission rebuilt.											
1967	**Toronado**		396877M603138	L	15-20.000 USD	12.109	17.328	15.157	02-04-16	Ft.Lauderdale	104	AA
	Body repainted and finished in pewter; original interior.											

F549: 1911 Oldsmobile Autocrat roadster

F550: 1953 Oldsmobile Fiesta 98 convertible

Year	Model	(Bodybuilder)	Chassis no.	Steering	Estimate	Hammer price £	$	€	Date	Place	Lot	Auc. H.
1970	Cutlass-Supreme SX convertible		342670E108614	L	40-45.000 USD		NS		02-04-16	Ft.Lauderdale	188	AA
	Red with white interior; restored. 455 engine with automatic transmission.											
1970	Cutlass-Supreme SX convertible		342670E108614	L	35-40.000 USD	28.842	41.800	36.579	07-05-16	Auburn	554	AA
	See lot 188 Auctions America 2.4.16.											
1972	442 convertible		3J67U2M140083	L	NA	48.934	77.500	68.138	31-10-15	Hilton Head	175	AA
	Black with white interior; restored. 455 engine with automatic transmission.											
1970	442 convertible		344670M335028	L	NA	215.508	308.000	282.036	30-01-16	Scottsdale	5094	R&S
	Red; stored for 28 years until 2004 and subsequently restored. W30 engine with 4-speed manual gearbox.											
1970	442 coupé		344870M175564	L	NA	49.280	64.000	57.811	09-07-16	Denver	S35	Mec
	Burgundy with white vinyl roof and parchment interior; 370bhp 455 W-30 engine with automatic transmission.											
1969	442 coupé		7344879M336338	L	90-120.000 USD	72.274*	94.600*	83.522*	19-08-16	Carmel	102	Bon
	White with gold trim; restored in 2004 (see lot 56 Gooding & Company 20.8.11 $95,700).											

OM (I) (1918-1968)

1926	665 S3 Superba	(Short Bros.)	25892	R	120-150.000 GBP	126.940	193.292	173.540	05-09-15	Beaulieu	128	Bon
	Red with black wings and black interior; sold new to the UK where it was bodied. Probably restored between the late 1970s and early 1980s; further works carried out in the 1990s; described as in good overall condition.											F551

OPEL (D) (1898-)

1964	Kapitan A 2.5L saloon		263113332	L	10-15.000 EUR	8.153	11.648	10.350	18-06-16	Wien	417	Dor
	Champagne with original light brown cloth interior; body repainted.											
1973	GT		793279817	L	14-20.000 EUR	9.886	15.268	13.440	17-10-15	Salzburg	309	Dor
	Red with black interior; restored at unspecified date. 37,143 kms on the odometer.											
1981	Ascona 2000 Group 2		8115071788	L	35-45.000 EUR	25.402*	32.989*	29.800*	09-07-16	Le Mans	185	Art
	White and yellow; prepared to Group 1 specification, the car was raced in period at some rallies in Italy. Later it was prepared to Group 2 specification for historic rallying.											

OSCA (I) (1947-1967)

1959	Tipo S-273		767	L	650-800.000 USD		NS		11-03-16	Amelia Island	54	G&Co
	White with blue stripes; built with a 1100 Type 273 engine, the car was bought new by Briggs Cunningham and immediately fitted by Alfred Momo with 750 Type 187N engine no.771. Raced at several events, among them the 1960 Sebring 12 Hours, in 1961 the car was acquired by A. Cecil Schoeneman who raced it until 1963. In 1971 it was bought by John Hunholz who had it fully restored. Bought in 2015 by the current owner; engine and gearbox recently restored.											
1959	Tipo S-273		767	L	650-800.000 USD	462.220	605.000	534.155	20-08-16	Pebble Beach	36	G&Co
	See lot 54 Gooding & Company 11.3.16.											
1961	1600 GT coupé	(Touring)	019	L	380-460.000 EUR		NS		05-09-15	Chantilly	10	Bon
	One of two examples built, the car was sold new in Italy. Later it was exported to France where it was restored under the supervision of Carlo Felice Bianchi Anderloni. Further restoration works were carried between 2004 and 2006. Offered with a spare engine.											
1963	1600 GT cabriolet	(Fissore)	00119	L	170-230.000 EUR	155.982	226.997	202.640	05-02-16	Paris	121	Art
	Burgundy with original black leatherette interior; described as in well-preserved original condition. Engine recently overhauled. 37,500 kms on the odometer. Displayed at the 1963 Turin Motor Show (see lot 134 Coys 24.3.12 $ 166,935).											F552

OSI (I) (1960-1968)

1963	Fiat 1200 S spider		118H035896	L	14-18.000 EUR	8.073	11.363	10.000	09-04-16	Essen	224	Coy
	Red; for 25 years on display in an Italian museum.											
1967	20M TS		EX54HB02648	L	22-24.000 GBP		NS		10-07-16	Chateau Impney	70	H&H
	Silver with red interior; described as in good overall condition. Currently fitted with a Burton Engines 2.8-litre Ford V6 engine (see lots 279 Sotheby's 18.9.95 $5,690, 933 Brooks 6.12.99 $3,792, and 325 Bonhams 28.4.14 $29,059).											

OVERLAND (USA) (1903-1939)

1910	Model 40 roadster		2060	R	NA		NS		14-10-15	Duxford	100	H&H
	Light grey with black interior; restored at unspecified date, the car is described as in good overall condition.											

F551: 1926 OM 665 S3 Superba (Short Bros.)

F552: 1963 Osca 1600 GT cabriolet (Fissore)

Year	Model	(Bodybuilder)	Chassis no.	Steering	Estimate	£	$	€	Date	Place	Lot	Auc. H.

PACKARD (USA) (1899-1958)

Year	Model	(Bodybuilder)	Chassis no.	Steering	Estimate	£	$	€	Date	Place	Lot	Auc. H.
1906	Model S touring		2425	R	300-350.000 USD		NS		20-08-16	Monterey	S56	Mec

Blue and black with black leather interior; described as in very good overall condition. From 1966 to 1986 it was part of the Bill Harrah's collection and later for 25 years it was in the Tom and Joann Goodlet Collection (see lot S108.1 Mecum 10.4.15 $300,000).

| 1911 | Thirty UE limousine | | 16476 | R | 150-200.000 USD | 96.195* | 137.500* | 123.984* | 12-03-16 | Amelia Island | 117 | RMS |

In the same ownership from 1947 for over 60 years, the car is described as in original condition except for the driver's seat retrimmed years ago. In working order (see lot 154 RM 10.10.13 NS).

| 1907 | Thirty touring | | 3634 | R | 375-425.000 USD | 233.020 | 305.000 | 269.285 | 20-08-16 | Monterey | S55 | Mec |

Maroon with gold pinstriping; fully restored in the 1970s.

| 1914 | 1-38 touring | | 39441 | L | 400-500.000 USD | 268.950* | 412.500* | 363.083* | 09-10-15 | Hershey | 254 | RMS |

Black and olive green with black leather interior; fully restored, the car is described as in very good driving order. Formerly in the Paine and Browning collections (see lots 37 Christie's 20.8.00 $ 171,000 and 115 Gooding 18.8.13 $ 467,500). **F553**

| 1915 | Twin Six 1-25 touring | | 80709 | L | 125-175.000 USD | 111.166 | 170.500 | 150.074 | 09-10-15 | Hershey | 270 | RMS |

Dark blue with black leather interior; acquired by the current owner in the late 1960s, the car was subjected to a long restoration started in the 1980s. In good driving order.

| 1918 | Twin Six 3-35 Ormonde roadster | (Rubay) | 158825(engine) | L | 200-250.000 USD | 114.839 | 162.500 | 149.663 | 10-03-16 | Amelia Island | 192 | Bon |

Red with black fenders; for the past 20 years at the America's Packard Museum in Dayton, Ohio. Engine rebuilt about a decade ago. Recently recommissioned (see lot 37 Bonhams 14.8.15 NS).

| 1926 | Eight 243 touring | | 200346 | L | 120-150.000 USD | | NS | | 05-06-16 | Greenwhich | 61 | Bon |

Green with black fenders; purchased by the current owner and restored that same year.

| 1929 | Eight 640 roadster | | 173197 | L | NA | | NS | | 26-09-15 | Las Vegas | 762 | B/J |

Two-tone blue with tan interior; restored about 15 years ago. In the same family ownership for the last 30 years.

| 1929 | DeLuxe Eight 645 sport phaeton | (Dietrich) | 176980 | L | 175-225.000 USD | 115.210 | 176.000 | 156.394 | 08-10-15 | Hershey | 170 | RMS |

Beige with scarlet accents; restored 14 years ago. Further mechanical and cosmetic works carried out two years ago.

| 1929 | Eight 640 phaeton | | 171752 | L | 130-160.000 USD | 87.263 | 125.000 | 115.650 | 23-01-16 | Kissimmee | F204 | Mec |

Burgundy with black fenders and tan interior; restored.

| 1929 | DeLuxe Eight 645 sport phaeton | (Dietrich) | 169841 | L | 150-200.000 USD | 219.325 | 313.500 | 282.683 | 12-03-16 | Amelia Island | 155 | RMS |

Two-tone red with red leather interior; restored in the late 1980s. In more recent years the car was acquired by Richard & Linda Kughn who refreshed the restoration and mechanicals (see RM lots 107 17.1.03 $ 121,000 and 279 22.1.10 $ 137,500).

| 1930 | DeLuxe Eight 7th series phaeton | | 187369 | L | NA | 115.597 | 176.000 | 158.030 | 05-09-15 | Auburn | 5134 | AA |

Silver and red with tan interior (see lot S186 Mecum 17.8.13 $ 165,000).

| 1930 | Eight 733 roadster | | 287705 | L | 80-100.000 USD | 43.204 | 66.000 | 58.648 | 08-10-15 | Hershey | 183 | RMS |

Two-tone brown; restored in the mid-1990s.

| 1930 | DeLuxe 8 745 convertible sedan | (Dietrich) | 179463 | L | 225-300.000 USD | | NS | | 10-03-16 | Amelia Island | 151 | Bon |

Light red and silver; restored.

| 1930 | Eight 734 Speedster Runabout | | 184100 | L | 1.200-1.500.000 USD | 1.596.760 | 2.090.000 | 1.845.261 | 20-08-16 | Pebble Beach | 30 | G&Co |

Two-tone grey; one of 18 examples known to survive. First restored in the early 1970s. In 1986 the car was purchased by Glen Mounger who in 1989 resold it and in 2000 repurchased it. Concours-quality restoration completed in 2002. From the Glen Mounger Collection. **F554**

| 1931 | DeLuxe Eight 845 convertible | (LeBaron) | 189776 | L | 325-375.000 USD | 205.380 | 315.000 | 277.263 | 09-10-15 | Hershey | 266 | RMS |

Orange and brown with light brown interior; from the early 1940s for 70 years in the same family ownership. Restored by Hill & Vaughn between 1977 and 1980, it is described as still in good overall condition.

| 1931 | Eight 840 roadster | | 189993 | L | 250-275.000 USD | | NS | | 28-01-16 | Scottsdale | 81 | Bon |

White and dark red with dark red interior; restored about 10 years ago.

| 1931 | DeLuxe Eight 840 convertible | | 4796 | L | 140-170.000 USD | 107.615 | 154.000 | 134.704 | 02-04-16 | Ft.Lauderdale | 511 | AA |

White with black fenders and black interior; for over 40 years in the current, second ownership. Restored approximately 30 years ago, engine rebuilt in the early 1990s.

| 1931 | Custom Eight 8th series phaeton | | 323319 | L | 75-95.000 USD | 52.371 | 75.900 | 66.420 | 07-05-16 | Auburn | 785 | AA |

Ivory with dark grey fenders and red leather interior.

| 1931 | DeLuxe Eight 840 convertible | | 191094 | L | 110-140.000 USD | 54.626* | 71.500* | 63.127* | 19-08-16 | Carmel | 115 | Bon |

White with red leather interior; restoration completed in 2002.

| 1932 | Eight 9th series sedan | | 563175 | L | NA | 107.754* | 154.000* | 141.018* | 29-01-16 | Scottsdale | 1374 | B/J |

Two-tone blue; fully restored at unspecified date.

F553: 1914 Packard 1-38 touring

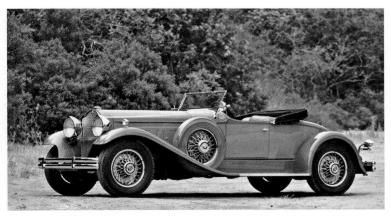

F554: 1930 Packard Eight 734 Speedster Runabout

Year	Model	(Bodybuilder)	Chassis no.	Steering	Estimate	Hammer Price £	Hammer Price $	Hammer Price €	Date	Place	Lot	Auc. H.
1932	Standard Eight 902 phaeton		50115	L	140-175.000 USD		NS		07-05-16	Auburn	783	AA
	Black with black interior and red wheels (see lot 279 RM 10.10.08 $ 82,500).											
1933	Eight 1001 roadster		60983	L	250-300.000 USD	163.878	214.500	189.382	20-08-16	Pebble Beach	4	G&Co
	Two-tone tan and maroon with maroon leather interior; in single ownership from 1960 circa to 1995. First restored in the 1970s and in the late 1990s again. In concours condition.											
1934	Eight 1101 coupé		376770	L	100-120.000 USD	69.211	99.000	90.793	28-01-16	Scottsdale	8	Bon
	White and maroon with brown interior; acquired by the current owner in 2008 and subsequently restored.											
1933	Eight 1101 coupé		76715	L	NA	100.057*	143.000*	130.945*	29-01-16	Scottsdale	1375	B/J
	Red and maroon with tan leather interior; restored.											
1935	Eight 12th series convertible victoria		807294	L	160-180.000 EUR		NS		26-09-15	Frankfurt	163	Coy
	Green with brown interior; described as in very good overall condition.											
1937	Super Eight 1501 convertible victoria		1007304	L	95-125.000 EUR		NS		03-02-16	Paris	158	RMS
	Dark green with original interior; since 1964 in the same family ownership. In good driving order.											
1937	Super 8 1507 convertible sedan		399089	L	115-145.000 USD		NS		05-06-16	Greenwhich	67	Bon
	Green with light brown interior; restored.											
1940	Eight 18th series 120 coupé		B314772	R	15-18.000 GBP	16.675	25.391	22.796	05-09-15	Beaulieu	162	Bon
	White with red leather interior; restored in 2007-08.											
1940	Super 8 1803 convertible sedan		13772026	L	90-120.000 USD	38.451*	55.000*	50.441*	28-01-16	Scottsdale	37	Bon
	Cream with dark red leather interior; restoration completed in early 2015. Engine rebuilt.											
1932	Twin Six sport phaeton		900202	L	2.300-3.000.000 DKK	209.559	318.061	285.298	26-09-15	Ebeltoft	36	Bon
	Cream and maroon with tan interior; restored in the late 1960s. From the Frederiksen Collection.											
1932	Twin Six 906 sport phaeton		900362	L	375-475.000 USD	288.024	440.000	390.984	08-10-15	Hershey	155	RMS
	Cream with brown interior; Dietrich style body built in 1981. The car was freshened in 2006 and subsequently exhibited at Concours d'Elegance events in the USA.											
1932	Twin Six 905 roadster		900471	L	650-800.000 USD	846.516	1.210.000	1.091.057	12-03-16	Amelia Island	118	RMS F555
	Dark blue with dark blue leather interior; long regarded as the Clark Gable Twin Six. After several ownership changes in 1997 circa the car was acquired by the late Tom Moretti who subsequently restored it to concours condition (see lot 146 Gooding 21.1.12 $ 737,000).											
1932	Twin Six 905 roadster		57693	L	650-800.000 USD	351.440	460.000	406.134	20-08-16	Monterey	S63	Mec
	Grey with black fenders and red leather interior; described as in very good overall condition. The car was acquired from its first owner in 1951 by the Kalinoff family who retained it for 63 years until 2014.											
1933	Twelve 1005 convertible victoria		901624	L	500-600.000 USD	461.802	660.000	604.362	29-01-16	Phoenix	224	RMS F556
	Black with scarlet leather interior; from 1986 to 2011 with the same owner who had it fully restored. Described as in excellent overall condition.											
1933	Twelve 1005 roadster		901615	L	400-475.000 USD	277.327	365.000	328.427	30-07-16	Plymouth	123	RMS
	Sage green with light green leather interior; fully restored in the 2000s (see lot 151 RM 29.7.12 $385,000).											
1934	Twelve 1107 roadster		73936	L	2.600-4.000.000 DKK	226.550	343.850	308.430	26-09-15	Ebeltoft	5	Bon
	Blue with blue leather interior; fully restored between the late 1980s-early 1990s. From the Frederiksen Collection (see lot 127 RM 20.3.99 $ 214,500).											
1934	Twelve 1107 formal sedan		73215	L	75-85.000 AUD	39.817	61.332	55.333	24-10-15	Melbourne	19	TBr
	For restoration.											
1934	Twelve 1108 sport sedan	(Derham)	110888	L	400-600.000 USD		NS		20-08-16	Pebble Beach	44	G&Co
	Beige with brown fenders and beige cloth interior; acquired in 1965 by Ken Vaughn who restored it to concours condition and retained it until 1998. Described as still in very good overall condition (see lot 42 Gooding & Company 21.10.06 $495,000).											
1934	Twelve 1107 dual cowl phaeton		73113	L	550-700.000 USD	378.180	495.000	437.036	21-08-16	Pebble Beach	133	G&Co
	Black with red leather interior; restored to concours condition between 1978 and 1980. Further works carried out in 2007; engine rebuilt in 2009.											
1936	Twelve 1407 roadster		939225	L	275-350.000 USD	251.020*	385.000*	338.877*	09-10-15	Hershey	259	RMS
	Blue with tan leather interior; first restored in the late 1960s, the car was acquired about 15 years ago by the current owner and subsequently restored again.											
1936	Twelve 1407 roadster		939201	L	225-275.000 USD	115.352	165.000	151.322	28-01-16	Phoenix	152	RMS
	Ivory with brown leather interior; restored in the late 1980s.											
1937	Twelve 1508 convertible sedan		1073214	L	150-175.000 USD	129.611*	198.000*	175.943*	08-10-15	Hershey	157	RMS
	Maroon with leather and cloth interior; acquired over 10 years ago by the current owner, the car was subsequently repainted and retrimmed. Engine rebuilt. Not used in the last two years.											
1937	Twelve 1508 convertible sedan		906221	L	200-225.000 USD	144.512	206.800	180.888	02-04-16	Ft.Lauderdale	726	AA
	Grey with grey cloth interior; restored.											

F555: 1932 Packard Twin Six 905 roadster

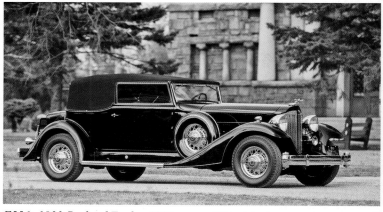

F556: 1933 Packard Twelve 1005 convertible victoria

Year	Model	(Bodybuilder)	Chassis no.	Steering	Estimate	Hammer price £	$	€	Date	Place	Lot	Auc. H.
1938	**Twelve 1607 roadster**		11392021	L	250-300.000 USD	250.734	330.000	296.934	30-07-16	Plymouth	153	**RMS**
Maroon with biscuit leather interior; since 1993 in the current ownership. Restoration completed in late 2015.												
1939	**Twelve 1708 convertible sedan**		12532017	L	NA		NS		05-09-15	Auburn	7068	**AA**
Silver metallic with red leather interior; fully restored at unspecified date (see lots 17 Gooding 12.3.10 $ 170,500 and 237 Bonhams 31.5.15 $ 160,600).												
1939	**Twelve 1707 convertible victoria**		B602466	L	225-325.000 USD	173.027	247.500	226.982	28-01-16	Phoenix	142	**RMS**
Dark blue with burgundy interior; bought in 2007 by the current owner and fully restored between 2010 and 2013 (see lot 230 RM 19.1.07 $ 165,000).												
1937	**15th series Six Model 115C convertible**		10892803	L	85-105.000 USD	48.411	74.250	65.355	09-10-15	Hershey	228	**RMS**
Dark red with red leather interior; fully restored in the 1990s.												
1937	**15th series Six 115C convertible**		T34319	L	75-100.000 USD	51.480	75.000	66.848	20-05-16	Indianapolis	S126	**Mec**
Dark blue with blue leather interior; restored.												
1939	**17th series Six convertible**		12893012	L	55-65.000 USD	21.381	30.800	27.246	11-06-16	Hershey	104	**TFA**
Black with red interior; always well maintained, the car is described as in largely original condition. The paintwork was redone in the past and the original leather interior have been covered with red vinyl.												
1941	**One-Ten 1900 Six convertible**		588895	L	NA	23.087	33.000	29.756	12-03-16	Kansas City	S113	**Mec**
White and red with red interior.												
1948	**Eight 22nd series station sedan**		G241516C	L	NA	53.453	77.000	68.114	11-06-16	Newport Beach	6102	**R&S**
Sand with wooden panels and beige interior; the car remained in a museum from 1949 circa to the mid-1990s, is described as in highly original condition and has covered approximately 19,000 miles since new.												
1948	**Eight 2201 station sedan**		22932212	L	75-90.000 USD	41.789*	55.000*	49.489*	30-07-16	Plymouth	154	**RMS**
Dark green with wooden panels and beige interior; restored in 2010 (see lot 707 Barrett-Jackson 28.9.13 $93,500).												
1949	**Eight Series 2301 station sedan**		229395098	L	40-50.000 USD	39.446*	60.500*	53.252*	09-10-15	Hershey	249	**RMS**
Brown with wooden panels and brown interior; in good overall condition (see lot 146 RM 27.7.13 $ 35.750).												
1950	**Custom 8 2333 convertible victoria**		H600707	L	55-75.000 USD	36.918	50.600	45.722	25-06-16	Santa Monica	2103	**AA**
Blue with red leather interior; restored.												
1955	**Caribbean convertible**		55881024	L	NA	49.268	75.000	69.683	13-11-15	Anaheim	S117.1	**Mec**
White with white interior; automatic transmission.												
1955	**Caribbean convertible**		55881356	L	NA	92.360*	132.000*	120.872*	29-01-16	Scottsdale	1315	**B/J**
White, red and black with red and white interior; restored. The engine and automatic transmission have covered less than 250 miles since the rebuild.												
1958	**Hawk hardtop**		58LS1312	L	NA	55.837	85.000	78.974	13-11-15	Anaheim	S175.1	**Mec** **F557**
Black with tan interior; full restoration completed in 2015. 275bhp 289 supercharged engine with automatic transmission (see lot F62 Mecum 14.8.15 NS).												

PAGANI (I) *(1999-)*

Year	Model	(Bodybuilder)	Chassis no.	Steering	Estimate	£	$	€	Date	Place	Lot	Auc. H.
2014	**Huayra**		76062	L	1.900-2.200.000 USD	1.423.686	2.035.000	1.834.960	12-03-16	Amelia Island	164	**RMS** **F558**
Dark blue with cream leather and alcantara interior; sold new to the USA, the car has covered less than 400 miles. With the seven-piece luggage set.												

PANHARD ET LEVASSOR (F) *(1891-1967)*

Year	Model	(Bodybuilder)	Chassis no.	Steering	Estimate	£	$	€	Date	Place	Lot	Auc. H.
1899	**M2E 4hp two-seater**		1862	R	300-350.000 GBP		NS		30-10-15	London	105	**Bon**
Acquired in 1999 by the current owner as a part restored project, the car received subsequently a full restoration and was fitted with the present, new body in a style different from that of the original. 1,201cc twin-cylinder Daimler-Phenix engine.												
1913	**X19 torpedo**		35771	R	30-50.000 EUR	29.280	44.325	40.800	07-11-15	Lyon	257	**Agu**
Green with black wings and black leather interior; restored many years ago. For over 30 years in the same family ownership, the car is unused from time and requires recommissioning prior to use.												
1953	**X90 Scarlette**		490153	L	15-20.000 EUR		NS		08-11-15	Lyon	227	**Ose**
Black; in original condition. One of 10 known survivors.												
1964	**CD**		258	L	50-70.000 EUR		NS		04-02-16	Paris	302	**Bon**
Restored some years ago.												

F557: 1958 Packard Hawk hardtop

F558: 2014 Pagani Huayra

Year	Model	(Bodybuilder)	Chassis no.	Steering	Estimate	Hammer Price £	Hammer Price $	Hammer Price €	Sale Date	Place	Lot	Auc. H.

PATHFINDER (USA) (1912-1917)

1913 Series XIII A touring — 1331 — R — 100-140.000 USD — 84.591* — 121.000* — 110.969* — 28-01-16 — Phoenix — 144 — **RMS F559**
Dark blue with black leather interior; in the same family ownership from new to 2006, the car was restored in the early 1980s. Believed to be the only surviving example of the model (see RM lots 161 30.7.11 $ 115,500 and 104 19.1.12 NS).

PEEL (GB) (1962-1967)

1964 P50 — D535 — C — 75-100.000 USD — 123.130* — 176.000* — 158.699* — 12-03-16 — Amelia Island — 198 — **RMS F560**
Red with black interior; fully restored when it was part of the Bruce Weiner Microcar Museum. One of 26 examples known to survive of 47 built (see lot 259 RM 15.2.13 $ 120,750).

PEGASO (E) (1951-1958)

1954 Z-102 coupé (Touring) — 01021500150 — L — 800-1.000.000 USD — 490.867 — 742.500 — 678.497 — 10-12-15 — New York — 205 — **RMS F561**
Dark green with green and brown interior; the car was exhibited by the factory at the 1954 San Remo Concours d'Elegance and then sold to the first of its four Spanish owners. In 1954 and 1955 it was raced at some Spanish hillclimb events, first with the original 2.8-litre engine and later with the new 3.2-litre unit. Since 1981 in the current, fourth ownership the car is described as in very good overall condition.

1954 Z-102 coupé (Saoutchik) — 01021500148 — L — 800-1.000.000 USD — 672.320 — 880.000 — 776.952 — 20-08-16 — Monterey — 238 — **RMS**
White pearl with metallic grey roof and light grey leather interior; exhibited at the 1954 Paris Motor Show, the car was later sold new in Spain. Imported into the USA, it was first restored in the early 1990s and later it received a further restoration completed in 2013 (see lots 626 Brooks 5.5.97 $119,015, 49 Christie's 31.8.03 NS, and 130 RM-Sotheby's 21.11.13 $797,500).

PETREL (USA) (1909-1912)

1909 Four 30hp roadster — 5318(engine) — R — 100-150.000 USD — NS — 09-10-15 — Hershey — 239 — **RMS**
Violet with black leather interior; restored in the early 1960s, the car is described as still in good overall condition. Only known survivor of the make. From the Harold Coker collection.

PEUGEOT (F) (1889-)

1904 Type 69 — 5311L — R — NA — 61.600 — 94.747 — 83.037 — 14-10-15 — Duxford — 114 — **H&H**
Black with black interior; described as in good overall condition. First entered for the London-Brighton Run in 1938.

1909 Lion Type VC racing voiturette — 2711 — R — 30-40.000 GBP — 46.000 — 70.044 — 62.887 — 05-09-15 — Beaulieu — 135 — **Bon**
Discovered in France in 2000 in rolling chassis form and restored over the next two years to racing voiturette specification. Replica of the 1909 Brooklands car; fitted with a 2.7-litre single-cylinder DeDion engine.

1914 Type 144A torpedo coloniale — KA20152 — R — 22-32.000 EUR — 26.080 — 38.661 — 34.500 — 04-02-16 — Paris — 394 — **Bon**
Yellow with black wings; acquired in 1962 by the current owner and restored.

1914 Bébé Type BP1 — 11290 — R — 55-75.000 USD — 48.411* — 74.250* — 65.355* — 09-10-15 — Hershey — 255 — **RMS F562**
Two-tone grey with black leather interior; the car remained in the Peter and Susan Williamson for 23 years until 2008 when it was acquired by the current owner and subsequently restored (see lot 26 Gooding 16.8.08 $ 44,000).

1925 Type 172 BC spider — 0414 — R — 15-20.000 EUR — NS — 14-05-16 — Monaco — 125 — **RMS**
Dark red with black wings and black interior; it requires some cosmetic attention. One of the 215 examples built in Italy. Since 1960 in the Quattroruote Collection.

1937 Type 201 M cabriolet — 532511 — L — 22-28.000 EUR — 25.691* — 37.388* — 33.376* — 05-02-16 — Paris — 106 — **Art**
Dark blue and light grey with blue interior; restored.

1934 Type 601 roadster — 712071 — L — 90-125.000 EUR — 63.277 — 91.837 — 84.000 — 03-02-16 — Paris — 104 — **RMS F563**
Dark blue with red interior; the car has covered 100 kms since the restoration.

1937 Type 402 Eclipse (Pourtout) — 478174 — L — 150-170.000 EUR — NS — 08-11-15 — Lyon — 211 — **Ose**
Restored circa 12 years ago, the car is described as in good overall condition.

1937 Type 402 roadster — 797280 — L — 450-600.000 USD — NS — 20-08-16 — Monterey — S157 — **Mec**
Black and silver; body built in France probably soon after WWII and fitted on the car's chassis purposely lengthened. Formerly in the Roger Baillon collection, the car was imported into the USA in the 1980s. Subjected to a restoration completed in 2010 and subsequently exhibited at Concours d'Elegance events.

1939 Type 202 cabriolet — 853981 — L — 18-24.000 EUR — 18.351* — 26.706* — 23.840* — 05-02-16 — Paris — 103 — **Art**
Dark green with cream leather interior; body restored some years ago, interior redone, mechanicals overhauled in recent years.

1951 203 Break — 1403051 — L — 23-28.000 EUR — 17.125 — 24.104 — 21.213 — 09-04-16 — Essen — 211 — **Coy**
Ivory; restored in 2014.

1953 203 coupé — 1299249 — L — 70-90.000 EUR — NS — 08-11-15 — Lyon — 234 — **Ose**
Black; reimported into France from Portugal 10 years ago and subsequently restored.

1955 203 C cabriolet — 1752810 — L — 60-80.000 EUR — 50.465* — 73.440* — 65.560* — 05-02-16 — Paris — 104 — **Art F564**
Black with red leather interior; restored some years ago. Engine overhauled in 2012.

1958 403 berline — 2233210 — L — 6-10.000 EUR — 6.884 — 9.836 — 8.740 — 18-06-16 — Wien — 416 — **Dor**
Burgundy with grey cloth interior; in good overall condition.

1959 403 cabriolet — 2320136 — L — 70-80.000 EUR — 55.868 — 79.848 — 72.000 — 12-03-16 — Lyon — 336 — **Agu**
Dark grey with beige interior; in good overall condition. Body restored 20 years ago, engine rebuilt 10 years ago.

1963 404 berline — 1345891 — L — 3-4.000 EUR — 3.363 — 4.873 — 4.320 — 20-03-16 — Fontainebleau — 373b — **Ose**
Dark blue; described as in good original condition.

1976 504 V6 cabriolet (Pininfarina) — B312266808 — L — 30-40.000 EUR — 30.483* — 39.586* — 35.760* — 09-07-16 — Le Mans — 152 — **Art F565**
Light metallic blue with beige leather interior; overhauled in 2013.

1987 205 GTI — 79505 — R — 10-15.000 GBP — 11.500 — 17.511 — 15.722 — 05-09-15 — Beaulieu — 146 — **Bon**
Black; in original condition. One owner and 19,051 miles covered.

1984 205 GTI — 82376 — L — 8-12.000 EUR — 10.090 — 14.618 — 12.960 — 20-03-16 — Fontainebleau — 377 — **Ose**
In very good working order.

F559: 1913 Pathfinder Series XIII A touring

F560: 1964 Peel P50

F561: 1954 Pegaso Z-102 coupé (Touring)

F562: 1914 Peugeot Bébé Type BP1

F563: 1934 Peugeot Type 601 roadster

F564: 1955 Peugeot 203 C cabriolet

F565: 1976 Peugeot 504 V6 cabriolet (Pininfarina)

F566: 1984 Peugeot 205 Turbo 16

Year	Model	(Bodybuilder)	Chassis no.	Steering	Estimate	Hammer Price £	Hammer Price $	Hammer Price €	Date	Place	Lot	Auc. H.
1984	**205 Turbo 16**		100152	L	120-150.000 GBP		NS		07-09-15	London	106	RMS
Dark grey with two-tone grey interior; the car was originally delivered to Peugeot's Italian office for press demonstration. Recently serviced and fitted with new shocks and brakes.												
1984	**205 Turbo 16**		100189	L	200-300.000 USD	151.272	198.000	174.814	19-08-16	Carmel	30	Bon F566
Grey; in highly original condition, less than 48,000 kms covered. For almost 30 years with its first owner in Belgium and subsequently imported into the USA.												
1984	**205 Turbo 16 Evolution 1 Groupe B**		5200012	L	600-800.000 EUR		NS		14-05-16	Monaco	250	RMS
Serial number C11; driven by Ari Vatanen, the car won the 1985 Monte Carlo Rally and Swedish Rally. Retired from competition at the end of the season, it was sold to Seydoux who retained it until 2001 when it was acquired by the current owner. During this time, it has not been rallied, only occasionally demonstrated. Recently recommissioned.												
2008	**908 HDi FAP**		90805	R	1.200-1.600.000 EUR		NS		14-05-16	Monaco	251	RMS
Raced by the factory during the 2008 and 2009 seasons, the car placed 2nd overall at the 2008 Le Mans 24 Hours driven by Nicolas Minassian, Marc Gene and Jacques Villeneuve. In 2010 it was entrusted to the Oreca team to compete in the LMS Championship and it was retired from competition at the end of the season (see lot 34 RM 5.2.14 NS).												

PIERCE-ARROW (USA) *(1901-1938)*

Year	Model	(Bodybuilder)	Chassis no.	Steering	Estimate	£	$	€	Date	Place	Lot	Auc. H.
1903	**6.5hp Stanhope**		302	R	75-100.000 USD	37.803*	57.750*	51.317*	08-10-15	Hershey	149	RMS
Black; in the same family ownership since 1948. Engine rebuilt in 2009.												
1916	**Model 38-C touring**		2803	R	90-130.000 USD	64.805*	99.000*	87.971*	08-10-15	Hershey	137	RMS
In largely original condition, the car needs servicing prior to use. From the estate of Richard Roy.												
1916	**Model 48-B touring**	(Wood & Son)	14727	R	165-185.000 USD	78.892*	121.000*	106.504*	09-10-15	Hershey	233	RMS
Dark green and black; several restoration works carried out in recent years, including an engine rebuild (see lot 449 Bonhams 17.8.12 NS).												
1913	**Model 48-B touring**		10431	R	400-600.000 USD	238.393*	341.000*	312.731*	28-01-16	Phoenix	150	RMS F567
Dark blue with black leather interior; in single ownership from 1952 to 1989, the car was restored in the early 1990s and is described as in very good overall condition. From the Craig McCaw Collection (see lots 49 Christie's 17.8.03 $ 222,000, 814 RM 25.2.12 $ 385,000 and 60 Gooding 7.3.14 NS).												
1913	**Model 66-A touring**		66667	R	550-650.000 USD	541.486	830.500	731.006	09-10-15	Hershey	267	RMS
Red with black leather interior; sold new to Chicago, in the early 1920s the car was bought by the Minneapolis Fire Department, which modified it and used it until the late 1940s. At unspecified date the car was fully restored recreating the original coachwork from the cowl back, including the front and rear fenders. Described as in good driving order. One of 14 examples of the model known to survive.												
1919	**Model 48 roadster**		514463	L	NA	73.119*	104.500*	95.691*	29-01-16	Scottsdale	1399.1	B/J
Red; restored at unspecified date.												
1925	**Model 33 runabout**		340988	L	80-120.000 USD	61.205*	93.500*	83.084*	08-10-15	Hershey	136	RMS
In original condition except for the top replaced at unspecified date; 31,703 miles on the odometer. The car requires servicing prior to use. From the estate of Richard Roy.												
1924	**Model 33 touring**		339177	L	70-90.000 USD	45.968*	60.500*	54.438*	30-07-16	Plymouth	122	RMS
Crimson with black fenders and black leather interior; restored at unspecified date.												
1925	**Model 80 touring**		8012580(engine)	L	60-80.000 USD	39.446	60.500	53.252	09-10-15	Hershey	243	RMS
Light grey with black fenders and red leather interior; restored in 1993-94. From the Harold Coker collection.												
1927	**Model 80 touring**		8022178	L	90-110.000 USD	45.968	60.500	54.438	30-07-16	Plymouth	131	RMS
Pale green with black fenders and green leather interior; recently serviced. "New York" headlamps (see lot 125 RM 27.7.13 $90,200).												
1930	**Model B tonneau cowl phaeton**		2025018	L	125-175.000 USD	63.005*	96.250*	85.528*	08-10-15	Hershey	145	RMS
Two-tone blue with dark blue leather interior; restored many years ago. The present body was installed in the early 1960s. From the estate of Richard Roy.												
1930	**Model A tourer**		3025617	L	30-50.000 USD	28.263*	42.900*	38.181*	05-10-15	Philadelphia	206	Bon
For restoration; unused since the late 1960s; in the same family ownership since the late 1940s.												
1931	**Model 42 convertible**		325585	L	NA	72.248	110.000	98.769	05-09-15	Auburn	7060	AA
Two-tone blue with dark blue leather interior; restored many years ago.												
1931	**Model 42 dual cowl phaeton**		2525010	L	1.000-1.300.000 DKK	96.284	146.136	131.083	26-09-15	Ebeltoft	42	Bon
Black with tan leather interior; restored at unspecified date. From the Frederiksen Collection.												
1931	**Model 42 convertible**		2525124	L	150-200.000 USD	147.700	209.000	192.489	10-03-16	Amelia Island	196	Bon
Two-tone red with tan interior; restored, the car is described as in very good overall condition.												
1933	**Model 1242 roadster**		3100014	L	350-400.000 USD	208.817	319.000	283.463	08-10-15	Hershey	167	RMS
Black with tan leather interior; uno of five examples built and three known surviving. Original engine. Known history since new (see lot 53 Sotheby's 5.10.96 $ 134,500).												
1933	**Model 836 sedan**		236N2342	L	70-90.000 USD	36.432*	52.800*	46.205*	07-05-16	Auburn	756	AA
Two-tone body with beige cloth interior.												

F567: 1913 Pierce-Arrow Model 48-B touring

F568: 1933 Pierce-Arrow Silver Arrow

Year	Model	(Bodybuilder)	Chassis no.	Steering	Estimate	Hammer price £	$	€	Date	Place	Lot	Auc. H.
1933	**Silver Arrow**		2575029	L	2.500-3.000.000 USD	**2.472.514**	**3.740.000**	**3.417.612**	10-12-15	New York	214	**RMS** F568

One of three known survivors of five originally built, the car is believed the one exhibited at the 1933 Chicago World's Fair. Formerly in the collections of Cameron Peck and Austin Clark Jr. First restored in the early 1950s and restored again in the early 1990s when the body was repainted in the present metallic pewter livery. For over 20 years in the current ownership.

Year	Model	Chassis no.	Steering	Estimate	£	$	€	Date	Place	Lot	Auc. H.
1934	**Model 840A coupé**	2080431	L	75-100.000 USD	100.408*	154.000*	135.551*	09-10-15	Hershey	282	**RMS**

Two-tone sand with brown leather interior; the car has covered less than 1,500 miles since a full restoration.

| 1934 | **Model 840A Silver Arrow** | 2580001 | L | 225-275.000 USD | 183.872 | 242.000 | 217.752 | 30-07-16 | Plymouth | 139 | **RMS** |

Two-tone green with green leather interior; restored to concours condition several years ago (see RM lots 89 2.8.03 $242,001, 445 19.8.06 NS and 670 9.10.09 $187,000).

| 1934 | **Model 840A coupé** | 2080431 | L | 120-150.000 USD | 100.848* | 132.000* | 116.543* | 19-08-16 | Carmel | 48 | **Bon** |

See lot 282 RM/Sotheby's 9.10.15 $154,000).

PININFARINA (I) (1930-)

| 1983 | **Spidereuropa** | 5502880 | L | 15-20.000 USD | 18.456* | 26.400* | 24.211* | 28-01-16 | Scottsdale | 104 | **Bon** |

Red with tan interior; described as in good, largely original condition. 15,000 miles on the odometer.

PLATÉ (I)

| 1949 | **Alfa Romeo 6C Speciale** | P002 | R | Refer Dpt. | 222.706* | 291.500* | 257.365* | 19-08-16 | Carmel | 41 | **Bon** F569 |

The car was built between 1948 and 1949 on a chassis designed by Luigi Platé fitted with an Alfa Romeo 6C 2300 engine. In 1951 it was entered at the Susa-Moncenisio hillclimb driven by Paolo Soprani. In 1959 the car was imported into the USA as an "Alfa Romeo Platé 2500, chassis no.002, engine no.700174". In 1984 it was acquired by the current owner, John Murphy, who in 1990 started a long restoration completed 20 years later. The car was exhibited at the 2011 Pebble Beach Concours d'Elegance and at the 2015 Amelia Island Concours.

PLYMOUTH (USA) (1928-2001)

Year	Model	Chassis no.	Steering	Estimate	£	$	€	Date	Place	Lot	Auc. H.
1931	**Model PA coupé**	PA17864	L	NA	10.511*	15.950*	14.304*	26-09-15	Las Vegas	51.1	**B/J**

Blue and black with tan interior; previously owned by same family for 35 years.

| 1933 | **Model PD DeLuxe coupé** | PD1701102011776 | L | 10-18.000 EUR | 8.696 | 12.424 | 11.040 | 18-06-16 | Wien | 414 | **Dor** |

Red and black with red leather interior; sold new to Austria. Since 1966 in the current ownership; stored for the past 48 tears; mechanicals in need of recommissioning.

| 1940 | **P10 DeLuxe station wagon** | 11083536 | L | 50-65.000 USD | 25.102* | 38.500* | 33.888* | 09-10-15 | Hershey | 225 | **RMS** |

Maroon with wooden panels and maroon interior; recent cosmetic restoration.

| 1940 | **P11 business coupé** | 15074936 | L | 16-18.000 GBP | 14.950 | 22.764 | 20.438 | 05-09-15 | Beaulieu | 161 | **Bon** |

Restored in the USA in 2013 and imported into the UK in 2015.

| 1948 | **Special DeLuxe convertible** | P15605096 | L | 35-45.000 USD | 21.740* | 33.000* | 29.370* | 05-10-15 | Philadelphia | 234 | **Bon** |

Ivory with red leather interior recently retrimmed; from the Evergreen Collection.

| 1949 | **Special DeLuxe convertible** | 12257225 | L | 20-25.000 USD | 14.801* | 21.450* | 18.771* | 07-05-16 | Auburn | 746 | **AA** |

Green with green and white interior and black soft-top.

| 1950 | **Special DeLuxe convertible** | 12480029 | L | 50-70.000 USD | 29.796 | 39.000 | 34.433 | 19-08-16 | Monterey | F62 | **Mec** |

Red; restored three decades ago. Engine rebuilt and fitted with a 1953 Plymouth 3-speed manual gearbox.

| 1956 | **Belvedere convertible** | 15970732 | L | 70-90.000 USD | 44.825* | 68.750* | 60.514* | 09-10-15 | Hershey | 251 | **RMS** F570 |

Turquoise and blue; the car remained with its first owner until 2006 and was later restored. 200bhp 276 engine with automatic transmission (see lot 117 RM 27.7.13 $ 90,750).

| 1963 | **Savoy 2-door sedan** | 3131167605 | L | 50-75.000 USD | 30.560 | 40.000 | 35.316 | 20-08-16 | Monterey | S187 | **Mec** |

Metallic blue with two-tone blue interior; 426 Max Wedge engine with automatic transmission.

| 1961 | **Fury hardtop** | 3319134334 | L | NQ | 33.634 | 49.000 | 43.674 | 20-05-16 | Indianapolis | F30.1 | **Mec** |

Coral with grey interior; 330bhp 383 engine with 4-speed manual gearbox.

| 1962 | **Fury hardtop** | 3321177385 | L | NA | 46.950* | 67.100* | 61.443* | 29-01-16 | Scottsdale | 1122 | **B/J** |

Black with black and red interior; restored. 413 Max Wedge engine with automatic transmission.

| 1966 | **Belvedere Satellite hardtop** | RP23H67271499 | L | NA | 35.208 | 54.000 | 47.531 | 09-10-15 | Chicago | S85.1 | **Mec** |

Silver with original black interior; body repainted. 425bhp 426 Hemi engine with 4-speed manual gearbox.

| 1967 | **Belvedere II hardtop** | R023J71202505 | L | NA | 59.265* | 84.700* | 77.560* | 29-01-16 | Scottsdale | 1294 | **B/J** |

White with black interior; 425bhp 426 Hemi engine with automatic transmission.

| 1966 | **Belvedere Satellite hardtop** | RP23H67250092 | L | 75-85.000 USD | 43.470 | 63.000 | 55.131 | 07-05-16 | Auburn | 763 | **AA** |

Black with black interior; fully restored in 2013. 425bhp 426 Hemi engine with 4-speed manual gearbox.

F569: 1949 Platé Alfa Romeo 6C Speciale

F570: 1956 Plymouth Belvedere convertible

Year	Model	(Bodybuilder)	Chassis no.	Steering	Estimate	Hammer Price £	$	€	Date	Place	Lot	Auc. H.
1966	**Belvedere I two-door sedan**		RL21H61233436	L	130-150.000 USD	87.860	115.000	101.534	19-08-16	Monterey	F57	Mec
Red with red interior; restored. 7,418 original miles. 426 Hemi engine with automatic transmission.												
1968	**Barracuda Super Stock**		B029M8B29912	L	NA	123.147	176.000	161.163	30-01-16	Scottsdale	5291	R&S
Acquired and raced in period by Arlen Vanke. Fully restored. 426 Cross Ram Hemi engine.												
1971	**Barracuda hardtop**		NQ	L	850-1.100.000 USD		NS		20-05-16	Indianapolis	F212	Mec
Red, white and blue; verified as the car which was used by the Sox & Martin team during the 1971 season. Driven by Ronnie Sox it won six NHRA Pro Stock events. Restored to 1971 race configuration. 426 Hemi engine with 4-speed manual gearbox. Sold on bill of sale.												
1969	**GTX convertible**		RS27J9G277476	L	150-200.000 USD	104.715	150.000	138.780	23-01-16	Kissimmee	F106	Mec **F571**
Black with black interior; restored in 2007. 43,822 miles. 425bhp 426 Hemi engine with 4-speed manual gearbox.												
1968	**GTX convertible**		RS27J8G165203	L	150-200.000 USD	104.715	150.000	138.780	23-01-16	Kissimmee	F110	Mec
Metallic blue with white interior; 45,590 miles. 425bhp 426 Hemi engine with automatic transmission.												
1969	**GTX hardtop**		23RSL9A142015	L	90-120.000 USD	50.263	72.000	66.614	23-01-16	Kissimmee	F123	Mec
Metallic platinum with black vinyl roof and black interior; fully restored. 375bhp 440 engine with automatic transmission.												
1969	**GTX hardtop**		RS23L9A119173	L	NA	38.180	50.000	45.395	23-07-16	Harrisburg	T211	Mec
Bronze with saddle interior; fully restored. 440 engine with automatic transmission.												
1970	**Road Runner convertible**		RM27V0G142174	L	175-225.000 USD	111.696	160.000	148.032	23-01-16	Kissimmee	F112	Mec
Metallic gold with black vinyl interior; 35,528 miles. Restored in 2007. 440 Six Pack engine with 4-speed manual gearbox.												
1971	**Road Runner hardtop**		RM23V1G154401	L	125-160.000 USD	80.282	115.000	106.398	23-01-16	Kissimmee	F175	Mec
Gold with black vinyl roof and black interior; fully restored. 390bhp 440 Six Pack engine with 4-speed manual gearbox.												
1970	**Road Runner hardtop**		RM23R0G131076	L	NA	105.445*	150.700*	137.996*	29-01-16	Scottsdale	1081	B/J
Black with black interior; older restoration. 426 Hemi engine with automatic transmission.												
1970	**Road Runner convertible**		RM27V0G196699	L	125-150.000 USD	73.788	107.500	95.815	20-05-16	Indianapolis	S148	Mec
Blue with white interior; fully restored. 390bhp 440 Six Pack engine with 4-speed manual gearbox.												
1968	**Road Runner hardtop**		RM21J8A183329	L	NA	64.906	85.000	77.172	23-07-16	Harrisburg	S159.1	Mec
Yellow with black interior; 426 Hemi engine with 4-speed manual gearbox.												
1970	**Road Runner Super Bird**		RM23V0A167049	L	NA	76.704	120.000	105.096	19-09-15	Dallas	S76	Mec
Yellow with black roof and black interior; 440 engine with automatic transmission.												
1970	**Road Runner Super Bird**		WM23U0A167071	L	300-450.000 USD	198.959	285.000	263.682	23-01-16	Kissimmee	F166	Mec **F572**
Blue with black roof and white interior; two owners and 671 miles covered. 375bhp 440 engine with automatic transmission.												
1970	**Road Runner Super Bird**		RM23R0A162318	L	350-375.000 USD		NS		23-01-16	Kissimmee	S166	Mec
White with black vinyl roof and black interior; body repainted in 2000. 24,925 actual miles. 425bhp 426 Hemi engine with automatic transmission (see lot S119 Mecum 16.5.15 NS).												
1970	**Road Runner Super Bird**		RM23V0A179738	L	NA		NS		12-03-16	Kansas City	S109	Mec
White with black vinyl roof and black interior; unrestored. 390bhp 440 engine with 4-speed manual gearbox.												
1970	**Road Runner Super Bird**		RM23V0A158621	L	200-250.000 USD	120.120	175.000	155.978	20-05-16	Indianapolis	S138	Mec
Yellow with black vinyl roof and black interior; restored. 390bhp 440 Six Pack egine with 4-speed manual gearbox.												
1970	**Road Runner Super Bird**		RM23R0A172593	L	NA		NS		24-06-16	Uncasville	650	B/J
White with black roof and black interior; 426 Hemi engine with 4-speed manual gearbox.												
1970	**Road Runner Super Bird**		RM23R0A162316	L	NA	240.768	330.000	298.188	24-06-16	Uncasville	676	B/J
White with black roof and black interior; restored. 425bhp 426 Hemi engine with automatic transmission.												
1970	**'Cuda hardtop**		BS23V0B157348	L	NA	92.684	145.000	126.991	19-09-15	Dallas	S126	Mec
Black with black interior; 5,644 actual miles. 440 Six Pack engine with automatic transmission.												
1970	**'Cuda hardtop**		BS23R0B257766	L	NA		NS		12-12-15	Austin	S38.1	Mec
Blue with original black interior; garage kept for 43 years. 16,802 original miles. Engine repaired in 1986. 425bhp 426 engine with automatic transmission.												
1971	**'Cuda hardtop**		BS23R1B345763	L	800-1.200.000 USD	663.195	950.000	878.940	23-01-16	Kissimmee	F100	Mec **F573**
Metallic Winchester grey with black leather interior; unrestored. 58,990 miles. Original 425bhp 426 Hemi engine with 4-speed manual gearbox.												
1970	**'Cuda hardtop**		BS23R0B349189	L	NA	173.176*	247.500*	226.636*	29-01-16	Scottsdale	1341	B/J
Orange with black vinyl roof and black interior; 425bhp 426 engine with 4-speed manual gearbox.												
1970	**'Cuda hardtop**		BS23R0B146392	L	NA	103.905	148.500	135.981	30-01-16	Scottsdale	5136	R&S
Violet; restored in 2005. 4-speed manual gearbox (see lot X2 Mecum 14.10.05 $ 267,750).												

F571: 1969 Plymouth GTX convertible

F572: 1970 Plymouth Road Runner Super Bird

F573: 1971 Plymouth 'Cuda hardtop

F574: 1970 Plymouth 'Cuda convertible

Year	Model (Bodybuilder)	Chassis no.	Steering	Estimate	£	$	€	Date	Place	Lot	Auc. H.
1971	**'Cuda hardtop**	BS23R1B405092	L	275-325.000 USD	230.604	330.000	288.651	02-04-16	Ft.Lauderdale	554	**AA**
	Black with white interior; fully restored. 425bhp 426 Hemi engine with 4-speed manual gearbox.										
1970	**'Cuda hardtop**	BS23R0B257766	L	NA	84.624	120.000	106.344	16-04-16	Houston	F141.1	**Mec**
	See lot S38.1 Mecum 12.12.15.										
1970	**'Cuda hardtop**	BS23R0B227013	L	425-525.000 USD	291.720	425.000	378.803	20-05-16	Indianapolis	S129	**Mec**
	Metallic orange with black interior; in original, unrestored condition. The car remained with its first owner until 2015 and has covered 10,945 miles. 425bhp 426 Hemi engine with 4-speed manual gearbox.										
1971	**'Cuda hardtop**	BS23R1B268379	L	700-850.000 USD		NS		20-05-16	Indianapolis	S164	**Mec**
	Black with black leather interior; restoration completed in 1999. 31,801 miles on the odometer. Formerly in the Otis Chandler Collection. 425bhp 426 Hemi engine with 4-speed manual gearbox.										
1970	**'Cuda hardtop**	BS23R0B234614	L	NA	132.981	190.000	168.815	18-06-16	Portland	S95	**Mec**
	Light metallic blue with black interior; the car has covered less than 600 miles since the restoration. 425bhp 426 engine with automatic transmission.										
1971	**'Cuda hardtop**	BS23R1B227275	L	500-600.000 USD		NS		19-08-16	Monterey	F127	**Mec**
	Red and black with black leather interior; for 29 years in the current ownership. 426 Hemi engine with 4-speed manual gearbox.										
1971	**'Cuda convertible**	BS27R1B126869	L	2.250-2.750.000 USD	1.605.630	2.300.000	2.127.960	23-01-16	Kissimmee	F102	**Mec**
	White with black interior; fully restored between 2003 and 2004. One of five examples built in 1971 with the 425bhp 426 Hemi engine with automatic transmission.										
1970	**'Cuda convertible**	BS27R0B156924	L	2.750-3.500.000 USD	1.867.418	2.675.000	2.474.910	23-01-16	Kissimmee	F109	**Mec**
	Yellow with black vinyl interior; less than 27,500 miles on the odometer. Refreshed in the early 2000s. One of five examples built in 1970 with the 425bhp 426 Hemi engine with the 4-speed manual gearbox.										**F574**
1970	**'Cuda convertible**	BS27V0B100004	L	500-750.000 USD	331.598	475.000	439.470	23-01-16	Kissimmee	F113	**Mec**
	White with black leather interior; restored in 2005. 390bhp 440 Six Pack engine with 4-speed manual gearbox.										
1970	**'Cuda convertible**	BS27U0B194936	L	500-600.000 USD	244.335	350.000	323.820	23-01-16	Kissimmee	S209	**Mec**
	Lime with white interior; fully restored. 375bhp 440 Super Commando engine with automatic transmission.										
1970	**Gran Coupé convertible**	BP27GOB212246	L	NA	70.810	101.200	92.669	30-01-16	Scottsdale	5402	**R&S**
	Red with white and black interior; originally built with the 230bhp 318 engine, the car has been recently restored and fitted with a 426 Hemi engine with 4-speed manual gearbox.										

PONTIAC (USA) *(1926-2009)*

Year	Model (Bodybuilder)	Chassis no.	Steering	Estimate	£	$	€	Date	Place	Lot	Auc. H.
1932	**Model 302 convertible**	311958P8	L	NA	39.145*	59.400*	53.270*	26-09-15	Las Vegas	412	**B/J**
	Two-tone brown with brown interior; restored in the 1970s.										
1957	**Star Chief Bonneville convertible**	P857H29747	L	150-200.000 USD	101.225	145.000	134.154	23-01-16	Kissimmee	S141	**Mec**
	White with red and white leather interior; 310bhp 347 fuel-injected engine with automatic transmission.										**F575**
1958	**Bonneville convertible**	K558H1951	L	125-150.000 USD	84.652*	121.000*	109.106*	12-03-16	Amelia Island	176	**RMS**
	Red and light grey with matching interior; restored several years ago, it is described as still in good overall condition. 310bhp 370 fuel-injected engine with automatic transmission.										
1958	**Bonneville hardtop**	C558H3252	L	90-110.000 USD	50.029*	71.500*	65.473*	29-01-16	Phoenix	271	**RMS**
	Two-tone green with green vinyl and cloth interior; restored. 300bhp 370 engine with automatic transmission (see lots 802 RM 25.2.12 $ 121,000 and 137 RM/Sotheby's 14.3.15 $ 82,500).										

F575: 1957 Pontiac Star Chief Bonneville convertible

F576: 1963 Pontiac Bonneville convertible

Year	Model	(Bodybuilder)	Chassis no.	Steering	Estimate	Hammer Price £	Hammer Price $	Hammer Price €	Date	Place	Lot	Auc. H.
1958	**Bonneville hardtop**		K558H2572	L	62-68.000 USD	46.121	66.000	57.730	02-04-16	Ft.Lauderdale	434	AA
	Green with green interior; 330bhp 370 engine with automatic transmission.											
1963	**Bonneville convertible**		863S02964	L	250-350.000 USD	203.619	308.000	281.450	10-12-15	New York	222	RMS
	One of the cars customized by Nudie Cohen, it is decorated with silver dollars, pistols, guns, a saddle over the transmission tunnel and a pair of Texas longhorns. For over 45 years in the ownership of Roy Rogers and Dale Evans, it was on display in their museum in Missouri until 2010 when it was acquired by the current owner. Described as in excellent original condition, never restored.											**F576**
1962	**Catalina hardtop**		362P12169	L	NA	49.759*	68.200*	61.626*	24-06-16	Uncasville	636	B/J
	Red with maroon and white interior; restored. 425A Tri-Power engine with 4-speed manual gearbox.											
1961	**Catalina convertible**		361P11998	L	35-45.000 USD	29.252*	38.500*	34.642*	30-07-16	Plymouth	171	RMS
	Gold; restored. Engine upgraded to Tri-Power specification.											
1958	**Parisienne convertible**		8786745646	L	90-110.000 USD	46.944	72.000	63.374	09-10-15	Hershey	284	RMS
	Black with white and red interior; restored about 10 years ago. 280bhp 348 Tri-power engine with 4-speed manual gearbox.											
1964	**Tempest station wagon**		804F11173	L	30-40.000 USD	11.766*	15.400*	13.597*	19-08-16	Carmel	92	Bon
	White with red interior; restored in the late 1990s and updated with front disc brakes and Turbo Hydra-Matic 400 transmission (see lot 159 Gooding & Company 17.1.15 $26,400).											
1965	**Grand Prix hardtop**		266575E1175745	L	32-34.000 USD		NS		02-04-16	Ft.Lauderdale	156	AA
	Light blue with black roof and black vinyl interior; older restoration. 325bhp 389 engine with automatic transmission.											
1962	**Grand Prix hardtop**		962P8232	L	375-425.000 USD		NS		20-05-16	Indianapolis	S191	Mec
	Burgundy with white interior; restored in the past and recently refreshed. 405bhp 421 Super Duty engine with 4-speed manual gearbox (see lot 243 RM 13.11.10 $181,500).											
1965	**Le Mans GTO hardtop**		237375P354025	L	NA	48.767	74.250	66.669	05-09-15	Auburn	4074	AA
	Gold with black interior; 360bhp 389 engine with 4-speed manual gearbox (see lot 282 Bonhams 14.8.09 NS).											
1965	**Le Mans GTO hardtop**		237375K109386	L	90-110.000 USD	52.358	75.000	69.390	23-01-16	Kissimmee	S152	Mec
	White with black roof and blue interior; restored 19 years ago. 360bhp 389 engine with 4-speed manual gearbox.											
1964	**Le Mans GTO convertible**		824F32414	L	70-100.000 USD	50.029*	71.500*	65.473*	30-01-16	Scottsdale	102	G&Co
	Dark blue with black interior; in good overall condition. 35,504 miles on the odometer. 348bhp 389 engine with 4-speed manual gearbox.											
1970	**GTO Judge hardtop**		242370Z123994	L	NA	104.320	160.000	140.832	09-10-15	Chicago	S99	Mec
	Black with black interior; concours-quality restoration completed in 2014. 370bp 400 Ram Air IV engine with 4-speed manual gearbox.											**F577**
1969	**GTO Judge hardtop**		242379R187730	L	NA	73.301	105.000	97.146	23-01-16	Kissimmee	W158.1	Mec
	Black with original black interior; concours restoration. 400 engine with 4-speed manual gearbox.											
1969	**GTO Judge hardtop**		242379A122614	L	NA	90.051*	128.700*	117.851*	29-01-16	Scottsdale	1282	B/J
	Red with parchment interior; recently restored. 400 Ram Air III 400 engine with 4-speed manual gearbox.											
1969	**GTO Judge hardtop**		242379B163075	L	NA	138.541*	198.000*	181.309*	29-01-16	Scottsdale	1346	B/J
	Red with black interior; fully restored. Ram Air IV engine with 4-speed manual gearbox.											
1967	**GTO hardtop**		242177K112896	L	NA	123.147*	176.000*	161.163*	29-01-16	Scottsdale	1350	B/J
	Gold with black vinyl roof and gold interior; recent full restoration. 400 Ram Air engine with 4-speed manual gearbox.											
1967	**GTO hardtop**		242177P302943	L	NA	60.034	85.800	78.567	30-01-16	Scottsdale	5242	R&S
	Ivory with black vinyl roof and red interior; restored. 360bhp 400 HO engine with 4-speed manual gearbox.											
1970	**GTO Judge hardtop**		242370P182366	L	NA	91.492	125.400	113.311	24-06-16	Uncasville	727	B/J
	Orange with black interior; concours-quality restoration. 400 Ram Air III engine with manual gearbox.											
1970	**GTO Judge hardtop**		242370R110551	L	NA	51.590	67.000	60.521	09-07-16	Denver	S160	Mec
	Gold with sandalwood interior; restored in 2010, engine detailed in 2015. 366bhp 400 engine with automatic transmission.											
1969	**GTO convertible**		242679R167185	L	NA	88.438*	134.200*	120.351*	26-09-15	Las Vegas	699	B/J
	Red with red interior; 1,250 miles covered since the restoration. 400 Ram Air IV engine with automatic transmission.											
1971	**GTO Judge convertible**		242671P110366	L	NA	134.692*	192.500*	176.272*	29-01-16	Scottsdale	1343	B/J
	Bronze; full restoration completed in 2009. 455 Ram Air engine with automatic transmission.											
1969	**GTO convertible**		242679B165939	L	NA	177.024*	253.000*	231.672*	29-01-16	Scottsdale	1344	B/J
	Black with black interior; fully restored. Ram Air IV engine with automatic transmission.											**F578**
1970	**GTO convertible**		242670P146985	L	NA	48.972	70.000	63.119	12-03-16	Kansas City	S105	Mec
	Black with black vinyl interior; until 2005 with its first owner. Restored in 2005; engine rebuilt in 2015. 350bhp 400 engine with automatic transmission.											

F577: 1970 Pontiac GTO Judge hardtop

F578: 1969 Pontiac GTO convertible

Year	Model	(Bodybuilder)	Chassis no.	Steering	Estimate	Hammer price £	$	€	Date	Place	Lot	Auc. H.

F579: 1969 Pontiac Firebird TransAm

F580: 1977 Pontiac Firebird TransAm Bandit

Year	Model	Chassis no.	Steering	Estimate	£	$	€	Date	Place	Lot	Auc. H.
1968	**Beaumont Sport DeLuxe coupé**	7383781107523	L	NA	25.186	36.000	32.461	12-03-16	Kansas City	F121	Mec
	Teal with white interior; Canadian market model. 325bhp 396 engine with automatico transmission.										
1974	**Firebird TransAm**	2V87X4N159682	L	NA	72.490*	110.000*	98.648*	26-09-15	Las Vegas	744	B/J
	Red with black interior; 9,500 actual miles. Restored. 455 Super Duty engine with 4-speed manual gearbox.										
1969	**Firebird TransAm**	223379N104712	L	NA	83.130	127.500	112.226	09-10-15	Chicago	S98	Mec F579
	White with parchment white interior; in original unrestored condition. 335bhp 400 Ram Air III engine with 4-speed manual gearbox.										
1969	**Firebird TransAm convertible**	223679N104810	L	NQ		NS		23-01-16	Kissimmee	F115	Mec
	White with blue stripes and parchment interior; one of eight examples built and one of four fitted with the 4-speed manual gearbox. First used as a company car, it was sold in April 1970 to its first private owner. Restored in the 1990s; fitted with a 335bhp 400 Ram Air III engine.										
1969	**Firebird TransAm convertible**	223679N106884	L	NA		NS		23-01-16	Kissimmee	F138	Mec
	White with blue stripes and blue interior; one of eight examples built and one of four with automatic transmission. 335bhp 400 Ram Air III engine.										
1974	**Firebird TransAm**	2V87X4N168278	L	NA	74.658*	106.700*	97.705*	29-01-16	Scottsdale	1131	B/J
	Blue with white interior; Super Duty 455 engine with automatic transmission.										
1973	**Firebird TransAm**	2V87X3N139660	L	NA	111.602*	159.500*	146.054*	29-01-16	Scottsdale	1275	B/J
	Brewster green with black interior; stored from 1980 to 2014 and subsequently restored. 455 Super Duty engine with automatic transmission.										
1977	**Firebird TransAm Bandit**	2W87Z7N139933	L	NA	384.835*	550.000*	503.635*	29-01-16	Scottsdale	7004	B/J F580
	Black; fully restored. The car was used by Universal Studios for the movie "Smokey and the Bandit". Presented by actor Burt Reynolds and previously titled "Burt Reynolds Institute for film and theater".										
1969	**Firebird TransAm**	223379N104394	L	NA	97.680*	137.500*	121.000*	09-04-16	Palm Beach	7001	B/J
	White with black vinyl interior; fully restored. 400 Ram Air III engine with automatic transmission.										

POPE-HARTFORD (USA) *(1903-1914)*

Year	Model	Chassis no.	Steering	Estimate	£	$	€	Date	Place	Lot	Auc. H.
1904	**Model D side-entrance tonneau**	543	R	75-85.000 GBP	82.140	130.077	114.372	30-10-15	London	107	Bon F581
	Dark red with black fenders and black interior; restored in 2005 and fitted with a new body. Paintwork and interior redone in 2014.										

POPE-TRIBUNE (USA) *(1904-1908)*

Year	Model	Chassis no.	Steering	Estimate	£	$	€	Date	Place	Lot	Auc. H.
1904	**Model II runabout**	369	R	NA	56.000	86.134	75.488	14-10-15	Duxford	22	H&H F582
	Green with black fenders and black interior; in good overall condition. Engine apparently overhauled in 2014 and fitted with a new cylinder block. Imported into the UK in 1992-1993.										

POPE-WAVERLEY (USA) *(1904-1908)*

Year	Model	Chassis no.	Steering	Estimate	£	$	€	Date	Place	Lot	Auc. H.
1906	**Model 21 runabout**	3774	L	30-40.000 GBP	44.800	64.525	57.084	11-06-16	Brooklands	259	His
	Black with black interior; imported into the UK in 2008 and subsequently fitted with modern batteries and charging system (see lot 155 RM 3.12.11 $ 77,000).										

F581: 1904 Pope-Hartford Model D side-entrance tonneau

F582: 1904 Pope-Tribune Model II runabout

F583: 1953 Porsche 356 coupé (Reutter)

F584: 1954 Porsche 356 cabriolet

PORSCHE (D) (1948-)

Year	Model (Bodybuilder)	Chassis no.	Steering	Estimate	£	$	€	Date	Place	Lot	Auc. H.
1953	356 coupé (Reutter)	50687	L	190-230.000 GBP	162.400*	247.855*	222.374*	07-09-15	London	158	RMS F583
Light blue; sold new in Germany, the car remained in the same family ownership for 50 years. In 2004 it was imported into the UK and subsequently restored. Original 1500 engine and gearbox.											
1953	356 coupé (Reutter)	50540	L	NA	101.486	154.000	138.107	26-09-15	Las Vegas	734	B/J
Black with tobacco interior; prepared years ago for historic racing. Engine enlarged to 1,640cc giving 120bhp. Recently restored.											
1954	356 coupé (Reutter)	52476	L	180-240.000 EUR	137.557	212.432	187.000	17-10-15	Salzburg	329	Dor
Pearl grey with blue/grey cloth interior; restored in the USA in the 1990s and fitted with a 60bhp type 616/1 engine.											
1955	356 Continental coupé (Reutter)	53344	L	140-180.000 USD	99.971	143.000	131.145	28-01-16	Scottsdale	114	Bon
Black with saddle leather interior; since 1971 in the current ownership. Between 2006 and 2010 the car was fully restored and fitted with the present 1963 1600 Super engine.											
1952	356 coupé (Reutter)	50089	L	190-200.000 EUR		NS		06-08-16	Schloss Dyck	131	Coy
Black with tan interior; described as in original condition except for the paintwork redone in the 1990s.											
1953	356 coupé (Reutter)	50894	L	250-290.000 EUR	220.799	290.441	260.345	06-08-16	Schloss Dyck	165	Coy
Silver with blue and white interior; fully restored. 1500 S engine.											
1954	356 coupé	51878	L	140-150.000 EUR		NS		06-08-16	Schloss Dyck	171	Coy
Silver; prepared for historic racing in 1993 and subsequently used at numerous events.											
1953	356 cabriolet (Reutter)	60236	L	140-180.000 GBP		NS		24-06-16	Goodwood	258	Bon
Light blue with blue leather interior; described as in good overall condition. Non-original but correct Type 546 1.5-litre engine.											
1954	356 cabriolet	60635	L	320-350.000 EUR	298.619	392.806	352.103	06-08-16	Schloss Dyck	160	Coy F584
Dark blue with blue/grey interior; first owned by the Swedish Royal Family. Fitted at unspecified date with a 1600 engine. 3,967 kms covered since a full restoration.											
1955	356 Speedster (Reutter)	80597	L	NA		NS		30-01-16	Scottsdale	5462	R&S
Blue with tan interior; restoration completed in 2007.											
1955	356 Speedster (Reutter)	80389	L	250-300.000 EUR	257.327	373.471	341.600	03-02-16	Paris	139	RMS F585
Metallic grey with red leather interior; recently restored and fitted with a 1958 1600 S engine.											
1955	356 Speedster	80354	L	350-400.000 USD	282.680	370.000	326.673	20-08-16	Monterey	S65	Mec
Red; recently restored. Engine rebuilt.											
1954	356 Speedster	80144	L	375-425.000 USD		NS		20-08-16	Monterey	S93	Mec
Red with original black interior; currently fitted with a later 356 engine, the car is offered with also its original 1500 type 546/2 engine and gearbox.											
1955	356 Speedster (Reutter)	80612	L	350-425.000 USD		NS		21-08-16	Pebble Beach	102	G&Co
White with black interior; used by the factory as a show car until mid-1956. Restored in the 1990s. Recently the restoration has been freshened and the car has been fitted with the present, unnumbered engine, rebuilt to Super specification.											
1955	550 Spyder (Wendler)	5500068	L	2.200-2.600.000 EUR	2.067.055	3.000.015	2.744.000	03-02-16	Paris	143	RMS
Silver; displayed at the Porsche stand at the 1955 Frankfurt Motor Show and then sold to the USA where it was raced until 1958. In 1989 it was imported into Italy and in 1999 it was acquired by the current owner. Described as ready to be used at historic events.											

F585: 1955 Porsche 356 Speedster (Reutter)

F586: 1955 Porsche 550 Spyder (Wendler)

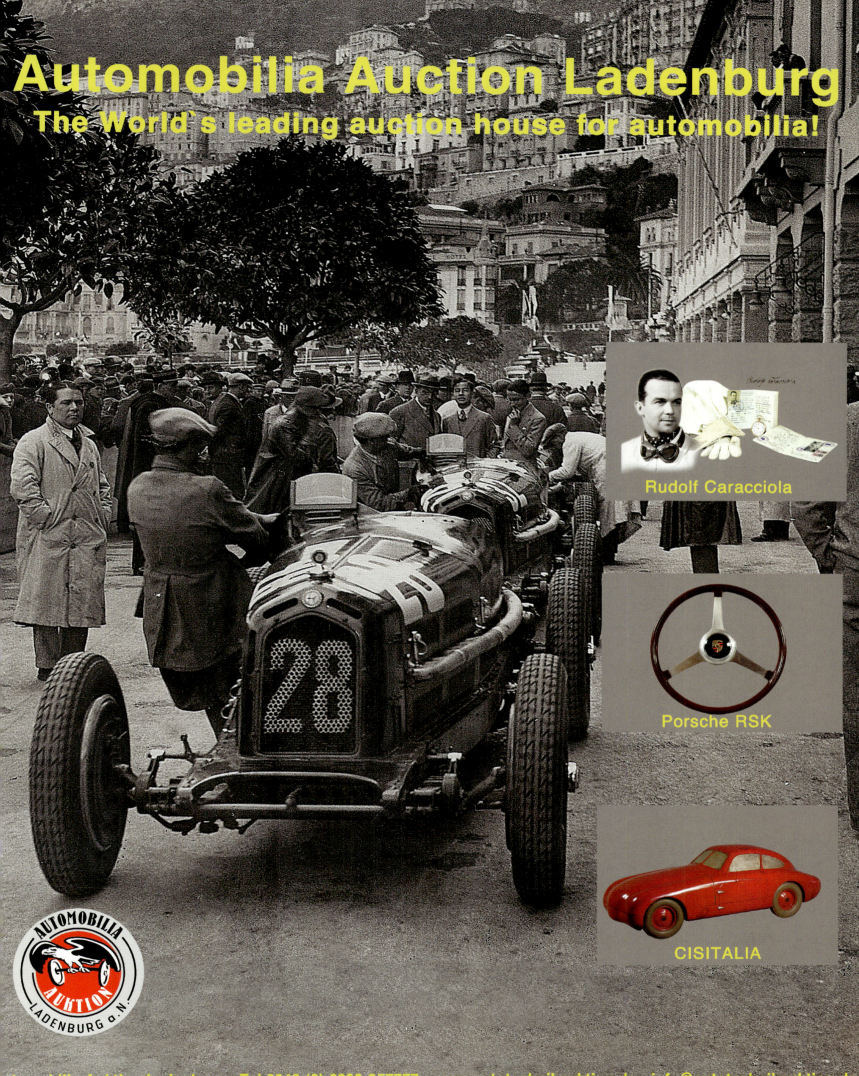

Year	Model	(Bodybuilder)	Chassis no.	Steering	Estimate	Hammer price £	$	€	Date	Place	Lot	Auc. H.

F587: 1958 Porsche Type 597 Jagdwagen

F588: 1958 Porsche 356A cabriolet (Reutter)

Year	Model	Chassis no.	Steer	Estimate	£	$	€	Date	Place	Lot	Auc. H.
1955	**550 Spyder (Wendler)**	5500060	L	5.000-6.000.000 USD	**3.732.366**	**5.335.000**	**4.810.570**	11-03-16	Amelia Island	34	G&Co F586
1958	**Type 597 Jagdwagen**	597000148	L	350-425.000 USD	**230.868**	**330.000**	**297.561**	11-03-16	Amelia Island	42	G&Co F587
1957	**356A coupé**	100814	L	NA		**NS**		26-02-16	Coventry	410	SiC
1956	**356A coupé**	57110	L	NA	**87.479**	**119.900**	**108.342**	24-06-16	Uncasville	696	B/J
1956	**356A cabriolet**	61347	R	170-200.000 GBP	**196.875**	**299.723**	**278.460**	14-11-15	Birmingham	330	SiC
1958	**356A cabriolet (Reutter)**	150523	L	175-225.000 USD	**83.772**	**120.000**	**111.024**	23-01-16	Kissimmee	S132	Mec F588
1959	**356A convertible D (Drauz)**	86509	L	130-160.000 GBP		**NS**		06-09-15	Hedingham Cas.	118	Coy
1956	**356A convertible D (Drauz)**	86509	L	130-160.000 EUR		**NS**		26-09-15	Frankfurt	148	Coy
1958	**356A convertible D (Drauz)**	85724	L	130-150.000 USD	**113.454***	**148.500***	**131.111***	19-08-16	Carmel	108	Bon F589
1959	**356A convertible D (Drauz)**	86090	L	325-375.000 USD	**247.918**	**324.500**	**286.501**	21-08-16	Pebble Beach	139	G&Co
1956	**356A Speedster (Reutter)**	82494	L	200-250.000 EUR	**189.791**	**288.038**	**258.307**	26-09-15	Frankfurt	136	Coy
1955	**356A Speedster (Reutter)**	80333	L	300-400.000 USD	**246.294**	**352.000**	**322.326**	29-01-16	Scottsdale	3	G&Co
1958	**356A Speedster (Reutter)**	83895	L	325-400.000 USD	**206.412**	**295.000**	**270.132**	29-01-16	Phoenix	253	RMS
1958	**356A Speedster (Reutter)**	84577	L	350-425.000 USD	**257.839**	**368.500**	**337.435**	30-01-16	Scottsdale	108	G&Co
1957	**356A Speedster (Reutter)**	83568	L	NA		**NS**		30-01-16	Scottsdale	5198	R&S

1955 550 Spyder (Wendler) — Blue with original beige vinyl interior; described as in original condition except for the paintwork redone in the late 1960s-early 1970s. While little is known about its first few years, in 1963 circa the car was acquired by Lou Hilton who retained it until 1998 when it was bought by Joel Horvitz. Since 2007 it is in the collection of Jerry Seinfeld who acquired it from the Mr. Horvitz's estate. 10,330 miles on the odometer.

1958 Type 597 Jagdwagen — Green with original light brown vinyl interior; sold new to the USA to Wendell Fletcher who retained it until 1987. Less than 24,000 kms covered. Since 2010 in the Jerry Seinfeld Collection.

1957 356A coupé — Blue; in good overall condition. Currently fitted with a 1600 S engine (see Silverstone Auctions lots 321 22.2.14 $ 101,659 and 813 25.7.15 NS).

1956 356A coupé — Dark green; in concours condition.

1956 356A cabriolet — Light blue; stored in the mid-1990s for 14 years, the car subsequently received a three year full restoration. For the past two years on display in the showroom of the Porsche Hong Kong, it has been recently imported into the UK.

1958 356A cabriolet (Reutter) — Green with tan interior; 1600 Super engine.

1959 356A convertible D (Drauz) — Silver with red interior; sold new to the USA, the car was reimported into Europe in 1992. Restored in the 2000s (see lot 151 Coys 23.10.10 NS).

1956 356A convertible D (Drauz) — See lot 118 Coys 6.9.15.

1958 356A convertible D (Drauz) — Red with black interior; for 25 years in the current ownership. Transmission replaced in 1989, body repainted in 1992, front drum brakes replaced with discs. Original Super 1600 engine.

1959 356A convertible D (Drauz) — Dark green with tan interior; at unspecified date fully restored to concours condition. 1600 engine.

1956 356A Speedster (Reutter) — White with red interior; restored in the USA prior to be reimported into Germany in 1996. 1600 engine.

1955 356A Speedster (Reutter) — White with black leatherette interior; since 1990 circa in the current ownership, the car was restored between 2013 and 2014. The pistons and cylinders have been replaced with 356C 1600 unit (the original 1500 components are included with the sale).

1958 356A Speedster (Reutter) — Light blue with navy blue interior; restored in the 1990s, the car was later fitted with the present Porsche 912 engine. Body repainted in more recent times (see lot 444 RM 16.8.08 NS).

1958 356A Speedster (Reutter) — Light blue; in good overall condition. Body repainted at unspecified date. Since 1967 for 45 years in the previous ownership. 1600 original engine. With hardtop.

1957 356A Speedster (Reutter) — Ivory with red interior; restored in the USA (see lot S743 Russo & Steele 17.1.15 $ 286,000).

F589: 1958 Porsche 356A convertible D (Drauz)

F590: 1956 Porsche 356A 1500 GS Carrera coupé (Reutter)

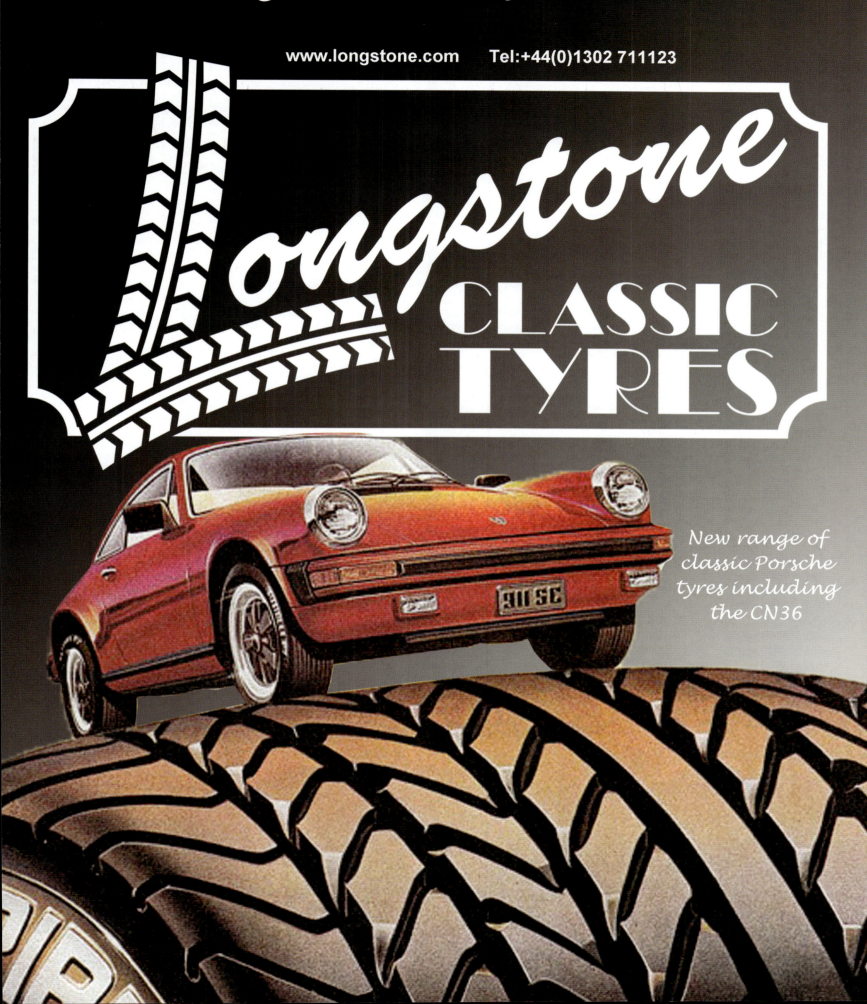

Year	Model (Bodybuilder)	Chassis No.	Steering	Estimate	Hammer Price £	Hammer Price $	Hammer Price €	Date	Place	Lot	Auc. H.
1957	**356A Speedster (Reutter)**	83124	L	500-600.000 USD	477.127	682.000	614.959	11-03-16	Amelia Island	35	**G&Co**
	Metallic aquamarine blue; sold new to the USA, the car remained with its second owner from 1958 to 2009 when it was acquired by Tom Scott who restored it to concours condition. 1600 original engine. Since 2010 in the Jerry Seinfeld Collection.										
1956	**356A Speedster**	82642	L	240-280.000 GBP		NS		20-03-16	Goodwood	44	**Bon**
	Black with red leather interior; in good working order. Fitted in the past with the present Super 90 engine no.85234 (see Bonhams lots 518 6.12.10 NS and 353 5.2.11 $ 188,108).										
1958	**356A Speedster**	84031	L	260-275.000 USD		NS		02-04-16	Ft.Lauderdale	505	**AA**
	Blue with red leatherette interior; restored in the early 2000s. 912 engine, 356B o C gearbox, all-around disc brakes.										
1958	**356A Speedster (Reutter)**	83832	L	260-300.000 USD		NS		25-06-16	Santa Monica	1071	**AA**
	Silver; restored and fitted with a period-correct 1600 Super engine.										
1956	**356A Speedster (Reutter)**	82561	L	400-450.000 USD	290.320	380.000	335.502	19-08-16	Monterey	143	**RMS**
	White with original red leatherette interior; sold new to the USA, the car has had just two registered owners until 2010. Body repainted in the 1970s. 1600 engine and gearbox rebuilt 6,000 miles ago.										
1956	**356A Speedster (Reutter)**	82623	L	400-500.000 USD	357.170	467.500	412.756	20-08-16	Pebble Beach	81	**G&Co**
	Red with black interior; described as in largely original condition. 1600 engine.										
1957	**356A Speedster (Reutter)**	83568	L	NQ		NS		20-08-16	Monterey	7029	**R&S**
	See lot 5198 Russo & Steele 30.1.16.										
1956	**356A 1500 GS Carrera coupé (Reutter)**	56118	L	Refer Dpt.	580.000	883.166	792.918	06-09-15	Hedingham Cas.	131	**Coy** F590
	Silver metallic with dark blue leatherette interior; imported in 2001 into Italy and subsequently restored. Described as in excellent overall condition. Recently serviced.										
1956	**356A 1500 GS Carrera coupé (Reutter)**	56417	L	300-350.000 GBP	302.400	461.523	414.076	07-09-15	London	142	**RMS**
	Metallic aquamarine blue with red leather interior; sold new to the USA, the car was reimported into Europe in 2004. Fully restored in Italy in 2005-2006; engine replaced with a Type 547/1 unit (see lot 328 RM 12.5.12 $ 304,443).										
1956	**356A 1500 GS Carrera coupé (Reutter)**	56118	L	Refer Dpt.		NS		26-09-15	Frankfurt	132	**Coy**
	See lot 131 Coys 6.9.15.										
1958	**356A 1500 GS/GT Carrera speedst (Reutter)**	84908	L	2.000-2.500.000 USD	1.077.384	1.540.000	1.388.618	11-03-16	Amelia Island	46	**G&Co** F591
	Green with black vinyl interior; it is believed the car was raced in the USA until the early 1970s. In 2009 it was acquired by European Collectibles, California, and fully restored over a three year period to concours condition. Original engine type 692/0 no.91015. From the Jerry Seinfeld Collection.										
1956	**356A 1500 GS Carrera speedster (Reutter)**	82243	L	800-1.100.000 USD	680.724	891.000	786.664	19-08-16	Carmel	52	**Bon**
	Black with red interior; restored in the early 1990s. In the late 1990s the engine was rebuilt and fitted with 550A Spyder camshafts. It should be noted that the original engine and gearbox were substituted at some point, though the current motor is stamped as a Type 547/2, which was used almost exclusively in the 550A Spyder racing cars (see lots 38 P.R.Group 27.11.99 NS and 346 Brooks 19.8.00 $167,500).										
1956	**356A 1500 GS Carrera Custom coupé**	56083	L	550-750.000 USD		NS		20-08-16	Pebble Beach	57	**G&Co**
	Built with Reutter body, in 1957 circa the car was purchased by Dean Jeffries who subsequently customized it. After some ownership changes in 1971 it was bought by the current owner. Restored to its original silver livery between 2008 and 2011. Currently fitted with Carrera 1600 GS engine no.93046.										
1958	**550A/1500RS**	550A0145	L	5.000-6.000.000 USD		NS		20-08-16	Pebble Beach	42	**G&Co**
	Bought by Count Carel Godin de Beaufort, the car raced as an entry Porsche at four events of the 1958 World Make Championship, including the Le Mans 24 Hours where it placed 5th overall and 2nd in class. Raced by de Beaufort until 1959 when it was sold to Canada where it was raced until the early 1960s. Reimported into Europe in 1991; bought in 2002 by Italian collector Bruno Ferracin and driven at 10 editions of the historic MM. Since 2013 in the current ownership. Currently fitted with a period 4-speed gearbox (the original 5-speed unit is included with the sale).										
1959	**718 RSK**	718019	L	3.800-4.200.000 USD	2.000.856	2.860.000	2.578.862	11-03-16	Amelia Island	48	**G&Co** F592
	Silver; sold new to the USA, the car was extensively raced until 1970 and was driven in 1959 and 1960 also by Roger Penske. In late 1970 it caught fire in the garage of the then owner, John Beam. After some ownership changes, it was acquired by Tom Trabue, who had it fully restored and fitted with a new body. Currently fitted with a 1.6-litre version of the type 547/3 engine, no.90322. Since 2001 in the Jerry Seinfeld Collection.										
1960	**356B coupé**	109041	L	NQ	58.500*	89.078*	79.975*	04-09-15	Woodstock	236	**SiC**
	Red with black leather interior; restoration recently completed in the UK.										
1963	**356B coupé**	214319	L	60-70.000 GBP		NS		06-09-15	Hedingham Cas.	157	**Coy**
	Dark grey with red leather interior; restored at unspecified date.										
1963	**356B coupé**	214319	L	60-70.000 GBP		NS		10-10-15	Ascot	142	**Coy**
	See lot 157 Coys 6.9.15.										
1960	**356B coupé**	110448	L	40-45.000 GBP		NS		25-10-15	Silverstone	204	**SiC**
	Red with black interior; the car has covered 8,000 kms since the restoration carried out in 1997, when it was fitted with the present Super 90 engine.										
1961	**356B coupé**	115118	R	60-70.000 GBP	68.625	105.717	95.375	25-10-15	Silverstone	224	**SiC**
	Blue with red leatherette and cloth interior; body repainted in the 1970s, interior retrimmed in more recent years, Super 90 engine rebuilt some time ago and recently serviced.										

F591: 1958 Porsche 356A 1500 GS/GT Carrera speedst (Reutter)

F592: 1959 Porsche 718 RSK

Year	Model (Bodybuilder)	Chassis no.	Steering	Estimate	Hammer price £	Hammer price $	Hammer price €	Date	Place	Lot	Auc. H.
1959	**356B coupé**	109849	L	35-55.000 EUR	42.805*	67.783*	59.600*	01-11-15	Paris	108	**Art**
	Green with beige leather interior; in good working order. 356C Super 90 engine.										**F593**
1960	**356B coupé**	109532	L	60-70.000 EUR		NS		07-11-15	Lyon	260	**Agu**
	Black with tan interior; restored about 10 years ago.										
1962	**356B coupé**	210289	L	50-60.000 EUR	47.365	71.702	66.000	08-11-15	Lyon	216	**Ose**
	Grey with red interior; restored in 1995 and fitted with a Super 90 engine.										
1962	**356B coupé**	212147	R	25-35.000 GBP	31.920	48.161	44.021	09-12-15	Chateau Impney	65	**H&H**
	Yellow with red vinyl interior; imported into Ireland in 1998 and converted to right-hand drive.										
1962	**356B coupé (Reutter)**	120976	L	90-120.000 USD	61.574*	88.000*	80.582*	30-01-16	Scottsdale	119	**G&Co**
	Blue with grey vinyl interior; stored for 20 years, the car is in largely original condition and has been recently serviced.										
1961	**356B coupé**	117401	L	50-70.000 EUR	49.789*	64.658*	58.408*	09-07-16	Le Mans	110	**Art**
	Dark blue with black vinyl interior; in good mechanical order. Non-original 1600 engine.										
1960	**356B cabriolet**	153241	L	NA		NS		05-09-15	Auburn	4113	**AA**
	Grey with red leather interior; cosmetically restored.										
1960	**356B cabriolet (Reutter)**	152913	R	140-160.000 GBP	153.000	232.973	209.166	06-09-15	Hedingham Cas.	115	**Coy**
	Silver grey; sold new to Australia. In good overall condition. 1600S engine.										
1961	**356B cabriolet (Reutter)**	155501	R	80-120.000 GBP	124.700	192.325	170.689	12-09-15	Goodwood	334	**Bon**
	Red with black interior; restored in 1993-94 circa. Super 90 engine; with hardtop.										
1960	**356B cabriolet (Reutter)**	154090	L	135-160.000 EUR		NS		26-09-15	Frankfurt	153	**Coy**
	Red with black leather interior; restored in Italy at unspecified date. 1600 Super engine (see lot 142 Coys 18.4.15 $ 130,276).										
1959	**356B cabriolet (Reutter)**	152823	L	140-180.000 EUR		NS		09-10-15	Zoute	10	**Bon**
	Grey with blue interior; sold new to the USA, the car was later imported into Belgium where it was restored in 2012-13. 1600 Super engine.										
1960	**356B cabriolet**	153241	L	NA		NS		09-10-15	Chicago	S150.1	**Mec**
	See lot 4113 Auctions America 5.9.15.										
1962	**356B cabriolet (Reutter)**	156055	L	90-110.000 GBP		NS		01-12-15	London	322	**Coy**
	Red with black interior; restored at unspecified date.										
1960	**356B cabriolet**	154172	L	120-150.000 EUR	100.472	143.999	131.940	16-01-16	Maastricht	425	**Coy**
	Silver with red interior; described as in good overall condition. 1600 Super engine.										
1960	**356B cabriolet**	154251	L	175-200.000 USD	117.274*	167.750*	153.844*	28-01-16	Phoenix	124	**RMS**
	Silver with dark blue leather interior; restored, the car is described as in good overall condition. 1600 engine (see lots S642 Russo & Steele 18.8.11 $ 105,270, S91 Mecum 16.8.12 NS, 145 RM 27.4.13 $ 148,500 and 2126 Auctions America 18.7.15 NS).										**F594**
1962	**356B cabriolet**	155921	L	NA	73.888	105.600	96.698	30-01-16	Scottsdale	5122	**R&S**
	Blue; restored. Two owners since new.										
1963	**356B cabriolet (Reutter)**	157771	L	140-160.000 USD	105.722	149.600	137.782	10-03-16	Amelia Island	171	**Bon**
	Black with black leather interior; restored approximately 20 years ago. Super 90 engine.										
1963	**356B cabriolet (Reutter)**	157310	L	175-225.000 USD	130.825*	187.000*	168.618*	11-03-16	Amelia Island	19	**G&Co**
	Champagne yellow with beige leather interior; restored in 1992.										
1960	**356B cabriolet (Reutter)**	152629	L	200-250.000 USD	169.303	242.000	218.211	12-03-16	Amelia Island	156	**RMS**
	Light ivory with red leather interior; in the same family ownership since 1960, the car was used until 1966 and then stored until 2011 when it was bought by a new owner who subjected it to a full restoration. 50 miles covered since.										
1961	**356B cabriolet**	155210	L	150-180.000 EUR	118.799	171.173	150.840	14-05-16	Monaco	186	**Coy**
	White with red interior; restored in 2012. Super 90 engine.										
1960	**356B cabriolet**	153241	L	NQ	106.392	155.000	138.152	20-05-16	Indianapolis	F81.1	**Mec**
	See lot S150.1 Mecum 10.09.15.										
1962	**356B cabriolet**	157070	L	86-96.000 GBP	118.720	170.992	151.273	11-06-16	Brooklands	273	**His**
	Red with black interior; recent full restoration. 1600 S engine.										
1961	**356B roadster**	89023	L	150-180.000 EUR	135.205	204.678	188.400	08-11-15	Lyon	214	**Ose**
	Red with black interior; in good overall condition. Interior retrimmed three years ago. Super 90 engine.										
1960	**356B roadster (Drauz)**	86950	L	175-225.000 USD	125.071*	178.750*	163.681*	29-01-16	Scottsdale	54	**G&Co**
	Red with tan interior; in the same family ownership since new. 29,000 miles covered. In largely original condition; the front fender and nose were replaced in 1978 following an accident.										

F593: 1959 Porsche 356B coupé

F594: 1960 Porsche 356B cabriolet

Year	Model	(Bodybuilder)	Chassis no.	Steering	Estimate	Hammer price £	Hammer price $	Hammer price €	Sale Date	Place	Lot	Auc. H.
1961	356B roadster	(Drauz)	88316	L	175-225.000 USD	111.602*	159.500*	146.054*	30-01-16	Scottsdale	148	G&Co
Grey with light grey leatherette interior; restored 25 years ago. 1961 1600 Super engine not original to the car.
1960	356B roadster	(Drauz)	87954	L	180-220.000 USD	123.130*	176.000*	158.699*	12-03-16	Amelia Island	191	RMS F595
Ivory with red interior; restored some years ago, recently the car has been repainted and the interior have been retrimmed. Currently fitted with a 1600 S engine.
1961	356B roadster	(D'Ieteren)	89097	L	240-260.000 EUR		NS		14-05-16	Monaco	237	RMS
Dark grey with red leather interior; the car has covered 1,000 kms since a recent restoration. 1600 S engine.
1960	356B roadster	(Drauz)	87746	L	185-200.000 USD		NS		20-08-16	Monterey	S62	Mec
Red with tan leather interior; full restoration completed in 2014. Super 90 engine (see lot S11 Mecum 15.8.15 $170,000).
1960	356B roadster		87299	L	NQ		NS		20-08-16	Monterey	7103	R&S
Red; restored several years ago. For over 50 years in the same family ownership.
1962	356B 2000 GS Carrera 2 coupé	(Reutter)	120915	L	350-400.000 GBP	386.400	589.724	529.098	07-09-15	London	163	RMS
Green with black leatherette interior; restored at unspecified date. Porsche Certificate of Authenticity included.
1962	356B 2000 GS Carrera 2 coupé	(Reutter)	120840	L	650-800.000 USD	438.336	627.000	575.022	28-01-16	Scottsdale	28	Bon F596
Red with black leatherette and grey cloth interior; sold new in Germany, the car was imported in the late 1960s into the USA where it remained in single ownership from 1971 to 2008. Fully restored between 2009 and 2013. The original engine was replaced early in its life at the factory with the present unit, no. 97311. Electric sunroof.
1963	356B 2000 GS/GT Carrera 2 coupé	(Reutter)	122561	L	1.100-1.400.000 USD	577.170	825.000	743.903	11-03-16	Amelia Island	39	G&Co
Silver with blue leatherette interior; sold new to Belgium, in 1964 the car returned at the factory where it was fitted with the present type 587/2 GT-specification engine, no.98016. In 1982 circa it was imported into the USA where later the engine was rebuilt. In 2002 it was reimported into Europe and in 2008 it returned to the USA. From the Jerry Seinfeld Collection (see lots 119 RM 25.5.02 $ 173,250 and 241 Bonhams 26.5.03 $ 178,376).
1965	356C coupé		219852	L	32-37.000 GBP	39.880*	60.725*	54.520*	06-09-15	Hedingham Cas.	117	Coy
Red with black interior; restored at unspecified date (see lot 128 Coys 18.4.15 $ 59,898).
1965	356SC coupé		129779	R	50-60.000 GBP	45.167	68.776	61.748	06-09-15	Hedingham Cas.	139	Coy
Red with black interior; in good overall condition. Body repainted in recent years.
1965	356SC coupé		129724	L	100-125.000 USD	62.829	90.000	83.268	23-01-16	Kissimmee	S183	Mec
Black with grey interior.
1964	356C coupé	(Karmann)	220576	L	80-100.000 USD	36.143*	51.700*	47.414*	28-01-16	Scottsdale	61	Bon
Red with black leatherette interior; sold new to the USA, the car remained with its first owner until 2012. The body was repainted in the mid-1970s and the car was stored in 1982. Acquired in 2014 by the current owner, it requires further mechanical works prior to use.
1964	356C coupé		216880	L	NA	67.731*	96.800*	88.640*	29-01-16	Scottsdale	1084	B/J
Red with black interior; restored (see lot 698 Barrett-Jackson 19.1.07 $ 77,000).
1964	356SC coupé	(Karmann)	216391	L	130-160.000 USD	67.346*	96.250*	88.136*	29-01-16	Scottsdale	40	G&Co
Red with black leatherette interior; restored in recent years.
1964	356SC coupé	(Reutter)	128987	L	140-180.000 USD	84.652*	121.000*	109.106*	12-03-16	Amelia Island	106	RMS F597
Champagne yellow with black leatherette interior; restored in 2003. Transmission recently replaced (see lots 142 RM 15.1.15 $ 159,500 and 1065 Auctions America 18.7.15 NS).
1964	356SC coupé		217063	L	80-90.000 USD	69.181	99.000	86.595	02-04-16	Ft.Lauderdale	559	AA
Black with red interior; restored.
1964	356C coupé		220716	L	75-85.000 EUR		NS		09-04-16	Essen	143	Coy
Green with light brown interior; restored a few years ago.
1965	356SC coupé	(Reutter)	131907	L	115-130.000 USD	100.320	137.500	124.245	25-06-16	Santa Monica	1143	AA
Grey with black leather interior recently retrimmed; engine rebuilt. Factory sunroof.
1964	356C coupé	(Karmann)	216729	L	70-90.000 USD	92.444*	121.000*	106.831*	19-08-16	Carmel	12	Bon
Black with red leatherette interior; full restoration completed in May 2016.
1965	356C coupé		131874	L	175-210.000 USD	48.132	63.000	55.623	20-08-16	Monterey	S151	Mec
White with red leatherette interior; recently serviced. Electric sunroof.
1965	356SC coupé		131469	L	200-250.000 USD		NS		20-08-16	Monterey	S27	Mec
White with black vinyl interior; fully restored. Electric sunroof.
1964	356SC coupé		216391	L	125-150.000 USD	72.580	95.000	83.876	20-08-16	Monterey	S60	Mec
See lot 40 Gooding & Company 29.1.16.
1965	356C coupé		219861	L	NQ	65.551	85.800	75.753	20-08-16	Monterey	7099	R&S
Red; in good overall condition. Repainted body, original interior.

F595: 1960 Porsche 356B roadster (Drauz)

F596: 1962 Porsche 356B 2000 GS Carrera 2 coupé (Reutter)

Year	Model	(Bodybuilder)	Chassis No.	Steering	Estimate	Hammer Price £	Hammer Price $	Hammer Price €	Date	Place	Lot	Auc. H.
1964	356SC cabriolet	(Reutter)	160371	L	400-600.000 USD	1.163.536	1.760.000	1.608.288	10-12-15	New York	206	RMS
	Bought in 1968 by the rock star Janis Joplin, the car was painted by Dave Richards to what he referred to as "The History of the Universe". Following the Janis' death in 1970, the car was used by her manager until 1973 when Michael Joplin and his sister, Laura, retrieved it. Years later it was repainted in its original grey livery, but in the early 1990s the Joplin brothers commissioned artists Jana Mitchell and Amber Owen to duplicate the original artwork. For the past 20 years on display at the Rock and Roll Hall of Fame and Museum in Cleveland.											SEASON CASE
1964	356SC cabriolet	(Reutter)	160751	L	200-250.000 USD	153.802	220.000	201.762	28-01-16	Scottsdale	30	Bon
	Black with red interior; restored in the USA in the mid-1990s, the car is described as still in very good overall condition.											
1965	356SC cabriolet	(Reutter)	161161	L	NA	73.119*	104.500*	95.691*	29-01-16	Scottsdale	1385	B/J
	Yellow with black interior; restored (see lot F194 Mecum 16.5.15 NS).											
1964	356C cabriolet	(Reutter)	160180	L	130-160.000 USD	83.829	121.000	108.477	05-06-16	Greenwhich	100	Bon
	Silver; restoration completed in 2001 and refreshed in 2015. The car was fitted at unspecified date with the present 1600 engine.											
1965	356C cabriolet		161632	L	NA		NS		11-06-16	Newport Beach	6051	R&S
	Red with retrimmed light brown interior; fitted with a period correct SC engine.											
1964	356SC cabriolet	(Reutter)	160633	L	110-150.000 GBP		NS		24-06-16	Goodwood	285	Bon
	Red with black leather interior; fully restored in Germany between 2013 and 2015.											
1963	356C cabriolet		157841	L	NA		NS		09-07-16	Denver	S114	Mec
	Red with black interior; fitted with disc brakes in the 1970s. In the same ownership from 1980 to 2015. Engine detailed in 2016.											
1969	911 T coupé		119122649	L	65-75.000 GBP	65.873	100.305	90.055	06-09-15	Hedingham Cas.	105	Coy
	Red with black interior; restored in 2013.											
1969	911 S Targa		119310538	L	90-110.000 GBP	87.670	133.495	119.854	06-09-15	Hedingham Cas.	109	Coy
	Silver with original black leatherette interior; body repainted at unspecified date, engine rebuilt in 2014. Three owners since new.											
1969	911 T coupé		119123097	L	35-38.000 GBP	31.873	48.533	43.574	06-09-15	Hedingham Cas.	112	Coy
	Red with black interior; body repainted in 2014. 5-speed 901 gearbox.											
1966	911 coupé		304575	L	95-120.000 GBP		NS		06-09-15	Hedingham Cas.	141	Coy
	White; imported from the USA into the UK in 1992 and subsequently restored for historic racing. Acquired in 2010 by the current owner and restored again.											
1968	911 T coupé		119120923	L	38-45.000 GBP	41.785	63.626	57.124	06-09-15	Hedingham Cas.	145	Coy
	Red with black interior; restored in the USA at unspecified date.											
1965	911 coupé		302285	L	65-85.000 GBP	56.000*	85.467*	76.681*	07-09-15	London	103	RMS
	Red; acquired in 1993 by the current owner and subsequently prepared for historic racing. Fitted with a 911 S engine enlarged to 2.5 litres (see lot 249 RM 31.10.07 NS).											
1969	911 T coupé		119123097	L	45-50.000 EUR	24.247	36.798	33.000	26-09-15	Frankfurt	129	Coy
	See lot 112 Coys 6.9.15.											
1968	911 T Targa		11870020	L	55-75.000 EUR		NS		26-09-15	Frankfurt	170	Coy
	Blue with black interior; restored in 2003.											
1969	911 E coupé		9119220161	L	60-80.000 USD		NS		05-10-15	Philadelphia	263	Bon
	Burgundy with black interior; in good overall condition.											
1968	911 S Targa		119319163	L	140-210.000 EUR	144.807	222.127	195.500	09-10-15	Zoute	25	Bon F598
	Green with beige interior; sold new to the USA, the car was imported into Switzerland in 1990 circa and subsequently fully restored. Currently registered in the Netherlands.											
1969	911 T coupé		119120008	L	65-95.000 EUR		NS		09-10-15	Zoute	6	Bon
	Described as in very good overall condition; engine rebuilt in 2008.											
1968	911 T Targa		11870310	L	140-200.000 EUR	93.053	143.704	126.500	17-10-15	Salzburg	323	Dor
	Orange with black interior; until 2011 with its first owner. Body repainted in 2010; recently serviced.											
1966	911 coupé		305368	L	70-80.000 GBP		NS		14-11-15	Birmingham	641	SiC
	Irish green with black leather interior; described as in very good overall condition. Imported into the UK from the USA in 2014 (see lot 290 Historics 7.3.15 NS).											
1969	911 T coupé		119123058	L	45-55.000 EUR	42.286	60.605	55.530	16-01-16	Maastricht	414	Coy
	Yellow with black interior; body repainted, gearbox rebuilt.											
1969	911 S Targa		119319587	L	135-165.000 USD	115.352*	165.000*	151.322*	28-01-16	Scottsdale	14	Bon
	Red; restored in the early 2000s. Three owners since new.											
1969	911 S coupé		119301410	L	175-225.000 USD	146.112*	209.000*	191.674*	28-01-16	Scottsdale	56	Bon
	Metallic blue with beige interior; recently restored. Electric sunroof.											
1967	911 S coupé		306058	L	160-200.000 USD	97.664*	139.700*	128.119*	28-01-16	Scottsdale	83	Bon
	Irish green with leatherette and cloth interior; sold new in Germany, later the car was imported into the USA. Some cosmetic and mechanical works carried out in recent years.											

F597: 1964 Porsche 356SC coupé (Reutter)

F598: 1968 Porsche 911 S Targa

Year	Model	(Bodybuilder)	Chassis no.	Steering	Estimate	Hammer price £	Hammer price $	Hammer price €	Date	Place	Lot	Auc. H.
1968	**911 Targa**		11880182	L	75-100.000 USD	48.448*	69.300*	63.555*	28-01-16	Scottsdale	91	**Bon**
Irish green with black leatherette interior; recent cosmetic restoration.												
1967	**911 S coupé**		307557	L	250-300.000 USD	157.647*	225.500*	206.806*	28-01-16	Phoenix	123	**RMS F599**
Beige with black interior; restored. Sunroof. From the Craig McCaw Collection.												
1968	**911 S Targa**		11850368	L	200-250.000 USD	96.209*	137.500*	125.909*	29-01-16	Phoenix	216	**RMS**
Tangerine with black interior; restoration recently completed. Engine and gearbox rebuilt.												
1965	**911 coupé**		300569	L	250-300.000 USD	173.176	247.500	226.636	30-01-16	Scottsdale	110	**G&Co**
Finished in red with leatherette and cloth interior, the car was sold new to the USA. Restored in recent years.												
1966	**911 S coupé**		306565	L	150-200.000 EUR	127.793	189.437	169.050	04-02-16	Paris	324	**Bon**
Light ivory with black interior; since 1991 in the current ownership, the car was restored in Italy between 1996 and 1999 and has covered 1,600 kms since. Electric sunroof.												
1965	**911 coupé**		302855	L	220-260.000 EUR		NS		04-02-16	Paris	327	**Bon**
Silver with burgundy leather interior; restored circa in 2004.												
1969	**911 T coupé**		119122652	L	60-90.000 EUR		NS		04-02-16	Paris	367	**Bon**
Orange with black interior; described as in good overall condition.												
1967	**911 S coupé**		306131	L	140-180.000 USD	89.398*	126.500*	116.507*	10-03-16	Amelia Island	138	**Bon**
Light ivory with black interior; restored in the USA between 2012 and 2014. Original engine replaced with another S unit of the same year.												
1966	**911 coupé**		304182	L	200-300.000 USD	192.390	275.000	247.968	11-03-16	Amelia Island	31	**G&Co**
Sand with light brown leatherette interior; described as in very good original condition. Less than 19,000 miles covered. From the Jerry Seinfeld Collection.												
1969	**911 T Targa**		9110110161	L	55-65.000 GBP		NS		12-03-16	Brooklands	187	**His**
Blue with black interior; cosmetically restored in Italy in 2014.												
1968	**911 coupé**		11830350	L	NA	43.375	62.000	55.905	12-03-16	Kansas City	S210	**Mec**
White with tan and white interior; restored.												
1968	**911 S coupé**		11800468	R	100-130.000 GBP	122.460	177.408	157.288	20-03-16	Goodwood	86	**Bon**
Red with black interior; restored at unspecified date, the car is described as in very good overall condition (see lot 229 Coys 3.10.09 $ 80,489).												
1969	**911 Targa**		119111255	L	75-95.000 EUR	95.295	138.055	122.400	20-03-16	Fontainebleau	355	**Ose**
Burgundy with black interior; 5-speed gearbox.												
1968	**911 T coupé**		11825343	L	110-125.000 EUR		NS		09-04-16	Essen	161	**Coy**
Light ivory with black leatherette interior; restored body, original interior.												
1965	**911 coupé**		300617	L	200-300.000 EUR	66.157*	95.323*	84.000*	14-05-16	Monaco	215	**RMS**
Some years ago the car was handed over to German artist Peter Klasen who completed his project, entitled "007", in 2009. Presented in race-prepared condition.												
1968	**911 S Targa**		11850368	L	180-200.000 USD	102.534	148.000	132.682	05-06-16	Greenwhich	51	**Bon**
See lot 216 RM-Sotheby's 29.1.16.												
1969	**911 E coupé**		119220908	L	70-90.000 EUR	71.460	102.096	90.720	19-06-16	Fontainebleau	373	**Ose**
Restored in 2014; original interior.												
1966	**911 coupé**		304193	L	NA	134.028	183.700	165.991	24-06-16	Uncasville	686	**B/J**
Green with tan interior; concours-quality restoration.												
1969	**911 T coupé**		119100158	L	90-120.000 EUR		NS		09-07-16	Le Mans	191	**Art**
Dark metallic red with black vinyl interior; sold new to the USA, at unspecified date the car was reimported into Europe and fully restored.												
1966	**911 coupé**		304507	L	130-150.000 GBP	103.500	136.278	122.886	28-07-16	Silverstone	109	**SiC**
Prepared for historic racing; with both FFSA and FIA HTTP papers.												
1969	**911 E coupé**		6298434	L	80-90.000 EUR	116.406	153.122	137.255	06-08-16	Schloss Dyck	106	**Coy**
Light beige with black interior; sold new to the USA, the car was then reimported into the UK and later restored in Germany.												
1965	**911 coupé**		303509	L	230-250.000 EUR	207.512	272.964	244.679	06-08-16	Schloss Dyck	146	**Coy**
Blue with leatherette and cloth interior; sold new to the USA and later reimported into Europe. Restoration recently completed.												
1965	**911 coupé**		302003	L	200-250.000 USD		NS		19-08-16	Carmel	18	**Bon**
Red with black interior; sold new to the USA, the car was acquired in the early 2000s by the current owner and subsequently fully restored.												
1969	**911 Targa**		119110448	L	90-110.000 USD		NS		19-08-16	Monterey	F38	**Mec**
Grey with vinyl and cloth interior; restored.												

F599: 1967 Porsche 911 S coupé

F600: 1967 Porsche 912 coupé

Year	Model	(Bodybuilder)	Chassis no.	Steering	Estimate	Hammer price £	Hammer price $	Hammer price €	Sale Date	Sale Place	Lot	Auc. H.
1967	911 coupé		306437	L	100-130.000 USD	55.008	72.000	63.569	19-08-16	Monterey	F78	Mec
Irish green with black interior; mechanicals refurbished 8,000 miles ago. Last serviced in 2015.											
1965	911 coupé		302610	L	160-200.000 USD		NS		20-08-16	Monterey	S105	Mec
Red with black leatherette interior; last serviced in 2016.											
1969	911 E Targa		119210147	L	145-175.000 USD		NS		20-08-16	Monterey	S133	Mec
Silver with black leatherette interior; since 1991 in the current ownership. Engine recently rebuilt.											
1967	911 DeLuxe RS coupé		304769	L	275-325.000 USD		NS		20-08-16	Monterey	S94	Mec
White with black interior; the car was first used by the factory for test and as a demonstrator. Fully restored over the last two years. With Porsche Certificate of Authenticity.											
1967	911 S Targa		500714S	L	NQ		NS		20-08-16	Monterey	7037	R&S
Yellow; restoration recently completed.											
1968	912 coupé		12803934	L	32-38.000 GBP		NS		06-09-15	Hedingham Cas.	119	Coy
Orange with black leatherette interior; described as in very good overall condition.											
1967	912 coupé		458842	L	20-30.000 GBP	63.400	96.539	86.674	06-09-15	Hedingham Cas.	138	Coy F600
Red with black interior; since 1979 with the present, second owner.											
1968	912 Targa		12870322	L	70-85.000 EUR		NS		26-09-15	Frankfurt	167	Coy
Orange; restored.											
1968	912 coupé		12803890	L	28-35.000 GBP		NS		16-01-16	Birmingham	319	Coy
Red; restored in the mid-1990s.											
1967	912 coupé		461936	L	28-35.000 GBP	39.320	55.870	50.664	08-03-16	London	108	Coy
Light ivory with tan interior; described as in good original condition. 53,000 kms covered.											
1966	912 coupé		353326	L	60-80.000 USD	46.174*	66.000*	59.512*	11-03-16	Amelia Island	9	G&Co
Blue; since 1972 for 38 years in the same ownership. Restored in 1990. Automatic transmission.											
1965	912 coupé		452853	L	28-35.000 GBP	33.350	48.314	42.835	20-03-16	Goodwood	48	Bon
Black with original black leatherette interior; imported into the UK from the USA in 2014 and subsequently subjected to several restoration works.											
1969	912 coupé		129022919	L	40-50.000 EUR		NS		09-04-16	Essen	181	Coy
Ivory; the car has covered 3,000 miles since a full restoration. The engine was rebuilt and bored out to 1776cc.											
1968	912 coupé		12803890	L	28-35.000 GBP	31.860	45.177	40.035	16-04-16	Ascot	107	Coy
See lot 319 Coys 16.1.16.											
1966	912 coupé		460304	L	45-50.000 EUR	31.741	46.492	41.630	28-05-16	Aarhus	214	SiC
Red; restored in the USA between 2012 and 2013 (see lot 87 Bonhams 14.8.15 $ 55,000).											
1965	912 coupé		13415	L	950-1.200.000 USD		NS		20-08-16	Monterey	S120	Mec
Light ivory with black leatherette interior; one of six development prototypes of the 912, and one of two known to survive. Offered with Porsche Authenticity Certificate which identifies it as a 1965 356B/912. Original engine no.821653 built to 356SC specification. Fully restored; exhibited at the 2014 Monterey Porsche Parade.											
1970	908/3 spider		90803011	R	2.200-2.500.000 GBP		NS		12-09-15	Goodwood	353	Bon
Delivered to the Gulf/JWA team, in 1970 the car raced the Targa Florio driven by Attwood/Waldegaard and the Nürburgring 1000 Kms driven by Rodriguez/Kinnunen. In 1974 it was modified at the factory, fitted with the 6-cylinder 2,142cc turbocharged engine, sold in Germany and raced at several 1975 events mainly driven by Leo Kinnunen and Herbert Muller. Later it was acquired by Sigi Brun, reassembled in the present form and raced until 1983. In ready to race condition, the car is offered with FIA Historic Technical Passport.											
1968	908 coupé		908011	R	3.000-3.300.000 USD		NS		11-03-16	Amelia Island	75	G&Co
White with red nose and red interior; ex-Works car raced in 1968 at the Spa 1000 KM, Watkings Glen 6 Hours and Zeltweg 500 KM. In 1970 it was sold to a Swiss racer who drove it at some hillclimbs and race events before to damage it in an accident. In 1974 it was sold to Germany where some parts were dismantled to use as spare for a similar car. In 1998 it was acquired by the previous owner, imported into the USA and fully restored. Engine recently rebuilt on a new magnesium case.											
1973	917/30 CanAm spyder		91730004	R	5.000-7.000.000 USD	2.098.800	3.000.000	2.705.100	11-03-16	Amelia Island	44	G&Co F601
Finished in white, the car was sold to the Porsche Australian importer, Alan Hamilton. Never seriously raced, in 1991 it was bought back by the factory and refinished in the blue, red and yellow livery of the Roger Penske's cars at the 1973 Can-Am Championship. In 1994 Porsche rebuilt the engine and resold the car to David Morse, in the USA. In 2001 it passed to the Drendel family and in 2012 it was acquired by the current owner, Jerry Seinfeld. Raced at several historic events (see lot 57 Gooding 9.3.12 $ 4,400,000).											
1970	911 S 2.2 coupé		9110301644	L	NA		NS		05-09-15	Auburn	5117	AA
Grey with black interior; restored in 2004.											
1971	911 E 2.2 coupé		9111200054	R	55-70.000 GBP		NS		06-09-15	Hedingham Cas.	108	Coy
Green; restored in 2007 and fitted with carburettors as replacement of the fuel injection system.											
1970	911 T 2.2 coupé		911021369	L	40-50.000 GBP	41.870	63.755	57.240	06-09-15	Hedingham Cas.	116	Coy
Irish green; recently reimported into the UK and restored.											

F601: 1973 Porsche 917/30 CanAm spyder

F602: 1971 Porsche 911 E 2.2 coupé

Year	Model	(Bodybuilder)	Chassis no.	Steering	Estimate	Hammer price £	Hammer price $	Hammer price €	Date	Place	Lot	Auc. H.
1970	911 2.2 coupé		9110120855	L	60-70.000 GBP		NS		06-09-15	Hedingham Cas.	122	Coy
Red with black interior; in good overall condition (see lot 167 Silverstone Auctions $ 60,244).												
1970	911 S 2.2 coupé		9110301339	L	Refer Dpt.		NS		06-09-15	Hedingham Cas.	124	Coy
Light ivory with black interior; originally owned by Porsche, the car was delivered to Vic Elford, Works driver at the time, for his personal use. Later Elford acquired the car which in 1972 was fitted at the factory with the new 2.4-litre engine, still today on it. Since 2004 with the current owner, it is described as in very good overall condition.												
1971	911 E 2.2 coupé		9111200168	L	70-80.000 GBP	125.000	190.338	170.888	06-09-15	Hedingham Cas.	155	Coy F602
Silver metallic with black leather interior; fully restored and fitted with a 2.4 engine (the original 2.2 unit is included in the sale).												
1970	911 S 2.2 Targa		9110310558	L	160-190.000 EUR		NS		26-09-15	Frankfurt	106	Coy
Black with black leatherette interior; described as in very good overall condition (see lot 288 Bonhams 13.9.14 NS).												
1971	911 T 2.2 coupé		9111100515	L	50-60.000 USD	32.611	49.500	44.055	05-10-15	Philadelphia	258	Bon
Silver with original black leatherette interior; engine recently rebuilt.												
1970	911 T 2.2 coupé		911110032	R	150-180.000 AUD	96.692	148.942	134.373	24-10-15	Melbourne	17	TBr
Red with original black interior; recently restored.												
1972	911 E 2.2 coupé		9111200935	L	50-70.000 EUR	28.282	43.056	40.000	14-11-15	Ladenburg	5219	Aut
For restoration; modified in 1987 to Carrera model aesthetical specification; de-registered in 2000.												
1970	911 T 2.2 coupé		9110121262	L	90-120.000 USD	77.670*	111.100*	101.890*	28-01-16	Scottsdale	24	Bon
Tangerine with black interior; restored to concours condition.												
1971	911 S 2.2 Targa		9111310022	L	170-200.000 USD	80.815*	115.500*	105.763*	29-01-16	Scottsdale	58	G&Co
Silver with black interior; approximately 69,000 miles recorded from new. Recently serviced.												
1969	911 S 2.2 coupé		119300783	L	200-250.000 EUR		NS		03-02-16	Paris	119	RMS
Light ivory with black interior; discovered in 2008 and subsequently restored.												
1970	911 T 2.2 coupé		9110101579	L	135-175.000 USD	115.434*	165.000*	148.781*	11-03-16	Amelia Island	53	G&Co
Tangerine with beige leatherette interior; until January 2016 with its first owner. 14,983 miles covered; for more than 33 years in storage.												
1970	911 S 2.2 Targa		9110310558	L	150-170.000 EUR	134.676	194.051	171.000	14-05-16	Monaco	145	Coy
See lot 106 Coys 26.9.15.												
1970	911 2.2 T coupé		9110122804	L	80-110.000 EUR	88.774	126.833	112.700	18-06-16	Wien	438	Dor
Ivory with black leatherette interior; restored in Italy about seven years ago.												
1970	911 S 2.2 Targa		9111310200	L	80-100.000 EUR	107.757	153.955	136.800	19-06-16	Fontainebleau	342	Ose
Light brown; fully restored.												
1970	911 E 2.2 coupé		9110200496	L	100-140.000 USD	53.186	70.000	62.986	30-07-16	Plymouth	115	RMS
Green with black leatherette interior; body repainted. 911 S front suspension (see lots 50 Gooding & Company 20.1.12 $63,250 and 77 RM 17.1.14 $71,500).												
1970	911 S/T		9110300949	L	1.100-1.400.000 USD		NS		11-03-16	Amelia Island	66	G&Co
Works car, it did its race debut winning the 1970 Austrian Alps Rally driven by Waldegard and Helmer. Used by factory as both a racing and support car, it was driven at the 1970 RAC Rally by Gerard Larrousse who later acquired it, repainted the body to the yellow and red Shell livery and raced it at several events. In 1972 the car was bought by Louis Meznarie and after some ownership changes it was imported into the USA in 1997. Restored and fitted with a 2.5-litre engine, it was used at several historic events also driven by Jurgen Barth.												
1972	911 T 2.4 coupé		9112500589	L	70-80.000 GBP	73.125	111.347	99.969	04-09-15	Woodstock	221	SiC
Yellow; imported into the UK in 1982 and restored in 2012.												
1972	911 S 2.4 coupé		9112301025	L	130-160.000 GBP		NS		06-09-15	Hedingham Cas.	128	Coy
Blue with beige leatherette interior; car overhauled and body repainted probably in the 2000s.												
1973	911 S 2.4 coupé		9113300934	L	120-150.000 GBP		NS		12-09-15	Goodwood	324	Bon
Blue with beige vinyl interior; restored in 2010.												
1973	911 S 2.4 coupé		9113301311	R	250-300.000 GBP		NS		12-09-15	Goodwood	347	Bon
Royal purple with black interior; two owners until 2012, 500 miles covered since a full restoration recently completed. Semi-automatic Sportomatic transmission; sunroof.												
1972	911 S 2.4 coupé prototype		9112300013	L	650-850.000 GBP		NS		12-09-15	Goodwood	364	Bon
Prototype built in July 1971 for homologation for the 2.4-litre model. In December 1971 returned to Porsche Competition Dept. to serve as a test and development mule. Registered in 1972; sold in 1973; bought in 1974 by Andre Herck and raced at Group 3 events; bought in 1976 by Jean-Pierre Gaban and raced at some rallies. Restored in the UK in the late 1990s for historic racing; again restored between 2008 and 2010; 270bhp circa engine rebuilt in 2013; chassis incorporating all RSR modifications including 917 brakes. With FIA HTTP Group IV 2.5 ST papers.												
1973	911 T 2.4 coupé		9113100753	L	60-80.000 USD		NS		05-10-15	Philadelphia	244	Bon
Yellow; in good overall condition.												
1973	911 S 2.4 coupé		9113301270	L	115-130.000 GBP		NS		25-10-15	Silverstone	220	SiC
The car was sold new to the USA where it remained until 2002 with its first owner. Engine rebuilt in 2007; car reimported into Europe in 2010 and into the UK in 2012.												
1973	911 T 2.4 coupé		9113500225	L	50-70.000 EUR	51.366	81.340	71.520	01-11-15	Paris	135	Art F603
Grey with black interior; in good overall condition. Electric sunroof (see lot 8 Artcurial 7.7.03 $ 13,841).												
1972	911 S 2.4 Targa		9112310135	L	140-180.000 EUR	115.573	183.014	160.920	01-11-15	Paris	136	Art
Grey with black interior; several restoration works carried out in 2011.												
1973	911 T 2.4 Targa		9113511295	L	65-75.000 EUR		NS		01-11-15	Paris	167	Art
White with black vinyl interior; engine rebuilt in 2009.												
1972	911 E 2.4 coupé		9112301549	L	155-195.000 EUR		NS		14-11-15	Ladenburg	5051	Aut
Light ivory with original black interior; 5-speed gearbox.												
1972	911 T 2.4 coupé		9112100438	L	260-330.000 EUR		NS		14-11-15	Ladenburg	5367	Aut
Yellow with brown interior; first owner actor Dean Martin.												
1973	911 T 2.4 Targa		9113111750	L	42-48.000 GBP	44.438	67.652	62.853	14-11-15	Birmingham	309	SiC
Sepia brown with black interior; engine rebuilt in the USA in 1993, car restored in the UK between 2010 and 2015.												
1973	911 S 2.4 Targa		9113310586	R	140-160.000 GBP	140.625	214.088	198.900	14-11-15	Birmingham	616	SiC
Yellow with black interior; several restoration works carried out between 1999 and 2010. The engine has covered 1,500 miles since the rebuild (see lot 324 Silverstone Auctions 24.5.14 $ 178,178).												

Year	Model	(Bodybuilder)	Chassis no.	Steering	Estimate	Hammer price £	$	€	Date	Place	Lot	Auc. H.
1973	**911 S 2.4 coupé**		911330676	L	155-185.000 EUR		NS		16-01-16	Maastricht	446	Coy
Blue with black interior; in very good condition. With sunroof.													
1973	**911 T 2.4 coupé**		9113100333	L	90-110.000 USD	55.801*	79.750*	73.027*	30-01-16	Scottsdale	101	G&Co
Tangerine with black vinyl interior; restored in 2013.													
1971	**911 S 2.4 coupé**		9112300294	L	130-180.000 EUR		NS		04-02-16	Paris	319	Bon
Gold with black leather interior; described as in good overall condition. Body repainted a few years ago.													
1971	**911 S 2.4 Targa**		9112310338	L	120-160.000 EUR	119.280	173.586	154.960	05-02-16	Paris	139	Art
Cherry red with black interior; the car has covered 25 kms since the restoration.													
1973	**911 S 2.4 Targa**		9113310775	L	170-220.000 USD	138.521*	198.000*	178.537*	11-03-16	Amelia Island	72	G&Co
Finished in yellow with black leatherette interior, the car was sold new to the USA. In the 2000s it received several restoration works and in 2013 the body was repainted.													
1973	**911 S 2.4 coupé**		911330676	L	110-140.000 EUR	137.907	194.108	170.825	09-04-16	Essen	199	Coy
See lot 446 Coys 16.1.16.													
1972	**911 S 2.4 Targa**		9112310826	L	150-200.000 EUR	153.972	221.853	195.500	13-05-16	Monaco	117	Bon **F604**
Jade green; offered with numerous invoices for service/repairs from 1998 to 2015.													
1972	**911 S 2.4 coupé**		9112300277	L	150-170.000 EUR	121.445	174.986	154.200	14-05-16	Monaco	141A	Coy
Aubergine with light brown interior; described as in good original condition. 80,000 kms on the odometer.													
1972	**911 S 2.4 coupé**		9112301612	L	90-120.000 GBP		NS		20-05-16	Silverstone	363	SiC
Metallic blue; some recent restoration works (see lot 355A Silverstone Auctions 17.5.13 NS).													
1973	**911 S 2.4 Targa**		9113310296	L	225-250.000 USD		NS		11-06-16	Hershey	146	TFA
Blue with black interior; the car was sold new to the USA and remained for 30 years with its first owner. Fully restored in the 2000s (see lot 273 RM 20.01.12 $88,000).													
1972	**911 T 2.4 coupé**		9112500773	R	50-70.000 GBP	70.940	97.216	87.845	24-06-16	Goodwood	286	Bon
Orange with black interior; since 1977 in the current, second ownership. In original condition; circa 62,000 miles recorded.													
1973	**911 S 2.4 coupé**		9113301183	L	100-140.000 EUR		NS		09-07-16	Le Mans	107	Art
Red with black interior; purchased in 1981 by the current, second owner. Body repainted in 1991; engine rebuilt in 2015.													
1972	**911 S 2.4 coupé**		9112300954	L	150-200.000 USD		NS		30-07-16	Plymouth	160	RMS
Blue with tan vinyl interior; since new in the same family ownership. Engine rebuilt in 1981; body repainted about 35 years ago; interior retrimmed in recent times.													
1972	**911 T 2.4 coupé**		9113500394	R	85-95.000 GBP	84.375	111.038	99.917	30-07-16	Silverstone	924	SiC
Royal purple; fully restored two years ago.													
1973	**911 S 2.4 coupé**		9113300934	L	140-160.000 EUR	123.998	163.109	146.207	06-08-16	Schloss Dyck	128	Coy
See lot 324 Bonhams 12.9.15.													
1972	**911 E 2.4 Targa**		9112210825	L	95-115.000 EUR	87.935	115.671	103.685	06-08-16	Schloss Dyck	156	Coy
Metallic grey; reimported into Germany from the USA in 2010 and subsequently restored.													
1973	**911 S 2.4 coupé**		9113301166	L	180-220.000 USD	100.848*	132.000*	116.543*	19-08-16	Carmel	4	Bon
Orange with black leatherette interior; several restoration works carried out over the years.													
1973	**911 T 2.4 Targa**		9113110260	L	90-110.000 USD	63.030*	82.500*	72.839*	19-08-16	Carmel	55	Bon
Tangerine with black interior; stored for many years, the car has been restored by the current, probably third owner.													
1973	**911 S 2.4 Targa**		9113310214	L	200-250.000 USD		NS		19-08-16	Monterey	F129	Mec
Silver with dark green leather and cloth interior; restored.													
1973	**911 T 2.4 coupé**		9113100811	L	175-200.000 USD		NS		20-08-16	Monterey	S109	Mec
Light blue with black leatherette and cloth interior; fully restored. Three owners.													
1972	**911 E 2.4 Targa**		9112210860	L	185-225.000 USD	131.790	172.500	152.300	20-08-16	Monterey	S47	Mec
Silver with red leather interior; described as in very good, unrestored condition. 11,600 miles covered.													
1973	**911 Carrera RS 2.7**		9113601175	L	450-550.000 GBP		NS		04-09-15	Woodstock	216	SiC
Touring version finished in yellow with black leatherette and cloth interior; restored between 1996 and 1999. Original engine and gearbox.													
1973	**911 Carrera RS 2.7**		9113600048	L	425-525.000 GBP		NS		07-09-15	London	145	RMS
Touring version finished in light ivory with black interior; sold new to Portugal, the car was later exported to Monaco and then to Switzerland. Original engine rebuilt; gearbox replaced. UK papers.													
1973	**911 Carrera RS 2.7**		9113600615	L	500-700.000 EUR	569.494	864.297	775.085	26-09-15	Frankfurt	150	Coy
Touring version finished in light ivory with black leather interior; the car has covered 7,500 kms since the restoration completed in 2012.													

F603: 1973 Porsche 911 T 2.4 coupé

F604: 1972 Porsche 911 S 2.4 Targa

Year	Model	(Bodybuilder)	Chassis no.	Steering	Estimate	Hammer Price £	$	€	Date	Place	Lot	Auc. H.
1973	911 Carrera RS 2.7		9113600235	L	375-425.000 GBP	410.625	632.568	570.687	25-10-15	Silverstone	230	SiC

Touring version finished in white; sold new in Germany, the car was exported in 1988 to Denmark where it was restored and remained for 26 years in the same ownership. Described as in very good driving order.

1973	911 Carrera RS 2.7		9113601018	L	900-1.100.000 USD	607.220	918.500	839.325	10-12-15	New York	218	RMS F605

Touring version finished in yellow; subjected to a full concours-quality restoration completed in 2008. Electric sunroof.

1973	911 Carrera RS 2.7		9113601446	L	600-800.000 USD	367.028	525.000	481.478	28-01-16	Scottsdale	46	Bon

Touring version finished in white with black interior; sold new in Germany, the car was later imported into the UK where it was restored in the mid-1990s. Imported into the USA in 2003 and used at historic events.

1973	911 Carrera RS 2.7		911360440	L	600-800.000 EUR		NS		05-02-16	Paris	206	Art

Touring version sold new to Italy; acquired in 2007 by the current owner and subsequently restored.

1972	911 Carrera RS 2.7		9113600805	L	470-570.000 EUR		NS		13-05-16	Monaco	133	Bon

Touring version finished in light yellow with black interior; modified to some Lightweight specification. Restored in Switzerland in 2004, acquired in 2005 by the current Italian owner.

1973	911 Carrera RS 2.7		9113601046	L	580-680.000 EUR	480.739	692.682	610.400	14-05-16	Monaco	244	RMS

Touring version finished in light yellow with black leatherette and cloth interior; electric sunroof. Sold new in Germany, the car was imported into France in 1995. Recently restored. Less than 30,000 kms.

1973	911 Carrera RS 2.7		9113601366	L	420-580.000 EUR	406.439	527.818	476.800	09-07-16	Le Mans	109	Art

Touring version finished in white with cloth and vinyl interior; used at several historic events in the 2000s. Engine rebuilt in recent years (see Artcurial lots 17 13.7.09 NS and 80 14.2.10 $184,484).

1973	911 Carrera RSH 2.7		9113601429	L	1.300-1.500.000 USD		NS		20-08-16	Pebble Beach	38	G&Co

Orange with black interior; one of 17 Homologation examples. Sold to France, the car did its race debut at the 1973 Tour de France and was raced until 1975. Original engine; restored in the 1990s; finished in the 1973 Tour de France livery; imported into the USA in 2014.

1972	916 coupé		9140430367	L	165.000 EUR		NS		20-05-16	Ladenburg	1458	Aut

White; one of 11 examples built. Experimental car built on the Volkswagen-Porsche 914 chassis, fitted with a 190bhp 2.4 S engine. The car remained in the Porsche ownership until 1974 when it was sold to private hands.

1974	Carrera RSR 3.0		9114600016	L	1.200-1.500.000 USD	1.616.076	2.310.000	2.082.927	11-03-16	Amelia Island	36	G&Co F606

Light yellow; one of the 15 examples built for Roger Penske's IROC Series. It was raced at three IROC events by Revson, Johncock and Follmer and then sold to Grey Egerton who raced it at several events until late 1975 when it was bought by Vasek Polak. The latter had the car restored, repainted in white and red with blue stripes and fitted with an earlier 2.8-litre engine. In 1998 it was acquired by Tom Linton, restored again to its original yellow livery and fitted with a correct Type 911/74 engine, no.6840034. Since 2005 in the Jerry Seinfeld Collection.

1975	911 2.7 coupé		9116300633	R	18-23.000 GBP	21.750	33.119	29.734	06-09-15	Hedingham Cas.	103	Coy

Black; unused from time, the car requires recommissioning prior to use. Sportomatic transmission.

1974	911 2.7 Targa		9115110341	L	95-145.000 EUR	93.699	143.729	126.500	09-10-15	Zoute	7	Bon

White and red with black interior; delivered new to the Dutch Police. Restored in 2015 to original specification; engine rebuilt.

1977	911 "50" coupé		9117301478	R	125-150.000 GBP	173.250	266.892	240.783	25-10-15	Silverstone	214	SiC

Originally a 911 2.7, the car was sold new to the UK and was taken off the road in 2006. In 2014 it was designed and built by Porsche Central Operations to compete in the "50 Years of 911" restoration competition. The body was restored and finished in viper green; the wiring would be replaced with modern electronic systems; the suspension would be to a full RS specification all round; the front brakes would come from a 930 Turbo 3.3, the rears from a Carrera 3.2; the original engine was replaced with a 993 unit giving 300bhp.

1974	911 S 2.7 coupé		9115200465	L	80-90.000 GBP	78.750	121.314	109.447	25-10-15	Silverstone	226	SiC

Beige with beige interior; described as in very good original condition, the car has covered 9,571 miles. Recommissioned in Germany in 2012 at 9,355 miles.

1977	911 2.7 coupé		9117301730	L	25-35.000 EUR	29.963*	47.448*	41.720*	01-11-15	Paris	134	Art

Body repainted some years ago, mechanicals recently overhauled.

1975	911 S 2.7 coupé		9115200301	L	70-90.000 USD	49.217*	70.400*	64.564*	28-01-16	Scottsdale	2	Bon

Silver with blue cloth and vinyl interior; in highly original condition. Two owners and less than 42,000 miles covered. Example of the Silver Anniversary special edition.

1977	911 S 2.7 Targa		9117211349	L	60-80.000 USD	31.529*	45.100*	41.361*	28-01-16	Scottsdale	68	Bon

Red with original cork interior; sold new to the USA, it is believed the car remained with its first owner until 2015. Less than 51,000 miles on the odometer.

1974	911 S 2.7 Targa		9114110930	L	40-45.000 EUR	34.982	46.015	41.247	06-08-16	Schloss Dyck	173	Coy

White with black leather interior; restored many years ago.

1975	911 S 2.7 Targa		9115211401	L	60-70.000 USD	30.560	40.000	35.316	20-08-16	Monterey	S163	Mec

Metallic brown with cinnamon leatherette interior; 19,000 miles covered. Recently serviced.

1975	911 S 2.7 coupé		9115200989	L	60-80.000 USD	56.307*	73.700*	65.070*	21-08-16	Pebble Beach	116	G&Co

Brown with cinnamon interior; in good overall condition. Just over 36,000 miles covered. In single ownership from 1975 to 2013.

F605: 1973 Porsche 911 Carrera RS 2.7

F606: 1974 Porsche Carrera RSR 3.0

Year	Model	(Bodybuilder)	Chassis no.	Steering	Estimate	Hammer Price £	$	€	Date	Place	Lot	Auc. H.
1975	**911 Carrera 2.7 Targa**		9115610050	R	80-100.000 GBP		NS		04-09-15	Woodstock	228	SiC
	Red with black interior; engine rebuilt in 1995. Body repainted.											
1974	**911 Carrera 2.7 coupé**		9114600823	R	90-110.000 GBP	87.440	133.145	119.539	06-09-15	Hedingham Cas.	127	Coy
	Yellow with blue leather interior; described as in largely original condition. Just one owner since 1982.											
1973	**911 Carrera 2.7 Targa**		9114610043	L	100-125.000 EUR		NS		26-09-15	Frankfurt	145	Coy
	Mexico blue with blue and black interior; restored in 2007.											
1974	**911 Carrera 2.7 coupé**		9114600459	L	170-220.000 EUR	151.621	232.580	204.700	09-10-15	Zoute	42	Bon **F607**
	Black with tan vinyl interior; sold new to Italy, probably the car was stored from 1995 until 2012 when it was acquired by the current owner and subjected to a full restoration completed in 2014.											
1976	**911 Carrera 2.7 coupé**		9116609056	L	220-300.000 EUR		NS		14-11-15	Ladenburg	5911	Aut
	Copper with leatherette and tartan interior; described as in good original condition.											
1975	**911 Carrera 2.7 coupé**		9115400113	L	130-150.000 USD	52.293*	74.800*	68.599*	28-01-16	Scottsdale	111	Bon
	Silver with original black leather interior; believed to have covered less than 47,000 miles since new. Sunroof.											
1975	**911 Carrera 2.7 Targa**		9115410127	L	75-100.000 USD	38.451*	55.000*	50.441*	28-01-16	Scottsdale	85	Bon
	Metallic beige with cinnamon leather interior; non original engine possibly from a 1978 911 SC.											
1974	**911 Carrera 2.7 coupé**		9114600628	L	300-375.000 USD		NS		29-01-16	Phoenix	259	RMS
	White with black interior; restored between 2009 and 2012. Engine recently rebuilt.											
1976	**911 Carrera 2.7 coupé**		9116609116	L	220-260.000 EUR		NS		05-02-16	Paris	140	Art
	Black with original leather and cloth interior; engine and gearbox rebuilt many years ago, body repainted in recent years. Recently serviced.											
1975	**911 Carrera 2.7 Targa**		9115610058	L	Refer Dpt.	183.075	257.684	226.775	09-04-16	Essen	111	Coy **F608**
	Silver with leather and cloth interior; example of the 25th Anniversary special edition, the car has covered 700 kms since a full restoration.											
1974	**911 Carrera 2.7 coupé**		9114600666	R	125-150.000 GBP	130.000	189.384	168.805	20-05-16	Silverstone	352	SiC
	Red; sold new to Japan, the car has been recntly imported into the UK. 42,000 kms on the odometer. Body repainted in recent years.											
1974	**911 Carrera 2.7 Targa**		9114410246	L	110-130.000 USD	66.468	87.000	76.812	20-08-16	Monterey	S75	Mec
	Jade green with cinnamon leather interior; recent restoration works to the mechanicals and interior.											
1975	**911 Carrera 2.7 coupé**		9115600482	L	NQ		NS		20-08-16	Monterey	7253	R&S
	White.											
1974	**911 Carrera 2.7 coupé**		9114600422	L	225-275.000 USD	155.474*	203.500*	179.670*	21-08-16	Pebble Beach	107	G&Co
	White with blue/black leatherette interior; in good overall condition. Body repainted.											
1974	**Carrera RS 3.0**		9114609089	L	375-525.000 USD	336.160	440.000	388.476	19-08-16	Carmel	39	Bon
	Sold new in Germany, the car was raced in period and in 1977 it was fitted at the factory with a 3.0 RSR engine. Later it was damaged in a fire and in 2003 it was sold to France in partially restored condition. Bought by the current owner, the car was restored in 2012 to race-ready condition. As the original engine was missing, it was replaced by a dual-ignition 3.0-liter based on a 930 crankcase.											
1977	**911 Turbo coupé**		930770053	R	75-85.000 GBP	99.576	151.624	136.130	06-09-15	Hedingham Cas.	135	Coy
	Martini livery with blue interior; for 16 years in the current ownership, the car has covered 22,000 miles since new.											
1976	**911 Turbo coupé**		9306800232	L	NA	135.435	214.500	188.588	31-10-15	Hilton Head	149	AA
	Metallic platinum with original cinnamon leather interior; in largely original condition. The engine has covered just over 300 miles since the rebuild carried out two years ago.											
1976	**911 Turbo coupé**		9306800084	L	NA		NS		13-11-15	Anaheim	F199	Mec
	Salmon with black interior; recently repainted. Believed to be 72,000 orignal miles.											
1977	**911 Turbo coupé**		9112100438	L	75-110.000 EUR		NS		14-11-15	Ladenburg	5959	Aut
	Black with black interior; sold new to the USA. Body repainted at unspecified date.											
1975	**911 Turbo coupé**		9305700163	L	350-450.000 USD	218.163	330.000	301.554	10-12-15	New York	229	RMS
	Copper brown metallic with tan leather and tartan cloth interior; sold new to Japan. The car has covered 20 since a full restoration carried out in Canada.											
1977	**911 Turbo coupé**		9307800362	L	225-275.000 USD	119.197*	170.500*	156.366*	28-01-16	Scottsdale	11	Bon
	Copper brown metallic; described as in very good overall condition. Less than 32,000 miles covered. Electric sunroof.											
1976	**911 Turbo coupé**		9306800074	L	225-275.000 USD	130.732	187.000	171.498	28-01-16	Phoenix	114	RMS
	White with cinnamon leather interior; sold new to the USA, the car remained with its first owner until 1997 and is described as in largely original condition. Engine rebuilt in recent times.											
1977	**911 Turbo coupé**		9307800254	L	NA	184.721*	264.000*	241.745*	29-01-16	Scottsdale	1367	B/J
	Metallic ice green with black leather interior; recent restoration.											
1976	**911 Turbo coupé**		9306800143	L	250-300.000 USD	138.541*	198.000*	181.309*	29-01-16	Scottsdale	16	G&Co
	Metallic ice green with cinnamon leather interior; in good overall condition (see lot 151 Auctions America 28.3.15 $ 165,000).											

F607: 1974 Porsche 911 Carrera 2.7 coupé

F608: 1975 Porsche 911 Carrera 2.7 Targa

Year	Model	(Bodybuilder)	Chassis no.	Steering	Estimate	Hammer Price £	$	€	Date	Place	Lot	Auc. H.
1976	911 Turbo coupé		9306800466	L	275-350.000 USD	178.398	255.000	229.934	12-03-16	Amelia Island	126	RMS
Metallic platinum with brown leather interior; described as in very good overall condition. 20,082 miles covered. Sunroof.												
1976	911 Turbo coupé		9306700626	L	170-220.000 EUR		NS		13-05-16	Monaco	123	Bon
Metallic blue; full restoration completed in 2015.												
1977	911 Turbo coupé		9307800715	L	170-200.000 USD		NS		25-06-16	Santa Monica	1086	AA
Copper metallic with tan interior.												
1977	911 Turbo coupé		9307700567	L	140-180.000 EUR	108.770	141.253	127.600	09-07-16	Le Mans	183	Art
Grey with green interior; bought in 2001 by the current owner and subsequently restored.												
1976	911 Turbo coupé		9306800292	L	180-240.000 USD	100.848*	132.000*	116.543*	19-08-16	Carmel	20	Bon
Silver with black interior; acquired in 2014 by the current owner and subsequently restored in Canada.												
1977	911 Turbo coupé		9307800305	L	250-325.000 USD	210.100*	275.000*	242.798*	19-08-16	Monterey	105	RMS F609
Silver with leather and tartan cloth interior; described as in very good original condition. 16,698 miles covered.												
1976	911 Turbo coupé		9306800054	L	200-250.000 USD	197.494*	258.500*	228.230*	20-08-16	Pebble Beach	72	G&Co
Silver with black leather interior; in original condition. Two owners and 33,000 miles on the odometer. Engine rebuilt in 2015.												
1977	911 Turbo coupé		9307800186	L	NQ	96.646	126.500	111.687	20-08-16	Monterey	7071	R&S
Silver with red leather and red tartan plaid interior; restored between June 2015 and July 2016.												
1976	Carrera 3.0 coupé		9117600644	L	95-155.000 EUR	80.921	124.130	109.250	09-10-15	Zoute	31	Bon F610
Orange with black interior; body repainted, engine and gearbox overhauled. Fitted with 5-speed gearbox and electric sunroof.												
1976	Carrera 3.0 Targa		9116610115	R	40-45.000 GBP	29.810	45.922	41.430	25-10-15	Silverstone	232	SiC
Light metallic green with black leather interior; described as in good original condition.												
1976	912 E coupé		91226000323	L	35-40.000 EUR	32.512	47.101	41.760	20-03-16	Fontainebleau	347	Ose
Brown; rebuilt engine and clutch. Sunroof.												
1986	924 S		401112	R	5.8-6.500 GBP	5.625	8.665	7.818	25-10-15	Silverstone	227	SiC
Metallic red; in good driving order. Last serviced in October 2014.												
1977	935 Turbo		9307700904	L	1.100-1.400.000 EUR	1.109.523	1.440.871	1.301.600	09-07-16	Le Mans	175	Art
One of 13 1977 "Competition Client" examples, the car was sold new in Germany and in early 1978 it was bought by Swiss Claude Haldi. Raced until 1980, it participated in three editions of the Le Mans 24 Hours, 1978, 1979 and 1980. Since 1990 in the current ownership, it is finished in the white "Sermati" livery of Le Mans 1980.												
1979	935 Turbo		0090030	L	4.500-5.500.000 USD	3.697.760	4.840.000	4.273.236	20-08-16	Pebble Beach	60	G&Co
Hawaiian Tropic red livery; acquired new by Dick Barbour Racing, the car did its race debut at the 1979 Le Mans 24 Hours where it placed 2nd overall driven by Rolf Stommelen, Dick Barbour and Paul Newman. Raced until 1987 and driven also, among others, by Brian Redman and Bobby Rahal, the car won the 1981 Daytona 24 Hours and 1983 Sebring 12 Hours. Between 2006 and 2007 it was restored to the 1979 Le Mans livery.												F611
1981	911SC coupé		121060	L	35-45.000 GBP	34.630	52.731	47.343	06-09-15	Hedingham Cas.	113	Coy
White with brown interior; described as in very good overall condition. Just over 90,000 miles covered.												
1983	911SC coupé		122426	L	32-40.000 GBP		NS		06-09-15	Hedingham Cas.	156	Coy
Bronze with brown interior; described as in very good working order.												
1982	911SC Targa		140339	R	30-40.000 GBP		NS		06-09-15	Hedingham Cas.	158	Coy
Metallic burgundy with tan interior; described as in very good overall condition.												
1982	911SC Targa		140339	R	30-40.000 GBP		NS		10-10-15	Ascot	161	Coy
See lot 158 Coys 6.9.15.												
1983	911SC cabriolet		150399	R	18-20.000 GBP	16.750	25.803	23.279	25-10-15	Silverstone	216	SiC
Red with black leather interior; in good overall condition. Last serviced in October 2014 at 110,242 miles.												
1979	911SC coupé		9118200479	L	NQ	39.375	60.657	54.723	25-10-15	Silverstone	221	SiC
Red; the car has had two owners in the USA and was imported into the UK in 2014. 29,500 miles covered; original interior.												
1979	911SC coupé		91A0130294	L	20-25.000 GBP	20.250	31.195	28.143	25-10-15	Silverstone	249	SiC
Light metallic blue with blue interior; body repainted eight years ago, engine rebuilt 16,000 miles ago.												
1984	911SC cabriolet		151965	L	35-40.000 EUR	30.285	45.846	42.200	08-11-15	Lyon	239	Ose
Red with black interior; the car has covered 15,000 kms since the restoration completed in 2009.												
1978	911SC coupé		9118301977	R	32-37.000 GBP		NS		30-07-16	Silverstone	909	SiC
Red with black leather interior; in good driving order.												

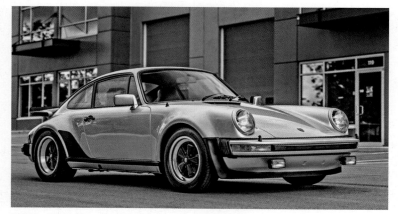

F609: 1977 Porsche 911 Turbo coupé

F610: 1976 Porsche Carrera 3.0 coupé

Year	Model	(Bodybuilder)	Chassis no.	Steering	Estimate	Hammer Price £	Hammer Price $	Hammer Price €	Sale Date	Sale Place	Lot	Auc. H.
1980	911SC Targa		140164	R	40-45.000 GBP	37.125	48.857	43.963	30-07-16	Silverstone	943	SiC
White; fully restored.												
1978	911SC coupé		9118202124	L	40-45.000 EUR	33.983	44.701	40.069	06-08-16	Schloss Dyck	179	Coy
Silver with brown leather interior; in good overall condition.												
1980	911SC Targa		91A0131697	L	50-75.000 USD	35.297*	46.200*	40.790*	19-08-16	Carmel	72	Bon
White with red/blue tartan dress interior; in good overall condition. Recently serviced.												
1978	911SC coupé		9118201816	L	80-100.000 USD	38.200	50.000	44.145	19-08-16	Monterey	F66	Mec
Brown with tan leather interior; restored in 2009. Electric sunroof.												
1979	911 Turbo 3.3 coupé		9309800333	L	NA	104.760*	159.500*	143.215*	05-09-15	Auburn	4112	AA
White with brown leather interior; just over 14,000 believed original miles. Formerly in the ownership of driver Peter Gregg.												
1986	911 Turbo S 3.3 slantnose coupé		5001154	R	75-95.000 GBP	NS			06-09-15	Hedingham Cas.	114	Coy
Red with tan interior; described as in largely original condition, the car is in the same family ownership since new and has covered 69.500 miles.												
1978	911 Turbo 3.3 coupé		9308700395	R	60-70.000 GBP	68.187	103.828	93.218	06-09-15	Hedingham Cas.	120	Coy
Red with black leather interior; two owners since 1984, fewer than 47,000 miles covered.												
1986	911 Turbo S 3.3 coupé		000062	L	150-180.000 GBP	146.420	222.954	200.171	06-09-15	Hedingham Cas.	121	Coy
White with original black leather interior; described as in very good overall condition. 86,000 kms covered.												
1985	911 Turbo 3.3 coupé		000964	L	40-50.000 GBP	47.720	72.663	65.238	06-09-15	Hedingham Cas.	126	Coy
Black with black interior; recently restored. The engine and gearbox have covered less than 1,000 miles since the rebuilt.												
1988	911 Turbo 3.3 Targa		93ZJS010123	R	45-55.000 GBP	NS			06-09-15	Hedingham Cas.	149	Coy
Red with black interior; in good working order. Gearbox rebuilt some years ago.												
1989	911 Turbo 3.3 slantnose cabriolet		070438	L	NA	NS			26-09-15	Las Vegas	713	B/J
Grey with black interior; 39,000 miles covered. Recently serviced.												
1989	911 Turbo SE 3.3 slantnose coupé		050485	L	125-140.000 EUR	92.292	140.068	125.610	26-09-15	Frankfurt	165	Coy
Silver with black interior; in very good overall condition.												
1988	911 Turbo 3.3 Targa		93ZJS010123	R	NQ	53.387*	81.890*	72.072*	10-10-15	Ascot	123	Coy
See lot 149 Coys 6.9.15.												
1986	911 Turbo 3.3 SE slantnose coupé		5001154	R	75-85.000 GBP	88.712	136.075	119.761	10-10-15	Ascot	146	Coy
See lot 114 Coys 6.9.15.												
1980	911 Turbo 3.3 coupé		93A0070429	R	58-64.000 GBP	60.000	92.430	83.388	25-10-15	Silverstone	203	SiC
Black with black interior; the car has covered 44,251 miles and has been always well cared for.												
1981	911 Turbo 3.3 coupé		000665	R	100-115.000 GBP	118.125	181.972	164.170	25-10-15	Silverstone	213	SiC
Red with black leather interior; stored for over 15 years, the car was fully restored by the Porsche Centre Leeds and exhibieted at the 2014 national "50 Years of the 911" restoration competition.												
1989	911 Turbo LE 3.3 coupé		000584	R	100-120.000 GBP	97.830	150.707	135.964	25-10-15	Silverstone	243	SiC
Red with cream leather interior; 49,435 miles covered. Acquired 12 years ago by the current owner who later had the paintwork and interior redone.												
1985	911 Turbo SE 3.3 slantnose coupé		001063	R	150-170.000 GBP	NS			25-10-15	Silverstone	244	SiC
Silver metallic with red leather interior; 33,500 miles covered. Acquired over 16 years ago by the current, fourth owner. 330bhp engine.												
1989	911 Turbo SE 3.3 slantnose coupé		000440	R	150-170.000 GBP	165.940	255.631	230.623	25-10-15	Silverstone	248	SiC
Light metallic blue with blue leather interior; engine tuned to 450bhp in Germany by Ruf Automobile GmbH at date unknown. Acquired in 2006 by the current owner who had later replaced the turbocharger, injectors, brakes among other.												
1981	911 Turbo 3.3 coupé		000224	R	40-45.000 GBP	39.380	60.665	54.730	25-10-15	Silverstone	256	SiC
Silver with dark blue leather interior; paintwork and interior redone in 2010. Sunroof.												
1986	911 Turbo 3.3 coupé		000588	L	80-100.000 EUR	66.775	105.742	92.976	01-11-15	Paris	138	Art
Red with black leather interior; always well maintained, the car has covered 66,000 kms.												
1988	911 Turbo 3.3 coupé		000616	L	190-240.000 EUR	195.190	309.091	271.776	01-11-15	Paris	166	Art F612
Blue; 7,778 kms covered. Since new in the same family ownership; road registered in 1991.												
1989	911 Turbo 3.3 cabriolet		070531	L	125-160.000 EUR	106.058	161.460	150.000	14-11-15	Ladenburg	5054	Aut
Metallic grey with light grey interior; sold new to Canada to ice hockey star Wayne Gretzky who retained it until 2002. 44,000 miles on the odometer.												
1987	911 Turbo 3.3 coupé		050748	L	90-125.000 EUR	NS			14-11-15	Ladenburg	5913	Aut
Black with black interior; body repainted in 2013, engine overhauled in 2015 and fitted with a K27 turbocharger.												

F611: 1979 Porsche 935 Turbo

F612: 1988 Porsche 911 Turbo 3.3 coupé

Year	Model	(Bodybuilder)	Chassis no.	Steering	Estimate	Hammer Price £	$	€	Sale Date	Place	Lot	Auc. H.
1988	911 Turbo 3.3 coupé		000299	R	NQ	112.500*	171.270*	159.120*	14-11-15	Birmingham	620	SiC

White with blue and white leather interior; in original condition, the car has had just one owner and has covered less than 31,000 miles.

| 1989 | 911 Turbo 3.3 cabriolet | | 070540 | R | 65-75.000 GBP | | NS | | 28-11-15 | Weybridge | 298 | His |

Silver with red leather interior; 36,768 miles on the odometer. The car was sold new in the USA to its first owner who that same year imported it in the UK. In the same family ownership since new; converted to right-hand drive in 1992.

| 1978 | 911 Turbo 3.3 coupé | | 9308700395 | R | 50-60.000 GBP | 73.480 | 110.698 | 104.430 | 01-12-15 | London | 306 | Coy |

See lot 120 Coys 6.9.15.

| 1987 | 911 Turbo 3.3 coupé | | 050503 | L | 110-120.000 EUR | 96.204 | 137.882 | 126.335 | 16-01-16 | Maastricht | 435 | Coy |

Recently reimported into Europe from the USA; less than 21,000 miles covered.

| 1984 | 911 Turbo 3.3 slantnose coupé | | 000740 | L | 70-90.000 EUR | 58.644 | 84.050 | 77.011 | 16-01-16 | Maastricht | 438 | Coy |

Black; paintwork redone. New clutch.

| 1989 | 911 Turbo 3.3 cabriolet | | 020106 | L | 175-225.000 USD | 111.696 | 160.000 | 148.032 | 23-01-16 | Kissimmee | S111 | Mec |

Black with green leather interior; modified in 1991 by Andial Racing, California. 3.4-litre engine.

| 1978 | 911 Turbo 3.3 coupé | | 9308800410 | L | 200-240.000 USD | 92.281* | 132.000* | 121.057* | 28-01-16 | Scottsdale | 88 | Bon |

White with brown leather interior; described as in largely original condition.

| 1988 | 911 Turbo 3.3 coupé | | 050455 | L | 175-225.000 USD | 96.209* | 137.500* | 125.909* | 29-01-16 | Scottsdale | 42 | G&Co |

Red with black leather interior; described as in very good overall condition, the car has covered less than 29,000 miles.

| 1983 | 911 Turbo 3.3 coupé | | 000673 | L | 175-225.000 USD | 115.451* | 165.000* | 151.091* | 30-01-16 | Scottsdale | 117 | G&Co |

Black with black leather interior; described as in very good original condition. 39,000 miles covered since new. First owner Jacky Ickx.

| 1979 | 911 Turbo 3.3 coupé | | 9309700373 | L | 175-225.000 USD | 82.740* | 118.250* | 108.282* | 30-01-16 | Scottsdale | 136 | G&Co |

Red; one owner until 2014. 26,000 miles covered. Unused for 15 years until 2015 and subsequently fully serviced.

| 1984 | 911 Turbo 3.3 coupé | | 000635 | L | NA | 59.649 | 85.250 | 78.063 | 30-01-16 | Scottsdale | 5162 | R&S |

Black with champagne leather interior; approximately 18,600 miles covered.

| 1989 | 911 Turbo S 3.3 slantnose cabriolet | | 070209 | L | 175-250.000 USD | 128.266* | 181.500* | 167.162* | 10-03-16 | Amelia Island | 136 | Bon |

White with red interior; described as in very good overall condition. Less than 35,000 miles covered. First owner Andre Agassi.

| 1979 | 911 Turbo 3.3 coupé | | 9309800724 | L | 240-280.000 USD | 140.445* | 200.750* | 181.016* | 11-03-16 | Amelia Island | 15 | G&Co |

Silver with red leather interior; less than 21,000 miles covered. Some restoration works carried out in 2013.

| 1989 | 911 Turbo 3.3 cabriolet | | 020210 | R | 55-65.000 GBP | 83.440 | 119.252 | 107.529 | 12-03-16 | Brooklands | 172 | His |

Black with ivory leather interior; recently serviced. 61,603 miles on the odometer.

| 1986 | 911 Turbo 3.3 slantnose coupé | | 001154 | R | 115-140.000 GBP | | NS | | 12-03-16 | Brooklands | 184 | His |

See lot 146 Coys 10.10.15.

| 1982 | 911 Turbo 3.3 coupé | | 000393 | R | 40-48.000 GBP | 49.280 | 70.431 | 63.507 | 12-03-16 | Brooklands | 189 | His |

Red with white leather interior; 72,285 miles on the odometer.

| 1988 | 911 Turbo 3.3 slantnose cabriolet | | 070324 | L | 225-275.000 USD | 230.868* | 330.000* | 297.561* | 12-03-16 | Amelia Island | 142 | RMS F613 |

Silver with blue interior; three owners and less than 9,000 miles covered. Major service in July 2013.

| 1989 | 911 Turbo 3.3 coupé | | 050623 | L | 240-280.000 USD | 215.477 | 308.000 | 277.724 | 12-03-16 | Amelia Island | 149 | RMS |

Red with beige interior; in original condition. 1,161 miles covered.

| 1979 | 911 Turbo 3.3 coupé | | 9309800848 | L | 300-375.000 USD | | NS | | 12-03-16 | Amelia Island | 186 | RMS |

Described as in very good original condition, the car has had three owners and has covered 548 miles. Last serviced in April 2015.

| 1989 | 911 Turbo 3.3 slantnose cabriolet | | 070080 | L | NA | 130.500 | 183.700 | 161.656 | 09-04-16 | Palm Beach | 417 | B/J |

Red with black interior.

| 1984 | 911 Turbo S 3.3 slantnose coupé | | 000743 | L | 160-210.000 EUR | 113.516 | 159.777 | 140.612 | 09-04-16 | Essen | 128 | Coy |

Dark metallic silver with black leather interior; 77,000 kms covered. Engine overhauled in 2015.

| 1988 | 911 Turbo 3.3 cabriolet | | 020118 | L | 110-130.000 GBP | | NS | | 16-04-16 | Ascot | 117 | Coy |

Black with black leather interior; the car received several restoration works.

| 1989 | 911 Turbo 3.3 cabriolet | | 020144 | L | 150-180.000 GBP | | NS | | 16-04-16 | Ascot | 144 | Coy |

Red with black interior; in good overall condition.

| 1987 | 911 Turbo 3.3 cabriolet | | 020067 | L | 150-200.000 EUR | | NS | | 13-05-16 | Monaco | 108 | Bon |

Pearlescent gold; acquired in 2013 by the current owner and subsequently recommissioned. Body repainted, gearbox and turbocharger rebuilt. Exhibited at the Porsche stand at the 1987 Frankfurt Motor Show.

F613: 1988 Porsche 911 Turbo 3.3 slantnose cabriolet

F614: 1994 Porsche 928 GTS

Year	Model (Bodybuilder)	Chassis no.	Steering	Estimate	Hammer price £	Hammer price $	Hammer price €	Date	Place	Lot	Auc. H.
1988	911 Turbo Ruf CTR coupé	000370	L	175-225.000 EUR	176.418	254.195	224.000	14-05-16	Monaco	213	RMS
	*Black; modified by Ruf in 1988 to BTR specification, in 1992 the car was updated to 469bhp CTR specification. Two owners since new and 51,000 kms covered.*
1979	911 Turbo 3.3 coupé	9309801156	L	NA	148.906	214.500	189.747	11-06-16	Newport Beach	6106	R&S
	*Pearl yellow; restored in 2014.*
1986	911 Turbo 3.3 coupé	001130	L	100-140.000 EUR	121.463	173.537	154.200	18-06-16	Wien	430	Dor
	*Red with black leather interior; since 1993 in the current ownership, the car is described as in good overall condition.*
1984	911 Turbo 3.3 coupé	000329	L	85-125.000 EUR	76.207	98.966	89.400	09-07-16	Le Mans	174	Art
	*Black with brown interior; described as in very good original condition.*
1986	911 Turbo 3.3 coupé	051217	L	NA	61.600	80.000	72.264	09-07-16	Denver	S170.1	Mec
	*Red with black interior; believed to be 68,000 miles. Engine rebuilt at 55,000 miles; serviced at 67,000 miles.*
1986	911 Turbo SE 3.3 slantnose coupé	001154	L	90-110.000 GBP	94.500	124.362	111.907	30-07-16	Silverstone	930	SiC
	*See lot 184 Historics 12.3.16.*
1989	911 Turbo 3.3 slantnose cabriolet	070402	L	175-200.000 USD	100.848*	132.000*	116.543*	19-08-16	Carmel	86	Bon
	*White with blue interior; sold new to the USA. Stored for more than 10 years, the car received recently an engine-out service. Less than 34,000 miles covered since new.*
1986	911 Turbo 3.3 coupé	050139	L	150-175.000 USD	103.140	135.000	119.192	19-08-16	Monterey	F140	Mec
	*Black with black interior; two owners, 15,970 miles covered, unrestored.*
1988	911 Turbo 3.3 slantnose cabriolet	070343	L	155-175.000 USD	99.320	130.000	114.777	19-08-16	Monterey	F148	Mec
	*White with navy blue leather interior; in good overall condition. 38,000 original miles.*
1989	911 Turbo 3.3 cabriolet	070197	L	325-375.000 USD		NS		20-08-16	Monterey	S116	Mec
	*Red with tan leather interior; 1,315 miles covered.*
1979	911 Turbo 3.3 coupé	800983	L	450-550.000 USD	275.040	360.000	317.844	20-08-16	Monterey	S131.1	Mec
	*Black with black leather interior; in original condition. 64 miles covered.*
1987	911 Turbo 3.3 slantnose cabriolet	070175	L	NQ	91.680	120.000	105.948	20-08-16	Monterey	7178	R&S
	*White; last serviced in August 2015.*
1990	928 GT S4	842440	R	20-25.000 GBP	27.140	41.326	37.103	06-09-15	Hedingham Cas.	106	Coy
	*Dark blue with grey leather interior; in good overall condition. Manual gearbox.*
1990	928	841231	R	14-16.000 GBP	19.125	29.462	26.580	25-10-15	Silverstone	242	SiC
	*Black with cream leather interior; 68,000 miles on the odometer. Last serviced in August 2015.*
1986	928 S2	840532	R	19-27.000 GBP	26.320	39.614	37.443	28-11-15	Weybridge	310	His
	*Silver; manual gearbox.*
1990	928 S4	840605	R	NA	14.400	20.386	18.585	06-03-16	Birmingham	366	SiC
	*Anthacite grey; imported into the UK from Japan.*
1994	928 GTS	820063	L	75-100.000 USD	93.284*	132.000*	121.572*	10-03-16	Amelia Island	150	Bon **F614**
	*Silver with light grey interior; in very good, highly original condition. Less than 24,000 miles covered. Manual gearbox.*
1987	928 S4	841653	L	13-18.000 EUR	17.226	24.620	22.200	12-03-16	Lyon	312	Agu
	*Dark blue with plum interior; bought in 2010 by the current, second owner. In good overall condition. Manual gearbox.*
1989	928 S4	840773	L	28-36.000 EUR		NS		09-04-16	Essen	203	Coy
	*Silver with black leather interior; one owner and 93,000 kms covered.*
1993	928 GTS	820061	L	60-75.000 USD	46.548	63.800	57.650	25-06-16	Santa Monica	1050	AA
	*Silver; described as in very good overall condition.*
1988	928 S4	842250	L	20-30.000 EUR	31.499*	40.906*	36.952*	09-07-16	Le Mans	102	Art
	*Metallic green with green leather interior; last serviced in late 2015. Manual gearbox.*
1989	928 S4	424764	R	14-18.000 GBP	26.320	34.448	30.413	20-08-16	Brooklands	233	His
	*Silver with black interior; described as in good overall condition and low mileage.*
1981	924 Carrera GT	700297	R	NA	34.875	48.741	44.288	26-02-16	Coventry	419	SiC
	*Black with black interior; in good, unrestored condition. Engine rebuilt in the late 1980s; last serviced 1,500 miles ago.*
1981	924 Carrera GTR	10	L	475-575.000 GBP	495.000	651.767	587.714	28-07-16	Silverstone	117	SiC **F615**
	*Red; sold new to Japan, the car has had just one owner and has covered 109 kms. In original condition; never raced. One of 17 examples built.*

F615: 1981 Porsche 924 Carrera GTR

F616: 1991 Porsche 944 S2 cabriolet

Year	Model	(Bodybuilder)	Chassis No.	Steering	Estimate	Hammer Price £	Hammer Price $	Hammer Price €	Date	Place	Lot	Auc. H.
1991	944 S2 cabriolet		432079	R	25-30.000 GBP	27.560	42.456	38.303	25-10-15	Silverstone	253	SiC F616
	Silver with dark blue interior; 18,900 miles covered. Last serviced in August 2015.											
1990	944 S2 cabriolet		430949	R	NQ	18.000*	27.403*	25.459*	14-11-15	Birmingham	305	SiC
	Red; described as in very good overall condition. Last serviced in 2014.											
1990	944 S2 cabriolet		430273	R	8-10.000 GBP	10.640	16.054	14.674	09-12-15	Chateau Impney	21	H&H
	White with leather interior; 58,000 miles on the odometer. Former Porsche Cars (GB) press car.											
1991	944 Turbo coupé		100875	L	13-18.000 GBP	22.400	32.014	28.867	12-03-16	Brooklands	137	His
	Red with black leather interior; stored from 2005 to 2013 and subsequently recommissioned.											
1989	944 cabriolet		431336	R	30-35.000 GBP	27.800	36.924	33.160	02-07-16	Woodstock	126	Coy
	White with black interior; one owner and 8,800 miles covered.											
1985	944 coupé		423030	R	9-11.000 GBP	10.304	13.567	12.234	28-07-16	Donington Park	31	H&H
	Red; in the same family ownership until 2015. 24,500 recorded miles; automatic transmission.											
1986	911 Carrera 3.2 Supersport coupé		103518	L	NQ	163.125*	248.390*	223.008*	04-09-15	Woodstock	205	SiC F617
	White with red leather interior; 743 kms covered since new. Recently serviced.											
1987	911 Carrera 3.2 Supersport cabriolet		150329	R	NQ	67.500*	102.782*	92.279*	04-09-15	Woodstock	208	SiC
	Bronze with brown interior; engine and gearbox overhauled in early 2015. Two owners and 20,251 miles covered (see Coys lots 445 3.12.13 NS and 117 26.4.14 $ 67,034).											
1985	911 Carrera 3.2 cabriolet		150534	R	30-35.000 GBP	43.700	66.542	59.742	05-09-15	Beaulieu	175	Bon
	Red with black and red leather interior; 40,641 miles covered. Since 1988 in the current ownership.											
1987	911 Carrera 3.2 Targa		140584	R	32-35.000 GBP	41.997	63.949	57.414	06-09-15	Hedingham Cas.	123	Coy
	Dark metallic grey; just one owner and 91,000 miles covered.											
1989	911 Carrera 3.2 coupé		102281	R	30-40.000 GBP	37.595	57.246	51.396	06-09-15	Hedingham Cas.	130	Coy
	Red with black interior; in good overall condition. Last serviced in July 2015.											
1984	911 Carrera 3.2 cabriolet		151494	R	27-30.000 GBP		NS		06-09-15	Hedingham Cas.	148	Coy
	Red with black interior; 73,000 miles covered.											
1986	911 Carrera 3.2 Supersport cabriolet		150754	R	40-45.000 GBP	38.250	58.924	53.160	25-10-15	Silverstone	207	SiC
	Grey; recently serviced. In the past the body was repainted and the gearbox overhauled.											
1989	911 Carrera 3.2 Supersport cabriolet		590466	R	45-55.000 GBP	52.310	80.584	72.700	25-10-15	Silverstone	236	SiC
	Black with grey interior; in largely original condition. 48,641 miles covered.											
1985	911 Carrera 3.2 cabriolet		151565	R	35-39.000 GBP		NS		28-11-15	Weybridge	236	His
	Red with cream leather interior; body repainted about 10 years ago. Recently serviced.											
1986	911 Carrera 3.2 Targa		141720	R	23-26.000 GBP		NS		09-12-15	Chateau Impney	45	H&H
	White; described as in very good overall condition.											
1985	911 Carrera 3.2 cabriolet		150534	R	30-35.000 GBP		NS		10-12-15	London	316	Bon
	See lot 175 Bonhams 5.9.15.											
1987	911 Carrera 3.2 coupé		121555	L	45-65.000 USD	39.989*	57.200*	52.458*	28-01-16	Scottsdale	32	Bon
	Red with black leather interior; 87,000 miles covered. Recently serviced. Electric sunroof.											
1987	911 Carrera 3.2 coupé		122352	L	80-100.000 USD	53.877*	77.000*	70.509*	30-01-16	Scottsdale	146	G&Co
	Blue with beige interior; in very good overall condition. Less than 11,900 miles covered.											
1987	911 Carrera 3.2 cabriolet		150214	R	29-35.000 GBP	31.360	44.820	40.414	12-03-16	Brooklands	155	His
	Silver with blue interior; body repainted in recent years. Recently serviced.											
1985	911 Carrera 3.2 cabriolet		151173	R	28-32.000 GBP	29.813	43.432	38.712	20-05-16	Silverstone	367	SiC
	Red with black interior; overhauled in March 2016.											
1984	911 Carrera 3.2 cabriolet		151707	R	32-38.000 GBP	37.520	54.040	47.808	11-06-16	Brooklands	290	His
	Ice blue with dark blue leather interior; 6,000 miles covered since the engine rebuild (see lot 250 Historics 3.7.15 $ 29,753).											
1986	911 Carrera 3.2 cabriolet		156202	R	35-45.000 GBP		NS		02-07-16	Woodstock	202	Coy
	White with blue leather interior; in good overall condition.											
1989	911 Carrera 3.2 Club Sport coupé		120507	L	350-425.000 USD	252.120	330.000	291.357	20-08-16	Pebble Beach	10	G&Co
	Irish green; original interior; less than 9,200 miles covered; two owners; one of 28 examples sold to the USA.											

F617: 1986 Porsche 911 Carrera 3.2 Supersport coupé

F618: 1990 Porsche 962C

Year	Model (Bodybuilder)	Chassis No.	Steering	Estimate	Hammer Price £	Hammer Price $	Hammer Price €	Date	Place	Lot	Auc. H.
1985	962	962108C2	R	2.500-3.000.000 USD		NS		23-01-16	Kissimmee	S98	Mec
	Campaigned by Jim Busby Racing and sponsored by BF Goodrich and Miller Brewing Company, the car won, among others events, the 1989 Daytona 24 Hours driven by Derek Bell, Bob Wolleck and John Andretti. Fitted during its race career with the present honeycomb tub built by Jim Chapman. Retired from competition at the end of the 1989 season.										
1990	962C	962012	R	1.500-2.000.000 USD	1.154.340	1.650.000	1.487.805	11-03-16	Amelia Island	38	G&Co
	Ex-Works car run by Joest Racing with factory support, it was raced at the 1990 FIA World Sports-Prototype and 1991 European Interserie Championships. Retired from competition, it remained in Joest Racing ownership and was restored in 2001 to the present white livery. Since 2006 in the Jerry Seinfeld Collection, its second owner.										F618
1989	962	962108C2	R	1.800-2.500.000 USD		NS		20-08-16	Monterey	S124	Mec
	See lot S98 Mecum 23.1.16.										
1986	962	962122	R	1.000-1.200.000 USD		NS		20-08-16	Monterey	S132	Mec
	Purchased new by the Dyson Racing, the car remained damaged in a race accident during a IMSA event at Watkins Glen. The damaged chassis was sold by Dyson Racing in 1989 and in 1992 it was acquired by the current owner. The car was full restored in the mid-2000s (see lot 249 RM 17.8.13 NS).										
1984	911SC/RS	110008	L	1.400-1.800.000 USD		NS		21-08-16	Pebble Beach	141	G&Co
	White and blue Rothmans livery; one of six examples of the Rothmans Porsche Team prepared in the UK by the David Richards Autosports. Raced at 13 international events from 1984 to 1987 driven by Henri Toivonen, Juha Kankkunen and Saeedi Al Hajri. Sold in late 1987 by the David Richards Autosports. Since 2015 circa in the current ownership. Recently serviced.										
1988	959	900191	L	1.100-1.400.000 USD		NS		29-01-16	Phoenix	213	RMS
	Komfort version finished in white with blue leather interior; 25,428 kms on the odometer. Last serviced in November 2014 in Switzerland (see lot 124 Bonhams 24.5.15 $ 781,480).										
1988	959	900032	L	1.200-1.400.000 EUR		NS		05-02-16	Paris	142	Art
	White with grey interior; 14,968 kms on the odometer. Last serviced in 2008 at the factory at 14,712 kms. First owner the former motocross World Champion André Malherbe.										
1988	959	900152	L	1.300-1.600.000 USD	783.552	1.120.000	1.009.904	11-03-16	Amelia Island	56	G&Co
	Komfort version finished in silver with black leather interior; sold new to France, the car was later imported into Germany, then into Italy and more recently into the USA. 29,299 kms on the odometer; major service in 2015.										
1988	959	900082	L	500-600.000 EUR	389.458	561.159	494.500	13-05-16	Monaco	135	Bon
	Komfort version finished in red with grey leather interior; acquired in 2008 by the current owner from the Freisinger Motorsport in Karlsruhe, Germany. Prior to sale, Freisinger had overhauled the engine and repainted the body. New Zealand papers. Should the car remain in the UE, local import taxes of 20% will be applied to the hammer price (see lot 132 Coys 27.8.06 NS).										
1988	959	900248	L	900-1.250.000 EUR	705.672	1.016.781	896.000	14-05-16	Monaco	253	RMS
	Komfort version finished in black with black interior; just under 9,500 kms covered. Upgraded to Stage-2 specification by the Porsche Classic Centre in Stuttgart. Body repainted.										F619
1988	959	900120	L	1.300-1.600.000 USD	912.000	1.250.000	1.129.500	25-06-16	Santa Monica	1100	AA
	Komfort version; two owners and 7,600 original kms.										
1988	959	900108	L	1.300-1.500.000 USD	1.008.480	1.320.000	1.165.428	20-08-16	Pebble Beach	19	G&Co
	Komfort version finished in silver with dark grey leather interior; described as in very good overall condition, the car has covered less than 8,200 kms. Imported in 2015 into the USA.										
1987	959	900036	n	1.000-1.300.000 USD		NS		20-08-16	Monterey	S127	Mec
	Komfort version finished in red with three-tone grey interior; sold new in Germany and later imported into the UK. Described as in very good overall condition.										
1989	**Carrera 3.2 Speedster**	173355	L	110-130.000 GBP		NS		06-09-15	Hedingham Cas.	152	Coy
	Black with original red interior; just over 60,000 miles covered. Recently serviced.										
1989	**Carrera 3.2 Speedster**	152342	L	180-220.000 GBP	173.600*	264.948*	237.710*	07-09-15	London	139	RMS
	Red with black interior; in original condition. 23,051 kms covered.										F620
1989	**Carrera 3.2 Speedster**	151974	L	130-150.000 GBP		NS		12-09-15	Goodwood	342	Bon
	"Turbo-look" finished in red with black leather interior; sold new to Spain, the car has had just one owner and has covered 16.600 kms.										
1989	**Carrera 3.2 Speedster**	173068	L	NA		NS		19-09-15	Dallas	S189.1	Mec
	Red with tan interior; turbo-look body.										
1989	**Carrera 3.2 Speedster**	152549	R	105-120.000 GBP		NS		25-10-15	Silverstone	235	SiC
	Black with black leather interior; since 1998 in the current ownership. Last serviced in December 2014 at 55,193 miles.										
1989	**Carrera 3.2 Speedster**	152150	L	190-230.000 EUR		NS		01-11-15	Paris	153	Art
	Silver with original black leather interior; Turbo-look version. 82,000 kms covered; last serviced in September 2015.										
1989	**Carrera 3.2 Speedster**	152161	L	190-210.000 EUR	141.090	213.586	196.600	07-11-15	Lyon	266	Agu
	Red with black leather interior; described as in very good overall condition. Engine and gearbox overhauled in 2015 (see Poulain lots 20 12.6.95 NS and 56 10.6.96 NS).										
1989	**Carrera 3.2 Speedster**	151335	L	140-170.000 GBP		NS		28-11-15	Weybridge	247	His
	Black with red leather interior; one owner and 18,929 kms covered.										
1989	**Carrera 3.2 Speedster**	151750	R	100-120.000 GBP	114.240	172.103	162.358	01-12-15	London	339	Coy
	Black with black leather interior; recently serviced.										

F619: 1988 Porsche 959

F620: 1989 Porsche Carrera 3.2 Speedster

Year	Model	(Bodybuilder)	Chassis no.	Steering	Estimate	Hammer Price £	$	€	Date	Place	Lot	Auc. H.
1989	**Carrera 3.2 Speedster**		173806	L	NA	126.996*	181.500*	166.200*	29-01-16	Scottsdale	1368	**B/J**
Black with black interior; 12,627 miles (see lot F182 Mecum 16.5.15 NS).												
1989	**Carrera 3.2 Speedster**		173142	L	175-225.000 USD	107.754*	154.000*	141.018*	29-01-16	Phoenix	233	**RMS**
Red with black interior; described as in very good overall condition, the car has covered just over 20,000 miles (see lot 3 Bonhams 14.8.15 $ 165,000).												
1989	**Carrera 3.2 Speedster**		151832	L	250-350.000 EUR	190.247	282.017	251.666	04-02-16	Paris	314	**Bon**
Turbo-look example finished in red with black interior; the car remained unregistered in the ownership of a French Porsche dealer until 2012. In original condition except for the paintwork redone in the original colour. Delivery mileage (see lot 257 Artcurial 5.7.14 $ 261,651).												
1989	**Carrera 3.2 Speedster**		173355	L	150-180.000 EUR		NS		04-02-16	Paris	380	**Bon**
See lot 152 Coys 6.9.15.												
1989	**Carrera 3.2 Speedster**		173287	L	250-325.000 USD	253.955	363.000	327.317	11-03-16	Amelia Island	37	**G&Co**
White with black leather interior; less than 3,800 original miles. Since 2013 in the Jerry Seinfeld Collection.												
1989	**Carrera 3.2 Speedster**		173273	L	220-250.000 USD	146.216*	209.000*	188.455*	11-03-16	Amelia Island	81	**G&Co**
White with beige leather interior; two owners and less than 6,400 miles covered.												
1989	**Carrera 3.2 Speedster slantnose**		151214	R	85-105.000 GBP	104.000	148.637	134.025	12-03-16	Brooklands	227	**His**
The car was sold new to Australia where the Turbo-look body was modified to slantnose front end. Last serviced in October 2014 at 8,760 kms.												
1989	**Carrera 3.2 Speedster**		151760	R	150-170.000 EUR	101.440*	146.162*	128.800*	14-05-16	Monaco	210	**RMS**
White with white leather interior; 26,300 miles covered. Exhibited at numerous concours d'elegance between 1999 and 2005.												
1989	**Carrera 3.2 Speedster**		173534	L	210-250.000 USD		NS		25-06-16	Santa Monica	1083	**AA**
White; approximately 7,000 miles covered.												
1989	**Carrera 3.2 Speedster**		173351	L	100-140.000 USD	77.848*	106.700*	96.414*	25-06-16	Santa Monica	2085	**AA**
Black; in good original condition. 78,000 miles covered.												
1989	**Carrera 3.2 Speedster**		173497	L	NA		NS		23-07-16	Harrisburg	S154.1	**Mec**
White with blue interior; 10,835 actual miles.												
1989	**Carrera 3.2 Speedster**		173247	L	195-235.000 USD		NS		20-08-16	Monterey	S68	**Mec**
Red with black interior; 8,800 miles covered.												
1990	**Carrera 4 3.6 coupé**		402906	L	45-55.000 EUR	37.980	49.960	44.783	06-08-16	Schloss Dyck	162	**Coy**
Red; in good overall condition. Manual gearbox.												
1993	**Carrera 2 3.6 cabriolet**		A51514	R	25-28.000 GBP	34.190	52.061	46.741	06-09-15	Hedingham Cas.	146	**Coy**
Light metallic blue with dark blue leather interior; the car has covered 2,000 miles since the rebuild.												
1993	**Carrera 2 3.6 cabriolet**		451973	R	25-28.000 GBP		NS		06-09-15	Hedingham Cas.	153	**Coy**
Metallic coral red with black leather interior; in good overall condition.												
1991	**Carrera 2 3.6 Targa**		411081	R	21-28.000 GBP	30.240	43.219	38.970	12-03-16	Brooklands	175	**His**
Black with black interior; in good overall condition.												
1992	**Carrera 2 3.6 America Roadster**		460750	L	NA	77.572	110.000	97.482	16-04-16	Houston	S180.1	**Mec** **F621**
White with red interior; 47,386 miles covered. Recently serviced.												
1992	**Carrera 2 3.6 America Roadster**		460750	L	120-140.000 USD		NS		25-06-16	Santa Monica	1097	**AA**
See lot S180.1 Mecum 16.4.16.												
1991	**Carrera 2 3.6 cabriolet**		453009	L	45-55.000 EUR	42.250	56.120	50.400	02-07-16	Lyon	334	**Agu**
Blue with light grey interior; in good overall condition.												
1992	**Carrera 2 3.6 cabriolet**		460519	L	150-175.000 USD	68.760	90.000	79.461	20-08-16	Monterey	S162	**Mec**
Black with black leather interior; 32,015 miles covered.												
1992	**Carrera 2 3.6 America Roadster**		460750	L	NQ		NS		20-08-16	Monterey	7190	**R&S**
See lot 1097 Auctions America 25.6.16.												
1992	**Carrera 2 3.6 America Roadster**		460839	L	140-180.000 USD	94.125*	123.200*	108.773*	21-08-16	Pebble Beach	151	**G&Co**
Black with black leather interior; less than 12,000 miles covered.												
1994	**Carrera 2 Speedster**		455411	R	160-180.000 GBP		NS		06-09-15	Hedingham Cas.	134	**Coy**
Dark green with black leather interior; in very good overall condition. 45,000 miles on the odometer.												
1993	**Carrera 2 Speedster**		455166	L	130-150.000 GBP	135.900	209.599	186.020	12-09-15	Goodwood	343	**Bon**
Black with black interior; just one owner and 19,050 kms covered.												
1994	**Carrera 2 Speedster**		465324	L	140-160.000 EUR	90.742	137.715	123.500	26-09-15	Frankfurt	162	**Coy**
Black with black interior; 45,000 miles covered. Tiptronic transmission (see lot 148 Coys 18.4.15 NS).												
1994	**Carrera 2 Speedster**		455411	R	120-140.000 GBP	154.512	237.006	208.591	10-10-15	Ascot	119	**Coy**
See lot 134 Coys 6.9.15.												
1994	**Carrera 2 Speedster**		465163	L	150-180.000 EUR	143.154	205.172	187.990	16-01-16	Maastricht	432	**Coy**
Black with black leather interior; described as in excellent overall condition, the car has had three owners and has covered 52,000 kms.												
1994	**Carrera 2 Speedster**		465399	L	285-325.000 USD	156.620	205.000	180.995	20-08-16	Monterey	S150	**Mec**
Red with black interior; one owner and 1,500 miles covered.												
1992	**Carrera RS**		490443	L	110-140.000 GBP		NS		04-09-15	Woodstock	244	**SiC**
Red with grey and black interior; 88,500 kms covered. Body repainted in recent years (see lot 627 Silverstone Auctions 16.11.14 $ 175,500).												
1991	**Carrera RS**		490353	L	140-160.000 GBP		NS		06-09-15	Hedingham Cas.	142	**Coy**
Black with black and grey interior; just over 60,000 miles covered.												
1992	**Carrera RS**		491262	L	160-180.000 GBP		NS		12-09-15	Goodwood	344	**Bon**
Light red with red and black interior; just one owner and 44,475 kms covered. With sunroof.												

Year	Model	(Bodybuilder)	Chassis No.	Steering	Estimate	Hammer Price £	Hammer Price $	Hammer Price €	Date	Place	Lot	Auc. H.
1991	**Carrera RS**		490353	L	160-180.000 EUR		NS		26-09-15	Frankfurt	119	**Coy**
See lot 142 Coys 6.9.15.												
1992	**Carrera RS**		491040	L	150-170.000 GBP		NS		25-10-15	Silverstone	217	**SiC**
Described as in very good overall condition; 21,500 miles covered. Recently imported into the UK.												
1994	**Carrera RS America**		419104	L	NA	75.866	115.000	105.018	12-12-15	Austin	S147	**Mec**
Black with black interior (see lot 160 RM 15.1.15 $ 104,500).												
1992	**Carrera RS**		490311	L	140-160.000 EUR	105.462	153.062	140.000	03-02-16	Paris	129	**RMS**
White with grey and black interior; sold to Italy, the car was raced in the past. Engine recently rebuilt.												
1992	**Carrera RS**		490451	L	150-200.000 EUR	155.982	226.997	202.640	05-02-16	Paris	221	**Art**
Grey with grey interior; last serviced in November 2015 (see lot 52 Artcurial 22.6.15 NS).												
1991	**Carrera RS**		490353	L	150-170.000 EUR	134.676	194.051	171.000	14-05-16	Monaco	134	**Coy**
See lot 119 Coys 26.9.15.												
1992	**Carrera RS**		490289	L	375-450.000 EUR		NS		14-05-16	Monaco	269	**RMS**
Red with three-tone grey leather interior; 12,088 kms covered.												
1992	**Carrera RS**		491040	L	120-140.000 GBP	134.400	193.576	171.252	11-06-16	Brooklands	251	**His**
See lot 217 Silverstone Auctions 25.10.15.												
1992	**Turbo S Leichtbau coupé**		479074	R	390-420.000 GBP		NS		04-09-15	Woodstock	247	**SiC**
Metallic electric blue with black leather interior; just one owner and approximately 23,000 miles covered. One of 86 examples built.												
1993	**Turbo 3.6 coupé**		470551	R	160-180.000 GBP		NS		04-09-15	Woodstock	241	**SiC**
Dark green; 77,725 miles covered. Extensive recommissioning carried out in 2013.												
1994	**Turbo 3.6 coupé**		480113	L	NA		NS		19-09-15	Dallas	S94	**Mec**
Red with black interior; believed to be 26,920 original miles. Recently serviced. Sunroof.												
1993	**Turbo 3.6 coupé**		470612	L	200-250.000 EUR	217.448	344.338	302.768	01-11-15	Paris	137	**Art**
Desctibed as in very good overall condition; 39,000 kms covered. 385bhp S engine.												
1994	**Turbo 3.6 S slantnose coupé**		480403	L	1.000-1.300.000 USD	711.843	1.017.500	917.480	11-03-16	Amelia Island	45	**G&Co** **F622**
Silver with grey leather interior; the car was sold new to the USA and remained until 2014 with its first owner. 12,545 miles covered. From the Jerry Seinfeld Collection.												
1994	**Turbo 3.6 coupé**		480349	L	195-225.000 EUR		NS		09-04-16	Essen	226	**Coy**
Red with tan interior; in good overall condition.												
1994	**Turbo 3.6 coupé**		480225	L	200-230.000 EUR	125.855	181.341	159.800	14-05-16	Monaco	165	**Coy**
Black; described as in very good overall condition.												
1995	**Turbo 3.6 coupé**		371046	L	145-155.000 EUR	116.406	153.122	137.255	06-08-16	Schloss Dyck	114	**Coy**
Black; described as in very good original condition. 19,409 kms covered.												
1994	**Turbo S 3.6 slantnose coupé**		480425	L	Refer Dpt.		NS		19-08-16	Carmel	70	**Bon**
Red with cashmere leather interior; sold new to the USA, the car has had two owners and has covered 2,310 miles. In 2011 it was displayed at the Porsche Museum in Germany at the Exclusive Department's 25th Anniversary exhibition.												
1994	**Turbo 3.6 S slantnose coupé**		480441	L	1.400-1.800.000 USD	840.400	1.100.000	971.190	20-08-16	Pebble Beach	45	**G&Co**
White with beige leather interior; sold new to the USA to the Blackhawk Collection in Danville, California, where it remained for more that two decades and from which it was acquired by the current owner. 37 miles covered; serviced in early 2016.												
1994	**Turbo 3.6 coupé**		480080	L	180-225.000 USD	148.980	195.000	172.166	20-08-16	Monterey	S42	**Mec**
Black with tan leather interior; 54,000 miles covered.												
1994	**968 coupé**		820075	L	50-60.000 USD	38.434	55.000	48.109	02-04-16	Ft.Lauderdale	176	**AA**
Red with black interior; original condition. Last serviced in 2014.												
1992	**968 Club Sport CS coupé**		815119	L	28-32.000 GBP	28.350	37.309	33.572	30-07-16	Silverstone	941	**SiC**
Blue with black interior; in good overall condition. 234,289 kms covered. Engine rebuilt in 2008.												
1997	**Carrera Targa**		381144	R	45-55.000 GBP	47.812	72.803	65.364	04-09-15	Woodstock	259	**SiC**
Dark metallic blue with grey leather interior; in good overall condition. Just over 47,300 miles covered.												
1996	**Carrera 4S coupé**		321262	L	140-180.000 USD	109.662*	156.750*	141.341*	11-03-16	Amelia Island	6	**G&Co**
Yellow with black leather interior; less than 8,000 miles covered.												
1996	**Carrera RS**		390411	L	150-170.000 GBP		NS		06-09-15	Hedingham Cas.	111	**Coy**
Black with black and grey leather interior; three owners and 166,000 kms covered. Regularly serviced.												

F621: 1992 Porsche Carrera 2 3.6 America Roadster

F622: 1994 Porsche Turbo 3.6 S slantnose coupé

Year	Model	(Bodybuilder)	Chassis No.	Steering	Estimate	Hammer Price £	$	€	Date	Place	Lot	Auc. H.
1995	**Carrera RS**		390154	L	250-300.000 EUR	224.798	327.143	292.040	05-02-16	Paris	205	Art
Yellow; described as in very good overall condition. 88,000 kms covered.												
1997	**Carrera Cup 3.8 RSR**		398070	L	1.200-1.500.000 USD	654.126	935.000	843.090	11-03-16	Amelia Island	41	G&Co
White; example built to European specification and sold new to japan fitted with a 340bhp type M64/75 engine. Never raced, it has covered less than 5,900 kms. From the Jerry Seinfeld Collection.												**F623**
1996	**Carrera RS**		390331	L	240-280.000 EUR		NS		09-04-16	Essen	135	Coy
Yellow; 41,000 kms covered. Sold new to Japan, reimported into Europe in 2015.												
1995	**Carrera RS**		390403	L	280-330.000 EUR		NS		14-05-16	Monaco	159	Coy
Black with black and grey interior; described as in excellent overall condition, the car has had two owners and has covered 50,082 kms. Fitted with RSR front and rear spoilers (see lot 118 Coys 18.4.15 $360,193).												
1995	**Carrera RS**		390746	L	190-230.000 GBP	214.300	293.677	265.368	24-06-16	Goodwood	261	Bon
Dark metallic blue with black and grey interior; described as in excellent overall condition. 51,862 kms covered.												
1996	**Carrera RS Clubsport**		390239	R	270-320.000 GBP	281.500	385.768	348.581	24-06-16	Goodwood	275	Bon
Silver; last serviced in May 2016 at 23,677 miles.												
1995	**Carrera RS**		390791	L	400-500.000 USD	277.332	363.000	320.493	20-08-16	Pebble Beach	28	G&Co
Silver with black and grey leather interior; sold new to Japan where it remained in single ownership for nearly two decades and then imported into the USA by the current, second owner. 66,258 kms covered.												
1997	**GT2 Evo**		394075	L	550-750.000 EUR		NS		05-02-16	Paris	208	Art
The car was raced at some events until 2002, including the 1998 and 1999 Le Mans 24 Hours. Since 2003 in the current ownership, it has been restored to the red and yellow 1998 Le Mans livery.												
1996	**GT2 Evo**		394062	L	1.250-1.750.000 USD		WD		20-08-16	Monterey	S76	Mec
White; one owner and 7,000 kms covered.												
1997	**Boxster**		604004	L	10-15.000 EUR	9.525*	14.456*	12.964*	26-09-15	Frankfurt	101	Coy
Red with black interior; one owner and 31,000 kms covered.												
1996	**Turbo 3.6 coupé**		371994	R	80-90.000 GBP		NS		06-09-15	Hedingham Cas.	150	Coy
Black pearl with beige leather interior; described as in very good original condition.												
1998	**Turbo S 3.6 coupé**		370716	R	250-280.000 GBP		NS		07-09-15	London	159	RMS
Dark metallic blue with grey leather interior; three owners and 71,700 miles covered. Last serviced in August 2014.												
1996	**Turbo 3.6 coupé**		371323	L	125-195.000 EUR	106.476	163.329	143.750	09-10-15	Zoute	37	Bon
Metallic black with grey interior; two owners and approximately 84,000 kms covered. Body repainted. 430bhp engine; electric sunroof.												
1993	**Turbo 3.6 prototype coupé**		310004	L	300-400.000 EUR	258.073	392.886	365.000	14-11-15	Ladenburg	5053	Aut
Black with red interior; development prototype of the new model, the car was registered by the factory in April 1993 and used until December 1994. Later it was fitted with a standard Turbo engine and sold to private hands. 75,000 kms on the odometer.												
1996	**Turbo 3.6 coupé**		376031	L	300-375.000 USD	212.921	305.000	282.186	23-01-16	Kissimmee	S150	Mec
Red with red leather interior; since new in the same family ownership. 5,866 miles covered.												**F624**
1997	**Turbo 3.6 coupé**		375867	L	175-250.000 USD	97.734	140.000	129.528	23-01-16	Kissimmee	S213	Mec
Red with black leather interior; 17,000 actual miles.												
1997	**Turbo 3.6 coupé**		375393	L	185-200.000 USD	109.602	157.000	145.256	23-01-16	Kissimmee	S252	Mec
Silver with tan leather interior; 28,083 actual miles.												
1996	**Turbo 3.6 coupé**		375623	L	200-250.000 USD	146.112*	209.000*	191.674*	28-01-16	Phoenix	134	RMS
Silver with blue leather interior; less than 10,000 miles covered. Recently serviced.												
1997	**Turbo S 3.6 coupé**		375793	L	450-500.000 USD	338.655	484.000	443.199	29-01-16	Scottsdale	11	G&Co
Metallic blue with tan leather interior; one owner until 2015. Approximately 22,000 miles covered since new.												
1997	**Turbo 3.6 coupé**		375501	L	275-325.000 USD	169.327	242.000	221.599	30-01-16	Scottsdale	141	G&Co
Yellow with black leather interior; in excellent overall condition. Three owners and less than 30,000 miles covered.												
1997	**Turbo S 3.6 coupé**		375774	L	400-475.000 USD	346.302	495.000	446.342	12-03-16	Amelia Island	133	RMS
Dark metallic green with beige leather interior; 13,379 miles covered.												
1997	**Turbo 3.6 S coupé**		375990	L	525-575.000 USD		NS		20-08-16	Pebble Beach	70	G&Co
Black with black leather interior; less than 6,300 miles covered.												

F623: 1997 Porsche Carrera Cup 3.8 RSR

F624: 1996 Porsche Turbo 3.6 coupé

Year	Model	(Bodybuilder)	Chassis no.	Steering	Estimate	£	$	€	Date	Place	Lot	Auc. H.
1997	Turbo 3.6 S coupé		375924	L	425-525.000 USD		NS		20-08-16	Monterey	S97.1	Mec
	Black with tan leather interior; 9,360 miles covered. Formerly owned by tennis player Pete Sampras.											
1997	GT1 Evolution		993117	L	2.700-3.000.000 EUR	2.183.172	3.145.666	2.772.000	14-05-16	Monaco	261	RMS
	Sold as a bare tub to Canadian Bytzek Motorsports team, the car was completed by the team using the drivetrain and suspension components from a their 1996 GT1 damaged in a race accident, and additional components, including an Evo upgrade package. Raced until 2002, the car won the Canadian GT Championship in 1999, 2000 and 2001. Fully restored in the UK between 2014 and 2015 and registered for road use. Two owners since new.											**F625**
2004	911 GT3		697083	R	60-70.000 GBP		NS		06-09-15	Hedingham Cas.	107	Coy
	Comfort model finished in red with black leather interior; two owners and 27,000 miles covered. Last serviced in July 2013.											
2003	911 GT3 RS		690932	R	145-165.000 GBP	142.875	220.099	198.568	25-10-15	Silverstone	219	SiC
	White; 3,277 miles covered. Sold new to Hong Kong and later imported into the UK.											
2003	911 GT3 RS		691123	R	120-140.000 GBP	112.500	173.306	156.353	25-10-15	Silverstone	240	SiC
	White; 26,889 miles covered. Last serviced in March 2014 at 26,639 miles.											
2004	911 GT3 RS		691626	R	140-160.000 GBP	148.500	216.335	192.827	20-05-16	Silverstone	308	SiC
	White; 9,722 miles on the odometer. Last serviced 500 miles ago in 2014.											
2003	911 GT2		695135	R	110-120.000 GBP		NS		06-09-15	Hedingham Cas.	137	Coy
	Silver with black leather interior; described as in excellent overall condition.											
2003	911 GT2		695130	R	115-130.000 GBP		NS		25-10-15	Silverstone	225	SiC
	Silver with black leather interior; 20,000 miles covered. Recently serviced.											
2003	911 GT2		695135	R	100-115.000 GBP		NS		25-10-15	Silverstone	247	SiC
	See lot 137 Coys 6.9.15.											
2002	911 GT2		696197	L	NA	108.348	171.600	150.871	31-10-15	Hilton Head	180	AA
	Silver with black interior; 5,585 actual miles.											
2005	911 Turbo cabriolet		670085	R	55-65.000 GBP		NS		06-09-15	Hedingham Cas.	129	Coy
	Black with beige interior; two owners and 23,500 miles covered.											
2005	911 Turbo cabriolet		670085	R	48-55.000 GBP		NS		25-10-15	Silverstone	223	SiC
	See lot 129 Coys 6.9.15.											
2006	Carrera GT		000206	L	500-550.000 GBP	617.800	940.724	844.594	06-09-15	Hedingham Cas.	143	Coy
	Black with Terracotta leather interior; three owners and 6,300 miles covered (see lot 324 Coys 14.5.05 NS).											
2006	Carrera GT		00158	L	475-550.000 GBP	448.000	683.738	613.446	07-09-15	London	125	RMS
	White with Terracotta leather interior; 12,300 miles covered. Clutch replaced in 2011; last serviced in January 2015.											
2005	Carrera GT		000145	L	650-950.000 EUR	477.011	731.713	644.000	09-10-15	Zoute	43	Bon
	Silver; bought new by the current owner, the car was immediately rebuilt as a GTR version by the GPR Racing. Subsequently it was never raced, as Porsche refused permission, but only used at track days. It is estimated it has covered around 2,000 kms. Unused for the past seven years, it received recently a major service. All the original parts are included with the sale.											
2005	Carrera GT		001159	L	900-1.100.000 USD		NS		23-01-16	Kissimmee	S153	Mec
	Black with dark grey interior; 909 miles covered.											
2005	Carrera GT		001525	L	900-1.100.000 USD		NS		23-01-16	Kissimmee	S190	Mec
	Red with black interior; two owners and 2,720 miles covered.											
2005	Carrera GT		001145	L	850-925.000 USD	555.785	795.000	729.095	28-01-16	Phoenix	115	RMS **F626**
	Silver; one owner and 1,600 miles covered. Recently serviced.											
2005	Carrera GT		001573	L	1.100-1.400.000 USD	685.706	980.000	897.386	29-01-16	Scottsdale	35	G&Co
	Finished in Rosso Scuderia with dark grey leather interior, the car was sold new to the USA; in original condition. Less than 450 miles covered; last serviced in 2015.											
2005	Carrera GT		000275	L	800-1.000.000 EUR		NS		04-02-16	Paris	343	Bon
	Dark blue with terracotta leather interior. Two owners. Last serviced in October 2014 at 9,126 miles.											
2004	Carrera GT		001068	L	NA	427.500	597.474	542.882	26-02-16	Coventry	423	SiC
	Silver with black leather interior; sold new to the USA, the car was imported into the UK in 2009. Last serviced in November 2015 al 18,018 miles.											
2005	Carrera GT		001107	L	800-900.000 USD		NS		10-03-16	Amelia Island	191	Bon
	Silver with black interior; until 2015 with its first owner, the car has covered less than 2,500 miles.											
2005	Carrera GT		001320	L	775-925.000 USD		NS		11-03-16	Amelia Island	24	G&Co
	Red with black interior; two owners. Full service in 2014 at just over 2,000 miles.											

F625: 1997 Porsche GT1 Evolution

F626: 2005 Porsche Carrera GT

Year	Model	(Bodybuilder)	Chassis No.	Steering	Estimate	Hammer Price £	Hammer Price $	Hammer Price €	Date	Place	Lot	Auc. H.
2000	**Carrera GT Prototype**		9R3M001	L	1.500-2.250.000 USD		NS		11-03-16	Amelia Island	40	**G&Co**
	One of two development prototypes built and the only one assembled as a running automobile. Presented at the Paris Motor Show driven by Walter Rohrl. In 2007 the car was acquired directly from the factory by Jerry Seinfeld in whose collection it remained since. The buyer of this car, as a condition of purchase, agrees that it may not be driven and that any future sale by such buyer is subject to a right of first refusal in favor of Porsche.												
2005	**Carrera GT**		001460	L	750-850.000 USD	500.214	715.000	644.716	12-03-16	Amelia Island	153	**RMS**
	Silver with brown leather interior; one owner and 1,184 miles covered. Recently serviced.												
2005	**Carrera GT**		001525	L	NA		NS		09-04-16	Palm Beach	400	**B/J**
	See lot S190 Mecum 23.1.16.												
2004	**Carrera GT**		001014	L	NA		NS		09-04-16	Palm Beach	428	**B/J**
	Silver with brown interior; 4,252 actual miles.												
2006	**Carrera GT**		000110	L	650-750.000 EUR	561.545	809.112	713.000	13-05-16	Monaco	111	**Bon**
	Silver; un proprietario e approximately 14,300 kms covered. Clutch replaced at 12,000 kms.												
2005	**Carrera GT**		000261	L	700-850.000 EUR		NS		14-05-16	Monaco	267	**RMS**
	Silver with black leather interior; less than 3,500 kms covered.												
2006	**Carrera GT**		000204	L	550-625.000 EUR	581.428	764.816	685.565	06-08-16	Schloss Dyck	152	**Coy**
	Silver; 31,000 kms covered (see lot 156 Artcurial 7.7.12 NS).												
2005	**Carrera GT**		001566	L	600-750.000 USD	487.432	638.000	563.290	19-08-16	Carmel	5	**Bon**
	Silver with terracotta leather interior; less than 2,200 miles covered.												
2005	**Carrera GT**		001107	L	700-800.000 USD		NS		19-08-16	Monterey	F133	**Mec**
	See lot 191 Bonhams 10.3.16.												
2005	**Carrera GT**		001302	L	1.100-1.400.000 USD		NS		20-08-16	Monterey	S74	**Mec**
	Black with dark grey leather interior; 152 miles covered.												
2004	**Carrera GT**		001034	L	700-900.000 USD	466.040	610.000	538.569	20-08-16	Monterey	S90	**Mec**
	Silver with dark grey leather interior; one owner and 1,334 miles covered. From the Modern Speed Collection.												
2004	**Carrera GT**		001183	L	650-700.000 USD	495.836	649.000	573.002	20-08-16	Monterey	247	**RMS**
	Silver with black interior; 3,500 miles covered. Recently serviced.												
2005	**Carrera GT**		001172	L	NQ		NS		20-08-16	Monterey	7114	**R&S**
	Silver; recently serviced.												
2005	**Carrera GT**		001109	L	NQ		NS		20-08-16	Monterey	7206	**R&S**
	Red.												
2011	**911 GT3 RS**		785350	L	250-300.000 GBP	281.250	428.259	384.497	04-09-15	Woodstock	218	**SiC** **F627**
	White with black leather and alcantara interior; 4,000 miles covered. Never used on the track. One of 600 examples built with the 4.0-litre engine.												
2007	**911 GT3 RS**		791260	R	130-150.000 GBP	168.750	259.959	234.529	25-10-15	Silverstone	218	**SiC**
	Orange with black wheels; since 2008 in the current ownership, the car has covered 5,527 miles.												
2008	**911 GT3 RS**		792253	L	285-315.000 USD	213.920	280.000	247.212	20-08-16	Monterey	S142	**Mec**
	Viper green; 16,965 miles covered.												
2007	**911 GT3 RS**		792655	L	200-275.000 USD	171.900	225.000	198.653	20-08-16	Monterey	S88	**Mec**
	White with black leather interior; one owner and 565 miles covered. From the Modern Speed Collection.												
2009	**911 GT2**		776176	L	100-120.000 GBP	112.500	173.306	156.353	25-10-15	Silverstone	212	**SiC**
	White with black leather interior; 22,000 miles covered. Just one owner until early 2015 when it was imported into the UK from Dubai. Taxes paid; to be registered.												
2010	**911 GT2 RS**		776350	R	300-350.000 GBP	315.000	479.651	430.637	04-09-15	Woodstock	249	**SiC**
	Red with black bonnet and black interior; just over 2,000 miles covered.												
2011	**911 GT2 RS**		778109	L	550-650.000 USD	411.796	539.000	475.883	20-08-16	Pebble Beach	13	**G&Co**
	Red with black bonnet and black leather and red alcantara interior; two owners and less than 1,250 miles covered.												
2010	**911 GT3 RS**		780358	L	130-150.000 GBP	135.000	207.968	187.623	25-10-15	Silverstone	209	**SiC**
	White with black interior; 1,500 kms covered. Recently serviced.												
2011	**911 GT3 RS**		783589	L	250-300.000 USD	200.114	286.000	261.890	30-01-16	Scottsdale	106	**G&Co**
	Black with leather and alcantara interior; two owners and less than 900 miles covered.												

F627: 2011 Porsche 911 GT3 RS

F628: 2015 Porsche 918 Spyder

Year	Model	(Bodybuilder)	Chassis no.	Steering	Estimate	Hammer price £	$	€	Date	Place	Lot	Auc. H.
2011	911 GT3 RS		785072	L	220-270.000 GBP		NS		11-06-16	Brooklands	304	His
White with black and red leather and alcantara interior; 2,980 kms on the odometer. Recently serviced. Russian documents.											
2011	911 GT3 RS		785714	L	500-600.000 USD	420.200	550.000	485.595	20-08-16	Monterey	S87	Mec
White with red and black interior; 426 miles covered. From the Modern Speed Collection.											
2011	Speedster		795643	L	300-330.000 EUR		NS		07-11-15	Lyon	272	Agu
Blue with blue leather interior; sold new to the USA, the car was reimported into Europe in 2014. About 5,000 kms covered since new.											
2011	Speedster		795554	L	300-400.000 USD	307.824	440.000	396.748	11-03-16	Amelia Island	32	G&Co
Blue; less than 5,000 miles covered. Since new in the Jerry Seinfeld Collection.											
2011	Speedster		795620	L	275-325.000 USD	214.302*	280.500*	247.653*	21-08-16	Pebble Beach	131	G&Co
White with black leather interior; the car remained unitil early 2016 with its first owner. Recently serviced.											
2015	918 Spyder		800804	L	1.300-1.600.000 USD	1.115.065	1.595.000	1.462.775	28-01-16	Phoenix	148	RMS
Metallic white with black interior; two owners and less than 1,500 miles covered. Fitted with the Weissach package.												F628
2015	918 Spyder		800561	L	NA	1.231.472	1.760.000	1.611.632	29-01-16	Scottsdale	1392	B/J
White with black interior; one owner and 595 original miles. Weissach package.											
2015	918 Spyder		800381	L	1.900-2.300.000 USD		NS		20-08-16	Monterey	S112	Mec
Matt black; 1,957 miles covered. Fitted with the Weissach Package.											
2015	918 Spyder		800489	L	NQ		NS		20-08-16	Monterey	7125	R&S
Viper green; manufactured with the Weissach Package.											

PROCTER (USA) *(1907)*

1907	Runabout		1771(engine)	R	10-15.000 USD	12.241*	18.700*	16.617*	08-10-15	Hershey	130	RMS
Only one ever built; in original condition. Powered by a Ford Model A engine, as when new. Mechanicals to be restored. From the Richard Roy estate.											

QVALE (USA)

2000	Mangusta		000064	L	20-30.000 USD	10.870*	16.500*	14.685*	05-10-15	Philadelphia	242	Bon
Metallic green with tobacco interior; in original condition. From the Evergreen Collection.											

RAILTON (GB) *(1933-1949)*

1934	Terraplane cabriolet (Berkeley)		75379	R	NA		NS		14-10-15	Duxford	136	H&H
Cherry red and silver with burgundy leather interior; currently fitted with a 1937 8-cylinder engine. Several restoration works carried out in the 1980s; several mechanical works carried out in the 2000s.											

RAINIER (USA) *(1905-1911)*

1908	Model D touring		1603	R	250-350.000 USD	166.676	253.000	225.170	05-10-15	Philadelphia	261	Bon
Bought new by the Asbury family, California; later it was laid up for a half shaft casing cracked. In the 1930s the family gave it to their chauffeur who retained it until 1947. Subsequently the car remained in the Buess collection for over 60 years until the late 1990s. In original condition, it was last used about five years ago. The radiator was rebuilt with a new core. The interior and soft top are in poor condition. The broken original axle is included with the lot. Sole survivor of the model.												F629

RALLY (F) *(1921-1933)*

1929	Type ABC 2-seater		635K	R	NA	81.760	125.755	110.212	14-10-15	Duxford	139	H&H
Blue with blue leather interior; imported new into the UK, the car has had a long race career. After WWII, it has been also part from 1973 for about 30 years of the collection of Douglas John Moray Stuart who had it restored. Since 2003 in the current ownership, the car is in working order and still fitted with its original 1.1-litre engine. Little used in the past 12 years.												F630

RAMBLER (USA) *(1902-1917)*

1904	Model H tonneau		3561	R	NA		NS		14-10-15	Duxford	126	H&H
Red with black interior; restored in the 1980s, the car is described as in good overall condition. Imported into the UK in 2007 (see lot 683 Bonhams 3.12.07 $ 100,704).											

F629: 1908 Rainier Model D touring

F630: 1929 Rally Type ABC 2-seater

Year	Model	(Bodybuilder)	Chassis no.	Steering	Estimate	Hammer price £	Hammer price $	Hammer price €	Date	Place	Lot	Auc. H.

RAUCH & LANG (USA) (1905-1928)

| 1920 | Coach Model C45 | | 90127 | L | 50-75.000 USD | 43.032 | 66.000 | 58.093 | 09-10-15 | Hershey | 237 | RMS F631 |

Dark blue with blue velour interior; acquired in 1970 by Harold Coker and subsequently restored. Included in the sale a Lestronic battery charger of recent vintage.

RAYNAUD (F)

| 1896 | Vis-a-vis | | NQ | R | 220-250.000 EUR | 101.244* | 146.940* | 134.400* | 03-02-16 | Paris | 115 | RMS F632 |

Ivory with black interior; discovered in France in 1975. Described as in original condition except for the paintwork redone in the original colour. Dated 1896 by the Veteran Car Club of Great Britain.

REGAL (USA) (1908-1918)

| 1913 | Twenty Model N roadster | | 4708(ENGINE) | R | 100-150.000 USD | 67.232 | 88.000 | 77.695 | 19-08-16 | Carmel | 78 | Bon F633 |

In single ownership from 1938 to 1999; restored in the early 2000s.

RENAULT (F) (1899-)

| 1909 | Type V1 Cape Top Victoria | (Brewster) | 14985 | R | 1.200-1.500.000 DKK | 79.293 | 120.348 | 107.951 | 26-09-15 | Ebeltoft | 29 | Bon F634 |

Dark blue with burgundy leather interior; restored in the 1990s, the car is described as still in very good overall condition.

| 1907 | Type X1 limousine | (Labourdette) | 27 | R | 30-40.000 EUR | 51.671 | 78.221 | 72.000 | 08-11-15 | Lyon | 207 | Ose |

For 23 years in the current ownership; engine dismantled for restoration.

| 1911 | Type CB limousine | (Labourdette) | 26929 | R | 70-80.000 EUR | 85.072 | 121.543 | 108.000 | 19-06-16 | Fontainebleau | 320 | Ose |

Black with original interior.

| 1911 | Type CC torpedo | | 28303 | R | 140-160.000 EUR | | NS | | 04-02-16 | Paris | 407 | Bon |

Red with black leather interior; sold new to Australia, in the mid-1980s the car was imported into the UK and restored. New Labourdette-style body.

| 1913 | Type DG torpedo | | 41838 | R | 40-50.000 EUR | 31.296 | 46.393 | 41.400 | 04-02-16 | Paris | 396 | Bon |

Red with black wings; acquired in 1968 by the current owner and restored.

| 1915 | Type EK spider | | 58748 | R | 20-30.000 EUR | 12.918 | 19.555 | 18.000 | 08-11-15 | Lyon | 206 | Ose |

For 38 years in the same ownership; body in good condition, engine lacking magneto and carburettor.

| 1914 | Type EE limousine | (Letourneur/Marchand) | 44265 | R | 180-240.000 EUR | | NS | | 04-02-16 | Paris | 340 | Bon |

Green with black wings; restored in the 1970s. For many years with the current owner who is in effect only its fourth owner.

| 1925 | Type NM torpedo | | 139416 | R | 175-225.000 GBP | | NS | | 07-09-15 | London | 174 | RMS |

Ivory with biscuit leather interior; at unspecified date the car was acquired in the UK by the Nethercutt Collection, who imported it in the USA, restored it, used it at several historic events and resold it in 2010 (see lots 109 Gooding 15.8.10 $ 292,210, 128 RM 26.7.14 $ 278,256 and 338 Bonhams 5.2.15 NS).

| 1925 | Type NM torpedo | | 139416 | R | NA | | NS | | 29-01-16 | Scottsdale | 1399 | B/J |

See lot 174 RM/Sotheby's 7.9.15.

| 1929 | Vivasix landaulette de ville | (Strakosch) | 475583 | R | 22-26.000 GBP | 23.000 | 34.788 | 31.788 | 10-12-15 | London | 383 | Bon |

Black and yellow; acquired in 2006 by the current owner and subsequently restored (see lot 432 Bonhams 9.9.06 $ 11,837).

| 1934 | Vivastella limousine | | 619646 | L | 30-40.000 EUR | 13.475* | 19.975* | 17.825* | 04-02-16 | Paris | 412 | Bon |

Black and grey with brown cloth interior; the car has covered less than 3,000 kms since the restoration (see lot 183 Artcurial 6.2.15 $ 30,541).

| 1934 | Monaquatre cabriolet | | 666109 | L | 30-40.000 EUR | 13.040* | 19.330* | 17.250* | 04-02-16 | Paris | 399 | Bon |

Dark blue with burgundy interior; restored in the early 1990s. Since 1992 in the current ownership.

| 1932 | Vivaquatre berline | | 561678 | L | 20-25.000 EUR | 15.648* | 23.196* | 20.700* | 04-02-16 | Paris | 433 | Bon |

Blue with black wings; restored.

| 1936 | Viva Grand Sport cabriolet | | 754545 | L | 80-120.000 EUR | 62.393* | 90.799* | 81.056* | 05-02-16 | Paris | 189 | Art F635 |

Cream with green leather interior; acquired in 1990s by the current owner and subsequently restored.

| 1961 | 4CV Resort Special | (Ghia) | 3607759 | L | 60-80.000 USD | 53.831* | 77.000* | 70.617* | 28-01-16 | Scottsdale | 43 | Bon F636 |

Mint green and cream with wicker seats; acquired some years ago by the current owner and subsequently fully restored in California.

| 1958 | 4CV berline | | 3159318 | L | 8-12.000 EUR | 7.287 | 10.557 | 9.360 | 20-03-16 | Fontainebleau | 341 | Ose |

Dark red; restored between 2013 and 2014.

| 1951 | 4CV Grand Luxe berline décapotable | | 1580776 | L | 20-25.000 EUR | 24.954 | 35.653 | 31.680 | 19-06-16 | Fontainebleau | 352 | Ose |

Red with original light brown leatherette interior; some recent overhaul works to the mechanicals. For over 50 years until 2009 in the same family ownership.

| 1953 | Fregate Ondine cabriolet | (Ghia) | 2434085 | L | 80-100.000 EUR | 59.640* | 86.793* | 77.480* | 05-02-16 | Paris | 105 | Art F637 |

One of four examples built and one of three with fiberglass body; probably the only survivor. Blue; restored in the 1990s (see lot 36 Poulain/Sotheby's 17.6.02 NS).

| 1963 | Dauphine 1093 | | 67145 | L | 30-40.000 EUR | 33.032* | 48.070* | 42.912* | 05-02-16 | Paris | 164 | Art |

Beige; bought in 1984 by Michel Hommell and subsequently restored. Little used since, it requires recommissioning prior to use it on the road.

| 1964 | Caravelle cabriolet | | 121104 | R | NA | | NS | | 24-02-16 | Donington Park | 76 | H&H |

Red with black interior; described as in good overall condition.

| 1981 | R5 Turbo | | 001651 | L | 60-70.000 GBP | 61.875 | 94.199 | 87.516 | 14-11-15 | Birmingham | 337 | SiC |

Red with red leather interior; described as in very good overall condition.

| 1982 | R5 Turbo Groupe 4 | | B0000454 | L | 250-350.000 EUR | 374.888 | 540.165 | 476.000 | 14-05-16 | Monaco | 273 | RMS |

Managed by Renault Chartres, the car was used in several rallies in France, won the 1982 French Rally Championship driven by Jean-Luc Thérier and placed 4th overall and 1st two-wheel drive car at the 1984 Monte Carlo Rally driven by Jean Ragnotti. Later it was sold to Guadeloupe and raced at several rallies. In 1999 it was acquired by the current owner and reimported into Europe. Presented in the 1984 Monte Carlo livery. Recently serviced. F638

| 1980 | R5 Turbo | | B0000331 | L | 90-110.000 EUR | 78.465 | 104.224 | 93.600 | 02-07-16 | Lyon | 343 | Agu |

Red with red interior; bought circa 10 years ago by the current owner and subsequently restored.

F631: 1920 Rauch & Lang Coach Model C45

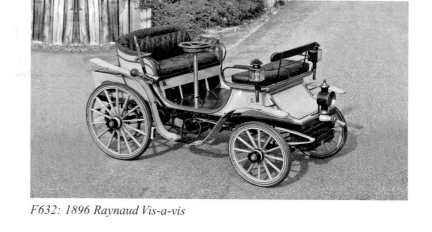
F632: 1896 Raynaud Vis-a-vis

F633: 1913 Regal Twenty Model N roadster

F634: 1909 Renault Type V1 Cape Top Victoria (Brewster)

F635: 1936 Renault Viva Grand Sport cabriolet

F636: 1961 Renault 4CV Resort Special (Ghia)

F637: 1953 Renault Fregate Ondine cabriolet (Ghia)

F638: 1982 Renault R5 Turbo Groupe 4

Year	Model	(Bodybuilder)	Chassis No.	Steering	Estimate	Hammer Price £	$	€	Date	Place	Lot	Auc. H.
1982	**R5 Turbo**		000316	L	90-110.000 EUR	89.416	116.120	104.896	09-07-16	Le Mans	146	Art
Red; acquired in 2015 by the current owner and subsequently restored.												
1984	**R5 Turbo 2**		000935	L	45-55.000 GBP	38.152	58.083	53.962	14-11-15	Birmingham	311	SiC
White; in original condition. The car was stored from 1999 to 2014 when it was acquired by the current owner and fully recommissioned.												
1984	**R5 Turbo 2**		001270	L	90-110.000 USD	46.180*	66.000*	60.436*	30-01-16	Scottsdale	134	G&Co
Red; imported into the USA in 1984. Body repainted.												
1983	**R5 Turbo 2**		000453	L	60-70.000 EUR		NS		12-03-16	Lyon	329	Agu
Red with black interior; restored in 2006. Engine rebuilt. Since 1992 in the current ownership. 26,000 kms covered since new.												
1984	**R5 Turbo 2**		10083	L	75-80.000 EUR	67.515	88.810	79.607	06-08-16	Schloss Dyck	170	Coy
White; in good overall condition. 58,000 kms covered.												
1983	**R5 Turbo 2**		000912	L	70-90.000 USD	100.848*	132.000*	116.543*	19-08-16	Carmel	111	Bon
Blue; from the mid-1990s with the present owner, who later commissioned some restoration works.												
1990	**Alpine GT Turbo**		23155	L	20-30.000 USD	11.397*	15.000*	13.497*	30-07-16	Plymouth	106	RMS
Dark blue with grey leather interior; in largely original condition. Japanese market version; about 28,000 kms covered.												
1999	**Spider**		434504	L	35-45.000 EUR	35.209	46.767	42.000	02-07-16	Lyon	360	Agu
Grey with grey and black interior; one owner, 3,390 kms on the odometer.												

REO (USA) *(1904-1936)*

Year	Model	(Bodybuilder)	Chassis No.	Steering	Estimate	£	$	€	Date	Place	Lot	Auc. H.
1905	**16hp detachable tonneau**		339	R	50-65.000 USD		NS		20-08-16	Monterey	S59	Mec
Red with black interior; restored. Formerly owned for over 50 years by the same family (see lot 38 RM 16.1.14 $60,500).												
1931	**Royale model 35 civtoria coupé**		2448	L	80-90.000 EUR		NS		28-05-16	Aarhus	107	SiC
Black and red; imported new into Denmark. Purchased in 1981 by the current owner and subsequently restored.												

REYNARD (GB) *(1973-)*

Year	Model	(Bodybuilder)	Chassis No.	Steering	Estimate	£	$	€	Date	Place	Lot	Auc. H.
2000	**Chrysler ISSC**		2KF010	M	22-28.000 GBP	76.840	110.127	100.899	16-01-16	Birmingham	361	Coy
Black and red; 3.5-litre 6-cylinder Chrysler engine rebuilt, Hewland NMT 6-speed gearbox recently overhauled.												

RILEY (GB) *(1898-1969)*

Year	Model	(Bodybuilder)	Chassis No.	Steering	Estimate	£	$	€	Date	Place	Lot	Auc. H.
1925	**Eleven-40 tourer**		3705	R	NA		NS		14-10-15	Duxford	115	H&H
Blue with black wings and blue interior; overhauled engine (see lot 1057 Bonhams 1.12.03 $ 16,868).												
1931	**Nine WD tourer**		6014408	R	22-28.000 GBP	20.700	31.520	28.299	05-09-15	Beaulieu	106	Bon
Since 1976 in the same family ownership; restored in 1993 and last used in 1995; recommissioned in 2014.												
1933	**Nine Kestrel saloon**		6022867	R	NA	16.240	24.979	21.892	14-10-15	Duxford	7	H&H
Cream and green with green leather interior; restored 15 years ago.												
1928	**Nine cabriolet**		60950	R	22-28.000 GBP	20.700	29.988	26.587	20-03-16	Goodwood	35	Bon
Black with original medium brown leather interior; restored in 1986.												
1933	**Nine Lynx Special tourer**		6021101	R	NA	41.440	58.762	52.388	20-04-16	Duxford	28	H&H **F639**
Red with brown interior; raced in period and retained by its first owner until 1956. Acquired in 1991 by the current owner, the car has covered 4,500 miles since a recent restoration.												
1935	**Imp Sports**		6027359	R	40-60.000 GBP	49.450	75.298	67.603	05-09-15	Beaulieu	107	Bon
For restoration. Since 1964 in the same family ownership, the car was last used many years ago, is complete and substantially original. The original engine (no. 55514) has at some stage been replaced with a Riley 9hp engine of similar vintage. Pre-war competition history.												
1935	**Imp Sports**		6027683	R	125-175.000 USD	97.546	140.800	126.227	05-06-16	Greenwhich	35	Bon
Red with red interior; over the years the car has had numerous owners in the UK and was first restored in 1955 and again in 1964 when it was refinished in the present red livery. In the 1960s it was fitted with the present engine no.47252. Imported in 2010 into the USA.												
1935	**MPH Sports**		44T2415	R	600-750.000 USD	621.896	880.000	810.480	10-03-16	Amelia Island	174	Bon
Originally finished in red, the car was sold new to Switzerland and raced at some events in the 1930s. In 1963 it was acquired by its third owner, Bob Lutz, who imported it into the USA and retained it for nearly 50 years. Probably fitted since new with the present, slightly later 15/6 engine; fully restored in the early 1970s; further restoration works carried out recently by its current owner. **F640**												
1936	**12/4/Sprite recreation**		46A2596	R	80-120.000 GBP	79.900	121.664	109.231	05-09-15	Beaulieu	130	Bon
Recreation built between 1998 and 2000 on a shortened Adelphi chassis. Subsequently it was driven at several historic events.												

F639: 1933 Riley Nine Lynx Special tourer

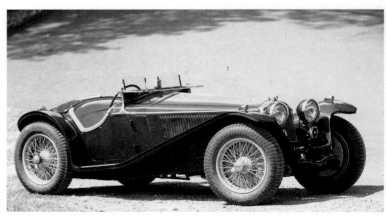

F640: 1935 Riley MPH Sports

Year	Model	(Bodybuilder)	Chassis no.	Steering	Estimate	Hammer price £	Hammer price $	Hammer price €	Sale Date	Place	Lot	Auc. H.
1934	12/4 Special		22T572	R	125-175.000 USD		NS		19-08-16	Carmel	75	Bon

Built as a Falcon saloon, probably before WWII the car was fitted with the present open two-seater body for competition use. Restored in the Netherlands in 2003, it is described as in good overall condition (see lot 149 Gooding & Company 22.1.11 $121,000).

Year	Model	(Bodybuilder)	Chassis no.	Steering	Estimate	£	$	€	Date	Place	Lot	Auc. H.
1936	Sprite two seater		S26S4920	R	200-300.000 EUR		NS		09-07-16	Le Mans	123	Art

The car was raced in period. In the late 1950s the engine was race-prepared and the body was fitted with the present wings previously fitted to a Delage and made by Figoni. In 1967 it was sold to the USA and in 1975 it was imported into France. Restoration completed in 1995. Since 2001 in the current ownership.

| 1949 | 2.5-litre RMC roadster | | 59SS5380 | R | 25-30.000 GBP | 42.550 | 64.357 | 58.808 | 10-12-15 | London | 350 | Bon |

Ivory with red interior; restored in 2004-05.

ROAMER (USA) (1916-1929)

| 1918 | C-6-54 touring | | 22960 | L | 90-110.000 USD | 46.180* | 66.000* | 60.436* | 29-01-16 | Phoenix | 270 | RMS |

White with red wheels and red leather interior; refreshed older restoration (see RM lots 660 9.10.09 $ 68,750 and 264 12.10.12 $ 93,500).

ROLLS-ROYCE (GB) (1904-)

| 1922 | Silver Ghost Salamanca town car (Willoughby) | 111BG | R | 100-120.000 GBP | 85.500 | 130.191 | 116.887 | 05-09-15 | Beaulieu | 127 | Bon |

Green with black wings and black leather interior to the front compartment and grey cloth to the rear; recently serviced. The car was used in the 1974 movie "The Great Gatsby", starring Robert Redford (see lot 329 Bonhams 7.12.14 $ 128,138).

| 1920 | Silver Ghost coupé chauffeur (Binder) | 60RE | R | 120-150.000 GBP | 123.200 | 188.028 | 168.698 | 07-09-15 | London | 116 | RMS |

Light blue with dark blue wings and black leather interior to the front compartment and beige cloth to the rear; built with Charpentier limousine body, in 1930 the car was fitted with the present body. Engine overhauled in 1991; chassis and body restored in 2003-04 (see lot 294 RM 29.10.08 $ 167,691).

| 1914 | Silver Ghost skiff (Schebera/Shapiro) | 54PB | R | 7.200-9.200.000 DKK | 736.288 | 1.117.513 | 1.002.398 | 26-09-15 | Ebeltoft | 20 | Bon |

Built with enclosed drive coachwork, the car was fitted with the present body between 1919 and 1923. Dark green bonnet and wings, body and side panels mahogany. Restored in the late 1950s; further works carried out in 2004 circa. From the Frederiksen Collection (see lots 36 Christie's 18.8.02 NS, and RM 175 16.1.09 NS and 268 28.10.09 $ 772,125).   F641

| 1910 | Silver Ghost "balloon car" | 1513 | R | 4.600-6.200.000 DKK | 424.781 | 644.719 | 578.306 | 26-09-15 | Ebeltoft | 25 | Bon |

Dark blue with beige leather interior; built with Barker landaulette body, the car was sold new to the USA. In 1969 it was acquired by Millard Newman who commissioned the present, new body replica of the "balloon car" coachwork built by H.J.Mulliner for Charles Stewart Rolls. From the Frederiksen Collection (see lots 129 Gooding 19.8.07 $ 1,430,000 and 145 RM 19.8.11 $ 484,000).

| 1912 | Silver Ghost cabriolet | 2145 | R | 4.200-5.600.000 DKK | 470.091 | 713.489 | 639.992 | 26-09-15 | Ebeltoft | 44 | Bon |

Dark green with leather and cloth interior; sold new in the UK and later exported to Australia, the car was restored in the 2000s and fitted with the present new body replica of the one originally fitted to it built in period by Barker. From the Frederiksen Collection (see lot 344 Bonhams 27.6.14 NS).   F642

| 1913 | Silver Ghost tourer (H.J.Mulliner) | 2517 | R | 4.200-5.600.000 DKK | 385.135 | 584.545 | 524.331 | 26-09-15 | Ebeltoft | 9 | Bon |

Red with black wings and tan interior; sold new to India to the Maharaja of Patiala, the car was rediscovered in 1970, reimported into the UK, fully restored and subsequently exported to the USA. Body repainted in recent years. From the Frederiksen Collection (see lots 122 Gooding 19.8.07 $ 1,870,000, 358 RM 14.8.10 NS, 145 Gooding 21.8.11 NS, and 239 RM 26.10.11 $ 491,968).

| 1914 | Silver Ghost landaulette (Barker) | 25EB | R | 500-700.000 USD | 378.032 | 577.500 | 513.166 | 08-10-15 | Hershey | 162 | RMS |

Cream with leather and cloth interior; the car remained with its first US owner until 1934 when it was acquired by the Ford Museum where it remained until 1971. In the years it was part, among others, of the Paul Moser, Richard Solove and John O'Quinn collections (see lots 85 Sotheby's 18.8.93 $ 134,500, 1082 Coys 21.6.03 $ 246,012, 132 Gooding 19.8.07 $ 1,155,000 and 221 RM 20.1.12 $ 550,000).

| 1914 | Silver Ghost landaulette (Barker) | 54AB | R | 750-950.000 AUD | 312.634 | 481.571 | 434.468 | 24-10-15 | Melbourne | 27 | TBr |

Dark green and black with leather interior to the front compartment and cloth to the rear; sold new in England, in 1972 the car was imported into Australia where in 1981 it received a cosmetic restoration. Exhibited at the York Motor Museum, the car was used over the years at several historic events.

| 1912 | Silver Ghost tourer | 2006 | R | 800-1.000.000 USD | | NS | | 28-01-16 | Scottsdale | 65 | Bon |

Red with brown interior; originally with landaulette body, the car was sold new to Australia where it remained until the mid-1960s when it was imported into the USA. Later it was sold to Denmark and and then later it was acquired by the current owner. In 1989 it was fitted with the present Roi des Belges style tourer body built by Wilkinsons.

| 1923 | Silver Ghost tourer | 23EM | R | 275-350.000 USD | 161.492* | 231.000* | 211.850* | 28-01-16 | Phoenix | 162 | RMS |

Dark green with tan leather interior; originally fitted with Million-Guiet cabriolet body coming from chassis JG6, the car was fully restored approximately in the 1970s and fitted with the present, new, Hooper style tourer body. Engine rebuilt in 2005 circa (see Coys lots 49 20.9.94 $ 105,289, 44 2.3.98 $ 99,087 and 53 10.5.99 $ 102,774).

| 1924 | Silver Ghost Pall Mall touring | 404MF | L | 225-275.000 USD | 151.587 | 214.500 | 197.555 | 10-03-16 | Amelia Island | 161 | Bon |

In good overall condition; recent mechanical works.

| 1911 | Silver Ghost tourer (Lawton/Goodman) | 1544 | R | 2.500-3.500.000 USD | | NS | | 12-03-16 | Amelia Island | 141 | RMS |

Cream with polished aluminium bonnet and red interior; sold new in the UK, in 1960 the car was acquired by Dr. Samuel Scher, who restored it in the UK, imported it into the USA and retained it until 1969. The body was repainted again in more recent years. For over two decades in the current ownership.

F641: 1914 Rolls-Royce Silver Ghost skiff (Schebera/Shapiro)

F642: 1912 Rolls-Royce Silver Ghost cabriolet

Year	Model	(Bodybuilder)	Chassis no.	Steering	Estimate	Hammer Price £	$	€	Date	Place	Lot	Auc. H.
1924	Silver Ghost cabriolet	(Barker)	135EM	R	170-230.000 GBP	264.700	383.471	339.981	20-03-16	Goodwood	53	Bon F643

Blue-grey with black wings; bought new by Lord Louis Mountbatten, the car had subsequently several owners in the UK and was discovered in France in 1966. Acquired in 1978 by the current owner, a friend of Lord Mountbatten, it was subsequently restored at the workshop of the National Motor Museum, Beaulieu. Little used following the restoration completed in the early 1980s, it has been recently recommissioned.

Year	Model	(Bodybuilder)	Chassis no.	Steering	Estimate	£	$	€	Date	Place	Lot	Auc. H.
1925	Silver Ghost Berwick sedan		S298PK	L	NA		NS		20-04-16	Duxford	26	H&H

Two-tone blue; restoration to be completed, interior to be reupholstered. The car is in running order (see lot 35 H&H 20.6.15 NS).

| 1923 | Silver Ghost cabriolet de ville | (Barker) | 35NK | R | NA | 100.800* | 142.934* | 127.431* | 20-04-16 | Duxford | 92 | H&H |

Green and black with green leather interior to the front compartment and beige cloth to the rear; restored in the USA in the 1980s, the car was reimported into the UK some years ago. Recently the interior were retrimmed and the mechanicals were overhauled (see lot S198 Mecum 17.8.13 $ 132,000).

| 1921 | Silver Ghost tourer | (Burnett & Reyner) | 94NE | R | 240-280.000 GBP | | NS | | 24-06-16 | Goodwood | 266 | Bon |

Red with black wings and black interior; built with Hooper cabriolet body, the car was fitted with the present body in the 1930s. Restored in 2000; engine rebuilt in 2013 (see lot 518 Bonhams/Brooks 26.7.01 $118,213).

| 1921 | Silver Ghost tourer | | 48CE | R | 340-390.000 GBP | | NS | | 02-07-16 | Woodstock | 163 | Coy |

Light grey with black leather interior; at unspecified date fitted with the present, new London-to-Edinburgh style tourer body.

| 1923 | Silver Ghost Pall Mall dual cowl phaeton | | 77JH | R | 325-375.000 USD | 252.120 | 330.000 | 291.357 | 20-08-16 | Pebble Beach | 18 | G&Co |

Black with grey leather interior; built with town car Pickwick body, the car was later fitted with the present body built by Rolls-Royce Custom Coachwork. Described as in very good overall condition (see lot 862 Bonhams 27.9.08 $315,000).

| 1908 | Silver Ghost tourer | | 60756 | R | 1.000-1.500.000 USD | 756.360 | 990.000 | 874.071 | 20-08-16 | Monterey | 236 | RMS F644 |

Red with brown leather interior; bodied by H.J. Mulliner when new, the car was discovered in 1958 as a bare chassis. In 1972 it was acquired by W.D.S. Lake who subsequently had it fully restored and fitted with the present new body built by Wilkinson. Since 1993 in the current ownership (see lot 1200 Sotheby's 6.12.93 $478,664).

| 1929 | 20hp shooting brake | (Alpe & Saunders) | GX03 | R | 70-90.000 USD | 43.204 | 66.000 | 58.648 | 08-10-15 | Hershey | 185 | RMS |

Black with wooden panels and maroon interior; originally built with Park Ward limousine body, the car was fitted in the 1950s with the present body built in the UK.

| 1926 | 20hp tourer | (Thrupp/Maberly) | GZK81 | R | 60-70.000 GBP | | NS | | 01-12-15 | London | 320 | Coy |

Burgundy with black wings and red leather interior; described as in good overall condition. Since 1994 in the current ownership.

| 1926 | 20hp tourer | (Thrupp/Maberly) | GZK81 | R | 55-65.000 GBP | | NS | | 08-03-16 | London | 121 | Coy |

See lot 320 Coys 1.12.15.

| 1923 | 20hp tourer | (Windovers) | 57S9 | R | 32-38.000 GBP | 48.300 | 69.972 | 62.037 | 20-03-16 | Goodwood | 11 | Bon |

Metallic grey; in working order. Body repainted probably in the 1950s. From the Kingsley Curtis Collection.

| 1927 | New Phantom tourer | | S168PM | L | 700-900.000 DKK | 62.301 | 94.559 | 84.818 | 26-09-15 | Ebeltoft | 13 | Bon |

Black with red interior; built with St. Martin Towncar body by Brewster, the car was later fitted with a Riviera Towncar body also by Brewster. At some point it was acquired by a Mr. McElroy who had it fitted with the present tourer body, designed by McElroy himself and probably built by Inskip. From the Frederiksen Collection.

| 1927 | New Phantom town car | (Brewster) | S178PM | L | 950-1.250.000 DKK | | NS | | 26-09-15 | Ebeltoft | 39 | Bon |

Black with leather and cloth interior; restored in Europe some years ago. From the Frederiksen Collection.

| 1931 | New Phantom Playboy roadster | (Brewster) | S186PR | L | 2.000-2.600.000 DKK | 226.550 | 343.850 | 308.430 | 26-09-15 | Ebeltoft | 4 | Bon F645 |

Pale yellow with red leather interior; fully restored in Europe between 2002 and 2006. From the Frederiksen Collection (see lot 313 Bonhams 17.8.02 $ 107,000).

| 1927 | New Phantom Pall Mall tourer | (Brewster) | S286RM | L | 125-150.000 EUR | | NS | | 26-09-15 | Frankfurt | 134 | Coy |

Black with black leather interior; restored many years ago (see lots 270 Bonhams 15.8.14 $ 192,500 and 139 Coys 18.4.15 NS).

| 1929 | New Phantom Ascot tourer | (Brewster) | S368LR | L | 300-350.000 USD | 198.017 | 302.500 | 268.802 | 08-10-15 | Hershey | 148 | RMS |

Brown and pewter with tan leather interior; several works carried out over the last 10 years. Engine recently rebuilt (see lots 615 Bonhams 13.8.10 $ 403,000 and 143 RM 26.7.14 NS).

| 1927 | New Phantom Pall Mall tourer | | S286RM | L | 125-150.000 EUR | 104.741 P | 150.117 P | 137.545 P | 16-01-16 | Maastricht | 431 | Coy |

See lot 134 Coys 26.9.15.

| 1927 | New Phantom Piccadilly roadster | | S285RM | L | 225-300.000 USD | | NS | | 28-01-16 | Scottsdale | 51 | Bon |

Maroon and black with black interior; restored at unspecified date, the car is described as in good overall condition (see lot 118 RM 8.9.14 NS).

| 1928 | New Phantom Newmarket convertible sedan | (Brewster) | S393KP | L | 150-200.000 USD | 69.211* | 99.000* | 90.793* | 28-01-16 | Phoenix | 170 | RMS |

Black with polished aluminium bonnet and chestnut leather interior; described as in good driving order (see lots 439 Bonhams 19.8.11 NS and 179 RM 10.3.12 NS).

| 1929 | New Phantom roadster | | 118KR | R | 70-100.000 EUR | 56.507 | 83.765 | 74.750 | 04-02-16 | Paris | 423 | Bon |

Built with Grose coupé body, the car was imported into Switzerland in 1963, restored and fitted with the present new body. In the same family ownership since 1963 and little used then.

| 1930 | New Phantom York roadster | | S111FR | L | 225-275.000 USD | 248.758 | 352.000 | 324.192 | 10-03-16 | Amelia Island | 193 | Bon |

Two-tone green; restored and fitted at unspecified date with the present, new body in the York roadster style.

| 1930 | Phantom II rolling chassis | | 141XJ | R | 10-15.000 GBP | 23.000* | 35.022* | 31.443* | 05-09-15 | Beaulieu | 169 | Bon |

Restoration project; since 1966 in the current ownership.

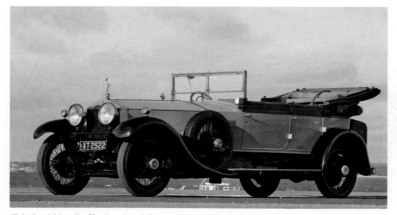

F643: 1924 Rolls-Royce Silver Ghost cabriolet (Barker)

F644: 1908 Rolls-Royce Silver Ghost tourer

Year	Model	(Bodybuilder)	Chassis no.	Steering	Estimate	Hammer price £	Hammer price $	Hammer price €	Date	Place	Lot	Auc. H.

F645: 1931 Rolls-Royce New Phantom Playboy roadster (Brewster)

F646: 1933 Rolls-Royce Phantom II Continental cabriolet (Park Ward)

Year	Model	(Bodybuilder)	Chassis no.	Steering	Estimate	£	$	€	Date	Place	Lot	Auc. H.
1933	Phantom II Continental cabriolet	(Park Ward)	55MW	R	250-300.000 GBP	270.300	416.884	369.987	12-09-15	Goodwood	361	Bon F646

Grey and black with grey interior; restored in the USA in 1977, the car was reimported into the UK about 15 years ago and subsequently it received further restoration works. From the late James Crickmay's collection.

| 1933 | Phantom II Continental sedanca coupé | (Gurney Nutting) | 64PY | R | 5.600-7.200.000 DKK | 486.590 | 738.530 | 662.454 | 26-09-15 | Ebeltoft | 27 | Bon F647 |

Dark blue and black; sold new in the UK, the car was exported to the USA probably in the 1940s. Reimported into Europe in 1996 it received a cosmetic restoration in the late 1990s and further works in 2012. It is believed the car was driven in the late 1930s by the then owner, Mrs Peta Fisher, to race the famous Le Train Bleu from Calais to Antibes. From the Frederiksen Collection.

| 1931 | Phantom II tourer | (Barker) | 115GY | R | 2.000-2.600.000 DKK | | NS | | 26-09-15 | Ebeltoft | 46 | Bon |

Black with burgundy leather interior; an older restoration. From the Frederiksen Collection (see lot 762 Coys 7.12.10 NS).

| 1935 | Phantom II limousine de ville | (Barker) | 147TA | R | 45-65.000 USD | 13.044* | 19.800* | 17.622* | 05-10-15 | Philadelphia | 210 | Bon |

Black and dark blue; sold new in Scotland, the car was imported into the USA in 1966. Unused from time.

| 1929 | Phantom II tourer | (Barker) | 50XJ | R | 550-650.000 USD | 284.424 | 434.500 | 386.097 | 08-10-15 | Hershey | 163 | RMS |

Dark blue; one-off sold new to India and imported into the USA in 1967. Later the car was dismantled for a long restoration completed in the mid-1990s. In more recent years the body was repainted again and the interior were retrimmed. Recently serviced (see lots 130 Gooding 15.8.10 $ 770,000 and 162 RM 26.7.14 NS).

| 1936 | Phantom II saloon | | GXM37 | R | NA | | NS | | 09-10-15 | Chicago | S136 | Mec |

Grey/maroon with grey/maroon interior; since 1968 in the current ownership. Restored many years ago.

| 1930 | Phantom II limousine | (Harrison) | 167XJ | R | 45-50.000 GBP | 51.750 | 78.272 | 71.524 | 10-12-15 | London | 337 | Bon |

Cream and brown with leather interior to the front compartment and cloth to the rear; described as in very good driving order. Engine rebuilt in the 2000s (see lots Bonhams 721 30.6.01 $ 32,251 and 319 30.4.12 $ 72,899, and H&H 29 20.6.15 NS).

| 1935 | Phantom II Continental saloon | (Barker) | 36UK | R | 70-90.000 GBP | 74.300 | 112.379 | 102.690 | 10-12-15 | London | 358 | Bon F648 |

Black and grey with red interior; reimported from the USA in 2012 and subsequently restored.

| 1932 | Phantom II Continental saloon | (Hooper) | 114MS | R | 200-275.000 USD | | NS | | 28-01-16 | Phoenix | 161 | RMS |

Blue and grey with grey leather interior; described as in good driving condition (see lot 145 Gooding 22.1.11 $ 192,500).

| 1934 | Phantom II cabriolet | (Kellner) | 164PY | R | NA | | NS | | 29-01-16 | Scottsdale | 1398 | B/J |

Two-tone brown with red interior; sold new to France, in the 1950s the car was imported into the USA where it was restored at unspecified date.

| 1934 | Phantom II Continental sedanca coupé | (Gurney Nutting) | 117RY | R | 800-1.000.000 USD | | NS | | 29-01-16 | Scottsdale | 39 | G&Co |

Taupe with red leather interior; sold new in the UK, the car was exported to the USA in 1967 and reimported in the late 1980s in the UK where it was restored. Imported again in the USA in 2010, it received subsequently a mechanical refreshening (see lots 423 Coys 4.12.08 NS and 44 Gooding 14.8.10 $ 528,000).

| 1930 | Phantom II two-seater sports | (Barker) | 179XJ | R | 2.500-3.500.000 USD | | NS | | 29-01-16 | Phoenix | 248 | RMS |

Streamlined body finished in scarlet with tan leather interior; acquired in the early 1990s by the current owner and subsequently restored. Believed to have been originally delivered to Maharaja Gulab Singh of Rewa. From 1932 to 1958 it remained in the same ownership in the UK. In 1960 it was imported into the USA where over the years it was also part of the collections of Vojta F. Mashek, Samuel Scher and Richard and Linda Kughn.

| 1935 | Phantom II cabriolet | | 37TA | R | 450-550.000 USD | | NS | | 10-03-16 | Amelia Island | 190 | Bon |

Cream with red interior; built with Windovers limousine body, the car received at unspecified date the present body already fitted to the car when it was in 1954 in the ownership of Vernon D. Jarvis in the USA.

| 1934 | Phantom II limousine | (Barker) | 178SK | R | 45-55.000 GBP | | NS | | 12-03-16 | Brooklands | 239 | His |

Ivory and tan with maroon leather interior; restored in 2002 (see lots Sotheby's 431 6.3.95 $ 45,842, Brooks 6.11.97 NS and 877 4.12.97 NS, and Coys 336 10.3.15 $ 63,871).

F647: 1933 Rolls-Royce Phantom II Continental sedanca coupé (Gurney Nutting)

F648: 1935 Rolls-Royce Phantom II Continental saloon (Barker)

Year	Model	(Bodybuilder)	Chassis no.	Steering	Estimate	Hammer Price £	Hammer Price $	Hammer Price €	Date	Place	Lot	Auc. H.
1934	Phantom II Continental sedanca cabriolet	(H.J.Mulliner)	120SK	R	450-650.000 USD	384.780	550.000	495.935	12-03-16	Amelia Island	170	RMS

Grey and black; sold new in the UK, in the late 1930s the car was imported into France where the wings were modernized probably by Chapron. Imported into the USA it has had two long-term owners from 1957 to 2002. Subsequently it was restored and recently refreshed (see lots 42 Christie's 18.8.02 NS, 255 RM 10.10.08 NS, 51 Worldwide Group 2.5.09 NS, and 258 RM 22.1.10 $ 357,500).

Year	Model	(Bodybuilder)	Chassis no.	Steering	Estimate	£	$	€	Date	Place	Lot	Auc. H.
1929	Phantom II sedanca de ville	(Hooper)	189XJ	R	100-140.000 EUR		NS		14-05-16	Monaco	131	RMS

Two-tone grey with leather interior to the front compartment and cloth to the rear; displayed at the 1929 Milan Motor Show, the car was sold new in Italy. An older restoration, it was refinished some years ago in the present livery. Since 1961 in the Quattroruote Collection.

| 1933 | Phantom II cabriolet | (Gurney Nutting) | 124MY | R | 1.100-1.600.000 USD | | WD | | 11-06-16 | Hershey | 134 | TFA |

Black with teal interior; the car was sold new in the UK and imported into the USA at unspecified date after WWII. From the JWR Collection.

| 1929 | Phantom II cabriolet de ville | (Barker) | 121XJ | R | 100-140.000 GBP | 107.900 | 147.866 | 133.613 | 24-06-16 | Goodwood | 233 | Bon |

Black with red leather interior; restored between 2000 and 2002. Built with Thrupp & Maberly limousine body, at unspecified date the car was fitted with the present body originally fitted to the New Phantom chassis 31HC.

| 1934 | Phantom II limousine | (J.Young) | 141RY | R | 80-100.000 GBP | | NS | | 10-07-16 | Chateau Impney | 44 | H&H |

Green and black with black leather interior to the front compartment and light brown cloth to the rear; restored many years ago, the car is described as in good overall condition.

| 1934 | Phantom II Continental sedanca coupé | (Gurney Nutting) | 117RY | R | 600-800.000 USD | 462.220 | 605.000 | 534.155 | 19-08-16 | Carmel | 87 | Bon |

See lot 39 Gooding & Company 29.1.16.

| 1933 | Phantom II Continental cabriolet | (Barker) | 186MY | R | 800-1.100.000 USD | | NS | | 20-08-16 | Pebble Beach | 58 | G&Co |

Garnet with black wings and tan leather interior; in very good overall condition.

| 1932 | Phantom II Continental Berline | (Figoni/Falaschi) | 2MS | R | 1.800-2.200.000 USD | 1.344.640 | 1.760.000 | 1.553.904 | 21-08-16 | Pebble Beach | 125 | G&Co |

Built with Windovers saloon body, the car was sold new to the Prince of Nepal, living in exile in England, who later had it rebodied by Figoni & Falaschi. In 1955 it was imported into the USA and in 1985 it was bought by Jeffrey Davis, living in India, who had it restored. In 2010 it was purchased by the current owner and finished in the present dark blue livery. **F649**

| 1932 | 20/25hp Sportsman's coupé | (Arnold) | GFT68 | R | 20-30.000 GBP | 18.400 | 28.018 | 25.155 | 05-09-15 | Beaulieu | 121 | Bon |

Red with black roof and wings; since 1978 in the current ownership. In working order, it is in need of refurbishment.

| 1935 | 20/25hp tourer | (Corsica) | GHF10 | R | 35-38.000 GBP | 32.200 | 49.031 | 44.021 | 05-09-15 | Beaulieu | 158 | Bon |

Dark green with black wings and dark green leather interior; recommissioned during the current ownership. Built with saloon body, the car was fitted with the present, pre-war body in the 1960s.

| 1934 | 20/25hp sedanca coupé | (Gurney Nutting) | GYD26 | R | 1.000-1.300.000 DKK | 135.930 | 206.310 | 185.058 | 26-09-15 | Ebeltoft | 45 | Bon |

Two-tone green with medium green leather interior; restored in 1998. From the Frederiksen Collection (see lot 354 Coys 7.12.11 NS).

| 1934 | 20/25hp saloon | | GED26 | R | NA | | NS | | 14-10-15 | Duxford | 70 | H&H |

Blue and black with blue interior; in working order, the car requires several restoration works.

| 1934 | 20/25hp cabriolet | | GWE40 | R | 42-45.000 GBP | | NS | | 10-12-15 | London | 342 | Bon |

White and grey with red interior; since 1993 in the current ownership. Re-bodied in the 1990s; engine rebuilt 5,000 miles ago.

| 1933 | 20/25hp sedanca coupé | (Freestone/Webb) | GBA64 | R | 100-130.000 GBP | 91.100 | 137.789 | 125.909 | 10-12-15 | London | 357 | Bon |

Black with burgundy interior; restored many years ago (see lots Coys 67 5.4.02 $ 85,892, 129 3.10.02 NS and 1032 21.6.03 NS, and Bonhams 701 3.12.07 $ 184,692).

| 1934 | 20/25hp special touring saloon | (Park Ward) | GRC28 | R | 28-34.000 GBP | | NS | | 12-03-16 | Brooklands | 238 | His |

Black with red leather interior; some works to the mechanicals and body carried out by the current owner (see lots 20 H&H 21.7.10 NS and 141 Coys 2.10.10 $ 59,365).

| 1936 | 20/25hp saloon | (Hooper) | GBK31 | R | 30-40.000 EUR | 29.149 | 42.229 | 37.440 | 20-03-16 | Fontainebleau | 309 | Ose |

Black and light yellow with leather interior to the front compartment and cloth to the rear; in good working order (see lots 22 Poulain 14.12.98 $ 28,604 and 1 Artcurial 16.6.03 NS).

| 1932 | 20/25hp roadster | | GAU66 | R | 35-50.000 EUR | 39.694* | 57.194* | 50.400* | 14-05-16 | Monaco | 129 | RMS **F650** |

Black and yellow with tan interior; built with Hooper limousine body, the car was fitted with the present body prior to 1970. Since then in the Quattroruote Collection.

| 1935 | 20/25hp coupé | (Barker) | GYH35 | R | 60-80.000 USD | 49.535 | 71.500 | 64.100 | 05-06-16 | Greenwhich | 36 | Bon |

Black and light brown with beige interior; sold new in the UK, the car was imported into the USA in the 1960s. Restored many years ago, it is in good driving order.

| 1936 | 20/25hp saloon | (Barker) | GTK11 | R | NA | 31.300* | 42.900* | 38.764* | 24-06-16 | Uncasville | 753 | B/J |

Silver with blue and grey interior; restored about six years ago.

| 1934 | 20/25hp saloon | (Park Ward) | GFE17 | R | 20-25.000 GBP | 20.160 | 26.545 | 23.936 | 28-07-16 | Donington Park | 67 | H&H |

Restored in the past.

| 1936 | 25/30hp sedanca de ville | (Park Ward) | GLU2 | R | 23-28.000 GBP | 26.880 | 38.417 | 34.640 | 12-03-16 | Brooklands | 201 | His |

Grey with grey interior; in sound mechanical order, the car requires some attention to the body. Entered by the factory in the 1936 JCC Rally in the USA and Canada and subsequently sold.

| 1935 | 25/30hp saloon | (Windovers) | GHL20 | R | 30-35.000 GBP | | NS | | 28-07-16 | Donington Park | 94 | H&H |

Cream and brown; since 1984 in the current ownership.

F649: 1932 Rolls-Royce Phantom II Continental Berline (Figoni/Falaschi)

F650: 1932 Rolls-Royce 20/25hp roadster

Year	Model (Bodybuilder)	Chassis no.	Steering	Estimate	Hammer price £	$	€	Date	Place	Lot	Auc. H.

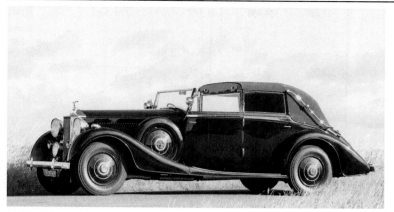

F651: 1937 Rolls-Royce Phantom III 4-door cabriolet (Vanden Plas)

F652: 1947 Rolls-Royce Silver Wraith 2-door saloon (Freestone/Webb)

Year	Model (Bodybuilder)	Chassis no.	Steering	Estimate	£	$	€	Date	Place	Lot	Auc. H.
1937	**Phantom III 4-door cabriolet (Vanden Plas)**	3BT185	R	4.000-5.200.000 DKK	407.790	618.930	555.174	26-09-15	Ebeltoft	34	Bon F651

Dark blue with light grey interior; full restoration completed in 2002. The car was acquired new by Austrian industrialist Fritz Mendl at the time married with actress Hedy Lamarr. Later it was exported to South America and in the 1980s it was imported into the USA. From the Frederiksen Collection (see lot 76 Gooding 20.8.06 $ 253,000).

1936	**Phantom III saloon (H.J.Mulliner)**	3AZ48	R	50-60.000 USD	37.683	57.200	50.908	05-10-15	Philadelphia	254	Bon

Black and yellow; imported into the USA in 1981. Body repainted decades ago. Stored for the past decade.

1937	**Phantom III touring limousine (Inskip)**	3AX85	R	100-130.000 USD	46.116	70.000	62.300	05-10-15	Philadelphia	260	Bon

One-off ordered by Mrs. Florence Adele Vanderbilt Twombly. In the mid-1950s it was bought by a collector who retained it for the next five decades. In 2010 it was acquired by the current owner. Described as in good, largely original condition; 18,800 miles on the odometer.

1937	**Phantom III limousine (Barker)**	3BU110	R	60-70.000 EUR		NS		16-01-16	Maastricht	418	Coy

Black and red; described as in good condition.

1936	**Phantom III sedanca de ville (Windovers)**	3AZ40	R	75-100.000 USD	49.986*	71.500*	65.573*	28-01-16	Scottsdale	3	Bon

Yellow and black with black leather interior; single ownership for over 50 years. Restored in the 1970s. The car was exhibited at the 1935 Scottish Motor Show presumably at the Windovers stand.

1954	**Silver Wraith saloon (J.Young)**	BLW65	R	40-50.000 GBP	29.900	45.529	40.876	05-09-15	Beaulieu	154	Bon

Cream with cream leather interior; restored between 2013 and 2015.

1952	**Silver Wraith saloon (Vincents)**	WVH3	R	40-50.000 USD	28.987	44.000	39.160	05-10-15	Philadelphia	255	Bon

Grey with original red leather interior; the car remained in Vincents' ownership until 1960. Imported into the USA in 1975. In good running order.

1947	**Silver Wraith 2-door saloon (Freestone/Webb)**	WVA74	R	80-120.000 EUR	59.927	94.896	83.440	01-11-15	Paris	131	Art F652

Black and sand with light brown leather interior; mechanicals overhauled in the 1990s, body repainted many years ago. Little used, the car requires servicing prior to use (see lot 67 Bonhams 11.10.10 NS).

1958	**Silver Wraith Empress limousine (Hooper)**	HLW6	R	50-70.000 GBP	49.333	76.086	67.527	12-09-15	Goodwood	357	Bon

Black and grey with red interior; restored in the late 1980s and subsequently always well maintained. From the late James Crickmay's collection.

1949	**Silver Wraith limousine (Hooper)**	WDC24	R	NQ	32.625*	47.528*	42.364*	20-05-16	Silverstone	324	SiC

Described as in highly original, never fully restored condition. Formerly owned by actress Gloria Swanson.

1954	**Silver Wraith limousine (J.Young)**	DLW125	R	100-130.000 USD	84.040*	110.000*	97.119*	21-08-16	Pebble Beach	114	G&Co

Black with leather interior to the front compartment and cloth to the rear; restored in the 1990s.

1947	**Silver Wraith cabriolet (Inskip)**	WYA26	R	1.250-2.000.000 USD		NS		20-08-16	Pebble Beach	65	G&Co

Violet with tan leather interior; the car was ordered by Thomas Franklyn Manville Jr., and was exhibited, finished in black with red interior, at the 1949 New York International Motor Show prior to be delivered to its owner. First restored in the 1960s, it received further restoration works in more recent years by its current owner.

1953	**Silver Wraith sedanca de ville (Hooper)**	ALW47	R	90-120.000 GBP		NS		12-09-15	Goodwood	358	Bon

Black and grey with leather interior to the front compartment and cloth to the rear; recently serviced. From the late James Crickmay's collection.

1948	**Silver Wraith sedanca de ville (H.J.Mulliner)**	WZB28	R	150-200.000 USD	89.650*	137.500*	121.028*	09-10-15	Hershey	246	RMS F653

Black with leather and cloth interior; restored in the 1990s. Described as in very good driving order (see lots 636 Bonhams 3.12.07 $ 93,894 and 154 RM 15.8.14 $ 110,000).

1954	**Silver Dawn saloon**	SPG85	R	30-40.000 GBP	41.400	63.851	56.668	12-09-15	Goodwood	356	Bon F654

Black and grey with grey interior; several services carried out in the past 12 years. From the late James Crickmay's collection.

F653: 1948 Rolls-Royce Silver Wraith sedanca de ville (H.J.Mulliner)

F654: 1954 Rolls-Royce Silver Dawn saloon

CLASSIC CAR AUCTION 2015-2016 YEARBOOK

Year	Model	(Bodybuilder)	Chassis no.	Steering	Estimate	Hammer price £	Hammer price $	Hammer price €	Date	Place	Lot	Auc. H.
1956	**Silver Cloud saloon**		SBC108	R	NA	22.400	34.453	30.195	14-10-15	Duxford	91	H&H
Two-tone green with stone interior; several mechanical works carried out in recent times.												
1957	**Silver Cloud (cabriolet/conversion)**		SSD172	L	140-180.000 EUR	108.509*	164.264*	151.200*	07-11-15	Lyon	261	Agu
Red with magnolia interior; conversion to left-hand drive cabriolet carried out at unspecified date. Cosmetically restored in 2005 (see lot 216 Bonhams 2.2.12 NS).												
1958	**Silver Cloud saloon**		SGE180	R	NA	18.563	26.280	23.957	06-03-16	Birmingham	305	SiC
Grey with green leather interior; recently serviced.												
1959	**Silver Cloud saloon lwb**	(J.Young)	CLC14	R	225-275.000 USD		NS		10-03-16	Amelia Island	173	Bon
Burgundy with magnolia interior; restored sone decades ago. Displayed at the 1959 Geneva Motor Show.												
1956	**Silver Cloud saloon**		SCC97	R	60-70.000 EUR	48.419	69.202	62.400	12-03-16	Lyon	338	Agu
Silver and brown with grey interior; acquired in 1995 by the current owner and subsequently restored in France by Lecoq.												
1959	**Silver Cloud saloon**		LSKG39	L	90-120.000 USD	63.489*	90.750*	81.829*	12-03-16	Amelia Island	114	RMS
Silver and claret; acquired in 1985 by the present, third owner and later restored.												
1958	**Silver Cloud saloon**		SHF149	R	70-90.000 GBP		NS		24-06-16	Goodwood	255	Bon
Light grey and dark green; restored between 2011 and 2015. Two owners; just over 28,000 miles covered since new; original interior.												
1959	**Silver Cloud (cabriolet/conversion)**		LSNH144	L	110-125.000 GBP	137.760	180.300	159.182	20-08-16	Brooklands	294	His
Metallic grey with maroon leather interior; conversion carried out in the UK. Described as in very good driving order.												
1959	**Silver Cloud cabriolet**	(H.J.Mulliner)	SNH14	R	175-200.000 GBP	218.400	333.322	299.055	07-09-15	London	160	RMS
White with red leather interior; acquired in 1975 by the current, second owner. Body repainted many years ago.												
1959	**Silver Cloud two-door saloon**	(J.Young)	LSHF111	L	275-350.000 USD		NS		29-01-16	Scottsdale	21	G&Co
Dark blue with red leather interior; one of two examples built. Body recently repainted; in concours condition.												
1961	**Silver Cloud II (cabriolet/conversion)**		SZD17S	L	130-150.000 EUR		NS		26-09-15	Frankfurt	112	Coy
Black with tan interior; between 2006 and 2008 fully restored and converted to cabriolet form.												
1962	**Silver Cloud II saloon lwb**		LLCA49	L	40-60.000 USD	30.603*	46.750*	41.542*	08-10-15	Hershey	186	RMS
Sand and sable with biscuit leather interior; in good overall condition. Two owners.												
1960	**Silver Cloud II saloon**		LSVB119	L	40-50.000 EUR		NS		08-11-15	Lyon	219	Ose
Grey and black with grey interior; in good overall condition.												
1960	**Silver Cloud II lwb saloon**	(Park Ward)	LCB4	R	50-70.000 EUR		NS		04-02-16	Paris	410	Bon
Silver and black with burgundy leather interior; sold new to Nigeria, the car was later reimported into Europe. Recently restored.												
1961	**Silver Cloud II saloon lwb**		LLCB80	L	40-60.000 USD	35.056	50.600	45.363	05-06-16	Greenwhich	6	Bon F655
Black with beige leather interior; since new in the same family ownership. Body repaired and repainted in the 2000s.												
1961	**Silver Cloud II saloon**		LSXC57	L	NA	32.836	47.300	41.842	11-06-16	Newport Beach	6049	R&S
Regal red with cream interior; in the same family ownership since new. Some works to the paintworl and interior carried out as needed over the years.												
1961	**Silver Cloud II saloon**		SAE55	R	22-28.000 GBP		NS		20-08-16	Brooklands	268	His
Two-tone grey with red leather interior; restored.												
1961	**Silver Cloud II cabriolet**	(Mulliner,Park Ward)	SXC123	R	380-420.000 GBP		NS		04-09-15	Woodstock	230	SiC
Sand with beige leather interior; restored.												
1960	**Silver Cloud II cabriolet**	(H.J.Mulliner)	SVB99	R	150-200.000 GBP	145.600	222.215	199.370	07-09-15	London	173	RMS
Tudor grey with red interior; the car remained in the same family ownership from new to 2003 circa and was restored in the late 1990s.												
1962	**Silver Cloud II cabriolet**	(Mulliner,Park Ward)	LSAE639	L	400-475.000 USD	269.154	385.000	353.084	28-01-16	Phoenix	146	RMS
Sand with magnolia leather interior; restored at unspecified date. Just over 42,000 miles on the odometer (see lot 135 RM/Sotheby's 23.5.15 $ 418,650).												
1962	**Silver Cloud II cabriolet**	(Mulliner,Park Ward)	LSAE281	L	340-370.000 GBP		NS		12-03-16	Brooklands	240	His
Gunmetal grey with beige interior; sold new to the USA, the car remained in the same family ownership from 1963 to 1997 when it was reimported into the UK and restored. 59,000 miles on the odometer.												
1962	**Silver Cloud II cabriolet**	(Mulliner,Park Ward)	LSAE281	L	330-360.000 GBP		NS		16-04-16	Ascot	128	Coy
See lot 240 Historics 12.3.16.												
1962	**Silver Cloud II cabriolet**	(Mulliner,Park Ward)	LSAE281	L	375-425.000 EUR	333.146	480.020	423.000	14-05-16	Monaco	156	Coy
See lot 128 Coys 16.4.16.												
1961	**Silver Cloud II cabriolet**	(Mulliner,Park Ward)	LSXC173	L	300-400.000 USD	183.592	265.000	237.573	05-06-16	Greenwhich	93	Bon
Dark blue with beige leather interior; sold new to the USA, the car was restored in the 1990s. In more recent years the body was repainted again to its original colour. Currently fitted with a rebuilt Silver Cloud III engine.												

F655: 1961 Rolls-Royce Silver Cloud II saloon lwb

F656: 1964 Rolls-Royce Silver Cloud III cabriolet (Mulliner,Park Ward)

Year	Model (Bodybuilder)	Chassis No.	Steering	Estimate	Hammer Price £	$	€	Date	Place	Lot	Auc. H.
1964	**Silver Cloud III (cabriolet/conversion)**	SGT89	R	240-260.000 GBP		NS		04-09-15	Woodstock	250	SiC
	Black with red leather interior; conversion carried out by Byrnes Motor Trust Restorations. In excellent overall condition.										
1965	**Silver Cloud III saloon**	LSJR267	L	NA	31.896*	48.400*	43.405*	26-09-15	Las Vegas	651	B/J
	Silver and black with black interior.										
1965	**Silver Cloud III saloon**	LSGT449	L	50-60.000 EUR		NS		04-02-16	Paris	329	Bon
	Blue with light grey interior; sold new to the USA, the car was reimported into Europe in 1998. The brakes require attention.										
1965	**Silver Cloud III saloon**	SKP233	R	28-32.000 GBP	30.975	44.012	39.911	08-03-16	London	144	Coy
	Green and grey; 87,000 miles recorded (see lot 226 Coys 11.10.14).										
1964	**Silver Cloud III saloon**	LSEV175	L	100-120.000 USD	79.838*	104.500*	92.263*	20-08-16	Pebble Beach	76	G&Co
	Black with black interior; in good overal condition.										
1966	**Silver Cloud III cabriolet (Mulliner,Park Ward)**	CSC81C	R	300-360.000 GBP		NS		28-11-15	Weybridge	281	His
	Dark blue with light grey leather interior; sold new to Malaysia, the car was reimported into the UK 10 years ago circa and subsequently fully restored.										
1964	**Silver Cloud III cabriolet (Mulliner,Park Ward)**	LSEV169	L	380-540.000 EUR	321.657	476.815	425.500	04-02-16	Paris	328	Bon F656
	The car remained with its first owner, Abraham van Leeuwen Prince de Lignac, until 2001; it passed subsequently to a charitable foundation founded by the Prince himself from which it was bought by the Louwman Museum. In 2008 it was acquired by the present, second private owner and fully restored between 2011 and 2014 and finished in the present black and regal red livery.										
1963	**Silver Cloud III cabriolet (Mulliner,Park Ward)**	SCX775	R	135-150.000 GBP	120.000	159.384	143.136	02-07-16	Woodstock	155	Coy
	Blue with grey leather interior; in the same ownership from 1983 to 2014. Recently restored.										
1963	**Silver Cloud III cabriolet (Mulliner,Park Ward)**	LSCX789	L	600-700.000 USD		NS		20-08-16	Pebble Beach	16	G&Co
	Shell grey with black leather interior; in single ownership from 1965 to 2005, the car received subsequently some restoration works in Belgium.										
1965	**Silver Cloud III coupé (Mulliner,Park Ward)**	LSGT641C	L	60-70.000 GBP		NS		08-03-16	London	138	Coy
	Dark mahogany with magnolia interior; recently discovered after 20 years in storage. Engine and transmission described as in good condition.										
1962	**Phantom V (Mulliner,Park Ward)**	5LCG79	L	NA		NS		26-09-15	Las Vegas	695	B/J
	Two-tone blue with grey leather interior to the front compartment and beige cloth to the rear; 36,450 miles.										
1962	**Phantom V (Mulliner,Park Ward)**	5LCG79	L	NA	57.725*	82.500*	75.545*	29-01-16	Scottsdale	1442	B/J
	See lot 695 Barrett-Jackson 26.9.15.										
1966	**Phantom V (J.Young)**	5LVF41	L	140-180.000 USD	99.503*	140.800*	129.677*	10-03-16	Amelia Island	166	Bon F657
	Dark burgundy with tan leather interior; cosmetically restored at unspecified date (see lot 151 Gooding 22.1.11 $ 154,000).										
1962	**Phantom V (Mulliner,Park Ward)**	5LBX4	L	125-175.000 USD	73.108*	104.500*	94.228*	12-03-16	Amelia Island	136	RMS
	Two-tone grey; in good overall condition. Less than 20,000 miles covered.										
1974	**Silver Shadow**	SRH19657	R	17-20.000 GBP		NS		09-12-15	Chateau Impney	85	H&H
	Metallic blue with magnolia interior; three owners since new.										
1976	**Silver Shadow**	SRH26377	R	8-12.000 EUR	12.105	17.300	15.600	12-03-16	Lyon	347	Agu
	Black with beige interior; in good overall condition. Recently serviced.										
1970	**Silver Shadow**	SRH8654	R	10-12.000 GBP	8.400	12.227	10.840	18-05-16	Donington Park	58	H&H
	Gold with beige interior; in good original condition. 78,600 miles covered.										
1979	**Silver Shadow II**	SRK36530	L	15-20.000 EUR	14.554	23.046	20.264	01-11-15	Paris	177	Art
	Plum and grey with burgundy leather interior; in good overall condition.										
1980	**Silver Shadow II**	SLR39777	L	20-30.000 EUR	16.793	25.422	23.400	08-11-15	Lyon	218	Ose
	Burgundy with biscuit interior; 43,000 miles on the odometer.										
1980	**Silver Shadow II**	SRH0040943	R	16-20.000 GBP		NS		18-05-16	Donington Park	84	H&H
	Gold with magnolia interior; 12,000 kms on the odometer. Described as in very good overall condition. Reimported into the UK in 2015.										
1968	**Silver Shadow cabriolet (Mulliner,Park Ward)**	CRH5023	R	30-40.000 GBP	28.175	42.902	38.518	05-09-15	Beaulieu	142	Bon F658
	Red with beige leather interior; described as in good overall condition.										
1970	**Silver Shadow 2-door (Mulliner,Park Ward)**	CRH8086	R	14-16.000 GBP	13.440	20.278	18.535	09-12-15	Chateau Impney	74	H&H
	Silver with dark blue Everflex roof and blue interior; some mechanical works carried out in 2014 (see lots 734 Brooks 5.6.99 NS, 334 Coys 20.10.07 $ 16,874 and 35 H&H 4.12.13 $ 19,258).										
1968	**Silver Shadow 2-door (Mulliner,Park Ward)**	CHR3931	R	20-30.000 GBP	16.387	24.785	22.648	10-12-15	London	311	Bon
	Burgundy with black vinyl roof and beige leather interior; restored in 2010 in France.										
1967	**Silver Shadow 2-door (Mulliner,Park Ward)**	CRH3399	R	40-50.000 GBP	40.320	57.625	51.960	12-03-16	Brooklands	141	His
	Regal red with grey leather interior; in very good overall condition. Believed a pre-production example used by the factory to test various mechanical components.										

F657: 1966 Rolls-Royce Phantom V (J.Young)

F658: 1968 Rolls-Royce Silver Shadow cabriolet (Mulliner,Park Ward)

Year	Model (Bodybuilder)	Chassis No.	Steering	Estimate	Hammer Price £	Hammer Price $	Hammer Price €	Date	Place	Lot	Auc. H.
1973	**Phantom VI cabriolet (Frua)**	PRX4705	L	2.000-2.600.000 DKK	**362.480**	**550.160**	**493.488**	26-09-15	Ebeltoft	24	Bon F659
	Light metallic green with white leather interior; one-off ordered by Consul Simon van Kempen who retained it until 1997. Described as in very good overall condition. From the Frederiksen Collection (see lot 121 Christie's 22.5.97 NS).										
1970	**Phantom VI (Mulliner,Park Ward)**	PRH4597	R	40-50.000 GBP	**54.050**	**81.751**	**74.703**	10-12-15	London	346	Bon
	The car was acquired new by Lady Beaverbrook who in 1999 donated it to the National Motor Museum Trust. In museum storage for 16 years, it requires recommissioning prior to use.										
1972	**Phantom VI (Mulliner,Park Ward)**	PRH4661	R	55-65.000 GBP	**80.640**	**116.146**	**102.751**	11-06-16	Brooklands	266	His
	Black with tan leather interior to the front compartment and beige cloth to the rear; in very good overall condition. 46,400 miles covered (see lot 30 Coys 24.1.95 $ 87,346).										
1971	**Phantom VI (Mulliner,Park Ward)**	PRH4609	R	130-150.000 USD		NS		25-06-16	Santa Monica	1091	AA
	Red and white; it is believed to have been delivered new to singer Tom Jones.										
1971	**Phantom VI four-door cabriolet (Frua)**	PRH4643	L	800-1.200.000 USD		NS		21-08-16	Pebble Beach	144	G&Co
	Metallic burgundy with cognac leather interior; delivered in rolling chassis form to Carrozzeria Frua in 1971. Following the death of Pietro Frua in 1983 the body building was stopped. The project was acquired by a new owner in the late 1980s and delivered for completion to Royle Cars Ltd. in the UK. The completed car was exhibited at the 1993 Geneva Motor Show. 75 miles covered (see lot 652 Brooks 5.5.97 NS).										
1972	**Corniche cabriolet (Mulliner,Park Ward)**	DRX13154	L	40-70.000 EUR	**39.538**	**60.201**	**54.050**	05-09-15	Chantilly	31	Bon
	Cream with habana leather interior; engine rebuilt in 2000, brakes restored in 2009. Since 1984 in the Alain Dominique Perrin collection.										
1985	**Corniche cabriolet (Mulliner,Park Ward)**	10281	L	30-40.000 USD	**23.402***	**35.750***	**31.767***	08-10-15	Hershey	187	RMS
	Ocean blue with beige interior; two owners and 50,156 miles covered.										
1972	**Corniche cabriolet (Mulliner,Park Ward)**	DRH12290	R	22-28.000 GBP	**30.114**	**46.192**	**40.654**	10-10-15	Ascot	141	Coy
	Light blue with beige interior; just one owner and 74,000 miles covered. Last serviced in April 2015.										
1985	**Corniche cabriolet (Mulliner,Park Ward)**	10326	L	60-70.000 EUR	**43.059**	**65.184**	**60.000**	08-11-15	Lyon	217	Ose
	Medium grey with tan interior; 20,000 miles covered.										
1980	**Corniche cabriolet (Mulliner,Park Ward)**	DRX50314	L	40-50.000 EUR	**34.447**	**52.147**	**48.000**	08-11-15	Lyon	238	Ose
	Black with tan interior; paintwork redone 15 years ago, gearbox replaced 10,000 kms ago.										
1978	**Corniche cabriolet (Mulliner,Park Ward)**	DRH31285	R	29-34.000 GBP	**31.000**	**46.658**	**44.101**	28-11-15	Weybridge	238	His
	White with parchment interior; in good overall condition. Recently serviced.										
1983	**Corniche cabriolet (Mulliner,Park Ward)**	07052	L	35-40.000 GBP	**25.833**	**39.072**	**35.704**	10-12-15	London	344	Bon
	Metallic red with beige leather interior; reimported from the USA in 2014.										
1986	**Corniche cabriolet (Mulliner,Park Ward)**	14219	L	75-85.000 EUR	**53.522**	**76.709**	**70.285**	16-01-16	Maastricht	450	Coy
	Dark blue with sand interior; imported into the Netherlands from the USA in 2009 and restored in 2011.										
1984	**Corniche cabriolet (Mulliner,Park Ward)**	07971	L	30-40.000 EUR	**27.819***	**41.238***	**36.800***	04-02-16	Paris	402	Bon
	White with dark blue interior; in good driving order.										
1981	**Corniche cabriolet (Mulliner,Park Ward)**	04226	L	26-28.000 GBP	**24.780**	**35.138**	**31.139**	16-04-16	Ascot	134	Coy
	White with red interior; described as in very good working order.										
1995	**Corniche cabriolet (Mulliner,Park Ward)**	50053	L	130-160.000 EUR	**105.851**	**152.517**	**134.400**	14-05-16	Monaco	279	RMS
	Red with magnolia leather interior; 14,600 kms covered.										
1985	**Corniche cabriolet (Mulliner,Park Ward)**	10112	L	30-40.000 GBP	**28.175***	**38.611***	**34.889***	24-06-16	Goodwood	204	Bon
	White with red interior; reimported into the UK from the USA in 2015. Mechanical restoration completed in January 2016.										
1992	**Corniche cabriolet (Mulliner,Park Ward)**	40023	L	125-140.000 USD		NS		25-06-16	Santa Monica	1064	AA
	Grey with grey interior; less than 20,000 miles on the odometer.										
1973	**Corniche cabriolet (Mulliner,Park Ward)**	DRA12467	L	40-60.000 EUR	**36.579***	**47.504***	**42.912***	09-07-16	Le Mans	170	Art
	White; for 20 years in the current ownership. Body repainted in the 2000s.										
1976	**Corniche cabriolet (Mulliner,Park Ward)**	DRX22381	L	35-45.000 EUR	**45.724***	**59.379***	**53.640***	09-07-16	Le Mans	211	Art F660
	Black and grey with black leather interior; some restoration works carried out in early 2016.										
1975	**Corniche cabriolet (Mulliner,Park Ward)**	DRX19718	L	40-50.000 EUR	**21.989***	**28.924***	**25.927***	06-08-16	Schloss Dyck	104	Coy
	Black and silver with tan interior; in good overall condition. Reimported into Europe from the USA some years ago.										
1973	**Corniche cabriolet (Mulliner,Park Ward)**	DRA13858	L	30-40.000 EUR	**19.990***	**26.295***	**23.570***	06-08-16	Schloss Dyck	141	Coy
	Brown with brown leather interior; sold new to the USA and later reimported into the UK (see lot 419 Bonhams 14.11.09 $23,400).										
1991	**Corniche cabriolet (Mulliner,Park Ward)**	30489	L	120-135.000 USD		NS		19-08-16	Monterey	F159	Mec
	Magnolia with tan leather interior; 23,931 miles covered.										

F659: 1973 Rolls-Royce Phantom VI cabriolet (Frua)

F660: 1976 Rolls-Royce Corniche cabriolet (Mulliner,Park Ward)

Year	Model	(Bodybuilder)	Chassis No.	Steering	Estimate	Hammer Price £	Hammer Price $	Hammer Price €	Sale Date	Sale Place	Lot	Auc. H.
1984	**Corniche 2-door**	**(Mulliner,Park Ward)**	CRH0050654	R	12-15.000 GBP	**34.500**	52.533	47.165	05-09-15	Beaulieu	115	**Bon** F661
	Dark green; the property of the late Lord Richard Attenborough. Not in running order; in needs of recommissioning.											
1974	**Corniche 2-door**	**(Mulliner,Park Ward)**	CRH17200	R	15-20.000 GBP	**23.520**	33.615	30.310	12-03-16	Brooklands	218	**His**
	Blue with magnolia interior; body repainted in 1981.											
1976	**Corniche 2-door**	**(Mulliner,Park Ward)**	CPE26154	L	35-45.000 USD	**35.056***	50.600*	45.363*	05-06-16	Greenwhich	26	**Bon**
	Sand and brown with tan leather interior; in good overall condition. Just over 26,000 recorded miles; body repainted.											
1973	**Corniche 2-door**	**(Mulliner,Park Ward)**	CRH16013	R	40-50.000 GBP	**44.000**	58.441	52.483	02-07-16	Woodstock	128	**Coy**
	Grey with grey interior; described as in very good overall condition. Several restoration works carried out in the 2000s.											
1983	**Camargue**	**(Pininfarina/Mulliner,Park Ward)**	05963	R	50-60.000 GBP		NS		01-12-15	London	307	**Coy**
	Crem with cream interior; reimported into the UK in 1996. Body repainted in 2014.											
1985	**Camargue**	**(Pininfarina/Mulliner,Park Ward)**	09039	R	33-36.000 GBP		NS		09-12-15	Chateau Impney	105	**H&H**
	Beige with stone interior; described as in very good overall condition (see lot 71 H&H 3.12.14 $ 50,669).											
1980	**Camargue**	**(Pininfarina/Mulliner,Park Ward)**	JRH50294	R	30-40.000 GBP		NS		08-03-16	London	120	**Coy**
	Blue with cream interior; in good overall condition. Body recently repainted (see lots 993 Brooks 6.12.99 $ 16,700, 63 Christie's 4.12.01 $ 36,766 and 119 Coys 11.7.15 NS).											
1980	**Camargue**	**(Pininfarina/Mulliner,Park Ward)**	JRL50667	L	50-60.000 EUR	**40.039**	57.224	51.600	12-03-16	Lyon	317	**Agu**
	Pale yellow with tan interior; body repainted years ago. Good mechanical condition (see lot 53 Brooks 7.9.98 $ 23,556).											
1982	**Camargue**	**(Pininfarina/Mulliner,Park Ward)**	BCX0251	L	45-55.000 USD	**38.104**	55.000	49.308	05-06-16	Greenwhich	63	**Bon** F662
	Blue with blue interior; in good original condition. Two owners.											
1979	**Camargue**	**(Pininfarina/Mulliner,Park Ward)**	JRK33115	L	25-35.000 GBP	**27.600***	37.823*	34.177*	24-06-16	Goodwood	202	**Bon**
	Dove grey; sold new to the USA. Bought in 2000 by the current, second owner. 16,624 miles covered. Body repainted in 2006.											
1980	**Camargue**	**(Pininfarina/Mulliner,Park Ward)**	JRH50294	R	25-30.000 GBP	**22.650**	30.084	27.017	02-07-16	Woodstock	147	**Coy**
	See lot 120 Coys 8.3.16.											
1976	**Camargue**	**(Pininfarina/Mulliner,Park Ward)**	JRX20784	L	40-50.000 EUR	**39.120***	50.802*	45.892*	09-07-16	Le Mans	155	**Art**
	Two-tone blue with light beige leather interior; in good overall condition.											
1994	**Silver Spur**		54422	R	17-21.000 GBP		NS		09-12-15	Chateau Impney	86	**H&H**
	Graphite grey with parchment interior; four owners.											
1987	**Silver Spur**		22737	L	15-25.000 EUR	**8.867***	13.145*	11.730*	04-02-16	Paris	430	**Bon**
	Dark blue with dark blue Everflex roof and parchment leather interior; paintwork refurbished in 1995-96.											
1984	**Silver Spur**		08434	R	16-20.000 GBP		NS		12-03-16	Brooklands	143	**His**
	White with cream leather interior; in very good overall condition. One owner.											
1998	**Silver Spur**		59598	L	5-8.000 GBP	**15.792**	22.570	20.351	12-03-16	Brooklands	265	**His**
	Black; in good overall condition. In the same family ownership since new.											
1984	**Silver Spur**		XOG011	L	60-70.000 EUR		NS		09-04-16	Essen	198	**Coy**
	Metallic silver and light blue with light blue leather interior; 1,545 miles covered.											
2000	**Silver Seraph**		04051	R	38-42.000 GBP		NS		09-12-15	Chateau Impney	136	**H&H**
	Silver with black interior; 31,000 miles covered.											
1998	**Silver Seraph**		01662	R	30-33.000 GBP	**29.666**	43.182	38.284	18-05-16	Donington Park	105	**H&H**
	Silver with dark blue leather interior; 45,800 recorded miles.											
2000	**Corniche**		68052	R	90-110.000 GBP		NS		08-03-16	London	123	**Coy**
	Blue with cream leather interior; 18,000 miles covered.											
2000	**Corniche**		68052	R	90-105.000 GBP	**93.640**	132.782	117.668	16-04-16	Ascot	115	**Coy**
	See lot 123 Coys 8.3.16.											

ROLUX (F) *(1947-1952)*

Year	Model		Chassis No.	Steering	Estimate	£	$	€	Date	Place	Lot	Auc. H.
1948	**VB 58**		25159	L	18-23.000 EUR		NS		02-07-16	Lyon	329	**Agu**
	Light green and white; recently restored and fitted with a 175cc Ydral engine.											

F661: 1984 Rolls-Royce Corniche 2-door (Mulliner,Park Ward)

F662: 1982 Rolls-Royce Camargue (Pininfarina/Mulliner,Park Ward)

Year	Model (Bodybuilder)	Chassis no.	Steering	Estimate	Hammer price £	Hammer price $	Hammer price €	Date	Place	Lot	Auc. H.

ROOSEVELT (USA) (1929-1930)

| 1929 | Eight sedan (Hayes) | S703951 | L | 10-15.000 USD | 6.841* | 10.450* | 9.286* | 08-10-15 | Hershey | 126 | RMS |

Black and green; in largely original condition. From the Richard Roy estate.

ROSENGART (F) (1928-1955)

| 1936 | LR4N2 coupé | 53922 | L | NA | 3.808 | 5.297 | 4.824 | 24-02-16 | Donington Park | 9 | H&H |

Two-tone blue with blue interior; restored in 2007, it requires mechanical overhaul prior to use.

ROVER (GB) (1904-)

| 1937 | 14 P1 saloon | 831153 | R | NQ | 6.160* | 8.804* | 7.938* | 12-03-16 | Brooklands | 111 | His |

Black; restored in 2006 and used until a couple of years ago. Since 1962 in the current ownership.

| 1955 | Land Rover 86 | 17060671 | R | NA | 39.760 | 61.155 | 53.596 | 14-10-15 | Duxford | 38 | H&H |

Bronze green with green interior; the car has covered 20 miles since the restoration.

| 1972 | Land Rover series 3 | 90102031A | R | 3-3.500 GBP | 3.100 | 4.788 | 4.214 | 17-10-15 | Cambridge | 2503 | Che |

Orange and white; in working order.

| 1951 | Land Rover 80 | 16103834 | R | 18-22.000 GBP | NS | | | 09-12-15 | Chateau Impney | 71 | H&H |

Green with green interior.

| 1952 | Land Rover 80 | 36100013 | R | 35-40.000 GBP | 43.700 | 66.096 | 60.398 | 10-12-15 | London | 370 | Bon |

Bronze green; fully restored between 2014 and 2015.

| 2015 | Land Rover Defender 90 | 2000000 | R | Refer Dpt. | 400.000 | 600.440 | 549.200 | 16-12-15 | London | 1 | Bon F663 |

One-off finished in silver with black interior; 2,000,000th example built of the Land Rover and Defender series, commissioned by the factory to celebrate 67 years of production. All proceeds from the sale will be donated in their entirety to the Born Free Foundation and the International Federation of Red Cross and Red Crescent Societies.

| 1995 | Land Rover Defender 90 | 962124 | L | NA | 76.362 | 110.000 | 97.306 | 11-06-16 | Newport Beach | 6254 | R&S |

Red with black roof; low mileage. Manual gearbox.

| 1970 | P5B 3.5 Coupé | 84503517D | R | 10-14.000 GBP | 12.880 | 18.408 | 16.598 | 12-03-16 | Brooklands | 185 | His F664 |

Dark blue with silver roof and buckskin leather interior; in good working order.

| 1970 | P5B 3.5 Coupé | 84800286D | L | 6-8.000 EUR | 14.179 | 20.257 | 18.000 | 19-06-16 | Fontainebleau | 365 | Ose |

Dark blue with silver roof and original grey leather interior; in good working order.

| 1975 | P6 3500 V8 | 48111151D | R | 7-9.000 GBP | 6.916 | 10.435 | 9.538 | 09-12-15 | Chateau Impney | 76 | H&H |

Maroon with fawn interior; body repainted in 2012. 54,150 miles on the odometer.

| 1983 | Range Rover 2-door | 136071 | R | 20-25.000 GBP | 22.500 | 34.254 | 31.824 | 14-11-15 | Birmingham | 306 | SiC |

Beige; recently restored.

| 1971 | Range Rover 2-door | 35501657A | R | 20-25.000 GBP | 18.760 | 28.305 | 25.872 | 09-12-15 | Chateau Impney | 9 | H&H |

Green; restored at unspecified date (see lot 437 Bonhams 1.7.11 $ 30,377).

| 1975 | Range Rover 2-door | 35814817D | L | 70-90.000 EUR | 54.769 | 81.187 | 72.450 | 04-02-16 | Paris | 330 | Bon |

Yellow with beige interior; fully restored in Italy between 2011 and 2012. Some 6,000 kms covered since.

| 1971 | Range Rover 2-door | 35801952A | L | 50-70.000 EUR | NS | | | 13-05-16 | Monaco | 137 | Bon |

Blue with beige interior; the car has covered 5-6,000 kms since the restoration carried out in the 2000s.

| 1985 | MG Metro 6R4 | 70011 | R | 85-95.000 GBP | NS | | | 16-01-16 | Birmingham | 349 | Coy |

White and blue Rothmans livery; the car was used by Rothmans for promotional purpose. Never rallied and never registered; 3,100 miles covered.

| 1991 | Mini | 034834 | R | 7-10.000 GBP | 7.269 | 11.150 | 9.813 | 10-10-15 | Ascot | 104 | Coy |

Dark blue with white roof; 48,000 miles covered. First owner the actress Britt Ekland.

| 1990 | Mini Cooper S | 010952 | R | 7-10.000 GBP | 11.200 | 16.857 | 15.933 | 28-11-15 | Weybridge | 255 | His |

Green with white roof; bought by the Pink Floyd drummer, Nick Mason, the car was delivered to John Cooper Garages for the fitting of their S Works kit. Engine overhauled in 2014 by Wood & Pickett. From the collection of Michael Standring.

| 1992 | Mini British Open Classic | 047191 | R | 5.5-9.500 GBP | 9.200* | 13.915* | 12.715* | 10-12-15 | London | 312 | Bon |

Metallic British racing green; one owner and 7,200 miles covered. Special Edition built in 1,000 examples.

F663: 2015 Rover Land Rover Defender 90

F664: 1970 Rover P5B 3.5 Coupé

Year	Model	(Bodybuilder)	Chassis no.	Steering	Estimate	Hammer price £	$	€	Date	Place	Lot	Auc. H.

F665: 1998 Rover Mini John Cooper Works

F666: 1932 Ruxton Eight sedan

1998	Mini John Cooper Works		153692	R	60-80.000 EUR	55.053*	80.117*	71.520*	05-02-16	Paris	151	Art

Dark blue with silver stripes and white roof; alcantara interior; electric sunroof. The car was delivered new to John Cooper who modified it and fitted it with a 138bhp 1,380cc engine. 2000 kms covered since new. **F665**

2001	Mini Cooper S Works		178913	R	40-60.000 EUR	41.289*	60.088*	53.640*	05-02-16	Paris	152	Art

Dark green with white roof and red interior; bought new by John Cooper's wife. 90bhp engine. 550 miles covered.

1995	MG RV8 roadster		001242	R	12-15.000 GBP	11.500	17.394	15.894	10-12-15	London	373	Bon

Dark green with stone interior; described as in very good overall condition.

RUXTON (USA) *(1929-1930)*

1930	Eight sedan		1005	L	450-600.000 USD		NS		28-01-16	Scottsdale	77	Bon

Six-tone blue with blue cloth interior; restored many years ago. Believed to be a car used by the factory for promotional purpose and shown at some Motor Shows.

1932	Eight sedan		10C112	L	375-450.000 USD	250.107	357.500	322.358	12-03-16	Amelia Island	130	RMS

One of five examples known finished in the "rainbow" paint scheme; the car was acquired from its first owner in 1952 by the Donlan family who retained it until 2013, when it was bought by the current owner, who commissioned a full restoration completed in 2014. Exhibited at several Concours d'Elegance. **F666**

SAAB (S) *(1950-)*

1966	96 Monte Carlo 850		348101	L	17-20.000 EUR	11.246	16.118	14.768	16-01-16	Maastricht	417	Coy

White and red with red interior; in good driving order.

SABRA (IL)

1964	GT coupé		GT4819	L	80-100.000 USD	66.076	93.500	86.114	10-03-16	Amelia Island	109	Bon

Pastel light blue with dark blue leatherette interior; restored at unspecified date. 1,701cc 4-cylinder engine. From the Italian Classic Cars Collection. **F667**

SALEEN (USA)

2005	S7 Twin Turbo		0046	L	550-650.000 USD	374.340	535.000	489.900	29-01-16	Phoenix	266	RMS

Metallic black with black interior; two owners and 941 miles covered. Upgraded by factory with the Competition Package. **F668**

2006	S7 Twin Turbo		0073	L	650-725.000 USD	480.574	632.500	569.124	30-07-16	Plymouth	158	RMS

Red; two owners and 300 miles covered. Last serviced in May 2016.

SALMSON (F) *(1921-1957)*

1925	D-Type Grand Sport torpedo		25855	R	NA		NS		20-04-16	Duxford	41	H&H

Grey with black leather interior; the car remained in the same family ownership and was used until the 1950s. Restored.

F667: 1964 Sabra GT coupé

F668: 2005 Saleen S7 Twin Turbo

Year	Model	(Bodybuilder)	Chassis no.	Steering	Estimate	Hammer Price £	$	€	Date	Place	Lot	Auc. H.
1925	VAL3 series 5 spider		11295	R	25-30.000 EUR		NS		08-11-15	Lyon	210	Ose
Blue; restored between 1994 and 2000.												
1925	VAL3 series 5 spider		11295	R	25-30.000 EUR	28.588	41.416	36.720	20-03-16	Fontainebleau	311	Ose
See lot 210 Osenat 8.11.15.												
1950	S4-61 cabriolet		62738	R	45-55.000 EUR		NS		08-11-15	Lyon	213	Ose
Green and cream; restored several years ago.												
1951	G 72 coupé	(Saoutchik)	72437	R	160-220.000 EUR	142.219	206.968	184.760	05-02-16	Paris	129	Art F669
Purple; one-off exhibited at the London Motor Show. Body repainted 25 years ago. Cotal electromagnetic gearbox. For over 35 years in the André Trigano Collection.												

SAXON (USA) (1913-1923)

Year	Model	(Bodybuilder)	Chassis no.	Steering	Estimate	£	$	€	Date	Place	Lot	Auc. H.
1914	Model A roadster		1420	L	11-13.000 GBP		NS		10-07-16	Chateau Impney	2	H&H
Grey and black with black leather interior; restored in the early 1970s. Imported into the UK in 2011.												

SCARAB (USA) (1958-1962)

Year	Model	(Bodybuilder)	Chassis no.	Steering	Estimate	£	$	€	Date	Place	Lot	Auc. H.
1958	Chevrolet Mark I sports		RAI003	L	650-900.000 GBP		NS		12-09-15	Goodwood	332	Bon
Recreation completed in the late 1990s by Don Orosco using new chassis and body, and original or reconstructed as-original mechanical parts. 577bhp engine.												
1959	F1		001	M	700-950.000 GBP	673.500	1.038.739	921.887	12-09-15	Goodwood	330	Bon F670
While on display at the Cunningham Museum, the car was acquired by Richard Reventlow (half-brother of the Scarab constructor and driver Lance) who in 1985-86 started the restoration. Prior to finish the works, he sold the car to Don Orosco, who fitted it with a 220 Meyer-Drake Offenhauser engine, completed the restoration and for many years drove it at numerous historic races. Described as in very good, ready to race condition.												
1959	F1		002	M	400-525.000 GBP	328.540	506.707	449.706	12-09-15	Goodwood	331	Bon
Recreation of the second Scarab single-seater raced during the 1960 and 1961 seasons carried out by Don Orosco during the restoration of the car chassis 001. New body and chassis; 220 CDI-derived Offenhauser engine. Completed in the late 1990s and raced at several historic events. In ready to race condition (see lots 172 Brooks 27.5.00 NS and 142 RM 20.8.05 NS).												

SCAT (I) (1906-1932)

Year	Model	(Bodybuilder)	Chassis no.	Steering	Estimate	£	$	€	Date	Place	Lot	Auc. H.
1914	18/30hp torpedo	(Solaro)	2878	R	50-70.000 EUR	33.519*	48.297*	42.560*	14-05-16	Monaco	138	RMS F671
Yellow with black wings and interior; from the Quattroruote Collection.												

SEARS (USA) (1908-1912)

Year	Model	(Bodybuilder)	Chassis no.	Steering	Estimate	£	$	€	Date	Place	Lot	Auc. H.
1909	Model H motor buggy		3399	L	30-50.000 USD	16.137*	24.750*	21.785*	09-10-15	Hershey	290	RMS
Black with black interior; restored 10-12 years ago.												

SHELBY AMERICAN (USA) (1962-1970)

Year	Model	(Bodybuilder)	Chassis no.	Steering	Estimate	£	$	€	Date	Place	Lot	Auc. H.
1962	Cobra 260		CS2030	R	250-350.000 GBP	371.100	561.808	515.309	06-12-15	London	002	Bon
First Cobra with rack-and-pinion steering, the car was first used as a factory demonstrator and sold in late 1963. In the late 1960s it was involved in a serious accident probably also resulted in a fire. The then owner obtained from the AC factory the necessary parts to effect a full repair of the chassis and acquired a new body. Probably in that same period the original 260 engine was replaced by the present 289 unit. Restored over a number of years, the car is for over 30 years in the current ownership and has seen virtually no use for the last 20 years.												
1962	Cobra 260		CSX2023	L	800-950.000 USD	523.376	748.000	684.944	30-01-16	Scottsdale	155	G&Co
Silver with black interior; built with 260 engine, at some point in its life the car was fitted with a 289 engine. Restored in the 1990s; body repainted in recent years (see lot 581 Auctions America 22.3.13 $ 533,500).												
1962	Cobra 260		CSX2000	L	Priceless!	10.505.000	13.750.000	12.139.875	19-08-16	Monterey	117	RMS TOP TEN
First Cobra built, the car was fitted with the 260 engine and for the first five months it was the sole example available for promotional purpose and press test. Currently finished in blue, in its early months the car was repainted more times and in various colours. In more recent years the car was used at events celebrating the history of the make. Offered from the Carroll Hall Shelby Trust.												
1963	Cobra 289		CSX2104	L	950-1.250.000 EUR	744.427	1.149.632	1.012.000	17-10-15	Salzburg	339	Dor
Blue with black leather interior; 9,674 miles covered. Sold new in the USA; from 1964 to 1989 in the same family ownership; acquired in 2008 by the current owner and imported into Germany. Described as in original condition.												
1965	Cobra 289		CSX2495	L	NA	558.011	797.500	730.271	29-01-16	Scottsdale	1396	B/J
Navy blue with silver stripes and black interior; restored in the 2000s.												
1964	Cobra 289		CSX2561	L	950-1.100.000 USD	750.428	1.072.500	982.088	29-01-16	Phoenix	219	RMS
White with red interior; recently sorted considerably and fitted with a 4-speed manual gearbox as replacement of the original automatic transmission (included in the sale) (see lot 800 Auctions America 1.8.13 $ 825,000).												

F669: 1951 Salmson G 72 coupé (Saoutchik)

F670: 1959 Scarab F1

Year	Model	(Bodybuilder)	Chassis no.	Steering	Estimate	£	$	€	Date	Place	Lot	Auc. H.

F671: 1914 Scat 18/30hp torpedo (Solaro)

F672: 1963 Shelby American Cobra 289

1963 Cobra 289 Dragonsnake — CSX2093 — L — 1.400-1.600.000 USD — **692.703** — **990.000** — **906.543** — 29-01-16 Phoenix — 251 — **RMS**
Prepared to Dragonsnake specification by Bruce Larson, the car was raced at drag racing events from late 1964 to 1969. Driven by Larson and Ed Hedrick, it won several National A, AA, B, and C Class Championships and the 1967 World Points Championship. Restored in 1991 to its metallic fuchsia racing livery, it was later bought by Bruce Larson who retained it for some years. Since 2010 in the current ownership (see Mecum lots S137 18.8.11 NS and S93.1 12.4.14 NS).

1964 Cobra 289 — CSX2433 — L — 950-1.100.000 USD — **923.472** — **1.320.000** — **1.190.244** — 11-03-16 Amelia Island — 14 — **G&Co**
Originally finished in green with black interior; prepared in 1966 for racing; restored in 1973 and returned to road trim; acquired in 2011 by Bruce Canepa and restored again to racing specification and finished in dark blue; driven by the current owner at the 2014 Goodwood Revival. Fitted with a Le Mans hardtop.

1963 Cobra 289 — CSX2188 — L — 950-1.200.000 USD — **808.038** — **1.155.000** — **1.041.464** — 12-03-16 Amelia Island — 179 — **RMS**
Black with red interior; the car received minor modifications in order to remain competitive in drag-race in period and was returned to street configuration in 1975. In 1979 it was acquired by Bill Collins who later restored and retained it for 37 years. *F672*

1964 Cobra 289 — CSX2271 — L — 800-1.000.000 USD — **686.400** — **1.000.000** — **891.300** — 20-05-16 Indianapolis — F163 — **Mec**
Silver with red leather interior; restoration completed in 2003 (see lot S90 Mecum 10.05.07 $630,000).

1965 Cobra 289 — CSX2524 — L — 725-825.000 USD — **672.320** — **880.000** — **776.952** — 19-08-16 Carmel — 71 — **Bon**
Black with red leather interior; in January 1965 the car was loaned to the Yamaha International Corporation to be used in a Yamaha motorcycle advertisement. During Yamaha's use, the car was involved in an accident and subsequently it was repaired by Hi-Performance Motors, Inc., Shelby's retail outlet. Probably during the repair works the car's square edged flares were rounded to the Cobra 427 style. In single ownership from 1981 to 2004. Described as in excellent working order.

1964 Cobra 289 — CSX2326 — L — 1.000-1.400.000 USD — **739.552** — **968.000** — **854.647** — 19-08-16 Monterey — 137 — **RMS**
Blue with white stripes; four private owners from new, owned by Jim Click on three occasions over 50 years. Modified in the mid-1990s for historic racing by Don Roberts for Click. In the Chip Connor's collection from 2002 to 2007 when it was bought back for the third time by Click. Engine rebuilt in 2012; 289 block bored out to 306c.i. From the Jim Click Ford Performance Collection.

1964 Cobra 289 Competition — CSX2473 — L — 2.200-2.600.000 USD — — **NS** — — 19-08-16 Monterey — 140 — **RMS**
Blue with white stripes; race-prepared and driven by Don Roberts, the car won the 1966, 1972 and 1973 the SCCA Southern Pacific Divisional B-Production Championships. Roberts himself won the 1966 SCCA B-Production National Champion title. Later the car was raced at historic events and since 2006 it is part of the Jim Click Ford Performance Collection. (see lot 159 RM 18.8.06 $ 1,237,500).

1964 Cobra 289 — CSX2549 — L — 1.000-1.250.000 USD — — **NS** — — 20-08-16 Monterey — S108 — **Mec**
Silver with red interior; described as in excellent overall condition. One of approximately 20 examples built with the Ford C4 automatic transmission (see lot F186 Mecum 16.5.15 NS).

1966 Cobra 427 — CSX3272 — L — NA — — **NS** — — 09-10-15 Chicago — S148 — **Mec**
Silver with black interior; restored in the 1970s. Since 1986 in the current ownership. Raced at historic events from 1987 to 1995.

1965 Cobra 427 Competition — CSX3010 — L — 2.500-3.300.000 USD — **1.576.471** — **2.255.000** — **2.068.061** — 28-01-16 Phoenix — 140 — **RMS**
Black with gold stripes; raced until 1971, the car won the 1968 U.S. SCCA A Production Championship and the 1971 Eastern Canadian Endurance Championship. Damaged at the last 1971 race, it was acquired in 1978 without engine by the current owner who had it restored, fitted with a new engine, and drove it at historic events. Subsequently he sold the car but in 2011 he reacquired it. Currently fitted with an over 600bhp 427 engine and ready to use. *F673*

1967 Cobra 427 — CSX3295 — L — 1.100-1.300.000 USD — **755.040** — **1.100.000** — **980.430** — 20-05-16 Indianapolis — F124 — **Mec**
White with black leather interior; body restored and repainted in 2008. 20,165 original miles. From the Joe McMurrey Collection.

1965 Cobra 427 — CSX3178 — L — 1.500-2.000.000 USD — **1.050.500*** — **1.375.000*** — **1.213.988*** — 19-08-16 Monterey — 119 — **RMS**
Red with black interior; its only known owner is Carroll Shelby. First restored in 1972 and in the early 2000s again. Offered from the Carroll Shelby Foundation.

1966 Cobra 427 — CSX3165 — L — 1.200-1.600.000 USD — — **NS** — — 21-08-16 Pebble Beach — 143 — **G&Co**
Road versione finished in dark green with black interior; the car has had several owners and was bought by the current vendor in 2001. Body subsequently repainted. Engine and gearbox believed original to the car.

F673: 1965 Shelby American Cobra 427 Competition

F674: 1999 Shelby American Series 1 roadster

Year	Model	(Bodybuilder)	Chassis no.	Steering	Estimate	Hammer Price £	Hammer Price $	Hammer Price €	Date	Place	Lot	Auc. H.

SHELBY AMERICAN (USA) (1995-)

| 1999 | Series 1 roadster | | 000064 | L | 175-225.000 USD | 105.050* | 137.500* | 121.399* | 19-08-16 | Monterey | 116 | RMS F674 |

Silver with metallic blue stripes; 2,637 miles covered. In 2005 the car was bought back by Carroll Shelby. Proceeds to benefit the Carroll Hall Shelby Trust.

SIATA (I) (1926-1970)

| 1953 | 300BC spider | (Bertone) | ST438BC | L | 200-250.000 USD | 138.521* | 198.000* | 178.537* | 12-03-16 | Amelia Island | 172 | RMS F675 |

Red; imported into the USA by Antonio Pompeo, the car was acquired by the current owner in 1956 and raced at hillclimbs and ice races in period. Registered for road use in 1989, it is described as in largely original condition and still fitted with its original Fiat 1100 engine.

| 1952 | 300BC spider | (Bertone) | ST403BC | L | 350-425.000 USD | 229.086 | 330.000 | 291.918 | 11-06-16 | Hershey | 132 | TFA |

Red with tan interior; the car was sold new to the USA where it was raced until the early 1960s with a 750cc Crosley engine. Later it was raced for three decades at historic events. Fully restored between 2010 and 2012 (see lot 53 Bonhams 14.08.15 $313,500).

| 1954 | 208S spider | (Motto) | BS535 | L | 1.500-1.900.000 USD | 1.090.815 | 1.650.000 | 1.507.770 | 10-12-15 | New York | 227 | RMS F676 |

Dark blue with red leather interior; sold new in Italy, the car was imported into the USA in 1955. Probably in the early 1970s it was fitted with a Ford V8 engine and in 1982 it was bought by Walter Eisenstark who had it restored and fitted again with the original engine. He retained the car until 2009 when it was acquired by the current owner who commissioned a concours-quality restoration completed in 2011 (see lot 261 Bonhams 7.6.09 NS).

SIGMA (F) (1913-1928)

| 1919 | 10hp torpedo | | 1340 | R | 15-18.000 GBP | 12.000 | 15.938 | 14.314 | 02-07-16 | Woodstock | 127 | Coy |

Brown with black wings.

SIMCA (F) (1934-1981)

| 1936 | 5 decouvrable | | 16885 | L | 1.5-3.000 EUR | 3.875 | 5.867 | 5.400 | 07-11-15 | Lyon | 285 | Agu |

Black with beige interior; since 1968 in the current ownership. For restoration.

| 1951 | 8 Sport coupé | | 902137 | L | 40-50.000 EUR | 50.465* | 73.440* | 65.560* | 05-02-16 | Paris | 179 | Art F677 |

Black; restored in the 1980s.

| 1971 | 1200 S coupé | (Bertone) | CA012445G | L | 17-20.000 EUR | 22.131 | 29.396 | 26.400 | 02-07-16 | Lyon | 328 | Agu |

Blue with black vinyl roof; bought in 2013 by the current owner and subsequently restored.

SIMPLEX (USA) (1907-1919)

| 1915 | Crane Model 5 limousine | (Brewster) | 2196 | L | 40-50.000 GBP | 21.458 | 32.455 | 29.657 | 10-12-15 | London | 356 | Bon |

Dark grey with black fenders and turquoise cloth interior; restored at unspecified date. Last used in 2014.

| 1916 | Crane Model 5 boattail roadster | | 2331 | L | 185-250.000 USD | 139.927 | 198.000 | 182.358 | 10-03-16 | Amelia Island | 163 | Bon F678 |

Ivory and dark green; the car remained until 1936 with its first owner who in the 1920 had the body modified to a more modern look. Described as in largely original condition. Six owners since new.

SINGER (GB) (1905-1970)

| 1919 | 10hp tourer | | C4413 | R | 9-12.000 GBP | 7.475* | 10.829* | 9.601* | 20-03-16 | Goodwood | 6 | Bon |

Used sparingly and stored since 2006. From the Kingsley Curtis Collection.

| 1933 | Nine saloon | | 40858 | R | 4-5.000 GBP | 6.500 | 8.685 | 7.805 | 16-07-16 | Cambridge | 1254 | Che |

Black and red; restored many years ago. Running condition unknown.

| 1933 | Nine Sports 4-seater | | 48462 | R | NA | 19.124 | 29.415 | 25.779 | 14-10-15 | Duxford | 31 | H&H |

Old English white with red interior; since 1979 in the current ownership, restored in 1980, engine overhauled in 2009, gearbox replaced in 2014.

| 1952 | 4AD roadster | | L4AD897V | L | NA | 19.791 | 30.000 | 27.396 | 12-12-15 | Austin | F100 | Mec |

Red with cream interior; restored.

SIZAIRE & NAUDIN (F) (1905-1921)

| 1908 | Type F1 8hp Sport | | 1368 | R | 70-90.000 EUR | 91.754* | 133.528* | 119.200* | 05-02-16 | Paris | 181 | Art F679 |

Sold new in France, in 1958 the car was imported into Belgium and in 1978 it was acquired by the current owner. Fitted with its original engine, it is described as in very good working order. Several mechanical works carried out over the years.

SS (GB) (1932-1945)

| 1935 | S.S.I tourer | | 248806 | R | 75-90.000 GBP | | NS | | 01-12-15 | London | 341 | Coy |

Dark green with beige interior; sold new in the UK, later the car was imported into Sweden where it was fitted with a replacement 1936 SS 2.5-litre engine. Stored for some 45 years, in 2011 it was reimported into the UK and restored (see lot 32 H&H 15.6.13 NS).

| 1934 | S.S.I 2.5l sports saloon | | 248788 | R | 50-70.000 GBP | 79.900 | 120.849 | 110.430 | 10-12-15 | London | 338 | Bon F680 |

Black with brown leather interior; fully restored between 1995 and 2002. Rebuilt 2.5-litre Standard engine.

| 1935 | S.S.I tourer | | 248806 | R | 65-70.000 GBP | | NS | | 08-03-16 | London | 117 | Coy |

See lot 341 Coys 1.12.15.

| 1935 | S.S.I tourer | | 248806 | R | 65-70.000 GBP | 58.820 | 78.125 | 70.160 | 02-07-16 | Woodstock | 177 | Coy |

See lot 117 Coys 8.3.16.

| 1937 | Jaguar 100 2.5l | | 18056 | R | Refer Dpt. | 326.000 | 500.051 | 440.100 | 10-10-15 | Ascot | 126 | Coy |

Red with tan interior; restored in the early 1990s, the car is described as in very good overall condition. Since 1997 in the current ownership.

F675: 1953 Siata 300BC spider (Bertone)

F676: 1954 Siata 208S spider (Motto)

F677: 1951 Simca 8 Sport coupé

F678: 1916 Simplex Crane Model 5 boattail roadster

F679: 1908 Sizaire & Naudin Type F1 8hp Sport

F680: 1934 SS S.S.I 2.5l sports saloon

F681: 1939 SS Jaguar 100 2.5l roadster (Van den Plas)

F682: 1938 SS Jaguar 100 3.5l

Year	Model	(Bodybuilder)	Chassis no.	Steering	Estimate	Hammer Price £	Hammer Price $	Hammer Price €	Date	Place	Lot	Auc. H.
1939	Jaguar 100 2.5l roadster	(Van den Plas)	49064	R	1.500-2.100.000 USD	981.329	1.402.500	1.284.269	29-01-16	Phoenix	231	RMS F681

Last chassis built in 1939, it was bought by Belgian coachbuilder Van den Plas that fitted it after WWII with the present one-off body and exhibited it at the 1948 Brussels Motor Show. For many years in the ownership of a Belgian enthusiast, it was later imported into the USA where it was restored in the early 1990s and finished in the present red and ebony livery with red interior.

| 1938 | Jaguar 100 2.5/3.5l | | 49049 | R | 600-800.000 USD | 437.008 | 572.000 | 505.019 | 20-08-16 | Monterey | 246 | RMS |

Gunmetal grey with red leather interior; sold new in the UK and later imported into the USA. In single ownership from 1971 to 2014. Less than 100 miles covered since its recent restoration. Upgraded at unspecified date with the 3.5-litre Jaguar engine no.T9528 (see lot 293 Bonhams 31.5.15 $215,000).

| 1938 | Jaguar 100 3.5l | | 39083 | R | 3.600-4.600.000 DKK | 328.498 | 498.583 | 447.224 | 26-09-15 | Ebeltoft | 7 | Bon F682 |

Gunmetal grey; sold new in the UK, the car was imported into the USA in 1940 circa and later into Switzerland, where it was first restored in the 1980s. Damaged in a fire, it was resold in 2000 and subsequently restored again. From the Frederiksen Collection (see lot 126 Coys 30.11.11 NS).

| 1938 | Jaguar 100 3.5l | | 39064 | R | 180-260.000 GBP | 337.500 | 462.510 | 417.926 | 24-06-16 | Goodwood | 219 | Bon |

British racing green with black interior; imported new into the Netherlands and since 1959 in the current ownership, the car requires several restoration works. Engine block replaced in 1960 circa with one taken from a 3.5-litre Jaguar Mark V; original cylinder head. Body repainted in 1967 circa, interior retrimmed in the 1970s.

| 1937 | Jaguar 2.5l roadster | | 12538 | R | 50-70.000 GBP | | NS | | 05-09-15 | Beaulieu | 117 | Bon |

Built with four-door saloon body, the car was fitted with the present aluminium body circa 40 years ago. Original un-shortened chassis. Polished aluminium body with black leather interior. Originally delivered with engine no.252253, the car is currently fitted with engine no.L1612E.

STANGUELLINI (I) (1947-1963)

| 1947 | 1100 Sport coupé | (Motto) | 508C209006 | L | 220-280.000 EUR | | NS | | 05-02-16 | Paris | 193 | Art |

Red with black interior; believed to be an unique example, the car was probably displayed at the 1947 Turin Motor Show. Sold new in Italy, in 1950/1951 it was imported into Switzerland where it has had several owners. The nose was rebuilt in the 1950s to Cisitalia style and the car was restored in 1969 circa. Since 1999/2000 in the current ownership, it is offered with the engine currently fitted and its original unit stored in a crate.

| 1959 | F Junior | | 00201 | M | 90-120.000 EUR | 54.614 | 79.264 | 72.500 | 03-02-16 | Paris | 159 | RMS F683 |

Red; described as in good overall condition. Bought in 1982 from the Stanguellini family and raced in historic events in the 1980s. Since then the car has been on static display in a private collection (see lot 165 Coys 8.8.15 NS).

STANLEY (USA) (1895-1931)

| 1903 | Model CX steam runabout | | 507 | R | 35-40.000 GBP | 40.250 | 63.740 | 56.044 | 30-10-15 | London | 104 | Bon |

Red with black fenders and black interior; imported from the USA in 2008 in partially dismantled state, the car was subsequently fully restored and is described as in excellent overall condition (see lot 136 Coys 8.10.11 NS).

| 1909 | Model E2 runabout | | 4520 | R | 80-100.000 USD | 34.630* | 49.500* | 44.634* | 12-03-16 | Amelia Island | 110 | RMS |

Green with black fenders and black leather interior; recently returned to running condition (see lot 120 RM 10.10.13 NS).

| 1911 | Model 63 10hp toy tonneau | | 6210 | R | 100-140.000 USD | 75.606* | 115.500* | 102.633* | 08-10-15 | Hershey | 164 | RMS |

Red with black fenders and black leather interior; bought in 2009 by the current owner and subsequently fully restored.

| 1911 | Model 63 10hp toy tonneau | | 6076 | R | 125-175.000 USD | 200.086* | 286.000* | 257.886* | 12-03-16 | Amelia Island | 165 | RMS F684 |

Dark green with yellow wheels and chassis and black leather interior; in the ownership of the Fodor family, Connecticut, from the 1930s to 1994, the car was fully restored in the second half of the 1990s. Later it was part of the collection of William Ruger Jr. who commissioned further mechanical works (see lots 330 Bonhams 6.5.06 $ 181,900 and 134 RM 29.7.12 $ 165,000).

| 1922 | Model 735 touring | | 22009 | L | 30-60.000 EUR | 18.351* | 26.706* | 23.840* | 05-02-16 | Paris | 188 | Art |

Red with black fenders; in working order.

| 1924 | Model 740 touring | | 24039 | L | 40-60.000 USD | 31.574 | 46.000 | 41.000 | 20-05-16 | Indianapolis | T204.1 | Mec |

Blue with black interior; restoration completed in 2007. Cruban burner installed in 1930.

STAR (GB) (1898-1932)

| 1899 | Benz 3.5hp vis-a-vis | | CE261(registration) | R | 60-70.000 GBP | 92.220 | 146.040 | 128.407 | 30-10-15 | London | 101 | Bon F685 |

Red with black wings and black interior; rediscovered in 1932, the car ran its first London-Brighton Run in 1938. Damaged by enemy action during the war, it was restored in the mid-1950s and fitted with a new body. Subsequently it ran several editions of the London-Brighton Run until the early 1970s. For the last 25-30 years on display in a private museum on the Isle of Man, it requires recommissioning prior to use.

| 1910 | 15hp tourer | | 2471 | R | 35-40.000 GBP | 27.600 | 42.027 | 37.732 | 05-09-15 | Beaulieu | 133 | Bon |

Maroon and black with black interior; restored in the mid-1980s. In good running order (see lot 610 Bonhams 8.9.12 $ 56,855).

STAR (USA) (1922-1928)

| 1926 | Four touring | | L202557 | L | 20-30.000 USD | 3.623* | 5.500* | 4.895* | 05-10-15 | Philadelphia | 229 | Bon |

Blue with black fenders; restored in the 1980s. From the Evergreen Collection.

F683: 1959 Stanguellini F Junior

F684: 1911 Stanley Model 63 10hp toy tonneau

F685: 1899 Star Benz 3.5hp vis-a-vis

F686: 1912 Stearns Knight 28hp toy tonneau runabout

STEARNS (USA) (1901-1929)

Year	Model	Chassis no.	Steering	Estimate	£	$	€	Date	Place	Lot	Auc. H.
1907	**Four 30/60hp touring**	350	R	650-850.000 USD		NS		05-10-15	Philadelphia	265	Bon

Red with red leather interior; the car was acquired in 1977 in partially restored form by Bill Harrah, who resold it in 1981 to Jim Conant. The latter had the restoration completed and the body repainted in the present red livery. Described as still in very good overall condition.

| 1912 | **Knight 28hp toy tonneau runabout** | 5662 | R | 175-275.000 USD | 75.306 | 115.500 | 101.663 | 09-10-15 | Hershey | 241 | RMS F686 |

The car was acquired by Harold Coker in 2011 in original condition. Subsequently it received a full mechanical restoration, the interior were retrimmed while the body, repainted in the 1920s, required only new wood and some metal repairs.

STEVENS-DURYEA (USA) (1901-1927)

| 1903 | **Model L runabout** | 326 | R | 150-180.000 USD | | NS | | 05-10-15 | Philadelphia | 249 | Bon |

Red with black seats; restored many years ago and later unused for many years. Once in the Indianapolis Motor Speedway Museum.

| 1913 | **Model C touring** | 26200 | R | 125-175.000 USD | 82.807* | 126.500* | 112.408* | 08-10-15 | Hershey | 160 | RMS F687 |

Light grey with black interior; acquired in 1997 by the current owner, who later had the body repainted and the engine rebuilt (see lot 234 RM 10.10.08 NS).

STEYR-PUCH (A) (1920-1977)

| 1939 | **Typ 55 "Baby"** | LV3551 | L | 10-15.000 EUR | 12.682 | 18.119 | 16.100 | 18-06-16 | Wien | 401 | Dor |

Red with light brown interior; since new in the same family ownership.

| 1965 | **500 D** | 5141968 | L | 10-16.000 EUR | 16.477 | 25.446 | 22.400 | 17-10-15 | Salzburg | 301 | Dor |

Light blue with two-tone brown interior; fully restored. Two owners.

| 1962 | **650 T** | 5133162 | L | 14-20.000 EUR | 12.229 | 17.472 | 15.525 | 18-06-16 | Wien | 407 | Dor |

Red with black cloth interior; in the past the car was modified in Finland for rallying and fitted with a 650 TR engine.

| 1968 | **Fiat 2300 DeLuxe** | 207437 | L | 14-20.000 EUR | 10.710 | 16.540 | 14.560 | 17-10-15 | Salzburg | 331 | Dor |

Blue with brown cloth interior; described as in good original condition.

STODDARD DAYTON (USA) (1904-1913)

| 1907 | **Model K runabout** | 1004K | R | 200-250.000 USD | | NS | | 20-05-16 | Indianapolis | S141 | Mec |

Black with black leather interior; fully restored. Engine rebuilt in 2015. One of only three examples known to exist.

| 1909 | **Model 9A touring** | A3724 | R | 100-125.000 USD | | NS | | 09-10-15 | Hershey | 232 | RMS |

Red with black leather interior; an older restoration, the car is described as still in very good overall condition.

STUDEBAKER (USA) (1902-1966)

| 1910 | **Garford Model G runabout** | G7239 | L | 80-120.000 USD | 96.646* | 126.500* | 111.687* | 19-08-16 | Carmel | 54 | Bon F688 |

Cream with red interior; an older restoration, the car requires recommissioning prior to use.

F687: 1913 Stevens-Duryea Model C touring

F688: 1910 Studebaker Garford Model G runabout

Year	Model	(Bodybuilder)	Chassis No.	Steering	Estimate	Hammer Price £	Hammer Price $	Hammer Price €	Date	Place	Lot	Auc. H.
1915	Model SD touring		431892	L	20-30.000 USD	10.801*	16.500*	14.662*	08-10-15	Hershey	132	RMS
Two-tone maroon with black fenders; restored a few years ago. From the Richard Roy estate.													
1914	Model SD touring		412644	R	8-12.000 GBP	8.580*	11.396*	10.234*	02-07-16	Woodstock	152	Coy
White with black fenders; since 1968 in the current ownership. For restoration.													
1936	Dictator sedan		5517156	L	NA	20.064*	27.500*	24.849*	24-06-16	Uncasville	76	B/J
Light green with light grey interior; fully restored.													
1938	Commander sedan		4114127	R	12-16.000 GBP		NS		10-12-15	London	324	Bon
Black; described as in original condition. Mechanicals recently overhauled.													
1939	Commander sedan (Richards)		4130704	R	10-14.000 GBP	12.320	16.124	14.236	20-08-16	Brooklands	243	His
Metallic green with maroon leather interior; sold new to Australia where it was bodied, the car remained with its first owner until the early 1990s. Restored in the mid-1990s; imported into the UK in 2007 (see lots 739 Bonhams 8.9.07 $15,814 and 298 Historics 31.8.13 $17,358).													
1939	Champion DeLuxe coupé		636480	L	18.5-21.500 GBP	19.550	29.769	26.727	05-09-15	Beaulieu	105	Bon
Beige; the car was imported new in Portugal where it was restored in the late 1990s.													
1951	Champion Business coupé		G1005268	L	NA	18.123*	27.500*	24.662*	26-09-15	Las Vegas	389	B/J
Blue with grey interior; restored.													
1948	Champion DeLuxe sedan		327597	L	18-25.000 EUR	4.851*	6.990*	6.160*	14-05-16	Monaco	126	RMS
Green; in original, unrestored condition. Purchased new by Gianni Mazzocchi, founder of the Quattroruote magazine. Since the mid-1970s on display at the Quattroruote Collection.													
1948	Champion convertible		G316329	L	NA	31.496	45.000	39.983	18-06-16	Portland	S62	Mec
Yellow with red leather interior; restored in 2006-07.													
1955	Champion Regal		1G935529	L	14-16.000 GBP	12.880	16.959	15.292	28-07-16	Donington Park	81	H&H
Yellow and black; fitted with a 5-speed manual gearbox.													
1950	Commander Starlight coupé		H432357	L	NA	17.192*	24.200*	21.296*	09-04-16	Palm Beach	40	B/J
Green with tan interior; 4-speed manual gearbox with overdrive.													
1953	Commander Regal Starliner hardtop		8342291	L	28-32.000 USD		NS		02-04-16	Ft.Lauderdale	765	AA
Two-tone green; described as in good working order.													
1955	Commander Regal hardtop		8420103	L	70-90.000 USD	37.752	55.000	49.022	20-05-16	Indianapolis	F204.1	Mec
Blue and white with blue leather interior; restored. Automatic transmission.													
1957	Golden Hawk hardtop		6100991	L	90-120.000 USD	65.221	99.000	88.110	05-10-15	Philadelphia	216	Bon
Gold and white; restoration completed two years ago. The original drum brakes were replaced with discs. Supercharged 289 engine with automatic transmission (see lot F481 Russo & Steele 18.1.14 $ 60,600).													
1957	Golden Hawk hardtop		6103678	L	50-70.000 USD	34.067*	52.250*	45.990*	09-10-15	Hershey	287	RMS
Gold with tan interior; since 1996 in the current ownership. Some mechanical works carried out in 2010. 275bhp 289 supercharged engine with automatic transmission.													
1963	Gran Turismo Hawk		63V32107	L	40-50.000 USD	17.930*	27.500*	24.206*	09-10-15	Hershey	283	RMS
Champagne gold with red vinyl interior; in very good original condition, the car has covered 93,500 miles. 210bhp 289 engine with automatic transmission.													
1963	Avanti		63R1908	L	22-28.000 USD	12.537*	16.500*	14.847*	30-07-16	Plymouth	107	RMS
White with orange interior; for over 40 years in the same family ownership. 240bhp R1 engine with automatic transmission.													

STUTZ (USA) (1911-1934)

Year	Model	(Bodybuilder)	Chassis No.	Steering	Estimate	£	$	€	Date	Place	Lot	Auc. H.
1921	Series K Bearcat		10555	R	Refer Dpt.	453.816	594.000	524.443	19-08-16	Carmel	84	Bon
The car was discovered in Georgia by Wayne Carini at the former estate of its original owner, where it had been stored for 80 years from the 1930s. Approximately 10,000 miles covered since new. The body and interior are original, the mechanicals has been overhauled. Exhibited at the 2015 Pebble Beach Concours d'Elegance, it won the FIVA award for the most significant original pre-war car.													
1930	Model M cabriolet (LeBaron)		M846CD25E	L	180-240.000 USD		NS		19-08-16	Carmel	89	Bon
Described as in highly original condition, the car received a conservative restoration in Italy in the late 2000s.													
1931	Model SV-16 convertible		MB461325	L	140-180.000 USD	93.608	143.000	127.070	08-10-15	Hershey	165	RMS
Red with black fenders and tan interior; restored in the late 1960s. In more recent years the body was repainted and the interior were reupholstered. Recently serviced (see lot 271 RM 12.10.12 $ 154,000).													
1930	Model SV-16 Monte Carlo sedan (Weymann)		M854CD27S	L	550-650.000 USD	384.780	550.000	495.935	12-03-16	Amelia Island	159	RMS
Beige and maroon with beige cloth interior; restored to concours condition in the early 2000s and refreshed in recent years. Formerly in the A.K. Miller collection (see lot 132 RM 9.3.13 $ 550,000).													

F689: 1957 Studebaker Golden Hawk hardtop

F690: 1921 Stutz Series K Bearcat

Year	Model	(Bodybuilder)	Chassis no.	Steering	Estimate	Hammer price £	Hammer price $	Hammer price €	Date	Place	Lot	Auc. H.
1933	Model DV-32 roadster	(LeBaron)	DV241505	L	3.300-4.600.000 DKK	373.808	567.353	508.910	26-09-15	Ebeltoft	26	Bon
	Two-tone tan with tan leather interior; full restoration completed in 1997. From the Frederiksen Collection (see lot 35 Christie's 7.9.96 $ 167,500).											
1931	Model DV-32 convertible sedan	(LeBaron)	DV421383	L	175-225.000 USD	103.994	159.500	140.392	09-10-15	Hershey	271	RMS
	Blue with cloth interior; from 1950 to 2012 in the Pettit family ownership, the car is described as in original condition except for the paintwork redone probably during the WWII years. Recently returned to running and driving order (see lot 6 Gooding 18.8.12 $ 154,000).											
1931	Mod.DV-32 convertible victoria	(Rollston)	DVPC1294	L	800-1.000.000 USD	769.560	1.100.000	991.870	12-03-16	Amelia Island	132	RMS F691
	Black with cream leather interior; known ownership history since new. Bought in 2010 by the current owner, Richard Mitchell, and fully restored to concours condition to its original colours.											

STUTZ (USA) (1969-1985)

Year	Model	Chassis no.	Steering	Estimate	£	$	€	Date	Place	Lot	Auc. H.
1976	Blackhawk	2J57W6P308891	L	NA	23.922*	36.300*	32.554*	26-09-15	Las Vegas	782	B/J
	Gold with tan interior; restored.										

SUBARU (J) (1958-)

Year	Model	Chassis no.	Steering	Estimate	£	$	€	Date	Place	Lot	Auc. H.
1968	360	K111L3787	L	NQ	9.545*	13.750*	12.163*	11-06-16	Hershey	121	TFA
	White with red interior; restored several years ago.										
1996	Impreza WRC	PR0WRC97001	R	NA	155.000	238.406	208.940	14-10-15	Duxford	112	H&H
	First example of the new model built by Prodrive, the car was tested during its development by several drivers, including Colin McRae, and did its race debut at the 1997 Monte Carlo Rally. Subsequently it has had a long race career until 2007. In 2009 it was bought by the current owner who had it restored by Prodrive (see lot 233 Coys 10.1.09 NS).										

SUNBEAM (GB) (1901-1935)

Year	Model	Chassis no.	Steering	Estimate	£	$	€	Date	Place	Lot	Auc. H.
1913	25/30hp tourer	5320	R	1.200-1.600.000 DKK	118.939	180.521	161.926	26-09-15	Ebeltoft	33	Bon F692
	Green with black wings and tan interior; an older restoration. From the Frederiksen Collection (see lot 645 Bonhams 3.12.07 NS).										
1919	16hp tourer	503019	R	35-45.000 GBP	40.825	62.164	55.812	05-09-15	Beaulieu	124	Bon
	Two-tone brown with beige leather interior; restored at unspecified date, it is described as in very good driving order (see lots 319 Bonhams 9.12.13 $ 60,286 and 150 Coys 11.7.15 $ 56,668).										
1927	30hp tourer	7001G	R	200-250.000 GBP	NS			07-09-15	London	166	RMS
	British racing green with green leather interior; built as a two-passenger tourer with twin dickie seats, the car was later fitted with a hearse body and used until 1961, when the body was removed and the chassis put in storage for several years. In 1997 the car was fitted with the present new body and subsequently it was driven at several historic events and exhibited at some Concourse d'Elegance events.										
1934	Twenty-Five tourer	81495	R	25-30.000 GBP	43.700	66.542	59.742	05-09-15	Beaulieu	138	Bon
	Red with black wings and black interior; fully restored between 1975 and 1979. Body repainted in 1993. Acquired in 2011 by the current owner and recommissioned.										
1933	Twenty-Five 4-door sports coupé	8035S	R	40-50.000 GBP	NS			10-07-16	Chateau Impney	24	H&H
	Dark blue and black with brown interior; restored in the mid-1990s. Described as in good mechanical order (see lot 40 H & H 28.7.04 $22,796).										
1933	Twenty-Five 4-door sports coupé	8035S	R	35-45.000 GBP	33.600	44.241	39.893	28-07-16	Donington Park	71	H&H
	See lot 24 H & H 10.7.16.										

SUNBEAM-TALBOT (GB) (1938-1975)

Year	Model	(Bodybuilder)	Chassis no.	Steering	Estimate	£	$	€	Date	Place	Lot	Auc. H.
1938	Ten cabriolet	(Abbott)	40030	R	7-8.000 GBP	11.760	15.484	13.963	28-07-16	Donington Park	38	H&H
	Two-tone body with green leather interior; in good overall condition.											
1954	Alpine Special		A3015176LRXS	L	45-60.000 USD	35.860*	55.000*	48.411*	09-10-15	Hershey	288	RMS F693
	Black; stored from 1970 to 2000 and subsequently fully restored. 43,000 original miles.											
1955	Alpine		A3502014	L	45-55.000 USD	32.007*	46.200*	41.418*	05-06-16	Greenwhich	81	Bon
	Light blue with beige leather interior; restored at unspecified date. From the Evergreen Collection.											
1961	Alpine		9108109HRO	R	5-8.000 GBP	7.952	11.969	11.313	28-11-15	Weybridge	322	His
	Light green with red interior; recently restored.											
1964	Tiger V8		B9470404LRXFE	L	30-35.000 GBP	NS			05-09-15	Beaulieu	118	Bon
	Red; sold new to the USA, the car was reimported in the UK in later 2014 and subsequently recommissioned.											
1965	Tiger V8		B9472154LRXFE	L	NA	94.007	142.500	130.131	12-12-15	Austin	S101	Mec
	Red with black interior; 310bhp 289 rebuilt engine. Rear disc brakes. With hardtop.											

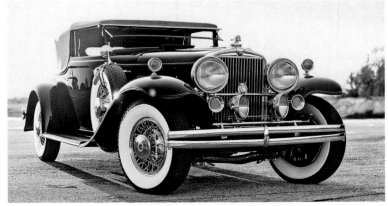

F691: 1931 Stutz Mod.DV-32 convertible victoria (Rollston)

F692: 1913 Sunbeam 25/30hp tourer

Year	Model	(Bodybuilder)	Chassis no.	Steering	Estimate	Hammer Price £	$	€	Sale Date	Place	Lot	Auc. H.
1967	Tiger V8		B382002093LRXFE	L	150-180.000 USD	103.905*	148.500*	135.981*	30-01-16	Scottsdale	105	G&Co
	Blue; recently restored. Just over 55,000 original miles (see lot 179 RM/Sotheby's 14.3.15 $ 137,500).											
1967	Tiger V8		B395011945LRX	L	85-95.000 EUR		NS		14-05-16	Monaco	157	Coy
	Red with black interior; described as in good overall condition.											
1967	Tiger V8		B382100231	L	150-200.000 USD	99.528	145.000	129.239	20-05-16	Indianapolis	F128	Mec
	Green with black interior; restored in 2015. From the Joe McMurrey Collection.											
1966	Tiger V8		B382000607LRXFE	L	125-150.000 USD	76.208	110.000	98.615	05-06-16	Greenwhich	44	Bon F694
	Black with red interior; mechanicals restored between 2008 and 2010, body and interior in 2012. Currently fitted with a 289 engine (the original 260 unit in included with the sale).											
1967	Tiger V8		B382100625	L	120-140.000 USD	76.400	100.000	88.290	19-08-16	Monterey	F79	Mec
	Red with black interior; since 1976 with the same owner.											
1964	Tiger Le Mans coupé		B9499999	R	300-400.000 GBP		NS		06-12-15	London	022	Bon
	One of the thees examples built by the Rootes Group's Competition Department for the 1964 Le Mans 24 Hours. The offered car was used as a test mule but not raced at the event. The cars were built by Brian Lister, the bodies by Williams & Pritchard and the 275bhp 260 Ford V8 engine were supplied by Carroll Shelby. In early 1965 the car was sold to the Alan Frazer Racing Team and raced for the next few seasons. Finished in British racing green, the car has been raced in the 2000s at several historic events. The 260 engine has been recently rebuilt.											

SURTEES (GB) *(1969-1978)*

Year	Model	(Bodybuilder)	Chassis no.	Steering	Estimate	Hammer Price £	$	€	Sale Date	Place	Lot	Auc. H.
1971	TS8		TS806	M	30-35.000 GBP	38.810	51.101	46.079	28-07-16	Silverstone	123	SiC
	Driven by Sam Posey, the car placed second at the 1971 Formula 5000 USA Championship. Raced until 1975; restored in the mid-2000s.											

SWALLOW DORETTI (GB) *(1954-1956)*

Year	Model	(Bodybuilder)	Chassis no.	Steering	Estimate	Hammer Price £	$	€	Sale Date	Place	Lot	Auc. H.
1954	Doretti		T5621E	L	70-90.000 USD	51.821*	74.800*	67.058*	05-06-16	Greenwhich	28	Bon F695
	White with grey and black interior; acquired in 2008 by the current owner and subsequently fully restored. The TR2 Triumph engine has been fitted with a competition supercharger.											

TALBOT (F) *(1920-1935)*

Year	Model	(Bodybuilder)	Chassis no.	Steering	Estimate	Hammer Price £	$	€	Sale Date	Place	Lot	Auc. H.
1929	M67 torpedo (Saoutchik)		72027	R	70-80.000 EUR		NS		08-11-15	Lyon	209	Ose
	White with black wings and burgundy leather interior; some works to the body and mechanicals carried out recently (see Osenat lots 309 9.12.12 $ 29,940 and 354 16.3.14 NS).											

TALBOT (GB) *(1902-1938)*

Year	Model	(Bodybuilder)	Chassis no.	Steering	Estimate	Hammer Price £	$	€	Sale Date	Place	Lot	Auc. H.
1929	14/45 Type AG tourer (Darracq)		25065	R	70-90.000 EUR	33.748*	48.980*	44.800*	03-02-16	Paris	132	RMS
	Dark blue with black wings; fully restored over a long period from the 1970s to 1996. In good working order (see lot 623 Bonhams 24.4.06 $ 40,076).											
1933	AV105 Alpine Speed Model (Vanden Plas)		31654	R	90-120.000 GBP	141.500	204.991	181.743	20-03-16	Goodwood	46	Bon F696
	Two-tone green; acquired as a dismantled restoration project in 1978 by the current owner and fully restored between 2000 and 2004. Little used in the past 3-4 years. Manual gearbox.											

TALBOT-LAGO (F) *(1935-1958)*

Year	Model	(Bodybuilder)	Chassis no.	Steering	Estimate	Hammer Price £	$	€	Sale Date	Place	Lot	Auc. H.
1938	T120 Baby 3l coach		91509	R	NQ	50.810	76.917	70.800	08-11-15	Lyon	212	Ose
	The car has covered 1,000 kms since the restoration completed 10 years ago.											
1939	T15 Baby cabriolet		91626	R	NA	384.835	550.000	503.635	29-01-16	Scottsdale	1378	B/J
	Brown with tan interior; restored in France in 1990 and imported into the USA in 1991.											
1950	T15 Baby berline		121524	R	3-4.000 EUR	9.866	14.293	12.672	20-03-16	Fontainebleau	303	Ose
	For restoration; since 1966 in the collection of Jacques Blomet, its second owner.											
1938	T23 Baby 4l cabriolet (Figoni/Falaschi)		93123	R	550-600.000 USD	394.988	517.000	456.459	19-08-16	Carmel	34	Bon F697
	Black with tan leather interior; exhibited at the Talbot-Lago stand at the 1938 London Motor Show, the car was acquired by Grant Barney Schley III and imported into the USA. In the late 1960s it was bought by the previous owner who retained it for 40 years or more. In recent times the body has been repainted and the front seats refurbished. The car was checked over mechanically and has been made to run, but it requires proper refurbishment of the technical aspect. The sale proceeds will be donated to the Simeone Foundation Museum.											
1939	T4 Minor berline		95300	R	12-16.000 EUR	14.209	21.511	19.800	07-11-15	Lyon	251	Agu
	Black with red leather interior; described as in good working order. Since 1990 in the current ownership.											
1947	T26 Lago Record cabriolet (Graber)		100007	R	145-185.000 GBP	145.600	222.215	199.370	07-09-15	London	148	RMS
	Pale yellow with red interior; described as in good overall condition. 55,000 kms on the odometer.											
1947	T26 Lago Record cabriolet (Worblaufen)		100089	R	NA	500.286	715.000	654.726	29-01-16	Scottsdale	1383	B/J F698
	Red with tan interior; restored.											
1950	T26 Lago Record cabriolet (Graber)		102028	R	180-300.000 EUR	155.982	226.997	202.640	05-02-16	Paris	131	Art
	Grey with tab interior; sold new to Switzerland, in 1965 the was imported into the USA where it was restored in the late 1990s. In the 2000s it was reimported into Europe (see lots Christie's 74 28.4.01 NS, and Bonhams 109 9.2.08 $ 298, 242 and 544 7.2.13 $ 389,448).											
1951	T26 Lago Record cabriolet (Dubos)		102017	R	240-320.000 EUR	201.859	293.761	262.240	05-02-16	Paris	224	Art
	White with original cream leather interior; body repainted about 40 years ago. Restored in 2005 (see lot 227 Osenat 13.12.09 NS).											
1954	T26 GSL Lago Grand Sport		111006	R	350-425.000 USD	294.140	385.000	339.917	19-08-16	Monterey	151	RMS
	Burgundy with cognac leather interior; restored approximately 25 years ago and recently refreshed (see lot 180 RM 12.3.11 $154,000).											
1956	T14 LS		140036	R	280-340.000 EUR	293.613	427.289	381.440	05-02-16	Paris	186	Art F699
	Metallic grey with blue leather interior; restored in the 1990s. 188 kms covered since.											
1956	T14 LS Spécial		140031	R	220-260.000 EUR		NS		13-05-16	Monaco	129	Bon
	Silver with grey interior; restored in 1994. When new a factory demonstrator used by Louis Rosier, then also a Talbot-Lago dealer (see Bonhams lots 102 5.9.03 $ 68,358 and 230 2.2.12 $ 210,813).											
1958	T14 LS		140010	R	200-250.000 EUR	187.978	244.116	220.520	09-07-16	Le Mans	149	Art
	Metallic blue with grey roof and beige and grey/blue interior; restored some years ago. Last serviced in 2014.											

F693: 1954 Sunbeam-Talbot Alpine Special

F694: 1966 Sunbeam-Talbot Tiger V8

F695: 1954 Swallow Doretti

F696: 1933 Talbot AV105 Alpine Speed Model (Vanden Plas)

F697: 1938 Talbot-Lago T23 Baby 4l cabriolet (Figoni/Falaschi)

F698: 1947 Talbot-Lago T26 Lago Record cabriolet (Worblaufen)

F699: 1956 Talbot-Lago T14 LS

F700: 1950 Tatra Type 87

Year	Model	(Bodybuilder)	Chassis no.	Steering	Estimate	Hammer price £	Hammer price $	Hammer price €	Date	Place	Lot	Auc. H.

TATRA (CS) (1899-1998)

| 1950 | **Type 87** | | 79233 | L | 100-125.000 USD | 95.260 | 137.500 | 123.269 | 05-06-16 | Greenwhich | 15 | **Bon** F700 |

Dark blue with ivory interior; restored in Czechoslovakia in the late 1990s and imported into the USA in 2000. Some mechanical works carried out in 2010.

| 1949 | **T600 Tatraplan** | | 70722 | L | 30-40.000 EUR | | NS | | 26-09-15 | Frankfurt | 149 | Coy |

Black with red interior; mechanicals restored in 2011.

| 1981 | **T613-3** | | TMT613003JP008931 | L | 6-8.000 EUR | 5.708* | 8.035* | 7.071* | 09-04-16 | Essen | 195 | Coy |

Black with grey interior; 23,445 kms on the odometer. From the Brundza Collection.

TECNO (I) (1962-1973)

| 1966 | **F3** | | 00204 | M | 35-45.000 GBP | 32.450 | 49.775 | 43.808 | 10-10-15 | Ascot | 111 | **Coy** F701 |

Red with gold nose; Works car for the 1966 and 1967 seasons, race debut at Mugello in July 1966 driven by Carlo Facetti. Restored in the UK in the 2000s. Most of the original Fantuzzi body included in the sale.

TEMPLAR (USA) (1917-1924)

| 1924 | **Model 4-45 touring** | | 6706 | L | 45-60.000 USD | | NS | | 05-06-16 | Greenwhich | 33 | **Bon** |

Dark green with black leather interior; restored in recent years (see lot 180 Bonhams 12.3.15 $ 60,500).

THOMAS (USA) (1903-1918)

| 1905 | **Flyer 40hp touring** | | B114(engine) | R | 375-500.000 USD | 143.440 | 220.000 | 193.644 | 09-10-15 | Hershey | 244 | RMS |

Red with tan leather interior; restored many years ago. Recently recommissioned after a period of inactivity. From the Harold Coker collection.

| 1907 | **Flyer 60hp runabout** | | D212(engine) | R | 450-600.000 USD | 215.160 | 330.000 | 290.466 | 09-10-15 | Hershey | 238 | RMS |

Grey with burgundy leather interior; acquired in 2004 by Harold Coker from the previous German owner. The latter searched the world for original Thomas vehicles and parts and subsequently assembled this vehicle. The body is new but nearly all chassis components are of genuine Thomas design and construction, except for the cylinder casting and transmission which where newly made.

| 1910 | **Model K-6-70 flyabout** | | 318 | R | 900-1.200.000 USD | 583.028 | 825.000 | 759.825 | 10-03-16 | Amelia Island | 142 | **Bon** F702 |

Red with red interior; bought new by the Fire Department of Chattanooga, the car remained the property of the city until 1956. In the mid-1960 it was acquired by Harold Coker, its third owner who had it restored and fitted with the present flyabout coachwork. Later the car passed to David Noran and then to the present owner who had it recommissioned and returned to the road.

TOYOTA (J) (1936-)

| 1982 | **FJ40 Land Cruiser** | | 810127 | L | 40-60.000 EUR | | NS | | 09-10-15 | Zoute | 18 | **Bon** |

Brown with white roof and black vinyl interior; described as in good overall condition.

| 1980 | **FJ43 Land Cruiser** | | FJ4365659 | L | 80-100.000 USD | 47.679* | 68.200* | 62.546* | 28-01-16 | Scottsdale | 96 | **Bon** |

Long-wheelbase version finished in green with tan soft-top; restored.

| 1978 | **FJ40 Land Cruiser** | | FJ40265788 | L | 80-100.000 USD | 57.676* | 82.500* | 75.661* | 28-01-16 | Phoenix | 102 | RMS |

Sky blue with white roof and grey interior; fully restored. Since new in the same family ownership.

| 1966 | **FJ40 Land Cruiser** | | FJ4041897 | L | 90-130.000 USD | 48.104* | 68.750* | 62.954* | 30-01-16 | Scottsdale | 115 | G&Co |

Red; fully restored (see lot 151 RM 27.4.13 $ 88,000).

| 1978 | **FJ40 Land Cruiser** | | 266294 | L | 65-85.000 USD | 50.147 | 66.000 | 59.387 | 30-07-16 | Plymouth | 128 | RMS |

Green with white roof; since 1989 in the current ownership. Restoration completed in 2013.

| 1981 | **FJ43 Land Cruiser** | | FJ43105510 | L | 70-90.000 USD | 134.464* | 176.000* | 155.390* | 20-08-16 | Pebble Beach | 78 | G&Co |

Green; restored in early 2016. Fitted with a 5-speed gearbox.

| 1967 | **2000 GT** | | MF1010100 | L | 800-1.000.000 USD | | NS | | 23-01-16 | Kissimmee | S200 | Mec |

Red with black interior; one of 62 US market cars built. Restored in 2007 (see lot S59 Mecum 15.8.15 $ 925,000).

| 1967 | **2000 GT** | | MF1010128 | R | 750-950.000 USD | | NS | | 29-01-16 | Scottsdale | 27 | G&Co |

Red with black interior; sold new to Mozambique. Fully restored in Costa Rica between 2013 and 2014 (see lot 217 RM 16.8.14 $ 1,045,000).

| 1967 | **2000 GT** | | MF1010158 | R | 800-900.000 USD | | NS | | 29-01-16 | Phoenix | 255 | RMS |

White with black leather interior; sold new in Japan, the car was imported into the USA in 2013 and subsequently fully serviced.

F701: 1966 Tecno F3

F702: 1910 Thomas Model K-6-70 flyabout

Year	Model	(Bodybuilder)	Chassis no.	Steering	Estimate	Hammer price £	Hammer price $	Hammer price €	Date	Place	Lot	Auc. H.
1967	**2000 GT**		MF1010088	L	800-950.000 USD	557.931	797.500	719.106	12-03-16	Amelia Island	125	RMS
	White with black interior; delivered new to a USA Toyota dealer, the car remained unsold for five years. First registered in 1973, it remained in the same family ownership until 2007. Engine rebuilt, body repainted. 46,859 miles covered. Since 2014 with the present, third owner (see lot 36 Gooding 16.8.14 $ 1,155,000).											**F703**
1967	**2000 GT**		MF1010128	L	600-700.000 USD	407.594	533.500	471.027	20-08-16	Pebble Beach	9	G&Co
	See lot 27 Gooding & Company 29.1.16.											

TRIUMPH (GB) (1923-1984)

Year	Model	(Bodybuilder)	Chassis no.	Steering	Estimate	£	$	€	Date	Place	Lot	Auc. H.
1932	**Southern Cross tourer**		90705	R	14-18.000 GBP	14.000	18.323	16.177	20-08-16	Brooklands	297	His
	Two-tone green with green leather interior; since 1963 in the same family ownership. Restored between 2004 and 2008.											
1937	**Dolomite saloon**		2311407	R	30-36.000 GBP	36.960	48.373	42.707	20-08-16	Brooklands	299	His
	Green with green leather interior; subjected to a long restoration started in 1998. Currently fitted with a pre-war 1767cc Triumph engine (see lots 343 Bonhams 3.7.09 $29,162 and 253 Historics 29.11.14 $59,405).											**F704**
1946	**1800 Roadster**		TRD255	R	22-25.000 GBP	23.063	30.351	27.311	30-07-16	Silverstone	958	SiC
	Gunmetal grey with blue leather interior; restored in the 1990s and recently refreshed.											
1947	**1800 Roadster**		TRD434	R	18-25.000 GBP	21.840	28.584	25.236	20-08-16	Brooklands	272	His
	Black with silver bonnet; restored in 2015.											
1954	**TR2**		TS349	R	NA	34.160	48.439	43.185	20-04-16	Duxford	12	H&H
	Red with blackberry leather interior; fully restored in 1994, the car is described as still in very good overall condition.											
1954	**TR2**		TS4719L	L	30-40.000 EUR	21.338*	27.710*	25.032*	09-07-16	Le Mans	111	Art
	Light blue; restored at unspecified date. In good mechanical condition.											
1960	**TR3A**		TS57907LO	L	20-22.500 USD	12.320	18.700	16.643	05-10-15	Philadelphia	214	Bon
	British racing green with white leather interior; in largely original condition. 61,000 miles covered.											
1959	**TR3A**		TS34754L	L	30-35.000 EUR	25.835	39.110	36.000	08-11-15	Lyon	244	Ose
	White with blue interior; restored in 2007.											
1959	**TR3A**		TS58901L	L	22-28.000 EUR	16.195	23.211	21.267	16-01-16	Maastricht	422	Coy
	Red with black interior; restored between 2013 and 2015.											
1959	**TR3A**		TS39531L	R	NA	22.400	31.161	28.376	24-02-16	Donington Park	39	H&H
	Red with black interior; in good overall condition. Reimported into the UK from the USA in 2005 and converted to right-hand drive in 2007 (see lot 403 Bonhams 1.12.11 $ 27,535).											
1959	**TR3A**		TS46190LO	L	20-30.000 EUR	20.984	29.981	26.640	19-06-16	Fontainebleau	358	Ose
	Light blue with blue interior; in good overall condition.											
1962	**TR3B**		TCF862L	L	35-45.000 USD	23.243	33.550	30.078	05-06-16	Greenwhich	4	Bon
	White with black interior; restored.											
1965	**Herald 2-door saloon** (Michelotti)		GA1813510L	R	1.5-1.800 GBP	1.400	1.985	1.759	16-04-16	Cambridge	3307	Che
	White with red interior; restored some years ago.											
1970	**Herald 13/60 saloon** (Michelotti)		GE75278DL	R	4-5.000 GBP	3.390	4.934	4.375	18-05-16	Donington Park	3	H&H
	Brown with beige vinyl interior; one owner from new to April 2016. 82,000 miles covered. Refurbished in the 1980s.											
1963	**Italia 2000** (Vignale)		TSF519LCO	L	80-100.000 EUR	68.816	100.146	89.400	05-02-16	Paris	123	Art
	Silver with black interior; restored many years ago, engine overhauled in recent years.											**F705**
1980	**Spitfire 1500**		FM95148	R	3.5-4.500 GBP	4.144	6.032	5.348	18-05-16	Donington Park	117	H&H
	White with black interior; restored in 2012.											
1967	**Spitfire MkIII**		FD6416	R	7-9.000 GBP		NS		28-07-16	Donington Park	51	H&H
	Red with black vinyl interior; restored in 2004.											
1965	**Spitfire MkII**		FC57784	R	19-24.000 GBP	22.400	29.317	25.883	20-08-16	Brooklands	331	His
	Dark green with black interior; in the same family ownership since new. 10,000 miles covered. Mechanicals overhauled and body repainted in recent years.											
1964	**TR4** (Michelotti)		26464CT	R	17-19.000 GBP	18.230	27.963	24.611	10-10-15	Ascot	137	Coy
	Black with black interior; body repainted. Used for club racing.											
1964	**TR4 Dové coupé** (Harrington)		CT20440	R	30-40.000 EUR		NS		07-11-15	Lyon	279	Agu
	Red with black interior; the car remained in the same ownership for circa 30 years and subsequently it was restored and later imported into France.											

F703: 1967 Toyota 2000 GT

F704: 1937 Triumph Dolomite saloon

Year	Model	(Bodybuilder)	Chassis no.	Steering	Estimate	Hammer price £	Hammer price $	Hammer price €	Date	Place	Lot	Auc. H.
1965	TR4A	(Michelotti)	CTC519220	R	18-22.000 GBP	20.160	30.343	28.680	28-11-15	Weybridge	216	His **F706**
	Red; in good overall condition. Engine overhauled in 2010.											
1965	TR4A IRS	(Michelotti)	CTC575140	R	18-22.000 GBP		NS		09-12-15	Chateau Impney	146	H&H
	Red with black interior; restored.											
1963	TR4 surrey top	(Michelotti)	CT21834LO	L	25-35.000 USD	19.225*	27.500*	25.220*	28-01-16	Phoenix	176	RMS
	Red with black interior; restored in 2008 (see lot 320 Bonhams 2.6.13 $ 36,850).											
1965	TR4A IRS	(Michelotti)	CTC54792	R	NA	20.720	28.824	26.248	24-02-16	Donington Park	36	H&H
	Old English white with black interior; from 1982 to 2014 with the same owner who restored it at unspecified date.											
1966	TR4A IRS	(Michelotti)	CTC60671	R	30-34.000 GBP	28.000	40.018	36.084	12-03-16	Brooklands	168	His
	Red with black leather interior; for 26 years in the current ownership. Restored.											
1962	TR4	(Michelotti)	CT2905	R	15.5-17.500 GBP	14.840	21.601	19.151	18-05-16	Donington Park	75	H&H
	Red with black interior; restored in 1992-93, new wings fitted in 2010 (see lot 9 H&H 26.7.06 $ 17,567).											
1964	TR4	(Michelotti)	CT325750	R	26-30.000 GBP	23.916	31.057	28.056	10-07-16	Chateau Impney	52	H&H
	White with red interior; restored two years ago.											
1965	TR4	(Michelotti)	CT55074L	R	18-22.000 GBP	*	NR	*	28-07-16	Donington Park	29	H&H
	Red with black interior; reimported into the UK from the USA and converted to right hand drive.											
1966	TR4A IRS	(Michelotti)	CTC65334	R	26-30.000 GBP	24.640	32.443	29.255	28-07-16	Donington Park	61	H&H
	White; restored.											
1968	TR5	(Michelotti)	CP26320	R	5-8.000 GBP	18.400*	28.018*	25.155*	05-09-15	Beaulieu	101	Bon
	Restoration project; acquired in 1976 by the current owner and last used in 1990.											
1968	TR5	(Michelotti)	CO18470	R	24-28.000 GBP	35.840	53.943	50.986	28-11-15	Weybridge	219	His
	Dark blue; stored from 1973 to 2003, the car was subsequently fully restored. Engine and gearbox rebuilt. With hardtop.											
1975	TR6		CR62090	R	24-28.000 GBP	29.680	44.671	42.223	28-11-15	Weybridge	239	His
	Yellow with black interior; in very good original condition. 19,419 miles covered.											
1971	TR6		CP54077	R	22-25.000 GBP		NS		09-12-15	Chateau Impney	37	H&H
	Restored at unspecified date.											
1972	TR6		CP757510	R	10-15.000 GBP		NS		10-12-15	London	322	Bon
	Red; major restoration work undertaken in 2002. For 20 years in the current ownership.											
1976	TR6		CF57938UO	L	40-50.000 USD	32.322*	46.200*	41.659*	11-03-16	Amelia Island	51	G&Co
	Yellow; in very good original condition. 8,250 miles on the odometer. Clutch replaced.											
1973	TR6		CR18610	R	19-24.000 GBP	20.160	28.813	25.980	12-03-16	Brooklands	124	His
	Yellow with black interior; restored in the 1990s.											
1974	TR6		CF24347U	R	13-16.000 GBP	12.040	15.853	14.295	28-07-16	Donington Park	42	H&H
	Red with black interior; reimported into the UK from the USA in 1991 and subsequently restored and converted to right hand drive.											
1976	Stag	(Michelotti)	LD363300	R	NA	18.480	28.424	24.911	14-10-15	Duxford	16	H&H
	Dark blue with black interior; restored in 1991.											
1976	Stag	(Michelotti)	LD409260	R	10-14.000 GBP	11.200	16.857	15.933	28-11-15	Weybridge	211	His
	Red with black vinyl interior; restored four years ago.											
1970	Stag	(Michelotti)	LD6BW	R	NA	15.750	22.297	20.327	06-03-16	Birmingham	355	SiC
	White; acquired 12 years ago by the current owner and subsequently restored.											
1973	Stag	(Michelotti)	LD24773D	R	12-15.000 GBP	12.880	18.408	16.598	12-03-16	Brooklands	203	His
	Green with beige leather interior; restored.											
1980	Dolomite Sprint		TWTLD5AT104779	R	5-7.000 GBP		NS		28-07-16	Donington Park	14	H&H
	Blue; restored.											
1980	TR7		TPADJ7AT210770	R	5-7.000 GBP		NS		12-03-16	Brooklands	112	His
	Silver; described as in good running order.											

F705: 1963 Triumph Italia 2000 (Vignale)

F706: 1965 Triumph TR4A (Michelotti)

384

Year	Model	(Bodybuilder)	Chassis no.	Steering	Estimate	Hammer Price £	Hammer Price $	Hammer Price €	Date	Place	Lot	Auc. H.

TROJAN (GB) *(1922-1974)*

1963 200 — 11247 — R — 15-18.000 GBP — 10.916 — 16.622 — 14.923 — 05-09-15 — Beaulieu — 188 — Bon
Dark blue; since new in the same family ownership. In good overall condition (see lot 457 Bonhams 20.6.15 NS).

TUCKER (USA) *(1947-1948)*

1948 Model 48 Torpedo — 1052 — L — 950-1.250.000 USD — NS — — — 02-04-16 — Ft.Lauderdale — 470 — AA
Chassis, fitted with firewall and suspension, left uncompleted at the factory. It had been built as the test chassis for the automatic transmission. Bought in 1950 at the Tucker bankruptcy auction, the car was completed over a number of years using original parts (as the front end, bumpers, front doors) and new built parts (as the roof, floor and rear doors). Fitted with original 335 engine and pre-selector transmission. Finished in maroon with beige cloth interior.

1948 Model 48 Torpedo — 1049 — L — 1.350-1.850.000 EUR — 1.058.508 — 1.525.171 — 1.344.000 — 14-05-16 — Monaco — 266 — RMS **F707**
One of the cars completed at the factory after production had officially ended. Formerly of the Nick Jenin, Gene Zimmerman and Bob Bahre collections. Between 2003 and 2007 it was fully restored and finished in its original blue livery. Immediately after the restoration it was acquired by the current owner and imported into the UK.

TURNER (GB) *(1951-1966)*

1960 Sports MkII — 60412 — R — NA — 15.400 — 23.687 — 20.759 — 14-10-15 — Duxford — 49 — H&H
Blue with grey interior; 450 miles covered since its recent restoration.

TVR (GB) *(1949-)*

1971 Vixen 2500 — 2061T — R — 19-24.000 GBP — 24.080 — 36.243 — 34.256 — 28-11-15 — Weybridge — 302 — His **F708**
Metallic blue with black interior; restored in the 1990s. Recently serviced.

1978 3000M — 4176FM — R — NA — 12.150 — 17.201 — 15.681 — 06-03-16 — Birmingham — 311 — SiC
White and brown with tan interior; one owner since new. Engine rebuilt in 2004.

1983 Tasmin V8 convertible — DH5503R1 — R — 12-15.000 GBP — 9.520 — 13.606 — 12.268 — 12-03-16 — Brooklands — 257 — His
In good overall condition.

1992 400 SE cabriolet — SDLDEN4PXMB011249 — R — 15-17.000 GBP — NS — — — 09-12-15 — Chateau Impney — 16 — H&H
Metallic red; restored.

1992 Griffith — 11005 — R — 14-16.000 GBP — 16.675 — 25.221 — 23.047 — 10-12-15 — London — 319 — Bon
One owner and 15,000 miles covered.

1997 Chimera 4.0 — 11233 — R — 13-16.000 GBP — 13.500 — 17.766 — 15.987 — 30-07-16 — Silverstone — 505 — SiC
Red with grey leather interior; described as in very good overall condition. 33,000 miles covered.

2002 Tamora — 001457 — R — 17-18.500 GBP — 18.760 — 28.305 — 25.872 — 09-12-15 — Chateau Impney — 24 — H&H
Light metallic grey.

UNIC (F) *(1904-1940)*

1924 Type L3 torpedo — 37025 — L — 25-30.000 EUR — NS — — — 19-06-16 — Fontainebleau — 313 — Ose
Pale yellow with black wings and black interior; described as in good overall condition.

VALLEE (F) *(1896-1901)*

1897 4hp Vis-a-vis — NQ — R — 150-170.000 EUR — 63.277* — 91.837* — 84.000* — 03-02-16 — Paris — 114 — RMS **F709**
Green with black interior; described as in original condition, but for a repaint and new black canvas. One of two Vallees known to survive. Dated 1897 by the Veteran Car Club of Great Britain.

VANDEN PLAS (GB) *(1960-1980)*

1967 Princess 4-Litre R — VDM416716 — R — 40-45.000 USD — 29.601 — 42.900 — 37.542 — 07-05-16 — Auburn — 881 — AA
Blue with tan leather interior; 3-speed manual gearbox.

1961 Princess 4-Litre R — VDM414784 — R — 55-7.500 GBP — 8.064 — 10.618 — 9.574 — 28-07-16 — Donington Park — 84 — H&H
Two-tone body; described as in very good overall condition.

F707: 1948 Tucker Model 48 Torpedo

F708: 1971 TVR Vixen 2500

Year	Model	(Bodybuilder)	Chassis No.	Steering	Estimate	Hammer price £	$	€	Date	Place	Lot	Auc. H.

F709: 1897 Vallee 4hp Vis-a-vis

F710: 1920 Vauxhall 30/98E tourer (Damyon Bros.)

VAUXHALL (GB) (1903-)

Year	Model	Chassis No.	Steering	Estimate	£	$	€	Date	Place	Lot	Auc. H.
1920	30/98E tourer (Damyon Bros.)	E267	R	180-220.000 GBP	169.500	258.098	231.723	05-09-15	Beaulieu	125	Bon F710

Burgundy with black wings, polished aluminium bonnet and black interior; sold new in rolling chassis form to Australia where it was bodied. Fully restored between 1966 and 1970; re-imported into the UK in the late 1980s; several mechanical works carried out between 1991 and 2003; body repainted in more recent years.

| 1925 | 14/40 Princeton tourer | LM2317 | R | 40-45.000 EUR | 31.952 | 46.289 | 41.040 | 20-03-16 | Fontainebleau | 310 | Ose |

Red with black wings and polished aluminium bonnet; in good working order (see lots 119 Coys 14.5.11 NS and 23 H&H 21.9.11 NS).

| 1929 | 20/60 tourer | R4444 | R | NA | 28.560 | 40.498 | 36.106 | 20-04-16 | Duxford | 34 | H&H |

Maroon with maroon interior; restored in the past, the car requires recommissioning prior to use.

| 1934 | Light Six saloon | 612715 | R | 5-7.000 GBP | 5.600 | 8.004 | 7.217 | 12-03-16 | Brooklands | 110 | His |

Black with blue interior; unused from several years. 12hp engine.

| 1961 | Cresta PA saloon | PADX159846 | R | NA | 8.512 | 11.841 | 10.783 | 24-02-16 | Donington Park | 83 | H&H |

Light blue and cream with cream and blue interior; restored. Described as in very good overall condition.

| 1956 | Cresta E saloon | E1PC215282 | R | 10-12.000 GBP | WD | | | 12-03-16 | Brooklands | 202 | His |

Described as in largely original condition; 60,000 miles on the odometer.

| 1962 | Victor DeLuxe saloon | FBE65791 | R | 6.5-7.500 GBP | NS | | | 09-12-15 | Chateau Impney | 14 | H&H |

White; unwarranted 38,500 miles on the odometer.

| 1977 | Firenza Magnum 2300 coupé | 9E37PCX10377 | R | 80-120.000 GBP | 93.340 | 135.222 | 119.886 | 20-03-16 | Goodwood | 23 | Bon F711 |

Prepared to Group 1 Touring Car specification, the car was entered by the Dealer Team Vauxhall (DTV) in the 1977 SPA 24 Hours where it placed 2nd overall and 1st in class driven by Peter Brock and Gerry Marshall. Discovered in 2005 after 15 years probably in a barn, it was fully restored to the DTV livery and raced at several historic events since 2006.

| 1982 | Chevette HSR DTV | 980DEY227924 | R | 70-85.000 GBP | 82.440 | 118.153 | 108.252 | 16-01-16 | Birmingham | 321 | Coy |

"Andrews - Heat for Hire" white and yellow livery; Ex-Works car driven by Russell Brookes at the Rothmans-RAC Series in 1982 and 1983. Sold to private hands it was rallied until 1989. Stored until 1999 and subsequently recommissioned.

| 1991 | Lotus Carlton | 1062159 | L | NA | 20.250 | 28.301 | 25.715 | 26-02-16 | Coventry | 440 | SiC |

Described as in good overall condition.

VELAM (F) (1955-1961)

| 1955 | Isetta | 100605 | L | 1-1.500 EUR | 5.606 | 8.121 | 7.200 | 20-03-16 | Fontainebleau | 301 | Ose |

For restoration; for 32 years in the Jacques Blomet collection.

VENTURI (F) (1985-)

| 1988 | Cup 221 | 00040 | L | 25-35.000 EUR | 26.419* | 34.308* | 30.992* | 09-07-16 | Le Mans | 130 | Art |

Grey with cognac leather interior; in good original condition. 75,000 kms covered.

| 1995 | 400 GT | CE0012 | L | 150-180.000 EUR | 214.162 | 306.084 | 276.000 | 12-03-16 | Lyon | 335 | Agu F712 |

Dark blue with black interior; in very good overall condition. Three owners.

F711: 1977 Vauxhall Firenza Magnum 2300 coupé

F712: 1995 Venturi 400 GT

Year	Model	(Bodybuilder)	Chassis No.	Steering	Estimate	Hammer Price £	$	€	Date	Place	Lot	Auc. H.

VERITAS (D) (1948-1952)

1950 Meteor F2 — 4211 — M — 210-240.000 EUR — NS — 04-02-16 Paris 354 **Bon**
Last example built, the car was raced at just one event in 1952. It remained in the same ownership from 1953 to 1977 when it was acquired by Don Williams and imported into the USA. First restored in 1989 and displayed at the 1992 Pebble Beach Concours d'Elegance. Back to Europe, it was restored again in 2010. The 2-litre Heinkel engine was rebuilt in 2015.

VICTOR (USA)

1907 Highwheel runabout — 33759 — C — 30-40.000 GBP — 38.080 — 54.847 — 48.522 — 11-06-16 Brooklands 260 **His**
See lot 134 Coys 07.11.15.

1907 Runabout — 38(engine) — R — 10-15.000 USD — 14.401* — 22.000* — 19.549* — 08-10-15 Hershey 131 **RMS**
Blue with black interior; restored in the 1960s. Twin-cylinder engine. From the Richard Roy engine.

VOISIN (F) (1919-1958)

1927 C12 torpedo (Duvivier) — 30032 — R — 200-250.000 GBP — 219.900 — 334.842 — 300.625 — 05-09-15 Beaulieu 139 **Bon** F713
Blue and grey; the car was imported into the UK in 1933 and later for many years it remained unrestored in a museum in the Channel Islands. Acquired by the current owner, it was subjected to a full restoration completed in 2004. 2,000 miles covered since.

1927 C14 Lumineuse coach — 28068 — R — 800-950.000 USD — NS — 12-03-16 Amelia Island 154 **RMS**
Black with red cloth interior; restored in France in the 1980s, the car was acquired in 1991 by the current owner. In 2000 the original engine no.28152 was reacquired, rebuilt and refitted to the car. More recently the interior were retrimmed.

1935 C28 Aérosport — 53034 — R — Refer Dpt. — WD — 20-08-16 Monterey 227 **RMS**
Silver with caramel leather interior; the car is described as the first of eight to ten examples built, one of two known to survive and the one displayed at the 1935 Paris Motor Show. Damaged by a bombing during WWII, it was later repaired and fitted with a conventional four-door saloon body. The remains of the car were discovered in 1980 and were acquired in 1998 by the current owner who in 2006 started a full restoration, completed in 2014, using original factory drawings and genuine parts.

1947 C31 Biscooter — NQ — L — 30-35.000 EUR — NS — 20-03-16 Fontainebleau 318 **Ose**
Grey with red interior; restored some years ago.

VOLKSWAGEN (D) (1936-)

1957 Beetle — 1379698 — L — NA — 14.136* — 21.450* — 19.236* — 26-09-15 Las Vegas 67 **B/J**
Blue with blue interior; not used since a full restoration.

1978 Beetle 1200L — 1182007364 — R — 12-16.000 GBP — 13.800 — 20.873 — 19.073 — 10-12-15 London 320 **Bon**
Silver metallic with blue velour interior; never registered, the car has covered 63 miles. Formerly also in the collections of Bernie Ecclestone and Jimi Heselden. Last Edition built in 300 examples (see lot 542 Sotheby's 7.7.97 $ 22,267).

1954 Beetle — 10773047 — L — 30-35.000 USD — 26.915* — 38.500* — 35.308* — 28-01-16 Scottsdale 102 **Bon**
Black with red vinyl interior; restored in 2008/9.

1952 Beetle — 10339587 — L — 60-80.000 USD — 46.180* — 66.000* — 60.436* — 29-01-16 Phoenix 211 **RMS** F714
Grey; restored to concours condition.

1960 Beetle — 2764371 — L — 35-55.000 USD — 84.652 — 121.000 — 109.106 — 11-03-16 Amelia Island 47 **G&Co**
Light grey with two-tone interior; in original condition, the car has covered less than 15,500 miles. Since 2008 in the Jerry Seinfeld Collection.

1951 Beetle — 10264265 — L — 55-65.000 USD — 44.634* — 63.800* — 57.528* — 11-03-16 Amelia Island 78 **G&Co**
Dark blue; full restoration completed in the USA in 2015.

1954 Beetle — 10661552 — R — 14-18.000 GBP — NS — 12-03-16 Brooklands 146 **His**
Maroon; recent full restoration.

1952 Beetle — 10307723 — L — 35-40.000 EUR — NS — 20-03-16 Fontainebleau 327 **Ose**
Black with grey cloth interior; restored some years ago.

1954 Beetle — 536042 — L — 18-24.000 EUR — 11.155 — 16.339 — 14.630 — 28-05-16 Aarhus 117 **SiC**
Beige with tan interior; body repainted in the 1980s.

1974 Beetle — 1342217262 — L — 35-40.000 EUR — 29.164 — 42.718 — 38.250 — 28-05-16 Aarhus 136 **SiC**
In original condition; 90 kms covered. Unused since 1978 and recently recommissioned.

1963 Beetle — 5494928 — L — 20-30.000 USD — 13.336* — 19.250* — 17.258* — 05-06-16 Greenwich 99 **Bon**
White with white and grey interior; restored. Sunroof.

F713: 1927 Voisin C12 torpedo (Duvivier)

F714: 1952 Volkswagen Beetle

Year	Model	(Bodybuilder)	Chassis no.	Steering	Estimate	Hammer Price £	$	€	Sale Date	Place	Lot	Auc. H.
1943	Beetle		1019477	L	275-350.000 USD		NS		11-06-16	Hershey	135	TFA
	Grey with grey interior; the car was delivered new in June 1943 to the German Red Cross in Berlin. Advertised for sale on a Polish newspaper in 2000, it was purchased by the current owner who had it fully restored in Europe and who imported it in the USA in 2013. Recently serviced.											
1958	Beetle		1805386	L	45-65.000 USD	54.626*	71.500*	63.127*	21-08-16	Pebble Beach	160	G&Co
	Green with green/grey interior; restored in the USA in 2010.											
1975	Beetle cabriolet		1552010298	L	4-6.000 EUR	13.698*	21.691*	19.072*	01-11-15	Paris	107	Art
	Dark blue with tan leather interior; in good working order.											
1979	Super Beetle cabriolet	(Karmann)	1592041475	L	50-100.000 USD	37.314*	52.800*	48.629*	10-03-16	Amelia Island	119	Bon
	Red with black vinyl interior; the car remained unregistered in the collection of the Seattle Volkswagen dealer, the late Wade Carter. 66 miles covered; recently serviced.											
1979	Beetle cabriolet		1592038235	L	40-60.000 USD	20.009*	28.600*	25.789*	11-03-16	Amelia Island	11	G&Co
	Black with black interior; in original condition. 14,000 miles covered.											
1979	Super Beetle cabriolet	(Karmann)	1592038538	L	25-35.000 USD	18.290	26.400	23.668	05-06-16	Greenwhich	52	Bon
	Light metallic blue with black interior; described as in very good overall condition, the car has had one owner and has covered 15,500 miles.											
1957	Beetle cabriolet	(Karmann)	14676143	L	55-65.000 USD	34.363	49.500	43.788	11-06-16	Hershey	116	TFA
	Light brown with light brown leatherette interior; restored at unspecified date.											
1960	Beetle cabriolet		3041319	L	30-40.000 EUR	23.552	33.649	29.900	18-06-16	Wien	425	Dor
	Coral red with grey leatherette interior; restored some time ago. Engine replaced.											
1957	Beetle cabriolet	(Karmann)	1371341	L	40-50.000 USD	25.073*	33.000*	29.693*	30-07-16	Plymouth	166	RMS
	Red; described as in highly original condition. Body repainted in the late 1960s.											
1949	Beetle Type 14A cabriolet	(Hebmüller)	10132694	L	300-350.000 USD		NS		19-08-16	Monterey	F179	Mec
	Green and ivory with cognac leather interior; fully restored, the car is currently fitted with a 50bhp engine and disc brakes. A period-correct engine will be delivered with the car. One of 696 examples built.											
1964	Beetle cabriolet		5718523	L	35-55.000 USD	21.010	27.500	24.280	19-08-16	Monterey	F181	Mec
	Red with grey and tan interior; recently restored.											
1979	Super Beetle Epilogue Edition cabriolet		1592033434	L	45-65.000 USD	25.976	34.000	30.019	19-08-16	Monterey	F28	Mec
	Black with black interior; one of 900 examples built. One owner and 2,525 miles covered.											
1965	Minibus		245030699	L	80-100.000 USD	66.341*	101.750*	89.560*	09-10-15	Hershey	250	RMS
	Red and silver/beige; restored at unspecified date, engine recently enlarged to 1,950cc giving 100bhp (see lot 66 Gooding 8.3.13 $ 99,000).											
1960	Minibus		605773	L	NA	60.034*	85.800*	78.567*	29-01-16	Scottsdale	1276.1	B/J
	White and grey with two-tone grey plaid interior; restored. 23-window version.											
1963	Minibus		1083449	L	125-175.000 USD	111.586*	159.500*	143.821*	12-03-16	Amelia Island	120	RMS F715
	"23 windows" model finished in turquoise and light blue; restored in the 1990s. Fitted with a rebuilt 50bhp 1600 engine. A 1967 Eriba Puck camping trailer, restored in the same colours of the Minibus, is included with the lot.											
1966	Minibus DeLuxe		246147867	L	90-110.000 USD	71.041	93.500	84.131	30-07-16	Plymouth	164	RMS
	21 window version finished in red with white roof; restored in 2000 (see lot 461 RM 18.8.00 $34,100).											
1970	Karmann Ghia cabriolet		1402200062	L	NA	19.547	28.000	25.906	23-01-16	Kissimmee	S30	Mec
	Silver with black interior; recently restored.											
1964	Karmann Ghia cabriolet		6337462	L	NA	26.569*	37.400*	32.912*	09-04-16	Palm Beach	344	B/J
	Black with tan interior; fully restored.											
1972	Karmann Ghia coupé		1422690120	L	6-8.000 GBP	6.215	9.377	8.571	09-12-15	Chateau Impney	28	H&H F716
	White; registered in the UK.											
1972	Porsche 914 2.0		4722918887	L	18-22.000 GBP		NS		06-09-15	Hedingham Cas.	110	Coy
	Green; described as in very good original condition, the car has covered 21,000 miles.											
1974	Porsche 914 2.0		4742909082	L	24-28.000 GBP		NS		25-10-15	Silverstone	234	SiC
	Red; restoration completed in 2014. Engine rebuilt on a new block bored to 2.1-litre; front brakes upgraded.											
1974	Porsche 914		4742908821	L	20-24.000 GBP		NS		25-10-15	Silverstone	258	SiC
	Yellow; fully restored in the USA at unspecified date and later reimported into Europe. Formerly owned by Arie Luyendik.											
1972	Porsche 914		4722909100	L	15-18.000 GBP	18.880	27.059	24.791	16-01-16	Birmingham	322	Coy
	Red; in good overall condition. Two owners and 41,000 miles covered.											

F715: 1963 Volkswagen Minibus

F716: 1972 Volkswagen Karmann Ghia coupé

Year	Model	(Bodybuilder)	Chassis no.	Steering	Estimate	£	$	€	Date	Place	Lot	Auc. H.

F717: 1972 Volkswagen Porsche 914/6   *F718: 1973 Volvo P1800ES*

Year	Model	Chassis no.	Steering	Estimate	£	$	€	Date	Place	Lot	Auc. H.
1970	**Porsche 914**	4702907299	L	14-18.000 EUR		NS		16-01-16	Maastricht	411	Coy
Metallic grey with black interior; in good overall condition.											
1970	**Porsche 914**	4712908012	L	30-40.000 USD	11.535*	16.500*	15.132*	28-01-16	Scottsdale	22	Bon
Green with original black interior; body repainted in 2012. For over 40 years with its first owner.											
1970	**Porsche 914/6**	9141430071	L	40-50.000 GBP	36.418	55.454	49.787	06-09-15	Hedingham Cas.	125	Coy
Blue with black interior; restored in 1999 (see lot 120 Bonhams 24.5.15 NS).											
1970	**Porsche 914/6**	9140432498	L	85-135.000 EUR		NS		04-02-16	Paris	375	Bon
Orange with black interior; sold new to the USA, the car was reimported into Germany in 2008. Engine and gearbox overhauled in 2014.											
1972	**Porsche 914/6**	9142430061	L	70-80.000 USD	49.196	70.400	61.579	02-04-16	Ft.Lauderdale	565	AA F717
Orange with black interior; a few miles covered since a full restoration.											
1970	**Porsche 914/6**	9140432237	L	120-130.000 USD	85.950	112.500	99.326	19-08-16	Monterey	F117	Mec
Tangerine with black leatherette interior; concours-quality restoration.											
1973	**Modell 181 "The Thing"**	1832652734	L	NA	8.336*	12.650*	11.345*	26-09-15	Las Vegas	33	B/J
Yellow with white hardtop and black interior; 55,770 original miles.											
1973	**Modell 181 "The Thing"**	1832840262	L	15-20.000 USD	17.457	25.300	22.140	07-05-16	Auburn	504	AA
Yellow with black interior; body repainted.											
1981	**Golf GTI**	17BW535827	R	15-20.000 GBP	16.100	24.515	22.010	05-09-15	Beaulieu	116	Bon
Since 1985 in the current ownership; restored in 2006; original interior; 65,000 miles covered since new.											
1982	**Golf GTI 16 S Oettinger**	573410	L	25-35.000 EUR	23.971	37.959	33.376	01-11-15	Paris	162	Art
Anthracite grey; fully restored in the 2000s.											

VOLVO (S) *(1926-)*

Year	Model	Chassis no.	Steering	Estimate	£	$	€	Date	Place	Lot	Auc. H.
1952	**PV 444**	36721	L	14-18.000 GBP		NS		10-07-16	Chateau Impney	13	H&H
Metallic blue with grey cloth interior; restored at unspecified date.											
1962	**122S saloon**	108303	R	4-6.000 GBP	3.136	4.732	4.325	09-12-15	Chateau Impney	57	H&H
Light blue with cream interior; clutch replaced in 2013.											
1973	**P1800ES**	1836353007626	L	20-25.000 EUR	20.668	31.288	28.800	08-11-15	Lyon	233	Ose
White with blue interior; imported into the Netherlands in 1995 from the USA and subsequently restored.											
1972	**P1800ES**	1834352000505	R	13-15.000 GBP	12.320	18.588	16.991	09-12-15	Chateau Impney	17	H&H
Light blue; in original, never restored condition.											
1971	**P1800E**	034931	R	NA	34.875	49.373	45.010	06-03-16	Birmingham	344	SiC
Gold with black interior; restored over the past four years. Two owners and 53,323 miles covered (see lot 73 H&H 15.4.15 NS).											
1973	**P1800ES**	1834351002874	L	25-30.000 EUR	20.485	29.278	26.400	12-03-16	Lyon	348	Agu F718
White with tan interior; restored two years ago.											

F719: 1936 Wanderer W25 K roadster (Wendler)   *F720: 1923 Wills Sainte Claire Model B-68 Gray Goose Special*

Year	Model	(Bodybuilder)	Chassis no.	Steering	Estimate	Hammer Price £	$	€	Sale Date	Place	Lot	Auc. H.
1973	P1800ES		6763	R	16-20.000 GBP		NS		18-05-16	Donington Park	72	H&H

Light metallic blue with black leather interior; restored in 2014. 51,725 miles covered since new.

| 1965 | P1800 S | | 12387 | L | NQ | 11.766 | 15.400 | 13.597 | 20-08-16 | Monterey | 7129 | R&S |

Red; body repainted. Fitted with disc brakes.

WANDERER (D) (1911-1939)

| 1936 | W25 K roadster | (Wendler) | 252702 | L | 350-450.000 USD | 210.157 | 319.000 | 283.910 | 05-10-15 | Philadelphia | 219 | Bon F719 |

Red with brown interior; an older restoration, the car is described as still in good overall condition (see lot 164 Bonhams 12.3.15 NS).

WHIPPET (USA) (1927-1931)

| 1927 | Model 96 sedan | | 96104308 | L | 20-25.000 USD | 15.061* | 23.100* | 20.333* | 09-10-15 | Hershey | 213 | RMS |

Blue and black; on display at the AACA Museum for some years, the car requires recommissioning prior to use.

WHITE (USA) (1900-1918)

| 1910 | Model G-A touring | | GA1628 | R | 30-50.000 USD | 24.639* | 37.400* | 33.286* | 05-10-15 | Philadelphia | 221 | Bon |

White with maroon leather interior; from the Evergreen Collection (see lot 661 Bonhams 13.8.10 $ 25,740).

| 1916 | Model Forty-Five GED touring | | GED75502 | L | 20-25.000 USD | 23.762* | 36.300* | 32.256* | 08-10-15 | Hershey | 141 | RMS |

Blue and black; paintwork and interior redone many years go. It requires some mechanical works prior to use. From the estate of Richard Roy.

WILLS SAINTE CLAIRE (USA) (1921-1927)

| 1923 | Model B-68 Gray Goose Special | | 06916 | L | 45-65.000 USD | 37.443* | 57.200* | 50.828* | 08-10-15 | Hershey | 140 | RMS F720 |

The car remained in the same family ownership from new to 1998 when it was acquired by Richard Roy, from whose estate it is offered. Some restoration works, including the engine rebuild, carried out in the 1950s. Not been run in the last half-century.

WILLYS (USA) (1914-1963)

| 1942 | MB Jeep | | 153355 | L | 19-23.000 GBP | 23.000 | 34.788 | 31.788 | 10-12-15 | London | 341 | Bon |

Olive green; in good overall condition.

| 1942 | MB Jeep | | 194076 | L | 35-40.000 EUR | 40.076* | 58.164* | 53.200* | 03-02-16 | Paris | 126 | RMS |

Olive green; restored to the 1942 US military specification.

| 1942 | MB Jeep | | 144118 | L | 15-18.000 EUR | 19.406* | 27.961* | 24.640* | 14-05-16 | Monaco | 117 | RMS |

Described as in original condition; from the Quattroruote Collection.

WINTON (USA) (1897-1925)

| 1904 | 20hp rear-entrance tonneau | | 3227 | R | 130-160.000 GBP | 130.000 | 205.868 | 181.012 | 30-10-15 | London | 106 | Bon F721 |

Red with black fenders and black interior; the car was part from the mid-1930s to 2006 of the US collection of Robert Stormont, who restored it soon after the purchase. In recent years it received several mechanical works and was last driven at the London-Brighton Run in 2012 (see Bonhams lots 322 6.5.06 $ 172,000 and 323 3.12.12 $ 218,527).

| 1916 | Six-33 touring | | 31395(engine) | L | 75-100.000 USD | 48.411 | 74.250 | 65.355 | 09-10-15 | Hershey | 242 | RMS |

Two-tone grey with black leather interior; restoration completed in 2007. New body. From the Harold Coker collection.

WOLSELEY (GB) (1896-1975)

| 1923 | Seven open 2-seater | | 50802 | R | 7-8.000 GBP | 11.500 | 15.366 | 13.809 | 16-07-16 | Cambridge | 1256 | Che |

Black; appearing to be thoroughly original.

| 1933 | Hornet Special cabriolet | (Swallow) | NQ | R | 40-45.000 EUR | 24.284 | 35.570 | 31.850 | 28-05-16 | Aarhus | 240 | SiC |

Old English white with red interior; first restored in the 1950s and between 1970 and 1986 again.

WOODS ELECTRIC (USA) (1899-1919)

| 1905 | Style 214A Queen Victoria brougham | | 2843 | L | 550-650.000 DKK | 62.301 | 94.559 | 84.818 | 26-09-15 | Ebeltoft | 15 | Bon F722 |

Wooden body; only example known to survive. In running order; new charging mechanism and batteries. From the Frederiksen Collection (see lot 546 RM 7.10.10 $ 77,000).

F721: 1904 Winton 20hp rear-entrance tonneau

F722: 1905 Woods Electric Style 214A Queen Victoria brougham

Twenty-three years of Top Five

This chapter is dedicated to the Top Five cars of the last 23 auction seasons.

1993-94

1 – 1912 ROLLS-ROYCE
Silver Ghost tourer
Sotheby's, Solvang (USA)
18.8.1993 – Lot 82
US$ 1.762.500

2 – 1927 DELAGE
1500 G.P.
Poulain Le Fur, Paris (F)
19.2.1994 – Lot 30
US$ 1.192.170

3 – 1931 BENTLEY
4½l supercharged tourer
Sotheby's, London (GB)
6.12.1993 – Lot 1152
US$ 593.662

4 – 1930 BENTLEY
4½l supercharged tourer
Sotheby's, London (GB)
16.5.1994 – Lot 560
US$ 580.403

5 – 1928 MERCEDES-BENZ
S 26/120/180 PS tourer
Sotheby's, London (GB)
6.12.1993 – Lot 1183
US$ 495.092

1994-95

1 – 1954 MASERATI
250F
Brooks, Monaco (MC)
24.5.1995 – Lot 242
US$ 884.969

2 – 1948 FERRARI
166MM barchetta
Sotheby's, Los Angeles (USA)
17.6.1995 – Lot 26
US$ 800.000

3 – 1927 DELAGE
1500 G.P.
Poulain Le Fur, Paris (F)
12.6.1995 – Lot 32
US$ 708.491

4 – 1964 FERRARI
250 LM
Coys, Silverstone (GB)
29.7.1995 – Lot 49
US$ 589.119

5 – 1931 BENTLEY
8l tourer
Coys, Silverstone (GB)
29.7.1995 – Lot 72
US$ 562.340

1995-96

1 – 1933 ALFA ROMEO
8C 2300 corto spider
Christie's, Pebble Beach (USA)
20.8.1995 – Lot 41
US$ 1.817.500

2 – 1935 ALFA ROMEO
8C-35
Brooks, London (GB)
4.12.1995 – Lot 767
US$ 1.319.763

3 – 1931 BENTLEY
4½l supercharged tourer
Christie's, Pebble Beach (USA)
20.8.1995 – Lot 44
US$ 717.500

4 – 1927 MERCEDES-BENZ
S 26/120/180 PS tourer
Brooks, Stuttgart (D)
20.4.1996 – Lot 111
US$ 710.902

5 – 1960 MASERATI
Tipo 61 Birdcage
Brooks, Monaco (MC)
15.5.1996 – Lot 152
US$ 705.032

1996-97

1 – 1949 FERRARI
166MM barchetta
Christie's, Pebble Beach (USA)
18.8.1996 – Lot 73
US$ 1.652.500

2 – 1952 FERRARI
225 Sport barchetta
Poulain Le Fur, Paris (F)
9.6.1997 – Lot 14
US$ 1.294.188

3 – 1953 FERRARI
625 TF barchetta
Christie's, Geneva (CH)
22.5.1997 – Lot 133
US$ 876.217

4 – 1956 MASERATI
300S
Christie's, London (GB)
14.7.1997 – Lot 413
US$ 745.516

5 – 1930 DUESENBERG
Model J convertible
Sotheby's, New York (USA)
5.10.1996 – Lot 59
US$ 662.500

ALL ABOUT ORIGINALITY

A classic Ferrari is more than simply a collectors' car. It is a testimony to Ferrari's heritage and each model represents the pinnacle of road-car engineering of its era. When you own a Ferrari, the most important aspect is originality. Since 2003, Ferrari has provided factory support for the collector car world, introducing a programme that testifies to the authenticity of cars and supplying a comprehensive range of services dedicated to the preservation of these historically significant motor vehicles.

Ferrari Classiche has certified over 5400 cars and carried out over 95 full restorations. Recent projects include the 1954 Ferrari 500 Mondial Spider PF (chassis no. 0438 MD) originally owned Porfirio Rubirosa who drove it at Santa Barbara in September 1954, finishing eighth overall and second in its category. In the hands of subsequent owner, American John Von Neumann, the 500 Mondial went on to win two races at Santa Barbara in 1955, then took victory at Pomona before triumphing again at Santa Barbara in 1956. Now owned by Californian Tom Peck, the vehicle was sent to the Ferrari Classiche Department for a full restoration that included the installation of a factory-produced replacement for its original engine. Just a week after the restoration was finished in 2015, it arrived in Pebble Beach for the legendary Concours d'Elegance, where it dominated the scene, winning three prizes in two days.

Equally noteworthy was the Ferrari Classiche Department's efforts in restoring the engine, bodywork, suspension and running gear of a 250 GT Berlinetta passo corto Competizione (chassis no. 2321 GT) to pristine condition. The car arrived in Maranello in March 2014 and work began in the summer of the same year, finishing 14 months later. The 250 GT Berlinetta Competizione's first owner was Dorino Serafini, a GT and Scuderia Ferrari Formula 1 driver. After many changes of livery, the colour chosen by the new owner is a Pininfarina grey (with brown interior) similar to the colour sported by many Prancing Horse cars in the late 1960s.

All restoration work carried out by Ferrari Classiche is underpinned by in-depth research using Ferrari's production archive, a treasure trove of invaluable technical information on every car built at the factory. This extensive archive allows us to offer our classic car clients a Certificate of Authenticity or an Attestation for vehicles of historic interest, and to supply all major mechanical components manufactured to the original specifications.

Ferrari Classiche
via Abetone Inferiore 4
41053 Maranello - Italy
Tel +39 0536 1935914, Fax +39 0536 949335
ferrariclassiche@ferrari.com   www.ferrari.com

1997-98

1 – 1938 DUESENBERG
Model SJ convertible sedan
Christie's, Tarrytown (USA)
25-04-1998 – Lot 91
US$ 1.267.500

2 – 1962 ASTON MARTIN
DB4 GT Zagato
Brooks, Goodwood (GB)
12.6.1998 – Lot 724
US$ 1.115.743

3 – 1953 FERRARI
340/375 MM spider
Christie's, Pebble Beach (USA)
17.8.1997 – Lot 95
US$ 1.080.500

4 – 1956 JAGUAR
D-Type
Christie's, Pebble Beach (USA)
17.8.1997 – Lot 54
US$ 1.014.500

5 – 1911 ROLLS-ROYCE
Silver Ghost landaulette
Sotheby's, London (GB)
24.11.1997 – Lot 526
US$ 840.575

1998-99

1 – 1967 FERRARI
275GTS/4 NART Spider
Christie's, Pebble Beach (USA)
16.8.1998 – Lot 47
US$ 2.092.500

2 – 1965 FERRARI
250 LM
Brooks, Gstaad (CH)
19.12.1998 – Lot 173
US$ 1.797.334

3 – 1935 ALFA ROMEO
8C-35
Christie's, Pebble Beach (USA)
16.8.1998 – Lot 45
US$ 1.322.500

4 – 1957 VANWALL
F1
Brooks, Nürburgring (D)
8.8.1998 – Lot 304
US$ 1.306.447

5 – 1960 MASERATI
Tipo 60 Birdcage
RM Auctions, Amelia Island (USA)
20.3.1999 – Lot 152
US$ 1.100.000

1999-2000

1 – 1937 ALFA ROMEO
8C 2900B cabriolet
Christie's, Pebble Beach (USA)
29.8.1999 – Lot 29
US$ 4.072.500

2 – 1954 FERRARI
250 Monza
RM Auctions, Monterey (USA)
27.8.1999 – Lot 452
US$ 2.970.000

3 – 1955 JAGUAR
D-Type
Christie's, London (GB)
1.11.1999 – Lot 219
US$ 2.809.496

4 – 1965 FERRARI
250 LM
RM Auctions, Amelia Island (USA)
11.3.2000 – Lot 249
US$ 2.310.000

5 – 1964 FERRARI
250 LM
Christie's, Pebble Beach (USA)
29.8.1999 – Lot 24
US$ 2.147.500

2000-01

1 – 1966 FERRARI
330 P3
Christie's, Pebble Beach (USA)
20.8.2000 – Lot 89
US$ 5.616.000

2 – 1964 SHELBY AMERICAN
Cobra Daytona Coupé
RM Auctions, Monterey (USA)
18.8.2000 – Lot 454
US$ 4.400.000

3 – 1938 ALFA ROMEO
8C 2900B berlinetta
Brooks, Carmel (USA)
19.8.2000 – Lot 336
US$ 3.082.500

4 – 1935 MERCEDES-BENZ
500K Spezial Roadster
RM Auctions, Amelia Island (USA)
10.3.2001 – Lot 61
US$ 2.970.000

5 – 1960 MASERATI
Tipo 60 Birdcage
Christie's, London (GB)
26.3.2001 – Lot 62
US$ 2.055.942

INTERNI AUTO MAIELI

REAL PASSION FOR REAL LOVERS
CLASSIC CAR INTERIOR RESTORATION

Via Francesco Baracca, 3
46048 CANEDOLE DI ROVERBELLA (MN)
Tel: +39 0376 695105
Fax: +39 0376 695300
E-mail: maieli@inwind.it

www.interniautomaieli.com

2001-02

1 – 1956 FERRARI
410 Sport
RM Auctions, Monterey (USA)
17.8.2001 – Lot 277
US$ 3.822.500

2 – 1937 MERCEDES-BENZ
540K Spezial Roadster
RM Auctions, Phoenix (USA)
18.1.2002 – Lot 73
US$ 3.630.000

3 – 1933 ALFA ROMEO
8C 2600 Monza
RM Auctions, Amelia Island (USA)
9.3.2002 – Lot 75
US$ 2.530.000

4 – 1934 DUESENBERG
Model J convertible coupé
RM Auctions, Rochester (USA)
4.8.2001 – Lot 37
US$ 1.980.000

5 – 1953 FERRARI
375 MM spider
RM Auctions, Amelia Island (USA)
9.3.2002 – Lot 118
US$ 1.925.000

2002-03

1 – 1962 FERRARI
330 TRI/LM
RM Auctions, Monterey (USA)
16.8.2002 – Lot 143
US$ 6.490.000

2 – 1929 MERCEDES-BENZ
SSK Rennwagen
Artcurial, Paris (F)
10.2.2003 – Lot 34
US$ 3.331.553

3 – 1932 BUGATTI
Type 55 roadster
Christie's, Paris (F)
8.2.2003 – Lot 51
US$ 1.812.822

4 – 1954 FERRARI
250 Monza
RM Auctions, Monterey (USA)
16.8.2002 – Lot 174
US$ 1.705.000

5 – 1963 JAGUAR
E-Type 3.8 Lightweight roadster
RM Auctions, Amelia Island (USA)
8.3.2003 – Lot 82
US$ 1.375.000

2003-04

1 – 1930 BENTLEY
6½l Speed Six tourer
Christie's, Le Mans (F)
23.7.2004 – Lot 83
US$ 5.105.896

2 – 1956 FERRARI
860 Monza
RM Auctions, Monterey (USA)
15.8.2003 – Lot 453
US$ 2.057.001

3 – 1928 BENTLEY
4½l tourer
Christie's, Le Mans (F)
23.7.2004 – Lot 86
US$ 2.021.573

4 – 2000 FERRARI
F1/2000
Bonhams, Monaco (MC)
15.5.2004 – Lot 272
US$ 1.690.637

5 – 1956 ASTON MARTIN
DB3S
Christie's, Le Mans (F)
23.7.2004 – Lot 91
US$ 1.646.090

2004-05

1 – 1929 MERCEDES-BENZ
SSK two-seater tourer
Bonhams, Goodwood (GB)
3.9.2004 – Lot 144
US$ 7.487.841

2 – 1935 DUESENBERG
Model SJ speedster special
Gooding & Company, Pebble Beach (USA)
15.8.2004 – Lot 37
US$ 4.455.000

3 – 1954 OLDSMOBILE
F-88 convertible concept car
Barrett & Jackson, Scottsdale (USA)
26.1.2005 – Lot 992
US$ 3.240.000

4 – 2004 FERRARI
F-2004
Sotheby's, Maranello (I)
28.6.2005 – Lot 133
US$ 3.205.175

5 – 1934 DUESENBERG
Model J convertible coupé
RM Auctions, Phoenix (USA)
28.1.2005 – Lot 53
US$ 2.750.000

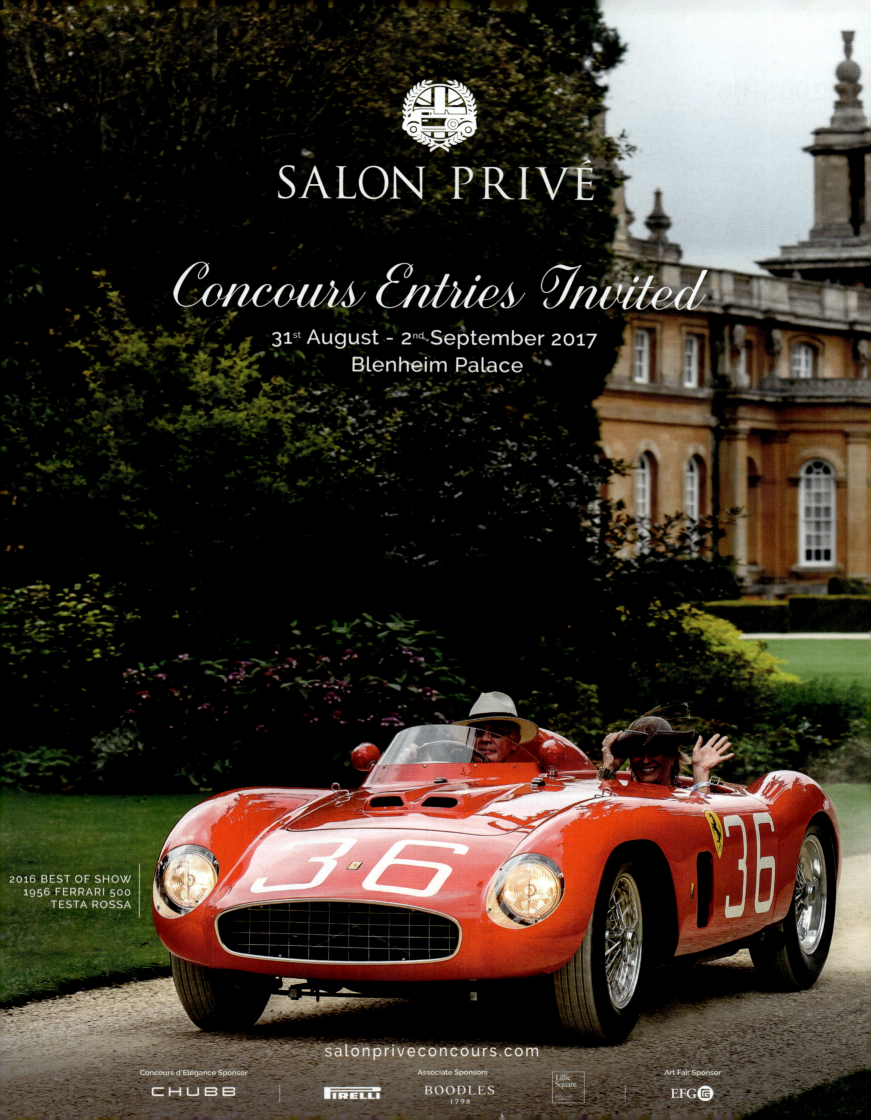

2005-06

1 – 1940 GENERAL MOTORS
Futurliner Bus
Barrett & Jackson, Scottsdale (USA)
17.1.2006 – Lot 1307
US$ 4.320.000

2 – 1967 FERRARI
275 GTS/4 NART Spider
Gooding & Company, Pebble Beach (USA)
21.8.2005 – Lot 37
US$ 3.960.000

3 – 1938 TALBOT-LAGO
T150 C SS Goutte d'Eau
Gooding & Company, Palm Beach (USA)
22.1.2006 – Lot 29
US$ 3.905.000

4 – 1938 TALBOT-LAGO
T150 C Speciale Goutte d'Eau
RM Auctions, Monterey (USA)
20.8.2005 – Lot 251
US$ 3.685.000

5 – 1937 TALBOT-LAGO
T150 C SS Goutte d'Eau
Christie's, Monterey (USA)
18.8.2005 – Lot 85
US$ 3.535.000

2006-07

1 – 1962 FERRARI
330 TRI/LM
RM Auctions, Maranello (I)
20.5.2007 – Lot 221
US$ 9.265.438

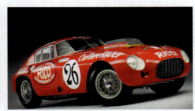

2 – 1953 FERRARI
340/375 Mille Miglia Berlinetta
RM Auctions, Maranello (I)
20.5.2007 – Lot 233
US$ 5.707.510

3 – 1958 FERRARI
412 S
RM Auctions, Monterey (USA)
19.8.2006 – Lot 465
US$ 5.610.000

4 – 1966 SHELBY AMERICAN
Cobra 427 "Supersnake"
Barrett & Jackson, Scottsdale (USA)
19.1.2007 – Lot 1301
US$ 5.500.000

5 – 1928 MERCEDES-BENZ
S torpedo roadster
Christie's, Monterey (USA)
17.8.2006 – Lot 52
US$ 3.645.000

2007-08

1 – 1961 FERRARI
250 GT Spyder California swb
RM Auctions, Maranello (I)
18.5.2008 – Lot 328
US$ 10.910.592

2 – 1937 MERCEDES-BENZ
540 K Spezial Roadster
RM Auctions, London (GB)
31.10.2007 – Lot 225
US$ 8.090.769

3 – 1904 ROLLS-ROYCE
10HP two-seater
Bonhams, London (GB)
3.12.2007 – Lot 604
US$ 7.266.967

4 – 1964 FERRARI
250 LM
RM Auctions, Maranello (I)
18.5.2008 – Lot 339A
US$ 6.989.598

5 – 1959 FERRARI
250 GT Spyder California lwb
RM Auctions, Monterey (USA)
18.8.2007 – Lot 560
US$ 4.950.000

2008-09

1 – 1957 FERRARI
250 Testa Rossa
RM Auctions, Maranello (I)
17.5.2009 – Lot 237
US$ 12.193.236

2 – 1937 BUGATTI
Type 57SC Atalante
Gooding & Company, Pebble Beach (USA)
16.8.2008 – Lot 27
US$ 7.920.000

3 – 1960 JAGUAR
E2A
Bonhams, Carmel (USA)
15.8.2008 – Lot 364
US$ 4.957.000

4 – 1960 FERRARI
250 GT Spyder California swb
Gooding & Company, Scottsdale (USA)
17.1.2009 – Lot 78
US$ 4.950.000

5 – 1939 TALBOT-LAGO
T150 C SS Aerocoupé
Bonhams, Carmel (USA)
15.8.2008 – Lot 330
US$ 4.847.000

2009-10

1 – 1965 SHELBY AMERICAN
Cobra Daytona Coupé
Mecum, Monterey (USA)
15.8.2009 – Lot S104
US$ 7.685.000

2 – 1962 FERRARI
250 GT Spyder California swb
Gooding & Company, Pebble Beach (USA)
16.8.2009 – Lot 135
US$ 5.115.000

3 – 1933 ALFA ROMEO
8C 2300 cabriolet
Gooding & Company, Pebble Beach (USA)
16.8.2009 – Lot 139
US$ 4.180.000

4 – 1955 JAGUAR
D-Type
Gooding & Company, Scottsdale (USA)
22.1.2010 – Lot 16
US$ 3.740.000

5 – 1962 FERRARI
400 Superamerica cabriolet
RM Auctions, Monaco (MC)
1.5.2010 – Lot 221
US$ 3.728.200

2010-11

1 – 1959 FERRARI
250 GT Spyder California lwb
Gooding & Company, Pebble Beach (USA)
14.8.2010 – Lot 46
US$ 7.260.000

2 – 1933 ALFA ROMEO
8C 2300 Monza
Gooding & Company, Pebble Beach (USA)
15.8.2010 – Lot 117
US$ 6.710.000

3 – 1961 FERRARI
250 GT Berlinetta Competizione
Gooding & Company, Pebble Beach (USA)
15.8.2010 – Lot 133
US$ 6.105.000

4 – 1955 FERRARI
375 MM coupé
RM Auctions, Villa d'Este (I)
21.5.2011 – Lot 120
US$ 4.783.632

5 – 1954 FERRARI
375 MM coupé
RM Auctions, Pebble Beach (USA)
14.8.2010 – Lot 351
US$ 4.620.000

2011-12

1 – 1957 FERRARI
250 Testa Rossa
Gooding & Company, Pebble Beach (USA)
20.8.2011 – Lot 18
US$ 16.390.000

2 – 1931 DUESENBERG
Model J coupé
Gooding & Company, Pebble Beach (USA)
21.8.2011 – Lot 123
US$ 10.340.000

3 – 1937 MERCEDES-BENZ
540 K Spezial Roadster
RM Auctions, Monterey (USA)
20.8.2011 – Lot 242
US$ 9.680.000

4 – 1929 BENTLEY
4½l Supercharged
Bonhams, Goodwood (GB)
29.6.2012 – Lot 204
US$ 7.867.261

5 – 1912 ROLLS-ROYCE 40/50hp
Silver Ghost double pullman limousine
Bonhams, Goodwood (GB)
29.6.2012 – Lot 272
US$ 7.342.933

2012-13

1 – 1954 MERCEDES-BENZ
W196R
Bonhams, Goodwood (GB)
12.7.2013 – Lot 320
US$ 29.598.265

2 – 1953 FERRARI
340/375 Mille Miglia Berlinetta
RM Auctions, Villa Erba (I)
25.5.2013 – Lot 130
US$ 12.752.678

3 – 1936 MERCEDES-BENZ
540 K Spezial Roadster
Gooding & Company, Pebble Beach (USA)
19.8.2012 – Lot 123
US$ 11.770.000

4 – 1960 FERRARI
250 GT Spyder California lwb
Gooding & Company, Pebble Beach (USA)
18.8.2012 – Lot 49
US$ 11.275.000

5 – 1968 FORD
GT40
RM Auctions, Monterey (USA)
17.8.2012 – Lot 139
US$ 11.000.000

2013-14   2014-15   2015-16

1 – 1962 FERRARI
250 GTO
Bonhams, Carmel (USA)
14.8.2014 – Lot 03
US$ 38.115.000

1 – 1961 FERRARI
250 GT Spyder California swb
Artcurial, Paris (F)
6.2.2015 – Lot 59
US$ 18.644.874

1 – 1957 FERRARI
335 S
Artcurial, Paris (F)
5.2.2016 – Lot 170
US$ 35.930.639

2 – 1964 FERRARI
275 GTB/C Speciale
RM Auctions, Monterey (USA)
16.8.2014 – Lot 239
US$ 26.400.000

2 – 1964 FERRARI
250 LM
RM Sotheby's, Monterey (USA)
13.8.2015 – Lot 113
US$ 17.600.000

2 – 1956 FERRARI
290 MM
RM Sotheby's, New York (USA)
10.12.2015 – Lot 221
US$ 28.050.000

3 – 1954 FERRARI
375 Plus spider
Bonhams, Goodwood (UK)
27.6.2014 – Lot 320
US$ 18.315.361

3 – 1961 FERRARI
250 GT Spyder California swb
Gooding & Company, Pebble Beach (USA)
16.8.2015 – Lot 129
US$ 16.830.000

3 – 1955 JAGUAR
D-Type
RM Sotheby's, Monterey (USA)
19.8.2016 – Lot 114
US$ 21.780.000

4 – 1961 FERRARI
250 GT Spyder California swb
Gooding & Company, Pebble Beach (USA)
16.8.2014 – Lot 18
US$ 15.180.000

4 – 1962 FERRARI
250 GT Berlinetta Speciale swb
Gooding & Company, Pebble Beach (USA)
15.8.2015 – Lot 39
US$ 16.500.000

4 – 1939 ALFA ROMEO
8C 2900B Spider
RM Sotheby's, Monterey (USA)
20.8.2016 – Lot 234
US$ 19.800.000

5 – 1964 FERRARI
250 LM
RM Sotheby's, New York (USA)
21.11.2013 – Lot 141
US$ 14.300.000

5 – 1998 McLAREN
F1
RM Sotheby's, Monterey (USA)
13.8.2015 – Lot 107
US$ 13.750.000

5 – 1959 FERRARI
250 GT Spyder California lwb
Gooding & Company, Pebble Beach (USA)
20.8.2016 – Lot 33
US$ 18.150.000

THE WORLD OF CLASSIC CARS PASSION

WWW.PETERAUTO.PETER.FR

Peter Auto - 103 rue Lamarck - 75018 PARIS - FRANCE - Tel.: +33 1 42 59 73 40 - Contact: info@peter.fr

The 1st August 1993
31st August 2016
"Top Five" for Makes

Alfa Romeo | Aston Martin | Ferrari | Jaguar

1 – 1939 8C 2900B Spider
RM Sotheby's, Monterey (USA)
20.8.2016 – Lot 234
US$ 19.800.000

1 – 1962 DB4 GT Zagato
RM Sotheby's, New York (USA)
10.12.2015 – Lot 215
US$ 14.300.000

1 – 1962 250 GTO
Bonhams, Carmel (USA)
14.8.2014 – Lot 03
US$ 38.115.000

1 – 1955 D-Type
RM Sotheby's, Monterey (USA)
19.8.2016 – Lot 114
US$ 21.780.000

2 – 1933 8C 2300 Monza
Gooding & Company, Pebble Beach (USA)
21.8.2016 – Lot 128
US$ 11.990.000

2 – 1955 DB3S
Gooding & Company, Pebble Beach (USA)
16.8.2014 – Lot 32
US$ 5.500.000

2 – 1957 335 S
Artcurial, Paris (F)
5.2.2016 – Lot 170
US$ 35.930.639

2 – 1953 C-Type
RM Sotheby's, Monterey (USA)
14.8.2015 – Lot 235
US$ 13.200.000

3 – 1935 8C-35
Bonhams, Goodwood (UK)
14.9.2013 – Lot 235
US$ 9.402.426

3 – 1960 DB4 GT Jet
Bonhams, Newport Pagnell (UK)
18.5.2013 – Lot 239
US$ 4.874.880

3 – 1956 290 MM
RM Sotheby's, New York (USA)
10.12.2015 – Lot 221
US$ 28.050.000

3 – 1955 D-Type
RM Auctions, Paris (F)
5.2.2014 – Lot 30
US$ 5.005.493

4 – 1933 8C 2300 Monza
Gooding & Company, Pebble Beach (USA)
15.8.2010 – Lot 117
US$ 6.710.000

4 – 1964 DB5 coupé
RM Auctions, London (UK)
27.10.2010 – Lot 197
US$ 4.607.658

4 – 1967 275 GTB/4 NART Spider
RM Auctions, Monterey (USA)
17.8.2013 – Lot 225
US$ 27.500.000

4 – 1960 E2A
Bonhams, Carmel (USA)
15.8.2008 – Lot 364
US$ 4.957.000

5 – 1948 6C 2500 Competizione
Gooding & Company, Pebble Beach (USA)
18.8.2013 – Lot 114
US$ 4.840.000

5 – 1935 Ulster
Bonhams, Goodwood (UK)
26.6.2015 – Lot 323
US$ 4.581.770

5 – 1964 275 GTB/C Speciale
RM Auctions, Monterey (USA)
16.8.2014 – Lot 239
US$ 26.400.000

5 – 1952 C-Type
Bonhams, London (UK)
1.12.2013 – Lot 005
US$ 4.762.116

ASTON MARTIN
ASSURED PROVENANCE

REST ASSURED

DISCOVER THE TRUE HERITAGE OF YOUR CAR

The Aston Martin Assured Provenance certification programme comprehensively assesses the background of its sports cars, offering a true blue riband service to owners and collectors. Drawing on the unrivalled knowledge of a committee of authoritative Aston Martin experts, the pioneering Assured Provenance certification programme is administered and run by the brand's world-renowned in-house heritage car facility – Aston Martin Works.

For further information please contact the Assured Provenance team.

ASTON MARTIN WORKS

Tickford Street, Newport Pagnell
Buckinghamshire MK16 9AN

Tel: +44 (0)1908 610 620
Email: assuredprovenance@astonmartin.com

www.astonmartinworks.com

EXPERIENCE MATTERS

Maserati | Mercedes-Benz | Porsche | Shelby American

1 – 1955 300 S
Bonhams, Goodwood (UK)
12.7.2013 – Lot 340
US$ 6.090.585

1 – 1954 W196R
Bonhams, Goodwood (GB)
12.7.2013 – Lot 320
US$ 29.598.265

1 – 1982 956
Gooding & Company, Pebble Beach (USA)
15.8.2015 – Lot 50
US$ 10.120.000

1 – 1962 Cobra 260
RM Sotheby's, Monterey (USA)
19.8.2016 – Lot 117
US$ 13.750.000

2 – 1956 250 F
Gooding & Company, Pebble Beach (USA)
17.8.2014 – Lot 115
US$ 4.620.000

2 – 1936 540 K Spezial Roadster
Gooding & Company, Pebble Beach (USA)
19.8.2012 – Lot 123
US$ 11.770.000

2 – 1972 917/10 spyder Can-Am
Mecum, Monterey (USA)
16.8.2012 – Lot S123
US$ 5.500.000

2 – 1965 Cobra Daytona Coupé
Mecum, Monterey (USA)
15.8.2009 – Lot S104
US$ 7.685.000

3 – 1955 A5G/54 spider
RM Sotheby's, New York (USA)
21.11.2013 – Lot 134
US$ 4.455.000

3 – 1937 540 K Spezial Roadster
RM Sotheby's, Phoenix (USA)
29.1.2016 – Lot 242
US$ 9.900.000

3 – 1960 RS60
Gooding & Company, Pebble Beach (USA)
16.8.2015 – Lot 143
US$ 5.400.000

3 – 1966 Cobra 427 "Supersnake"
Barrett & Jackson, Scottsdale (USA)
19.1.2007 – Lot 1301
US$ 5.500.000

4 – 1972 Boomerang
Bonhams, Goodwood (UK)
5.9.2015 – Lot 11
US$ 3.714.523

4 – 1937 540 K Spezial Roadster
RM Auctions, Monterey (USA)
20.8.2011 – Lot 242
US$ 9.680.000

4 – 1955 550 Spyder
Gooding & Company, Amelia Island (USA)
11.3.2016 – Lot 34
US$ 5.335.000

4 – 1966 Cobra 427 "Supersnake"
Barrett & Jackson, Scottsdale (USA)
17.1.2015 – Lot 2509
US$ 5.115.000

5 – 1961 Tipo 61 Birdcage
Gooding & Company, Pebble Beach (USA)
19.8.2012 – Lot 146
US$ 3.520.000

5 – 1928 S Torpedo Roadster
RM Auctions, Monterey (USA)
17.8.2013 – Lot 216
US$ 8.250.000

5 – 1979 935 Turbo
Gooding & Company, Pebble Beach (USA)
20.8.2016 – Lot 60
US$ 4.840.000

5 – 1964 Cobra Daytona Coupé
RM Auctions, Monterey (USA)
18.8.2000 – Lot 454
US$ 4.400.000

HORTONS
BOOKS

Hortons Books are the leading suppliers of new and out-of-print motoring literature

We are exhibiting at the following events next year:

Autosport International: The Racing Car Show, UK

Retromobile: Paris, France

Race Retro: International Historic Motorsport Show, UK

Amelia Island Concours D'Elegance: USA

Goodwood Members' Meeting: UK

Techno Classica Essen: Germany

Goodwood Festival of Speed: UK

F1 British Grand Prix: UK

Silverstone Classic: UK

Automobilia Monterey: USA

Pebble Beach RetroAuto: USA

Pebble Beach Concours D'Elegance: USA

Goodwood Revival: UK

email: contact@hortonsbooks.co.uk **tel:** +44 (0) 1672 514 777

www.hortonsbooks.co.uk

The 1st August 1993 - 31st August 2016 "Top Twenty"

1 – 1962 FERRARI
250 GTO
Bonhams, Carmel (USA)
14.8.2014 – Lot 03
US$ 38.115.000

2 – 1957 FERRARI
335 S
Artcurial, Paris (F)
5.2.2016 – Lot 170
US$ 35.930.639

3 – 1954 MERCEDES-BENZ
W196R
Bonhams, Goodwood (GB)
12.7.2013 – Lot 320
US$ 29.598.265

4 – 1956 FERRARI
290 MM
RM Sotheby's, New York (USA)
10.12.2015 – Lot 221
US$ 28.050.000

5 – 1967 FERRARI
275 GTB/4 NART Spider
RM Auctions, Monterey (USA)
17.8.2013 – Lot 225
US$ 27.500.000

6 – 1964 FERRARI
275 GTB/C Speciale
RM Auctions, Monterey (USA)
16.8.2014 – Lot 239
US$ 26.400.000

7 – 1955 JAGUAR
D-Type
RM Sotheby's, Monterey (USA)
19.8.2016 – Lot 114
US$ 21.780.000

8 – 1939 ALFA ROMEO
8C 2900B Spider
RM Sotheby's, Monterey (USA)
20.8.2016 – Lot 234
US$ 19.800.000

9 – 1961 FERRARI
250 GT Spyder California swb
Artcurial, Paris (F)
6.2.2015 – Lot 59
US$ 18.644.874

10 – 1954 FERRARI
375 Plus spider
Bonhams, Goodwood (UK)
27.6.2014 – Lot 320
US$ 18.315.361

11 – 1959 FERRARI
250 GT Spyder California lwb
Gooding & Company, Pebble Beach (USA)
20.8.2016 – Lot 33
US$ 18.150.000

12 – 1964 FERRARI
250 LM
RM Sotheby's, Monterey (USA)
13.8.2015 – Lot 113
US$ 17.600.000

13 – 1961 FERRARI
250 GT Spyder California swb
Gooding & Company, Amelia Island (USA)
11.3.2016 – Lot 69
US$ 17.160.000

14 – 1961 FERRARI
250 GT Spyder California swb
Gooding & Company, Pebble Beach (USA)
16.8.2015 – Lot 129
US$ 16.830.000

15 – 1962 FERRARI
250 GT Berlinetta Speciale swb
Gooding & Company, Pebble Beach (USA)
15.8.2015 – Lot 39
US$ 16.500.000

16 – 1957 FERRARI
250 Testa Rossa
Gooding & Company, Pebble Beach (USA)
20.8.2011 – Lot 18
US$ 16.390.000

17 – 1961 FERRARI
250 GT Spyder California swb
Gooding & Company, Pebble Beach (USA)
16.8.2014 – Lot 18
US$ 15.180.000

18 – 1964 FERRARI
250 LM
RM Sotheby's, New York (USA)
21.11.2013 – Lot 141
US$ 14.300.000

19 – 1962 ASTON MARTIN
DB4 GT Zagato
RM Sotheby's, New York (USA)
10.12.2015 – Lot 215
US$ 14.300.000

20 – 1998 McLAREN
F1
RM Sotheby's, Monterey (USA)
13.8.2015 – Lot 107
US$ 13.750.000

Concours d'Elegance Suisse

CHATEAU DE COPPET

THE CELEBRATION OF THE FINEST
COLLECTIBLE AUTOMOBILES

23-25 JUNE, 2017
COPPET, SWITZERLAND

+41 22 320 4678
info@projectA.ae
www.ConcoursdEleganceSuisse.com

© Photograph by Michael Furman

Advertisers:

	page
Abarth	25
Alfa Romeo	8
Artcurial Motorcars	167
Aston Martin	39
Aston Martin Works	407
Audemars Piguet	10
Automobilia Ladenburg	333
Axel Schuette	179
BMW	115
Bonhams	17
Carrozzeria Autosport	177
CARS	21
Christoph Grohe	261
CHUBB	33
Concorso d'Eleganza Villa d'Este	45
Concours d'Elegance Suisse	411
Cooper Technica	61
Coys	239
Credit Suisse	2
Cremonini Carrozzeria	171
Dino Cognolato Snc	73
Egon Zweimueller	283
Elettrauto Franco	77
Emil Frey Classics	237
Ferrari Classiche	393
Fiskens	69
Gallery Aaldering	279
Girardo & Co.	23
Gooding & Company	13
Gran Premio Nuvolari	75
Hagerty	137
Hall & Hall	271
Historica Selecta	6
HK Engineering	293
Hortons Books	409
Interni Auto Maieli	395
Italdesign	62
J.D. Classics	183
Jean Lain Vintage	175
JSWL	53
Lamborghini PoloStorico	255
Longstone	335
Lukas Huni	71
Maserati Classiche	275
McGrath Maserati	281
Mecum	221
Mercedes-Benz Classic	291
Niki Hasler	169
Opus	35
Padova Auto e Moto d'Epoca - Verona Legend Cars	51

	page
Pagani	31
Passione Italia	59
Paul Russell and Company	173
Peter Auto	403
Peter Wiesner	277
Quality Cars	181
Renè Grosse Restaurierungen	155
Retromobile	401
Richard Mille	15
RM Sotheby's	163
Salon Privé	397
Sport Auto Modena	165
Stefano Ricci	40
Techno Classica Essen	57
The Houtkamp Collection	89
The Peninsula Hotels	47
Thiesen Automobile	289
Tom Fischer	399
Touring Superleggera	49
Vredestein	64
Zenith	19
ZF Friedrichshafen AG	55

Photo credits

Images copyright and courtesy of Aguttes
297, 412, 535, 712, 718

Images copyright and courtesy of Artcurial
Top Ten 1, 12,16, 21, 24, 28, 38, 40, 46, 58, 59, 64, 82, 120, 122, 124, 127, 129, 134, 143, 189, 191, 192, 193, 194, 195, 196, 197, 199, 221, 232, 241, 251, 281, 283, 285, 291, 294, 302, 306, 315, 332, 356, 386, 391, 407, 411, 413, 425, 439, 457, 462, 468, 476, 491, 502, 503, 511, 529, 542, 552, 564, 565, 593, 603, 612, 635, 637, 652, 660, 665, 669, 677, 679, 699, 705

Images copyright and courtesy of Auctions America
158, 160, 172, 174, 180, 227, 270, 301, 329, 373, 385, 415, 471, 472, 546, 550, 717

Images copyright and courtesy of Barrett-Jackson
166, 168, 172, 174, 180, 227, 270, 301, 329, 373, 385, 415, 471, 472, 546, 550, 717

Images copyright and courtesy of Bonhams
5, 7, 8, 13, 14, 17, 18, 19, 20, 23, 25, 26, 27, 34, 36, 37, 39, 42, 43, 44, 48, 49, 51, 52, 54, 55, 56, 57, 61, 65, 66, 67, 68, 70, 71, 72, 73, 75, 77, 83, 85, 88, 91, 93, 94, 95, 96, 97, 98, 101, 102, 103, 104, 110, 111, 112, 113, 115, 118, 121, 123, 126, 128, 131, 133, 135, 138, 140, 141, 144, 153, 163, 185, 198, 200, 212, 202, 203, 211, 212, 213, 220, 222, 234, 235, 253, 263, 267, 275, 282, 286, 299, 313, 317, 325, 326, 327, 328, 335, 346, 350, 351, 352, 359, 360, 363, 367, 368, 369, 370, 374, 375, 376, 378, 379, 382, 387, 388, 389, 392, 393, 398, 400, 401, 403, 405, 410, 414, 419, 420, 422, 424, 428, 429, 430, 434, 437, 438, 441, 442, 446, 451, 454, 455, 461, 464, 469, 470, 477, 478, 479, 480, 481, 482, 486, 487, 489, 493, 495, 499, 500, 501, 503, 509, 510, 512, 514, 515, 516, 518, 519, 521, 522, 523, 524, 526, 527, 528, 530, 534, 537, 538, 539, 540, 541, 544, 545, 551, 566, 569, 581, 589, 596, 598, 604, 607, 610, 614, 629, 633, 634, 636, 640, 641, 642, 643, 645, 646, 647, 648, 651, 654, 655, 656, 657, 658, 659, 661, 662, 663, 667, 670, 678, 680, 682, 685, 688, 689, 690, 692, 694, 695, 696, 697, 700, 702, 710, 711, 713, 719, 721, 722
Photos by
Theo Civitello, Jeremy Cliff, Simon Clay, Jasen Delgado, Patrick Ernzen, Anthony Fraser, Jonathan Harper, JSB Photo - John Bryan, Pawel Litwinski, Gabor Mayer, Chadsee Photography, Clint David Photography, David Bush Photography, Greg Keysar Photography, Noggs Photography, Sean Smith Photography, Dan Savinelli, Lucas Scarfone, Deyan Sokolovski, Joshua Sweeney, Rich Truesdell, Randy Wells

Images copyright and courtesy of Coys
35, 79, 89, 100, 117, 210, 223, 226, 240, 242, 296, 330, 354, 355, 357, 377, 421, 431, 445, 447, 458, 484, 504, 543, 584, 590, 600, 602, 608, 701

Images copyright and courtesy of Gooding & Company
Photos by
Mike Daly: 303
Brian Henniker: Top Ten 5, Top Ten 10, 137, 257, 268, 295, 453, 456, 497, 554, 591, 606
Mathieu Heurtault: Top Ten 6, Top Ten 9, 10, 139, 243, 452, 473, 586, 587, 592, 601, 611, 618, 622, 623
Mike Maez: 53, 236, 649

Images copyright and courtesy of H & H
15, 207, 254, 265, 284, 292, 362, 381, 394, 397, 399, 406, 582, 630, 639, 716

Images copyright and courtesy of Historics at Brooklands
29, 81, 114, 204, 233, 333, 365, 423, 507, 664, 704, 706, 708

Images copyright and courtesy of Mecum Auctions
32, 142, 147, 149, 157, 164, 165, 171, 175, 176, 177, 178, 188, 216, 228, 229, 230, 231, 238, 280, 288, 305, 314, 318, 339, 340, 342, 344, 345, 371, 372, 390, 408, 416, 557, 571, 572, 573, 574, 575, 577, 579, 588, 621, 624

Images copyright and courtesy of Osenat
214, 218, 332, 383, 444

Images copyright and courtesy of RM Sotheby's
Top Ten 2, Top Ten 3, Top Ten 4, Top Ten 7, Top Ten 8, Season Case, 1, 2, 3, 4, 6, 11, 22, 30, 32, 33, 41, 45, 47, 50, 60, 62, 69, 76, 78, 80, 84, 86, 87, 90, 92, 99, 105, 106, 107, 108, 109, 116, 119, 125, 130, 132, 136, 145, 146, 148, 150, 151, 152, 154, 155, 156, 159, 161, 162, 169, 173, 179, 183, 184, 186, 187, 190, 205, 206, 208, 209, 215, 217, 219, 225, 237, 244, 245, 246, 247, 248, 249, 250, 252, 255, 258, 260, 261, 262, 264, 266, 269, 271, 272, 273, 274, 276, 277, 278, 279, 287, 289, 290, 293, 300, 304, 307, 308, 309, 310, 316, 319, 320, 321, 323, 324, 331, 334, 336, 337, 338, 353, 364, 380, 384, 395, 396, 402, 404, 409, 417, 418, 426, 427, 432, 433, 435, 436, 440, 443, 448, 449, 450, 459, 460, 463, 465, 474, 475, 483, 485, 488, 490, 492, 494, 496, 498, 506, 508, 513, 517, 520, 525, 531, 532, 533, 536, 547, 548, 549, 553, 555, 556, 558, 559, 560, 561, 562, 563, 567, 568, 570, 576, 583, 585, 594, 595, 597, 599, 605, 609, 613, 619, 620, 625, 626, 628, 631, 632, 638, 644, 650, 653, 666, 668, 671, 672, 673, 674, 675, 676, 681, 683, 684, 686, 687, 691, 693, 703, 707, 709, 714, 715, 720
Photos by
Robin Adams, Boris Adolf, Ravi Angard, John Black, David Bush, Don Chang, Bernard Canonne, Steve Chesler, Theo Civitello, Simon Clay,Chris Clewell, Jeremy Cliff, Remi Dargegen, Clint Davis, Dirk De Jager, Piotr Degler, Patrick Ernzen, Nick Fancher, Owen Fitter, Erik Fuller, Tom Gidden, Phil Greatorex, Jonathan Green, Nicole Hains, Karissa Hosek, Ned Jackson, Gary Kessler, Greg Keysar, Stephen Kim, Ron Kimball, Alison Langley, Nathan Leach-Proffer, Marcel Lech, Pawel Litwinski, Philip Lohmann, Travis Massey, Gabor Mayer, Michael McConnell, Scott, McGuigan, David McNeese, Ryan Merill, Calvin Miller, Rick Minor, Motorcar Studios, Phil Parrish, Dino Petrocelli, Teddy Pieper, Joshua Rainey, Rasy Ran, Ronnie Renaldi, Brian Regan, Ben Sarles, Darin Schnabel, Tim Scott, Drew Shipley, Juan Silva, Corey Silvia, Sean Smith, Cymon Taylor, Trace Taylor, Josh Sweeney, Randy Wells, Tom Wood, Pepper Yandell, Jeff Yardis, Glenn Zanotti

Images copyright and courtesy of Russo & Steele
312, 349

Images copyright and courtesy of Silverstone Auctions
63, 74, 256, 259, 311, 615, 616, 617, 627

Images copyright and courtesy of Theodore Bruce
358

By the same authors, previous Yearbooks still available:

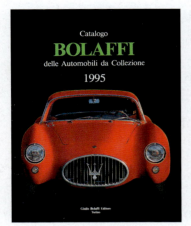

1993-1994 season
All the Makes
Italian text
p. 208 hard-bound
€ 46,00

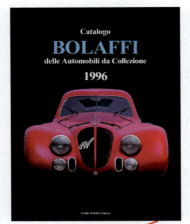

1994-1995 season
All the Makes
Italian/English text
p. 208 hard-bound
€ 46,00

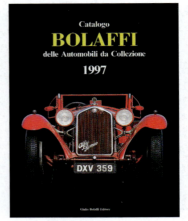

1995-1996 season
All the Makes
Italian/English text
p. 206 hard-bound
€ 49,00

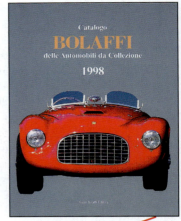

1996-1997 season
All the Makes
Italian/English text
p. 254 hard-bound
€ 57,00

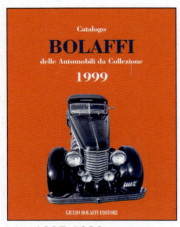

1997-1998 season
All the Makes
Italian/English text
p. 238 hard-bound
€ 46,00

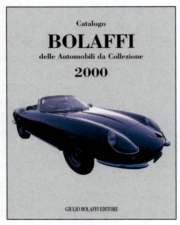

1998-1999 season
All the Makes
Italian/English text
p. 248 hard-bound
€ 46,00

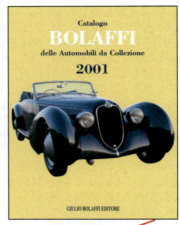

1999-2000 season
All the Makes
Italian/English text
p. 236 hard-bound

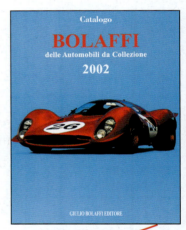

2000-2001 season
All the Makes
Italian/English text
p. 254 soft-bound

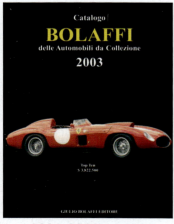

2001-2002 season
All the Makes
Italian/English text
p. 272 soft-bound
€ 46,00

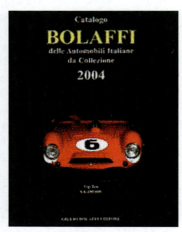

2002-2003 season
Only Italian Makes
Italian/English text
p. 102 soft-bound
€ 29,90

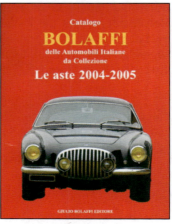

2003-2005 (2 seasons)
Only Italian Makes
Italian/English text
p. 158 soft-bound
€ 29,90

2005-2006 season
Only Italian Makes
Italian/English text
p. 126 soft-bound
€ 29,90

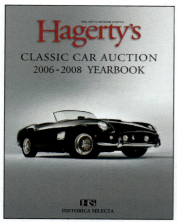
2006-2008 (2 seasons)
All the Makes
English text
p. 390 hard-bound
€ 39,90

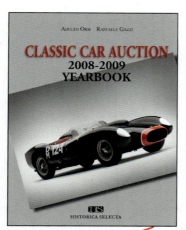
2008-2009 season
All the Makes
English text
p. 286 hard-bound
€ 39,90

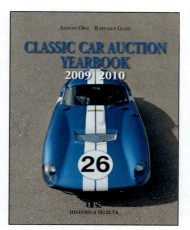
2009-2010 season
All the Makes
English text
p. 320 hard-bound
€ 39,90

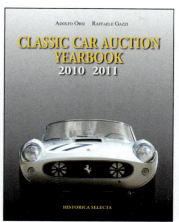
2010-2011 season
All the Makes
English text
p. 320 hard-bound
€ 44,90

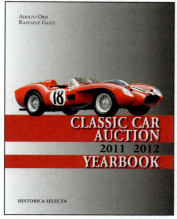
2011-2012 season
All the Makes
English text
p. 336 hard-bound
€ 44,90

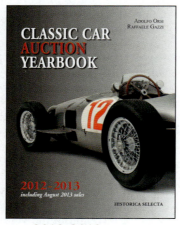
2012-2013 season
All the Makes
English text
p. 400 hard-bound
€ 52,00

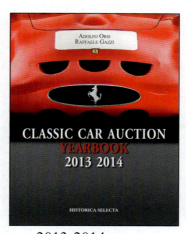
2013-2014 season
All the Makes
English text
p. 392 hard-bound
€ 60,00

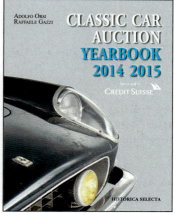
2014-2015 season
All the Makes
English text
p. 424 hard-bound
€ 70,00

HISTORICA SELECTA SRL

41012 CARPI (MODENA) - VIA PAUSSOLO, 14/A - ITALY
TEL +39 059 663955
info@historicaselecta.it
www.classiccarauctionyearbook.com

About the authors

Adolfo Orsi's passion for motorcars was honed throughout his teenage years. In fact, as the grandson of Adolfo and son of Omar Orsi, who held the reins of Maserati between 1937 and 1968, he grew up surrounded by cars.

In 1986 he decided to dedicate himself full-time to his passion and, from 1988 to 1991, he organized auctions of collector cars, motorcycles and automobilia, in association with Finarte Casa d'Aste, in Modena and Monza.

In 1990 he established the company **HISTORICA SELECTA** and Raffaele Gazzi, a long-time friend and fellow enthusiast, joined the company in 1991.

As leading specialists in the international collector car market, HISTORICA SELECTA often advises many of the world's most prestigious Manufacturers, Museums and collectors.

In detail, HISTORICA SELECTA:
- **Organizes historical exhibitions:** "*Maserati 100 – A Century of pure Italian Luxury Sports Cars*", MEF (Museo Enzo Ferrari), Modena 2014; "*The history of the automobile in Modena 1895-1970*", MEF (Museo Enzo Ferrari), Modena 2012 (still part of the Museum exhibit); "*Quando scatta Nuvolari*", Palazzo Te, Mantova, 2009-2010; "*Mitomacchina*", MART, Rovereto, 2006-2007, which had 130.000 visitors and was described by Thoroughbred & Classic Cars as "the most braintingling exhibition of cars ever assembled in the name of art"; "*Cuando el hombre es mas que el mito*" (Fangio), Modena, 2005; "*Maserati, la macchina sublime*", Modena, 1996; "*Maserati ottantanni: 1914-1994*", Motorshow Bologna, 1994; "*Lo sviluppo della tecnica automobilistica dagli inizi del secolo a oggi: Bugatti*", Fiera Bologna, 1993; "*Bugatti e Lotus*", Motorshow Bologna, 1993;
- **Advises manufacturers on Heritage collections and programs:** FCA, Lamborghini and Maserati;
- **Advises Museums** and **private collectors;**
- **Organizes celebrations and forums:** in 2014, HISTORICA SELECTA ran the Concorso d'Eleganza for the Maserati Centennial Gathering; in 2013 for the 50th Anniversary of Lamborghini; in 2009, it coordinated the "XI World Forum for Motor Museums" in Emilia-Romagna; in 2007, it ran the Concorso d'Eleganza for the Ferrari 60th celebration; and in 2001, it organized the 75th Anniversary Celebration of the Modena Automobile Club;
- **Publishes** the "*Classic Car Auction Yearbook*" from 2008; from 1994 to 2006 HISTORICA SELECTA edited the "*Catalogo Bolaffi delle automobili da collezione*".

The President of Historica Selecta is Doctor **Adolfo Orsi,** who is an:
- **Automobile historian**, one of the leading experts in the field of Italian Sports and Racing Cars and discoverer of the unpublished history of the Carrozzeria Emilia in Modena, Enzo Ferrari's first entrepreneurial activity;
- **Expert in the problems of the authenticity** by the Modena Court;
- **Expert in restoration**, having coordinated the restoration of several Italian cars winning the most prestigious Awards in many Concours d'Elegance;
- **Judge in Concours d'Elegance,** since 1997 at Pebble Beach; convinced of the importance of preserving cars in their original condition, in 1999 he inspired the FIVA Award for the best preserved car in the field, for which he has been chief class judge ever since; he served as chief judge of the 2016 Swiss Concours, 2014 Maserati Centennial Gathering, 2013 Concorso Lamborghini 50th, 2007 Concorso Ferrari 60th, Uniques Special Ones in Florence and St. Petersburg; he was a member of the Louis Vuitton Classic Concours Award jury and in 2016 of The Peninsula Classics Best of the Best Award; throughout the years, he has also judged at many other significant events including Amelia Island, Bund Classic in Shanghai, Cavallino Classic, Chantilly, Villa d'Este, Salon Privé, The Legend of Motorcycles, Schloss Dyck, Zoute, Techno Classica, Hurlingham and Schwetzingen;
- **Lecturer,** in Italy and abroad, on automobile history and car collecting;
- **Writer**, for the financial newspaper "Il Sole-24 Ore Domenicale" (from 1989 to 2008) and for "The Official Ferrari Magazine";
- **Honorary member** of the Maserati Club UK, Maserati Club Japan, Maserati Club Italia, Gruppo Anziani Maserati, Club Castiglionese Auto e Moto d'Epoca, **charter member** of ICJAG (International Chief Judge Advisory Group), consulting member of the IAC-PFA (International Advisory Council for the Preservation of Ferrari Automobiles) and FIVA Technical Committee Advisor.

Raffaele Gazzi, a long-time enthusiast of automotive history and of vintage cars in general, was still a bank manager in 1988 when he began dedicating a few of his weekends to working with Adolfo Orsi to create the most important auctions for classic cars and memorabilia in Italy.
At the end of 1991, Raffaele joined HISTORICA SELECTA as a part owner. In addition to co-organizing numerous ongoing events and exhibitions for the company, Raffaele often serves as Secretary of Jury or Judge at various, leading Concours d'Elegance.